新疆统计年鉴

XINJIANG STATISTICAL YEARBOOK

2008

新疆

统计年鉴

XINJI

STATISTICA

新疆维吾尔自治区统计局·编

Compiled by Statistics Bureau of Xinjiang Uygur Autonomous Region

新疆
统计年鉴

XINJIANG

STATISTICAL YEARBOOK

2008

中国统计出版社

China Statistics Press

(京)新登字 041 号

图书在版编目(CIP)数据

新疆统计年鉴. 2008 / 新疆维吾尔自治区统计局编
——北京:中国统计出版社,2008.7
ISBN 978-7-5037-5408-1

Ⅰ.新…
Ⅱ.新…
Ⅲ.统计资料 - 新疆 -2008- 年鉴
Ⅳ.C832.45-54

中国版本图书馆 CIP 数据核字 (2008) 第 054626 号

新疆统计年鉴 -2008

作　　者 / 新疆维吾尔自治区统计局
责任编辑 / 郑淼淼　刘金成　韦 红
E-mail　/ yearbook@stats.gov.cn
封面设计 / 黄永中
出版发行 / 中国统计出版社
通信地址 / 北京市西城区三里河月坛南街 57 号　中国统计出版社
邮　　编 / 100826
电　　话 / (010)63376907
正文印刷 / 新疆统计印刷厂
彩色印刷 / 新疆新华华龙印务有限责任公司
经　　销 / 新疆统计信息咨询服务中心总发行
开　　本 / 890 × 1240 毫米 1/16 开本
字　　数 / 160 万字
印　　张 / 40.75 印张　彩插 2.88 印张
印　　数 / 1-3000 册
版　　别 / 2008 年 7 月第 1 版
版　　次 / 2008 年 7 月第 1 次印刷
书　　号 / ISBN 978-7-5037-5408-1/F·2649
定　　价 / 298.00 元(含光盘)

《新疆统计年鉴—2008》编辑委员会

XINJIANG STATISTICAL YEARBOOK–2008
NAME LIST OF EDITORIAL BOARD

《新疆统计年鉴—2008》特邀编委

（排名不分先后）

编者说明

一、《新疆统计年鉴—2008》(中英文对照)，是一部信息高度密集的统计资料书。本书收录了2007年新疆经济和社会等各方面的统计数据，以及重要年份和改革开放以来的主要统计数据，是一部全面反映新疆经济和社会发展情况的资料性年刊。

二、全书内容分为：特载（新疆维吾尔自治区2007年国民经济和社会发展统计公报）；综合；国民经济核算；人口与就业；固定资产投资；财政、金融和保险；物价指数；人民生活和社会保障；城市概况；自然资源和环境保护；农业；工业；建筑业；运输和邮电；批发和零售、住宿和餐饮业；能源生产和消费；对外经济贸易和旅游；教育、科技和文化；体育、卫生及其他；企业集团和企业景气指数；各地、州、市主要经济指标排序；附录（各省、市、区主要经济指标排序）等，各篇末均附有《主要统计指标解释》。

三、与2007年版《新疆统计年鉴》相比较，在统计内容和编辑上主要做了如下修订：

1、对篇章内容进行了规范化调整。将原来《行政区划和自然资源》篇中内容进行了分解，行政区划内容划归到《综合》篇，自然资源的相关内容归纳到《自然资源和环境保护》篇；将社会保障内容划归到《人民生活和社会保障》篇。

2、在《人民生活和社会保障》篇增加了离休、退休、退职人员数及相关费用等内容；在《工业》篇增加了主要工业产品生产能力。

3、为了体现改革开放30年以来新疆经济建设和社会发展取得的突出成就，在《综合》篇列示了1978年的相关数据，并进行了相应的计算和比较。

四、资料中所使用的计算单位均采用国家法定计量单位。

五、本《年鉴》总量指标计算所采用的价格均为现行价格。

六、本《年鉴》伊犁哈萨克自治州的数据包括伊犁州直属县（市）、塔城地区和阿勒泰地区。

七、本《年鉴》使用符号说明：

“#”表示其中项；

“...”表示不足小数位的数据；

“空”表示没有或未掌握该指标数据。

八、本《年鉴》在编辑过程中得到自治区内外许多单位和同志们的大力支持，在此深表谢意。限于我们的水平，加之时间仓促，不足之处，敬请各级领导、各界人士和统计战线的同仁批评指正。

Editor's Explanatory Notes

Ⅰ. Xinjiang Statistical Yearbook-2008 (in both Chinese and English) is an annual statistic publication of comprehensive information with highly density. The yearbook covers very comprehensive data in 2007 and some selected data series in important years and the data since reform and opening of Xinjiang, reflects various aspects of Xinjiang's social and economic development.

Ⅱ. The yearbook comprises such sections as: Special Article (Statistical Communique on National Economy and Social Development of Xinjiang Uygur Autonomous Region in the year 2007); general survey; national accounts; population and employment; investment in fixed assets;government finance,financial intermediation and insurance; price indices; people's livelihood and social security;general survey of cities;natural resources and environment protection;agriculture;industry; construction; transport, post and telecommunication services;wholesale & retail trades,hotels and catering services; production and consumption of energy;foreign trade & economic cooperation and tourism;education,science & technology and culture;sports,public health and others; enterprises group and prosperity index on enterprises;ranking of main economic indicators by region of Xinjiang; appendix (ranking of main economic indicators by region),etc.Each section is equipped with Explanatory Notes on Main Statistical Indicators at the end.

Ⅲ.Compared with the China Statistical Yearbook 2007,some changes are made in contents and in editing mode, including the following:

1)The chapter concered in this yearbook have been adjusted.Data on divisions of administrative concluded in the chapter of general survey,data on natural resources concluded in the chapter of natural resources and environment protection and data on social security concluded in the chapter of people's living conditions and social security.

2)In the chapter of people's livelihood and social security,there are new tables on leave office for rest,retire and related fees.in the chapter of industry increased production capacity of major industrial products.

3)In order to reflect economic and social development since reform and opening of Xinjiang 30,in the chapter of general survey,there are new tables on data on 1978.

Ⅳ.The units of measurement used in this yearbook are internationally standard measurement units.

Ⅴ.The computation of all the indicators in the *Yearbook* is equipped with current prices.

Ⅵ.The data about Ili Kazak Autonomous Prefecture in the present Xinjiang Statistical Yearbook covers counties (cities) direct under Ili Prefecture, Tacheng Prefecture and Altay Prefecture..

Ⅶ.Description of signs or symbols in the yearbook:

"# "stands for interim item; "..." for data with insufficient decimal place; "blank" for absence of data indicators or ignorance of them.

Ⅷ.In the course of compilation, the yearbook has received great support from many units and comrades in and out of Autonomous Region, we acknowledge their help to the book. Mistakes and faults are inevitable to take place for inadequate proficiency and limited time. Leaders, personnel from all walks of life and colleagues from statistical sector are welcome to make their critical comments and suggestions.

目 录 CONTENTS

第一篇 综 合

CHAPTER 1 GENERAL SURVEY

1-1 行政区划......3
Divisions of Administrative Areas in Xinjiang Uygur Autonomous Region

1-2 县级以上行政区划......4
Divisions of Administrative Areas at and above County Level

1-3 各部门机构数......5
Grass-roots Units in Various Sectors

1-4 平均每天主要社会经济活动......7
Selected Indicators on Average Daily Social and Economic Activities

1-5 国民经济和社会发展总量与速度指标......8
Principal Aggregate Indicators on National Economic and Social Development and Grouth Rates

1-6 国民经济和社会发展结构指标......16
Composition Indicators on National Economic and Social Development

1-7 国民经济和社会发展比例和效益指标......19
Indicators on Proportions and Efficiency in National Economic and Social Development

1-8 人均主要工农业产品产量......22
Per capita Output of Major Industrial and Agricultural Products

1-9 人均国民经济主要指标......23
Per Capita Main Indicators on National Economy

1-10 各时期社会经济主要指标......24
Major Social and Economic Indicators of Each Period

1-11 各时期社会经济主要指标平均增长率......25
Growth Rate of Major Social and Economic Indicators of Each Period

1-12 天山北坡经济带主要经济指标......26
Main Economic Indicators for Economic Belt on the Northern Slope of the Tianshan Mountains

主要统计指标解释......30
Explanatory Notes on Main Statistical Indicators

第 二 篇　国民经济核算

CHAPTER 2 NATIONAL ACCOUNTS

2-1 新疆生产总值......35
Gross Domestic Product in Xinjiang
2-2 新疆生产总值构成......36
Composition of Gross Domestic Product in Xinjiang
2-3 新疆生产总值指数(上年=100)......37
Indices of Gross Domestic Product in Xinjiang (preceding year=100)
2-4 新疆生产总值指数(1978 年=100)......38
Indices of Gross Domestic Product in Xinjiang (1978=100)
2-5 分行业新疆生产总值......39
Gross Domestic Product by Sector in Xinjiang
2-6 新疆生产总值项目结构......40
Components of Gross Domestic Product in Xinjiang
2-7 支出法新疆生产总值......41
Gross Domestic Product by Expenditure Approach in Xinjiang
2-8 资本形成总额及其构成......42
Gross Capital Formation and Its Composition
2-9 最终消费及其构成......43
Final Consumption Expenditure and Its Composition
2-10 各地、州、市、县(市)地区生产总值......44
Gross Regional Product by Prefecture, Autonomous Prefecture, City and County
2-11 各地、州、市、县(市)地区生产总值构成......48
Composition of Gross Domestic Product by Prefecture, Autonomous Prefecture, City and County
2-12 各地、州、市、县(市)地区生产总值指数(上年=100)......52
Indices of Gross Domestic Product by Prefecture, Autonomous Prefecture, City and County(preceding year=100)
2-13 居民消费水平及指数......56
Household Consumption Expenditure and Its Indices
2-14 居民消费支出......57
Household Consumption Expenditure
主要统计指标解释......58
Explanatory Notes on Main Statistical Indicators

第 三 篇　人口与就业

CHAPTER 3 POPULATION AND EMPLOYMENT

3-1 人口数及构成......65
Population and Its Composition
3-2 人口出生率、死亡率、自然增长率......65
Birth Rate, Death Rate and Natural Growth Rate of Population
3-3 新疆人口普查基本情况......66
Basic Statistics on National Population Census in Xinjiang
3-4 婚姻登记情况......66
Number of Marriages Registry

3-5 各地、州、市、县(市)户数、人口数、土地面积......67
Household, Population, Land Area by Prefecture, Autonomous Prefecture City and County

3-6 各地、州、市、县(市)按城镇、乡村和农业、非农业分人口数......71
Population of Urban and Rural, Agriculture and Non-Agriculture by Prefecture, Autonomous Prefecture, City and County

3-7 各地、州、市、县(市)民族人口数......74
Population of Major Nationalities by Prefecture, Autonomous Prefecture, City and County

3-8 主要年份分民族人口数......80
Population by Nationality in Main Years

3-9 各地、州、市、县(市)人口自然变动情况......81
Statistics on Population Natural Changes by Prefecture, Autonomous Prefecture, City and County

3-10 各地、州、市采取各种避孕措施情况......84
Condition of Adopting Various Contraceptions by Prefecture, Autonomous Prefecture, City and County

3-11 各地、州、市计划生育及领证情况......85
Family Planning and Certificate Receiving by Prefecture, Autonomous Prefecture and City

3-12 新疆生产建设兵团人口情况......85
Population of Xinjiang Production and Construction Group

3-13 按县、市分列的团场户数、人口数......86
Household and Population of Regiment Farms by City and County

3-14 就业基本情况......89
Employment

3-15 城镇失业人数及失业率......90
Number of Urban Unemployed Persons and Unemployment Rate

3-16 各地、州、市城镇失业率......90
Urban Unemployment Rate by Prefecture , Autonomous Prefecture and City

3-17 按三次产业分的就业人员......91
Number of Employed Persons by Three Strata of Industry

3-18 按城乡分的年底就业人员数......92
Number of Employed Persons at the Year-end by Urban and Rural Areas

3-19 各地区按行业分城镇单位就业人员(年底数)......94
Number of Employed Persons in Urban Units at the Year-end by Sectors and Region

3-20 各地区年底单位在岗职工人数......95
Number of Staff and Workers at the Year-end by Region

3-21 分行业年底单位在岗职工人数......96
Number of Staff and Workers at the Year-end by Sectors

3-22 各地、州、市分行业年底单位在岗职工人数......99
Number of Staff and Workers at the Year-end by Sector and Prefecture, Autonomous Prefecture and City

3-23 分行业城镇单位年底女性就业人员......101
Number of Female Employed in Urban Units at the Year-end by Sectors

3-24 单位在岗职工工资总额及构成......102
Total Wages of Staff and Workers and Its Composition

3-25 在岗职工工资总额指数......103
Indices of Total Wages of Staff and Workers

3-26 在岗职工工资情况......103
Wages of Full-Employed Staff and Workers

3-27 在岗职工平均货币工资......104
Average Money Wage of Staff and Workers

3-28 在岗职工平均工资指数......104
Indices of Average Wage of Staff and Workers

3-29 各地、州、市分行业单位在岗职工平均货币工资......105
Average Money Wage of Staff and Workers by Sector and by Prefecture, Autonomous Prefecture and City
3-30 各地、州、市、县(市)在岗职工平均货币工资......107
Average Money Wages of Fully Employed Staff and Workers by Prefecture, Autonomous Prefecture, City and County
主要统计指标解释......110
Explanatory Notes on Main Statistical Indicators

第 四 篇 固定资产投资

CHAPTER 4 INVESTMENT IN FIXED ASSETS

4-1 各时期全社会固定资产投资......115
Total Investment in Fixed Assets in the Whole Country by Period
4-2 全社会固定资产投资......116
Total Investment in Fixed Assets in the Whole Country
4-3 按登记注册类型分全社会固定资产投资......118
Total Investment in Fixed Assets in the Whole Country by Ownership
4-4 按构成分全社会固定资产投资......119
Total Investment in Fixed Assets by Composition of Funds
4-5 全社会固定资产投资资金来源情况......120
Sources of Funds of Total Investment in Fixed Assets in the Whole Country
4-6 按行业分全社会固定资产投资......121
Total Investment in Fixed Assets in the Whole Country by Sector
4-7 全社会房屋施工面积、竣工面积......124
Floor Space of Buildings under Construction and Completed in Whole Country
4-8 按登记注册类型分城镇固定资产投资......125
Investment in Fixed Assets in Urban Area by Ownership
4-9 按构成及建设性质分城镇固定资产投资......126
Investment in Fixed Assets in Urban Area by Composition of Funds and Type of Construction
4-10 分行业城镇固定资产投资主要指标......128
Main Indicators of Investment in Fixed Assets in Urban Area by Sector
4-11 各地、州、市、县(市)城镇固定资产投资和新增固定资产......132
Total Investment and Newly Increased Fixed Assets in Urban Area by Prefecture, Autonomous Prefecture, City and County
4-12 各地、州、市分行业城镇固定资产投资......136
Investment in Fixed Assets in Urban Area by Sectors in Prefecture, Autonomous Prefecture and City
4-13 城镇固定资产投资效果指标......138
Investment Result of Urban Investment
4-14 房地产开发企业基本情况......139
Basic Condition of Enterprises for Real Estate Development
4-15 房地产投资主要指标......140
Main Indicators of Real Estate Investment
4-16 按用途分房地产开发企业（单位）投资完成额......141
Investment Actually Completed by Enterprises for Real Estate Development by Use
4-17 房地产开发企业（单位）资金来源......143
Sources of Funds of Enterprises for Real Estate Develpment
4-18 房地产开发企业（单位）施工、销售和空置情况......144
Condition of Under Construction, Sale and Idle of Enterprises for Real Estate Development

4-19 新增主要产品生产能力......147
Newly Increased Production Capacity of Major Products
4-20 农村非农户固定资产投资情况......149
Investment in Fixed Assets of Non-Rural Households in Rural Areas
4-21 农户固定资产投资情况......150
Investment in Fixed Assets of Rural Households in Rural Areas
主要统计指标解释......151
Explanatory Notes on Main Statistical Indicators

第五篇 财政、金融、保险

CHAPTER 5 GOVERNMENT FINANCE, FINANCIAL INTERMEDIATION AND INSURANCE

5-1 地方财政一般预算收支及增长速度......157
The General Budgetary Revenue & Expenses and Growth Rate of Local Finance
5-2 地方财政一般预算收入占新疆生产总值的比重......157
Percentage of the General Budgetary Revenue in Local Finance to GDP of Xinjiang
5-3 地方财政收支情况......158
Statistics on Total Government Revenue and Expenditures in Local Finance
5-4 各地、州、市、县(市)地方财政一般预算收支......159
Government Revenue and Expenditures by Prefecture, Autonomous Prefecture, City and County
5-5 金融机构各项存款和各项贷款余额......162
Balance of Deposits and Loans of National Banking System
5-6 金融机构和人员数......163
Number of Financial Institutions and Staff
5-7 金融机构信贷资金平衡表......165
Credit Funds Balance Sheet of Financial Institutions by Sources
5-8 国有商业银行信贷资金平衡表......166
Credit Funds Balance Sheet of State-owned Commercial Banks
5-9 金融机构现金收支表......167
Cash Income and Expenditure of Financial Institutions
5-10 保险机构......167
Number of Insurance Institutions
5-11 国内保险业务情况......168
Conditions of Domestic Insurance Service
5-12 保险事业发展情况......168
Statistics on Development of Insurance
5-13 各地区保险业务情况......169
Conditions of Insurance Service by Region
5-14 保险业务经济技术指标......170
Main Economic and Technological Indicators of Insurance Company
5-15 新疆辖区证券、期货经营机构和人员数......170
Operators and Staff of Securities and Futures in Xinjiang
5-16 上市公司基本情况表......171
Basic Condition of Listed Companies
主要统计指标解释......172
Explanatory Notes on Main Statistical Indicators

第六篇 物价指数

CHAPTER 6 PRICE INDICES

6-1 各种物价指数......175
Price Indices
6-2 居民消费价格分类指数......176
Consumer Price Indices by Category
6-3 各市县居民消费价格分类指数......178
Consumer Price Indices by Category in Cities and Counties
6-4 商品零售价格分类指数......182
Retail Price Indices by Category of Commodities
6-5 各市县商品零售价格分类指数......184
Retail Price Indices by Category in Cities and Counties
6-6 农业生产资料价格分类指数......188
Price Indices of Agricultural Means of Production by Category
6-7 各市县农业生产资料价格指数......188
Price Indices of Agricultural Means of Production by Category in Cities and Counties
6-8 历年房屋销售价格指数......189
Selling Price Indices of Houses by Period
6-9 房屋销售价格指数......189
Selling Price Indices of Houses
6-10 工业品出厂价格分类指数......190
Ex-Factory Price Indices of Industrial Products by Category
6-11 原材料、燃料、动力购进价格分类指数......191
Indices of Purchasing Prices of Raw Material, Fuels and Power by Category
6-12 固定资产投资价格指数......191
Price Indices of Investment in Fixed Assets
主要统计指标解释......192
Explanatory Notes on Main Statistical Indicators

第七篇 人民生活和社会保障

CHAPTER 7 PEOPLE'S LIVELIHOOD AND SOCIAL SECURITY

7-1 人民物质文化生活情况......195
People's Material and Cultural Life
7-2 城乡居民储蓄存款年底余额和年增加额......196
Savings Deposit in Urban and Rural Areas (Year-end)
7-3 城乡居民家庭人均收入及指数......196
Per Capita Annual Income of Urban and Rural Households and the Related Index
7-4 城镇居民家庭生活基本情况......197
Basic Living Conditions of Urban Households
7-5 城镇居民家庭基本情况......198
Basic Conditions of Urban Households
7-6 城镇居民家庭平均每人全年消费性支出......199
Per Capita Annual Living Expenditure of Urban Households
7-7 城镇居民家庭平均每人全年消费性支出构成......200
Composition of Per Capita Annual Consumption Expenditure of Urban Households

7-8 城镇居民家庭年人均购买的主要商品数量......201
Per Capita Annual Purchases of Major Commodities of Urban Households

7-9 城镇居民家庭平均每百户年底耐用消费品拥有量......201
Number of Major Durable Consumer Goods Owned Per-100 Urban Households at Year-end

7-10 按收入等级分的城镇居民家庭平均每人全年购买商品数量......202
Per Capita Annual Purchases of Major Commodities of Urban Households by Level of Income

7-11 按收入等级分城镇居民家庭平均每百户年底耐用消费品拥有量......203
Ownership of Durable Consumer Goods Per100 Urban Households at Year-end by Level of Income

7-12 农村居民家庭基本情况......204
Basic Conditions of Rural Households

7-13 农村居民家庭人均年总收入、纯收入和构成......205
Per Capita Annual Gross and Net Income and Its Composition of Rural Households

7-14 农村居民家庭平均每人总收入和纯收入......205
Per Capita Annual Gross and Net Income of Rural Households

7-15 主要年份农村居民家庭人均主要消费品消费量......206
Per Capita Consumption of Major Consumer Goods of Rural Households in Main Years

7-16 主要年份农村居民家庭平均每百户耐用消费品拥有量......206
Number of Durable Consumer Goods Owned by Per100 Rural Households in Main Years

7-17 农村居民人均生活消费支出及构成......207
Per Capita Annual Living Expendture and Its Composition of Rural Households

7-18 农村居民家庭平均每百户耐用消费品拥有量......207
Number of Durable Consumer Goods Owned by Per100 Rural Households

7-19 农村居民家庭人均商品性和自给性生活消费品支出......208
Per Capita Self-Sufficiency and Consumption on Commodity Goods of Living Expenditure in Rural Households

7-20 农村居民家庭人均纯收入分组......209
Rural Households Grouped by Per Capita Annual Net Income

7-21 分地区农村居民家庭人均总收入和纯收入......210
Per Capita Annual Gross and Net Income of Rural Households by Region

7-22 分地区农村居民家庭平均每人总支出......212
Per Capita Total Expenditure of Rural Household by Region

7-23 分地区农村居民家庭人均现金收支......214
Per Capita Income and Expenditure in Cash of Rural Household by Region

7-24 农村居民家庭房屋使用情况......218
Housing Conditions of Rural Households

7-25 城乡新建住宅面积和居民住房情况......218
Floor Space Completed and Housing Conditions of Urban and Rural Residents

7-26 分地区农村居民家庭平均每人粮食收支平衡表......219
Per Capita Grain Banlance of Debit and Credit by Region

7-27 农村居民家庭平均每户饲养畜禽、其他小动物生产情况......220
Output of Livestock, Poultry and Other Small Animals Per Rural Households

7-28 农村居民家庭平均每户饲养畜禽、其他小动物出售量......220
Quantities of Livestock, Poultry and Other Small Animals Sold Per Rural Households

7-29 社会保险基本情况......221
Basic Conditions on Social Insurance

7-30 各地、州、市社会保险年末参保人数......222
Number of Social Insured Persons at the Year-end by Prefecture, Autonomous Prefecture and City

7-31 离休、退休、退职人员年底人数......222
Number of Retired and Resigned Persons at the Year-end

7-32 离休、退休、退职费 223
Pensions for Retired and Resigned Persons
7-33 离休、退休、退职人员保险福利费用情况 223
Condition of Total Social Insurance and Welfare Fund of Retire and Resigned Persons
主要统计指标解释 224
Explanatory Notes on Main Statistical Indicators

第 八 篇 城市概况

CHAPTER 8 GENERAL SURVEY OF CITIES

8-1 城市公用事业基本情况 229
Basic Statistics on Urban Public Utilities
8-2 各城市主要经济指标 230
Major Economic Indicators by Cities
8-3 各城市市区设施水平 232
Level of Urban Public Facilities in Cities
8-4 城市自来水情况 232
Basic Statistics on Tap Water Supply in Cities
8-5 城市公用交通情况 233
Basic Statistics on Public Transportation in Cities
8-6 城市市政建设情况 233
Basic Statistics on Municipal Construction in Cities
8-7 城市园林绿化情况 233
Basic Statistics on Urban Gardens and Green Areas in Cities
8-8 城市环境卫生情况 234
Basic Statistics on Urban Environment and Sanitation in Cities
8-9 城市煤气、液化石油气、天然气情况 234
Basic Statistics on Supply of Gas, Liquefied Petroleum Gas and Natural Gas in Cities
8-10 城市集中供热情况 234
Basic Statistics on Heating in Cities
主要统计指标解释 235
Explanatory Notes on Main Statistical Indicators

第 九 篇 自然资源和环境保护

CHAPTER 9 NATURAL RESOURCES AND ENVIRONMENT PROTECTION

9-1 自然资源 239
Natural Resources
9-2 主要山脉基本情况 241
Main Mountain Ranges
9-3 主要湖泊基本情况 241
Major Lakes
9-4 主要河流基本情况 241
Major Rivers
9-5 主要城市平均气温 242
Monthly Average Temperature of Major Cities
9-6 主要城市降水量 243
Monthly Precipitation of Major Cities

9-7 主要城市日照时数......244
Monthly Sunshine Hours of Major Cities
9-8 环境保护基本情况......245
Basic Statistics on Environmental Protection
9-9 水资源情况......248
Water Resources
9-10 供水用水情况......249
Water Supply and Water Used
9-11 环保系统机构、人员数......250
Number of Environmental Protection Agencies and Persons Engaged
9-12 自然保护区基本情况......250
Basic Situation of Natural Protection
9-13 环境污染与破坏事故情况......251
Environment Pollution and Destruction Accidents
9-14 环境污染治理投资......251
Investment in the Treatment of Environment Pollution
9-15 工业污染治理投资完成情况......252
Investment Completed in the Treatment of Industrial Pollution
9-16 工业污染治理投资来源......252
Sources of Investment in the Treatment of Industrial Pollution
9-17 分行业重点调查企业工业废水及污染物排放量......253
Discharge of Industrial Waste Water and Pollutants in Major Investigated Enterprises by Sector
9-18 分行业重点调查企业工业废气及污染物排放量......253
Emission of Industrial Waste Gas and Pollutants in Major Investigated Enterprises by Sector
9-19 分行业重点调查企业固体废物产生量及处理利用......254
Production,Treatment and Utilization of Solid Wastes in Major Investigated Enterprises by Sector
9-20 主要城市空气质量指标......254
Ambient Air Quality in Main Cities
9-21 主要城市道路交通噪声监测情况......255
Monitoring of Urban Road Traffic Noise in Major Cities
9-22 国控主要城市区域环境噪声监测情况......255
Monitoring of Urban Environment Noise in Major Cities under National Control Programme
9-23 各地区城市生活垃圾清运和处理情况......256
Collection, Transport and Disposal of Consumption Wastes in Cities by Region
9-24 地质灾害及防治情况......258
Geological Disasters and Prevention and Cure
9-25 各地区土地利用情况......259
Land Use by Region
9-26 造林面积......260
Area of Afforestation
9-27 林业重点工程造林面积......261
Area of Key Afforestation Projects
9-28 各地区天然湿地面积......262
Area of Wetlands by Region

9-29 森林火灾情况......263
Forest Fires
9-30 森林病虫害防治情况......264
Prevention of Forest Diseases and Pests
9-31 地震灾害情况......265
Earthquake Disasters
9-32 林业系统营林固定资产投资资金来源......266
Sources of Funds of Investment in Fixed Assets for Afforestation in Forest System
9-33 林业系统营林固定资产投资完成情况......267
Completed Investment in Fixed Assets for Afforestation in Forest System
主要统计指标解释......268
Explanatory Notes on Main Statistical Indicators

第十篇 农 业

CHAPTER 10 AGRICULTURE

10-1 农村基层组织情况......275
Basic Conditions of Rural Grass-roots Unit
10-2 国有农林牧渔场基本情况......275
Basic Conditions of State Agriculture, Forestry, Animal Husbandry and Fishery
10-3 各地、州、市、县(市)农村基层组织情况......276
Basic Conditions of Rural Grass-roots Units by Prefecture, Autonomous Prefecture, City and County
10-4 各地、州、市、县(市)耕地面积......280
Area of Cultivated land by Prefecture, Autonomous Prefecture, City and County
10-5 农、林、牧、渔业总产值......282
Gross Output Value of Agriculture, Forestry, Animal Husbandry and Fishery
10-6 农、林、牧、渔业总产值指数......283
Indices of Gross Output Value of , Forestry, Animal Husbandry and Fishery
10-7 各地、州、市、县(市)农林牧渔业总产值......284
Gross Output Value of , Forestry, Animal Husbandry and Fishery by Prefecture, Autonomous Prefecture, City and County
10-8 各地、州、市、县(市)农业机械拥有量......287
Agricultural Machinery by Prefecture, Autonomous Prefecture, City and County
10-9 各地、州、市、县(市)农村电气化和农田水利情况......291
Statistics on Water Conservancy and Electrification in Rural Areas by Prefecture, Autonomous Prefecture, City and County
10-10 灌溉、水库和除涝、治水情况......295
Irrigation, Reservoirs, Flood Prevention, Water and Soil Conservation
10-11 各地、州、市水利设施和除涝面积......296
Water Conservancy Facilities and Area with Flood Prevention Measures by Prefecture, Autonomous Prefecture and City
10-12 各地、州、市农村饮水安全情况......296
Basic Statistics on Security of Drinking Water in Rural Area by Prefecture, Autonomous Prefecture and City
10-13 主要年份农作物播种面积......297
Total Sown Areas of Farm Crops in Main Years
10-14 各地、州、市、县(市)农作物播种面积......298
Sown Areas of Farm Crops by Prefecture, Autonomous Prefecture, City and County
10-15 主要农作物种植结构......302
Planting Structure of Major Farm Crops

10-16 主要年份农作物产品产量......303
Output of Major Farm Crops in Main Years
10-17 各地、州、市、县(市)主要农产品产量......304
Output of Major Farm Crops by Prefecture, Autonomous Prefecture, City and County
10-18 各地、州、市、县(市)农作物单位面积产量......308
Output of Major Farm Crops Per Hectare by Prefecture, Autonomous Prefecture, City and County
10-19 各地、州、市林业生产情况......310
Condition on Forest Products by Prefecture, Autonomous Prefecture, City
10-20 各地、州、市水果种植面积......311
Planted Area of Fruits by Prefecture, Autonomous Prefecture, City
10-21 各地、州、市水果产量......312
Output of Fruits by Prefecture, Autonomous Prefecture, City
10-22 牲畜饲养情况......313
Number of Livestock
10-23 各地、州、市、县(市)牲畜年底头数......314
Number of Livestock at the Year-end by Prefecture, Autonomous Prefecture, City and County
10-24 主要年份畜产品产量......316
Output of Livestock Products in Main Years
10-25 各地、州、市、县(市)总产肉量......317
Total Output of Meat by Prefecture, Autonomous Prefecture, City and County
10-26 水产品产量和养殖面积......320
Output of Aquatic Products and Cultured Area
10-27 受灾面积情况......321
Areas Covered by Natural Disaster
10-28 乡镇企业主要指标......322
Main Indicators of Township Enterprises
主要统计指标解释......324
Explanatory Notes on Main Statistical Indicators

第十一篇 工 业

CHAPTER 11 INDUSTRY

11-1 工业总产值......329
Gross Industrial Output Value
11-2 工业总产值指数(1978 年=100)......329
Indices of Gross Industrial Output Value(1978=100)
11-3 规模以上工业企业主要经济指标......330
Main Economic Indicators of Industrial Enterprises above Designated Size
11-4 按行业分规模以上工业企业主要经济指标......334
Main Economic Indicators of Industrial Enterprises above Designated Size by Sectors
11-5 各地、州、市、县(市)规模以上工业企业主要经济指标......338
Main Economic Indicators of Industrial Enterprises above Designated Size by Prefecture, Autonomous Prefecture, City and County
11-6 规模以上工业企业主要经济效益指标......350
Main Indicators on Economic Efficiency of Industrial Enterprises above Designated Size
11-7 分行业规模以上工业企业主要经济效益指标......352
Main Indicators on Economic Efficiency of Industrial Enterprises above Designated Size by Sectors

11-8 各地、州、市、县(市)规模以上工业企业主要经济效益指标 354
Main Indicators on Economic Benefit of Industrial Enterprises above Designated Size By Prefecture, Autonomous Prefecture, City and County

11-9 国有及国有控股工业企业主要经济指标 360
Main Economic Indicators Efficiency of State-owned and State-holding Industrial Enterprises

11-10 分行业国有及国有控股工业企业主要经济指标 364
Main Economic Indicators of State-owned and State-holding Industrial Enterprises by Sectors

11-11 各地、州、市、县(市)国有及国有控股工业企业主要经济指标 368
Main Economic Indicators of State-owned and State-holding Industrial Enterprises by Prefecture, Autonomous Prefecture, City and County

11-12 国有及国有控股工业企业主要经济效益指标 380
Main Indicators on Economic Efficiency of State-owened and State-holding Industrial Enterprises

11-13 分行业国有及国有控股工业企业主要经济效益指标 382
Main Indicators on Economic Efficiency of State-owened and State-holding Industrial Enterprises by Sectors

11-14 各地、州、市、县(市)国有及国有控股工业企业主要经济效益指标 384
Main Indicators on Economic Efficiency of State-owened and State-holding Industrial Enterprises
by Prefecture, Autonomous Prefecture, City and County

11-15 分行业大中型工业企业主要经济指标 390
Main Indicators of Large-scale and Medium-scale Industrial Enterprises by Sectors

11-16 分行业大中型工业企业主要经济效益指标 394
Main Indicators on Economic Efficiency of Large-scale and Medium-scale Industrial Enterprises by Sectors

11-17 主要工业产品产量 396
Output of Major Industrial Products

11-18 各地、州、市主要工业产品产量 400
Output of Major Industrial Products by Prefecture, Autonomous Prefecture and City

11-19 国有及国有控股企业主要指标占全区规模以上工业比重 404
Percentage of Main Indicators in State-owned and State-holding Enterprises to Enterprises above Designated Size

11-20 重点行业主要指标占全区规模以上工业比重 405
Percentage of Main Indicators in Key Industrial Sectors to Xinjiang's Industry above Designated Size

11-21 规模以上工业主要产品生产能力 407
Production Capacity of Major Industrial Products above Designated Size

主要统计指标解释 408
Explanatory Notes on Main Statistical Indicators

第 十二 篇 建筑业

CHAPTER 12 CONSTRUCTION

12-1 建筑企业概况 415
Main Indicators on Construction Enterprises Status

12-2 按登记注册类型分建筑业总产值 416
Total Output Value of Construction by Registration

12-3 按构成分建筑业总产值 417
Total Output Value of Construction by Composition

12-4 按行业和登记注册类型分建筑业总产值 418
Total Output Value of Construction by Registration Status and Sectors

12-5 建筑企业增加值 419
Value-added of Construction Enterprises

12-6 建筑企业利税总额 420
Total Pre-tax Profits of Construction Enterprises

12-7 建筑企业劳动生产率......421
Labor Productivity of Construction Enterprises

12-8 建筑企业技术装备情况......422
Number and Power of Machinery and Equipment Owned by Construction Enterprises

12-9 按登记注册类型分的建筑企业技术装备情况......423
Number and Power of Machinery and Equipment Owned by Registration Status

12-10 建筑企业签订合同情况......424
Contracts Signed by Construction Enterprises

12-11 建筑企业承包工程完成情况......425
Completion of Contracted Projects by Construction Enterprises

12-12 建筑企业资产及资本金......426
Assets and Capital Principal of Construction Enterprises

12-13 建筑企业负债及所有者权益......427
Liability and Owner's Equity of Construction Enterprises

12-14 建筑企业总收入......428
Total Income of Construction Enterprises

12-15 建筑企业亏损额及从业人数......429
Losses and Employed Persons of Construction Enterprises

12-16 建筑企业工程施工情况......430
Condition of Building Works by Construction Enterprise

12-17 按登记注册类型分建筑企业工程施工情况......431
Condition of Building Works by Construction Enterprise by Registration Status

12-18 建筑企业竣工房屋建筑面积......432
Floor Space of Completed Building of Construction Enterprises

主要统计指标解释......433
Explanatory Notes on Main Statistical Indicators

第 十三 篇 运输和邮电

CHAPTER 13 TRANSPORT, POSTAL AND TELECOMMUNICATION SERVICES

13-1 运输业基本情况......437
Basic Conditions of Transport

13-2 运输线路长度......438
Length of Transport Routes

13-3 运输线路质量......438
Quality of Transport Routes

13-4 客运量及周转量......439
Passenger Traffic and Passenger -kilometers

13-5 货运量及货物周转量......440
Freight Traffic and Ton-kilometers

13-6 货物运输平均运距......441
Average Transport Distance of Freight

13-7 铁路运输主要财务指标......441
Main Financial Indicators of Railway Transport

13-8 铁路运输技术经济主要指标......442
Main Technical and Economic Indicators of Railway Transport

13-9 民用车辆拥有量......442
Number of Civil Vehicles Owned

13-10 邮电事业情况......443
Basic Conditions of Postal and Telecommunication Services

13-11 主要年份邮电业务情况......444
Conditions of Postal and Telecommunication Services in Main Years

主要统计指标解释......446
Explanatory Notes on Main Statistical Indicators

第十四篇 批发和零售业、住宿和餐饮业

CHAPTER 14 WHOLESALE & RETAIL TRADES, HOTELS AND CATERING SERVICES

14-1 限额以上批发和零售业、住宿和餐饮业基本情况......451
Basic Conditions of Enterprises above Designated Size of Wholesale and Retail Trades, Hotels and Catering Services

14-2 社会消费品零售总额......452
Total Retail Sales of Consumer Goods

14-3 分类型、分地区限额以上批发和零售业、住宿和餐饮业基本情况......453
Basic Conditions of Enterprises above Designated Size in Wholesale and Retail Trades, Hotels and Catering Services by Category and Region

14-4 分行业、分地区限额以上批发零售业商品销售额......455
Total Sales Values of Enterprises above Designated Size of Wholesale and Retail Trade by Sector and Region

14-5 限额以上餐饮企业销售情况......457
Sales Values of Enterprises Above Designated Size of Catering Services

14-6 限额以上住宿企业经营情况......458
Operation of Enterprises Above Designated Size in Hotels services

14-7 各地、州、市、县(市)社会消费品零售总额......460
Total Retail Sales of Consumer Goods by Prefecture, Autonomous Prefecture, City and County

14-8 各地、州、市、县(市)社会消费品零售总额(按行业分)......462
Total Retail Sales of Consumer Goods by Sector and Prefecture, Autonomous Prefecture, City and County

14-9 限额以上批发企业资产及负债情况......464
Assets and Liabilities of Enterprises above Designated Size of Wholesale Trade

14-10 限额以上零售企业资产及负债情况......465
Assets and Liabilities of Enterprises above Designated Size of Retail Trade

14-11 限额以上餐饮企业资产及负债情况......466
Assets and Liabilities of Enterprises above Designated Size of Catering Services

14-12 限额以上住宿企业资产及负债情况......467
Assets and Liabilities of Enterprises above Designated Size of Accommodation Services

14-13 限额以上批发企业主要财务指标......468
Main Financial Indicators of Wholesale Enterprises above Designated Size

14-14 限额以上零售企业主要财务指标......469
Main Financial Indicators of Retail Enterprises above Designated Size

14-15 限额以上餐饮企业主要财务指标......470
Main Financial Indicators of Catering Enterprises above Designated Size

14-16 限额以上住宿企业主要财务指标......471
Main Financial Indicators of Hotels Enterprises above Designated Size

14-17 限额以上批发零售业商品销售类值......472
Total Sales of Enterprises above Designated Size in Wholesale and Retail Trades by Category of Commodities

主要统计指标解释......473
Explanatory Notes on Main Statistical Indicators

第 十五 篇 能源生产和消费

CHAPTER 15 PRODUCTION AND CONSUMPTION OF ENERGY

15-1 能源生产总量及构成......477
Total Production of Energy and Its Composition
15-2 能源消费总量及构成......477
Total Consumption of Energy and Its Composition
15-3 综合能源平衡表......478
Overall Energy BalanceSheet
15-4 石油平衡表......479
Petroleum Balance Sheet
15-5 煤炭平衡表......480
Coal Balance Sheet
15-6 电力平衡表......481
Electricity Balance Sheet
15-7 分行业能源消费总量和主要能源消费量......482
Consumption of Total Energy and Its Main Varieties by Sector
15-8 能源生产弹性系数......486
Elasticity Ration of Energy Production
15-9 能源消费弹性系数......486
Elasticity Ration of Energy Consumption
15-10 能源加工转换效率......487
Efficiency of Energy Conversion
15-11 平均每天各种能源消费量......487
Average Daily Energy Consumption by Type of Energy
15-12 分品种生活能源年消费总量......488
Average Annual Energy Consumption for Households by Variety
15-13 每人年平均生活用能源......488
Annual Average Per Capital Energy Consumption of Households
15-14 各地、州、市规模以上工业能源消费量......489
Energy Consumption of Industry above Designated Size by Prefecture, Autonomous Prefecture and City
主要统计指标解释......491
Explanatory Notes on Main Statistical Indicators

第 十六 篇 对外经济贸易和旅游

CHAPTER 16 FOREIGN TRADE & ECONOMIC COOPERATION AND TOURISM

16-1 进出口贸易总额......495
Total Value of Imports and Exports
16-2 主要进出口商品数量和金额......496
Main Imports and Exports in Volume and Value
16-3 新疆同各国(地区)海关进出口总额......497
Volume of Xinjiang's Imports and Exports with Related Countries and Territories (Customs Statistics)
16-4 按贸易方式和登记注册类型分的海关进出口额......500
Total Imports and Exports by Trade Mode and Registration (Customs Statiatics)
16-5 人民币对主要外币年平均汇价(中间价)......500
Average Exchange Rate of RMB Yuan Against Main Convertible Currences (Medium Rate)

16-6 对外承包工程和劳务合作......501
Contracted Projects in Foreign Countries or Territories
16-7 外商直接投资......501
Foreign Direct Investments
16-8 外国和港澳台地区在华直接投资情况......502
Basic Conditions of Direct Investment in China by Foreign Countries and Compatriots From Hongkong Macao and Taiwan
16-9 各地、州、市利用外商直接投资情况......503
Conditions of Foreign Direct Investment Used by Prefecture, Autonomous Prefecture and City
16-10 新疆在外国和港澳台地区直接投资......503
Direct Investment in Foreign Countries and Hong Kong, Macao and Talwan Made by Xinjiang Partner
16-11 经济技术开发(合作)区主要情况......504
Main Conditions of Economic and Technological Development and Cooperation Zones
16-12 旅游事业发展情况......505
Development of Tourism
16-13 各地、州、市国际旅行社及旅游宾馆(酒店)基本情况......506
Accommodation of International Travel Agencies and Tourist Hotels by Prefecture, Autonomous Prefecture and City
16-14 各地、州、市旅游收入情况......507
Income of Tourism by Prefecture, Autonomous Prefecture and City
16-15 国际旅游外汇收入及构成......508
Foreign Exchange Earnings and Its Composition
16-16 接待外国旅游人数(按国别分)......508
Number of Foreign Tourists Received by Country
主要统计指标解释......509
Explanatory Notes on Main Statistical Indicators

第 十七 篇 教育、科技和文化

CHAPTER 17 EDUCATION, SCIENCE & TECHNOLOGY AND CULTURE

17-1 各级各类学校数......513
Number of Schools by Level and Type
17-2 各级各类学校教师数......513
Number of Teachers by Level and Type of School
17-3 各级各类学校在校学生数......514
Number of Students Enrollment by Level and Type of School
17-4 各级各类学校招生数......514
Number of New Students Enrollment by Level and Type of School
17-5 各级各类学校毕业生数......515
Number of Graduates by Level and Type of School
17-6 研究生数......516
Number of Postgraduates
17-7 高等学校基本情况......516
Basic Statistics on Institutions of Higher Education
17-8 中等专业学校基本情况......517
Basic Statistics on Specialized Secondary Schools
17-9 普通中学和其他学校基本情况......517
Basic Statistics on Regular Secondary Schools and Other Schools
17-10 各类成人教育情况......518
Basic Statistics on Adult Education by Type

17-11 教育发展水平......518
Development Level of Education

17-12 各级学校教师负担学生数......519
Student-Teacher Ratio by Level of School

17-13 各级学校女学生和女教师数......519
Number of Female Students and Teachers by Level of School

17-14 初中毕业生和小学生升学率及小学学龄儿童入学率......520
Percentage of Graduates of Junior Secondary Schools and Primary Schools Entering Higher Level Schools, Enrollment Rate of School-age Children

17-15 各级各类学校少数民族在校学生数......520
Number of Students Enrollment of Minority Nationalities by Level and Type of School

17-16 各地、州、市各级各类学校数......521
Number of Schools by Level, Type and by Prefecture, Autonomous Prefecture and City

17-17 各地、州、市各级各类学校教职工数......522
Number of Teachers and Staff by Level and Type of School and by Prefecture, Autonomous Prefecture and City

17-18 各地、州、市各级各类学校教师数......523
Number of Teachers by Level and Type of School and by Prefecture, Autonomous Prefecture and City

17-19 各地、州、市各级各类学校在校学生数......524
Number of Students Enrollment by Level and Type of School and by Prefecture, Autonomous Prefecture and City

17-20 各地、州、市各级各类学校招生数......525
Number of New Students Enrollment by Level and Type of School and by Prefecture, Autonomous Prefecture and City

17-21 各地、州、市各级各类学校毕业生数......526
Number of Graduates by Level and Type of School and by Prefecture, Autonomous Prefecture and City

17-22 各类学校教育经费情况......527
Educational Funds in Various Schools

17-23 科技活动基本情况......528
Basic Statistics on Scientific and Technological Activities

17-24 县级以上政府部门属研究与开发机构及科技信息与文献机构数、人员数......528
State-Owned Research and Development Institutions and Information and Literature Institutions at and Above County Level and Persons Engaged

17-25 重大科学技术研究成果及奖励数......529
Number of Major Achievements in Scientific and Technological Research and Awarded Prizes

17-26 专利申请和批准数......529
Number of Patent Applications Accepted and Approved

17-27 高等学校科技活动情况......530
Basic Statistics on Scientific and Technological Activities of Higher Education School

17-28 企事业单位主要专业技术人员数......531
Number of Main Scientific and Technical Personnel in Enterprises and Institutions

17-29 企事业单位主要专业技术人员比重......531
Proportion of Scientific and Technical Personnel in Enterprises and Institutions

17-30 大中型工业企业科技活动情况......532
Statistics on Science and Technical Activities of Large and Medium-Sized Industrial Enterprises

17-31 各类技术合同签定及执行情况......536
Statistics on Signing and Implementing Technical Contracts by Type

17-32 各级技术计划项目进入技术市场情况......536
Statistics on Projects for Technical Plan Entering Technical Market by Level

17-33 技术流向地域情况......537
Statistics on Location of Technical Contract

17-34 技术经济合同成交情况......538
Statistics on Transaction in Technical and Economic Contract
17-35 文化产业基本情况......538
Basic Statistics on Culture
17-36 文化艺术、文物事业机构和人员情况......539
Number of Institutions and Personnel in Culture, Art and Cultural Relics
17-37 电影、电视、广播事业基本情况......540
Basic Statistics on Feature Film, Television and Broadcasting
主要统计指标解释......541
Explanatory Notes on Main Statistical Indicators

第 十八 篇 体育、卫生及其他

CHAPTER 18 SPORTS, PUBLIC HEALTH AND OTHERS

18-1 体育局系统从业人员数......547
Number of Staff and Workers in Sports Bureau
18-2 按项目分等级裁判员发展人数......548
Number of Referees in Levels by Type of Sports
18-3 按项目分等级运动员发展人数......548
Number of Athletes at Levels by Type of Sports
18-4 各地、州、市体育局系统机构数......549
Number of Institutions in Sports Committees by Region
18-5 各地、州、市体育局系统机构从业人员数......550
Number of Staff & Workers in Sports Bureau by Region
18-6 主要年份卫生机构数......551
Number of Health Institutions in Main Years
18-7 主要年份卫生人员数......551
Number of Persons Engaged in Health Institutions in Main Years
18-8 卫生机构、床位、人员数......552
Number of Health Institutions, Beds and Persons Engaged by Type of Institutons
18-9 卫生机构床位数......554
Number of Beds in Health Institutions
18-10 医疗机构病床使用情况......554
Utilization of Beds in Medical Institutions
18-11 医疗机构、诊疗人次及入院出院人数......555
Number of Visits Inpatients and Patients Discharged in Medical Institutions
18-12 各地、州、市卫生机构、床位和人员数......556
Number of Health Institutions, Beds and Personnel by Prefecture, Autonomous Prefecture and City
18-13 各地、州、市卫生技术人员数......557
Number of Medical Technical Personnel by Prefecture, Autonomous Prefecture and City
18-14 分市县医院床位和专业卫生技术人员数......558
Hospital Beds and Medical Technical Personnel by City and County Areas
18-15 全区法定报告传染病发病及死亡情况......558
Confirmed Incidence and Death from Infectious Diseases in Xinjiang
18-16 城市前十位疾病死亡原因及构成......559
Death Causes and Percentage of Top10 Diseases in Urban Areas
18-17 安全生产情况......559
Basic Statistics on work Safety

18-18 社会福利事业单位基本情况......560
Basic Statistics on Social Welfare Institutions

18-19 社会福利事业、企业单位数和工作人员数......560
Number of Social Welfare Institutions and Enterprises and Persons Engaged

18-20 社会救济情况......561
Basic Statistics on Social Relief Funds

18-21 工会组织情况......561
Basic Statistics on Trade Unions

18-22 残疾人事业基本情况......562
Basic Information of Person with Disabilities

18-23 历届全区人民代表大会代表人数......564
Number of Deputies to all the Previous People's Congresses of Xinjiang

18-24 历届全区政治协商会议委员人数......564
Number of Deputies to all the Previous People's Political Consultative Conferences of Xinjiang

18-25 律师、公证、调解工作基本情况......565
Basic Statistics on Lawyers, Notarization and Mediation

18-26 调解民间纠纷分类......566
Number of Civil Disputes Mediated by Type

18-27 火灾事故发生情况......566
Basic Statistics on Fire Accidents

18-28 交通事故发生情况......566
Basic Statistics on Traffic Accidents

18-29 公安机关受理查处治安案件情况......567
Cases of Offense Against Public Order Handled by Public Security Organs

18-30 刑事案件中青少年犯罪情况......567
Juvenile Delinquency Among Criminal Cases

主要统计指标解释......568
Explanatory Notes on Main Statistical Indicators

第 十九 篇　企业集团及企业景气指数

CHAPTER 19 ENTERPRISES GROUP AND PROSPERITY INDEX ON ENTERPRISES

19-1 企业集团基本情况......573
Basic Condition of Enterprise Group

19-2 企业集团主要财务指标......574
Main Indicators in Finance of Enterprises Group

19-3 企业家信心指数......578
Entrepreneur Confidence Index

19-4 企业景气指数......580
Prosperity Index on Enterprises

主要统计指标解释......582
Explanatory Notes on Main Statistical Indicators

第 二十 篇　各地州市主要经济指标排序

CHAPTER 20 RANKING OF MAIN ECONOMIC INDICATORS BY REGION OF XINJIANG

20-1 各地、州、市生产总值......587
Gross Domestic Product by Prefecture, Autonomous Prefecture and City

20-2 各地、州、市人口状况......588
Population Status by Prefecture, Autonomous Prefecture and City

20-3 各地、州、市城镇固定资产投资......589
Investmment in Fixed Assets by Prefecture, Autonomous Prefecture City and Town

20-4 各地、州、市农林牧渔业总产值......590
Gross Output Value of Agriculture, Forestry, Animal Husbandry and Fishery by Prefecture, Autonomous Prefecture and City

20-5 各地、州、市主要农产品产量......591
Yield of Major Farm Crops by Prefecture, Autonomous Prefecture and City

20-6 各地、州、市规模以上工业总产值和工业增加值......591
Out put Industrial Ouput Value and Added-Value of Industrial Enterprises above Designated Size by Prefecture, Autonomous Prefecture and City

20-7 各地、州、市规模以上工业企业主要经济效益指标......592
Main Indicators on Economic Benefit of Industrial Enterprises above Designated Size By Prefecture, Autonomous Prefecture and City

20-8 各地、州、市主要工业产品产量......594
Output of Major Industrial Products by Prefecture, Autonomous Prefecture and City

20-9 各地、州、市社会消费品零售总额......596
Total Retail Sales of Consumer Goods by Prefecture, Autonomous Prefecture and City

20-10 各地、州、市海关进出口总额......597
Total Value of Imports and Exports by Prefecture, Autonomous Prefecture and City

20-11 各地、州、市在岗职工工资总额和平均工资......597
Total Wages of Employed Staff and Workers and Average Wage by Prefecture, Autonomous Prefecture and City

20-12 各地、州、市地方财政一般预算收支......598
The General Budgetary Revenue and Expenditures of Local Finance by Prefecture, Autonomous Prefecture and City

20-13 分城镇居民消费价格指数和商品零售价格指数......598
General Retail Price and Consumer Price Index by City/County

20-14 各地、州、市各类学校在校学生数......599
Number of Students Enrollment by Type of School and by Prefecture, Autonomous Prefecture and City

20-15 各地、州、市每万人口医院床位数和医生数......600
Number of Doctors and Hospital Beds Per 10 000 Population by Prefecture, Autonomous Prefecture and City

20-16 各地、州、市卫生技术人员和医生数......600
Medical Technical Personnel and Doctors by Prefecture, Autonomous Prefecture and City

附录： 各省市区主要经济指标排序

APPENDIX: RANKING OF MAIN ECONOMIC INDICATORS BY REGION

各省市区主要经济指标排序......603
Ranking of Main Economic Indicators by Region

特 载

SPECIAL ARTICLE

新疆统计年鉴

XINJIANG STATISTICAL YEARBOOK 2008

新疆维吾尔自治区
2007年国民经济和社会发展
统 计 公 报

2007年，在自治区党委和人民政府的正确领导下，全区各族人民深入贯彻党的十七大和自治区第七次党代会精神，全面落实科学发展观，着力推进国务院32号文件的各项战略部署，深化改革、开拓奋进，取得了国民经济和社会事业和谐发展的新成就。

一、综 合

初步核算，全区实现生产总值（GDP）3523.16亿元（经国家审定通过），比上年增长12.2%。人均生产总值16950元，增长9.9%，以当年平均汇率折算，达到2229美元/人，首次突破2000美元大关。

表 1: 2007 年居民消费价格上涨幅度

单位: %

指 标	2007 年
居民消费价格指数（上年 = 100）	5.5
#食 品	12.6
粮 食	8.5
肉禽及其制品	25.7
油 脂	34.9
蛋	24.8
水产品	9.0
菜	1.4
干鲜瓜果	6.3
烟酒及用品	2.4
衣 着	0.8
家庭设备用品及服务	0.8
医疗保健和个人用品	1.3
交通和通信	0.9
娱乐教育文化用品及服务	0.1
居 住	6.2

在三次产业中，第一产业增加值628.72亿元，增长7.1%；第二产业增加值1647.55亿元，增长12.7%；第三产业增加值1246.89亿元，增长14.3%。三次产业结构为17.8∶46.8∶35.4。

居民消费价格比上年上涨5.5%，其中，食品价格上涨12.6%，居住类价格上涨6.2%。商品零售价格上涨5.1%。农业生产资料价格上涨6.2%。农产品生产价格上涨14.7%。原材料、燃料、动力购进价格上涨3.8%。工业品出厂价格上涨6.3%。固定资产投资价格上涨4.4%。房屋销售价格上涨9.0%。

二、农 业

粮食作物播种面积137.90万公顷（2068.50万亩），比上年下降5.9%；棉花播种面积178.26万公顷（2673.90万亩），增长7.1%；油料播种面积17.64万公顷（264.60万亩），增长16.3%；甜菜播种面积9.4万公顷（141万亩），与上年基本持平。

全年粮食产量867.04万吨，比上年下降3.1%，棉花产量290万吨，增长8.4%；油料产量40.30万吨，增长22.8%；甜菜产量586.93万吨，增长5.7%，水果产量 750.65万吨，增长29.3%，其中，园林水果411.98万吨，增长20.1%。

年末牲畜存栏5023.37万头（只），比上年下降5.9%；全年牲畜出栏4108.28万头（只），增长1.1%；肉类总产量160.58万吨，增长1.5%，其中，猪肉产量31.73万吨，增长10.3%，牛肉产量42.25万吨，增长7.6%，羊肉产量65.02万吨，下降2.9%；牛奶产量196.23万吨，增长9.1%；水产品产量8.89万吨，增长5.1%。

年末农业机械总动力1274.74万千瓦，比上年增长7.1%。拥有大中型拖拉机15.30万台，增长18.4%，小型拖拉机36.38万台，增长1.5%。化肥施用量（折纯）131.53万吨，增长11.4%。新增有效灌溉面积13.93万公顷（208.95万亩），增长14.3%。

三、工业和建筑业

工业增加值1405.11亿元，比上年增长14.1%。其中，规模以上工业增加值1396.68亿元，增长15.2%。分轻重工业看，轻工业增加值125.38亿元，增长15.5%；重工业增加值1271.30亿元，增长15.2%。

表2：2007年主要工业产品产量

产品名称	单 位	绝对数	比上年增长%
原 煤	万吨	5018.64	11.1
原 油	万吨	2604.31	5.2
原油加工量	万吨	1705.45	5.5
天然气	亿立方米	210.33	28.1
发电量	亿千瓦小时	416.87	16.7
粗 钢	万吨	447.24	13.5
钢 材	万吨	470.94	14.5
生 铁	万吨	394.97	21.9
水 泥	万吨	1536.77	15.2
纱	万吨	40.89	14.4
成品糖	万吨	64.94	20.7
化肥(折100%)	万吨	138.53	7.3
变压器	万千伏安	1781.28	34.2
乙 烯	万吨	23.92	-3.2
机制纸及纸板	万吨	25.23	-14.6
罐 头	万吨	63.74	17.3

在规模以上工业中，石油和天然气开采业增加值897.63亿元，增长12.4%；石油加工及炼焦业增加值49.70亿元，增长19.2%；电力、热力的生产和供应业增加值72.99亿元，增长15.8%；黑色金属冶炼及压延加工业增加值46.92亿元，增长18.6%；化学原料及化学制品制造业增加值41.07亿元，增长11.2%；纺织业增加值33.85亿元，增长20.2%。

规模以上工业企业销售产值3277.99亿元，比上年增长23.7%，工业产品销售率99.4%，增长0.6个百分点。出口交货值61.59亿元，增长74.1%。实现利润691.57亿元，增长18.1%。

具有建筑业资质等级的总承包和专业承包建筑企业完成建筑业总产值454.10亿元，扣除物价上涨因素，比上年实际增长10.0%。完成房屋建筑施工面积3552.36万平方米，增长22.9%，其中，新开工面积2421.17万平方米，增长30.5%，竣工面积1849.64万平方米，增长12.4%。

四、固定资产投资

全社会固定资产投资总额1850.84亿元，比上年增长18.1%。其中，城镇固定资产投资1659.19亿元，增长17.0%；农村固定资产投资191.65亿元，增长28.6%。

第一产业投资147.64亿元，增长11.5%；第二产业投资953.15亿元，增长36.1%，其中，工业投资931.35亿元，增长36.6%；第三产业投资750.05亿元，增长2.2%。三次产业的投资结构为8.0∶51.5∶40.5。

房地产开发投资168.32亿元，比上年增长39.2%。房屋施工面积2053.76万平方米，增长31.0%。竣工面积890.55万平方米，增长31.1%。商品房销售面积1144.34万平方米，增长28.2%，销售额238.15亿元，增长43.6%。商品房空置面积289.22万平方米，下降28.8%。

五、批发零售业和住宿餐饮业

社会消费品零售总额847.70亿元，比上年增长16.5%，增幅创1995年以来新高。

分地域看，城市消费品零售额599.80亿元，增长17.8%，农村消费品零售额247.90亿元，增长13.5%。分行业看，批发零售业零售额678.10亿元，增长17.4%；住宿餐饮业零售额129.02亿元，增长16.5%；其他行业零售额40.58亿元，增长3.9%。

在限额以上批发零售业零售额中，食品、饮料、烟酒类零售增长20.5%，服装鞋帽、针、纺织品类增长34.8%，汽车类零售增长35.1%，石油及制品类零售增长18.7%，家用电器及音像器材类零售增长27.8%，金银珠宝类零售增长71.4%。

六、对外经济

货物进出口总额137.16亿美元，比上年增长50.7%。其中，出口额115.03亿美元，增长61.1%，进口额22.13亿美元，增长12.7%。

使用外商直接投资额1.25亿美元，增长20.4%。实际完成对外承包工程营业额3.66亿美元，增长2.4倍。

表 3： 2007 年货物进出口总额及增速

单位：亿美元

指　标	绝对数	比上年增长%
货物进出口总额	137.16	50.7
出口额	115.03	61.1
#一般贸易	29.40	85.1
加工贸易	3.67	35.6
边境小额贸易	80.69	54.6
#机电产品	20.27	74.4
高新技术产品	1.06	2.2 倍
进口额	22.13	12.7
#一般贸易	7.54	21.8
加工贸易	0.29	-38.8
边境小额贸易	13.48	6.6
#机电产品	3.74	54.3
高新技术产品	0.99	83.1

七、交通、邮电和旅游

各种运输方式累计完成货物运输周转量1264.31亿吨公里，增长10.6%，其中，铁路运输678.53亿吨公里，增长4.9%；公路运输468.80亿吨公里，增长10.1%；民航运输0.91亿吨公里，增长1.8%；管道运输116.07亿吨公里，增长66.7%。

旅客运输周转量548.10亿人公里，增长10.0%。其中，铁路144.46亿人公里，增长4.0%；公路326.70亿人公里，增长11.8%；民航76.94亿人公里，增长14.3%。

年末全区民用汽车保有量81.77万辆（包括三轮车和低速货车），比上年增长14.0%，其中，私人汽车保有量43.68万量，增长19.5%。私人轿车保有量19.26万辆。

完成邮政电信业务总量303.65亿元，比上年增长32.6%。其中，邮政业务总量10.05亿元，增长6.7%；电信业务总量293.60亿元，增长33.7%。年末电话交换机总容量517.50万门，下降10.0%。固定电话用户678.10万户，下降4.1%；移动电话用户808.30万户，增长20.4%；互联网用户157.80万户，增长27.6%。电话普及率72.0部/百人，增长7.1%，其中，固定电话普及率33.4部/百人，下降3.2%；移动电话普及率38.6部/百人，增长18.0%。

年末，全区共有星级宾馆432家，其中，五星级宾馆8家。各类旅行社426家，其中，国际旅行社51家，国内旅行社375家。接待国际旅游入境人数43.84万人次，增长21.0%。国际旅游外汇收入1.62亿美元，增长26.5%。接待国内旅游者2126万人次，增长28.0%，国内旅游收入192.92亿元，增长29.4%。

八、财政、金融和保险业

全口径财政收入640亿元，比上年增长32.2%。地方财政收入369亿元，增长39.1%。地方财政一般预算收入286亿元，增长30.1%，其中，各项税收收入221亿元，增长26.4%。地方财政支出875亿元，增长20.1%。地方财政一般预算支出795亿元，增长17.3%。

年末全区金融机构人民币各项存款余额4614.62亿元，比上年增长14.2%，其中，企业存款余额1452.25亿元，增长31.3%，城乡居民储蓄存款余额2054.91亿元，增长0.9%。金融机构人民币各项贷款余额2685.00亿元，增长11.3%，其中，个人消费贷款余额194.60亿元，增长12.2%。

截至年末全区累计发行A股30只，H股2只。本年新发行A股6只（包括增发、可转债及非公开发行股票），募集66.50亿元人民币。新发行H股1只，募集46.30亿港元。上市公司数量位居西北第1位，全国第16位。

保费收入105.62亿元，比上年增长23.7%，其中，寿险收入58.84亿元，健康险和意外伤害险收入12.11亿元，财产险收入34.67亿元。支付各类保险赔款及给付37.42亿元，其中，寿险给付13.81亿元，健康险和意外伤害险赔款及给付4.83亿元，财产险赔款18.78亿元。

九、教育和科学技术

本专科招生6.55万人，在校生21.64万人，其中，少数民族在校生8.08万人，毕业生4.61万人。研究生招生3491人，在校研究生9623人，其中，少数民族研究生1185人，毕业生2244人。

各类中等职业教育招生9.71万人，在校生19.31万人，其中，少数民族在校生8.28万人，毕业生3.71万人。

普通高中招生14.64万人，在校生41.35万人，毕业生12.71万人。初中招生36.36万人，在校生111.56万人，毕业生38.84万人。普通小学招生34.01万人，在校学生205.89万人，毕业生36.19万人。

特殊教育招生1158人，在校学生6396人，毕业生716人。

幼儿园招生25.89万人，在园幼儿36.21万人。

“两基”人口覆盖率99.8%。小学学龄儿童入学率99.3%，初中阶段适龄少年入学率93.9%。初中毕业升入普通高中升学率62.7%。

安排自治区级各类科技计划项目771项。承担国家级各类科技计划项目（课题）249项。县以上部门属研究与技术开发机构116个，自治区科技成果转化基地31个，高新技术园区7个，自治区高新技术企业166家，生产力促进中心22个，国家级创新型试点企业5家。共取得省部级以上科技成果220项。受理专利申请2270项，获得专利授权1534项。签订技术合同3049项，技术合同成交额7.17亿元。

十、文化和体育

年末全区共有文化馆、群众艺术馆109个，公共图书馆94个，博物馆32个，广播电台6座，电视台9座，广播电视台31座，中短波广播发射台和转播台47座，电视发射及转播台934座。广播综合人口覆盖率93.5%，电视综合人口覆盖率93.5%，有线电视用户162.04万户，有线数字电视用户17.67万户。拍摄故事片1部，译制少数民族语故事片157部。出版各类图书8239万册、音像制品350余种、电子出版物25种。年末全区共有档案馆114个，已开放各类档案51.61万卷（件）。

全区运动健儿在国际、国内大赛中共取得44个第一名、49个第二名和45个第三名。其中，在国际大赛中荣获3个第三名。

十一、安全生产

据自治区安全生产监督部门统计，全区共发生各类伤亡事故13114起，比上年减少9.8%；死亡2632人，减少16.3%；受伤7628人，减少14.9%；直接经济损失6005.68万元，减少21.3%。其中，发生一次死亡3-9人事故63起，减少6.0%；死亡人数245人，减少1.6%，未发生一次死亡10人以上的重特大事故。

全区亿元GDP生产安全事故死亡0.77人，比上年下降23.8%；工矿商贸企业就业人员十万人生产安全事故死亡8.64人，下降14.4%；道路交通万车死亡11.0人，下降22.5%；煤矿百万吨死亡2.71人，下降5.6%。

十二、人口与人民生活

年末全区总人口2095.19万人，比上年增长2.2%。其中，城镇人口820.27万人，乡村人口1274.92万人，城镇化率为39.2%。男性人口1072.53万人，女性人口1022.66万人，性别比为51.2∶48.8。出生人口35.18万人，出生率16.79‰；死亡人口10.50万人，死亡率5.01‰；自然增长率11.78‰。

城镇居民人均可支配收入10313.44元，扣除物价上涨因素，比上年实际增长11.2%。农村居民人均纯收入3182.97元，实际增长10.1%。城镇居民家庭恩格尔系数35.1%，农村居民家庭恩格尔系数39.9%。

十三、劳动就业和社会保险

年末全区就业人员830.42万人，比上年末增加18.67万人。其中，城镇就业人员375.59万人，净增加5.49万人。通过各种途径实现城镇就业再就业43.62万人。城镇登记失业率为3.9%。

据劳动和社会保障部门统计，全区参加城镇失业保险人数151.55万人，比上年末增加6.28万人。参加基本养老保险205万人，增加13.03万人，其中，参保职工156.89万人，增加10.79万人；参保离退休人员48.10万人，增加2.23万人。参加城镇居民基本医疗保险人数244.78万人，增加17.63万人。参加工伤保险人数127万人，增加24.6万人。参加生育保险人数150万人，增加14.1万人。

城镇居民中有61.50万人得到政府最低生活保障救济。全区共有2.26万人得到国家抚恤和优抚补助。年末各类收养性社会福利单位拥有床位1.39万张，收养各类人员1.14万人。销售社会福利彩票13.45亿元，筹集社会福利资金4.7亿元。

开展新型农村合作医疗试点工作的县（市）87个，比上年增长64.2%；覆盖农牧业人口973.99万人，增长53.3%；实际参加农村合作医疗的农牧民847.25万人，增长47.6%。

十四、资源与环境

新增建设用地6126.23公顷（9.19万亩），其中，农用地转为建设用地3003.74公顷（4.51万亩），农用地中耕地963.18公顷（1.44万亩）；未利用土地3122.49公顷（4.68万亩）。

非油气矿产勘查新发现矿产地22处，其中，煤矿9处，铁矿2处，金矿3处，铜矿3处，铅锌矿2处，钼矿1处，石墨矿2处；煤、铁、镍、铅锌、钠硝石等矿产勘查取得重要进展。

削减废气污染物二氧化硫排放量0.42万吨，削减废水污染物化学需氧量排放量2.42万吨。

在监测的20个城市中，有8个城市空气质量达到国家Ⅱ级标准，6个城市达到Ⅲ级标准，6个城市超过Ⅲ级标准，全区城市空气质量好于Ⅱ级的优良天数占83.8%，比上年提高0.6个百分点。首府乌鲁木齐市空气质量好于Ⅱ级的优良天数占69.0%，比上年提高1.6个百分点。

在监测的57条河流的144个断面中，Ⅰ～Ⅲ类优良水质断面占72.2%，Ⅳ～Ⅴ类轻、中度污染水质断面占24.3%，超过Ⅴ类的重度污染水质断面占3.5%；湖库水质达标率为38.9%；城市集中式饮用水源地水质达标率为85.3%。

全区已建立各类自然保护区34个，保护区总面积22.58万平方公里，占全区国土面积的13.6%。

注：1、新疆生产总值、各产业增加值及农林牧渔业总产值指标绝对数按现价计算，增长速度按可比价计算。

2、农业部分指标2006年基数根据农业普查结果作了调整。

3、规模以上工业是指年主营业务收入500万元以上的工业企业。

4、2003年以后社会消费品零售总额口径有所调整。

Statistical Communique on the 2007 National Economic & Social Development of the Xinjiang Uygur Autonomous Region

In2007,under the correct leadership of the Autonomous Region Party Committee and the People's Government, the people in different nationalities of the Autonomous Region followed the guidance of the 17th national people's congress of CPC and the 7th Xinjiang congress of CPC sprit, fulfilled the scientific concept of development strategy in full swing, focus on promoting the state council document NO.32 of the strategies deployment, deepening reform, opening up, and march to the national economy and social undertakings in the harmonious development of the new achievements.

I. General Outlook

According to the Preliminary statistics, the gross domestic product (GDP) of Xinjiang was 352.316 billion yuan (passed through the co-census of the National Bureau of Statistics of China), up by 12.2 percent over the previous year. The permanent-population-based per-capita GDP reached 16950 yuan, up by 9.9 percent over the previous year, equivalent to US$2229 at current exchange rate.

Table 1: Span of rise and decrease on the consumer price indices

unit: %

Items	2007
Consumer price index	5.5
#Food	12.6
Grain	8.5
Meal poultry and processed products	25.7
Oil and Fat	34.9
Eggs	24.8
Aquatic products	9.0
Vegetables	1.4
Dried and Fresh Melons and Fruits	6.3
Articles for Smoking and Drinking	2.4
Clothing	0.8
Household Facilities, Articles and Services	0.8
Health Care and Personal Articles	1.3
Transportation and Communication	0.9
Recreation, Education and Culture Articles	0.1
Residence	6.2

In the three industries, The value-added of the primary industry was 62.872 billion yuan, up by 7.1 percent over the previous year. The value-added of the secondary industry was 164.755 billion yuan, up by 12.7percent over the previous year. The value-added of the tertiary industry was 124.689 billion yuan, up by 14.3 percent over the previous year. The composition of three industries was 17.8:46.8:35.4.

The total consumer price index of the year was up by 5.5 percent over the previous year, of which, the price of food was up by 12.6 percent, the price of the residence was up by 6.2 percent. Retail price indices was up by 5.1 percent. the price index of agriculture products was by 6.2 percent. Index of producers' price for farm products was up by 14.7 percent。 Index of purchasing price of raw material, fuels and power was up by 3.8 percent, The total Ex-Factory price index of industrial product of the year was up by 6.3 percent, Price index of investment in fixed asset was up by 4.4 percent. Selling price index of house was up by 9.0 percent.

II. Agriculture

The planting area of grain was 1.3790 million hectares (20.6850 million acres), down by 5.9 percent over the previous year; The planting area of cotton was 1.7826 million hectares (26.7390 million acres), up by 7.1 percent; The planting area of oil bearing was 176.4 thousand hectares (2.646 million acres), up by 16.3 percent; The planting area of sugar was 94.0 thousand hectares (1.41 million acres), and basically the same as the previous year.

The total output of grain in 2007 was 867.04 ten thousand tons, down by 3.1 percent over the previous year; The output of cotton was 290 ten thousand tons, up by 8.4 percent over the previous year; The output of oil-bearing crops was 403.0 thousand tons, an increase of 22.8 percentage points; The output of beetroot was 586.93 ten thousand tons, an increase of 5.7 percentage points over the previous year; The output of fruit was 750.65 ten thousand tons, an increase of 29.3 percentage points, of which, the output of garden fruit was 411.98 ten thousand, an increase of 20.1 percentage points.

The year-end domesticated animals in stock numbered 50.2337 million heads, down by 5.9 percent over the previous year ;the domesticated animal out of stock 41.0828 million heads, up by 1.1 percent; the total output of meat reached 1.6058 million tons, up by 1.5 percent; of which, the output of pork 31.73 ten thousand tons, up by 10.3 percent, the output of poultry 42.25 ten thousand tons, up by 7.6 percent; the output of mutton 65.02 ten thousand, down by 2.9 percent, the output of milk 1.9623 million tons, up by 9.1 percent; the output of aquatic product reached 8.89 ten thousand tons, up by 5.1 percent.

Total agricultural machinery power was 12.7474 million kilowatt, up by 7.1 percent over the previous year. There were 15.30 ten thousand large and medium-size tractors, up by 18.4 percent; and 36.38 ten thousand small-size tractors, up by 1.5 percent. The consumption of chemical fertilizer was 131.53 ten thousand tons(100 percent equivalent), up by 11.4 percent. Over 13.93 ten thousand hectares (2.0895 million acres equivalent) of land were converted into farmland with effective irrigation system, up by 14.3 percent.

III. Industry and Construction

The total value-added of the industrial sector was 140.511 billion yuan, up by 14.1 percentage points over the previous year. Of which, the added value of industrial enterprises above designated size was 139.668 billion yuan, up by 15.2 percent. The added value of light industry was 12.538 billion yuan, up by 15.5 percentage points; the added value of heavy industry was 127.130 billion yuan, up by 15.2 percentage points.

Among the industrial enterprises above designated size, the added value of the extraction of petroleum and natural gas was 89.763 billion yuan, up by 12.4 percent; the added value of the processing of petroleum, coking was 4.970 billion yuan, up by 19.2 percent; the added value of production and supply of electric power and heat power was 7.299 billion yuan, up by 15.8 percent; the added value of smelting and pressing of ferrous metals was 4.692 billion yuan, up by 18.6 percent; the added value of the manufacture of raw chemical materials and chemical products was 4.107 billion yuan, up by 11.2 percent; the added value of the manufacture of textile was 3.385 billion yuan, up by 20.2 percent.

The sales of industrial enterprises above designated size of the output value was 327.799 billion yuan,up by 23.7 percent .The proportion of industrial products sold was 99.4 percent, an increase of 0.6 percentage points. The value of delivered exported goods creat by industrial enterprises above designated size was 6.159 billion yuan, up by 74.1 percent. The profits were achieved reached to 69.157 billion yuan, up by 18.1 percent.

Total output value of all general construction contractors and professional contractors which possess qualification grades was 45.410 billion yuan, up by 10.0 percent; floor space under construction was 35.5236 million sq.m, up by 22.9 percent, of which, floor space under construction was 24.2117 million sq.m, up by 30.5 percent, floor space completed was 18.4964 million sq.m, up by 12.4 percent.

Table2: Output of Major Industrial Products 2007

Item	Unit	Output	Increase over 2006(%)
Coal	10000 tons	5018.64	11.1
Crude oil	10000 tons	2604.31	5.2
Processed oil	10000 tons	1705.45	5.5
Natural gas	100 million cubic meters	210.33	28.1
Electricity	100million kilowatt-hours	416.87	16.7
Crude steel	10000 tons	447.24	13.5
Rolled steel	10000 tons	470.94	14.5
Pig Iron	10000tons	394.97	21.9
Cement	10000 tons	1536.77	15.2
Yarn	10000 tons	40.89	14.4
Machine-made sugar	10000 tons	64.94	20.7
Chemical fertilizers(100 percent equivalent)	10000 tons	138.53	7.3
Transformer	10000 kilovolt-amper	1781.28	34.2
Ethylene	10000 tons	23.92	-3.2
Machine-made paper and paperbord	10000 tons	25.23	-14.6
Can	10000 tons	63.74	17.3

IV. Investment in Fixed Asset

The completed investment in fixed assets in 2007 was 185.084 billion yuan, up by 18.1 percent over the previous year. Of the total investment, that in urban areas was 165.919 billion yuan, up by 17.0 percent; and that in rural areas was 19.165 billion yuan, up by 28.6 percent.

The investment in the primary industry was 14.764 billion yuan, up by 11.5 percent; The investment in the secondary industry was 93.135 billion yuan, up by 36.6 percent, The third industry investment was 75.005 billion yuan, up by 2.2 percent. The composition of three industries was 8.0:51.5:40.5.

The investment in real estate development was 16.832 billion yuan, up by 39.2 percent over the previous year. The floor space of buildings under construction was 20.5376 million square meters, up by 31.0 percent. The floor space of building completed was 8.9055 million square meters, up by 31.1 percent. The total sales area of commercial buildings for the whole year reached 11.4434 million square meters, up by 28.2 percent. The total sales of commercial building was 23.815 billion yuan, up by 43.6percent. The vacancy area of commercial buildings was 2.8932 million square meters, down by 28.8 percent.

V. Wholesale and Retail Trades & Hotels and Catering Service

In 2007, the total retail sales of consumer goods reached 84.77 billion yuan, up by 16.5 percent over the previous year, or creat a new high since 1995.

In terms of different areas, the retail sales of consumer goods in urban areas reached 59.980 billion yuan, up by 17.8 percent; and the retail sales of consumer goods in rural areas reached 24.790 billion yuan, up by 13.5 percent. In terms of different sectors, the sales of the wholesale and retail trade reached 67.810 billion yuan, up by 17.4 percent; the sales of the accommodation and catering service was 12.902 billion yuan, up by 16.5 percent; and the sales of others were 4.058 billion yuan, up by 3.9 percent.

Of the retail sales created by wholesale and retail enterprises above designated size, the retail sales of food, beverage, tobacco and alcoholic drinks grew 20.5 percent, that of clothing grew 34.8 percent, that of automobiles grew 35.1 percent, that of petroleum and related products grew 18.7 percent, that of household appliance as well as audiovisual equipment grew 27.8 percent and that of jewelries grew 71.4 percent.

VI. Foreign Economic Cooperation

The total value of import and export in 2007 reached US$ 13.716 billion, up by 50.7 percent over the previous year. Of which, the value of export was US$ 11.503 billion, up by 61.1 percent; and the value of import was US$ 2.213 billion, up by 12.7 percent.

Table3: Total Value of Imports and Exports and Growth Rates

unit: US$ 100 million

Item	2007	Increase over 2006(%)
Total value of imports and exports	137.16	50.7
Total exports	115.03	61.1
#Ordinary trade	29.40	85.1
Processing trade	3.67	35.6
Frontier small trade	80.69	54.6
#mechanical and electrical products	20.27	74.4
New and high-tech products	1.06	2.2times
Total imports	22.13	12.7
# Ordinary trade	7.54	21.8
Processing trade	0.29	-38.8
Frontier small trade	13.48	6.6
#mechanical and electrical products	3.74	54.3
New and high-tech products	0.99	83.1

Foreign directly investment actually utilized this year stood at US$ 125 million, up by 20.4 percent; the contracted value of overseas engineering projects was US$ 366 million, up by 2.4 times.

VII. Transportation, Postal & Telecommunication and Tourism

The total freight turnover reached 126.431 billion ton-kilometers in 2007, up by 10.6 percent over the previous year. Of the total, the freight turnover by railways was 67.853 billion ton-kilometers, up by 4.9 percent; that by highways 46.880 billion ton-meters, up by 10.1 percent; that by civil aviation 91 million ton-kilometers, up by 1.8 percent; that by pipelines 11.607 billion ton-kilometers, up by 66.7 percent.

Total passenger traffic by various means reached 54.810 billion passenger-kilometers, up by 10.0 percent. Of which, passenger traffic by railways was 14.446 billion passenger-kilometers, up by 4.0 percent; that by highways 32.670 billion passenger-kilometers, up by 11.8 percent; that by civil aviation 7.694 billion passenger-kilometers, up by 14.3 percent.

At the end of the year, there were 81.77 ten thousand civilian automobiles, up by 14.0 percent over the end of the previous year, of which, there were 43.68 ten thousand private automobiles, up by 19.5 percent. 19.26 ten thousand were sedans.

The total volume of post and telecommunication was 30.365 billion yuan, up by 32.6 percent over the previous year. Of which, the volume of post stood at 1005 million yuan, up by 6.7 percent .the volume of telecommunication stood at 29.360 billion yuan, up by 33.7 percent; By the end of 2007, The capacity of office exchanges reached 5.175 million gates, down by 10.0 percent. the number of fixed telephone subscribers reached 6.781 million, down by 4.1 percent. Number of mobile phone users 8.083 million, up by 20.4 percent. Year-end Internet customer 1.578 million, up by 27.6 percent. Popularization rate of telephone was 72.0 sets per 100 persons, up by 7.1percent. Of which, there were fixed telephone 33.4 sets per 100 persons, down by 3.2 percent; and, there were 38.6 mobile phones per 100 persons, up by 18.0 percent..

In 2007, there were 432 star-rated hotel, of which, there were 8 five-stared-rated hotel. There were 426 travel agencies, of which, there were 51 international travel agencies, domestic travel agencies were 375.overseas visitor arrivals to Xinjiang numbered 438.4 thousand, up by 21.0 percent over the previous year; Foreign exchange earnings from international tourism stood at US$ 162 million, up by 26.5 percent. Domestic visitor arrivals to Xinjiang numbered 2126 ten thousand, up by 28.0 percent over the previous year; incomes from domestic tourists were 19.292 billion yuan, up by 29.4 percent.

VIII. Finance, Banking and Insurance

The overall-caliber financial revenue stood at 64.0 billion yuan, up by 32.2 percent over the previous year. Local government revenue was 36.90 billion yuan, up by 39.1 percent. the general budgetary revenue was 28.6 billion yuan, up by 30.1 percent. Of which, total taxes were 22.1 billion yuan, up by 26.4 percent over the previous year. Local government expenditure reached 87.5 billion yuan, up by 20.1 percent, the general budgetary expenditure was 79.5 billion yuan, up by 17.3 percent.

By the end of 2006, savings deposits of all kinds in financial institutions reached 461.462 billion yuan, up by 14.2 percent over the previous year. Of which, enterprise savings deposits were 145.225 billion yuan, up by 31.3percent; Urban and rural household savings deposits were 205.491 billion yuan,up by 0.9 percent. Loans of all kinds in financial institutions were 268.50 billion yuan, up by 11.3; of which, individual consumption loans were 19.460 billion yuan, up by 12.2 percent.

At the end of 2007,30 A-shares and 2 H-shares were issued.6 A-shares were newly issued, raising 6.650 billion yuan. H-shares were newly issued, raising 4.630 billion yuan. The number of listed companies ranked No.1 in northwest region and ranked No.16 in nation.

The total premium of insurance companies reached 10.562 billion yuan, up by 23.7 percent over the previous year. Of the total, life insurance premium was 5.884 billion yuan, health and casualty insurance premium 1.211 billion yuan, property insurance premium 3.467 billion yuan. The insurance companies paid an indemnity of 3.742 billion yuan, of which, the indemnity against life insurance was 1.381 billion yuan, that against health and accidental injury, 483 million yuan, and that against property was 1.878 billion yuan.

IX. Education and Scientific Technology

By the end of 2007, there were 65.5 thousand new entrants of undergraduate and associate graduate; The enrollment of undergraduates and associate graduates was 216.4 thousand, of which, number of ethnic minority graduates were 80.8 thousand, 46.1 thousand graduates. The enrollment of postgraduate students was 3.491thousand, the enrollment of postgraduate students was 9.623 thousand, of which, number of ethnic minority were 1.185 thousand, 2.244 thousand graduates.

The enrollment of vocational secondary education was97.1 thousand, enrollment were 193.1thousand, of which, number of ethnic minority graduates were 82.8 thousand, and 37.1thousand graduates.

The enrollment of regular senior secondary schools were 146.4 thousand, enrollment were 413.5 thousand, with 127.1 thousand graduates. Students enrolled in junior secondary schools totaled 36.36 ten thousand, enrollment were 111.56 ten thousand, with 388.4 thousand graduates. Regular primary schools had an enrollment of 34.01 ten thousand, enrollment were 2.0589 million, with 361.9 thousand graduates.

There were1.158 thousand students in special education schools, enrollment were 6.396 thousand, with 0.7 thousand graduates.

There were 258.9 thousand children in Kindergartens, enrollment were 362.1 thousand .

The enrollment rate of school-age children reached 99.8 percent, enrollment rate of junior secondary school-age youth was 99.3%, 62.7 percent of junior secondary school graduates continued their study in senior secondary school.

X. Culture and Sports

At the end of 2007, there were 109 culture centers, 94 public libraries, 32 museums and 6 radio broadcasting stations, 9 television stations, 31 broadcasting television stations, and 47 radio transmission stations and relaying stations, 934 television transmission stations and relaying stations. Radio broadcasting coverage rate was 93.5 percent and television broadcasting coverage rate was 93.5 percent. Subscribers to cable television programs reached 1.6204 million. Number of Users of digital TV was 17.67 ten thousand. The Autonomous Region shot 1 feature movie, translated and edited 157 feature movies of minority language; A total of 82.39 million copies of newspapers and 25 copies of magazines of all kinds were issued. There were 114 archives, opening 51.61 ten thousand volumes of file of different types.

Athletes from the Autonomous Region won 44 first, 49 second and 45 third prizes in international and intercontinental matches. Of which, and 3 first prizes in international matches.

XI. Safe production

According to Xinjiang Uygur Autonomous Region Administration of Work Safety statistic, there were 13114 accidents occurred, down 9.8 percent over the previous year.2632 persons were killed in these accident, down by 16.3 percent; 7628 persons were injured in these accident, down by 14.9 percent; the direct economic loss hit 60.0568 million yuan, down by 21.3 percent. of which, there were 63 accidents occurred, down by 6.0 percent;245 persons were killed, down by 1.6 percent.

The 100-million-GDP-based death rate in production safety accidents was 0.77, down by 23.8 percent over the previous year; among every 100000 employees in industrial sector, mines, business and trade sectors, 8.64 persons died, down by 14.4 percent; for every 10000 vehicles, 11.0 persons were killed in road traffic accidents, down by 22.5 percent; for every one million output of coal mines, 2.71 persons were killed, down by 5.6 percent.

XII. Population and People's Living

The year-end population of the Autonomous Region was 20.9519 million, an increase of 2.2 percent over the previous year. Of this total, urban population was 8.2027 million, rural population was 12.7492 million, urbanization rate was 39.2 percent; the male reached 10.7253 million, and the female numbered10.2266 million, sex rate was 51.2:48.8. This year birth persons were 35.18 ten thousand, saw a birth rate of 16.79 per thousand, a death rate of 10.5 per thousand, death rate of 5.01 per thousand, and thus the natural growth rate 11.78 per thousand.

By the end of 2007, the per capital disposable income of urban residents reached 10313.44 yuan, up by 11.2 percent over the previous year; the per capital annual net income of rural households was 3182.97 yuan, up by10.1 percent; Engle coefficient of urban households was 35.1 percent, Engle coefficient of rural households was39.9.

XIII.Employment and Social Security

Number of employed person was 8.3042 million at year-end, an increase of 18.7 ten thousand as compared with the previous year. of which, number of urban employed persons were 3.7559 million, net increase of 5.49 ten thousand. Number of employed persons were 43.62 ten thousand. Registered unemployment rate in urban areas was 3.9 percent.

According to the statistics of department of labor and social securities, a total of 1.5155 million people participated in unemployment insurance programs, or an increase of 6.28 ten thousand as compared with the previous year. 2.05 million people participated in the basic pension programs, or an increase of 13.03 ten thousand people as compared with the previous year. Among them, 1.569 million were employees, an increase of 10.8 ten thousand people;481.0 thousand were retirees, an increase of 2.23 ten thousand people ;The population covered by basic health insurance programs was 2.448 thousand, an increase of 17.63 ten thousand people, 1270 thousand people participated in work injury insurance, an increase of 24.60 ten thousand people, 1500 thousand covered maternity insurance, an increase of 14.1 ten thousand people.

A total 61.50 ten thousand urban residents have been covered by a government system of guaranteeing their minimum standard of living. Social welfare institutions of various types has possessed 13.9 thousand beds and accommodating 11.4 thousand inmates. The Autonomous Region sold 1.345 billion yuan worth of social welfare lottery tickets, raising about 470 million yuan of social welfare funds.

There are 87 countries(cities) which participated in the new rural cooperative medical service,64.2 percent points higher than the previous year, covered total rural population was 9.7399 million, up by 53.3 percentage;8.4725 million people participated in the new rural cooperative medical service, up by 47.6 percent.

XIV. Resources and Environment

Newly construction land were6.126 thousand hectares (91.9 thousand acres). of this total, 3.004 thousand hectares (45.1 thousand acres) of land for farming purpose were changed for the purpose of construction, of which 0.963 thousand hectares (14.4 million acres) were farmland. that of undeveloped land was 3122.49 hectares (0.468million acres).

22 mineral products were founded in non-oil mineral exploration of new mineral, of which, coal mine were 9,iron mine were 2,golden mine were 3,copper mine were 3,lead and zinc mine were 2,prospecting of mineral products made an important progress.

Reduction of pollutant emissions of sulphur dioxide were 0.42 ten thousand tons and pollutant emissions of waste water were 2.42 ten thousand tons.

In the 20 monitored cities, 8 cities had their air quality reach national standard Grade II, 6 cities attained GradeIIIand 6 cities exceeded GradeIII. In the Autonomous Region about 83.8 percent of the year the air quality was better than Grade II, up by 0.6 percent over the previous year. And 69.0 percent of the year in Urmqi the air quality was better than Grade II, up by 1.6 percent over the previous year.

Monitoring of water quality on 144 sections of the 57 rivers showed that good quality water of standard Grade I ~III accounted for 72.2 percent; slightly and moderately polluted water meeting standard Grade IV ~ V accounted for 24.3 percent; heavy polluted water below standard Grade V accounted for 3.5 percent. The lake water quality standard rate was 38.9 percent, urban centralized source of drinking water quality standard rate was 85.3 percent.

The Autonomous Region has established 34 natural reserves, the area of natural reserves totaled 225.8 thousand square kilometers, accounting for 13.6 percent of the surface area of the Autonomous Region.

Note: 1.Figures in absolute value terms on gross domestic product of Xinjiang, value-added of various industries and total output value of Farming, Forestry, Animal husbandry, Fishery were at current prices, whereas growth rate was calculated at comparable prices.

2.part of Figures in agriculture in 2006 were adjusted on the basis of agriculture census.

3.Industry above designated size are those with annual revenue from principal business over 5 million yuan.

4. Since 2003, the statistical caliber of total retail sales of consumer goods have been made adjustment.

第一篇 综 合

CHAPTER 1 General Survey

简要说明
Brief Introduction

本篇资料的主要内容及来源

综合篇资料包括行政区划、部门机构数及国民经济和社会发展综合资料四部分。

行政区划划分资料由新疆维吾尔自治区民政厅提供。部门机构数、国民经济和社会发展综合资料由新疆维吾尔自治区统计局综合处根据各篇主要指标加工整理而成。

Main Content and Source of Data

This chapter mainly covers four parts: the data of division of administrative areas, grass-roots units and summary data on the national economy and social development.

Data on division of administrative areas are provided by the Bureau of Civil Affairs of Xinjiang Uygur Autonomous Region。Data on grass-roots units and the national economy and social development are compiled and processed by the Department of Comprehensive statistics of the Xinjiang Bureau of Statistics using relevant

1-1 行 政 区 划

Divisions of Administrative Areas in Xinjiang Uygur Autonomous Region

单位：个 (2007 年) (unit)

区划名称	Region	市、地、州数 Number of Regions				市 数 Cities			市辖区数 Districts under City Administration
		合计 Total	地级市 Cities at Prefecture Level	地区 Administrative Offices	自治州 Autonomous Prefectures	合计 Total	区直辖市 Cities under the Autonomous Region	地州辖市 Cities under the Prefectures	
总　计	**Total**	**14**	**2**	**7**	**5**	**19**	**4**	**15**	**11**
乌鲁木齐市	Urumqi City	1	1						7
克拉玛依市	Karamay City	1	1						4
石河子市	Shihezi City					1	1		
阿拉尔市	Aral City					1	1		
图木舒克市	Tumxuk City					1	1		
五家渠市	Wujiaqu City					1	1		
吐鲁番地区	Turpan Administrative Offices	1		1		1		1	
哈密地区	Hami [Kumul] Administrative Offices	1		1		1		1	
昌吉回族自治州	Changji Hui Autonomous Prefecture	1			1	2		2	
伊犁哈萨克自治州	Ili Kazak Autonomous Prefecture	3		2	1	5		5	
伊犁州直属县(市)	Counties (Cities) Direct Under Ili Prefecture	1			1	2		2	
塔城地区	Tacheng [Tarbagatai] Administrative Offices	1		1		2		2	
阿勒泰地区	Altay Administrative Offices	1		1		1		1	
博尔塔拉自治州	Bortala Mongol Autonomous Prefecture	1			1	1		1	
巴音郭楞自治州	Bayangol Mongol Autonomous Prefecture	1			1	1		1	
阿克苏地区	Aksu Administrative Offices	1		1		1		1	
克孜勒苏自治州	Kizilsu Kirgiz Autonomous Prefecture	1			1	1		1	
喀什地区	Kashgar [Kaxgar] Administrative Offices	1		1		1		1	
和田地区	Hotan Administrative Offices	1		1		1		1	

区划名称	Region	县数 Number of Counties			乡镇数 Number of Townships and Towns				
		合计 Total	县 County	自治县 Autonomous County	合计 Total	街道办事处 Urban Subdistrict Office	镇 Town	乡 Township	民族乡 National Township
总　计	**Total**	**68**	**62**	**6**	**1000**	**147**	**229**	**581**	**43**
乌鲁木齐市	Urumqi City	1	1		72	56	3	13	
克拉玛依市	Karamay City				14	12		2	
石河子市	Shihezi City				7	5	1	1	
阿拉尔市	Aral City				5	4		1	
图木舒克市	Tumxuk City				3	3			
五家渠市	Wujiaqu City								
吐鲁番地区	Turpan Administrative Offices	2	2		28	2	10	15	1
哈密地区	Hami [Kumul] Administrative Offices	2	1	1	42	5	10	24	3
昌吉回族自治州	Changji Hui Autonomous Prefecture	5	4	1	89	12	41	23	13
伊犁哈萨克自治州	Ili Kazak Autonomous Prefecture	19	17	2	241	24	59	141	17
伊犁州直属县(市)	Counties (Cities) Direct Under Ili Prefecture	8	7	1	110	13	19	68	10
塔城地区	Tacheng [Tarbagatai] Administrative Offices	5	4	1	74	8	27	34	5
阿勒泰地区	Altay Administrative Offices	6	6		57	3	13	39	2
博尔塔拉自治州	Bortala Mongol Autonomous Prefecture	2	2		20	4	7	9	
巴音郭楞自治州	Bayangol Mongol Autonomous Prefecture	8	7	1	90	5	23	61	1
阿克苏地区	Aksu Administrative Offices	8	8		88	5	31	50	2
克孜勒苏自治州	Kizilsu Kirgiz Autonomous Prefecture	3	3		39	2	5	31	1
喀什地区	Kashgar [Kaxgar] Administrative Offices	11	10	1	172	4	28	137	3
和田地区	Hotan Administrative Offices	7	7		90	4	11	73	2

1-2 县级以上行政区划

Divisions of Administrative Areas at and above County Level

(2007 年)

<table>
<tr><th colspan="2">地、州、市名称
Name of Administrative Offices, Autonomous Prefectures, Cities</th><th>市 县 (市辖区)名称
Names of Cities and Counties (Districts under Cities)</th></tr>
<tr><td colspan="2">乌鲁木齐市
Urumqi City</td><td>天山区、沙依巴克区、新市区、水磨沟区、头屯河区、达坂城区、米东区、乌鲁木齐县
Tianshan District, Shayibak District, Xinshi District, Shui Mogou District, Tou Tunhe District, Da Bancheng District, Midong District, Urumqi County</td></tr>
<tr><td colspan="2">克拉玛依市
Karamay City</td><td>克拉玛依区、独山子区、白碱滩区、乌尔禾区
Karamay District, Dushanzi District, Bai Jiantan District, Urhe District</td></tr>
<tr><td rowspan="4">自治区直辖县级市
Municpa-lity Country-Level City directly under the Central Govern-ment</td><td>石河子市
Shihezi City</td><td></td></tr>
<tr><td>阿拉尔市
Aral City</td><td></td></tr>
<tr><td>图木舒克市
Tumxuk City</td><td></td></tr>
<tr><td>五家渠市
Wujiaqu City</td><td></td></tr>
<tr><td colspan="2">吐鲁番地区
Turpan Administrative Offices</td><td>吐鲁番市、鄯善县、托克逊县
Turpan City, Shanshan [Piqan] County, Toksun County</td></tr>
<tr><td colspan="2">哈密地区
Hami [Kumul] Administrative Offices</td><td>哈密市、巴里坤哈萨克自治县、伊吾县
Hami [Kumul] City, Barkol Kazak Autonomous County, Yiwu[Araturuk] County</td></tr>
<tr><td colspan="2">昌吉回族自治州
Changji Hui Autonomous Prefecture</td><td>昌吉市、阜康市、呼图壁县、玛纳斯县、奇台县、吉木萨尔县、木垒哈萨克自治县
Changji City, Fukang City, Hutubi County, Manas County, Qitai County, Jimsar County, Mori Kazak Autonomous County</td></tr>
<tr><td rowspan="3">伊犁哈萨克自治州
Ili Kazak Autonomous Prefecture</td><td>伊犁州直属县(市)
Counties (Cities) Direct Under Ili Prefecture</td><td>伊宁市、奎屯市、伊宁县、察布查尔锡伯自治县、霍城县、巩留县、新源县、昭苏县、特克斯县、尼勒克县
Yining [Gulja] City, Kuytun City , Yining [Gulja] County, Qapqal Xibe AutonomousCounty, Huocheng [Korgas] County, Gongliu [Tokkuzlara] County, Xinyuan [Kunes] County, Zhaosu [Mongolkure] County, Tekes County, Nilka County</td></tr>
<tr><td>塔城地区
Tacheng [Tarbagatai] Administrative Offices</td><td>塔城市、乌苏市、额敏县、沙湾县、托里县、裕民县、和布克赛尔蒙古自治县
Tacheng [Qoqek] City, Usu City, Emin [Dorbiljin] County, Shawan County, Toli County, Yumin [Qagantokay] County, Hoboksar Mongol Autonomous County</td></tr>
<tr><td>阿勒泰地区
Altay Administrative Offices</td><td>阿勒泰市、布尔津县、富蕴县、福海县、哈巴河县、青河县、吉木乃县
Altay City, Burqin County, Fuyun [Koktokay] County, Fuhai [Burultokay] County, Habahe [Kaba] County, Qinghe [Qinggil] County, Jeminay county</td></tr>
<tr><td colspan="2">博尔塔拉蒙古自治州
Bortala Mongol Autonomous Prefecture</td><td>博乐市、精河县、温泉县
Bole [Bortala] City, Jinghe [Jing] County, Wenquan [Arxang] County</td></tr>
<tr><td colspan="2">巴音郭楞蒙古自治州
Bayangol Mongol Autonomous Prefecture</td><td>库尔勒市、轮台县、尉犁县、若羌县、且末县、焉耆回族自治县、和静县、和硕县、博湖县
Korla City, Luntai [Bugur] County, Yuli [Lopnur] County, Ruoqiang [Qarkilik] County, Qiemo [Qarqan] County, Yanqi Hui Autonomous County, Hejing County, Bohu [Bagrax] County</td></tr>
<tr><td colspan="2">阿克苏地区
Aksu Administrative Offices</td><td>阿克苏市、温宿县、库车县、沙雅县、新和县、拜城县、乌什县、阿瓦提县、柯坪县
Aksu City, Wensu [Onsu] County, Kuqa County, Xayar County, Xinhe [Toksu] County, Baicheng [Bay] County, Wushi [Uqturpan] County, Awat County, Kalpin County</td></tr>
<tr><td colspan="2">克孜勒苏柯尔克孜自治州
Kizilsu Kirgiz Autonomous Prefecture</td><td>阿图什市、阿克陶县、阿合奇县、乌恰县
Artux City, Akto County, Akqi County, Wuqia [Ulugqat] County</td></tr>
<tr><td colspan="2">喀什地区
Kashgar [Kaxgar] Administrative Offices</td><td>喀什市、疏附县、疏勒县、英吉沙县、泽普县、莎车县、叶城县、麦盖提县、岳普湖县、伽师县、巴楚县、塔什库尔干塔吉克自治县
Kashgar [Kaxgar] City, Shufu County, Shule County, Yengisar County, Zepu [Poskam] County, Shache [Yarkant] County, Yecheng [Kagilik] County, Makit County, Yopurga County, Jiashi [Payzawat] County, Bachu [Maralbexi] County, Taxkorgan Tajik Aotonomous County</td></tr>
<tr><td colspan="2">和田地区
Hotan Administrative Offices</td><td>和田市、和田县、墨玉县、皮山县、洛浦县、策勒县、于田县、民丰县
Hotan City, Hotan County, Moyu [Karakax] County, Pishan [Guma] County, Lop County, Qira County, Yutian [Keriya] County, Minfeng [niya] County</td></tr>
</table>

1-3 各部门机构数
Grass-roots Units in Various Sectors

单位：个 (unit)

部门	Sector	机构数 Grass-roots Units 2006	2007	2007年比上年增长(%) Increase Rate % in 2007 over 2006
农村基层单位	**Rural Grass-root Units**			
基层组织	Grass-roots Organization			
乡政府	Township Governments	626	798	27.5
镇政府	Town Governments	170	172	1.2
村民委员会	Village Committees	8965	8965	持平
乡村户数(万户)	Numbers of Rural Households (10 000 household)	229.00	233.37	1.9
乡镇企业	Township Enterprises	368724	377385	2.3
国营农场	State-owned Farms	485	478	-1.4
规模以上工业企业	**Industrial Enterprises above Designated Size**	**1481**	**1575**	**6.3**
内资企业	Domestic Funded Enterprises	1421	1507	6.1
#国有企业	State-owned Enterprises	302	147	-51.3
集体企业	Collective-owned Enterprises	31	30	-3.2
股份合作企业	Cooperative Enterprises	6	8	33.3
联营企业	Joint Ownership Enterprises	6	6	持平
有限责任公司	Limited Liability Corporations	613	701	14.4
股份有限公司	Share Holding Corporation Ltd.	53	54	1.9
私营企业	Private Enterprises	408	560	37.3
港澳台商投资企业	Enterprises with Funds from Hong Kong, Macao and Taiwan	21	23	9.5
外商投资企业	Foreign Funded Enterprises	39	45	15.4
建筑业企业	**Construction Enterprises and Units**	**914**	**967**	**5.8**
#国有企业	State-owned Enterprises	102	103	1.0
城镇集体企业	Urban Collective-owned Enterprises	39	35	-10.3
邮电业	**Postal and Telecommunication Services**			
邮政局营业网点	Business Outlets of Post-office	1444	1418	-1.8
卫生事业	**Health Care**	**8175**	**7465**	**-8.7**
#医院、卫生院	Hospitals and Health Centers	1560	1629	4.4
疗养院	Sanatoriums	6	7	16.7
门诊部	Clinics	220	240	9.1
专科防治所、站	Specialized Prevention & Treatment Stations	7	7	持平
疾病防控中心	Epidemic Prevention Stations	211	214	1.4
妇幼保健所、站	Maternity and Child Care Centers	92	87	-5.4
社会福利事业	**Social Welfare Establishments**			
社会福利事业单位	Social Welfare Institutions	928	866	
#收养性福利事业单位	Adopting Social Welfare Institutions	471	498	
社会福利企业	Social Welfare Enterprises	130	109	
社区服务中心	Community Services Units	128	50	

1-3 续表 Continued

部门	Sector	机构数 Grass-roots Units 2006	2007	2007年比上年增长(%) Increase Rate % in 2007 Over 2006
教育事业(所)	**Education (unit)**			
普通高等学校	Regular Institutions of Higher Education	31	32	3.2
中等学校	Secondary Schools	2101	2040	-2.9
#中等专业学校	Specialized Schools	67	74	10.4
普通中学	Regular Secondary Schools	1891	1830	-3.2
职业中学	Vocational Secondary Schools	84	75	-10.7
小学	Primary Schools	4815	4589	-4.7
盲聋哑学校	Special Schools	9	9	持平
艺术事业	**Art Institutions**	**161**	**150**	**-6.8**
艺术表演团体	Art Performance Troupes	118	120	1.7
艺术表演场所	Art Show Centers	43	30	-30.2
#剧场、影剧院	· Theaters	43	29	-32.6
公共图书馆	**Public Libraries**	**98**	**94**	**-4.1**
群众文化事业	**Mass Cultural Establishments**	**1221**	**1160**	**-5.0**
群众艺术馆	Mass Art Centers	15	15	0.0
文化馆	Cultural Centers	94	94	0.0
文化站	Cultural Stations	1112	1051	-5.5
#乡镇文化站	Township Cultural Centers	1004	941	-6.3
艺术教育事业	**Arts Education Establishments**	**3**	**3**	**持平**
其他文化事业	**Other Cultural Establishments**	**8**	**17**	**1.1倍**
#艺术创作机构	Art Creation Institutions	2	2	持平
艺术研究机构	Art Research Institutions	2	1	-50.0
文化市场经营单位	**Entertainment Operators**	**10950**	**10385**	**-5.2**
文物事业	**Cultural Relic Establishments**	**117**	**121**	**3.4**
博物馆	Museums	28	32	14.3
文物机构	Cultural Relic Agencies	88	88	持平
文物商店	Cultural Relic Shops	1	1	持平
广播电视台站(座)	**Broadcasting and Television Stations (unit)**			
广播电台	Radio Stations	6	6	持平
电视台	Television Stations	10	9	-10.0
广播电视台	Radio and TV Stations	30	31	3.3
#县级广播电视台	Number of Wire Broadcasting and Television Stations in County Level	24	23	-4.2
金融、保险业	**Banking and Insurance**	**3991**	**4620**	**15.8**
金融机构	Banking System	3578	3493	-2.4
保险机构	Insurance System	413	1127	1.7倍

1-4 平均每天主要社会经济活动
Selected Indicators on Average Daily Social and Economic Activities

指　　标	Item	1978	1990	2000	2006	2007
每天创造的财富	**Daily Production**					
新疆生产总值(万元)	Gross Domestic Product (10 000 yuan)	1070.4	7150.7	37369.9	83424.7	96524.9
第一产业	Primary Industry	382.7	2849.3	7890.4	14465.8	17225.2
第二产业	Secondary Industry	502.7	2274.0	14739.7	39972.6	45138.4
工　业	Industry	396.7	1945.2	11479.5	34000.0	38496.2
建筑业	Construction	106.0	328.8	3260.3	5972.6	6642.2
第三产业	Tertiary Industry	184.9	2027.4	14739.7	28986.3	34161.4
#交通运输仓储和邮政业	Transport, Storage and Post	32.6	411.0	4082.2	4548.0	4857.0
批发和零售业	Wholesale and Retail Trades	56.7	548.0	3013.7	4465.8	5126.0
地方财政一般预算收入(万元)	General Budgetary Revenue in Local Finance (10 000 yuan)	195.6	596.7	2166.4	6012.7	7831.8
地方财政一般预算支出(万元)	General Budgetary Expenditure in Local Finance (10 000 yuan)	466.3	1304.7	5231.6	18588.3	21785.0
粮食(吨)	Grain (ton)	10137.3	18544.9	22153.4	24526.6	23754.5
棉花(吨)	Cotton (ton)	150.7	1284.4	4109.6	7329.6	7945.2
油料(吨)	Oil-bearing Crops (ton)	283.0	1067.4	1647.7	899.2	1104.1
肉类(吨)	Meat (ton)	264.4	834.5	2465.8	4334.5	4399.5
水产品(吨)	Aquatic Products (ton)	15.6	63.6	164.6	231.6	243.5
布(万米)	Cloth (10 000 m)	76.7	82.2	76.9	42.2	43.8
原煤(吨)	Coal (ton)	29561.9	57534.3	76682.1	123795.0	137497.0
发电量(万千瓦小时)	Electricity (10 000 kwh)	580.0	1912.1	5013.2	9784.9	11421.0
原油(吨)	Crude Oil (ton)	9672.6	19041.1	50641.9	67801.2	71351.0
粗钢(吨)	Crude Steel (ton)	231.8	999.7	3005.4	10799.8	12253.1
钢材(吨)	Steel Products (ton)	187.1	780.3	3596.1	11272.6	12902.4
水泥(吨)	Cement (ton)	2141.1	7808.2	24538.9	36561.6	42109.6
每天消费量	**Daily National Consumption**					
最终消费(万元)	Final Consumption Expenditure (10 000 yuan)	757.3	4569.1	20827.4	43313.8	52897.3
居民消费	Resident Consumption	619.5	3318.4	13488.1	23296.1	27766.4
农村居民	Rural Household	331.0	1251.1	4382.8	6928.9	8096.4
城镇居民	Urban Household	288.5	2067.3	9105.3	16367.2	19670.0
政府消费	Government Consumption Expenditure	137.8	1250.7	7339.3	20017.7	25130.9
能源消费量(万吨标准煤)	Energy Consumption (10 000 tons of SCE)		5.4	9.1	16.6	
社会消费品零售总额(万元)	Total Retail Sales of Consumer Goods (10 000 yuan)	599.7	2857.7	10260.3	19933.9	23224.7
每天其他经济活动	**Other Daily Economic Activities**					
资本形成总额(万元)	Gross Capital Formation (10 000 yuan)	504.9	3867.6	16934.9	52949.0	57255.1
固定资产形成	Fixed Capital Formation	363.0	2506.7	17756.8	50020.5	54931.2
存货增加	Increase in Stock	141.9	1360.9	-821.9	2928.5	2324.0
城镇新建住宅面积(万平方米)	Residential Buildings Completed in Urban Areas (10 000 sq.m)		1.1	3.6	4.6	4.6
农民个人新建住宅面积(万平方米)	Private Residential Buildings Completed in Rural Areas (10 000 sq.m)		1.6	1.4	3.9	4.6
货运量(万吨)	Freight Traffic (10 000 tons)	16.6	38.1	90.7	118.1	134.3
客运量(万人)	Passenger Traffic (10 000 persons)	2.6	26.3	63.5	94.4	105.3
邮电业务总量(万元)	Business Volume of Post and Telecommunication Services (10 000 yuan)	13.0	47.6	1295.9	6271.8	8319.2
进出口总额(万美元)	Total Value of Imports and Exports (USD 10 000)	6.4	112.4	620.3	2494.1	3757.9
出口额	Exports	2.6	91.9	329.9	1956.0	3151.5
进口额	Imports	3.9	20.5	290.4	538.1	606.3
实际利用外资额(万美元)	Foreign Capital Actually Used (USD 10 000)		20.9	5.3	28.4	34.2
入境旅游人数(人)	Number of Tourists from Abroad (person)	…	219	702	993	1201
居民新增储蓄额(万元)	Outstanding Amount of Savings Deposit (10 000 yuan)	13.0	977.4	2297.6	6006.9	528.2
每天人口变动和婚姻	**Daily Population Changes and Marriages**					
出　生(人)	Birth (person)	754	839	782	888	953
死　亡(人)	Death (person)	257	330	238	280	284
结　婚(对)	Marriages (couple)		434	445	548	620
离　婚(对)	Divorces (couple)		155	162	211	237

1-5 国民经济和社会发展总量与速度指标

指标	Item	1978
人口与就业	**Population and Employment**	
人口(万人)	**Population (10 000 persons)**	
年末总人口	Population at the Year-end	1233.01
城镇	Urban	321.40
乡村	Rural	911.61
男性	Male	630.18
女性	Female	602.83
就业(万人)	**Employment (10 000 persons)**	
就业人员数	Employment	491.25
#在岗职工人数	Staff and Workers	226.69
城镇登记失业人数	Urban Registeration Unemployment	
宏观经济	**Macro Economy**	
国民经济核算(亿元)	**National Accounting (100 million yuan)**	
新疆生产总值	Gross Domestic Product	39.07
第一产业	Primary Industry	13.97
第二产业	Secondary Industry	18.35
第三产业	Tertiary Industry	6.75
支出法新疆生产总值	Gross Domestic Expenditure	
#最终消费	Total Consumption	27.64
居民消费	Resident Consumption	22.61
政府消费	Public Consumption	5.03
资本形成总额	Total of Capital Formation	18.43
固定资本形成	Fixed Assets	13.25
存货增加	Increase in Stock	5.18
固定资产投资(亿元)	**Investment in Fixed Assets (100 million yuan)**	
全社会固定资产投资总额	Total Investment in Fixed Assets	13.00
城镇	Urban	13.00
#房地产	Real Estate Development	
农村	Rural	
财政(亿元)	**Public Finance (100 million yuan)**	
地方财政一般预算收入	Local Financial Governments Intrabudgetary Ordinary Revenue	7.14
#各项税收	Various Taxes	4.34
地方财政一般预算支出	Local Financial Governments Intrabudgetary Ordinary Expenditures	17.02
#一般公共服务	General Common Service	
教育与科学技术	Operating Expenses for Education and Operating Expenses for Science and Technology	
社会保障和就业	Operating Expenses for Medical Treatment and Sanitation	
环境保护	Operating Expenses for Environmental Conservation	
城乡社区事务	Expenses of Community	
农林水事务	Expenses of Agriculture, Forest and Irrigation	
物价总指数(上年=100)	**Price Indices (preceding year=100)**	
商品零售价格总指数	Retail Price Index	101.4
居民消费价格总指数	Consumer Price Index	101.2
利用外资(万美元)	**Utilization of Foreign Capital (USD 10 000)**	
签订利用外资协议额	Amount of Foreign Capital for Utilization through Signed Contracts or Agreements	
实际利用外资额	Amount of Foreign Capital Actually Utilized	
能源生产与消费(万吨标准煤)	**Production and Consumption of Energy (10 000 tons of SCE)**	
能源生产总量	Total Energy Production	1410.75
能源消费总量	Total Energy Consumption	979.27

注：2000 年及以后城镇人口和乡村人口按“五普”城乡划分口径计算，其余年份按公安年报口径计算。

Principal Aggregate Indicators on National Economic and Social Development and Growth Rates

总量指标 Aggregate Data				速度指标(%) Indices and Growth Rates						
				指数(2007 年比以下各年) Index (2007 as percentuage of the following years)				平均增长速度 Average Annual Growth Rate		
1990	2000	2006	2007	1978	1990	2000	2006	1979-2007	1991-2007	2001-2007
1529.16	1849.41	2050.00	2095.19	169.9	137.0	113.3	102.2	1.8	1.9	1.8
685.96	624.18	777.77	820.27	255.2	119.6	131.4	105.5	3.3	1.1	4.0
843.20	1225.23	1272.23	1274.92	139.9	151.2	104.1	100.2	1.2	2.5	0.6
785.06	957.07	1050.01	1072.53	170.2	136.6	112.1	102.1	1.9	1.9	1.6
744.10	892.34	999.99	1022.66	169.6	137.4	114.6	102.3	1.8	1.9	2.0
617.70	672.50	811.75	830.42	169.0	134.4	123.5	102.3	1.8	1.8	3.1
300.53	255.75	238.95	239.45	105.6	79.7	93.6	100.2	0.2	-1.3	-0.9
9.60	11.00	11.98	11.70		121.9	106.4	97.7		1.2	0.9
261.44	1363.56	3045.26	3523.16	1765.9	508.0	201.0	112.2	10.4	10.0	10.5
104.09	288.18	527.80	628.72	854.0	272.5	148.8	107.1	7.7	6.1	5.8
83.18	537.58	1459.30	1647.55	1547.1	572.6	211.8	112.7	9.9	10.8	11.3
74.17	537.80	1058.16	1246.89	4558.6	724.9	220.1	114.3	14.1	12.4	11.9
166.77	760.19	1584.53	1930.75							
121.12	492.31	853.88	1013.47							
45.65	267.88	730.65	917.28							
141.17	618.12	1778.51	2089.81							
91.50	648.12	1719.96	2004.99							
49.67	-30.00	58.55	84.82							
88.78	610.38	1567.05	1850.84	14237.2	2084.7	303.2	118.1	18.6	19.6	17.2
79.16	556.85	1418.01	1659.19	12763.0	2096.0	298.0	117.0	18.2	19.6	16.9
0.95	57.43	120.88	168.32		17717.9	293.1	139.2		35.6	16.6
9.62	53.53	149.04	191.65		1992.2	358.0	128.6		19.2	20.0
21.78	79.07	219.46	285.86	4003.6	1312.5	361.5	130.3	13.6	16.4	20.2
20.45	64.53	174.54	220.65	5084.1	1079.0	341.9	126.4	14.5	15.0	19.2
47.62	190.95	678.47	795.15	4671.9	1669.8	416.4	117.2	14.2	18.0	22.6
		125.98	148.41				117.8			
		122.06	155.61				127.5			
		75.22	90.93				120.9			
		19.08	21.49				112.6			
		41.58	59.37				142.8			
		69.26	98.43				142.1			
104.1	98.3	101.8	105.1							
105.0	99.4	101.3	105.5							
4463	9212	36439	45679		1023.5	495.9	125.4		14.7	25.7
7629	1923	10366	12484		163.6	649.2	120.4		2.9	30.6
2801.57	5419.77	9528.72								
1924.45	3316.03	6047.27								

Note: The urban and rural population after 2000 is calculated on the 5th National population census and others are calculated on the annals of public security.

1-5 续表 1

指　　标	Item	1978
产　业	**Industry**	
农　业	**Agriculture**	
耕地面积(千公顷)	Cultivated Areas (1 000 hectares)	3184.69
农林牧渔业劳动力(万人)	Labor Force of Farming, Forestry, Animal Husbandry and Fishery (10 000 persons)	256.80
农林牧渔业总产值(亿元)	Gross Output Value of Farming, Forestry, Animal Husbandry and Fishery (100 million yuan)	19.12
主要农产品产量(万吨)	Output of Major Farm Products (10 000 tons)	
粮　食	Grain	370.01
棉　花	Cotton	5.50
油　料	Oil-bearing Crops	10.33
甜　菜	Beet Roots	16.37
水　果	Fruits	13.98
肉　类	Meat	9.65
水产品	Aquatic Products	0.57
工　业	**Industry**	
主要工业产品产量	Output of Major Industrial Products	
纱(万吨)	Yarn (10 000 tons)	2.80
布(亿米)	Cloth (100 million meter)	1.56
绒线(吨)	Knitting Wool (ton)	1239
呢绒(万米)	Woolen Goods (10 000 meter)	189
原盐(万吨)	Crude Salt (10 000 tons)	51.71
机制纸及纸板(万吨)	Machine-Made Paper and Paperboards (10 000 tons)	1.99
成品糖(万吨)	Refined Sugar (10 000 tons)	2.08
原煤(万吨)	Natural Crude Petroleum Coal (10 000 tons)	1079.01
原油(万吨)	Crude Oil (10 000 tons)	353.05
天然气(亿立方米)	Natural Gas (100 million cu.m)	2.51
发电量(亿千瓦小时)	ElectriCity (100 million kwh)	21.17
粗钢(万吨)	Crude Steel (10 000 tons)	8.46
钢材(万吨)	Steel Products (10 000 tons)	6.83
水泥(万吨)	Cement (10 000 tons)	78.15
全部工业总产值(亿元)	Gross industrial Output Value (100 million yuan)	33.91
规模以上工业企业主要经济指标	Principal Financial Indicators of Industrial Enterprises Above Designated Size	
固定资产原值(亿元)	Original Value of Fixed Assets (100 million yuan)	45.92
固定资产净值年平均余额(亿元)	Annual Average Balance of Net Value of Fixed Assets (100 million yuan)	
利润总额(亿元)	Profits (100 million yuan)	4.28
建筑业	**Construction**	
建筑业企业从业人员(万人)	Number of Employed Persons (10 000 persons)	
建筑业总产值(亿元)	Gross Output Value (100 million yuan)	
施工房屋面积(万平方米)	Floor Space of Buildings under Construction (10 000 sq.m)	
竣工房屋面积(万平方米)	Floor Space of Buildings Completed (10 000 sq.m)	
交通运输	**Transportation**	
货运量(万吨)	Freight Traffic (10 000 tons)	6065
铁　路	Railways	923
公　路	Highways	4843
管　道	Pipelines	298
航　空	Civil Aviation	0.12
客运量(万人)	Passenger Traffic Volume (10 000 persons)	941
铁　路	Railways	148
公　路	Highways	786
航　空	Civil Aviation	7

Continued

总量指标 Aggregate Data				速度指标(%) Indices and Growth Rates						
				指数(2007 年比以下各年) Index (2007 as percentage of the following years)				平均增长速度 Average Annual Growth Rate		
1990	2000	2006	2007	1978	1990	2000	2006	1979-2007	1991-2007	2001-2007
3086.89	3416.52	3640.43	3787.28	118.9	122.7	110.9	104.0	0.6	1.2	1.5
250.93	314.45	350.18	354.34	138.0	141.2	112.7	101.2	1.1	2.1	1.7
144.65	487.20	883.54	1063.46	5562.0	735.2	218.3	120.4	14.9	12.5	11.8
676.89	808.60	895.22	867.04	234.3	128.1	107.2	96.9	3.0	1.5	1.0
46.88	150.00	267.53	290.00	5272.7	618.6	193.3	108.4	14.7	11.3	9.9
38.96	60.14	32.82	40.30	390.1	103.4	67.0	122.8	4.8	0.2	-5.6
224.37	292.65	555.53	586.93	3585.4	261.6	200.6	105.7	13.1	5.8	10.5
79.88	151.87	343.14	411.98	2946.9	515.7	271.3	120.1	12.4	10.1	15.3
30.46	90.00	158.21	160.58	1664.0	527.2	178.4	101.5	10.2	10.3	8.6
2.32	6.01	8.45	8.89	1559.6	383.2	147.9	105.2	9.9	8.2	5.8
10.19	33.43	35.73	40.89	1460.4	401.3	122.3	114.4	9.7	8.5	2.9
3.00	2.81	1.54	1.60	102.6	53.3	56.9	103.9	0.1	-3.6	-7.7
2179	1184	799	637	51.4	29.2	53.8	79.7	-2.3	-7.0	-8.5
1230	754	327	368	194.3	29.9	48.8	112.5	2.3	-6.9	-9.7
159.00	31.78	153.21	85.54	165.4	53.8	269.2	55.8	1.8	-3.6	15.2
9.09	17.65	29.53	25.23	1267.8	277.6	142.9	85.4	9.2	6.2	5.2
16.84	30.76	53.79	64.94	3122.1	385.6	211.1	120.7	12.6	8.3	11.3
2100.00	2798.90	4518.52	5018.64	465.1	239.0	179.3	111.1	5.4	5.3	8.7
695.00	1848.43	2474.74	2604.31	737.7	374.7	140.9	105.2	7.1	8.1	5.0
5.02	35.39	164.21	210.33	8379.7	4189.8	594.3	128.1	16.5	24.6	29.0
69.79	182.98	357.15	416.87	1969.2	597.3	227.8	116.7	10.8	11.1	12.5
36.49	109.70	394.19	447.24	5286.5	1225.7	407.7	113.5	14.7	15.9	22.2
28.48	131.26	411.45	470.94	6895.2	1653.6	358.8	114.5	15.7	17.9	20.0
285.00	895.67	1334.50	1536.77	1966.4	539.2	171.6	115.2	10.8	10.4	8.0
219.92	1061.29	2894.88	3471.51	2322.8	610.8	232.2	112.9	11.5	11.2	12.8
233.86	1387.56	2860.59	3592.91	7824.3	1536.4	258.9	125.6	16.2	17.4	14.6
	891.27	1637.65	2010.83			225.6	122.8			12.3
3.13	90.49	585.63	691.57	16158.2	22094.9	764.3	118.1	19.2	37.4	33.7
22.86	26.16	33.84	37.02		161.9	141.5	109.4		2.9	5.1
27.39	234.95	385.62	454.10		1657.9	193.3	117.8		18.0	9.9
578.05	2241.48	2889.64	3552.36		614.5	158.5	122.9		11.3	6.8
282.88	1261.42	1645.02	1849.64		653.9	146.6	112.4		11.7	5.6
13920	33091	43096	49010	808.1	352.1	148.1	113.7	7.5	7.7	5.8
1691	4199	6001	7430	805.0	439.4	176.9	123.8	7.5	9.1	8.5
11551	27048	34835	34427	710.9	298.0	127.3	98.8	7.0	6.6	3.5
677	1840	2256	3149	1056.7	465.1	171.1	139.6	8.5	9.5	8.0
0.87	3.50	3.40	3.62	3016.7	416.1	103.4	106.5	12.5	8.7	0.5
9602	23191	34471	38434	4084.4	400.3	165.7	111.5	13.6	8.5	7.5
388	1147	1272	1873	1265.5	482.7	163.3	147.2	9.1	9.7	7.3
9161	21877	32835	36159	4600.4	394.7	165.3	110.1	14.1	8.4	7.4
53	167	364	402	5742.9	758.5	240.7	110.4	15.0	12.7	13.4

1-5 续表 2

指　　标	Item	1978
邮电通信业	**Postal and Telecommunication Services**	
邮电业务总量(亿元)	Total Business Revenue (100 million yuan)	0.21
函　件(万件)	Number of Letters Delivered (10 000 pieces)	4843
报刊期发数(万份)	Number of Newspapers and Magazines Distributed (10 000 copies)	224
局用交换机容量(万门)	CapaCity of Office Telephone Exchanges (10 000 lines)	
固定电话年末用户(万部)	Local Telephone Subscribers at Year-end (10 000 subscribers)	2.90
移动电话用户(万户)	Number of Mobile Telephone Subscribers (10 000 subscribers)	
国内商业	**Domestic Trades**	
社会消费品零售总额(亿元)	Total Retail Sales of Consumer Goods (100 million yuan)	21.89
对外经济贸易	**Foreign Trades**	
进出口总额(万美元)	Total Value of Exports and Imports (USD 10 000)	2346
出口额	Exports	937
进口额	Imports	1409
国际旅游	**International Tourism**	
入境旅游人数(万人)	Number of Tourists from Abroad (10 000 persons)	0.01
旅游外汇收入(万美元)	Foreign Exchange Earnings from Tourism (USD 10 000)	5
金　融	**Finance and Insurance**	
金融机构各项存款(亿元)	Deposits of National Banking System (100 million yuan)	32.07
金融机构各项贷款(亿元)	Loans of National Banking System (100 million yuan)	18.26
教育、科技、文化	**Education, Science & Technology and Culture**	
教　育	**Education**	
专任教师数(人)	Full-time Teachers (person)	
普通高等学校	Institutions of Higher Education	2458
中等学校	Secondary Schools	44417
小　学	Primary Schools	82616
在校学生数(万人)	Students Enrollment (10 000 persons)	
普通高等学校	Institutions of Higher Education	1.02
中等学校	Secondary Schools	83.86
小　学	Primary Schools	202.88
科　技	**Science and Technology**	
科学家、工程师数(人)	Number of Scientists and Engineers (persons)	
研究与发展经费支出(万元)	Expenditures on Research and Development (10 000 yuan)	
技术市场成交额(万元)	Volume of Transaction in Technical Markets (10 000 yuan)	
文　化	**Culture**	
电视节目制作时间(小时)	Time for TV Programs Production (hour)	

Continued

总量指标 Aggregate Data				速度指标(%) Indices and Growth Rates						
				指数(2007 年比以下各年) Index (2007 as percentage of the following years)				平均增长速度 Average Annual Growth Rate		
1990	2000	2006	2007	1978	1990	2000	2006	1979-2007	1991-2007	2001-2007
1.74	47.30	228.92	303.65	144595.2	17451.1	642.0	132.6	28.5	35.5	30.4
7381	7148	4130	3177	65.6	43.0	44.4	76.9	-1.4	-4.8	-10.9
806	535	342	305	136.2	37.8	57.0	89.2	1.1	-5.6	-7.7
	241.67	912.00	940.60			389.2	103.1			21.4
8.94	191.03	706.90	678.10	23382.8	7585.0	355.0	95.9	20.7	29.0	19.8
	78.00	671.10	808.30			1036.3	120.4			39.7
104.30	374.50	727.59	847.70	3872.5	812.8	226.4	116.5	13.4	13.1	12.4
41025	226399	910327	1371623	58466.5	3343.4	605.8	150.7	24.6	22.9	29.3
33530	120408	713923	1150311	122765.3	3430.7	955.3	161.1	27.8	23.1	38.0
7495	105991	196404	221312	15707.0	2952.8	208.8	112.7	19.0	22.0	11.1
7.98	25.61	36.25	43.84	438400.0	549.4	171.2	120.9	33.5	10.5	8.0
1212	9494	12800	16190	323800.0	1335.8	170.5	126.5	32.1	16.5	7.9
221.80	1863.48	4040.78	4614.62	14389.2	2080.5	247.6	114.2	18.7	19.5	13.8
233.72	1403.13	2412.69	2685.00	14704.3	1148.8	191.4	111.3	18.8	15.4	9.7
7002	7924	13783	15096	614.2	215.6	190.5	109.5	6.5	4.6	9.6
78596	89211	120777	123246	277.5	156.8	138.2	102.0	3.6	2.7	4.7
95060	131259	134718	133626	161.7	140.6	101.8	99.2	1.7	2.0	0.3
3.13	7.41	20.77	22.60	2215.7	722.0	305.0	108.8	11.3	12.3	17.3
101.52	131.18	173.94	174.29	207.8	171.7	132.9	100.2	2.6	3.2	4.1
185.72	247.74	209.80	205.89	101.5	110.9	83.1	98.1	0.1	0.6	-2.6
	16018	18924	20976			131.0	110.8			3.9
	32381	84764	100174			309.4	118.2			17.5
	66168	76084	71724			108.4	94.3			1.2
3699	29261	51401	53984		1459.4	184.5	105.0		17.1	9.1

1-5 续表 3

指　　标	Item	1978
家庭、生活、环境	**Family, People's Livelihood and Environment**	
家 庭	**Family**	
家庭总户数(万户)	Total Number of Households (10 000 households)	
城镇居民平均每户家庭人口(人)	Average Household Size in Urban Areas (person)	
农村居民平均每户家庭人口(人)	Average Household Size in Rural Areas (person)	
婚 姻	**Marriages and Divorces**	
结婚数(万对)	Number of Marriages (10 000 couples)	
离婚数 (万对)	Number of Divorces (10 000 couples)	
居 住	**Housing**	
城镇居民人均使用面积(平方米)	Per capita Gross Floor Space of Urban Residents (sq.m)	
城镇居民人均建筑面积(平方米)	Per capita Gross Living Space in Urban Areas (sq.m)	
农村居民人均居住面积(平方米)	Per capita Net Floor Space of Rural Residents (sq.m)	
生 活	**People's Livelihood**	
城镇居民人均可支配收入(元)	Per Capita Annual Disposable Income of Urban Households (yuan)	319
农村居民人均纯收入(元)	Per Capita Net Income of Rural Residents (yuan)	119
城乡储蓄存款余额(亿元)	Outstanding Amount of Saving Deposits in Urban and Rural Areas (100 million yuan)	6.42
工 资	**Wages and Welfare**	
工资总额 (亿元)	Total Wages (100 million yuan)	15.94
在岗职工平均工资(元)	Average Wage of Staff and Workers (yuan)	717
离休、退休、退职费(亿元)	Pensions for Retired Staff and Workers(100 million yuan)	
卫 生	**Health Care**	
医院、卫生院(个)	Number of Hospitals (unit)	806
医生(人)	Number of Doctors (person)	16898
医院、卫生院床位数(张)	Number of Hospital Beds (unit)	39179
市政建设	**Municipal Works**	
自来水供应量(亿吨)	Volume of Tapping Water Supply (100 million tons)	
下水道长度(公里)	Length of Sewer Pipelines (km)	
年末营运公交车辆(辆)	Year-end Operating Vehicles (vehicle)	
铺装道路长度(公里)	Length of Paved Roads (km)	
环境、灾害	**Environment and Disaster**	
工业污染治理项目当年完成投资额(万元)	Investment Completed in Pollution Treatment Projects (10 000 yuan)	
火灾发生数(起)	Number of Fire Disasters (times)	
火灾损失(万元)	Fire Loss (10 000 yuan)	
交通事故发生数(起)	Number of Traffic Accidents (times)	
交通事故损失(万元)	Loss of Traffic Accidents (10 000 yuan)	

Continued

总量指标 Aggregate Data				速度指标(%) Indices and Growth Rates						
				指数(2007 年比以下各年) Index (2007 as percentage of the following years)				平均增长速度 Average Annual Growth Rate		
1990	2000	2006	2007	1978	1990	2000	2006	1979-2007	1991-2007	2001-2007
356.67	481.91	592.48	614.43		172.3	127.5	103.7		3.3	3.5
3.92	3.15	2.98	3.02		77.0	95.9	101.3		-1.5	-0.6
5.37	5.33	4.72	4.67		87.0	87.6	98.9		-0.8	-1.9
15.84	16.25	20.00	22.63		142.9	139.3	113.2		2.1	4.8
5.65	5.90	7.69	8.65		153.1	146.6	112.5		2.5	5.6
13.55	20.06	20.33	20.38		150.4	101.6	100.2		2.4	0.2
18.07	26.75	26.31	27.17		150.4	101.6	103.3		2.4	0.2
14.04	17.25	21.96	22.45		159.9	130.1	102.2		2.8	3.8
1314	5645	8871	10313	3232.9	784.9	182.7	116.3	12.7	12.9	9.0
684	1618	2737	3183	2674.8	465.4	196.7	116.3	12.0	9.5	10.1
128.42	908.55	2035.63	2054.91	32007.9	1600.1	226.2	100.9	22.0	17.7	12.4
66.88	234.47	443.00	533.24	3345.3	797.3	227.4	120.4	12.9	13.0	12.5
2272	8717	17819	21434	2989.4	943.4	245.9	120.3	12.4	14.1	13.7
9.43	75.99	94.92	124.13		1316.3	163.4	130.8		16.4	7.3
1049	1352	1560	1629	202.1	155.3	120.5	104.4	2.5	2.6	2.7
33683	45402	42775	43551	257.7	129.3	95.9	101.8	3.3	1.5	-0.6
60707	65916	80090	87131	222.4	143.5	132.2	108.8	2.8	2.1	4.1
1.57	5.00	5.12	6.30		401.3	126.0	123.0		8.5	3.4
533	2008	3194	3441		645.6	171.4	107.7		11.6	8.0
788	5678	7822	8512		1080.2	149.9	108.8		15.0	6.0
970	2809	4044	4276		440.8	152.2	105.7		9.1	6.2
5138	22311	45229	60138		1170.5	269.5	133.0		15.6	15.2
	3050	4753	6215			203.8	130.8			10.7
	2329	3680	2385			102.4	64.8			0.3
	10048	7427	6487			64.6	87.3			-6.1
	4443	1663	1261			28.4	75.8			-16.5

1-6 国民经济和社会发展结构指标

Composition Indicators on National Economic and Social Development

单位: % (%)

指 标	Item	1978	1990	2000	2006	2007
人口与就业	**Population and Employment**					
人 口	**Population**					
城乡结构	Urban and Rural Composition					
城 镇	Urban	26.1	44.9	33.8	37.9	39.2
乡 村	Rural	73.9	55.1	66.2	62.1	60.8
性别结构	Sexual Composition					
男	Male	51.1	51.3	51.8	51.2	51.2
女	Female	48.9	48.7	48.2	48.8	48.8
就 业	**Employment**					
产业结构	Industrial Composition					
第一产业	Primary Industry	72.1	61.3	57.7	51.1	50.3
第二产业	Secondary Industry	14.3	17.4	13.8	13.7	14.3
第三产业	Tertiary Industry	13.6	21.3	28.5	35.2	35.4
宏观经济	**Macro Economy**					
国民核算	**National Accounting**					
新疆生产总值产业结构	Industrial Composition					
第一产业	Primary Industry	35.8	34.7	21.1	17.3	17.8
第二产业	Secondary Industry	47.0	30.6	39.5	48.0	46.8
#工 业	Industry	37.1	27.3	30.7	40.7	39.9
第三产业	Tertiary Industry	17.2	34.7	39.4	34.7	35.4
固定资产投资	**Investment**					
全社会固定资产投资结构	Composition of Total Investment in Fixed Assets					
城 镇	Urban	100.0	89.2	91.2	90.5	89.6
#房地产	Real Estate Development		1.2	10.3	8.5	9.1
农 村	Rural		10.8	8.8	9.5	10.4
资金来源结构	Composition of Funded Sources					
国家预算内资金	State Budgetary Appropriation	79.0	11.9	8.3	13.4	11.8
国内贷款	Domestic Loans		33.2	22.1	11.8	13.0
利用外资	Foreign Investment		4.6	1.6	0.6	0.6
自筹和其他投资	Fundraising and Other Investment	21.0	50.3	68.0	74.2	74.6
财 政	**Government Finance**					
地方财政一般预算收入结构	Composition of Government Revenue					
税收收入	Various Taxes	60.8	93.9	81.6	79.5	77.2
非税收入	Nontax Revenues	39.2	6.1	18.4	20.5	22.8
地方财政一般预算支出结构	Composition of Government Expenditures					
一般公共服务	General Common Service				18.6	18.7
教育与科学技术	Operating Expenses for Education and Operating Expenses for Science and Technology				18.0	19.6
社会保障和就业	Operating Expenses for Medical Treatment and Sanitation				11.1	11.4
环境保护	Operating Expenses for Environmental Conservation				2.8	2.7
城乡社区事务	Expenses of Community				6.1	7.5
农林水事务	Expenses of Agriculture, Forest and Irrigation				10.2	12.4
其他各项支出	Other Expense				33.2	27.7
能源生产与消费	**Energy Production and Consumption**					
能源生产总量结构	Composition of Total Energy Production					
原 煤	Coal	60.0	58.8	40.6	37.3	
原 油	Petroleum Crude Oil	35.8	35.8	48.7	37.1	
天然气	Natural Gas	2.4	2.4	7.9	22.9	
水风电	Water, Wind and Electricity	1.8	3.0	2.8	2.7	
能源消费总量结构	Composition of Total Energy Consumption					
煤 炭	Coal	72.5	69.6	63.6	56.7	
石 油	Petroleum Oil	21.5	22.5	23.3	24.7	
天然气	Natural Gas	3.4	3.5	8.6	14.3	
水风电	Water, Wind and Electricity	2.6	4.4	4.5	4.3	

1-6 续表 1 Continued

单位: % (%)

指　标	Item	1978	1990	2000	2006	2007
产　业	**Industrial**					
农 业	**Agriculture**					
农林牧渔业产值结构	Composition of Gross Output Value of Agriculture,Forestry,Animal Husbandry, Fishery					
农　业	Farming	74.5	76.4	74.0	72.3	72.1
林　业	Forestry	1.8	2.6	1.7	2.0	2.0
牧　业	Animal Husbandry	23.5	20.4	23.5	21.4	21.8
渔　业	Fishery	0.2	0.6	0.8	0.5	0.6
农林牧渔服务业	Agricultural, Forestry, Animal Husbandry, Fishery and Their Services				3.8	3.5
工 业	**Industry**					
工业总产值规模结构	Composition of Gross Output Value of Industry					
大型企业	Large Enterprises		27.5	53.7	65.5	61.0
中型企业	Medium-sized Enterprises		17.4	10.1	18.8	22.7
小型企业	Small Enterprises		55.1	36.2	15.7	16.3
建筑业	**Construction**					
建筑业总产值结构	Composition of Gross Output Value of Construction Industry					
建筑工程	Construction Projects		88.2	88.3	83.3	84.2
安装工程	Installation Projects		10.3	9.1	13.2	12.4
其　他	Others		1.5	2.6	3.5	3.4
交通运输业	**Transportation**					
货运量结构按运输方式分	By Means of Transportation					
铁　路	Railways	15.2	12.1	12.7	13.9	15.2
公　路	Highways	79.9	83.0	81.7	80.8	78.4
民用航空	Civil Aviation	…	…	…	…	…
管道输油(气)	Pipelines	4.9	4.9	5.6	5.3	6.4
国内商业	**Domestic Trades**					
社会消费品零售总额结构	Composition of Retail Sales of Consumer Goods					
市	Cities	33.9	54.8	62.4	70.0	70.8
县	Counties	21.9	23.3	17.4	14.7	14.4
县以下	Below Counties	44.2	21.9	20.2	15.3	14.8
对外经济贸易	**Foreign Trades**					
进出口总额结构	Composition of Total Value of Exports and Imports					
出口额	Exports	39.9	81.7	53.2	78.4	83.9
进口额	Imports	60.1	18.3	46.8	21.6	16.1
国际旅游	**International Tourism**					
来华旅游人数结构	Composition of Tourists					
外国人	Foreigners	100.0	80.4	81.4	86.4	91.8
港澳台同胞	Compatriots form Hong Kong, Macao and Taiwan		19.6	18.6	13.6	8.2
金　融	**Finance**					
金融机构资金来源结构	Composition of Sources of Funds in State Banks					
各项存款	Various Deposits			122.8	99.8	108.8
应付及暂收款	Payable and Temporary Collection			…	1.4	1.9
所有者权益	Owner's Right and Interest			0.1	1.2	2.1
其　他	Others			-22.9	-2.4	-12.8
金融机构资金运用结构	Composition of Fund Uses in State Banks					
各项贷款	Loans			92.5	59.6	63.3
有价证券及投资	Securities and Investment			4.4	3.7	3.1
行内资金往来	Funds Tranfer inward Banks			1.6	27.2	30.3
库存现金	Cash in Stock			1.1	0.8	0.8
其　他	Others			0.4	8.7	2.5

1-6 续表 2 Continued

单位: % (%)

指　标	Item	1978	1990	2000	2006	2007
教育、科技	**Education and Science**					
教 育	**Education**					
在校学生结构	Composition of Student Enrollment					
大学生	College and University Students	0.4	1.1	2.0	5.2	5.4
中学生	Secondary School Students	29.1	31.4	30.8	42.5	43.4
小学生	Primary School Students	70.5	67.5	67.2	52.3	51.2
专任教师结构	Full-time Teachers by Type					
大　学	Colleges and Universities	1.9	3.9	3.5	5.1	5.6
中　学	Secondary Schools	34.3	43.5	39.1	44.7	45.3
小　学	Primary Schools	63.8	52.6	57.4	50.2	49.1
科 技	**Science and Technology**					
科技经费筹集额结构	Composition of Funding for Scientific and Technological Income					
政府资金	Government Fund			25.6	17.9	24.1
企业资金	Enterprises Fund			58.2	68.2	63.3
银行贷款	Loans from Banks			5.7	4.1	4.4
其　他	Others			10.5	9.8	8.2
科技经费内部支出结构	Composition of Internal Expenditures on Scientific and Technological Activities					
#劳务费	Service Fees			34.3	25.6	26.5
固定资产购建	Purchases of Fixed Assets			28.5	33.2	34.3
#研究与发展经费支出	Research and Development Expenses			23.9	30.3	30.5
生活、环境	**People's Livelihood and Environment**					
生 活	**People's Livelihood**					
城镇居民消费结构	Consumption Composition of Urban Residents					
食品类	Food		47.8	36.4	35.5	35.1
衣着类	Clothing		15.6	13.1	14.2	15.0
家庭设备、用品及其他	Articles for Daily Use and Others		32.0	42.7	39.9	40.5
居　住	Residence		4.6	7.8	10.4	9.4
农村居民消费结构	Consumption Composition of Rural Residents					
食品类	Food		53.7	50.0	39.9	40.0
衣着类	Clothing		15.2	9.2	9.2	9.3
家庭设备、用品及其他	Articles for Daily Use and Others		17.4	27.0	32.6	31.8
居　住	Residence		13.7	13.8	18.3	18.9
卫 生	**Health Care**					
医生结构	Doctors by Types					
执业医师(西医师)	(Doctors of Western Medicine)	43.6	64.9	68.0	79.5	80.0
执业助理医师(西医士)	(Paramedics of Western Medicine)	56.4	25.9	23.1	20.5	20.0
医院床位结构	Hospital Beds by Area					
市医院	Hospitals at City Level		40.6	58.3	62.7	62.4
县医院	Hospitals at County Level		59.4	41.7	37.3	37.6
环境、灾害	**Environment and Disasters**					
治理工业污染资金使用结构	Uses of Funds Inindustrial Pollution Treatment					
治理废水	Waste Water Treatment		55.3	38.2	59.4	49.8
治理废气	Waste Gas Treatment		32.4	40.9	26.6	39.7
治理固体废物	Solid Wastes Treatment		10.6	1.6	5.7	2.8
治理噪声	Noise Abatement		0.9	18.4	0.1	0.4
其　他	Others		0.8	0.9	8.2	7.3
火灾事故损失额结构	Composition of Fire Losses Converted into Cash					
特　大	Extraordinarily Serious Fires			15.7	52.0	9.1
重　大	Serious Fires			14.3	11.4	14.3
一　般	Ordinary Fires			70.0	36.6	76.6

1-7 国民经济和社会发展比例和效益指标
Indicators on Proportions and Efficiency in National Economic and Social Development

指　　标	Item	1978	1990	2000	2006	2007
人口与就业	**Population and Employment**					
人 口	**Population**					
出生率(‰)	Birth Rate (‰)	22.55	26.41	17.57	15.97	16.79
死亡率(‰)	Death Rate (‰)	7.69	7.81	5.40	5.03	5.01
自然增长率(‰)	Natural Growth Rate (‰)	14.86	18.60	12.17	10.94	11.78
就 业	**Employment**					
就业者负担人口	Dependency Ratio		1.48	1.67	1.53	1.47
三次产业从业者比例(以第一产业为 100)	Employment Ratio by Type of Industry (Employment in primary industry=100)					
第一产业	Primary Industry	100	100	100	100	100
第二产业	Secondary Industry	19.9	28.4	25.2	26.9	28.3
第三产业	Tertiary Industry	18.9	34.8	53.6	69.0	70.5
城镇登记失业率(%)	Unemployment Rate in Urban Areas (%)		3.8	3.8	3.9	3.9
宏观经济	**Macro Economy**					
国民经济核算	**National Accounting**					
三次产业增加值比例(以第一产业为 100)	Ratio of Value-added by Type of Industry (Value added in primary industry=100)					
第一产业	Primary Industry	100	100.0	100	100	100
第二产业	Secondary Industry	131.4	79.8	186.8	276.3	262.0
第三产业	Tertiary Industry	48.3	71.2	186.8	200.4	198.3
全社会劳动生产率(元/人)	Overall Labor Productivity (yuan/person)	795	4225	20283	37515	42426
第一产业	Primary Industry	395	2748	7425	12735	15051
第二产业	Secondary Industry	2606	7727	58037	131138	139222
第三产业	Tertiary Industry	1010	5614	28035	36996	42361
人均生产总值(元/人)	Per capita GDP (yuan/person)	313	1713	7372	15000	16950
固定资产投资	**Investment in Fixed Assets**					
全社会固定资产投资相当于新疆生产总值比例(%)	Proportion of Investment in Fixed Assets to GDP of Xinjiang (%)	33.3	34.0	44.8	51.5	52.5
全社会房屋建筑面积竣工率(%)	Rate of Total Floor Space of Buildings Completed in Construction (%)		76.8	58.7	60.8	67.8
财 政	**Finance**					
地方财政一般预算收入相当于新疆生产总值比例(%)	Proportion of Local Financial Revenue to GDP of Xinjiang (%)	18.3	8.3	5.8	7.2	8.1
地方财政一般预算支出相当于新疆生产总值比例(%)	Proportion of Local Financial Expenditure to GDP of Xinjiang (%)	43.6	18.2	14.0	22.3	22.6
利用外资	**Utilization of Foreign Capital**					
实际利用外资额相当于签订利用外资额比例(%)	Proportion of Actually Foreign Direct Investment for Foreign Direct Investment (%)		80.94	20.87	28.45	27.33
能源生产与消费	**Production and Consumption of Energy**					
能源生产弹性系数	Elasticity Ratio of Energy Production	1.20	0.50	0.40	1.51	
能源消费弹性系数	Elasticity Ratio of Energy Consumption	0.74	0.79	0.38	0.89	
每万元新疆生产总值消耗的能源(吨标准煤)	Energy Consumption per 10 000 yuan GDP (ton of SCE)		7.37	2.43	2.09	2.03

1-7 续表 1 Continued

指　　标	Item	1978	1990	2000	2006	2007
产　业	**Industries**					
农 业	**Agriculture**					
农业从业者人均农产品产量（公斤）	Output of Farm Corps per Agricultural Laborer (kg)					
粮　食	Grain		2514.5	2571.5	2556.5	2446.9
棉　花	Cotton		237.6	477.0	646.8	818.4
油　料	Oil-bearing Crops		144.7	191.3	93.7	113.7
肉　类	Meat		113.2	286.2	451.8	453.2
水产品	Aquatic Products		8.6	19.1	24.1	25.1
每公顷播种面积农产品产量（公斤）	Output of Farm Crops per Hectare of Sown Area (kg)					
粮　食	Grain	1650	3705	5595	6107	6287
棉　花	Cotton	375	1080	1485	1607	1627
油　料	Oil-bearing Crops	510	1440	1935	2163	2284
工业企业经济效益(规模以上)	**Economic Efficiency of Industrial Enterprises above Designated Size**					
总资产贡献率（%）	Rate of Total Assets to Industrial Output Value (%)			11.2	26.9	25.9
资产负债率（%）	Assets-Liability Ratio (%)			62.7	51.6	50.6
成本费用利润率（%）	Rate of Profits to Industrial Cost (%)		2.6	12.8	28.4	25.6
流动资产周转次数（次/年）	Number of Times of Annual of Turnover Circulating Funds (times/year)		1.5	1.6	2.8	2.8
全员劳动生产率(按增加值计算)(元/人.年)	Overall Labor Productivity(yuan/person-year) (in terms of value-added per employee)		14226	35645	242002	259636
建筑业	**Construction**					
技术装备率（元/人）	Value of Machinery per Laborer (yuan/person)		2511	8582	11187	10650
动力装备率（千瓦/人）	Power of Machines Per Laborer (kw/person)		5	7	6	6
全员劳动生产率(按总产值计算)(元/人)	Overall Labor Productivity (yuan/person) (in terms of gross output value per employee)		12014	74994	121506	126303
交通运输业	**Transportation**					
客运量弹性系数	Elasticity of Passenger Traffic	2.88	0.85	0.22	0.34	0.94
货运量弹性系数	Elasticity of Freight Traffic	2.14	1.54	0.37	0.56	1.12
铁路网密度（公里/万平方公里）	Railway Density (km/10 000 sq.km)	6.19	9.48	18.08	17.57	17.57
公路网密度（公里/万平方公里）	Highway Density (km/10 000 sq.km)	143	153	208	863	872
邮电通信业	**Post and Communications**					
邮电业务总量弹性系数	Elasticity of Postal and Telecommunications Services	0.52	0.74	4.17	2.98	2.68
固定电话普及率(部/百人)	PopularizationRate of Telephones (set/100 persons)		0.6	15.0	34.5	33.4
移动电话普及率(部/百人)	Popularization Rate of Mobile Telephone (set/100 persons)				32.7	38.6
国内商业	**Domestic Trades**					
人均社会消费品零售额(元)	Per capita Retail Sales of Consumer Goods (yuan)	179	699	2066	3584	4090
对外经济贸易	**Foreign Trades**					
进出口总额相当于新疆生产总值比例(%)	Proportion of Total Value Imports & Exports to GDP (%)	1.01	7.52	13.74	23.83	29.60
国际旅游	**International Tourism**					
每一来华游客花费(美元)	Expenditure per International Tourist in China (USD)		152	371	353	369

1-7 续表 2 Continued

指　　标	Item	1978	1990	2000	2006	2007
金　融	**Finance**					
金融机构存款相当于新疆生产总值比例(%)	Bank Deposits as Percentage of GDP in Xinjiang (%)	82.08	84.98	136.62	132.70	130.98
金融机构贷款相当于新疆生产总值比例(%)	Bank Loans as Percentage of GDP in Xinjiang (%)	46.74	89.55	102.87	79.23	76.21
金融机构现金支出相当于收入比例(%)	Proportion of Cash Outlay to Cash Receipt in Bank (%)		105.71	101.65	101.11	101.07
教育、科技、文化	**Education, Science and Technology and Culture**					
教 育	**Education**					
学龄儿童入学率(%)	Rate of School-age Children Enrollment (%)	96.00	97.50	97.03	99.15	99.28
小学升学率(%)	Rate of Graduates of Primary Schools Entering Junior Secondary Schools (%)	88.67	82.17	92.01	101.53	100.47
初中升学率(%)	Rate of Graduates of Junior Secondary Schools Entering Senior Secondary Schools (%)	48.22	39.12	30.30	36.98	37.71
学校每一专任教师负担学生数(人)	Student-teacher (full-time)Ratio (person)					
高等学校	Colleges and Universities	4.16	4.47	9.34	15.07	14.33
普通中等	Secondary Schools	19.36	13.12	14.92	14.70	14.13
小学学校	Primary Schools	24.56	19.54	18.87	15.57	15.41
科 技	**Science and Technology**					
研究与开发经费支出相当于新疆生产总值比例(%)	R&D Expenditures as Percentage of GDP (%)			0.24	0.28	0.28
文 化	**Culture**					
每百万人有艺术表演团体(个)	Number of Troupes per Million Persons(unit)	5.24	6.21	4.76	5.76	5.79
每百万人有公共图书馆(个)	Number of Public Libraries per Million Persons(unit)	0.41	4.05	4.33	4.78	4.54
每百万人有博物馆(个)	Number of Museums per Million Persons(unit)	0.08	0.52	1.24	1.37	1.54
家庭、生活、环境	**Family, People's Livelihood and Environment**					
家 庭	**Family**					
负担少儿系数(%)	Dependency Ratio of Children (%)		52.43	40.06	31.15	39.71
负担老年系数(%)	Dependency Ratio of the Aged (%)		6.20	6.86	9.18	7.35
婚 姻	**Marriages and Divorces**					
离婚率(‰)	Divorce Rate (‰)		7.4	6.4	7.5	8.3
生 活	**People's Livelihood**					
城镇与农村居民收入增长率比例(以农村居民收入指数为 1)(1978 年=100)	Proportion of Growth Rate of Annual Income of Urban Residents to the Growth Rate of Annual Net Income of Rural Residents (1978=100)	1.00	0.72	1.17	1.16	1.16
卫 生	**Health Care**					
每万人医院、卫生院数(个)	Number of Hospitals and Health Centers per 10 000 Persons (unit)	0.66	0.69	0.73	0.76	0.78
每万人医生数(人)	Number of Doctors per 10 000 Persons (unit)	13.70	22.03	24.59	20.87	20.79
每万人医院、卫生院床位数(张)	Number of Hospital and Health Centers Beds per 10 000 Persons (unit)	31.8	40.5	35.7	39.1	41.6
医院病床使用率(%)	Utilization Rate of Hospital Beds (%)		77.20	66.31	71.36	75.77
市政建设	**City Construction**					
城市自来水普及率(%)	Percentage of Households with Access to Tap Water (%)	59.0	80.9	98.8	99.4	99.1
城市燃气普及率(%)	Percentage of Households with Access to Tap Gas (%)	11.0	49.8	92.8	91.5	92.8
建成区绿化覆盖率(%)	Green Covrage Rate in Completed Area(%)		26.0	29.1	30.0	32.0
灾害	**Disasters**					
平均每起火灾损失(元)	Average Loss of per Fire Disaster (yuan)			7635	7742	3837
平均每起交通事故损失(元)	Average Loss of per Traffic Accident (yuan)			4775	2239	1943

1-8 人均主要工农业产品产量
Per capita Output of Major Industrial and Agricultural Products

年份 Year	粮食（公斤） Grain (kg)	棉花（公斤） Cotton (kg)	油料（公斤） Oil-bearing Crops (kg)	甜菜（公斤） Sugar Crops (kg)	水果（公斤） Fruits (kg)	猪牛羊肉（公斤） Pork, Beef and Mutton (kg)	水产品（公斤） Aquatic Products (kg)
1978	303.0	4.5	8.5	13.4	11.4	7.9	0.5
1980	304.1	6.2	13.9	30.3	12.3	9.4	0.5
1985	367.2	13.9	25.3	30.1	36.4	12.8	0.7
1990	453.8	31.4	26.1	150.4	53.6	18.6	1.6
1995	443.3	56.8	30.0	174.9	69.4	27.9	2.7
1996	488.4	56.1	18.5	211.6	69.2	31.4	2.9
1997	484.4	67.5	17.6	228.2	72.6	32.7	3.1
1998	479.0	80.8	21.7	296.1	70.1	37.7	3.1
1999	476.3	79.9	34.3	201.1	77.5	39.9	3.2
2000	446.2	82.8	33.2	161.5	83.8	42.4	3.3
2001	427.3	84.3	22.9	244.3	82.8	44.5	3.3
2002	463.3	79.3	23.5	246.9	104.8	46.9	3.4
2003	417.6	83.4	26.1	198.8	113.7	50.4	3.5
2004	425.2	89.9	22.9	176.7	135.6	55.2	3.8
2005	441.5	98.5	19.6	211.0	146.6	60.5	4.0
2006	441.0	131.8	16.2	273.6	169.0	66.5	4.1
2007	418.3	139.9	19.4	283.2	198.8	67.1	4.3

年份 Year	布（米） Cloth (m)	机制纸及纸板（公斤） Machine-made Paper and Paperboard (kg)	纱（公斤） Yarn (kg)	原煤（公斤） Coal (kg)	原油（公斤） Crude Oil (kg)	发电量（千瓦小时） Electricity (kwh)	粗钢（公斤） Steel (kg)	水泥（公斤） Cement (kg)
1978	13	1.6	2.3	884	289	173	7	64
1980	13	1.9	2.5	895	308	186	8	72
1985	16	3.1	2.9	1183	369	282	15	149
1990	20	6.1	6.8	1408	466	468	23	191
1995	18	11.0	14.9	1652	770	731	43	297
1996	16	10.1	12.5	1782	870	812	52	336
1997	18	9.5	14.5	1773	956	884	57	369
1998	15	9.7	12.7	1689	940	910	62	421
1999	16	10.2	16.7	1577	988	961	60	458
2000	15	9.7	18.5	1546	1021	1011	61	495
2001	14	10.4	16.3	1514	1045	1061	72	527
2002	11	12.0	16.7	1639	1077	1123	93	545
2003	8	12.2	15.3	1814	1116	1222	106	588
2004	7	13.5	15.0	1924	1156	1367	128	623
2005	7	14.6	17.2	1962	1212	1545	154	625
2006	8	14.5	17.6	2226	1219	1759	194	657
2007	8	12.2	19.7	2421	1257	2011	216	741

1-9 人均国民经济主要指标

Per Capita Main Indicators on National Economy

指　　标	Item	1978	1990	2000	2006	2007
新疆生产总值(元)	Gross Domestic Product of Xinjiang (yuan)	313	1713	7372	15000	16950
工农业总产值(元)	Gross Output Value of Industry and Agriculture (yuan)	450	2444	8544	18611	21881
工业总产值	Gross Industrial Output Value	278	1474	5856	14259	16750
农林牧渔业总产值	Gross Output Value of Agriculture, Forestry, Animal Husbandry and Fishery	172	970	2688	4352	5131
固定资产投资总额(元)	Total Investment in Fixed Assets (yuan)	106	595	3368	7719	8930
#国有经济	State-owned Economic	106	506	2540	3322	3331
地方财政一般预算收入(元)	General Budgetary Revenue in Local Finance (10 000 yuan)	58	146	436	1081	1379
地方财政一般预算支出(元)	General Budgetary Expenditure in Local Finance (10 000 yuan)	139	319	1054	3342	3837
耕地面积(公顷)	Cultivated Area (hectare)	0.26	0.20	0.18	0.18	0.18
主要工农业产品产量	Output of Major Industrial and Agriculturd Produts					
粮食(公斤)	Grain Yield (kg)	303.0	453.8	446.2	441.0	418.3
棉花(公斤)	Cotton Yield (kg)	4.5	31.4	82.8	131.8	139.9
油料(公斤)	Oil-bearing Crops Yield (kg)	8.5	26.1	33.2	16.2	19.4
甜菜(公斤)	Beet Roots Yield (kg)	13.4	150.4	161.5	273.6	283.2
猪牛羊肉(公斤)	Pork, Beef and Mutton Yield (kg)	7.9	18.6	42.4	66.5	67.1
水产品(公斤)	Aquatic Products Yield (kg)	0.5	1.6	3.3	4.1	4.3
水果(公斤)	Fruits Yield (kg)	11.4	53.6	83.8	169.0	198.8
果用瓜(公斤)	Fruit Melon Yield (kg)	36.1	62.6	83.3	116.8	163.4
布(米)	Cloth (m)	12.8	20.0	15.0	8.0	7.7
机制纸和纸板(公斤)	Machine-made Paper and Paperboard (kg)	1.6	6.1	9.7	14.5	12.2
纱(公斤)	Yarn (kg)	2.3	6.8	18.5	17.6	19.7
原煤(公斤)	Coal Output (kg)	884	1408	1546	2226	2421
原油(公斤)	Crude Oil Output (kg)	289	466	1021	1219	1257
发电量(千瓦小时)	Electric Power (kwh)	173	468	1011	1759	2011
水泥(公斤)	Cement (kg)	64	191	495	657	741
社会消费品零售总额(元)	Total Retail Sales of Consumer Goods (yuan)	179	699	2066	3584	4090
海关出口总额(美元)	Value of Exports (USD)	0.8	23.2	66.5	351.7	555.0
高等学校在校学生数(人/万人)	Students Enrollment in Institions of Higher Education (person/10 000 persons)	8.3	20.5	41.1	97.2	103.3
中等职业学校在校学生数(人/万人)	Students Enrollment in Specialized Secondary Schools (person/10 000 persons)	19.2	30.0	56.9	52.7	67.4
普通中学在校学生数(人/万人)	Students Enrollment in Regular Secondary Schools (person/10 000 persons)	654.0	564.0	638.0	767.0	729.8
医院、卫生院床位数(人/万人)	Beds of Medical and Health Centers (person/10 000 persons)	31.8	40.5	35.7	39.1	41.6
卫生技术人员数(人/万人)	Medical Technical Personnel (person/10 000 persons)	41.4	52.2	53.0	48.7	50.5
#医　生	Doctors	13.7	22.0	24.6	20.9	20.8
城乡储蓄存款余额(元)	Urban and Rural Savings Deposits (yuan)	57	746	4913	9930	9915

1-10 各时期社会经济主要指标
Major Social and Economic Indicators of Each Period

时 期	Period	新疆生产总值(亿元) Gross Domestic Product of Xinjiang (100 million yuan)	第一产业 Primary Industry	第二产业 Secondary Industry	#工 业 Industry	第三产业 Tertiary Industry	全社会固定资产投资总额(亿元) Total Investment in Fixed Assets (100 million yuan)
"一五"时期	"First Five-Year Plan" Period	60.35	33.86	15.54	8.82	10.95	
"二五"时期	"Second Five-Year Plan" Period	102.65	43.27	39.48	28.37	19.90	31.42
	1963—1965	64.76	33.56	19.27	13.64	11.93	10.43
"三五"时期	"Third Five-Year Plan" Period	111.94	53.53	38.02	27.84	20.39	18.82
"四五"时期	"Fourth Five-Year Plan" Period	128.37	54.38	50.55	36.84	23.42	24.72
"五五"时期	"Fifth Five-Year Plan" Period	205.39	77.27	91.75	72.34	36.37	69.12
"六五"时期	"Sixth Five-Year Plan" Period	405.19	165.70	146.99	117.51	92.50	149.13
"七五"时期	"Seventh Five-Year Plan" Period	948.99	356.55	318.96	263.20	273.48	331.97
"八五"时期	"Eighth Five-Year Plan" Period	2710.64	781.61	993.78	755.30	935.25	1162.22
"九五"时期	"Ninth Five-Year Plan" Period	5574.46	1376.78	2052.88	1574.58	2144.80	2499.46
"十五"时期	"Tenth Five-Year Plan" Period	9398.72	1962.15	3975.87	3168.48	3865.81	5034.95

时 期	Period	住宅竣工建筑面积(万平方米) Floor Space of Building Completed (10 000 sq.m)	地方财政一般预算收入(亿元) General Budgetary Revenue in Local Finance (100 million yuan)	地方财政一般预算支出(亿元) General Budgetary Expenditure in Local Finance (100 million yuan)	进出口总额(万美元) Total Imports And Exports (USD 10 000)	#出口额 Exports	社会消费品零售总额(亿元) Total Retail Sales of Consumer Goods (100 million yuan)
"一五"时期	"First Five-Year Plan" Period		8.65	9.50	20819	10945	31.38
"二五"时期	"Second Five-Year Plan" Period		21.39	27.16	26197	17976	53.43
	1963—1965		12.20	11.61	4806	4632	31.92
"三五"时期	"Third Five-Year Plan" Period		15.38	21.78	1243	633	63.75
"四五"时期	"Fourth Five-Year Plan" Period		11.11	39.78	2922	1217	76.26
"五五"时期	"Fifth Five-Year Plan" Period		18.24	54.80	10255	4310	113.51
"六五"时期	"Sixth Five-Year Plan" Period	3279.57	27.35	100.30	81536	57445	215.35
"七五"时期	"Seventh Five-Year Plan" Period	4175.39	75.48	197.04	190173	142124	323.14
"八五"时期	"Eighth Five-Year Plan" Period	4928.74	155.63	338.64	460033	265704	878.89
"九五"时期	"Ninth Five-Year Plan" Period	8341.78	318.60	741.45	841181	425462	1655.20
"十五"时期	"Tenth Five-Year Plan" Period	12466.98	675.80	1933.02	2281284	1260601	2471.83

1-11 各时期社会经济主要指标平均增长率

Growth Rate of Major Social and Economic Indicators of Each Period

单位：% (%)

时　期	Period	新疆生产总值 Gross Domestic Product of Xinjiang	第一产业 Primary Industry	第二产业 Secondary Industry	#工业 Industry	第三产业 Tertiary Industry	全社会固定资产投资总额 Total Investment in Fixed Assets
"一五"时期	"First Five-Year Plan" Period	9.0	5.1	12.6	8.8	18.8	
"二五"时期	"Second Five-Year Plan" Period	4.5	2.8	11.0	24.5	-1.3	-14.8
	1963—1965	12.9	17.9	8.4	3.3	5.4	28.4
"三五"时期	"Third Five-Year Plan" Period	0.3	-3.1	3.8	4.3	4.8	2.2
"四五"时期	"Fourth Five-Year Plan" Period	2.9	…	7.2	7.3	-0.5	6.3
"五五"时期	"Fifth Five-Year Plan" Period	10.5	7.4	11.6	14.3	14.5	34.1
"六五"时期	"Sixth Five-Year Plan" Period	12.5	13.0	9.2	9.3	17.6	10.9
"七五"时期	"Seventh Five-Year Plan" Period	9.8	7.9	8.2	9.2	14.7	14.8
"八五"时期	"Eighth Five-Year Plan" Period	11.8	6.7	14.2	13.5	15.0	30.3
"九五"时期	"Ninth Five-Year Plan" Period	7.7	5.8	6.8	5.9	10.3	12.9
"十五"时期	"Tenth Five-Year Plan" Period	10.0	5.6	10.6	11.3	11.2	17.2

时　期	Period	住宅竣工建筑面积 Floor Space of Building Completed	地方财政一般预算收入 General Budgetary Revenue in Local Finance	地方财政一般预算支出 General Budgetary Expenditure in Local Finance	进出口总额 Total Imports And Exports	#出口额 Exports	社会消费品零售总额 Total Retail Sales of Consumer Goods
"一五"时期	"First Five-Year Plan" Period		25.0	30.7	17.8	17.8	18.5
"二五"时期	"Second Five-Year Plan" Period		4.7	-0.4	-12.5	-9.6	4.3
	1963—1965		16.8	30.5	-20.4	-13.8	2.3
"三五"时期	"Third Five-Year Plan" Period		-4.7	4.3	-34.4	-50.3	3.2
"四五"时期	"Fourth Five-Year Plan" Period		-22.3	7.9	40.6	58.0	5.0
"五五"时期	"Fifth Five-Year Plan" Period		31.9	12.9	28.4	35.5	11.7
"六五"时期	"Sixth Five-Year Plan" Period		16.0	12.0	56.0	60.2	14.3
"七五"时期	"Seventh Five-Year Plan" Period	2.3	20.8	10.7	7.0	13.2	12.7
"八五"时期	"Eighth Five-Year Plan" Period	3.1	11.9	15.1	28.3	18.1	19.4
"九五"时期	"Ninth Five-Year Plan" Period	12.1	15.6	14.6	9.7	9.4	8.1
"十五"时期	"Tenth Five-Year Plan" Period	14.0	17.9	22.1	28.5	33.2	11.2

1-12 天山北坡经济带主要经济指标

(2007 年)

指 标	Item	全区合计 Total of the whole region	北坡经济带合计 Total of the economic belt	北坡经济带占全区比重(%) ratio of the economic belt (%)	乌昌合计 Total of Urmqi and Changji	乌昌占全区比重(%) Pencent-age of Urmqi and Changji to total(%)	乌鲁木齐市 Urumqi City
人口(万人)	**Population and Labor force (10 000 persons)**						
年末总人口	Year-end Population	2095.19	484.58	23.1	366.67	17.5	231.30
#少数民族人口	Population of Ethnic minority	1271.27	110.21	8.7	97.19	7.6	62.52
城镇人口	Population of cities and Towns	820.27	468.54	57.1	336.78	41.1	224.42
乡村人口	Rural population	1274.92	16.04	1.3	29.89	2.3	6.88
综合	**General**						
新疆生产总值(亿元)	Gross Domestic Produc in Xinjiang (100 million yuan)	3523.16	1837.43	52.2	1133.48	32.2	820.28
第一产业	First Industry	628.72	148.78	23.7	113.66	18.1	16.26
第二产业	Second Industry	1647.55	984.93	59.8	436.26	26.5	316.59
工 业	Industry	1405.11	875.98	62.3	355.16	25.3	261.86
建筑业	Building Sector	242.44	108.95	44.9	81.10	33.5	54.73
第三产业	Tertiary Industry	1246.89	703.72	56.4	583.56	46.8	487.43
#交通运输、仓储和邮政业	Communication, Storage and Telecom	177.28	112.28	63.3	90.48	51.0	71.60
批发和零售贸易业	Wholesale &Retail and Catering Sectoring	187.10	115.09	61.5	97.99	52.4	82.89
新疆生产总值构成(%)	Composition of Gross Domestic Produc in Xinjiang (%)	100	100		100		100
第一产业	First Industry	17.8	8.1		10.0		2.0
第二产业	Second Industry	46.8	53.6		38.5		38.6
工 业	Industry	39.9	47.7		31.3		31.9
建筑业	Construction	6.9	5.9		7.2		6.7
第三产业	Tertiary Industry	35.4	38.3		51.5		59.4
#交通运输、仓储和邮政业	Communication, Storage and Telecom	5.0	6.1		8.0		8.7
批发和零售贸易业	Wholesale &Retail and Catering Sectoring	5.3	6.3		8.6		10.1
财政收入占新疆生产总值比重(%)	Ratio of GDP covered by financial Expenditure (%)	8.1	7.3		7.7		9.0
财政支出占新疆生产总值比重(%)	Ratio of GDP covered by financial Expenditure (%)	22.6	8.1		9.1		8.3
固定资产投资(亿元)	**Fixed Asset Investment (100 million yuan)**						
#城镇固定资产投资总额	Fixed Asset Value of the town	1490.87	665.29	44.6	303.99	20.4	223.47
财政、金融(亿元)	**Finance and Public Money(100 million yuan)**						
地方财政一般预算收入	Local Financial Income	285.86	134.17	46.9	87.23	30.5	73.43
#各项税收	Various Tax Incomes	220.65	119.92	54.3	77.89	35.3	66.34
地方财政一般预算支出	Expenditure of Local Finance	795.15	148.59	18.7	102.73	12.9	68.32
#一般公共服务	General Common Service	148.41	25.85	17.4	20.17	13.6	13.99
教 育	Operating Expenses for Education	142.77	30.51	21.4	20.17	14.1	12.97
社保和就业	Operating Expenses for Medical Treatment and Sanitation	90.93	10.67	11.7	10.41	11.4	6.06
金融机构年末存款余额	Year-end Loan Balance of Finance	4614.62	2795.46	60.6	2320.67	50.3	2056.09
金融机构年末贷款余额	Year-end Deposit Balance of Finance	2685.00	1506.78	56.1	1323.05	49.3	1145.54
物价(上年=100)	**Commodity Price (Preceding year=100)**						
商品零售价格指数	Index of Commodity Retail Price	105.1					104.6
居民消费价格指数	Index of Price for Residents' Consumption	105.5					104.6
人民生活	**People's life**						
职工工资总额(亿元)	Total Sum of Staff's Salary (100 million yuan)	533.24	264.51	49.6	185.39	34.8	146.36
职工平均货币工资(元)	Average Staff''s Money Wage (yuan)	21434					29483
农村居民家庭人均纯收入(元)	Annual Per capita Net Income of Rural Residents (yuan)	3183					5662
城乡储蓄存款余额(亿元)	Balance of Both Urban and Rural Deposit(100 million yuan)	2054.91	1073.93	52.3	840.05	40.9	679.53

Main Economic Indicators for Economic Belt on the Northern Slope of the Tianshan Mountains

克拉玛依市 Karamay City	石河子市 Shihezi City	奎屯市 Kuitun City	乌苏市 Usu City	沙湾县 Shawan County	昌吉市 Changji City	阜康市 Fukang City	呼图壁县 Hu Tubi County	玛纳斯县 Manas County	农六师 XJPCC No.6 Division	农七师 XJPCC No.7 Division	农八师 XJPCC No.8 Division	农十二师 XJPCC No.12 Division	建工师 XJPCC architectural engineer Division
26.72	63.61	30.76	21.54	20.70	34.78	16.62	21.36	17.19					
6.55	3.52	1.58	7.70	6.56	9.13	4.53	4.87	3.25					
26.72	63.61	30.76	21.54	17.72	34.78	14.65	20.65	13.69					
				2.98		1.97	0.71	3.50					
515.13	73.25	40.16	52.66	73.85	108.03	47.22	45.93	60.92					
2.54	5.09	1.77	21.03	30.65	16.96	6.61	19.88	27.99					
461.51	34.92	20.29	18.74	22.01	42.72	31.82	14.88	21.45					
449.71	28.48	17.01	13.47	17.41	31.42	28.99	9.19	18.44					
11.80	6.44	3.28	5.27	4.60	11.30	2.83	5.69	3.01					
51.08	33.24	18.10	12.89	21.19	48.35	8.79	11.17	11.48					
10.57	3.11	3.93	2.16	3.49	11.80	1.42	2.59	1.61					
5.55	4.35	1.27	4.04	5.12	6.49	1.47	2.07	1.84					
100	100	100	100	100	100	100	100	100					
0.5	6.9	4.4	39.9	41.5	15.7	14.0	43.3	45.9					
89.6	47.7	50.5	35.6	29.8	39.5	67.4	32.4	35.2					
87.3	38.9	42.4	25.6	23.6	29.1	61.4	20.0	30.3					
2.3	8.8	8.1	10.0	6.2	10.5	6.0	12.4	4.9					
9.9	45.4	45.1	24.5	28.7	44.8	18.6	24.3	18.9					
2.1	4.2	9.8	4.1	4.7	10.9	3.0	5.6	2.6					
1.1	5.9	3.2	7.7	6.9	6.0	3.1	4.5	3.0					
7.1	9.1	8.1	3.2	2.2	4.3	6.7	2.9	3.1					
8.3	11.5	10.1	8.2	5.6	6.4	7.0	6.6	5.4					
279.52	50.52	14.10	12.83	14.79	29.16	14.88	11.02	15.00					
36.48	6.67	3.24	1.70	1.66	4.62	3.15	1.33	1.89					
32.70	5.89	2.79	1.35	1.20	4.03	2.83	1.10	1.69					
42.82	8.44	4.06	4.34	4.10	6.88	3.30	3.05	3.28					
5.18	1.09	0.50	1.11	0.95	1.51	0.52	0.48	0.52					
9.10	1.25	1.02	1.18	1.38	1.26	0.76	0.88	0.71					
1.77	0.25	0.49	0.25	0.18	0.65	0.35	0.24	0.43					
285.88	159.44	81.24	21.99	22.61	96.51	23.75	25.42	22.53					
49.79	104.12	52.96	16.09	22.03	62.73	11.81	17.75	23.96					
105.5	105.1	103.5	105.0		104.1								
106.1	104.8	103.6	104.4		103.7								
42.43	18.58	5.28	7.49	11.38	13.54	3.85	4.78	10.82					
29706	19215	19180	13055	14853	26577	19979	16667	19119					
6569	6061		6167	7183	6585	6200	7006	8277					
120.28	101.10	34.59	15.23	22.61	51.85	15.07	18.24	15.43					

1-12 续表 1

指　　标	Item	全区合计 Total of the whole region	北坡经济带合计 Total of the economic belt	北坡经济带占全区比重(%) ratio of the economic belt (%)	乌昌合计 Total of Urmqi and Changji	乌昌占全区比重(%) Pencentage of Urmqi and Changji to total(%)	乌鲁木齐市 Urumqi City
农　业	**Agriculture**						
农林牧渔业总产值(亿元)	Value of Farm, Forestry, Herding and Fishery (100 million yuan)	1063.46	302.31	28.4	138.24	13.0	18.99
农　业	Farming	766.95	208.38	27.2	68.67	9.0	8.67
林　业	Forestry	20.86	3.43	16.4	2.30	11.0	0.16
牧　业	Animal Husbandry	231.51	72.15	31.2	63.10	27.3	8.87
渔　业	Fishery	7.01	2.45	35.0	1.37	19.5	0.39
农林牧渔服务业	Services for Farming, Forestry, Animal Husbandary and Fishery	37.13	15.90	42.8	2.80	7.5	0.90
主要农产品产量(万吨)	Main Rural Products Output (10 000 tons)						
粮　食	Grain	867.04	105.41	12.2	93.71	10.8	11.72
棉　花	Cotton	290.00	92.58	31.9	16.10	5.6	0.25
油　料	Oil-bearing Crops	40.30	3.79	9.4	4.00	9.9	0.59
甜　菜	Beet	586.93	74.30	12.7	49.16	8.4	1.04
水　果	Fruit	411.98	28.69	7.0	14.58	3.5	1.63
肉　类	Meat	160.58	34.57	21.5	29.48	18.4	4.70
工　业	**Industry**						
工业总产值(规模以上)(亿元)	Total Value of Industrial Products (100 million yuan)	3296.61	2240.64	68.0	1151.68	34.9	970.15
轻工业	Light Industry	446.70	280.59	62.8	207.73	46.5	132.49
重工业	Heavy Industry	2849.91	1960.05	68.8	943.95	33.1	837.65
国有工业	State-owned Industry	2637.79	1857.27	70.4	856.73	32.5	800.39
集体工业	Collective-owned industry	70.76	46.12	65.2	20.62	29.1	10.54
其他工业	Other Industrial Sectors	588.06	337.25	57.4	274.33	46.7	159.22
主要工业产品产量(全口径)	Output of Main Industrial Products						
纱(万吨)	Cotton Yarn (10 000 tons)	40.89	24.41	59.7	11.60	28.4	6.90
布(万米)	Cloth (10 000 m)	15999.61	10295.33	64.3	4953.92	31.0	4690.20
绒线(吨)	Woolen knitting wool (ton)	637.30	375.00	58.8	375.00	58.8	375.00
呢绒(万米)	Woolen Goods (10 000 m)	367.51	367.51	100.0	183.61	50.0	0.38
原盐(万吨)	Crude Salt (10 000 tons)	85.54	12.29	14.4	12.50	14.6	12.30
成品糖(万吨)	Sugar (10 000 tons)	64.94	4.67	7.2	4.30	6.6	
原煤(万吨)	Crude Coal (10 000 tons)	5018.64	2384.30	47.5	2449.20	48.8	1706.70
原油(万吨)	Crude Oil (10 000 tons)	2604.31	1753.31	67.3	536.30	20.6	536.30
发电量(亿千瓦小时)	Volume of Electric Generation (100 million kwh)	416.87	257.94	61.9	186.40	44.7	121.20
粗钢(万吨)	Grude steel (10 000 tons)	447.24	418.46	93.6	415.50	92.9	415.50
钢材(万吨)	Steel Rolled (10 000 tons)	470.94	446.47	94.8	441.20	93.7	441.00
水泥(万吨)	Cement (10 000 tons)	1536.77	665.94	43.3	518.60	33.8	372.30
运输邮电业	**Traffic and Telecommunication Sector**						
公路客运量(万人)	Highway Passenger Volume (10 000 persons)	36159	5442	15.0	6977	19.3	2414
公路货运量(万吨)	Highway Cargo Volume (10 000 tons)	38427	13007	33.8	12652	32.9	8677
公路货物周转量(亿吨公里)	Turnover of Highway Cargo (100million tons-km)	468.80	162.75	34.7	152.62	32.6	104.34
邮电业务总量(亿元)	Volume of Postal-Telecommunication (100 million yuan)	303.70	52.74	17.4	40.49	13.3	32.04
国内商业	**Domestic Trades**						
社会消费品零售总额(亿元)	Retail Volume of Social Commodities (100 million yuan)	847.70	503.32	59.4	388.41	45.8	321.76
教育、文化、卫生	**Education, Culture and Health**						
在校学生数(人)	Number of Registered Students (person)						
高等学校	Institutions of Higher Education	216389	149043	68.9	143544	66.3	126923
中等专业学校	Specialized Secondary School	141162	103351	73.2	76375	54.1	68750
普通中学	Ordinary Middle School	1529092	339532	22.2	222698	14.6	141627
小　学	Elementary School	2058884	426502	20.7	271274	13.2	180967
毕业生数(人)	Number of Graduates (person)						
高等学校	Institutions of Higher Education	46128	32965	71.5	31062	67.3	26955
中等专业学校	Specialized Secondary School	25735	20312	78.9	14675	57.0	12286
普通中学	Ordinary Middle School	515494	104283	20.2	70374	13.7	44128
小　学	Elementary School	361921	71097	19.6	43603	12.0	28627
医院床位数(张)	Number of Sick Beds (unit)	87131	33425	38.4	27807	31.9	20204
卫生技术人员数(人)	Number of Hygiene Technicians (person)	104671	38919	37.2	33389	31.9	24410

Continued

克拉玛依市 Karamay City	石河子市 Shihezi City	奎屯市 Kuitun City	乌苏市 Usu City	沙湾县 Shawan County	昌吉市 Changji City	阜康市 Fukang City	呼图壁县 Hu Tubi County	玛纳斯县 Manas County	农六师 XJPCC No.6 Division	农七师 XJPCC No.7 Division	农八师 XJPCC No.8 Division	农十二师 XJPCC No.12 Division	建工师 XJPCC architectural engineer Division
5.91	9.57	0.48	20.76	26.35	22.80	8.82	22.68	25.12	42.07	31.07	61.59	6.10	
2.30	7.85	0.30	16.24	19.41	11.25	4.32	10.39	15.69	31.57	24.48	51.33	4.58	
0.51	0.04	0.01	0.30	0.08	0.37	0.30	0.29	0.30	0.30	0.34	0.37	0.06	
1.47	1.06	0.02	3.64	6.43	10.28	4.11	11.09	8.40	6.39	3.57	5.62	1.20	
0.05	0.24		0.16	0.09	0.62	0.01	0.19	0.09	0.18	0.10	0.26	0.07	
1.58	0.38	0.15	0.42	0.34	0.28	0.08	0.72	0.64	3.63	2.58	4.01	0.19	
0.11	0.53	0.01	11.44	14.20	11.12	5.76	7.76	8.05	22.17	6.11	5.26	1.17	
1.51	3.80	0.16	7.32	6.64	4.22	0.93	3.86	6.56	14.54	12.70	29.78	0.31	
	0.02	0.01	0.56	1.06	0.23	0.31	0.21	0.36	0.42		0.02		
	0.28		3.90	14.02	11.71	0.35	11.15	3.42	4.73	21.11	0.42	2.17	
	1.57		0.17	0.50	3.63	0.55	0.59	7.15	2.28	1.86	3.52	5.24	
0.68	0.54	0.02	2.54	3.89	4.45	3.17	3.52	3.34	3.61	1.29	2.19	0.63	
942.98	89.54	30.07	14.35	23.29	87.48	32.16	20.35	30.27					
2.33	35.61	24.07	4.48	14.63	33.26	0.77	14.02	18.92					
940.65	53.93	6.00	9.87	8.66	54.22	31.39	6.33	11.35					
901.97	68.36	22.19	2.03	7.62	23.38	19.07	2.22	10.05					
23.67	0.61		1.32	0.27	0.06	4.44	4.89	0.31					
17.34	20.57	7.88	11.00	15.40	64.04	8.65	13.24	19.91					
	8.24	2.74	0.44	1.35	0.83		2.86	1.05					
	3341.41	1090.00	176.00	734.00			261.48	2.28					
	183.90				183.23								
		2.51			2.16								
		16.20	164.08	52.60	145.11	119.03	143.08	37.52					
1217.06													
27.34	36.15	5.79	1.83	1.06	14.74	4.76		45.09					
				2.97									
				5.26	0.02			0.21					
	29.44	0.53		117.41	106.88	39.37							
422	602	478	726	800									
1686	1526	332	206	580									
31.41	10.93	7.64	3.50	4.93									
11.19	4.51	3.49	1.06	0.45									
23.07	26.57	8.40	5.84	6.29	28.63	8.66	7.85	8.19	16.99	8.83	25.48	6.76	
5075	1864	394			14787								
1350	16358	855			4458	3227	609		1339	855	3361	525	1664
23932	17347	13068	15841	15538	13456	8205	9049	7949	20524	13939	28522	5510	5025
26451	13723	10575	19297	17256	24954	9480	12487	11400	27618	18536	39713	6866	7179
1482	137				4391								
774	2212	297			2360	523	116		491	204	761		288
7038	4289	3520	5023	5555	4171	2617	3013	2671	6356	3997	9030	1780	1095
4164	2262	2020	3215	2947	4096	1597	1882	1851	4894	3430	7778	1273	1061
1582	4161	1668	650	750	2512	635	575	688					
2739	4937	2120	836	724	974	770	497	912					

主要统计指标解释

行政区划 指国家对行政区域的划分.根据宪法规定,我国的行政区域划分如下: (1)全国分为省、自治区、直辖市; (2)省、自治区分为自治州、县、自治县、市; (3)自治州分为县、自治县、市; (4)县、自治县分为乡、民族乡、镇; (5)直辖市和较大的市分为区、县; (6)国家在必要时设立的特别行政区。

平均增长速度 我国计算平均增长速度有两种方法: 一种是习惯上经常使用的"水平法", 又称几何平均法, 是以间隔期最后一年的水平同基期水平对比来计算平均每年增长(或下降)速度; 另一种是"累计法", 又称代数平均法或方程法, 是以间隔期内各年水平的总和同基期水平对比来计算平均每年增长(或下降)速度。在一般正常情况下, 两种方法计算的平均每年增长速度比较接近; 但在经济发展不平衡、出现大起大落时, 两种方法计算的结果差别较大。

本《年鉴》内所列的平均增长速度, 均用"水平法"计算。从某年到某年平均增长速度的年份, 均不包括基期年在内。如建国四十三年的平均增长速度是以 1949 年为基期计算的, 则写为 1950-1992 年平均增长速度, 其余类推。

国民经济行业分类 自 2003 年定期报表开始使用新的《国民经济行业分类》(GB/T4754-2002), 该分类是由国家统计局组织修订, 经国家质量监督检验检疫总局批准, 于 2002 年 5 月 10 日发布实施。这次修订是在 1994 年分类标准的基础上, 参照联合国《全部经济活动的国际标准产业分类》(ISIC/Rev.3) 进行的。修订后的《国民经济行业分类》(GB/T4754-2002) 共有门类 20 个, 大类 95 个, 中类 396 个, 小类 913 个。新增门类 4 个, 大类增加 3 个, 中类增加 28 个, 小类增加 67 个。

企业(单位)登记注册类型 是以在工商行政管理机关登记注册的各类企业为划分对象, 以工商行政管理部门对企业登记注册的类型为依据, 将企业登记注册类型分为内资企业、港澳台商投资企业和外商投资企业三大类。内资企业包括国有企业、集体企业、股份合作企业、联营企业、有限责任公司、股份有限公司、私营公司和其他企业; 港澳台商投资企业和外商投资企业分别包括合资经营企业、合作经营企业、独资经营企业和股份有限公司。对不在工商行政管理部门进行登记注册的行政机关、事业单位和社会团体, 主要按其经费来源和管理方式进行划分。

国有企业 指企业全部资产归国家所有, 并按《中华人民共和国企业法人登记管理条例》规定登记注册的非公司制的经济组织。不包括有限责任公司中的国有独资公司。

集体企业 指企业资产归集体所有, 并按《中华人民共和国企业法人登记管理条例》规定登记注册的经济组织。

股份合作企业 指以合作制为基础, 由企业职工共同出资入股, 吸收一定比例的社会资产投资组建, 实行自主经营, 自负盈亏, 共同劳动, 民主管理, 按劳分配与按股分红相结合的一种集体经济组织。

联营企业 指两个及两个以上相同或不同所有制性质的企业法人或事业单位法人, 按自愿、平等、互利的原则, 共同投资组成的经济组织。联营企业包括国有联营企业、集体联营企业、国有与集体联营企业和其他联营企业。

有限责任公司 指根据《中华人民共和国公司登记管理条例》规定登记注册, 由两个以上、五十个以下的股东共同出资, 每个股东以其所认缴的出资额对公司承担有限责任, 公司以其全部资产对其债务承担责任的经济组织。有限责任公司包括国有独资公司以及其他有限责任公司。

股份有限公司 指根据《中华人民共和国公司登记管理条例》规定登记注册, 其全部注册资本由等额股份构成并通过发行股票筹集资本, 股东以其认购的股份对公司承担有限责任, 公司以其全部资产对其债务承担责任的经济组织。

私营企业 指由自然人投资设立或由自然人控股, 以雇佣劳动为基础的营利性经济组织。包括按照《公司法》、《合伙企业法》、《私营企业暂行条例》规定登记注册的私营有限责任公司、私营股份有限公司、私营合伙企业和私营独资企业。

其他内资企业 指上述企业之外的其他内资经济组织。

与港澳台商合资经营企业 指港澳台地区投资者与内地企业依照《中华人民共和国中外合资经营企业法》及有关法律的规定, 按合同规定的比例投资设立、分享利润和分担风险的企业。

与港澳台商合作经营企业 指港澳台地区投资者与内地企业依照《中华人民共和国中外合作经营企业法》及有关法律的规定, 依照合作合同的约定进行投资或提供条件设立、分配利润和分担风险的企业。

港澳台商独资经营企业 指依照《中华人民共和国外资企业法》及有关法律的规定, 在内地由港澳台地区投资者全额投资设立的企业。

港澳台商投资股份有限公司 指根据国家有关规定, 经外经贸部依法批准设立, 其中港、澳、台商的股本占公司注册资本的比例达 25% 以上的股份有限公司。凡其中港、澳、台商的股本占公司注册资本的比例小于 25%的, 属于内资企业中的股份有限公司。

中外合资经营企业 指外国企业或外国人与中国内地企业依照《中华人民共和国中外合资经营企业法》及有关法律的规定, 按合同规定的比例投资设立、分享利润和分担风险的企业。

中外合作经营企业 指外国企业或外国人与中国内地企业依照《中华人民共和国中外合作经营企业法》及有关法律的规定, 依照合作合同的约定进行投资或提供条件设立、分配利润和分担风险的企业。

外资企业 指依照《中华人民共和国外资企业法》及有关法律的规定, 在中国内地由外国投资者全额投资设立的企业。

外商投资股份有限公司 指根据国家有关规定, 经外经贸部依法批准设立, 其中外资的股本占公司注册资本的比例达 25% 以上的股份有限公司。凡其中外资股本占公司注册资本的比例小于 25%的, 属于内资企业中的股份有限公司。

行政机关、事业单位和社会团体 **参照企业登记注册类型, 主要按其经费来源和管理方式划分。具体规定如下:**

⑴行政机关: 包括国家机关和政党机关, 原则上均列为"国有"。但有特殊规定的, 如供销社等, 则列为"集体"。

⑵事业单位: 包括经国家机构编制部门和有关业务主管部门批准成立的各类事业单位, 不包括实行企业化管理的事业单位。事业单位的划分办法如下:

①由国家财政预算拨款或列入财政预算外资金管理以及经费主要来源于国有主管部门或国有上级单位的事业单位, 列为"国有"。

②经费主要来源于集体单位的事业单位, 列为"集体"。

③公民个人(或个人合伙)开办的事业单位, 列为"私营"。

④上述以外的其他事业单位, 如果其经费来源不明确, 按管理方式进行归类。

⑶社会团体: 包括经民政部门批准成立以及未纳入社会团体管理条例范围的工会、妇联等各类社会团体。社会团体的划分办法如下:

①未纳入民政部社会团体管理条例范围的工会、妇联、共青团、青联、工商联、科协、侨联等社会团体, 国家拨款设立的基金会或基金管理组织以及经费主要来源于国有业务主管部门或国有上级单位的社会团体, 列为"国有"。

②经费主要来源于集体单位的社会团体, 列为"集体"。

③公民个人(或个人合伙)开办的社会团体, 划为"私营"。

④上述以外的其他社会团体, 如果其经费来源不明确, 改按管理方式进行归类。

Explanatory Notes on Main Statistical Indicators

Administrative Division refers to the division of administrative areas by the state. The Constitution of the People's Republic of China stipulates that the administrative areas in China are divided as: 1) The whole Country is divided into provinces, autonomous regions and municipalities directly under the central government; 2) Provinces and autonomous regions are divided into autonomous prefectures, counties, autonomous counties and cities; 3) Autonomous prefectures are divided into counties, autonomous counties and cities; 4) Counties and autonomous counties are divided into townships, nationality townships and towns; 5) Municipalities and large cities are divided into districts and counties, 6) The state shall, when necessary, establish special administrative regions.

Average Annual Growth Rate Two methods for calculating average annual growth rate are applied in China,one is often called level approachor the method of calculating geometric average,which is derived by comparing the level of the last year of the interval with that of the beginning year;the other is calledaccumulative approach or algebraic average or equation method,which is derived by the summation of the actual figure of each year in the interval divided by the figure in the base year.Usually the results calculated by the two methods are fairly close, but they differed sharply when uneven economic development occurred with striking fluctuations in growth.

The average annual growth rates listed in this statistical yearbook are calculated by level approach except for the growth rate of investment in fixed assets. The base years are not listed when the years are listed for average annual growth rates. For instance,the average annual growth rate of 43 years since 1949 is listed as average annual growth rate of 1950-1992 without listing the base year 1949.And the analogy of this is also the same for the rest of the years.

Industrial Classification of the National Economy The new Industrial Classification of the National Economy (GB/T 4754-2002) is introduced starting from the compilation of 2003 annual statistics. The new revision was based on the 1994 classification and organized by the National Bureau of Statistics taking into consideration of the International Standards of the Industrial Classification of All Economic Activities (ISIC/Rev.3) of the United Nations, and the new Classification was promulgated by the National Administration of Quality Supervision, Inspection and Quarantine on May 10, 2002. The revised version of the Industrial Classification of the National Economy (GB/T 4754-2002) is composed of 20 major divisions, 95 divisions, 396 major groups and 913 groups, including 4 new major divisions, 3 new divisions, 28 major groups and 67 groups.

Registration Status of Enterprises Enterprises are classified into 3 categories, namely domestic-funded enterprises, enterprises with investment from Hong Kong, Macau and Taiwan, and enterprises with foreign investment, in the light of the registration status of an enterprise in industrial and commercial administration agencies. Domestic-funded enterprises include state-owned enterprises, collective-owned enterprises, cooperative enterprises, joint ownership enterprises, limited liability corporations, share-holding corporations Ltd., private enterprises and other enterprises. Included in the enterprises with investment from Hong Kong, Macau and Taiwan and enterprises with foreign investment are joint-venture enterprises, cooperative enterprises, sole investment enterprises and share-holding corporations Ltd. For government agencies, institutions and social organizations which are not requested to be registered in industrial and commercial administration agencies, they are classified mainly by their sources of funds and way of management.

State-owned Enterprises refer to non-corporation economic units where the entire assets are owned by the state and which have registered in accordance with the Regulation of the Peoples Republic of China on the Management of Registration of Corporate Enterprises. Excluded from this category are sole state-funded corporations in the limited liability corporations.

Collective-owned Enterprises refer to economic units where the assets are owned collectively and which have registered in accordance with the Regulation of the Peoples Republic of China on the Management of Registration of Corporate Enterprises.

Cooperative Enterprises refer to a form of collective economic units (enterprises) where capitals come mainly from employees as their shares, with certain proportion of capital from the outside, where production is organized on the basis of independent operation, independent accounting for profits and losses, joint work, democratic management, and a distribution system that integrates remuneration according to work with dividend according to capital share.

Joint Ownership Enterprises refer to economic units established by two or more corporate enterprises or corporate institutions of the same or different ownership, through joint investment on the basis of equality, voluntary participation and mutual benefits. They include state joint ownership enterprises, collective joint ownership enterprises, joint state-collective enterprises, other joint ownership enterprises.

Limited Liability Corporations refer to economic units established with investment from 2-50 investors and registered in accordance with the Regulation of the Peoples Republic of China on the Management of Registration of Corporations, each investor bearing limited liability to the corporation depending on its share of investment, and the corporation bearing liability to its debt to the maximum of its total assets. Limited liability corporations include exclusive state-funded limited liability corporations and other limited liability corporations.

Share-holding Corporations Ltd. refer to economic units registered in accordance with the Regulation of the Peoples Republic of China on the Management of Registration of Corporations, with total registered capitals divided into equal shares and raised through issuing stocks. Each investor bears limited liability to the corporation depending on the holding of shares, and the corporation bears liability to its debt to the maximum of its total assets.

Private Enterprises refer to profit-making economic units invested and established by natural persons, or controlled by natural persons using employed labour. Included in this category are private limited liability corporations, private share-holding corporations Ltd., private partnership enterprises and private-funded enterprises registered in accordance with the Corporation Law, Partnership Enterprises Law and Interim Regulations on Private Enterprises .

Other Domestic-funded Enterprises refer to domestic-funded economic units other than those mentioned above.

Joint-venture Enterprises with Funds from Hong Kong, Macau and Taiwan refer to enterprises jointly established by investors from Hong Kong, Macau and Taiwan with enterprises in the mainland of China in accordance with the Law of the Peoples Republic of China on Sino-foreign Joint Venture Enterprises and other relevant laws, where the share of investment, profits and risks is stipulated in the contract.

Cooperative Enterprises with Funds from Hong Kong Macau and Taiwan , established by investors from Hong Kong, Macau and Taiwan with enterprises in the mainland of China in accordance with the Law of the Peoples Republic of China on Sino-foreign Cooperative Enterprises and other relevant laws, where the investment or provision of facilities, and the share of profits and risks is stipulated in the cooperative contract.

Enterprises with Sole (exclusive) Investment from Hong Kong, Macau and Taiwan refer to enterprises established in the mainland of China with exclusive investment from investors from Hong Kong, Macau and Taiwan in accordance with the Law of the Peoples Republic of China on Foreign-Funded Enterprises and other relevant laws.

Share-holding Corporations Ltd. with Investment from Hong Kong, Macau and Taiwan refer to share-holding corporations Ltd. established with the approval from the Ministry of Foreign Trades and Economic Relations in line with relevant state regulations, where the share of investment from Hong Kong, Macau or Taiwan businessmen exceeds 25% of the total registered capital of the corporation. In case the share of investment from Hong Kong, Macau or Taiwan is less than 25% of the total registered capital, the enterprise is to be classified as domestic-funded share-holding corporation Ltd.

Joint-venture Enterprises with Foreign Investment refer to enterprises jointly established by foreign enterprises or foreigners with enterprises in the mainland of China in accordance with the Law of the Peoples Republic of China on Sino-foreign Joint Venture Enterprises and other relevant laws, where the share of investment, profits and risks is stipulated in the contract.

Cooperation Enterprises with Foreign Investment refer to enterprises jointly established by foreign enterprises or foreigners with enterprises in the mainland of China in accordance with the Law of the Peoples Republic of China on Sino-foreign Cooperative Enterprises and other relevant laws, where the investment or provision of facilities, and the share of profits and risks is stipulated in the cooperative contract.

Enterprises with Sole (exclusive) Foreign Investment refer to enterprises established in the mainland of China with exclusive investment from foreign investors in accordance with the Law of the Peoples Republic of China on Foreign-Funded Enterprises and other relevant laws.

Share-holding Corporations Ltd. with Foreign Investment refer to share-holding corporations Ltd. established with the approval from the Ministry of Foreign Trades and Economic Relations in line with relevant state regulations, where the share of investment from foreign investors exceeds 25% of the total registered capital of the corporation. In case the share of foreign investment is less than 25% of the total registered capital, the enterprise is to be classified as domestic-funded share-holding corporation Ltd.

Government Agencies, Institutions and Social Organizations are classified into following categories by source of funds and way of management taking reference of the registration status of enterprises:

(1) Government agencies: include state and party agencies, classified in principle as "state-owned". There are exceptions, such as supply and marketing cooperatives which are classified as "collective".

(2) Institutions: include institutions of various types established with the approval by organization and staffing departments of the government, but exclude institutions where enterprise management system is introduced. Institutions are further classified as follows:

(a) Institutions whose main budget is listed in the government budget appropriations or extra-budget funds, or allocated from the budget of their competent government agencies. Such institutions are classified as "state-owned".

(b) Institutions whose budget mainly comes from collective units. Such institutions are classified as "collective".

(c) Institutions other than those mentioned above whose source of budget is not clear. Such institutions are classified by way of management.

(3) Social organizations: include social organizations established with the approval from the Ministry of Civil Affairs, and organizations that are not covered by social organization management regulations such as Trades unions, women's federations etc.. Social organizations are further classified as follows:

(a) Social organizations that are not covered by social organization management regulations of the Ministry of Civil Affairs such as Trades unions, women's federations, communist youth leagues, youth associations, industrial and commerce associations, scientists associations, overseas Chinese associations, etc., foundations and fund management organizations established with funds from the state, and social organizations whose funds mainly come from the budget of their competent government agencies. Such institutions are classified as "state-owned".

(b) Social organizations whose budget mainly comes from collective units. Such institutions are classified as "collective".

(c) Social organizations established by individual or a group of citizens, which are classified as "private".

(d) Social organizations other than those mentioned above whose source of budget is not clear. Such organizations are classified by way of management.

第二篇
国民经济核算

CHAPTER 2
National Accounts

简要说明
Brief Introduction

本篇资料的主要内容及来源

国民经济核算篇资料主要包括新疆维吾尔自治区历年生产总值的绝对值、构成和指数，居民消费水平，各地、州、市、县生产总值、构成和指数等资料。以上资料是由新疆维吾尔自治区统计局核算处根据不同产业部门、不同支出构成的特点和资料来源，严格按照国家国民经济核算制度计算的。

新疆生产总值的1993年以后数据已按照国家统计局制定的统一方案，根据2004年经济普查资料采用国际上通用的"趋势离差法"进行了调整。

关于数据使用的说明。本篇表2-1、表2-4中三次产业数据使用的是国家1994年国民经济行业分类标准；2-5、2-6表使用的是国家2002年国民经济行业分类标准。若做历史数据分析比较请使用表2-1表中公布的数据资料；若只使用当年数据，请用表2-5表或2-6表中公布的数据。

Main Content and Source of Data

Statistics on national accounts include mainly gross domestic product of Xinjiang Bureau of Statistics, it´s composition and indices of gross domestic product, household consumption level, composition and indices of gross domestic product by prefecture, autonomous prefecture, city and county. Data on GDP are calculated by the Department of National Accounts Statistics of the Xinjiang Bureau of Statistics with various approaches in the light of the features of various sectors, various expenditure structures and the data sources and National Accounts system.

Historical data of GDP were recompiled in accordance with the uniform plan of NBS and revised by trend deviation approach.

Data on the table 2-1 and 2-4 use the Industrial Classification of National Economy of 1994;The table 2-5 and 2-6 use the Industrial Classification of National Economy of 2002.If analyze the historical data ,you could use the data of table 2-1.If use the present data, you use the data of 2-5 or 2-6.

2-1 新疆生产总值
Gross Domestic Product in Xinjiang

单位：亿元 (100 million yuan)

年 份 Year	新疆生产总值 Gross Domestic Product	第一产业 Primary Industry	第二产业 Secondary Industry	工 业 Industry	建筑业 Construction	第三产业 Tertiary Industry	#交通运输仓储和邮政业 Transport, Storage and Post	#批发和零售业 Wholesale, and Retail Trades	人均新疆生产总值(元/人) Per Capita GDP (yuan/person)
1978	39.07	13.97	18.35	14.48	3.87	6.75	1.19	2.07	313
1979	45.63	16.32	21.43	17.16	4.27	7.88	1.52	2.34	359
1980	53.24	21.53	21.44	17.48	3.96	10.27	1.91	2.91	410
1981	59.41	25.18	22.39	17.93	4.46	11.84	2.25	3.41	450
1982	65.24	28.11	23.35	18.66	4.69	13.78	2.53	3.84	488
1983	78.55	32.84	29.10	23.33	5.77	16.61	3.01	4.75	583
1984	89.75	36.68	31.65	25.45	6.20	21.42	4.01	6.29	661
1985	112.24	42.89	40.50	32.14	8.36	28.85	4.59	8.97	820
1986	129.04	46.00	45.63	36.79	8.84	37.41	5.98	10.48	924
1987	148.50	56.18	50.30	41.16	9.14	42.02	7.73	12.45	1053
1988	192.72	72.27	66.02	53.53	12.49	54.43	11.60	16.11	1347
1989	217.29	78.01	73.83	60.21	13.62	65.45	12.90	17.59	1493
1990	261.44	104.09	83.18	71.50	11.68	74.17	14.63	20.48	1713
1991	335.91	111.86	107.99	84.07	23.92	116.06	22.63	36.88	2101
1992	402.31	114.50	147.64	106.29	41.35	140.17	28.32	39.85	2477
1993	495.25	126.85	205.07	155.92	49.15	163.33	32.58	43.46	2964
1994	662.32	187.69	249.11	190.00	59.11	225.52	44.40	57.67	3888
1995	814.85	240.71	283.97	219.01	64.96	290.17	59.63	73.78	4701
1996	900.93	249.31	313.70	239.07	74.63	337.92	73.74	87.25	5102
1997	1039.85	279.73	385.37	302.50	82.87	374.75	85.70	94.23	5848
1998	1106.95	291.05	395.75	298.53	97.22	420.15	106.87	98.06	6174
1999	1163.17	268.51	420.48	315.86	104.62	474.18	129.60	102.26	6443
2000	1363.56	288.18	537.58	418.63	118.95	537.80	148.63	110.10	7372
2001	1491.60	288.12	573.91	445.60	128.31	629.57	148.38	118.45	7945
2002	1612.65	305.00	603.15	463.59	139.56	704.50	168.58	123.88	8457
2003	1886.35	412.90	719.54	563.57	155.97	753.91	159.43	141.32	9828
2004	2209.09	446.13	914.47	734.10	180.37	848.49	186.70	160.30	11337
2005	2604.14	510.00	1164.80	961.62	203.18	929.34	149.61	145.10	13108
2006	3045.26	527.80	1459.30	1241.33	217.97	1058.16	165.60	163.15	15000
2007	3523.16	628.72	1647.55	1405.11	242.44	1246.89	177.28	187.10	16950

注：1.本表绝对数按当年价格计算。2.1993 年以后数据根据经济普查资料采用趋势离差法（国际上通用的调整历史数据的方法）修订。3. 2004 年及以前年份第一产业不包括农林牧渔服务业，交通运输和邮政业包括电信业，但不包括城市公共交通业，批发和零售业包括餐饮业（下表同）

Note: a) Data in value terms in this table are calculated at current prices. b) The data since 1993 were revised by trend deviation approach accordance with the economic census.c) In 2004 and preceding years the primary industry did not include service of farming,forestry,animal husbandry and fishery;transport,storage and post include telecommunication services,but did not include urban public transport;wholesale and retail Trades include catering servites.(The same as in the following table)

2-2 新疆生产总值构成
Composition of Gross Domestic Product in Xinjiang

单位：% (%)

年 份 Year	新疆生产总值 Gross Domestic Product	第一产业 Primary Industry	第二产业 Secondary Industry	工 业 Industry	建筑业 Construction	第三产业 Tertiary Industry	#交通运输仓储和邮政业 Transport, Storage and Post	#批发和零售业 Wholesale, and Retail Trades
1978	100	35.8	47.0	37.1	9.9	17.2	3.0	5.3
1979	100	35.7	47.0	37.6	9.4	17.3	3.3	5.1
1980	100	40.4	40.3	32.9	7.4	19.3	3.6	5.5
1981	100	42.4	37.7	30.2	7.5	19.9	3.8	5.7
1982	100	43.1	35.8	28.6	7.2	21.1	3.9	5.9
1983	100	41.8	37.1	29.8	7.3	21.1	3.8	6.0
1984	100	40.9	35.2	28.3	6.9	23.9	4.5	7.0
1985	100	38.2	36.1	28.7	7.4	25.7	4.1	8.0
1986	100	35.6	35.4	28.5	6.9	29.0	4.6	8.1
1987	100	37.8	33.9	27.7	6.2	28.3	5.2	8.4
1988	100	37.5	34.3	27.8	6.5	28.2	6.0	8.4
1989	100	35.9	34.0	27.7	6.3	30.1	5.9	8.1
1990	100	39.8	31.8	27.3	4.5	28.4	5.6	7.8
1991	100	33.3	32.1	25.0	7.1	34.6	6.7	11.0
1992	100	28.5	36.7	26.4	10.3	34.8	7.0	9.9
1993	100	25.6	41.4	31.5	9.9	33.0	6.6	8.8
1994	100	28.3	37.6	28.7	8.9	34.1	6.7	8.7
1995	100	29.5	34.9	26.9	8.0	35.6	7.3	9.1
1996	100	27.7	34.8	26.5	8.3	37.5	8.2	9.7
1997	100	26.9	37.1	29.1	8.0	36.0	8.2	9.1
1998	100	26.3	35.7	27.0	8.7	38.0	9.7	8.9
1999	100	23.1	36.1	27.1	9.0	40.8	11.1	8.8
2000	100	21.1	39.4	30.7	8.7	39.5	10.9	8.1
2001	100	19.3	38.5	29.9	8.6	42.2	9.9	7.9
2002	100	18.9	37.4	28.7	8.7	43.7	10.5	7.7
2003	100	21.9	38.1	29.8	8.3	40.0	8.5	7.5
2004	100	20.2	41.4	33.2	8.2	38.4	8.5	7.3
2005	100	19.6	44.7	36.9	7.8	35.7	5.7	5.6
2006	100	17.3	47.9	40.7	7.2	34.8	5.4	5.4
2007	100	17.8	46.8	39.9	6.9	35.4	5.0	5.3

注：本表按当年价格计算。
Note: Data in value terms in this table are calculated at current prices.

2-3 新疆生产总值指数

Indices of Gross Domestic Product in Xinjiang

(上年=100) (preceding year=100)

年份 Year	新疆生产总值 Gross Domestic Product	第一产业 Primary Industry	第二产业 Secondary Industry	工业 Industry	建筑业 Construction	第三产业 Tertiary Industry	#交通运输仓储和邮政业 Transport, Storage and Post	#批发和零售业 Wholesale, and Retail Trades	人均新疆生产总值 Per Capita GDP
1978	109.8	110.2	110.3	112.8	101.8	107.2	102.1	109.3	106.9
1979	112.4	109.8	111.5	111.2	112.6	120.8	121.6	117.5	110.2
1980	107.3	106.0	105.2	108.5	93.1	116.6	115.6	125.5	105.0
1981	108.5	115.2	99.3	99.1	100.3	113.4	119.4	117.9	106.6
1982	109.9	111.2	104.3	104.6	102.8	117.1	118.9	119.8	108.5
1983	113.5	112.1	111.9	112.4	109.8	118.7	113.3	108.8	112.5
1984	114.1	113.6	114.7	115.1	112.9	114.0	100.0	109.2	113.2
1985	116.9	112.9	116.6	116.1	119.0	125.0	100.3	126.6	115.9
1986	111.7	108.3	109.5	111.0	102.5	120.7	124.7	110.0	109.2
1987	110.0	110.7	105.6	108.5	91.4	114.7	119.3	111.0	108.7
1988	109.6	103.3	114.6	113.6	120.2	112.9	118.8	114.7	108.0
1989	106.1	101.8	105.0	106.9	94.5	113.5	112.7	107.5	104.1
1990	111.7	116.0	106.7	106.4	108.6	112.0	106.7	104.5	106.8
1991	114.4	111.2	117.0	113.1	140.6	115.7	128.8	101.6	109.0
1992	113.1	105.5	119.4	112.6	152.8	115.7	124.6	112.6	111.3
1993	110.2	101.1	113.3	111.4	120.3	117.7	118.3	121.3	106.9
1994	112.1	111.2	110.2	111.3	106.3	115.3	109.7	105.6	110.2
1995	109.1	104.9	111.5	113.3	105.0	110.9	119.5	108.9	107.4
1996	106.5	103.5	107.8	107.4	109.5	108.0	113.0	109.6	104.5
1997	108.4	110.8	105.2	103.4	112.0	109.7	119.6	105.8	107.6
1998	107.5	107.2	105.7	103.0	115.0	109.6	117.5	104.9	106.6
1999	107.4	102.7	106.8	106.5	107.7	112.3	114.7	107.9	106.6
2000	108.7	104.8	108.6	109.1	107.3	112.1	114.4	109.6	106.2
2001	108.6	102.8	108.1	107.8	109.0	112.1	109.5	105.0	107.0
2002	108.2	105.0	107.4	107.7	106.3	110.4	114.3	110.3	106.5
2003	111.2	108.2	111.6	111.2	112.8	112.3	115.1	110.9	110.5
2004	111.4	105.7	114.0	114.5	112.2	111.5	115.1	112.6	109.7
2005	110.9	106.5	114.4	115.7	109.7	109.4	109.0	111.9	108.8
2006	111.0	105.7	111.2	112.5	105.0	113.6	107.2	110.5	108.7
2007	112.2	107.1	112.7	114.1	105.4	114.3	106.1	109.1	109.9

注：本表按可比价计算。

Note: Data in this table are calculated at constante prices.

2-4 新疆生产总值指数
Indices of Gross Domestic Product in Xinjiang

(1978 年=100)

年 份 Year	新疆生产总值 Gross Domestic Product	第一产业 Primary Industry	第二产业 Secondary Industry	工 业 Industry	建筑业 Construction	第三产业 Tertiary Industry	#交通运输仓储和邮政业 Transport, Storage and Post	#批发和零售业 Wholesale, and Retail Trades	人均新疆生产总值 Per Capita GDP
1978	100.0	100.0	100.0	100.0	100.0	100.0	100.0	100.0	100.0
1979	112.4	109.8	111.5	111.2	112.6	120.8	121.6	117.5	110.2
1980	120.6	116.4	117.3	120.7	104.8	140.9	140.6	147.5	115.7
1981	130.9	134.1	116.5	119.6	105.1	159.8	167.9	173.9	123.3
1982	143.9	149.1	121.5	125.1	108.0	187.1	199.6	208.3	133.8
1983	163.3	167.1	136.0	140.6	118.6	222.1	226.1	226.6	150.6
1984	186.3	189.8	156.0	161.8	133.9	253.2	226.1	247.4	170.4
1985	217.8	214.3	181.9	187.8	159.3	316.5	226.8	313.2	197.5
1986	243.3	232.1	199.2	208.5	163.3	382.0	282.8	344.5	215.7
1987	267.6	256.9	210.4	226.2	149.3	438.2	337.4	382.4	234.5
1988	293.3	265.4	241.1	257.0	179.5	494.7	400.8	438.6	253.2
1989	311.2	270.2	253.2	274.7	169.6	561.5	451.7	471.5	263.6
1990	347.6	313.4	270.2	292.3	184.2	628.9	482.0	492.7	281.5
1991	397.7	348.5	316.1	330.6	259.0	727.6	620.8	500.6	306.9
1992	449.8	367.7	377.4	372.3	395.8	841.8	773.5	563.7	341.6
1993	495.7	371.7	427.6	414.7	476.1	990.8	915.1	683.8	365.1
1994	555.7	413.3	471.2	461.6	506.1	1142.4	1003.9	722.1	402.4
1995	606.3	433.6	525.4	523.0	531.4	1266.9	1199.7	786.4	432.1
1996	645.7	448.8	566.4	561.7	581.9	1368.3	1355.7	861.9	451.6
1997	699.9	497.3	595.9	580.8	651.7	1501.0	1621.4	911.9	485.9
1998	752.4	533.1	629.9	598.2	749.5	1645.1	1905.1	956.6	518.0
1999	808.1	547.5	672.7	637.1	807.2	1847.4	2185.1	1032.2	552.2
2000	878.4	573.8	730.6	695.1	866.1	2070.9	2499.8	1131.3	586.4
2001	953.9	589.9	789.8	749.3	944.0	2321.5	2737.3	1187.9	627.4
2002	1032.1	619.4	848.2	807.0	1003.5	2562.9	3128.7	1310.3	668.2
2003	1147.7	670.2	946.6	897.4	1131.9	2878.1	3601.1	1453.1	738.4
2004	1278.5	708.4	1079.1	1027.5	1270.0	3209.1	4144.9	1636.2	810.0
2005	1417.9	754.4	1234.5	1188.8	1393.2	3510.8	4517.9	1830.9	881.3
2006	1573.9	797.4	1372.8	1337.4	1462.9	3988.3	4843.2	2023.1	958.0
2007	1765.9	854.0	1547.1	1526.0	1541.9	4558.6	5138.6	2207.2	1052.8

注：本表按可比价计算。
Note: Data in this table are calculated at constant prices.

2-5 分行业新疆生产总值

Gross Domestic Product by Sector in Xinjiang

指 标	Item	增加值(亿元) Added Value (100 million yuan)		构成(%) Composition (%)		指数(上年=100) Indices (preceding year=100)	
		2006	2007	2006	2007	2006	2007
新疆生产总值(亿元)	**Gross Domestic Product (100 million yuan)**	**3045.26**	**3523.16**	**100.0**	**100.0**	**111.0**	**112.2**
第一产业	Primary Industry	527.80	628.72	17.3	17.8	105.7	107.1
第二产业	Secondary Industry	1459.30	1647.55	47.9	46.8	111.2	112.7
工 业	Industry	1241.33	1405.11	40.8	39.9	112.5	114.1
建筑业	Construction	217.97	242.44	7.1	6.9	105.0	105.4
第三产业	Tertiary Industry	1058.16	1246.89	34.8	35.4	113.6	114.3
交通运输、仓储和邮政业	Transport, storage and Post	165.60	177.28	5.4	5.0	107.2	106.1
信息传输、计算机服务和软件业	Information Transmission, Computer Service and Software	70.31	73.37	2.3	2.1	121.9	115.6
批发和零售业	Wholesale and Retail Trades	163.15	187.10	5.4	5.3	110.5	109.1
住宿和餐饮业	Hotels and Catering Services	51.77	57.69	1.7	1.6	112.6	105.4
金融业	Financial Intermediation	99.25	149.22	3.3	4.3	121.3	140.9
房地产业	Real Estate	68.90	91.28	2.3	2.6	121.2	124.9
租赁和商务服务业	Leasing and Business Service	36.32	40.36	1.2	1.1	106.8	108.5
科学研究、技术服务和地质勘查业	Scientific Research, Technology Service and Geological Prospecting	30.38	35.24	1.0	1.0	113.1	112.9
水利、环境和公共设施管理业	Water Conservancy, Environment and Public Facility Management	17.82	23.31	0.6	0.7	113.7	124.0
居民服务和其他服务业	Community Service and Other Services	30.47	34.43	1.0	1.0	115.4	110.0
教 育	Education	101.57	119.84	3.3	3.4	115.0	115.6
卫生、社会保障和社会福利业	Health, Social Security and Social Welfare	56.78	64.86	1.9	1.8	114.8	112.1
文化、体育和娱乐业	Culture, Sports and Entertainment	13.37	15.06	0.4	0.4	115.8	110.7
公共管理和社会组织	Public Management and Social Organizations	152.47	177.85	5.0	5.1	112.6	110.6

注：本表按当年价格计算，采用 GB/T4754-2002 国民经济行业分类标准。
Note: Data in value terms in this table are calculated at current prices and adopted the new Industrial Classification of National Economy (GB/T4754-2002).

2-6 新疆生产总值项目结构
Components of Gross Domestic Product in Xinjiang

(2007 年)

指 标	Item	新疆生产总值 Gross Domestic Product	劳动者报酬 Compensation of Employees	固定资产折旧 Depreciation of Fixed Assets	生产税净额 Net Taxes on Production	营业盈余 Operating Surplus
新疆生产总值(亿元)	**Gross Domestic Product (100 million yuan)**	**3523.16**	**1566.80**	**494.69**	**456.62**	**1005.05**
第一产业	Primary Industry	628.72	609.23	19.49		
第二产业	Secondary Industry	1647.55	354.67	250.88	316.38	725.62
工 业	Industry	1405.11	210.17	231.69	280.91	682.34
建筑业	Construction	242.44	144.50	19.19	35.47	43.28
第三产业	Tertiary Industry	1246.89	602.90	224.32	140.24	279.43
交通运输、仓储和邮政业	Transport, storage and Post	177.28	65.81	37.28	17.49	56.70
信息传输、计算机服务和软件业	Information Transmission, Computer Service and Software	73.37	27.64	33.28	4.30	8.15
批发和零售业	Wholesale and Retail Trades	187.10	50.10	21.27	58.49	57.24
住宿和餐饮业	Hotels and Catering Services	57.69	15.18	8.12	5.23	29.16
金融业	Financial Intermediation	149.22	49.52	7.58	25.79	66.33
房地产业	Real Estate	91.28	11.46	50.28	16.46	13.08
租赁和商务服务业	Leasing and Business Service	40.36	16.66	8.62	5.47	9.61
科学研究、技术服务和地质勘查业	Scientific Research, Technology Service and Geological Prospecting	35.24	26.99	3.47	2.14	2.64
水利、环境和公共设施管理业	Water Conservancy, Environment and Public Facility Management	23.31	10.74	11.52	0.28	0.77
居民服务和其他服务业	Community Service and Other Services	34.43	8.79	2.77	2.80	20.07
教 育	Education	119.84	106.91	9.32	0.07	3.54
卫生、社会保障和社会福利业	Health, Social Security and Social Welfare	64.86	48.87	5.45	0.44	10.10
文化、体育和娱乐业	Culture, Sports and Entertainment	15.06	10.05	2.02	0.95	2.04
公共管理和社会组织	Public Management and Social Organizations	177.85	154.18	23.34	0.33	

注：本表按当年价格计算。
Note: Data in value terms in this table are calculated at current prices.

2-7 支出法新疆生产总值

Gross Domestic Product by Expenditure Approach in Xinjiang

单位：万元 (10 000 yuan)

年 份 Year	支出法新疆生产总值 Gross Domestic Product by Expenditure	最终消费 Final Consumption Expenditures	资本形成总额 Gross Capital Formation	货物和服务净出口 Net Export of Goods and Services	最终消费率(消费率)(%) Final Consumption Rate (%)	资本形成率(投资率)(%) Capital Formation Rate (%)
1978	390667	276393	184279	-70005	70.7	47.2
1980	532441	398217	231515	-97291	74.8	43.5
1985	1122379	780423	584289	-242333	69.5	52.1
1986	1290398	923792	602593	-235987	71.6	46.7
1987	1485104	1037723	699416	-252035	69.9	47.1
1988	1927224	1260879	983051	-316706	65.4	51.0
1989	2172907	1374960	1178441	-380494	63.3	54.2
1990	2614402	1667725	1411667	-464990	63.8	54.0
1991	3359147	1965753	1691482	-298088	58.5	50.4
1992	4023096	2215692	2492589	-685185	55.1	61.9
1993	4952509	2699236	3561561	-1308288	54.5	71.9
1994	6623239	3369417	4875542	-1621720	50.9	73.6
1995	8148512	4446226	4737079	-1034793	54.6	58.1
1996	9009288	5539010	4569575	-1099297	61.5	50.7
1997	10398462	6118128	5649193	-1368859	58.8	54.3
1998	11069485	6424751	6858461	-2213727	58.0	62.0
1999	11631711	6905712	5815889	-1089890	59.4	50.0
2000	13635631	7601990	6181229	-147588	55.8	45.3
2001	14916046	8590024	7714187	-1388165	57.6	51.7
2002	16126539	9637142	8642721	-2153324	59.8	53.6
2003	18863541	10272223	11192144	-2600826	54.5	59.3
2004	22090869	11251138	13504699	-2664968	50.9	61.1
2005	26041353	12665161	16068046	-2691854	48.6	61.7
2006	30452623	15845278	17785089	-3177744	52.0	58.4
2007	35231620	19307527	20898127	-4974034	54.8	59.3

注：1993 年以后数据依据 2004 年经济普查资料已修订。
Note: Since 1993 the data has adjusted according to the economic census in 2004.

2-8 资本形成总额及其构成
Gross Capital Formation and Its Composition

年 份	Year	资本形成总额(万元) Gross Capital Formation (10 000 yuan)	固定资本形成 Gross Fixed Capital Formation	存货增加 Increase in Inventories	以资本形成总额为100 Gross Capital Formation=100 固定资本形成(%) Gross Fixed Capital Formation (%)	存货增加(%) Increase in Inventories (%)
	1978	184279	132469	51810	71.9	28.1
	1980	231515	181385	50130	78.3	21.7
	1985	584289	467807	116482	80.1	19.9
	1990	1411667	914955	496712	64.8	35.2
	1991	1691482	1247717	443765	73.8	26.2
	1992	2492589	1811739	680850	72.7	27.3
	1993	3561561	2648981	912580	74.4	25.6
	1994	4875542	3769512	1106030	77.3	22.7
	1995	4737079	3779069	958010	79.8	20.2
	1996	4569575	4228684	340891	92.5	7.5
	1997	5649193	4614059	1035134	81.7	18.3
	1998	6858461	5437824	1420637	79.3	20.7
	1999	5815889	5517222	298667	94.9	5.1
	2000	6181229	6481229	-300000	104.9	-4.9
	2001	7714187	7201155	513032	93.3	6.7
	2002	8642721	8567008	75713	99.1	0.9
	2003	11192144	10792366	399778	96.4	3.6
	2004	13504699	12395034	1109666	91.8	8.2
	2005	16068046	14851729	1216317	92.4	7.6
	2006	17785089	17199644	585445	96.7	3.3
	2007	20898127	20049873	848254	95.9	4.1
“一五”时期	"First Five-Year Plan" Period	162638	143262	19376	88.1	11.9
“二五”时期	"Second Five-Year Plan" Period	363925	266883	97042	73.3	26.7
	1963—1965	193986	143430	50556	73.9	26.1
“三五”时期	"Third Five-Year Plan" Period	306461	209622	96839	68.4	31.6
“四五”时期	"Fourth Five-Year Plan" Period	516970	321276	195694	62.1	37.9
“五五”时期	"Fifth Five-Year Plan" Period	877599	624988	252611	71.2	28.8
“六五”时期	"Sixth Five-Year Plan" Period	1913818	1584755	329063	82.8	17.2
“七五”时期	"Seventh Five-Year Plan" Period	4875168	3616395	1258773	74.2	25.8
“八五”时期	"Eighth Five-Year Plan" Period	17358253	13257018	4101235	76.4	23.6
“九五”时期	"Ninth Five-Year Plan" Period	29074347	26279018	2795329	90.4	9.6
“十五”时期	"Tenth Five-Year Plan" Period	57121797	53807292	3314506	94.2	5.8

注：本表按当年价格计算。
Note: Data in value terms in this table are calculated at current prices.

2-9 最终消费及其构成

Final Consumption Expenditure and Its Composition

单位：% (%)

年 份	Year	最终消费（万元） Final Consumption Expenditures (10 000yuan)	居民消费 Household Consump-tion	农村居民 Rural Household	城镇居民 UrbanHou-sehold	政府消费 Governme-nt Consu-mption	最终消费=100 Final Consumption Expenditure=100 居民消费 House-hold Consum-ption	政府消费 Govern-ment Consum-ption	居民消费=100 Houshold Consumption=100 农村居民 Rural House-hold	城镇居民 Urban House-hold
	1978	276393	226066	120791	105275	50327	81.8	18.2	53.4	46.6
	1980	398217	327835	161988	165847	70382	82.3	17.7	49.4	50.6
	1985	780423	585134	264111	321023	195289	75.0	25.0	45.1	54.9
	1990	1667725	1211211	456657	754554	456514	72.6	27.4	37.7	62.3
	1991	1965753	1455536	522958	932578	510217	74.0	26.0	35.9	64.1
	1992	2215692	1592023	551827	1040196	623669	71.9	28.1	34.7	65.3
	1993	2699236	1977837	639604	1338233	721399	73.3	26.7	32.3	67.7
	1994	3369417	2427922	830385	1597537	941495	72.1	27.9	34.2	65.8
	1995	4446226	3206963	1084307	2122656	1239263	72.1	27.9	33.8	66.2
	1996	5539010	3976132	1560749	2415383	1562878	71.8	28.2	39.3	60.7
	1997	6118128	4366716	1648365	2718351	1751412	71.4	28.6	37.7	62.3
	1998	6424751	4573797	1757168	2816629	1850954	71.2	28.8	38.4	61.6
	1999	6905712	4757427	1589784	3167643	2148285	68.9	31.1	33.4	66.6
	2000	7601990	4923159	1599716	3323443	2678831	64.8	35.2	32.5	67.5
	2001	8590024	5454878	1759959	3694919	3135146	63.5	36.5	32.3	67.7
	2002	9637142	6154672	1908516	4246156	3482470	63.9	36.1	31.0	69.0
	2003	10272223	6236144	2026744	4209400	4036079	60.7	39.3	32.5	67.5
	2004	11251138	6712767	2099911	4612856	4538371	59.7	40.3	31.3	68.7
	2005	12665161	7642601	2389831	5252770	5022560	60.3	39.7	31.3	68.7
	2006	15845278	8538825	2535773	6003052	7306453	53.9	46.1	29.7	70.3
	2007	19307527	10134750	2955193	7179557	9172777	52.5	47.5	29.2	70.8
“一五”时期	"First Five-Year Plan" Period	429668	386161	238855	147306	43507	89.9	10.1	61.9	38.1
“二五”时期	"Second Five-Year Plan" Period	713994	640202	393021	247181	73792	89.7	10.3	61.4	38.6
	1963—1965	470001	424240	309298	114942	45761	90.3	9.7	72.9	27.1
“三五”时期	"Third Five-Year Plan" Period	800945	729723	491304	238419	71222	91.1	8.9	67.3	32.7
“四五”时期	"Forth Five-Year Plan" Period	974596	837494	517784	319710	137102	85.9	14.1	61.8	38.2
“五五”时期	"Fifth Five-Year Plan" Period	1497660	1231107	650165	580942	266553	82.2	17.8	52.8	47.2
“六五”时期	"Sixth Five-Year Plan" Period	2892722	2269952	1079305	1190647	622770	78.5	21.5	47.5	52.5
“七五”时期	"Seventh Five-Year Plan" Period	6265079	4641659	1864681	2776978	1623420	74.1	25.9	40.2	59.8
“八五”时期	"Eighth Five-Year Plan" Period	14696324	10660281	3629081	7031200	4036043	72.5	27.5	34.0	66.0
“九五”时期	"Ninth Five-Year Plan" Period	32589591	22597231	8155782	14441449	9992360	69.3	30.7	36.1	63.9
“十五”时期	"Tenth Five-Year Plan" Period	52415688	32201062	10184961	22016101	20214626	61.4	38.6	31.6	68.4

注：本表按当年价格计算。
Note: Data in value terms in this table are calculated at current prices.

2-10 各地、州、市、县(市)地区生产总值

单位：万元 (2007 年)

地 区	Region	地区生产总值 Gross Regional Product	第一产业 Primary Industry
乌鲁木齐市	**Urumqi City**	**8202800**	**162659**
#乌鲁木齐县	Urumqi County	106297	37385
克拉玛依市	**Karamay City**	**5151297**	**25445**
石河子市	**Shihezi City**	**732468**	**50878**
吐鲁番地区	**Turpan Administrative Offices**	**1720268**	**164631**
吐鲁番市	Turpan City	355586	73242
鄯善县	Shanshan [Piqan] County	1196928	58102
托克逊县	Toksun County	161288	35029
哈密地区	**Hami [Kumul] Administrative Offices**	**919912**	**142197**
哈密市	Hami [Kumul] City	779560	94058
巴里坤哈萨克自治县	Barkol Kazak Autonomous County	91297	31770
伊吾县	Yiwu [Araturuk] County	48970	16369
昌吉回族自治州	**Changji Hui Autonomous Prefecture**	**3131995**	**973960**
昌吉市	Changji City	1080307	169573
阜康市	Fukang City	472183	66059
呼图壁县	Hutubi County	459337	198777
玛纳斯县	Manas County	609173	279867
奇台县	Qitai County	275597	144632
吉木萨尔县	Jimsar County	159625	71851
木垒哈萨克自治县	Mori Kazak Autonomous County	76411	36800
伊犁哈萨克自治州	**Ili Kazak Autonomous Prefecture**	**5396630**	**1559727**
伊犁州直属县(市)	**Counties (Cities) Direct Under Ili Prefecture**	**2364705**	**592900**
伊宁市	Yining [Gulja] City	569160	37114
奎屯市	Kuytun City	401569	17654
伊宁县	Yining [Gulja] County	274455	97743
察布查尔锡伯自治县	Qapqal Xibe Autonomous County	113987	54115
霍城县	Huocheng [Korgas] County	296128	116959
巩留县	Gongliu [Tokkuztara] County	109116	44515
新源县	Xinyuan [Kunes] County	320774	99306
昭苏县	Zhaosu [Mongolkure] County	122959	58223
特克斯县	Tekes County	79284	33681
尼勒克县	Nilka County	113873	35078
塔城地区	**Tacheng [Tarbagatai] Administrative Offices**	**2039121**	**748599**
塔城市	Tacheng [Qoqek] City	263133	66520
乌苏市	Usu City	526645	210360
额敏县	Emin [Dorbiljin] County	261632	95727
沙湾县	Shawan County	738473	306460
托里县	Toli County	114302	16870
裕民县	Yumin [Qagantokay] County	55241	24305
和布克赛尔蒙古自治县	Hoboksar Mongol Autonomous County	106380	28357

注：阿克苏市数据不包括阿拉尔市。(表 2-11、表 2-12 同)

Gross Regional Product by Prefecture, Autonomous Prefecture, City and County

(10 000 yuan)

第二产业 Secondary Industry	工业 Industry	建筑业 Construction	第三产业 Tertiary Industry	#交通运输、仓储和邮政业 Transport,storage And Post	#批发和零售业 Wholesale, and Retail Trades	人均地区生产总值(元/人) Per Capita GDP (yuan/person)
3165857	**2618574**	**547283**	**4874284**	**715974**	**828925**	**31140**
21721	14628	7093	47191	5152	5492	11997
4615056	**4497053**	**118003**	**510796**	**105653**	**55500**	**98398**
349172	**284772**	**64400**	**332418**	**31099**	**43490**	**23797**
1174061	**1061661**	**112400**	**381576**	**105914**	**66446**	**28907**
88686	72285	16401	193658	55683	42131	13557
1003634	922534	81100	135192	47439	13369	55285
71553	56653	14900	54706	7688	16105	14349
318520	**252975**	**65545**	**459195**	**165889**	**47580**	**16910**
281249	227159	54090	404253	160863	44355	18469
23402	16687	6715	36125	3729	2038	9039
16045	11306	4739	16556	561	657	23431
1196734	**932987**	**263747**	**961301**	**188848**	**151006**	**20893**
427170	314192	112978	483564	118048	64929	25042
318221	289887	28334	87903	14204	14677	29365
148785	91908	56877	111775	25874	20677	21187
214516	184371	30145	114790	16099	18370	23233
46113	26906	19207	84852	11634	16410	13424
34917	23268	11649	52857	3651	7576	12549
9013	4087	4926	30598	2099	4077	10054
1896660	**1457861**	**438799**	**1940243**	**276720**	**255556**	**12349**
806274	**637675**	**168599**	**965531**	**157619**	**63914**	**9534**
157322	108460	48862	374724	67431	39849	13073
202922	170133	32789	180993	39266	12723	28683
108573	97390	11183	68139	7852	5583	7251
23589	15471	8118	36283	2295	1117	6301
73376	62826	10550	105793	22219	4916	7801
32170	21831	10339	32431	2475	1039	6241
127181	105174	22007	94287	13399	17250	10394
19394	14044	5350	45342	5122	2504	7355
13077	9608	3469	32526	1011	1879	4986
48712	32781	15931	30083	2026	964	6636
635049	**457649**	**177400**	**655473**	**87462**	**151206**	**15451**
55460	32749	22711	141153	19614	41399	15947
187379	134729	52650	128906	21644	40355	16165
71164	47243	23921	94741	16100	22848	12597
220109	174067	46042	211904	34885	51234	18064
66155	49536	16619	31277	5665	3051	12173
12003	6150	5853	18933	2346	1104	9953
44195	29993	14202	33828	8129	3242	16886

Note: The data of Aksu city did not include data on Aral city.(the same as in the following table 2-11,2-12)

2-10 续表

单位：万元

地　　区	Region	地区生产总值 Gross Regional Product	第一产业 Primary Industry
阿勒泰地区	**Altay Administrative Offices**	**992804**	**218228**
阿勒泰市	Altay City	239060	49941
布尔津县	Burqin County	81377	20167
富蕴县	Fuyun [Koktokay] County	237391	40788
福海县	Fuhai [Burultokay] County	120155	47610
哈巴河县	Habahe [Kaba] County	230463	30543
青河县	Qinghe [Qinggil] County	50300	17196
吉木乃县	Jeminay County	27487	10094
博尔塔拉蒙古自治州	**Bortala Mongolian Autonomous Prefecture**	**770414**	**246439**
博乐市	Bole [Bortala] City	541860	138585
精河县	Jinghe [Jing] County	162090	73419
温泉县	Wenquan [Araxang] County	69824	34040
巴音郭楞蒙古自治州	**Bayangol Mongol ian Autonomous Prefecture**	**4690028**	**688644**
库尔勒市	Korla City	3538604	186144
轮台县	Luntai [Bugur] County	205883	58081
尉犁县	Yuli [Lopnur] County	217049	135614
若羌县	Ruoqiang [Qarkilik] County	62524	20963
且末县	Qiemo [Qarqan] County	70550	30698
焉耆回族自治县	Yanqi Hui Autonomous County	172073	62023
和静县	Hejing County	250759	88986
和硕县	Hoxud County	106483	59483
博湖县	Bohu [Bagrax] County	81034	41615
阿克苏地区	**Aksu Administrative Offices**	**2315179**	**850624**
阿克苏市	Aksu City	985453	338383
温宿县	Wensu [Onsu] County	177068	95187
库车县	Kuqa County	416627	87500
沙雅县	Xayar County	157390	71829
新和县	Xinhe [Toksu] County	98207	57653
拜城县	Baicheng [Bay] County	173690	47288
乌什县	Wushi [Uxturpan] County	89380	42767
阿瓦提县	Awat County	189837	102632
柯坪县	Kalpin County	27527	7385
克孜勒苏柯尔克孜自治州	**Kizilsu Kirgiz Autonomous Prefecture**	**237132**	**59928**
阿图什市	Artux City	119571	29901
阿克陶县	Akto County	59724	19820
阿合奇县	Akqi County	20312	4584
乌恰县	Wuqia [Ulugqat] County	31062	5861
和田地区	**Hotan Administrative Offices**	**636962**	**255785**
和田市	Hotan City	146478	22661
和田县	Hotan County	89226	46979
墨玉县	Moyu [Karakax] County	117636	58538
皮山县	Pishan [Guma] County	63093	30173
洛浦县	Lop County	69799	27748
策勒县	Qira County	48640	20608
于田县	Yutian [Keriya] County	75189	34260
民丰县	Minfeng [Niya] County	26901	9482

Continued

(10 000 yuan)

第二产业 Secondary Industry	工 业 Industry	建筑业 Construction	第三产业 Tertiary Industry	#交通运输、仓储和邮政业 Transport,storage And Post	#批发和零售业 Wholesale, and Retail Trades	人均地区生产总值(元/人) Per Capita GDP (yuan/person)
455337	**362537**	**92800**	**319239**	**31639**	**40436**	**17412**
49179	32479	16700	139940	19225	13003	13244
23720	8720	15000	37490	2246	5980	12676
156866	140966	15900	39737	4203	4107	28740
36356	11356	25000	36189	3004	5385	16392
171794	162194	9600	28126	2912	3046	29890
11460	5460	6000	21644	1463	2604	8934
5969	1969	4000	11424	447	1029	7721
104095	**57294**	**46801**	**419880**	**80637**	**128548**	**16437**
76239	42662	33577	327036	59069	119759	21166
18518	10904	7614	70153	20572	7252	11729
9370	3760	5610	26414	2214	1744	9487
3184905	**2816032**	**368873**	**816479**	**120723**	**110843**	**37466**
2877934	2582352	295582	474525	67294	86174	72074
96053	88149	7904	51749	10342	4880	19758
40293	27759	12534	41142	1640	4885	18148
22668	17321	5347	18893	3151	342	19817
10424	5093	5331	29428	2120	2866	11888
52952	34624	18328	57098	8363	1513	13496
80092	67068	13024	81681	21251	3039	13621
19574	13694	5880	27426	3854	2784	15752
15494	9545	5949	23925	3299	2463	13650
618047	**412117**	**205930**	**846508**	**77299**	**134747**	**9898**
238662	156465	82197	408408	39339	83737	16198
30327	17073	13254	51554	3994	8667	7615
207313	147517	59796	121814	16389	11197	9684
26074	15032	11042	59487	2414	9193	6909
11674	5979	5695	28880	4535	2802	6351
65206	51488	13718	61196	4854	6211	7913
9442	4825	4617	37171	990	2956	4552
25556	12728	12828	61649	2921	9467	8430
3793	1010	2783	16349	1863	517	6197
43512	**20594**	**22918**	**133692**	**12212**	**3909**	**4712**
20385	8870	11515	69285	8901	2834	5272
14113	6464	7649	25791	1230	737	3283
1917	134	1784	13811	1045	708	5091
10265	6644	3621	14936	1314	799	7785
111942	**40330**	**71612**	**269235**	**8933**	**11301**	**3405**
44555	15599	28956	79262	14217	12453	5218
20405	6125	14280	21842	684	325	3612
15956	2976	12980	43142	2491	6400	2474
10578	3031	7547	22342	647	1013	2630
15245	4925	10320	26806	1210	2634	3170
7161	466	6695	20871	635	1434	3360
8501	692	7809	32428	2040	4298	3197
7444	3944	3500	9975	679	285	7330

2-11 各地、州、市、县(市)地区生产总值构成

单位：%　　　　(2007 年)

地　　区	Region	地区生产总值 Gross Regional Product	第一产业 Primary Industry
乌鲁木齐市	**Urumqi City**	**100.0**	**2.0**
#乌鲁木齐县	Urumqi County	100.0	35.2
克拉玛依市	**Karamay City**	**100.0**	**0.5**
石河子市	**Shihezi City**	**100.0**	**6.9**
吐鲁番地区	**Turpan Administrative Offices**	**100.0**	**9.6**
吐鲁番市	Turpan City	100.0	20.6
鄯善县	Shanshan [Piqan] County	100.0	4.9
托克逊县	Toksun County	100.0	21.7
哈密地区	**Hami [Kumul] Administrative Offices**	**100.0**	**15.5**
哈密市	Hami [Kumul] City	100.0	12.1
巴里坤哈萨克自治县	Barkol Kazak Autonomous County	100.0	34.8
伊吾县	Yiwu [Araturuk] County	100.0	33.4
昌吉回族自治州	**Changji Hui Autonomous Prefecture**	**100.0**	**31.1**
昌吉市	Changji City	100.0	15.7
阜康市	Fukang City	100.0	14.0
呼图壁县	Hutubi County	100.0	43.3
玛纳斯县	Manas County	100.0	45.9
奇台县	Qitai County	100.0	52.5
吉木萨尔县	Jimsar County	100.0	45.0
木垒哈萨克自治县	Mori Kazak Autonomous County	100.0	48.2
伊犁哈萨克自治州	**Ili Kazak Autonomous Prefecture**	**100.0**	**28.9**
伊犁州直属县(市)	**Counties (Cities) Direct Under Ili Prefecture**	**100.0**	**25.1**
伊宁市	Yining [Gulja] City	100.0	6.5
奎屯市	Kuytun City	100.0	4.4
伊宁县	Yining [Gulja] County	100.0	35.6
察布查尔锡伯自治县	Qapqal Xibe Autonomous County	100.0	47.5
霍城县	Huocheng [Korgas] County	100.0	39.5
巩留县	Gongliu [Tokkuztara] County	100.0	40.8
新源县	Xinyuan [Kunes] County	100.0	31.0
昭苏县	Zhaosu [Mongolkure] County	100.0	47.4
特克斯县	Tekes County	100.0	42.5
尼勒克县	Nilka County	100.0	30.8
塔城地区	**Tacheng [Tarbagatai] Administrative Offices**	**100.0**	**36.7**
塔城市	Tacheng [Qoqek] City	100.0	25.3
乌苏市	Usu City	100.0	39.9
额敏县	Emin [Dorbiljin] County	100.0	36.6
沙湾县	Shawan County	100.0	41.5
托里县	Toli County	100.0	14.8
裕民县	Yumin [Qagantokay] County	100.0	44.0
和布克赛尔蒙古自治县	Hoboksar Mongol Autonomous County	100.0	26.7

Composition of Gross Domestic Product by Prefecture, Autonomous Prefecture, City and County

(%)

第二产业 Secondary Industry	工业 Industry	建筑业 Construction	第三产业 Tertiary Industry	#交通运输、仓储和邮政业 Transport,storage And Post	#批发和零售业 Wholesale, and Retail Trades
38.6	**31.9**	**6.7**	**59.4**	**8.7**	**10.1**
20.4	13.8	6.6	44.4	4.8	5.2
89.6	**87.3**	**2.3**	**9.9**	**2.1**	**1.1**
47.7	**38.9**	**8.8**	**45.4**	**4.2**	**5.9**
68.2	**61.7**	**6.5**	**22.2**	**6.2**	**3.9**
24.9	20.3	4.6	54.5	15.7	11.8
83.9	77.1	6.8	11.2	4.0	1.1
44.4	35.1	9.3	33.9	4.8	10.0
34.6	**27.5**	**7.1**	**49.9**	**18.0**	**5.2**
36.1	29.2	6.9	51.8	20.6	5.7
25.6	18.2	7.4	39.6	4.1	2.2
32.8	23.1	9.7	33.8	1.1	1.3
38.2	**29.8**	**8.4**	**30.7**	**6.0**	**4.8**
39.5	29.1	10.5	44.8	10.9	6.0
67.4	61.4	6.0	18.6	3.0	3.1
32.4	20.0	12.4	24.3	5.6	4.5
35.2	30.3	4.9	18.9	2.6	3.0
16.7	9.7	7.0	30.8	4.2	6.0
21.9	14.6	7.3	33.1	2.3	4.7
11.8	5.4	6.4	40.0	2.7	5.3
35.1	**27.0**	**8.1**	**36.0**	**5.1**	**4.7**
34.1	**27.0**	**7.1**	**40.8**	**6.7**	**2.7**
27.6	19.1	8.5	65.9	11.8	7.0
50.5	42.4	8.1	45.1	9.8	3.2
39.6	35.5	4.1	24.8	2.9	2.0
20.7	13.6	7.1	31.8	2.0	1.0
24.8	21.2	3.6	35.7	7.5	1.7
29.5	20.0	9.5	29.7	2.3	1.0
39.6	32.8	6.9	29.4	4.2	5.4
15.8	11.4	4.4	36.8	4.2	2.0
16.5	12.1	4.4	41.0	1.3	2.4
42.8	28.8	14.0	26.4	1.8	0.8
31.1	**22.4**	**8.7**	**32.2**	**4.3**	**7.4**
21.1	12.4	8.5	53.6	7.5	15.7
35.6	25.6	10.0	24.5	4.1	7.7
27.2	18.1	9.1	36.2	6.2	8.7
29.8	23.6	6.2	28.7	4.7	6.9
57.9	43.4	14.5	27.3	5.0	2.7
21.7	11.1	10.6	34.3	4.2	2.0
41.5	28.1	13.4	31.8	7.6	3.0

2-11 续表

单位：%

地　　区	Region	地区生产总值 Gross Regional Product	第一产业 Primary Industry
阿勒泰地区	**Altay Administrative Offices**	**100.0**	**22.0**
阿勒泰市	Altay City	100.0	20.9
布尔津县	Burqin County	100.0	24.8
富蕴县	Fuyun [Koktokay] County	100.0	17.2
福海县	Fuhai [Burultokay] County	100.0	39.6
哈巴河县	Habahe [Kaba] County	100.0	13.3
青河县	Qinghe [Qinggil] County	100.0	34.2
吉木乃县	Jeminay County	100.0	36.7
博尔塔拉蒙古自治州	**Bortala Mongolian Autonomous Prefecture**	**100.0**	**32.0**
博乐市	Bole [Bortala] City	100.0	25.6
精河县	Jinghe [Jing] County	100.0	45.3
温泉县	Wenquan [Araxang] County	100.0	48.8
巴音郭楞蒙古自治州	**Bayangol Mongol ian Autonomous Prefecture**	**100.0**	**14.7**
库尔勒市	Korla City	100.0	5.3
轮台县	Luntai [Bugur] County	100.0	28.2
尉犁县	Yuli [Lopnur] County	100.0	62.4
若羌县	Ruoqiang [Qarkilik] County	100.0	33.5
且末县	Qiemo [Qarqan] County	100.0	43.5
焉耆回族自治县	Yanqi Hui Autonomous County	100.0	36.0
和静县	Hejing County	100.0	35.5
和硕县	Hoxud County	100.0	55.8
博湖县	Bohu [Bagrax] County	100.0	51.4
阿克苏地区	**Aksu Administrative Offices**	**100.0**	**36.7**
阿克苏市	Aksu City	100.0	34.3
温宿县	Wensu [Onsu] County	100.0	53.8
库车县	Kuqa County	100.0	21.0
沙雅县	Xayar County	100.0	45.6
新和县	Xinhe [Toksu] County	100.0	58.7
拜城县	Baicheng [Bay] County	100.0	27.3
乌什县	Wushi [Uxturpan] County	100.0	47.8
阿瓦提县	Awat County	100.0	54.0
柯坪县	Kalpin County	100.0	26.8
克孜勒苏柯尔克孜自治州	**Kizilsu Kirgiz Autonomous Prefecture**	**100.0**	**25.3**
阿图什市	Artux City	100.0	25.0
阿克陶县	Akto County	100.0	33.2
阿合奇县	Akqi County	100.0	22.6
乌恰县	Wuqia [Ulugqat] County	100.0	18.9
和田地区	**Hotan Administrative Offices**	**100.0**	**40.1**
和田市	Hotan City	100.0	15.5
和田县	Hotan County	100.0	52.6
墨玉县	Moyu [Karakax] County	100.0	49.8
皮山县	Pishan [Guma] County	100.0	47.8
洛浦县	Lop County	100.0	39.8
策勒县	Qira County	100.0	42.4
于田县	Yutian [Keriya] County	100.0	45.6
民丰县	Minfeng [Niya] County	100.0	35.2

Continued

(%)

第二产业 Secondary Industry	工业 Industry	建筑业 Construction	第三产业 Tertiary Industry	#交通运输、仓储和邮政业 Transport,storage And Post	#批发和零售业 Wholesale, and Retail Trades
45.9	**36.5**	**9.4**	**32.1**	**3.2**	**4.1**
20.6	13.6	7.0	58.5	8.0	5.4
29.1	10.7	18.4	46.1	2.8	7.3
66.1	59.4	6.7	16.7	1.8	1.7
30.3	9.5	20.8	30.1	2.5	4.5
74.5	70.3	4.2	12.2	1.3	1.3
22.8	10.9	11.9	43.0	2.9	5.2
21.7	7.2	14.5	41.6	1.6	3.7
13.5	**7.4**	**6.1**	**54.5**	**10.5**	**16.7**
14.1	7.9	6.2	60.4	10.9	22.1
11.4	6.7	4.7	43.3	12.7	4.5
13.4	5.4	8.0	37.8	3.2	2.5
67.9	**60.0**	**7.9**	**17.4**	**2.6**	**2.4**
81.3	73.0	8.3	13.4	1.9	2.4
46.7	42.8	3.7	25.1	5.0	2.4
18.6	12.8	5.8	19.0	0.8	2.3
36.3	27.7	8.6	30.2	5.0	0.5
14.8	7.2	7.6	41.7	3.0	4.1
30.8	20.1	10.7	33.2	4.9	0.9
31.9	26.7	5.2	32.6	8.5	1.2
18.4	12.9	5.5	25.8	3.6	2.6
19.1	11.8	7.3	29.5	4.1	3.0
26.7	**17.8**	**8.9**	**36.6**	**3.3**	**5.8**
24.2	15.9	8.3	41.4	4.0	8.5
17.1	9.6	7.5	29.1	2.3	4.9
49.8	35.4	14.4	29.2	3.9	2.7
16.6	9.6	7.0	37.8	1.5	5.8
11.9	6.1	5.8	29.4	4.6	2.9
37.5	29.6	7.9	35.2	2.8	3.6
10.6	5.4	5.2	41.6	1.1	3.3
13.5	6.7	6.8	32.5	1.5	5.0
13.8	3.7	10.1	59.4	6.8	1.9
18.3	**8.7**	**9.6**	**56.4**	**5.1**	**1.6**
17.0	7.4	9.6	57.8	7.4	2.4
23.6	10.8	12.8	43.2	2.1	1.2
9.4	0.7	8.7	68.0	5.1	3.5
33.0	21.3	11.7	48.1	4.2	2.6
17.6	**6.4**	**11.2**	**42.3**	**1.4**	**1.8**
30.4	10.6	19.8	54.1	9.7	8.5
22.9	6.9	16.0	24.5	0.8	0.4
13.5	2.5	11.0	36.7	2.1	5.4
16.8	4.8	12.0	35.4	1.0	1.6
21.8	7.0	14.8	38.4	1.7	3.8
14.7	1.0	13.7	42.9	1.3	2.9
11.3	0.9	10.3	43.1	2.7	5.7
27.7	14.7	13.0	37.1	2.5	1.1

2-12 各地、州、市、县(市)地区生产总值指数

(上年=100) (2007 年)

地　　区	Region	地区生产总值 Gross Regional Product	第一产业 Primary Industry
乌鲁木齐市	**Urumqi City**	**115.0**	**107.6**
#乌鲁木齐县	Urumqi County	114.9	111.7
克拉玛依市	**Karamay City**	**112.0**	**126.0**
石河子市	**Shihezi City**	**114.4**	**103.5**
吐鲁番地区	**Turpan Administrative Offices**	**111.0**	**109.2**
吐鲁番市	Turpan City	113.5	110.7
鄯善县	Shanshan [Piqan] County	109.3	109.2
托克逊县	Toksun County	121.8	108.5
哈密地区	**Hami [Kumul] Administrative Offices**	**116.4**	**111.6**
哈密市	Hami [Kumul] City	116.3	112.7
巴里坤哈萨克自治县	Barkol Kazak Autonomous County	116.8	109.3
伊吾县	Yiwu [Araturuk] County	117.4	111.2
昌吉回族自治州	**Changji Hui Autonomous Prefecture**	**114.9**	**109.5**
昌吉市	Changji City	116.0	107.0
阜康市	Fukang City	109.0	112.4
呼图壁县	Hutubi County	116.5	107.1
玛纳斯县	Manas County	117.0	109.7
奇台县	Qitai County	114.6	112.4
吉木萨尔县	Jimsar County	115.8	107.5
木垒哈萨克自治县	Mori Kazak Autonomous County	110.4	105.2
伊犁哈萨克自治州	**Ili Kazak Autonomous Prefecture**	**112.5**	**103.4**
伊犁州直属县(市)	**Counties (Cities) Direct Under Ili Prefecture**	**113.9**	**107.0**
伊宁市	Yining [Gulja] City	115.0	103.7
奎屯市	Kuytun City	114.6	101.9
伊宁县	Yining [Gulja] County	116.2	113.3
察布查尔锡伯自治县	Qapqal Xibe Autonomous County	112.2	110.5
霍城县	Huocheng [Korgas] County	116.1	107.7
巩留县	Gongliu [Tokkuztara] County	110.6	106.9
新源县	Xinyuan [Kunes] County	113.4	106.7
昭苏县	Zhaosu [Mongolkure] County	114.4	111.2
特克斯县	Tekes County	112.4	104.8
尼勒克县	Nilka County	112.9	107.5
塔城地区	**Tacheng [Tarbagatai] Administrative Offices**	**114.4**	**106.2**
塔城市	Tacheng [Qoqek] City	113.8	111.3
乌苏市	Usu City	114.4	105.3
额敏县	Emin [Dorbiljin] County	114.2	105.3
沙湾县	Shawan County	113.1	106.8
托里县	Toli County	126.2	107.8
裕民县	Yumin [Qagantokay] County	114.1	109.8
和布克赛尔蒙古自治县	Hoboksar Mongol Autonomous County	115.6	98.5

Indices of Gross Domestic Product by Prefecture, Autonomous Prefecture, City and County

(preceding year=100)

第二产业 Secondary Industry	工业 Industry	建筑业 Construction	第三产业 Tertiary Industry	#交通运输、仓储和邮政业 Transport,storage And Post	#批发和零售业 Wholesale, and Retail Trades
115.3	**117.0**	**108.0**	**115.1**	**110.2**	**115.0**
122.9	133.4	106.2	114.1	108.0	109.2
112.6	**112.8**	**104.5**	**107.0**	**99.3**	**109.0**
116.4	**118.1**	**109.4**	**114.2**	**116.5**	**112.4**
110.6	**111.4**	**104.3**	**113.1**	**102.7**	**111.7**
112.1	121.3	89.0	115.1	113.1	112.8
109.3	108.7	115.5	109.5	94.5	107.8
140.2	178.7	87.6	113.8	110.4	111.9
121.3	**123.8**	**112.0**	**114.7**	**108.3**	**110.0**
119.6	121.7	111.1	115.0	109.0	109.7
124.6	134.5	106.3	119.5	108.7	107.6
128.6	126.4	134.3	114.1	77.6	111.1
117.9	**121.0**	**108.6**	**117.1**	**114.3**	**115.9**
120.0	125.0	108.5	116.2	114.0	122.3
105.3	106.9	92.9	119.3	120.0	115.7
131.5	138.9	121.2	116.5	114.5	113.8
128.5	133.2	106.3	116.6	113.0	108.2
120.2	122.2	117.3	115.0	118.6	117.2
131.6	136.4	123.3	118.8	115.7	116.3
111.0	121.2	102.8	117.3	114.8	110.2
121.3	**127.2**	**107.3**	**113.1**	**110.9**	**112.7**
118.8	**123.5**	**104.0**	**114.1**	**107.9**	**119.3**
114.0	118.5	105.0	116.6	110.0	111.1
115.5	118.1	103.4	114.9	106.4	111.4
119.5	121.8	102.6	115.3	107.4	109.1
111.3	117.1	102.3	115.2	106.4	107.5
129.8	135.0	106.0	117.2	107.3	131.0
114.3	121.1	101.9	111.9	103.3	111.6
119.8	123.5	105.5	112.6	106.9	107.4
121.1	130.4	103.2	115.7	105.1	101.0
129.6	143.7	102.9	114.6	109.0	109.1
114.4	121.5	101.8	116.8	109.3	105.9
131.5	**145.4**	**107.4**	**110.7**	**116.3**	**110.0**
113.7	124.4	101.6	115.0	112.1	117.1
130.7	146.2	105.1	110.6	115.0	108.5
128.4	136.3	116.0	114.2	116.2	119.2
125.7	134.1	103.2	111.8	112.1	113.3
140.3	180.2	87.5	113.7	116.0	105.1
128.9	132.5	125.4	111.7	105.1	107.6
137.8	167.7	102.4	108.1	101.9	142.5

2-12 续表 1

(上年=100)

地　　区	Region	地区生产总值 Gross Regional Product	第一产业 Primary Industry
阿勒泰地区	**Altay Administrative Offices**	**112.0**	**104.2**
阿勒泰市	Altay City	112.6	106.4
布尔津县	Burqin County	112.0	102.2
富蕴县	Fuyun [Koktokay] County	125.4	101.8
福海县	Fuhai [Burultokay] County	108.9	105.2
哈巴河县	Habahe [Kaba] County	107.1	108.5
青河县	Qinghe [Qinggil] County	109.9	104.4
吉木乃县	Jeminay County	103.1	101.4
博尔塔拉蒙古自治州	**Bortala Mongolian Autonomous Prefecture**	**112.8**	**107.8**
博乐市	Bole [Bortala] City	113.3	109.1
精河县	Jinghe [Jing] County	112.1	106.7
温泉县	Wenquan [Araxang] County	112.3	105.0
巴音郭楞蒙古自治州	**Bayangol Mongol ian Autonomous Prefecture**	**113.0**	**110.8**
库尔勒市	Korla City	112.7	108.1
轮台县	Luntai [Bүgur] County	114.6	113.7
尉犁县	Yuli [Lopnur] County	113.1	111.2
若羌县	Ruoqiang [Qarkilik] County	114.2	113.1
且末县	Qiemo [Qarqan] County	115.2	112.5
焉耆回族自治县	Yanqi Hui Autonomous County	113.0	114.0
和静县	Hejing County	110.8	101.5
和硕县	Hoxud County	113.4	117.7
博湖县	Bohu [Bagrax] County	113.4	114.4
阿克苏地区	**Aksu Administrative Offices**	**114.0**	**109.0**
阿克苏市	Aksu City	114.3	109.1
温宿县	Wensu [Onsu] County	114.3	115.7
库车县	Kuqa County	117.1	106.5
沙雅县	Xayar County	114.0	107.2
新和县	Xinhe [Toksu] County	111.2	108.6
拜城县	Baicheng [Bay] County	115.9	106.3
乌什县	Wushi [Uxturpan] County	110.8	107.4
阿瓦提县	Awat County	108.0	108.8
柯坪县	Kalpin County	112.5	111.0
克孜勒苏柯尔克孜自治州	**Kizilsu Kirgiz Autonomous Prefecture**	**113.5**	**103.9**
阿图什市	Artux City	112.8	101.7
阿克陶县	Akto County	112.2	101.3
阿合奇县	Akqi County	112.3	116.7
乌恰县	Wuqia [Ulugqat] County	118.5	101.4
和田地区	**Hotan Administrative Offices**	**111.0**	**109.8**
和田市	Hotan City	120.2	135.6
和田县	Hotan County	107.6	101.6
墨玉县	Moyu [Karakax] County	109.6	105.1
皮山县	Pishan [Guma] County	110.5	105.6
洛浦县	Lop County	100.4	92.9
策勒县	Qira County	109.6	107.0
于田县	Yutian [Keriya] County	109.1	103.0
民丰县	Minfeng [Niya] County	112.7	103.5

Continued

(preceding year=100)

第二产业 Secondary Industry	工业 Industry	建筑业 Construction	第三产业 Tertiary Industry	#交通运输、仓储和邮政业 Transport,storage And Post	#批发和零售业 Wholesale, and Retail Trades
115.5	**116.4**	**113.5**	**114.4**	**107.9**	**113.2**
113.4	113.1	113.9	114.7	106.4	114.5
119.0	118.3	119.4	113.7	104.8	113.6
137.4	141.5	116.0	121.4	131.6	118.6
108.3	100.4	112.4	115.0	107.9	112.0
101.9	102.6	97.7	120.3	116.9	113.7
119.0	127.6	113.8	110.7	104.0	104.4
92.9	104.4	88.2	110.8	108.1	106.1
115.9	**115.6**	**116.2**	**114.7**	**116.5**	**107.9**
112.7	108.8	117.8	115.1	122.4	107.9
129.2	139.5	116.6	113.7	106.0	108.5
118.9	142.9	107.3	118.1	111.9	106.6
113.2	**115.2**	**101.1**	**113.7**	**106.5**	**110.2**
112.9	114.9	99.3	113.6	106.9	110.4
115.5	116.1	109.8	114.2	107.7	110.3
119.2	126.2	106.6	113.7	105.7	109.0
113.3	118.1	101.1	116.1	105.3	98.4
117.2	127.8	108.7	117.1	105.2	113.8
110.2	111.1	108.5	114.7	108.0	110.7
117.5	118.8	111.6	114.7	120.6	103.4
111.4	115.3	103.2	107.7	106.5	102.8
111.0	113.7	107.0	113.5	106.4	118.4
121.5	**128.3**	**109.9**	**114.2**	**115.3**	**111.8**
122.9	130.6	110.6	114.1	117.1	114.0
119.7	129.1	109.7	109.2	105.6	108.0
125.4	132.0	113.0	113.8	112.6	111.4
126.2	143.9	109.2	118.9	113.9	107.1
110.6	105.3	116.7	117.3	113.3	109.1
127.6	134.7	100.6	110.3	118.5	107.7
106.3	98.6	115.7	116.2	114.2	109.5
85.2	73.4	99.2	118.7	126.0	106.2
114.7	126.6	111.1	112.6	113.5	104.3
119.0	**149.3**	**102.5**	**116.6**	**127.3**	**109.7**
121.5	141.3	110.6	115.7	123.4	116.2
131.8	207.9	101.4	111.9	112.1	106.9
117.2	134.5	116.1	110.1	106.7	100.8
131.1	156.3	102.8	118.8	233.4	111.2
114.8	**127.7**	**108.5**	**110.5**	**108.1**	**116.8**
117.7	123.5	114.8	118.0	110.2	120.2
113.4	116.8	112.1	116.9	111.1	123.7
111.0	205.7	101.7	115.7	109.7	131.9
111.3	101.4	115.8	117.3	109.3	117.9
89.9	96.4	87.2	117.2	97.9	98.3
105.8	103.0	106.0	113.5	101.2	112.4
111.5	102.7	112.4	115.7	104.1	120.3
94.0	101.4	86.9	145.6	104.3	120.3

2-13 居民消费水平及指数
Household Consumption Expenditure and Its Indices

年份 Year	居民消费水平(元) Household Consumption (yuan)	农村居民 Rural Households	城镇居民 Urban Households	居民消费水平指数(1952年=100) Index of Residents' Consumption Level (1952=100)	农村居民 Rural Households	城镇居民 Urban Households	居民消费水平指数(上年=100) Index of Residents' Consumption Level (preceding year=100)	农村居民 Rural Households	城镇居民 Urban Households
1978	181	131	323	140.5	144.5	99.0	104.7	102.3	102.8
1980	252	180	417	182.4	184.4	119.3	111.9	107.6	113.1
1985	428	280	755	267.0	252.3	183.8	110.5	105.9	114.6
1990	796	447	1508	299.5	236.3	226.4	103.8	98.8	105.0
1995	1852	977	3414	344.1	246.5	257.4	109.0	102.3	112.3
1996	2266	1387	3836	377.1	312.6	260.7	109.6	126.8	101.3
1997	2455	1445	4261	384.6	313.9	268.5	102.0	100.4	103.0
1998	2539	1520	4364	396.1	339.3	268.5	103.0	108.1	100.0
1999	2606	1358	4841	413.1	319.3	297.8	104.3	94.1	110.9
2000	2662	1308	5131	415.2	299.2	315.7	100.5	93.7	106.0
2001	2905	1427	5743	434.3	307.6	338.7	104.6	102.8	107.3
2002	3228	1525	6483	484.7	325.4	386.8	111.6	105.8	114.2
2003	3249	1603	6427	488.6	338.1	386.8	100.8	103.9	100.0
2004	3445	1652	6808	502.3	339.8	396.1	102.8	100.5	102.4
2005	3864	1889	7349	556.0	386.0	421.1	110.7	113.6	106.3
2006	4206	2000	7875	596.0	399.9	445.5	107.2	103.6	105.8
2007	4890	2320	8986	660.4	431.9	489.2	110.8	108.0	109.8

2-14 居民消费支出
Household Consumption Expenditure

单位：万元 (10 000 yuan)

项目	Item	2006	2007
居民消费支出	**Household Consumption Expenditure**	**8538825**	**10134750**
食品类支出	Foods	2847520	3401777
衣着类支出	Clothes	963633	1223662
居住类支出	Residence	747798	680435
家庭设备、用品及服务类支出	Family Facilities and Servises	370170	496187
医疗保健类支出	Medical and Hygiencic Expenditure	600578	746768
公共医疗消费支出	Public Health	138412	166902
交通和通信类支出	Traffic and Telecommunications	849283	1010277
文教娱乐用品及服务类支出	Teathing, Entertainment and Services	823936	928311
金融中介服务虚拟支出	Imaginary Expenditure of Middle Finance Services	436291	523200
自有住房服务虚拟支出	Imaginary Expenditure of Freeform Resident Services	376582	491862
实物消费支出	Reality Consumption	136301	142625
其他商品和服务类支出	Other Goods and Services	248321	322744
按城乡分	**By Residence**		
农村居民支出	Agricaltural Households Expenditure	2535773	2955193
食品类支出	Foods	1027909	1195930
衣着类支出	Clothes	237129	277870
居住类支出	Residence	215202	261517
家庭设备、用品及服务类支出	Family Facilities and Servises	92605	116469
医疗保健类支出	Medical and Hygiencic Expenditure	240501	268331
交通和通信类支出	Traffic and Telecommunications	265567	298909
文教娱乐用品及服务类支出	Teathing, Entertainment and Services	199055	211758
金融中介服务虚拟支出	Imaginary Expenditure of Middle Finance Services	74286	89315
自有住房服务虚拟支出	Imaginary Expenditure of Freeform Resident Services	140602	177465
其他商品和服务类支出	Other Goods and Services	42917	57629
城镇居民支出	Non-agricaltural Households Expenditure	6003052	7179557
食品类支出	Foods	1819611	2205847
衣着类支出	Clothes	726504	945792
居住类支出	Residence	532596	418918
家庭设备、用品及服务类支出	Family Facilities and Servises	277565	379718
医疗保健类支出	Medical and Hygiencic Expenditure	360077	478437
公共医疗消费支出	Public Health	138412	166902
交通和通信类支出	Traffic and Telecommunications	583716	711368
文教娱乐用品及服务类支出	Teathing, Entertainment and Services	624881	716553
金融中介服务虚拟支出	Imaginary Expenditure of Middle Finance Services	362005	433885
自有住房服务虚拟支出	Imaginary Expenditure of Freeform Resident Services	235980	314397
实物消费支出	Reality Consumption	136301	142625
其他商品和服务类支出	Other Goods and Services	205404	265115

主要统计指标解释

国内生产总值(GDP) 指按市场价格计算的一个国家(或地区)所有常住单位在一定时期内生产活动的最终成果。国内生产总值有三种表现形态，即价值形态、收入形态和产品形态。从价值形态看，它是所有常住单位在一定时期内生产的全部货物和服务价值超过同期投入的全部非固定资产货物和服务价值的差额，即所有常住单位的增加值之和；从收入形态看，它是所有常住单位在一定时期内创造并分配给常住单位和非常住单位的初次收入之和；从产品形态看，它是所有常住单位在一定时期内最终使用的货物和服务价值减去货物和服务进口价值。在实际核算中，国内生产总值有三种计算方法，即生产法、收入法和支出法。三种方法分别从不同的方面反映国内生产总值及其构成。

三次产业 三产业的划分是世界上较为常用的产业结构分类，但各国的划分不尽一致。我国的三次产业划分是：

第一产业是指农、林、牧、渔业。

第二产业是指采矿业，制造业，电力、煤气及水的生产和供应业，建筑业。

第三产业是指除第一、二产业以外的其他行业。

劳动者报酬 指劳动者因从事生产活动所获得的全部报酬。包括劳动者获得的各种形式的工资、奖金和津贴，既包括货币形式的，也包括实物形式的，还包括劳动者所享受的公费医疗和医药卫生费、上下班交通补贴、单位支付的社会保险费、住房公积金等。对于个体经济来说，其所有者所获得的劳动报酬和经营利润不易区分，这两部分统一作为劳动者报酬处理。

生产税净额 指生产税减生产补贴后的余额。生产税指政府对生产单位从事生产、销售和经营活动以及因从事生产活动使用某些生产要素(如固定资产、土地、劳动力)所征收的各种税、附加费和规费。生产补贴与生产税相反，指政府对生产单位的单方面转移支出，因此视为负生产税，包括政策亏损补贴、价格补贴等。

固定资产折旧 指一定时期内为弥补固定资产损耗按照规定的固定资产折旧率提取的固定资产折旧，或按国民经济核算统一规定的折旧率虚拟计算的固定资产折旧。它反映了固定资产在当期生产中的转移价值。各类企业和企业化管理的事业单位的固定资产折旧是指实际计提的折旧费；不计提折旧的政府机关、非企业化管理的事业单位和居民住房的固定资产折旧是按照统一规定的折旧率和固定资产原值计算的虚拟折旧。原则上，固定资产折旧应按固定资产当期的重置价值计算，但是目前我国尚不具备对全社会固定资产进行重估价的基础，所以暂时只能采用上述办法。

营业盈余 指常住单位创造的增加值扣除劳动者报酬、生产税净额和固定资产折旧后的余额。它相当于企业的营业利润加上生产补贴，但要扣除从利润中开支的工资和福利等。

支出法国内生产总值 是从最终使用的角度反映一个国家(或地区)一定时期内生产活动最终成果的一种方法，包括最终消费、资本形成总额及货物和服务净出口三部分。计算公式为：

支出法国内生产总值=最终消费+资本形成总额+货物和服务净出口

最终消费 指常住单位为满足物质、文化和精神生活的需要，从本国经济领土和国外购买的货物和服务的支出。它不包括非常住单位在本国经济领土内的消费支出。最终消费分为居民消费和政府消费。

居民消费 指常住住户在一定时期内对于货物和服务的全部最终消费支出。居民消费除了直接以货币形式购买的货物和服务的消费支出外，还包括以其他方式获得的货物和服务的消费支出，即所谓的虚拟消费支出。居民虚拟消费支出包括如下几种类型：单位以实物报酬及实物转移的形式提供给劳动者的货物和服务；住户生产并由本住户消费了的货物和服务，其中的服务仅指住户的自有住房服务和付酬的家庭雇员提供的家庭和个人服务；金融机构提供的金融媒介服务；保险公司提供的保险服务。

政府消费 指政府部门为全社会提供的公共服务的消费支出和免费或以较低的价格向居民住户提供的货物和服务的净支出，前者等于政府服务的产出价值减去政府单位所获得的经营收入的价值，后者等于政府部门免费或以较低价格向居民住户提供的货物和服务的市场价值减去向住户收取的价值。

资本形成总额 指常住单位在一定时期内获得减去处置的固定资产和存货的净额，包括固定资本形成总额和存货增加两部分。

固定资本形成总额 指生产者在一定时期内获得的固定资产减处置的固定资产的价值总额。固定资产是通过生产活动生产出来的，且其使用年限在一年以上、单位价值在规定标准以上的资产，不包括自然资产。可分为有形固定资本形成总额和无形固定资本形成总额。有形固定资本形成总额包括一定时期内完成的建筑工程、安装工程和设备工器具购置(减处置)价值，以及土地改良、新增役、种、奶、毛、娱乐用牲畜和新增经济林木价值。无形固定资本形成总额包括矿藏的勘探、计算机软件等获得减处置。

存货增加 指常住单位在一定时期内存货实物量变动的市场价值，即期末价值减期初价值的差额，再扣除当期由于价格变动而产生的持有收益。存货增加可以是正值，也可以是负值，正值表示存货上升，负值表示存货下降。存货包括生产单位购进的原材料、燃料和储备物资等存货，以及生产单位生产的产成品、在制品和半成品等存货。

货物和服务净出口 指货物和服务出口减货物和服务进口的差额。出口包括常住单位向非常住单位出售或无偿转让的各种货物和服务的价值；进口包括常住单位从非常住单位购买或无偿得到的各种货物和服务的价值。由于服务活动的提供与使用同时发生，一般把常住单位从非常住单位得到的服务作为进口，非常住单位从常住单位得到的服务作为出口。货物的出口和进口都按离岸价格计算。

直接消耗系数 也称为投入系数，记为aij(ij=1,2,…,n)它是指在生产经营过程中第 j 产品(或产业)部门的单位总产出所直接消耗的第 i 产品部门货物或服务的价值量，将各产品(或产业)部门的直接消耗系数用表的形式表现，就是直接消耗系数表或直接消耗系数矩阵，通常用字母A表示。

完全消耗系数 指第 j 产品部门每提供一个单位最终使用时，对第 i 产品部门货物或服务的直接消耗和间接消耗之和。将各产品部门的完全消耗系数用表的形式表现，就是完全消耗系数表或完全消耗系数矩阵，通常用字母B表示。

机构单位 指有权拥有资产和承担负债，能够独立地从事经济活动并与其他实体进行交易的经济实体。

机构部门 将相同性质的机构单位归并在一起，就形成机构部门。资金流量核算将常住机构单位划分为以下四个机构部门：非金融企业部门、金融机构部门、政府部门、住户部门。与常住单位发生经济往来关系的非常住单位组成国外部门，在资金流量核算中也视同机构部门。

非金融企业与非金融企业部门 非金融企业指主要从事市场货物生产和提供非金融市场服务的常住企业，它主要包括从事上述活动的各类法人企业。所有非金融企业归并在一起，就形成非金融企业部门。

金融机构与金融机构部门 金融机构指主要从事金融媒介以及与金融媒介密切相关的辅助金融活动的常住单位，它主要包括中央银行、商业银行和政策性银行、非银行信贷机构和保险公司。所有金融机构归并在一起，就形成金融机构部门。

政府单位与政府部门 政府单位指在我国境内通过政治程序建立的、在一特定区域内对其他机构单位拥有立法、司法和行政权的法律实体及其附属单位。政府单位的主要职能是利用征税和其他方式获得的资金向社会和公众提供公共服务。通过转移支付，对社会收入和财产进行再分配。它主要包括各种行政单位和非营利性事业单位。所有政府单位归并在一起，就形成政府部门。

住户与住户部门 住户指共享同一生活设施、部分或全部收入和财产集中使用、共同消费住房、食品和其他消费品与消费服务的常住个人或个人群体。所有住户归并在一起，就形成住户部门。

非常住单位与国外部门 所有不具有常住性的机构单位都是非常住单位。将所有与我国常住单位发生交易的非常住单位归并在一起，就形成国外部门。

初次分配总收入 初次分配是生产活动形成的净成果在参与生产活动的生产要素的所有者及政府之间的分配。生产活动的净成果是增加值。生产要素包括劳动力、土地、资本。劳动力所有者因提供劳动而获得劳动报酬；土地所有者因出租土地而获得地租；资本的所有者因资本的形态不同而获得不同形式的收入：借贷资本所有者获得利息收入；股权所有者获得红利或未分配利润；政府因直接或间接介入生产过程而获得生产税或支付补贴。初次分配的结果形成各个机构部门的初次分配总收入。各部门的初次分配总收入之和就等于国民总收入，亦即国民生产总值。

经常转移 转移是一个机构单位向另一个机构单位提供货物、服务或资产，而同时并没有从后一机构单位获得任何货物、服务或资产作为回报的一种交易。经常转移包括扣除资本转移外的所有转移。其形式有收入税、社会保险付款、社会补助和其他经常转移。

可支配总收入 在初次分配总收入的基础上，通过经常转移的形式对初次分配总收入进行再次分配。再分配的结果形成各个机构部门的可支配总收入。各部门的可支配总收入之和称为国民可支配总收入。

总储蓄 指可支配总收入用于最终消费后的余额。各部门的总储蓄之和称为国民总储蓄。

资本转移 指一个部门无偿地向另一个部门支付用于非金融投资的资金，是一种不从对方获取任何对应物作为回报的交易。资本转移具有不同于经常转移的两个特征，一是转移的目的是用于投资，而不是用于消费；二是资本转移其实物形式往往涉及除存货和现金以外资产所有权的转移；其现金形式往往涉及除存货以外的资产的处置。资本转移包括投资性补助和其他资本转移。

净金融投资 它反映机构部门或经济总体资金富余或短缺的状况。从实物交易角度看，它是指总储蓄加资本转移收入减资本转移支出减非金融投资后的差额。从金融交易角度看，它是金融资产的增加额减金融负债的增加额之后的差额。

通货 指以现金形式存在于市场流通中的货币，包括本币和外币。

存款 指金融机构接受客户存入的货币款项，存款人可随时或按约定时间支取款项的信用业务。包括活期存款、定期存款、住户储蓄存款、财政存款、外汇存款和其他存款等。

贷款 指金融机构将其所吸收的资金，按一定的利率贷放给客户并约期归还的信用业务。包括短期贷款、中长期贷款、财政贷款、外汇贷款和其他贷款。

证券（不含股票） 由债券购买者承购的或因销售产品而拥有的，可在金融市场上交易并代表一定债权的书面证明。包括政府债券、金融债券、企业债券、商业票据、支付固定收入但不提供法人企业残余价值分享权的优先股等。

股票及其他股权 指股票购买者及直接投资者对其投资企业净资产所拥有的权益。股票是股份公司签发的证明股东投资并按其所持股份享有权益和承担义务的权益性证券。其他股权是机构单位以直接投资的方式用除股票、债权性证券以外的土地、房屋及建筑物、机器设备、存货、资源资产等实物资产，商标、专利权、土地使用权、特许使用权、商誉等无形资产及货币资金直接向其他单位进行的投资。通常以股权证、出资证明书、参与证或类似的单据为凭证。

保险准备金 指对人寿保险准备金和养恤基金的净权益、保险费预付款和未结索赔准备金。

结算资金 指金融机构用于结算目的汇兑在途的资金。

金融机构往来 指各金融机构之间的资金往来，包括同业存放款和同业拆借款。

准备金 指各金融机构在中央银行的存款及缴存中央银行的法定准备金。

中央银行贷款 指中央银行向各金融机构的贷款。

经常项目 包括货物、服务、收益及经常性转移。

货物进出口 指通过我国海关进出口的货物。货物的进出口值都按离岸价格估价。离岸价格可视为进口商在出口商边境领取货物时支付的购买者价格。当进口商领取该货物时，该货物已装载到进口商自己的运载工具或其他运载工具，出口商已为该货物支付了出口税或获得了出口退税。

服务进出口 指常住单位与非常住单位之间相互提供的服务。包括运输服务、旅游服务、通讯服务、建筑服务、保险服务、金融服务、计算机和信息服务、咨询服务、广告、宣传服务、电影音像服务、专有权力使用费和特许费、其他商务服务、政府服务。

收益 指常住单位与非常住单位之间因相互提供生产要素而产生的收入，包括劳动者报酬和投资收益。其中投资收益包括直接投资、证券投资和其他投资的收益和支出，以及直接投资收益的再投资。

资本项目 包括移民转移、债务减免等资本性转移。

金融项目 包括直接投资、证券投资和其他投资。

直接投资 指外国、港澳台地区在我国和我国在外国、港澳台地区以独资、合资、合作及合作勘探开发方式进行的投资。

证券投资 指我国对外国、港澳台地区发行的股票、债券等有价证券和我国购买外国、港澳台地区发行的股票、债券等有价证券。

其他投资 指除直接投资和证券投资以外的所有对外金融资产与负债交易项目。包括外国提供给我国和我国提供给外国的贸易信贷、贷款、货币和存款以及其他资产。

储备资产增减额 指我国在黄金储备、外汇储备、在国际货币基金组织的储备头寸、特别提款权、使用基金信贷等方面本年末与上年末余额之间的差额。负号表示储备资产增加，正号表示储备资产减少。

Explanatory Notes on Main Statistical Indicators

Gross Domestic Product (GDP) refers to the final products at market prices produced by all resident units in a country (or a region) during a certain period of time. Gross domestic product is expressed in three different forms, i.e. value, income, and products respectively. GDP in its value form refers to the total value of all goods and services produced by all resident units during a certain period of time, minus the total value of input of goods and services of the nature of non-fixed assets; in other term, it is the sum of the value-added of all resident units. GDP in the form of income includes the income created by all resident units and distributed to resident and non-resident units. GDP in the form of products refers to the value of all goods and services for final consumption by all resident units minus the net exports of goods and services during a given period of time. In the practice of national accounting, gross domestic product is calculated with three approaches, i.e. production approach, income approach and expenditure approach, which reflect gross domestic product and its composition from different aspects.

Three Industries Classification of economic activities into three branches of industries is a common practice in the world, although the grouping varies to some extent form country to country. In China economic activities are categorized into following industries:

Primary industry: refers to agriculture, forestry, animal husbandry and fishery.

Secondary industry: refers to mining and quarrying, manufacturing, production and supply of electricity, water and gas, and construction.

Tertiary industry: refers to all other economic activities not included in primary or secondary industry.

Labourers Remuneration refers to the whole payment of various forms earned by the labourers from the productive activities they are engaged in. It includes wages, bonuses and allowances the labourers earned in monetary form and in kind. It also includes the free medical services provided to the labourers and the medicine expenses, traffic subsidies and social insurance, housing fund paid by the employers. As the individual economy is concerned, since the labourers remuneration is not easily distinguished from the operating profit, both are treated as labourers remuneration.

Net Taxes on Production refers to the difference of the taxes on production minus the subsidies on production. The taxes on production refers to the various taxes, extra charges and fees levied on the production units on their production, sale and business activities as well as on the use of some factors of production, such as fixed assets, land and labour force in the production activities they are engaged in. In contrast to the taxes on production, the subsidies on production refer to the unilateral government transfer to the production units and are therefore regarded as negative taxes on production. They include subsidies on the loss due to implementation of government policies, price subsidies, etc.

Depreciation of Fixed Assets refers to the depreciation of fixed assets of a given period, drawn in accordance with the stipulated depreciation rate for the purpose of compensating the wear loss of the fixed assets or the depreciation of fixed assets calculated in a fictitious way in accordance with the stipulated unified depreciation rate in the national economic accounting system. It reflects the value of transfer of the fixed assets in the production of the current period. The depreciation of fixed assets in various enterprises and institutions managed as enterprises refers to the depreciation expenses actually drawn. In government agencies and institutions not managed as enterprises which do not draw the depreciation expenses, as well as for the houses of residents, the depreciation of fixed assets is the imputed depreciation, which is calculated in accordance with the stipulated unified depreciation rate. In principle, the depreciation of fixed assets should be calculated on the basis of the re-purchased value of the fixed assets. However, there is no actual condition to re-evaluate all the fixed assets in China. Therefore, the above-mentioned methods are temporarily adopted at present.

Operating Surplus refers to the balance of the value added created by the resident units deducting the labourers remuneration, net taxes on production and the depreciation of fixed assets. It is equivalent to the business profit of the enterprises plus subsidies on production, but the wages and welfare expenses paid from the profits should be deducted.

GDP by Expenditure Approach refers to the method of measuring the final results of production activities of a country (region) during a given period from the perspective of final use. It includes final consumption, total capital formation and net export of goods and services, i.e.:

GDP by expenditure approach = final consumption + total capital formation + net export of goods and services

Final Consumption refers to the total expenditure of resident units for purchases of goods and services from domestic economic territory and abroad to meet the requirements of material, cultural and spiritual life. It excludes the expenditure of non-resident units on consumption in the economic territory of the country. The final consumption is broken down into household consumption and government consumption.

Households Consumption refers to the total expenditure of resident households on the final consumption of goods and services. In addition to the consumption of goods and services bought by the households directly with money, the households consumption also includes expenditure on goods and services obtained by the households in other ways, i.e. the so-called imputed consumption expenditure, which includes the following: (a) the goods and services provided to the households by the employer in the form of payment in kind and transfer in kind; (b) goods and services produced and consumed by the households themselves, in which the services refer only to the owner-occupied housing and domestic and individual services provided by the paid household workers; (c) financial intermediate services provided by financial institutions; (d) insurance services provided by insurance companies.

Government Consumption refers to the expenditure on the consumption of the public services provided by the government to the whole society and the net expenditure on the goods and services provided by the government to the households free of charge or at low prices. The former equals to the output value of the government services minus the value of operating income obtained by the government departments. The latter equals to the market value of the goods and services provided by the government free of charge or at low prices to the households minus the value received by the government from the households.

Total Capital Formation refers to the fixed assets acquired minus those disposed of and the net value of inventory, including the total fixed capital formation and the increase in inventory.

Total Fixed Capital Formation refers to the value of fixed assets acquired minus those disposed of during a given period. Fixed assets are the assets produced through production activities with specified unit value which could be used for over one year, excluding natural assets. Total fixed capital formation can be categorized into total tangible capital formation and total intangible capital formation. The total tangible capital formation include the value of the construction projects, installation projects completed and the equipment, apparatus and instruments purchased as well as the value of land improved, the value of draught animals, breeding stock, animals for milk, wool and for recreational purpose, and the newly increased forest with economic value during a given period. The total intangible capital formation includes the prospecting of minerals, the acquisition of computer software minus the disposal of them.

Increase in Inventory refers to the market value of the change in inventory of resident units during a given period, i.e. the difference of value between the beginning and the end of the period minus the current gains due to the change in prices. The increase in inventory can be positive or negative. A positive value indicates the increase in inventory while a negative value indicates the decrease in stock. The inventory includes the raw materials, fuels and reserve materials purchased by the production units as well as the inventory of finished products, semi-finished products, work-in-progress, etc.

Net Export of Goods and Services refers to the difference of the exports of goods and services minus the imports of goods and services. The imports include the value of various goods and services sold or gratuitously transferred by the resident units to the non-resident units. The imports include the value of various goods and services purchased or gratuitously acquired by the resident units from the non-resident units. Because the provision of services and the use of them happen simultaneously, the acquisition of services by the resident units from abroad is usually treated as import while the acquisition of services by non-resident units in this country is usually treated as export. The export and import of goods are calculated at FOB.

Direct Input Coefficient refers to the volume of products and services of industry i, which is consumed directly by industry j in the course of its production or business, recorded as aij (i,j=1,2, … ,n). The direct input coefficient table or direct input coefficient matrix, usually denoted as A, is a table that presents direct input coefficients of all industries.

Total Input Coefficient refers to the volume of products and services of industry i which is consumed directly and indirectly by industry j in producing each unit of final use. The total input coefficient table or total input coefficient matrix, usually denoted as B, is a table that presents total input coefficients of all industries.

Institutional Units refer to economic entities that are in a position to own assets and incur liabilities, to engage independently in economic activities, and to conduct transactions with other entities.

Institutional Sectors refer groups of institutional units that are homogenous in nature. Following 4 institutional sectors are identified in the flow of fund accounts: non-financial corporations, financial institutions, governments and households, Also treated as an institutional sector is the rest of the world, which is composed of non-resident units that have economic relations with the resident units.

Non-Financial Corporations and the Sector of Non-Financial Corporations Non-financial corporations refer to resident corporations that are engaged in the production of goods and the provision of non financial services in the market, mainly covering corporate enterprises of various types engaged in the above-mentioned activities. All non-financial corporations make up the sector of non-financial corporations.

Financial Institutions and the Sector of Financial Institutions Financial institutions refer to resident institutions that are engaged in the financial intermediate services or auxiliary financial activities that are closed related with financial intermediate services, mainly covering central banks, commercial banks, policy-related banks, non-banking credit institutions and insurance companies. All financial institutions make up the sector of financial institutions.

Government Units and the Sector of Governments Government units refer to legal entities and their auxiliary units within the territory of China that are established through political process and are empowered with legislative, administrative or judicial rights over other institutional units in a given region. The main function of government units is to acquire funds through taxation or other means, to provide public services to the society and households, and to conduct redistribution of income and properties of the society through transfer payment. Government units cover mainly administrative and non-profit institutional units of various types. All government units make up the sector of governments.

Households and the Sector of Households Households refer to resident individuals or groups of resident individuals who share common living facilities, pool together entire or part of their income and properties at their common disposal, and share their housing, food and other consumer goods and services. All households make up the sector of households.

Non-resident Units and the Rest of the World Non-resident units refer to of units that are of a non-resident nature. All non-resident units that have transactions with resident units make up the sector the rest of the world.

Total Income of Primary Distribution Primary distribution refers to the distribution of net results from production activities among the owners of factors of production and the governments. Factors of production include labour force, land and capitals. Owners of labour force gain remuneration by providing labour. Owners of land receive rents from leasing of land. Owners of capitals get income of various forms depending on the type of capitals: bankers receive income from interest and share holders receive dividends or non-distributed profits. Governments either gain production tax or pay for subsidies by participating directly or indirectly in the production process. Results of primary distribution generate the total income of primary distribution of each sector, and the sum of the total income of primary distribution of all sectors make up the gross national income, or the gross national product.

Current Transfers Transfer refers to the transaction of provision of goods, services or assets by an institutional unit to another institutional unit without receiving any goods, services or assets in return from the recipient. Current transfers refer to all kinds of transfers other than capital transfers, including income tax, payment to social securities, social allowances and other current transfers.

Total Disposable Income Total income of primary distribution is re-distributed through current transfer, resulting in the total disposable income of various institutional sectors. The sum of total disposable income of all institutional sectors makes up the total national disposable income.

Total Savings refer to the total disposable income minus the final consumption. Total savings of all sectors make up the total national savings.

Capital Transfer refers to the free payment from one sector to another sector for non-financial capital formation, and is a transaction that seeks no return from the recipient. The capital transfer differs from the current transfer in 2 aspects: 1) The purpose of the capital transfer is investment rather than consumption. 2) The capital transfer features the transfer of the ownership of the assets other than inventory and cash, and the capital transfer in its monetary form involves the disposal of assets other than inventory. Capital transfer includes investment subsidies and other capital transfers.

Net Financial Investment reflects the surplus or shortage of capitals of institutional sectors or of the economy in general. It refers to total savings plus the income from capital transfer minus payment for capital transfer and the non-financial investment from the point of view of physical transaction. In terms of monetary transaction, it is the difference between the increase in financial assets minus the increase of the financial liabilities.

Currency in Circulation refers to currency that is in circulation in the market, including local and foreign currencies.

Deposits refer to credit transactions by which financial institutions accept deposits from clients who could withdraw their deposit at any time or by agreed time frame. They include current deposit, fixed deposit, household savings deposit, government deposit, foreign exchange deposit and other deposits.

Loans refer to credit transactions by which financial institutions lend their capital to clients at certain level of interest rates, which the latter will repay by agreed time frame. They include short-term loans, medium and long-term loans, government loans, foreign exchange loans and other loans.

Securities (excluding stocks) refer to written certificates representing creditors' rights, purchased by bond holders or owned by selling products, which can be transacted at the financial markets. They include government bonds, financial bonds, corporation bonds, commercial drafts, preferential stocks that provide fixed income without the right to share the residual value of corporations, etc.

Stocks and Other Holding Rights refer to the rights by stockholders and direct investors on the net assets of corporations they invested in. Stocks refer to negotiable securities on creditor's rights, issued by stock companies certifying the investment by stockholders and their rights and duties depending on their stocks. Other holding rights refer to the direct investment by institutional units to other units in forms other than stocks and negotiable securities on creditor's rights, including tangible assets such as land, buildings, machines and equipment, inventory, resources, etc., and intangible assets such as Trades marks, patents, rights on land use, licenses, commodity credit, and the capitals. Documents on holding rights usually include certificates on creditor's right, certificates on investment or on participation, etc.

Insurance Reserve Funds refer to reserve fund for life insurance, the net pension fund, advance payment of premium and non-claimed reserves.

Settlement Fund refers to bank fund of financial institutions for settlement that is in the process of remittance.

Transactions Between Financial Institutions refer to flow of capital between financial institutions, including inter-bank deposits and loans.

Reserve Funds refer to savings of financial institutions in the central bank and designated reserves to the central bank.

Loans from the Central Bank refer to loans from the central bank to financial institutions.

Current Account includes goods, services, earnings and current transfers.

Import and Export of Goods refer to imported or exported goods through Chinese customs. Both import and export of goods are valued at free on board (f.o.b.) prices. Free on board prices can be regarded as the purchaser's prices paid by importers when claiming goods at the boarder of the exporters. When the importer claim the imported goods, the goods have been loaded in importer's carriers or other carriers, and the exporter has paid export duty or received export redeem.

Import and Export of Services refers services provided between resident and non-resident units, including services on transportation, tourism, communications, construction, insurance, banking, computer and information, consultation, advertisements and publicity, as well as film, audio and video services, royalty for patents, Tradesmarks and other special rights, other commercial services, and government services.

Earnings refers income from provision of factors of production between resident and non-resident units, including compensation of labours and earnings from investment. Earnings from investment include earnings from and expenses on direct investment, security investment and other investment, as well as reinvestment of earnings from direct investment.

Capital Account includes capital transfers such as immigration transfer, reduction or exemption of debts, etc.

Financial Account includes direct investment, security investment and other investments.

Direct Investment refers to investment by foreign investors or investors from Hong Kong, Macao and Taiwan in China, or by Chinese investors in foreign countries or in Hong Kong, Macao and Taiwan, in forms of exclusive investment, joint investment, contracted operation and cooperative development,.

Security Investment refers to the issue of stocks and securities by China in foreign countries or in Hong Kong, Macao and Taiwan, and the purchase by Chinese units of stocks and securities issued in foreign countries or in Hong Kong, Macao and Taiwan.

Other Investment refers to all external transactions on financial assets and liabilities other than direct investment and security investment, including Trades credits, loans, currency, savings and other assets, provided by foreign countries to China and by China to foreign countries.

Reserve Assets, Net Increase refers to the net balance between the end of the reference year and the end of the previous year, in the gold reserve, foreign exchange reserve, special drawing rights in the International Monetary Fund, and the use of the Funds credits. The increase in the reserve assets is expressed in negative figure and the decrease in the reserve assets is expressed in positive figure.

第三篇 人口与就业

CHAPTER 3 Population and Employment

简要说明
Brief Introduction

本篇资料的主要内容及来源

本篇内容主要包括人口、计划生育、就业、工资等资料。人口资料包括全区、各地、州、市、县及兵团人口情况、第五次人口普查的主要数据。

分地区人口数据为户籍人口，由新疆维吾尔自治区公安厅提供；计划生育资料由新疆维吾尔自治区计划生育委员会提供；失业资料由新疆维吾尔自治区社会劳动保障局提供；全区人口为常住人口由新疆维吾尔自治区统计局人口与社会科技处根据 2007 年人口变动情况抽样调查数据推算；人口普查主要数据、就业和工资资料由新疆维吾尔自治区统计局人口与社会科技处提供。

Main Content and Source of Data

Data in this chapter show the basic condition of population, employment, wages of staff and workers, family planning. Data of population mainly include the condition of population by whole region, prefecture, autonomous prefecture, city, country and Xinjiang Production and Construction Group, and the data of 5 national population censuses.

The data on household registered population are provided by Municipal Bureau of Public Security of Xinjiang Uygur Autonomous Region; Data on family planning come from Municipal Family Planning Commission. Data on unemployment are provided by Bureau of Labor and Social Security. Total region population are estimated by the Department of Population and Social Science Technology Statistics of the Xinjiang Bureau of Statistics in accordance with the annual national sample survey on population changes in 2007; The data of population census, employment and wages are provided by the Department of Population and Social Science and Technology Statistic of the Xinjiang Bureau of Statistics.

3-1 人口数及构成
Population and Its Composition

单位：万人、% (10 000 persons,%)

年 份 Year	年 末 总人口 Total Population (Year-end)	按性别分 By Sex				按城乡分 By Residence			
		男 Male		女 Female		城镇人口 Urban		乡村人口 Rural	
		人口数 Population	比 重 Proportion	人口数 Population	比 重 Proportion	人口数 Population	比 重 Proportion	人口数 Population	比 重 Proportion
1978	1233.01	630.18	51.11	602.83	48.89	321.40	26.07	911.61	73.93
1980	1283.24	654.90	51.03	628.34	48.97	372.74	29.05	910.50	70.95
1985	1361.14	696.81	51.19	664.33	48.81	582.24	42.78	778.90	57.22
1990	1529.16	785.06	51.34	744.10	48.66	685.96	44.86	843.20	55.14
1995	1661.35	848.12	51.05	813.23	48.95	822.53	49.51	838.82	50.49
1996	1689.29	869.59	51.48	819.70	48.52	846.17	50.09	843.12	49.91
1997	1718.08	883.03	51.40	835.05	48.60	860.76	50.10	857.32	49.90
1998	1747.35	897.90	51.39	849.45	48.61	875.42	50.10	871.93	49.90
1999	1775.00	910.98	51.32	864.02	48.68	929.00	52.34	846.00	47.66
2000	1849.41	957.07	51.75	892.34	48.25	624.18	33.75	1225.23	66.25
2001	1876.19	954.23	50.86	921.96	49.14	633.21	33.75	1242.98	66.25
2002	1905.19	975.46	51.20	929.73	48.80	644.72	33.84	1260.47	66.16
2003	1933.95	994.24	51.41	939.71	48.59	665.11	34.39	1268.84	65.61
2004	1963.11	1008.02	51.30	955.09	48.70	690.11	35.15	1273.00	64.85
2005	2010.35	1029.70	51.22	980.65	48.78	746.85	37.15	1263.50	62.85
2006	2050.00	1050.01	51.22	999.99	48.78	777.77	37.94	1272.23	62.06
2007	2095.19	1072.53	51.19	1022.66	48.81	820.27	39.15	1274.92	60.85

注：2000 年及以后城镇人口和乡村人口按“五普”城乡划分口径，其余年份按公安年报口径。
Note: Since 2000 the total uban and rural population is caculated on the 5th national population censuses, data of population is caculated on the annals of public secutity in oters year.

3-2 人口出生率、死亡率、自然增长率
Birth Rate, Death Rate and Natural Growth Rate of Population

单位：‰ (‰)

年 份 Year	出生率 Birth Rate	死亡率 Death Rate	自然增长率 Natural Growth Rate	年 份 Year	出生率 Birth Rate	死亡率 Death Rate	自然增长率 Natural Growth Rate
1978	22.55	7.69	14.86	1996	19.45	6.60	12.85
1980	21.28	7.62	13.66	1997	19.66	6.55	13.11
1985	19.80	6.39	13.41	1998	19.74	6.93	12.81
1986	20.54	6.13	14.41	1999	18.76	6.96	11.80
1987	21.03	5.96	15.07	2000	17.57	5.40	12.17
1988	19.72	5.99	13.73	2001	16.82	5.69	11.13
1989	21.15	5.77	15.38	2002	16.30	5.43	10.87
1990	26.41	7.81	18.60	2003	16.01	5.23	10.78
1991	24.45	7.86	16.59	2004	16.00	5.09	10.91
1992	22.80	7.84	14.96	2005	16.42	5.04	11.38
1993	21.53	7.68	13.85	2006	15.97	5.03	10.94
1994	20.82	7.43	13.39	2007	16.79	5.01	11.78
1995	18.90	6.45	12.45				

3-3 新疆人口普查基本情况
Basic Statistics on National Population Census in Xinjiang

单位：万人 (10 000 persons)

指 标	Items	第二次普查 (1964 年) 1964 Census	第三次普查 (1982 年) 1982 Census	第四次普查 (1990 年) 1990 Census	第五次普查 (2000 年) 2000 Census
总人口	**Total Population**	**727.01**	**1308.15**	**1515.69**	**1845.95**
男	Male	389.47	673.22	782.32	955.22
女	Female	337.54	634.93	733.37	890.73
总户数(万户)	**Total Number of Households (10000 households)**	**178.00**	**293.79**	**337.41**	**491.66**
家 庭 户	Family Households		292.70	334.89	479.38
集 体 户	Non-family Households		1.09	2.52	12.28
各年龄组人口	**Population by Age**				
0-5 岁	Age 0-5	121.86	186.70	218.85	165.12
6-14 岁	Age 6-14	146.77	330.85	282.12	338.18
15-64 岁	Age 15-64	428.73	742.42	955.49	1256.40
65 岁及以上	Population Aged 65 and Over	29.65	48.18	59.23	86.25
民族人口	**Nationality Population**				
汉 族	Han Nationality	232.12	528.40	569.54	748.99
少数民族	Minority Nationalities	494.89	779.75	946.15	1096.96
各种文化程度人口	**Population by Educational Level**				
大专及以上	College and Above	4.10	8.37	27.98	94.65
高中和中专	Senior Secondary School and Specialized Secondary School	15.51	84.28	157.42	224.79
初 中	Junior Secondary School	50.37	228.63	313.51	508.59
小 学	Primary School	197.34	442.57	552.55	699.78
不识字或识字很少	Illiterate and Semi-iliterate	249.03	265.39	198.11	103.68

注：不识字或识字很少除 1964 年包含 12-14 岁人口外，其他均为 15 岁及以上人口。
Note:Illiterate or semi-illiterate population refers to the population aged above 15 except for the population aged between 12 and 14 in 1964

3-4 婚姻登记情况
Number of Marriages Registry

指 标	Item	1995	2000	2007
登记结婚(对)	**Registered Marriages (couple)**	**166363**	**162527**	**226288**
初婚(人)	First Marriage (person)	249428	250461	331005
再婚(人)	Remarriage (person)	83298	74593	121571
#男	Male	46996	38484	57622
#再婚中恢复结婚(对)	Resumed Marriages (couple)	5194	3954	6498
登记离婚(对)	**Registered Divorces (couple)**	**53500**	**59000**	**86510**
民政部门批准	Approved by the Civil Administration	26759	26003	55403
法院调判	Mediated by the court	26741	32997	26107
涉外及华侨港澳台居民婚姻	**Marital status of OverseasChinese ,Foreigner and Hong Kong, Macao and Taiwan Compatriots**			
登记结婚(对)	Registered Marriages (couple)	136	172	256
国内公民(人)	Citizen (person)	136	172	256
港澳台居民(人)	Compatriots of Hong Kong, Macao and Taiwan (person)	77	78	57
华 侨(人)	Overseas Chinese (person)	33	34	45
外国人(人)	Foreigner (person)	26	60	154
登记离婚(对)	Registered Divorces (couple)	1	6	34

3-5 各地、州、市、县(市)户数、人口数、土地面积

Household, Population, Land Area by Prefecture, Autonomous Prefecture City and County

(2007 年)

地区	Region	户数 (万户) Number of Households (10 000 households)	年末人口 (万人) Year-end Population (10 000 persons)	#男 Male	平均每户人口 (人) Average Persons Per Household (person)	土地面积 (平方公里) Land Area (sq.km)
总计	**Total**	**614.43**	**2095.19**	**1072.53**	**3.41**	**1664897.17**
乌鲁木齐市	**Urumqi City**	**74.17**	**231.30**	**120.30**	**3.12**	**15173.13**
天山区	Tianshan District	16.16	51.54	25.96	3.19	47.31
沙依巴克区	Shayibak District	16.74	52.27	27.07	3.12	38.60
新市区	Xinshi District	14.84	48.32	25.49	3.26	57.07
水磨沟区	Shui Mogou Distric	8.28	23.56	12.75	2.85	10.76
头屯河区	Tou Tunhe District	4.59	12.79	6.74	2.79	20.11
达坂城区	Da Bancheng District	1.40	4.24	2.29	3.03	1111.85
米东区	Midong District	9.34	29.58	15.40	3.17	4086.85
乌鲁木齐县	Urumqi County	2.82	9.00	4.60	3.19	9800.58
克拉玛依市	**Karamay City**	**9.76**	**26.72**	**13.77**	**2.74**	**8654.08**
独山子区	Dushanzi District	1.81	5.29	2.79	2.92	379.11
克拉玛依区	Karamay District	6.12	16.41	8.38	2.68	4231.56
乌尔河区	Urhe District	1.75	4.79	2.48	2.74	1424.65
白碱滩区	Bai Jiantan District	0.08	0.23	0.12	2.88	2618.76
吐鲁番地区	**Turpan Administrative Offices**	**17.33**	**60.06**	**30.53**	**3.47**	**67562.91**
吐鲁番市	Turpan City	7.64	26.92	13.62	3.52	13589.22
鄯善县	Shanshan [Piqan] County	6.48	21.82	11.15	3.37	38281.46
托克逊县	Toksun County	3.21	11.32	5.76	3.53	15692.23
哈密地区	**Hami [Kumul] Administrative Offices**	**17.88**	**54.62**	**27.92**	**3.05**	**142094.88**
哈密市	Hami [Kumul] City	13.93	42.38	21.69	3.04	85587.23
巴里坤哈萨克自治县	Barkol Kazak Autonomous County	3.22	10.13	5.15	3.15	36988.55
伊吾县	Yiwu [Araturuk] County	0.73	2.11	1.08	2.89	19519.10

注：1.全区总计中"户数、年末人口、男"均根据 2007 年人口变动抽样调查数据推算，各地州市此部分数据为 2007 年公安年报数据。因此，各地州市此部分数据合计不等于全区总计。2.全疆各地州市土地面积为国土资源厅 2007 年数据。

Note: a) Households, Year-end population and Male in the census are calculated on the data of surveyed population variation in 2007. The data in this part come from the annual data of Public Security for the year 2007 in prefectures and cities. Therefore, the total of data in this part is not equal to the total in this region. b) The land area of different prefectures and cities is from the date dated 2007 in the Bureau of State Land.

3-5 续表 1 Continued

地　区	Region	户 数 (万户) Number of Households (10 000 households)	年末人口 (万人) Year-end Population (10 000 persons)	#男 Male	平均每户人口 (人) Average Persons Per Household (person)	土地面积 (平方公里) Land Area (sq.km)
昌吉回族自治州	**Changji Hui Autonomous Prefecture**	**44.11**	**135.37**	**69.53**	**3.07**	**73139.75**
昌吉市	Changji City	11.18	34.78	17.90	3.11	7505.12
阜康市	Fukang City	5.85	16.62	8.57	2.84	8534.97
呼图壁县	Hutubi County	7.37	21.36	10.92	2.90	9421.03
玛纳斯县	Manas County	5.62	17.19	8.75	3.06	9597.27
奇台县	Qitai County	6.98	23.14	11.89	3.32	16635.92
吉木萨尔县	Jimsar County	4.33	13.56	7.00	3.13	8144.58
木垒哈萨克自治县	Mori Kazak Autonomous County	2.78	8.72	4.50	3.14	13300.86
伊犁哈萨克自治州	**Ili Kazak Autonomous Prefecture**	**132.36**	**434.22**	**221.39**	**3.28**	**268778.72**
伊犁州直属县(市)	**Counties (Cities) Direct Under Ili Prefecture**	**81.24**	**270.23**	**137.66**	**3.33**	**56381.53**
伊宁市	Yining [Gulja] City	13.77	44.59	22.16	3.24	524.94
奎屯市	Kuytun City	10.90	30.76	15.73	2.82	1109.89
伊宁县	Yining [Gulja] County	10.19	38.83	19.94	3.81	4681.90
察布查尔锡伯自治县	Qapqal Xibe Autonomous County	5.84	18.41	9.40	3.15	4471.95
霍城县	Huocheng [Korgas] County	11.66	38.45	19.77	3.30	5429.83
巩留县	Gongliu [Tokkuztara] County	5.16	17.82	9.21	3.45	4326.90
新源县	Xinyuan [Kunes] County	9.01	30.95	15.79	3.44	6813.74
昭苏县	Zhaosu [Mongolkure] County	5.34	16.95	8.57	3.17	11127.91
特克斯县	Tekes County	4.67	16.31	8.29	3.49	7764.10
尼勒克县	Nilka County	4.70	17.16	8.80	3.65	10130.37
塔城地区	**Tacheng [Tarbagatai] Administrative Offices**	**32.03**	**99.48**	**50.89**	**3.11**	**94698.18**
塔城市	Tacheng [Qoqek] City	5.25	16.36	8.26	3.12	3991.25
乌苏市	Usu City	6.89	21.54	11.31	3.13	14299.86
额敏县	Emin [Dorbiljin] County	7.18	20.77	10.58	2.89	9448.37
沙湾县	Shawan County	6.44	20.70	10.54	3.21	12676.58
托里县	Toli County	2.62	9.40	4.73	3.59	19977.34
裕民县	Yumin [Qagantokay] County	1.75	5.55	2.84	3.17	6112.13
和布克赛尔蒙古自治县	Hoboksar Mongol Autonomous County	1.90	5.16	2.63	2.72	28192.65

3-5 续表 2 Continued

地　　区	Region	户 数（万户） Number of Households (10 000 households)	年末人口（万人） Year-end Population (10 000 persons)	#男 Male	平均每户人口（人） Average Persons Per Household (person)	土地面积（平方公里） Land Area (sq.km)
阿勒泰地区	**Altay Administrative Offices**	**19.09**	**64.51**	**32.84**	**3.38**	**117699.01**
阿勒泰市	Altay City	7.11	23.00	11.73	3.23	10829.06
布尔津县	Burqin County	2.03	6.89	3.49	3.39	10357.35
富蕴县	Fuyun [Koktokay] County	2.45	9.05	4.60	3.69	32186.11
福海县	Fuhai [Burultokay] County	2.18	7.28	3.77	3.34	33250.74
哈巴河县	Habahe [Kaba] County	2.39	8.38	4.26	3.51	8166.58
青河县	Qinghe [Qinggil] County	1.60	6.03	3.04	3.77	15756.87
吉木乃县	Jemnay County	1.33	3.88	1.95	2.92	7152.30
博尔塔拉蒙古自治州	**Bortala Mongol Autonomous Prefecture**	**16.37**	**47.29**	**24.25**	**2.89**	**24934.33**
博乐市	Bole [Bortala] City	9.20	25.96	13.29	2.82	7877.34
精河县	Jinghe [Jing] County	4.69	13.96	7.20	2.98	11175.25
温泉县	Wenquan [Araxang] County	2.48	7.37	3.76	2.97	5881.74
巴音郭楞蒙古自治州	**Bayangol Mongol Autonomous Prefecture**	**43.14**	**122.41**	**64.46**	**2.84**	**470954.25**
库尔勒市	Korla City	18.98	47.21	25.86	2.49	7215.90
轮台县	Luntai [Bugur] County	2.92	10.42	5.28	3.57	14156.61
尉犁县	Yuli [Lopnur] County	4.01	11.46	5.92	2.86	59234.48
若羌县	Ruoqiang [Qarkilik] County	1.08	3.20	1.69	2.96	198793.52
且末县	Qiemo [Qarqan] County	1.75	6.10	3.13	3.49	137831.05
焉耆回族自治县	Yanji Hui Autonomous County	4.01	12.99	6.64	3.24	2440.73
和静县	Hejing County	6.05	18.32	9.37	3.03	34886.74
和硕县	Hoxud County	2.53	6.86	3.56	2.71	12816.49
博湖县	Bohu [Bagrax] County	1.81	5.85	3.01	3.23	3578.73
阿克苏地区	**Aksu Administrative Offices**	**57.26**	**220.31**	**112.76**	**3.85**	**127144.91**
阿克苏市	Aksu City	13.09	45.24	23.11	3.46	13987.61
温宿县	Wensu [Onsu] County	6.17	23.46	12.05	3.80	14202.46
库车县	Kuqa County	10.37	43.74	22.23	4.22	14602.95
沙雅县	Xayar County	6.01	23.01	11.85	3.83	31955.15
新和县	Xinhe [Toksu] County	4.51	15.61	8.03	3.46	5817.82
拜城县	Baicheng [Bay] County	5.89	22.13	11.32	3.76	15553.70
乌什县	Wushi [Uxturpan] County	5.04	19.92	10.21	3.95	9082.00
阿瓦提县	Awat County	5.23	22.71	11.64	4.34	13233.57
柯坪县	Kalpin County	0.95	4.49	2.32	4.73	8709.65

3-5 续表 3 Continued

地　　区	Region	户数(万户) Number of Households (10 000 households)	年末人口(万人) Year-end Population (10 000 persons)	#男 Male	平均每户人口(人) Average Persons Per Household (person)	土地面积(平方公里) Land Area (sq.km)
克孜勒苏柯尔克孜自治州	**Kizilsu Kirgiz Autonomous Prefecture**	**12.14**	**50.00**	**25.46**	**4.12**	**72468.08**
阿图什市	Artux City	5.15	22.51	11.43	4.37	16151.17
阿克陶县	Akto County	4.40	18.10	9.26	4.11	24539.86
阿合奇县	Akqi County	1.05	3.99	2.01	3.79	12737.09
乌恰县	Wuqia [Ulugqat] County	1.54	5.40	2.76	3.51	19039.96
喀什地区	**Kashgar [Kaxgar] Administrative Offices**	**89.16**	**369.43**	**187.09**	**4.14**	**137578.51**
喀什市	Kashgar [Kaxgar] City	12.71	44.01	22.01	3.46	199.38
疏附县	Shufu County	7.00.	30.88	15.81	4.41	3323.12
疏勒县	Shule County	7.77	31.48	15.97	4.05	2485.31
英吉沙县	Yengisar County	5.39	24.08	12.33	4.47	3223.87
泽普县	Zepu [Poskam] County	5.46	18.67	9.43	3.42	826.90
莎车县	Shache [Yarkant] County	15.55	71.47	36.09	4.60	9066.86
叶城县	Yecheng [Kagilik] County	9.64	40.41	20.52	4.19	29359.29
麦盖提县	Makit County	5.91	23.45	11.84	3.97	10276.57
岳普湖县	Yopurga County	3.84	14.85	7.54	3.87	2700.48
伽师县	Jiashi [Payzawat] County	7.89	36.86	18.76	4.67	6668.59
巴楚县	Bachu [Maralbexi] County	7.09	29.81	15.00	4.20	18903.70
塔什库尔干塔吉克自治县	Taxkorgan Tajik Autonomous County	0.91	3.46	1.79	3.80	50544.44
和田地区	**Hotan Administrative Offices**	**49.65**	**188.39**	**96.22**	**3.79**	**249146.59**
和田市	Hotan City	7.77	28.19	14.22	3.63	495.84
和田县	Hotan County	5.77	24.77	12.66	4.29	40876.80
墨玉县	Moyu [Karakax] County	12.05	47.90	24.48	3.98	25624.02
皮山县	Pishan [Guma] County	6.33	23.79	12.22	3.76	39819.75
洛浦县	Lop County	5.77	22.07	11.31	3.82	14286.97
策勒县	Qira County	4.45	14.48	7.36	3.25	31342.58
于田县	Yutian [Keriya] County	6.35	23.52	12.10	3.70	39126.14
民丰县	Minfeng [Niya] County	1.16	3.67	1.87	3.16	57574.49
自治区直辖市	**Municpality Country-LevelCity directly under the Central Govern-ment**					
石河子市	Shihezi City	22.98	63.61	32.52	2.77	459.94
阿拉尔市	Aral City	6.16	16.65	8.81	2.70	4196.00
图木舒克市	Tumxuk City	4.20	14.78	7.81	3.52	1901.10
五家渠市	Wujiaqu City	2.78	7.28	3.66	2.61	710.00

3-6 各地、州、市、县(市)按城镇、乡村和农业、非农业分人口数

Population of Urban and Rural, Agriculture and Non-Agriculture by Prefecture, Autonomous Prefecture, City and County

单位：万人 (2007 年) (10 000 persons)

地区	Region	城镇人口 Urban Population	#非农业人口 Non-agricultural Population	乡村人口 Rural Population	农业人口 Agricultural Population	非农业人口 Non-agricultural Population
总 计	**Total**	**820.27**	**562.22**	**1274.92**	**1187.53**	**907.66**
乌鲁木齐市	**Urumqi City**	**224.41**	**172.71**	**6.88**	**57.94**	**173.35**
天山区	Tianshan District	51.54	44.40		7.14	44.40
沙依巴克区	Shayibak District	52.27	42.73		9.54	42.73
新市区	Xinshi District	48.32	37.95		10.37	37.95
水磨沟区	Shui Mogou Distric	23.56	16.87		6.69	16.87
头屯河区	Tou Tunhe District	12.79	11.23		1.56	11.23
达坂城区	Da Bancheng District	3.30	1.84	0.94	2.33	1.91
米东区	Midong District	29.12	17.08	0.46	12.45	17.13
乌鲁木齐县	Urumqi County	3.51	0.61	5.48	7.86	1.13
克拉玛依市	Karamay City	**26.72**	**26.24**		**0.48**	**26.24**
独山子区	Dushanzi District	5.29	5.29			5.29
克拉玛依区	Karamay District	16.41	16.13		0.28	16.13
乌尔河区	Urhe District	4.79	4.74		0.05	4.74
白碱滩区	Bai Jiantan District	0.23	0.08		0.15	0.08
吐鲁番地区	**Turpan Administrative Offices**	**43.27**	**13.57**	**16.80**	**43.21**	**16.85**
吐鲁番市	Turpan City	26.92	6.91		18.38	8.54
鄯善县	Shanshan [Piqan] County	14.14	4.69	7.68	16.50	5.32
托克逊县	Toksun County	2.21	1.97	9.11	8.33	2.99
哈密地区	**Hami [Kumul] Administrative Offices**	**48.02**	**30.02**	**6.60**	**21.74**	**32.88**
哈密市	Hami [Kumul] City	42.38	27.94		13.44	28.94
巴里坤哈萨克自治县	Barkol Kazak Autonomous County	4.69	1.49	5.44	6.99	3.14
伊吾县	Yiwu [Araturuk] County	0.95	0.59	1.16	1.31	0.80
昌吉回族自治州	**Changji Hui Autonomous Prefecture**	**112.37**	**66.48**	**23.00**	**67.04**	**68.33**
昌吉市	Changji City	34.78	22.05		12.53	22.25
阜康市	Fukang City	14.65	9.31	1.97	6.99	9.63
呼图壁县	Hutubi County	20.65	12.91	0.71	8.33	13.03
玛纳斯县	Manas County	13.69	7.26	3.50	9.60	7.59
奇台县	Qitai County	16.01	8.51	7.13	14.30	8.84
吉木萨尔县	Jimsar County	8.04	4.55	5.52	8.82	4.74
木垒哈萨克自治县	Mori Kazak Autonomous County	4.55	1.89	4.17	6.47	2.25

注：1.全区城镇、乡村人口，农业、非农业人口根据2007年人口变动抽样调查数据推算，各地、州、市城镇人口、乡村人口为公安年报按行政建制划分的人口数。2.各地、州、市农业人口数均含未落常住户口人员。

Note: a) The Total urban and rural population in Xinjiang is calculated on the data of surveyed population variation in 2007, the urban and rural population of different prefectures is calculated on the annals of Public Security. b) The figure of rural population refers to resident population in rural areas.

3-6 续表 1 Continued

单位：万人 (10 000 persons)

地区	Region	城镇人口 Urban Population	#非农业人口 Non-agri-cultural Population	乡村人口 Rural Population	农业人口 Agricul-tural Population	非农业人口 Non-agri-cultural Population
伊犁哈萨克自治州	**Ili Kazak Autonomous Prefecture**	**246.91**	**152.61**	**187.30**	**233.68**	**200.53**
伊犁州直属县(市)	**Counties (Cities) Direct Under Ili Prefecture**	**137.94**	**83.50**	**132.29**	**155.24**	**114.99**
伊宁市	Yining [Gulja] City	44.59	26.16		14.72	29.87
奎屯市	Kuytun City	30.76	27.74		3.02	27.74
伊宁县	Yining [Gulja] County	7.66	4.67	31.17	32.16	6.67
察布查尔锡伯自治县	Qapqal Xibe Autonomous County	5.83	4.27	12.58	12.04	6.37
霍城县	Huocheng [Korgas] County	18.86	5.52	19.59	23.29	15.16
巩留县	Gongliu [Tokkuztara] County	3.79	2.99	14.03	13.66	4.16
新源县	Xinyuan [Kunes] County	16.91	4.82	14.04	22.19	8.76
昭苏县	Zhaosu [Mongolkure] County	2.64	2.18	14.31	10.09	6.86
特克斯县	Tekes County	3.57	2.58	12.74	11.66	4.65
尼勒克县	Nilka County	3.33	2.57	13.83	12.41	4.75
塔城地区	**Tacheng [Tarbagatai] Administrative Offices**	**73.56**	**44.35**	**25.91**	**46.17**	**53.30**
塔城市	Tacheng [Qoqek] City	16.36	8.93		5.92	10.44
乌苏市	Usu City	21.54	7.37		13.80	7.74
额敏县	Emin [Dorbiljin] County	9.26	8.94	11.51	8.26	12.51
沙湾县	Shawan County	17.72	11.84	2.98	7.80	12.90
托里县	Toli County	4.35	3.49	5.04	5.42	3.97
裕民县	Yumin [Qagantokay] County	1.94	1.90	3.61	2.66	2.89
和布克赛尔蒙古自治县	Hoboksar Mongol Autonomous County	2.39	1.88	2.77	2.31	2.85
阿勒泰地区	**Altay Administrative Offices**	**35.41**	**24.76**	**29.10**	**32.27**	**32.24**
阿勒泰市	Altay City	23.00	13.42		8.06	14.94
布尔津县	Burqin County	1.88	1.87	5.01	4.27	2.62
富蕴县	Fuyun [Koktokay] County	3.06	2.72	5.99	5.27	3.78
福海县	Fuhai [Burultokay] County	2.55	2.50	4.73	3.41	3.87
哈巴河县	Habahe [Kaba] County	1.90	1.78	6.48	5.35	3.03
青河县	Qinghe [Qinggil] County	1.73	1.36	4.30	3.93	2.10
吉木乃县	Jemnay County	1.29	1.11	2.59	1.98	1.90
博尔塔拉蒙古自治州	**Bortala Mongol Autonomous Prefecture**	**37.95**	**22.69**	**9.35**	**22.14**	**25.16**
博乐市	Bole [Bortala] City	25.96	15.24		10.45	15.51
精河县	Jinghe [Jing] County	7.58	4.44	6.39	7.84	6.13
温泉县	Wenquan [Araxang] County	4.41	3.01	2.96	3.85	3.52
巴音郭楞蒙古自治州	**Bayangol Mongol Autonomous Prefecture**	**94.80**	**54.25**	**27.61**	**61.70**	**60.71**
库尔勒市	Korla City	47.21	26.96		17.19	30.02
轮台县	Luntai [Bugur] County	6.15	2.27	4.27	7.74	2.68
尉犁县	Yuli [Lopnur] County	7.00	5.22	4.46	5.73	5.73
若羌县	Ruoqiang [Qarkilik] County	1.75	1.41	1.45	1.60	1.60
且末县	Qiemo [Qarqan] County	1.95	1.60	4.15	3.93	2.17
焉耆回族自治县	Yanji Hui Autonomous County	8.99	5.04	4.00	7.43	5.56
和静县	Hejing County	15.08	7.67	3.24	10.06	8.26
和硕县	Hoxud County	3.66	2.55	3.20	3.86	3.00
博湖县	Bohu [Bagrax] County	3.01	1.53	2.84	4.16	1.69

3-6 续表 2 Continued

单位：万人 (10 000 persons)

地　　区	Region	城　镇人　口 Urban Population	#非农业人　口 Non-agri-cultural Population	乡　村人　口 Rural Population	农　业人　口 Agricul-tural Population	非农业人　口 Non-agri-cultural Population
阿克苏地区	**Aksu Administrative Offices**	**138.55**	**61.10**	**81.76**	**152.12**	**68.19**
阿克苏市	Aksu City	45.24	23.51		20.84	24.40
温宿县	Wensu [Onsu] County	15.80	5.78	7.66	16.71	6.75
库车县	Kuqa County	31.34	13.37	12.40	28.94	14.80
沙雅县	Xayar County	16.28	4.65	6.73	18.09	4.92
新和县	Xinhe [Toksu] County	4.71	2.38	10.90	12.48	3.13
拜城县	Baicheng [Bay] County	8.38	3.91	13.75	17.47	4.66
乌什县	Wushi [Uxturpan] County	3.59	2.74	16.33	16.54	3.38
阿瓦提县	Awat County	12.48	4.18	10.23	17.69	5.02
柯坪县	Kalpin County	0.73	0.58	3.76	3.36	1.13
克孜勒苏柯尔克孜自治州	**Kizilsu Kirgiz Autonomous Prefecture**	**28.86**	**9.78**	**21.14**	**35.94**	**14.06**
阿图什市	Artux City	22.51	5.60		15.11	7.40
阿克陶县	Akto County	3.58	1.69	14.52	15.27	2.83
阿合奇县	Akqi County	1.13	0.85	2.85	2.48	1.50
乌恰县	Wuqia [Ulugqat] County	1.64	1.64	3.77	3.08	2.33
喀什地区	**Kashgar [Kaxgar] Administrative Offices**	**134.03**	**63.56**	**235.42**	**286.87**	**82.58**
喀什市	Kashgar [Kaxgar] City	44.01	18.42		18.10	25.91
疏附县	Shufu County	2.99	1.86	27.90	27.98	2.91
疏勒县	Shule County	9.71	3.75	21.78	26.97	4.52
英吉沙县	Yengisar County	2.56	2.56	21.52	20.43	3.65
泽普县	Zepu [Poskam] County	5.35	4.50	13.32	13.00	5.67
莎车县	Shache [Yarkant] County	31.23	9.29	40.24	60.38	11.09
叶城县	Yecheng [Kagilik] County	10.73	6.60	29.68	32.84	7.57
麦盖提县	Makit County	6.74	6.14	16.71	16.39	7.06
岳普湖县	Yopurga County	4.21	2.11	10.64	11.85	3.00
伽师县	Jiashi [Payzawat] County	4.16	2.84	32.70	32.75	4.11
巴楚县	Bachu [Maralbexi] County	11.04	4.57	18.77	23.86	5.95
塔什库尔干塔吉克自治县	Taxkorgan Tajik Autonomous County	1.30	0.92	2.16	2.32	1.14
和田地区	**Hotan Administrative Offices**	**60.16**	**24.15**	**128.23**	**157.31**	**31.08**
和田市	Hotan City	28.20	11.01		15.96	12.24
和田县	Hotan County	5.30	0.31	19.46	23.67	1.09
墨玉县	Moyu [Karakax] County	6.04	2.26	41.86	44.00	3.90
皮山县	Pishan [Guma] County	6.72	3.84	17.07	18.47	5.32
洛浦县	Lop County	3.52	2.71	18.55	19.59	2.48
策勒县	Qira County	2.76	1.39	11.72	12.34	2.14
于田县	Yutian [Keriya] County	6.31	1.98	17.21	20.55	2.97
民丰县	Minfeng [Niya] County	1.31	0.65	2.36	2.73	0.94
自治区直辖市	**Municpality Country-LevelCity directly under the Central Govern-ment**					
石河子市	Shihezi City	63.61	52.61		11.00	52.61
阿拉尔市	Aral City	16.65	11.67		4.96	11.69
图木舒克市	Tumxuk City	14.78	13.47		1.31	13.47
五家渠市	Wujiaqu City	7.28	7.08		0.20	7.08

3-7 各地、州、市、县(市)民族人口数

单位：人 (2007 年)

地 区	Region	合 计 Total	#少数民族 Minority Nationalities	维吾尔族 Uygur	汉 族 Han	哈萨克族 Kazak
总 计	**Total**	**20951900**	**12712655**	**9650629**	**8239245**	**1483883**
乌鲁木齐市	**Urumqi City**	**2312964**	**625172**	**284058**	**1687792**	**63275**
天山区	Tianshan District	515356	168172	101634	347184	13632
沙依巴克区	Shayibak District	522747	129571	75745	393176	7079
新市区	Xinshi District	483210	93762	48184	389448	5131
水磨沟区	Shui Mogou Distric	235646	39686	25046	195960	2682
头屯河区	Tou Tunhe District	127860	33879	15464	93981	1292
达坂城区	Da Bancheng District	42416	22127	2480	20289	6198
米东区	Midong District	295801	89291	11273	206510	4682
乌鲁木齐县	Urumqi County	89928	48684	4232	41244	22579
克拉玛依市	**Karamay City**	**267174**	**65486**	**40512**	**201688**	**10684**
独山子区	Dushanzi District	52902	13681	8469	39221	2281
克拉玛依区	Karamay District	164100	37869	23009	126231	6366
乌尔河区	Urhe District	47917	12922	8681	34995	1955
白碱滩区	Bai Jiantan District	2255	1014	353	1241	82
吐鲁番地区	**Turpan Administrative Offices**	**600610**	**462865**	**423212**	**137745**	**270**
吐鲁番市	Turpan City	269152	211725	191180	57427	29
鄯善县	Shanshan [Piqan] County	218164	155958	144770	62206	34
托克逊县	Toksun County	113294	95182	87262	18112	207
哈密地区	**Hami [Kumul] Administrative Offices**	**546169**	**182057**	**110220**	**364112**	**49663**
哈密市	Hami [Kumul] City	423781	131928	101207	291853	11245
巴里坤哈萨克自治县	Barkol Kazak Autonomous County	101310	36445	150	64865	34406
伊吾县	Yiwu [Araturuk] County	21078	13684	8863	7394	4012
昌吉回族自治州	**Changji Hui Autonomous Prefecture**	**1353742**	**346707**	**61646**	**1007035**	**132582**
昌吉市	Changji City	347818	91295	11749	256523	18557
阜康市	Fukang City	166183	45303	9691	120880	13668
呼图壁县	Hutubi County	213631	48696	5861	164935	24467
玛纳斯县	Manas County	171896	32535	5540	139361	18638
奇台县	Qitai County	231414	58023	16828	173391	24061
吉木萨尔县	Jimsar County	135571	41243	7013	94328	10766
木垒哈萨克自治县	Mori Kazak Autonomous County	87229	29612	4964	57617	22425

注：总计根据 2007 年人口变动抽样调查数据推算，各地、州、市民族人口为公安年报数据，因此，总计不等于各地州市合计。

Note: The total have been estimated on the base of the annual national sample survey on population changes in 2007. The nationalites population refer to data of Public Security for the year in prefecture and cities.Therefore,the total data is not equal to the sum of each of prefectures,autonomous prefectures and cities.

Population of Major Nationalities by Prefecture, Autonomous Prefecture, City and County

(person)

回 族 Hui	柯尔克孜族 Kirgiz	蒙古族 Mongolian	锡伯族 Xibo	俄罗斯族 Russion	塔吉克族 Tajik	乌孜别克族 Uzbek	塔塔尔族 Tatar	满 族 Manchu	达斡尔族 Daur	其 它 Others
942956	**181862**	**177120**	**42444**	**11609**	**44824**	**16138**	**4728**	**25626**	**6678**	**124158**
237730	**1514**	**9088**	**4757**	**3353**	**198**	**1869**	**923**	**9774**	**524**	**8109**
41259	669	2460	1532	1142	92	1004	490	2414	178	1666
36656	346	2480	1207	894	40	426	161	2453	126	1958
31409	317	1968	1144	753	30	276	148	2543	150	1709
8932	86	754	329	254	21	64	28	890	27	573
15102	11	337	351	90	4	13	5	663	6	541
13197	7	30	6	12		2	3	87	3	102
69829	52	922	171	199	9	16	22	680	29	1407
21346	26	137	17	9	2	68	66	44	5	153
6352	**123**	**2293**	**868**	**589**	**24**	**245**	**85**	**1055**	**133**	**2523**
1438	10	437	157	148	4	60	9	212	19	437
3853	67	1022	580	377	16	161	38	667	93	1620
1047	44	280	128	64	4	24	36	176	21	462
14	2	554	3				2			4
37778	**1**	**186**	**36**	**57**		**20**	**5**	**322**	**3**	**975**
19547		114	22	45		7	1	164	3	613
10654	1	60	10	12		13	4	118		282
7577		12	4					40		80
16226	**17**	**2452**	**171**	**104**		**8**	**28**	**1745**	**9**	**1414**
15196	16	1023	161	88		7	3	1693	9	1280
290	1	1424	8	16			25	44		81
740		5	2			1		8		53
130793	**152**	**6544**	**598**	**675**	**7**	**2278**	**918**	**3133**	**49**	**7332**
54967	84	1444	370	287	7	106	98	1267	23	2336
19735	17	394	71	105		36	50	207	9	1320
16047	2	301	37	97		2	27	175	4	1676
7197	32	111	29	99		20	8	167	12	682
12484	6	1724	63	58		600	474	1139	1	585
19542	8	2542	21	18		474	171	128		560
821	3	28	7	11		1040	90	50		173

3-7 续表 1

单位：人

地 区	Region	合 计 Total	#少数民族 Minority Nationalities	维吾尔族 Uygur	汉 族 Han	哈萨克族 Kazak
伊犁哈萨克自治州	**Ili Kazak Autonomous Prefecture**	**4342166**	**2438415**	**702219**	**1903751**	**1139293**
伊犁州直属县(市)	**Counties (Cities) Direct Under Ili Prefecture**	**2702333**	**1645744**	**652110**	**1056589**	**561549**
伊宁市	Yining [Gulja] City	445944	292125	221754	153819	20214
奎屯市	Kuytun City	307583	15816	1016	291767	5319
伊宁县	Yining [Gulja] County	388307	317470	175233	70837	47102
察布查尔锡伯自治县	Qapqal Xibe Autonomous County	184057	119425	48450	64632	37433
霍城县	Huocheng [Korgas] County	384502	211463	78921	173039	33665
巩留县	Gongliu [Tokkuztara] County	178190	122877	40259	55313	51670
新源县	Xinyuan [Kunes] County	309476	191489	29983	117987	137712
昭苏县	Zhaosu [Mongolkure] County	169522	120721	16268	48801	80510
特克斯县	Tekes County	163137	125724	17855	37413	70172
尼勒克县	Nilka County	171615	128634	22371	42981	77752
塔城地区	**Tacheng [Tarbagatai] Administrative Offices**	**994776**	**418924**	**40332**	**575852**	**249134**
塔城市	Tacheng [Qoqek] City	163606	58855	4985	104751	24879
乌苏市	Usu City	215430	77030	16342	138400	21943
额敏县	Emin [Dorbiljin] County	207735	94376	7765	113359	70728
沙湾县	Shawan County	206968	65588	8810	141380	35080
托里县	Toli County	93896	68167	1192	25729	65078
裕民县	Yumin [Qagantokay] County	55507	21764	204	33743	16868
和布克赛尔蒙古自治县	Hoboksar Mongol Autonomous County	51634	33144	1034	18490	14558
阿勒泰地区	**Altay Administrative Offices**	**645057**	**373747**	**9777**	**271310**	**328610**
阿勒泰市	Altay City	229960	90976	5013	138984	74399
布尔津县	Burqin County	68900	47820	1018	21080	39614
富蕴县	Fuyun [Koktokay] County	90456	70008	1974	20448	65405
福海县	Fuhai [Burultokay] County	72792	32484	637	40308	28672
哈巴河县	Habahe [Kaba] County	83811	57873	341	25938	50036
青河县	Qinghe [Qinggil] County	60322	49128	576	11194	46101
吉木乃县	Jemnay County	38816	25458	218	13358	24383
博尔塔拉蒙古自治州	**Bortala Mongol Autonomous Prefecture**	**472918**	**154656**	**60149**	**318262**	**44664**
博乐市	Bole [Bortala] City	259557	82433	39844	177124	18636
精河县	Jinghe [Jing] County	139661	42234	17096	97427	13021
温泉县	Wenquan [Araxang] County	73700	29989	3209	43711	13007
巴音郭楞蒙古自治州	**Bayangol Mongol Autonomous Prefecture**	**1224080**	**520830**	**400528**	**703250**	**1197**
库尔勒市	Korla City	472147	143057	123118	329090	87
轮台县	Luntai [Bugur] County	104152	85946	85351	18206	7
尉犁县	Yuli [Lopnur] County	114601	32791	31746	81810	15
若羌县	Ruoqiang [Qarkilik] County	32016	13135	11864	18881	6
且末县	Qiemo [Qarqan] County	61001	44811	44499	16190	2
焉耆回族自治县	Yanji Hui Autonomous County	129897	73032	39276	56865	39
和静县	Hejing County	183170	84899	45101	98271	1001
和硕县	Hoxud County	68622	23027	10490	45595	30
博湖县	Bohu [Bagrax] County	58474	20132	9083	38342	10

Continued

(Person)

回 族 Hui	柯尔克孜族 Kirgiz	蒙古族 Mongolian	锡伯族 Xibo	俄罗斯族 Russion	塔吉克族 Tajik	乌孜别克族 Uzbek	塔塔尔族 Tatar	满 族 Manchu	达斡尔族 Daur	其 它 Others
368474	**19371**	**72570**	**33884**	**5566**	**152**	**6957**	**2539**	**5043**	**5702**	**76645**
273347	**17082**	**33090**	**31844**	**1580**	**147**	**6365**	**1119**	**3892**	**535**	**63084**
33850	599	1250	4288	784	79	3887	462	1977	53	2928
6426	20	1060	289	102	4	19	19	431	38	1073
63459	349	268	244	26	5	555	56	371	32	29770
9585	305	511	20804	106	1	110	6	112	10	1992
75065	295	769	3114	241	5	184	85	347	350	18422
22717	454	2234	1569	114		278	98	290	7	3187
20132	424	161	451	94	5	548	136	154	3	1686
4681	4670	13334	76	43	12	320	232	31	1	543
20891	9311	4610	246	4	16	253	20	82	3	2261
16541	655	8893	763	66	20	211	5	97	38	1222
72274	**2079**	**33590**	**1939**	**3546**	**3**	**372**	**471**	**799**	**5152**	**9233**
12030	1702	1704	1490	2412		144	238	241	4983	4047
29240	2	8110	151	140		49	20	126	33	874
6539	317	6002	89	584		118	60	143	55	1976
19643	11	466	35	118	3	20	23	162	17	1200
1046	19	523	70	18		21	42	52	9	97
3299	5	139	49	241			13	44	35	867
477	23	16646	55	33		20	75	31	20	172
22853	**210**	**5890**	**101**	**440**	**2**	**220**	**949**	**352**	**15**	**4328**
6580	181	2580	41	207	1	145	308	195	3	1323
4095	5	1551	9	143		2	294	40	1	1048
1761	14	295	25	42		15	90	40	7	340
2451		187	9	33			33	35	2	425
6139	7	436	6			7	45	5	1	850
1154		817	9	9	1	50	166	9		236
673	3	24	2	6		1	13	28	1	106
17814	**90**	**27833**	**409**	**185**	**5**	**149**	**16**	**386**	**33**	**2923**
9463	35	12522	298	146	5	87	11	286	15	1085
5595	19	5075	59	36		37	4	60		1232
2756	36	10236	52	3		25	1	40	18	606
61892	**216**	**48886**	**191**	**245**	**3**	**127**	**1**	**1117**	**20**	**6407**
11156	11	5328	167	211	3	68	1	845	12	2050
387		47	9	3		5		22		115
597		29		4		16		22	6	356
869	1	15						6		374
193		23	2			10		6		76
29570	104	3171		2		23		82	1	764
6724	88	30273	11	17		5		91	1	1587
6304	1	5622	1	8				28		543
6092	11	4378	1					15		542

3-7 续表 2

单位：人

地　区	Region	合　计 Total	#少数民族 Minority Nationalities	维吾尔族 Uygur	汉　族 Han	哈萨克族 Kazak
阿克苏地区	**Aksu Administrative Offices**	**2203077**	**1748101**	**1718270**	**454976**	**190**
阿克苏市	Aksu City	452388	236120	228801	216268	49
温宿县	Wensu [Onsu] County	234595	180832	175031	53763	8
库车县	Kuqa County	437402	389685	386542	47717	59
沙雅县	Xayar County	230080	191884	189457	38196	5
新和县	Xinhe [Toksu] County	156133	146327	145831	9806	8
拜城县	Baicheng [Bay] County	221319	192096	190208	29223	22
乌什县	Wushi [Uxturpan] County	199178	187491	180703	11687	29
阿瓦提县	Awat County	227096	179995	178088	47101	10
柯坪县	Kalpin County	44886	43671	43609	1215	
克孜勒苏柯尔克孜自治州	**Kizilsu Kirgiz Autonomous Prefecture**	**500007**	**463150**	**317540**	**36857**	**126**
阿图什市	Artux City	225054	204389	177115	20665	62
阿克陶县	Akto County	181049	174371	130010	6678	10
阿合奇县	Akqi County	39863	35955	1129	3908	27
乌恰县	Wuqia [Ulugqat] County	54041	48435	9286	5606	27
喀什地区	**Kashgar [Kaxgar] Administrative Offices**	**3694349**	**3423137**	**3367013**	**271212**	**230**
喀什市	Kashgar [Kaxgar] City	440074	366343	362202	73731	72
疏附县	Shufu County	308867	303589	302805	5278	6
疏勒县	Shule County	314871	293890	293114	20981	4
英吉沙县	Yengisar County	240808	236256	235564	4552	7
泽普县	Zepu [Poskam] County	186671	152166	146777	34505	14
莎车县	Shache [Yarkant] County	714708	687730	681073	26978	59
叶城县	Yecheng [Kagilik] County	404065	380424	375521	23641	30
麦盖提县	Makit County	234535	185681	184707	48854	9
岳普湖县	Yopurga County	148486	139245	139051	9241	1
伽师县	Jiashi [Payzawat] County	368553	361625	361360	6928	9
巴楚县	Bachu [Maralbexi] County	298099	283635	283080	14464	17
塔什库尔干塔吉克自治县	Taxkorgan Tajik Autonomous County	34612	32553	1759	2059	2
和田地区	**Hotan Administrative Offices**	**1883894**	**1818716**	**1814785**	**65178**	**82**
和田市	Hotan City	281958	247316	246189	34642	24
和田县	Hotan County	247646	246412	246152	1234	1
墨玉县	Moyu [Karakax] County	479015	468064	467882	10951	5
皮山县	Pishan [Guma] County	237938	234141	232301	3797	1
洛浦县	Lop County	220702	216481	216337	4221	32
策勒县	Qira County	144756	142381	142305	2375	1
于田县	Yutian [Keriya] County	235197	230739	230468	4458	18
民丰县	Minfeng [Niya] County	36682	33182	33151	3500	
自治区直辖市	**Municpality Country-LevelCity directly under the Central Govern-ment**					
石河子市	Shihezi City	636090	35238	7648	600852	3957
阿拉尔市	Aral City	166544	11332	6719	155212	206
图木舒克市	Tumxuk City	147804	94279	93053	53525	
五家渠市	Wujiaqu City	72782	2433	72	70349	103

Continued

(person)

回 族 Hui	柯尔克孜族 Kirgiz	蒙古族 Mongolian	锡伯族 Xibo	俄罗斯族 Russion	塔吉克族 Tajik	乌孜别克族 Uzbek	塔塔尔族 Tatar	满 族 Manchu	达斡尔族 Daur	其 它 Others
14826	**9422**	**760**	**107**	**128**	**75**	**194**	**25**	**470**		**3634**
4606	221	522	54	66	69	38		259		1435
822	4155	34	2	1	3		1	9		766
2459	146	69	28	26	2	46	14	110		184
1976	9	8	8	16		6		29		370
326	4	11	3	12				19		113
873	847	25	6		1	12	2	18		82
2465	3999	13	4	1		70	4	7		196
1286	8	74	2	6		22	4	19		476
13	33	4								12
594	**139042**	**70**	**27**	**5**	**5199**	**141**	**23**	**89**	**2**	**292**
238	26618	38	12	5	28	15		72	2	184
175	38865	23	5		5141	77	23			42
101	34670	3	2					3		20
80	38889	6	8		30	49		14		46
5805	**6438**	**534**	**113**	**99**	**37084**	**3668**	**38**	**507**	**9**	**1599**
1515	313	116	53	58	184	1137	23	240	4	426
81	585	8	1		3	11	1	5		83
283	309	64	2	3		10		21		80
62	528	3	1	5	17	19	2	28	1	19
880	509	93	9	13	3355	76	2	53		385
997	1136	89	22	7	2588	1592	5	47	1	114
752	1006	33	8	9	2179	697		34	2	153
650	4	31	2	1	3	35	2	27	1	209
103	1	54	1	1	3		2			28
37	57	18	4			61		29		50
428	4	22	5	2	1	30	1	14		31
17	1986	3	5		28751			9		21
1471	**795**	**106**	**10**	**8**	**919**	**33**	**6**	**97**		**404**
774	13	47	5	8	3	23	2	55		173
256								3		
91		13	2					14		57
91	778	5			915	5				45
51		19	1					12		29
36		5				1		1		32
163	4	14	2		1			12		57
9		3				4	4			11
16402	60	838	179	236	23	11	2	961	25	4896
996	33	272	10	16	6			77		2997
586		32	1	5		30		36		536
1475	9	196	14	46		2		169	1	346

3-8 主要年份分民族人口数
Population by Nationality in Main Years

单位：万人 (10 000 persons)

年 份 Year	维吾尔族 Uygur	汉 族 Han	哈萨克族 Kazak	回 族 Hui	柯尔克孜族 Kirgiz	蒙古族 Mongolian	锡伯族 Xibo
1978	555.53	512.90	82.10	53.12	10.40	10.74	2.55
1980	576.46	531.03	87.68	56.56	10.89	11.32	2.59
1985	629.44	534.92	98.72	59.96	12.35	12.33	2.93
1990	724.95	574.66	113.92	68.89	14.44	14.28	3.42
1991	736.28	584.21	116.13	70.37	14.69	14.47	3.51
1992	747.41	594.00	118.20	72.18	15.09	14.76	3.58
1993	758.95	603.67	119.64	73.23	15.42	14.92	3.68
1994	769.73	616.48	121.70	74.04	15.62	15.20	3.74
1995	780.00	631.81	123.77	74.76	15.78	15.28	3.82
1996	791.60	643.28	125.70	76.02	16.05	15.54	3.89
1997	802.00	660.13	127.08	77.06	16.27	15.75	3.90
1998	813.95	674.11	128.70	78.20	16.41	15.91	3.95
1999	825.03	687.15	130.45	79.26	16.64	16.13	4.00
2000	852.33	725.08	131.87	83.93	16.47	16.20	4.05
2001	860.56	742.20	131.92	84.42	17.01	16.19	4.13
2002	869.23	759.57	133.35	85.46	17.13	16.38	4.10
2003	882.35	771.10	135.21	86.67	17.37	16.69	4.03
2004	897.67	780.25	138.16	87.63	17.12	16.96	4.08
2005	923.50	795.66	141.39	89.35	17.15	17.17	4.15
2006	941.38	812.16	143.50	90.96	17.59	17.46	4.19
2007	965.06	823.93	148.39	94.30	18.19	17.71	4.24

年 份 Year	俄罗斯族 Russian	塔吉克族 Tajik	乌孜别克族 Uzbek	塔塔尔族 Tatar	满 族 Manchu	达斡尔族 Daur	其他民族 Others
1978	0.06	2.28	0.77	0.31	0.42	0.41	1.42
1980	0.06	2.41	0.79	0.31	0.50	0.40	2.24
1985	0.43	2.89	0.93	0.33	0.95	0.48	4.49
1990	0.75	3.44	1.14	0.40	1.66	0.56	6.65
1991	0.80	3.45	1.17	0.44	1.75	0.55	6.75
1992	0.85	3.60	1.21	0.42	1.84	0.57	6.92
1993	0.86	3.61	1.28	0.44	1.89	0.58	7.09
1994	0.86	3.68	1.29	0.43	1.93	0.59	7.41
1995	0.90	3.82	1.33	0.47	1.99	0.62	7.00
1996	0.92	3.89	1.35	0.47	2.05	0.63	7.90
1997	0.92	3.90	1.35	0.46	2.06	0.63	6.56
1998	0.93	3.96	1.37	0.47	2.09	0.64	6.66
1999	0.94	4.01	1.39	0.48	2.12	0.65	6.75
2000	1.09	4.09	1.36	0.48	2.31	0.66	9.48
2001	1.08	4.12	1.37	0.47	2.30	0.67	9.75
2002	1.12	4.07	1.39	0.48	2.35	0.67	9.89
2003	1.11	4.09	1.46	0.49	2.39	0.67	10.32
2004	1.13	4.35	1.42	0.47	2.41	0.67	10.79
2005	1.12	4.40	1.51	0.47	2.46	0.65	11.37
2006	1.14	4.47	1.60	0.47	2.52	0.66	11.91
2007	1.16	4.48	1.61	0.47	2.56	0.67	12.42

3-9 各地、州、市、县(市)人口自然变动情况

Statistics on Population Natural Changes by Prefecture, Autonomous Prefecture, City and County

单位：‰ (2007 年) (‰)

地　区	Region	出生率 Birth Rate	#少数民族 Minority Nationalities	死亡率 Death Rate	#少数民族 Minority Nationalities	自然增长率 Natural Growth Rate	#少数民族 Minority Nationalities
总　计	**Total**	**16.79**	**22.19**	**5.01**	**5.24**	**11.78**	**16.95**
乌鲁木齐市	**Urumqi City**	**8.92**	**13.39**	**3.50**	**4.26**	**5.42**	**9.13**
天山区	Tianshan District	8.42	11.83	3.14	3.48	5.28	8.35
沙依巴克区	Shayibak District	8.36	10.53	3.47	3.83	4.89	6.70
新市区	Xinshi District	8.36	10.28	2.54	2.20	5.82	8.08
水磨沟区	Shui Mogou Distric	8.22	15.23	2.64	3.78	5.58	11.45
头屯河区	Tou Tunhe District	9.30	15.24	4.82	6.11	4.48	9.13
达坂城区	Da Bancheng District	12.38	17.57	10.53	14.83	1.85	2.74
米东区	Midong District	9.93	17.19	4.14	4.19	5.79	13.00
乌鲁木齐县	Urumqi County	14.19	19.88	5.64	6.26	8.55	13.62
克拉玛依市	**Karamay City**	**8.63**	**13.85**	**3.42**	**3.46**	**5.21**	**10.39**
独山子区	Dushanzi District	9.97	13.90	2.62	3.82	7.35	10.08
克拉玛依区	Karamay District	9.08	15.14	3.74	3.12	5.34	12.02
乌尔河区	Urhe District	5.68	10.14	3.29	4.10	2.39	6.04
白碱滩区	Bai Jiantan District	8.79	12.80	2.20	2.95	6.59	9.85
吐鲁番地区	**Turpan Administrative Offices**	**20.29**	**23.24**	**4.23**	**4.38**	**16.06**	**18.86**
吐鲁番市	Turpan City	20.89	23.76	4.76	4.69	16.13	19.07
鄯善县	Shanshan [Piqan] County	21.31	25.64	3.34	3.73	17.97	21.91
托克逊县	Toksun County	16.94	18.19	4.70	4.81	12.24	13.38
哈密地区	**Hami [Kumul] Administrative Offices**	**12.04**	**19.35**	**4.17**	**4.86**	**7.87**	**14.49**
哈密市	Hami [Kumul] City	9.88	14.92	3.85	4.65	6.03	10.27
巴里坤哈萨克自治县	Barkol Kazak Autonomous County	13.36	23.59	3.24	2.91	10.12	20.68
伊吾县	Yiwu [Araturuk] County	14.56	16.23	2.92	3.32	11.64	12.91
昌吉回族自治州	**Changji Hui Autonomous Prefecture**	**10.36**	**18.77**	**3.61**	**4.01**	**6.75**	**14.76**
昌吉市	Changji City	10.96	16.79	2.81	3.07	8.15	13.72
阜康市	Fukang City	9.37	16.62	3.94	3.94	5.43	12.68
呼图壁县	Hutubi County	10.96	20.70	3.35	4.07	7.61	16.63
玛纳斯县	Manas County	10.06	20.36	5.03	4.66	5.03	15.70
奇台县	Qitai County	11.39	21.65	4.33	4.68	7.06	16.97
吉木萨尔县	Jimsar County	10.61	18.23	3.72	4.66	6.89	13.57
木垒哈萨克自治县	Mori Kazak Autonomous County	10.23	19.05	3.40	4.15	6.83	14.90

注：此表来源于 2007 年公安人口年报资料。
Note: Data in this table are from Public Security annual bulletin in 2007.

3-9 续表 1 Continued

单位：‰ (‰)

地区	Region	出生率 Birth Rate	#少数民族 Minority Nationalities	死亡率 Death Rate	#少数民族 Minority Nationalities	自然增长率 Natural Growth Rate	#少数民族 Minority Nationalities
伊犁哈萨克自治州	**Ili Kazak Autonomous Prefecture**	**19.30**	**26.18**	**4.20**	**4.60**	**15.10**	**21.58**
伊犁州直属县(市)	**Counties (Cities) Direct Under Ili Prefecture**	**22.19**	**28.82**	**4.45**	**4.66**	**17.74**	**14.16**
伊宁市	Yining [Gulja] City	20.27	26.09	5.09	5.94	15.18	20.15
奎屯市	Kuytun City	5.87	12.44	4.50	4.91	1.37	7.53
伊宁县	Yining [Gulja] County	22.63	22.78	3.10	2.87	19.53	19.91
察布查尔锡伯自治县	Qapqal Xibe Autonomous County	27.71	33.93	4.28	4.25	23.43	29.68
霍城县	Huocheng [Korgas] County	24.64	31.46	4.19	3.74	20.45	27.72
巩留县	Gongliu [Tokkuztara] County	27.19	30.30	3.44	3.38	23.75	26.92
新源县	Xinyuan [Kunes] County	21.42	29.39	5.71	6.94	15.71	22.45
昭苏县	Zhaosu [Mongolkure] County	24.66	29.84	5.59	6.54	19.07	23.30
特克斯县	Tekes County	30.95	35.49	4.71	4.70	26.24	30.79
尼勒克县	Nilka County	29.99	34.88	3.95	3.96	26.04	30.92
塔城地区	**Tacheng [Tarbagatai] Administrative Offices**	**13.22**	**18.68**	**3.54**	**4.21**	**9.68**	**14.47**
塔城市	Tacheng [Qoqek] City	10.65	14.31	3.45	4.05	7.20	10.26
乌苏市	Usu City	13.99	19.10	2.79	3.67	11.20	15.43
额敏县	Emin [Dorbiljin] County	12.56	17.32	3.55	3.78	9.01	13.54
沙湾县	Shawan County	11.84	19.68	3.66	3.83	8.18	15.85
托里县	Toli County	22.33	25.73	4.46	5.27	17.87	20.46
裕民县	Yumin [Qagantokay] County	11.42	18.07	3.87	4.60	7.55	13.47
和布克赛尔蒙古自治县	Hoboksar Mongol Autonomous County	11.75	13.34	4.45	5.33	7.30	8.01
阿勒泰地区	**Altay Administrative Offices**	**16.62**	**23.07**	**4.13**	**4.82**	**12.49**	**18.25**
阿勒泰市	Altay City	12.24	21.05	4.72	6.43	7.52	14.62
布尔津县	Burqin County	17.84	21.60	3.91	4.54	13.93	17.06
富蕴县	Fuyun [Koktokay] County	22.43	27.16	4.25	4.54	18.18	22.62
福海县	Fuhai [Burultokay] County	13.42	19.76	3.34	4.04	10.08	15.72
哈巴河县	Habahe [Kaba] County	19.66	24.25	3.39	3.97	16.27	20.28
青河县	Qinghe [Qinggil] County	22.72	23.44	3.51	3.45	19.21	19.99
吉木乃县	Jemnay County	16.91	22.65	4.69	5.90	12.22	16.75
博尔塔拉蒙古自治州	**Bortala Mongol Autonomous Prefecture**	**12.38**	**19.53**	**2.89**	**3.50**	**9.49**	**16.03**
博乐市	Bole [Bortala] City	11.70	18.95	2.18	2.38	9.52	16.57
精河县	Jinghe [Jing] County	13.62	24.65	2.25	2.34	11.37	22.31
温泉县	Wenquan [Araxang] County	12.45	13.85	6.59	8.18	5.86	5.67
巴音郭楞蒙古自治州	**Bayangol Mongol Autonomous Prefecture**	**14.87**	**22.64**	**4.39**	**5.68**	**10.48**	**16.96**
库尔勒市	Korla City	11.74	20.80	3.13	3.65	8.61	17.15
轮台县	Luntai [Bugur] County	32.11	35.29	10.84	12.30	21.27	22.99
尉犁县	Yuli [Lopnur] County	13.80	23.67	3.39	3.90	10.41	19.77
若羌县	Ruoqiang [Qarkilik] County	11.97	16.89	4.00	4.47	7.97	12.42
且末县	Qiemo [Qarqan] County	15.76	17.64	2.75	3.10	13.01	14.54
焉耆回族自治县	Yanji Hui Autonomous County	17.45	20.92	4.61	4.56	12.84	16.36
和静县	Hejing County	14.21	20.31	5.86	6.57	8.35	13.74
和硕县	Hoxud County	12.10	19.59	4.03	4.60	8.07	14.99
博湖县	Bohu [Bagrax] County	11.53	14.11	2.37	2.35	9.16	11.76

3-9 续表 2 Continued

单位：‰ (‰)

地　　区	Region	出生率 Birth Rate	#少数民族 Minority Nationalities	死亡率 Death Rate	#少数民族 Minority Nationalities	自然增长率 Natural Growth Rate	#少数民族 Minority Nationalities
阿克苏地区	**Aksu Administrative Offices**	**21.44**	**24.02**	**4.25**	**4.61**	**17.19**	**19.41**
阿克苏市	Aksu City	12.95	17.12	4.04	5.56	8.91	11.56
温宿县	Wensu [Onsu] County	18.15	21.44	4.67	4.68	13.48	16.76
库车县	Kuqa County	32.03	34.80	5.14	5.44	26.89	29.36
沙雅县	Xayar County	16.92	16.90	3.13	3.56	13.79	13.34
新和县	Xinhe [Toksu] County	21.78	21.56	5.02	5.10	16.76	16.46
拜城县	Baicheng [Bay] County	18.36	19.78	5.88	6.28	12.38	13.50
乌什县	Wushi [Uxturpan] County	25.34	25.37	3.30	3.09	22.04	22.28
阿瓦提县	Awat County	24.79	25.16	2.38	2.22	22.41	22.94
柯坪县	Kalpin County	24.29	24.52	4.05	4.05	20.24	20.47
克孜勒苏柯尔克孜自治州	**Kizilsu Kirgiz Autonomous Prefecture**	**24.23**	**24.88**	**5.01**	**5.26**	**19.22**	**19.62**
阿图什市	Artux City	33.23	34.62	5.22	5.51	28.01	29.11
阿克陶县	Akto County	15.30	15.56	4.98	5.15	10.32	10.41
阿合奇县	Akqi County	18.69	19.00	4.79	5.16	13.90	13.84
乌恰县	Wuqia [Ulugqat] County	21.68	22.87	4.23	4.53	17.45	18.34
喀什地区	**Kashgar [Kaxgar] Administrative Offices**	**21.68**	**22.47**	**5.63**	**5.84**	**16.05**	**16.63**
喀什市	Kashgar [Kaxgar] City	14.79	16.18	7.11	7.64	7.68	8.54
疏附县	Shufu County	33.68	33.68	7.05	7.03	26.63	26.65
疏勒县	Shule County	27.73	28.98	3.31	3.30	24.42	25.68
英吉沙县	Yengisar County	21.07	21.08	4.45	4.49	16.62	16.59
泽普县	Zepu [Poskam] County	21.20	22.55	6.61	7.46	14.59	15.09
莎车县	Shache [Yarkant] County	20.56	20.76	5.38	5.41	15.18	15.35
叶城县	Yecheng [Kagilik] County	20.14	19.96	5.46	5.55	14.68	14.41
麦盖提县	Makit County	16.07	17.58	3.52	3.94	12.55	13.64
岳普湖县	Yopurga County	16.94	17.30	5.02.	5.19	11.92	12.11
伽师县	Jiashi [Payzawat] County	20.37	20.56	7.21	7.29	13.16	13.27
巴楚县	Bachu [Maralbexi] County	32.36	32.62	7.15	7.41	25.21	25.21
塔什库尔干塔吉克自治县	Taxkorgan Tajik Autonomous County	22.07	21.07	4.72	4.75	17.35	16.32
和田地区	**Hotan Administrative Offices**	**18.36**	**18.70**	**7.60**	**7.75**	**10.76**	**10.95**
和田市	Hotan City	13.58	14.31	7.21	7.74	6.37	6.57
和田县	Hotan County	15.09	15.15	11.89	11.95	3.20	3.20
墨玉县	Moyu [Karakax] County	18.35	18.62	6.51	6.57	11.84	12.05
皮山县	Pishan [Guma] County	17.79	17.92	6.30	6.36	11.49	11.56
洛浦县	Lop County	25.31	25.60	6.47	6.53	18.84	19.07
策勒县	Qira County	18.82	18.92	7.17	7.25	11.65	11.67
于田县	Yutian [Keriya] County	21.82	21.96	8.58	8.67	13.24	13.29
民丰县	Minfeng [Niya] County	15.18	16.08	5.90	6.44	9.28	9.64
自治区直辖市	**Municpality Country-LevelCity directlyunder the Central overn-ment**						
石河子市	Shihezi City	5.70	11.07	5.19	4.52	0.51	6.55
阿拉尔市	Aral City	7.32	9.78	3.94	4.39	3.38	5.39
图木舒克市	Tumxuk City	5.21	5.35	1.78	1.57	3.43	3.78
五家渠市	Wujiaqu City	5.20	10.90	4.70	3.30	0.50	7.60

3-10 各地、州、市采取各种避孕措施情况

Condition of Adopting Various Contraceptions by Prefecture, Autonomous Prefecture, City and County

单位：% (2007年) (%)

地 区	Region	男性绝育 Masculine Sterilization	女性绝育 Femirvie Sterilization	宫内绝育器 Contraceptive	皮下埋植 Cutinization
总 计	**Total**	**0.30**	**7.61**	**76.11**	**0.52**
城 镇	Urban	0.20	4.78	73.38	0.40
农 村	Rural	0.36	9.28	77.71	0.60
乌鲁木齐市	Urumqi City	0.27	4.46	57.97	0.54
克拉玛依市	Karamay City	0.73	4.58	65.06	1.01
石河子市	Shihezi City	0.79	13.26	56.14	0.56
吐鲁番地区	Turpan Administrative Offices	0.02	2.26	87.75	0.49
哈密地区	Hami [Kumul] Administrative Offices	0.05	3.76	72.97	0.77
昌吉回族自治州	Changji Hui Autonomous Prefecture	0.33	9.96	72.69	0.53
伊犁州直属县(市)	Counties (Cities) Direct Under Ili Prefecture	0.22	6.67	77.96	0.29
塔城地区	Tacheng [Tarbagatai] Administrative Offices	0.34	10.62	70.87	1.42
阿勒泰地区	Altay Administrative Offices	0.19	5.11	71.18	0.82
博尔塔拉蒙古自治州	Bortala Mongol Autonomous Prefecture	1.00	11.84	66.95	1.13
巴音郭楞蒙古自治州	Bayangol Mongol Autonomous Prefecture	0.99	7.01	79.36	0.60
阿克苏地区	Aksu Administrative Offices	0.30	8.31	81.27	0.76
克孜勒苏柯尔克孜自治州	Kizilsu Kirgiz Autonomous Prefecture	0.02	3.81	84.90	0.24
喀什地区	Kashgar [Kaxgar] Administrative Offices	0.11	5.88	87.30	0.27
和田地区	Hotan Administrative Offices	0.06	13.04	79.98	0.05

地 区	Region	口服药及注射针 Medicine and Entry Needle	避孕套 Condom	外用药 Drug for Exterior Use	其 他 Other
总 计	**Total**	**1.43**	**12.57**	**1.09**	**0.37**
城 镇	Urban	1.46	18.46	0.68	0.64
农 村	Rural	1.41	9.11	1.32	0.21
乌鲁木齐市	Urumqi City	1.91	32.38	0.87	1.60
克拉玛依市	Karamay City	0.58	25.85	0.64	1.55
石河子市	Shihezi City	2.53	24.88	0.77	1.07
吐鲁番地区	Turpan Administrative Offices	1.67	7.48	0.29	0.04
哈密地区	Hami [Kumul] Administrative Offices	1.22	20.73	0.32	0.18
昌吉回族自治州	Changji Hui Autonomous Prefecture	0.98	15.14	0.27	0.10
伊犁州直属县(市)	Counties (Cities) Direct Under Ili Prefecture	1.03	12.97	0.40	0.46
塔城地区	Tacheng [Tarbagatai] Administrative Offices	0.95	15.60	0.16	0.04
阿勒泰地区	Altay Administrative Offices	1.11	21.30	0.21	0.08
博尔塔拉蒙古自治州	Bortala Mongol Autonomous Prefecture	1.52	17.09	0.46	0.01
巴音郭楞蒙古自治州	Bayangol Mongol Autonomous Prefecture	0.71	11.08	0.25	…
阿克苏地区	Aksu Administrative Offices	2.43	4.64	2.03	0.26
克孜勒苏柯尔克孜自治州	Kizilsu Kirgiz Autonomous Prefecture	4.09	4.33	2.05	0.56
喀什地区	Kashgar [Kaxgar] Administrative Offices	1.45	2.70	2.23	0.06
和田地区	Hotan Administrative Offices	0.52	4.48	1.82	0.05

注：表3-10、3-11根据自治区计生委2007年计划生育统计年报整理。
Note: In table 3-10 and 3-11,data are compiled on statistic annals of the family planning in Xinjiang Uygur Autonomous Region in 2007.

3-11 各地、州、市计划生育及领证情况

Family Planning and Certificate Receiving by Prefecture, Autonomous Prefecture and City

(2007 年)

地　区	Region	计划生育率 (%) Family Planning Rate (%)	领证率 (%) Coverage of One-child Certificate (%)	领取计划生育证人数 (人) Number of Persons Receiving Certificates of Honor (person)	领取独生子女证人数 (人) Number of Married Couples with One-child Certificate (person)
总　计	**Total**	**99.83**	**21.82**	**318078**	**633878**
城　镇	Urban	99.82	43.10	167016	506562
农　村	Rural	99.83	9.94	151062	127316
乌鲁木齐市	Urumqi City	99.94	47.27	47139	168797
克拉玛依市	Karamay City	100.00	54.39	6896	34854
石河子市	Shihezi City	99.93	41.39	1618	66295
吐鲁番地区	Turpan Administrative Offices	100.00	19.73	13401	12310
哈密地区	Hami [Kumul] Administrative Offices	99.70	43.74	9833	38983
昌吉回族自治州	Changji Hui Autonomous Prefecture	99.79	33.73	17484	88778
伊犁州直属县(市)	Counties (Cities) Direct Under Ili Prefecture	99.88	19.03	59582	53770
塔城地区	Tacheng [Tarbagatai] Administrative Offices	99.83	25.35	19707	36699
阿勒泰地区	Altay Administrative Offices	99.82	23.60	19014	18065
博尔塔拉蒙古自治州	Bortala Mongol Autonomous Prefecture	99.80	23.70	7504	14042
巴音郭楞蒙古自治州	Bayangol Mongol Autonomous Prefecture	99.33	21.25	23511	34882
阿克苏地区	Aksu Administrative Offices	99.78	12.08	30172	27196
克孜勒苏柯尔克孜自治州	Kizilsu Kirgiz Autonomous Prefecture	99.74	10.01	7993	3564
喀什地区	Kashgar [Kaxgar] Administrative Offices	99.87	8.24	36383	26259
和田地区	Hotan Administrative Offices	99.88	6.53	17841	9384

3-12 新疆生产建设兵团人口情况

Population of Xinjiang Production and Construction Group

单位：人　　(person)

年份 Year	总人口 Total Population	男 Male	女 Female	农业人口 Agricultural Population	非农业人口 Non-Agricultural Population	出生人口 Birth Population	死亡人口 Death Population	出生率 (‰) Birth Rate (‰)	死亡率 (‰) DeathRate (‰)	自然增长率 (‰) Natural Growth Rate (‰)
1978	2119835	1090674	1029161			32749	6203	16.56	3.14	13.42
1980	2200755	1127050	1073705			26972	7162	12.27	3.26	9.01
1985	2222350	1142630	1079720	1182415	1039935	16893	7977	7.55	3.57	3.98
1990	2143528	1110475	1033053	1132435	1044093	24589	9305	11.48	4.35	7.13
1995	2287896	1194166	1093730	1230151	1057745	22519	10044	9.98	4.45	5.53
2000	2427920	1272719	1155201	1379913	1048007	22674	12525	9.40	5.20	4.20
2001	2453575	1289954	1163621	1325998	1127577	19061	9014	7.80	3.70	4.10
2002	2501189	1311750	1189439	1355526	1145663	18179	9842	7.37	3.99	3.38
2003	2542170	1330666	1211504	1377224	1164946	17218	9914	6.84	3.94	2.90
2004	2563837	1341213	1222624	1413197	1150640	15860	9864	6.21	3.86	2.35
2005	2569756	1346901	1222855	1332458	1237298	16381	11934	6.38	4.65	1.73
2006	2579435	1352541	1226894	1312908	1266527	14687	11858	5.71	4.61	1.10
2007	2584732	1353053	1231679	1316590	1268142	13289	10131	5.15	3.92	1.23

3-13 按县、市分列的团场户数、人口数

Household and Population of Regiment Farms by City and County

(2007 年)

团　场	Regiment Farm	户数(户) Number of Households (household)	人口数(人) Population (person)	团　场	Regiment Farm	户数(户) Number of Households (household)	人口数(人) Population (person)
总　计	**Total**	**621473**	**1888446**	军户农场	Junhu Farm	4043	11997
乌鲁木齐市	**Urumqi City**	**23420**	**73520**	呼图壁县	Hutubi County	27776	76111
市辖区	Areas under Municipality	21538	67975	105 团	No.105 Regiment Farm	4966	14113
102 团	No.102 Regiment Farm	6596	16932	106 团	No.106 Regiment Farm	2642	6907
104 团	No.104 Regiment Farm	6016	20210	芳草湖农场	Fang Caohu Farm	20168	55091
三坪农场	Sanping Farm	2970	9890	玛纳斯县	Manas County	44228	119533
五一农场	May Ist Farm	3010	10378	147 团	No.147 Regiment Farm	6795	16808
头屯河农场	Tou Tunhe Farm	2946	10565	148 团	No.148 Regiment Farm	11624	28277
乌鲁木齐县	Urumqi County	1882	5545	149 团	No.149 Regiment Farm	7145	18923
西山农场	Xishan Farm	1882	5545	150 团	No.150 Regiment Farm	5623	19869
克拉玛依市	**Karamay City**	**7132**	**18952**	新湖农场	Xinhu Farm	13041	35656
136 团	No.136 Regiment Farm	3991	10648	奇台县	Qitai County	12061	36833
137 团	No.137 Regiment Farm	3141	8304	奇台农场	Qitai Farm	11285	33500
石河子市	**Shihezi City**	**22175**	**60080**	北塔山牧场	Bei Tashan Ranch	776	3333
152 团	No.152 Regiment Farm	3540	10535	阜康市	Fukang City	8701	24151
石河子总场	General Shihezi Farm	18635	49545	222 团	No.222 Regiment Farm	4430	11839
吐鲁番地区	**Turpan Administrative Offices**	**1875**	**5856**	土墩子农场	Tu Dunzi Farm	1983	5427
吐鲁番市	Turpan City	1875	5856	六运湖农场	Liu Yunhu Farm	2288	6885
221 团	No.221 Regiment Farm	1875	5856	吉木萨尔县	Jimsar County	5459	16973
哈密地区	**Hami [Kumul] Administrative Offices**	**21405**	**70326**	红旗农场	Red Flag Farm	5459	16973
哈密市	Hami [Kumul] City	17063	55239	**伊犁哈萨克自治州**	**Ili Kazak Autonomous Prefecture**	**229655**	**660227**
红星一场	Red Star No.1 Farm	2415	7330	**伊犁州直属县(市)**	**Counties (Cities) Direct UnderIli Prefecture**	**70637**	**212314**
红星二场	Red Star No.2 Farm	2221	7003	奎屯市	Kuytun City	6710	19812
红星四场	Red Star No.4 Farm	2526	8047	131 团	No.131 Regiment Farm	6710	19812
黄田农场	Huangtian Farm	2676	10032	伊宁县	Yining [Gulja] County	3918	12704
火箭农场	Huojian Farm	4324	13082	70 团	No.70 Regiment Farm	3918	12704
柳树泉农场	Liu Shuquan Farm	2901	9745	察布查尔锡伯自治县	Qapqal Xibe Autonomous County	9145	24865
巴里坤哈萨克自治县	Barkol Kazak AutonomousCounty	3719	12735	67 团	No.67 Regiment Farm	2752	8691
红山农场	Hongshan Farm	3719	12735	68 团	No.68 Regiment Farm	3398	8757
伊吾县	Yiwu [Araturuk] County	623	2352	69 团	No.69 Regiment Farm	2995	7417
淖毛湖农场	Zhuo Maohu Farm	623	2352	霍城县	Huocheng [Korgas] County	28252	88647
昌吉回族自治州	**Changji Hui Autonomous Prefecture**	**118499**	**331472**	61 团	No.61 Regiment Farm	4132	13270
昌吉市	Changji City	20274	57871	62 团	No.62 Regiment Farm	5158	17021
101 团	No.101 Regiment Farm	6877	18975	63 团	No.63 Regiment Farm	3364	9726
103 团	No.103 Regiment Farm	6594	16934	64 团	No.64 Regiment Farm	6759	22424
共青团农场	Communist League Farm	2760	9965	66 团	No.66 Regiment Farm	8839	26206

3-13 续表 1 Continued

团　场	Regiment Farm	户数(户) Number of Households (household)	人口数(人) Population (person)	团　场	Regiment Farm	户数(户) Number of Households (household)	人口数(人) Population (person)
巩留县	Gongliu [Tokkuztara] County	2313	6214	141 团	No.141 Regiment Farm	4515	11262
73 团	No.73 Regiment Farm	2313	6214	142 团	No.142 Regiment Farm	11900	31582
新源县	Xinyuan [Kunes] County	8140	23405	143 团	No.143 Regiment Farm	14388	41323
71 团	No.71 Regiment Farm	4375	13321	144 团	No.144 Regiment Farm	5412	13591
72 团	No.72 Regiment Farm	3765	10084	托里县	Toli County	1304	3486
昭苏县	Zhaosu [Mongolkure] County	8837	26842	170 团	No.170 Regiment Farm	1304	3486
74 团	No.74 Regiment Farm	1241	3631	裕民县	Yumin [Qagantokay] County	1750	5148
75 团	No.75 Regiment Farm	1453	3928	161 团	No.161 Regiment Farm	1750	5148
76 团	No.76 Regiment Farm	3775	11307	和布克赛尔蒙古自治县	Hoboksar Mongol Autonomous County	1936	5983
77 团	No.77 Regiment Farm	2368	7976	184 团	No.184 Regiment Farm	1936	5983
特克斯县	Tekes County	1613	4761	**阿勒泰地区**	**Altay Administrative Offices**	**15574**	**45918**
78 团	No.78 Regiment Farm	1613	4761	阿勒泰市	Altay City	3824	10681
尼勒克县	Nilka County	1709	5064	181 团	No.181 Regiment Farm	3824	10681
79 团	No.79 Regiment Farm	1709	5064	福海县	Fuhai [Burultokay] County	9445	28003
塔城地区	**Tacheng [Tarbagatai] Administrative Offices**	**143444**	**401995**	182 团	No.182 Regiment Farm	1633	5172
塔城市	Tacheng City	5122	15223	183 团	No.183 Regiment Farm	2863	8210
163 团	No.163 Regiment Farm	3137	9195	187 团	No.187 Regiment Farm	2485	7306
164 团	No.164 Regiment Farm	1985	6028	188 团	No.188 Regiment Farm	2464	7315
额敏县	Emin [Dorbiljin] County	10317	33210	哈巴河县	Habahe [Kaba] County	1336	4216
165 团	No.165 Regiment Farm	1617	5042	185 团	No.185 Regiment Farm	1336	4216
166 团	No.166 Regiment Farm	2413	8095	吉木乃县	Jeminay County	969	3018
167 团	No.167 Regiment Farm	2012	6162	186 团	No.186 Regiment Farm	969	3018
168 团	No.168 Regiment Farm	3236	10574	**博尔塔拉蒙古自治州**	**Bortala Mongol Autonomous Prefecture**	**28911**	**92516**
团结农场	Tuanjie Farm	1039	3337	博乐市	Bole [Bortala] City	17001	56857
乌苏市	Usu City	52549	153698	81 团	No.81 Regiment Farm	3229	10832
123 团	No.123 Regiment Farm	15107	40677	84 团	No.84 Regiment Farm	2578	8576
124 团	No.124 Regiment Farm	5503	20207	86 团	No.86 Regiment Farm	3921	13793
125 团	No.125 Regiment Farm	7845	21378	89 团	No.89 Regiment Farm	4122	14056
126 团	No.126 Regiment Farm	4632	14618	90 团	No.90 Regiment Farm	3151	9600
128 团	No.128 Regiment Farm	5716	16671	精河县	Jinghe [Jing] County	8617	25782
129 团	No.129 Regiment Farm	6301	17136	83 团	No.83 Regiment Farm	7153	21751
130 团	No.130 Regiment Farm	7445	23011	91 团	No.91 Regiment Farm	1464	4031
沙湾县	Shawan County	70466	185247	温泉县	Wenquan [Araxang] County	3293	9877
121 团	No.121 Regiment Farm	16198	41567	87 团	No.87 Regiment Farm	1672	5369
133 团	No.133 Regiment Farm	9257	25052	88 团	No.88 Regiment Farm	1621	4508
134 团	No.134 Regiment Farm	8796	20870				

3-13 续表 2 Continued

团　场	Regiment Farm	户数(户) Number of Households (household)	人口数(人) Population (person)	团　场	Regiment Farm	户数(户) Number of Households (household)	人口数(人) Population (person)
巴音郭楞蒙古自治州	**Bayangol Mongol Autonomous Prefecture**	**49924**	**149262**	阿瓦提县	Awat County	4744	14811
库尔勒市	Korla City	11085	32990	3 团	No.3 Regiment Farm	4744	14811
29 团	No.29 Regiment Farm	7805	22838	**克孜勒苏柯尔克孜自治州**	**Kizilsu Kirgiz Autonomous Prefecture**	**1070**	**4442**
30 团	No.30 Regiment Farm	3280	10152	阿图什市	Artux City	753	3455
尉犁县	Yuli [Lopnur] County	13387	40466	红旗农场	Red Flag Farm	753	3455
31 团	No.31 Regiment Farm	3143	9110	乌恰县	Wuqia [Ulugqat] County	317	987
33 团	No.33 Regiment Farm	5201	16104	托云牧场	Tuoyun Ranch	317	987
34 团	No.34 Regiment Farm	5043	15252	**喀什地区**	**Kashgar [Kaxgar] Administrative Offices**	**45285**	**181648**
若羌县	Ruoqiang [Qarkilik] County	2712	8411	疏勒县	Shule County	1996	6091
36 团	No.36 Regiment Farm	2712	8411	41 团	No.41 Regiment Farm	1996	6091
焉耆回族自治县	Yanji Hui Autonomous County	3753	12016	英吉莎县	Yengisar County	414	1470
27 团	No.27 Regiment Farm	3753	12016	东风农场	Dong Feng Farm	414	1470
和静县	Hejing County	13064	37527	叶城县	Yecheng [Kagilik] County	495	1460
21 团	No.21 Regiment Farm	4170	11120	叶城牧场	Yechen Ranch	495	1460
22 团	No.22 Regiment Farm	6877	19121	麦盖提县	Makit County	8455	27683
223 团	No.223 Regiment Farm	2017	7286	45 团	No.45 Regiment Farm	7436	23962
和硕县	Hoxud County	4078	12341	46 团	No.46 Regiment Farm	1019	3721
24 团	No.24 Regiment Farm	4078	12341	岳普湖县	Yopurga County	1665	4782
博湖县	Bohu [Bagrax] County	1845	5511	42 团	No.42 Regiment Farm	1665	4782
25 团	No.25 Regiment Farm	1845	5511	伽师县	Jiashi [Payzawat] County	2940	11062
阿克苏地区	**Aksu Administrative Offices**	**55665**	**184755**	伽师总场	General Jiashi Farm	2940	11062
阿克苏市	Aksu City	40072	133711	巴楚县	Bachu [Maralbexi] County	29320	129100
1 团	No.1 Regiment Farm	6571	21940	44 团	No.44 Regiment Farm	6281	28112
2 团	No.2 Regiment Farm	3966	11098	48 团	No.48 Regiment Farm	2072	7076
7 团	No.7 Regiment Farm	3914	12380	49 团	No.49 Regiment Farm	4798	17147
8 团	No.8 Regiment Farm	3292	11133	50 团	No.50 Regiment Farm	4069	17950
10 团	No.10 Regiment Farm	5360	18360	51 团	No.51 Regiment Farm	8173	41010
11 团	No.11 Regiment Farm	3005	10771	53 团	No.53 Regiment Farm	3927	17805
12 团	No.12 Regiment Farm	2462	8125	**和田地区**	**Hotan Administrative Offices**	**9202**	**31065**
13 团	No.13 Regiment Farm	4183	15345	墨玉县	Moyu [Karakax] County	2996	8818
14 团	No.14 Regiment Farm	3202	11329	47 团	No.47 Regiment Farm	1480	4137
16 团	No.16 Regiment Farm	4117	13230	224 团	No.224 Regiment Farm	1516	4681
温宿县	Wensu [Onsu] County	8073	28575	皮山县	Pishan [Guma] County	5454	20120
5 团	No.5 Regiment Farm	5167	18124	皮山农场	Pishan Farm	5454	20120
6 团	No.6 Regiment Farm	2906	10451	策勒县	Qira County	752	2127
乌什县	Wushi [Uxturpan] County	2776	7658	一牧场	No.1Ranch	752	2127
4 团	No.4 Regiment Farm	2776	7658				

3-14 就业基本情况
Employment

项　　目	Item	1995	2000	2007
就业人员合计(万人)	**Total Number of Employed Persons (10 000 persons)**	**676.00**	**672.50**	**830.42**
第一产业	Primary Industry	388.16	387.90	417.73
第二产业	Secondary Industry	124.21	92.70	118.34
第三产业	Tertiary Industry	163.63	191.90	294.35
就业人员构成(合计=100)	**Composition of Employed Persons (total=100)**			
第一产业	Primary Industry	57.42	57.68	50.30
第二产业	Secondary Industry	18.37	13.78	14.25
第三产业	Tertiary Industry	24.21	28.54	35.45
按城乡分就业人员(万人)	**Number of Employed Persons by Urban and Rural Areas (10 000 persons)**		**672.50**	**830.42**
城镇就业人员	Urban Employed Persons		318.40	375.59
国有单位	State-owned Units		223.36	186.77
城镇集体单位	Urban Collective-owned Units		15.58	4.64
股份合作单位	Cooperatire Units		1.43	0.64
联营单位	Joint Ownership Units		0.33	0.42
有限责任公司	Limited Liability Corporations		12.32	36.46
股份有限公司	Share-holding Corporations Ltd.		5.87	14.40
私营企业	Private Enterprises		17.15	68.79
其　他	Others			1.95
港澳台商投资单位	Units With Funds From Hong Kong, Macao&Taiwan		0.92	1.32
外商投资单位	Foreign Funded Units		0.51	1.23
个　体	Self-employed Individuals		40.93	58.97
乡村就业人员	Rural Employed Persons		354.10	454..83
#乡镇企业	Township and Village Enterprises		80.64	103.70
私营企业	Private Enterprises		5.24	9.64
个　体	Self-employed Individuals		19.82	19.93
在岗职工人数(万人)	**Number of Staff and Workers (10 000 persons)**	**311.93**	**255.75**	**239.45**
国有单位	State-owned Units	278.49	219.41	181.46
城镇集体单位	Urban Collective-owned Units	29.95	15.28	4.58
其他单位	Units of Other Types of Ownership	3.49	21.06	53.41
城镇单位女性就业人员(万人)	**Number of Female Employment in Urban Units (10 000 persons)**		**107.89**	**104.27**
城镇登记失业人数(万人)	**Number of Registered Unemployed Persons in Urban Areas (10 000 persons)**	**10.24**	**11.00**	**11.70**
城镇登记失业率(%)	**Registered Unemployment Rate in Urban Areas (%)**	**3.9**	**3.8**	**3.9**

3-15 城镇失业人数及失业率

Number of Urban Unemployed Persons and Unemployment Rate

单位：万人 (10 000 persons)

年 份 Year	城镇登记失业人数 Registered Unemployment	城镇登记失业率(%) Registered Unemployment Rate in Urban Areas (%)	年 份 Year	城镇登记失业人数 Registered Unemployment	城镇登记失业率(%) Registered Unemployment Rate in Urban Areas (%)
1980	13.55	7.5	1998	11.06	3.9
1985	4.04	1.9	1999	10.30	3.7
1990	9.60	3.8	2000	11.00	3.8
1991	9.95	3.8	2001	12.07	3.7
1992	9.81	3.7	2002	12.68	3.6
1993	9.50	3.6	2003	12.75	3.8
1994	10.00	3.8	2004	10.87	3.8
1995	10.24	3.9	2005	11.13	3.9
1996	9.81	3.8	2006	11.98	3.9
1997	10.20	3.8	2007	11.70	3.9

3-16 各地、州、市城镇失业率

Urban Unemployment Rate by Prefecture, Autonomous Prefecture and City

单位：% (%)

地 区	Region	2006	2007
总 计	**Total**	**3.87**	**3.88**
乌鲁木齐市	Urumqi City	3.13	3.20
克拉玛依市	Karamay City	2.00	1.56
石河子市	Shihezi City	2.64	
吐鲁番地区	Turpan Administrative Offices	3.44	3.79
哈密地区	Hami [Kumul] Administrative Offices	3.92	3.87
昌吉回族自治州	Changji Hui Autonomous Prefecture	3.53	3.50
伊犁州直属县(市)	Counties (Cities) Direct Under Ili Prefecture	3.39	3.10
塔城地区	Tacheng [Tarbagatai] Administrative Offices	2.06	2.18
阿勒泰地区	Altay Administrative Offices	2.50	3.61
博尔塔拉蒙古自治州	Bortala Mongol Autonomous Prefecture	3.60	2.40
巴音郭楞蒙古自治州	Bayangol Mongol Autonomous Prefecture	3.38	2.71
阿克苏地区	Aksu Administrative Offices	2.00	2.02
克孜勒苏柯尔克孜自治州	Kizilsu Kirgiz Autonomous Prefecture	2.99	4.00
喀什地区	Kashgar [Kaxgar] Administrative Offices	3.75	3.51
和田地区	Hotan Administrative Offices	3.68	3.26

3-17 按三次产业分的就业人员

Number of Employed Persons by Three Strata of Industry

单位：万人 (10 000 persons)

年份 Year	经济活动人口 Economically Active Population	就业人员合计 Total Employed persons	第一产业 Primary Industry	第二产业 Secondary Industry
1978		491.25	353.99	70.42
1980	519.90	506.35	354.49	75.12
1985	569.85	565.81	363.24	89.64
1990	627.30	617.70	378.47	107.42
1995	686.24	676.00	388.16	124.21
1996	693.81	684.00	390.98	119.39
1997	725.60	715.40	421.30	105.40
1998	691.98	680.92	387.80	106.22
1999	704.64	694.34	385.57	104.51
2000	683.50	672.50	387.90	92.70
2001	697.45	685.38	388.19	92.19
2002	714.17	701.49	391.84	95.82
2003	734.02	721.27	397.20	95.69
2004	755.36	744.49	403.31	98.49
2005	802.75	791.62	408.00	122.81
2006	823.73	811.75	414.45	111.28
2007	842.12	830.42	417.73	118.34

年份 Year		构成(合计=100) (%) Composition in Percentage (total=100)(%)		
	第三产业 Tertiary Industry	第一产业 Primary Industry	第二产业 Secondary Industry	第三产业 Tertiary Industry
1978	66.84	72.06	14.33	13.61
1980	76.74	70.01	14.84	15.15
1985	112.93	64.20	15.84	19.96
1990	131.81	61.27	17.39	21.34
1995	163.63	57.42	18.37	24.21
1996	173.63	57.16	17.45	25.39
1997	188.70	58.89	14.73	26.38
1998	186.90	56.95	15.60	27.45
1999	204.26	55.53	15.05	29.42
2000	191.90	57.68	13.78	28.54
2001	205.00	56.64	13.45	29.91
2002	213.83	55.86	13.66	30.48
2003	228.38	55.07	13.27	31.66
2004	242.69	54.17	13.23	32.60
2005	260.81	51.54	15.51	32.95
2006	286.02	51.06	13.71	35.23
2007	294.35	50.30	14.25	35.45

3-18 按城乡分的年底就业人员数

单位：万人

年份 Year	地区 Region	总计 Total	城镇 Urban Area	国有单位 State-owned Units	集体单位 Collective-owned Units	股份合作单位 Cooperative Units	联营单位 Joint Ownership Units
	2000	672.50	318.40	223.36	15.58	1.43	0.33
	2001	685.38	319.92	201.10	12.03	0.93	0.41
	2002	701.49	327.37	193.57	9.68	0.77	0.43
	2003	721.27	339.00	188.89	8.02	0.64	0.27
	2004	744.49	349.43	188.18	6.86	0.82	0.33
	2005	791.62	358.78	186.96	6.05	0.79	0.33
	2006	811.75	370.10	187.19	5.32	0.64	0.33
	2007	830.42	375.59	186.77	4.64	0.64	0.42
乌鲁木齐市	Urumqi City	116.95	101.99	31.67	1.12	0.12	0.25
克拉玛依市	Karamay City	22.71	22.56	9.02	0.66	0.02	0.06
石河子市	Shihezi City	14.08	12.29	5.04	0.02		
吐鲁番地区	Turpan Administrative Offices	35.71	11.15	6.43	0.07	0.06	0.01
哈密地区	Hami [Kumul] Administrative Offices	20.62	10.02	5.63	0.08		0.03
昌吉回族自治州	Changji Hui Autonomous Prefecture	68.43	28.23	14.84	0.26	0.01	0.01
伊犁哈萨克自治州	Ili Kazak Autonomous Prefecture	183.39	74.62	48.66	0.62	0.18	0.05
伊犁州直属县(市)	Counties (Cities) Direct Under Ili Prefecture	103.02	35.91	19.86	0.34	0.15	0.02
塔城地区	Tacheng [Tarbagatai] Administrative Offices	55.25	25.64	19.57	0.19	0.02	
阿勒泰地区	Altay Administrative Offices	25.12	13.07	9.23	0.09	0.01	0.03
博尔塔拉蒙古自治州	Bortala Mongol Autonomous Prefecture	21.29	11.61	7.73	0.17	0.01	
巴音郭楞蒙古自治州	Bayangol Mongol Autonomous Prefecture	49.49	27.58	13.65	0.27	0.03	
阿克苏地区	Aksu Administrative Offices	91.42	30.75	17.72	0.45	0.12	0.01
克孜勒苏柯尔克孜自治州	Kizilsu Kirgiz Autonomous Prefecture	18.00	5.00	3.43	0.06	0.01	
喀什地区	Kashgar [Kaxgar] Administrative Offices	117.79	26.58	15.60	0.76	0.08	
和田地区	Hotan Administrative Offices	70.54	13.21	7.35	0.10		

Number of Employed Persons at Year-end by Urban and Rural Areas

(10 000 persons)

有限责任公司 Limited Liability Corporations	股份有限公司 Share-Holding Corporations Ltd.	私营企业 Private Enterprises	其 他 Others	港澳台商投资单位 Units With Funds from Hong Kong Macao and Taiwan	外商投资单位 Foreign Funded Units	个 体 Self-employed Individuals	乡 村 Rural Area	#乡镇企业 Township and Village Enterprises	#私营企业 Private Enterprises	#个 体 Self-employed Individuals
12.32	5.87	17.15		0.92	0.51	40.93	354.10	80.64	5.24	19.82
26.54	9.01	23.16		0.96	0.55	45.23	365.46	82.44	4.93	19.10
33.35	7.81	34.44		1.06	0.65	45.61	373.41	86.67	4.26	20.01
34.26	10.09	42.35	1.13	0.64	0.73	51.98	382.98	88.09	6.82	18.68
34.96	9.70	50.75	1.16	0.66	0.84	55.17	395.06	93.35	6.50	19.01
35.37	12.01	58.55	1.59	0.71	0.89	57.12	431.25	95.44	8.55	18.77
34.92	12.85	66.36	1.99	0.77	1.14	58.59	441.65	99.04	8.88	19.16
36.46	14.40	68.79	1.95	1.32	1.23	58.97	454.83	103.70	9.64	19.93
10.86	3.44	37.17	0.36	0.94	0.87	15.19	14.96	6.49	1.32	0.57
3.40	4.44	1.80		0.03	0.01	3.12	0.15	0.14		
1.47	1.22	1.87	0.03	0.03	0.13	2.48	1.79	1.02	0.09	0.68
0.63	0.70	1.46	0.01	0.04	0.07	1.67	24.56	4.14	0.60	1.29
1.57	0.14	0.84	0.01	0.06	0.03	1.63	10.60	3.25	0.18	0.51
3.25	0.89	4.91	0.03	0.03		4.02	40.20	10.99	2.46	1.54
6.25	1.00	6.51	0.76	0.04	0.08	10.47	108.77	27.97	1.80	4.39
4.19	0.78	3.81	0.51	0.02	0.08	6.15	67.11	14.14	0.90	2.36
1.43	0.02	1.59		0.02		2.80	29.61	8.85	0.74	1.42
0.63	0.20	1.11	0.25			1.52	12.05	4.98	0.16	0.61
0.61	0.02	1.71		0.11		1.25	9.68	2.72	0.20	0.81
2.76	1.58	3.94	0.04	0.04	0.03	5.24	21.91	6.13	0.68	1.82
2.60	0.49	3.46	0.09		0.01	5.80	60.67	10.23	1.33	1.85
0.08	0.07	0.52	0.04			0.79	13.00	2.86	0.20	0.23
2.55	0.34	2.91				4.34	91.21	15.09	0.60	4.01
0.44	0.07	1.69	0.59			2.97	57.33	12.68	0.18	2.23

3-19 各地区按行业分城镇单位就业人员(年底数)

Number of Employed Persons in Urban Units at Year-end by Sectors and Region

单位：万人 (2007 年) (10 000 persons)

项 目	Item	合 计 Total	国有单位 State-owned Units	城镇集体 Urban Collective-Owned Units	其他单位 Units of Other Types Of Ownership
总 计	**Total**	**247.83**	**186.77**	**4.64**	**56.42**
按国民经济行业分组	**Grouped by Sectors**				
农林牧渔业	Farming, Forestry, Animal Husbandry and Fishery	60.24	59.82	0.11	0.32
采矿业	Mining	18.43	9.71	0.07	8.65
制造业	Manufacturing	25.02	4.23	0.55	20.24
电力、燃气及水的生产和供应业	Production and Distribution of Electricity, Gas and Water	5.99	2.14	0.05	3.80
建筑业	Construction	14.33	4.83	0.74	8.76
交通运输、仓储和邮政业	Transport, Storage and Post	11.03	8.54	0.09	2.40
信息传输、计算机服务和软件业	Information Transmission, Computer Servcie and Software	1.82	1.05		0.77
批发和零售业	Wholesale and Retail Trades	6.97	2.20	1.07	3.70
住宿和餐饮业	Hotels and Catering Services	2.65	1.31	0.15	1.19
金融业	Financial Intermediation	6.04	3.32	0.84	1.88
房地产业	Real Estate	2.64	1.09	0.06	1.49
租赁和商务服务业	Leasing and Business Services	5.05	2.17	0.59	2.29
科学研究、技术服务和地质勘查业	Scientific Research, Technology Service and Geological Prospecting	4.52	4.06	0.02	0.44
水利、环境和公共设施管理业	Water Conservancy, Environment and Public Facility Management	4.47	4.20	0.11	0.16
居民服务和其他服务业	Services to households and Other Services	0.29	0.21	0.03	0.05
教育	Education	33.08	32.88	0.02	0.17
卫生、社会保障和社会福利业	Health, Social Security and Social Welfare	11.60	11.41	0.14	0.05
文化、体育和娱乐业	Culture, Sports and Entertainment	2.50	2.44		0.06
公共管理和社会组织	Public Management and Social Organizations	31.16	31.16		
按地区分	**By Region**				
乌鲁木齐市	Urumqi City	49.62	31.67	1.12	16.84
克拉玛依市	Karamay City	17.64	9.02	0.66	7.96
石河子市	Shihezi City	7.94	5.05	0.02	2.87
吐鲁番地区	Turpan Administrative Offices	8.02	6.44	0.07	1.51
哈密地区	Hami [Kumul] Administrative Offices	7.55	5.63	0.08	1.84
昌吉回族自治州	Changji Hui Autonomous Prefecture	19.30	14.84	0.26	4.19
伊犁哈萨克自治州	Ili Kazak Autonomous Prefecture	57.64	48.65	0.63	8.36
伊犁州直属县(市)	Counties (Cities) Direct Under Ili Prefecture	25.95	19.86	0.34	5.75
塔城地区	Tacheng [Tarbagatai] Administrative Offices	21.25	19.57	0.20	1.48
阿勒泰地区	Altay Administrative Offices	10.44	9.22	0.09	1.13
博尔塔拉蒙古自治州	Bortala Mongol Autonomous Prefecture	8.65	7.73	0.17	0.75
巴音郭楞蒙古自治州	Bayangol Mongol Autonomous Prefecture	18.40	13.65	0.27	4.48
阿克苏地区	Aksu Administrative Offices	21.50	17.72	0.45	3.33
克孜勒苏柯尔克孜自治州	Kizilsu Kirgiz Autonomous Prefecture	3.69	3.43	0.06	0.20
喀什地区	Kashgar [Kaxgar] Administrative Offices	19.33	15.59	0.76	2.98
和田地区	Hotan Administrative Offices	8.55	7.35	0.09	1.11

3-20 各地区年底单位在岗职工人数

Number of Staff and Workers at Year-end by Region

单位：万人 (10 000 persons)

年份 Year	地区 Region	合计 Total	国有单位 State-owned Units	城镇集体 Urban Collective-owned Units	其他单位 Units of Other Types of Ownership
	2002	242.26	189.26	9.31	43.69
	2003	237.94	184.02	7.55	46.37
	2004	235.97	182.80	6.43	46.74
	2005	237.84	181.92	5.96	49.96
	2006	238.95	182.91	5.19	50.85
	2007	239.45	181.46	4.58	53.41
乌鲁木齐市	Urumqi City	47.87	30.12	1.09	16.66
克拉玛依市	Karamay City	14.16	6.82	0.64	6.70
石河子市	Shihezi City	7.91	5.03	0.02	2.86
吐鲁番地区	Turpan Administrative Offices	7.97	6.42	0.07	1.48
哈密地区	Hami [Kumul] Administrative Offices	7.36	5.51	0.08	1.77
昌吉回族自治州	Changji Hui Autonomous Prefecture	18.93	14.74	0.26	3.93
伊犁哈萨克自治州	Ili Kazak Autonomous Prefecture	57.00	48.31	0.63	8.06
伊犁州直属县(市)	Counties (Cities) Direct Under Ili Prefecture	25.63	19.75	0.34	5.54
塔城地区	Tacheng [Tarbagatai] Administrative Offices	21.09	19.44	0.20	1.45
阿勒泰地区	Altay Administrative Offices	10.28	9.12	0.09	1.07
博尔塔拉蒙古自治州	Bortala Mongol Autonomous Prefecture	8.44	7.59	0.17	0.68
巴音郭楞蒙古自治州	Bayangol Mongol Autonomous Prefecture	17.96	13.38	0.27	4.31
阿克苏地区	Aksu Administrative Offices	21.21	17.47	0.44	3.30
克孜勒苏柯尔克孜自治州	Kizilsu Kirgiz Autonomous Prefecture	3.45	3.27	0.07	0.11
喀什地区	Kashgar [Kaxgar] Administrative Offices	18.71	15.45	0.76	2.50
和田地区	Hotan Administrative Offices	8.48	7.35	0.08	1.05

3-21 分行业年底单位在岗职工人数
Number of Staff and Workers at Year-end by Sectors

单位：万人　　(2007 年)　　(10 000 persons)

项　目	Item	合 计 Total	国有单位 State-owned Units	城镇集体 Urban Collective-owned Units	其他单位 Units of Other Types of Ownership
总　计	**Total**	**239.45**	**181.46**	**4.58**	**53.41**
农林牧渔业	**Farming, Forestry, Animal Husbandry and Fishery**	**59.87**	**59.46**	**0.11**	**0.30**
农　业	Farming	47.30	47.18	0.02	0.10
林　业	Forestry	1.01	1.01		
畜 牧 业	Animal Husbandry	7.84	7.75		0.09
渔　业	Fishery	0.03	0.02		0.01
农林牧渔服务业	Farming, forestry, stock-breeding and fishing	3.69	3.50	0.09	0.10
采 矿 业	**Mining**	**15.89**	**7.67**	**0.07**	**8.15**
#煤炭开采和洗选业	Coal Mining and Dressing	4.35	1.05	0.04	3.26
石油和天然气开采业	Petroleum and Natural Gas Extraction	10.22	6.12		4.10
制 造 业	**Manufacturing**	**24.18**	**4.15**	**0.54**	**19.49**
#农副食品加工业	Farming, Non-staple Food Processing	2.02	0.18	0.02	1.82
食品制造业	Food Manufacturing	1.22	0.34	0.02	0.86
饮料制造业	Beverage Manufacturing	1.08	0.03	0.03	1.02
纺织业	Textile Industry	3.86	0.87	0.02	2.97
造纸及纸制品业	Papermaking and Paper Products	0.43	0.04	0.01	0.39
印刷业和记录媒介的复制	Printing and Record Medium Reproduction	0.42	0.28	0.02	0.12
石油加工、炼焦及核燃料加工业	Oil processing, Refining and Nuclear-fuel processing	3.08	1.08		2.00
化学原料及化学制品制造业	Raw Chemical Materials and Chemical Products	2.77	0.20	0.03	2.54
塑料制品业	Plastic Products	0.86	0.05	0.09	0.72
非金属矿物制品业	Nonmetal Mineral Products	2.46	0.30	0.12	2.05
黑色金属冶炼及压延加工业	Smelting and Pressing of Ferrous Metals	1.75	0.04	0.06	1.64
有色金属冶炼及压延加工业	Smelting and Pressing of Nonferrous Metals	0.42	0.12	0.04	0.26
通用设备制造业	Manufacturing of Equipment for General Purpose	0.23			0.23
电力、燃气及水的生产和供应业	**Production and Distribution of Electricity, Gas and Water**	**5.92**	**2.13**	**0.05**	**3.74**
电力、热力的生产和供应业	Production and Distribution of Electric Power, Thermal Power	5.07	1.68	0.03	3.36
燃气生产和供应业	Production and Distribution of Gas	0.18	0.02		0.16
水的生产和供应业	Production and Distribution of Water	0.67	0.43	0.02	0.22
建 筑 业	**Construction**	**13.53**	**4.74**	**0.72**	**8.07**
房屋和土木工程建筑业	Construction of Buildings and Civil Engineering	12.04	4.42	0.44	7.18
建筑安装业	Building and Installation	1.32	0.23	0.28	0.81
建筑装饰业	Building and Decoration	0.06	0.01		0.05

3-21 续表 1 Continued

单位：万人 (10 000 persons)

项　目	Item	合 计 Total	国有单位 State-owned Units	城镇集体 Urban Collective-owned Units	其他单位 Units of Other Types of Ownership
其他建筑业	Other Construction	0.11	0.08		0.03
交通运输、仓储和邮政业	**Transport Storage and Post**	**10.22**	**7.77**	**0.08**	**2.37**
铁路运输业	Railway Transport	3.46	3.46		
道路运输业	Road Transportat	2.82	2.15	0.02	0.65
城市公共交通业	Urban Public Transport	1.30	0.13		1.17
航空运输业	Air Transportat	0.76	0.43		0.33
管道运输业	Pipe Transportat	0.06			0.06
装卸搬运和其他运输服务业	Loading and Discharging; Other Transportation Service	0.36	0.28	0.06	0.02
仓储业	Storage	0.23	0.19		0.04
邮政业	Post	1.23	1.13		0.10
信息传输、计算机服务和软件业	**Information Transmission, Computer Service And Software**	**1.76**	**1.00**		**0.76**
电信和其他信息传输服务业	Telecommunication and Other I.T Transmission Service	1.66	0.98		0.68
计算机服务业	Computer Service	0.04	0.02		0.02
软件业	Software	0.06			0.06
批发和零售业	**Wholesale and Retail Trades**	**6.83**	**2.13**	**1.05**	**3.65**
批发业	Wholesale Trades	4.57	1.45	0.93	2.19
零售业	Retail Trades	2.26	0.68	0.12	1.46
住宿和餐饮业	**Hotels and Catering Services**	**2.49**	**1.15**	**0.15**	**1.19**
住宿业	Hotels	2.10	1.03	0.14	0.93
餐饮业	Catering Services	0.39	0.12	0.01	0.26
金融业	**Financial Intermediation**	**4.87**	**2.89**	**0.84**	**1.14**
银行业	Banking	3.82	2.52	0.83	0.48
证券业	Security Activities	0.05	0.01		0.04
保险业	Insurance	0.97	0.36		0.61
其他金融活动	Other Finance Activities	0.02		0.01	0.01
房地产业	**Real Estate**	**2.43**	**0.91**	**0.06**	**1.46**
#房地产开发经营	Development and Management of Real Estate	0.85	0.09	0.02	0.74
物业管理	Real Estate Management	0.91	0.28	0.02	0.60
房地产中介服务	Agency Service for Real Estate	0.47	0.42		0.04
租赁和商务服务业	**Leasing and Business Service**	**4.96**	**2.15**	**0.59**	**2.23**
租赁业	Leasing	0.05	0.03		0.02
商务服务业	Business Service	4.91	2.11	0.59	2.21

3-21 续表 2 Continued

单位：万人 (10 000 persons)

项　　目	Item	合 计 Total	国有单位 State-owned Units	城镇集体 Urban Collective-owned Units	其他单位 Units of Other Types of Ownership
科学研究、技术服务和地质勘查业	**Scientific Research, Technology Service and Geological Prospecting**	**4.33**	**3.90**	**0.02**	**0.41**
研究与试验发展	Research and Experiment Development	0.56	0.55		0.01
专业技术服务业	Professional Technique Service	2.10	1.72	0.02	0.36
科技交流和推广服务业	Services of Science and Technology Exchanges and Promotion	0.82	0.79		0.03
地质勘查业	Geologica Prospecting	0.85	0.84		0.01
水利、环境和公共设施管理业	**Management ofWater Conservancy, Environment and Public Facility**	**4.39**	**4.13**	**0.11**	**0.15**
水利管理业	Management of Water Conservance	2.11	2.09		0.02
环境管理业	Environmental Management	1.35	1.22	0.11	0.02
公共设施管理业	Management of Public Facilities	0.93	0.82		0.11
居民服务和其他服务业	**Service to Households and Other Services**	**0.28**	**0.21**	**0.03**	**0.04**
居民服务业	Services to Households	0.22	0.18	0.02	0.02
其他服务业	Other Services	0.06	0.03	0.01	0.02
教　育	**Education**	**32.85**	**32.67**	**0.02**	**0.16**
#初等教育	Junior Education	14.42	14.37		0.05
中等教育	Secondary Education	14.38	14.34		0.04
高等教育	Senior Education	2.61	2.60		0.01
卫生、社会保障和社会福利业	**Health, Social Security and Social Welfare**	**11.37**	**11.18**	**0.13**	**0.05**
卫　生	Health	10.93	10.75	0.13	0.05
社会保障业	Social Security	0.20	0.20		
社会福利业	Social Welfare	0.24	0.24		
文化、体育和娱乐业	**Culture, Sports and Entertainment**	**2.46**	**2.40**		**0.06**
新闻出版业	Journalism and Publishing Activities	0.45	0.41		0.04
广播、电影、电视和音像业	Broadcasting, Movies, Televisions and Audiovisual Activities	0.98	0.98		
文化艺术业	Culture and Art Activities	0.88	0.88		
体　育	Sports	0.10	0.10		
娱乐业	Entertainment	0.05	0.03		0.02
公共管理和社会组织	**Public Management and Social Organization**	**30.82**	**30.82**		
#中国共产党机关	Organs of Communist Party of China	1.83	1.83		
国家机构	Government Agencies	27.51	27.51		
人民政协和民主党派	People's Political Consultative Conference and Democratic Parties	0.22	0.22		
群众团体、社会团体和宗教组织	Non-Governmental Organizations, Social Organizations and Religion Organizations	1.02	1.02		

3-22 各地、州、市分行业年底单位在岗职工人数

Number of Staff and Workers at Year-end by Sector and Prefecture, Autonomous Prefecture and City

单位：万人 (10 000 persons)

年份 Year	地区 Region	合计 Total	农林牧渔业 Farming, Forestry, Animal Husbandry and Fishery	采矿业 Mining	制造业 Manufacturing	电力、燃气及水的生产和供应业 Power, Gas and Water Production and Distribution
	2005	237.84	60.99	14.30	24.34	5.61
	2006	238.95	61.12	15.56	23.41	5.77
	2007	239.45	59.87	15.89	24.18	5.92
乌鲁木齐市	Urumqi City	47.87	1.26	1.95	8.06	1.04
克拉玛依市	Karamay City	14.16	0.90	5.10	2.86	0.01
石河子市	Shihezi City	7.91	1.21		1.89	0.55
吐鲁番地区	Turpan Administrative Offices	7.97	0.39	3.36	0.52	0.23
哈密地区	Hami [Kumul] Administrative Offices	7.36	1.88	1.14	0.53	0.20
昌吉回族自治州	Changji Hui Autonomous Prefecture	18.93	7.03	0.48	2.25	0.60
伊犁哈萨克自治州	Ili Kazak Autonomous Prefecture	57.00	25.07	1.58	3.98	1.30
伊犁州直属县(市)	Counties (Cities) Direct Under Ili Prefecture	25.63	7.78	0.20	3.04	0.74
塔城地区	Tacheng [Tarbagatai] Administrative Offices	21.09	12.73	0.85	0.70	0.30
阿勒泰地区	Altay Administrative Offices	10.28	4.56	0.53	0.24	0.26
博尔塔拉蒙古自治州	Bortala Mongol Autonomous Prefecture	8.44	4.08	0.02	0.47	0.22
巴音郭楞蒙古自治州	Bayangol Mongol Autonomous Prefecture	17.96	6.05	1.57	0.85	0.34
阿克苏地区	Aksu Administrative Offices	21.21	7.33	0.46	1.53	0.47
克孜勒苏柯尔克孜自治州	Kizilsu Kirgiz Autonomous Prefecture	3.45	0.29	0.09	0.09	0.05
喀什地区	Kashgar [Kaxgar] Administrative Offices	18.71	3.25	0.01	0.81	0.69
和田地区	Hotan Administrative Offices	8.48	1.13	0.13	0.34	0.22

年份 Year	地区 Region	建筑业 Construction	交通运输、仓储和邮政业 Transport Storage and Post	信息传输、计算机服务和软件业 Information Transmission, Computer Servcie and Software	批发和零售业 Wholesale and Retail Trades	住宿和餐饮业 Hotels and Catering Services
	2005	15.21	10.70	2.04	7.47	2.59
	2006	13.83	10.41	1.86	7.37	2.70
	2007	13.53	10.22	1.76	6.83	2.49
乌鲁木齐市	Urumqi City	5.89	6.25	0.48	2.06	1.21
克拉玛依市	Karamay City	1.37	0.17	0.05	0.30	0.07
石河子市	Shihezi City	1.31	0.17	0.08	0.12	0.03
吐鲁番地区	Turpan Administrative Offices	0.04	0.16	0.06	0.13	0.06
哈密地区	Hami [Kumul] Administrative Offices	0.16	0.11	0.08	0.11	0.11
昌吉回族自治州	Changji Hui Autonomous Prefecture	0.50	0.42	0.14	0.33	0.02
伊犁哈萨克自治州	Ili Kazak Autonomous Prefecture	1.28	1.17	0.36	1.18	0.52
伊犁州直属县(市)	Counties (Cities) Direct Under Ili Prefecture	0.92	0.69	0.21	0.81	0.34
塔城地区	Tacheng [Tarbagatai] Administrative Offices	0.11	0.24	0.06	0.23	0.06
阿勒泰地区	Altay Administrative Offices	0.25	0.24	0.09	0.14	0.12
博尔塔拉蒙古自治州	Bortala Mongol Autonomous Prefecture	0.13	0.10	0.04	0.22	0.04
巴音郭楞蒙古自治州	Bayangol Mongol Autonomous Prefecture	0.76	0.45	0.09	0.53	0.16
阿克苏地区	Aksu Administrative Offices	0.93	0.32	0.12	0.77	0.10
克孜勒苏柯尔克孜自治州	Kizilsu Kirgiz Autonomous Prefecture	0.03	0.11	0.03	0.06	0.02
喀什地区	Kashgar [Kaxgar] Administrative Offices	0.68	0.56	0.16	0.85	0.12
和田地区	Hotan Administrative Offices	0.45	0.23	0.07	0.17	0.03

3-22 续表 Continued

单位：万人 (10 000 persons)

年份 Year	地区 Region	金融业 Financial Intermedia-tion	房地产业 Real Estate	租赁和商务服务业 Leasing and Business Services	科学研究、技术服务和地质勘查业 Scientific Research, Technology Service and Geological Prospecting	水利、环境和公共设施管理业 Management of Water Conservancy, Environment and Public Facility
	2005	4.84	2.20	3.94	4.25	4.20
	2006	4.89	1.95	4.73	4.29	4.25
	2007	4.87	2.43	4.96	4.33	4.39
乌鲁木齐市	Urumqi City	1.42	1.25	1.29	1.67	0.64
克拉玛依市	Karamay City	0.18	0.13	1.16	0.16	0.01
石河子市	Shihezi City	0.24	0.03	0.27	0.10	0.21
吐鲁番地区	Turpan Administrative Offices	0.15	0.02	0.02	0.21	0.10
哈密地区	Hami [Kumul] Administrative Offices	0.16	0.05	0.05	0.19	0.16
昌吉回族自治州	Changji Hui Autonomous Prefecture	0.37	0.16	0.23	0.33	0.50
伊犁哈萨克自治州	Ili Kazak Autonomous Prefecture	0.91	0.35	0.33	0.61	0.91
伊犁州直属县(市)	Counties (Cities) Direct Under Ili Prefecture	0.50	0.29	0.25	0.31	0.45
塔城地区	Tacheng [Tarbagatai] Administrative Offices	0.25	0.04	0.05	0.13	0.34
阿勒泰地区	Altay Administrative Offices	0.16	0.02	0.03	0.17	0.12
博尔塔拉蒙古自治州	Bortala Mongol Autonomous Prefecture	0.12	0.03	0.42	0.10	0.15
巴音郭楞蒙古自治州	Bayangol Mongol Autonomous Prefecture	0.32	0.14	0.68	0.24	0.32
阿克苏地区	Aksu Administrative Offices	0.31	0.12	0.31	0.23	0.57
克孜勒苏柯尔克孜自治州	Kizilsu Kirgiz Autonomous Prefecture	0.08	0.01	0.03	0.17	0.06
喀什地区	Kashgar [Kaxgar] Administrative Offices	0.43	0.13	0.14	0.21	0.53
和田地区	Hotan Administrative Offices	0.18	0.01	0.03	0.11	0.23

年份 Year	地区 Region	居民服务和其他服务业 Service to Households and Other Services	教育 Education	卫生、社会保障和社会福利业 Health, Social Security and Social Welfare	文化、体育和娱乐业 Culture, Sports and Entertainment	公共管理和社会组织 Public Management and Social Organizations
	2005	0.29	31.78	10.70	2.42	29.97
	2006	0.34	32.54	11.07	2.41	30.45
	2007	0.28	32.85	11.37	2.46	30.82
乌鲁木齐市	Urumqi City	0.04	4.47	2.30	0.90	5.69
克拉玛依市	Karamay City	0.02	0.66	0.30	0.04	0.67
石河子市	Shihezi City	0.02	0.75	0.37	0.03	0.53
吐鲁番地区	Turpan Administrative Offices		1.06	0.31	0.04	1.11
哈密地区	Hami [Kumul] Administrative Offices	0.01	0.94	0.43	0.09	0.96
昌吉回族自治州	Changji Hui Autonomous Prefecture		2.43	0.87	0.10	2.17
伊犁哈萨克自治州	Ili Kazak Autonomous Prefecture	0.05	7.48	2.57	0.50	6.85
伊犁州直属县(市)	Counties (Cities) Direct Under Ili Prefecture	0.03	4.13	1.32	0.24	3.38
塔城地区	Tacheng [Tarbagatai] Administrative Offices	0.02	2.18	0.82	0.11	1.87
阿勒泰地区	Altay Administrative Offices		1.17	0.43	0.15	1.60
博尔塔拉蒙古自治州	Bortala Mongol Autonomous Prefecture	0.01	0.94	0.36	0.06	0.93
巴音郭楞蒙古自治州	Bayangol Mongol Autonomous Prefecture	0.02	2.15	0.84	0.10	2.35
阿克苏地区	Aksu Administrative Offices	0.02	3.23	0.97	0.16	3.26
克孜勒苏柯尔克孜自治州	Kizilsu Kirgiz Autonomous Prefecture	0.07	0.97	0.28	0.09	0.92
喀什地区	Kashgar [Kaxgar] Administrative Offices	0.01	5.43	1.13	0.24	3.33
和田地区	Hotan Administrative Offices	0.01	2.34	0.64	0.11	2.05

3-23 分行业城镇单位年底女性就业人员

Number of Female Employed in Urban Units at Year-end by Sectors

单位：万人 (2007 年) (10 000 persons)

项目	Item	合计 Total	国有单位 State-owned Units	城镇集体 Urban Collective-owned Units	其他单位 Units of Other Types of Ownership
总计	**Total**	**104.27**	**82.52**	**1.65**	**20.10**
农林牧渔业	Farming, Forestry, Animal Husbandry and Fishery	26.17	26.05	0.03	0.09
采矿业	Mining	5.39	2.93	0.01	2.45
制造业	Manufacturing	9.97	1.82	0.22	7.93
电力、燃气及水的生产和供应业	Production and Distribution of Electricity, Gas and Water	2.14	0.73	0.02	1.39
建筑业	Construction	2.73	1.06	0.11	1.56
交通运输、仓储和邮政业	Transport, Storage and Post	3.68	2.80	0.05	0.83
信息传输、计算机服务和软件业	Information Transmission, Computer Servcie and Software Industries	0.79	0.43		0.36
批发和零售业	Wholesale and Retail Trades	2.97	0.95	0.40	1.62
住宿和餐饮业	Hotels and Catering Services	1.53	0.79	0.08	0.66
金融业	Financial Intermediation	3.22	1.69	0.34	1.19
房地产业	Real Estate	1.15	0.47	0.03	0.65
租赁和商务服务业	Leasing and Business Services	1.92	0.81	0.14	0.97
科学研究、技术服务和地质勘查业	Scientific Research, Technology Service And Geological Prospecting	1.58	1.45	0.01	0.12
水利、环境和公共设施管理业	Management of Water Conservancy, Environment and Public Facility	1.87	1.73	0.06	0.08
居民服务和其他服务业	Services to households and Other Services	0.16	0.12	0.02	0.02
教育	Education	19.76	19.63	0.02	0.11
卫生、社会保障和社会福利业	Health, Social Security and Social Welfare	7.59	7.46	0.10	0.03
文化、体育和娱乐业	Culture, Sports and Entertainment	1.15	1.12		0.03
公共管理和社会组织	Public Management and Social Organizations	10.49	10.49		

3-24 单位在岗职工工资总额及构成
Total Wages of Staff and Workers and Its Composition

年份 Year	地区 Region	工资总额（万元）Total wages (10 000yuan) 合计 Total	国有单位 State-owned Units	城镇集体单位 Urban Collective-owned Units	其他单位 Units of Other Types of Ownership	构成(总计=100)(%) composition in percentage(total=100)(%) 国有单位 State-owned Units	城镇集体单位 Urban Collective-owned Units	其他单位 Units of Other Types of ownership
	1978	159409	148278	11131		93.0	7.0	
	1980	212446	196711	15735		92.6	7.4	
	1985	339110	304999	33789	322	89.9	10.0	0.1
	1990	668808	601300	65858	1650	90.0	9.8	0.2
	1991	746910	666971	78026	1913	89.3	10.4	0.3
	1992	856020	763348	89408	3265	89.2	10.4	0.4
	1993	1027934	905289	115639	7006	88.1	11.2	0.7
	1994	1327539	1200161	114011	13367	90.4	8.6	1.0
	1995	1677257	1521670	135990	19597	90.7	8.1	1.2
	1996	1897561	1719504	148059	29998	90.6	7.8	1.6
	1997	2098467	1898582	163748	36137	90.5	7.8	1.7
	1998	2095963	1852330	147334	96299	88.4	7.0	4.6
	1999	2118609	1857722	137261	123626	87.7	6.5	5.8
	2000	2344694	2007823	125510	211361	85.6	5.4	9.0
	2001	2677431	2092155	105861	479415	78.1	4.0	17.9
	2002	2915398	2211411	93605	610382	75.9	3.2	20.9
	2003	3315399	2497369	77460	740570	75.3	2.3	22.4
	2004	3563312	2691462	78224	793626	75.5	2.2	22.3
	2005	3874068	2871542	75971	926555	74.1	2.0	23.9
	2006	4429959	3318694	77978	1033287	74.9	1.8	23.3
	2007	5332395	3951882	82215	1298298	74.1	1.5	24.4
乌鲁木齐市	Urumqi City	1463601	960360	20877	482364	65.6	1.4	33.0
克拉玛依市	Karamay City	424259	213064	12208	198987	50.2	2.9	46.9
石河子市	Shihezi City	185790	113260	505	72025	61.0	0.3	38.7
吐鲁番地区	Turpan Administrative Offices	231334	189904	1623	39807	82.1	0.7	17.2
哈密地区	Hami [Kumul] Administrative Offices	165900	118775	1589	45536	71.6	1.0	27.4
昌吉回族自治州	Changji Hui Autonomous Prefecture	390283	300516	5185	84582	77.0	1.3	21.7
伊犁哈萨克自治州	Ili Kazak Autonomous Prefecture	944421	786854	11613	145954	83.3	1.2	15.5
伊犁州直属县(市)	Counties (Cities) Direct Under Ili Prefecture	430600	331854	5615	93131	77.1	1.3	21.6
塔城地区	Tacheng [Tarbagatai] Administrative Offices	330023	295981	4088	29954	89.7	1.2	9.1
阿勒泰地区	Altay Administrative Offices	183798	159019	1910	22869	86.6	1.0	12.4
博尔塔拉蒙古自治州	Bortala Mongol Autonomous Prefecture	131984	119147	3129	9708	90.2	2.4	7.4
巴音郭楞蒙古自治州	Bayangol Mongol Autonomous Prefecture	360358	250758	5772	103828	69.6	1.6	28.8
阿克苏地区	Aksu Administrative Offices	397962	335645	8270	54047	84.3	2.1	13.6
克孜勒苏柯尔克孜自治州	Kizilsu Kirgiz Autonomous Prefecture	78788	76836	574	1378	97.6	0.7	1.7
喀什地区	Kashgar [Kaxgar] Administrative Offices	377626	325320	9732	42574	86.1	2.6	11.3
和田地区	Hotan Administrative Offices	180089	161443	1138	17508	89.7	0.6	9.7

3-25 在岗职工工资总额指数
Indices of Total Wages of Staff and Workers

年 份 Year	指数(上年=100) Index (preceding year=100) 合 计 Total	国有单位 State-owned Units	城镇集体单位 Urban Collective-owned Units	其他单位 Units of Other Types of Ownership	指数(1978 年=100) Index (1978=100) 合 计 Total	国有单位 State-owned Units	城镇集体单位 Urban Collective-owned Units	其他单位 Units of Other Types of Ownership
1978	114.2	114.5	109.6		100.0	100.0	100.0	
1980	120.5	120.1	125.2		133.3	132.7	141.4	
1985	117.4	117.5	116.0	167.5	212.7	205.7	303.6	100.0
1990	116.6	116.3	126.9	132.6	419.6	405.5	591.7	513.4
1995	126.3	126.8	119.3	146.6	1052.2	1026.2	1221.7	6097.7
1996	113.1	113.0	108.8	153.1	1190.4	1159.6	1330.2	9333.5
1997	110.6	110.4	110.6	120.5	1316.4	1280.4	1471.1	11244.0
1998	99.9	97.6	90.0	266.5	1314.8	1249.2	1323.6	29962.3
1999	101.1	100.3	93.2	128.4	1329.0	1252.9	1233.1	38464.9
2000	110.7	108.1	91.4	171.0	1470.9	1354.1	1127.6	65762.7
2001	114.2	104.2	84.3	226.8	1679.6	1411.0	951.0	149164.7
2002	108.9	105.7	88.4	127.3	1828.9	1491.4	840.9	189913.4
2003	113.7	112.9	82.8	121.3	2079.8	1684.2	695.9	230420.0
2004	107.5	107.8	101.0	107.2	2235.3	1815.1	702.8	246927.8
2005	108.7	106.7	97.1	116.7	2430.3	1936.6	682.5	288287.3
2006	114.3	115.6	102.6	111.5	2779.0	2238.2	700.5	321896.3
2007	120.4	119.1	105.4	125.6	3345.1	2665.2	738.6	403198.1

注：2000 年起职工工资总额指数由在岗职工工资总额计算而得。
Note: The indice of total sum of wages for the staff workers fom the year 2000 are calculated on the basis of on-the-job staff.

3-26 在岗职工工资情况
Wages of Full-Employed Staff and Workers

年 份 Year	在岗职工工资总额(万元) Total Wages of staff and workers (10 000 yuan)	国有单位 State-owned Units	城镇单位 Urban Collective-owned Units	其他单位 Units of Other Types of Ownership	在岗职工平均工资(元) Average Wage of Staff and Workers (yuan)	国有单位 State-owned Units	城镇单位 Urban Collective-owned Units	其他单位 Units of Other Types of Ownership
1999	2118609	1857722	137261	123626	7611	7614	6815	8681
2000	2344694	2007823	125510	211361	8717	8731	7489	9498
2001	2677431	2092155	105861	479415	10278	10145	8197	11594
2002	2915398	2211411	93605	610382	11605	11435	9353	12767
2003	3315399	2497369	77460	740570	13255	13199	9966	13937
2004	3563312	2691462	78224	793626	14484	14477	11594	14870
2005	3874068	2871542	75971	926555	15558	15364	12738	16503
2006	4429959	3318694	77978	1033287	17819	17704	14209	18566
2007	5332395	3951882	82215	1298298	21434	21369	17780	21921

3-27 在岗职工平均货币工资
Average Money Wage of Staff and Workers

单位：元 (yuan)

年份 Year	全部职工 Full Employees	国有单位 State-owned Units	城镇集体单位 Urban Collective-owned Units	其他单位 Units of Other Types of Ownership
1978	717	726	614	
1980	882	904	676	
1985	1277	1310	1038	1707
1990	2272	2345	1765	2498
1995	5348	5431	4509	5973
2000	8717	8731	7489	9498
2001	10278	10145	8197	11594
2002	11605	11435	9353	12767
2003	13255	13199	9966	13937
2004	14484	14477	11594	14870
2005	15558	15364	12738	16503
2006	17819	17704	14209	18566
2007	21434	21369	17780	21921

3-28 在岗职工平均工资指数
Indices of Average Wage of Staff and Workers

(上年=100) (preceding year=100)

年份 Year	货币工资 Average Money Wage				实际工资 Average Real Wage			
	合计 Total	国有单位 State-owned Units	城镇集体单位 Urban Collective-owned Units	其他单位 Units of Other Types of Ownership	合计 Total	国有单位 State-owned Units	城镇集体单位 Urban Collective-owned Units	其他单位 Units of Other Types of Ownership
1978		105.2				103.9		
1980	114.5	115.3	108.3		109.3	110.0	103.4	
1985	115.7	116.0	112.5	124.6	105.9	106.0	102.7	113.7
1990	113.2	113.3	113.6	96.5	108.3	108.4	108.7	92.3
1995	125.8	125.7	125.8	120.9	105.7	105.6	105.7	101.6
2000	114.5	114.7	109.9	109.4	115.2	115.4	110.6	110.1
2001	117.9	116.2	109.5	122.1	113.4	111.7	105.3	117.4
2002	112.9	112.7	114.1	110.1	113.6	113.4	114.8	110.8
2003	114.2	115.4	106.6	109.2	113.6	114.8	106.1	108.7
2004	109.3	109.7	116.3	106.7	107.0	107.4	113.9	104.5
2005	107.4	106.1	109.9	111.0	106.7	105.4	109.1	110.2
2006	114.5	115.2	111.5	112.5	113.7	114.4	110.7	111.7
2007	120.3	120.7	125.1	118.1	114.0	114.4	118.6	111.9

3-29 各地、州、市分行业单位在岗职工平均货币工资
Average Money Wage of Staff and Workers by Sector and by Prefecture, Autonomous Prefecture and City

单位：元 (yuan)

年份 Year	地区 Region	合计 Total	农林牧渔业 Farming, Forestry, Animal Husbandry and Fishery	采矿业 Fishery	制造业 Manufacturing	电力、燃气及水的生产和供应业 Power, Gas and Water Production and Distribution
	2005	15558	9896	23337	14871	21920
	2006	17819	11306	27985	16781	23290
	2007	21434	13013	34044	20513	28897
乌鲁木齐市	Urumqi City	29483	12842	36138	26822	42005
克拉玛依市	Karamay City	29706	13248	37663	30589	33436
石河子市	Shihezi City	19215	19689		16776	20589
吐鲁番地区	Turpan Administrative Offices	29415	20100	42372	15522	42161
哈密地区	Hami [Kumul] Administrative Offices	22422	14435	30731	16447	55173
昌吉回族自治州	Changji Hui Autonomous Prefecture	19085	15610	21899	14158	34360
伊犁哈萨克自治州	Ili Kazak Autonomous Prefecture	15888	10732	19667	14388	25469
伊犁州直属县(市)	Counties (Cities) Direct Under Ili Prefecture	16590	10624	14340	14844	24762
塔城地区	Tacheng [Tarbagatai] Administrative Offices	14534	11250	18338	13657	29178
阿勒泰地区	Altay Administrative Offices	17049	9409	23530	11127	23019
博尔塔拉蒙古自治州	Bortala Mongol Autonomous Prefecture	15456	10873	21072	11763	20860
巴音郭楞蒙古自治州	Bayangol Mongol Autonomous Prefecture	19345	14187	28524	15737	26417
阿克苏地区	Aksu Administrative Offices	18207	16323	26344	15982	20745
克孜勒苏柯尔克孜自治州	Kizilsu Kirgiz Autonomous Prefecture	22990	18394	8395	11121	19608
喀什地区	Kashgar [Kaxgar] Administrative Offices	19897	14847	12787	10165	17340
和田地区	Hotan Administrative Offices	20936	11016	15966	8672	24389

年份 Year	地区 Region	建筑业 Construction	交通运输、仓储和邮政业 Transport, Storage and Post	信息传输、计算机服务和软件业 Information Transmission, Computer Servcie and Software	批发和零售业 Wholesale and Retail Trades	住宿和餐饮业 Hotels and Catering Services
	2005	14005	23634	27544	15127	12417
	2006	16183	25802	28513	17115	13153
	2007	17990	32486	35284	20492	15041
乌鲁木齐市	Urumqi City	19797	41875	51931	28332	17710
克拉玛依市	Karamay City	23702	25076	32649	27382	17460
石河子市	Shihezi City	15756	23545	35007	25552	8915
吐鲁番地区	Turpan Administrative Offices	15777	13468	23261	22225	10968
哈密地区	Hami [Kumul] Administrative Offices	13249	16845	34612	20621	18244
昌吉回族自治州	Changji Hui Autonomous Prefecture	19089	14070	24630	17812	12480
伊犁哈萨克自治州	Ili Kazak Autonomous Prefecture	14711	17954	27627	15069	12069
伊犁州直属县(市)	Counties (Cities) Direct Under Ili Prefecture	16554	15629	30626	13008	11091
塔城地区	Tacheng [Tarbagatai] Administrative Offices	9758	21775	25541	19218	9770
阿勒泰地区	Altay Administrative Offices	15540	20637	22031	19653	15282
博尔塔拉蒙古自治州	Bortala Mongol Autonomous Prefecture	12668	21191	35137	17197	13428
巴音郭楞蒙古自治州	Bayangol Mongol Autonomous Prefecture	16289	16974	24408	19989	12358
阿克苏地区	Aksu Administrative Offices	16659	16484	19993	15735	10555
克孜勒苏柯尔克孜自治州	Kizilsu Kirgiz Autonomous Prefecture	15602	22607	21273	11420	10914
喀什地区	Kashgar [Kaxgar] Administrative Offices	14652	16972	43217	13846	10111
和田地区	Hotan Administrative Offices	14095	17853	20443	16326	14676

3-29 续表 Continued

单位：元 (yuan)

年份 Year	地区 Region	金融业 Financial Intermedition	房地产业 Real Estate	租赁和商务服务业 Leasing and Business Services	科学研究、技术服务和地质勘查业 Scientific Research, Technology Service and Geological Prospecting	水利、环境和公共设施管理业 Management of Water Conservancy, Environment and Public Facility
	2005	25149	14517	14176	19077	13419
	2006	28647	15425	16430	21220	15220
	2007	38137	20313	16140	26631	17824
乌鲁木齐市	Urumqi City	60103	25917	20511	29723	20940
克拉玛依市	Karamay City	39140	20048	15895	35232	35788
石河子市	Shihezi City	32148	23109	18083	27192	17620
吐鲁番地区	Turpan Administrative Offices	26468	11328	11551	27343	14987
哈密地区	Hami [Kumul] Administrative Offices	32910	12213	15162	24130	14116
昌吉回族自治州	Changji Hui Autonomous Prefecture	33833	17531	14647	23603	16872
伊犁哈萨克自治州	Ili Kazak Autonomous Prefecture	28598	13362	12959	24390	15068
伊犁州直属县(市)	Counties (Cities) Direct Under Ili Prefecture	27152	12639	12735	22047	14001
塔城地区	Tacheng [Tarbagatai] Administrative Offices	28976	16289	12060	21812	16181
阿勒泰地区	Altay Administrative Offices	32481	15352	16482	30831	15774
博尔塔拉蒙古自治州	Bortala Mongol Autonomous Prefecture	34319	12509	10017	23806	17120
巴音郭楞蒙古自治州	Bayangol Mongol Autonomous Prefecture	32486	11920	17070	23406	14017
阿克苏地区	Aksu Administrative Offices	22559	13907	9812	21079	24154
克孜勒苏柯尔克孜自治州	Kizilsu Kirgiz Autonomous Prefecture	24252	15320	16705	26747	20798
喀什地区	Kashgar [Kaxgar] Administrative Offices	21454	12869	13879	19280	15595
和田地区	Hotan Administrative Offices	23972	14755	15935	25139	18631

年份 Year	地区 Region	居民服务和其他服务业 Service to households and Other Services	教育 Education	卫生、社会保障和社会福利业 Health, Social Security and Social Welfare	文化、体育和娱乐业 Culture, Sports and Entertainment	公共管理和社会组织 Public Administration and Social Organizations
	2005	12159	17183	17297	16972	17661
	2006	14044	19663	20053	19308	20356
	2007	15978	23680	23518	23492	25145
乌鲁木齐市	Urumqi City	23187	26294	29633	27197	32646
克拉玛依市	Karamay City	21845	28520	29590	33247	29486
石河子市	Shihezi City	20216	23169	24407	20653	25865
吐鲁番地区	Turpan Administrative Offices	8586	22243	18599	18236	19888
哈密地区	Hami [Kumul] Administrative Offices	20016	25811	22493	22841	23902
昌吉回族自治州	Changji Hui Autonomous Prefecture	4038	24424	21232	23785	24015
伊犁哈萨克自治州	Ili Kazak Autonomous Prefecture	13031	22413	20963	20425	22674
伊犁州直属县(市)	Counties (Cities) Direct Under Ili Prefecture	12333	21804	20983	19025	21896
塔城地区	Tacheng [Tarbagatai] Administrative Offices	13814	21422	18983	19688	21882
阿勒泰地区	Altay Administrative Offices	16478	26417	24746	23321	25268
博尔塔拉蒙古自治州	Bortala Mongol Autonomous Prefecture	14407	23723	21601	21109	23069
巴音郭楞蒙古自治州	Bayangol Mongol Autonomous Prefecture	17102	24327	22043	22341	23607
阿克苏地区	Aksu Administrative Offices	16481	20225	21153	19122	20091
克孜勒苏柯尔克孜自治州	Kizilsu Kirgiz Autonomous Prefecture	11029	25617	25842	22392	25429
喀什地区	Kashgar [Kaxgar] Administrative Offices	10872	22951	21902	19653	26215
和田地区	Hotan Administrative Offices	22265	25581	23614	24064	24672

3-30 各地、州、市、县(市)在岗职工平均货币工资
Average Money Wages of Fully Employed Staff and Workers by Prefecture, Autonomous Prefecture, City and County

单位：元 (2007 年) (yuan)

地区	Region	合计 Total	国有单位 State-owned Units	城镇集体单位 Urban Collective-owned Units	其他单位 Units of Other Types of Ownership
总　计	**Total**	**21434**	**21369**	**17780**	**21921**
乌鲁木齐市	**Urumqi City**	**29483**	**31831**	**18797**	**26270**
#乌鲁木齐县	Urumqi County	27759	27759		
克拉玛依市	**Karamay City**	**29706**	**31914**	**20023**	**28443**
石河子市	**Shihezi City**	**19215**	**20462**	**30048**	**17495**
吐鲁番地区	**Turpan Administrative Offices**	**29415**	**30061**	**20266**	**27133**
吐鲁番市	Turpan City	19404	20193	17891	16942
鄯善县	Shanshan [Piqan] County	36950	36839	30494	37643
托克逊县	Toksun County	20212	21393	17719	14455
哈密地区	**Hami [Kumul] Administrative Offices**	**22422**	**21377**	**19477**	**25857**
哈密市	Hami [Kumul] City	23785	22835	24513	25996
巴里坤哈萨克自治县	Barkol Kazak Autonomous County	16387	16287	22000	18852
伊吾县	Yiwu [Araturuk] County	20557	21405	11962	11500
昌吉回族自治州	**Changji Hui Autonomous Prefecture**	**19085**	**19362**	**20090**	**18110**
昌吉市	Changji City	26577	32504	23266	17758
阜康市	Fukang City	19979	20682	26771	18227
呼图壁县	Hutubi County	16667	16486	19537	17181
玛纳斯县	Manas County	19119	18342	19979	24179
奇台县	Qitai County	19507	19149	16263	21499
吉木萨尔县	Jimsar County	19498	19972	16047	17604
木垒哈萨克自治县	Mori Kazak Autonomous County	22229	25299	14488	11939
伊犁哈萨克自治州	**Ili Kazak Autonomous Prefecture**	**15558**	**15803**	**18590**	**16170**
伊犁州直属县(市)	**Counties (Cities) Direct Under Ili Prefecture**	**16590**	**16761**	**16721**	**16001**
伊宁市	Yining [Gulja] City	18557	20995	13875	15635
奎屯市	Kuytun City	19180	19684	19656	16799
伊宁县	Yining [Gulja] County	13374	12812	13652	15893
察布查尔锡伯自治县	Qapqal Xibe Autonomous County	14575	14793	26361	10446
霍城县	Huocheng [Korgas] County	13510	13084	18246	16948
巩留县	Gongliu [Tokkuztara] County	17279	17627	32535	
新源县	Xinyuan [Kunes] County	16675	15911	19157	18643
昭苏县	Zhaosu [Mongolkure] County	17891	18306	19653	12461
特克斯县	Tekes County	18471	19062	16368	15864
尼勒克县	Nilka County	15883	16240	15345	12824

3-30 续表 1 Continued

单位：元 (yuan)

地　　区	Region	合　计 Total	国　有 单　位 State-owned Units	城镇集体 单　位 Urban Collective-owned Units	其　他 单　位 Units of Other Types of Ownership
塔城地区	**Tacheng [Tarbagatai] Administrative Offices**	**14534**	**14362**	**19644**	**15846**
塔城市	Tacheng [Qoqek] City	18004	17445	19161	20954
乌苏市	Usu City	13055	12513	13254	19294
额敏县	Emin [Dorbiljin] County	11664	11222	23822	15861
沙湾县	Shawan County	14853	15225	24972	7852
托里县	Toli County	20731	20670	28000	18000
裕民县	Yumin [Qagantokay] County	15239	15338	13930	10102
和布克赛尔蒙古自治县	Hoboksar Mongol Autonomous County	15296	15022	22125	15294
阿勒泰地区	**Altay Administrative Offices**	**17049**	**16946**	**23642**	**17383**
阿勒泰市	Altay City	18306	18360	25818	17707
布尔津县	Burqin County	16260	16648	14512	14885
富蕴县	Fuyun [Koktokay] County	15575	14730	26526	21660
福海县	Fuhai [Burultokay] County	14874	15005	26189	12887
哈巴河县	Habahe [Kaba] County	18203	17986	45058	18541
青河县	Qinghe [Qinggil] County	19683	19552	22441	20669
吉木乃县	Jeminay County	15239	15436	14426	12003
博尔塔拉蒙古自治州	**Bortala Mongol Autonomous Prefecture**	**15456**	**15647**	**13027**	**14174**
博乐市	Bole [Bortala] City	17316	17735	12267	14523
精河县	Jinghe [Jing] County	13353	13428	12672	13020
温泉县	Wenquan [Araxang] County	12006	11881	34519	12988
巴音郭楞蒙古自治州	**Bayangol Mongol Autonomous Prefecture**	**19345**	**18690**	**21105**	**21029**
库尔勒市	Korla City	20442	19983	14546	21158
轮台县	Luntai [Bugur] County	20666	19958	31729	31498
尉犁县	Yuli [Lopnur] County	19494	19408	27437	14889
若羌县	Ruoqiang [Qarkilik] County	23433	20284	24272	38696
且末县	Qiemo [Qarqan] County	22718	22409	40590	10240
焉耆回族自治县	Yanji Hui Autonomous County	19405	19586	26079	16572
和静县	Hejing County	15362	15323	19485	15199
和硕县	Hoxud County	14832	14879	27869	11888
博湖县	Bohu [Bagrax] County	18907	19204	21111	15517
阿克苏地区	**Aksu Administrative Offices**	**18207**	**18445**	**18718**	**16795**
阿克苏市	Aksu City	19588	19909	18908	17716
温宿县	Wensu [Onsu] County	13192	13261	15286	9512
库车县	Kuqa County	15019	16167	16999	11651

3-30 续表 2 Continued

单位：元 (yuan)

地 区	Region	合 计 Total	国有单位 State-owned Units	城镇集体单位 Urban Collective-owned Units	其他单位 Units of Other Types of Ownership
沙雅县	Xayar County	16360	16915	23661	14072
新和县	Xinhe [Toksu] County	18793	20055	17041	14489
拜城县	Baicheng [Bay] County	23407	21150	23652	28162
乌什县	Wushi [Uxturpan] County	18860	19178	18000	13581
阿瓦提县	Awat County	17943	19233	22164	10049
柯坪县	Kalpin County	21179	21303	12159	
克孜勒苏柯尔克孜自治州	**Kizilsu Kirgiz Autonomous Prefecture**	**22990**	**23567**	**10751**	**12149**
阿图什市	Artux City	23730	24489	9588	12766
阿克陶县	Akto County	23557	24208	11035	10894
阿合奇县	Akqi County	23887	23970	15871	
乌恰县	Wuqia [Ulugqat] County	19384	19654	13818	9657
喀什地区	**Kashgar [Kaxgar] Administrative Offices**	**19897**	**20957**	**13069**	**15702**
喀什市	Kashgar [Kaxgar] City	20161	22985	14654	16479
疏附县	Shufu County	21755	22600	8503	
疏勒县	Shule County	21434	24119	13677	13255
英吉沙县	Yengisar County	21970	22498	18615	12587
泽普县	Zepu [Poskam] County	20283	20483	23043	8881
莎车县	Shache [Yarkant] County	18076	18503	12849	10958
叶城县	Yecheng [Kagilik] County	23305	24392	11425	8902
麦盖提县	Makit County	18282	18635	16781	3447
岳普湖县	Yopurga County	20052	20136	14991	
伽师县	Jiashi [Payzawat] County	20753	22051	8677	10239
巴楚县	Bachu [Maralbexi] County	16636	16900	12437	15595
塔什库尔干塔吉克自治县	Taxkorgan Tajik Autonomous County	30046	30240	10974	
和田地区	**Hotan Administrative Offices**	**20936**	**21958**	**12791**	**15086**
和田市	Hotan City	21053	22798	10154	15956
和田县	Hotan County	22531	22981	17413	16481
墨玉县	Moyu [Karakax] County	19045	19291	8900	15832
皮山县	Pishan [Guma] County	17741	18566	12635	11371
洛浦县	Lop County	20411	22650	12898	12476
策勒县	Qira County	24113	24535	14518	21263
于田县	Yutian [Keriya] County	24192	24912	15344	13304
民丰县	Minfeng [Niya] County	26396	26638	17250	22438

主要统计指标解释

人口数 指一定时点、一定地区范围内的有生命的个人的总和。

年度统计的年末人口数指每年 12 月 31 日 24 时的人口数。

市、镇、县人口 其定义有两种口径:

第一种口径(按行政建制)

市人口：市管辖区域内的全部人口(含市辖镇，不含市辖区县);

镇人口：县辖镇的全部人口(不含市辖镇);

县人口：县辖乡人口。

第二种口径(按常住人口划分)

市人口：设区的市的区人口和不设区的市所辖的街道人口;

镇人口：不设区的市所辖镇的居民委员会人口和县辖镇的居民委员会人口;

县人口：除上述两种人口以外的全部人口。

出生率(又称粗出生率) 指在一定时期内(通常为一年)平均每千人所出生的人数的比率，一般用千分率表示。计算公式为:

出生率＝年出生人数／年平均人数×1000‰

式中：出生人数指活产婴儿，即胎儿脱离母体时(不管怀孕月数)，有过呼吸或其他生命现象。年平均人数指年初、年底人口数的平均数，也可用年中人口数代替。

死亡率(又称粗死亡率) 指在一定时期内(通常为一年)一定地区的死亡人数与同期平均人数(或期中人数)之比，一般用千分率表示。计算公式为:

死亡率＝年死亡人数／年平均人数×1000‰

人口自然增长率 指在一定时期内(通常为一年)人口自然增加数(出生人数减死亡人数)与该时期内平均人数(或期中人数)之比，一般用千分率表示。计算公式为:

人口自然增长率＝(本年出生人数－本年死亡人数)／年平均人数×1000‰＝人口出生率－人口死亡率

在业人口(又称就业人口) 指十五周岁及十五周岁以上人口中从事一定的社会劳动并取得劳动报酬或经营收入的人口。

不在业人口 指十五周岁及十五周岁以上人口中未从事社会劳动的人口，包括在校学生、料理家务、待升学、市镇待业、离退休、退职、丧失劳动能力等非在业人口。

经济活动人口 指在 16 岁以上，有劳动能力，参加或要求参加社会经济活动的人口；包括就业人员和失业人员。

各单位的就业人员 指在各级国家机关、政党机关、社会团体及企业、事业单位中工作，取得工资或其他形式的劳动报酬的全部人员。包括在岗职工、再就业的离退休人员、民办教师以及在各单位中工作的外方人员和港澳台方人员、兼职人员、借用的外单位人员和第二职业者。不包括离开本单位仍保留劳动关系的职工。各单位的从业人员反映了各单位实际参加生产或工作的全部劳动力。

城镇私营和个体就业人员 城镇私营就业人员指在工商管理部门注册登记，其经营地址设在县城关镇(含城关镇)以上的私营企业从业人员；包括私营企业投资者和雇工。城镇个体就业人员指在工商管理部门注册登记，并持有城镇户口或在城镇长期居住，经批准从事个体工商经营的从业人员；包括个体经营者和在个体工商户劳动的家庭帮工和雇工。

城镇登记失业人员 指有非农业户口，在一定的劳动年龄内，有劳动能力，无业而要求就业，并在当地就业服务机构进行求职登记的人员。

城镇登记失业率 指城镇登记失业人数同城镇从业人数与城镇登记失业人数之和的比。计算公式为:

城镇登记失业率=城镇登记失业人数／(城镇从业人数+城镇登记失业人数)×100%

职工 指在国有经济、城镇集体经济、联营经济、股份制经济、外商和港、澳、台投资经济、其他经济单位及其附属机构工作，并由其支付工资的各类人员，不包括返聘的离退休人员、民办教师、在国有经济单位工作的外方人员和港、澳、台人员(1998 年以后的数据均为在岗职工数据，其他相关指标如职工工资总额，职工平均工资等指标也从 1998 年按此口径进行了相应调整)。

国有单位职工 指在国有经济单位及其附属机构工作，并由其支付工资的各类人员。

城镇集体单位职工 指在城镇集体经济单位及其管理部门工作，并由其支付工资的各类人员。

其他单位职工 指在联营经济、股份制经济、外商投资经济、港、澳、台投资经济单位工作，并由其支付工资的各类人员。

在岗职工 指在本单位工作并由单位支付工资的人员，以及有工作岗位，但由于学习、病伤产假等原因暂未工作，仍由单位支付工资的人员。

工资总额 指各单位在一定时期内直接支付给本单位全部职工的劳动报酬总额。工资总额的计算原则应以直接支付给职工的全部劳动报酬为根据。各单位支付给职工的劳动报酬以及其他根据有关规定支付的工资，不论是计入成本的还是不计入成本的，不论是按国家规定列入计征奖金税项目的，还是未列入计征奖金税项目的，不论是以货币形式支付的还是以实物形式支付的，均包括在工资总额内。

奖金 指支付给职工的超额劳动报酬和增收节支的劳动报酬。

津贴和补贴 指为了补偿职工特殊或额外的劳动消耗和因其他特殊原因支付给职工的津贴，以及为了保证职工工资水平不受物价影响支付给职工的物价补贴。

平均工资 指企业、事业、机关单位的职工在一定时期内平均每人所得的货币工资额。它表明一定时期职工工资收入的高低程度，是反映职工工资水平的主要指标。计算公式为:

职工平均工资＝报告期实际支付的全部职工工资总额／报告期全部职工平均人数

平均工资指数 指报告期职工平均工资与基期职工平均工资的比率，是反映不同时期职工货币工资水平变动情况的相对数。计算公式为:

职工平均工资指数＝报告期职工平均工资／基期职工平均工资

平均实际工资指数 职工平均实际工资指扣除物价变动因素后的职工平均工资。职工平均实际工资指数是反映实际工资变动情况的相对数，表明职工实际工资水平提高或降低的程度。计算公式为:

职工平均实际工资指数＝报告期职工平均工资指数／报告期城镇居民消费价格指数×100%

Explanatory Notes on Main Statistical Indicators

Total Population refers to the total number of people alive at a certain point of time within a given area.

The annual statistics on total population is taken at midnight,the 3lst of December.

City,Town and County Population Urban Population and Rural Population.

There are two definitions.The first definition (according to the administrative organizational system):

City Population: Total population under the jurisdiction of City (including population of the town under the jurisdiction of City. excluding the population of counties under the jurisdiction of City).

Town Population: Total population of town under the jurisdiction of County (excluding the population of town under the jurisdiction of City).

County Population: Total population of country under the jurisdiction of County).

The second definition (classified by the permanent population):

City Population: Total population of districts under the jurisdiction of City with district establishment and the population of street under the jurisdiction of City without district establishment.

Town Population: Total resident-committees population of towns under the jurisdiction of City without district establishment and the resident-committees population of towns under the jurisdiction of County.

County Population: Total population except City population and town population.

Birth Rate(or Crude Birth Rate) refers to the ratio of the number of births to the average population during a certain period of time(usually a year) which is often expressed in‰. The following formula is used:

Brith Rate= Number of Births/Annual Average Number of Population

Number of births refers to live births i.e. the births when babies had showed any vital phenomena regardless of the length of pregnancy.

Annual average number of population is the average of the number of population at the beginning of the year and that at the end of the year. Sometimes it is substituted for with the mid year population.

Death Rate(or Crude Death Rate) refers to the ratio of the number of deaths to the average population (or mid year population) during a certain period of time (usually a year) which is often expressed in‰. The following formula is used:

Death Rate =Number of Deaths/ Annual Average Number of Population

Natural Growth Rate of Population refers to the ratio of natural increase in population(number of births minus number of deaths)in a certain period of time(usually a year)to the average population(or mid year population)of the same period which is often expressed in‰. The following formula is applied:

Natural Growth Rate of Population= Number of Births-Number of Deaths / Average Number of Population

Natural Growth Rate of Population=Birth Rate-Death Rate

Employed Population refers to population aged 15 or over engaging in social labour which generates income.

Unemployed Population refers to population aged 15 or over not engaging in any social labour which generates income, including students enrolled in schools, house wives,students waiting for entering schools with higher level, urban job seekers, retirees, job quitters, disabled, etc.

Economically Active Population refers to the population aged 16 and over who are capable to work, are participating in or willing to participate in economic activities, including employed persons and unemployed persons.

Persons Employed in Various Units refer to all the persons working in government agencies of various levels, political and party organizations, social organizations, enterprises and institutions, and receiving wages or other forms of payment. They include fully-employed staff and workers, re-employed retirees, teachers in schools run by the local people, foreigners and Chinese compatriots from Hong Kong, Macao, and Taiwan working in various units, part-time employees, employees of other units working temporarily at current posts, and employees holding the second job, but exclude staff and workers who have left their working units while keeping their labour contract (employment relation) unchanged. This indicator reflects the total number of laborers actually engaged in production or other operations in various units.

Persons Employed in Private Enterprises and Self-Employed Individuals in Urban Areas Persons employed in private enterprises refer to the persons employed in the private enterprises which have been registered at the departments of industrial and commercial administration and are situated at a County town (i.e. a town where the County government is located) for business operation or at urban areas with the level higher than a County town. The self-employed individuals in urban areas refer to persons who hold the certificates of residence in urban areas or have resided in the urban areas for a long time and have been registered at the departments of industrial and commercial administration and approved to be engaged in individual industrial or commercial business, including self-employed persons as well as helpers and hired labourers who work in the individual households engaged in industrial or commercial business.

Registered Urban Unemployed Persons The registered unemployed persons in urban areas refer to the persons who are registered as permanent residents in the urban areas engaged in non-agricultural activities, aged within the range of working age, capable to labour, unemployed but desirous to be employed and have been registered at the local employment service agencies to apply for a job.

Registered Urban Unemployment Rate Registered unemployment rate in urban areas refers to the ratio of the number of the registered unemployed persons to the sum of the number of employed persons and the registered unemployed persons . The formula is as follows:

Registered urban unemployment rate = number of registered urban unemployed persons/(number of urban employed persons + number of registered urban unemployed persons) ×100%

Staff and Workers refer to the persons who work in(and receive payment therefrom)enterprises and institutions of state ownership, collective ownership, joint ownership, share holding, foreign ownership, and ownership by entrepreneurs from Hong Kong, Macao, and Taiwan, and other types of ownership and their affiliated units, excluding the retired persons invited to work in the units again, teachers in the schools run by the local people and foreigners and persons coming from Hong Kong, Macao and Taiwan and working in the state-owned economic units. (Number of staff and workers in this yearbook include only fully employed staff and workers, excluding those who have left their working units while keeping their labour contract/employment relation unchanged).

Staff and Workers in State-owned Economic Units refer to the persons who work in the state-owned economic units or their attached units and are listed in their payrolls.

Staff and Workers of Collective Owned Units in Urban Areas refer to the persons who work in collective owned units in urban areas and their administration departments and receive payment therefrom.

Staff and Workers in Units of Other Types of Ownership refer to those who work in(and receive payment therefrom)enterprises and institutions of joint ownership, share holding, foreign ownership, and ownership by entrepreneurs from Hong Kong, Macao, and Taiwan.

Fully Employed Staff and Workers refer to persons who work in, and receive wages from their working units, as well as persons who have their work posts, but are temporarily absent from work for reasons of study or on sick, injury or maternal leave and still receive wages from their working units.

Total Wages refer to the total remuneration payment to staff and workers in various units during a certain period of time. The calculation of total wages is based on the total remuneration payment to the staff and workers. Therefore, all the wages and salaries and other payments to staff and workers are included in the total wages regardless of their sources, category, and forms (in kind or cash). (Total wages of staff and workers in this yearbook include only total wages of fully employed staff and workers, excluding the living allowances distributed to those who have left their working units while keeping their labour contract/employment relation unchanged).

Bonus refers to remuneration payment to workers for extra work and for increasing earnings and practicing economy.

Subsidies and Allowances refer to subsidies paid to staff and workers for compensating special or extra labour and allowances paid to staff and workers to offset the impact of inflation on real wages.

Average Wage refers to the average wage in money terms per person during a certain period of time for staff and workers in enterprises, institutions, and government agencies, which reflects the general level of wage income during a certain period of time and is calculated as follows:

Average Wage of Staff and Workers =Total Wages of Staff and Workers in Reference Period/Average Number of Staff and Workers in Reference Period

Index of Average Wage refers to the ratio of average wage of staff and workers at the report time to that at the reference time. It reflects the relative changing degree of average wage in money terms at the various of time, which is calculated as following:

Index of Average Wage of Staff and Worker = average wage of staff and workers at the report time/average wage of staff and workers at the reference time

Index of Average Real Wage refers to the average wage which has removed the factor of price change. Index of average real wage of staff and worker reflects the relative changing degree of average real wage, and indicates the degree of the rising or declining degree of real wage of staff and worker, which is calculated as following:

Index of Average Real Wage of Staff and Worker = Index of Average Wage of Staff and Worker at the Report Time/Urban Consumer Prices Index at the Report Time

第四篇
固定资产投资

CHAPTER 4
Investment in Fixed Assets

简要说明
Brief Introduction

本篇资料的主要内容及来源

本篇资料包括历年全社会固定资产投资及其主要分组；2007 年及同期的全区固定资产投资及其细化分组；2007 年自治区主要新增生产能力(或效益)；房地产开发企业基本情况。

农户固定资产投资来自国家统计局新疆调查总队商业和投资建筑业调查处；其余资料均来自新疆维吾尔自治区统计局固定资产投资处。

本篇的统计调查方法除农户固定资产投资统计采用抽样调查方法外，其他均为全面调查。

Main Content and Source of Data

Statistics in this chapter cover the total investment in fixed assets of the whole society and its composition, total investment in fixed assets and its refining grouping by region in 2007; newly increased production capacity of major production in 2007; basic condition of enterprises for real estate development.

The data of individual investment in fixed assets in rural areas come from the Trade and Fixed Assets and Construction Census Division of NBS Survey Office in Xinjiang; Others data come from the Division of Investment in Fixed Assets, Xinjiang Bureau of Statistics.

Method of data collection: All data on the investment in fixed assets are collected by the statistical reporting system with complete enumeration, except data on the investment in fixed assets in rural areas which are collected through sample surveys.

4-1 各时期全社会固定资产投资
Total Investment in Fixed Assets in the Whole Country by Period

单位：万元 (10 000 yuan)

年份 Year	合计 Total	城镇 Urban	#房地产 Real Estate Development	农村 Rural	非农户 Non-Rural Households	农村个人 Rural Individuals
1978	129999	129999				
1979	138253	138253				
1980	204652	203489		1163		1163
1981	183986	171706		12280	10000	2280
1982	247382	233668		13714	9693	4021
1983	277923	262027		15896	8804	7092
1984	337250	305713		31537	11089	20448
1985	444758	408435		36323	11528	24795
1986	484658	443631		41027	13934	27093
1987	512479	469898		42581	14714	27867
1988	684119	622041		62078	16848	45230
1989	750698	664243		86455	18841	67614
1990	887775	791555	9456	96220	20578	75642
1991	1249325	1130155	16886	119170	26946	92224
1992	1700326	1571456	23941	128870	33202	95668
1993	2484352	2336810	53616	147542	40738	106804
1994	2854786	2614211	86244	240575	70349	170226
1995	3333404	3035386	171238	298018	92118	205900
1996	3878472	3495942	156232	382530	111936	270594
1997	4468148	3987127	169906	481021	131063	349958
1998	5197673	4709794	148577	487879	136402	351477
1999	5346468	4847597	234481	498871	150744	348127
2000	6103843	5568492	574347	535351	171862	363489
2001	7059970	6469753	979184	590217	210040	380177
2002	8130223	7474024	877060	656199	252891	403308
2003	10021256	9213289	1024908	807967	327137	480830
2004	11615245	10608048	1125577	1007197	463358	543839
2005	13522757	12232255	1016618	1290502	573585	716917
2006	15670521	14180110	1208786	1490411	699084	791327
2007	18508415	16591894	1683160	1916521	1080611	835910

4-2 全社会固定资产投资
Total Investment in Fixed Assets in the Whole Country

单位：万元 (2007 年) (10 000 yuan)

项 目	Item	合 计 Total	城 镇 Urban	#房地产 Real Estate Development
投资总额	**Total Investment**	**18508415**	**16591894**	**1683160**
#住 宅	Residential Buildings	2851187	2258008	1390360
#国有经济控股	State-holding	13199474	12540182	188460
按构成分	**Grouped by Use of Funds**			
建筑工程	Construction	10667717	9497550	1232041
安装工程	Installation	1517359	1469851	89113
设备工器具购置	Purchase of Equipment and Instruments	4312525	3767687	21211
其他费用	Other Expenses	2010814	1856806	340795
按三次产业分	**Grouped by Three Strata of Industry**			
第一产业	Primary Industry	1476457	846093	
第二产业	Secondary Industry	9531482	9118036	
第三产业	Tertiary Industry	7500476	6627765	1683160
按登记注册类型分	**Grouped by Types of Registration**			
内 资	Domestic Fund	18166732	16252497	1600034
国 有	State-owned	6904003	6246911	40697
集 体	Collective-owned	52683	34139	5474
股份合作	Share-holding Cooperative	24229	23979	2962
国有联营	State Joint Ownership	8470	8470	7860
集体联营	Collective Joint Ownership Ownership	3806	3806	
国有与集体联营	Joint State-collective	7327	7327	
其他联营	Others	3230	3130	
国有独资公司	State-funded Corporations	188312	186112	14543
其他有限责任公司	Other Limited Liability Corporations	2919159	2702166	597535
股份有限公司	Share-holding Corporations Ltd	5117940	5114373	19885
私营个体	Private	2818243	1820438	911078
#个体户	Self-employment	176771	152517	
个体合伙	Individual Partenership	10121	6341	
其 他	Others	119330	101646	
港澳台商投资	Enterprises With Funds from Hong Kong, Macao and Taiwan	173382	173382	82828
外商投资	Foreign Funded Enterprises	168301	166015	298
按隶属关系分	**By administrative relationship**			
中 央	Central Government	7643650	7623736	54198
地 方	Local Regions	10864765	8968158	1628962
资金来源小计	**All Sources**	**19070184**	**17152480**	**2243755**
国家预算内资金	State Budget Funds	2258779	1975941	
国内贷款	Domestic Loans	2480410	2352960	217380
债 券	Bonds	5526	5526	
利用外资	Foreign Investment	110034	99056	
自筹资金	Self-raising Funds	11293073	10018160	766344
其他资金来源	Others	2922362	2700837	1260031
本年新增固定资产	**Newly Increased Fixed Assets**	**14303865**	**11303169**	**1164833**
房屋施工面积(万平方米)	**Floor Space of Buildings (10 000 sq.m)**	**8028.33**	**5695.76**	**2053.76**
#住 宅	Residential Buildings	5915.83	3765.45	1715.00
房屋竣工面积(万平方米)	**Floor Space of Buildings Completed (10 000 sq.m)**	**5441.23**	**3327.06**	**890.55**
#住 宅	Residential Buildings	4458.77	2491.60	798.12

4-2 续表 Continued

单位：万元 (10 000 yuan)

项 目	Item	农 村 Rural	非农户 Non-Rural Households	农村个人 Rural Individuals
投资总额	**Total Investment**	**1916521**	**1080611**	**835910**
#住 宅	Residential Buildings	593179	243887	349292
#国有经济控股	State-holding	659292	659292	
按构成分	**Grouped by Use of Funds**			
建筑工程	Construction	1170167	773848	396319
安装工程	Installation	47508	47508	
设备工器具购置	Purchase of Equipment and Instruments	544838	187317	357521
其他费用	Other Expenses	154008	71938	82070
按三次产业分	**Grouped by Three Strata of Industry**			
第一产业	Primary Industry	630364	187462	442902
第二产业	Secondary Industry	413446	326791	86655
第三产业	Tertiary Industry	872711	566358	306353
按登记注册类型分	**Grouped by Types of Registration**			
内 资	Domestic Fund	1914235	1078325	835910
国 有	State-owned	657092	657092	
集 体	Collective-owned	18544	18544	
股份合作	Share-holding Cooperative	250	250	
国有联营	State Joint Ownership			
集体联营	Collective Joint Ownership Ownership			
国有与集体联营	Joint State-collective			
其他联营	Others	100	100	
国有独资公司	State-funded Corporations	2200	2200	
其他有限责任公司	Other Limited Liability Corporations	216993	216993	
股份有限公司	Share-holding Corporations Ltd	3567	3567	
私营个体	Private	997805	161895	835910
#个体户	Self-employment	24254	24254	
个体合伙	Individual Partenership	3780	3780	
其 他	Others	17684	17684	
港澳台商投资	Enterprises With Funds from Hong Kong, Macao and Taiwan			
外商投资	Foreign Funded Enterprises	2286	2286	
按隶属关系分	**By administrative relationship**			
中 央	Central Government	19914	19914	
地 方	Local Regions	1896607	1060697	835910
资金来源小计	**All Sources**	**1917704**	**1081794**	**835910**
国家预算内资金	State Budget Funds	282838	282838	
国内贷款	Domestic Loans	127450	54667	72783
债 券	Bonds			
利用外资	Foreign Investment	10978	10978	
自筹资金	Self-raising Funds	1274913	557401	717512
其他资金来源	Others	221525	175910	45615
本年新增固定资产	**Newly Increased Fixed Assets**	**3000696**	**2164786**	**835910**
房屋施工面积(万平方米)	**Floor Space of Buildings (10 000 sq.m)**	**2332.57**	**799.29**	**1533.28**
#住 宅	Residential Buildings	2150.38	669.70	1480.68
房屋竣工面积(万平方米)	**Floor Space of Buildings Completed (10 000 sq.m)**	**2114.17**	**619.62**	**1494.55**
#住 宅	Residential Buildings	1967.17	524.37	1442.80

4-3 按登记注册类型分全社会固定资产投资
Total Investment in Fixed Assets in the Whole Country by Ownership

单位：万元 (10 000 yuan)

年份 Year	地区 Region	合计 Total	国有经济 State-owned Units	集体经济 Collective -owned Units	股份制经济 Share Holding Economic Units	私营个体经济 Private and Individual Economic Units	其他经济 Others Ownership
	1978	129999	129577	422			
	1985	444758	394075	20962		29721	
	1990	887775	754469	46966		86340	
	1995	3333404	2632775	228951	64695	277981	129002
	1996	3878472	3118118	221641	98490	346949	93274
	1997	4468148	3632454	212601	126912	420005	76176
	1998	5197673	4345893	214143	119361	437207	81069
	1999	5346468	4291067	172851	194894	532104	155552
	2000	6103843	4602642	124466	548224	638511	190000
	2001	7059970	4955062	107561	1084893	820956	91498
	2002	8130223	5623113	78573	1219111	966931	242495
	2003	10021256	6712609	93639	1734211	1284477	196320
	2004	11615245	7599491	86434	2124033	1587304	217983
	2005	13522757	8647683	91172	2733901	1770207	279794
	2006	15670521	9670007	77934	3401195	2213858	307527
	2007	18508415	10086156	80718	5051728	2818243	471570
乌鲁木齐市	Urumqi City	3150310	1312521	20531	823801	742795	250662
克拉玛依市	Karamay City	2861913	1586081	829	1260595	14110	298
石河子市	Shihezi City	549008	438597		65631	34764	10016
吐鲁番地区	Turpan Administrative Offices	613575	176668	3730	402132	27045	4000
哈密地区	Hami [Kumul] Administrative Offices	397082	185550	1099	132207	55999	22227
昌吉回族自治州	Changji Hui Autonomous Prefecture	1125342	383360	14085	528693	191711	7493
伊犁哈萨克自治州	Ili Kazak Autonomous Prefecture	1940315	1027660	11745	579232	288091	33587
伊犁州直属县(市)	Counties (Cities) Direct Under Ili Prefecture	881789	483133	4100	217606	162876	14074
塔城地区	Tacheng [Tarbagatai] Administrative Offices	676355	308034	6655	260294	81859	19513
阿勒泰地区	Altay Administrative Offices	382171	236493	990	101332	43356	
博尔塔拉蒙古自治州	Bortala Mongol Autonomous Prefecture	264830	173397	1202	48340	36935	4956
巴音郭楞蒙古自治州	Bayangol Mongol Autonomous Prefecture	2100681	1413978	1680	428009	239720	17294
阿克苏地区	Aksu Administrative Offices	1133263	580675	4952	353741	163472	30423
克孜勒苏柯尔克孜自治州	Kizilsu Kirgiz Autonomous Prefecture	121096	55221	9205	42005	14415	250
喀什地区	Kashgar [Kaxgar] Administrative Offices	1158147	689185	10374	275218	135396	47974
和田地区	Hotan Administrative Offices	434951	300721	1286	52674	37880	42390
跨地区投资	Trans-regional Investment	1821992	1762542		59450		

注：1.1998 年起国有经济包括国有单位以及国有独资公司、纯国有联营和中国石油天然气公司新疆分公司的投资额。2.股份制经济包括股份有限公司和其他有限责任公司的投资额，但扣除了中石油股份的投资额,以下同。3.各地区按经济类型分的投资中不包括农村个人投资。

Note: a) Since 1998, the state-owned units includes the investment sum of state-owned units and state-owned sole-funded company, state-owned joint-operated and China Petroleum Company. b) Share-holding units includes investment sum from stock limited company and other Limited Liability Corporations,but with investment sum from petroleum share deducted, the same as below. c) Investment classified by economic types in different regions does not include rural individual investment.

4-4 按构成分全社会固定资产投资

Total Investment in Fixed Assets by Composition of Funds

单位：万元 (10 000 yuan)

年份 Year	地区 Region	建筑工程 Construction Works	安装工程 Installation Works	设备工具器具购置 Purchase of Equipment and Instruments	其他费用 Others
	1978	86667		35686	7646
	1985	323395		93254	28109
	1990	571461		274647	41667
	1995	2145762		810995	376647
	1996	2245924	278445	929463	424640
	1997	2725428	310687	988070	443963
	1998	3435120	278895	920992	562666
	1999	3245779	344130	1039617	716942
	2000	3833328	416759	1254077	599679
	2001	4232768	454765	1616907	755530
	2002	4815707	593242	1787899	933375
	2003	6075091	690459	2030335	1225371
	2004	7133323	806705	2304931	1370286
	2005	8499303	993311	2637777	1392366
	2006	9776613	1014851	3166617	1712440
	2007	10667717	1517359	4312525	2010814
乌鲁木齐市	Urumqi City	1678220	229341	847196	395553
克拉玛依市	Karamay City	1152721	581814	803659	323719
石河子市	Shihezi City	202860	96848	202534	46766
吐鲁番地区	Turpan Administrative Offices	362835	46786	139705	64249
哈密地区	Hami [Kumul] Administrative Offices	209449	21138	122427	44068
昌吉回族自治州	Changji Hui Autonomous Prefecture	638433	102910	297197	86802
伊犁哈萨克自治州	Ili Kazak Autonomous Prefecture	1171221	85494	430146	253454
伊犁州直属县(市)	Counties (Cities) Direct Under Ili Prefecture	559600	39629	184558	98002
塔城地区	Tacheng [Tarbagatai] Administrative Offices	386130	34179	180976	75070
阿勒泰地区	Altay Administrative Offices	225491	11686	64612	80382
博尔塔拉蒙古自治州	Bortala Mongol Autonomous Prefecture	165391	12403	67804	19232
巴音郭楞蒙古自治州	Bayangol Mongol Autonomous Prefecture	1433059	140723	362348	164551
阿克苏地区	Aksu Administrative Offices	682357	52559	265842	132505
克孜勒苏柯尔克孜自治州	Kizilsu Kirgiz Autonomous Prefecture	76556	12997	29233	2310
喀什地区	Kashgar [Kaxgar] Administrative Offices	836813	44781	214999	61554
和田地区	Hotan Administrative Offices	324187	23782	26841	60141
跨地区投资	Trans-regional Investment	1337296	65783	145073	273840

4-5 全社会固定资产投资资金来源情况

Sources of Funds of Total Investment in Fixed Assets in the Whole Country

单位：万元 (10 000 yuan)

年 份 Year	地 区 Region	合 计 Total	国家预算内资金 State Budget Funds	国内贷款 Domestic Loans	债 券 Bonds	利用外资 Foreign Investment	自筹及其他资金 Self-raising And Other Funds
	1978	129999	102693				27306
	1985	444758	117439	72227		7708	247384
	1990	887775	105423	294985		40927	446440
	1995	3333404	98004	818914		307619	2108867
	1996	3878472	128725	756412		324532	2668803
	1997	4468148	269106	749345		109629	3340068
	1998	5197673	384195	1116497		133936	3563045
	1999	5346468	512364	1097949	12376	93895	3629884
	2000	6103843	506867	1346175	19429	99942	4131430
	2001	7059970	545176	1321317	8340	64834	5120303
	2002	8130223	1323660	1607535	30504	62992	5105532
	2003	10021256	1626261	1896104	21586	95287	6382018
	2004	11490824	1799593	1555105	46095	87388	8002643
	2005	13543432	2093022	1677020	15428	109968	9647994
	2006	15773966	2119253	1854512	8193	88675	11703333
	2007	19070184	2258779	2480410	5526	110034	14215435
乌鲁木齐市	Urumqi City	3749967	200224	875886		34385	2639472
克拉玛依市	Karamay City	2813631	155096	93265			2565270
石河子市	Shihezi City	570317	26303	231533		15894	296587
吐鲁番地区	Turpan Administrative Offices	613658	52311	22296	1729	1354	535968
哈密地区	Hami [Kumul] Administrative Offices	393914	64413	33571		9584	286346
昌吉回族自治州	Changji Hui Autonomous Prefecture	1145449	86996	199952		4216	854285
伊犁哈萨克自治州	Ili Kazak Autonomous Prefecture	1965825	431487	118626		31140	1384572
伊犁州直属县(市)	Counties (Cities) Direct Under Ili Prefecture	909796	190180	80040		17153	622423
塔城地区	Tacheng [Tarbagatai] Administrative Offices	680591	115292	17949		13897	533453
阿勒泰地区	Altay Administrative Offices	375438	126015	20637		90	228696
博尔塔拉蒙古自治州	Bortala Mongol Autonomous Prefecture	262155	56032	24249			181874
巴音郭楞蒙古自治州	Bayangol Mongol Autonomous Prefecture	2033833	139870	158848		3374	1731741
阿克苏地区	Aksu Administrative Offices	1167950	173505	160472	3797	7913	822263
克孜勒苏柯尔克孜自治州	Kizilsu Kirgiz Autonomous Prefecture	115637	28602	7550			79485
喀什地区	Kashgar [Kaxgar] Administrative Offices	1124417	321846	10633		2174	789764
和田地区	Hotan Administrative Offices	509036	174058	15000			319978
跨地区投资	Trans-regional Investment	1768485	348036	455746			964703

注：1.自 2004 年起资金来源为本年实际到位资金；2.各地区资金来源中不包括农村个人投资额。

Note: a) Sources of capital caculated on actual arrived investment from 2004. b) Sources of Capital from different regions excludes rural individdual investment.

4-6 按行业分全社会固定资产投资
Total Investment in Fixed Assets in the Whole Country by Sector

单位：万元 (10 000 yuan)

行　业	Sector	2006	2007
总　计	**Total**	**15670521**	**18508415**
农、林、牧、渔业	**Agriculture, Forestry, Animal Husbandry and Fishing**	**1324232**	**1476457**
农　业	Agriculture	288521	293873
林　业	Forestry	97286	107118
畜牧业	Animal Husbandry	57756	65698
渔　业	Fishing	1780	1922
农、林、牧、渔服务业	Services Activities for Agriculture, Forestry, Animal Husbandry and Fishing	459632	564944
采矿业	**Mining and Quarrying**	**3745316**	**4548851**
#煤炭开采和洗选业	Mining and Washing of Coal	374026	482247
石油和天然气开采业	Extraction of Petroleum and Natural Gas	3084665	3607573
#天然原油和天然气开采	Extraction of Ores Crude Oil and Natural Gas Extraction	2787675	3360024
黑色金属矿采选业	Mining and Processing of Ferrous Metals Ores	121493	137138
#铁矿采选	Mining and Processing of Iron Ore	117358	135508
有色金属矿采选业	Mining and Processing of Nonferrous Metals Ores	93443	163680
#常用有色金属矿采选	Mining and Processing of Common Non-ferrous Metal	57665	118942
非金属矿采选业	Processing of Nonmetal Ores	70839	156563
#土砂石开采	Mining of Earth and Gravel	13175	11759
化学矿采选	Extracting of Chemical Ore	51745	139765
采　盐	Extracting of Salt	1670	889
制造业	**Manufacturing**	**2303622**	**3551861**
#农副食品加工业	Processing of Food from Agricultural Products	142314	201327
#制　糖	Sugar Making	4618	11355
食品制造业	Manufacture of Food	94725	117432
#液体乳及乳制品制造	Manufacture of Liquid Milk and Dairy Products	25941	27068
饮料制造业	Manufacture of Beverage	59303	70015
烟草加工业	Manufacture of Tobacco		17036
纺织业	Manufacture of Textile	171142	167260
#棉、化纤纺织及印染精加工	Cotton, Chemical Fiber, Dyeing, Printing and Processing	165096	150295
毛纺织和染整精加工	Dyeing and Printing of Wool Textile	106	1414
麻纺织	Manufacture of Flax Textile	1350	2000
纺织服装、鞋、帽制造业	Textile Wearing Apparel,Footware and Caps Manufacturing	1231	14724
皮革、毛皮、羽绒及其制品业	Leather, Fur, Feather and Related Products Manufacturing	5422	3245
木材加工及竹、藤、棕、草制品业	Processing of Timber, Wood, Bamboo, Cane, Grass Products	19967	18172
家具制造业	Furniture Manufacturing	3981	6012
造纸及纸制品业	Paper and Paper Products Manufacturing	47600	37548
印刷业、记录媒介的复制	Printing and Copying of Medium for Record	6363	6968
石油加工及炼焦业	Oil Processing, Coking and Nuclear Fuel Processing	813342	1412818
#精炼石油产品的制造	Manufacture of Oil Products	779480	1252354
炼　焦	Coking	33862	160464
化学原料及化学制品制造业	Raw Chemical Material and Chemical Products	321591	584141
#基础化学原料制造	Basic Chemical Material	183164	374014
肥料制造	Fertilizer Making	58398	40869
医药制造业	Medicine Manufacturing	32023	18079
#中药饮片加工	Processing of Chinese Herbs and Tablet	3372	7210
中成药制造	Manufacture of Chinese Herbs and Patent Medicine	4930	3223
化学纤维制造业	Chemical Fiber Manufacturing	13492	49509

注：该表大类包括农村个人投资，中类未包括。
Note: The major category contains rural individual investment while sub-category excludes it.

4-6 续表 1 Continued

单位：万元 (10 000 yuan)

行　业	Sector	2006	2007
橡胶制品业	Rubber Products Manufacturing	4670	4520
塑料制品业	Plastic Products Manufacturing	70387	84066
非金属矿物制品业	Manufacture of Plastics	129065	238022
#水泥、石灰和石膏的制造	Cement Manufacturing	39323	138170
黑色金属冶炼及压延加工业	Smelting and Pressing of Ferrous Metals	206315	311163
#钢压延加工	Steel Rolling	153769	14471
有色金属冶炼及压延加工业	Smelting and Pressing of Nonferrous Metals	37901	44646
#常用有色金属冶炼	Smeltering of Common Non-ferrous Metal	30318	35750
金属制品业	Metal Products Manufacturing	40443	37865
通用设备制造业	General Purpose Machinery Manufacturing	14053	20832
专用设备制造业	Special Purpose Machinery Manufacturing	15943	31717
交通运输设备制造业	Transport Equipment Manufacturing	4411	13137
#汽车制造	Manufacture of Car	4011	10635
电气机械及器材制造业	Electric Equipment and Machinery Manufacturing	32850	24915
工艺品及其他制造业	Art work and Other Manufacturing Sector	2270	1410
电力、燃气及水的生产和供应业	**Electric Power and Thermal Production and Supply**	**769735**	**1212767**
电力、热力的生产和供应业	Production and Distribution of Electric Power and Heat Power	648201	1053987
电力生产	Production of Electric Power	468077	641489
电力供应	Distribution of Electric Power	103668	319204
热力生产和供应	Production and Distribution of Heat Power	76456	93294
燃气生产和供应业	Gas Production and Supply	69248	74512
水的生产和供应业	Water Production and Supply	51506	84268
#自来水的生产和供应	Production and Distribution of Running Water	46168	73400
污水处理及其再生利用	Treatment and Recycle of Waste Water	5338	10868
建筑业	**Construction**	**186357**	**218003**
#房屋和土木工程建筑业	Buildings and Givil Engineering Construction	97910	129272
建筑安装业	Construction and Installation	4480	2316
交通运输、仓储和邮政业	**Transportation, Storage, Post and Telecommunications Services**	**1825662**	**1679270**
铁路运输业	Railway Transport	287458	319248
道路运输业	Road Transport	1137561	938963
城市公共交通业	Urban Public Transport	35459	5385
航空运输业	Air Transportation	75358	153380
管道运输业	Pipeline Transport	136787	51751
装卸搬运和其他运输服务业	Loading, Discharging and Other Transport Services	1418	1062
仓储业	Storage	41401	91945
邮政业	Post	2887	1004
信息传输、计算机服务和软件业	**Information Transmission, Computer Services and Software**	**395616**	**416007**
#电信和其他信息传输服务业	Telecommunication and Other Information Transmission Services	385275	407166
#电　信	Telecommunication	365117	385508
批发和零售业	**Wholesal&Retail Trades**	**180358**	**238693**
批发业	Wholesale Trades	83660	142032
零售业	Retail Trades	96698	96661
住宿和餐饮业	**Hotel and Catering Services**	**159086**	**119367**
住宿业	Hotels	109903	93028
#旅游饭店	Tourist Restaurant	94290	69183
餐饮业	Catering Service	27871	10250
金融业	**Financial Intermediation**	**35717**	**37935**
银行业	Banks	33880	33986

4-6 续表 2 Continued

单位：万元 (10 000 yuan)

行 业	Sector	2006	2007
保险业	Insurance	1649	3449
其他金融活动	Other Financial Activities	188	500
房地产业	**Real Estate**	**2274944**	**2581400**
#房地产开发与经营业	Real Estate Development and Operation	1299451	1752841
物业管理	Real Estate Management	2898	10488
租赁和商务服务业	**Leasing and Business Services**	**58240**	**61471**
租赁业	Leasing	1509	9080
商务服务业	Business Service	56731	52391
#旅行社	Travel Service	150	1000
科学研究、技术服务和地质勘查业	**Scientific Research, Technical Service and Geological Prospecting**	**138630**	**86693**
研究与试验发展	Research and Experiment Development	8653	12403
专业技术服务业	Professional Technical Service	11366	8656
科技交流和推广服务业	Services of Science and Technology Exchanges and Promotion	4556	6983
地质勘查业	Geologic Prospection	114055	58651
水利、环境和公共设施管理业	**Management of Water Conservancy, Environment and Public Facilities**	**996095**	**1158637**
水利管理业	Management of Water Conservancy	451098	429975
环境管理业	Environmental Management	30550	26018
公共设施管理业	Public Facilities Management	509631	698404
市政公共设施管理	Public Facilities Management	406951	552705
城市绿化管理	Urban Greening Management	25292	87413
游览景区管理	Scenic-Spot Management	77388	58286
居民服务和其他服务业	**Services to Household and Other Services**	**101327**	**47841**
教 育	**Education**	**294301**	**285468**
#初等教育	Junion Education	53563	45250
中等教育	Secondary Education	132173	125592
高等教育	Senior Education	85018	83651
卫生、社会保障和社会福利业	**Health, Social Security and Social Welfare**	**177303**	**147896**
卫 生	Health Care	169829	133321
#医 院	Hospital	147596	111342
专科疾病防治活动	Control Over Special Diseases	165	232
疾病预防控制及防疫活动	Prevention and Control of Diseases	3780	1351
社会保障业	Social Security	1150	2951
社会福利业	Social Welfare	6324	11624
文化、体育和娱乐业	**Culture, Sport and Entertainment**	**96242**	**135064**
新闻出版业	Journalism and Publishing Activities	8915	3680
广播、电视、电影和音像业	Broadcasting,Movies,Televisionsand Audiovisual Activites	9604	15943
文化艺术业	Culture and Art Activities	39733	59527
体 育	Sports	8466	23509
娱乐业	Entertainment	25333	27037
公共管理和社会组织	**Public Management and Social Organization**	**607738**	**504734**
中国共产党机关	Orgars of Communist Party of China	15951	18211
国家机构	Govemment Agencies	575384	453554
人民政协和民主党派	People's Political Consultative Conference and Democratic Parties	3385	1628
群众团体、社会团体和宗教组织	Non-Govemmental Institutions,Social Organizations and Religion Organizations	638	12166
基层群众自治组织	Grassroot Self-governing Organizations	12380	19175

4-7 全社会房屋施工面积、竣工面积
Floor Space of Buildings under Construction and Completed in Whole Country

单位：万平方米 (10 000 sq.m)

年 份 Year	地 区 Region	施工面积 Floor Space under Construction of Buildings	#住 宅 Residential Buildings	竣工面积 Floor Space of Building Completed	#住 宅 Residential Buildings	房屋建筑面积竣工率(%) Completion Rate of Area for House Structure (%)	#住 宅 Residential Buildings
	1985	1670.30	945.76	1327.69	816.26	79.5	86.3
	1990	1740.94	1074.98	1337.06	912.57	76.8	84.9
	1995	2420.38	1368.84	1634.33	1064.14	67.5	77.7
	1996	2952.02	1901.01	2095.58	1441.22	71.0	75.8
	1997	2574.79	1732.19	1903.96	1393.11	73.9	80.4
	1998	2946.76	2057.08	2148.75	1604.68	72.9	78.0
	1999	3439.11	2470.41	2618.98	2020.89	76.2	81.8
	2000	4485.77	2509.17	2633.23	1881.88	58.7	75.0
	2001	4940.70	3282.51	3386.60	2411.78	68.5	73.5
	2002	3986.81	2358.04	2706.44	1790.82	67.9	75.9
	2003	5004.13	2863.92	3599.74	2347.04	71.9	82.0
	2004	5290.77	2999.85	4273.02	2298.56	80.8	76.6
	2005	6677.06	4522.20	4705.07	3618.78	70.5	80.0
	2006	7854.43	5694.75	4773.93	3785.46	60.8	66.5
	2007	8028.32	5915.83	5441.23	4458.77	67.8	75.4
乌鲁木齐市	Urumqi City	1392.39	926.67	597.42	405.07	42.9	43.7
克拉玛依市	Karamay City	138.95	82.83	34.33	28.55	24.7	34.5
石河子市	Shihezi City	174.13	60.01	58.39	41.73	33.5	69.5
吐鲁番地区	Turpan Administrative Offices	63.24	23.84	30.85	11.59	48.8	48.6
哈密地区	Hami [Kumul] Administrative Offices	108.71	62.13	64.46	46.87	59.3	75.4
昌吉回族自治州	Changji Hui Autonomous Prefecture	411.42	231.52	248.93	146.34	60.5	63.2
伊犁哈萨克自治州	Ili Kazak Autonomous Prefecture	742.86	425.60	493.90	313.79	66.5	73.7
伊犁州直属县(市)	Counties (Cities) Direct Under Ili Prefecture	412.01	246.14	278.62	177.47	67.6	72.1
塔城地区	Tacheng [Tarbagatai] Administrative Offices	191.09	113.55	141.27	93.97	73.9	82.8
阿勒泰地区	Altay Administrative Offices	139.76	65.91	74.01	42.35	53.0	64.3
博尔塔拉蒙古自治州	Bortala Mongol Autonomous Prefecture	99.43	70.19	80.31	63.44	80.8	90.4
巴音郭楞蒙古自治州	Bayangol Mongol Autonomous Prefecture	396.91	236.36	240.75	151.30	60.7	64.0
阿克苏地区	Aksu Administrative Offices	569.60	392.22	250.88	160.32	44.0	40.9
克孜勒苏柯尔克孜自治州	Kizilsu Kirgiz Autonomous Prefecture	154.29	44.87	49.41	17.36	32.0	38.7
喀什地区	Kashgar [Kaxgar] Administrative Offices	953.06	729.13	752.99	628.31	79.0	86.2
和田地区	Hotan Administrative Offices	582.79	445.47	453.07	410.38	77.7	92.1
跨地区投资	Trans-regional Investment	707.26	704.31	590.99	590.92	83.6	83.9

注：分地区房屋施工面积、竣工面积未包括农村个人。
Note: Floor space under construction and completed floor space by sectors exclude those in rural areas.

4-8 按登记注册类型分城镇固定资产投资

Investment in Fixed Assets in Urban Area by Ownership

单位：万元 (10 000 yuan)

年份 Year	地区 Region	合计 Total	国有经济 State-owned units	集体经济 Collective-units	股份经济 Share Holding Economic Units	私营个体经济 Private and self-employed Individual Units	其他经济 Others units
	1978	129999	129577	422			
	1985	408435	394075	9434		4926	
	1990	782099	745013	26388		10698	
	1995	2864148	2557165	110671	50452	52330	93530
	1996	3339710	3053423	95182	67620	59513	63972
	1997	3817221	3563371	72775	77859	56774	46442
	1998	4561217	4335338	68840	85200	60390	11449
	1999	4613116	4193644	119262	156254	123414	20542
	2000	4994145	4355629	61316	420926	127630	28644
	2001	5490569	4362352	56558	806119	192431	73109
	2002	6596964	4866673	46269	1293668	269888	120466
	2003	8188381	6009120	71120	1546577	464983	96581
	2004	9482471	6804046	66305	1855399	601094	155627
	2005	11215637	8144930	46375	2144636	672492	207204
	2006	12971324	9248627	63450	2684531	733046	241670
	2007	14908734	9363764	53488	4213748	909360	368374
乌鲁木齐市	Urumqi City	2234568	1260408	12695	613625	180101	167739
克拉玛依市	Karamay City	2795166	1584596	829	1208135	1606	
石河子市	Shihezi City	505194	437222		49371	8585	10016
吐鲁番地区	Turpan Administrative Offices	605481	175618	1950	397018	26895	4000
哈密地区	Hami [Kumul] Administrative Offices	344375	163909	1099	125131	32009	22227
昌吉回族自治州	Changji Hui Autonomous Prefecture	805338	315054	10130	371504	103470	5180
伊犁哈萨克自治州	Ili Kazak Autonomous Prefecture	1495561	919507	3174	392469	159307	21104
伊犁州直属县(市)	Counties (Cities) Direct Under Ili Prefecture	604377	415299	1465	113114	62070	12429
塔城地区	Tacheng [Tarbagatai] Administrative Offices	532523	267715	719	187652	67762	8675
阿勒泰地区	Altay Administrative Offices	358661	236493	990	91703	29475	
博尔塔拉蒙古自治州	Bortala Mongol Autonomous Prefecture	236855	166297	1202	44949	19451	4956
巴音郭楞蒙古自治州	Bayangol Mongol Autonomous Prefecture	1934072	1397535	80	399039	120740	16678
阿克苏地区	Aksu Administrative Offices	951407	549142	4952	275139	92201	29973
克孜勒苏柯尔克孜自治州	Kizilsu Kirgiz Autonomous Prefecture	97553	40436	8955	37925	9987	250
喀什地区	Kashgar [Kaxgar] Administrative Offices	675598	310162	7522	194875	119178	43861
和田地区	Hotan Administrative Offices	405574	281336	900	45118	35830	42390
跨地区投资	Trans-regional Investment	1821992	1762542		59450		

注：城镇投资额未含房地产业，以下同。
Note: Urban Investment exclude real estate, the following the same as follows.

4-9 按构成及建设性质分城镇固定资产投资

Investment in Fixed Assets in Urban Area by Composition of Funds and Type of Construction

单位：万元 (10 000 yuan)

年 份 Year	地 区 Region	合 计 Total	按构成分 By Use of Funds			
			建筑安装工程 Construction and Installation	设备工具器具购置 Purchase of Equipment, Tools and Apparatuses	#用于更新的设备 Update Equipment	其他费用 Others
	1978	129999	86667	35686		7646
	1985	408435	314651	67295	5499	26489
	1990	782099	516443	224673	25153	40983
	1995	2864148	1817364	754369	64612	292415
	1996	3339710	2167304	825067	66119	347339
	1997	3817221	2600884	858958	61094	357379
	1998	4561217	3333948	792449	71986	434820
	1999	4613116	3294346	831951	82363	486819
	2000	4994145	3531280	1103399	104850	359466
	2001	5490569	3638754	1392920	186605	458895
	2002	6596964	4379556	1558818	181920	658590
	2003	8188381	5599787	1718853	105728	869741
	2004	9482471	6451184	2047000	232343	984287
	2005	11215637	7926905	2230165	145514	1058567
	2006	12971324	8943879	2686125	188170	1341320
	2007	14908734	9646247	3746476	177062	1516011
乌鲁木齐市	Urumqi City	2234568	1227477	813076	50678	194015
克拉玛依市	Karamay City	2795166	1676356	803259	10213	315551
石河子市	Shihezi City	505194	261942	202204	1928	41048
吐鲁番地区	Turpan Administrative Offices	605481	403256	138844	1923	63381
哈密地区	Hami [Kumul] Administrative Offices	344375	188868	119383	3052	36124
昌吉回族自治州	Changji Hui Autonomous Prefecture	805338	506117	244226	10008	54995
伊犁哈萨克自治州	Ili Kazak Autonomous Prefecture	1495561	919268	374420	25212	201873
伊犁州直属县(市)	Counties (Cities) Direct Under Ili Prefecture	604377	390116	150060	11857	64201
塔城地区	Tacheng [Tarbagatai] Administrative Offices	532523	312123	159748	12359	60652
阿勒泰地区	Altay Administrative Offices	358661	217029	64612	996	77020
博尔塔拉蒙古自治州	Bortala Mongol Autonomous Prefecture	236855	157163	65248	11839	14444
巴音郭楞蒙古自治州	Bayangol Mongol Autonomous Prefecture	1934072	1450477	351068	4419	132527
阿克苏地区	Aksu Administrative Offices	951407	595662	261029	35299	94716
克孜勒苏柯尔克孜自治州	Kizilsu Kirgiz Autonomous Prefecture	97553	70109	25946		1498
喀什地区	Kashgar [Kaxgar] Administrative Offices	675598	463703	176209	12039	35686
和田地区	Hotan Administrative Offices	405574	322770	26491	4675	56313
跨地区投资	Trans-regional Investment	1821992	1403079	145073	5777	273840

4-9 续表 Continued

单位：万元 (10 000 yuan)

年份 Year	地区 Region	按建设性质分 By Type of Construction 新建 New Construction	扩建 Expansion	改建 Reconstruction	其他 Others
	1978	93462	34399		2138
	1985	110236	160639	116006	21554
	1990	299356	148222	277007	57514
	1995	1067281	886882	646081	263904
	1996	1240585	820966	967022	311137
	1997	1405259	911902	1155121	344939
	1998	1648622	1017786	1338994	555815
	1999	1381764	1226797	1326775	677780
	2000	1410065	1424339	1558514	601227
	2001	891146	2373927	1614961	610535
	2002	1429874	2687996	1984657	494437
	2003	2207269	3128374	2237752	614986
	2004	2358662	3595847	2781101	746861
	2005	3397472	3657464	3063457	1097244
	2006	3633284	5436397	2430373	1471270
	2007	3759028	7439715	2386806	1323185
乌鲁木齐市	Urumqi City	177810	1333024	341859	381875
克拉玛依市	Karamay City	139165	2540941	99637	15423
石河子市	Shihezi City	265897	191790	32728	14779
吐鲁番地区	Turpan Administrative Offices	139820	336760	123270	5631
哈密地区	Hami [Kumul] Administrative Offices	94062	149298	72602	28413
昌吉回族自治州	Changji Hui Autonomous Prefecture	188688	277383	250427	88840
伊犁哈萨克自治州	Ili Kazak Autonomous Prefecture	419474	538211	363739	174137
伊犁州直属县(市)	Counties (Cities) Direct Under Ili Prefecture	96761	235524	187323	84769
塔城地区	Tacheng [Tarbagatai] Administrative Offices	233147	107609	135111	56656
阿勒泰地区	Altay Administrative Offices	89566	195078	41305	32712
博尔塔拉蒙古自治州	Bortala Mongol Autonomous Prefecture	24991	140338	30658	40868
巴音郭楞蒙古自治州	Bayangol Mongol Autonomous Prefecture	1402002	345367	133345	53358
阿克苏地区	Aksu Administrative Offices	429972	175470	254077	91888
克孜勒苏柯尔克孜自治州	Kizilsu Kirgiz Autonomous Prefecture	45616	29145	6019	16773
喀什地区	Kashgar [Kaxgar] Administrative Offices	255941	154895	104612	160150
和田地区	Hotan Administrative Offices	23590	178871	56723	146390
跨地区投资	Trans-regional Investment	152000	1048222	517110	104660

4-10 分行业城镇固定资产投资主要指标

Main Indicators of Investment in Fixed Assets in Urban Area by Sector

(2007 年)

行 业	Sector	投资额 (万元) Total Investment (10 000 yuan)	#地 方 Local	施工项目个数 (个) Number of Projects under Construction (unit)	竣工项目个数 (个) Number of Projects Completed (unit)	本年新增固定资产 (万元) Newly Increased Fixed Assets (10 000 yuan)
总 计	**Total**	**14908734**	**7339196**	**6734**	**4807**	**10138336**
农、林、牧、渔业	**Agriculture, Forestry, Animal Husbandry and Fishery**	**846093**	**534378**	**1049**	**872**	**748962**
农 业	Agriculture	234108	143784	248	192	204626
林 业	Forestry	90501	75621	159	132	74751
畜牧业	Animal Husbandry	37492	31727	87	68	42628
渔 业	Fishing	1072	962	4	2	720
农、林、牧、渔服务业	Activities for Agriculture, Forestry, Animal Husbandry and Fishing	482920	282284	551	478	426237
采矿业	**Mining and Quarrying**	**4444101**	**653509**	**386**	**190**	**3558453**
#煤炭开采和洗选业	Mining and Washing of Coal	410485	361020	167	75	269818
石油和天然气开采业	Extraction of Petroleum and Natural Gas	3605552	15065	16	11	3113598
#天然原油和天然气开采	Extraction of Ores Crude Oil and Natural Gas Extraction	3358003	700	9	6	2894825
黑色金属矿采选业	Processing of Ferrous Metals Ores	114425	114425	66	37	75935
#铁矿采选	Mining and Processing of Iron Ore	114295	114295	66	37	75805
有色金属矿采选业	Processing of Nonferrous Metals Ores	157504	142092	107	53	87964
#常用有色金属矿采选	Mining and Processing of Common Non-ferrous Metal	113331	102076	62	26	54010
非金属矿采选业	Processing of Nonmetal Ores	155657	20429	28	13	10795
#土砂石开采	Mining of Earth and Gravel	11303	11303	13	7	7108
化学矿采选	Extracting of Chemical Ore	139765	5080	3	1	80
采 盐	Extraction of Salt	439	439	2	2	1359
制造业	**Manufacturing**	**3380868**	**1870457**	**985**	**588**	**1157338**
#农副食品加工业	Processing of Food from Agricultural Products	182705	166706	174	130	128636
食品制造业	Manufacture of Food	110827	101627	69	45	73869
#液体乳及乳制品制造	Manufacture of Liquid Milk and Dairy Products	25449	24379	16	10	12588
饮料制造业	Manufacture of Beverage	65730	58915	59	37	51109
纺织业	Manufacture of Textile	163989	136757	64	37	118029
#棉、化纤纺织及印染精加工	Cotton, Chemical Fiber Dyeing, Printing and Processing	147152	120469	51	28	103230
麻纺织	Manufacture of Flax Textile	2000	2000	2	1	900
皮革、毛皮、羽绒及其制品业	Leather, Fur, Feather and Related Products Manufacturing	3245	3245	7	5	3670
木材加工及竹、藤、棕、草制品业	Processing of Timber, Wood, Bamboo, Cane, Grass Products	13743	13293	23	14	12292
家具制造业	Furniture Manufacturing	5732	5732	13	8	4390
造纸及纸制品业	Paper and Paper Products Manufacturing	30391	29603	29	19	28991
印刷业、记录媒介的复制	Printing and Copying of Medium for Record	6228	6119	5	1	4651
石油加工及炼焦业	Oil Processing, Coking and Nuclear Fuel Processing	1397414	249607	41	17	158511
#精炼石油产品的制造	Manufacture of Oil Products	1247093	99414	26	10	122392
炼 焦	Coking	150321	150193	15	7	36119

4-10 续表 1 Continued

行业	Sector	投资额（万元）Total Investment (10 000 yuan)	#地方 Local	施工项目个数（个）Number of Projects under Construction (unit)	竣工项目个数（个）Number of Projects Completed (unit)	本年新增固定资产（万元）Newly Increased Fixed Assets (10 000 yuan)
化学原料及化学制品制造业	Raw Chemical Material and Chemical Products	581405	373140	89	37	165882
#基础化学原料制造	Basic Chemical Material	372948	167143	31	9	33101
肥料制造	Fertilizer Making	39799	39649	23	10	16943
医药制造业	Medicine Manufacturing	18079	18079	17	10	18497
#中药饮片加工	Processing of Chinese Herbs and Tablet	7210	7210	4	3	3841
中成药制造	Manufacture of Chinese Herbs and Patent Medicine	3223	3223	4	3	4170
橡胶制品业	Rubber Products Manufacturing	4320	4320	4	1	832
塑料制品业	Plastic Products Manufacturing	74631	46594	73	49	98093
非金属矿物制品业	Manufacture of Plastics	198946	153877	115	65	83438
#水泥、石灰和石膏的制造	Cement Manufacturing	131162	86996	27	13	29315
黑色金属冶炼及压延加工业	Smelting and Pressing of Ferrous Metals	289213	288782	33	19	40471
#钢压延加工	Steel Rolling	13801	13801	8	6	7543
有色金属冶炼及压延加工业	Smelting and Pressing of Nonferrous Metals	42586	42586	22	12	27686
#常用有色金属冶炼	Smeltering of Common Non-ferrous Metal	35400	35400	16	6	17642
金属制品业	Metal Products Manufacturing	32145	31855	35	24	29803
通用设备制造业	General Purpose Machinery Manufacturing	19372	19372	26	16	15155
专用设备制造业	Special Purpose Machinery Manufacturing	31267	30760	28	15	16261
交通运输设备制造业	Transport Equipment Manufacturing	12627	11355	10	3	4517
#汽车制造	Manufacture of Car	10125	8853	7	3	4517
电气机械及器材制造业	Electric Equipment and Machinery Manufacturing	23950	23113	21	10	19829
电力、燃气及水的生产和供应业	**Electric Power and Thermal Production and Supply**	**1158069**	**496727**	**438**	**285**	**785670**
电力、蒸汽、热水的生产和供应业	Production and Distribution of Electric Power and Heat Power	1003369	370081	256	175	693510
电力生产	Production of Electric Power	634139	219876	59	27	380399
电力供应	Distribution of Electric Power	275996	87341	123	95	260984
热力生产和供应	Production and Distribution of Heat Power	93234	62864	74	53	52127
燃气生产和供应业	Gas Production and Supply	74137	69222	41	19	32910
水的生产和供应业	Water Production and Supply	80563	57424	141	91	59250
#自来水的生产和供应	Production and Distribution of Running Water	69895	48074	125	83	51147
污水处理及其再生利用	Treatment and Recycle of Waste Water	10668	9350	16	8	8103
建筑业	**Construction**	**134998**	**123162**	**88**	**56**	**81933**
#房屋和土木工程建筑业	Buildings and Givil Engineering Construction	129132	118708	84	53	76307
建筑安装业	Construction and Installation	2316	1452			2316

4-10 续表 2 Continued

行　业	Sector	投资额 (万元) Total Investment (10 000 yuan)	#地 方 Local	施工项目个数 (个) Number of Projects under Construction (unit)	竣工项目个数 (个) Number of Projects Completed (unit)	本年新增固定资产 (万元) Newly Increased Fixed Assets (10 000 yuan)
交通运输、仓储和邮政业	**Transportation, Storage, Post and Telecommunications Services**	**1458349**	**898822**	**484**	**335**	**736441**
铁路运输业	Railway Transport	319248	3000	9	4	51179
道路运输业	Road Transport	840239	663340	373	263	471256
城市公共交通业	City Public Transport	5385	4055	5	5	5133
航空运输业	Air Transportation	153380	141340	20	12	109593
管道运输业	Pipeline Transport	51751	5581	4	3	29781
仓储业	Storage	86580	80854	70	46	68543
邮政业	Post	704	400	1	1	704
信息传输、计算机服务和软件业	**Information Transmission, Computer Services and Software**	**407281**	**194300**	**94**	**80**	**381761**
#电信和其他信息传输服务业	Telecommunication and Other Information Transmission Services	402744	190234	89	75	373957
#电　信	Telecommunication	382286	178708	71	61	364456
批发和零售业	**Wholesale&Retail Trades**	**220206**	**195068**	**177**	**139**	**206958**
批发业	Wholesale Trades	132776	122339	83	64	116718
零售业	Retail Trades	87430	72729	94	75	90240
住宿和餐饮业	**Hotels and Catering Services**	**93973**	**87463**	**111**	**80**	**143183**
#住宿业	Hotels	84123	77613	95	69	129154
#旅游饭店	Tourist Restaurant	62743	58395	51	34	110510
金融业	**Financial Intermediation**	**37935**	**16152**	**30**	**24**	**44866**
银行业	Banks	33986	14692	26	22	41743
保险业	Insurance	3449	960	4	2	2623
其他金融活动	Others	500	500			500
房地产业	**Real Estate**	**537995**	**406019**	**482**	**402**	**518159**
#房地产开发与经营业	Real Estate Development and Operation	68811	68811	69	48	71828
物业管理	Real Estate Management	488	238	2	1	488
租赁和商务服务业	**Leasing and Business Services**	**58246**	**53372**	**49**	**26**	**31582**
租赁业	Leasing	6992	6992			6992
商务服务业	Business Service	51254	46380	49	26	24590
#旅行社	Travel Service	1000	1000	1	1	1000
科学研究、技术服务和地质勘查业	**Scientific Research, Technical Service and Geological Prospecting**	**71860**	**59580**	**80**	**50**	**57000**
研究与试验发展	Research and Experiment Development	12403	3620	10	4	3213
专业技术服务业	Professional Technical Service	8656	6825	20	12	5771
科技交流和推广服务业	Services of Science and Technology Exchanges and Difussion	3400	2970	10	7	4385

4-10 续表 3 Continued

行　业	Sector	投资额（万元）Total Investment (10 000 yuan)	#地方 Local	施工项目个数（个）Number of Projects under Construction (unit)	竣工项目个数（个）Number of Projects Completed (unit)	本年新增固定资产（万元）Newly Increased Fixed Assets (10 000 yuan)
地质勘查业	Geologic Prospection	47401	46165	40	27	43631
水利、环境和公共设施管理业	**Management of Water Conservancy, Environment and Public Facilities**	**1040220**	**882499**	**743**	**549**	**686842**
水利管理业	Management of Water Conservancy	352637	270932	219	137	162073
环境管理业	Environmental Management	24188	20460	47	26	20491
公共设施管理业	Management of Public Facilities	663395	591107	477	386	504278
市政公共设施管理	Management of Public Facilities	529077	460015	349	281	388606
城市绿化管理	Management of Urban Greening	87413	84885	70	62	73746
游览景区管理	Scenic-Spot Management	46905	46207	58	43	41926
居民服务和其他服务业	**Resident Service and Other Services**	**13984**	**13347**	**36**	**23**	**10498**
教　育	**Education**	**269064**	**221266**	**455**	**345**	**235968**
#初等教育	Elementary Education	37408	32492	114	92	39392
中等教育	Secondary Education	119808	87619	243	189	109451
高等教育	Higher Education	83651	74353	43	25	70860
卫生、社会保障和社会福利业	**Health, Social Security and Social Welfare**	**142415**	**115549**	**244**	**180**	**213505**
卫　生	Health Care	128668	103767	208	156	204567
#医　院	Hospital	111192	91463	137	98	183244
专科疾病防治活动	Prerention and Control of Special Diseases	232	232			232
疾病预防控制及防疫活动	Prevention and Control of Diseases	1351	1070	7	5	4805
社会保障业	Social Security	2951	1360	10	7	1849
社会福利业	Social Welfare	10796	10422	26	17	7089
文化、体育和娱乐业	**Culture, Sport and Entertainment**	**125672**	**113553**	**188**	**136**	**73191**
新闻出版业	Journalism and Publishing Activities	3680	3586	3	2	1301
广播、电视、电影和音像业	Broadcasting,Movies,Televisions and Audiovisual Activites	15943	13581	33	28	10856
文化艺术业	Culture and Art Activities	57108	47445	105	80	35290
体　育	Sports	23409	23409	19	9	15309
娱乐业	Entertainment	25532	25532	28	17	10435
公共管理和社会组织	**Public Management and Social Organization**	**467405**	**403973**	**615**	**447**	**466026**
中国共产党机关	Orgars of Communist Party of China	8838	8838	18	15	10408
国家机构	Govemment Agencies	431616	368184	551	400	438367
人民政协和民主党派	People's Political Consultative Conference and Democratic Parties	1554	1554	4	3	604
群众团体、社会团体和宗教组织	Non-Govemmental Institutions,Social Organizations and Religion Organizations	12166	12166	11	7	8546
基层群众自治组织	Grassroot Self-governing Organizations	13231	13231	31	22	8101

4-11 各地、州、市、县(市)城镇固定资产投资和新增固定资产

Total Investment and Newly Increased Fixed Assets in Urban Area by Prefecture, Autonomous Prefecture, City and County

单位：万元 (2007 年) (10 000 yuan)

地 区 Region	投资总额 Total Investment	第一产业 Primary Industry	第二产业 Secondary Industry	第三产业 Tertiary Industry	新增固定资产 Newly Increased Fixed Assets	房屋建筑面积(万平方米) Floor Space of Buildings (10 000sq.m) 施工面积 Floor Space Under Construction	竣工面积 Floor Space Completed
总 计 Total	**14908734**	**846093**	**9118036**	**4944605**	**10138336**	**3642.00**	**2436.51**
按隶属关系分 By administrative relationship							
中 央 Central government	7569538	311715	5974181	1283642	5131201	511.39	332.80
地 方 Local	7339196	534378	3143855	3660963	5007135	3130.61	2103.71
按区域分 Grouped by Region							
乌鲁木齐市 Urumqi City	**2234568**	**12863**	**1090032**	**1131673**	**1630580**	**463.00**	**254.15**
#乌鲁木齐县 Urumqi County	22596		19387	3209	4340	1.60	1.60
克拉玛依市 Karamay City	**2795166**	**9491**	**2627185**	**158490**	**1628176**	**46.02**	**6.13**
石河子市 Shihezi City	**505194**	**3837**	**433223**	**68134**	**192924**	**119.27**	**22.30**
吐鲁番地区 Turpan Administrative Offices	**605481**	**30918**	**500327**	**74236**	**423368**	**55.20**	**26.04**
吐鲁番市 Turpan City	103311	10845	69655	22811	32875	16.22	4.41
鄯善县 Shanshan [Piqan] County	432420	10337	395390	26693	367987	22.87	21.63
托克逊县 Toksun County	69750	9736	35282	24732	22506	16.11	
哈密地区 Hami [Kumul] Administrative Offices	**344375**	**27633**	**208979**	**107763**	**208063**	**67.66**	**36.43**
哈密市 Hami [Kumul] City	238499	25087	122800	90612	176456	55.38	34.91
巴里坤哈萨克自治县 Barkol Kazak Autonomous County	34998	1984	21395	11619	26833	11.33	0.63
伊吾县 Yiwu [Araturuk] County	70878	562	64784	5532	4774	0.95	0.89
昌吉回族自治州 Changji Hui Autonomous Prefecture	**805338**	**84671**	**431297**	**289370**	**682198**	**196.69**	**134.32**
昌吉市 Changji City	291618	29147	133219	129252	238790	101.43	66.09
阜康市 Fukang City	148847	3076	108110	37661	76895	7.75	5.82
呼图壁县 Hutubi County	110226	18265	44626	47335	105123	35.36	28.97
玛纳斯县 Manas County	150039	21841	87502	40696	172064	27.59	14.95
奇台县 Qitai County	48524	9865	25718	12941	50270	6.48	4.60
吉木萨尔县 Jimsar County	48572	1967	29658	16947	31319	12.20	8.75
木垒哈萨克自治县 Mori Kazak Autonomous County	7512	510	2464	4538	7737	5.89	5.14

4-11 续表 1 Continued

单位：万元 (10 000 yuan)

地区 Region	投资总额 Total Investment	第一产业 Primary Industry	第二产业 Secondary Industry	第三产业 Tertiary Industry	新增固定资产 Newly Increased Fixed Assets	房屋建筑面积(万平方米) Floor Space of Buildings (10 000sq.m) 施工面积 Floor Space Under Construction	竣工面积 Floor Space Completed
伊犁哈萨克自治州 Ili Kazak Autonomous Prefecture	**1495561**	**207625**	**637320**	**650616**	**1299864**	**424.50**	**305.45**
伊犁州直属县(市) Counties (Cities) Direct Under Ili Prefecture	**604377**	**46768**	**249381**	**308228**	**547392**	**203.78**	**156.41**
伊宁市 Yining [Gulja] City	118066		34501	83565	110709	46.39	35.70
奎屯市 Kuytun City	141020	120	72412	68488	115613	25.43	20.61
伊宁县 Yining [Gulja] County	30254	2631	18250	9373	29709	19.60	9.05
察布查尔锡伯自治县 Qapqal Xibe Autonomous County	71630	10708	45234	15688	56558	19.53	15.71
霍城县 Huocheng [Korgas] County	111891	11117	50615	50159	79090	32.38	19.66
巩留县 Gongliu [Tokkuztara] County	15995	2017	4334	9644	20351	3.76	3.29
新源县 Xinyuan [Kunes] County	44300	7890	5135	31275	49269	16.61	15.34
昭苏县 Zhaosu [Mongolkure] County	21428	4628	6287	10513	19638	13.74	11.73
特克斯县 Tekes County	25604	5791	2954	16859	30931	16.06	16.06
尼勒克县 Nilka County	24189	1866	9659	12664	35524	10.28	9.26
塔城地区 Tacheng [Tarbagatai] Administrative Offices	**532523**	**108424**	**256996**	**167103**	**492751**	**117.95**	**89.79**
塔城市 Tacheng [Qoqek] City	46219	11036	8579	26604	34417	10.51	4.93
乌苏市 Usu City	128342	28580	68468	31294	148091	27.26	24.05
额敏县 Emin Ciunty	77967	15170	33537	29260	61146	20.64	19.35
沙湾县 Shawan County	147888	38576	63745	45567	142023	33.80	29.39
托里县 Toli County	48626	2643	41470	4513	51459	5.01	2.11
裕民县 Yumin [Qagantokay] County	14972	1360	2938	10674	16502	10.08	5.97
和布克赛尔蒙古自治县 Hoboksar Mongol Autonomous County	68509	11059	38259	19191	39113	10.65	3.99
阿勒泰地区 Altay Administrative Offices	**358661**	**52433**	**130943**	**175285**	**259721**	**102.77**	**59.25**
阿勒泰市 Altay City	69785	8293	17999	43493	55839	20.81	14.26
布尔津县 Burqin County	69820	5756	26650	37414	58455	25.41	9.35
富蕴县 Fuyun [Koktokay] County	96749	10666	52150	33933	49767	12.69	8.04
福海县 Fuhai [Burultokay] County	30334	9272	7133	13929	29499	8.94	6.38
哈巴河县 Habahe [Kaba] County	47807	10558	19106	18143	31854	17.11	9.80

4-11 续表 2 Continued

单位：万元 (10 000 yuan)

地区 Region	投资总额 Total Investment	第一产业 Primary Industry	第二产业 Secondary Industry	第三产业 Tertiary Industry	新增固定资产 Newly Increased Fixed Assets	房屋建筑面积(万平方米) Floor Space of Buildings (10 000sq.m) 施工面积 Floor Space Under Construction	竣工面积 Floor Space Completed
青河县 Qinghe [Qinggil] County	28250	4945	6734	16571	24498	11.16	7.83
吉木乃县 Jeminay County	15916	2943	1171	11802	9809	6.65	3.59
博尔塔拉蒙古自治州 Bortala Mongol Autonomous Prefecture	**236855**	**23864**	**72921**	**140070**	**186713**	**68.53**	**54.56**
博乐市 Bole [Bortala] City	165845	12209	45886	107750	120621	34.47	24.39
精河县 Jinghe [Jing] County	53323	6267	24047	23009	48544	27.91	24.87
温泉县 Wenquan [Araxang] County	17687	5388	2988	9311	17548	6.15	5.30
巴音郭楞蒙古自治州 Bayangol Mongol Autonomous Prefecture	**1934072**	**102246**	**1532515**	**299311**	**1329023**	**188.95**	**133.63**
库尔勒市 Korla City	1367009	29259	1187638	150112	1006114	75.18	53.96
轮台县 Luntai [Bugur] County	88249	11277	44474	32498	81019	24.32	21.61
尉犁县 Yuli [Lopnur] County	76706	13573	9482	53651	98450	33.62	26.45
若羌县 Ruoqiang [Qarkilik] County	152325	3729	137773	10823	12563	4.30	2.54
且末县 Qiemo [Qarqan] County	24065	3349	13570	7146	9710	7.19	0.97
焉耆回族自治县 Yanqi Hui Autonomous County	52497	10273	28139	14085	45725	17.25	10.40
和静县 Hejing County	128134	17209	101166	9759	37289	13.77	9.11
和硕县 Hoxud County	31702	8958	8360	14384	31517	8.47	7.57
博湖县 Bohu [Bagrax] County	13385	4619	1913	6853	6636	4.85	1.02
阿克苏地区 Aksu Administrative Offices	**951407**	**153207**	**466839**	**331361**	**674670**	**275.63**	**169.03**
阿克苏市 Aksu City	378674	78065	152800	147809	265639	88.01	53.56
温宿县 Wensu [Onsu] County	92179	24809	38932	28438	88115	28.75	27.70
库车县 Kuqa County	237976	15852	137068	85056	99386	52.81	16.18
沙雅县 Xayar County	61295	2970	39092	19233	30786	13.10	4.30
新和县 Xinhe [Toksu] County	27074	8407	15983	2684	20927	5.62	4.78
拜城县 Baicheng [Bay] County	72228	1282	56483	14463	110732	36.16	15.36
乌什县 Wushi [Uxturpan] County	27917	9209	4719	13989	27167	38.45	38.45
阿瓦提县 Awat County	45868	11610	16874	17384	25587	4.80	4.02
柯坪县 Kalpin County	8196	1003	4888	2305	6331	7.93	4.68

4-11 续表 3 Continued

单位：万元 (10 000 yuan)

地区 Region	投资总额 Total Investment	第一产业 Primary Industry	第二产业 Secondary Industry	第三产业 Tertiary Industry	新增固定资产 Newly Increased Fixed Assets	房屋建筑面积(万平方米) Floor Space of Buildings (10 000sq.m) 施工面积 Floor Space Under Construction	竣工面积 Floor Space Completed
克孜勒苏柯尔克孜自治州 Kizilsu Kirgiz Autonomous Prefecture	**97553**	**1853**	**42671**	**53029**	**98353**	**142.71**	**41.07**
阿图什市 Artux City	42978	1280	12512	29186	60970	115.61	32.03
阿克陶县 Akto County	30535	340	17816	12379	25846	7.26	5.18
阿合奇县 Akqi County	6685	233	3358	3094	2628	7.83	1.23
乌恰县 Wuqia [Ulugqat] County	17355		8985	8370	8909	12.01	2.63
喀什地区 Kashgar [Kaxgar] Administrative Offices	**675598**	**46468**	**208400**	**420730**	**610558**	**321.44**	**220.97**
喀什市 Kashgar [Kaxgar] City	266389	17339	64237	184813	255014	124.39	67.04
疏附县 Shufu County	16706		3345	13361	17900	15.10	10.58
疏勒县 Shule County	93642	5811	35415	52416	76678	41.89	32.48
英吉沙县 Yengisar County	5409	64	3297	2048	4759	3.17	1.85
泽普县 Zepu [Poskam] County	26161	1063	14350	10748	16660	18.42	12.92
莎车县 Shache [Yarkant] County	26228	2000	7962	16266	27752	16.75	14.86
叶城县 Yecheng [Kagilik] County	43746	167	28609	14970	28349	16.87	15.18
麦盖提县 Makit County	42699	11178	16840	14681	52588	12.86	11.06
岳普湖县 Yopurga County	25193	749	4858	19586	24528	21.50	21.50
伽师县 Jiashi [Payzawat] County	23922	5994	6124	11804	20238	21.84	10.82
巴楚县 Bachu [Maralbexi] County	59797	2103	13863	43831	75975	26.00	20.03
塔什库尔干塔吉克自治县 Taxkorgan Tajik Autonomous County	45706		9500	36206	10117	2.65	2.65
和田地区 Hotan Administrative Offices	**405574**	**37524**	**105875**	**262175**	**297144**	**565.12**	**441.45**
和田市 Hotan City	112258	1310	22085	88863	85486	161.51	63.88
和田县 Hotan County	68065	3322	40650	24093	36578	57.23	55.90
墨玉县 Moyu [Karakax] County	89918	17632	29344	42942	54384	81.50	70.57
皮山县 Pishan [Guma] County	46739	5849	3543	37347	49278	139.09	134.23
洛浦县 Lop County	38896	5059	5212	28625	30887	73.32	67.36
策勒县 Qira County	7667	1260	168	6239	6008	2.45	1.34
于田县 Yutian [Keriya] County	33841	2171	3646	28024	26983	44.63	43.64
民丰县 Minfeng [Niya] County	8190	921	1227	6042	7540	5.39	4.53
跨地区投资 Trans-regional Investment	**1821992**	**103893**	**760452**	**957647**	**876702**	**707.27**	**590.97**

4-12 各地、州、市分行业城镇固定资产投资

单位：万元 (2007 年)

行业 Sector	合计 Total	乌鲁木齐市 Urumqi City	克拉玛依市 Karamay City	石河子市 Shihezi City	吐鲁番地区 Turpan Administrative Offices	哈密地区 Hami [Kumul] Administrative Offices	昌吉回族自治州 Changji Hui Autonomous Prefecture
总计 Total	**14908734**	**2234568**	**2795166**	**505194**	**605481**	**344375**	**805338**
农、林、牧、渔业 Farming, Forestry, Animal Husbandry and Fishery	846093	12863	9491	3837	30918	27633	84671
采矿业 Mining and Quarrying	4444101	92461	1396051		405433	137935	93744
制造业 Manufacturing	3380868	701780	1201187	259788	53553	51284	174011
电力、燃气及水的生产和供应业 Electric Power, Gas and Water Production and Supply	1158069	273291	7999	172293	41016	19760	160214
建筑业 Construction	134998	22500	21948	1142	325		3328
交通运输、仓储及邮政业 Transportation, Storage, Postal and Telecommunications Services	1458349	212914	6254	14660	17575	39170	63776
信息传输、计算机服务和软件业 Message Transmission, Computer and Software Service	407281	216065		5019	2876	3364	6179
批发和零售业 Wholesale&Retail Trades	220206	46647	794	5487	1110	3202	30799
住宿和餐饮业 Hotels and Catering Services	93973	10852	7168	483	3273	3602	5042
金融业 Financial Intermediation	37935	30455	558			305	160
房地产业 Real Estate	537995	40013	2567	3937	4493	10630	47418
租赁和商务服务业 Leasing and Business Services	58246	5740	2592		600	52	4030
科学研究、技术服务和地质勘查业 Scientific Research, Technical Service and Geological Prospection	71860	13634		90	2070	606	3843
水利、环境和公共设施管理业 Water Conservancy, Environment and Public Facilities	1040220	229209	75607	13883	29008	22291	85635
居民服务和其他服务业 Service to Households and Others Services	13984	7631	1005	58		326	1265
教育 Education	269064	95717	23430	18940	4519	3599	9655
卫生、社会保障和社会福利业 Health, Social Security and Social Welfare	142415	62569	1897	1450	4006	4395	9120
文化、体育和娱乐业 Culture, Sports and Entertainment	125672	18718	16852	2011	2028	11029	8937
公共管理和社会组织 Public Management and Social Organization	467405	141509	19766	2116	2678	5192	13511

Investment in Fixed Assets in Urban Area by Sectors in Prefecture, Autonomous Prefecture and City

(10 000 yuan)

伊犁哈萨克自治州 Ili Kazak Autonomous Prefecture	伊犁州直属县(市) Counties (Cities) Direct Under Ili Prefecture	塔城地区 Tacheng [Tarbagatai] Administrative Offices	阿勒泰地区 Altay Administrative Offices	博尔塔拉蒙古自治州 Bortala Mongol Autonomous Prefecture	巴音郭楞蒙古自治州 Bayangol Mongol Autonomous Prefecture	阿克苏地区 Aksu Administrative Offices	克孜勒苏柯尔克孜自治州 Kizilsu Kirgiz Autonomous Prefecture	喀什地区 Kashgar [Kaxgar] Administrative Offices	和田地区 Hotan Administrative Offices	跨地区投资 Trans-regional Investment
1495561	**604377**	**532523**	**358661**	**236855**	**1934072**	**951407**	**97553**	**675598**	**405574**	**1821992**
207625	46768	108424	52433	23864	102246	153207	1853	46468	37524	103893
183101	53133	53900	76068	1021	1215987	74930	31682	43586	7718	760452
266186	125686	125521	14979	57538	234510	183683	4086	134906	58356	
177914	62333	76925	38656	14137	82018	145768	3240	22507	37912	
10119	8229	650	1240	225		62458	3663	7401	1889	
126014	39014	34571	52429	17477	71976	71993	10667	36765	17061	752047
18966	6478	7619	4869	7506	3549	9989	3106	30415	4647	95600
28269	20184	3572	4513	17177	9259	17566	3500	51241	5155	
35071	5874	15053	14144	2178	4376	3262	1060	9917	7689	
1668	400	1028	240	91	800	518		1458	1922	
97810	49257	33922	14631	22458	36660	41217	9734	83223	137835	
18464	17107	1257	100	322	12005	2250	1120	11071		
37715	2218		35497	189	2221	2618	630	7676	568	
154998	92954	40278	21766	45418	95225	74546	2092	78495	23813	110000
541	123	291	127			1338		310	1510	
25430	12596	6968	5866	5036	13261	26104	5634	24616	13123	
20412	10021	7406	2985	3060	8414	11317	2832	7150	5793	
20675	5572	8954	6149	2647	3670	12576	732	16543	9254	
64583	46430	6184	11969	16511	37895	56067	11922	61850	33805	

4-13 城镇固定资产投资效果指标

Investment Result of Urban Investment

指 标	Item	2006	2007
建设周期(年)	Construction Cycle (year)	2.2	2.3
计划总投资(万元)	Total Planned Investment (10 000 yuan)	28883016	34418795
本年完成投资(万元)	Completed Invetsment for the Current Year (10 000 yuan)	12971324	14908734
本年新增固定资产(万元)	Newly Increased Fixed Assets for the Current Year (10 000 yuan)	10831849	10138336
固定资产交付使用率(%)	Rate of Project of Fixed Assets Put into Operation (%)	83.5	68.0
施工项目个数(个)	Number of Projects under Construction (unit)	6459	6734
竣工项目个数(个)	Number of Projects Completed (unit)	4627	4807
建设项目投产率(%)	Rate of Projects Completed Put into Use (%)	71.6	71.4
施工面积(万平方米)	Construction Area (10 000 sq.m)	4297.87	3642.00
#住 宅	Residential Buildings	2785.74	2050.45
竣工面积(万平方米)	Completed Area (10 000 sq.m)	2380.65	2436.51
#住 宅	Residential Buildings	1660.46	1693.49
房屋面积竣工率(%)	Rate of Floor Space of Buildings Completed (%)	55.4	66.9
#住 宅	Residential Buildings	59.6	82.6

4-14 房地产开发企业基本情况

Basic Condition of Enterprises for Real Estate Development

指 标	Item	2000	2005	2007
企业单位数(个)	**Number of Enterprises (unit)**	**209**	**756**	**909**
#亏损企业	Loss- Suffering Enterprises	101	410	461
从业人员数(人)	**Number of Persons Engaged in the Sector (person)**	**10311**	**15558**	**19589**
从业人员劳动报酬(万元)	**Work Pay for Employees (10 000 yuan)**	**10706**	**27184**	**41589**
主要财务指标 (万元)	**Main Financial Indices (10 000 yuan)**			
年末资产负债情况	Situation of Year-end Liabilities			
资产总计	Total Assets	1332444	4861415	5782980
固定资产累计折旧	Accumulated Depreciation of Fixed Assets	15027	81096	108464
#本年折旧	Depreciation for the Current Year	4450	17981	23043
负债总计	Total Liabilities	1081934	2932694	3867190
所有者权益合计	Total of Owner's Right and Interest	250510	1928721	1915790
实收资本合计	Total of Actual Capital	200762	970103	1257459
#国家资本	State-owned Capital	21344	59976	85659
损益情况	Situation of Profit and Loss			
经营收入总计	Total Income of Business	342400	1084796	2020930
土地转让收入	Income of Land Transfer		11295	1140
商品房销售收入	Sales Income of Commercial Flat	319460	1047965	1972731
房屋出租收入	Income of Renting House	2558	15773	24446
其他收入	Other Income	20382	9763	22613
经营成本	Cost of Business	272611	871320	1586881
经营税金及附加	Tax and Extra Charges on Business	17697	63562	126986
销售费用	Expenses of sales	9711	27319	61032
其他业务利润	Other Business Profits	2167	9161	12332
管理费用及财务费用	Expenses of both Management and Finance	34988	80949	148877
投资收益及营业外收入	Income of Investment earnings and Extra-business	2395	7829	15907
营业外支出	Expenditure of Extra-business	2060	3456	7529
利润总额	Total Profits	9895	55180	117864

注：2004 年以后，企业个数包括了没有开发量的企业数，而往年未包括。
Note: Since 2004, the number of enterprises yet to be developed while the previous years fail to contain those.

4-15 房地产投资主要指标
Main Indicators of Real Estate Investment

指标	Item	2000	2005	2007
本年购置土地面积(万平方米)	**Land Area Purchased for the Current Year (10 000 Sq. m)**	**496.02**	**447.30**	**672.47**
#完成开发土地面积	Land Area Completed for Development	248.21	478.54	611.50
房地产开发投资额(万元)	**Total Investment of Real-Estate Development (10 000 yuan)**	**574347**	**1016618**	**1683160**
#商品房建设投资	Investment in Commercial Flat	510144	874232	
土地开发投资	Investment in Land Development	34057	50588	146796
按中央和地方分	Classified by Central and Local			
中央企业	Central Enterprises	50536	54128	54198
地方企业	Local Enterprises	523811	962490	1628962
按经济类型分	Classified by Economic Ownership			
国有单位	State-owned Enterprises	126304	37243	63100
集体单位	Collective-owned Enterprises	13618	3971	8436
私营及个体	Private-owned and Self-employed	131935	332644	911078
其他单位	Other Enterprises	302490	642760	700546
按投资构成分	Classified by Use of Funds			
建筑工程	Construction Works	419216	810003	1232041
安装工程	Works of Installation	7568	49559	89113
设备工器具购置	Purchase of Equipment and Instruments	21845	14135	21211
其他费用	Other Expenses	125718	142921	340795
#土地购置费	Expenses of Land Purchase	73811	94230	249430
按工程用途分	Classified by Purpose of Projects			
住　宅	Residential buildings	500381	679521	1390360
办公楼	Office Building	13171	40977	27629
商业营业用房	Houses for Commercial and Business Purpose	42601	247033	205590
其　他	Others	18194	49087	59581
本年资金来源小计 (万元)	**Sub-total of Capital Sources for the Current Year (10 000 yuan)**	**701332**	**1137693**	**2243755**
国内贷款	Domestic Loans	113823	113887	217380
利用外资	Foreign Investment	600	160	
自筹资金	Self-raising Funds	232768	479948	766344
其它资金	Others	354141	543698	1260031

4-16 按用途分房地产开发企业（单位）投资完成额

Investment Actually Completed by Enterprises for Real Estate Development by Use

单位：万元 (10 000 yuan)

年份 Year	地区 Region	企业个数(个) Number of Enterprises (unit)	本年完成投资 Investment Completed This Year	住宅 Residential Buildings	#别墅、高档公寓 Villas, High-grade Apartments	#经济适用房 Economically Affordable Housing
	1996	139	156232	80728		4489
	1997		169906	81886	1668	21474
	1998		148577	95225	1000	27388
	1999	165	234481	174446	2994	55345
	2000	209	574347	500381	2390	236923
	2001	293	979184	757490	3126	350362
	2002	335	877060	570643	11001	236731
	2003	492	1024908	547770	20212	243651
	2004	709	1125577	599276	29585	207447
	2005	756	1016618	679521	26634	245022
	2006	824	1208786	899482	48542	304890
	2007	909	1683160	1390360	57776	164429
乌鲁木齐市	Urumqi City	302	817958	677793	27523	69716
克拉玛依市	Karamay City	32	66447	53857	4277	32883
石河子市	Shihezi City	28	41916	38489	156	1998
吐鲁番地区	Turpan Administrative Offices	12	5780	3327	250	
哈密地区	Hami [Kumul] Administrative Offices	35	33725	29289		4273
昌吉回族自治州	Changji Hui Autonomous Prefecture	83	117539	98234	1792	1437
伊犁哈萨克自治州	Ili Kazak Autonomous Prefecture	156	205431	169376	7047	25573
伊犁州直属县(市)	Counties (Cities) Direct Under Ili Prefecture	85	135083	111426	7047	10261
塔城地区	Tacheng [Tarbagatai] Administrative Offices	48	46838	40824		7761
阿勒泰地区	Altay Administrative Offices	23	23510	17126		7551
博尔塔拉蒙古自治州	Bortala Mongol Autonomous Prefecture	36	23360	20560		4073
巴音郭楞蒙古自治州	Bayangol Mongol Autonomous Prefecture	82	142138	119805	16131	6523
阿克苏地区	Aksu Administrative Offices	96	152283	124899	400	13458
克孜勒苏柯尔克孜自治州	Kizilsu Kirgiz Autonomous Prefecture	7	3010	2827	200	
喀什地区	Kashgar [Kaxgar] Administrative Offices	39	66052	46158		4495
和田地区	Hotan Administrative Offices	1	7521	5746		

4-16 续表 Continued

单位：万元 (10 000 yuan)

年份 Year	地区 Region	办公楼 Office buildings	商业营业用房 Houses for Business Use	其他 Other
	1996	18108	42562	14834
	1997	25347	41935	20738
	1998	17394	22027	13931
	1999	9133	27068	23834
	2000	13171	42601	18194
	2001	41911	111028	68755
	2002	81119	153498	71800
	2003	81497	286896	108745
	2004	77843	390566	57892
	2005	40977	247033	49087
	2006	28233	236945	44126
	2007	27629	205590	59581
乌鲁木齐市	Urumqi City	15912	91738	32515
克拉玛依市	Karamay City	1708	6684	4198
石河子市	Shihezi City	549	2782	96
吐鲁番地区	Turpan Administrative Offices		2035	418
哈密地区	Hami [Kumul] Administrative Offices	342	3775	319
昌吉回族自治州	Changji Hui Autonomous Prefecture	1744	12788	4773
伊犁哈萨克自治州	Ili Kazak Autonomous Prefecture	1983	27274	6798
伊犁州直属县(市)	Counties (Cities) Direct Under Ili Prefecture	838	19334	3485
塔城地区	Tacheng [Tarbagatai] Administrative Offices	263	3146	2605
阿勒泰地区	Altay Administrative Offices	882	4794	708
博尔塔拉蒙古自治州	Bortala Mongol Autonomous Prefecture		1919	881
巴音郭楞蒙古自治州	Bayangol Mongol Autonomous Prefecture	3909	15462	2962
阿克苏地区	Aksu Administrative Offices	151	20691	6542
克孜勒苏柯尔克孜自治州	Kizilsu Kirgiz Autonomous Prefecture	56	127	
喀什地区	Kashgar [Kaxgar] Administrative Offices	1275	18568	51
和田地区	Hotan Administrative Offices		1747	28

4-17 房地产开发企业（单位）资金来源

Sources of Funds of Enterprises for Real Estate Develpment

单位：万元 (10 000 yuan)

年份 Year	地区 Region	合计 Total	国家预算内资金 State Budget Funds	国内贷款 Domestic Loans	利用外资 Foreign Investment	自筹资金 Self-raising Funds	其他资金来源 Others
	1996	154995	502	51048	742	45104	57599
	1997	161399		51443	500	60573	48883
	1998	151094		22419	500	49427	78748
	1999	244252		29665	5770	73899	134918
	2000	701332		113823	600	232768	354141
	2001	890102	405	106794	1278	303975	477650
	2002	1064031	348	158511		455707	449465
	2003	1117659		208348		448441	460870
	2004	1215850	2290	125553		546282	541725
	2005	1137693		113887	160	479948	543698
	2006	1446593		145340		478871	822382
	2007	2243755		217380		766344	1260031
乌鲁木齐市	Urumqi City	1345744		135548		410826	799370
克拉玛依市	Karamay City	70139		2245		27563	40331
石河子市	Shihezi City	51511		350		6060	45101
吐鲁番地区	Turpan Administrative Offices	7372				5094	2278
哈密地区	Hami [Kumul] Administrative Offices	35371		3700		9788	21883
昌吉回族自治州	Changji Hui Autonomous Prefecture	131960		16625		36693	78642
伊犁哈萨克自治州	Ili Kazak Autonomous Prefecture	207249		27530		85110	94609
伊犁州直属县(市)	Counties (Cities) Direct Under Ili Prefecture	140664		24732		52735	63197
塔城地区	Tacheng [Tarbagatai] Administrative Offices	45466		1548		21155	22763
阿勒泰地区	Altay Administrative Offices	21119		1250		11220	8649
博尔塔拉蒙古自治州	Bortala Mongol Autonomous Prefecture	22567		624		8655	13288
巴音郭楞蒙古自治州	Bayangol Mongol Autonomous Prefecture	144590		11924		43136	89530
阿克苏地区	Aksu Administrative Offices	153176		15434		91258	46484
克孜勒苏柯尔克孜自治州	Kizilsu Kirgiz Autonomous Prefecture	3090					3090
喀什地区	Kashgar [Kaxgar] Administrative Offices	63465		3400		34640	25425
和田地区	Hotan Administrative Offices	7521				7521	

4-18 房地产开发企业（单位）施工、销售和空置情况

单位：万平方米

年 份 Year	地 区 Region	本年施工房屋面积 Floor Space of Building under Construction This Year	#住宅 Residential Buildings	#商业营业用房 Houses for Business Use	本年新开工房屋面积 Floor Space Started This Year	#住宅 Residential Buildings	#商业营业用房 Houses for Business Use
	1996	224.90	150.80	41.67	103.87	69.84	19.52
	1997	222.20	144.50	47.68	90.24	70.08	12.81
	1998	252.61	188.38	40.72	133.26	120.95	6.35
	1999	343.38	295.62	34.33	212.73	194.77	12.48
	2000	771.86	665.30	74.20	453.63	397.77	43.00
	2001	1433.54	1207.89	150.63	912.06	778.55	97.24
	2002	1246.89	946.11	204.52	577.04	433.57	98.13
	2003	1382.14	962.89	298.51	782.78	557.28	175.73
	2004	1333.03	863.19	357.53	771.47	550.66	178.43
	2005	1371.15	941.58	340.63	793.55	639.98	130.90
	2006	1567.70	1188.61	307.19	1035.59	875.99	131.90
	2007	2053.76	1715.00	271.52	1347.11	1216.39	101.82
乌鲁木齐市	Urumqi City	915.34	771.28	102.56	546.31	498.40	33.91
克拉玛依市	Karamay City	92.94	80.61	8.60	77.85	66.80	7.34
石河子市	Shihezi City	53.26	48.88	3.61	42.09	38.66	2.66
吐鲁番地区	Turpan Administrative Offices	7.82	4.03	3.79	6.76	3.05	3.71
哈密地区	Hami [Kumul] Administrative Offices	39.83	35.83	3.47	25.97	23.49	2.38
昌吉回族自治州	Changji Hui Autonomous Prefecture	166.76	143.45	16.72	126.23	115.01	9.11
伊犁哈萨克自治州	Ili Kazak Autonomous Prefecture	269.56	219.24	45.83	180.59	161.73	15.37
伊犁州直属县(市)	Counties (Cities) Direct Under Ili Prefecture	180.66	146.28	32.49	106.33	97.69	7.22
塔城地区	Tacheng [Tarbagatai] Administrative Offices	51.91	46.21	4.81	45.66	40.65	4.32
阿勒泰地区	Altay Administrative Offices	36.99	26.75	8.53	28.59	23.40	3.82
博尔塔拉蒙古自治州	Bortala Mongol Autonomous Prefecture	30.39	27.91	2.45	20.53	19.00	1.53
巴音郭楞蒙古自治州	Bayangol Mongol Autonomous Prefecture	195.41	159.22	30.20	141.59	130.01	8.22
阿克苏地区	Aksu Administrative Offices	169.12	151.41	17.18	123.84	111.33	11.98
克孜勒苏柯尔克孜自治州	Kizilsu Kirgiz Autonomous Prefecture	3.06	2.94	0.04	3.06	2.94	0.04
喀什地区	Kashgar [Kaxgar] Administrative Offices	104.53	67.33	34.20	49.39	43.27	5.37
和田地区	Hotan Administrative Offices	5.74	2.87	2.87	2.90	2.70	0.20

Condition of Under Construction, Sale and Idle of Enterprises for Real Estate Development

(10 000sq.m)

本年竣工房屋面积 Floor Space of Buindings Completed This Year	#住宅 Residential Buildings	#商业营业用房 Houses for Business Use	本年房屋销售面积 Floor Space of Building Sold This Year	#住宅 Residential Buildings	#商业营业用房 Houses for Business Use	房屋空置面积 Floor Space At Idle	#住宅 Residential Buildings	#商业营业用房 Houses for Business Use
81.19	64.51	8.14	45.60	41.29	2.91	33.20	27.41	4.44
93.56	73.32	6.93	55.43	52.48	0.98	36.33	25.58	3.76
94.28	79.92	6.23	83.29	75.97	3.46	27.20	20.33	2.78
159.99	143.93	13.52	127.48	120.44	4.67	63.01	49.00	8.91
330.11	298.79	23.07	262.52	250.95	9.82	69.75	58.92	6.35
633.25	559.91	57.01	419.87	381.67	31.77	200.46	169.78	20.26
727.21	616.12	85.03	506.66	455.68	46.34	353.23	285.87	51.33
791.14	626.50	126.42	587.02	516.48	53.44	422.11	313.93	84.81
704.25	511.61	156.54	635.53	538.33	81.27	400.40	248.38	125.31
717.43	553.48	121.37	687.20	606.48	68.16	460.99	269.07	151.02
679.06	551.63	104.13	892.41	806.46	73.96	406.25	208.02	157.83
890.55	798.12	72.07	1144.34	1078.28	51.57	289.22	115.39	150.68
330.46	301.61	17.17	498.68	468.09	18.78	97.37	35.74	45.30
28.20	26.94	0.95	59.90	57.53	1.77	12.72	3.48	8.61
34.49	32.11	2.05	44.82	41.53	3.18	10.46	3.58	6.87
4.63	3.19	1.44	8.50	7.03	1.47	1.24	1.08	0.16
27.68	25.18	1.98	29.17	27.72	1.43	7.10	3.59	2.87
84.07	77.00	5.31	114.36	108.86	4.73	28.15	9.68	16.48
148.61	134.63	11.88	159.76	151.64	7.38	52.73	22.91	27.49
99.20	89.60	9.25	104.62	100.26	4.36	42.89	17.97	22.58
34.65	33.05	1.36	36.10	34.40	1.51	6.63	3.24	3.39
14.76	11.98	1.26	19.04	16.98	1.51	3.22	1.69	1.52
25.32	24.08	1.21	21.90	21.10	0.75	7.20	4.74	2.46
100.73	85.17	12.62	87.80	83.06	4.61	26.68	11.93	14.47
69.80	64.09	5.71	86.80	81.66	4.98	37.77	15.28	21.55
			4.67	4.37	0.22	1.41	0.26	1.15
36.56	24.12	11.75	26.14	23.96	2.17	4.09	2.38	1.71
			1.84	1.73	0.10	2.30	0.74	1.56

4-18 续表 Continued

单位：万平方米 (10 000sq.m)

年份 Year	地区 Region	房屋销售额(万元) Sales Value of Buildings (10 000 yuan)	#住宅 Residential Buildings	#商业营业用房 Houses for Business Use	房屋平均销售价格(元) Average Selling Price of House (yuan)	#住宅 Residential Buildings	#商业营业用房 Houses for Business Use
	1996	67514	57024	5883	1481	1381	2019
	1997	75110	67585	1569	1355	1288	1604
	1998	118386	98803	8544	1421	1301	2471
	1999	177683	158304	12599	1394	1314	2695
	2000	373801	333166	35153	1424	1328	3578
	2001	643814	537818	90441	1533	1409	2847
	2002	879287	658157	208821	1735	1444	4506
	2003	1066640	768012	224579	1817	1487	4202
	2004	1106143	784408	281856	1741	1457	3468
	2005	1235410	915191	288747	1798	1509	4237
	2006	1658176	1358136	265450	1858	1684	3589
	2007	2381520	2113425	211508	2081	1960	4101
乌鲁木齐市	Urumqi City	1330081	1183526	95690	2667	2528	5095
克拉玛依市	Karamay City	96100	87989	6618	1604	1529	3747
石河子市	Shihezi City	75626	66724	8704	1687	1607	2739
吐鲁番地区	Turpan Administrative Offices	12282	8914	3368	1445	1268	2290
哈密地区	Hami [Kumul] Administrative Offices	44671	38385	6217	1532	1385	4359
昌吉回族自治州	Changji Hui Autonomous Prefecture	186308	170387	14490	1629	1565	3062
伊犁哈萨克自治州	Ili Kazak Autonomous Prefecture	260780	229740	30233	1632	1515	4096
伊犁州直属县(市)	Counties (Cities) Direct Under Ili Prefecture	185174	164922	20252	1770	1645	4650
塔城地区	Tacheng [Tarbagatai] Administrative Offices	49596	45210	4139	1374	1314	2738
阿勒泰地区	Altay Administrative Offices	26010	19608	5842	1366	1155	3860
博尔塔拉蒙古自治州	Bortala Mongol Autonomous Prefecture	31111	29498	1566	1421	1398	2091
巴音郭楞蒙古自治州	Bayangol Mongol Autonomous Prefecture	160809	141258	19305	1832	1701	4186
阿克苏地区	Aksu Administrative Offices	137997	119303	17501	1590	1461	3515
克孜勒苏柯尔克孜自治州	Kizilsu Kirgiz Autonomous Prefecture	5951	4908	805	1274	1123	3662
喀什地区	Kashgar [Kaxgar] Administrative Offices	37101	30478	6623	1420	1272	3048
和田地区	Hotan Administrative Offices	2703	2315	388	1471	1335	3767

4-19 新增主要产品生产能力
Newly Increased Production Capacity of Major Products

项　　目	Item	2006	2007
原煤开采(万吨/年)	Coal Mining (10 000 tons/year)	732.10	1154.44
洗煤(万吨/年)	Washer coal (10 000 tons/year)	126	12
焦炭(万吨/年)	Coke (10 000 tons/year)	324.30	134.00
天然原油(万吨/年)	Petroleum Extractin (10 000 tons/year)	273.60	511.68
天然气开采(亿立方米/年)	Natural Gas Extraction (100 million cubic meters/year)	34.00	25.78
石油加工：(处理万吨/年)	Oil Processing (10 000 tons/year)		
蒸馏设备能力	Distilloction Equipment Dressing	2	
裂化设备能力	Coking Equipment Capacity		6
铁矿石原矿开采(万吨/年)	Iron-Ore Mining (10 000 tons/year)	541.00	269.50
铁矿选矿处理量(万吨/年)	Iron-ore Dressing (10 000 tons/year)	5	347
钢材(万吨/年)	Steel Material (10 000 tons/year)	92.30	30.50
热轧钢材	Hot-rolled Steel Material	92.20	27.50
冷加工钢材	Non-hot-processed Steel Material		2
焊接钢管	Weld Steel Pipe		2
铜采矿(原矿)(万吨/年)	Copper Ore Mining (10 000 tons/year)	79.30	82.16
铜选矿(万吨 / 年)	Copper Ore Dressing (10 000 ton/year)		
处理原矿	Raw Ore Treatment	70	62
铝加工(吨/年)	Aluminium Processing (ton/year)	500	14000
黄金(公斤/年)	Gold (kg/year)	2169.31	2867.00
发电机组装机容量(万千瓦)	Capacity of Generating Setes (10 000 kw/year)	14.51	94.63
水力发电	Hydropower	8.14	23.76
火力发电	Thermal Power	0.30	64.08
其他发电	Others	6.07	5.59
输电线路长度(11 万伏及以上)(公里)	Transmission Line (110 000V)(km)	1146.31	3295.60
水泥(万吨/年)	Cement (10 000 tons/year)	67.70	253.90
平板玻璃(万重量箱/年)	Plate Glass (10 000 weight-box/year)	100	20
烧碱(吨/年)	Caustic Soda (ton/year)	100000	120000
农用氮、磷、钾化学肥料(吨/年)	Farm-use Nitrogen, Phosphorus and Potassium Fertilizer (ton/year)	134000	80100
#氮肥	Nitrogen fertilizer	51000	30100
塑料树脂及共聚物(吨/年)	Plastic Colophony and Polymer (ton/year)	164710	218436
棉纺锭(锭)	Cotton Spindle (spindle)	630120	617260
酒(万吨/年)	Liquors (10 000 tons/year)	16.70	31.36
啤酒	Beer	10	28
白酒	Liquor	6.35	2.98
其他酒	Others	0.35	0.38

4-19 续表 Continued

项 目	Item	2006	2007
机制纸板(万吨/年)	Machine-made Paperboard (10 000 tons/year)	3	1
移动通信基站设备(个/年)	Mobile Communicating Base Station Equipment (unit/year)	221	884
程控交换机(万线/年)	Program-Controlled Telephone Exchange (10 000 lines/year)	18.64	17.01
新建公路(公里)	Length of New Highways (km)	1792.85	1382.81
改建公路(公里)	Length of Reconstructed Highways(km)	8367.97	7710.49
#一级公路	First Class Highway	515.53	
二级公路	Second Class highway	1363.29	982.40
新建独立公路桥梁(延长米)	New-Built Separate Highway and Bridge (Extended Length)	2151.69	1002.00
(座)	(unit)	4	12
新(扩)建客、货运站(个)	Number of newly-Built or Expanded Passenger and Freight Stations	61	49
(平方米)	(sq.m)	45376	25145
民航机场跑道(条)	Length of runway(unit)	2	2
(米)	(m)	2900	5300
候机楼(座)	Terminal Building (unit)	2	2
(平方米)	(sq.m)	3083	8500
耕地面积(万公顷)	Tilled land Area (10 000 hectares)	1.62	1.37
造林面积(万公顷)	Afforested Area (10 000 hectares)	1024.23	11.24
水库容量(亿立方米)	Reservoir Capacity (100 million cu.m)	0.66	4.17
有效灌溉面积(万公顷)	Effective Irrigated Area (10 000 hectares)	12.46	13.42
各类院校:学生席位(个)	Number of Student Seat of University and College (unit)	216974	130253
建筑面积(平方米)	Floor Space (sq.m)	1094173	801774
医院病床(张)	Sick Beds (unit)	4914	10544
宾馆、旅馆、招待所客房数(间)	Number of Rooms in Guest Houses, Hotels and Hostels (unit)	2556	2732
(平方米)	(sq.m)	103134	134112
城市自来水供水能力(万吨/日)	Capacity of City Tap Water Supply (10 000 tons/day)	40.17	248.95
城市公共交通车辆购置(辆)	Purchase of City Communiting Vehicles (unit)	630	227
城市道路扩建长度(公里)	Length of City Road Extended (km)	479.06	544.36
城市道路扩建面积(万平方米)	Area of City Road Extended (10 000 sq.m)	457.75	576.03
城市排水管道铺设长度(公里)	Length of Sewer Pipelines (km)	151.03	235.79
城市污水处理能力(万吨/日)	Disposal Capacity of Sewer (10 000 tons/day)	7.30	46.30
城市永久性桥梁(座)	City Permanent Bridge (unit)	1	3
城市防洪堤长度(公里)	Length of City Embarkment (km)	24.00	68.95

4-20 农村非农户固定资产投资情况

Investment in Fixed Assets of Non-Rural Households in Rural Areas

单位：万元　　(2007 年)　　(10 000 yuan)

指标	Item	合计 Total 数量 Amount	合计 Total 构成(%) Composition(%)
新增固定资产	**Newly Increased Investment in Fixed Assets**	**2164786**	
固定资产投资完成额	**Completed Investment in Fixed Assets**	**1080611**	**100**
按投资构成分	By Use of Funds		
建筑工程	Construction Works	773848	71.61
安装工程	Installation Works	47508	4.40
设备工器具购置	Purchase of Equipment and Instruments	187317	17.33
#用于更新的设备	Renew of Equipment and Instruments	8681	0.80
其　他	Others	71938	6.66
按投资方向分	By Sector of Investment		
农、林、牧、渔业	Activities for Agriculture, Forestry, Animal Husbandry and Fishing	187462	17.35
采矿业	Mining and Quarrying	103578	9.59
制造业	Manufacturing	168185	15.56
电力燃气及水的生产及供应业	Production and Supply of Power and Gas	54698	5.06
建筑业	Construction	330	0.03
交通运输仓储和邮政业	Transportation, Logistics and Post Industries	104389	9.66
信息传输、计算机服务和软件业	Information Transmission, Computer Servcie and Software Industries	4422	0.41
批发和零售业	Retail and Wholesale Trades	18487	1.71
住宿和餐饮业	Hotel and Catering Service	9305	0.86
金融业	Financial Intermediation		
房地产业	Real Estate	233772	21.63
租赁和商务服务业	Leasing and Business Service Industries	3225	0.30
科学研究、技术服务和地质勘查业	Scientific Research, Technology Service and Geological Prospecting	14833	1.37
水利、环境和公共设施管理业	Water Conservancy, Environment and Public Facility Management	114177	10.57
居民服务和其他服务业	Community Service and Other Services	1146	0.11
教　育	Education	15768	1.46
卫生、社会保障和社会福利业	Health, Social Security and Welfare	5481	0.51
文化、体育和娱乐业	Culture, Sports and Entertainment	4024	0.37
公共管理和社会组织	Public Management and Social Organizations	37329	3.45
资金来源小计	**All Sources**	**1081794**	**100**
国家预算内资金	State Budgetary Appropriation	282838	26.15
国内贷款	Domestic Loans	54667	5.05
债　券	Bonds		
利用外资	Application of Foreign Capital	10978	1.01
自筹资金	Self-raising Capital	557401	51.53
其他资金	Other Funds	175910	16.26
本年施工房屋面积(万平方米)	**Floor Space of Buildings Under Construction (10 000 sq.m)**	**799.29**	
#住　宅	Residential Building	669.70	
本年竣工房屋面积(万平方米)	**Floor Space of Completed Building (10 000 sq.m)**	**619.62**	
#住　宅	Residential Building	524.37	

4-21 农户固定资产投资情况
Investment in Fixed Assets of Rural Households in Rural Areas

单位:万元　　(抽样调查 Sampled Survey)　　(10 000 yuan)

指　　标	Item	2006	2007
新增固定资产原值	**Newly Increased Investment in Fixed Assets**	**791327.43**	**835909.72**
固定资产投资完成额	**Complete Investment in Fixed Assets**	**791327.43**	**835909.72**
按投资来源分	By Source of Fund		
国内贷款	Domestic Loans	79376.69	72782.99
自筹资金	Self-raising Capital	683421.28	717511.46
其他资金	Others	28529.46	45615.27
按投资构成分	By Use of Fund		
建筑工程	Construction	375712.83	396318.65
#水　利	Water Conservancy	9882.50	4239.45
房　屋	Building	365697.00	392079.20
#住　宅	Residential Building	321040.63	349292.20
安装工程	Installation	135.69	
设备工、器具购置	Purchase of Equipment And Instruments	334606.42	357521.19
#生产设备	Production of Equipment	188900.85	230322.59
其　它	Others	80872.49	82069.88
按投资方向分	By Sector of Funds		
农　业	Farming	419256.71	442902.13
采矿业	Mining and Quarrying		1172.12
制造业	Manufacturing		2807.48
电力燃气及水的生产及供应业	Production and Supply of Power and Gas	780.22	
建筑业	Construction	78338.76	82675.28
交通运输仓储和邮政业	Transportation, Logistics and Post Industries	107333.36	116532.31
信息传输、计算机服务和软件业	Information Transmission, Computer Servcie and Software Industries	6200.00	4303.82
住宿和餐饮业	Hotel and Catering Services	21312.31	16088.44
房地产业	Real Estate	97856.43	126473.38
水利、环境和公共设施管理业	Water Conservancy, Environment and Public Facility Management	4816.21	4239.45
居民服务和其他服务业	Community Service and Other Service	51242.69	32711.19
教　育			635.89
文化、体育和娱乐业	Culture, Sports and Entertainment	4190.74	5368.23
按具体投资项目分	By Project of Investment		
房　屋	Building	365697.00	392079.20
#住　宅	Residential Building	321040.63	349292.20
桥　梁	Bridge	269.02	
设　备	Equipment	334606.42	357521.19
水　利	Water Conservancy	9882.50	4239.45
其　他	Others	80872.49	82069.88
本年施工房屋面积 (万平方米)	Floor Space of Buildings Under Construction (10 000 sq.m)	1506.34	1533.28
#住　宅	Residential Building	1439.13	1480.68
本年竣工房屋面积(万平方米)	Floor Space of Completed Building (10 000 sq.m)	1461.15	1494.55
#住　宅	Residential Building	1403.67	1442.80
调查户总人口(人)	**Total Number of Households (person)**	**7309**	**7239**

主要统计指标解释

全社会固定资产投资 以货币形式表现的在一定时期内全社会建造和购置固定资产的工作量以及与此有关的费用的总称。该指标是反映固定资产投资规模、结构和发展速度的综合性指标,又是观察工程进度和考核投资效果的重要依据。全社会固定资产投资按登记注册类型可分为国有、集体、个体、联营、股份制、外商、港澳台商、其他等。

城镇固定资产投资 指城镇各种登记注册类型的企业、事业、行政单位及个体户进行的计划总投资(或实际需要总投资)50 万元及 50 万元以上的建设项目投资、房地产开发投资、城镇和工矿区私人建房投资。县城及以上区域内发生的投资，县及县以上各级政府及主管部门直接领导、管理的建设项目和企业事业单位的投资均为城镇固定资产投资。

房地产开发投资 指各种登记注册类型的房地产开发公司、商品房建设公司及其他房地产开发法人单位和附属于其他法人单位实际从事房地产开发或经营活动的单位统一开发的包括统代建、拆迁还建的住宅、厂房、仓库、饭店、宾馆、度假村、写字楼、办公楼等房屋建筑物和配套的服务设施，土地开发工程(如道路、给水、排水、供电、供热、通讯、平整场地等基础设施工程)的投资;不包括单纯的土地交易活动。

城镇和工矿区私人建房投资 包括市、县城、城关镇、工矿区所辖范围内的全部私人建房，不论其房主是否系本地的常住户口均应包括。

农村投资 包括在农村区域范围内进行固定资产投资活动的企业、事业、行政单位及农村个人投资。

建设总规模 是指在报告期内所有施工项目的计划总投资。这个指标和施工项目相对应。

在建总规模 是指在报告期末所有在建项目的计划总投资。

在建净规模 是指报告期末所有在建项目建成投产尚需的投资总量。在建净规模＝在建总规模－累计完成投资。

固定资产投资的资金来源 根据固定资产投资的资金来源不同，分为国家预算内资金、国内贷款、利用外资、自筹资金和其他资金来源。(1)国家预算内资金:分为财政拨款和财政安排的贷款两部分。包括中央财政的基本建设基金(分经营性基金和非经营性基金两部分)、专项支出(如煤代油专项等)、收回再贷、贴息资金，财政安排的挖潜改造和新产品试制支出、城建支出、商业部门简易建筑支出、不发达地区发展基金等资金中用于固定资产投资的资金;地方财政中由国家统筹安排的资金等。(2)国内贷款:指报告期固定资产投资单位向银行及非银行金融机构借入的用于固定资产投资的各种国内借款，包括银行利用自有资金及吸收的存款发放的贷款、上级主管部门拨入的国内贷款、国家专项贷款(包括煤代油贷款、劳改煤矿专项贷款等)、地方财政专项资金安排的贷款、国内储备贷款、周转贷款等。(3)利用外资:指报告期收到的用于固定资产建造和购置的国外资金(包括设备、材料、技术在内)。包括对外借款(外国政府、国际金融组织贷款、出口信贷、外国银行商业贷款、对外发行债券和股票)、外商直接投资及外商其他投资。不包括我国自有外汇资金(国家外汇、地方外汇、留成外汇、调剂外汇和中国银行自有资金发行的外汇贷款等)。计算利用外资时，需要折算成人民币，折算中所使用的外汇汇率按现汇计算，即按使用外汇时的汇率计算。(4)自筹资金:指固定资产投资单位报告期收到的，由各地区、各部门及企、事业单位筹集用于固定资产投资的预算外资金，包括中央各部门、各级地方和企、事业单位的自筹资金。(5)其他资金来源:指在报告期收到的除以上各种资金之外其他用于固定资产投资的资金，包括企业或金融机构通过发行各种债券筹集到的资金、群众集资、个人资金、无偿捐赠的资金及其他单位拨入的资金等。

固定资产投资按国民经济行业分 建设项目归哪个行业，按其建成投产后的主要产品或主要用途及社会经济活动性质来确定。基本建设按建设项目划分国民经济行业，更新改造、其他固定资产投资根据整个企业、事业单位所属的行业来划分。一般情况下，一个建设项目或一个企业、事业单位只能属于一种国民经济行业。为了更准确地反映国民经济各行业之间的比例关系，联合企业(总厂)所属分厂属于不同行业的，原则上按分厂划分行业。

固定资产投资按建设性质分 建设项目的性质一般分为新建、扩建、改建、迁建、恢复。房地产开发单位、农村投资、城镇工矿区私人建房投资不划分建设性质。基本建设按建设项目划分建设性质，更新改造、国有经济中其他固定资产投资及城镇集体投资等按整个企业、事业单位的建设情况确定建设性质。(1)新建:一般指从无到有“平地起家”开始建设的企业、事业和行政单位或独立的工程。现有企业、事业、行政单位一般不属于新建。但如有的单位原有基础很小，经过建设后新增的固定资产价值超过该企、事业、行政单位原有固定资产价值(原值)三倍以上的也应作为新建。(2)扩建:指在厂内或其他地点，为扩大原有产品的生产能力(或效益)或增加新的产品生产能力，而增建主要的生产车间(或主要工程)、分厂、独立的生产线。行政、事业单位在原单位增建业务用房(如学校增建教学用房、医院增建门诊部、病房等)也作为扩建。现有企、事业单位为扩大原有主要产品生产能力或增加新的产品生产能力，增建一个或几个主要生产车间(或主要工程)、分厂，同时进行一些更新改造工程的，也应作为扩建。(3)改建:指对原有设施进行技术改造或更新(包括相应配套的辅助性生产、生活福利设施)，没有增建主要生产车间、分厂等。现有企、事业单位为适应市场变化的需要，而改变企业的主要产品种类(如军工企业转产民品等)，或原有产品生产作业线由于各工序(车间)之间能力不平衡，为填平补齐充分发挥原有生产能力而增建不增加本企业主要产品设计能力的车间，也应作为改建。

固定资产投资按构成分 固定资产投资活动按其工作内容和实现方式分为建筑安装工程，设备、工具、器具购置，其他费用三个部分。(1)建筑安装工程(建筑安装工作量):指各种房屋、建筑物的建造工程和各种设备、装置的安装工程。包括各种房屋建造工程，各种用途设备基础和各种工业窑炉的砌筑工程及金属结构工程;为施工而进行的各种准备工作和临时工程以及完工后的清理工作等;铁路、道路的铺设，矿井的开凿及石油管道的架设等;水利工程;防空地下建筑等特殊工程;列入房屋工程预算内的暖气、卫生、通风、照明、煤气等设备的价值及装设油饰工程;列入建筑工程预算内的各种管道(蒸汽、压缩空气、石油、给排水等管道)、电力、电讯电缆导线等的敷设工程;以及各种机械设备的安装工程;为测定安装工程质量，对设备进行的试运工作;房地产开发单位进行的商品房屋开发建设工程、土地开发工程。在安装工程中，不包括被安装设备本身的价值。(2)设备、工具、器具购置:指建设单位或企、事业单位购置或自制的，达到固定资产标准的设备、工具、器具的价值。新建单位及扩建单位的新建车间，按照设计或计划要求购置或自制的全部设备、工具、器具，不论是否达到固定资产标准均计入“设备、工具、器具购置”中。(3)其他费用:指在固定资产建造和购置过程中发生的，除上述几项内容以外的各种应分摊计入固定资产的费用。

施工项目 指报告期内进行过建筑或安装施工活动的项目。凡是报告期内施过工的建设项目，不论施工时间长短，均作为施工项目统计。施工项目个数可以反映一定时期固定资产投资的实际规模，与同期建成投产的建设项目个数相比，可以从建设速度的角度反映固定资产投资的效果。根据建设项目施工活动的不同性质，施工项目又分为:本年正式施工项目、本年收尾项目和以前年度全部停缓建项目。

全部建成投产项目 工业项目指设计文件规定形成生产能力的主体工程及其相应配套的辅助设施全部建成，经负荷试运转，证明具备生产设计规定合格产品的条件，并经过验收鉴定合格或达到竣工验收标准，与生产性工程配套的生活福利设施可以满足近期正常生产的需要，正式移交生产的建设项目。非工业项目指设计文件规定的主体工程和相应的配套工程全部建成，能够发挥设计规定的全部效益，经验收鉴定合格或达到竣工验收标准，正式移交使用的建设项目。新增生产能力(或工程效益)指通过固定资产投资活动而增加的设计能力(或工程效益)，该指标是以实物形态表现的反映固定资产投资成果的指标，也是考核投资经济效果的重要依据之一。

新增生产能力(或工程效益)　指通过固定资产投资活动而增加的设计能力(或工程效益)，该指标是以实物形态表现的反映固定资产投资成果的指标，也是考核投资经济效果的重要依据之一。新增生产能力(或工程效益)一般有以下几种表现形式:

(1)用产品数量表示，以工程在单位时间内(一般是一年)所能生产的产品数量(即年产量)表示。如原煤开采用万吨／年表示，化学农药用吨／年表示，拖拉机制造用台／年表示等。某些化工产品由于含量差别较大，按其设计含量计算折合量表示，如硫酸、纯碱、烧碱等。(2)用单位时间内所能处理的原料数量表示，以工程每天(或小时)所能处理原料的数量表示。如机制糖工程日处理原料吨，食用植物油日处理原料吨，城市污水处理能力用万吨／日表示等。(3)用新增加的主要设备的数量或容量表示，如新增棉布织机、丝织机等台数，毛纺锭等锭数，发电厂新增发电机组容量用千瓦表示等。(4)用建筑物容积、容量、面积、长度表示，是非工业项目或工程新增效益的一种表现形式。如铁路投产里程、新建公路、水库容量、粮食仓库、学校学生席位、医院病床、有效灌溉面积等。

根据工程的特点，有时需要用两种或两种以上的复合计量单位表示新增生产能力(或工程效益)，如新增内燃机生产能力同时用年产台数、千瓦数表示等。

为了规范新增生产能力(或工程效益)的名称和计算单位，国家统计局制订了《新增生产能力(或工程效益)目录及代码》。各固定资产投资单位在统计新增生产能力(或工程效益)时，必须按目录中规定的名称、计量单位和代码填报。

房屋建筑面积　指房屋建筑物勒脚以上外墙外围的水平截面面积，包括房屋建筑物的有效面积和结构面积。该指标是从实物形态上反映建设规模和建设成果的重要指标之一，也是检查工程形象进度、计算工程造价、分析投资效果、研究施工任务和建筑材料之间平衡情况的重要依据。

住宅建筑面积　指施工和竣工房屋建筑面积中供居住用的房屋建筑面积。

施工面积　指报告期内施工的全部房屋建筑面积。包括本期新开工的面积和上期开工跨入本期继续施工的房屋面积，以及上期已停建在本期恢复施工的房屋面积。本期竣工和本期施工后又停缓建的房屋，其建筑面积仍计入本期房屋施工面积中。

竣工面积　指在报告期内房屋建筑按照设计要求已经全部完工，达到住人和使用条件，经验收鉴定合格(或达到竣工验收标准)，正式移交使用单位的各栋房屋建筑面积的总和。

房屋建筑面积竣工率　指一定时期内房屋竣工面积占同期房屋施工面积的比率。该指标从房屋建筑施工速度的角度反映投资效果的指标。

新增固定资产　指报告期内已经完成建造和购置过程，并已交付生产或使用单位的固定资产价值。该指标是表示固定资产投资成果的价值指标，也是反映建设进度，计算固定资产投资效果的重要指标。

建设项目投产率　指一定时期内全部建成投产项目个数与同期施工项目个数的比率。该指标是从建设单位建设速度的角度反映投资效果的指标。

固定资产交付使用率　指一定时期新增固定资产与同期完成投资额的比率。该指标是反映固定资产动用速度，衡量建设过程中宏观投资效果的综合指标。由于新增固定资产是较长时期内形成的结果，而投资额则是当年完成的，因此，该指标一般适宜于反映较长时期内固定资产的动用情况。

竣工房屋住宅套数　指报告期内按照设计要求全部完工，经验收合格，达到居住和使用条件并正式交付使用的成套住宅数量。包括独立厨房、独立卫生间、若干卧室、室内走廊等设施在内的供一户居住和使用的房屋。该指标可以反映住宅建设的产业化程度和城市化进程以及人民居住水平提高的情况。

别墅、高档公寓　指建筑造价和销售价格明显高于一般商品住宅的商品住宅。别墅一般指地处郊区，独立成栋的商品住宅;高档公寓一般指地处市内高尚社区，高层或多层的商品住宅。别墅、高档公寓的确定标准:一是经有房地产投资计划审批权的主管部门审批建设的别墅、高档公寓开发项目;二是销售价格高于当地同等地段商品住宅平均销售价格一倍以上的别墅、公寓开发项目。该指标可以分析房地产投资结构，反映高收入家庭商品住宅的供求平衡情况。

经济适用房　指根据国家经济适用房计划安排建设的政策性住宅。经济是指房屋建筑造价和销售价格低于一般商品住宅;适用是指适合中低收入家庭购买使用。经济适用房主要是由国家统一下达投资计划，房地产公司开发，对外销售;用地一般采用行政划拨或招标投标方式，免收土地出让金;对各种经批准的收费减半征收，开发利润不超过3%;销售价格实行政府指导价。该指标可以分析房地产投资结构，反映中低收入家庭商品住宅的供求平衡情况。

Explanatory Notes on Main Statistical Indicators

Total Investment in Fixed Assets in the Whole Country refers to the volume of activities in construction and purchases of fixed assets and related fees, expressed in monetary terms. It is a comprehensive indicatorwhich shows the size, structure and growth of the investment in fixed assets, providing basis for observing the progress of construction projects and evaluating results of investment. Total investment in fixed assets in the whole country includes, by type of ownership, the investment by the state-owned units, collective units, individuals, joint ownership units, share-holding units, as well as investment by businessmen from foreign countries and from Hong Kong, Macau and Taiwan, and by other units.

Urban Investment in Fixed Assets refer to construction projects involving a total planned (or required) investment of 500,000 yuan and over by urban enterprises and institutions of various types of ownership, by administrative units and by individuals, investment in real estate development, and housing investment by individuals in urban areas and in industrial and mining areas. In other words, all investments that take place in county towns and urban areas, investment in construction projects under the direct leadership and management of government agencies at and above county levels and investments by enterprises and institutions at and above county levels are covered in urban investment in fixed assets.

Investment in Real Estate Development refers to the investment by the real estate development companies, commercial buildings construction companies and other real estate development units of various types of ownership in the construction of house buildings, such as residential buildings, factory buildings, warehouses, hotels, guesthouses, holiday villages, office buildings, and the complementary service facilities and land development projects, such as roads, water supply, water drainage, power supply, heating, telecommunications, land leveling and other projects of infrastructure. It excludes the activities in pure land transactions.

Investment in Housing Construction in Urban Areas and in Industrial and Mining Areas refers to all private housing construction under the jurisdictionof cities, county towns and industrial and mining areas, no matter whether the owner of the house is registered as the permanent resident in the locality or not.

Investment in Rural Areas refers to investment in fixed assets by enterprises, institutions and individuals in rural areas.

Total Size of Construction refers to the planned total investment for all construction projects during the reference period.

Total Size of Investment in Projects under Construction refers to the planned total investment of all projects under construction at the end of the reference period.

Net Size of Investment in Projects under Construction refers to the required investment of all projects under construction at the end of the reference period.

Net Size of Investment = Total Size of Investment – accumulated completed investment

Sources of Funds for Investment in Fixed Assets include fund from state budget, domestic loans, foreign investment, self-raised funds, and others depending on the source of investment. (1) Fund from state budget consists of budgetary appropriation and loans from state budget. More specifically, it includes, from the budget of the central government, capital construction fund (operation fund and non-operational fund), special expenses (e.g. expenses on substituting petroleum with coal), loans from repayment, discount fund, expenses on innovation and trial production of new products, expenses on urban construction, expenses on temporary construction by Trades departments, development fund for less developed areas, as well as local budgetary fund transferred from the central budget. (2) Domestic loans refer to loans of various forms borrowed by investing units from banks and non-bank financial institutions during the reference period for the purpose of investment in fixed assets, including loans issued by banks from their self-owned funds and deposit, loans appropriated by higher responsible authorities, special loans by government (including loan for substituting petroleum with coal, special loan for reform-through-labour coal mines), loans arranged by local government from special funds, domestic reserve loan, and working loan, etc. (3) Foreign Investment refers to foreign funds received during the reference period for the construction and purchase of investment in fixed assets (covering equipment, materials and technology), including foreign borrowings (loans from foreign governments and international financial institutions, export credit, commercial loans from foreign banks, issue of bonds and stocks overseas), foreign direct investment and other foreign investment. Excluded in this category are capitals in foreign exchanges owned by China (foreign exchanges owned by the central and local governments, foreign exchanges retained by enterprises, foreign exchanges by enterprises through regulating mechanism, loans in foreign exchanges issued by the Bank of China with its own fund, etc.). In calculating the utilization of foreign capitals, foreign currencies are converted into Chinese Renminbi applying the current exchange rate when the foreign capitals are actually used. (4) Self-raised funds refer to extra-budgetary funds for investment in fixed assets received by investing units from central government ministries, local governments, enterprises and institutions, including their self-raised funds. (5) Others refer to funds for investment in fixed assets received from the sources other than those listed above, including capitals raised through issuing bonds by enterprises or financial institutions, funds raised from individuals and through donations, and funds transferred from other units.

Investment in Fixed Assets by Sector The classification of construction projects by sector is determined by the major products or the purpose of the projects when they are put into production or use, and by the nature of their social economic activities. In general, one project or one enterprise or institution can only be classified into one sector.

Investment in Fixed Assets by Type of Construction The construction projects in general can be classified, by the type of construction, into new construction, expansion, reconstruction and technical transformation, moving and restoration. However, investment by type of construction is not applied to investment by real-estate development units, investment in rural areas and investment in housing by urban individuals. (1) New construction in general refers to newly constructed enterprises, institutions, administrative agencies or independent projects from scratch. Construction in the existing enterprises, institutions or agencies is not considered as new construction. In case the assets of the existing unit is quite small, and the value of newly added fixed assets exceeds the original value of assets by three times, the expansion will be considered as new construction.(2) Expansion refers to construction of new major production workshop, branch factory or independent production line within a factory or in other locations, for the purpose of increasing the production capacity (or improving efficiency) of the original products. Newly constructed houses for the operation of institutions and administrative organizations (such as the newly constructed buildings for teaching in schools, buildings for clinics or wards in hospitals, etc.) are also classified as expansion.Also included in the expansion are investments by existing enterprises or institutions in building major production line(s) or branch factory(ies) along with some work on innovation, for the purpose of expending the production capacity of original products or producing new products. (3) Reconstruction refers to construction projects by existing enterprises or institutions in innovation or technical transformation of the old facilities (including auxiliary production equipment and welfare facilities). Also considered as reconstruction is the construction of new workshops by the existing enterprises or institutions to change the variety of products to meet the market demand (such as the production of civil products by defence industries), or to bring the designed production capacity into full play through a more balanced production process on production lines. Technical transformation refers to replacement of old technology or equipment by new technology or equipment, in order to expand the reproduction through improvement of technology contents in production, to improve product quality, to promote new products, to save energy and reduce consumption and to improve overall social-economic efficiency. Contents of technical transformation include: updating of machinery, equipment and tools; reforming production process by using energy or materials saving technology; construction of factory workshops and transformation of public facilities; improvement of working conditions and environment, etc.

Investment in Fixed Assets by Structure By their contents, investment activities are classified into 3 categories, i.e. construction and installation, purchase of equipment and instrument, and other expenses.(1) Construction and installation (work volume of construction and installation) refers to the construction of various houses and buildings and installation of various kinds of equipment and instruments. They include construction of various houses; equipment foundations, industrial kilns and stoves, and metal structure work; preparation works for project construction, and clearing up works post project construction; pavement of railways and roads, drilling of mines and putting up of oil pipes; construction of projects of water conservancy; construction of underground air-raid shelters and construction of other special projects; value of equipment for heating, sanitation, ventilation, lighting, gas, painting, etc. that are covered by the budget of housing projects; laying out of various pipelines (for steam, compressed air, petroleum, tap water and sewage) and lines for electric power and for communications; installation of various machinery equipment, testing operation for pre-testing the quality of installation projects, and land and other development work conducted by real estate developers for commercial housing. The value of equipment installed is not included in the value of installation projects.(2) Purchase of equipment and instruments refers to the total value of equipment, tools, and instruments purchased or self-produced which come up to standards for fixed assets by the construction units or investing enterprises or institutions. Equipment, tools and instruments purchased or self-produced for new workshops by newly established or expanded units are categorized as "purchase of equipment and instruments" no matter whether they come up to the standards for fixed assets.(3) Other expenses refer to expenses occurring during the construction or purchase of fixed assets other than those mentioned above.

Projects under Construction refer to projects with construction and installation activities undertaken in the reference period. All projects that have construction activities undertaken during the reference period are reported as projects under construction irrespective of the length of construction work. The number of projects under construction can reflect the actual size of investment in fixed assets during a given period, and when compared with the number of projects completed and put into use during the same period, it demonstrates the results of investment in fixed assets. Depending on the nature of const ruction activities, projects under construction can also be classified into projects under construct ion in current y ear, winding-up projects in current year and stopped or suspended projects in previous years (with preservation work in current year).

Projects Completed and Put into Use Industrial projects refer to the major projects and accessory facilities completed which result in forming production capaCity and have been checked and accepted while the living and welfare facilities have been completed and can ensure normal production and formally put into production. Non-industrial projects refer to the major project s and accessory facilities completed which possess the designed capaCity and have been checked, accepted and formally put into production.

Newly Increased Production CapaCity (or Project Efficiency) refers to the increase of designed capaCity (or project efficiency) through investment in fixed assets, which reflects the accomplishment of investment in fixed assets in kind and serves as important basis for evaluating the economic efficiency of in-vestment.

The newly increased product ion capaCity (project efficiency) are usually expressed in one of the following forms: (1) output of products, i.e. the output that the project can produce during a given period (usually a year). For instance, the capaCity in coal mining is expressed in 10, 000 tons/year , the capaCity in producing chemical pesticides expressed in ton/year, the capaCity in producing tractors in tractor/year, etc. For some chemical products where the effective contents differ significantly, the production capaCity is expressed as the designed effective content equivalent, such as in the case of sulphuric acid, soda ash, caustic soda, etc; (2) raw materials processing capaCity, i.e. the volume of raw materials that could be processed by the project per day (or per hour), such as tons of materials processed per day by a sugar refining project or edible vegetable oil project, or tons of urban sewage processed per day; (3) number or capaCity of major equipment increased, such as number of cotton or silk looms increased, wool spindles in-creased, or capaCity (in kilowatt s) of power generators increased; (4) saved raw materials, fuels or power, which are mainly used for the efficiency of innovation and transformation projects; and (5) physical measures (volume, capaCity, area, and length) of construction, which is typical for non industrial projects, for instance, the length of new railways or highways, the capaCity of reservoirs, the floor space of housing projects, capaCity f or new students in schools or beds in hospitals, areas under new irrigation project, etc. Features of projects sometimes call for combined use of two or more measurement to reflect the increased production capaCity (or project efficiency), for instance, the new capaCity for the production of internal combustion engines are expressed in set s per year and kilowatts per year simultaneously. To standardize the nomenclature and unit of measurement for new production capaCity (or project efficiency), the National Bureau of Statistics has developed Nomenclature for New Production CapaCity (Project Efficiency) and Nomenclature for Saving Raw Materials, Fuels and Power. All reporting units with investment activities are required to follow these two nomenclatures in reporting statistics on new production capaCity (project efficiency).

Floor Space of Buildings under Construction refers to total floor space of the horizontal section of outer walls above the plinth of the building, including the effective area and the area occupied by the structure. This indicator is one of the important indicators in physical terms to reflect the scale and accomplishment of the construction industry, and important basis for monitoring the pr ogress, calculating the cost, analyzing the efficiency and studying the sup ply of building materials in relation with the construction projects.

Floor Space of Residential Buildings refers to the floor space of the residential buildings among the total space of buildings under construction or completed.

Floor Space under Construction refers to total floor space of all buildings under construct ion during the reference period, including floor space of newly start ed buildings during the reference period, floor space of construction extended from the previous period to the current period, and floor space of construction suspended during the previous period and resumed in the current period. Floor space of const ruction completed in the current period, and floor space of const ruction started and then suspended in the current period are also included in the floor space under const ruction of the current year.

Floor Space of Buildings Completed refers to the floor space of all buildings completed in the reference period, which have been appraised and accepted (or come up to the designed standards) and have been transferred to the owners for use.

Completion Rate of Floor Space of Buildings refers to the ratio of the floor space of buildings completed in certain period of time to the floor space of buildings under const ruction in the same period. This indicator reflects the investment result from the perspective of t he speed of construction.

Newly Increased Fixed Assets refer to the newly in-creased value of fixed assets, constructed or purchased, that have been transfer red to the investors. This is an indicator that demonstrates the results of investment in fixed assets in monetary terms, and an important indicator to reflect the speed of construct ion and to calculate the efficiency of investment.

Rate of Construction Projects Completed and Put into Use refers to the ratio of the number of construction projects completed and put into use in certain period of time to the number of projects under construction in the same period. This reflects the investment efficiency from the perspective of the speed of projects construction.

Rate of Projects of Fixed Assets Completed and Put into Operation refers to the ratio of the newly increased fixed assets to the total investment made in the same period. This is a comprehensive indicator reflecting the speed of the employment of fixed assets and the investment efficiency at the macro-level. As the newly increase fixed assets is the result of a long period while the investment is completed in the current year, this indicator is expected to be used to reflect the employment of fixed assets over a long period of time.

Number of Flats in Completed Residential Buildings refers to total number of flats completed during the reference period, appraised and accepted as meeting the standards for living, and transfer red for use. A flat includes separate kitchen and bathroom, several bedrooms and corridor, suitable for one household. This indicator reflects the degree of industrialization of the residential building construction, the process of urbanization and the improvement of the living standard of people.

Villas, High-Grade Apartments refers to commercial houses whose const ruction costs and marketing pr ices are significantly higher than ordinary housing. Villas are independent structures generally located in the suburbs; high-grade apartments are multi-story buildings located in elegant urban neighborhoods. Criteria for villas and high-grade apartments include: 1) projects for the construction of villas or high-grade apartments have to be approved by competent departments in charge of real estate development and investment plans, and 2) pr ices f or projects on villas or high- grade apartments are higher by over 100% com-pared with the aver age prices of ordinary commercial housing projects in similar location. This indicator helps to analyze the investment structure of the real estate industry and the demand and supply of housing for high-income households.

Economically Affordable Housing refers to housing constructed according to the state plan for economically affordable housing. Houses of this category featured in low cost in construct ion and low prices, and therefore are affordable to mid-income or low-income households. Economically affordable housing projects are developed by real estate companies under the state investment plan, with the land provided through government allocation or tendering procedures. Developers are exempted from land utilization fees and enjoy another 50% exemption of all other legitimate fees, while their profits are limited to less than 3%, and the completed houses are sold under the government guided prices. This indicator helps to analyze the investment structure of the real estate industry and the demand and supply of housing for mid or low income households.

第五篇
财政、金融和保险

CHAPTER 5
Government finance, Financial Intermediation and insurance

简要说明

Brief Introduction

本篇资料的主要内容及来源

本篇反映自治区财政、金融、证券和保险业发展情况,有以下四个部分:一是地方财政预算收支情况;二是金融机构存贷及现金收支等活动情况;三是保险业务情况;四是证券上市情况。

地方财政预算收支情况取自新疆维吾尔自治区财政厅年度决算,2007年度由于财政科目进行了调整,部分指标数据无法取得,取消了一张表格;金融资料来自中国人民银行乌鲁木齐中心支行金融机构信贷统计月报;保险业务情况资料取自中国保险监督管理委员会新疆监管局编制的保险统计资料;证券及上市公司情况来自新疆证监会。

本篇章数据由新疆维吾尔自治区统计局综合处根据上述部门所提供的资料整理。

Main Content and Source of Data

The data in this chapter show the development of Xinjiang Uygur Autonomous region government finance, banking, securities and insurance, in the following 4 aspects (1)The government revenue and expenditure; (2)The financial activities of banking institutions; (3) The business of insurance; (4)The condition of listed securities.

Data on the government revenue and expenditure come from the final state financial accounts of the Buteau of Finance. Because of financial figures have beer adjusted in 2007,pevrt of figures did not obtainted, So a table was canceled. Data on financial intermediation come from the credit funds sheet of financial institutions of Urumqi municipal sub-branches, People´s Bank of China; Data on insurance come from Xinjiang Insurance Regulatory Bureau of CIRC. Data on listed securities are from Xinjiang Security Regulatory Bureau of CSRC.

Data in this chapter are compiled and collected by the Division of comprehensive of the Xinjiang Bureau of Statistics on the basis of data from the relative departments.

5-1 地方财政一般预算收支及增长速度
The General Budgetary Revenue & Expenses and Growth Rate of Local Finance

单位：万元 (10 000 yuan)

年 份 Year	地方财政一般预算收入 General Budgetary Revenue in Local Finance	地方财政一般预算支出 General Budgetary Expenditure in Local Finance	收支差额 Balance	指数(上年=100) Indices (precding year=100)	
				地方财政一般预算收入 General Budgetary Revenue in Local Finance	地方财政一般预算支出 General Budgetary Expenditure in Local Finance
1978	71416	170169	-98753	196.5	153.3
1980	40309	162159	-121850	73.4	95.4
1985	84663	286031	-201368	117.2	122.6
1990	217784	476210	-258426	118.9	114.2
1995	382818	964021	-581203	133.4	135.6
1996	483051	1148790	-665739	126.2	119.2
1997	545248	1233534	-688286	112.9	107.4
1998	653928	1459933	-806005	119.9	118.4
1999	713110	1662788	-949678	109.1	113.9
2000	790724	1909529	-1118805	110.9	114.8
2001	950933	2633232	-1682299	120.3	137.9
2002	1164724	3611729	-2447005	122.5	137.2
2003	1282218	3684676	-2402458	110.1	102.0
2004	1557040	4210446	-2653406	121.4	114.3
2005	1803184	5190179	-3386995	115.8	123.3
2006	2194628	6784723	-4590095	121.7	130.7
2007	2858600	7951540	-5092940	130.3	117.2

5-2 地方财政一般预算收入占新疆生产总值的比重
Percentage of the General Budgetary Revenue in Local Finance to GDP of Xinjiang

单位：亿元 (100 million yuan)

年 份 Year	地方财政一般预算收入 General Budgetary Revenue in Local Finance	新疆生产总值 Gross Domestic Product in Xinjiang	地方财政一般预算收入占新疆生产总值的比重(%) Percentage of Budgetary Revenue to Xinjiang GDP (%)
1978	7.14	39.07	18.27
1980	4.03	53.24	7.57
1985	8.47	112.24	7.56
1990	21.78	261.44	8.34
1995	38.28	814.85	4.70
1996	48.31	900.93	5.36
1997	54.52	1039.85	5.24
1998	65.39	1106.95	5.91
1999	71.31	1163.17	6.13
2000	79.07	1363.56	5.80
2001	95.09	1491.60	6.37
2002	116.47	1612.65	7.22
2003	128.22	1886.35	6.79
2004	155.70	2209.09	7.05
2005	180.32	2604.14	6.92
2006	219.46	3045.26	7.21
2007	285.86	3523.16	8.11

5-3 地方财政收支情况

Statistics on Total Government Revenue and Expenditures in Local Finance

单位：万元 (10 000 yuan)

项　目	Item	2006	2007
收入合计	**Total Revenue**	**2656543**	**3695618**
地方财政一般预算收入	General Budgetary Revenue in Local Finance	2194628	2858600
税收收入	Taxes Revenue	1745372	2206460
增值税	Value-added Tax	549722	666160
营业税	Business Tax	550497	682275
企业所得税（含退税）	Company Income Tax	100054	140539
个人所得税	Individual Income Tax	107113	153247
资源税	Resources Tax	79542	94741
城市维护建设税	Tax on City Maintenance and Construction	163841	229299
房产税	Tax on Real Estates	73501	78381
契　税	Contract Tax	61230	82801
其他税收收入	Other Revenues	59872	79017
非税收入	Nontax Revenues	449256	652140
专项收入	Special Project Revenues	165168	284588
行政性收费收入	Revenues of Administrative and Institutional Units	150175	166874
罚没收入	Revenues of Penalty and Confiscatory	86094	100457
其他收入	Other Revenues	47819	100221
基金预算收入	Fund Budgetary Revenues	461915	837018
支出合计	**Total Expenditures**	**7278622**	**8745625**
地方财政一般预算支出	General Budgetary Expenditure in Local Finance	6784723	7951540
一般公共服务	General Common Service	1259785	1484113
教　育	Operating Expenses for Education	1137167	1427688
科学技术	Operating Expenses for Science and Technology	83468	128401
文化体育与传媒	Operating Expenses for Culture Sporrts and Broadcast	152062	233506
社会保障和就业	Operating Expenses for Medical Treatment and Sanitation	752189	909273
医疗卫生	Operating Expenses for Medical Treatment and Sanitation	335646	458154
环境保护	Operating Expenses for Environmental Conservation	190873	214918
城乡社区事务	Expenses of Community	415836	593730
农林水事务	Expenses of Agriculture, Forest and Irrigation	692632	984255
交通运输	Operating Expenses for Transportation	188835	342721
工业商业金融等事务	Operating Expenses for Industry, Trade and Finance	876117	389902
其他各项支出	Other Various Expenditures	700113	784915
基金预算支出	Fund Budgetary Expenditure	493899	794085

5-4 各地、州、市、县(市)地方财政一般预算收支

Government Revenue and Expenditures by Prefecture, Autonomous Prefecture, City and County

单位：万元 (2007 年) (10 000 yuan)

地　区	Region	收　入 Revenue	支　出 Expenditures
总　计	**Total**	**2858600**	**7951540**
自治区本级	Autonomous regional Level	427965	2700701
乌鲁木齐市	**Urumqi City**	**734279**	**683153**
天山区	Tianshan District	72107	58946
沙依巴克区	Shayibak District	51071	50763
新市区	Xinshi District	45618	42344
水磨沟区	Shui Mogou District	38258	39212
头屯河区	Tou Tunhe District	20137	19874
米东区	Midong District	60705	83928
达坂城区	Da Bancheng District	6028	12386
乌鲁木齐县	Urumqi County	8038	23417
市本级	City Level	432317	352283
克拉玛依市	**Karamay City**	**364826**	**428248**
独山子区	Dushanzi District	64500	78993
克拉玛依区	Karamay District	38042	58843
白碱滩区	Bai Jiantan District	12604	30926
乌尔河区	Urhe District	3296	12779
市本级	City Level	246384	246707
吐鲁番地区	**Turpan Administrative Offices**	**93214**	**165740**
吐鲁番市	Turpan City	24552	42173
鄯善县	Shanshan [Piqan] County	54701	59144
托克逊县	Toksun County	11679	35335
地区本级	Regional Level	2282	29088
哈密地区	**Hami [Kumul] Administrative Offices**	**60955**	**163823**
哈密市	Hami [Kumul] City	47963	64930
巴里坤县	Barkol Kazak Autonomous County	4834	34400
伊吾县	Yiwu [Araturuk] County	3655	17739
地区本级	Prefecture Level	4503	46754
昌吉回族自治州	**Changji Hui Autonomous Prefecture**	**138018**	**344146**
昌吉市	Changji City	46226	68818
阜康市	Fukang City	31525	33030
呼图壁县	Hutubi County	13337	30482
玛纳斯县	Manas County	18865	32815
奇台县	Qitai County	6641	40497
吉木萨尔县	Jimsar County	11401	32174
木垒哈萨克自治县	Mori Kazak Autonomous County	2143	27667
州本级	Autonomous Prefecture Level	7880	78663
伊犁哈萨克自治州	**Ili Kazak Autonomous Prefecture**	**335217**	**1134352**
州本级	Autonomous Prefecture Level	48031	201410
伊犁州直属县(市)	**Counties (Cities) Direct Under Ili Prefecture**	**146961**	**555788**
伊宁市	Yining [Gulja] City	39531	76354
奎屯市	Kuytun City	32388	40629
伊宁县	Yining [Gulja] County	9419	58833
察布查尔县	Qapqal Xibe Autonomous County	4726	37469

5-4 续表 1 Continued

单位：万元 (10 000 yuan)

地 区	Region	收入 Revenue	支出 Expenditures
霍城县	Huocheng [Korgas] County	9318	47355
巩留县	Gongliu [Tokkuztara] County	4702	33875
新源县	Xinyuan [Kunes] County	13854	44572
昭苏县	Zhaosu [Mongolkure] County	2594	34673
特克斯县	Tekes County	2720	38145
尼勒克县	Nilka County	7919	36367
州直属县(市)本级	Counties (Cities) Direct under the Prefecture	19790	107516
塔城地区	**Tacheng [Tarbagatai] Administrative Office**	**125913**	**323630**
塔城市	Tacheng [Qoqek] City	8602	36025
乌苏市	Usu City	16999	43424
额敏县	Emin [Dorbiljin] County	6523	36406
沙湾县	Shawan County	16609	41039
托里县	Toli County	6403	29929
裕民县	Yumin [Qagantokay] County	1527	22513
和布克赛尔蒙古自治县	Hoboksar Mongol Autonomous County	66530	76796
地区本级	Prefecture Level	2720	37498
阿勒泰地区	**Altay Administrative Offices**	**62343**	**254934**
阿勒泰市	Altay City	7524	44892
布尔津县	Burqin County	5124	24404
富蕴县	Fuyun [Koktokay] County	16505	37206
福海县	Fuhai [Burultokay] County	6312	26361
哈巴河县	Habahe [Kaba] County	18555	37836
青河县	Qinghe [Qinggil] County	1499	23184
吉木乃县	Jeminay County	1241	18327
地区本级	Prefecture Level	5583	42724
博尔塔拉蒙古自治州	**Bortala Mongol Autonomous Prefecture**	**48082**	**153008**
博乐市	Bole [Bortala] City	14371	41559
精河县	Jinghe [Jing] County	6346	32958
温泉县	Wenquan [Araxang] County	1844	22095
州本级	Autonomous Prefecture Level	25521	56396
巴音郭楞蒙古自治州	**Bayangol Mongol Autonomous Prefecture**	**196444**	**396809**
库尔勒市	Korla City	76699	84621
轮台县	Luntai [Bugur] County	47251	55303
尉犁县	Yuli [Lopnur] County	8863	28021
若羌县	Ruoqiang [Qarkilik] County	3860	17049
且末县	Qiemo [Qarqan] County	20191	29201
焉耆回族自治县	Yanqi Hui Autonomous County	9217	28218
和静县	Hejing County	10193	41343
和硕县	Hoxud County	3865	20253
博湖县	Bohu [Bagrax] County	3188	18042
州本级	Autonomous Prefecture Level	13117	74758
阿克苏地区	**Aksu Administrative Offices**	**255818**	**538450**
阿克苏市	Aksu City	38026	66594
温宿县	Wensu [Onsu] County	11947	43176

5-4 续表 2 Continued

单位：万元 (10 000 yuan)

地　　区	Region	收 入 Revenue	支 出 Expenditures
库车县	Kuqa County	102595	120544
沙雅县	Xayar County	44507	57715
新和县	Xinhe [Toksu] County	13921	37708
拜城县	Baicheng [Bay] County	27548	57357
乌什县	Wushi [Uxturpan] County	1566	31236
阿瓦提县	Awat County	4100	32562
柯坪县	Kalpin County	572	17303
地区本级	Prefecture Level	11036	74255
克孜勒苏柯尔克孜自治州	**Kizilsu Kirgiz Autonomous Prefecture**	**12294**	**178392**
阿图什市	Artux City	4970	43875
阿克陶县	Akto County	2371	38566
阿合奇县	Akqi County	847	20076
乌恰县	Wuqia [Ulugqat] County	2303	25703
地区本级	Prefecture Level	1803	50172
喀什地区	**Kashgar [Kaxgar] Administrative Offices**	**81220**	**607616**
喀什市	Kashgar [Kaxgar] City	30647	69234
疏附县	Shufu County	2327	43860
疏勒县	Shule County	4125	42871
英吉沙县	Yengisar County	1547	36626
泽普县	Zepu [Poskam] County	6191	30284
莎车县	Shache [Yarkant] County	7878	88699
叶城县	Yecheng [Kagilik] County	7724	64811
麦盖提县	Makit County	4042	33829
岳普湖县	Yopurga County	1501	25911
伽师县	Jiashi [Payzawat] County	2910	47476
巴楚县	Bachu [Maralbexi] County	6480	48261
塔什库尔干塔吉克自治县	Taxkorgan Tajik Autonomous County	1853	20554
地区本级	Prefecture Level	3995	55200
和田地区	**Hotan Administrative Offices**	**31843**	**351057**
和田市	Hotan City	12538	45623
和田县	Hotan County	2824	39598
墨玉县	Moyu [Karakax] County	3770	60972
皮山县	Pishan [Guma] County	2293	39076
洛浦县	Lop County	2942	37560
策勒县	Qira County	1593	30144
于田县	Yutian [Keriya] County	2396	43806
民丰县	Minfeng [Niya] County	1489	15527
地区本级	Prefecture Level	1998	38751
自治区直辖市	**Municpality Country-LevelCity directly under the Central Govern-ment**		
石河子市	Shihezi City	66656	84440
阿拉尔市	Aral City	4112	6738
图木舒克市	Tumxuk City	1606	7083
五家渠市	Wujiaqu City	6051	7784

5-5 金融机构各项存款和各项贷款余额

Banlance of Deposits and Loans of National Banking System

单位：亿元 (100 million yuan)

年 份 Year	各项存款合计 Total Deposits	#企业存款 Deposits by Enterprises	#储蓄存款 Savings Deposit	各项贷款合计 Total Loans	#工业贷款 Industrial Loans	#商业贷款 Commercial Loans	#农业贷款 Agricultural Loans
1978	32.07	6.86	6.42	18.26	5.11	12.15	1.00
1979	33.44	7.03	7.21	21.19	6.48	12.21	2.49
1980	38.56	9.60	9.52	24.74	5.65	16.09	2.26
1981	45.59	12.21	12.29	28.84	5.05	19.48	2.46
1982	53.47	15.23	15.30	32.86	5.23	21.37	3.65
1983	61.94	17.95	19.01	38.85	6.27	24.03	3.47
1984	73.63	23.35	24.31	52.02	8.91	27.47	6.49
1985	82.96	29.87	29.55	72.68	12.78	35.82	7.38
1986	102.75	38.15	40.37	93.18	18.21	40.43	10.07
1987	124.93	44.13	53.25	111.14	21.33	44.52	12.61
1988	141.10	47.41	66.25	139.43	26.80	54.73	14.97
1989	167.03	52.76	83.33	173.02	36.55	68.48	17.46
1990	221.80	71.23	114.13	233.72	46.82	100.17	18.66
1991	282.21	92.78	145.01	299.59	60.39	134.28	22.58
1992	336.58	119.51	175.62	380.26	75.06	165.36	29.76
1993	397.39	129.98	220.45	467.81	98.65	191.17	23.93
1994	634.44	214.13	347.71	632.32	123.93	230.54	31.53
1995	838.42	274.24	477.18	843.38	155.23	327.38	43.34
1996	1012.47	364.51	575.79	1016.20	197.94	392.26	54.51
1997	1180.78	442.76	676.13	1215.39	238.72	444.88	51.31
1998	1336.58	461.02	759.14	1318.41	258.31	485.03	83.41
1999	1548.72	544.22	824.68	1386.78	270.20	471.45	91.51
2000	1863.48	702.21	908.55	1403.13	243.03	392.01	84.13
2001	1972.55	691.74	994.00	1584.73	298.91	433.27	99.46
2002	2225.31	705.82	1137.87	1801.15	311.01	397.44	114.45
2003	2661.65	763.49	1371.59	2099.09	319.51	411.22	123.03
2004	2959.78	832.50	1534.67	2214.66	309.38	471.42	149.20
2005	3427.48	909.45	1816.38	2272.08	248.59	496.99	169.78
2006	4040.78	1106.42	2035.63	2412.69	272.90	443.03	175.86
2007	4614.62	1452.25	2054.91	2685.00	281.14	462.15	189.24

5-6 金融机构和人员数
Number of Financial Institutions and Staff

单位：个、人　　(2007 年)　　(unit, person)

项　目	Item	合计 Total 机构 Institutions	合计 Total 人员 Employees	自治区级 Level of Autonomous Region 机构 Institutions	自治区级 Level of Autonomous Region 人员 Employees	地区级 Prefectural Level 机构 Institutions	地区级 Prefectural Level 人员 Employees
总　计	**Total**	**3493**	**54145**	**14**	**3293**	**120**	**13506**
人民银行	**The People's Bank of China**	**68**	**3264**	**1**	**399**	**14**	**1579**
银监会新疆监管局	**China Banking Regulatory Commission Xingjiang Bureau**	**63**	**936**	**1**	**163**	**14**	**594**
政策性银行	**Policy Bank**	**91**	**2072**	**2**	**230**	**18**	**581**
国家开发银行	The Bank of State Development	1	80	1	80		
农业发展银行	The Bank of Agricultural Development	90	1992	1	150	18	581
国有商业银行	**State Sole-funded Commercial Bank**	**1309**	**29783**	**5**	**2180**	**60**	**9087**
工商银行	Industrial and Commercial Bank	302	8773	1	620	15	3061
农业银行	Agricultural Bank	386	8815	1	349	15	2435
农业银行兵团分行	Agricultural Bank, XPCG Branch	263	3523	1	205	3	305
中国银行	Bank of China	161	3268	1	619	13	1022
建设银行	Bank of Construction	197	5404	1	387	14	2264
股份制商业银行	**Share-Holding Commercial Bank**	**46**	**1484**			**5**	**712**
交通银行	Bank of Communication	26	743			1	290
招商银行	Merchants Bank	9	339			1	141
华夏银行	Hua Xia Bank	6	178			1	100
上海浦东发展银行	Shanghai PuDong Development Bank	3	124			1	95
兴业银行	XinYe Bank	2	100			1	86
城市商业银行	**City Commercial Bank**	**80**	**1224**			**2**	**391**
乌鲁木齐市商业银行	Urumqi Commercial Bank	70	1064			1	302
克拉玛依市商业银行	Karamay Commercial Bank	10	160			1	89
城市信用社	**City Credit Cooperative**	**34**	**429**				
农村信用社	**Rural Credit Cooperative**	**1062**	**10079**	**1**	**92**		
资产管理公司	**Assets Management Company**	**3**	**178**	**3**	**178**		
信达公司	Xinda Firm	1	51	1	51		
华融公司	Huarong Firm	1	74	1	74		
长城公司	Great Wall Firm	1	53	1	53		
信托投资公司	**Trust and Investment Company**	**1**	**50**			**1**	**50**
金融租赁公司	**Financial Leasing Company**	**1**	**47**			**1**	**47**
邮政储汇	**Postal Remittence**	**735**	**4599**	**1**	**51**	**5**	**465**

5-6 续表 Continued

单位：个、人 (unit, person)

项 目	Item	县 级 County Level		营业网点 Business Outlets	
		机 构 Institutions	人 员 Employees	机 构 Institutions	人 员 Employees
总 计	**Total**	**778**	**18054**	**2581**	**19292**
人民银行	**The People's Bank of China**	**53**	**1286**		
银监会新疆监管局	**China Banking Regulatory Commission Xingjiang Bureau**	**48**	**179**		
政策性银行	**Policy Bank**	**68**	**1222**	**3**	**39**
国家开发银行	The Bank of State Development				
农业发展银行	The Bank of Agricultural Development	68	1222	3	39
国有商业银行	**State Sole-funded Commercial Bank**	**403**	**10737**	**841**	**7779**
工商银行	Industrial and Commercial Bank	144	3387	142	1705
农业银行	Agricultural Bank	127	3629	243	2402
农业银行兵团分行	Agricultural Bank, XPCG Branch	29	1086	230	1927
中国银行	Bank of China	59	986	88	641
建设银行	Bank of Construction	44	1649	138	1104
股份制商业银行	**Share-Holding Commercial Bank**			**41**	**772**
交通银行	Bank of Communication			25	453
招商银行	Merchants Bank			8	198
华夏银行	Hua Xia Bank			5	78
上海浦东发展银行	Shanghai PuDong Development Bank			2	29
兴业银行	XinYe Bank			1	14
城市商业银行	**City Commercial Bank**	**9**	**71**	**69**	**762**
乌鲁木齐市商业银行	Urumqi Commercial Bank			69	762
克拉玛依市商业银行	Karamay Commercial Bank	9	71		
城市信用社	**City Credit Cooperative**	**3**	**237**	**31**	**192**
农村信用社	**Rural Credit Cooperative**	**163**	**3730**	**898**	**6257**
资产管理公司	**Assets Management Company**				
信达公司	Xinda Firm				
华融公司	Huarong Firm				
长城公司	Great Wall Firm				
信托投资公司	**Trust and Investment Company**				
金融租赁公司	**Financial Leasing Company**				
邮政储汇	**Postal Remittence**	**31**	**592**	**698**	**3491**

5-7 金融机构信贷资金平衡表

Credit Funds Balance Sheet of Financial Institutions by Sources

单位：亿元 (100 million yuan)

项目	Item	2006	2007
资金来源合计	**All Sources**	**4050.75**	**4241.00**
各项存款	Deposits	4040.78	4614.62
企业存款	Deposits of Enterprises	1106.42	1452.25
活期存款	Current Deposits	840.21	1073.21
定期存款	Time Deposits	266.21	379.04
财政存款	Treasury Deposits	76.24	136.64
机关团体存款	Deposits of Government Agencies and Organizations	368.59	435.70
储蓄存款	Savings Deposits	2035.63	2054.91
活期存款	Current Deposits	765.47	901.73
定期存款	Time Deposits	1270.16	1153.18
农业存款	Agricultural Deposits	85.20	114.90
委托存款	Commission Deposits	10.36	9.28
其他存款	Others	358.34	410.94
应付及暂收款	Payable and Temporary Collection	58.61	81.45
各项准备金	Various Preparations	43.38	44.53
所有者权益	Owner's Right and Interest	48.92	87.18
其他	Others	-140.94	-586.78
资金运用合计	**All Uses**	**4050.75**	**4241.00**
各项贷款	Loans	2412.69	2685.00
短期贷款	Short-term Loans	1168.22	1227.84
工业贷款	Industrial Loans	272.90	281.14
商业贷款	Commercial Loans	443.03	462.15
建筑业贷款	Construction Loans	27.43	27.47
农业贷款	Agricultural Loans	175.86	189.24
乡镇企业贷款	Loans to Township Enterprises	10.69	11.12
三资企业贷款	Loans to Sino-foreign Joint Venture and Cooperative Enterprises and Foreign-funded Enterprises	4.29	5.66
私营企业及个体贷款	Loans to Private Enterprises and Individuals	17.17	19.63
其他短期贷款	Other Short-term Loans	216.85	231.43
#个人短期消费贷款	Individual Short-term Loans	4.98	9.37
中长期贷款	Medium-term & Long-term Loans	1066.99	1270.43
基本建设贷款	Capital Construction	601.50	620.46
技术改造贷款	Technical Innovation	15.79	13.33
其他中长期贷款	Other Medium-term & Long-term Loans	449.70	636.64
#个人中长期消费贷款	Individual Medium and Long-term Loans	168.36	185.23
信托贷款	Credit Loans	0.03	0.03
其他贷款	Other Loans	177.45	186.70
有价证券及投资	Securities & Investment	151.43	133.31
同业往来	Inter-bank Debts	5.73	5.96
系统内资金往来	Funds Transfer Inward Banks	1103.73	1282.91
外汇占款	Position for Foreign Exchange	0.20	1.06
库存现金	Vault Cash	30.89	34.49
其他	Others	346.08	98.27

5-8 国有商业银行信贷资金平衡表

Credit Funds Balance Sheet of State-owned Commercial Banks

单位：亿元 (100 million yuan)

项　　目	Item	2006	2007
资金来源合计	**All Sources**	**2906.59**	**3255.00**
各项存款	Deposits	2838.40	3109.48
企业存款	Deposits of Enterprises	780.69	987.61
活期存款	Current Deposits	586.65	741.20
定期存款	Time Deposits	194.04	246.41
机关团体存款	Deposits of Government Agencies and Organizations	323.43	383.57
储蓄存款	Savings Deposits	1426.39	1395.18
活期存款	Current Deposits	510.62	583.56
定期存款	Time Deposits	915.77	811.62
农业存款	Agricultural Deposits	2.33	3.71
其他存款	Other Deposits	305.56	339.41
应付及暂收款	Payable and Temporary Collection	39.63	48.52
同业往来	Inter-bank Debts	29.27	68.65
各项准备	Various Preparations	32.27	27.43
所有者权益	Owner's Right and Interest	-6.64	17.03
其　他	Others	-26.34	-16.11
资金运用合计	**Total of Capital Application**	**2906.59**	**3255.00**
各项贷款	Loans	1258.25	1308.12
短期贷款	Short-term Loans	510.28	488.80
工业贷款	Industrial Loans	223.61	218.57
商业贷款	Commercial Loans	78.27	76.07
建筑业贷款	Construction Loans	18.87	19.32
农业贷款	Agricultural Loans	103.75	95.91
三资企业贷款	Loans to Industrial Enterprises with HongKong,Macao,Taiwan and Foreign Funds	3.51	4.61
私营企业及个体贷款	Loans to Private Enterprises and Individuals	7.27	5.25
其他短期贷款	Other Short-term Loans	75.00	69.07
#个人短期消费贷款	Individual Short-term Loans	2.51	6.60
中长期贷款	Medium-term & Long-term Loans	632.77	704.88
基本建设贷款	Capital Construction	290.99	252.01
技术改造贷款	Technical Innovation	12.54	11.44
其他中长期贷款	Other Medium-term & Long-term Loans	329.24	441.43
#个人中长期消费贷款	Individual Medium and Long-term Loans	156.55	165.23
其他贷款	Other Loans	115.20	114.44
有价证券及投资	Securities & Investment	18.96	41.70
应收及预付款	Payable and Pre-payment	11.39	3.43
同业往来	Inter-bank Debts	6.46	4.80
系统内资金往来	Funds Transfer Inward Banks	1338.92	1834.50
外汇占款	Position for Foreign Exchange	0.19	0.61
库存现金	Vault Cash	18.33	20.31
其　他	Others	254.09	41.53

5-9 金融机构现金收支表

Cash Income and Expenditure of Financial Institutions

单位：亿元 (100 million yuan)

项　目	Item	2006	2007	2007 年比 2006 年增减(%) Increase Rate in 2007over 2006
收入合计	**Total Income**	**9962.68**	**12073.58**	**21.2**
商品销售收入	Income from Commodity Sales	706.89	772.46	9.3
服务业收入	Income from Service Trades	413.28	512.08	23.9
行政税款收入	Income from Taxes	32.79	53.94	64.5
城乡个体经营收入	Income from Urban and Rural Individual Business	168.31	167.43	-0.5
储蓄存款收入	Income from Savings Deposits	7168.74	8864.27	23.7
居民归还贷款收入	Income from Repayment of Loans by Residents	164.00	169.39	3.3
汇兑收入	Income from Remittances	142.01	75.91	-46.6
有价证券及其他投资性收入	Income from Securities	31.51	50.36	59.8
其他收入	Other Income	1135.15	1407.74	24.0
支出合计	**Total Expenditure**	**10073.58**	**12202.49**	**21.1**
工资性支出	Wages	585.56	635.16	8.5
农副产品采购支出	Purchases of Agricultural and Sideline Products	416.72	488.40	17.2
工矿及其他产品采购支出	Expenditure for Purchases of Industrial and Mineral Products	52.88	51.01	-3.5
行政事业管理和经营费支出	Government and Enterprises Overhead	333.08	406.70	22.1
城乡个体经营支出	Expenditure for Individual Business	229.32	213.24	-7.0
储蓄存款支出	Expenditure for Savings Deposits	7064.17	8630.59	22.2
居民提取贷款支出	Expenditure for Loans withdrawn by Residents	140.29	153.92	9.7
汇兑支出	Expenditure for Remittances	27.94	25.51	-8.7
有价证券及其他投资性支出	Expenditure for Securities	30.11	66.88	122.1
其他支出	Other Expenditures	1193.51	1531.08	28.3
投放(+)、回笼(-)	**Monetary Issues (+) Cash Withdrawn (-)**	**110.90**	**128.91**	**16.2**

5-10 保险机构

Number of Insurance Institutions

单位：个 (2007 年) (unit)

项　目	Item	机构数 Number of Institution	总公司 General Corporation	自治区分公司 Xinjiang Branch Company	地区级中心支公司 Branch Company at Prefecture Level	县级支公司 Branch Company at County Level	营销服务部 Marketing Department
总　计	**Total**	**1127**	**1**	**15**	**105**	**310**	**696**
中国人民财产保险公司新疆分公司	The People's Insurance Corporation of China	238		1	16	84	137
中华联合财产保险公司	The Property Insurance Corporation, XPCG	231	1		14	145	71
中国平安财产保险公司	The Ping An Insurance Corporation, Property Insurance Company	35		1	11	4	19
中国太平洋财产保险公司	The Pacific Insurance Corporation, Property Insurance Company	12		1	5	4	2
永安财产保险公司	Yong An Property Insurance Corporation	55		1	12	1	41
天安财产保险公司	Tian An Property Insurance Corporation	14		1	6		7
安邦财产保险公司	An Bang Property Insurance Corporation	20		1	2		17
大地财产保险公司	Da Di Property Insurance Corporation	12		1			11
阳光财产保险公司	Sunshine Property Insurance Corporation	1		1			
中国人寿保险公司新疆分公司	The Life Insurance Corporation of China	368		1	15	68	284
中国平安人寿保险公司	The Ping An Insurance Corporation, Life Insurance Company	55		1	9	3	42
中国太平洋人寿保险公司	The Pacific Insurance Corporation, Life Insurance Company	32		1	5	1	25
新华人寿保险公司	Xin Hua Life Insurance Corporation	28		1	4		23
泰康人寿保险公司	Tai Kang Life Insurance Corporation	24		1	6		17
中国平安养老保险公司	Ping An Endowment Insurance Corporation	1		1			
中国人民人寿保险公司	PICC Life Insurance Corporation	1		1			

5-11 国内保险业务情况
Conditions of Domestic Insurance Service

单位：亿元 (100 million yuan)

年份 Year	承保额 Amount Insured		保费 Premium		赔款及给付 Claim and Payment	
	财产险 Property Insurance	人身险 Life Insurance	财产险 Property Insurance	人身险 Life Insurance	财产险 Property Insurance	人身险 Life Insurance
1980	4		0.01			
1985	70	2	0.40	0.01	0.15	…
1990	241	41	1.04	0.53	0.47	0.08
1995	613	168	4.59	2.06	2.38	0.41
2000	1612	1711	12.49	15.72	5.99	3.72
2001	2112	1371	14.17	19.98	7.43	4.37
2002	2283	3524	16.48	35.25	7.84	5.02
2003	5588	1362	19.12	43.06	10.36	7.10
2004	6401	1735	20.04	48.09	10.65	7.70
2005	8949	9418	20.93	51.57	12.60	7.65
2006	8333	27028	24.61	60.79	12.92	10.34
2007	12188	13081	34.67	70.95	18.78	18.64

5-12 保险事业发展情况
Statistics on Development of Insurance

(2007 年)

项目	Item	承保额(亿元) Amount Insured (100 million yuan)	保费(万元) Premium (10 000 yuan)	赔款及给付(万元) Claim and Payment (10 000 yuan)
总计	**Total**	**25269.37**	**1056178**	**374191**
中国人民财产保险公司新疆分公司	The People's Insurance Corporation of China	4368.17	182816	98803
中华联合财产保险公司	The Property Insurance Corporation, XPCG	3482.46	136307	79225
中国平安财产保险公司	The Ping An Insurance Corporation, Property Insurance Company	540.60	18121	11064
中国太平洋财产保险公司	The Pacific Insurance Corporation, Property Insurance Company	2670.27	14684	6549
永安财产保险公司	Yong An Property Insurance Corporation	437.93	13246	5905
天安财产保险公司	Tian An Property Insurance Corporation	141.73	4595	1709
安邦财产保险公司	An Bang Property Insurance Corporation	225.09	8336	1757
大地财产保险公司	Da Di Property Insurance Corporation	295.27	2725	495
阳光财产保险公司	Sunshine Property Insurance Corporation	26.86	1047	70
中国人寿保险公司新疆分公司	The Life Insurance Corporation of China	10035.66	372854	136450
中国平安人寿保险公司	The Ping An Insurance Corporation, Life Insurance Company	1553.42	109454	16856
中国太平洋人寿保险公司	The Pacific Insurance Corporation, Life Insurance Company	687.17	97651	13099
新华人寿保险公司	Xin Hua Life Insurance Corporation	119.43	38378	1484
泰康人寿保险公司	Tai Kang Life Insurance Corporation	685.03	55545	725
中国人民人寿保险公司	PICC Life Insurance Corporation	0.28	419	

5-13 各地区保险业务情况
Conditions of Insurance Service by Region

单位：万元 (2007 年) (10 000 yuan)

地 区	Region	全部业务 All Insurance Business		财产保险公司业务 Property Insurance Business	
		保费收入 Premium Income	比上年增长(%) Increase Rate Over preceding year(%)	保费收入 Premium Income	比上年增长(%) Increase Rate Over preceding year(%)
总 计	**Total**	**1056178**	**23.7**	**381878**	**39.1**
乌鲁木齐市	Urumqi City	316144	20.9	88303	30.8
克拉玛依市	Karamay City	78051	15.9	23035	16.8
石河子市	Shihezi City	48862	24.2	25265	36.9
吐鲁番地区	Turpan Administrative Offices	25384	12.7	11482	14.6
哈密地区	Hami [Kumul] Administrative Offices	34145	6.1	10044	43.0
昌吉回族自治州	Changji Hui Autonomous Prefecture	113906	27.3	33271	50.9
伊犁州直属县(市)	Counties (Cities) Direct Under Ili Prefecture	73333	31.1	28102	46.5
塔城地区	Tacheng [Tarbagatai] Administrative Offices	37760	22.8	12767	52.9
阿勒泰地区	Altay Administrative Offices	23269	11.4	8760	33.2
博尔塔拉蒙古自治州	Bortala Mongol Autonomous Prefecture	22314	22.5	11483	38.6
巴音郭楞蒙古自治州	Bayangol Mongol Autonomous Prefecture	97361	38.2	40219	54.1
阿克苏地区	Aksu Administrative Offices	69031	31.2	33491	54.2
克孜勒苏柯尔克孜自治州	Kizilsu Kirgiz Autonomous Prefecture	4189	9.6	1885	26.8
喀什地区	Kashgar [Kaxgar] Administrative Offices	57096	26.1	29275	45.1
和田地区	Hotan Administrative Offices	14012	25.2	7563	43.6
奎屯市	Kuytun City	27365	27.7	15943	43.8
区本级	Prefecture Level	13956	24.9	990	-38.7

地 区	Region	人寿保险公司业务 Life Insurance Business		保险密度(元) Insurance Density (yuan)	保险深度(%) Insurance Depth(%)
		保费收入 Premium Income	比上年增长(%) Increase Rate Over preceding year(%)		
总 计	**Total**	**674300**	**16.4**	**504**	**3.02**
乌鲁木齐市	Urumqi City	227841	17.5	1515	3.91
克拉玛依市	Karamay City	55016	15.6	2930	1.52
石河子市	Shihezi City	23597	13.0	807	7.00
吐鲁番地区	Turpan Administrative Offices	13902	11.2	423	1.48
哈密地区	Hami [Kumul] Administrative Offices	24101	-4.2	713	4.23
昌吉回族自治州	Changji Hui Autonomous Prefecture	80635	19.6	736	3.65
伊犁州直属县(市)	Counties (Cities) Direct Under Ili Prefecture	45231	23.1	271	3.10
塔城地区	Tacheng [Tarbagatai] Administrative Offices	24993	11.6	393	1.92
阿勒泰地区	Altay Administrative Offices	14509	1.4	361	2.34
博尔塔拉蒙古自治州	Bortala Mongol Autonomous Prefecture	10831	9.0	472	2.90
巴音郭楞蒙古自治州	Bayangol Mongol Autonomous Prefecture	57142	28.8	795	2.08
阿克苏地区	Aksu Administrative Offices	35540	15.0	313	2.98
克孜勒苏柯尔克孜自治州	Kizilsu Kirgiz Autonomous Prefecture	2304	-1.4	84	1.77
喀什地区	Kashgar [Kaxgar] Administrative Offices	27821	10.8	155	
和田地区	Hotan Administrative Offices	6449	8.9	74	2.20
奎屯市	Kuytun City	11422	10.5	906	6.86
区本级	Prefecture Level	12966	35.7		

5-14 保险业务经济技术指标

Main Economic and Technological Indicators of Insurance Company

单位：万元　　(2007 年)　　(10 000 yuan)

项　目	Item	保　费 Premium	赔款及给付 Claim and Payment
财产保险业务	**Property Insurance Corporation**	**346723**	**187771**
企业财产险	Insurance of Enterprise Property	27138	15878
家庭财产险	Insurance of Family Property	2219	917
机动车辆险	Insurance of Mobile Vehicles	212193	108819
工程保险	Engineering Insurance	2929	2295
责任保险	Insurance of Liability	12220	4070
信用保险	Insurance of Credit	9	-14
保证保险	Insurance of Guaranty	3929	2067
货物运输险	Insurance of Cargo Transportation	5516	1377
特殊风险保险	Special insurance against risk	4874	2084
农业保险	Insurance of Agriculture	75689	50277
其他险	Other Insurance	7	1
人身保险业务	**Life Insurance Companies**	**709455**	**186421**
寿　险	Life Insurance	588429	141992
健康险	Health Insurance	86453	32655
人身意外伤害险	Unforeseen Human Injury Insurance	34573	11774

5-15 新疆辖区证券、期货经营机构和人员数

Operators and Staff of Securities and Futures in Xinjiang

单位：个、人　　(2007 年)　　(unit, person)

公司名称	Name of Enterprise	机构数 Number of Institution	人员 Staff	营业部数量 Number of Business Department	人员 Staff	服务部数量 Number of Service Department	人员 Staff
总　计	**Total**	**3**	**602**	**35**	**617**	**19**	**76**
新疆辖区证券机构	**Stock Instituions in the Territory of Xinjiang**	**1**	**529**	**19**	**330**	**16**	**60**
宏源证券股份有限公司	Hongyuan Securities Stock Limited Company	1	529	19	330	16	60
异地证券公司乌鲁木齐营业部	**Urumqi Business Department, Yidi Stock Company**			**12**	**257**		
金元证券公司	Jinyuan Securities Company			1	24		
平安证券有限责任公司	Pin'An Securities Liability Ltd. Co.			1	19		
中国银河证券有限责任公司	China Yinhe Securities Liability Ltd. Co.			1	29		
湘财证券有限责任公司	Xiangcai Securities Liability Ltd. Co.			1	25	1	3
长江证券有限责任公司	Dapeng Securities Liability Ltd. Co.			1	40		
光大证券有限责任公司	Everbright Securities Liability Ltd. Co.			1	11		
国泰君安证券股份有限公司	Jun"an Securities Stock Ltd. Co.			1	14		
申银万国股份有限公司	Shenyin Universal Stock Ltd. Co.			1	10		
海通证券公司	Haitong Securities Company			1	18		
华融证券公司	Deheng Securities Company			1	46	2	13
民族证券公司	Nationality Securities Company			1	21		
新疆期货经纪公司	**Xinjiang Futures Broker's Company**	**2**	**73**	**4**	**30**		
新疆天利期货经纪有限公司	Xinjiang Tianli Futures Broker's Company	1	34	1	3		
新天期货经纪有限公司	Xin Tian Futures Broker's Company	1	39	2	7		
河南万达期货经纪有限公司乌鲁木齐营业部	**Urumqi Business Department, Henan Wanda Futures Broker's Company**			**1**	**20**		

5-16 上市公司基本情况表
Basic Condition of Listed Companies

公司简称 Names of Businesses		上市时间 Listed Time	上市交易所 Listing Stock Exchange	发行时股本(万股) Total Capital Stock (10 000 share)		发行募集资金(万元) Floated Raised Funds (10 000 yuan)	2007年末股本(万股) Stock Capital by 2007 (10 000 share)		2007年累计募集资金(万元) Capital Raised by 2007 (10 000 yuan)
				总股本 Total Stock Capital	流通股本 Circulating Capital Stock		总股本 Total Stock Capital	流通股本 Circulating Stock Capital	
总　计	**Total**			**483216**	**140065**	**984710**	**1163602**	**596175**	**2088609**
宏源信托	Hongyuan Trust	1994	深交所 SZSE	17500	4500	10550	146120	50524	320952
新疆众和	Xijiang Zhonghe	1996	上交所 SHSE	7953	2025	9690	29806	13550	9690
百花村	Bai Huacun	1996	上交所 SHSE	6128	2700	11800	9480	4650	20676
汇通水利	Huitong Water Conservancy	1996	深交所 SZSE	5000	1250	7062	30034	19478	17262
友好集团	Youhao Group	1996	上交所 SHSE	10700	2700	10607	31149	26310	61238
新疆屯河	Xinjiang Tunhe	1997	上交所 SHSE	7000	1750	9400	80560	40629	44400
啤酒花	Hop	1997	上交所 SHSE	8000	3000	11523	36792	21575	11523
新疆天业	Xinjiang Tianye	1997	上交所 SHSE	6300	2430	16896	43859	24883	63900
特变电工	Toban Electric Engineering	1997	上交所 SHSE	8168	3000	14820	85404	57619	86421
新天国际	Suntime International	1997	上交所 SHSE	8600	2700	24071	47036	27168	33278
天山纺织	Tianshan Textile	1998	深交所 SZSE	18782	4230	20783	36346	15620	40459
天山股份	Tianshan Stock	1999	上交所 SHSE	12946	4500	26394	20802	14069	44044
新农开发	Xinnong Development	1999	上交所 SHSE	29400	9000	32905	32100	15795	32905
伊力特	Yilite	1999	上交所 SHSE	22050	7500	45375	44100	20937	45375
新中基	Xin Zhongji	2000	上交所 SHSE	12459	4500	21011	32236	26679	59701
广汇股份	Guanghui Stock	2000	上交所 SHSE	35378	5000	31652	86606	42867	31652
国际实业	Industry International	2000	深交所 SZSE	17179	7000	39837	20455	11276	39837
美克股份	Markor Stock	2000	上交所 SHSE	9208	4000	50923	28367	13340	172713
天利高科	Tianli High-Tech	2000	上交所 SHSE	17000	6000	42653	40430	18246	93113
新疆天宏	Xinjinag Tianhong	2001	上交所 SHSE	8016	3000	16633	8016	4484	16633
香梨股份	Fragrant Pear Stock	2001	上交所 SHSE	16050	5000	23141	14771	10132	23141
天富热电	Tianfu Thermoelectricity	2002	上交所 SHSE	16909	6000	42000	32785	17400	153331
八一钢铁	August 1st Steel	2002	上交所 SHSE	40943	13000	92254	58958	27638	92254
冠农股份	Guannong Stock	2003	上交所 SHSE	12000	4000	21610	18000	10655	21610
青松建化	Qubgsibg Cement	2003	上交所 SHSE	18493	6000	24265	24593	14344	95208
新疆城建	Xinjiang Urban Construction	2003	上交所 SHSE	16054	6000	33546	20354	9376	63775
新赛股份	Xinsai Stock	2003	上交所 SHSE	15000	5000	31441	18000	9128	31441
中泰化学	ZhongTai Chemical	2006	深交所 SZSE	23600	8000	66000	26843	21403	166209
天康生物	TianKang Animal	2006	深交所 SZSE	6400	1280	15868	9600	2400	15868
金风科技	Goldwind	2007	深交所 SZSE	50000	5000	180000	50000	4000	180000

主要统计指标解释

地方财政收入 属于地方财政的收入包括营业税，地方企业所得税，个人所得税，城镇土地使用税，固定资产投资方向调节税，城镇维护建设税，房产税，车船使用税，印花税，屠宰税，农牧业税，农业特产税，耕地占用税，契税，增值税25%部分，证券交易税(印花税)50%部分和除海洋石油资源税以外的其他资源税。

地方财政支出 地方财政支出主要包括地方行政管理和各项事业费，地方统筹的基本建设、技术改造支出，支援农村生产支出，城市维护和建设经费，价格补贴支出等。

信贷资金 指金融机构以信用方式积聚和分配的货币资金。金融机构信贷资金的来源有各项存款、对国际金融机构负债、流通中货币、银行自有资金及当年结益等；信贷资金的运用有各项贷款、黄金占款、外汇占款、财政借款及在国际金融机构中的资产等。

存款 指企业、机关、团体或居民根据资金必须收回的原则，把货币资金存入银行或其他信用机构保管并取得一定利息的一种信用活动形式。根据存款对象的不同可划分为企业存款、财政存款、机关团体存款、基本建设存款、城镇储蓄存款、农村存款等科目。它是银行信贷资金的主要来源。

贷款 指银行或其他信用机构根据资金必须归还的原则，按一定利率，为企业、个人等提供资金的一种信用活动形式。我国银行贷款分为流动资金贷款、固定资产贷款、城乡个体工商户贷款以及农业贷款等科目。

保险金额 指保险人承担赔偿或者给付保险金责任的最高限额。

保费 指投保人为取得保险人在约定范围内所承担赔偿责任而支付给保险人的费用。

赔款 指保险人根据保险合同的规定，向被保险人支付的赔偿保险责任损失的金额。

给付 包括死伤医疗给付和满期给付。死伤医疗给付是指保险人根据人寿保险及长期健康保险合同的规定，因被保险人在保险期内发生保险责任范围内的保险事故支付给被保险人(或受益人)的金额。满期给付是指被保险人生存期满，保险人按人寿保险合同规定支付给被保险人的满期保险金额。

Explanatory Notes on Main Statistical Indicators

Revenue of the Local Governments The revenue of the local governments includes business tax, income tax of the enterprises subordinate to the local government, personal income tax, tax on the use of urban land, tax on the adjustment of the investment in fixed assets, tax on town maintenance and construction, tax on real estates, tax on the use of vehicles and ships, stamp tax, slaughter tax, tax on agriculture and animal husbandry, tax on special agricultural products, tax on the occupancy of cultivated land, contract tax, 25% of the value added tax, 50% of the tax on stock dealing (stamp tax) and tax on resources other than the ocean petroleum resources.

Expenditure of the Local Governments The expenditure of the local governments includes mainly the administrative expenses and various operating expenses at the vel of local governments, the expenditure for capital construction and technological innovation with the funds raised by the local government, expenditure for supporting rural production, expenditure for City maintenance and construction and expenditure for price subsidies, etc.

Credit Funds refer to the funds issued as loans by banking institutions. The sources of credit funds of the banking institutions included deposits, liabilities to international financial institutions, currency in circulation, self-owned funds and current retained profits, etc. The credit funds can be used in forms of loans, gold, foreign exchange, government debt and assets in the international financial institutions.

Deposit is a form of credit by which enterprises, institutions, organizations or households can put money into banks and other credit institutions for safekeeping and interest earning under the principle of free withdrawal. According to different depositors, deposits are divided into enterprise deposits,treasury deposits, deposits of government agencies and organizations,capital construction deposits, urban savings deposits, rural deposits and other deposits. Deposits are major sources of the credit funds of banks.

Loan is a form of credit by which banks and other credit institutions provide funds at certain interest rate to enterprises and individuals in the light of the principle of unconditional repayment. Loans from Chinese banks include circulating capital loans, fixed assets loans, loans to urban and rural individuals engaged in industrial and commercial business and agricultural loans.

Amount Insured refers to the maximum that the insurant will get for the claim of the case insured.

Premium is the fee paid by the insurant to the insurer to obtain the obligation of compensation from the insurance within the agreed terms.

Settled Claim is the compensation paid by the insurer to the insurant in accordance with the insurance contract.

Payment includes payment for death, injury or medical treatment and mature payment. Payment for death, injury or medical treatment refers to the money paid to the insurant (or the beneficiary) in accordance with the life or health insurance contract when the insurant encounters accidents within the insured period covered in the contract. Mature payment refers to the mature payment to the insurant in accordance with the life insurance contract at the end of the insured period.

第六篇 价格指数

CHAPTER 6 Price Indices

简要说明
Brief Introduction

本篇资料的主要内容及来源

本篇价格指数资料，反映生产、流通、消费与投资环节的价格变动趋势和变动幅度，主要包括居民消费价格指数、商品零售价格指数、农业生产资料价格指数、工业品出厂价格指数（生产价格指数）、原材料、燃料、动力购进价格指数、固定资产投资价格指数、房屋销售价格指数。

居民消费价格指数、商品零售价格指数和农业生产资料价格指数出自出国家统计局新疆调查总队消费价格调查处；工业品出厂价格指数（生产价格指数）、原材料、燃料、动力购进价格指数、固定资产投资价格指数、房屋销售价格指数出自国家统计局新疆调查总队生产投资价格调查处。

Main Content and Source of Data

Data on the price indices in this chapter show the changing trend and the change rates in production, circulation, consumption and investment, including mainly consumer price indices of residents, retail price indices, price indices of agricultural means of production, purchasing price indices of farm products, producers´ price indices of industrial products, purchasing price indices of raw materials, fuels and power, price indices of investment in fixed assets, and real estate price indices.

Data on the consumer price index, retail price index and price indices of agriculture production come from Division of Consumer Price of NBS Survey Office in Xinjiang; Data on the price indices of industrial products, indices of purchasing price of raw materials, fuels and power, price indices of investment in fixed assets, price indices for real estate come from Division of Consumer Price of NBS Survey Office in Xinjiang.

6-1 各种物价指数
Price Indices

年 份 Year	居民消费价格指数 Consumer Price Index	城市居民消费价格指数 Urban Areas	农村居民消费价格指数 Rural Areas	商品零售价格指数 Retail Price Index
上年=100 Preceding year=100				
1978	101.2	101.4	100.3	101.4
1980	102.8	104.1	102.0	104.2
1985	107.8	109.5	106.4	108.1
1990	105.0	104.5	105.9	104.1
1995	119.7	118.4	122.5	116.7
1996	110.5	110.4	110.6	108.8
1997	103.7	103.5	103.9	101.8
1998	100.2	99.9	100.8	99.7
1999	97.4	97.7	96.8	96.2
2000	99.4	100.1	97.6	98.3
2001	104.0	104.0	103.8	102.5
2002	99.4	98.9	100.9	97.9
2003	100.4	100.5	100.2	99.2
2004	102.7	102.1	104.5	100.7
2005	100.7	100.6	101.2	99.4
2006	101.3	101.0	102.0	101.8
2007	105.5	104.6	107.2	105.1
1978 年=100 Year 1978 =100				
1978	100.0	100.0	100.0	100.0
1980	105.1	106.6	103.8	107.8
1985	120.9	125.6	117.9	124.2
1990	194.3	206.0	184.0	197.6
1995	392.7	422.7	364.2	381.0
1996	433.9	466.7	402.9	414.6
1997	450.0	483.0	418.6	422.0
1998	450.9	482.5	421.9	420.8
1999	439.2	471.4	408.4	404.8
2000	436.5	471.9	398.6	397.9
2001	454.0	490.8	413.8	407.8
2002	451.3	485.4	417.5	399.3
2003	453.1	487.8	418.3	396.1
2004	465.3	498.1	437.1	398.9
2005	468.6	501.1	442.3	396.5
2006	474.7	506.1	451.1	403.6
2007	500.8	529.4	483.6	424.2

6-2 居民消费价格分类指数
Consumer Price Indices by Category

(上年=100) (2007 年) (preceding year=100)

项目	Item	全区 Autonomous Region	城市 Urban Areas	农村 Rural Areas
居民消费价格总指数	**Consumer Price Index**	**105.5**	**104.6**	**107.2**
食品	**Food**	**112.6**	**111.6**	**114.7**
粮食	Grain	108.5	108.7	108.1
大米	Rice	107.1	108.9	104.9
面粉	Flour	111.3	111.4	111.3
粮食制品	Grain Products	105.9	106.3	102.7
其它	Others	109.1	108.8	106.6
淀粉	Starches	106.6	109.0	103.8
干豆类及豆制品	Bean and Its Products	109.2	110.7	105.1
油脂	Oil or Fat	134.9	135.9	133.4
肉禽及其制品	Meat, Poultry and Their Products	125.7	124.8	127.3
蛋	Eggs	124.8	125.7	123.5
水产品	Aquatic Products	109.0	107.4	110.9
菜	Vegetables	101.4	102.6	99.2
鲜菜	Fresh Vegetables	100.8	101.8	98.9
干菜及菜制品	Dried Vegetables and Vegetable Products	115.3	118.1	106.3
薯类	Tubers	107.4	100.3	112.1
调味品	Flavoring	111.9	112.9	110.7
糖	Carbohydrate	101.5	101.8	100.7
食糖	Sugar	95.9	98.4	92.5
糖果	Candy	104.1	103.9	104.2
巧克力制品	Chocolate Goods	104.5	102.9	107.1
糖类小食品	Carbohydrate Products	103.1	101.8	107.0
茶及饮料	Tea and Beverages	102.3	101.4	103.8
干鲜瓜果	Dried and Fresh Melons and Fruits	106.3	105.8	106.6
鲜瓜果	Fresh Fruits	103.2	102.2	104.2
干(坚)果	Drie (nut) Fruits	114.5	114.0	116.9
糕点饼干	Cake and Biscuit	104.9	102.7	109.1
液体乳及乳制品	Milk and Its Products	108.2	108.5	107.6
在外用膳食品	Outward Dinner	106.4	104.7	112.8
主食	Staple Food	107.8	105.9	114.1
炒菜	Fried Dishes	104.7	102.3	113.2
地方小吃	Local Snack	108.4	108.3	108.5
其他食品	Other Foods	105.7	106.9	103.3
烟酒及用品	**Tobacco, Liquor and Articles**	**102.4**	**103.4**	**100.7**
烟草	Tobacco	101.1	101.0	101.4
酒	Liquor	104.2	106.5	100.2
吸烟饮酒用品	Articles for Smoking and Drinking	100.0	100.0	100.0
衣着	**Clothing**	**100.8**	**100.2**	**102.2**
服装	Garments	101.3	100.8	102.5
衣着材料	Clothing Material	100.7	100.3	101.2
棉布	Cotton Cloth	101.8	102.0	101.6

6-2 续表 Continued

(上年=100) (preceding year=100)

项　　目	Item	全　区 Autonomous Region	城　市 Urban Areas	农　村 Rural Areas
棉混纺布	Blend Cloth	100.4	99.9	100.9
化纤布	Chemical Fiber Cloth	100.9	100.6	101.2
毛　线	Wool	99.3	98.0	100.9
鞋袜帽	Footwear and Hats	99.5	99.0	100.7
鞋	Shoes	99.1	98.6	100.9
袜　子	Socks and Stockings	100.3	100.3	100.2
帽　子	Hats	108.0	113.1	101.3
衣着加工服务费	Clothing Processing	105.4	101.5	115.9
家庭设备及用品及维修服务	**Household Facilities and Articles**	**100.8**	**100.4**	**101.7**
耐用消费品	Durable Consumer Goods	99.8	99.2	101.0
家　具	Furniture	99.4	98.6	101.1
家庭设备	Household Facilities	100.1	99.6	100.9
室内装饰品	Interior Decorations	101.2	100.6	102.4
床上用品	Bed Articles	100.3	99.9	101.0
家庭日用杂品	Daily Use Household Articles	101.0	100.7	102.1
家庭服务及加工维修服务	Household Service	105.5	105.7	104.8
医疗保健和个人用品	**Health Care and Personal Articles**	**101.3**	**100.6**	**102.4**
医疗保健	Health Cares	100.4	99.9	101.0
医疗器具及用品	Medical Instruments and Articles	96.4	97.4	95.3
中药材及中成药	Traditional Chinese Medicine	102.6	102.9	102.2
西　药	Western Medicine	99.5	98.6	100.6
保健器具及用品	Constitutional Appliances and Articles	99.1	99.0	99.3
医疗保健服务	Medical and Health Service	100.5	100.1	101.4
个人用品及服务	Personal Articles and Services	102.8	101.7	104.8
交通和通信	**Transportation and Communication**	**100.9**	**100.2**	**102.3**
交　通	Transportation	102.9	102.0	104.0
通　信	Communication	98.8	98.7	98.8
娱乐教育文化用品及服务	**Recreation, Education, Culture Articles**	**100.1**	**99.7**	**101.1**
文娱用耐用消费品及服务	Durable Consumer Goods for Cultural and Recreationl Use and Services	95.8	95.2	97.9
教　育	Education	101.1	100.9	101.6
文化娱乐	Culture and Recreation	100.9	100.9	100.7
文化娱乐用品	Cultural and Recreational Articles	99.2	99.2	99.8
书报杂志	Newspapers and Magazines	100.4	100.1	101.1
文娱费	Recreation	102.6	102.6	101.3
旅　游	Touristry	101.5	101.6	103.1
居　住	**Housing**	**106.2**	**105.3**	**107.9**
建房及装修材料	Building and Building Decoration Materials	108.4	107.9	109.0
租　房	Rent	102.5	101.8	104.7
自有住房	Private Housing	107.8	107.7	108.9
水、电、燃料	Water, Electricity and Fuels	104.3	103.2	106.5
服务项目价格指数	**Services**	**102.4**	**101.9**	**103.6**

6-3 各市县居民消费价格分类指数

(上年=100) (2007 年)

项目	Item	乌鲁木齐市 Urumqi City	喀什市 Kashgar [Kaxgar] City	伊宁市 Yining [Gulja] City	和田市 Hotan City	克拉玛依市 Karamay City	哈密市 Hami [Kumul] City
居民消费价格总指数	**Consumer Price Index**	**104.6**	**104.3**	**104.5**	**104.5**	**106.1**	**103.8**
食　品	**Food**	**112.0**	**110.5**	**112.9**	**110.8**	**113.5**	**109.3**
粮　食	Grain	105.2	114.7	110.3	108.9	111.2	106.6
大　米	Rice	104.9	110.5	110.2	109.0	105.5	108.7
面　粉	Flour	105.4	120.0	111.3	109.6	113.6	105.5
粮食制品	Grain Products	103.6	106.7	108.5	103.3	115.6	104.9
其　它	Others	112.7	100.0	107.8	111.8	107.2	104.3
淀　粉	Starches	113.1	100.0	100.0	119.6	108.7	101.5
干豆类及豆制品	Bean and Its Products	111.3	120.3	108.5	105.1	117.6	112.9
油　脂	Oil or Fat	134.7	149.7	140.5	131.1	126.4	141.7
肉禽及其制品	Meat, Poultry and Their Products	126.2	117.9	127.8	121.7	122.2	122.8
蛋	Eggs	127.6	119.4	126.5	122.1	123.2	120.7
水产品	Aquatic Products	108.8	110.5	105.6	101.5	106.7	106.4
菜	Vegetables	104.1	95.9	98.3	100.1	109.6	97.0
鲜　菜	Fresh Vegetables	103.1	95.0	97.9	100.0	109.1	95.6
干菜及菜制品	Dried Vegetables and Vegetable Products	127.3	105.3	100.0	100.6	128.8	122.5
薯　类	Tubers	94.0	116.1	101.2	102.9	100.4	98.7
调味品	Flavoring	121.3	101.7	99.8	104.6	102.7	102.2
糖	Carbohydrate Products	103.4	100.8	100.3	99.8	108.4	99.1
食　糖	Sugar	100.6	94.2	100.5	99.4	112.0	90.7
糖　果	Candy	104.2	101.5	99.9	100.0	111.3	104.2
巧克力制品	Chocolate Goods	105.7	100.0	100.0	100.0	104.0	100.0
糖类小食品	Carbohydrate	97.7	120.0	100.0	100.0	103.9	100.0
茶及饮料	Tea and Beverages	101.3	100.2	100.1	101.4	103.4	101.6
干鲜瓜果	Dried and Fresh Melons and Fruits	106.9	101.7	105.6	114.7	112.2	98.4
鲜瓜果	Fresh Fruits	101.3	98.6	103.6	117.8	111.4	95.0
干(坚)果	Dried(nut)Fruits	119.8	107.9	111.7	107.5	116.3	104.0
糕点饼干	Cake, Cookie	103.4	102.5	100.0	101.1	102.6	100.7
液体乳及乳制品	Milk and Its Products	108.7	108.7	104.8	102.0	102.2	102.9
在外用膳食品	Outward Dinner	103.3	103.5	109.3	101.8	110.5	106.1
主　食	Staple Food	105.9	101.9	100.8	93.1	113.3	110.8
炒　菜	Fried Dishes	101.0	102.9	111.2	107.0	100.9	100.4
地方小吃	Local Snack	104.9	107.0	120.9	114.6	119.2	109.5
其他食品	Other Foods	110.2	100.0	101.8	98.1	103.3	105.4
烟酒及用品	**Tobacco, Liquor and Articles**	**104.3**	**104.0**	**100.0**	**101.4**	**102.2**	**100.9**
烟　草	Tobacco	100.0	100.0	100.0	100.0	102.9	100.0
酒	Liquor	111.1	108.5	99.9	102.8	101.8	102.0
吸烟饮酒用品	Articles for Smoking and Drinking	100.0	100.0	100.0	99.5	100.0	100.0
衣　着	**Clothing**	**99.3**	**100.1**	**95.6**	**99.6**	**105.3**	**101.6**
服　装	Garments	101.2	100.0	96.0	99.4	103.9	101.3
衣着材料	Clothing Material	98.1	100.0	99.5	98.5	100.6	102.4
棉　布	Cotton Cloth	100.0	100.0	100.0	100.0	102.4	104.8

Consumer Price Indices by Category in Cities and Counties

(preceding year=100)

昌吉市 Changji City	库尔勒市 Korla City	阿克苏市 Aksu City	焉耆回族自治县 Yanqi Hui Autonomous County	塔城市 Tacheng [Qoqek] City	阿勒泰市 Altay City	乌苏市 Usu City	博乐市 Bole [Bortala] City	吐鲁番市 Turpan City	库车县 Kuqa County	阿图什市 Artux City	莎车县 Shache [Yarkant] County	奎屯市 Kuytun City	石河子市 Shihezi City
103.7	**105.2**	**106.5**	**106.3**	**103.8**	**104.8**	**104.4**	**105.6**	**106.4**	**108.4**	**106.1**	**108.5**	**103.6**	**104.8**
108.6	**111.7**	**115.0**	**115.1**	**109.4**	**111.4**	**109.9**	**109.2**	**113.4**	**113.7**	**114.6**	**119.9**	**108.9**	**111.0**
109.0	110.3	127.0	106.6	100.3	104.3	105.7	103.1	105.9	110.0	110.8	109.9	103.0	110.4
109.2	104.7	134.2	104.1	100.5	103.2	104.4	100.7	105.4	105.9	102.7	109.0	103.8	112.7
109.5	123.7	126.2	109.7	103.3	105.7	106.7	103.4	108.9	115.5	117.2	115.8	102.4	113.8
103.4	103.0	109.7	106.4	97.7	102.2	105.5	103.3	100.0	105.4	105.8	103.9	102.3	104.3
115.4	106.6	118.6	103.8	94.4	111.0	114.3	111.5	105.4	105.4	109.2	108.2	106.1	102.1
108.4	102.5	99.6	102.8	107.0	81.9	102.6	93.4	100.0	112.7	100.0	106.5	100.0	100.0
104.8	106.2	100.3	100.2	104.8	112.4	114.8	107.6	105.0	100.9	116.5	99.5	104.4	107.3
141.0	122.9	133.5	145.0	146.2	127.7	123.9	132.2	137.5	126.4	149.3	138.1	122.1	146.4
118.1	127.3	123.2	130.7	122.2	119.5	122.3	120.1	126.8	130.8	128.0	130.6	125.6	122.8
116.7	129.9	124.4	125.3	118.2	122.4	116.6	116.5	133.4	109.2	118.3	128.1	120.9	123.0
103.4	99.5	114.1	107.8	105.8	106.9	109.6	113.3	109.1	111.6	128.5	111.5	108.1	110.4
92.6	99.1	99.5	100.0	98.7	105.1	104.1	104.0	106.5	101.4	98.9	92.7	96.8	99.4
91.3	98.1	98.0	98.9	99.7	103.7	104.2	101.4	100.8	102.6	99.1	91.5	96.4	99.7
104.3	100.9	109.1	105.3	104.4	100.0	106.8	109.0	112.0	109.1	103.0	101.9	101.9	105.6
107.2	114.1	130.9	105.2	89.3	114.2	94.3	109.6	136.9	79.6	77.7	105.4	117.1	88.5
107.8	111.9	107.8	119.9	103.5	97.8	119.1	106.7	104.8	118.2	98.0	105.7	106.2	103.0
97.9	98.3	102.0	93.8	100.3	102.0	100.8	96.3	94.1	104.9	96.9	109.5	98.3	101.1
88.0	89.5	94.2	87.5	94.5	98.7	98.9	85.1	86.0	98.3	92.3	92.1	95.4	92.0
102.6	100.6	108.0	94.4	100.6	104.5	102.3	103.0	99.7	112.0	100.0	111.3	100.0	114.9
102.1	100.0	97.7	102.4	100.0	101.6	100.0	100.6	100.0	100.0	100.0	126.0	100.5	100.0
101.4	100.0	103.8	100.0	102.7	100.0	101.8	100.1	100.0	95.7	100.0	122.4	100.0	100.0
103.6	100.7	99.3	103.1	108.5	100.6	100.0	104.2	97.8	104.6	100.4	100.2	100.0	104.4
104.8	106.2	91.3	106.0	99.5	109.7	98.9	97.9	100.6	109.1	102.0	121.4	113.1	100.5
104.3	104.4	86.7	105.4	96.6	108.1	95.7	96.3	97.6	98.6	104.8	117.0	118.4	99.0
106.4	112.6	104.4	106.7	109.8	115.9	107.8	101.4	109.7	133.9	99.2	134.4	102.4	107.0
102.4	100.9	102.9	106.0	101.8	100.8	101.0	101.9	101.8	106.5	100.4	130.9	104.0	103.1
118.1	104.3	116.9	112.8	117.5	105.5	110.7	102.2	104.8	102.2	101.5	106.4	100.9	112.5
106.7	102.2	107.5	103.3	105.0	115.4	102.7	106.9	104.5	112.3	106.5	137.2	101.4	104.7
110.4	103.3	114.2	101.1	106.0	108.1	105.6	105.0	109.2	105.9	102.8	144.0	104.2	108.2
103.9	101.9	104.2	105.1	101.9	124.5	100.4	103.7	100.6	119.1	106.4	139.8	100.0	103.3
104.5	100.0	103.4	101.8	114.1	109.7	102.2	117.0	104.2	108.9	114.8	114.7	110.6	102.6
100.4	99.7	101.5	106.9	100.0	102.8	100.0	100.4	101.4	100.0	102.2	114.3	100.2	113.2
106.7	**101.6**	**101.0**	**102.9**	**98.3**	**101.4**	**100.0**	**100.9**	**100.7**	**103.1**	**100.1**	**100.1**	**100.4**	**101.3**
106.1	103.0	100.0	104.6	100.0	100.8	100.0	100.0	100.0	104.2	100.0	100.8	100.0	103.0
108.1	100.2	102.4	100.9	95.8	102.2	100.0	102.2	101.7	101.6	100.4	99.2	101.0	99.4
97.6	100.9	100.0	99.3	100.0	100.0	100.0	100.0	100.0	100.0	100.0	100.0	100.0	100.0
100.7	**101.3**	**100.9**	**100.9**	**100.2**	**101.1**	**99.4**	**102.6**	**101.7**	**112.3**	**101.3**	**101.0**	**101.0**	**101.4**
101.6	101.3	99.0	100.3	100.1	101.7	98.7	105.1	102.6	114.1	98.6	100.7	100.9	101.6
99.4	103.0	100.7	101.6	100.0	100.0	100.0	104.1	101.1	100.0	102.0	101.2	101.2	104.9
99.2	106.6	100.0	100.0	100.0	100.0	100.0	104.0	102.4	100.0	106.7	100.0	100.0	117.5

6-3 续表

(上年=100)

项　目	Item	乌鲁木齐市 Urumqi City	喀什市 Kashgar [Kaxgar] City	伊宁市 Yining [Gulja] City	和田市 Hotan City	克拉玛依市 Karamay City	哈密市 Hami [Kumul] City
棉混纺布	Blend Cloth	100.0	100.0	100.0	93.6	99.6	101.5
化纤布	Chemical Fiber Cloth	100.0	100.0	100.0	101.0	100.0	103.4
毛　线	Wool	93.3	100.0	98.0	100.0	103.2	99.0
鞋袜帽	Footwear and Hats	94.8	100.0	93.1	100.1	109.5	101.5
鞋	Shoes	94.2	100.0	91.8	100.2	108.1	101.9
袜　子	Socks and Stockings	101.0	100.0	100.0	100.0	98.5	100.0
帽　子	Hats	100.0	100.0	100.4	100.0	136.4	99.9
衣着加工服务费	Clothing Processing	100.8	104.8	99.7	100.0	104.6	103.3
家庭设备及用品及维修服务	**Household Facilities and Articles and Services**	**100.2**	**101.4**	**100.3**	**99.7**	**100.8**	**100.4**
耐用消费品	Durable Consumer Goods	96.8	100.4	100.6	99.3	101.5	100.2
家　具	Furniture	96.1	100.0	100.0	99.5	100.1	100.0
家庭设备	Household Facilities	97.2	100.6	100.9	99.2	102.5	100.2
室内装饰品	Interior Decorations	100.0	100.0	100.0	100.0	102.8	100.0
床上用品	Bed Articles	99.6	98.7	100.1	100.5	100.4	100.0
家庭日用杂品	Daily Use Household Articles	103.2	102.2	100.0	99.9	99.0	100.0
家庭服务及加工维修服务	Household Service	112.7	108.1	100.0	100.0	100.0	102.1
医疗保健和个人用品	**Health Care and Personal Articles**	**100.0**	**101.9**	**98.9**	**101.2**	**101.9**	**100.7**
医疗保健	Health Cares	100.1	102.0	98.1	99.7	98.5	99.9
医疗器具及用品	Medical Appliances and Articles	91.8	105.4	100.3	100.0	92.5	100.0
中药材及中成药	Traditional Chinese Medicine	102.1	104.4	94.2	100.6	105.5	100.0
西　药	Western Medicine	99.5	101.3	98.9	99.0	93.5	99.7
保健器具及用品	Constitutional Appliances and Articles	98.1	99.2	99.1	99.4	100.1	99.8
医疗保健服务	Medical and Health Service	100.0	99.2	99.8	100.0	100.0	100.0
个人用品及服务	Personal Articles and Services	99.9	101.8	100.0	104.3	105.6	101.7
交通和通信	**Transportation and Communication**	**98.5**	**101.5**	**100.3**	**101.7**	**101.7**	**99.0**
交　通	Transportation	100.5	102.1	100.6	101.0	103.0	100.1
通　信	Communication	96.7	100.8	100.1	101.9	100.4	97.3
娱乐教育文化用品及服务	**Recreation, Education, Culture Articles and Services**	**99.3**	**100.0**	**100.5**	**99.9**	**101.6**	**99.1**
文娱用耐用消费品及服务	Durable Consumer Goods for Cultural and Recreationl Use and Services	88.9	99.4	97.5	99.8	98.4	94.8
教　育	Education	101.3	99.8	101.5	100.0	101.7	98.8
文化娱乐	Culture and Recreation	99.5	101.6	99.6	99.7	101.3	100.4
文化娱乐用品	Cultural and Recreational Articles	96.6	100.0	100.2	99.4	102.7	100.0
书报杂志	Newspapers and Magazines	100.0	100.0	100.0	100.0	100.0	99.7
文娱费	Recreation	102.9	105.7	98.8	100.0	100.0	102.1
旅　游	Touring	101.2	100.0	101.5	100.0	108.3	109.4
居　住	**Housing**	**106.1**	**101.0**	**104.0**	**104.5**	**102.4**	**103.8**
建房及装修材料	Builing and Building Decoration	112.9	100.1	107.2	104.5	102.7	107.6
租　房	Rent	105.6	100.0	100.0	103.8	101.3	100.0
自有住房	Private Housing	106.7	103.5	104.5	104.3	108.5	104.2
水、电、燃料	Water, Electricity and Fuels	103.7	101.1	103.0	104.1	100.6	102.2
服务项目价格指数	**Services**	**101.5**	**101.8**	**101.2**	**101.9**	**104.4**	**101.9**

Continued

(preceding year=100)

昌吉市 Changji City	库尔勒市 Korla City	阿克苏市 Aksu City	焉耆回族自治县 Yanqi Hui Autonomous County	塔城市 Tacheng [Qoqek] City	阿勒泰市 Altay City	乌苏市 Usu City	博乐市 Bole [Bortala] City	吐鲁番市 Turpan City	库车县 Kuqa County	阿图什市 Artux City	莎车县 Shache [Yarkant] County	奎屯市 Kuytun City	石河子市 Shihezi City
97.1	102.4	100.0	100.0	100.0	100.0	100.0	105.1	100.8	100.0	100.8	100.0	104.5	100.0
100.0	101.4	100.0	104.1	100.0	100.0	100.0	103.8	100.0	100.0	100.0	101.6	99.1	84.4
100.0	103.0	103.9	100.0	100.0	100.0	100.0	102.8	100.0	100.0	100.0	103.4	100.4	96.9
99.0	100.8	106.6	102.1	99.9	100.3	100.0	97.2	100.0	99.5	109.5	101.5	102.0	100.2
99.0	100.5	108.5	100.0	99.9	100.2	100.0	97.4	100.0	98.5	111.2	101.7	101.8	99.7
98.8	104.2	100.0	115.4	99.6	100.0	100.0	96.4	100.0	100.0	100.0	100.0	100.3	101.1
100.6	103.9	100.0	102.1	100.0	100.7	100.0	103.3	100.0	100.0	100.0	102.3	104.4	103.5
100.0	100.0	100.0	100.0	109.3	100.0	102.5	102.5	100.0	144.3	100.0	105.2	96.0	100.2
100.7	**101.2**	**102.0**	**100.0**	**101.9**	**102.7**	**100.0**	**101.5**	**102.6**	**102.0**	**104.4**	**102.7**	**100.1**	**100.8**
100.2	101.1	102.0	99.5	98.9	101.0	100.1	99.4	100.7	100.1	104.9	101.4	99.6	98.0
111.8	100.5	103.9	100.0	98.6	100.0	100.0	99.0	99.9	100.2	110.6	99.7	100.4	97.9
99.5	101.3	100.7	99.2	98.9	101.7	100.1	99.6	101.0	100.0	100.2	102.6	99.2	98.1
102.3	100.5	100.3	100.0	98.9	102.0	100.0	102.5	100.0	103.4	103.4	100.3	100.6	103.4
99.7	101.3	100.4	100.0	100.0	100.0	100.0	104.0	96.4	102.3	100.0	104.8	99.3	104.9
100.0	100.9	103.0	101.0	103.6	101.0	100.0	102.8	101.9	100.0	101.5	103.9	100.0	101.7
106.3	103.2	102.5	100.0	106.6	121.2	100.0	105.9	118.1	108.3	110.7	108.9	103.0	101.9
99.5	**101.6**	**101.3**	**100.2**	**101.8**	**100.3**	**103.5**	**101.1**	**104.2**	**103.3**	**100.9**	**100.4**	**101.5**	**100.4**
99.4	99.3	100.4	99.5	101.7	100.5	100.0	98.3	104.8	99.7	101.1	100.1	100.4	100.8
100.2	100.0	100.0	93.0	102.5	100.0	100.0	92.1	93.2	96.6	84.6	94.7	100.0	92.8
107.4	99.3	99.8	100.4	112.6	107.5	100.0	104.2	107.2	100.0	102.9	96.7	98.7	104.8
94.9	97.8	101.5	98.8	95.7	94.5	99.8	95.2	108.6	99.6	101.8	100.0	100.0	100.8
101.5	100.0	101.5	102.2	96.1	97.7	98.7	100.5	100.0	100.0	102.0	99.1	107.7	97.9
100.0	102.5	100.0	99.8	100.0	100.6	101.1	101.3	100.0	100.0	99.3	103.5	100.0	100.0
99.7	105.0	102.7	101.4	101.9	100.0	107.7	104.7	102.7	108.4	100.5	101.1	102.9	99.6
101.1	**103.8**	**100.6**	**101.3**	**100.2**	**102.0**	**100.3**	**103.6**	**99.7**	**99.4**	**97.8**	**101.4**	**100.0**	**101.7**
101.3	105.0	100.9	102.1	101.2	105.9	100.7	103.6	104.5	101.7	101.5	106.2	100.4	103.9
100.9	101.7	100.3	100.8	98.6	98.2	100.0	103.5	97.0	95.5	94.0	96.8	99.7	98.9
100.0	**100.9**	**101.2**	**103.4**	**100.4**	**99.0**	**100.0**	**100.2**	**100.3**	**102.2**	**100.1**	**99.4**	**98.6**	**97.7**
99.5	99.7	101.7	98.9	97.9	95.9	99.2	96.9	97.5	99.5	100.0	97.8	99.7	90.0
100.1	101.6	101.3	107.1	100.4	100.0	100.0	100.2	102.4	100.0	100.0	100.0	100.3	99.7
101.4	100.7	101.0	100.0	101.8	100.6	101.2	100.8	99.2	99.6	100.4	99.9	101.1	100.8
102.1	99.9	100.0	100.0	100.3	100.0	100.0	101.4	98.4	98.8	100.0	99.8	100.1	98.2
100.1	100.2	101.4	100.0	101.7	100.0	104.4	100.0	100.1	100.0	101.6	99.9	100.0	108.7
102.5	103.2	101.7	100.0	103.1	102.4	100.0	100.6	100.0	100.0	100.0	100.0	103.4	98.0
98.5	101.6	100.0	100.0	100.0	101.1	100.0	106.4	98.9	113.5	100.0	100.0	91.1	102.0
103.4	**102.4**	**105.8**	**103.0**	**103.3**	**104.1**	**105.1**	**110.4**	**106.2**	**114.4**	**105.1**	**108.9**	**103.6**	**104.0**
110.5	102.1	103.8	101.2	104.6	106.2	104.1	110.2	103.1	103.8	106.5	115.4	103.8	107.3
101.8	100.0	100.0	100.0	100.0	100.0	100.0	105.2	100.0	125.4	101.9	99.8	100.0	100.0
105.3	106.0	110.9	105.5	100.0	107.3	105.8	107.2	112.1	142.9	109.8	111.1	113.5	103.7
100.3	101.6	103.6	103.2	103.4	102.5	107.3	113.7	104.9	109.6	102.0	104.6	101.4	103.3
101.6	**103.8**	**103.7**	**104.4**	**102.4**	**103.6**	**103.2**	**104.9**	**104.6**	**111.4**	**100.8**	**103.5**	**101.2**	**101.9**

6-4 商品零售价格分类指数
Retail Price Indices by Category of Commodities

(上年=100) (2007 年) (preceding year=100)

项 目	Item	全 区 Autonomous Region	城 市 Urban Areas	农 村 Rural Areas
商品零售价格总指数	**General Retail Price Index**	**105.1**	**104.7**	**105.9**
食 品	**Food**	**112.8**	**112.7**	**113.0**
粮 食	Grain	107.7	108.4	107.1
油 脂	Oil or Fat	136.8	137.5	136.1
肉禽及其制品	Meat, Poultry and Their Products	124.8	124.4	125.7
猪 肉	Pork	128.9	130.1	126.6
牛 肉	Beef	130.1	129.0	132.2
羊 肉	Lamb	135.1	135.0	133.9
鸡	Chicken	118.5	116.9	121.3
鲜 蛋	Fresh Egg	125.6	126.3	125.0
水产品	Aquatic Products	109.0	107.6	112.5
鲜瓜果	Fresh Fruits	102.1	101.6	104.2
糕 点	Cake	104.7	104.8	104.5
饮料、烟酒	**Beverages, Tobacco and Liquor**	**102.6**	**103.1**	**101.4**
茶及饮料	Tea and Beverages	101.8	101.5	102.4
#饮 料	Beverages	100.9	101.1	100.1
烟 草	Tobacco	100.7	100.5	101.2
酒	Liquor	104.9	106.8	100.8
服装鞋帽	**Garments, Shoes and Hats**	**100.2**	**99.6**	**102.0**
服 装	Garments	101.2	100.5	103.0
鞋袜帽	Shoes, Stocks and Hats	98.5	98.2	100.4
#鞋	Shoes	97.6	97.0	100.3
纺织品	**Textiles**	**99.8**	**99.2**	**101.0**
棉 布	Cotton Cloth	101.1	100.7	101.7
棉混纺布	Blend Cloth	100.2	99.7	101.0
化纤布	Chemical Fiber Cloth	100.4	100.1	101.1
毛 线	Wool	97.0	95.3	101.1
家用电器及音响器材	**Household Appliances Music and Video Equipment**	**97.6**	**96.9**	**99.2**
家庭设备	Household Facilities	99.4	99.0	100.5
文娱用耐用消费品	Durable Consuming Goods for Entertainment	95.2	93.9	97.8
音响器材	Sound Apparatus	100.0	100.0	100.0

6-4 续表 Continued

(上年=100) (preceding year=100)

项目	Item	全区 Autonomous Region	城市 Urban Areas	农村 Rural Areas
文化办公用品	**Cultural and Office Goods**	**97.8**	**97.2**	**99.6**
日用品	**Articles for Daily Use**	**101.6**	**101.5**	**101.7**
日用百货	Merchandiles for Daily Use	102.0	101.6	102.7
日用杂品	Sundries for Daily Use	101.4	101.1	102.0
洗涤用品	Washing and Cleaning Goods	102.8	103.0	101.1
其他日用品	Other Daily-use Goods	99.5	99.2	100.3
体育娱乐用品	**Sports and Entertainment Goods**	**99.7**	**99.7**	**99.8**
体育用品	Sports Goods	99.9	99.9	99.8
娱乐用品	Recreational Goods	99.7	99.6	99.8
交通、通信用品	**Traffic and Telecommunication Goods**	**94.0**	**93.7**	**94.3**
交通运输机械	Traffic and Transport Machinery	98.4	97.8	99.7
通信器材	Telecommunication Apparatus	89.2	89.5	88.7
家具	**Furniture**	**99.4**	**99.0**	**100.4**
化妆品	**Cosmetics**	**99.9**	**99.7**	**100.8**
金银珠宝	**Gold and Silver Jewelry**	**105.4**	**105.1**	**106.4**
中西药品及医疗保健用品	**Chinese and Western Medicine, Medical-care and Healthy Goods**	**100.2**	**99.7**	**101.2**
医疗器具及用品	Medical-care Apparatus and Goods	94.3	93.5	95.3
中药材及中成药	Chinese Herbs and Patent Medicine	102.8	101.8	105.0
西药	Western Medicine	99.5	99.2	99.8
保健品及器具	Healthy Devices and Goods	99.0	98.8	99.4
书报杂志及电子出版物	**Books, Magazines and Electronic Publications**	**101.4**	**101.8**	**100.6**
教材及参考书	Texts and Reference Books	101.5	101.9	100.5
书报杂志	Newspapers and Magazines	100.2	100.1	100.7
电子音像制品	Electronic Audio and Video Products	102.2	102.6	100.4
燃料	**Fuels**	**107.7**	**106.4**	**108.2**
煤炭及制品	Coal and Its Products	115.7	118.2	111.7
石油及制品	Oil and Its Products	103.4	102.8	104.3
建筑材料及五金电料	**Building Apparatus, Hardwares and Electrical Apparatus**	**107.3**	**107.1**	**107.5**
建筑装璜材料	Building Decoration Materials	108.1	108.4	107.6
五金电料	Hardwares and Electrical Apparatus	105.2	104.0	107.2

6-5 各市县商品零售价格分类指数

(上年=100) (2007 年)

项目	Item	乌鲁木齐市 Urumqi City	喀什市 Kashgar [Kaxgar] City	伊宁市 Yining [Gulja] City	和田市 Hotan City	克拉玛依市 Karamay City	哈密市 Hami [Kumul] City
商品零售价格总指数	**General Retail Price Index**	**104.6**	**104.4**	**104.6**	**104.8**	**105.5**	**103.7**
食　品	**Food**	**112.4**	**110.7**	**113.3**	**111.5**	**114.0**	**110.1**
粮　食	Grain	105.2	115.0	110.3	109.2	111.2	106.7
油　脂	Oil or Fat	135.7	150.0	141.1	129.5	126.4	142.4
肉禽及其制品	Meat, Poultry and Their Products	125.7	118.4	127.7	121.1	121.8	124.1
猪　肉	Pork	132.2	121.6	129.1	121.4	127.8	142.0
牛　肉	Beef	132.8	119.9	123.5	122.5	126.8	113.2
羊　肉	Lamb	137.6	118.7	135.7	125.9	131.9	133.3
鸡	Chicken	114.5	119.7	132.1	123.7	116.1	113.3
鲜　蛋	Fresh Egg	128.8	119.2	128.1	123.1	124.5	121.4
水产品	Aquatic Products	108.8	107.8	105.4	101.5	106.5	106.7
鲜瓜果	Fresh Fruits	101.3	98.6	103.6	117.8	111.4	95.0
糕　点	Cake	106.3	102.2	100.0	101.4	102.5	100.1
饮料、烟酒	**Beverages, Tobacco and Liquor**	**104.6**	**102.1**	**100.0**	**101.6**	**102.7**	**101.1**
茶及饮料	Tea and Beverages	101.3	100.2	100.1	101.8	103.4	101.6
#饮 料	Beverages	101.7	100.4	100.2	100.9	101.2	102.2
烟　草	Tobacco	100.0	100.0	100.0	100.0	102.9	100.0
酒	Liquor	111.3	107.8	99.9	102.8	101.8	102.0
服装鞋帽	**Garments, Shoes and Hats**	**99.0**	**100.0**	**95.0**	**99.7**	**105.6**	**101.1**
服　装	Garments	101.2	100.0	96.0	99.4	103.9	101.0
鞋袜帽	Shoes, Stocks and Hats	94.8	100.0	93.1	100.1	109.2	101.4
#鞋	Shoes	94.2	100.0	91.8	100.2	108.1	101.8
纺织品	**Textiles**	**98.9**	**99.5**	**99.8**	**99.2**	**100.5**	**101.2**
棉　布	Cotton Cloth	100.0	100.0	100.0	100.0	102.4	104.8
棉混纺布	Blend Cloth	100.0	100.0	100.0	93.6	99.6	101.5
化纤布	Chemical Fiber Cloth	100.0	100.0	100.0	101.0	100.0	103.4
毛　线	Wool	93.3	100.0	98.0	100.0	103.2	99.0
家用电器及音响器材	**Electric Household Appliances and Sound Apparatus**	**94.3**	**100.3**	**99.3**	**99.2**	**100.6**	**98.6**
家庭设备	Household Facilities	97.2	101.3	100.9	99.2	102.5	100.1
文娱用耐用消费品	Durable Consuming Goods for Entertainment	89.9	99.3	96.9	99.3	98.1	97.1
音响器材	Sound Apparatus	100.0	100.0	100.0	99.4	101.0	100.0

Retail Price Indices by Category in Cities and Counties

(receding year=100)

昌吉市 Changji City	库尔勒市 Korla City	阿克苏市 Aksu City	焉耆回族自治县 Yanqi Hui Autonomous County	塔城市 Tacheng [Qoqek] City	阿勒泰市 Altay City	乌苏市 Usu City	博乐市 Bole [Bortala] City	吐鲁番市 Turpan City	库车县 Kuqa County	阿图什市 Artux City	莎车县 Shache [Yarkant] County	奎屯市 Kuytun City	石河子市 Shihezi City
104.1	**104.2**	**106.4**	**105.5**	**103.9**	**104.4**	**105.0**	**104.2**	**106.4**	**105.6**	**105.9**	**107.4**	**103.5**	**105.1**
109.7	**110.0**	**115.9**	**114.7**	**108.8**	**111.3**	**110.9**	**109.1**	**113.7**	**114.1**	**114.5**	**118.3**	**109.1**	**111.1**
109.4	112.0	126.8	106.5	100.3	103.9	105.7	104.1	105.9	109.2	110.9	109.8	103.1	110.8
141.4	127.6	133.5	141.8	146.2	127.1	122.7	131.1	137.5	125.7	144.2	140.1	123.0	145.1
117.3	119.4	123.2	126.8	122.2	118.3	119.8	118.0	125.7	127.0	126.8	129.9	121.9	122.0
123.5	121.4	123.7	131.8	127.4	135.1	113.6	127.6	132.9	131.3	116.9	126.4	133.3	128.7
115.9	138.7	129.6	138.6	123.0	127.1	130.3	119.9	134.8	130.1	135.6	139.3	133.7	127.1
121.5	137.0	130.7	133.7	134.4	133.6	134.3	132.3	135.8	141.4	130.2	134.2	134.0	129.2
115.7	113.0	120.7	120.2	108.5	108.4	117.9	120.6	114.8	138.1	121.4	134.7	122.7	117.6
117.6	131.7	124.5	125.7	121.1	127.1	118.4	121.5	134.3	108.5	119.2	132.2	122.7	124.0
103.3	100.1	113.9	108.3	105.8	108.3	110.1	111.9	109.1	110.7	134.4	111.8	107.5	110.5
104.3	104.4	86.7	105.4	96.6	108.1	95.7	96.3	97.6	98.6	104.8	117.0	118.4	99.0
102.0	100.4	100.8	115.0	103.0	102.0	100.8	104.3	102.9	102.6	100.0	112.0	108.7	110.0
105.3	**101.2**	**100.3**	**103.0**	**100.8**	**101.8**	**100.0**	**101.0**	**99.3**	**104.2**	**100.2**	**100.3**	**100.3**	**103.5**
104.9	100.5	100.3	102.5	108.5	101.0	100.0	104.1	97.7	104.8	100.3	100.2	100.0	104.1
102.1	100.8	101.4	103.8	105.6	102.5	100.0	100.1	96.8	99.3	100.6	100.4	100.0	101.1
104.8	102.5	100.0	104.7	100.0	100.5	100.0	100.0	100.0	104.3	100.0	100.9	100.0	105.3
106.4	100.1	100.6	101.1	95.8	103.2	100.0	99.9	101.7	101.8	100.3	99.6	101.1	101.6
100.5	**100.8**	**101.9**	**101.3**	**100.1**	**101.2**	**99.6**	**102.0**	**101.7**	**106.8**	**101.6**	**100.6**	**101.1**	**100.6**
101.8	101.1	99.2	100.3	100.1	102.0	99.1	104.0	102.6	114.6	99.1	100.7	100.7	101.4
99.0	101.4	106.2	104.4	99.9	100.1	100.0	98.8	100.0	99.5	105.4	101.5	101.6	100.3
99.0	100.5	108.5	100.0	99.9	100.4	100.0	98.2	100.0	98.5	109.7	101.7	101.8	99.5
98.8	**102.4**	**100.8**	**100.8**	**100.0**	**100.0**	**100.0**	**103.1**	**98.8**	**100.9**	**101.4**	**102.4**	**100.1**	**104.3**
99.2	106.6	100.0	100.0	100.0	100.0	100.0	104.0	102.4	100.0	106.7	100.0	100.0	117.5
97.1	102.4	100.0	100.0	100.0	100.0	100.0	105.1	100.8	100.0	100.8	100.0	104.5	100.0
100.0	101.4	100.0	104.1	100.0	100.0	100.0	103.8	100.0	100.0	100.0	101.6	99.1	84.4
100.0	103.0	103.9	100.0	100.0	100.0	100.0	102.8	100.0	100.0	100.0	103.4	100.4	96.9
100.0	**100.8**	**100.1**	**99.2**	**98.0**	**98.8**	**99.7**	**99.9**	**99.4**	**99.8**	**100.2**	**100.2**	**99.0**	**92.5**
99.5	101.7	100.7	99.2	98.9	101.9	100.1	99.8	101.1	100.2	100.3	103.1	99.3	97.8
101.2	99.7	99.5	99.1	97.5	94.3	99.1	99.8	96.9	99.4	100.0	96.6	99.0	86.8
89.8	100.0	100.0	100.0	100.0	100.0	100.0	100.0	100.0	100.0	100.0	100.0	98.2	100.0

6-5 续表

(上年=100)

项　　目	Item	乌鲁木齐市 Urumqi City	喀什市 Kashgar [Kaxgar] City	伊宁市 Yining [Gulja] City	和田市 Hotan City	克拉玛依市 Karamay City	哈密市 Hami [Kumul] City
文化办公用品	**Cultural and Office Goods**	**95.1**	**99.6**	**99.0**	**100.5**	**101.3**	**97.2**
日用品	**Articles for Daily Use**	**102.2**	**101.1**	**99.0**	**99.5**	**99.9**	**102.4**
日用百货	Merchandiles for Daily Use	102.6	101.1	98.4	98.8	100.6	99.7
日用杂品	Sundries for Daily Use	101.5	100.0	100.0	99.9	101.8	100.0
洗涤用品	Washing and Cleaning Goods	103.3	102.0	100.1	99.7	98.4	107.9
其他日用品	Other Daily-use Goods	99.0	99.9	98.0	100.1	99.3	100.0
体育娱乐用品	**Sports and Entertainment Goods**	**99.1**	**100.0**	**96.5**	**100.0**	**101.6**	**100.0**
体育用品	Sports Goods	100.0	100.0	96.9	100.0	101.3	100.0
娱乐用品	Recreational Goods	98.2	100.0	96.0	100.0	101.9	100.0
交通、通信用品	**Traffic and Telecommunication Goods**	**90.7**	**98.8**	**96.6**	**99.9**	**98.1**	**96.4**
交通运输机械	Traffic and Transport Machinery	96.1	100.5	98.8	100.0	97.7	98.7
通信器材	Telecommunication Apparatus	83.7	96.3	94.7	99.8	98.5	92.5
家　具	**Furniture**	**95.9**	**100.0**	**100.0**	**99.2**	**100.1**	**100.0**
化妆品	**Cosmetics**	**99.0**	**99.6**	**100.2**	**100.3**	**99.2**	**102.1**
金银珠宝	**Gold and Silver Jewelry**	**105.0**	**105.9**	**104.1**	**110.2**	**103.7**	**104.9**
中西药品及医疗保健用品	**Chinese and Western Medicine, Medical-care and Healthy Goods**	**99.4**	**102.0**	**97.5**	**99.5**	**97.7**	**99.8**
医疗器具及用品	Medical-care Apparatus and Goods	91.8	105.4	100.3	100.0	92.5	100.0
中药材及中成药	Chinese Herbs and Patent Medicine	102.1	104.4	94.1	100.6	105.5	100.0
西　药	Western Medicine	99.5	101.0	98.9	99.0	93.5	99.4
保健品及器具	Healthy Devices and Goods	98.1	99.7	99.1	99.2	100.1	99.8
书报杂志及电子出版物	**Books, Magazines and Electronic Publications**	**101.9**	**99.7**	**99.0**	**99.7**	**100.4**	**98.5**
教材及参考书	Texts and Reference Books	104.0	99.3	97.8	100.0	100.8	98.0
书报杂志	Newspapers and Magazines	100.0	100.0	100.0	100.0	100.0	99.7
电子音像制品	Electronic Audio and Video Products	104.6	100.0	99.7	98.7	100.0	97.1
燃　料	**Fuels**	**104.5**	**103.3**	**104.7**	**109.4**	**113.4**	**103.4**
煤炭及制品	Coal and Its Products	125.9	98.3	112.3	122.1	130.6	105.2
石油及制品	Oil and Its Products	102.6	104.6	103.6	103.1	102.8	102.5
建筑材料及五金电料	**Building Apparatus, Hardwares and Electrical Apparatus**	**109.8**	**102.9**	**107.4**	**103.7**	**102.7**	**104.7**
建筑装璜材料	Building Decoration Materials	111.4	102.3	109.0	104.2	102.7	105.3
五金电料	Hardwares and Electrical Apparatus	105.1	105.0	102.1	102.5	102.6	103.5

Continued

(preceding year=100)

昌吉市 Changji City	库尔勒市 Korla City	阿克苏市 Aksu City	焉耆回族自治县 Yanqi Hui Autonomous County	塔城市 Tacheng [Qoqek] City	阿勒泰市 Altay City	乌苏市 Usu City	博乐市 Bole [Bortala] City	吐鲁番市 Turpan City	库车县 Kuqa County	阿图什市 Artux City	莎车县 Shache [Yarkant] County	奎屯市 Kuytun City	石河子市 Shihezi City
94.1	**99.9**	**99.5**	**99.7**	**100.0**	**99.3**	**100.0**	**97.5**	**98.3**	**99.5**	**100.0**	**100.2**	**99.4**	**97.7**
99.5	**100.7**	**100.6**	**100.8**	**102.6**	**100.0**	**100.5**	**103.1**	**102.1**	**101.1**	**99.7**	**101.6**	**101.4**	**99.9**
97.4	101.2	100.5	99.8	102.4	100.3	101.3	104.7	103.6	103.2	97.8	102.1	102.9	100.6
100.7	100.1	102.2	100.0	104.9	100.0	100.0	103.8	102.4	100.0	100.0	106.1	100.0	99.0
100.6	100.7	100.7	102.6	107.2	99.9	100.0	104.2	100.6	100.0	101.3	100.0	100.8	99.9
98.6	100.4	100.1	100.0	100.0	100.0	100.0	100.5	101.2	100.0	100.0	100.3	100.3	99.5
97.7	**99.9**	**100.0**	**100.0**	**99.9**	**98.7**	**100.0**	**100.1**	**99.0**	**100.0**	**100.0**	**99.3**	**100.0**	**99.3**
99.5	100.0	100.0	100.0	99.6	96.4	100.0	100.4	99.2	100.0	100.0	100.0	100.5	99.3
95.6	99.9	100.0	100.0	100.0	100.0	100.0	99.8	98.6	100.0	100.0	98.5	99.6	99.2
95.9	**99.9**	**99.7**	**89.1**	**96.0**	**98.4**	**100.0**	**98.4**	**91.1**	**89.2**	**96.3**	**88.0**	**99.2**	**96.5**
96.5	100.1	99.8	100.0	98.0	100.6	100.0	97.8	99.4	99.1	102.2	100.6	99.9	100.2
95.1	99.6	99.6	84.0	84.5	96.1	100.0	98.9	86.6	79.3	91.5	78.8	98.7	90.6
107.7	**100.4**	**104.0**	**100.0**	**98.6**	**100.0**	**100.0**	**98.7**	**100.1**	**100.1**	**110.8**	**99.9**	**99.4**	**97.3**
102.0	**100.1**	**99.3**	**100.0**	**100.0**	**100.3**	**100.0**	**98.6**	**99.0**	**106.9**	**99.7**	**98.4**	**101.2**	**102.4**
108.4	**107.8**	**106.0**	**104.7**	**102.8**	**107.9**	**112.2**	**112.0**	**107.0**	**100.0**	**108.9**	**104.2**	**103.4**	**108.0**
100.9	**98.7**	**100.1**	**99.2**	**104.1**	**99.5**	**99.9**	**98.2**	**105.8**	**99.6**	**99.8**	**98.2**	**100.3**	**101.4**
100.2	100.0	100.0	93.0	102.5	100.0	100.0	92.1	93.2	96.6	84.6	94.7	100.0	92.8
108.5	99.4	97.7	100.4	112.6	105.3	100.0	103.3	106.7	100.0	101.9	96.4	98.7	104.8
95.9	97.8	101.5	98.7	95.7	94.7	100.1	95.3	108.6	99.7	101.7	99.3	100.0	100.8
101.5	100.0	101.5	102.0	96.1	97.6	98.7	100.5	100.0	100.0	102.1	99.1	105.5	96.7
99.6	**100.5**	**100.5**	**100.0**	**102.3**	**100.0**	**101.4**	**100.8**	**99.9**	**99.8**	**102.3**	**100.0**	**100.0**	**103.2**
98.7	102.0	100.0	100.0	102.0	100.0	100.0	100.0	100.8	99.7	103.2	100.0	100.0	100.3
100.1	100.1	101.4	100.0	101.7	100.0	104.0	100.0	100.1	100.0	102.3	99.9	100.0	107.7
100.0	100.0	100.0	100.0	105.0	99.8	100.0	103.6	96.3	99.6	100.0	100.7	100.0	100.0
104.8	**106.0**	**106.2**	**108.1**	**103.0**	**104.0**	**108.6**	**111.2**	**112.3**	**102.8**	**100.3**	**107.4**	**104.7**	**111.3**
106.7	114.4	112.0	111.8	100.7	104.7	115.5	114.3	124.7	105.6	97.6	109.8	102.9	132.6
103.5	103.5	104.3	105.7	104.0	103.6	102.9	105.7	103.2	100.1	101.1	105.4	105.6	103.2
108.5	**102.6**	**102.5**	**109.5**	**104.0**	**104.0**	**103.4**	**107.8**	**112.1**	**102.7**	**104.5**	**109.1**	**105.3**	**111.0**
111.0	102.4	103.1	101.1	104.8	106.5	103.9	109.6	102.8	105.4	105.7	112.4	104.5	105.4
102.4	103.1	100.2	129.0	96.6	101.0	102.7	103.9	128.2	100.0	102.3	100.0	108.9	118.5

6-6 农业生产资料价格分类指数

Price Indices of Agricultural Means of Production by Category

(上年=100) (preceding year=100)

项　　目	Item	2000	2005	2007
农业生产资料价格指数	**General Index**	**97.9**	**105.3**	**106.2**
农用手工工具	Farm-oriented Handwork Implement	99.1	104.9	106.9
饲料类	Forage	93.5	101.3	114.7
产品畜	Animals for Products	94.4	89.4	163.3
半机械化农具	Semi-mechanized Farm Tools	97.8	100.9	100.8
机械化农具	Mechanized Farm Machinery	97.7	102.5	100.6
化学肥料	Chemical Fertilizer	92.8	110.2	99.0
农药及农药械	Pesticide and Its Appliances	98.5	102.8	100.6
农机用油	Oil for Farm Machinery	110.3	111.0	105.9
其他农业生产资料	Others	98.4	105.5	102.5
农业生产服务	Agriculture Production Service			109.1

6-7 各市县农业生产资料价格指数

Price Indices of Agricultural Means of Production by Category in Cities and Counties

(上年=100) (2007 年) (preceding year=100)

项　　目	Item	塔城市 Kashgar [Kaxgar] City	阿勒泰市 Altay City	乌苏市 Usu City	博乐市 Bole [Bortala] City	吐鲁番市 Turpan City	库车县 Kuqa County	阿图什市 Artux City	莎车县 Shache [Yarkant] County	焉耆回族自治县 Yanqi Hui Autonomous County
农业生产资料价格指数	**General Index**	**104.4**	**102.8**	**102.2**	**104.7**	**105.8**	**107.5**	**105.0**	**108.7**	**105.2**
农用手工工具	Farm-oriented Handwork Implement	100.0	100.0	100.0	103.9	100.0	108.3	100.0	110.7	112.3
饲料类	Forage	117.2	125.7	101.9	113.2	103.2	125.1	115.1	112.3	117.0
产品畜	Animals for Products	154.3	119.5	150.6	119.0	116.3	105.5	123.8	208.3	140.2
半机械化农具	Semi-mechanized Farm Tools	97.7	100.5	100.0	100.0	100.0	106.4	103.8	100.4	100.0
机械化农具	Mechanized Farm Machinery	98.4	97.3	100.0	102.1	103.2	102.5	98.2	101.7	100.2
化学肥料	Chemical Fertilizer	99.4	100.4	96.5	101.8	98.5	99.0	101.4	96.4	101.5
农药及农药械	Pesticide and Its Appliances	96.7	100.3	96.6	100.3	104.0	102.1	100.0	100.2	101.2
农用机油	Oil for Farm Machinery	103.1	103.1	103.1	107.9	103.5	104.9	115.9	108.0	104.9
其他农业生产资料	Others	99.6	95.3	103.8	101.9	110.7	100.8	99.7	99.1	113.2
农业生产服务	Agriculture Production Service	100.0	100.0	100.0	102.3	139.2	126.4	107.4	102.2	100.0

6-8 历年房屋销售价格指数
Selling Price Indices of Houses by Period

(上年=100) (preceding year=100)

项 目	Item	2005	2006	2007
房屋销售价格指数	**Selling Price Indices of Houses**	**100.9**	**101.2**	**109.0**
商品房	Commercial Houses	100.8	101.1	109.9
住 宅	Residential Buildings	100.6	101.0	111.1
经济适用房	Economical Houses	100.7	101.4	110.1
普通住宅	General Residential Buildings	101.0	100.9	112.4
高档住宅	Luxury Residential Buildings	98.8	100.7	110.3
非住宅	Non-Residential Buildings	101.3	101.3	105.1

6-9 房屋销售价格指数
Selling Price Indices of Houses

(上年=100) (2007 年) (preceding year=100)

项 目	Item	一季度 First Quarter	二季度 Second Quarter	三季度 Third Quarter	四季度 Fourth Quarter
房屋销售价格指数	**Selling Price Indices of Houses**	**102.1**	**104.0**	**112.3**	**117.7**
商品房	Commercial Houses	102.2	104.1	114.2	119.1
住 宅	Residential Buildings	102.1	104.4	116.2	121.6
经济适用房	Economical Houses	102.8	103.8	114.0	119.8
普通住宅	General Residential Buildings	101.9	105.3	118.4	123.8
多层住宅	Multilayer Buildings	102.1	105.3	119.2	124.5
高层住宅	High-layer Buildings	100.7	105.5	114.7	123.2
高档住宅	Luxury Residential Buildings	101.4	103.0	117.2	119.6
非住宅	Non-Residential Buildings	102.2	103.2	106.2	108.8
办公楼	Office Buildings	104.0	103.4	103.2	111.1
商业用房	Houses for Business Use	100.7	102.9	108.3	107.7

6-10 工业品出厂价格分类指数

Ex-Factory Price Indices of Industrial Products by Category

(上年=100) (preceding year=100)

项 目	Item	2000	2005	2007
全部工业品	**Total Industrial Products**	**129.4**	**116.6**	**106.3**
轻工业	Light Industry	97.3	99.6	105.6
以农产品为原料	Using Farm Produces as Raw Materials	97.1	98.4	105.8
以非农产品为原料	Using Non-farm Produces as Raw Materials	103.5	101.9	105.2
重工业	Heavy Industry	141.8	122.5	106.4
采 掘	Mining and Quarrying	164.2	136.2	104.4
原 料	Raw Materials	114.3	114.2	106.3
加 工	Manufacturing	98.6	104.1	115.1
生产资料	Means of Production	138.0	118.4	106.1
采 掘	Mining and Quarrying	164.0	136.0	104.4
原 料	Raw Materials	113.7	114.3	106.1
加 工	Manufacturing	97.7	100.4	109.0
生活资料	Consumer Goods	96.6	101.3	108.4
食 品	Food	93.0	101.7	109.4
衣 着	Clothing	100.3	96.4	100.3
一般日用品	Articles for Daily Use	98.1	101.1	104.8
耐用消费品	Durable Consumer Goods	99.7	99.2	100.3
按工业部门分	**Division of Industrial Setors**			
冶金工业	Metallurgical Industry	103.9	101.9	115.5
电力工业	Power Industry	104.8	100.9	101.2
煤炭及炼焦工业	Coal and Coking Industry	98.2	109.4	112.5
石油工业	Petroleum Industry	162.2	130.5	104.9
化学工业	Chemical Industry	102.6	106.1	106.2
机械工业	Machine Building Industry	97.4	112.4	120.7
建筑材料工业	Building Materials Industry	98.4	99.4	103.3
森林工业	Timber Industry	99.7	99.9	100.7
食品工业	Food Industry	92.2	101.1	109.7
纺织工业	Textile Industry	101.8	92.1	99.4
缝纫工业	Tailoring Industry	101.7	96.3	100.3
皮革工业	Leather Industry	95.7	100.0	108.6
造纸工业	Paper Industry	98.4	102.6	104.6
文教艺术用品工业	Cultural, Educational and Handicrafts Articles	98.2	99.7	100.6
其他工业	Other Industry	98.8	104.0	106.5

6-11 原材料、燃料、动力购进价格分类指数
Indices of Purchasing Prices of Raw Material, Fuels and Power by Category

(上年=100) (preceding year=100)

项目	Iterm	2000	2005	2007
全部原材料价格指数	**Total of Raw Material**	**115.2**	**110.7**	**103.8**
燃料、动力类	Fuel and Power	137.9	132.0	102.4
黑色金属材料类	Material of Black Metal	100.5	113.8	105.7
#钢　材	Rolled Steel	104.8	112.9	103.2
其　他	Other	95.5	114.9	110.4
有色金属材料和电线类	Material of Coloured Metal	112.2	108.5	103.8
化工原料类	Material of Chemistry	104.4	113.0	104.1
木材及纸浆类	Timber and Paper Pulp	100.5	102.0	102.2
建筑材料及非金属矿类	Building Material and Non-metal Ore	100.4	103.9	103.7
其他工业原材料及半成品类	Other Industrial Raw Material and Semi-finished Category	111.4	105.5	108.4
农副产品类	Agricultural Produces	97.2	91.9	104.6
纺织原料类	Textile Raw Material	95.2	93.0	103.4

6-12 固定资产投资价格指数
Price Indices of Investment in Fixed Assets

(上年=100) (preceding year=100)

项目	Item	2000	2005	2007
固定资产投资价格指数	**Investment in Fixed Assets**	**103.6**	**102.8**	**104.4**
建筑安装工程	**Construction and Installtion**	**105.5**	**102.7**	**105.5**
人工费	Manpower Expenses	108.2	103.8	109.4
材料费	Material Expenses	104.9	102.3	104.2
#钢　材	Rolled Steel	108.3	101.7	105.5
木　材	Timber	102.2	102.5	101.3
水　泥	Cement	100.6	100.1	103.6
地方材料	Local Material	102.8	102.0	104.6
化工材料	Chemical Material	107.4	109.1	101.0
电　料	Electrical Wire	99.2	104.0	103.2
其他材料	Other Material	102.9	99.9	103.3
机械使用费	Expenses of Machine Use	104.4	102.3	103.8
设备工器具	**Purchase of Equipment,Tools and Instruments**	**97.4**	**104.8**	**101.6**
其他费用	**Others**	**103.2**	**100.0**	**102.8**

主要统计指标解释

居民消费价格指数 是反映一定时期内城乡居民所购买的生活消费品价格和服务项目价格变动趋势和程度的相对数，是对城市居民消费价格指数和农村居民消费价格指数进行综合汇总计算的结果。利用居民消费价格指数，可以观察和分析消费品的零售价格和服务价格变动对城乡居民实际生活费支出的影响程度。

城市居民消费价格指数 是反映城市居民家庭所购买的生活消费品价格和服务项目价格变动趋势和程度的相对数。城市居民消费价格指数可以观察和分析消费品的零售价格和服务项目价格变动对职工货币工资的影响，作为研究职工生活和确定工资政策的依据。

农村居民消费价格指数 是反映农村居民家庭所购买的生活消费品价格和服务项目价格变动趋势和程度的相对数。农村居民消费价格指数可以观察农村消费品的零售价格和服务项目价格变动对农村居民生活消费支出的影响，直接反映农民生活水平的实际变化情况，为分析和研究农村居民生活问题提供依据。

商品零售价格指数 是反映城乡商品零售价格变动趋势的一种经济指数。零售物价的调整变动直接影响到城乡居民的生活支出和国家的财政收入，影响居民购买力和市场供需平衡，影响消费与积累的比例。因此，计算零售价格指数，可以从一个侧面对上述经济活动进行观察和分析。

工业品出厂价格指数 是反映一定时期内全部工业产品出厂价格总水平的变动趋势和程度的相对数，包括工业企业售给本企业以外所有单位的各种产品和直接售给居民用于生活消费的产品。该指数可以观察出厂价格变动对工业总产值及增加值的影响。

农业生产资料价格指数 指反映一定时期内农业生产资料价格变动趋势和程度的相对数。农业生产资料价格指数分为小农具、饲料、产品畜、役畜、半机械化农具、机械化农具、化学肥料、农药及农药械、农机用油、其他农业生产资料十大类。其编制目的是了解农业生产中物质资料投入价格的变动状况，服务于国民经济核算。1994年以前，农业生产资料价格指数仅仅是商品零售价格指数的一个类别，此后，从商品零售价格指数中分离出来，单独编制。

固定资产投资价格指数 是反映固定资产投资额价格变动趋势和程度的相对数。固定资产投资额是由建筑安装工程投资完成额、设备、工器具购置投资完成额和其他费用投资完成额三部分组成的。编制固定资产投资价格指数应首先分别编制上述三部分投资的价格指数，然后采用加权算术平均法求出固定资产投资价格总指数。

编制固定资产投资价格指数可以准确地反映固定资产投资中涉及的各类商品和取费项目价格变动趋势和变动幅度，消除按现价计算的固定资产投资指标中的价格变动因素，真实地反映固定资产投资的规模、速度、结构和效益，为国家科学地制定、检查固定资产投资计划并提高宏观调控水平，为完善国民经济核算体系提供科学的、可靠的依据。

Explanatory Notes on Main Statistical Indicators

Consumer Price Indices reflect the trend and degree of changes in prices of consumer goods and services purchased by urban households during a given period,and is a composite index derived from the urban consumer price index and the rural consumer price index. Consumer price index can be used to analyze the impact of consumer price change on actual expenditure for living cost of urban and rural residents.

Urban Consumer Price Indices reflect the trend and degree of changes in prices of consumer goods and services purchased by urban households. It can be used to observe and analyze the impact of price changes in consumer goods and services on money wages of staff and workers, and provide basis for policymaking concerning the living cost and wages of staff and workers.

Rural Consumer Price Indices reflect the trend and degree of changes in prices of consumer goods and services purchased by rural households. It can be used to observe the impact of change in retail prices of consumer goods and service prices in rural areas on living expenditure of rural households, and to show the changes in the living standard of peasants. It provides basis for analysis and research on condition of life in rural areas.

Ex-factory Price Indices of Industrial Products reflect the trend and degree of changes in general ex-factory prices of all industrial products during a given period,including sales of industrial products by an industrial enterprise to all units outside the enterprise,as well as sales of consumer goods to residents.It can be used to analyze the impact of ex-factory prices on gross output value and value-added of the industrial sector.

Indices of Purchasing Prices of Farm Products reflects the trend and degree of changes in purchasing prices of farm products purchased by state-owned, collective-owned,and individual commercial enterprises,foreign Trades sectors,government agencies,social organizations and other units of various types of ownership. It is used to observe the impact of change in purchasing prices of farm products on the cash income of peasants, and serves as basis for the formulation and supervision of pricing policies for farm products.

Indices of Producers' Prices for Farm Products reflect the trend and degree of changes in producers' prices received by farmers when they sell farm products during a given period. These indices depict the change in the level and structure of producers' prices of farm products of the country and meet the needs of agriculture statistics and national account statistics. The producers' price index of a given product is calculated through geometrical mean of individual indices of all surveyed units who sell such product, and the indices of a product category is obtained through weighted mean of price indices of all products in the category. Method for calculating accumulative quarterly indices is the same as for calculating the distinctive quarterly indices.

Price Indices of Investment in Fixed Assets reflects the trend and degree of changes in prices of investment in fixed assets. The investment in fixed assets consists of three components, namely the investment in construction and installation, the investment in purchases of equipment and instrument,and the investment in other items. Price index of investment in fixed assets is calculated as the weighted arithmetic mean of the price indices of the three components of investment in fixed assets. Removing the factor of price change in the aggregates of investment at current prices, this indicator shows the changes in the prices of commodities and fees involved in the investment of fixed assets, and can be used to observe the actual size, growth, structure,and efficiency of investment in fixed assets and provides reliable and scientific data for government planning, management, decision making, and further improving the current national accounting system..

第七篇

人民生活和社会保障

CHAPTER 7

People's livelihood and social security

简要说明

Brief Introduction

本篇资料的主要内容及来源

本篇资料反映新疆城乡人民生活现状及变化以及城镇居民社会保障情况，分为城镇居民生活和农村居民生活两部分，主要包括居民家庭基本情况、家庭收入、支出情况、主要商品购买数量及支出金额、居住状况和耐用消费品的拥有量等。

城镇居民生活状况的数据来源于国家统计局新疆调查总队城镇住户调查处。

农村居民生活状况的数据来源于国家统计局新疆调查总队农村住户调查处。

城镇居民社会保障情况数据来源于新疆维吾尔自治区劳动和社会保障局。

Main Content and Source of Data

Data in this chapter show the condition of people´s livelihood in Xinjiang and social security in urban and rural, consisting of two parts on the life of urban and rural house-holds respectively, including mainly basic condition of people´s household, income of households, income and expenditure of the household, the quantity and the expenditure on major commodities purchased, the housing condition and the possession of the durable consumer goods, etc.

Data on the livelihood of the urban residents come from the Department of Urban households Survey , NBS Survey office in Xinjiang.

Data on the livelihood of the rural residents come from the Department of Rural households Surveys, NBS Survey Office in Xinjiang.

Data on the social security of the rural residerts come from the Department of Labor and Social Security of Xinjiang Uygur Autonomous Region.

7-1 人民物质文化生活情况
People's Material and Cultural Life

项目	Item	1990	1995	2000	2006	2007
就 业	**Employment**					
每一农村劳动力负担人数(人)	Number of Dependents Per Rural Laborer (person)	1.94	1.84	1.74	1.62	1.58
每一城镇就业者负担人数(人)	Number of Dependents Per Urban Employee (person)	2.11	1.82	2.03	1.92	1.89
城镇登记失业率(%)	Registered Urban Unemployment Rate (%)	3.8	3.9	3.8	3.9	3.9
收 入	**Income of Rural and Urban Residents**					
农村居民家庭人均纯收入(元)	Annual Per capita Net Income of Rural Residents (yuan)	684	1137	1618	2737	3183
农村居民家庭人均纯收入指数 (1978 年=100)	Index of Annual Per capita Net Income of Rural Residents (1978=100)	574.8	955.5	1359.3	2300.0	2674.8
城镇居民家庭人均可支配收入(元)	Annual Per capita Disposable Income of Urban Residents (yuan)	1314	4163	5645	8871	10313
城镇居民家庭人均可支配收入指数 (1978 年=100)	Index of Annual Per capita Disposable Income of Urban Residents (1978=100)	411.8	1172.3	1589.4	2679.0	3114.5
在岗职工年平均工资(元)	Annual Average Wages of Staff and Workers (yuan)	2272	5348	8717	17819	21434
消费水平（元）	**Annual Per capita Consumption (yuan)**					
全区居民	All Residents	796	1852	2662	4206	4890
农村居民	Rural Residents	447	977	1308	2000	2320
城镇居民	Urban Residents	1508	3414	5131	7875	8986
储 蓄	**Savings**					
城乡居民年底储蓄存款余额(亿元)	Balance of Savings Deposit of Rural and Urban Residents (Year-end) (100 million yuan)	114.13	477.18	908.55	2035.63	2054.91
平均每人储蓄存款余额(元)	Per capita Balance of Saving Deposit (yuan)	746	2872	4913	9930	9915
住房面积（平方米）	**Per Capita Floor Space of Residential Buildings (sq.m)**					
农村居民人均住房面积	Per-capital Living Space in Rural Areas	14.04	16.12	17.25	21.96	22.45
城镇居民人均使用面积	Per-capital Using Space in Urban Areas	13.55	16.57	20.06	20.33	20.38
交 通	**Traffic**					
城镇每百户拥有摩托车(辆)	Number of Motorcycle per 100 Households in Urban Areas (unit)	3.22	6.33	8.53	16.59	19.99
城镇每万人拥有营运公交车辆(标台)	Number of Public Transportation Vehicles per 10000 Population in City (unit)	3.5	10.8	13.8	14.7	11.4
城镇公用事业	**Public Utilities in Urban Areas**					
用水普及率（%）	Rate of Access to Tap Water (%)	80.9	97.1	98.8	99.4	94.4
燃气普及率（%）	Rate of Access to Gas (%)	49.8	86.2	92.8	91.5	84.8
每万人拥有绿地面积（公顷）	Green Area per 10 000 Population (hectare)	21.6	41.5	53.4	36.9	55.2
文 化	**Culture**					
城镇每百户拥有彩色电视机(台)	Number of Color TV Sets per 100 Households in Urban Areas (set)	67.80	85.50	102.57	107.97	105.34
农村每百户拥有电视机(台)	Number of TV Sets per 100 Households in Rural Areas (set)	33.95	69.42	91.20	100.38	99.16
广播综合人口覆盖率（%）	Broadcast Covering Rate of Population (%)	70.00	78.41	89.77	93.36	93.50
电视综合人口覆盖率（%）	TV Covering Rate of Population (%)	65.00	80.48	92.15	93.11	93.50
教 育	**Education**					
学龄儿童入学率(%)	Enrollment Ratio of School-Age Children (%)	97.50	97.03	97.03	99.15	99.28
每万人口中在校大学生数(人)	Number of University Students per 10 000 Population (person)	20.45	26.84	41.05	97.20	103.20
卫 生	**Public Health**					
每万人有医院、卫生院床位(张)	Number of Hospital Beds per 10 000 Population (unit)	40.5	40.1	35.7	39.1	41.6
每万人有医生数(人)	Number of Doctors per 10 000 Population (person)	22.0	23.9	24.6	20.9	20.8

注：2002 年以后的城镇人均拥有指标按城镇人口计算。以前按非农业人口计算。
Note: Per Capita Ownership is calculated on the population in cities for the year 2002.Prior to 2002, it was based on non-agricultural Population.

7-2 城乡居民储蓄存款年底余额和年增加额
Savings Deposit in Urban and Rural Areas (Year-end)

单位: 亿元 (100 million yuan)

年份 Year	年底余额 Outstanding Amount			年增加额 Increased Amount		
	总计 Total	定期 Fixed Deposits	活期 Current Deposits	总计 Total	定期 Fixed Deposits	活期 Current Deposits
1978	6.42					
1980	9.52	8.26	1.26	2.31		
1985	29.55	24.76	4.79	5.24	4.60	0.64
1990	128.43	108.15	20.27	35.68	28.72	6.96
1995	477.18	382.61	94.57	129.47	107.90	21.57
2000	908.55	653.58	254.97	83.86	22.50	61.36
2001	994.00	722.85	271.15	85.46	39.32	48.59
2002	1137.87	760.32	377.55	143.85	68.39	75.46
2003	1371.59	879.93	491.66	233.81	119.59	114.23
2004	1534.67	991.62	543.05	162.85	111.61	51.24
2005	1816.38	1170.89	645.49	281.71	179.27	102.44
2006	2035.63	1270.16	765.47	219.25	99.27	119.98
2007	2054.91	1153.18	901.73	19.29	-116.97	136.26

7-3 城乡居民家庭人均收入及指数
Per Capita Annual Income of Urban and Rural Households and the Related Index

年份 Year	农村居民家庭人均纯收入 Per capita Annual Net Income of Rural Households		城镇居民家庭人均年可支配收入 Per capita Annual Disposable Income of Urban Households		农村居民家庭恩格尔系数 (%) Engle Coefficient of Rural Households (%)	城镇居民家庭恩格尔系数 (%) Engle Coefficient of Urban Households (%)
	绝对数（元） Value (yuan)	指数(1978=100) Index	绝对数（元） Value (yuan)	指数(1978=100) Index		
1978	119	100.0	319	100.0		
1980	201	168.9	427	133.9	60.8	57.3
1985	394	331.1	735	230.4	57.9	46.8
1990	684	574.8	1314	411.8	53.7	47.8
1995	1137	955.5	4163	1172.3	50.1	44.8
2000	1618	1359.3	5645	1589.4	50.0	36.4
2001	1710	1437.0	6215	1749.9	50.4	34.8
2002	1863	1564.9	6554	1979.1	49.0	33.9
2003	2106	1768.3	7006	2115.7	45.5	35.9
2004	2245	1885.0	7503	2265.9	45.2	36.1
2005	2482	2084.0	7990	2412.9	41.8	36.4
2006	2737	2300.0	8871	2679.0	39.9	35.5
2007	3183	2674.8	10313	3114.5	39.9	35.1

注: 1992 年以前城镇居民人均年可支配收入为人均年生活费收入。
Note: Per capita disposal income of urban houscholds before the year 1992 is Per capita annual income as life expense.

7-4 城镇居民家庭生活基本情况
Basic Living Conditions of Urban Households

(抽样调查 Sampled Survey)

项目	Item	1990	1995	2000	2006	2007
调查户数（户）	**Number of Households Surveyed (household)**	**590**	**590**	**790**	**1380**	**1560**
平均每户家庭人口(人)	**Average Household Size (person)**	**3.92**	**3.37**	**3.15**	**2.98**	**3.02**
平均每户就业人口(人)	**Average Number of Employed Persons Per Household (person)**	**1.86**	**1.85**	**1.55**	**1.55**	**1.60**
平均每户就业面 (%)	**Proportion of Employment per Household (%)**	**47.45**	**54.90**	**49.21**	**52.01**	**52.98**
平均每一就业者负担人数(包括就业者本人)(人)	**Number of Dependents Per Employee (including the employee himself or herself) (person)**	**2.11**	**1.82**	**2.03**	**1.92**	**1.89**
平均每人全部年收入(元)	**Per Capita Annual Income (yuan)**	**1432.38**	**4183.81**	**5686.52**	**9689.07**	**11378.32**
#可支配收入	Disposable Income	1313.54	4163.44	5644.86	8871.27	10313.44
工薪收入	Income from Wages and Salaries	1166.64	3509.20	4128.29	7490.69	9012.19
工资及补贴收入	Salary & Subsidy	1146.15	3468.37	4027.36	7335.50	8901.01
其他劳动收入	Part-time Income	20.49	40.83	100.93	155.19	111.18
经营净收入	Net Business Income	21.75	85.43	230.29	594.81	681.66
财产性收入	Income from Porperties	8.81	54.94	38.03	58.39	67.97
转移性收入	Income from Transfer	235.18	501.71	1243.55	1545.18	1616.49
平均每人消费性支出(元)	**Per Capita Annual Consumption Expenditures (yuan)**	**1104.42**	**3186.75**	**4422.92**	**6730.01**	**7874.27**
食　品	Food	527.74	1428.47	1609.17	2386.97	2760.69
衣　着	Clothing	172.17	562.41	577.40	953.03	1183.69
家庭设备用品及服务	Household Applianances and Service	121.51	248.07	410.88	364.11	475.23
医疗保健	Health Care and Medical Service	27.39	133.84	330.54	472.35	598.78
交通通讯	Transport and Communication	17.88	175.95	331.03	765.72	890.30
娱乐教育文化服务	Recreation, Education and Cultural Services	123.95	290.78	600.34	819.72	896.79
居　住	Housing	51.22	179.06	343.25	698.66	736.99
杂项商品与服务	Miscellaneous Commodities and Service	62.56	168.17	220.31	269.45	331.80
平均每人消费性支出构成(%)(人均消费支出=100)	**Composition of Per Capita Annual Consumption (%)**	**100**	**100**	**100**	**100**	**100**
食　品	Food	47.78	44.83	36.38	35.47	35.06
衣　着	Clothing	15.59	17.65	13.05	14.16	15.03
家庭设备用品及服务	Household Appliances and Service	11.01	7.78	9.29	5.41	6.04
医疗保健	Health Care and Medical Service	2.48	4.20	7.48	7.02	7.60
交通通讯	Transport and Communication	1.62	5.52	7.48	11.38	11.31
娱乐教育文化服务	Recreation, Education and Cultural Services	11.22	9.12	13.58	12.18	11.39
居　住	Housing	4.64	5.62	7.76	10.38	9.36
杂项商品与服务	Miscellaneous Commodities and Services	5.66	5.28	4.98	4.00	4.21

7-5 城镇居民家庭基本情况
Basic Conditions of Urban Households

(2007 年) (抽样调查 Sampled Survey)

项目	Item	全区 Whole Region	最低收入户 Lowest Income Households	#困难户 Poor Households	低收入户 Low Income Households
调查户数(户)	Number of Households Surveyed (household)	1560	156	78	156
比重(%)	Proportion (%)	100	10	5	10
平均每户家庭人口(人)	Average Household Size (person)	3.02	3.69	3.93	3.22
平均每户就业人口(人)	Average Number of Employees per Household (person)	1.60	1.11	1.17	1.46
平均每户就业面(%)	Proportion of Employed Persons per Household (%)	52.98	30.08	29.77	45.34
平均每一就业者负担人数(包括就业者本人)(人)	Number of Dependents per Employee (Including the employee himself or herself) (person)	1.89	3.32	3.36	2.21
平均每人全部年收入(元)	Per Capita Annual Income (yuan)	11378.32	3733.16	2598.69	6450.91
平均每人可支配收入(元)	Per Capita Disposable Income (yuan)	10313.44	3258.57	2244.45	5668.41
平均每人消费性支出(元)	Per Capita Annual Consumption Expenditure (yuan)	7874.27	3481.40	2719.45	4828.37

项目	Item	中等偏下户 Lower Middle Income Households	中等收入户 Middle Income Households	中等偏上户 Upper Middle Income Households	高收入户 High Income Households	最高收入户 Highest Income Households
调查户数(户)	Number of Households Surveyed (household)	312	312	312	156	156
比重(%)	Proportion (%)	20	20	20	10	10
平均每户家庭人口(人)	Average Household Size (person)	3.10	3.04	2.93	2.78	2.20
平均每户就业人口(人)	Average Number of Employees per Household (person)	1.72	1.69	1.71	1.87	1.36
平均每户就业面(%)	Proportion of Employed Persons per Household (%)	55.48	55.59	58.36	67.27	61.82
平均每一就业者负担人数(包括就业者本人)(人)	Number of Dependents per Employee (Including the employee himself or herself) (person)	1.80	1.80	1.71	1.49	1.62
平均每人全部年收入(元)	Per Capita Annual Income (yuan)	8729.40	11293.26	14357.80	18164.01	24599.98
平均每人可支配收入(元)	Per Capita Disposable Income (yuan)	7813.01	10264.05	13064.33	16491.18	22872.33
平均每人消费性支出(元)	Per Capita Annual Consumption Expenditure (yuan)	6363.28	7867.17	9763.73	12102.63	14675.58

7-6 城镇居民家庭平均每人全年消费性支出
Per Capita Annual Living Expenditure of Urban Households

单位：元　　(2007 年) (抽样调查 Sampled Survey)　　(yuan)

项目	Item	总平均 Total Average	最低收入户 Lowest Income Households	#困难户 Poor Households	低收入户 Low Income Households
消费性支出	**Consumption Expenditures**	**7874.27**	**3481.40**	**2719.45**	**4828.37**
食 品	Food	2760.69	1586.18	1186.22	2084.51
#粮 食	Grain	269.59	268.75	233.82	290.25
肉禽及其制品	Meat, Poultry and Related Products	569.42	388.63	290.41	447.25
蛋 类	Eggs	51.73	38.14	30.01	51.18
水产品	Aquatic Products	63.72	20.69	9.21	52.53
奶及奶制品	Milk and Dairy Products	132.77	59.21	46.07	101.41
衣 着	Clothing	1183.69	410.11	334.08	652.24
#服 装	Garments	833.30	254.91	205.36	434.89
家庭设备用品及服务	Household Appliances and Services	475.23	135.93	104.82	229.87
#耐用消费品	Durable Consumer Goods	201.08	19.54	6.39	81.85
医疗保健	Health Care and Medical Services	598.78	186.87	119.66	343.01
交通通讯	Transport and Communication Services	890.30	265.28	209.36	414.31
娱乐教育文化服务	Recreation, Education and Cultural Services	896.79	331.80	211.54	492.70
#文化娱乐用品	Recreation Articles	241.16	36.72	27.85	99.90
居 住	Housing	736.99	482.42	489.84	461.63
#住 房	House	224.08	169.22	234.18	34.24
杂项商品与服务	Miscellaneous Commodities and Services	331.80	82.81	63.92	150.09

项目	Item	中等偏下户 Lower Middle Income Households	中等收入户 Middle Income Households	中等偏上户 Upper Middle Income Households	高收入户 High Income Households	最高收入户 Highest Income Households
消费性支出	**Consumption Expenditures**	**6363.28**	**7867.17**	**9763.73**	**12102.63**	**14675.58**
食 品	Food	2579.79	2712.88	3065.56	3761.03	4549.92
#粮 食	Grain	261.30	262.40	265.31	260.08	311.78
肉禽及其制品	Meat, Poultry and Related Products	571.63	596.71	625.70	682.81	708.72
蛋 类	Eggs	48.14	54.05	52.38	55.12	77.81
水产品	Aquatic Products	58.80	64.16	71.22	86.78	126.45
奶及奶制品	Milk and Dairy Products	132.20	136.41	155.05	162.30	211.58
衣 着	Clothing	957.25	1269.37	1488.74	1875.19	2159.17
#服 装	Garments	656.12	896.77	1051.32	1384.48	1573.38
家庭设备用品及服务	Household Appliances and Services	298.45	510.98	661.97	827.21	952.08
#耐用消费品	Durable Consumer Goods	97.75	227.00	293.55	401.35	452.13
医疗保健	Health Care and Medical Services	395.21	642.61	893.63	763.77	1239.29
交通通讯	Transport and Communication Services	679.29	825.88	1170.27	1618.98	1879.71
娱乐教育文化服务	Recreation, Education and Cultural Services	742.66	868.14	1083.71	1565.10	1732.03
#文化娱乐用品	Recreation Articles	183.38	225.36	284.75	475.91	637.20
居 住	Housing	480.44	715.09	937.11	1193.58	1324.15
#住 房	House	37.18	216.23	349.40	456.47	552.93
杂项商品与服务	Miscellaneous Commodities and Services	230.21	322.22	462.75	497.76	839.22

7-7 城镇居民家庭平均每人全年消费性支出构成
Composition of Per Capita Annual Consumption Expenditure of Urban Households

单位：% (2007 年) (抽样调查 Sampled Survey) (%)

项目	Item	总平均 Total Average	最低收入户 Lowest Income Households	#困难户 Poor Households	低收入户 Low Income Households
消费性支出	**Consumption Expenditures**	**100**	**100**	**100**	**100**
食 品	Food	35.06	45.56	43.62	43.17
衣 着	Clothing	15.03	11.78	12.29	13.51
家庭设备用品及服务	Household Appliances and Services	6.04	3.90	3.85	4.76
医疗保健	Health Care and Medical Services	7.60	5.37	4.40	7.10
交通通讯	Transport and Communication Services	11.31	7.62	7.70	8.58
娱乐教育文化服务	Recreation, Education and Cultural Services	11.39	9.53	7.78	10.21
居 住	Housing	9.36	13.86	18.01	9.56
杂项商品与服务	Miscellaneous Commodities and Services	4.21	2.38	2.35	3.11

项目	Item	中等偏下户 Lower Middle Income Households	中等收入户 Middle Income Households	中等偏上户 Upper Middle Income Households	高收入户 High Income Households	最高收入户 Highest Income Households
消费性支出	**Consumption Expenditures**	**100**	**100**	**100**	**100**	**100**
食 品	Food	40.54	34.48	31.40	31.08	31.00
衣 着	Clothing	15.04	16.13	15.25	15.49	14.71
家庭设备用品及服务	Household Appliances and Services	4.69	6.50	6.78	6.84	6.49
医疗保健	Health Care and Medical Services	6.21	8.17	9.15	6.31	8.45
交通通讯	Transport and Communication Services	10.68	10.50	11.98	13.38	12.81
娱乐教育文化服务	Recreation, Education and Cultural Services	11.67	11.03	11.10	12.93	11.80
居 住	Housing	7.55	9.09	9.60	9.86	9.02
杂项商品与服务	Miscellaneous Commodities and Services	3.62	4.10	4.74	4.11	5.72

7-8 城镇居民家庭年人均购买的主要商品数量
Per Capita Annual Purchases of Major Commodities of Urban Households

(抽样调查 Sampled Survey)

项 目	Item	1990	1995	2000	2006	2007
粮食(千克)	Grain (kg)	139.73	95.97	81.91	86.21	50.63
鲜菜(千克)	Fresh Vegetables (kg)	132.96	113.41	90.56	102.17	93.39
食用植物油(千克)	Edible Vegetable Oil (kg)	10.09	9.01	9.69	10.58	10.28
猪肉(千克)	Pork (kg)	5.56	6.34	5.17	6.31	5.19
牛肉(千克)	Beef (kg)	13.51	2.95	3.62	4.33	4.51
羊肉(千克)	Mutton(kg)		10.43	13.06	11.61	12.41
家禽(千克)	Poultry (kg)	2.12	4.65	6.11	6.20	5.38
鲜蛋(千克)	Fresh Eggs (kg)	4.46	5.11	7.39	7.66	6.95
水产品(千克)	Aquatic Products (kg)	3.73	4.89	4.35	5.01	4.35
鲜乳品(千克)	Fresh Dairy Products (kg)	12.70	12.98	18.44	27.55	26.74
鲜瓜果(千克)	Fresh Fruits & Melons(kg)	59.47	43.54	64.31	68.67	61.00
服装(件)	Clothes(piece)	2.12	5.84	6.36	7.81	8.31
液化石油气(千克)	Liquefied Petrolum Gas (kg)	11.40	21.62	24.77	13.47	9.87
天然气(立方米)	Natural Gas (cu.m)		0.08	1.93	30.58	32.85
煤炭(千克)	Coal (kg)	90.10	180.46	123.78	132.51	89.04

注: 2007 年粮食购买量仅指面粉和大米，不包括其他粮食及制品。
Note: In 2007 purchase of grain only refer to flour and rice, does not include miscellaneous grain and processed products.

7-9 城镇居民家庭平均每百户年底耐用消费品拥有量
Number of Major Durable Consumer Goods Owned Per-100 Urban Households at Year-end

项 目	Item	1990	1995	2000	2006	2007
摩托车(辆)	Motorcycle (unit)	3.22	6.33	8.53	16.59	19.99
家用汽车(辆)	Automobil (unit)			0.82	2.08	1.80
家用电脑(台)	Household Computer (set)			5.68	28.70	34.70
组合音响(套)	Hi-Fi Stereo Component System (set)	0.51	7.38	17.53	18.86	21.12
摄相机(架)	Pickug Camera (set)			1.02	3.12	3.58
钢琴(架)	Piano (set)		1.20	1.38	1.96	1.38
其他中高档乐器(件)	Other Medium and High Grade Musical Instrument (piece)	11.53	11.84	9.09	6.78	7.02
微波炉(台)	Oven (unit)			5.39	24.15	27.80
空调器(台)	Air Conditioner (unit)	0.17	0.93	2.78	8.62	6.70
淋浴热水器(台)	Shower (unit)		32.46	47.91	65.73	69.63
消毒碗柜(台)	Disinfectant Machine (unit)				5.38	6.08
健身器材(台)	Healthy Equipment (unit)			2.35	3.33	2.58
普通电话(部)	Telephone (unit)			71.69	87.70	90.15
移动电话(部)	Mobile phone (unit)			4.81	126.56	140.12
洗衣机(台)	Washing Machine (unit)	79.66	92.10	95.48	92.97	93.02
电冰箱(台)	Refrigerator (unit)	32.20	60.36	81.76	82.65	88.34
彩色电视机(台)	Color TV Set (set)	67.80	85.50	102.57	107.97	105.34
照相机(架)	Camera (set)	20.00	37.15	33.71	39.15	33.39

7-10 按收入等级分城镇居民家庭平均每人全年购买商品数量

Per Capita Annual Purchases of Major Commodities of Urban Households by Level of Income

(2007 年) (抽样调查 Sampled Survey)

项 目	Item	总平均 Total Average	最低收入户 Lowest Income Households	#困难户 Poor Households	低收入户 Low Income Households
粮 食(千克)	Grain (kg)	50.63	70.78	65.99	55.87
食用植物油(千克)	Edible Vegetable Oil (kg)	10.28	12.10	10.89	11.00
猪 肉(千克)	Pork (kg)	5.19	2.08	0.87	4.87
牛 肉(千克)	Beef (kg)	4.51	2.39	1.89	3.55
羊 肉(千克)	Mutton (kg)	12.41	12.12	10.72	9.30
家 禽(千克)	Poultry (kg)	5.38	2.27	1.15	5.01
鲜 蛋(千克)	Fresh Eggs (kg)	6.95	5.60	4.26	7.09
鱼 (千克)	Fish (kg)	3.94	1.41	0.66	3.65
虾 (千克)	Shrimp (kg)	0.41	0.13	0.06	0.30
鲜 菜(千克)	Fresh Vegetables (kg)	93.39	79.82	66.50	92.51
白 酒(千克)	Liquor (kg)	1.24	0.56	0.43	0.92
果 酒(千克)	Fruit Wine (kg)	0.32	0.08	0.07	0.18
啤 酒(千克)	Beer (kg)	1.80	0.83	0.51	1.35
鲜瓜果(千克)	Fresh Melons & Fruits (kg)	61.00	39.92	30.43	59.11
糕 点(千克)	Cake (kg)	3.91	2.18	1.79	3.50
鲜乳品(千克)	Fresh Dairy Products (kg)	26.74	15.81	13.03	23.01
奶 粉(千克)	Milk Powder (kg)	0.17	0.09	0.11	0.07
酸 奶(千克)	Sour Milk (kg)	2.99	1.00	0.79	2.25
服 装(件)	Clothing (piece)	8.31	4.60	4.34	5.79

项 目	Item	中等偏下户 Lower Middle Income Households	中等收入户 Middle Income Households	中等偏上户 Upper Middle Income Households	高收入户 High Income Households	最高收入户 Highest Income Households
粮 食(千克)	Grain (kg)	48.79	48.16	47.67	37.64	42.06
食用植物油(千克)	Edible Vegetable Oil (kg)	9.92	10.14	10.36	8.17	9.76
猪 肉(千克)	Pork (kg)	5.23	5.17	5.51	6.66	8.85
牛 肉(千克)	Beef (kg)	5.08	5.13	4.38	5.93	5.08
羊 肉(千克)	Mutton (kg)	12.66	13.21	14.11	12.26	9.90
家 禽(千克)	Poultry (kg)	5.03	5.73	6.02	7.01	8.06
鲜 蛋(千克)	Fresh Eggs (kg)	6.59	7.24	6.92	7.00	9.74
鱼 (千克)	Fish (kg)	4.08	3.93	4.40	4.74	6.54
虾 (千克)	Shrimp (kg)	0.36	0.39	0.48	0.59	0.94
鲜 菜(千克)	Fresh Vegetables (kg)	91.76	89.44	91.73	101.28	131.62
白 酒(千克)	Liquor (kg)	1.00	1.33	1.61	1.98	1.56
果 酒(千克)	Fruit Wine (kg)	0.28	0.29	0.41	0.70	0.43
啤 酒(千克)	Beer (kg)	1.94	1.98	2.13	2.06	2.16
鲜瓜果(千克)	Fresh Melons & Fruits (kg)	57.84	56.76	66.86	74.68	91.34
糕 点(千克)	Cake (kg)	3.77	3.91	4.99	3.83	5.41
鲜乳品(千克)	Fresh Dairy Products (kg)	27.12	27.72	30.78	30.87	32.56
奶 粉(千克)	Milk Powder (kg)	0.15	0.25	0.19	0.16	0.28
酸 奶(千克)	Sour Milk (kg)	2.97	2.95	3.31	4.42	5.36
服 装(件)	Clothing (piece)	7.17	8.71	9.48	12.16	13.30

7-11 按收入等级分城镇居民家庭平均每百户年底耐用消费品拥有量
Ownership of Durable Consumer Goods Per100 Urban Households at Year-end by Level of Income

(2007 年) (抽样调查 Sampled Survey)

项 目	Item	总平均 Total Average	最低收入户 Lowest Income Households	#困难户 Poor Households	低收入户 Low Income Households
摩托车(辆)	Motorcycle(unit)	19.99	22.30	23.10	14.56
家用汽车(辆)	Automobile(unit)	1.80	0.95	1.94	0.39
洗衣机(台)	Washing Machine (unit)	93.02	72.11	67.37	88.78
电冰箱(台)	Refrigerator (unit)	88.34	55.64	54.16	76.08
彩色电视机(台)	Color TV (set)	105.34	96.32	92.45	104.04
家用电脑(台)	Household Computer (set)	34.70	6.04	3.87	19.90
组合音响(套)	Hi-Fi Stereo Sound System (set)	21.12	5.35	3.44	12.62
摄相机(架)	Pickup Camera (set)	3.58	0.55	0.75	2.14
照相机(架)	Camera (set)	33.39	11.72	11.42	22.97
钢 琴(架)	Piano (set)	1.38			1.07
中高档乐器(件)	Other Medium and High Grade Musical Instrument (piece)	7.02			5.72
微波炉(台)	Microwave Oven (unit)	27.80	5.75	3.87	16.33
空调器(台)	Air Conditioner (unit)	6.70	0.36	0.37	1.66
淋浴热水器(台)	Shower (unit)	69.63	30.75	20.06	46.16
健身器材(件)	Healthy Equipment (unit)	2.58			0.41
移动电话(部)	Mobile Phone (unit)	140.12	65.78	53.24	110.78

项 目	Item	中等偏下户 Lower Middle Income Households	中等收入户 Middle Income Households	中等偏上户 Upper Middle Income Households	高收入户 High Income Households	最高收入户 Highest Income Households
摩托车(辆)	Motorcycle(unit)	13.87	19.71	31.55	25.63	5.95
家用汽车(辆)	Automobile(unit)	2.54	1.57	3.19	0.40	1.54
洗衣机(台)	Washing Machine (unit)	95.81	95.74	94.59	100.95	98.30
电冰箱(台)	Refrigerator (unit)	92.09	92.30	94.35	99.59	97.92
彩色电视机(台)	Color TV (set)	103.77	106.88	107.39	109.84	108.40
家用电脑(台)	Household Computer (set)	34.07	33.54	40.22	55.63	52.87
组合音响(套)	Hi-Fi Stereo Sound System (set)	19.22	23.24	23.07	41.37	22.34
摄相机(架)	Pickup Camera (set)	2.05	3.21	3.16	5.95	11.19
照相机(架)	Camera (set)	31.66	28.93	36.79	45.95	61.55
钢 琴(架)	Piano (set)	1.02	1.92	1.32	2.50	1.97
中高档乐器(件)	Other Medium and High Grade Musical Instrument (piece)	6.64	9.10	9.87	7.40	6.66
微波炉(台)	Microwave Oven (unit)	23.62	27.13	35.10	37.41	50.07
空调器(台)	Air Conditioner (unit)	2.51	6.07	8.69	12.70	19.33
淋浴热水器(台)	Shower (unit)	72.19	75.58	76.53	88.57	86.47
健身器材(件)	Healthy Equipment (unit)	2.31	1.44	3.14	2.02	10.15
移动电话(部)	Mobile Phone (unit)	141.07	149.28	151.64	182.97	165.99

7-12 农村居民家庭基本情况
Basic Conditions of Rural Households

(抽样调查 Sampled Survey)

项目	Item	1990	1995	2000	2007
调查户数(户)	**Number of Households Surveyed(household)**	**1240**	**1550**	**1500**	**1550**
调查户人口(人)	**Number of Residents Surveyed (person)**	**6659**	**8711**	**7999**	**7239**
平均每户常住人口	Average Number of Permanent Residents per Household	5.37	5.62	5.33	4.67
平均每户整半劳动力	Average Number of Full/semi Laborers per Household	2.76	3.06	3.06	2.96
平均每个劳动力负担人口(含本人)	Average Number of Dependents per Employee (Including oneself)	1.94	1.84	1.74	1.58
户均经营耕地面积(亩)	Per Household Area of Cultivated Land Managed(mu)	21.80	25.68	22.39	20.22
平均每人经营耕地面积(亩)	Per Capita Area of Cultivated Land Managed(mu)	4.06	4.57	4.20	4.30
年内每户新建房屋面积(平方米)	Space of Rooms per Household Newly Built Within the Year (sq.m)	4.18	2.49	2.03	4.32
年底人均居住面积(平方米)	Per Capita Net Living Rooms Space in Rural Area (sq.m)	14.04	16.12	17.25	22.45
平均每人年收入(元)	**Per Capita Annual Income(yuan)**				
总收入	Total Income	1112.01	2414.59	3129.35	6068.79
工资性收入	Income from Wages and Salaries	56.53	64.47	104.58	330.75
家庭经营收入	Income from Household Business	1034.69	2238.71	2926.75	5482.77
财产性收入	Income from Properties		65.30	40.42	116.55
转移性收入	Income from Transfers	20.79	46.11	57.60	138.72
#现金收入	Cash Income	830.88	1876.61	2444.30	5248.76
工资性收入	Income from Wages and Salaries	55.50	64.41	104.46	330.75
家庭经营收入	Income from Household Business	750.34	1700.93	2245.31	4675.59
财产性收入	Income from Properties		59.19	37.87	103.69
转移性收入	Income from Transfers	25.04	52.08	56.66	138.73
平均每人年支出(元)	**Per Capita Annual Expenditure(yuan)**				
总支出	Total Expenditure	971.46	2363.45	2819.77	5774.06
家庭经营费用支出	Expenditure for Household Business	325.97	1035.08	1198.23	2630.31
购置生产性固定资产	Purchase of Productive Fixed Assets	57.71	144.33	115.19	457.72
税费支出	Expenditure for Tax	62.07	173.36	177.24	17.30
生活消费支出	Expenditure for Consumption	506.82	941.58	1236.45	2350.58
转移性和财产性支出	Expenditure for Transfer and Property	18.89	69.10	92.66	318.15
#现金支出	Cash Expenditure	716.73	2009.15	2353.45	5289.98
家庭经营费用支出	Expenditure for Household Business	236.36	940.40	1100.43	2531.23
购置生产性固定资产	Purchase of Productive Fixed Assets	57.71	144.33	115.19	457.72
税费支出	Expenditure for Tax	58.19	172.55	177.22	17.30
生活消费支出	Expenditure for Consumption	333.88	682.13	871.37	1965.58
转移性和财产性支出	Expenditure for Transfer and Property	30.59	69.74	89.24	318.15
平均每人年纯收入(元)	**Per Capita Annual Net Income (yuan)**	**683.47**	**1136.45**	**1618.08**	**3182.97**
工资性收入	Income from Wages and Salaries	56.53	64.47	104.58	330.75
家庭经营纯收入	Income from Household Business	612.70	967.59	1451.33	2625.66
财产性收入	Income from Properties		65.30	40.43	116.54
转移性收入	Income from Transfers	14.24	39.09	21.74	110.02

7-13 农村居民家庭人均年总收入、纯收入和构成
Per Capita Annual Gross and Net Income and Its Composition of Rural Households

单位：元 (抽样调查 Sampled Survey) (yuan)

项目	Item	2006	2007	构成(%) Composition 2006	构成(%) Composition 2007
全年总收入	**Annual Gross Income**	**5166.20**	**6068.79**	**100.00**	**100.00**
工资性收入	Income from Wages and Salaries	254.07	330.75	4.92	5.45
家庭经营收入	Income from Household Business	4737.37	5482.77	91.70	90.34
财产性收入	Income from Transfers	58.69	116.55	1.14	1.92
转移性收入	Income from Properties	116.07	138.72	2.24	2.29
全年总支出	**Annual Gross Expenditure**	**4758.17**	**5774.06**	**100.00**	**100.00**
#家庭经营费用支出	Expenditure for Household Business	2226.80	2630.31	46.80	45.55
生活消费支出	Expenditure for Consumption	2032.36	2350.58	42.71	40.71
全年纯收入	**Annual Net Income**	**2737.28**	**3182.97**	**100.00**	**100.00**
基本纯收入	Basic Net Income	2577.08	2956.41	94.15	92.88
转移性纯收入	Transfer Net Income	58.69	110.02	2.14	3.46
财产性纯收入	Property Net Income	101.51	116.54	3.71	3.66

7-14 农村居民家庭平均每人总收入和纯收入
Per Capita Annual Gross and Net Income of Rural Households

单位：元 (抽样调查 Sampled Survey) (yuan)

项目	Item	1990	1995	2000	2006	2007
总 收 入	**Gross Income**	**1112.01**	**2414.59**	**3129.35**	**5166.20**	**6068.79**
基本收入	Basic Income	1091.22	2303.18	3031.33	4991.44	5813.52
工资性收入	Income from Wages and Salaries	56.53	64.47	104.58	254.07	330.75
家庭经营收入	Income from Household Business	1034.69	2238.71	2926.75	4737.37	5482.77
转移性和财产性收入	Income from Transfers and Properties	20.79	111.41	98.02	174.76	255.27
纯收入	**Net Income**	**683.47**	**1136.45**	**1618.08**	**2737.28**	**3182.97**
按收入来源分	By source					
基本收入	Basic Income	669.23	1032.06	1555.91	2577.08	2956.41
工资性收入	Income from Wages and Salaries	56.53	64.47	104.58	254.07	330.75
家庭经营纯收入	Income from Household Business	612.70	967.59	1451.33	2323.01	2625.66
农业收入	Agriculture	541.84	724.06	1109.39	1750.73	1943.59
林业收入	Forestry	8.80	27.69	22.51	82.33	106.45
牧业收入	Animal Husbandry	25.39	113.88	171.18	261.54	322.58
渔业收入	Fishery		3.49			
工业收入	Industry	1.05	0.73	6.35	26.15	47.54
建筑业收入	Construction	2.51	4.33	4.31	10.02	12.16
交通、运输和邮电业收入	Transportation, Post and Telecommunications Services	12.29	12.09	26.48	29.50	28.53
批发和零售贸易业、饮食业收入	Wholesale, Retail Trades and Catering Services	14.13	15.93	23.80	77.99	75.49
社会服务业收入	Services Trades	4.17	23.80	15.01	23.76	29.26
文教卫生业收入	Cultural, Education, Medicines and Medical Services				6.40	5.82
其他行业收入	Others	2.52	41.59	72.30	54.61	54.25
转移性和财产性收入	Income from Transfers and Properties	14.24	104.39	62.17	160.20	226.56

7-15 主要年份农村居民家庭人均主要消费品消费量

Per Capita Consumption of Major Consumer Goods of Rural Households in Main Years

单位:公斤　　(抽样调查 Sampled Survey)　　(kg)

项　目	Item	1990	1995	2000	2006	2007
粮食(原粮)	Grain(Unprocessed)	249.71	206.68	244.83	225.23	222.02
#小 麦	Wheat	201.37	162.52	199.83	182.13	179.10
稻 谷	Rice	13.39	8.44	15.19	17.97	20.90
豆类及豆制品	Soybeans and Related Products		0.10	0.50	0.47	0.10
蔬 菜	Fresh Vegetable	121.56	64.02	89.24	63.68	70.77
食 油	Edible Oil	7.87	6.38	9.64	10.76	10.82
#植物油	Vegetable Oil	7.41	6.14	9.56	10.72	10.79
肉禽及制品	Meats,Poultry and Related Products	9.02	8.11	12.41	15.26	14.49
#猪 肉	Pork	2.25	1.58	1.95	0.60	0.59
牛 肉	Beef	6.77	2.09	1.95	3.12	2.70
羊 肉	Mutton		3.22	7.03	9.82	9.18
家 禽	Poultry	0.90	1.00	1.36	1.39	1.62
蛋及制品	Eggs and Related Products	1.77	0.80	1.20	1.21	1.09
食 糖	Sugar	0.63	0.51	0.42	0.45	0.39
酒	Liquor	1.04	0.92	1.12	1.22	1.18
水果及制品	Fruits and Related Products	41.94	21.78	46.89	22.46	22.19
茶 叶	Tea	5.96	0.56	0.37	0.48	0.45

7-16 主要年份农村居民家庭平均每百户耐用消费品拥有量

Number of Durable Consumer Goods Owned by Per100 Rural Households in Main Years

(抽样调查 Sampled Survey)

项　目	Item	1990	1995	2000	2006	2007
洗衣机(台)	Washing Machine (unit)	12.58	16.39	20.87	32.32	36.65
电冰箱(台)	Refrigerator (unit)	0.40	2.26	9.93	25.10	28.32
空调机(台)	Air Conditioner (unit)				0.32	0.32
抽油烟机(台)	Smoke Absorber (unit)		0.13	1.13	1.16	1.48
自行车(辆)	Bicycle (unit)	111.21	151.29	136.60	83.42	84.06
摩托车(辆)	Motorcycle (unit)	1.37	4.90	18.33	49.29	49.74
电话机(部)	Telephone(unit)			15.07	40.97	41.48
移动电话(部)	Mobile phone (unit)			0.33	29.29	42.19
黑白电视机(台)	Black and White TV (set)	28.79	55.03	59.33	32.06	22.84
彩色电视机(台)	Color TV (set)	5.16	14.39	31.87	68.32	76.32
照像机(架)	Camera (set)	0.73	1.16	2.20	3.55	2.65
影碟机(台)	Video Disc Player (set)			3.60		21.94
微波炉(台)	Microwave Oven (unit)					1.42

7-17 农村居民人均生活消费支出及构成
Per Capita Annual Living Expendture and Its Composition of Rural Households

单位：元 (抽样调查 Sampled Survey) (yuan)

项　目	Item	2006	2007	构成(%) Composition(%) 2006	构成(%) Composition(%) 2007
生活消费支出	**Expenditure for Consumption**	**2032.36**	**2350.58**	**100.00**	**100.00**
食 品	Food	810.74	939.03	39.89	39.95
#主 食	Staple Food	282.08	305.67	13.88	13.00
副 食	Non-staple Food	433.69	535.84	21.34	22.80
衣 着	Clothing	187.03	218.18	9.20	9.28
居 住	Housing	371.56	445.02	18.28	18.93
家庭设备、用品及服务	Household Appliances and Services	73.04	91.45	3.59	3.89
医疗保健	Health Care and Medical Services	189.69	210.69	9.33	8.96
交通和通讯	Transportation and Communications	209.46	234.70	10.31	9.98
文教娱乐用品及服务	Cultural, Education ,Recreation and Services	157.00	166.27	7.73	7.07
其他商品和服务	Other Commodities and Services	33.85	45.24	1.67	1.92

7-18 农村居民家庭平均每百户耐用消费品拥有量
Number of Durable Consumer Goods Owned by Per100 Rural Households

(抽样调查 Sampled Survey)

项　目	Item	2006	2007
自行车(辆)	Bicycle (unit)	83.42	84.06
黑白电视机(台)	Black and White TV (set)	32.06	22.84
彩色电视机(台)	Color TV (set)	68.32	76.32
抽油烟机(台)	Smoke Absorber (unit)	1.16	1.48
照像机(架)	Camera (set)	3.55	2.65
移动电话(部)	Mobile phone (unit)	29.29	42.19
洗衣机(台)	Washing Machine (unit)	32.32	36.65
电冰箱(台)	Refrigerator (unit)	25.10	28.32
摩托车(辆)	Motorcycle (unit)	49.29	49.74
影碟机(台)	Video Disc Player (set)	21.35	21.94
微波炉(台)	Microwave Oven (unit)	0.58	1.42

7-19 农村居民家庭人均商品性和自给性生活消费品支出
Per Capita Self-Sufficiency and Consumption on Commodity Goods of Living Expenditure in Rural Households

(抽样调查 Sampled Survey)

项目	Item	2006			2007		
		合计 Total	货币性 In Money	实物性 In Kind	合计 Total	货币性 In Money	实物性 In Kind
生活消费支出合计(元/人)	**Expenditure for Consumption (yuan/person)**	**2032.36**	**1696.40**	**335.96**	**2350.58**	**1965.58**	**385.00**
食品	Food	810.74	494.47	316.27	939.03	591.82	347.21
衣着	Clothing	187.03	182.85	4.18	218.18	211.69	6.49
居住	Housing	371.56	358.29	13.27	445.02	418.61	26.41
家庭设备、用品及服务	Household Appliances and Services	73.04	70.79	2.25	91.45	86.56	4.89
医疗保健	Health Care and Medical Services	189.69	189.69		210.69	210.69	
交通和通讯	Transportation and Communications	209.46	209.46		234.70	234.7	
文教娱乐用品及服务	Cultural, Education and Recreational Articles and Services	157.00	157.00		166.27	166.27	
其他商品和服务	Other Commodities and Services	33.85	33.85		45.24	45.24	
生活消费支出构成(%)	**Composition of Living Expenditures (%)**	**100**	**100**	**100**	**100**	**100**	**100**
食品	Food	39.89	29.15	94.14	39.96	30.11	90.18
衣着	Clothing	9.20	10.78	1.24	9.28	10.77	1.69
居住	Housing	18.28	21.12	3.95	18.93	21.30	6.86
家庭设备、用品及服务	Household Appliances and Services	3.59	4.17	0.67	3.89	4.40	1.27
医疗保健	Health Care and Medical Services	9.33	11.18		8.96	10.72	
交通和通讯	Transportation and Communications	10.31	12.35		9.98	11.94	
文教娱乐用品及服务	Cultural, Education and Recreational Articles and Services	7.73	9.25		7.07	8.46	
其他商品和服务	Other Commodities and Services	1.67	2.00		1.93	2.30	
生活消费支出中货币性和实物性比重(%)	**Percentage of Expenditure for Consumption in Money and Kind (%)**	**100**	**83.47**	**16.53**	**100**	**83.62**	**16.38**
食品	Food	100	60.99	39.01	100	63.02	36.98
衣着	Clothing	100	97.77	2.23	100	97.03	2.97
居住	Housing	100	96.43	3.57	100	94.07	5.93
家庭设备、用品及服务	Household Appliances and Services	100	96.92	3.08	100	94.65	5.35
医疗保健	Health Care and Medical Services	100	100		100		
交通和通讯	Transportation and Communications	100	100		100		
文教娱乐用品及服务	Cultural, Education and Recreational Articles and Services	100	100		100		
其他商品和服务	Other Commodities and Services	100	100		100		

7-20 农村居民家庭人均纯收入分组
Rural Households Grouped by Per Capita Annual Net Income

(2007 年) (抽样调查 Sampled Survey)

项　目	Item	合 计 Total	0-400 元 0-400 yuan	400-600 元 400-600 yuan	600-800 元 600-800 yuan	800-1000 元 800-1000 yuan	1000-1200 元 1000-1200 yuan
调查户数(户)	**Number of Households Surveyed (household)**	**1550**	**25**	**26**	**54**	**64**	**78**
构成(%)	Percentage (%)	100	1.61	1.68	3.48	4.13	5.03
常住人口(人)	**Number of Permanent Residents in the Households Surveyed (person)**	**7239**	**120**	**143**	**282**	**330**	**404**
构成(%)	Percentage (%)	100	1.66	1.98	3.90	4.56	5.58
人均纯收入(元)	**Per Capita Net Income (yuan)**	**3182.97**	**-18.02**	**512.77**	**717.81**	**924.49**	**1106.29**

项　目	Item	1200-1500 元 1200-1500 yuan	1500-1700 元 1500-1700 yuan	1700-2000 元 1700-2000 yuan	2000-2500 元 2000-2500 yuan	2500-3000 元 2500-3000 yuan
调查户数(户)	**Number of Households Surveyed (household)**	**111**	**72**	**125**	**163**	**136**
构成(%)	Percentage (%)	7.16	4.65	8.06	10.52	8.77
常住人口(人)	**Number of Permanent Residents in the Households Surveyed (person)**	**543**	**354**	**639**	**830**	**660**
构成(%)	Percentage (%)	7.50	4.89	8.83	11.47	9.12
人均纯收入(元)	**Per Capita Net Income (yuan)**	**1342.56**	**1597.96**	**1843.93**	**2248.81**	**2745.80**

项　目	Item	3000-3500 元 3000-3500 yuan	3500-4000 元 3500-4000 yuan	4000-4500 元 4000-4500 yuan	4500-5000 元 4500-5000 yuan	5000 元以上 over 5000 yuan
调查户数(户)	**Number of Households Surveyed (household)**	**129**	**100**	**104**	**68**	**295**
构成(%)	Percentage (%)	8.32	6.45	6.71	4.39	19.04
常住人口(人)	**Number of Permanent Residents in the Households Surveyed (person)**	**620**	**447**	**444**	**297**	**1126**
构成(%)	Percentage (%)	8.56	6.17	6.13	4.10	15.55
人均纯收入(元)	**Per Capita Net Income (yuan)**	**3252.66**	**3745.78**	**4236.12**	**4724.54**	**7894.48**

7-21 分地区农村居民家庭人均总收入和纯收入

Per Capita Annual Gross and Net Income of Rural Households by Region

单位：元 (2007 年) (抽样调查 Sampled Survey) (yuan)

项目 Item	自治区 Autonomous Region	昌吉州 Changji Hui Autonomous Prefecture	伊犁州直属县(市) Counties (Cities) Direct Under Ili Prefecture	塔城地区 Tacheng [Tarbagatai] Administrative Offices
调查县、市 Number of Counties and Cities Surveyed	**30**	**4**	**5**	**4**
调查户数(户) Number of Households Surveyed (household)	**1550**	**160**	**260**	**145**
常住人口(人) Number of Permanent Residents In the Households Surveyed (person)	**7239**	**550**	**1228**	**660**
总收入 Annual Gross Income	**6068.79**	**12498.25**	**6412.71**	**9906.53**
工资性收入 Income from Wages and Salaries	330.76	489.12	440.30	268.56
在非企业组织中劳动得到的 From Non-enterprise Organization	96.29	131.89	162.57	184.11
在本地企业中劳动得到的 From Local Enterprise	141.51	157.59	234.61	63.69
常住人口外出从业得到的 Out of Migrant Workers	92.96	199.64	43.12	20.76
家庭经营收入 Income From Household Business	5482.77	11777.51	5560.54	9278.84
农业收入 Agriculture	4009.38	9250.18	3688.58	6889.26
林业收入 Forestry	123.92	20.00	89.98	12.62
牧业收入 Animal Husbandry	892.93	1750.43	1085.69	2323.80
渔业收入 Fishery		141.25		
工业收入 Industry	58.12	5.09	16.21	26.76
建筑业收入 Construction	19.76	13.50	89.88	
交通、运输和邮电业收入 Transportation, Post and Telecommunications Services	144.36	437.33	131.03	2.92
批发和零售贸易、餐饮业收入 Wholesale, Retail Trades and Catering Services	119.55	56.27	342.83	23.48
社会服务业收入 Social Services	34.05	3.73	59.07	
文教卫生业收入 Cultural, Education, Medicines and Medical Services	9.96	2.18	44.82	
其他家庭经营收入 Others	70.74	97.55	12.45	
财产性收入 Property Income	116.54	39.77	152.11	191.02
#利 息 Interest	2.77	7.65	0.94	2.19
租 金 Rent	3.87	15.64	4.76	2.50
转移性收入 Transfer Income	138.72	191.85	259.76	168.12
可支配收入 Disposable Income	2893.53	3434.68	3367.41	4033.31
全年家庭人均纯收入 Annual Net Income	**3182.97**	**5436.69**	**3583.55**	**4300.89**

7-21 续表 Continued

单位：元 (yuan)

项目 Item	阿勒泰地区 Altay Administrative Offices	巴音郭楞蒙古自治州 Bayangol Mongol Autonomous Prefecture	阿克苏地区 Aksu Administrative Offices	喀什地区 Kashgar [Kaxgar] Administrative Offices	和田地区 Hotan Administrative Offices
调查县、市 Number of Counties and Cities Surveyed	**4**	**6**	**5**	**6**	**4**
调查户数(户) Number of Households Surveyed (household)	**130**	**235**	**235**	**325**	**235**
常住人口(人) Number of Permanent Residents In the Households Surveyed (person)	**630**	**1108**	**1136**	**1605**	**1139**
总收入 Annual Gross Income	**5124.42**	**10272.89**	**6394.17**	**3461.26**	**2665.06**
工资性收入 Income from Wages and Salaries	364.03	469.26	240.71	198.40	325.59
在非企业组织中劳动得到的 From Non-enterprise Organization	203.95	131.26	61.54	30.35	26.68
在本地企业中劳动得到的 From Local Enterprise	53.57	273.83	174.28	79.97	112.61
常住人口外出从业得到的 Out of Migrant Workers	106.51	64.17	4.89	88.08	186.30
家庭经营收入 Income From Household Business	4614.15	9462.20	5995.33	3204.75	2222.16
农业收入 Agriculture	2136.65	7495.27	4950.13	2246.45	1065.34
林业收入 Forestry		26.21	77.91	174.51	181.82
牧业收入 Animal Husbandry	2025.39	1536.68	562.94	601.62	397.48
渔业收入 Fishery		1.81			
工业收入 Industry	19.05	15.94	0.76		319.38
建筑业收入 Construction	42.79	22.37	11.24	11.28	13.76
交通、运输和邮电业收入 Transportation, Post and Telecommunications Services	99.84	166.23	209.35	18.44	7.14
批发和零售贸易、餐饮业收入 Wholesale, Retail Trades and Catering Services	113.03	124.73	67.27	85.53	55.12
社会服务业收入 Social Services	14.25	48.72	65.58	0.87	15.12
文教卫生业收入 Cultural, Education, Medicines and Medical Services		1.94			
其他家庭经营收入 Others	163.15	22.30	50.15	66.05	167.00
财产性收入 Property Income	39.45	182.02	117.36	9.71	4.59
#利息 Interest	9.76	8.59			
租金 Rent		32.70	0.22	3.12	
转移性收入 Transfer Income	106.79	159.41	40.77	48.40	112.72
可支配收入 Disposable Income	3639.21	4856.26	3689.83	2347.47	1710.56
全年家庭人均纯收入 Annual Net Income	**3721.59**	**5210.08**	**3826.54**	**2393.84**	**1757.45**

7-22 分地区农村居民家庭平均每人总支出
Per Capita Total Expenditure of Rural Household by Region

单位：元　(2007 年)(抽样调查 Sampled Survey)　(yuan)

项　目 Item	自治区 Autonomous Region	昌吉州 Changji Hui Autonomous Prefecture	伊犁州直属县(市) Counties (Cities) Direct Under Ili Prefecture	塔城地区 Tacheng [Tarbagatai] Administrative Offices
全年总支出 Annual Total Expenditure	**5774.06**	**11986.23**	**5502.22**	**8640.81**
家庭经营费用支出 Expenditure for Household Business	**2630.31**	**6454.42**	**2538.65**	**4845.70**
农业生产 Agriculture	1937.71	4943.95	1564.44	3869.23
林业生产 Forestry	17.09	42.47	8.81	0.14
牧业生产 Animal Husbandry	501.01	927.82	579.09	969.50
渔业生产 Fishery		117.36	0.05	
工业生产 Industry	9.86		4.70	6.21
建筑业生产 Construction	6.99		76.60	
交通、运输和邮电业支出 Transportation, Post and Telecommunications Services	93.09	225.55	66.36	
批发和零售贸易、餐饮业支出 Wholesale, Retail Trades and Catering Services	42.10	18.18	213.65	0.62
社会服务业支出 Social Services	4.67	1.82	3.67	
文教卫生业支出 Cultural, Education, Medicines and Medical Services	3.66		21.03	
其他经营支出 Others	14.12	177.27	0.25	
购置生产用固定资产支出 Expenditure for Productive Fixed Assets	**457.72**	**220.11**	**283.16**	**221.46**
税费支出 Taxes and Fee	**17.30**	**3.64**	**0.51**	
生活消费支出 Expenditure for Consumption	**2350.59**	**4112.93**	**2434.24**	**3241.77**
食　品 Food	939.03	1510.03	842.51	1396.74
#主　食 Staple Food	305.67	289.04	225.81	311.12
副　食 Non-staple Food	449.53	857.24	442.51	774.56
其他食品 Others Food	86.30	167.73	102.56	123.92
衣　着 Clothing	218.18	340.94	228.37	365.08
居　住 Housing	445.02	537.48	527.88	406.64
家庭设备、用品及服务 Household Facilities, Articles and Services	91.45	193.21	103.95	90.57
医疗保健 Health Care and Medical Services	210.69	286.48	191.98	279.40
交通和通讯 Transportation and Communications	234.70	318.40	260.17	326.43
文化教育娱乐用品及服务 Cultural, Education and Recreational Articles and Services	166.27	760.66	237.60	329.78
其他商品和服务 Other Commodities and Services	45.25	165.72	41.78	47.13
附：生产用固定资产折旧 Depreciation Charge for Productive Fixed Assets	209.50	387.89	260.48	309.89

7-22 续表 Continued

单位：元 (yuan)

项 目 Item	阿勒泰地区 Altay Administrative Offices	巴音郭楞蒙古自治州 Bayangol Mongol Autonomous Prefecture	阿克苏地区 Aksu Administrative Offices	喀什地区 Kashgar [Kaxgar] Administrative Offices	和田地区 Hotan Administrative Offices
全年总支出 Annual Total Expenditure	**3775.10**	**9358.75**	**5400.07**	**2478.97**	**2310.22**
家庭经营费用支出 Expenditure for Household Business	**1296.06**	**4732.07**	**2260.70**	**1010.04**	**822.98**
农业生产 Agriculture	699.24	3776.80	1867.58	807.18	399.10
林业生产 Forestry		25.46	58.10	4.25	9.75
牧业生产 Animal Husbandry	483.18	803.51	213.13	193.17	276.89
渔业生产 Fishery		0.41			
工业生产 Industry	3.17	5.02			50.49
建筑业生产 Construction	5.59	4.63			3.66
交通、运输和邮电业支出 Transportation, Post and Telecommunications Services	38.13	101.37	95.26	2.29	4.09
批发和零售贸易、餐饮业支出 Wholesale, Retail Trades and Catering Services	41.17	3.96	9.77	2.28	23.96
社会服务业支出 Social Services	0.95	8.03	0.28		6.43
文教卫生业支出 Cultural, Education, Medicines and Medical Services		1.26			
其他经营支出 Others	24.63	1.62	16.58	0.87	48.61
购置生产用固定资产支出 Expenditure for Productive Fixed Assets	**115.17**	**401.85**	**898.18**	**128.65**	**54.93**
税费支出 Taxes and Fee	**47.78**	**2.51**	**53.46**	**0.93**	**9.37**
生活消费支出 Expenditure for Consumption	**2240.82**	**3839.55**	**2061.15**	**1296.68**	**1351.75**
食 品 Food	1187.64	1552.95	758.40	621.15	656.00
#主 食 Staple Food	333.24	332.35	303.41	289.79	249.62
副 食 Non-staple Food	748.45	893.82	349.42	244.53	266.49
其他食品 Others Food	91.11	151.49	55.39	38.84	92.12
衣 着 Clothing	279.64	290.31	218.67	153.66	148.53
居 住 Housing	310.28	596.67	506.29	284.21	252.21
家庭设备、用品及服务 Household Facilities, Articles and Services	106.98	138.37	79.59	43.66	55.01
医疗保健 Health Care and Medical Services	93.59	287.82	195.63	93.60	97.77
交通和通讯 Transportation and Communications	157.87	442.31	225.73	75.62	119.63
文化教育娱乐用品及服务 Cultural, Education and Recreational Articles and Services	80.17	453.71	54.13	16.23	10.80
其他商品和服务 Other Commodities and Services	24.65	77.41	22.71	8.55	11.80
附：生产用固定资产折旧 Depreciation Charge for Productive Fixed Assets	266.91	299.27	263.60	60.15	50.96

7-23 分地区农村居民家庭人均现金收支

Per Capita Income and Expenditure in Cash of Rural Household by Region

单位：元　　(2007 年)(抽样调查 Sampled Survey)　　(yuan)

项　　目	Item	自治区 Autonomous Region	昌吉州 Changji Hui Autonomous Prefecture	伊犁州直属县(市) Counties (Cities) Direct Under Ili Prefecture	塔城地区 Tacheng [Tarbagatai] Administrative Offices
期内现金收入	**Annual Total Income In Cash**	**5248.76**	**10455.80**	**5811.61**	**9344.76**
工资性收入	Income from Wages and Salaries	330.75	533.67	440.30	268.55
在非企业组织中劳动得到的	From Non-enterprise Organization	96.29	207.35	162.57	184.11
在本地企业中劳动得到的	From Local Enterprises	141.51	139.41	234.61	63.69
常住人口外出从业得到的	Out of Migrant Workers	92.96	186.92	43.12	20.76
家庭经营收入	Income of Household Operation	4675.59	9641.78	5002.65	8735.22
农业现金收入	Cash Income from Farming	3296.89	7380.85	3223.17	6572.51
#出售农产品收入	Sale of Agricultural Products	3127.61	7206.41	2868.43	6465.82
林业现金收入	Cash Income from Forestry	109.60	18.87	60.75	12.62
#出售林业产品收入	Sale of Forestry Products	104.01	18.87	36.78	12.62
牧业现金收入	Cash Income from Animal Husbandry	812.56	1474.98	1022.45	2096.93
#出售牧业产品收入	Sale of Animal Husbandry Products	802.71	1469.07	969.64	2096.93
渔业现金收入	Cash Income from Fishery		120.07		
#出售渔业产品收入	Sale of Fishery Products		120.07		
工业收入	Income from Industry	58.12	5.09	16.21	26.76
#出售工业产品收入	Sale of Industrial Products	45.59			
工业服务性收入	Income from Industrial services	12.53	5.09	16.21	26.76
建筑业收入	Income from Construction	19.76	27.13	89.88	
#出售建筑业产品收入	Sale of Constructive Products				
建筑业服务性收入	Income from Constructive services	19.76	27.13	89.88	
交通、运输、邮电业收入	Income from Transport,Post and Telecommunication Servies	144.36	443.69	131.03	2.92
批零贸易业、饮食业收入	Income from Wholesale and Retail Trades and Catering Servies	119.55	67.36	342.83	23.48
社会服务业收入	Income from Social Services	34.05	3.73	59.07	
文教卫生业收入	Income from Culture,Edcuation and Health Care	9.96	2.18	44.82	
其他行业收入	Others	70.74	97.83	12.45	
财产性收入	Property Income	103.69	40.86	108.90	173.17
#利 息	Interest	2.77	7.65	0.94	2.19
租 金	Rent	3.87	15.64	4.76	2.50
转移性收入	Transfer Income	138.72	239.49	259.76	167.82
非收入所得	**Non-income Gain**	**1386.19**	**2138.29**	**986.85**	**1915.89**
#从银行信用社得到的贷款	Credit	662.95	969.09	472.56	739.29
借入款	Borrowed Money	219.14	141.82	184.57	195.23
收回借出款	Recall Loaned Money	48.37	51.27	30.13	222.01
从银行信用社取回存款	Take Deposit back	253.26	826.36	160.13	720.38
出售财产所得款	Sold Property	86.37	9.20	42.09	17.03
期内现金支出	**Annual Expenditure in Cash**	**5289.98**	**11080.17**	**5200.63**	**8333.70**
生产费用支出	Producing Expenditure	2988.95	6479.97	2750.41	5015.20
家庭经营费用支出	Expenditure for Household Business	2531.23	6238.05	2467.25	4793.74
农业生产支出	Agriculture	1900.97	4814.06	1562.00	3867.41
林业生产支出	Forestry	17.09	11.56	8.81	0.14
牧业生产支出	Animal Husbandry	438.68	872.25	510.14	919.36

7-23 续表 1Continued

单位：元 (yuan)

项目	Item	自治区 Autonomous Region	昌吉州 Changji Hui Autonomous Prefecture	伊犁州直属县(市) Counties (Cities) Direct Under Ili Prefecture	塔城地区 Tacheng [Tarbagatai] Administrative Offices
渔业生产支出	Fishery		117.36	0.05	
工业生产支出	Industry	9.86		4.70	6.21
建筑业生产支出	Construction	6.99		76.60	
交通运输支出	Transportation	93.09	225.55	66.36	
批发和零售贸易、餐饮业	Wholesale Retail Trades and Catering services	42.10	18.18	213.65	0.63
社会服务业支出	Social Services	4.67	1.82	3.67	
文教卫生业	Cultural, Education, Medicines and Medical Services	3.66		21.03	
其他经营支出	Others	14.12	177.27	0.24	
购置生产性固定资产支出	Expenditure for Productive Fixed Assets	457.72	241.93	283.16	221.46
税费支出	Taxes and Fee	17.30	3.64	0.51	
生活消费支出	Expenditure for Consumption	1965.58	3400.70	2204.06	2986.62
财产性支出	Expenditure for Property	116.30	614.54	47.89	225.52
转移性支出	Expenditure for Transfer	201.84	581.32	197.78	106.36
非消费性现金付出	**Expenditure for Non-consumption**	**1295.13**	**2363.14**	**959.92**	**2007.54**
#归还银行信用社贷款	Loan Returned to Bank	566.06	950.67	332.60	989.99
借出款	Lending Money	61.85	8.58	8.58	48.47
归还借款	Return Borrowed Money	173.74	384.81	145.64	291.93
存入银行信用社	Deposit	297.90	713.43	285.02	479.85
期末金融资产余额	**Balance of Financial Assets in Year-end**	**1589.09**	**3569.87**	**1383.23**	**3961.92**
#银行存款	Deposit	992.37	3101.82	879.56	3592.73
手存现金	Cash	587.46	468.05	503.67	369.20
期末债务余额	**Balance of Debt in Year-end**	**602.68**	**1146.91**	**526.83**	**470.55**
#银行、信用社贷款	Loan from Bank and Credit Cooperatives	386.04	485.45	400.41	335.64
乡村集体组织、企业借(欠)款	Borrowed Money from Collective Units and Enterprises	6.11	90.91	8.06	
个人借(欠)款	Borrowed Money from Individual	210.53	570.55	118.36	134.91
生活消费支出的现金	**Expenditure for Consumption**	**1965.58**	**3400.70**	**2204.06**	**2986.62**
食品	Food	591.82	909.97	664.72	1141.59
#主食	Staple Food	119.33	126.39	169.95	277.41
副食	Non-staple Food	318.75	463.98	337.03	554.62
衣着	Clothing	211.69	315.31	228.37	365.08
居住	Housing	418.61	544.30	475.49	406.64
家庭设备、用品及服务	Household Facilities, Articles and Services	86.56	204.67	103.95	90.57
医疗保健	Health Care and Medical Services	210.69	263.03	191.98	279.53
交通和通讯	Transportation and Communications	234.70	304.77	260.17	326.43
文化教育、娱乐用品及服务	Cultural, Education and Recreational Articles and Services	166.27	699.06	237.60	329.78
#文化教育、娱乐用品	Cultural, Education and Recreational Articles	20.73	52.63	25.17	25.10
文化教育、娱乐服务	Cultural, Education and Recreational Services	145.54	646.43	212.44	304.68
#学杂费	Tuition	100.39	596.89	128.30	281.57
技术培训费	Charge for Training	8.66	3.13	14.95	6.75
其他商品和服务	Other Commodities and Services	45.25	159.60	41.77	46.99
商品性支出	Commodities	24.43	54.12	22.50	22.93
服务支出	Services	20.82	105.48	19.27	24.06

7-23 续表 2 Continued

单位：元 (yuan)

项目	Item	阿勒泰地区 Altay Adminis-trative Offices	巴音郭楞蒙古自治州 Bayangol Mongol Autono-mous Prefecture	阿克苏地区 Aksu Adminis-trative Offices	喀什地区 Kashgar [Kaxgar] Adminis-trative Offices	和田地区 Hotan Adminis-trative Offices
期内现金收入	**Annual Total Income In Cash**	**4070.68**	**9834.80**	**5320.17**	**2642.07**	**1923.49**
工资性收入	Income from Wages and Salaries	364.03	469.26	240.71	198.40	325.58
在非企业组织中劳动得到的	From Non-enterprise Organization	203.95	131.26	61.54	30.35	26.68
在本地企业中劳动得到的	From Local Enterprises	53.57	273.83	174.28	79.97	112.61
常住人口外出从业得到的	Out of Migrant Workers	106.51	64.17	4.89	88.08	186.30
家庭经营收入	Income of Household Operation	3571.52	9043.09	4964.94	2389.62	1481.12
农业现金收入	Cash Income from Farming	1749.96	7269.20	3977.31	1503.61	428.52
#出售农产品收入	Sale of Agricultural Products	1712.07	6997.65	3783.53	1468.21	410.67
林业现金收入	Cash Income from Forestry		22.14	71.40	163.61	143.65
#出售林业产品收入	Sale of Forestry Products		22.14	68.67	158.62	143.65
牧业现金收入	Cash Income from Animal Ausbandry	1369.45	1347.71	511.88	540.23	331.42
#出售牧业产品收入	Sale of Animal Husbandry Products	1345.63	1342.38	507.80	540.23	331.41
渔业现金收入	Cash Income from Fishery		1.81			
#出售渔业产品收入	Sale of Fishery Products					
工业收入	Income from Industry	19.05	15.94	0.76		319.38
#出售工业产品收入	Sale of Industrial Products	19.05				287.60
工业服务性收入	Income from Industrial services		15.94	0.76		31.78
建筑业收入	Income from Construction	42.79	22.37	11.24	11.28	13.76
#出售建筑业产品收入	Sale of Constructive Products					
建筑业服务性收入	Income from Constructive services	42.79	22.37	11.24	11.28	13.76
交通、运输、邮电业收入	Income from Transport,Post and Telecommunication Servies	99.84	166.23	209.35	18.44	7.14
批零贸易业、饮食业收入	Income from Wholesale and Retail Trades and Catering Servies	113.03	124.73	67.27	85.53	55.12
社会服务业收入	Income from Social Services	14.25	48.72	65.58	0.87	15.12
文教卫生业收入	Income from Culture,Edcuation and Health Care		1.94			
其他行业收入	Others	163.14	22.31	50.15	66.05	167.00
财产性收入	Property Income	28.33	163.04	73.74	5.65	4.07
#利 息	Interest	9.76	8.59			
租 金	Rent		32.70	0.22	3.12	
转移性收入	Transfer Income	106.79	159.41	40.77	48.40	112.72
非收入所得	**Non-income Gain**	**267.90**	**2881.30**	**1782.65**	**297.77**	**203.39**
#从银行信用社得到的贷款	Credit	171.59	777.95	1116.15	221.95	65.14
借入款	Borrowed Money	16.51	183.53	238.01	37.97	27.38
收回借出款	Recall Loaned Money	1.59	84.61	15.40	4.36	3.95
从银行信用社取回存款	Take Deposit back	74.60	1702.39	203.75	16.99	27.39
出售财产所得款	Sold Property		39.26	131.35	3.49	32.68
期内现金支出	**Annual Expenditure in Cash**	**2968.71**	**8918.63**	**5039.81**	**1931.24**	**1766.27**
生产费用支出	Producing Expenditure	1247.23	5114.05	3132.10	993.76	753.97
家庭经营费用支出	Expenditure for Household Business	1132.06	4712.21	2233.92	865.11	699.04
农业生产支出	Agriculture	636.57	3764.29	1858.72	747.55	346.63
林业生产支出	Forestry		25.46	58.10	4.25	9.75
牧业生产支出	Animal Husbandry	382.97	796.15	195.21	107.87	205.42

7-23 续表 3 Continued

单位：元 (yuan)

项　目	Item	阿勒泰地区 Altay Administrative Offices	巴音郭楞蒙古自治州 Bayangol Mongol Autonomous Prefecture	阿克苏地区 Aksu Administrative Offices	喀什地区 Kashgar [Kaxgar] Administrative Offices	和田地区 Hotan Administrative Offices
渔业生产支出	Fishery		0.41			
工业生产支出	Industry	3.17	5.02			50.49
建筑业生产支出	Construction	5.59	4.63			3.66
交通运输支出	Transportation	37.49	101.37	95.26	2.29	4.09
批发和零售贸易、餐饮业	Wholesale, Retail Trades and Catering services	41.17	3.96	9.77	2.28	23.96
社会服务业支出	Social Services	0.95	8.03	0.28		6.43
文教卫生业	Cultural, Education, Medicines and Medical Services		1.26			
其他经营支出	Others	24.16	1.63	16.58	0.87	48.60
购置生产性固定资产支出	Expenditure for Productive Fixed Assets	115.17	401.85	898.18	128.65	54.93
税费支出	Taxes and Fee	48.42	2.51	53.46	0.93	9.37
生活消费支出	Expenditure for Consumption	1597.78	3419.29	1727.67	893.89	932.31
财产性支出	Expenditure for Property	5.71	147.80	96.65	17.87	9.02
转移性支出	Expenditure for Transfer	69.57	234.98	29.93	24.80	61.61
非消费性现金付出	**Expenditure for Non-consumption**	**851.94**	**2797.56**	**1441.78**	**540.63**	**233.36**
#归还银行信用社贷款	Loan Returned to Bank	130.16	613.76	967.04	272.75	96.74
借出款	Lending Money	8.41	19.07	38.34	6.60	8.88
归还借款	Return Borrowed Money	7.14	190.92	163.81	37.54	45.27
存入银行信用社	Deposit	693.65	1693.79	185.48	153.27	62.16
期末金融资产余额	**Balance of Financial Assets in Year-end**	**5815.48**	**5050.08**	**1412.99**	**896.19**	**357.80**
#银行存款	Deposit	4066.34	4370.65	743.76	493.29	38.85
手存现金	Cash	1749.14	679.43	669.23	402.90	318.95
期末债务余额	**Balance of Debt in Year-end**		**906.67**	**210.80**	**172.42**	**44.30**
#银行、信用社贷款	Loan from Bank and Credit Cooperatives		706.49	109.60	130.81	32.85
乡村集体组织、企业借(欠)款	Borrowed Money from Collective Units and Enterprises		2.71	4.84	0.44	
个人借(欠)款	Borrowed Money from Individual		197.47	96.36	41.18	11.45
生活消费支出的现金	**Expenditure for Consumption**	**1597.78**	**3419.29**	**1727.67**	**893.89**	**932.31**
食 品	Food	552.56	1135.03	434.99	288.42	276.59
#主 食	Staple Food	207.15	210.61	88.43	33.74	29.44
副 食	Non-staple Food	279.29	638.87	275.92	182.16	179.64
衣 着	Clothing	277.64	287.96	217.91	144.35	134.68
居 住	Housing	305.20	596.67	497.86	236.05	240.19
家庭设备、用品及服务	Household Facilities, Articles and Services	106.98	138.37	78.71	31.07	40.85
医疗保健	Health Care and Medical Services	93.59	287.82	195.63	93.60	97.77
交通和通讯	Transportation and Communications	158.03	442.31	225.73	75.62	119.63
文化教育、娱乐用品及服务	Cultural, Education and Recreational Articles and Services	79.14	453.71	54.13	16.23	10.80
#文化教育、娱乐用品	Cultural, Education and Recreational Articles	26.83	56.47	18.19	3.65	4.88
文化教育、娱乐服务	Cultural, Education and Recreational Services	52.31	397.25	35.94	12.59	5.91
#学杂费	Tuition	51.41	287.11	22.21	9.85	5.09
技术培训费	Charge for Training		3.35	5.92	1.06	
其他商品和服务	Other Commodities and Services	24.63	77.41	22.72	8.55	11.81
商品性支出	Commodities	17.05	50.03	18.22	2.11	7.39
服务支出	Services	7.59	27.37	4.50	6.44	4.41

7-24 农村居民家庭房屋使用情况
Housing Conditions of Rural Households

(抽样调查 Sampled Survey)

项 目	Item	1990	1995	2000	2006	2007
本年新建房屋	**Newly-built House Within the Year**					
面积(平方米/人)	Per Capita Floor Space of Houses (sq.m/person)	0.78	0.44	0.38	1.43	0.93
价值(元/平方米)	Value of Houses (yuan/sq.m)	51.25	140.33	169.37	215.67	288.31
住房结构(平方米/人)	Structure of House (sq.m/person)					
#钢筋混凝土结构	Reinforced Concrete Structure	0.08	0.05	0.03	0.05	0.12
砖木结构	Brick and Wood Structure	0.44	0.18	0.16	1.09	0.65
生活用房面积(平方米/人)	Per Capita Living Rooms Space (sq.m/person)	0.55	0.34	0.38	1.43	0.93
年末住房情况	**Houses at the End of Year**					
住房面积(平方米/人)	Per Capita Floor Space of Houses (sq.m/person)	14.04	16.12	17.25	21.96	22.45
住房价值(元/平方米)	Value of Houses (yuan/sq.m)	22.16	51.63	120.86	168.41	187.27
住房结构(平方米/人)	Structure of House (sq.m/person)					
#钢筋混凝土结构	Reinforced Concrete Structure	0.29	0.30	0.53	1.14	1.18
砖木结构	Brick and Wood Structure	3.97	6.71	2.75	7.63	8.60

7-25 城乡新建住宅面积和居民住房情况
Floor Space Completed and Housing Conditions of Urban and Rural Residents

年 份 Year	城镇新建住宅面积 (万平方米) Floor Space of New Residential Buildings in Urban Areas (10 000 sq.m)	农村新建住宅面积 (万平方米) Floor Space of Newly-Built Houses in Rural Areas (10 000 sq.m)	城镇人均使用面积 (平方米) Per Capita Gross Living Space in Urban Areas (sq.m)	城镇人均建筑面积 (平方米) Per Capita Floor Space in Urban Areas (sq.m)	农村人均居住面积 (平方米) Per Capita Net Living Space in Rural Areas (sq.m)
1985	353.26	463.00	10.70	14.27	12.75
1990	381.61	593.96	13.55	18.07	14.04
1995	567.54	496.60	16.57	22.09	16.12
1996	683.51	757.71	17.61	23.48	16.12
1997	673.58	719.53	13.62	18.16	16.13
1998	874.97	729.71	18.95	25.27	16.20
1999	1315.89	705.00	19.76	26.35	16.90
2000	1327.29	554.59	20.06	26.75	17.25
2001	1517.22	894.56	20.60	27.47	18.04
2002	1256.72	534.10	18.17	23.78	18.56
2003	1546.23	800.81	17.91	23.36	18.62
2004	1565.16	732.84	18.82	24.44	19.10
2005	1673.49	1391.81	20.15	26.02	21.23
2006	1660.45	1573.38	20.33	26.31	21.96
2007	1693.48	1697.17	20.38	27.17	22.45

7-26 分地区农村居民家庭平均每人粮食收支平衡表

Per Capita Grain Banlance of Debit and Credit by Region

单位：公斤 (2007 年)(抽样调查 Sampled Survey) (kg)

项 目	Item	自治区 Autonomous Region	昌吉州 Changji Hui Autonomous Prefecture	伊犁州直属县(市) Counties (Cities) Direct Under Ili Prefecture	塔城地区 Tacheng [Tarbagatai] Administrative Office
年初粮食结存	**Inventory of Grain at Beginning of Year**	**479.19**	**607.08**	**706.92**	**197.00**
粮食收入合计	**Total of Debit**	**992.65**	**3009.56**	**1683.95**	**1405.15**
家庭经营生产的	From Household Business	869.26	2745.64	1428.59	1145.45
购 入	Purchases	123.39	248.47	255.36	259.70
其他粮食收入	Others		15.45		
粮食支出合计	**Total of Expenditure**	**793.03**	**2407.11**	**1444.79**	**1302.09**
主食用粮	Staple Food	222.02	187.15	154.53	170.54
出 售	Sales	430.36	1987.29	1080.06	966.46
种 籽	Seeds	24.02	40.33	20.08	51.21
饲 料	Fodder	114.54	192.34	190.12	113.88
其他粮食支出	Others	2.09			
年末粮食结存(实际数)	**Inventory of Grain at Year-end**	**472.01**	**540.53**	**712.22**	**204.19**

项 目	Item	阿勒泰地区 Altay Adminis-trative Offices	巴音郭楞蒙古自治州 Bayangol Mongol Autonomous Prefecture	阿克苏地区 Aksu Adminis-trative Offices	喀什地区 Kashgar [Kaxgar] Adminis-trative Offices	和田地区 Hotan Adminis-trative Offices
年初粮食结存	**Inventory of Grain at Beginning of Year**	**215.56**	**103.87**	**475.79**	**415.08**	**323.25**
粮食收入合计	**Total of Debit**	**1023.49**	**641.07**	**815.93**	**796.67**	**512.07**
家庭经营生产的	From Household Business	859.19	423.51	752.82	761.39	488.84
购 入	Purchases	164.30	217.56	63.11	35.28	23.23
其他粮食收入	Others					
粮食支出合计	**Total of Expenditure**	**970.78**	**631.96**	**584.89**	**558.07**	**404.89**
主食用粮	Staple Food	217.62	205.21	223.22	227.36	203.69
出 售	Sales	685.42	297.85	323.55	179.77	87.40
种 籽	Seeds	17.39	11.28	12.69	23.62	16.87
饲 料	Fodder	50.35	117.62	25.43	118.98	94.97
其他粮食支出	Others				8.34	1.96
年末粮食结存(实际数)	**Inventory of Grain at Year-end**	**240.57**	**204.86**	**509.35**	**437.67**	**456.60**

7-27 农村居民家庭平均每户饲养畜禽、其他小动物生产情况

Output of Livestock, Poultry and Other Small Animals Per Rural Households

单位：公斤　　(抽样调查)(Sampled Surrey)　　(kg)

年份 Year	出售自宰猪肉产量 Output of Pork Sold and Self-slaugutered	出售自宰羊肉产量 Output of Mutton Sold and Self-slaughtered	羊毛产量 Output of Wool	牛羊奶产量 Output of Cow and Sheep Milk	出售自宰家禽产量 Output of Poultry Sold and Self-slaughtered	禽蛋产量 Output of Poultry and Eggs	蚕茧产量 Output of Silkworm
1980	14.46	20.35	6.16			7.23	
1985	16.76	47.54	10.51	51.53		13.95	0.26
1990	24.97	45.72	15.86	67.16		17.68	1.26
1995	23.42	61.41	14.86	66.16	28.86	23.14	1.69
1996	23.10	62.09	7.61	34.93	7.61	8.20	0.89
1997	12.46	73.78	7.37	33.57	9.87	7.97	1.08
1998	10.18	84.42	5.40	42.53	7.39	8.78	1.58
1999	12.91	100.45	4.06	34.92	7.65	13.90	1.38
2000	16.48	94.55	5.49	34.27	13.03	25.26	1.01
2001	13.24	91.54			16.92	35.71	
2002	11.01	110.97			16.09	41.07	
2003	13.16	86.23	4.51	91.91	12.48	37.10	0.66
2004	10.30	105.20	4.09	89.54	12.75	6.03	0.23
2005	8.29	107.11	6.28	134.36	14.95	49.14	0.23
2006	4.28	114.78	6.91	112.72	12.33	71.07	0.14
2007	2.70	112.08	7.05	144.28	12.25	40.59	0.02

注：因调查户调整部分指标数据与往年相比变动较大。
Note:Beceucse of Households Surveyed adjustment, Parts of Index sign data quite changed from 7-28,7-29 compared to last yesr.

7-28 农村居民家庭平均每户饲养畜禽、其他小动物出售量

Quantities of Livestock, Poultry and Other Small Animals Sold Per Rural Households

(抽样调查) (Sampled Surrey)

年份 Year	猪(头) Pork (head)	牛(头) Cattle (head)	羊(只) Sheep (head)	家禽(只) Poultry (head)	蛋类(公斤) Eggs (kg)	羊毛(公斤) Wool (kg)	牛羊奶(公斤) Milk (kg)
1985	0.10		1.94	3.30	7.68	6.87	5.68
1990	0.22	0.11	1.50	4.15	8.25	9.63	17.47
1995	0.17	0.22	2.21	11.69	17.28	5.80	26.76
1996	0.24	0.14	2.14	1.98	3.08	3.13	12.43
1997	0.11	0.16	2.74	3.00	3.51	4.16	11.56
1998	0.07	0.15	3.47	2.14	4.30	2.23	18.04
1999	0.08	0.25	3.89	2.70	9.23	1.67	12.75
2000	0.14	0.39	3.81	4.89	21.27	1.82	21.30
2001	0.12	0.37	3.85	7.55	31.60	1.43	39.77
2002	0.11	0.35	4.61	6.64	34.55	1.95	55.33
2003	0.18	0.35	4.14	3.60	33.55	1.81	73.94
2004	0.12	0.32	4.55	4.28	3.01	1.86	77.30
2005	0.09	0.39	6.03	4.42	46.51	4.54	117.65
2006	0.06	0.59	7.21	4.12	68.19	5.19	91.42
2007	0.03	0.65	6.03	3.54	38.11	5.43	123.35

7-29 社会保险基本情况
Basic Conditions on Social Insurance

单位：万元 (10 000 yuan)

指 标	Item	2006	2007
基本养老保险	**Basic Endowment Insurance**		
年末参保人数(万人)	Year-end Contributors (10 000 persons)	191.97	205.00
#参保职工	Staff and Workers	146.10	156.89
#企 业	Enterprises	104.19	110.10
养老保险当年实际缴纳保险金	Actual Revenue of Urban Basic Endowment Insurance in Current Year	611687	739301
应发养老金额	Retirement Pension Supposed to Provide	489299	586590
实发养老金额	Retirement Pension Actually Provided	489299	586590
失业保险	**Unemployment Insurance**		
年末参保人数(万人)	Year-end Contributors (10 000 persons)	145.27	151.55
企 业	Enterprises	89.68	93.94
#国有企业	State-owned	58.20	58.00
集体企业	Collective-owned	3.30	3.21
事业单位	Institutions	54.40	56.10
其 他	Others	1.19	1.51
失业保险当年实际缴纳保险金	Actual Revenue of Unemployment Insurance in Current Year	71699	93297
失业保险实际支付人数(万人)	Actual Payees of Unemployment Insurance (10 000 persons)	7.11	6.49
失业保险基金当年支出额	Expenses of Unemployment Insurance in Current Year	30500	42858
失业保险基金当年末结余额	Balance of Unemployment Insurance in Current Year	230700	284066
年末城镇登记失业人员数(万人)	Year-end Urban Registered Unemployees (10 000 persons)	11.60	11.70
城镇登记失业人员就业人数(万人)	Employment of Urban Registered Unemployees (10 000 persons)	28.06	28.14
领取失业保险金人数(万人)	Beneficiaries of Unemployment Insurance in Current Year (10 000 persons)	7.11	6.49
基本医疗保险	**Basic Medical Insurance**		
年末参保人数(万人)	Year-end Contributors (10 000 persons)	227.15	244.78
#职 工	Staff and Workers	162.56	183.54

7-30 各地、州、市社会保险年末参保人数

Number of Social Insured Persons at the Year-end by Prefecture, Autonomous Prefecture and City

单位：万人 (10 000 persons)

年 份 Year	地 区 Region	基本养老保险 Basic Endowment Insurance	失业保险 Unemployment Insurance	基本医疗保险 Basic Medical Insurance
	2005	181.87	140.84	211.85
	2006	191.97	145.27	227.15
	2007	205.00	151.55	244.78
乌鲁木齐市	Urumqi City	44.45	46.74	60.99
克拉玛依市	Karamay City	1.87	1.69	16.84
石河子市	Shihezi City		5.69	
吐鲁番地区	Turpan Administrative Offices	2.41	3.16	5.83
哈密地区	Hami [Kumul] Administrative Offices	5.18	4.99	8.08
昌吉回族自治州	Changji Hui Autonomous Prefecture	10.60	9.35	18.19
伊犁州直属县(市)	Counties (Cities) Direct Under Ili Prefecture	13.29	11.73	21.28
塔城地区	Tacheng [Tarbagatai] Administrative Offices	6.28	6.59	10.48
阿勒泰地区	Altay Administrative Offices	3.98	4.64	9.27
博尔塔拉蒙古自治州	Bortala Mongol Autonomous Prefecture	2.92	2.89	4.56
巴音郭楞蒙古自治州	Bayangol Mongol Autonomous Prefecture	11.32	10.79	16.07
阿克苏地区	Aksu Administrative Offices	8.36	8.09	14.71
克孜勒苏柯尔克孜自治州	Kizilsu Kirgiz Autonomous Prefecture	1.12	2.40	4.90
喀什地区	Kashgar [Kaxgar] Administrative Offices	5.59	10.18	19.40
和田地区	Hotan Administrative Offices	2.95	4.95	8.63

7-31 离休、退休、退职人员年底人数

Number of Retired and Resigned Persons at the Year-end

单位：人 (person)

年 份 Year	总 计 Total				#企 业 Enterprises			
	合 计 Total	离休人员 Retired Veterans	退休人员 Retired Persons	退职人员 Resigned Persons	合 计 Total	离休人员 Retired Veterans	退休人员 Retired Persons	退职人员 Resigned Persons
1990	535736	63742	443669	28326	399764	47008	331514	21242
1995	773688	76834	668482	28372	611054	61399	526236	23419
2000	1003360	63260	905390	34710	783148	49083	703058	31007
2001	995882	54990	907178	33714	754933	41937	683293	29703
2002	1002836	52272	920401	30163	739035	39606	673844	25585
2003	1027896	50995	946583	30318	803436	39813	737054	26569
2004	1062388	47238	980378	34772	778236	35626	713634	28976
2005	1144548	46181	1062430	35937	908126	36480	839449	32197
2006	668209	14358	643614	10237	412787	6960	398978	6849
2007	732303	14546	702347	15410	486524	7590	467498	11436

注：19-20、19-21、19-22 表自 2006 年起数据不包括兵团。
Note: Since 2006 data in 19-20、19-21、19-22 table exclude Xinjiang Production and Construction Group.

7-32 离休、退休、退职费

Pensions for Retired and Resigned Persons

年份 Year	合计(万元) Total (10 000 yuan)	国有单位 Funds of State-Owned Units	城镇集体单位 Funds of Urban Collective Owned Units	其他单位 Funds of Other Ownership Units	平均每人(元) Per Capita Funds (yuan)	#国有单位 State-Owned Units
1990	94304	90341	3908	55	1871	1837
1995	331522	321199	9882	441	4615	4667
1996	377782	363217	13631	934	5014	5059
1997	456596	443124	12970	502	5802	5904
1998	585609	568726	13462	3421	6860	6949
1999	681553	661271	14971	5311	7383	7478
2000	759880	740782	14005	5093	7774	7878
2001	837082	816689	13989	6404	8374	8464
2002	952163	928137	15187	8839	9495	9582
2003	1005081	958106	17464	29511	9778	9891
2004	1098304	1049375	18868	30061	10338	10531
2005	1233797	1170938	17051	45808	10780	11106
2006	949162	859497	19387	70278	14205	14710
2007	1241316	1126756	20650	93910	16951	18011

7-33 离休、退休、退职人员保险福利费用情况

Condition of Total Social Insurance and Welfare Fund of Retire and Resigned Persons

单位：万元 (10 000 yuan)

年份 Year	合计 Total	离休金 Pensions for Termination	退休金 Retirement Pensions	退职生活费 Resignation Allowances For Living Expenses	医疗卫生费 Medical Care Expenses	其他 Others
1990	118560	16566	76102	1637	9665	14590
1995	394514	40535	286032	4955	39423	23569
1996	450345	42148	330166	5467	46043	26521
1997	545914	55033	394642	6921	49566	39752
1998	680074	65655	509711	10243	69431	25034
1999	789707	71871	597636	12177	81602	26421
2000	867925	77968	667698	14214	79834	28210
2001	950373	87574	736007	13502	77711	35579
2002	1055177	90010	847886	14268	64262	38753
2003	1129407	93408	895009	16664	83722	40604
2004	1202102	102193	977478	18634	50596	53202
2005	1346276	115803	1102101	15893	60694	51785
2006	949162	38634	804370	6875	50519	48764
2007	1241316	45860	1091931	14460	19007	70058

主要统计指标解释

城镇就业者负担人数 指家庭人口与就业人口之比。

城镇家庭总收入 指家庭成员得到的工薪收入、经营净收入、财产性收入、转移性收入之和，不包括出售财物收入和借贷收入。

城镇家庭可支配收入 指家庭成员得到可用于最终消费支出和其它非义务性支出以及储蓄的总和，即居民家庭可以用来自由支配的收入。它是家庭总收入扣除交纳的所得税、个人交纳的社会保障支出以及记账补贴后的收入。计算公式为:

可支配收入=家庭总收入-交纳所得税-个人交纳的社会保障支出-记帐补贴

城镇家庭消费性支出 指家庭用于日常生活的支出，包括食品、衣着、家庭设备用品及服务、医疗保健、交通和通信、娱乐教育文化服务、居住、杂项商品和服务等八大类支出。

城镇家庭服务性消费支出 指家庭用于支付社会提供的各种非商品性服务费用。

城镇家庭收入分组方法 将所有调查户依户人均可支配收入由低到高排队，按10%，10%，20%，20%，20%，10%，10%的比例依次分成：最低收入户、低收入户、中等偏下收入户、中等收入户、中等偏上收入户、高收入户、最高收入户等七组。总体中最低5%的户为困难户。

农村家庭经营收入 指农村住户以家庭为生产经营单位进行生产筹划和管理而获得的收入。农村住户家庭经营活动按行业划分为农业、林业、牧业、渔业、工业、建筑业、交通运输业邮电业、批发和零售贸易餐饮业、社会服务业、文教卫生业和其他家庭经营。

财产性收入 指金融资产或有形非生产性资产的所有者向其他机构单位提供资金或将有形非生产性资产供其支配，作为回报而从中获得的收入。

转移性收入 指农村住户和住户成员无须付出任何对应物而获得的货物、服务、资金或资产所有权等，不包括无偿提供的用于固定资本形成的资金。一般情况下，是指农村住户在二次分配中的所有收入。

现金收入 指农村住户和住户成员在调查期内得到以现金形态表现的收入。按来源分成工资性收入、家庭经营现金收入、财产性收入、转移性收入。

农村家庭纯收入 指农村住户当年从各个来源得到的总收入相应地扣除所发生的费用后的收入总和。计算方法:

纯收入=总收入-税费支出-家庭经营费用支出-税费支出-生产性固定资产折旧-调查补贴-赠送农村外部亲友支出

纯收入主要用于再生产投入和当年生活消费支出，也可用于储蓄和各种非义务性支出。“农民人均纯收入”按人口平均的纯收入水平，反映的是一个地区或一个农户农村居民的平均收入水平。

恩格尔系数 指食物支出金额在消费性总支出金额中所占的比例。计算公式为:

恩格尔系数=食品支出金额/消费性总支出金额 × 100%

基本养老保险

1.参加保险人数：指报告期末按照国家法律、法规和有关政策规定参加基本养老保险的职工人数。包括不能正常缴费、已中断缴费但未终止保险关系的职工人数。

2.社会统筹基金收入：指根据国家规定，由纳入基本养老保险范围的单位，按照国家规定的缴费基数和缴费比例缴纳的社会统筹基金，以及通过其他方式取得的形成基金来源的收入，包括：单位缴纳的社会统筹基金收入、财政补贴收入、利息收入、其他收入。

3.社会统筹基金支出：指按照国家政策规定的开支范围和开支标准从社会统筹基金中支付给参加基本养老保险的离休、退休、退职人员个人的养老金、丧葬抚恤补助，以及由于保险关系转移、上下级之间调剂资金等原因而发生的支出。包括：基础性养老金、过渡性养老金、离休金、退休金、退职金、补贴、丧葬抚恤补助、其他支出。

4.社会统筹基金结余：指截止报告期末基本养老保险的社会统筹基金结余金额。包括银行存款、财政专户、债券投资和其他。

基本医疗保险

1.参保人数：指报告期末按国家有关规定参加基本医疗保险的人数。包括参加保险的职工人数和退休人员人数。

2.基金收入：指根据国家有关规定，由纳入基本医疗保险范围的缴费单位和个人，按国家规定的缴费基数和缴费比例缴纳的基金，以及通过其他方式取得的形成基金来源的款项，包括：单位缴纳的社会统筹基金收入、个人缴纳的个人账户基金收入、财政补贴收入、利息收入、其他收入。

3.基金支出：指按照国家政策规定的开支范围和开支标准从社会统筹基金中支付给参加基本医疗保险的职工和退休人员的医疗保险待遇支出，和从个人帐户基金中支付给参加基本医疗保险的职工和退休人员的医疗费用支出，以及其他支出。包括：住院医疗费用支出、门急诊医疗费用支出、个人账户基金支出、其他支出。

4.基金累计结余：指截止报告期末基本医疗保险的社会统筹和个人帐户基金累计结余金额。包括银行存款、财政专户、债券投资和其他。

失业保险

1.参加保险人数：指报告期末按照国家法律、法规和有关政策规定参加了失业保险的城镇企业事业单位的职工及地方政府规定参加失业保险的其他人员的人数。

2.失业保险金：指为保障失业人员的基本生活而按规定支付的失业保险金金额。保险福利费用总额指各单位在工资以外支付给职工和离休、退休、退职人员个人和用于集体的保险福利费用，不包括用于职工的劳动保护费用，由保险福利费用开支的医务人员工资，集体福利机构工作人员和病伤休息期满6个月以上人员的工资。

Explanatory Notes on Main Statistical Indicators

Number of Dependents per Urban Employee refers to the ratio between number of persons in an urban household and the number of employed persons.

Total Income of Urban Households refers to the sum of wage and salary, net business income, income from properties, and income from transfers of members of the households, excluding income from selling of properties and income from borrowings.

Disposable Income of Urban Households refers to the actual income at the disposal of members of the households which can be used for final consumption, other non-compulsory expenditure and savings. This equals to total income minus income tax, personal contribution to social security and sample household subsidy for keeping diaries. Following formula is used:

Disposable income = total household income - income tax - personal contribution to social security - sample household subsidy for keeping diaries

Consumption Expenditure of Urban Households refers to total expenditure of the sample households for consumption in daily life, including expenditure on eight categories such as food, clothing, household appliances and services, health care and medical services, transport and communications, recreation, education and cultural services, housing, miscellaneous goods and services.

Expenditure of Urban Households on Consumption of Services refers to expenditure of households on services of various kinds provided by the society.

Urban Households by Income Group All households in the sample are grouped, by per capita disposable income of the household, into groups of lowest income, low income, lower middle income, middle income, upper middle income, high income and highest income, each group consisting of 10%, 10%, 20%, 20%, 20%, 10% and 10% of all households respectively. The lowest 5% of households are also referred to as poor households.

Income from Rural Household Operations refers to income by the rural households as units of production and operations. Operations by rural households are classified by economic activities as agriculture, forestry, animal husbandry, fishery, manufacturing, construction, transportation, post and telecommunications, wholesale, retail and catering, social service, culture, education, health, and other household operations.

Income from Properties refers to the income received as returns by owners of financial assets or tangible non-productive assets by providing capitals or tangible non-productive assets to other institutional units.

Income from Transfers refers to the receipt by rural households and their members of goods, services, capital or rights of assets without giving or repaying accordingly, excluding capital provided to them for the formation of fixed assets. In general, it refers to all income received by rural households through redistribution.

Cash Income refers to income received by rural households and their members in the form of cash during the reference period. It is classified, by source of income, into income from wages and salaries, cash income from household operations, income from properties and income from transfers.

Net Income from Rural household refers to the total income of rural households from all sources minus all corresponding expenses. The formula for calculation is as follows:

Net income = total income – taxes and fees paid - household operation expenses – taxes and fees – depreciation of fixed assets for production – subsidy for participating in household survey – gifts to non-rural relatives

Net income is mainly used as input for reproduction and as consumption expenditure of the year, and also used for savings and non-compulsory expenses of various forms.Per capita net income of farmers is the level of net income averaged by population which reflects the average income level of rural households in a given area.

Engel Coefficient refers to the percentage of expenditure on food in the total consumption expenditure,using the following formula:

Engel Coefficient=(expenditure on food/total consumption expenditure) × 100%

Basic Endowment Insurance

1. Number of people participating in the insurance program: by the end of reference period, number of staff and workers participating in the insurance program in line with national laws, regulations and related policies, including those who can not make regular payment or interrupt payment but not terminate the insurance program.

2. Revenue of social comprehensive funds: according to national provision, payments made by units covered in basic endowment insurance program, and income from other resources, including: income of social comprehensive funds paid by unites, financial subsidies, interest income and others.

3. Expenditure of social comprehensive funds: refer to payment made to those retired and resigned people covered in endowment insurance program in terms of pens ion or compensation within the expenditure scope and standards according to related national policies, and the expenditure occurred due to shift of the insurance relationship or adjustment funds among agencies, including: basic pension, transitional pension, pension for resigned people, pension for retired people, pension for people quitting jobs, subsidies, funeral subsidies and other expenditure.

4. Balance of social comprehensive funds: refer to the balance of basic endowment insurance of social comprehensive funds at the end of the reference period, including: bank savings, special fiscal account, investment in bonds and others.

Basic Medical Care Insurance:

1. Number of people participated in the insurance program: refer to number of people participated in the basic medical care insurance program according to related regulation by the end of reference period, including: number of staff and workers and retired persons participated in this insurance program.

2. Revenue of social comprehensive funds: according to national provision, payments made by units covered in basic medical care insurance program, and income from other resources, including: income of social comprehensive funds paid by unites, financial subsidies, interest income and others.

3. Expenditure of social comprehensive funds: refer to payment made to those retired and resigned people covered in basic medical care insurance within the expenditure scope and standards according to related national policies, including: expenditure on fee-for-service in hospital, expenditure on fee-for-service in clinic and other expenditure.

4. Balance of social comprehensive funds: refer to the balance of medical care insurance of social comprehensive funds at the end of the reference period, including: bank savings, special fiscal account, investment in bonds and others.

Unemployment Insurance

1. Number of people participated in unemployment insurance program: number of staff and workers in urban enterprises or institutions and other people according to local government regulations participated in unemployment insurance program in line with national law, regulations and related policies by the end of the reference period.

2. Sum of Unemployment Insurance: refer to total amount of insurance paid to un-employees to guarantee their basic lives according to related regulations.

第八篇
城市概况

CHAPTER 8
General Survey of Cities

简要说明
Brief Introduction

本篇资料的主要内容及来源

本篇资料反映新疆城市社会、经济发展和城市建设的基本情况。

城市概况资料主要包括城市公用事业基本情况、主要经济指标、市政设施、园林绿化、环境卫生、供水供气、公用交通等。

本篇资料由新疆维吾尔自治区统计局综合处根据新疆维吾尔自治区建设厅和新疆维吾尔自治区统计局相关处室提供的年度数据整理。

Main Content and Source of Data

Data in this chapter show the social and economic development and the basic condition of Xinjiang.

Data on the general survey cities include the basic condition of urban public facilities, main economic indicators, civil facilities, urban greenery, environment and sanitation, supply of gas and heating, public transportation, etc.

Data on this chapter are compiled by the Department of National Accounts of the Xinjiang Bureau of Statistics according to the data of yearly statistics, which are provided by the Construction Bureau of Xinjiang Uygur Autonomous Region and related departments of Statistics Bureau of Xinjiang Uygur Autonomous Region.

8-1 城市公用事业基本情况
Basic Statistics on Urban Public Utilities

项 目	Item	2006	2007
城市及建筑物面积	**Urban Areas and Floor Space of Buildings**		
建成区面积(平方公里)	Completed Areas (sq.km)	674	1109
征用土地面积(平方公里)	Land Put in Requisition for State Construction Projects (sq. km)	5.6	15.8
城市人口密度(人/平方公里)	Population Density of Urban Area (persons/sq.km)	4925	4836
供水、供气及供热	**Water Supply, Gas Supply and Heating**		
自来水年供水量(亿吨)	Annual Supply of Tap Water (100 million tons)	5.1	6.3
#生活用水量	Water Consumption for Residential use	2.1	2.3
平均每人日生活用水量(升)	Per -Capita Water Consumption for Residential Use (litre)	172.9	165.8
用水普及率(%)	Percentage of Population with Access to Tap Water (%)	99.4	99.1
人工煤气供气量(万立方米)	Coal Gas Supply (10 000 cu.m)	597267	579036
#家庭用量	Consumption of Coal Gas for Residential Use	1752	1752
天然气供气量(万立方米)	Natural Gas Supply (10 000 cu.m)	57463	70603
#家庭用量	Consumption of Coal Gas for Residential Use	18565	21849
液化石油气供气量(吨)	Liquefied Petroleum Gas (ton)	126396	114262
#家庭用量	Consumption of Liquefied Gas for Residential Use	80264	75430
天然气、煤气管道长度(公里)	Length of Gas Pipelines (km)	4092	4633
燃气普及率(%)	Percentage of Population with Access to Gas (%)	91.5	92.8
集中供热面积(万平方米)	Area of Centralized Heating (10 000 sq.m)	12978	14472
#住 宅	Residential Buildings	8629	10132
市政工程	**Municipal Engineering**		
铺装道路长度(公里)	Length of Paved Roads (km)	4044	4276
平均每万人拥有 (公里)	Length of Paved Roads per 10 000 Population (km)	8.3	5.3
铺装道路面积(万平方米)	Area of Paved Roads (10 000 sq.m)	6500	6954
平均每人拥有(平方米)	Area of Paved Roads per Population (sq.m)	13.3	13.3
下水道长度(公里)	Length of Sewer Pipelines (km)	3194	3441
平均每万人拥有 (公里)	Length of Sewer Pipelines per 10 000 Population (km)	6.5	4.2
公共交通	**Public Traffic**		
年末运营公交车辆(辆)	Number of Public Transportation Vehicles at the Year-end (unit)	7822	8512
平均每万人拥有(标台)	Number of Public Transportation Vehicles per 10 000 Population (unit)	14.7	15.6
出租汽车数量(辆)	Taxi (unit)	23409	25465
城市绿化	**Afforestation in Cities**		
建成区绿地面积(公顷)	Green Areas of Completed Area (hectare)	17886	19233
每万人建成区绿地面积(公顷)	Green Areas of Completed Area per 10 000 Population (hectare)	22.9	28.7
公园数(个)	Number of Parks (unit)	123	120
公园面积(公顷)	Area of Parks (hectare)	2885	2879
环境卫生	**Environmental Sanitation**		
清运生活垃圾(万吨)	Volume of Garbage Disposal (10 000 tons)	278	340
清运粪便(万吨)	Volume of Disposal of Excrement and Urine (10 000 tons)	5.4	20.1
每万人拥有公共厕所(座)	Number of Public Lavatories per 10 000 Population (unit)	5.1	3.0

8-2 各城市主要经济指标
Major Economic Indicators by Cities

单位: 万元 (2007 年) (10 000 yuan)

城市名称	City	年底总人口(万人) Total Population (Year-end) (10 000 persons)	地区生产总值(当年价格) Gross Region Production (current-year price)	第一产业 Primary Industry	第二产业 Secondary Industry
乌鲁木齐市	Urumqi City	231.30	8202800	162659	3165857
克拉玛依市	Karamay City	26.72	5151297	25445	4615056
吐鲁番市	Turpan City	26.92	355586	73242	88686
哈 密 市	Hami [Kumul] City	42.38	779560	94058	281249
昌 吉 市	Changji City	34.78	1080307	169573	427170
阜 康 市	Fukang City	16.62	472183	66059	318221
伊 宁 市	Yining [Gulja] City	44.59	569160	37114	157322
奎 屯 市	Kuytun City	30.76	401569	17654	202922
塔 城 市	Tacheng [Qoqek] City	16.36	263133	66520	55460
乌 苏 市	Usu City	21.54	526645	210360	187379
阿勒泰市	Altay City	23.00	239060	49941	49179
博 乐 市	Bole [Bortala] City	25.96	541860	138585	76239
库尔勒市	Korla City	47.21	3538604	186144	2877934
阿克苏市	Aksu City	45.24	985453	338383	238662
阿图什市	Artux City	22.51	119571	29901	20385
喀 什 市	Kashgar [Kaxgar] City	44.01			
和 田 市	Hotan City	28.19	146478	22661	44555
石河子市	Shi Hezi City	63.61	732468	50878	349172
阿拉尔市	Aral City	16.65			
图木舒克市	Tumxuk City	14.78			
五家渠市	Wujiaqu City	7.28			

城市名称	City	#工 业 Industry	第三产业 Tertiary Industry	#交通运输、仓储和邮政业 Transport, Storage and Post	人均地区生产总值(元/人) Per Capita GDP (yuan/person)
乌鲁木齐市	Urumqi City	2618574	4874284	715974	31140
克拉玛依市	Karamay City	4497053	510796	105653	98398
吐鲁番市	Turpan City	72285	193658	55683	13557
哈 密 市	Hami [Kumul] City	227159	404253	160863	18469
昌 吉 市	Changji City	314192	483564	118048	25042
阜 康 市	Fukang City	289887	87903	14204	29365
伊 宁 市	Yining [Gulja] City	108460	374724	67431	13073
奎 屯 市	Kuytun City	170133	180993	39266	28683
塔 城 市	Tacheng [Qoqek] City	32749	141153	19614	15947
乌 苏 市	Usu City	134729	128906	21644	16165
阿勒泰市	Altay City	32479	139940	19225	13244
博 乐 市	Bole [Bortala] City	42662	327036	59069	21166
库尔勒市	Korla City	2582352	474525	67294	72074
阿克苏市	Aksu City	156465	408408	39339	16198
阿图什市	Artux City	8870	69285	8901	5272
喀 什 市	Kashgar [Kaxgar] City				
和 田 市	Hotan City	15599	79262	14217	5218
石河子市	Shi Hezi City	284772	332418	31099	23797
阿拉尔市	Aral City				
图木舒克市	Tumxuk City				
五家渠市	Wujiaqu City				

8-2 续表 Continued

单位: 万元 (10 000 yuan)

城市名称	City	固定资产投资总额 Investment in Fixed Assets	工业经济效益综合指数(%) Comprehensive Index of Industry Ecnomic Results (%)	地方财政一般预算收入 General Budgetary Revenue in Local Finance	地方财政一般预算支出 General Budgetary Expenditure in Local Finance
乌鲁木齐市	Urumqi City	2234718	235.19	734279	683153
克拉玛依市	Karamay City	2795166	545.42	364826	428248
吐鲁番市	Turpan City	103311	180.50	24552	42173
哈密市	Hami [Kumul] City	238499	212.54	47963	64930
昌吉市	Changji City	291468	153.10	46226	68818
阜康市	Fukang City	148847	246.72	31525	33030
伊宁市	Yining [Gulja] City	118066	122.44	39531	76354
奎屯市	Kuytun City	141020	253.61	32388	40629
塔城市	Tacheng [Qoqek] City	46219	60.46	8602	36025
乌苏市	Usu City	128342	202.99	16999	43424
阿勒泰市	Altay City	69785	154.25	7524	44892
博乐市	Bole [Bortala] City	165845	109.23	14371	41559
库尔勒市	Korla City	1367009	1323.77	76699	84621
阿克苏市	Aksu City	378674	142.18	38026	66594
阿图什市	Artux City	42978	243.31	4970	43875
喀什市	Kashgar [Kaxgar] City	266389	131.09	30647	69234
和田市	Hotan City	112258	35.90	12538	45623
石河子市	Shi Hezi City	505194	176.96	66656	84440
阿拉尔市	Aral City		165.22	4112	6738
图木舒克市	Tumxuk City		105.42	1606	7083
五家渠市	Wujiaqu City		132.71	6051	7784

城市名称	City	居民消费价格指数(上年=100) Consumer Price Index (preceding year=100)	社会消费品零售总额 Total Retail Sales of Consumer Goods	在岗职工人数(万人) Number of Fully-employed Staff and Workers (10 000 persons)	在岗职工平均货币工资(元) Average Money Wage of Staff and Workers (yuan)
乌鲁木齐市	Urumqi City	104.6	3217648	47.87	29483
克拉玛依市	Karamay City	106.1	230656	14.16	29706
吐鲁番市	Turpan City	106.4	89229	2.70	19404
哈密市	Hami [Kumul] City	103.8	228240	5.81	23785
昌吉市	Changji City	103.7	286323	4.71	26577
阜康市	Fukang City		86581	1.92	19979
伊宁市	Yining [Gulja] City	104.5	202407	6.88	18557
奎屯市	Kuytun City	103.6	83997	2.76	19180
塔城市	Tacheng [Qoqek] City	103.8	59497	2.66	18004
乌苏市	Usu City	104.4	58355	5.66	13055
阿勒泰市	Altay City	104.8	73418	3.91	18306
博乐市	Bole [Bortala] City	105.6	87169	4.94	17316
库尔勒市	Korla City	105.2	256402	8.99	20442
阿克苏市	Aksu City	106.5	180461	10.26	19588
阿图什市	Artux City	106.1	32602	1.86	23730
喀什市	Kashgar [Kaxgar] City	104.3	211600	4.96	20161
和田市	Hotan City	104.5	87766	2.57	21053
石河子市	Shi Hezi City	104.8		7.91	19215
阿拉尔市	Aral City				
图木舒克市	Tumxuk City				
五家渠市	Wujiaqu City				

8-3 各城市市区设施水平
Level of Urban Public Facilities in Cities

(2007 年)

城市名称 City		城市用水普及率(%) Percentage of Population with Access to Tap Water (%)	城市燃气普及率(%) Percentage of Population with Access to Gas (%)	每万人拥有公交营运车辆(标台) Number of Public Transportation Vehicles per 10 000 Population (unit)	人均铺装道路面积(平方米) PerCapital Area of Paved Roads (sq.m)	人均公园绿地面积(平方米) PerCapital Public Green Areas (sq.m)	生活垃圾处理率(%) Ratio of disposal Garbage (%)
总　计	**Total**	**99.12**	**92.77**	**15.60**	**13.32**	**8.09**	**78.85**
乌鲁木齐市	Urumqi City	99.78	99.50	20.11	7.50	6.94	56.85
克拉玛依市	Karamay City	100.00	100.00	11.35	20.75	8.24	98.59
石河子市	Shihezi City	100.00	91.08	16.07	22.61	9.88	94.31
吐鲁番市	Turpan City	98.60	97.00	13.00	17.20	2.40	100.00
哈密市	Hami [Kumul] City	99.72	92.64	7.64	13.36	8.24	100.00
昌吉市	Changji City	100.00	100.00	19.14	11.01	8.69	100.00
阜康市	Fukang City	86.96	65.22	6.52	16.96	7.17	100.00
伊宁市	Yining [Gulja] City	100.00	88.53	13.60	16.36	8.00	98.17
奎屯市	Kuytun City	100.00	86.26	4.41	12.91	5.81	100.00
塔城市	Tacheng [Qoqek] City	91.15	69.84	6.03	13.67	16.22	96.94
乌苏市	Usu City	95.81	59.88	7.19	24.55	6.23	85.14
阿勒泰市	Altay City	99.24	59.54	11.76	9.31	18.63	97.74
博乐市	Bole [Bortala] City	99.46	90.01	14.67	11.52	11.88	95.16
库尔勒市	Korla City	100.00	100.00	22.04	28.40	8.83	100.00
阿克苏市	Aksu City	100.00	98.08	10.88	15.92	9.15	100.00
阿图什市	Artux City	92.78	92.78	6.70	19.24	2.23	100.00
喀什市	Kashgar [Kaxgar] City	100.00	72.37	10.61	18.41	8.80	100.00
和田市	Hotan City	94.91	97.50	10.27	13.81	9.92	80.90
五家渠市	Wujiaqu City	98.26	86.81	4.17	14.76	11.63	
图木舒克市	Tumxuk City	69.12	65.20	21.57	30.88	9.80	
阿拉尔市	Aral City	91.88		5.78	13.28	11.88	

8-4 城市自来水情况
Basic Statistics on Tap Water Supply in Cities

指　标	Item	1995	2000	2007
年末水厂生产能力(万吨/日)	Production Capacity of TapWater Supply (10 000tons/day)	69	292	340
年末供水管道总长度(公里)	Length of Water Supply Piplines (km)	1032	4448	5184
全年供水总量(亿立方米)	Total Annual Volume of Water supply (100 millon.cu.m)	3.1	5.0	6.3
#生活用水	For Residential Use	1.4	2.5	2.3
生产用水	For Productive Use	1.7	2.0	1.5
平均每人日生活用水量(升)	Per-Capitall Daily Consumption of Tap Water for Residential Use (litre)	158.3	165.1	165.8
用水人口(万人)	Number of Residents with Access to Tap Water (10 000 persons)	231	418	518

8-5 城市公用交通情况
Basic Statistics on Public Transportation in Cities

指　标	Item	1995	2000	2007
年末运营公交车辆(辆)	Number of Public Vehicles for Business Transportation (unit)	3324	5678	8512
平均每万人拥有公交车辆(标台)	Number of Public Vehicles for Business Transportation per 10 000 population(unit)	10.8	13.8	15.6
公交运营线路网长度(公里)	Length of Business Transportation Routes (km)	3203	1700	2410
公交客运总量(亿人次)	Number of Passengers Carried of Bus, Trolley Bus (100 millon person-times)	6.7	9.5	11.7
公交车辆平均每日运客数(万人次)	Number of Passengers Carried of Bus per day (10 000 person-times)	183.1	260.3	320.79
年末运营出租汽车(辆)	Number of Taxis (unit)	11762	22193	25465
出租汽车客运总量(亿人次)	Number of Passengers Carried of Taxi.s (100 millon person-times)			5.60

8-6 城市市政建设情况
Basic Statistics on Municipal Construction in Cities

指　标	Item	1995	2000	2007
实有道路长度(公里)	Length of Paved Roads (km)	2403	2809	4276
实有道路面积(万平方米)	Area of Paved Roads (10 000 sq.m)	2589	3654	6954
城市桥梁(座)	Number of City Bridges (unit)	165	253	339
防洪堤长度(公里)	Length of Dyke for Control of Flood (km)	112	130	238
城市下水道总长度(公里)	Length of Sewer Pipelines (km)	1557	2008	3441
城市污水日处理能力(万立方米)	Daily Disposal Capacity of Sewage (10 000 cu.m)	34	46	137
城市路灯盏数(千盏)	Number of Street Light (1 000 units)	28.8	72.9	300

注：城市污水日处理能力指污水处理厂处理能力，不包括其他污水处理设施处理量。
Note: The daily treatment capacity in urban area refers to the treatment capacity of a waste- water treatment plant, excluding the volume handled by other polluted-water treatment facility.

8-7 城市园林绿化情况
Basic Statistics on Urban Gardens and Green Areas in Cities

指　标	Item	1995	2000	2007
城市园林绿地面积(公顷)	Area of Urban Green Areas (hectare)	13481	19124	32648
#建成区绿地面积	Green Areas of Completed Area			19233
每万人建成区绿地面积(公顷)	Green Areas of Completed Area Per 10 000 Population (hectare)	41.5	53.4	28.7
建成区绿化覆盖率(%)	Green Covrage Rate in Completed Area (%)	24.2	29.1	32.0
平均每人公园绿地面积(平方米)	PerCapita Parks Green Areas (sq.m)	5.1	6.4	8.1
公园数(个)	Number of Parks(unit)	55	84	120
公园面积(公顷)	Area of Parks (hectare)	1331	1568	2879

8-8 城市环境卫生情况
Basic Statistics on Urban Environment and Sanitation in Cities

指　标	Item	1995	2000	2007
环卫专用车辆设备数量(辆)	Environmental Special Purpose Vehicle Equipment (unit)	566	767	1222
公共厕所(座)	Number of Public Lavatories (unit)	1147	1684	2458
每万人拥有公共厕所(座)	Number of Public Lavatories Per 10 000 Population (unit)	3.5	4.7	3.0
道路清扫面积(万平方米)	Area under Cleaning Program (10 000 sq.m)	1743	3224	6133
#机械化	Mechanization			1467
清运生活垃圾(万吨)	Volum of Garbage Disposal (10 000 tons)	198	259	340
清运粪便 (万吨)	Volum of Excrement and Urine Disposal (10 000 tons)	26	16	20

8-9 城市煤气、液化石油气、天然气情况
Basic Statistics on Supply of Gas, Liquefied Petroleum Gas and Natural Gas in Cities

指　标	Item	2000	2006	2007
人工煤气生产能力(万立方米/日)	Production Capacity of Coal Gas (10 000 cu.m/day)		1526	1586
管道长度(公里)	Length of Gas Pipelines (km)	385	4092	4633
人工煤气	Coal Gas		90	100
液化石油气	Liquefied Petroleum Gas		63	62
天然气	Natural Gas	385	3939	4471
全年供气总量(万立方米)	Total Gas Supply (10 000 cu.m)			
人工煤气	Coal Gas		597267	579036
液化石油气(吨)	Liquefied Petroleum Gas (ton)	244018	126396	114262
天然气	Natural Gas	5385	57463	70603
用气人口(万人)	Population with Access to Gas (10 000 persons)		449.53	484.47
人工煤气	Coal Gas		5.95	6.18
液化石油气	Liquefied Petroleum Gas	305.70	167.92	171.12
天然气	Natural Gas	27.00	275.66	307.17

8-10 城市集中供热情况
Basic Statistics on Heating in Cities

指　标	Item	2000	2006	2007
供应能力	**Heating Capacity**			
蒸汽(吨/小时)	Steam (ton/hour)	1638	1119	1700
热水(兆瓦)	Hot Water (1 billion kw)	6145	13478	14472
供热总量(万吉焦)	**Quantity of Heating Supplied (10 000 gigajoules)**			
蒸 汽	Steam		808	856
热 水	Hot Water		11968	12609
管道长度(公里)	**Length of Heating Pipelines (km)**			
蒸 汽	Steam	250	177	127
热 水	Hot Water	2064	4302	4352
供热面积(万平方米)	**Area of Centralized Heating (10 000 sq.m)**	**5170**	**12978**	**14472**
#住 宅	Residential Buildings		8629	10132

主要统计指标解释

供水综合生产能力 指按供水设施取水、净化、送水、出厂输水干管等环节设计能力计算的综合生产能力。包括在原设计能力的基础上，经挖、革、改增加的生产能力。计算时，以四个环节中最薄弱的环节为主确定能力。

年末供水管道长度 指从送水泵到用户水表之间所有管道的长度。

全年供水总量 指报告期供水企业(单位)供出的全部水量。包括有效供水量和漏损水量。

生活用水量 包括公共服务用水和居民家庭用水。公共服务用水指为城市社会公共生活服务的用水。包括行政事业单位、部队营区和公共设施服务、社会服务业、批发零售贸易业、旅馆饮食业以及其他公共服务业等单位的用水。居民家庭用水指城市范围内所有居民家庭的日常生活用水。包括城市居民、农民家庭、公共供水站用水。

城市人口用水普及率 指城市用水的非农业人口数(不包括临时人口和流动人口)与城市非农业人口总数之比。计算公式为:

用水普及率＝城市用水的非农业人口数／城市非农业人口数×100%

人工煤气生产能力 指城市煤气厂制气、净化、输送等环节的综合实际生产能力。

供气管道长度 指报告期末从气源厂压缩机的出口或门站出口至各类用户引入管之间的全部已经通气投入使用的管道长度。不包括煤气生产厂、输配站、液化气储存站、灌瓶站、储配站、气化站、混气站、供应站等厂(站)内的管道。

全年供气总量 指全年燃气企业(单位)向用户供应的燃气数量。包括销售量和损失量。

城市用气普及率 指使用煤气(包括人工煤气、液化石油气、天然气)的城市非农业人口数(不包括临时人口和流动人口)与城市非农业人口总数之比。计算公式为:

城市煤气普及率＝城市用气的非农业人口数／城市非农业人口总数×100%

城市供热能力 指热电厂、热力公司和达到标准的集中采暖锅炉房向城市输送的供热源的设计能力，即每小时向城市输送蒸汽、热水的能力。

城市供热总量 指热电厂、热力公司和达到标准的集中采暖锅炉房向城市输送的全部蒸汽、热水量。

城市供热管道长度 指热电厂、热力公司和达到标准的集中采暖锅炉房管理的集中供热热源到用户之间的全部供气、供热水的管道长度。

年底实有铺装道路长度 指除土路外，路面经过铺装宽度在3.5米以上的道路，包括高级、次高级道路和普通道路。

城市桥梁 指城市范围内，修建在河道上的桥梁和道路与道路立交、道路跨越铁路的立交桥及人行天桥。包括永久性桥和半永久性桥，不包括临时性桥、铁路桥、涵洞。

城市下水道总长度 指所有排水总管、干管、支管及暗渠、检查井、连接井进出水口等长度之和。

城市污水日处理能力 指污水处理厂每昼夜处理污水量的设计能力。

年末实有公共汽(电)车 指年底可参加营运的全部车辆数，包括营运车辆数和库存查封未参加营运的车辆。不包括非营运车辆，如架线车、油罐车、工程车、货车及其他专用车辆和借入的客运车辆。

城市园林绿地面积 指城市公共绿地、专用绿地、生产绿地、防护绿地、郊区风景名胜区的全部面积。

公共绿地 指供游览休息的各种公园、动物园、植物园、陵园以及花园、游园和供游览休息用的林荫道绿地、广场绿地，不包括一般栽植的行道树及林荫道的面积。

Explanatory Notes on Main Statistical Indicators

Production Capacity of Water Supply refers to the designed comprehensive production capacity of water facilities, covering the 4 links of water collection, purification, conveyance, and outflow through trunk pipelines. Increase capacity through transformation and innovation projects are included as well. The capacity is determined mainly on the weakest of the above-mentioned 4 links.

Length of Water Supply Pipelines at the Year-end refers to the total length of all the pipelines between the water pumps and the user扭 water meters, excluding pipelines newly installed but not used yet.

Annual Volume of Water Supply refers to the total volume of water supplied by water-works (units) during the reference period, including both the effective water supply and loss during the water supply.

Consumption of Water for Residential Use refers to the water consumption of households for daily life and the water consumption of public service facilities. The latter refers to water consumption for urban public services, including the consumption of government agencies and public institutions, military barracks, public facilities, wholesale and retail outlets, restaurants, hotels, and other units providing public services. Household water consumption refers to consumption of water for daily life of all households in the boundary of cities, including households of urban residents and farmers, and public water supply stations.

Percentage of Urban Population with Access to Tap Water refers to the ratio of the urban non-agricultural population (excluing temporary and mobile population) with access to tap water to the total urban non-agricultural population.The formula is:

Percentage of Population with Access to Tap Water = Urban Non-agricultural Population with Access to Tap Water ÷Urban Non-agricultural Population×100%

Production Capacity of Gaswork Gas refers to the actual comprehensive production capaCity of the urban gasworks in gas generation, purification and delivery.

Length of Gas Pipelines refers to the total length of pipelines between the outlet of the compressor, blower or gas tank and the gas meters of users.

Volume of Gas Supply refers to the total volume of gas sold to users in a year, including the volume for industrial use, residential use and other uses.

Percentage of Urban Population with Access to Gas refers to the ratio of the urban non-agricultural population with access to gas (including gas, liquefied petroleum gas and natural gas) to the urban non-agricultural population(excluding temporary and mobile population). The formula is:

Percentage of Population with Access to Gas =Urban Non-agricultural Population with Access to Gas÷Urban Non-agricultural Population×100%

Heating Capacity in Urban Area refers to the capaCity of hourly supply of steam and hot water to cities by thermal power plants,heating corporations and centralized heating boiler rooms which meet certain standard.

Quantity of Heat Supplied in Urban Area refers to the total quantity of heat from steam and hot water supplied to cities every year by thermal power plants,heating corporations and centralized heating boiler rooms which meet certain standard.

Length of Heating Pipelines refers to the total length of pipelines for centralized supply of steam and hot water from the thermal power plants,heating corporations and centralized heating boiler rooms which meet certain standard to the users.

Length of Paved Roads at the Year-end refers to the length of roads with a paved surface, and with a width of more than 3-5 meters, including high quality,medium quality and ordinary roads.

Urban Bridges refer to bridges over river courses, great separated junctions and overpasses in urban areas.Permanent bridges and semi-permanent bridges are included.Temporary bridges,railway bridges and culverts are excluded.

Length of Urban Sewage Pipes refers to the total length of general drainage, trunks. branch and blind drainage, inspection wells, connection wells, inlets and outlets, etc.

Daily Disposal Capacity of Urban Sewage refers to the designed 24 hour capaCity of sewage disposal at the sewage treatment works.

Number of Public Vehicles (Buses and Trolley buses) at the Year-end refers to the total number of operational buses available at the year-end, including the year-end operational vehicles and vehicles in stock.Non-operational vehicles such as stringing cars,tank cars,machine shop cars,trucks and other special vehicles and the borrowed passenger vehicles are excluded.

Area of Urban Gardens and Green Areas refers to the total area of urban public green land,special green land,production green land,protection green land and suburban scenic spots.

Public Green Area refers to green areas of various parks, zoos, botanical gardens, cemeteries, amusement parks, tree-flanked boulevards greenland squares for tourism and relaxing.Areas with trees planted along-side the streets and boulevards are excluded.

第九篇
自然资源和环境保护

CHAPTER 9
Natural Resources and Environment Protection

XINJIANG STATISTICAL YEARBOOK 2008

简要说明
Brief Introduction

本篇资料的主要内容及来源

本篇主要反映新疆维吾尔自治区自然资源、自然状况及环境保护事业发展情况等资料。主要内容包括自然资源储量和自然状况及水环境、大气环境、固体废物、声环境、生态环境、自然灾害和环境污染治理投资等内容。

水资源、城市生活垃圾清运及处理、地质灾害与防治、矿产资源资料、土地资源和土地利用情况、林木资源等资料分别由新疆维吾尔自治区水利厅、建设厅、地震局、国土资源厅、林业厅提供;气象资料由新疆维吾尔自治区气象局提供。环境污染与治理、声环境、工业污染治理投资等情况由新疆维吾尔自治区环境保护局依据年报资料整理提供。

Main Content and Source of Data

This chapter contain information that reflect the natural conditions and natural resources and data on development of environment protection in Xinjiang Uygur Autonomous Region, including natural resources and natural condition, total water resources, atmosphere environment, solid wastes, environmental noise, eco-environment protection, natural disaster and investments in the treatment of environmental pollution etc.

Data on water resource, collection and disposal of urban consumption wastes, geological disasters, land use, forest resource, etc. are provided respectively by Bureau of Water Conservancy, Bureau of Construction, Seismological Bureau, Bureau of Land and Resources, Forestry Bureau in Xinjiang Uygur Autonomous Region; Meteorological data are provided by the Xinjiang Uygur Autonomous Region Meteorological Bureau. Data on environment pollution and treatment, noise monitoring and on investment in the treatment of industrial pollution are provided by the Xinjiang Environmental Protection Bureau.

9-1 自 然 资 源
Natural Resources

指　　标	Item	2007
自然状况	**State of the Nature**	
经纬度	Longitude and Latitude	
东　经	East Longitude	73°40′～96°23′
北　纬	North Latitude	34°25′～49°10′
气　候	Climate	
年平均气温(摄氏度)	Annual Average Temperature (℃)	10.9
北　疆	North Xinjiang	8.6
南　疆	South Xinjiang	13.7
东　疆	East Xinjiang	13.8
年平均降水量(毫米)	Annual Average Precipitation (mm)	165.6
北　疆	North Xinjiang	262.6
南　疆	South Xinjiang	43.8
东　疆	East Xinjiang	34.0
平均日照时数(小时)	Average Sunny Hours (hour)	2045.3
北　疆	North Xinjiang	2764.9
南　疆	South Xinjiang	2929.0
东　疆	East Xinjiang	3188.0
自然资源	**Natural Resources**	
土地资源(万公顷)	Land Resources (10 000 hectares)	
土地总面积	Total Land Area	16648.97
农用地	Land for farm use	6308.05
耕地面积	Area of Cultivated Land	411.42
园地面积	Garden Area	36.45
林地面积	Woodland Area	676.54
牧草地面积	Pastureland Area	5111.93
其他农用地	Other Land for Agriculture	71.71
建设用地	Land for Construction	123.43
未利用地	Land yet to be Used	10217.49
土地利用率(%)	Land utilization rate (%)	38.63
林木资源	Forest resources	
活立木总蓄积量(万立方米)	Total Standing Stock Volume (10 000 cu.m)	31419.68
林地蓄积量(万立方米)	Woodland Stock Volume (10 000 cu.m)	28039.68

9-1 续表 Continued

指　　标	Item	2007
有林地面积(万公顷)	Woodland Area (10 000 hectares)	180.73
灌木林地面积(万公顷)	Bush Woodland Area (10 000 hectares)	304.90
四旁树(万株)	Surrounding Woods (10 000)	23067
森林覆盖率(%)	Forest-coverage Rate (%)	2.94
水资源(亿立方米)	Water Resources (100 million cu.m)	
水资源总量	Total Water Resources Volume	953.12
地表水水资源量	Surface Water Volume	903.84
地下水水资源量	Underground Water Volume	554.13
重复计算量	Volume of Repeated Computation	504.85
主要矿产资源保有储量	**Reserve of Main Mineral Resources**	
铁矿(万吨)	Iron ore (10 000 tons)	88175.54
铬矿(万吨)	Chromium ore (10 000 tons)	178.87
铜矿(万吨)	Copper ore (10 000 tons)	244.11
铅矿(万吨)	Lead ore (10 000 tons)	88.80
锌矿(万吨)	Zinc ore (10 000 tons)	181.51
铝土矿(万吨)	Bauxite(10 000 tons)	55.32
镍矿(万吨)	Nickel ore (10 000 tons)	97.97
煤(亿吨)	Coal (100 million tons)	1726.61
耐火粘土(万吨)	Fire-proof Clay (10 000 tons)	703.40
钠硝石(万吨)	Nitratite (10 000 tons)	6169.04
芒硝(Na_2SO_4) (万吨)	Mirabilite(Na_2SO_4) (10 000 tons)	3777801.28
盐矿(NaCl) (万吨)	Solidum Salt(NaCI) (10 000 tons)	745935.57
钾盐(KCl) (万吨)	Potassium(KCl) (10 000 tons)	9205.89
石棉(万吨)	Asbest (10 000 tons)	931.26
云母(吨)	Mica (ton)	54416.87
蛭石(万吨)	Roseite (10 000 tons)	1789.32
水泥用灰岩(万吨)	Limestone Used for Cement (10 000 tons)	156300.71
澎润土(万吨)	Bentonite (10 000 tons)	36086.15
饰面用花岗岩(万立方米)	Granite as Veneer (10 000 cu.m)	11776.30

注：1.水资源为 2006 年数据。2.林木资源为 2001 年自治区森林资源第四次清查数据。
Note: a).Water-resources is based on the data in 2006.b). Figures of 2001 forest resources were form the Fourth Autonomous Region Forest Survey.

9-2 主要山脉基本情况
Main Mountain Ranges

山脉名称	Mountain Range	山峰高程(米) Height of Mountain Peak (m)	雪线高程(米) Height of Snow Line (m)	冰川面积(平方公里) Glacier Area (sq.km)	冰川储量(亿立方米) Glacier Storage (100 million cu.m)	冰川年融水量(亿立方米) Annual Glacier Melting Water Volume (100 million cu.m)
合　计	**Total**			**23020**	**21349**	**198.50**
天　山	Tianshan Mountains	7435	3600-4400	9548	10106	96.20
阿尔泰山	Altay Mountains	4374	3000-3200	290	164	3.64
喀喇昆仑山及昆仑山	Karakorum Mountains and Kunlun Mountains	8611	5100-5400	3265	14365	79.09
帕米尔	Pamirs	7579	5500-5700	2258	2487	16.25

9-3 主要湖泊基本情况
Major Lakes

湖泊名称	Lake	湖水面积(平方公里) Lake Area (sq. m)	湖面高程(米) Height of Lake Surface (m)	水质类型 Water Type
博斯腾湖	The Bosten Lake [Bagrax]	972	1048	微咸 slight salty
乌伦古湖	The Ulunggur Lake	736	468	盐 salt
赛里木湖	The Sayram Lake	454	2073	咸 alkaline
艾比湖	The Aybi Lake [Eynur]	898	189	盐 salt

9-4 主要河流基本情况
Major Rivers

(2006 年)

河流名称	River	流域面积(平方公里) Drainage Area (sq.km)	河长(公里) Length (km)	年径流量(亿立方米) Annual Flow (100 million cu.m)
玛纳斯河	Manas River	5156	190	13.15
开都河	Kaidu River	19022	530	40.33
渭干河	Ugan River	16660	256	27.62
克孜河	Kizil River	15710	233	26.83
乌伦古河	Ulunggur River	32040	821	10.41
塔里木河	Tarim River	194210	2437	57.08

9-5 主要城市平均气温
Monthly Average Temperature of Major Cities

单位：摄氏度 (2007 年) (℃)

城 市	City	一月 Jan.	二月 Feb.	三月 Mar.	四月 Apr.	五月 May	六月 June	七月 July
乌鲁木齐市	Urumqi City	-10.4	-5.0	0.4	13.6	16.4	22.4	23.9
克拉玛依市	Karamay City	-15.5	-7.9	1.6	15.5	19.6	25.4	27.4
石河子市	Shihezi City	-14.5	-6.9	1.8	15.5	19.1	24.4	25.8
阜康市	Fukang City	-15.7	-8.9	0.4	15.1	18.5	24.9	25.8
伊宁市	Yining [Gulja] City	-6.8	0.1	5.1	16.1	18.7	22.2	23.0
塔城市	Tacheng [Qoqek] City	-7.9	-3.9	0.6	13.5	16.7	22.0	23.6
阿勒泰市	Altay City	-13.4	-8.2	-2.7	11.4	15.0	20.4	22.5
博乐市	Bole [Bor tala] City	-15.5	-7.8	-0.4	13.8	17.9	22.1	24.0
库尔勒市	Korla City	-7.2	3.2	8.8	17.5	22.6	26.2	27.7
阿克苏市	Aksu City	-6.9	2.1	8.2	18.1	21.8	24.7	24.9
阿图什市	Artux City	-3.7	4.7	9.8	19.8	24.3	27.2	27.4
喀什市	Kashgar [Kaxgar] City	-3.5	4.6	9.4	19.2	23.5	26.1	26.4
和田市	Hotan City	-2.4	5.9	10.8	20.1	23.7	26.3	26.8
吐鲁番市	Turpan City	-5.5	4.2	11.6	21.9	26.8	32.3	33.6
哈密市	Hami [Kumul] City	-8.9	1.1	5.9	15.2	21.5	26.4	26.9

城 市	City	八月 Aug.	九月 Sept.	十月 Oct.	十一月 Nov.	十二月 Dec.	全年平均 Annual Average
乌鲁木齐市	Urumqi City	22.1	18.6	7.8	1.0	-9.0	8.5
克拉玛依市	Karamay City	25.3	21.2	9.7	1.5	-9.5	9.5
石河子市	Shi Hezi City	23.4	18.8	8.3	0.2	-11.5	8.7
阜康市	Fukang City	23.4	19.1	8.5	-0.1	-12.1	8.2
伊宁市	Yining [Gulja] City	22.5	17.9	8.1	4.3	-5.8	10.5
塔城市	Tacheng [Qoqek] City	22.3	18.0	7.2	2.5	-6.4	9.0
阿勒泰市	Altay City	20.4	15.8	5.4	-1.0	-10.3	6.3
博乐市	Bole [Bor tala] City	21.8	17.7	7.3	-0.2	-10.5	7.5
库尔勒市	Korla City	27.1	20.6	11.0	4.0	-3.6	13.2
阿克苏市	Aksu City	23.7	19.2	10.9	3.8	-4.2	12.2
阿图什市	Artux City	26.2	21.4	12.7	6.3	-2.3	14.5
喀什市	Kashgar [Kaxgar] City	25.2	20.3	12.1	6.0	-1.9	14.0
和田市	Hotan City	25.8	20.8	13.1	7.0	-0.7	14.8
吐鲁番市	Turpan City	30.9	24.9	13.9	4.6	-3.6	16.3
哈密市	Hami [Kumul] City	24.7	19.0	8.5	1.6	-7.2	11.2

9-6 主要城市降水量

Monthly Precipitation of Major Cities

单位：毫米 (2007 年) (milli meter)

城 市	City	一月 Jan.	二月 Feb.	三月 Mar.	四月 Apr.	五月 May	六月 June	七月 July
乌鲁木齐市	Urumqi City	17.2	11.0	7.6	33.3	107.7	16.8	107.6
克拉玛依市	Karamay City	3.3	0.8	3.7	14.7	16.4	9.0	34.7
石河子市	Shi Hezi City	11.2	6.9	7.8	28.0	57.4	23.1	24.6
阜康市	Fukang City	13.2	7.3	3.8	18.1	64.1	15.7	54.3
伊宁市	Yining [Gulja] City	21.8	4.5	26.0	19.7	52.9	46.7	49.6
塔城市	Tacheng [Qoqek] City	13.9	19.2	25.0	12.6	38.4	28.0	33.2
阿勒泰市	Altay City	3.0	5.5	7.2	11.5	22.0	16.1	52.9
博乐市	Bole [Bortala] City	7.1	9.0	3.6	5.1	58.4	19.9	50.2
库尔勒市	Korla City	0.2				2.8	0.6	23.8
阿克苏市	Aksu City			0.7		1.7	0.2	6.8
阿图什市	Artux City	0.8		4.6		1.0	20.6	2.3
喀什市	Kashgar [Kaxgar] City	0.6		2.4		2.4	10.0	1.3
和田市	Hotan City			6.3		1.1	5.3	2.1
吐鲁番市	Turpan City				1.0	1.9	0.8	3.3
哈密市	Hami [Kumul] City	1.0		1.2	8.8	7.1	1.8	29.8

城 市	City	八月 Aug.	九月 Sept.	十月 Oct.	十一月 Nov.	十二月 Dec.	全 年 Annual Total
乌鲁木齐市	Urumqi City	53.5	27.1	15.3	5.4	17.0	419.5
克拉玛依市	Karamay City	33.3	2.8	1.3		5.2	125.2
石河子市	Shihezi City	29.1	23.5	13.3	11.2	21.2	257.3
阜康市	Fukang City	57.2	23.3	16.0	4.1	14.7	291.8
伊宁市	Yining [Gulja] City	10.7	20.3	6.7	18.1	15.6	292.6
塔城市	Tacheng [Qoqek] City	19.8	1.2	8.9	30.9	17.1	248.2
阿勒泰市	Altay City	25.1	3.4	33.7	23.1	11.4	214.9
博乐市	Bole [Bortala] City	14.0	4.6	3.0		11.8	186.7
库尔勒市	Korla City	4.1	15.1	0.4			47.0
阿克苏市	Aksu City	7.5	2.8	8.6		0.8	29.1
阿图什市	Artux City	13.9	7.4	28.1		1.0	79.7
喀什市	Kashgar [Kaxgar] City	2.3	2.8	16.0		1.6	39.4
和田市	Hotan City		8.9			0.1	23.8
吐鲁番市	Turpan City	4.7	0.6				12.3
哈密市	Hami [Kumul] City	0.8	2.5	0.2		2.5	55.7

9-7 主要城市日照时数
Monthly Sunshine Hours of Major Cities

单位：小时　　(2007 年)　　(hour)

城　市	City	一月 Jan.	二月 Feb.	三月 Mar.	四月 Apr.	五月 May	六月 June	七月 July
乌鲁木齐市	Urumqi City	115.8	134.6	230.2	291.9	280.6	338.3	307.9
克拉玛依市	Karamay City	153.6	144.8	237.2	242.1	272.5	301.2	274.1
石河子市	Shi Hezi City	110.9	109.0	238.4	287.1	277.6	330.4	317.1
阜康市	Fukang City	53.1	73.8	253.7	279.4	274.4	336.1	311.4
伊宁市	Yining [Gulja] City	173.9	124.1	190.1	270.5	291.6	292.5	301.8
塔城市	Tacheng [Qoqek] City	170.1	146.3	262.0	264.5	293.7	332.2	291.6
阿勒泰市	Altay City	196.4	181.6	278.8	292.2	310.1	338.6	325.6
博乐市	Bole [Bortala] City	158.4	104.3	216.1	247.4	277.4	284.4	280.5
库尔勒市	Korla City	195.1	207.7	259.4	263.4	294.1	313.0	316.4
阿克苏市	Aksu City	219.2	199.3	210.5	219.3	287.4	288.3	258.5
阿图什市	Artux City	204.2	210.8	176.3	214.5	264.7	329.5	304.0
喀什市	Kashgar [Kaxgar] City	199.2	217.9	208.4	239.0	282.6	348.3	317.5
和田市	Hotan City	239.0	193.8	218.1	187.4	266.7	280.3	271.9
吐鲁番市	Turpan City	153.5	185.4	218.5	279.6	294.3	314.1	309.5
哈密市	Hami [Kumul] City	223.2	252.2	301.0	308.6	362.0	366.1	338.5

城　市	City	八月 Aug.	九月 Sept.	十月 Oct.	十一月 Nov.	十二月 Dec.	全　年 Annual Total
乌鲁木齐市	Urumqi City	318.2	282.9	252.9	200.8	99.3	2853.4
克拉玛依市	Karamay City	318.2	283.2	226.6	182.2	103.4	2739.1
石河子市	Shi Hezi City	334.8	294.3	249.8	192.2	109.2	2850.8
阜康市	Fukang City	310.0	273.3	239.3	181.7	47.7	2633.9
伊宁市	Yining [Gulja] City	326.9	268.7	238.6	164.8	104.6	2748.1
塔城市	Tacheng [Qoqek] City	343.4	301.1	204.9	171.0	89.6	2870.4
阿勒泰市	Altay City	347.1	289.6	187.1	175.0	115.8	3037.9
博乐市	Bole [Bortala] City	308.7	264.8	221.8	149.7	88.9	2602.4
库尔勒市	Korla City	313.5	223.3	286.9	234.2	185.3	3092.3
阿克苏市	Aksu City	268.8	257.9	285.3	244.2	178.9	2917.6
阿图什市	Artux City	281.2	233.2	262.0	225.2	128.6	2834.2
喀什市	Kashgar [Kaxgar] City	311.7	285.6	251.7	229.5	140.0	3031.4
和田市	Hotan City	185.3	225.2	248.1	259.1	194.6	2769.5
吐鲁番市	Turpan City	298.7	262.2	268.5	194.9	80.5	2859.7
哈密市	Hami [Kumul] City	347.0	292.8	276.4	241.0	207.4	3516.2

9-8 环境保护基本情况
Basic Statistics on Environmental Protection

项 目	Item	2006	2007
水环境	**Water**		
废水排放总量(亿吨)	Waste Water Discharge (100 million tons)	6.54	6.86
工业废水排放量	Industry	2.06	2.10
城镇生活废水排放量	Non-industrial	4.49	4.77
工业废水排放达标量(亿吨)	Industrial Waste Water Meeting Discharge Standards (100 million tons)	1.26	1.36
工业废水排放达标率(%)	Percentage of Industrial Waste Water Meeting Discharge Standards (%)	61.08	65.03
化学需氧量排放量(万吨)	Discharge Amount of COD (10 000 tons)	28.67	28.95
工业化学需氧量排放量	Industry	16.54	16.70
城镇生活化学需氧量排放量	Non-industrial	12.13	12.25
氨氮排放量(万吨)	Ammonia Nitrogen Discharge (10 000 tons)	2.31	2.31
工业氨氮排放量	Industry	0.46	0.42
城镇生活氨氮排放量	Non-industrial	1.85	1.89
大气环境	**Atmosphere Environment**		
工业废气排放量(亿标立方米)	Industrial Waste Air Emission (100 million cu.m)	5052.97	5797.21
燃料燃烧	Fuels Burning	3470.29	3752.28
生产工艺	Production Process	1582.68	2044.93
二氧化硫排放量(万吨)	Sulphur Dioxide Emission (10 000 tons)	54.93	57.99
工 业	Industry	42.89	47.25
生 活	Non-industrial	12.04	10.74
烟尘排放量(万吨)	Soot Emission (10 000 tons)	28.18	29.18
工 业	Industry	18.84	20.82
生 活	Non-industrial	9.34	8.36
工业粉尘排放量(万吨)	Industrial Dust Emission (10 000 tons)	17.48	18.53

9-8 续表 1 Continued

项　　目	Item	2006	2007
固体废物	**Solid Wastes**		
工业固体废物产生量(万吨)	Industrial Solid Wastes Produced (10 000 tons)	1581.23	2136.64
#危险废物	Hazardous Wastes	12.26	64.26
工业固体废物综合利用量(万吨)	Industrial Solid Wastes Utilized (10 000 tons)	751.42	1010.32
工业固体废物综合利用率(%)	Ratio of Industrial Solid Wastes Utilized (%)	47.93	47.27
工业固体废物排放量(万吨)	Industrial Solid Wastes Discharged (10 000 tons)	126.33	68.02
"三废" 综合利用产品产值(亿元)	Output Value of Products Made from Waste Gas, WasteWater & Solid Wastes (100 million yuan)	6.7	9.12
生态环境	**Eco-Environment Protection**		
当年造林面积(万公顷)	Area of Reforestation of the Year (10 000 hectares)		
自然保护区数(个)	Number of Nature Reserves (unit)	28	34
#国家级	National Level	9	9
自然保护区面积(万公顷)	Area of Nature Reserves (10 000 hectares)	2162.49	2257.60
自然保护区面积占辖区面积比重(%)	Area of Nature Reserves in Regions (%)	13.0	13.6
生态示范区数(个)	Number of Demonstration Zones of Ecology (unit)	8	8
#国家级	National Level	8	8
天然湿地面积(万公顷)	Area of Wetland (10 000 hectares)	126.74	126.74
天然湿地面积占土地总面积比重(%)	Proportion of natural wetland in Total area of Territory (%)	0.76	0.76
自然灾害	**Natural Disaster**		
发生地质灾害起数(次)	Geological Disaster (case)	46	30
#滑　坡	Landslide	30	12
崩　塌	Collapse	1	4
泥石流	Mudflow	8	9
发生地震灾害次数(次)	Seismic Disaster (case)	2	1
#5.0 级以上	Magnitude above 5 Richter scale	2	1
森林火灾次数(次)	Forest Fire (case)	35	47
森林火灾受灾面积 (公顷)	Fire-Affected Forest Area (hectare)	94.10	75.34
森林病虫害发生面积(万公顷)	Forest Area Affected by Disease and Pests (10 000 hectares)	40.01	78.71
森林病虫害防治面积(万公顷)	Forest Area Provented and Cured from Disease and Pests (10 000 hectares)	34.41	44.15
森林病虫害防治率(%)	Rate of Prevention and Cure (%)	86.00	56.10

9-8 续表 2 Continued

项　　目	Item	2006	2007
环境污染治理投资	**Investment in the Treaiment of Environmental Pollution**		
环境污染治理投资总额(万元)	Total Investment in Pollution Treatment (10 000 yuan)	318991	411676
城镇环境基础设施建设投资额	Investment in Urban Environment Infrastructure	210335	264037
#污水处理	Volume of Waste Water	5055	15608
垃圾处理	Volume of Garbage Disposal	8141	2714
燃　气	Gas Supply	74837	43689
集中供热	Central Heating	45795	70169
园林绿化	Landscape and Greening	49200	90052
工业污染治理项目年完成投资总额	Investment Completed in Industrial Pollution TreatmentProjects	45229	60138
治理废水	Waste Water	26876	29958
治理废气	Waste Gas	12036	23891
治理固体废物	Solid Wastes	2582	1676
治理噪声	Noise Pollution	32	219
治理其他	Others	3703	4394
实际执行"三同时"项目环保投资总额	Investment in "Three Simultaneity" Projects	63427	87501
治理废水	Waste Water	9654	30546
治理废气	Waste Gas	11782	23208
治理固体废物	Solid Wastes	1321	5469
治理噪声	Noise Pollution	1406	2517
其　他	Others	39264	25761
环境污染治理投资总额占新疆生产总值比重(%)	Investment in Pollution Treatment Out of XJ GDP (%)	1.05	1.18
当年施工工业污染治理项目数(个)	Number of Projects in Industrial Pollution Treatment under Construction of The Year (unit)	143	117
当年竣工工业污染治理项目数(个)	Number of Projects Completed in Industrial Pollution Treatment of the Year Projects (unit)	132	103

9-9 水资源情况
Water Resource

年份 Year	地区 Region	水资源总量(亿立方米) Total Amount Of Water Resources (100 million cu.m)	地表水资源量 Surface Water	地下水资源量 Ground Water	地下水与地下水资源重复量 Duplicated Measurement Between surface Water and Groundwater	人均水资源量(立方米/人) Per Capita Water Resources (cu.m/person)
	2000	952.40	897.10	636.29	580.99	5255
	2001	1024.40	966.90	692.31	634.81	5500
	2002	1068.60	1006.00	724.85	662.25	5652
	2003	920.10	863.20	604.30	547.40	4793
	2004	855.40	809.20	502.60	456.40	4390
	2005	962.82	910.66	562.57	510.41	4789
	2006	953.12	903.84	554.13	504.85	4695
乌鲁木齐市	Urumqi City	9.52	9.18	5.15	4.81	481
克拉玛依市	Karamay City	0.42	0.05	1.14	0.77	162
石河子市	Shihezi City	0.12	0.05	0.76	0.69	19
吐鲁番地区	Turpan Administrative Offices	7.82	5.90	7.31	5.39	1332
哈密地区	Hami [Kumul] Administrative Offices	13.20	10.86	8.32	5.98	2441
昌吉回族自治州	Changji Hui Autonomous Prefecture	33.99	30.09	20.62	16.72	2139
伊犁州直属县(市)	Counties (Cities) Direct Under Ili Prefecture	166.30	163.00	84.83	81.53	6363
塔城地区	Tacheng [Tarbagatai] Administrative Offices	65.18	61.04	38.81	34.67	6700
阿勒泰地区	Altay Administrative Offices	111.77	107.20	46.20	41.63	17629
博尔塔拉蒙古自治州	Bortala Mongol Autonomous Prefecture	31.28	28.97	17.43	15.12	6781
巴音郭楞蒙古自治州	Bayangol Mongol Autonomous Prefecture	143.68	137.10	79.29	72.71	12175
阿克苏地区	Aksu Administrative Offices	72.10	65.44	77.44	70.78	3152
克孜勒苏柯尔克孜自治州	Kizilsu Kirgiz Autonomous Prefecture	72.78	71.58	38.83	37.63	15156
喀什地区	Kashgar [Kaxgar] Administrative Offices	93.96	88.38	70.48	64.90	2520
和田地区	Hotan Administrative Offices	131.00	125.00	57.52	51.52	7114

9-10 供水用水情况
Water Supply and Water Used

单位：亿立方米 (2006 年) (100 million cu.m)

年 份 Year	地 区 Region	供水总量 Water Supply	地表水 Surface Water	地下水 Ground Water	其 他 Others	用水总量 Water Used	生 产 Production
总 计	**Total**	**513.73**	**454.00**	**58.93**	**0.80**	**513.73**	**483.66**
乌鲁木齐市	Urumqi City	9.22	5.77	2.87	0.58	9.22	7.62
克拉玛依市	Karamay City	4.69	4.30	0.29	0.10	4.69	2.49
石河子市	Shihezi City	16.54	13.13	3.41		16.54	15.93
吐鲁番地区	Turpan Administrative Offices	11.40	5.95	5.45		11.40	11.06
哈密地区	Hami [Kumul] Administrative Offices	10.87	4.79	6.08		10.87	10.36
昌吉回族自治州	Changji Hui Autonomous Prefecture	32.31	18.79	13.45	0.07	32.31	31.82
伊犁州直属县(市)	Counties (Cities) Direct Under Ili Prefecture	53.58	50.98	2.60		53.58	52.82
塔城地区	Tacheng [Tarbagatai] Administrative Offices	21.17	15.88	5.29		21.07	19.15
阿勒泰地区	Altay Administrative Offices	43.39	43.23	0.11	0.05	43.39	33.74
博尔塔拉蒙古自治州	Bortala Mongol Autonomous Prefecture	13.78	10.36	3.42		13.78	13.64
巴音郭楞蒙古自治州	Bayangol Mongol Autonomous Prefecture	42.47	38.57	3.90		42.57	36.81
阿克苏地区	Aksu Administrative Offices	99.20	95.81	3.39		99.20	98.62
克孜勒苏柯尔克孜自治州	Kizilsu Kirgiz Autonomous Prefecture	7.69	6.89	0.80		7.69	7.51
喀什地区	Kashgar [Kaxgar] Administrative Offices	106.92	101.44	5.48		106.92	104.86
和田地区	Hotan Administrative Offices	40.50	38.11	2.39		40.50	37.23

年 份 Year	地 区 Region	第一产业 Primary Industry	第二产业 Secondary Industry	第三产业 Tertiary Industry	居民生活 Consumption	生态环境 Biological Protection	人均用水量(立方米/人) Per Capita Water Used (cu · m/person)
总 计	**Total**	**471.44**	**10.59**	**1.63**	**5.87**	**24.20**	**2530**
乌鲁木齐市	Urumqi City	5.94	1.41	0.27	1.33	0.27	466
克拉玛依市	Karamay City	1.49	0.96	0.04	0.19	2.01	1813
石河子市	Shihezi City	14.76	0.97	0.20	0.27	0.34	2576
吐鲁番地区	Turpan Administrative Offices	10.59	0.42	0.05	0.16	0.18	1942
哈密地区	Hami [Kumul] Administrative Offices	9.73	0.58	0.05	0.17	0.34	2010
昌吉回族自治州	Changji Hui Autonomous Prefecture	30.35	1.27	0.20	0.40	0.09	2033
伊犁州直属县(市)	Counties (Cities) Direct Under Ili Prefecture	51.45	1.26	0.11	0.62	0.14	2050
塔城地区	Tacheng [Tarbagatai] Administrative Offices	18.61	0.45	0.09	0.26	1.66	2166
阿勒泰地区	Altay Administrative Offices	33.39	0.25	0.10	0.15	9.50	6844
博尔塔拉蒙古自治州	Bortala Mongol Autonomous Prefecture	13.44	0.15	0.05	0.13	0.01	2987
巴音郭楞蒙古自治州	Bayangol Mongol Autonomous Prefecture	36.00	0.70	0.11	0.34	5.42	3607
阿克苏地区	Aksu Administrative Offices	97.44	1.08	0.10	0.53	0.05	4337
克孜勒苏柯尔克孜自治州	Kizilsu Kirgiz Autonomous Prefecture	7.43	0.06	0.02	0.12	0.06	1601
喀什地区	Kashgar [Kaxgar] Administrative Offices	103.97	0.74	0.15	0.88	1.18	2868
和田地区	Hotan Administrative Offices	36.85	0.29	0.09	0.32	2.95	2199

9-11 环保系统机构、人员数

Number of Environmental Protection Agencies and Persons Engaged

年 份 Year	机构数 (个) Number of Agencies (unit)	人员数 (人) Total Number of Staff & Workers (person)	#科技人员 Scientific and Technical Personnel	#监测人员 Monitoring Personnel	#监察人员 Supervising and Administrative Personnel
2000	208	1965	110	654	416
2001	208	2096	109	636	420
2002	238	2386	99	692	523
2003	275	2588	107	766	671
2004	288	2694	107	763	701
2005	304	2796	120	758	790
2006	326	2968	125	777	923
2007	326	2962	77	786	955

9-12 自然保护区基本情况

Basic Situation of Natural Protection

年 份 Year	自然保护区 Nature Reserves			国家级生态示范区 National-level Ecological Demonstration Zones		
	个 数 (个) Number (unit)	面 积 (万公顷) Area (10 000hectares)	占辖区面积比重 (%) Percentage of Nature Reserves in the Region (%)	个 数 (个) Number (unit)	面 积 (万公顷) Area (10 000 hectares)	占辖区面积比重 (%) Percentage of Ecdogical Demonstration Zones in the Region (%)
2000	23	1594.05	9.6	5	869.08	5.2
2001	26	2042.40	12.3	7	1105.50	6.6
2002	26	2042.40	12.3	7	1105.50	6.6
2003	26	2042.40	12.3	8	1105.96	6.6
2004	26	2042.40	12.3	8	1105.96	6.6
2005	28	2183.49	13.1	8	1275.86	7.7
2006	28	2162.49	13.0	8	1275.86	7.7
2007	34	2257.60	13.6	8	1275.86	7.7

注：2007 年,自然保护区包括兵团及地县级保护区。

Note: In 2007,natural reserve include reserve of Xinjiang prodution and construction Group and cities at country level.

9-13 环境污染与破坏事故情况
Environment Pollution and Destruction Accidents

年份 Year	环境污染与破坏事故次数(次) Number of Pollution andDestruction Accidents (times)	水污染 Water Pollution	大气污染 Air Pollution	固体废物 Solid Wastes Pollution	噪声与振动危害 Noise and Vibration Pollution	其 他 Others	污染直接经济损失(万元) Direct Economic Losses (10 000yuan)	污染事故赔、罚款总额(万元) Reparations and Fines on Pollution Accidents (10 000 yuan)
2000	9	3	3	1		2	16.0	26.7
2001	5	5					13.2	13.3
2002	21	10	6		4	1	29.6	61.0
2003	7	4		1		2	156.2	12.0
2004	13	10	1			2	111.2	102.4
2005	5	5					41.6	41.6
2006	3	1				2	23.0	68.6

注：2007 年，全区未发生较大环境污染和破坏事故,故无数据。
Note: In 2007,serious pollution auidents were not oaurred,so there is no data in this table.

9-14 环境污染治理投资
Investment in the Treatment of Environment Pollution

项 目	Item	2006	2007
环境污染治理投资总额(亿元)	**Total Investment in the Treatment of Environment Pollution (100 million yuan)**	**31.90**	**41.17**
城镇环境基础设施建设投资	Investment in Urban Environment Infrastructure Facilities	21.04	26.40
#污水处理	Volume of Waste Water	0.51	1.56
垃圾处理	Volume of Garbage Disposal	0.81	0.27
燃 气	Gas Supply	7.48	4.37
集中供热	Centralized Heating	4.58	7.02
园林绿化	Gardening and Greening	4.92	9.01
工业污染源治理投资	Investment in the Treatment of Industrial Pollution	4.52	6.01
建设项目“三同时”环保投资	“Three Simultaneities” Environmental Investment for New Project	6.34	8.75
环境污染治理投资总额占新疆生产总值比重(%)	**Investment in the Treatment of Environmental Pollution as Percent of GDP (%)**	**1.05**	**1.18**

9-15 工业污染治理投资完成情况
Investment Completed in the Treatment of Industrial Pollution

年 份 Year	汇总工业企业数(个) Number of Industrial Enterprises (unit)	污染治理项目本年完成投资(万元) Investment In the Treatment of Industrial Pollution (10 000 yuan)	治理废水 Treatment of Waste Water	治理废气 Treatment of Waste Gas	治理固体废物 Treatment of Solid Waste	治理噪声 Treatment of Noise Pollution	治理其他 Treatment of Other Pollution	本年施工项目数(个) Projects Under Construction (unit)	本年竣工项目数(个) Projects Completed (unit)
2000	154	22311	8528	9116	349	4109	209	203	198
2001	113	32009	25917	4886	723	66	416	113	106
2002	89	16952	5015	8241	2206	261	1229	129	85
2003	83	26509	9298	9514	4865	21	2811	104	94
2004	94	29622	12334	13114	2756	92	1327	146	110
2005	97	44008	23549	9656	371	321	10111	162	153
2006	92	45229	26876	12036	2582	32	3703	143	132
2007	90	60138	29958	23891	1676	219	4394	117	103

9-16 工业污染治理投资来源
Source of Investment in the Treatment of Industrial Pollution

单位：万元 (10 000 yuan)

项 目	Item	2006	2007
施工项目本年投资来源	Source of Current Investment	45229	60138
排污费补助	Pollution Charges Subsidies	824	8139
政府其他补助	Other Government Subsidies	1328	330
企业自筹	Self-raising Funds	43077	51669
#银行贷款	Bank Loans	3055	100

9-17 分行业重点调查企业工业废水及污染物排放量

Discharge of Industrial Waste Water and Pollutants in Major Investigated Enterprises by Sector

(2007 年)

行业	Sector	工业废水排放量(万吨) Volume Of Waste Water Discharged (10 000 tons)	工业废水中化学需氧量排放量(吨) COD Discharge From Industral WasteWater (ton)	工业废水中氨氮排放量(吨) Ammonia Nitrogen Discharge Form Industrial Waste Water (ton)	工业废水排放达标量(万吨) Industrial WasteWater Meeting Discharge Standards (10 000 tons)
合　计	**Total**	**30056.71**	**277332**	**5856**	**21206.06**
煤炭开采和洗选业	Mining and Washing of Coal	1212.87	2984	184	1186.27
石油和天然气开采业	Extraction of Petroleum and Natural Gas	1382.17	1689	220	1363.38
农副食品加工业	Processing of Food from Agricultural Products	1233.49	27368	319	182.47
食品制造业	Food Manufacturing	733.72	3886	192	262.17
饮料制造业	Beverage Manufacturing	207.24	1845	43	89.90
纺织业	Textile Industry	304.95	1975	26	227.91
造纸及纸制品业	Paper and Paper Products Manufacturing	2033.92	60004	439	1101.15
化学原料及化学制品制造业	Raw Chemical Material and Chemical Products	1453.62	2186	346	1031.49
化学纤维制造业	Chemical Fiber Manufacturing	1640.80	32412	85	1080.80
黑色金属冶炼及压延加工业	Smelting and Pressing of Ferrous Metals	2282.70	2517	668	2007.20
其他行业	Ohters	17571.23	140466	3334	12673.32

9-18 分行业重点调查企业工业废气及污染物排放量

Emission of Industrial Waste Gas and Pollutants in Major Investigated Enterprises by Sector

单位：吨　　(2007 年)　　(ton)

行业	Sector	工业废气排放总量(亿标立方米) Total Volume of Industrial Waste Gas Emission (100 million cu.m)	工业二氧化硫排放量 Volume of Sulphur Dioxide Emission by Industry	工业烟尘排放量 Volume of Industrial Soot Emission	工业粉尘排放量 Volume of Industrial Dust Emission	工业废气污染物排放达标量 Industrial Waste Gas Meeting Discharge Standards
合　计	**Total**	**5102.40**	**418082**	**177357**	**157471**	**603966**
煤炭开采和洗选业	Mining and Washing of Coal	39.29	5349	4508	9772	6430
黑色金属矿采选业	Processing of Ferrous Metals Ores	89.20	13586	755	12465	21849
有色金属矿采选业	Processing of Nonferrous Metals Ores	8.67	40099	374	2195	140
农副产品加工业	Processing of Food from Agricultural Products	55.83	6080	2496	3238	5162
石油加工炼焦及核燃料加工业	Oil Processing, Coking and Nuclear Fuel Processing	475.52	53050	15799	4276	79856
化学原料及化学制品制造业	Raw Chemical Material and Chemical Products	284.73	20650	7378	2281	28875
非金属矿物制品业	Nonmetal Mineral Products Manufacturing	848.03	20998	41384	104449	82153
黑色金属冶炼及压延加工业	Smelting and Pressing of Ferrous Metals	859.53	24249	4042	15059	33787
有色金属冶炼及压延加工业	Smelting and Pressing of Nonferrous Metals	157.05	20513	4027	209	3875
电力、热力的生产和供应业	Electricity and Thermal Production and Supply	1819.36	195919	86086	485	313966
其他行业	Ohters	465.19	17589	10508	3042	27873

9-19 分行业重点调查企业固体废物产生量及处理利用

Production,Treatment and Utilization of Solid Wastes in Major Investigated Enterprises by Sector

单位：万吨 (2007 年) (10 000 tons)

行业	Sector	工业固体废物产生量 Volume of Industrial SolidWastes Produced	工业固体废物综合利用量 Volume of Industrial SolidWastes Utilized	工业固体废物贮存量 Volume of Industrial SolidWastes in Stocks	工业固体废物处置量 Volume of Industrial SolidWastes Treated	工业固体废物排放量 Volume of Industrial SolidWastes Discharged
合 计	**Total**	**1834.09**	**871.00**	**689.01**	**218.20**	**56.86**
煤炭开采和洗选业	Mining and Washing of Coal	182.92	110.54	55.17	14.19	3.21
黑色金属矿采选业	Processing of Ferrous Metals Ores	301.58	104.72	159.13	7.52	30.71
有色金属矿采选业	Processing of Nonferrous Metals Ores	387.65	26.63	297.34	63.59	0.15
食品制造业	Food Manufacturing	5.47	4.07		1.12	0.28
造纸及纸制品业	Paper and Paper Products Manufacturing	5.35	4.86		0.12	0.38
化学原料及化学制品制造业	Raw Chemical Material and Chemical Products	120.67	78.78	16.75	24.22	0.92
塑料制品业	Manufacture of Plastic Products	0.08				0.08
非金属矿物制品业	Nonmetal Mineral Products Manufacturing	75.83	53.15	4.02	1.58	17.07
工艺品及其他制造业	Art Work and Other Manufacturing Sector	0.19	0.07			0.12
电力、热力的生产和供应业	Electricity and Thermal Production and Supply	341.98	215.23	76.42	46.56	3.80
其他行业	Ohters	412.37	272.95	80.18	59.30	0.14

9-20 主要城市空气质量指标

Ambient Air Quality in Main Cities

单位:毫克/立方米 (2007 年) (milligram/cu.m)

城市	City	可吸入颗粒物 (PM10) Paticulate Matters	二氧化硫 (SO_2)	二氧化氮 (NO_2)	空气质量达到及好于二级的天数(天) Days of Air Quality Equal to or Above Grade II (days)
乌鲁木齐市	Urumqi City	0.137	0.088	0.067	252
克拉玛依市	Karamay City	0.066	0.014	0.036	363
石河子市	Shihezi City	0.069	0.028	0.019	353
吐鲁番市	Turpan City	0.115	0.011	0.015	308
哈 密 市	Hami [Kumul] City	0.075	0.009	0.030	327
昌 吉 市	Changji City	0.103	0.020	0.025	316
阜 康 市	Fukang City	0.100			304
奎 屯 市	Kuytun City	0.081	0.005	0.019	328
伊 宁 市	Yining [Gulja] City	0.087	0.035	0.031	349
塔 城 市	Tacheng [Qoqek] City	0.047	0.005	0.010	360
乌 苏 市	Usu City	0.076	0.007	0.021	316
阿勒泰市	Altay City	0.025	0.003	0.010	362
博 乐 市	Bole [Bortala] City	0.065	0.004	0.005	361
库尔勒市	Korla City	0.120	0.019	0.039	293
阿克苏市	Aksu City	0.193	0.028	0.038	220
阿图什市	Artux City	0.199	0.009	0.001	213
喀 什 市	Kashgar [Kaxgar] City	0.137			286
和 田 市	Hotan City	0.234	0.035	0.027	145

9-21 主要城市道路交通噪声监测情况
Monitoring of Urban Road Traffic Noise in Key Cities

(2007 年)

城市	City	路段总长度 (米) Total Length of Roads (m)	超标路段 (米) Roads with Excess Noise (m)	路段超标率 (%) Percentage of Roads with Excess Noise (%)	路段平均宽度 (米) Average Width of Roads (m)	平均车流量 (辆/小时) AverageTraffic Volume (car/hour)	噪声均值 (LeqdBA) Average NoiseValue (LeqdBA)
乌鲁木齐市	Urumqi City	209580	116970	55.8	43.0	2202	70.0
克拉玛依市	Karamay City	452000	29500	6.5	17.7	754	65.8
石河子市	Shihezi City	45600	4200	9.2	16.5	871	66.4
吐鲁番市	Turpan City	31236	6830	21.9	18.5	745	68.2
哈密市	Hami [Kumul] City	15100	4400	29.1	25.6	1409	68.5
昌吉市	Changji City	48500			17.9	386	59.1
奎屯市	Kuytun City	7225	2210	30.6	18.4	819	68.5
伊宁市	Yining [Gulja] City	73310	1850	2.5	17.3	1200	66.4
塔城市	Tacheng [Qoqek] City	10520			24.7	609	60.5
阿勒泰市	Altay City	43110	17605	40.8	14.9	512	68.0
博乐市	Bole [Bortala] City	16620	750	4.5	17.3	170	60.1
库尔勒市	Korla City	33518	6051	18.1	43.6	1625	67.6
阿克苏市	Aksu City	32750	17424	53.2	21.5	1023	70.3
阿图什市	Artux City	16100	3800	23.6	35.0	563	67.8
喀什市	Kashgar [Kaxgar] City	32560	4720	14.5	24.0	1907	64.6
和田市	Hotan City	27310	18360	67.2	40.5	1099	71.8

9-22 国控主要城市区域环境噪声监测情况
Monitoring of Urban Environment Noise in Major Cities under National Control Programme

(2007 年)

城市	City	网格长度 (米) Grid Length (m)	网格宽度 (米) Grid Width (m)	网格总数 (个) Total number of Grids (unit)	等效声级 (LeqdBA) Sound Level (LeqdBA)
乌鲁木齐市	Urumqi City	750	750	209	54.7
克拉玛依市	Karamay City	317	317	111	53.2
石河子市	Shihezi City	250	250	267	54.1
吐鲁番市	Turpan City	300	300	110	48.2
哈密市	Hami [Kumul] City	500	500	100	52.2
昌吉市	Changji City	400	400	194	52.1
奎屯市	Kuytun City	400	400	102	48.8
伊宁市	Yining [Gulja] City	500	500	108	46.9
塔城市	Tacheng [Qoqek] City	250	250	106	52.3
阿勒泰市	Altay City	250	250	123	53.6
博乐市	Bole [Bortala] City	250	250	140	51.4
库尔勒市	Korla City	500	500	292	51.8
阿克苏市	Aksu City	500	500	110	55.2
阿图什市	Artux City	250	250	110	60.4
喀什市	Kashgar [Kaxgar] City	250	250	97	52.5
和田市	Hotan City	250	250	134	58.4

9-23 各地区城市生活垃圾清运和处理情况
Collection, Transport and Disposal of Consumption Wastes in Cities by Region

(2007 年)

地　　区	Region	生活垃圾清运量（万吨）Consumption Wastes Collected and Transported (10 000 tons)	无害化处理厂数（座）Number of Factories for Wastes Treatment (unit)	#卫生填埋 Landfill	无害化处理能力（吨/日）Treatment Capacity (ton/day)	#卫生填埋 Landfill
总　计	**Total**	**340.19**	**9**	**9**	**3238**	**3238**
乌鲁木齐市	Urumqi City	141.60	1	1	2000	2000
克拉玛依市	Karamay City	12.81	3	3	450	450
吐鲁番市	Turpan City	10.70				
哈 密 市	Hami [Kumul] City	13.20				
昌 吉 市	Changji City	14.00	1	1	450	450
阜 康 市	Fukang City	3.69				
伊 宁 市	Yining [Gulja] City	24.60				
奎 屯 市	Kuytun City	3.70	1	1	198	198
塔 城 市	Tacheng [Qoqek] City	8.50				
乌 苏 市	Usu City	7.40				
阿勒泰市	Altay City	3.99	1	1	140	140
博 乐 市	Bole [Bortala] City	9.10				
库尔勒市	Korla City	27.30	1	1		
阿克苏市	Aksu City	10.30				
阿图什市	Artux City	3.00				
喀 什 市	Kashgar [Kaxgar] City	18.25				
和 田 市	Hotan City	7.54	1	1		
石河子市	Shihezi City	14.42				
阿拉尔市	Aral City	3.00				
图木舒克市	Tumxuk City	0.19				
五家渠市	Wujiaqu City	2.90				

注：1.表中无害化处理数据均为二级以上无害化处理厂数据。
　　2.本表数据由自治区建设厅提供。

9-23 续表 Continued

地区	Region	无害化处理量（万吨） Volume of Wastes Disposed (10 000 tons)	#卫生填埋 Landfill	粪便清运量（万吨） Collection and Transport of Excrement and Urine (10 000 tons)	粪便处理量（万吨） Disposal of Excrement and Urine (10 000 tons)	生活垃圾无害化处理率(%) Treatment Rate of Consumption Wastes (%)
总　计	**Total**	**95.79**	**95.79**	**20.11**	**3.40**	**28.16**
乌鲁木齐市	Urumqi City	39.68	39.68	1.21		28.02
克拉玛依市	Karamay City	9.61	9.61	0.50		75.02
吐鲁番市	Turpan City					
哈 密 市	Hami [Kumul] City					
昌 吉 市	Changji City	14.00	14.00	14.70	0.70	100.00
阜 康 市	Fukang City					
伊 宁 市	Yining [Gulja] City			1.00		
奎 屯 市	Kuytun City	3.70	3.70			100.00
塔 城 市	Tacheng [Qoqek] City					
乌 苏 市	Usu City			2.70	2.70	
阿勒泰市	Altay City	3.90	3.90			97.74
博 乐 市	Bole [Bortala] City					
库尔勒市	Korla City	18.80	18.80			68.86
阿克苏市	Aksu City					
阿图什市	Artux City					
喀 什 市	Kashgar [Kaxgar] City					
和 田 市	Hotan City	6.10	6.10			80.90
石河子市	Shihezi City					
阿拉尔市	Aral City					
图木舒克市	Tumxuk City					
五家渠市	Wujiaqu City					

Note: a) Data on wastes disposed are provided by secondary and above factories for wastes treatment.
b) Data on this table are provided by Xinjiang Bureau of Construction.

9-24 地质灾害及防治情况
Geological Disasters and Prevention and Cure

年 份 Year	地 区 Region	发生地质灾害起数(次) Geological Disasters (case)	滑 坡 Land-slide	崩 塌 Collapse	泥石流 Mud-rock Flow	地面塌陷 Land Subside
	2000	10	2	1	6	1
	2005	91	28	12	48	3
	2007	30	12	4	9	5
乌鲁木齐市	Urumqi City	1				1
克拉玛依市	Karamay City					
石河子市	Shihezi City					
吐鲁番地区	Turpan Administrative Offices					
哈密地区	Hami [Kumul] Administrative Offices	1		1		
昌吉回族自治州	Changji Hui Autonomous Prefecture	3	3			
伊犁州直属县(市)	Counties (Cities) Direct Under Ili Prefecture	16	8	3	5	
塔城地区	Tacheng [Tarbagatai] Administrative Offices	5			3	2
阿勒泰地区	Altay Administrative Offices					
博尔塔拉蒙古自治州	Bortala Mongol Autonomous Prefecture	1	1			
巴音郭楞蒙古自治州	Bayangol Mongol Autonomous Prefecture					
阿克苏地区	Aksu Administrative Offices					
克孜勒苏柯尔克孜自治州	Kizilsu Kirgiz Autonomous Prefecture					
喀什地区	Kashgar [Kaxgar] Administrative Offices	3			1	2
和田地区	Hotan Administrative Offices					

年 份 Year	地 区 Region	人员伤亡(人) Casualties (person)	#死亡人数 Deaths	直接经济损失(万元) Direct Economic Loss (10 000 yuan)	地质灾害防治 Projects of prevention of Geological Disasters	
					项目数(个) Projects (unit)	投资(万元) Investment (10 000 yuan)
	2000	8	8	1000		
	2005	5	2	384	12	238
	2007	11	9	310	38	1665
乌鲁木齐市	Urumqi City	2		40	3	347
克拉玛依市	Karamay City					
石河子市	Shihezi City					
吐鲁番地区	Turpan Administrative Offices				2	132
哈密地区	Hami [Kumul] Administrative Offices					
昌吉回族自治州	Changji Hui Autonomous Prefecture	7	7	6	2	53
伊犁州直属县(市)	Counties (Cities) Direct Under Ili Prefecture	2	2	44	6	321
塔城地区	Tacheng [Tarbagatai] Administrative Offices			80	3	202
阿勒泰地区	Altay Administrative Offices				2	82
博尔塔拉蒙古自治州	Bortala Mongol Autonomous Prefecture			134		
巴音郭楞蒙古自治州	Bayangol Mongol Autonomous Prefecture				2	44
阿克苏地区	Aksu Administrative Offices				6	189
克孜勒苏柯尔克孜自治州	Kizilsu Kirgiz Autonomous Prefecture				2	93
喀什地区	Kashgar [Kaxgar] Administrative Offices			6	3	53
和田地区	Hotan Administrative Offices				7	149

9-25 各地区土地利用情况
Land Use by Region

单位:万公顷 (10 000 hectares)

年份 地区 Year Region	土地调查面积 Area under Land Survey	农用地 Land for Agriculture Use	#园地 Garden Land	#牧草地 Grazing and Pasture Land	建设用地 Land for Construction	居民点及工矿用地 Land for Living Quarters, Mining and Manufacturing Sites	交通用地 Land for Transport Facilities	水利设施用地 Land for Water Conservancy Facilities
2000	16648.97	6346.21	19.22	5136.05	154.38	88.69	22.30	43.39
2001	16648.97	6295.64	19.68	5135.35	112.11	88.88	5.25	17.98
2002	16648.97	6297.36	22.21	5135.75	118.20	94.63	5.49	18.08
2003	16648.97	6301.54	29.58	5131.49	119.96	96.12	5.76	18.08
2004	16648.97	6304.57	33.59	5121.58	121.05	97.02	5.89	18.14
2005	16648.97	6306.07	35.43	5116.07	122.07	97.62	6.12	18.33
2006	16648.97	6307.61	36.37	5112.47	122.66	98.15	6.16	18.35
2007	16648.97	6308.05	36.45	5111.92	123.43	98.86	6.21	18.36
乌鲁木齐市 Urumqi City	151.73	122.65	0.36	104.24	5.54	4.67	0.42	0.45
克拉玛依市 Karamay City	86.54	36.00	0.04	23.13	6.42	5.85	0.35	0.22
石河子市 Shihezi City	4.60	3.46	0.07	0.61	0.60	0.55	0.05	
吐鲁番地区 Turpan Administrative Offices	675.63	84.29	2.19	72.97	2.93	2.47	0.35	0.11
哈密地区 Hami [Kumul] Administrative Offices	1420.95	443.02	1.34	374.22	18.54	17.92	0.50	0.12
昌吉回族自治州 Changji Hui Autonomous Prefecture	738.50	571.10	0.85	471.69	10.39	8.93	0.63	0.83
伊犁州直属县(市) Counties (Cities) Direct Under Ili Prefecture	563.82	476.16	2.11	360.57	9.12	8.29	0.50	0.33
塔城地区 Tacheng [Tarbagatai] Administrative Offices	946.98	765.28	0.56	643.22	9.86	8.12	0.52	1.22
阿勒泰地区 Altay Administrative Offices	1176.99	1069.71	0.04	962.98	4.40	3.06	0.31	1.03
博尔塔拉蒙古自治州 Bortala Mongol Autonomous Prefecture	249.34	192.61	0.36	159.74	2.21	1.91	0.18	0.12
巴音郭楞蒙古自治州 Bayangol Mongol Autonomous Prefecture	4709.54	970.85	7.44	824.32	11.34	8.86	0.84	1.64
阿克苏地区 Aksu Administrative Offices	1313.41	542.42	6.34	403.71	12.60	7.95	0.39	4.26
克孜勒苏柯尔克孜自治州 Kizilsu Kirgiz Autonomous Prefecture	724.68	324.75	0.63	298.11	1.54	1.20	0.16	0.18
喀什地区 Kashgar [Kaxgar] Administrative Offices	1394.80	302.41	10.55	160.61	18.59	13.06	0.53	5.00
和田地区 Hotan Administrative Offices	2491.46	403.34	3.57	251.80	9.35	6.02	0.48	2.85

9-26 造林面积
Area of Afforestation

单位:公顷 (hectare)

年份 地区 Year Region	造林总面积 Total Area of Afforestation	按造林方式分 By Approach 人工造林 Manual Planting	飞机播种 Airplane Planting	无林地和疏林地新封 Woodless Area and Dispersive Woodland	按林种用途分 By Function of Forest 用材林 Timber Forests	经济林 By-product Forests	防护林 Protection Forests	薪炭林 Fuel Forests	特种用途林 Forests for Special Purpose
2000	64173	63793	200		1605	44564	16512	1012	480
2001	106771	106771			2149	78203	24536	1424	459
2002	216924	216924			3034	78302	134723	706	159
2003	263781	253781	10000		10152	59777	191380	2390	82
2004	176540	176540			3897	73103	96897	2638	5
2005	136990	130323	6667		3226	40523	92449	738	54
2006	97424	97424			1780	38495	56548	588	13
2007	146632	124642		21990	2991	71667	71325	589	60
乌鲁木齐市 Urumqi City	1845	1078		767			1845		
克拉玛依市 Karamay City	483	483				46	437		
石河子市 Shihezi City	203	203				133	70		
吐鲁番地区 Turpan Administrative Offices	8600	8600			1	7103	1496		
哈密地区 Hami [Kumul] Administrative Offices	5367	5367				2667	2700		
昌吉回族自治州 Changji Hui Autonomous Prefecture	15100	9767		5333	292	2001	12807		
伊犁州直属县(市) Counties (Cities) Direct Under Ili Prefecture	8073	8073			2025	2600	3447		1
塔城地区 Tacheng [Tarbagatai] Administrative Offices	6589	6589			13	392	6184		
阿勒泰地区 Altay Administrative Offices	10045	8312		1733	55	21	9969		
博尔塔拉蒙古自治州 Bortala Mongol Autonomous Prefecture	654	654				168	486		
巴音郭楞蒙古自治州 Bayangol Mongol Autonomous Prefecture	13297	5766		7531	344	3831	9122		
阿克苏地区 Aksu Administrative Offices	25567	25567				16117	9450		
克孜勒苏柯尔克孜自治州 Kizilsu Kirgiz Autonomous Prefecture	3694	2694		1000	161	351	3182		
喀什地区 Kashgar [Kaxgar] Administrative Offices	36982	33249		3733		31648	5190	144	
和田地区 Hotan Administrative Offices	8736	8069		667	100	4589	3602	445	
自治区林业厅 Xinjiang Forestry Bureau	1397	171		1226			1338		59

9-27 林业重点工程造林面积

Area of Key Afforestation Projects

单位:公顷 (hectare)

年份 Year	地区 Region	造林总面积 Total Area of Afforestation	退耕还林工程 Grain for Green Projects	三北及长江流域等防护林工程 Protection Forests in North China and Yangtze River Basin
	2001	102317	13173	
	2002	199324	113010	
	2003	235924	175314	
	2004	152967	82838	70129
	2005	133778	62457	71321
	2006	88744	38160	50584
	2007	138700	32926	105774
乌鲁木齐市	Urumqi City	1845	333	1512
克拉玛依市	Karamay City	468		468
吐鲁番地区	Turpan Administrative Offices	8377	1260	7117
哈密地区	Hami [Kumul] Administrative Offices	5367	1133	4234
昌吉回族自治州	Changji Hui Autonomous Prefecture	14154	4452	9702
伊犁州直属县(市)	Counties (Cities) Direct Under Ili Prefecture	5609	2323	3286
塔城地区	Tacheng [Tarbagatai] Administrative Offices	6589	5211	1378
阿勒泰地区	Altay Administrative Offices	9379	7010	2369
博尔塔拉蒙古自治州	Bortala Mongol Autonomous Prefecture	654		654
巴音郭楞蒙古自治州	Bayangol Mongol Autonomous Prefecture	13272	870	12402
阿克苏地区	Aksu Administrative Offices	25567	8000	17567
克孜勒苏柯尔克孜自治州	Kizilsu Kirgiz Autonomous Prefecture	3361	2334	1027
喀什地区	Kashgar [Kaxgar] Administrative Offices	36649		36649
和田地区	Hotan Administrative Offices	7409		7409

9-28 各地区天然湿地面积
Area of Wetlands by Region

单位:百公顷 (2007 年) (100 hectare)

地区 Region	天然湿地面积 Area of Natural Wetlands	河流 Rivers	湖泊 Lakes	沼泽 Marshland	天然湿地面积占土地总面积比重(%) Proportion of Natural Wetlands in Total Area of Territory(%)
总计 Total	**12673.70**	**4733.00**	**4763.92**	**3176.78**	**0.76**
乌鲁木齐市 Urumqi City	75.58	21.62	39.37	14.59	0.50
克拉玛依市 Karamay City	214.69	23.59	154.59	36.51	2.48
石河子市 Shihezi City	4.92	4.77		0.15	1.07
吐鲁番地区 Turpan Administrative Offices	127.85	5.99	0.19	121.67	0.19
哈密地区 Hami [Kumul] Administrative Offices	179.00	35.73	122.34	20.93	0.13
昌吉回族自治州 Changji Hui Autonomous Prefecture	263.60	49.63	2.58	211.39	0.36
伊犁州直属县(市) Counties (Cities) Direct Under Ili Prefecture	543.92	246.61	6.59	290.72	0.96
塔城地区 Tacheng [Tarbagatai] Administrative Offices	352.75	113.36	5.98	233.41	0.37
阿勒泰地区 Altay Administrative Offices	1353.84	353.78	845.49	154.57	1.15
博尔塔拉蒙古自治州 Bortala Mongol Autonomous Prefecture	1331.27	28.88	1176.41	125.98	5.34
巴音郭楞蒙古自治州 Bayangol Mongol Autonomous Prefecture	4034.70	979.74	2098.16	956.80	0.86
阿克苏地区 Aksu Administrative Offices	1018.87	709.20	68.68	240.99	0.78
克孜勒苏柯尔克孜自治州 Kizilsu Kirgiz Autonomous Prefecture	326.89	94.18	46.61	186.10	0.45
喀什地区 Kashgar [Kaxgar] Administrative Offices	1056.95	556.60	88.54	411.81	0.76
和田地区 Hotan Administrative Offices	1788.87	1509.32	108.39	171.16	0.72

9-29 森林火灾情况
Forest Fires

年 份 Year	地 区 Region	森林火灾次数(次) Forest Fires (case)	森林火警 Fire Alarms	一般火灾 Ordinary Fires	重大火灾 Major Fires	特大火灾 Severe Fires
	2001	41	33	8		
	2002	38	34	2	2	
	2003	25	16	9		
	2004	27	17	10		
	2005	28	27	1		
	2006	35	30	5		
	2007	47	34	13		
乌鲁木齐市	Urumqi City					
克拉玛依市	Karamay City					
吐鲁番地区	Turpan Administrative Offices					
哈密地区	Hami [Kumul] Administrative Offices	2	2			
昌吉回族自治州	Changji Hui Autonomous Prefecture	1	1			
伊犁州直属县(市)	Counties (Cities) Direct Under Ili Prefecture	15	12	3		
塔城地区	Tacheng [Tarbagatai] Administrative Offices	2	1	1		
阿勒泰地区	Altay Administrative Offices	23	16	7		
博尔塔拉蒙古自治州	Bortala Mongol Autonomous Prefecture					
巴音郭楞蒙古自治州	Bayangol Mongol Autonomous Prefecture	2	2			
阿克苏地区	Aksu Administrative Offices	1		1		
克孜勒苏柯尔克孜自治州	Kizilsu Kirgiz Autonomous Prefecture					
喀什地区	Kashgar [Kaxgar] Administrative Offices	1		1		
和田地区	Hotan Administrative Offices					

年 份 Year	地 区 Region	火场总面积(公顷) Total Area of Fires (hectare)	受灾森林总面积(公顷) Destructed Forest Area (hectare)	#天然林 Natural Forest	#人工林 Manmade Forest	经济损失(万元) Economic Loss (10 000yuan)
	2001	287.00	253.00	251.00	2.00	17.00
	2002	4134.58	1256.19	913.65	0.10	317.39
	2003	370.10	129.27	46.71	82.56	43.81
	2004	291.74	139.64	120.29	19.35	451.31
	2005	42.33	11.62	10.63	0.99	12.52
	2006	258.27	94.10	78.28	1.39	9.26
	2007	137.09	75.34	31.44	39.37	19.47
乌鲁木齐市	Urumqi City					
克拉玛依市	Karamay City					
吐鲁番地区	Turpan Administrative Offices					
哈密地区	Hami [Kumul] Administrative Offices	0.003	0.003	0.003		
昌吉回族自治州	Changji Hui Autonomous Prefecture	0.005	0.005	0.005		
伊犁州直属县(市)	Counties (Cities) Direct Under Ili Prefecture	40.118	24.568	12.008	12.560	6.72
塔城地区	Tacheng [Tarbagatai] Administrative Offices	4.004	4.001	0.001	0.300	2.50
阿勒泰地区	Altay Administrative Offices	78.114	34.247	13.887	19.530	10.25
博尔塔拉蒙古自治州	Bortala Mongol Autonomous Prefecture					
巴音郭楞蒙古自治州	Bayangol Mongol Autonomous Prefecture	0.618	0.550	0.500	0.050	
阿克苏地区	Aksu Administrative Offices	7.300	5.040	5.040		
克孜勒苏柯尔克孜自治州	Kizilsu Kirgiz Autonomous Prefecture					
喀什地区	Kashgar [Kaxgar] Administrative Offices	6.930	6.930		6.930	
和田地区	Hotan Administrative Offices					

9-30 森林病虫害防治情况
Prevention of Forest Diseases and Pests

单位：公顷 (hectare)

年 份 Year	地 区 Region	合 计 Total 发生面积 Area of Occurrence	合 计 Total 防治面积 Area of Prevention	合 计 Total 防治率(%) Prevention Rate (%)	森林病害 Forest Diseases 发生面积 Area of Occurrence	森林病害 Forest Diseases 防治面积 Area of Prevention	森林病害 Forest Diseases 防治率(%) Prevention Rate (%)
	2001	151213	133120	88.0	4213	3020	71.7
	2002	173067	147467	85.2	4920	3613	73.4
	2003	171908	146173	85.0	1940	1780	91.8
	2004	181473	152467	84.0	3286	2687	81.7
	2005	241713	221720	91.7	4467	3440	77.0
	2006	400127	344146	86.0	21993	19273	87.6
	2007	787087	441533	56.1	30194	23393	77.5
乌鲁木齐市	Urumqi City	6913	14333	207.3			
吐鲁番地区	Turpan Administrative Offices	7360	8427	114.5			
哈密地区	Hami [Kumul] Administrative Offices	11627	10760	92.5			
昌吉回族自治州	Changji Hui Autonomous Prefecture	380394	63007	16.6			
伊犁州直属县(市)	Counties (Cities) Direct Under Ili Prefecture	10547	8386	79.5	433	613	141.6
塔城地区	Tacheng [Tarbagatai] Administrative Offices	2220	2240	100.9	27	27	100.0
阿勒泰地区	Altay Administrative Offices	14900	14860	99.7	20	20	100.0
博尔塔拉蒙古自治州	Bortala Mongol Autonomous Prefecture	7820	7774	99.4			
巴音郭楞蒙古自治州	Bayangol Mongol Autonomous Prefecture	15147	18567	122.6	187	200	107.0
阿克苏地区	Aksu Administrative Offices	86187	101487	117.8	3060	2880	94.1
克孜勒苏柯尔克孜自治州	Kizilsu Kirgiz Autonomous Prefecture	4452	7133	160.2	593	793	133.7
喀什地区	Kashgar [Kaxgar] Administrative Offices	111360	97794	87.8	15387	12620	82.0
和田地区	Hotan Administrative Offices	89400	54500	61.0	4467	2827	63.3
自治区林业厅	Xinjiang Forestry Bureau	38760	32265	83.2	6020	3413	56.7

年 份 Year	地 区 Region	森林虫害 Forest Pest Plague 发生面积 Area of Occurrence	森林虫害 Forest Pest Plague 防治面积 Area of Prevention	森林虫害 Forest Pest Plague 防治率(%) Prevention Rate (%)	森林鼠害 Forest Rat Plague 发生面积 Area of Occurrence	森林鼠害 Forest Rat Plague 防治面积 Area of Prevention	森林鼠害 Forest Rat Plague 防治率(%) Prevention Rate (%)
	2001	133207	117687	88.3	13793	12413	90.0
	2002	132133	118133	89.4	36007	25693	71.4
	2003	152427	130593	85.7	17540	13807	78.7
	2004	165520	138140	83.5	12667	11640	91.9
	2005	221500	199700	89.9	21747	18580	85.4
	2006	340320	290693	85.4	37813	34180	90.4
	2007	350592	331735	94.6	406301	86405	21.3
乌鲁木齐市	Urumqi City	6853	14273	208.3	60	60	100.0
吐鲁番地区	Turpan Administrative Offices	7360	8427	114.5			
哈密地区	Hami [Kumul] Administrative Offices	7060	6460	91.5	4567	4300	94.2
昌吉回族自治州	Changji Hui Autonomous Prefecture	5867	5407	92.2	374527	57600	15.4
伊犁州直属县(市)	Counties (Cities) Direct Under Ili Prefecture	8687	6713	77.3	1427	1060	74.3
塔城地区	Tacheng [Tarbagatai] Administrative Offices	1873	1900	101.4	320	313	97.8
阿勒泰地区	Altay Administrative Offices	13087	13127	100.3	1793	1713	95.5
博尔塔拉蒙古自治州	Bortala Mongol Autonomous Prefecture	1113	1067	95.9	6707	6707	100.0
巴音郭楞蒙古自治州	Bayangol Mongol Autonomous Prefecture	12873	16247	126.2	2087	2120	101.6
阿克苏地区	Aksu Administrative Offices	83127	98607	118.6			
克孜勒苏柯尔克孜自治州	Kizilsu Kirgiz Autonomous Prefecture	3406	5567	163.4	453	773	170.6
喀什地区	Kashgar [Kaxgar] Administrative Offices	81633	73427	89.9	14340	11747	81.9
和田地区	Hotan Administrative Offices	84933	51673	60.8			
自治区林业厅	Xinjiang Forestry Bureau	32720	28840	88.1	20	12	60.0

注：自治区林业厅数据中包括石河子市和克拉玛依市的数据。
Note: The data on Bureau of Forestry include the data of Shihezi city and Karamay city.

9-31　地震灾害情况
Earthquake Disasters

年 份 Year	地 区 Region	地震次数（次）Number of Earthquakes (case)	5.0-5.9 级 5.0-5.9 Richterscale	6.0-6.9 级 6.0-6.9 Richterscale	7.0 级以上 Over 7.0 Richterscale
	2002	**1**	**1**		
乌恰县	Wuqia [Ulugqat] County	1	1		
	2003	**8**	**5**	**2**	**1**
伽师县	Jiashi [Payzawat] County	1	1		
石河子市	Shihezi City	2	2		
巴楚县 伽师县	Bachu [Maralbexi] County Jiashi [Payzawat] County	1		1	
岳普湖县	Yopurga County	1	1		
阿克陶县	Akto County	1	1		
阿勒泰市	Altay City	1			1
昭苏县	Zhaosu [Mongolkure] County	1		1	
	2004	**1**	**1**		
温泉县	Wenquan [Araxang] County	1	1		
	2005	**4**	**3**	**1**	
乌什县	Wushi [Uxturpan] County	2	1	1	
阿瓦提县	Awat County	1	1		
墨玉县	Moyu [Karakax] County	1	1		
	2006	**2**	**2**		
和田县	Hotan County	1	1		
乌苏市	Usu City	1	1		
	2007	**1**	**1**		
特克斯县		1	1		

年 份 Year	地 区 Region	人员伤亡（人）Casualties (person)	#死亡人数 Deaths	经济损失（万元）Economic Loss (10 000 yuan)	失去住所（户）Homeless (household)	牲畜死亡数（只）Deaths of Domestic Animals (head)
	2002	**3**	**1**	**3046**	**666**	
乌恰县	Wuqia [Ulugqat] County	3	1	3046	666	
	2003	**7261**	**279**	**174531**	**64220**	**78404**
伽师县	Jiashi [Payzawat] County			3122	1738	1119
石河子市	Shihezi City			50		
巴楚县	Bachu [Maralbexi] County	7179	268	137131	49656	62341
伽师县	Jiashi [Payzawat] County					
岳普湖县	Yopurga County	4	1	7720	5409	1112
阿克陶县	Akto County			847	240	1991
阿勒泰市	Altay City			7636	2460	75
昭苏县	Zhaosu [Mongolkure] County	78	10	18026	4717	11766
	2004					
温泉县	Wenquan [Araxang] County					
	2005			**16316**	**5823**	
乌什县	Wushi [Uxturpan] County			15758	5823	
阿瓦提县	Awat County					
墨玉县	Moyu [Karakax] County			558		
	2006			**126**		
和田县	Hotan County					
乌苏市	Usu City			126		
	2007			**11060**	**5074**	
特克斯县				11060	5074	

注：本表数据由自治区地震局提供。
Note: The data in this table is Provided by theBureau of Earthquake.

9-32 林业系统营林固定资产投资资金来源
Source of Funds of Investment in Fixed Assets for Afforestation in Forest System

单位:万元 (10 000 yuan)

年 份 Year	地 区 Region	合 计 Source of Funds This Year	上年底结余资金 Unspent Capitals From Last Year	国家预算内资金 State Budget	#国债资金 National Debts
	2001	44669	359	23835	11892
	2002	47718	2439	35930	19693
	2003	60179	1338	51933	21954
	2004	58111	2015	42074	17035
	2005	78919	1573	57553	17992
	2006	103671	6942	79265	20632
	2007	117405	11106	88233	14651
乌鲁木齐市	Urumqi City	2995	65	710	200
克拉玛依市	Karamay City	8072		8072	500
石河子市	Shihezi City	5376			
吐鲁番地区	Turpan Administrative Offices	2438		2013	64
哈密地区	Hami [Kumul] Administrative Offices	6220		3553	105
昌吉回族自治州	Changji Hui Autonomous Prefecture	8678	181	6392	2665
伊犁州直属县(市)	Counties (Cities) Direct Under Ili Prefecture	8651	3239	5302	80
塔城地区	Tacheng [Tarbagatai] Administrative Offices	6118		5512	705
阿勒泰地区	Altay Administrative Offices	7974	3366	4362	1053
博尔塔拉蒙古自治州	Bortala Mongol Autonomous Prefecture	5619		4670	395
巴音郭楞蒙古自治州	Bayangol Mongol Autonomous Prefecture	5708		5669	1662
阿克苏地区	Aksu Administrative Offices	11264	151	11070	3833
克孜勒苏柯尔克孜自治州	Kizilsu Kirgiz Autonomous Prefecture	2180		2180	145
喀什地区	Kashgar [Kaxgar] Administrative Offices	7034		7034	2227
和田地区	Hotan Administrative Offices	6905		6905	587
自治区林业厅	Xinjiang Forestry Bureau	22173	4104	14789	430

年 份 Year	地 区 Region	#中央财政专项资金 Special Funds of Central Finance	国内贷款 Domestic Loans	利用外资 Foreign Capitals	自筹资金 Self-raising Funds	其他资金 OtherFunds
	2001	7322	487		16763	3225
	2002	12503			6131	3218
	2003	18979			3919	2989
	2004	22491		234	12578	1210
	2005	32556			17857	1936
	2006	43320			11217	6247
	2007	50619	50	25	11161	6830
乌鲁木齐市	Urumqi City	510			2202	18
克拉玛依市	Karamay City	150				
石河子市	Shihezi City				5376	
吐鲁番地区	Turpan Administrative Offices	1949		25		400
哈密地区	Hami [Kumul] Administrative Offices	3448			20	2647
昌吉回族自治州	Changji Hui Autonomous Prefecture	3081			740	1365
伊犁州直属县(市)	Counties (Cities) Direct Under Ili Prefecture	4546			110	
塔城地区	Tacheng [Tarbagatai] Administrative Offices	3049	50		393	163
阿勒泰地区	Altay Administrative Offices	999			80	166
博尔塔拉蒙古自治州	Bortala Mongol Autonomous Prefecture	3950			174	775
巴音郭楞蒙古自治州	Bayangol Mongol Autonomous Prefecture	3123				39
阿克苏地区	Aksu Administrative Offices	6401			43	
克孜勒苏柯尔克孜自治州	Kizilsu Kirgiz Autonomous Prefecture	2035				
喀什地区	Kashgar [Kaxgar] Administrative Offices	1775				
和田地区	Hotan Administrative Offices	5742				
自治区林业厅	Xinjiang Forestry Bureau	9861			2023	1257

9-33 林业系统营林固定资产投资完成情况

Completed Investment in Fixed Assets for Afforestation in Forest System

单位：万元 (10 000 yuan)

年 份 Year	地 区 Region	本年完成投资 Investment Completed During the Year	#国家投资 State Investment	#国债资金 National Debt	本年新增固定资产 Newly Increased Fixed Assets
	2000	23582	11686	5170	4542
	2001	45890	23725	5433	12492
	2002	68861	35835	21369	
	2003	71277	40821	20448	27223
	2004	60631	43475	15748	23047
	2005	80150	57680	17224	24988
	2006	96062	82235	19937	31047
	2007	115523	94094	15698	33091
乌鲁木齐市	Urumqi City	3949	275	150	
克拉玛依市	Karamay City	8072	8072	650	8072
石河子市	Shihezi City	5376			
吐鲁番地区	Turpan Administrative Offices	3579	1930	64	1185
哈密地区	Hami [Kumul] Administrative Offices	6220	2707	105	5001
昌吉回族自治州	Changji Hui Autonomous Prefecture	10816	7756	4002	3325
伊犁州直属县(市)	Counties (Cities) Direct Under Ili Prefecture	7791	7681	255	164
塔城地区	Tacheng [Tarbagatai] Administrative Offices	6118	5512	705	511
阿勒泰地区	Altay Administrative Offices	9435	9435	1870	1352
博尔塔拉蒙古自治州	Bortala Mongol Autonomous Prefecture	4418	3629	395	1782
巴音郭楞蒙古自治州	Bayangol Mongol Autonomous Prefecture	5744	5744	1162	300
阿克苏地区	Aksu Administrative Offices	11264	11221	3326	7118
克孜勒苏柯尔克孜自治州	Kizilsu Kirgiz Autonomous Prefecture	2414	2414	40	
喀什地区	Kashgar [Kaxgar] Administrative Offices	6047	6047	2227	
和田地区	Hotan Administrative Offices	6905	6905	607	
自治区林业厅	Xinjiang Forestry Bureau	17375	14766	140	4281

主要统计指标解释

国土 指一个主权国家管辖下的领土、领海和领空。

气候 指地球与大气之间长期能量交换与质量交换所形成的一种自然环境状态，它是多种因素综合作用的结果。气候既是人类生活和生产的环境要素之一，又是供给人类生活和生产的重要资源。气温、降水、湿度等气象要素的多年平均值是用来描述一个地区气候状况的主要参数，而各种气象要素某年、某月的平均值(或总量)则可以反映出该时期天气气候状况的重要特征。

自然资源 指人类可以直接从自然界获得，并用于生产和生活的物质资源。自然资源一般可以分成可再生资源和非再生资源两大类。可再生资源指在较短时间内可以再生、可以循环利用的资源，包括土地资源、水资源、气候资源、生物资源和海洋资源等。非再生资源指在使用后不能再生的资源，包括矿产资源和地热能源。

土地资源 土地指陆地的表层部分，它主要由岩石、岩石的风化物和土壤构成。土地资源按利用类型可以分为农用地、建筑用地和未利用地。农用地包括耕地、园地、林地、牧草地和水面。建筑用地包括居民点及工矿用地、交通用地和水利设施用地。未利用地指农用地和建筑用地以外的土地，包括滩涂、荒漠、戈壁、冰川和石山等。

耕地面积 指种植各种农作物的土地面积，包括灌溉水田、望天田、水浇地、旱地、菜地等。

林业用地面积 指生长乔木、竹类、灌木、沿海红树林等林木的土地面积，包括有林地、灌木林、疏林地、未成造林地、迹地、苗圃等。

草地面积 指牧区和农区用于放牧牲畜或割草，植被盖度在5%以上的草原、草坡、草山等面积。包括天然的和人工种植或改良的草地面积。

森林资源 指森林、林木、林地以及依托森林、林木、林地生存的野生动物、植物和微生物。林木指树木和竹子。森林指以乔木为主体的植物群落，是集生的乔木及与共同作用的植物、动物、微生物和土壤、气候等的总体。

活立木总蓄积量 指一定范围内土地上全部树木蓄积的总量，包括森林蓄积、疏林蓄积、散生木蓄积和四旁树蓄积。

森林面积 指由乔木树种构成，郁闭度0.2以上(含0.2)的林地或冠幅宽度10米以上的林带的面积，即有林地面积。森林面积包括天然起源和人工起源的针叶林面积、阔叶林面积、针阔混交林面积和竹林面积，不包括灌木林地面积和疏林地面积。

森林蓄积量 指一定森林面积上存在着的林木树干部分的总材积。它是反映一个国家或地区森林资源总规模和水平的基本指标之一，也是反映森林资源的丰富程度、衡量森林生态环境优劣的重要依据。

森林覆盖率 指一个国家或地区森林面积占土地面积的百分比。在计算森林覆盖率时，森林面积包括郁闭度0．2以上的乔木林地面积和竹林地面积，国家特别规定的灌木林地面积、农田林网以及四旁(村旁、路旁、水旁、宅旁)林木的覆盖面积。森林覆盖率是反映森林资源的丰富程度和生态平衡状况的重要指标。计算公式为：

森林覆盖率(%)=森林面积／土地总面积×100%

水资源 水在自然界中以固体、液体和气态三种聚集状态存在，分布于海洋、陆地(包括土壤)以及大气之中，通过水循环形成水资源。水资源包括经人类控制并直接可供灌溉、发电、给水、航运、养殖等用途的地表水和地下水，以及江河、湖泊、井、泉、潮汐、港湾和养殖水域等。水资源是发展国民经济不可缺少的重要自然资源。

地表水和地下水 陆地上的水因空间分布不同，可以分为地表水和地下水。地表水指分别存在于河流、湖泊、沼泽、冰川和冰盖等水体中水分的总称，又称陆地水。地下水指储存在地面以下饱和岩土孔隙、裂隙及溶洞中的水。

内陆水域总面积 指江、河、湖泊、池塘、塘堰、水库等各种流水或蓄水的水面占地面积。

径流量 指在一定时段内通过河流某一过水断面的水量，用以反映一个国家或地区水资源的丰歉程度。计算公式为：

径流量=降水量-蒸发量

矿产资源 矿产指由地质作用形成，富集于地壳中或出露于地表达到工农业利用要求的有用矿物。矿产是一种重要的自然资源，是社会发展的重要物质基础。从某种意义上讲，一个国家对矿产资源开发利用的广度和深度，可以作为这个国家经济发展水平的标志。

矿产保有储量 指探明的矿产储量(包括工业储量和远景储量)，扣除已开采部分和地下损失量后的年末实有储量，是反映国家矿产资源现状的重要指标。

气温 指空气的温度，我国一般以摄氏度(℃)为单位表示。气象观测的温度表是放在离地面约1.5米处通风良好的百叶箱里测量的，因此，通常说的气温指的是离地面1.5米处百叶箱中的温度。其统计计算方法为：

降水量 指从天空降落到地面的液态或固态(经融化后)水，未经蒸发、渗透、流失而在地面上积聚的深度。

月降水量 是将全月各日的降水量累加而得。

年降水量 是将12个月的月降水量累加而得。

日照时数 指太阳实际照射地面的时间。其统计方法与降水量相同。

水资源总量 一定区域内的水资源总量指当地降水形成的地表和地下产水量，即地表径流量与降水入渗补给量之和，不包括过境水量。

地表水资源量 指河流、湖泊、冰川等地表水体中由当地降水形成的、可以逐年更新的动态水量，即天然河川径流量。

地下水资源量 指当地降水和地表水对饱水岩土层的补给量。

地表水与地下水资源重复计算量 指地表水和地下水相互转化的部分，即在河川径流量中包括一部分地下水排泄量，地下水补给量中包括一部分来源于地表水的入渗量。

供水总量 指各种水源工程为用户提供的包括输水损失在内的毛供水量。

地表水源供水量 指地表水体工程的取水量，按蓄、引、提、调四种形式统计。从水库、塘坝中引水或提水，均属蓄水工程供水量；从河道或湖泊中自流引水的，无论有闸或无闸，均属引水工程供水量；利用扬水站从河道或湖泊中直接取水的，属提水工程供水量；跨流域调指水资源一级区或独立流域之间的跨流域调配水量，不包括在蓄、引、提水量中。

地下水源供水量 指水井工程的开采量，按浅层谈水、深层承压水和微咸水分别统计。城市地下水源供水量包括自来水厂的开采量和工矿企业自备井的开采量。

用水总量 指分配给用户的包括输水损失在内的毛用水量。按用户特性分为农业、工业、生活和生态用水四大类。

农业用水 包括农田灌溉和林牧渔业用水。林牧渔业用水指林果地灌溉、草地灌溉和鱼塘补水。

工业用水 按新水取用量计，不包括企业内部的重复利用水量。

生活用水 包括城镇生活用水和农村生活用水。城镇生活用水由居民用水和公共用水(含服务业、商饮业、货运邮电业及建筑业等用水)组成；农村生活用水除居民生活用水外，还包括畜用水在内。

生态用水 仅包括河湖人工补水和城市环境用水。

工业废水排放量 指经过企业厂区所有排放口排到企业外部的工业废水量。包括生产废水、外排的直接冷却水、超标排放的矿井地下水和与工业废水混排的厂区生活污水，不包括外排的间接冷却水(清污不分流的间接冷却水应计算在内)。

工业废水排放达标量 指报告期内废水中各项污染物指标都达到国家或地方排放标准的外排工业废水量，包括未经处理外排达标的，经废水处理设施处理后达标排放的，以及经污水处理厂处理后达标排放的。

工业废水排放达标率 指工业废水排放达标量占工业废水排放量的百分率，计算公式为：

工业废水排放达标率=工业废水排放达标量/工业废水排放量×100%

化学需氧量(COD) 测量有机和无机物质化学所消耗氧的质量浓度的水污染指数。

工业废气排放量 指报告期内企业厂区内燃料燃烧和生产工艺过程中产生的各种排入大气的含有污染物的气体的总量，以标准状态(273K, 101325Pa)计算。测算公式为：

工业废气排放量=燃料燃烧过程中废气排放量+生产工艺过程中废气排放量

工业烟尘排放量 指企业厂区内燃料燃烧过程中产生的烟气中夹带的颗粒物排放量。

工业粉尘排放量 指企业在生产工艺过程中排放的能在空气中悬浮一定时间的固体颗粒物排放量。如钢铁企业的耐火材料粉尘、焦化企业的筛焦系统粉尘、烧结机的粉尘、石灰窑的粉尘、建材企业的水泥粉尘等。不包括电厂排入大气的烟尘。

工业固体废物产生量 指报告期内企业在生产过程中产生的固体状、半固体状和高浓度液体状废弃物的总量，包括危险废物、冶炼废渣、粉煤灰、炉渣、煤矸石、尾矿、放射性废物和其他废物等；不包括矿山开采的剥离废石和掘进废石(煤矸石和呈酸性或碱性的废石除外)。酸性或碱性废石指采掘的废石其流经水、雨淋水的 pH 值小于 4 或 pH 值大于 10.5 者。

工业固体废物综合利用量 指报告期内企业通过回收、加工、循环、交换等方式，从固体废物中提取或者使其转化为可以利用的资源、能源和其他原材料的固体废物量(包括当年利用往年的工业固体废物贮存量)，如用作农业肥料、生产建筑材料、筑路等。综合利用量由原产生固体废物的单位统计。

工业固体废物综合利用率 指工业固体废物综合利用量占工业固体废物产生量(包括综合利用往年贮存量)的百分率。计算公式为：

工业固体废物综合利用率=工业固体废物综合利用量/(工业固体废物产生量+综合利用往年贮存量)×100%

工业固体废物贮存量 指报告期内企业以综合利用或处置为目的，将固体废物暂时贮存或堆存在专设的贮存设施或专设的集中堆存场所内的数量。专设的固体废物贮存场所或贮存设施必须有防扩散、防流失、防渗漏、防止污染大气、水体的措施。

工业固体废物处置量 指报告期内企业将固体废物焚烧或者最终置于符合环境保护规定要求的场所，并不再回取的工业固体废物量(包括当年处置往年的工业固体废物贮存量)。处置方式有填埋(其中危险废物应安全填埋)、焚烧、专业贮存场(库)封场处理、深层灌注、回填矿井及海洋处置(经海洋管理部门同意投海处置)等。

工业固体废物排放量 指报告期内企业将所产生的固体废物排到固体废物污染防治设施、场所以外的数量，不包括矿山开采的剥离废石和掘进废石(煤矸石和呈酸性或碱性的废石除外)。

生活垃圾清运量 指报告期内收集和运送到垃圾处理厂(场)的生活垃圾数量。生活垃圾指城市日常生活或为城市日常生活提供服务的活动中产生的固体废物以及法律行政规定的视为城市生活垃圾的固体废物。包括：居民生活垃圾、商业垃圾、集市贸易市场垃圾、街道清扫垃圾、公共场所垃圾和机关、学校、厂矿等单位的生活垃圾。

生活垃圾无害化处理率 指报告期生活垃圾无害化处理量与生活垃圾产生量比率。在统计上，由于生活垃圾产生量不易取得，可用清运量代替。计算公式为：

生活垃圾无害化处理率=生活垃圾无害化处理量/生活垃圾产生量×100%

农用地 指直接用于农业生产的土地，包括耕地、园地、林地、牧草地及其他农用地。

人工林面积 指由人工播种、植苗或扦插造林形成的生长稳定，(一般造林 3-5 年后或飞机播种 5-7 年后)每公顷保存株数大于或等于造林设计植树株数 80%或郁闭度 0.20 以上(含 02.0)的林分面积。

造林总面积 指报告期内在荒山、荒地、沙丘、退耕地等一切可以造林的土地上，采用人工播种、飞机播种、植苗造林、分植造林等方法新植成片乔木林和灌木林，经过检查验收符合《造林技术规程》要求的单位面积株数，并按《中华人民共和国森林法实施条例》规定，成活率达 85%以上(含 85%，年降雨量在 400 毫米以下且无浇灌条件的地区造林成活率达 70%以上)的总面积。四旁植树如一侧在四行以上，连片面积 0.066 公顷(一亩)以上，应统计在造林面积内。造林面积，通常按所有制(国有、国有集体合作、集体和个人)、造林方式(人工、飞机播种)、主要林种用途(用材林、经济林、防护林、薪炭林、特种用途林)分组进行统计。

用材林 指以生产木材为主要目的的森林和林木，包括以生产竹材为主要目的的竹林。

经济林 指以生产果品，食用油料、饮料、调料，工业原料和药材为主要目的的林木。经济林是人们为了取得林木的果实、叶片、皮层、胶液等产品作为工业原料或者供食用所营造的林木，如油茶、油桐、核桃、樟树、花椒、茶、桑、果等。

防护林 指以防护为主要目的的森林、林木和灌木丛。包括水源涵养林，水土保持林，防风固沙林，农田、牧场防护林，护岸林，护路林等。

薪炭林 指以生产燃料为主要目的的林木。

天然林保护工程 是我国林业的“天”字号工程、一号工程,也是投资最大的生态工程。具体包括三个层次:全面停止长江上游、黄河上中游地区天然林采伐；大幅度调减东北、内蒙古等重点国有林区的木材产量；同时保护好其他地区的天然林资源。主要解决这些区域天然林资源的休养生息和恢复发展问题。

退耕还林还草工程 是我国林业建设上涉及面最广、政策性最强、工序最复杂、群众参与度最高的生态建设工程。主要解决重点地区的水土流失问题。

三北和长江流域等重点防护林体系建设工程 三北和长江中下游地区等重点防护林体系建设工程,是我国涵盖面最大、内容最丰富的防护林体系建设工程。具体包括三北防护林四期工程、长江中下游及淮河太湖流域防护林二期工程、沿海防护林二期工程、珠江防护林二期工程、太行山绿化二期工程和平原绿化二期工程。主要解决三北地区的防沙治沙问题和其他区域各不相同的生态问题。

野生动植物保护及自然保护区建设工程 野生动植物保护及自然保护区建设工程,是一个面向未来,着眼长远,具有多项战略意义的生态保护工程,也是呼应国际大气候、树立中国良好国际形象的“外交工程”。主要解决基因保存、生物多样性保护、自然保护、湿地保护等问题。

湿地 指天然或人工、长久或暂时性的沼泽地、泥炭地或水域地带，包括静止或流动、淡水、半咸水、咸水体，低潮时水深不超过 6 米的水域以及海岸地带地区的珊瑚滩和海草床、滩涂、红树林、河口、河流、淡水沼泽、沼泽森林、湖泊、盐沼及盐湖。

自然保护区 指对有代表性的自然生态系统、珍稀濒危野生动植物物种的天然分布区、水源涵养区、有特殊意义的自然历史遗迹等保护对象所在的陆地、陆地水体或海域，依法划出一定面积进行特殊保护和管理的区域。以县及县以上各级人民政府正式批准建立的自然保护区为准(包括“六五”以前由部门或“革委会”批准且现仍存在的自然保护区)。风景名胜区、文物保护区不计在内。

生态示范区 指省级以上环境保护行政主管部门批准，以省、地、县政府为主按批准的生态示范区建设规划实施的行政区域。包括已经过国家或省级环境保护行政主管部门验收的和正在开展试点工作的。

滑坡 指斜坡上不稳定的岩土体在重力作用下沿一定软面(或滑动带)整体向下滑动的物理地质现象。地表水和地下水的作用以及人为的不合理工程活动对斜坡岩、土体稳定性的破坏，经常是促使滑坡发生的主要因素。在露天采矿、水利、铁路、公路等工程中，滑坡往往造成严重危害。

崩塌 指陡坡上大块的岩土体在重力作用下突然脱离母体崩落的物理地质现象。它可因多裂隙的岩体经强烈的物理风化、雨水渗入或地震而造成，往往毁坏建筑物，堵塞河道或交通路线。

泥石流 指山地突然爆发的包含大量泥沙、石块的特殊洪流，多见于半干旱山地高原地区。其形成条件是地形陡峻，松散堆积物丰富，有特大暴雨或大量冰融水的流出。

地面塌陷 指地表岩、土体在自然或人为因素作用下向下陷落，并在地面形成塌陷坑(洞)的一种动力地质现象。由于其发育的地质条件和作用因素的不同，地面塌陷可分为：岩溶塌陷、非岩溶塌陷。

环境污染与破坏事故 指由于违反环境保护法规的经济、社会活动与行为，以及意外因素的影响或不可抗拒的自然灾害等原因，致使环境受到污染，国家重点保护的野生动植物、自然保护区受到破坏，人体健康受到危害，社会经济和人民财产受到损失，造成不良社会影响的突发性事件。

环境污染治理投资 指在工业污染源治理和城市环境基础设施建设的资金投入中，用于形成固定资产的资金。包括工业新老污染源治理工程投资、建设项目“三同时”环保投资，以及城市环境基础设施建设所投入的资金。

营林固定资产投资 指在报告期内进行的营林基本建设和营林更新改造活动投资。

Explanatory Notes on Main Statistical Indicators

Territory refers to territorial land, sea and air space under the administration of a sovereign state.

Climate refers to the natural environmental status formed by the long-time exchange of energy and mass between the earth and the air, and is the results of interaction of many factors. Climate is both one of the environment factors and the important resources for the living and production activities of the human being. The average values across several years of meteorological factors such as temperature, rainfall and humidity are used as important parameters to describe the climate of a region, while the average values (or total values) of a given year or month of meteorological factors reflect the key characteristics of climate for that period of time.

Natural Resources refer to material resources that could be obtained from the nature by human being and used for production and living. Natural resources in general can be classified as renewable resources and non-renewable resources. Renewable resources refer to resources that could be renewed and recycled during a relatively short period of time, including land resource, water resource, climate resource, biology resource and marine resource. Non-renewable resources include resources that could not be renewed, such as minerals and geothermal resource.

Land Resource Land refers to the surface of the earth, consisting of mainly rocks and its whethering and earth. Land resource can be classified, by its utilization, as land for agriculture, land for construction and unused land. Land for agriculture includes cultivated land, plantation land, forestland, grassland and waters. Land for construction includes land for residential purpose, for manufacturing and mining, for transportation and for water-conservancy projects. Unused land refers to land other than land for agriculture and construction, including beaches, deserts, Gobi, glaciers and rock mountains.

Area of Cultivated Land refers to land for the cultivation of various farm crops, including irrigated land, manual-watered land, dry land and vegetable land.

Area of Afforestated Land refer to land for trees bamboo, bushes and mangrove, including forest-cover land, bush-covered land, sparse forest land, land planned for afforestation and nurseries of young trees.

Area of Grassland refers to areas of grassland, grass-slopes and grass-covered hills with a vegetation-covering rate of over 5% that are used for animal husbandry or harvesting of grass. It includes natural, cultivated and improved grassland areas.

Forest Resource refers to forests, trees, forestland and wild animals, plants and microorganism that live on forest and trees. Trees include trees and bamboo. Forest refers to the population of clusters of trees and other plants, animals and microorganism as well as the earth and climate that have interactions with the trees.

Total Standing Stock Volume refers to the total stock volume of trees growing in land，including trees in forest， tress in sparse forest, scattered trees and trees planted by the side of farm houses and along the roads, rivers and fields.

Forest Area refers to the area of forest land where trees and bamboo grow with canopy density above 0.2，including land of natural woods and planted woods, but excluding bush land and thin forest land. It reflects the total areas of afforestation.

Stock Volume of Forest refers to total stock volume of wood growing in forest area，which shows the total size and level of forest resources of a Country or a region. It is also an important indicator illustrating the richness of forest resource and the status of forest ecological environment.

Forest Coverage Rate refers to the ratio of area of afforested land to total land area. This indicator shows the forest resources and afforestation progress of a Country or a region. According to regulations of the government， in addition to afforested land，the area of bush forest, the area of forest land inside farm land and the area of trees planted by the side of farm houses and along the roads, rivers and fields should also be included in the area of afforested land in the calculation of the forest coverage-rate. The formula for calculating forest coverage rate is as follows：

Forestry coverage rate (%)= (Area of Afforested Land/Area of Total Land)×100%

Water Resource Water exists in the nature in solid, liquid and gaseous states, is distributed in the ocean, land (including earth) and air, and constitutes the water resource through the circulation of water. Water resource includes the surface water and underground water that is controlled by the human being for irrigation, power-generation, water supply, navigation and cultivation. It also includes rivers, lakes, wells, springs, tides, gulf and water area for cultivation. Water resource as an important natural resource is indispensable for the development of the national economy.

Surface Water and Underground Water. Water on earth can be divided into surface water and underground water according to its distribution. Surface water refers to moisture exists in rivers, lakes, swamps, glaciers, icecaps and so on. It is also called land water. The underground water refers to water deposited underground in the cranny and the hole of saturated rock soil and in the water-eroded cave.

Inland Water Area refers to water area of rivers，lakes，ponds，reservoir，etc.

Volume of Runoff refers to the total volume of water running through a certain cross section of a river during a certain period of time, reflecting the water resource condition in a country or a region. The formula for calculating volume or runoff is as follows：

Runoff =Precipitation-Evaporation

Mineral Resources refer to useful minerals that can be used for industrial or agricultural purposes enriched in lithosphere or on earth due to the geological process.

Ensured Mineral Reserves refer to the actual mineral reserves, which equal to the proven mineral reserves (including industrial reserves and prospective reserves) minus extracted parts and underground losses. This indicator shows the current condition of the mineral resources of a Country.

Temperature refers to the air temperature. China uses centigrade as the unit. The thermometry used for weather observation is put in a breezy shutter, which is 1.5 meters high from the ground. Therefore, the commonly used temperature refers to the temperature in the breezy shutter 1.5 meters away from the ground. The calculation method is as follows:

Monthly average temperature is the summation of average daily temperature of one month divided by the actual days of that particular month.

Annual average temperature is the summation of monthly average of a year divided by 12 months.

Relative Humidity refers to the ratio of actual water vapor pressure to the saturation water vapor density under the current temperature. The calculation method is the same as that of temperature.

Volume of Precipitation refers to the deepness of liquid state or solid state (thawed) water falling from the sky to the ground that has not been evaporated, infiltrated or run off.

Sunshine Hours refer to the actual hours of sun irradiating the earth. The calculation method is the same as that of the precipitation.

Total Water Resources refers to total volume of water resources measured as run-off for surface water from rainfall and recharge for groundwater in a given area, excluding transit water.

Surface Water Resources refers to total renewable resources which exist in rivers, lakes, glaciers and other collectors from rainfall and are measured as run-off of rivers.

Groundwater Resources refers to replenishment of aquifers with rainfall and surface water.

Duplicated Measurement Between Surface Water and Groundwater refers to mutual exchange between surface water and groundwater, i.e. run-off of rivers includes some depletion with groundwater while groundwater includes some replenishment with surface water.

Water Supply refers to gross water supply by supply systems from sources to consumers, including losses during distribution.

Surface Water Supply refers to withdrawals by surface water supply system, broken down with storage, flow, pumping and transfer. Supply from storage projects includes withdrawals from reservoirs ; supply from flow includes withdrawals from rivers and lakes with natural flows no matter if there are locks or not; supply from pumping projects includes withdrawals from rivers or lakes with pumping stations; and supply from transfer refers to water supplies transferred from first-level regions of water resources or independent river drainage areas to others, and should not be covered under supplies of storage, flow and pumping.

Groundwater Supply refers to withdrawals from supplying wells, broken down with shallow layer freshwater, deep layer freshwater and slightly brackish water. Groundwater supply for urban areas includes water mining by both waterworks and own wells of enterprises.

Other Water Supply Sources include supplies by waste water treatment, rain collection, seawater desalinization and other water projects.

Water Use refers to gross water use distributed to users, including loss during transportation, broken down with use by agriculture, industry, living consumption and biological protection.

Water Use by Agriculture includes uses of water by irrigation of farming fields and by forestry, animal husbandry and fishing. Water use by forestry, animal husbandry and fishing includes irrigation of forestry and orchards, irrigation of grassland and replenishment of fishing pools.

Water Use by Industry refers to new withdrawals of water, excluding reuse of water within enterprises.

Water Use by Living Consumption includes use of water for living consumption in both urban and rural areas. Urban water use by living consumption is composed of household use and public use (including services, commerce, restaurants, cargo transportation, posts, telecommunication and construction). Rural water use by living consumption includes both households and animals.

Water Use by Biological Protection includes replenishment of rivers and lakes and use for urban environment.

Waste Water Discharged by Industry refers to the volume of waste water discharged by industrial enterprises through all their outlets, including waste water from production process, directly cooled water, groundwater from mining wells which does not meet discharge standards and sewage from households mixed with waste water produced by industrial activities, but excluding indirectly cooled water discharged (It should be included if the discharge is not separated with waste water).

Industrial Waste Water Meeting Discharge Standards refers to volume of industrial waste water discharge which, with or without treatment, reaches national or local standards with regard to all pollutants.

Ratio of Industrial Waste Water Meeting Discharge Standards refers to percentage of industrial waste water meeting discharge standards over total industrial waste water discharge. Its calculation formula is:

Ratio=industrial waste water meeting discharge standards/total industrial waste water discharge×100%

Chemical Oxygen Demand (COD) refers to index of water pollution measuring the mass concentration of oxygen consumed by the chemical breakdown of organic and inorganic matter.

Industrial Waste Air Emission refers to discharge into atmosphere of waste air containing pollutants generated from fuel burning and production process in enterprises within a given period of time. It is converted into standard (273K, 101325Pa) with the following formula:

Emission=emission from fuel burning+ emission through production process

Industrial SO_2 Emission refers to volume of sulphur dioxide emission from fuel burning and production process by enterprises during a given period of time. Its calculation formula is:

Emission=SO_2 Emission from fuel burning+ SO_2 Emission form production process

Industrial Soot Emission refers to volume of soot in smoke emitted in process of fuel burning in premises of enterprises.

Industrial Dust Emission refers to volume of dust emitted by production process of enterprises and suspended in the air for a given period of time, including dust from refractory material of iron and steel works, dust from coke-screening systems and sintering machines of coke plants, dust from lime kilns and dust from cement production in building material enterprises, but excluding soot and dust emitted from power plants.

Industrial Solid Wastes Produced refers to total volume of solid, semi-solid and high concentration liquid residues produced by industrial enterprises from production process in a given period of time, including hazardous wastes, slag, coal ash, gangue, tailings, radioactive residues and other wastes, but excluding stones stripped or dug out in mining (gangue and acid or alkaline stones not included). A stone is acid or alkaline depending on the pH value of the water below 4 or above 10.5 when the stone is in, or soaked by, the water.

Industrial Solid Wastes Utilized refers to volume of solid wastes from which useful materials can be extracted or which can be converted into usable resources, energy or other materials by means of reclamation, processing, recycling and exchange (including utilizing in the year the stocks of industrial solid wastes of the previous year). Examples of such utilizations include fertilizers, building materials and road materials. The information shall be collected by the producing units of the wastes.

Ratio of Industrial Solid Wastes Utilized refers to the percentage of industrial solid wastes utilized over industrial solid wastes produced (including stocks of the previous year). Its calculation formula is:

Ratio = Volume of industrial solid wastes utilized/(industrial solid wastes produced+stocks of previous year utilized)×100%

Stocks of Industrial Solid Wastes refers to volume of solid wastes placed in special facilities or special sites for purposes of utilization or disposal. The sites or facilities should take measures against dispersion, loss, seepage, and air and water contamination.

Industrial Solid Wastes Disposed refers to quantity of industrial solid wastes which are burnt or placed ultimately in the sites meeting the requirements for environmental protection and not salvaged or recycled (including disposition in the year of those wastes of previous years). The disposition includes landfill (Safe landfills should be conducted for hazardous wastes), incineration, containment spaces, deep underground disposal, backfill in mining pits and disposal at sea.

Industrial Solid Wastes Discharged refers to volume of industrial solid wastes discharged by producing enterprises to disposal facilities or to other sites. The wastes exclude stones stripped or dug from mining (gangue and acid or alkaline waste stones not included).

Consumption Wastes Transported refers to volume of consumption wastes collected and transported to disposal factories or sites. Consumption wastes are solid wastes produced from urban households or from service activities for urban households, and solid wastes regarded by laws and regulations as urban consumption wastes, including those from households, commercial activities, markets, cleaning of streets, public sites, offices, schools, factories, mining units and other sources.

Ratio of Consumption Wastes Treated refers to consumption wastes treated over that produced. In practical statistics, as it is difficult to estimate, the volume of consumption wastes produced is replaced with that transported. Its calculation formula is:

Ratio=consumption wastes treated/consumption wastes produced × 100%

Land for Agriculture Use refers to land directly used for agriculture production, including land for cultivation, gardening, forests, herbage and other agriculture activities.

Area of Man-made Forests refer to the area of stable growing forests, planted manually or by airplanes, with a survival rate of 80% or higher of the designed number of trees per hectare, or with a canopy density of or above 0.20 after 3-5 years of manual planting or 5-7 years of airplane planting.

Total Area of Afforestation refers to the total area of land suitable for afforestation, including barren hills, idle land, sand dunes, "grain for green" land, on which acres of arbores or bushes are planted through manual planting, airplane planting, plant seedlings, etc. in accordance with the required density standards of the Technical Procedures of Afforestation, and with a survival rate of over 85% in line with the Implementing Rules of the Forest Law of the People's Republic of China (or a survival rate of 75% in areas with less that 400 mm of annual rainfall and without irrigation facilities). Included in the this category are trees planted alone the roadsides, riversides, or next to houses that occupy an area over 0.066 hectares, or where more than 4 lines of trees are planted. Total area of afforestation is further classified by ownership (state-owned, state-collective, collective or private), by approach of planting (manual, airplane), and by type of forests (timber, by-products, protection, fuel, special use, etc.).

Timber Forests refer to forests which is mainly for the production of timber, including bamboo groves planted to harvest bamboos.

By-product Forests refer to forests that mainly produce fruits, nuts, edible oil, beverages, indigents, raw materials and medicine materials. By-product forests are planted to harvest the fruits, leaves, bark or liquid of trees, and consume them as food or raw materials for the manufacturing industry, such as tea-oil trees, tung oil trees, walnut trees, camphor trees, tea bushes, mulberry trees, fruit trees, etc.

Protection Forests refer to forests, trees and bushes planted mainly for protection or preservation purpose, including water resource conservation forests, water and soil conservation forests, windbreak and dune-fixing forests, farmland and pasture protection forests, riverside protection forests, roadside protection forests, etc.

Fuel Forests refer to forests planted mainly for fuels.

Project on Preservation of Natural Forests is the Number One ecological project in China's forest industry that involves the largest investment. It consists of 3 components: 1) Complete halt of all cutting and logging activities in the natural forests at the upper stream of Yangtze River and the upper and middle streams of the Yellow River. 2) Significant reduction of timber production of key state forest zones in northeast provinces and in Inner Mongolia. 3) Better protection of natural forests in other regions through rehabilitation programmes.

Projects on Converting Cultivated Land to Forests and Grassland (Grain for Green Projects) aiming at preventing soil erosion in key regions, these projects are ecological construction projects in the development of forest industry that have the widest coverage and most sophisticated procedures, with strong policy implications and most active participation of the people.

Projects on Protection Forests in North China and Yangtze River Basin covering the widest areas in China with a rich variety of contents, these projects aim at solving the problem of sand and dust in northeastern China, northern China and northwestern China and the ecological issues in other areas. More specifically, they include phase IV of project on North China protection forests, phase II of project on protection forests at the middle and lower streams of Yangtze River and at the Huihe River and Taihu Lake valley, phase II of project on coastal protection forests, phase II of project on Pearl River protection forests, phase II project on greenery of Taihang Mountain and phase II projects on greenery of plains.

Projects on Preserving Wild Animals and Plants and on Construction of Nature Reserves aiming at gene preservation and protection of bio-diversity, nature and wetlands, these projects look into the future with strategic perspective and are integrated with international trends.

Wetlands refer to marshland and peat bog, whether natural or man-made, permanent or temporary; water covered areas, whether stagnant or flowing, with fresh or semi-fresh or salty water that is less than 6 metres deep at low tide; as well as coral beach, weed beach, mud beach, mangrove, river outlet, rivers, fresh-water marshland, marshland forests, lakes, salty bog and salt lakes along the coastal areas.

Nature Reserves refer to certain areas of land, waters or sea that are representative in natural ecological systems, or are natural habitats for rare or endangered wild animals or plants, or water conservation zones, or the location of important natural or historic relics, which are demarked by law and put under special protection and management. Nature reserves are designated by the formal approval of governments at and above county level (including those approved by relevant departments or "revolutionary committees" before 1980). Scenic spots and cultural preservation zones are not included.

Ecological Demonstration Zones refer to administrative areas approved by the environment protection agencies of central and provincial governments and established by provincial, prefecture or county governments in line with the approved programme for ecological demonstration zones. They include those evaluated and accepted by the environment protection agencies of central and provincial governments and those under pilot development stage.

Landslides refer to the geological phenomenon of unstable rocks and earth on slopes sliding down along certain soft surface as a result of gravitational force. Role of surface water and underground water, and destruction of the stability of slopes by irrational construction work are usually main factors triggering the landslides. Several damages are often caused by landslides in open mining, in water conservancy projects, and in the construction of railways and highways.

Collapse refers to the geological phenomenon of large mass of rocks or earth suddenly collapsing from the mountain or cliff as a result of gravitational force. Usually caused by weathering of rocks, permeance of rain or earthquakes, collapse often destructs buildings and blocks river course or transport routes.

Mud-rock Flow refers to the sudden rush of flood torrents containing large amount of mud and rocks in mountainous areas. It is found mostly in semi-arid hills or plateaus. High and precipitous topographic features, loose soil mass, heavy rains or melting water contribute to the mud-rock flow.

Environment Pollution and Destruction Accidents refer to sudden accidents, due to economic or social activities that are in contrast to environment protection laws or due to unforeseen factors or natural disasters, that lead to the environment pollution, the destruction of protected wild animals, plants or nature reserves, the damage to human health, the economic and property losses, and the negative impact on the society.

Investment in Environment Pollution Harnessing Projects refers to the proportion of investment in fixed assets in the total investment in harnessing industrial pollution and in the construction of urban environment infrastructure facilities. It includes investment in harnessing sources of industrial pollution, investment in environment protection facilities designed concurrently with construction projects, and investment in urban environment infrastructure facilities.

Investment in Fixed Assets for Afforestation refers to the investment in capital construction and updating projects in afforestation during the reference period.

第十篇
农　业

CHAPTER 10
Agriculture

简要说明
Brief Introduction

本篇资料的主要内容及来源

本篇资料反映新疆维吾尔自治区农业生产和农村经济基本情况，主要内容包括农村基层组织情况、乡村从业人员、国有农、林、牧、渔场情况、主要农业生产条件、耕地、农林牧渔业产值、主要农产品生产情况、乡镇企业情况等。

农林牧渔业统计范围包括全社会除军马生产及农业科研机构进行的试验型农业生产以外的所有农林牧渔业生产活动。即农村各种经济组织和农户经营的农林牧渔业生产活动；各种专业性农、林、牧、渔场的生产活动；国家各级机关、团体、学校、部队进行的农业生产活动；集体所有制的乡、镇、村办农场的农林牧渔业生产活动；工矿企业经营的农、林、牧、渔业生产活动。

本篇资料除表10-10、10-11、10-12来自新疆维吾尔自治区水利厅，表10-27来自新疆维吾尔自治区民政厅，乡镇企业主要指标来自新疆维吾尔自治区乡镇企业局外，其余资料均由新疆维吾尔自治区统计局农村处提供。

Main Content and Source of Data

The data in this chapter show the basic conditions of agricultural production and rural economy in Xinjiang Uygur Autonomous Region, including mainly rural grassroots units rural population, rural employed labor force, basic conditions of township enterprises, statistic on forest products, cultivated land, gross output value farming, forest, animal husbandry and fishery, output of major farm products and condition on the township enterprises, ect.

Statistics on agriculture cover all agriculture production activities expect horse raising for military purpose and activities undertaken by agriculture research institutions. Included in agriculture statistics are production activities in crop cultivation, forestry, animal husbandry and fishery undertaken by rural economic units of various types and by rural households, production activities of farms specializing in crop cultivation, forestry, animal husbandry and fishery undertaken by rural economic units of various types and by rural households, production activities of farms specializing in crop cultivation, forestry, animal husbandry and fishery; production activities undertaken by government agencies, institutions, schools and military units, production activities in agriculture undertaken by collective farms run by townships and villages, and production activities in crop cultivation, forest, animal husbandry and fishery undertaken by manufacturing and mining enterprises.

Data on this chapter are provided by the Xinjiang Bureau of Water Resources except 10-10,10-11,10-12,the data on table 10-27 are provided by the Xinjiang Bureau of Civil Affairs. the data on the township enterprises are from the Xinjiang Bureau of Township Enterprises. Others are provided by the Department of Rural statistics, Xinjiang Bureau of Statistics.

10-1 农村基层组织情况
Basic Conditions of Rural Grass-roots Unit

指　　标	Item	1995	2000	2007
乡镇政府(个)	**Number of Township and Town Governments (unit)**	**798**	**794**	**798**
#镇政府	Number of Township Governments		124	172
村民委员会(个)	Number of Villagers' Committees (unit)	8943	9378	8965
乡村户数(户)	Number of Rural Households (household)	1811804	2008794	2333739
乡村人口(人)	Rural Population (person)	8664329	9131922	10161682
乡村从业人员(人)	**Number of Rural Laborers (person)**	**3124888**	**3540789**	**4252584**
按性别分	Grouped by Gender			
男	Male	1725300	1950559	2353333
女	Female	1399588	1590230	1899251
按行业分	Grouped by Sector			
农林牧渔业	Agriculture, Forestry, Animal Husbandry & Fishery	2835581	3144461	3543386
工　业	Industry	77948	84766	131942
建筑业	Construction	35535	49126	116747
交通运输、仓储和邮政业	Transportation,Storage, Postal and Telecommunication Services			120885
信息传输、计算机服务和软件业	Information Transmission, Computer Service and Software Sector			6954
批发与零售业	Wholesale and Retail Trades		76727	134794
住宿和餐饮业	Hotels and Catering Serives		109217	87086
其　他	Others		76492	110790

10-2 国有农林牧渔场基本情况
Basic Conditions of State Agriculture, Forestry, Animal Husbandry and Fishery

指　　标	Item	2006	2007
场数合计(个)	**Total (unit)**	**485**	**478**
农 场	Number of Farms	291	290
林 场	Number of Forest Farms	44	43
牧 场	Number of Ranch	133	131
渔 场	Number of Fishing Ground	17	14
场内户数(户)	**Number of Households on a Farm (household)**	**768075**	**779940**
#牧业户数	Number of Stock-breeding Household	60516	63648
场内人口(人)	**Farm Population (person)**	**2498046**	**2507935**
#牧业人口	Stock-breeding Population	240673	248354
场内实有从业人员(人)	**Persons Actually Engaged on a Farm (person)**	**991498**	**990763**
男	Male	554082	554753
女	Female	437416	436010
农　业	Employed Persons in Agriculture	740076	739707
工　业	Employed Persons in Industry	55973	52290
建筑业	Employed Persons in Construction	26588	24953
交通运输、仓储和邮政业	Transportation,Storage, Post and Telecommunications Services	26887	27481
信息传输、计算机服务和软件业	Information Transmission, Computer Service and Software Sector	523	446
批发与零售业	Wholesale and Retail Trades	41371	42879
住宿和餐饮业	Hotels and Catering Serives	19179	19688
其　他	Others	80901	83319

10-3 各地、州、市、县(市)农村基层组织情况

(2007 年)

地区	Region	乡镇数(个) Number of Township and Town Govern-ments (unit)	#镇 town	村民委员会(个) Number of Villagers' Committees (unit)	乡村户数(户) Number of Rural House-Holds (household)	#牧业户数 Stock-breeding households
总 计	**Total**	**798**	**172**	**8965**	**2333739**	**256192**
一、地 方	**Local Regions**	**796**	**172**	**8936**	**2326415**	**255885**
乌鲁木齐市	**Urumqi City**	**23**	**8**	**176**	**56131**	**5925**
#乌鲁木齐县	Urumqi County	9	2	59	16653	2975
克拉玛依市	**Karamay City**	**2**		**6**	**545**	**52**
吐鲁番地区	**Turpan Administrative Offices**	**23**	**7**	**174**	**93488**	**3194**
吐鲁番市	Turpan City	8	1	60	37709	1736
鄯善县	Shanshan [piqan]County	9	4	67	35650	352
托克逊县	Toksun County	6	2	47	20129	1106
哈密地区	**Hami [Kumul]Administrative Offices**	**31**	**5**	**171**	**48155**	**13355**
哈密市	Hami [Kumul]City	15	2	92	28432	7120
巴里坤哈萨克自治县	Barkol KazakAutonomous County	10	2	47	17296	5610
伊吾县	Yiwu [Araturuk]County	6	1	32	2427	625
昌吉回族自治州	**Changji Hui Autonomous Prefecture**	**67**	**32**	**728**	**162055**	**23737**
昌吉市	Changji City	10	6	88	28783	4927
阜康市	Fukang City	6	3	106	16188	2108
呼图壁县	Hutubi County	6	5	53	18892	3413
玛纳斯县	Manas County	11	6	152	23837	3423
奇台县	Qitai County	15	6	102	33970	3498
吉木萨尔县	Jimsar County	9	4	167	23189	1913
木垒哈萨克自治县	Mori Kazak Autonomous County	10	2	60	17196	4455
伊犁哈萨克自治州	**Ili Kazak Autonomous Prefecture**	**212**	**51**	**1965**	**482892**	**76670**
伊犁州直属县(市)	**Counties (Cities) Direct Under Ili Prefecture**	**100**	**20**	**666**	**296670**	**41685**
伊宁市	Yining [Gulja]City	9	1	46	28979	889
奎屯市	Kuytun City	1		4	421	
伊宁县	Yining [Gulja]County	18	2	129	62648	5715
察布查尔锡伯自治县	Qapqal Xibe Autonomous County	14	2	62	27318	1710
霍城县	Huocheng [korgas]County	10	5	75	43482	2463
巩留县	Gongliu [Tokkuzlara]County	8	1	52	24826	2902
新源县	Xinyuan [kunes]County	11	6	89	43042	7591
昭苏县	Zhaosu [mongolkure]County	10	1	75	21342	5518
特克斯县	Tekes County	8	1	59	20786	6648
尼勒克县	Nilka County	11	1	75	23826	8249
塔城地区	**Tacheng [Tarbagatai] Administrative Offices**	**61**	**21**	**793**	**122815**	**14158**
塔城市	Tacheng [Qoqek] City	6	1	115	17948	1624
乌苏市	Usu City	14	7	135	25302	412
额敏县	Emin [Dorbiljin] County	11		139	19075	1228
沙湾县	Shawan County	12	9	237	36645	1339
托里县	Toli County	7	3	66	12661	6727
裕民县	Yumin [Qagantokay] County	5		45	6795	1530
和布克赛尔蒙古自治县	Hoboksar Mongol Autonomous County	6	1	56	4389	1298
阿勒泰地区	**Altay Administrative Offices**	**51**	**10**	**506**	**63407**	**20827**
阿勒泰市	Altay City	10	2	97	14112	2891
布尔津县	Burqin County	7	1	63	10992	4017
富蕴县	Fuyun [Koktokay] County	9	3	73	8153	2839
福海县	Fuhai [Burultokay] County	5		65	9238	3140
哈巴河县	Habahe [Kaba] County	7	1	113	8476	3012
青河县	Qinghe [Qinggil] County	7	2	54	7195	3942
吉木乃县	Jeminay County	6	1	41	5241	986

Basic Conditions of Rural Grass-roots Units by Prefecture, Autonomous Prefecture, City and County

乡村人口数(人) Rural Population (person)	#牧业人口数 Population Engaged in Livestocks	乡村从业人员(人) Number of Rural Laborers (person)	#男 Male	农林牧渔业 Agriculture, Forestry, Animal Husbandry & Fishery	工业 Industry	建筑业 Construction	交通仓储和邮政业 Transport, Storage, Post and Telecommunication Services	信息传输、计算机服务和软件业 Information Transmission, Computer Servcie and Software Industries	批发与零售业 Retail and Wholesale Trades	住宿和餐饮业 Hotels and Catering Serives	其他 Others
10161682	**1109271**	**4252584**	**2353333**	**3543386**	**131942**	**116747**	**120885**	**6954**	**134794**	**87086**	**110790**
10138387	**1107435**	**4241109**	**2347602**	**3533456**	**131558**	**116715**	**120713**	**6954**	**134438**	**87041**	**110234**
217505	**24884**	**130724**	**68357**	**82182**	**9474**	**1950**	**10876**	**128**	**6811**	**8135**	**11168**
65365	12181	38784	20418	30312	764	211	1155	40	873	945	4484
1784	**278**	**1478**	**980**	**1388**	**30**	**20**	**15**	**16**	**9**		
406605	**11034**	**226714**	**127065**	**193222**	**3929**	**4223**	**7229**	**332**	**10819**	**5427**	**1533**
172966	5634	89531	49118	74033	1075	1380	2551	64	6327	3105	996
149479	1308	90897	50212	80578	1536	1168	2268	226	2882	1747	492
84160	4092	46286	27735	38611	1318	1675	2410	42	1610	575	45
178643	**52711**	**99054**	**54071**	**75242**	**4379**	**3306**	**5406**	**291**	**4377**	**3099**	**2954**
103456	26011	61726	32687	49928	1562	1250	3488	188	2160	1342	1808
67648	24225	33446	19238	21892	2800	2026	1880	101	2050	1668	1029
7539	2475	3882	2146	3422	17	30	38	2	167	89	117
647282	**101140**	**362021**	**194448**	**308402**	**9178**	**5367**	**9878**	**320**	**9668**	**6062**	**13146**
107123	17219	60426	32109	49210	2841	1170	1906	120	1966	785	2428
62843	9973	36983	20168	29573	1688	1379	1185	22	1035	851	1250
79131	15949	41559	22855	36640	762	94	1636	27	1049	802	549
89472	12707	53109	29329	46878	1158	326	1384	31	1146	1023	1163
146594	16849	78878	42109	67004	859	1111	2038	24	2378	1672	3792
91961	8430	52781	27464	44985	1044	692	1198	20	1379	638	2825
70158	20013	38285	20414	34112	826	595	531	76	715	291	1139
2205784	**373547**	**1025833**	**588138**	**830571**	**43084**	**31715**	**33078**	**3073**	**36472**	**21789**	**26051**
1434111	**207909**	**638545**	**369635**	**502636**	**29889**	**24713**	**22370**	**2339**	**25543**	**14347**	**16708**
135741	4912	62642	35674	38817	6188	3388	4312	114	5085	2504	2234
1256		672	351	641					6	20	5
306524	23109	153916	89241	122908	8237	5596	5141	452	5721	3835	2026
125405	8793	47308	28356	40184	3046	1054	1003	134	1637	87	163
205646	11832	114650	62833	94142	3211	2633	4190	717	3715	3022	3020
115780	16848	36610	21965	32002	1075	714	1143	10	1496	112	58
218999	40807	89141	54557	69542	4131	4043	3038	369	3448	1898	2672
103288	28762	36298	23263	27751	1793	1672	1341	104	1359	659	1619
106131	35672	53756	29447	41152	1118	3832	573	295	1333	1332	4121
115341	37174	43552	23948	35497	1090	1781	1629	144	1743	878	790
494817	**62546**	**274514**	**151782**	**237588**	**8417**	**2414**	**7145**	**600**	**7521**	**4740**	**6089**
61153	7063	38134	20241	30791	780	480	866	60	2095	619	2443
105237	1613	56395	31067	50380	1855	504	631		815	1500	710
81315	5054	47762	27117	42312	1057	314	1161	95	1249	542	1032
139039	5466	76230	40038	65960	3347	637	1570	133	2312	1375	896
56978	30093	29828	18865	24971	987	366	2227	261	495	179	342
31802	7796	16682	8785	14931	255	75	314	4	363	277	463
19293	5461	9483	5669	8243	136	38	376	47	192	248	203
276856	**103092**	**112774**	**66721**	**90347**	**4778**	**4588**	**3563**	**134**	**3408**	**2702**	**3254**
58289	13978	21939	13450	18266	1006	718	591	34	629	300	395
45261	17635	20938	12160	17072	290	434	419		647	926	1150
39073	14390	15406	8994	10826	1429	689	430	34	414	263	1321
36331	15688	17304	10005	13013	979	1720	799	16	360	260	157
44359	16082	16318	10394	13498	575	519	789	15	651	271	
37487	21353	15555	8708	12695	470	508	533	35	594	536	184
16056	3966	5314	3010	4977	29		2		113	146	47

10-3 续表

地　区	Region	乡镇数（个）Number of Township and Town Governments (Unit)	#镇 town	村民委员会（个）Number of Villagers' Committees (Unit)	乡村户数（户）Number of Rural Households (unit)	#牧业户数 Stock-Breeding households
博尔塔拉蒙古自治州	**Bortala Mongol Autonomous Prefecture**	**14**	**5**	**254**	**48598**	**5410**
博乐市	Bole [Bortala] City	5	3	134	18676	2115
精河县	Jinghe [Jing] County	4	1	55	19946	1754
温泉县	Wenquan [Araxang] County	5	1	65	9976	1541
巴音郭楞蒙古自治州	**Bayangol Mongol Autonomous Prefecture**	**73**	**11**	**390**	**108244**	**10001**
库尔勒市	Korla City	10	1	56	18202	362
轮台县	Luntai [Bugur] County	10	3	65	16388	907
尉犁县	Yuli [Lopnur] County	7		52	12168	1987
若羌县	Ruoqiang [Qarkilik] County	5		17	3652	201
且末县	Qiemo [Qarqan] County	11		52	7803	1033
焉耆回族自治县	Yanqi Hui Autonomous County	7	3	46	17550	582
和静县	Hejing County	11	3	54	17421	3674
和硕县	Hoxud County	6		22	6790	782
博湖县	Bohu [Bagrax] County	6	1	26	8270	473
阿克苏地区	**Aksu Administrative Offices**	**73**	**21**	**1104**	**302344**	**21151**
阿克苏市	Aksu City	6	2	122	30037	4755
温宿县	Wensu [Onsu] County	9	4	104	28958	2190
库车县	Kuqa County	13	7	211	61387	2055
沙雅县	Xayar County	7	3	147	40980	1605
新和县	Xinhe [Toksu] County	7	1	112	30800	3890
拜城县	Baicheng [Bay] County	12	2	150	31848	2650
乌什县	Wushi [Uxturpan] County	8		107	38361	1337
阿瓦提县	Awat County	7	2	118	32226	1249
柯坪县	Kalpin County	4		33	7747	1420
克孜勒苏柯尔克孜自治州	**Kizilsu Kirgiz Autonomous Prefecture**	**35**	**3**	**234**	**83525**	**21658**
阿图什市	Artux City	7		72	35893	6127
阿克陶县	Akto County	13	2	106	34215	7495
阿合奇县	Akqi County	6	1	22	6295	3540
乌恰县	Wuqia [Ulugqat] County	9		34	7122	4496
喀什地区	**Kashgar [Kaxgar] Administrative Offices**	**157**	**18**	**2344**	**571786**	**49254**
喀什市	Kashgar [Kaxgar] City	8		106	37633	2179
疏附县	Shufu County	12		165	57000	9100
疏勒县	Shule County	14	2	223	54404	2300
英吉沙县	Yengisar County	13		164	46218	285
泽普县	Zepu [Poskam] County	11	1	130	24576	771
莎车县	Shache [Yarkant] County	28	6	498	116425	10342
叶城县	Yecheng [Kagilik] County	19	2	305	61028	7076
麦盖提县	Makit County	9		128	26030	1250
岳普湖县	Yopurga County	8	1	87	25542	2396
伽师县	Jiashi [Payzawat] County	13	2	296	68970	4856
巴楚县	Bachu [Maralbexi] County	11	3	195	49352	5639
塔什库尔干塔吉克自治县	Taxkorgan Tajik Autonomous County	11	1	47	4608	3060
和田地区	**Hotan Administrative Offices**	**86**	**11**	**1390**	**368652**	**25478**
和田市	Hotan City	7	2	111	33574	4033
和田县	Hotan County	11	1	212	56469	3459
墨玉县	Moyu [Karakax] County	16	1	364	98079	6052
皮山县	Pishan [Guma] County	15	2	169	39531	1640
洛浦县	Lop County	8	1	207	50168	3228
策勒县	Qira County	8	1	124	32274	3041
于田县	Yutian [Keriya] County	15	2	174	52465	3156
民丰县	Minfeng [Niya] County	6	1	29	6092	869
二、生产建设兵团	**Xinjiang Production and Construction Group**	**2**		**29**	**7324**	**307**

Continued

乡村人口数(人) Rural Population (person)	#牧业人口数 Population Engaged in Livestocks	乡村从业人员(人) Number of Rural Laborers (person)	#男 Male	农林牧渔业 Agriculture, Forestry, Animal Husbandry & Fishery	工业 Industry	建筑业 Construction	交通仓储和邮政业 Transport, Storage, Post and Telecommunication Services	信息传输、计算机服务和软件业 Information Transmission, Computer Servcie and Software Industries	批发与零售业 Retail and Wholesale Trades	住宿和餐饮业 Hotels and Catering Serives	其他 Others
186054	**21978**	**86700**	**46918**	**68324**	**4502**	**2226**	**2194**	**173**	**3471**	**2401**	**3409**
78981	10057	36801	19962	26161	3230	1059	1411	73	1839	1156	1872
69244	6030	31075	16545	26710	702	615	442	27	1033	887	659
37829	5891	18824	10411	15453	570	552	341	73	599	358	878
434295	**39539**	**194102**	**110330**	**167849**	**4579**	**3662**	**5234**	**277**	**6891**	**2729**	**2881**
69846	1067	31370	18419	26592	216	328	1083	35	2371	401	344
63964	2524	29422	16447	26318	571	338	347	39	928	396	485
47131	8400	18161	10798	16875	60	116	258	38	425	161	228
13157	768	8669	4852	7781	84	133	106		348	94	123
37014	4609	12339	6768	10742	446	305	446		280	89	31
70706	2405	27005	16309	21084	2020	860	1059	6	831	578	567
73932	14515	37884	20421	32598	704	1314	1148	39	895	601	585
25028	3293	12581	7073	10833	162	132	349	105	450	212	338
33517	1958	16671	9243	15026	316	136	438	15	363	197	180
1348660	**79730**	**573593**	**312502**	**507578**	**11421**	**10304**	**10979**	**1018**	**14408**	**8783**	**9102**
137692	14722	57092	32216	51286	763	889	1861	120	823	977	373
127131	11315	42117	23582	39080	448	245	292	73	797	243	939
296861	9197	139311	76346	112584	4677	5491	5150	372	4742	3083	3212
170610	8246	70830	37960	61965	1590	622	316	54	2396	1489	2398
123856	8697	56049	30626	52962	301	340	620	163	1152	379	132
147337	11800	64338	36614	60649	250	480	645	21	1203	640	450
159850	6287	55300	29168	49197	1436	814	906	110	1393	744	700
150723	5582	71489	37633	64592	1525	947	933	105	1488	1001	898
34600	3884	17067	8357	15263	431	476	256		414	227	
374470	**98160**	**125671**	**73896**	**100225**	**6025**	**3930**	**3784**	**53**	**4767**	**3870**	**3017**
164500	27493	58995	32915	40200	4277	2615	2848	53	3184	3475	2343
149355	34421	48741	31563	43601	1412	1106	620		1023	395	584
28430	16104	6778	3728	6228	44	143	53		220		90
32185	20142	11157	5690	10196	292	66	263		340		
2620325	**207923**	**866011**	**473766**	**740073**	**13820**	**28097**	**20703**	**405**	**25818**	**16153**	**20942**
177298	8262	64099	40400	29849	1326	6403	3741		5112	6619	11049
265500	32200	82000	47250	65050	2010	4500	2310	59	4050	1700	2321
252948	10980	55300	32700	50000	800	1400	1450	20	1100	150	380
204277	317	94840	50010	91070	585	880	670		710	815	110
103191	3708	29224	14574	24986	558	1185	768		681		1046
536994	40879	194390	103880	170204	4271	5075	4342		5539	1200	3759
291613	31997	87659	49189	76277	1246	4428	2613	31	805	1745	514
119931	4507	48662	26016	45934	119	343	227	74	745	495	725
113522	8608	45414	23662	40996	308	948	561	96	750	1284	471
326806	24500	90219	47930	80769	1100	1600	2300	100	2000	2100	250
203433	27502	66456	33761	58432	1081	1033	1424	25	4176	35	250
24812	14463	7748	4394	6506	416	302	297		150	10	67
1516980	**96511**	**549208**	**297131**	**458400**	**21137**	**21915**	**11337**	**868**	**10927**	**8593**	**16031**
152362	17825	52011	28639	35213	4546	2970	2466	269	1442	1407	3698
232401	12143	89459	48371	70969	4320	3781	1570	62	2878	1979	3900
417736	20623	131334	72819	105016	6370	8284	3339	313	2920	2475	2617
166620	6141	63280	33484	55596	781	815	653		705	327	4403
194600	15596	83290	46394	73666	3174	2518	1349	62	1239	295	987
123094	11337	44726	23438	40195	1133	1033	403	46	856	860	200
205490	9763	78676	40439	72786	578	2332	1081	107	676	1044	72
24677	3083	6432	3547	4959	235	182	476	9	211	206	154
23295	**1836**	**11475**	**5731**	**9930**	**384**	**32**	**172**		**356**	**45**	**556**

10-4 各地、州、市、县(市)耕地面积

Area of Cultivated land by Prefecture, Autonomous Prefecture, City and County

单位：千公顷 (2007 年) (1 000 hectares)

地区	Region	年末耕地面积 Cultivated Land (Year-end)	年内增加的耕地面积 Newly Increased Cultivated Land in Current year	#新开荒地面积 Newly Reclaimed Wildland Land
总计	**Total**	**3787.28**	**191.13**	**40.92**
一、地方	**Local Regions**	**2708.80**	**160.88**	**40.92**
乌鲁木齐市	**Urumqi City**	**55.71**	**1.09**	**0.99**
#乌鲁木齐县	Urumqi County	21.05	0.78	0.69
克拉玛依市	**Karamay City**	**15.48**		
吐鲁番地区	**TurpanAdministrative Offices**	**34.80**	**0.10**	**0.10**
吐鲁番市	Turpan City	11.69		
鄯善县	Shanshan [piqan]County	10.08	0.10	0.10
托克逊县	Toksun County	13.03		
哈密地区	**Hami [Kumul]Administrative Offices**	**52.35**	**1.88**	**0.06**
哈密市	Hami [Kumul]City	25.17	0.02	
巴里坤哈萨克自治县	Barkol KazakAutonomous County	22.84	1.86	0.06
伊吾县	Yiwu [Araturuk]County	4.34		
昌吉回族自治州	**Changji Hui Autonomous Prefecture**	**337.77**	**19.59**	**13.92**
昌吉市	Changji City	53.45	3.37	2.60
阜康市	Fukang City	24.21	2.83	2.83
呼图壁县	Hutubi County	54.90	4.05	3.99
玛纳斯县	Manas County	54.30	1.67	1.03
奇台县	Qitai County	82.34	4.20	
吉木萨尔县	Jimsar County	31.23		
木垒哈萨克自治县	Mori Kazak Autonomous County	37.34	3.47	3.47
伊犁哈萨克自治州	**Ili Kazak Autonomous Prefecture**	**828.83**	**66.89**	**12.44**
伊犁州直属县(市)	**Counties (Cities) Direct Under Ili Prefecture**	**312.20**	**26.74**	**6.96**
伊宁市	Yining [Gulja]City	15.44	0.01	
奎屯市	Kuytun City	2.37	0.10	0.10
伊宁县	Yining [Gulja]County	61.82	1.20	
察布查尔锡伯自治县	Qapqal Xibe Autonomous County	41.07	6.86	6.86
霍城县	Huocheng [korgas]County	32.83		
巩留县	Gongliu [Tokkuzlara]County	27.43		
新源县	Xinyuan [kunes]County	43.69	5.33	
昭苏县	Zhaosu [mongolkure]County	45.60	6.33	
特克斯县	Tekes County	23.20	5.92	
尼勒克县	Nilka County	18.75	0.99	
塔城地区	**Tacheng [Tarbagatai] Administrative Offices**	**377.59**	**33.62**	**0.42**
塔城市	Tacheng [Qoqek] City	84.76	3.44	
乌苏市	Usu City	64.72	1.37	
额敏县	Emin [Dorbiljin] County	87.00	18.15	
沙湾县	Shawan County	78.06	0.23	0.05
托里县	Toli County	15.33		
裕民县	Yumin [Qagantokay] County	36.67	10.06	
和布克赛尔蒙古自治县	Hoboksar Mongol Autonomous County	11.05	0.37	0.37
阿勒泰地区	**Altay Administrative Offices**	**139.04**	**6.53**	**5.06**
阿勒泰市	Altay City	22.64	0.61	0.61
布尔津县	Burqin County	20.58	1.71	1.71
富蕴县	Fuyun [Koktokay] County	19.92	0.90	0.90
福海县	Fuhai [Burultokay] County	24.79	1.30	1.30
哈巴河县	Habahe [Kaba] County	22.53	0.33	0.33
青河县	Qinghe [Qinggil] County	12.60	1.68	0.21
吉木乃县	Jeminay County	15.98		

10-4 续表 Continued

单位：千公顷 (1 000 hectares)

地区	Region	年末耕地面积 Cultivated Land (Year-end)	年内增加的耕地面积 Newly Increased Cultivated Land in Current year	#新开荒地面积 Newly Reclaimed Wildland Land
博尔塔拉蒙古自治州	**Bortala Mongol Autonomous Prefecture**	**78.44**	**3.30**	**0.79**
博乐市	Bole [Bortala] City	28.74	0.79	0.79
精河县	Jinghe [Jing] County	24.95	1.25	
温泉县	Wenquan [Araxang] County	24.75	1.26	
巴音郭楞蒙古自治州	**Bayangol Mongol Autonomous Prefecture**	**204.68**	**19.16**	**6.13**
库尔勒市	Korla City	44.27	3.15	0.31
轮台县	Luntai [Bugur] County	19.31	0.67	
尉犁县	Yuli [Lopnur] County	40.44	2.72	2.65
若羌县	Ruoqiang [Qarkilik] County	4.61	0.78	0.78
且末县	Qiemo [Qarqan] County	12.84	1.19	1.19
焉耆回族自治县	Yanqi Hui Autonomous County	22.70	0.51	0.51
和静县	Hejing County	20.15	1.61	
和硕县	Hoxud County	26.31	8.41	0.69
博湖县	Bohu [Bagrax] County	14.05	0.12	
阿克苏地区	**Aksu Administrative Offices**	**379.30**	**11.42**	**4.79**
阿克苏市	Aksu City	48.31	2.20	
温宿县	Wensu [Onsu] County	51.84	1.13	1.10
库车县	Kuqa County	59.48	0.20	0.08
沙雅县	Xayar County	53.82	0.11	0.11
新和县	Xinhe [Toksu] County	39.19	4.50	3.50
拜城县	Baicheng [Bay] County	39.85		
乌什县	Wushi [Uxturpan] County	23.80		
阿瓦提县	Awat County	55.70	3.28	
柯坪县	Kalpin County	7.31		
克孜勒苏柯尔克孜自治州	**Kizilsu Kirgiz Autonomous Prefecture**	**30.83**	**0.80**	**0.70**
阿图什市	Artux City	9.23	0.60	0.53
阿克陶县	Akto County	16.49	0.20	0.17
阿合奇县	Akqi County	2.73		
乌恰县	Wuqia [Ulugqat] County	2.38		
喀什地区	**Kashgar [Kaxgar] Administrative Offices**	**515.71**	**32.11**	
喀什市	Kashgar [Kaxgar] City	12.00	1.22	
疏附县	Shufu County	33.81	0.97	
疏勒县	Shule County	41.47	4.63	
英吉沙县	Yengisar County	23.57	1.92	
泽普县	Zepu [Poskam] County	24.41	0.15	
莎车县	Shache [Yarkant] County	104.67	4.54	
叶城县	Yecheng [Kagilik] County	53.36	5.75	
麦盖提县	Makit County	54.67		
岳普湖县	Yopurga County	26.50	3.15	
伽师县	Jiashi [Payzawat] County	54.15	0.87	
巴楚县	Bachu [Maralbexi] County	83.16	8.73	
塔什库尔干塔吉克自治县	Taxkorgan Tajik Autonomous County	3.94	0.18	
和田地区	**Hotan Administrative Offices**	**174.90**	**4.54**	**1.00**
和田市	Hotan City	10.58	0.58	
和田县	Hotan County	24.02	0.39	0.39
墨玉县	Moyu [Karakax] County	34.85	0.05	0.04
皮山县	Pishan [Guma] County	29.76	0.08	0.08
洛浦县	Lop County	22.30	0.05	0.02
策勒县	Qira County	16.79	0.73	0.07
于田县	Yutian [Keriya] County	30.76	2.40	0.37
民丰县	Minfeng [Niya] County	5.84	0.26	0.03
二、生产建设兵团	**Xinjiang Production and Construction Group**	**1078.48**	**30.25**	

10-5 农、林、牧、渔业总产值

Gross Output Value of Agriculture, Forestry, Animal Husbandry and Fishery

单位：万元 (10 000 yuan)

年份 Year	地区 Region	农林牧渔业总产值 Total	农业产值 Farming	林业产值 Forestry	牧业产值 Animal Husbandry	渔业产值 Fishery	农林牧渔服务业产值 Output Value of Services for Farming, Forestry, Animal Husbandary and Fishery
1978		191184	142460	3397	44990	337	
1980		220135	164187	5394	50148	406	
1985		565699	429519	25906	108598	1676	
1990		1446535	1104742	38152	294963	8678	
1995		4057332	3150055	56381	823351	27545	
1996		4309617	3340735	61940	875560	31382	
1997		4764743	3738602	64913	925923	35305	
1998		4992355	3873616	74394	1008783	35562	
1999		4611503	3409380	75565	1092279	34279	
2000		4872005	3605405	83451	1145142	38007	
2001		4968125	3488409	100847	1340236	38633	
2002		5250446	3627669	110897	1480382	31498	
2003		6883187	4827597	136936	1619823	32065	266766
2004		7506792	5150018	138204	1874660	42985	300925
2005		8310614	5958464	152851	1835206	43405	320688
2006		8835409	6385954	171994	1890700	46945	339816
2007		10634648	7669468	208623	2315097	70149	371311
一、地　方	**Local Regions**	**8396841**	**5245494**	**284614**	**2547378**	**56677**	**262678**
乌鲁木齐市	Urumqi City	189911	86706	1570	88672	3962	9001
克拉玛依市	Karamay City	59070	23015	5133	14677	466	15779
吐鲁番地区	Turpan Administrative Offices	267171	207266	2652	52359	307	4587
哈密地区	Hami [Kumul] Administrative Offices	159272	97442	4354	53416	1257	2803
昌吉回族自治州	Changji Hui Autonomous Prefecture	1192472	600042	21362	542356	9755	18957
伊犁哈萨克自治州	Ili Kazak Autonomous Prefecture	1936796	1087816	30541	760813	16051	41575
伊犁州直属县(市)	Counties (Cities) Direct Under Ili Prefecture	819352	415061	14236	362840	7968	19247
塔城地区	Tacheng [Tarbagatai] Administrative Offices	805674	531388	8919	247537	3446	14384
阿勒泰地区	Altay Administrative Offices	311770	141367	7387	150437	4637	7942
博尔塔拉蒙古自治州	Bortala Mongol Autonomous Prefecture	267120	192689	2832	63316	1662	6621
巴音郭楞蒙古自治州	Bayangol Mongol Autonomous Prefecture	912405	656675	11050	204652	6802	33226
阿克苏地区	Aksu Administrative Offices	1055780	787950	41327	163410	5884	57209
克孜勒苏柯尔克孜自治州	Kizilsu Kirgiz Autonomous Prefecture	115514	62858	2034	41523	168	8931
喀什地区	Kashgar [Kaxgar] Administrative Offices	1723347	1096608	110079	453068	8758	54834
和田地区	Hotan Administrative Offices	517983	346427	51680	109116	1605	9155
二、生产建设兵团	**Xinjiang Production and Construction Group**	**3415178**	**2748722**	**33475**	**367703**	**18238**	**247040**

注：本表按当年价格计算；全区合计不等于各地、州汇总数。

Note : The number in this form is caculated by current price. Gross output value of autonomous region is not equal to the sum of output value of every prefecture.

10-6 农、林、牧、渔业总产值指数

Indices of Gross Output Value of Agriculture, Forestry, Animal Husbandry and Fishery

年 份 Year	农林牧渔业总产值 Total	#农业产值 Farming	#林业产值 Forestry	#牧业产值 Animal Husbandry	#渔业产值 Fishery
(上年=100) (preceding year=100)					
1978	113.0	118.6	108.8	105.4	106.7
1980	108.9	108.4	151.2	104.4	112.7
1985	110.9	111.5	131.3	104.6	135.1
1990	115.1	119.2	95.2	102.0	111.3
1991	108.0	109.2	99.6	103.4	105.8
1992	105.6	106.0	96.0	104.8	107.3
1993	102.3	101.6	108.3	104.6	113.8
1994	110.9	111.6	110.4	108.1	119.0
1995	107.1	107.0	88.5	109.0	127.0
1996	104.2	103.3	101.0	107.7	112.3
1997	109.5	109.6	100.5	110.2	108.6
1998	110.8	111.5	105.5	109.0	102.0
1999	104.8	103.9	100.9	108.1	106.3
2000	105.3	104.2	110.3	108.0	116.4
2001	104.5	103.9	116.1	105.8	104.2
2002	105.2	103.9	111.5	108.9	102.1
2003	106.3	105.2	120.7	108.7	101.7
2004	106.4	104.5	100.7	112.0	108.2
2005	107.4	107.0	105.8	109.0	105.3
2006	107.5	107.7	106.5	107.8	105.3
2007	108.2	108.9	108.6	106.0	115.2
(1978 年=100) (1978=100)					
1978	100.0	100.0	100.0	100.0	100.0
1980	115.9	115.5	158.8	111.1	120.5
1985	188.4	194.3	245.4	160.0	140.9
1990	303.7	322.6	244.4	243.7	442.4
1991	328.0	352.3	243.5	251.9	468.0
1992	346.3	373.4	233.8	264.1	502.1
1993	354.2	379.4	253.2	276.2	571.3
1994	392.8	423.6	279.6	298.5	680.0
1995	420.7	453.3	247.4	325.5	863.7
1996	438.4	468.1	249.8	350.6	970.0
1997	480.2	512.8	251.1	386.4	1053.2
1998	531.8	571.7	265.1	421.1	1073.9
1999	557.1	593.8	267.5	455.3	1141.6
2000	586.3	618.8	295.0	491.9	1328.4
2001	612.9	642.8	342.5	520.6	1384.1
2002	644.8	668.1	381.9	566.9	1413.2
2003	685.4	702.6	460.9	616.0	1437.2
2004	729.3	734.2	464.1	689.9	1555.1
2005	783.3	785.6	491.0	752.0	1637.5
2006	842.0	846.1	522.9	810.7	1724.3
2007	911.0	921.4	567.9	859.3	1986.4

10-7 各地、州、市、县(市)农林牧渔业总产值
Gross Output Value of Agriculture, Forestry, Animal Husbandry and Fishery by Prefecture, Autonomous Prefecture, City and County

单位：万元 (2007 年) (10 000 yuan)

地 区	Region	农林牧渔业总产值 Total	农业产值 Farming	林业产值 Forestry	牧业产值 Animal Husbandry	渔业产值 Fishery	农林牧渔服务业产值 Output Value of Services for Farming, Forestry, Animal Husbandary and Fishery
总 计	**Total**	**10634648**	**7669468**	**208623**	**2315097**	**70149**	**371311**
一、地 方	**Local Regions**	**8396841**	**5245494**	**284614**	**2547378**	**56677**	**262678**
乌鲁木齐市	**Urumqi City**	**189911**	**86706**	**1570**	**88672**	**3962**	**9001**
#乌鲁木齐县	Urumqi County	60080	33858	608	21224	1790	2600
克拉玛依市	**Karamay City**	**59070**	**23015**	**5133**	**14677**	**466**	**15779**
吐鲁番地区	**TurpanAdministrative Offices**	**267171**	**207266**	**2652**	**52359**	**307**	**4587**
吐鲁番市	Turpan City	108652	87283	1084	18290	178	1817
鄯善县	Shanshan [piqan]County	98125	78081	932	17867	55	1190
托克逊县	Toksun County	60395	41902	636	16202	74	1580
哈密地区	**Hami [Kumul]Administrative Offices**	**159272**	**97442**	**4354**	**53415**	**1258**	**2803**
哈密市	Hami [Kumul]City	88466	66114	1553	18383	921	1495
巴里坤哈萨克自治县	Barkol KazakAutonomous County	45422	15761	1030	27954	319	358
伊吾县	Yiwu [Araturuk]County	25384	15567	1771	7078	18	950
昌吉回族自治州	**Changji Hui Autonomous Prefecture**	**1192472**	**600042**	**21362**	**542356**	**9755**	**18957**
昌吉市	Changji City	227981	112494	3680	102820	6238	2749
阜康市	Fukang City	88175	43145	3006	41060	135	829
呼图壁县	Hutubi County	226776	103900	2924	110863	1886	7203
玛纳斯县	Manas County	251214	156877	3015	84003	942	6377
奇台县	Qitai County	220684	101346	4889	114244		205
吉木萨尔县	Jimsar County	106826	52942	2822	49588	554	920
木垒哈萨克自治县	Mori Kazak Autonomous County	70816	29338	1026	39778		674
伊犁哈萨克自治州	**Ili Kazak Autonomous Prefecture**	**1936796**	**1087816**	**30542**	**760814**	**16051**	**41573**
伊犁州直属县(市)	**Counties (Cities) Direct Under Ili Prefecture**	**819352**	**415061**	**14236**	**362840**	**7968**	**19247**
伊宁市	Yining [Gulja]City	61432	33187	625	23848	1917	1855
奎屯市	Kuytun City	4828	3043	66	259		1460
伊宁县	Yining [Gulja]County	183121	89178	3688	81089	4569	4597
察布查尔锡伯自治县	Qapqal Xibe Autonomous County	69464	44479	1344	21113	362	2166
霍城县	Huocheng [korgas]County	116203	65110	2765	45657	545	2126
巩留县	Gongliu [Tokkuzlara]County	76391	38802	965	36142	272	210
新源县	Xinyuan [kunes]County	136637	71586	2417	59963	223	2448
昭苏县	Zhaosu [mongolkure]County	56086	28997	549	25494	40	1006
特克斯县	Tekes County	54311	20833	629	32109	40	700
尼勒克县	Nilka County	60879	19846	1188	37166		2679

注： 1.本表按当年价格计算。 2.全区农林牧渔业总产值不等于各地汇总数。
Note: a) The number in this form is caculated by current price. b) Gross output value of autonomous region is not equal to the sum of output value of every prefecture.

10-7 续表 1 Continued

单位：万元 (10 000 yuan)

地　区	Region	农林牧渔业总产值 Total	农业产值 Farming	林业产值 Forestry	牧业产值 Animal Husbandry	渔业产值 Fishery	农林牧渔服务业产值 Output Value of Services for Farming, Forestry, Animal Husbandary and Fishery
塔城地区	**Tacheng [Tarbagatai] Administrative Offices**	**805674**	**531388**	**8919**	**247537**	**3446**	**14384**
塔城市	Tacheng [Qoqek] City	103862	72739	1328	28300	711	784
乌苏市	Usu City	207572	162369	3035	36405	1567	4196
额敏县	Emin [Dorbiljin] County	124698	62068	1183	58720	224	2503
沙湾县	Shawan County	263515	194077	864	64292	899	3383
托里县	Toli County	31522	9101	1055	19607		1759
裕民县	Yumin [Qagantokay] County	39077	19206	1430	17831	29	581
和布克赛尔蒙古自治县	Hoboksar Mongol Autonomous County	35428	11828	24	22382	16	1178
阿勒泰地区	**Altay Administrative Offices**	**311770**	**141367**	**7387**	**150437**	**4637**	**7942**
阿勒泰市	Altay City	66018	34140	669	29716	325	1168
布尔津县	Burqin County	35376	16290	1414	16667	171	834
富蕴县	Fuyun [Koktokay] County	62897	22502	766	38383	64	1182
福海县	Fuhai [Burultokay] County	59660	29049	1193	22940	3978	2500
哈巴河县	Habahe [Kaba] County	46632	23080	2368	20314	43	827
青河县	Qinghe [Qinggil] County	26538	10352	864	14517	41	764
吉木乃县	Jeminay County	14649	5954	113	7900	15	667
博尔塔拉蒙古自治州	**Bortala Mongol Autonomous Prefecture**	**267120**	**192689**	**2832**	**63316**	**1662**	**6621**
博乐市	Bole [Bortala] City	110348	74856	1999	30336	1178	1979
精河县	Jinghe [Jing] County	108122	87347	536	16269	428	3542
温泉县	Wenquan [Araxang] County	48650	30486	297	16711	56	1100
巴音郭楞蒙古自治州	**Bayangol Mongol Autonomous Prefecture**	**912405**	**656675**	**11050**	**204652**	**6802**	**33226**
库尔勒市	Korla City	250116	179718	917	62205	426	6850
轮台县	Luntai [Bugur] County	94664	76492	285	16099	52	1736
尉犁县	Yuli [Lopnur] County	136142	113160	1395	12287	85	9215
若羌县	Ruoqiang [Qarkilik] County	30072	24433	399	4619	8	613
且末县	Qiemo [Qarqan] County	53129	34566	1044	12853	154	4512
焉耆回族自治县	Yanqi Hui Autonomous County	98854	57796	875	36044	519	3620
和静县	Hejing County	86182	44456	1793	37327	136	2470
和硕县	Hoxud County	94582	77748	3640	10234	515	2445
博湖县	Bohu [Bagrax] County	68664	48306	702	12984	4907	1765
阿克苏地区	**Aksu Administrative Offices**	**1055781**	**787950**	**41328**	**163410**	**5884**	**57209**
阿克苏市	Aksu City	174647	130189	6683	27398	2186	8191
温宿县	Wensu [Onsu] County	156152	107404	7548	22633	747	17820
库车县	Kuqa County	173165	132093	7354	31588	268	1862

10-7 续表 2 Continued

单位：万元 (10 000 yuan)

地 区	Region	农林牧渔业总产值 Total	农业产值 Farming	林业产值 Forestry	牧业产值 Animal Husbandry	渔业产值 Fishery	农林牧渔服务业产值 Output Value of Services for Farming, Forestry, Animal Husbandary and Fishery
沙雅县	Xayar County	136556	113253	3745	16186	421	2951
新和县	Xinhe [Toksu] County	104758	74000	7799	12150	95	10714
拜城县	Baicheng [Bay] County	84307	56968	3740	20175	2007	1417
乌什县	Wushi [Uxturpan] County	67381	46955	2756	14733	72	2865
阿瓦提县	Awat County	143181	115861	1398	15356	88	10478
柯坪县	Kalpin County	15634	11227	305	3191		911
克孜勒苏柯尔克孜自治州	**Kizilsu Kirgiz Autonomous Prefecture**	**115514**	**62858**	**2034**	**41523**	**168**	**8931**
阿图什市	Artux City	52817	30929	945	16237	151	4555
阿克陶县	Akto County	44316	27709	931	12628	17	3031
阿合奇县	Akqi County	8722	1851	73	6193		605
乌恰县	Wuqia [Ulugqat] County	9659	2369	85	6465		740
喀什地区	**Kashgar [Kaxgar] Administrative Offices**	**1723347**	**1096608**	**110079**	**453068**	**8758**	**54834**
喀什市	Kashgar [Kaxgar] City	80949	43788	1006	32150	716	3289
疏附县	Shufu County	141806	78571	5871	53779	785	2800
疏勒县	Shule County	156415	106152	2063	47155	450	595
英吉沙县	Yengisar County	99693	69070	4088	19943	89	6503
泽普县	Zepu [Poskam] County	94760	53858	8797	28425	1800	1880
莎车县	Shache [Yarkant] County	300410	175285	38097	66315	3099	17614
叶城县	Yecheng [Kagilik] County	212889	113344	35093	61282	625	2545
麦盖提县	Makit County	127010	94300	842	25967	235	5666
岳普湖县	Yopurga County	64689	48252	1214	13603	172	1448
伽师县	Jiashi [Payzawat] County	212058	151305	3479	51867	507	4900
巴楚县	Bachu [Maralbexi] County	222760	160429	9502	44955	280	7594
塔什库尔干塔吉克自治县	Taxkorgan Tajik Autonomous County	9908	2254	27	7627		
和田地区	**Hotan Administrative Offices**	**517983**	**346427**	**51680**	**109116**	**1605**	**9155**
和田市	Hotan City	50410	28738	7124	12531	822	1195
和田县	Hotan County	91556	56468	20194	13398	283	1213
墨玉县	Moyu [Karakax] County	114438	79197	7103	26103	188	1847
皮山县	Pishan [Guma] County	61350	42236	7871	9490	24	1729
洛浦县	Lop County	60959	43893	3565	12465	151	885
策勒县	Qira County	44569	29401	2476	12011	20	661
于田县	Yutian [Keriya] County	74571	52202	2755	18251	97	1266
民丰县	Minfeng [Niya] County	20130	14292	592	4867	20	359
二、生产建设兵团	**Xinjiang Production and ConstructionGroup**	**3415178**	**2748722**	**33475**	**367703**	**18238**	**247040**

10-8 各地、州、市、县(市)农业机械拥有量

Agricultural Machinery by Prefecture, Autonomous Prefecture, City and County

(2007 年)

地区	Region	农业机械总动力(千瓦) Total Power of Agricultural Machinery (kw)	农用大中型拖拉机 Large and Medium Agricultural Tractors		小型拖拉机 Mini-Tractors	
			数量(台) Number (unit)	动力(千瓦) Capacity (kw)	数量(台) Number (unit)	动力(千瓦) Capacity (kw)
总 计	**Total**	**12747404**	**152985**	**4776233**	**363800**	**4314605**
一、地 方	**Local Regions**	**9758544**	**125951**	**3488267**	**327480**	**3860046**
乌鲁木齐市	**Urumqi City**	**255331**	**827**	**30916**	**7472**	**88665**
#乌鲁木齐县	Urumqi County	75165	219	9652	3282	38661
克拉玛依市	**Karamay City**	**25053**	**161**	**9634**	**398**	**6021**
吐鲁番地区	**TurpanAdministrative Offices**	**449647**	**1568**	**51494**	**12086**	**138824**
吐鲁番市	Turpan City	165612	423	11468	3755	42151
鄯善县	Shanshan [piqan]County	197236	578	21577	5610	66916
托克逊县	Toksun County	86799	567	18449	2721	29757
哈密地区	**Hami [Kumul]Administrative Offices**	**247829**	**1508**	**50113**	**10521**	**124013**
哈密市	Hami [Kumul]City	112170	656	20904	4616	55334
巴里坤哈萨克自治县	Barkol KazakAutonomous County	114889	714	23841	5114	59127
伊吾县	Yiwu [Araturuk]County	20770	138	5368	791	9552
昌吉回族自治州	**Changji Hui Autonomous Prefecture**	**1452597**	**10815**	**399103**	**55493**	**653952**
昌吉市	Changji City	224923	1373	58708	8112	100448
阜康市	Fukang City	118791	750	28503	4025	46546
呼图壁县	Hutubi County	250774	2067	81773	10227	124945
玛纳斯县	Manas County	245463	3160	94298	9673	116369
奇台县	Qitai County	350452	1843	78813	11406	123904
吉木萨尔县	Jimsar County	148149	716	28874	6264	73774
木垒哈萨克自治县	Mori Kazak Autonomous County	114045	906	28134	5786	67966
伊犁哈萨克自治州	**Ili Kazak Autonomous Prefecture**	**2739457**	**32520**	**1059946**	**82367**	**1006725**
伊犁州直属县(市)	**Counties (Cities) Direct Under Ili Prefecture**	**973509**	**11153**	**414541**	**26301**	**318825**
伊宁市	Yining [Gulja]City	52873	808	22565	1140	13467
奎屯市	Kuytun City	3030	15	1350	81	1370
伊宁县	Yining [Gulja]County	194658	2331	97579	5001	62487
察布查尔锡伯自治县	Qapqal Xibe Autonomous County	123396	1937	52577	2744	33478
霍城县	Huocheng [korgas]County	159000	1931	67585	5233	55486
巩留县	Gongliu [Tokkuzlara]County	108567	793	35993	4291	52853
新源县	Xinyuan [kunes]County	120173	1358	56765	2272	27721
昭苏县	Zhaosu [mongolkure]County	82667	699	29649	2333	32407
特克斯县	Tekes County	57387	769	24138	1367	15649
尼勒克县	Nilka County	71758	512	26340	1839	23907
塔城地区	**Tacheng [Tarbagatai] Administrative Offices**	**1355139**	**16470**	**484391**	**41954**	**517373**
塔城市	Tacheng [Qoqek] City	203941	1477	62750	5567	61023
乌苏市	Usu City	386213	3550	121299	15325	201756
额敏县	Emin [Dorbiljin] County	178792	1531	52316	4970	64563
沙湾县	Shawan County	403306	8434	201104	11668	133280
托里县	Toli County	59128	168	8850	1235	16969
裕民县	Yumin [Qagantokay] County	95584	945	28257	2357	29651
和布克赛尔蒙古自治县	Hoboksar Mongol Autonomous County	28175	365	9815	832	10131
阿勒泰地区	**Altay Administrative Offices**	**410809**	**4897**	**161014**	**14112**	**170527**
阿勒泰市	Altay City	119328	1623	57329	3585	45599
布尔津县	Burqin County	62795	842	23272	2473	30013
富蕴县	Fuyun [Koktokay] County	55083	587	20197	1738	22636
福海县	Fuhai [Burultokay] County	63236	587	23684	2210	21678
哈巴河县	Habahe [Kaba] County	58240	601	17083	2508	31070
青河县	Qinghe [Qinggil] County	34025	452	12603	1031	12780
吉木乃县	Jeminay County	18102	205	6846	567	6751

10-8 续表 1 Continued

地 区	Region	农业机械总动力(千瓦) Total Power of Agricultural Machinery (kw)	农用大中型拖拉机 Large and Medium Agricultural Tractors		小型拖拉机 Mini-Tractors	
			数量(台) Number (unit)	动力(千瓦) Capacity (kw)	数量(台) Number (unit)	动力(千瓦) Capacity (kw)
博尔塔拉蒙古自治州	**Bortala Mongol Autonomous Prefecture**	**366693**	**5289**	**134973**	**12992**	**158529**
博乐市	Bole [Bortala] City	156979	2458	62448	4833	58654
精河县	Jinghe [Jing] County	123585	1757	42237	6071	74753
温泉县	Wenquan [Araxang] County	86129	1074	30288	2088	25122
巴音郭楞蒙古自治州	**Bayangol Mongol Autonomous Prefecture**	**902257**	**10960**	**316500**	**30842**	**370213**
库尔勒市	Korla City	262220	2860	77220	11029	129039
轮台县	Luntai [Bugur] County	90764	825	19939	4531	55183
尉犁县	Yuli [Lopnur] County	87043	1243	39498	1700	19040
若羌县	Ruoqiang [Qarkilik] County	25519	467	10675	322	4508
且末县	Qiemo [Qarqan] County	60775	960	27811	2091	28824
焉耆回族自治县	Yanqi Hui Autonomous County	98306	1406	46742	3108	35068
和静县	Hejing County	120871	1703	50951	3141	40833
和硕县	Hoxud County	72722	630	16972	1570	19617
博湖县	Bohu [Bagrax] County	84037	866	26692	3350	38101
阿克苏地区	**Aksu Administrative Offices**	**1340356**	**18377**	**479808**	**58137**	**696881**
阿克苏市	Aksu City	172788	2188	61459	8152	101859
温宿县	Wensu [Onsu] County	242441	4177	119283	7690	88609
库车县	Kuqa County	181142	1420	36118	9001	114946
沙雅县	Xayar County	177348	3234	71002	6626	81760
新和县	Xinhe [Toksu] County	84365	1413	24981	4270	51240
拜城县	Baicheng [Bay] County	135821	1496	41911	5905	71644
乌什县	Wushi [Uxturpan] County	133169	2168	58141	5589	65889
阿瓦提县	Awat County	182146	1657	53306	10209	112707
柯坪县	Kalpin County	31136	624	13607	695	8227
克孜勒苏柯尔克孜自治州	**Kizilsu Kirgiz Autonomous Prefecture**	**172102**	**2977**	**75047**	**4485**	**56058**
阿图什市	Artux City	71720	1023	28756	1544	18675
阿克陶县	Akto County	81801	1437	35493	2692	34071
阿合奇县	Akqi County	8190	308	5782	110	1452
乌恰县	Wuqia [Ulugqat] County	10391	209	5016	139	1860
喀什地区	**Kashgar [Kaxgar] Administrative Offices**	**1398513**	**36289**	**750648**	**40891**	**488402**
喀什市	Kashgar [Kaxgar] City	44636	758	13449	1716	19707
疏附县	Shufu County	159308	3036	59091	6111	73167
疏勒县	Shule County	155456	3734	76527	5430	64261
英吉沙县	Yengisar County	75962	1545	30592	3025	36574
泽普县	Zepu [Poskam] County	92468	2734	55478	2824	33455
莎车县	Shache [Yarkant] County	225896	4480	105008	8109	98000
叶城县	Yecheng [Kagilik] County	131498	3498	66007	2855	33633
麦盖提县	Makit County	117045	3660	78007	2355	28303
岳普湖县	Yopurga County	73850	2259	49879	1772	20599
伽师县	Jiashi [Payzawat] County	153161	4740	91160	4352	52453
巴楚县	Bachu [Maralbexi] County	161271	5571	120180	2128	25558
塔什库尔干塔吉克自治县	Taxkorgan Tajik Autonomous County	7962	274	5270	214	2692
和田地区	**Hotan Administrative Offices**	**408709**	**4660**	**130085**	**11796**	**142691**
和田市	Hotan City	38857	371	9705	1254	15134
和田县	Hotan County	62053	534	13950	1443	18759
墨玉县	Moyu [Karakax] County	85976	843	21818	2296	26548
皮山县	Pishan [Guma] County	41408	611	14106	1228	14245
洛浦县	Lop County	64197	889	24830	1474	18956
策勒县	Qira County	42617	520	16056	1780	20598
于田县	Yutian [Keriya] County	58141	625	22900	1850	22200
民丰县	Minfeng [Niya] County	15460	267	6720	471	6251
二、生产建设兵团	**Xinjiang Production and Construction Group**	**2988860**	**27034**	**1287966**	**36320**	**454559**

10-8 续表 2 Continued

地 区	Region	大中型拖拉机配套农具(部) Number of Large and Medium Tractor Towing Farm Machinery (unit)	小型拖拉机配套农具(部) Number of Small Tractor Towing Farm Machinery (unit)	农用排灌柴油机 Diesel Engines	
				数 量(台) Number (unit)	动 力(千瓦) Capacity (kw)
总 计	**Total**	**272352**	**512600**	**8218**	**124264**
一、地 方	**Local Regions**	**211340**	**485246**	**6584**	**89257**
乌鲁木齐市	**Urumqi City**	**3202**	**5245**	**5**	**153**
#乌鲁木齐县	Urumqi County	1668	2213		
克拉玛依市	**Karamay City**	**380**	**578**	**2**	**40**
吐鲁番地区	**TurpanAdministrative Offices**	**3193**	**19106**	**28**	**363**
吐鲁番市	Turpan City	519	4786	4	71
鄯善县	Shanshan [piqan]County	1487	5846		
托克逊县	Toksun County	1187	8474	24	292
哈密地区	**Hami [Kumul]Administrative Offices**	**3743**	**17158**	**14**	**252**
哈密市	Hami [Kumul]City	1640	6020		
巴里坤哈萨克自治县	Barkol KazakAutonomous County	1785	10527	14	252
伊吾县	Yiwu [Araturuk]County	318	611		
昌吉回族自治州	**Changji Hui Autonomous Prefecture**	**23620**	**55793**	**43**	**616**
昌吉市	Changji City	3009	9736		
阜康市	Fukang City	1588	2730		
呼图壁县	Hutubi County	6307	13373		
玛纳斯县	Manas County	4802	16341	15	183
奇台县	Qitai County	5494	6651		
吉木萨尔县	Jimsar County	1232	4346		
木垒哈萨克自治县	Mori Kazak Autonomous County	1188	2616	28	433
伊犁哈萨克自治州	**Ili Kazak Autonomous Prefecture**	**75288**	**112350**	**3389**	**48511**
伊犁州直属县(市)	**Counties (Cities) Direct Under Ili Prefecture**	**26092**	**20305**	**629**	**7103**
伊宁市	Yining [Gulja]City	1983	712	18	219
奎屯市	Kuytun City	35	35		
伊宁县	Yining [Gulja]County	4056	4710	183	1619
察布查尔锡伯自治县	Qapqal Xibe Autonomous County	4640	3617	45	793
霍城县	Huocheng [korgas]County	4441	5953	195	1857
巩留县	Gongliu [Tokkuzlara]County	1812	2390	61	983
新源县	Xinyuan [kunes]County	3622	1899	37	458
昭苏县	Zhaosu [mongolkure]County	1346	66	11	121
特克斯县	Tekes County	2422	473	5	239
尼勒克县	Nilka County	1735	450	74	814
塔城地区	**Tacheng [Tarbagatai] Administrative Offices**	**40138**	**87832**	**1783**	**28060**
塔城市	Tacheng [Qoqek] City	4890	5417	56	1059
乌苏市	Usu City	11790	45624	482	5873
额敏县	Emin [Dorbiljin] County	4468	9778	1110	18359
沙湾县	Shawan County	14626	22939	7	77
托里县	Toli County	942	712	90	2180
裕民县	Yumin [Qagantokay] County	3212	3165	10	248
和布克赛尔蒙古自治县	Hoboksar Mongol Autonomous County	210	197	28	264
阿勒泰地区	**Altay Administrative Offices**	**9058**	**4213**	**977**	**13348**
阿勒泰市	Altay City	2680	1045	51	601
布尔津县	Burqin County	2028	896	86	997
富蕴县	Fuyun [Koktokay] County	1480	490	270	4190
福海县	Fuhai [Burultokay] County	1110	236	273	3146
哈巴河县	Habahe [Kaba] County	889	828	72	794
青河县	Qinghe [Qinggil] County	587	632	207	3307
吉木乃县	Jeminay County	284	86	18	313

10-8 续表 3 Continued

地　区	Region	大中型拖拉机配套农具（部）Number of Large and Medium Tractor Towing Farm Machinery (unit)	小型拖拉机配套农具（部）Number of Small Tractor Towing Farm Machinery (unit)	农用排灌柴油机 Diesel Engines 数量（台）Number (unit)	农用排灌柴油机 Diesel Engines 动力（千瓦）Capacity (kw)
博尔塔拉蒙古自治州	**Bortala Mongol Autonomous Prefecture**	**5138**	**14247**	**8**	**187**
博乐市	Bole [Bortala] City	1569	5169	3	33
精河县	Jinghe [Jing] County	1861	8168		
温泉县	Wenquan [Araxang] County	1708	910	5	154
巴音郭楞蒙古自治州	**Bayangol Mongol Autonomous Prefecture**	**20561**	**55237**	**2024**	**23841**
库尔勒市	Korla City	3526	16371	1501	15761
轮台县	Luntai [Bugur] County	1174	6454	26	368
尉犁县	Yuli [Lopnur] County	2256	6316	358	4158
若羌县	Ruoqiang [Qarkilik] County	862	1695	98	2940
且末县	Qiemo [Qarqan] County	1652	3033		
焉耆回族自治县	Yanqi Hui Autonomous County	2086	8081	2	22
和静县	Hejing County	2863	5725	39	592
和硕县	Hoxud County	4968	3454		
博湖县	Bohu [Bagrax] County	1174	4108		
阿克苏地区	**Aksu Administrative Offices**	**41341**	**106170**	**651**	**7913**
阿克苏市	Aksu City	10108	9497	39	504
温宿县	Wensu [Onsu] County	5365	8570	22	254
库车县	Kuqa County	3879	18017	40	536
沙雅县	Xayar County	7761	14443	381	4253
新和县	Xinhe [Toksu] County	2463	8833	80	882
拜城县	Baicheng [Bay] County	3930	15328		
乌什县	Wushi [Uxturpan] County	3217	6358	4	44
阿瓦提县	Awat County	4143	23630	46	721
柯坪县	Kalpin County	475	1494	39	719
克孜勒苏柯尔克孜自治州	**Kizilsu Kirgiz Autonomous Prefecture**	**3000**	**7121**	**33**	**575**
阿图什市	Artux City	1028	2022	31	560
阿克陶县	Akto County	1636	4810		
阿合奇县	Akqi County	228	106	1	11
乌恰县	Wuqia [Ulugqat] County	108	183	1	4
喀什地区	**Kashgar [Kaxgar] Administrative Offices**	**26933**	**76578**	**328**	**5141**
喀什市	Kashgar [Kaxgar] City	162	3553		
疏附县	Shufu County	1590	21992		
疏勒县	Shule County	1817	24	16	235
英吉沙县	Yengisar County	456	2612		
泽普县	Zepu [Poskam] County	1972	7718		
莎车县	Shache [Yarkant] County	3147	15787	7	585
叶城县	Yecheng [Kagilik] County	3000	6855		
麦盖提县	Makit County	2188	3185		
岳普湖县	Yopurga County	3209	3298	216	3276
伽师县	Jiashi [Payzawat] County	3934	8628	4	58
巴楚县	Bachu [Maralbexi] County	4887	2498	85	987
塔什库尔干塔吉克自治县	Taxkorgan Tajik Autonomous County	571	428		
和田地区	**Hotan Administrative Offices**	**4941**	**15663**	**59**	**1665**
和田市	Hotan City	532	1073	4	48
和田县	Hotan County	827	1343	7	77
墨玉县	Moyu [Karakax] County	654	2217	23	329
皮山县	Pishan [Guma] County	408	4170	1	13
洛浦县	Lop County	972	2592		
策勒县	Qira County	513	2201	20	1051
于田县	Yutian [Keriya] County	890	1810		
民丰县	Minfeng [Niya] County	145	257	4	147
二、生产建设兵团	**Xinjiang Production and Construction Group**	**61012**	**27354**	**1634**	**35007**

10-9 各地、州、市、县(市)农村电气化和农田水利情况
Statistics on Water Conservancy and Electrification in Rural Areas by Prefecture, Autonomous Prefecture, City and County

(2007 年)

地 区	Region	有效灌溉面积(千公顷) Effective Irrigated Area (1000 hectares)	化肥施用量(吨)(折纯) Consumption of Chemical Fertilizer (ton) (100% Purity)	#氮 肥 Nitrogenous Fertilizer	#磷 肥 Phosphate Fertilizer	#钾 肥 Potash Fertilizer
总 计	**Total**	**3465.40**	**1315273**	**635454**	**339287**	**65079**
一、地 方	**Local Regions**	**2444.82**	**842723**	**415541**	**251786**	**37369**
乌鲁木齐市	**Urumqi City**	**42.15**	**8578**	**5238**	**1730**	**648**
#乌鲁木齐县	Urumqi County	18.12	3418	1843	796	293
克拉玛依市	**Karamay City**	**9.64**	**1928**	**964**	**366**	**174**
吐鲁番地区	**TurpanAdministrative Offices**	**30.44**	**13247**	**7277**	**1223**	**254**
吐鲁番市	Turpan City	10.22	7028	2915	518	138
鄯善县	Shanshan [piqan]County	10.08	4245	2930	179	100
托克逊县	Toksun County	10.14	1974	1432	526	16
哈密地区	**Hami [Kumul]Administrative Offices**	**44.04**	**9303**	**4793**	**1479**	**310**
哈密市	Hami [Kumul]City	22.31	6108	3409	1164	297
巴里坤哈萨克自治县	Barkol KazakAutonomous County	16.65	2010	985		
伊吾县	Yiwu [Araturuk]County	5.08	1185	399	315	13
昌吉回族自治州	**Changji Hui Autonomous Prefecture**	**301.95**	**88455**	**46105**	**19810**	**3773**
昌吉市	Changji City	60.26	17121	8404	4791	291
阜康市	Fukang City	20.00	5025	3158	1283	87
呼图壁县	Hutubi County	50.34	21047	12827	4276	681
玛纳斯县	Manas County	53.20	21060	9254	4498	1367
奇台县	Qitai County	72.88	13990	6976	3279	275
吉木萨尔县	Jimsar County	27.05	8049	4638	978	873
木垒哈萨克自治县	Mori Kazak Autonomous County	18.22	2163	848	705	199
伊犁哈萨克自治州	**Ili Kazak Autonomous Prefecture**	**690.41**	**175634**	**81929**	**35597**	**5205**
伊犁州直属县(市)	**Counties (Cities) Direct Under Ili Prefecture**	**242.31**	**61251**	**22683**	**8719**	**1916**
伊宁市	Yining [Gulja]City	15.44	2812	1404		
奎屯市	Kuytun City	2.37	1637	654	654	44
伊宁县	Yining [Gulja]County	60.48	13557	5621	1300	726
察布查尔锡伯自治县	Qapqal Xibe Autonomous County	30.62	7302	3217	2130	
霍城县	Huocheng [korgas]County	32.43	12160	4016	1706	772
巩留县	Gongliu [Tokkuzlara]County	23.93	5260	2070		
新源县	Xinyuan [kunes]County	29.91	7709	2252	1047	238
昭苏县	Zhaosu [mongolkure]County	15.49	4882	1679	491	126
特克斯县	Tekes County	16.10	2621	679	803	
尼勒克县	Nilka County	15.54	3311	1091	588	10
塔城地区	**Tacheng [Tarbagatai] Administrative Offices**	**326.43**	**98509**	**48758**	**22522**	**2726**
塔城市	Tacheng [Qoqek] City	78.86	16206	7492	6147	616
乌苏市	Usu City	64.72	20143	11368	2680	932
额敏县	Emin [Dorbiljin] County	69.38	21655	7494	6763	156
沙湾县	Shawan County	78.45	32077	18845	5966	952
托里县	Toli County	7.00	534	315	130	
裕民县	Yumin [Qagantokay] County	17.50	4174	1787	558	
和布克赛尔蒙古自治县	Hoboksar Mongol Autonomous County	10.52	3720	1457	278	70
阿勒泰地区	**Altay Administrative Offices**	**121.67**	**15874**	**10488**	**4356**	**563**
阿勒泰市	Altay City	22.64	4309	2756	1470	43
布尔津县	Burqin County	13.00	2459	1894	565	
富蕴县	Fuyun [Koktokay] County	13.87	863	596	230	5
福海县	Fuhai [Burultokay] County	25.04	3387	2246	556	323
哈巴河县	Habahe [Kaba] County	26.66	3173	1817	1050	172
青河县	Qinghe [Qinggil] County	11.88	1227	865	362	
吉木乃县	Jeminay County	8.58	456	313	123	20

10-9 续表 1 Continued

地区	Region	有效灌溉面积(千公顷) Effective Irrigated Area(1000 hectares)	化肥施用量(吨)(折纯) Consumption of Chemical Fertilizer (ton) (100% Purity)	#氮肥 Nitrogenous Fertilizer	#磷肥 Phosphate Fertilizer	#钾肥 Potash Fertilizer
博尔塔拉蒙古自治州	**Bortala Mongol Autonomous Prefecture**	**77.90**	**25561**	**12150**	**7583**	**1928**
博乐市	Bole [Bortala] City	28.21	10896	4651	4305	980
精河县	Jinghe [Jing] County	24.95	6973	3634	899	173
温泉县	Wenquan [Araxang] County	24.74	7692	3865	2379	775
巴音郭楞蒙古自治州	**Bayangol Mongol Autonomous Prefecture**	**196.84**	**95169**	**48560**	**29843**	**4459**
库尔勒市	Korla City	44.27	17938	10163	6224	580
轮台县	Luntai [Bugur] County	19.31	14186	7339	2957	308
尉犁县	Yuli [Lopnur] County	35.47	24301	10153	10139	1776
若羌县	Ruoqiang [Qarkilik] County	3.67	1758	901	215	135
且末县	Qiemo [Qarqan] County	12.84	4649	3185	298	
焉耆回族自治县	Yanqi Hui Autonomous County	22.70	8791	5446	1250	390
和静县	Hejing County	18.58	7530	3443	3085	627
和硕县	Hoxud County	25.95	8185	4238	3479	95
博湖县	Bohu [Bagrax] County	14.05	7831	3691	2196	548
阿克苏地区	**Aksu Administrative Offices**	**347.15**	**152665**	**74333**	**49297**	**7345**
阿克苏市	Aksu City	33.00	24900	13226	7262	1449
温宿县	Wensu [Onsu] County	49.74	20067	9482	6123	576
库车县	Kuqa County	54.08	28917	13981	9350	695
沙雅县	Xayar County	48.57	26614	11231	12710	2181
新和县	Xinhe [Toksu] County	38.31	7373	3116	2500	473
拜城县	Baicheng [Bay] County	36.64	12064	4225	4504	1444
乌什县	Wushi [Uxturpan] County	23.80	10302	7418	639	
阿瓦提县	Awat County	55.70	19749	10272	4912	527
柯坪县	Kalpin County	7.31	2679	1382	1297	
克孜勒苏柯尔克孜自治州	**Kizilsu Kirgiz Autonomous Prefecture**	**30.38**	**12917**	**7387**	**5530**	
阿图什市	Artux City	9.23	5590	2903	2687	
阿克陶县	Akto County	16.04	7267	4441	2826	
阿合奇县	Akqi County	2.73	16	7	9	
乌恰县	Wuqia [Ulugqat] County	2.38	44	36	8	
喀什地区	**Kashgar [Kaxgar] Administrative Offices**	**508.97**	**209260**	**97370**	**85550**	**10392**
喀什市	Kashgar [Kaxgar] City	12.00	22108	8755	13353	
疏附县	Shufu County	33.81	18690	10100	8500	90
疏勒县	Shule County	41.47	18000	10000	6100	1600
英吉沙县	Yengisar County	22.33	7735	3935		
泽普县	Zepu [Poskam] County	24.63	11586	7356	4224	
莎车县	Shache [Yarkant] County	104.67	28052	12456	9738	1449
叶城县	Yecheng [Kagilik] County	48.13	19892	8478	6877	3664
麦盖提县	Makit County	54.67	12267	8142	3341	74
岳普湖县	Yopurga County	26.50	16460	7082	4641	2270
伽师县	Jiashi [Payzawat] County	54.15	21454	11905	7085	496
巴楚县	Bachu [Maralbexi] County	82.67	33016	9161	21691	749
塔什库尔干塔吉克自治县	Taxkorgan Tajik Autonomous County	3.94				
和田地区	**Hotan Administrative Offices**	**164.95**	**50006**	**29437**	**13778**	**2881**
和田市	Hotan City	10.51	4165	2473	1394	145
和田县	Hotan County	20.36	8422	4708	2880	822
墨玉县	Moyu [Karakax] County	34.59	10871	5177	1715	947
皮山县	Pishan [Guma] County	29.54	7252	4929	1522	572
洛浦县	Lop County	20.81	6916	4454	2462	
策勒县	Qira County	15.74	2749	1619	1130	
于田县	Yutian [Keriya] County	27.96	7505	4699	1992	344
民丰县	Minfeng [Niya] County	5.44	2126	1379	683	51
二、生产建设兵团	**Xinjiang Production and Construction Group**	**1020.58**	**472550**	**219913**	**87501**	**27710**

10-9 续表 2 Continued

地　区	Region	乡村及村以下办水电站 Hydropower Station inVillage or Below		农村用电量（万千瓦小时） Electricity Consumed in Rural Areas (10 000 kwh)
		装机容量(万千瓦) Installed Capacity (10 000 kw)	发电量(万千瓦) Generating Capacity (10 000 kw)	
总　计	**Total**	**10.00**	**24284.65**	**458431**
一、地 方	**Local Regions**	**4.67**	**6639.65**	**257962**
乌鲁木齐市	**Urumqi City**			**13575**
#乌鲁木齐县	Urumqi County			3584
克拉玛依市	**Karamay City**			**450**
吐鲁番地区	**TurpanAdministrative Offices**	**1.14**	**19.27**	**30729**
吐鲁番市	Turpan City	0.19	15.47	9237
鄯善县	Shanshan [piqan]County			15520
托克逊县	Toksun County	0.95	3.80	5972
哈密地区	**Hami [Kumul]Administrative Offices**	**0.26**	**454.00**	**12737**
哈密市	Hami [Kumul]City			9912
巴里坤哈萨克自治县	Barkol KazakAutonomous County	0.10	76.00	2190
伊吾县	Yiwu [Araturuk]County	0.16	378.00	635
昌吉回族自治州	**Changji Hui Autonomous Prefecture**	**0.10**	**120.00**	**59227**
昌吉市	Changji City			14024
阜康市	Fukang City			3601
呼图壁县	Hutubi County			12000
玛纳斯县	Manas County			6655
奇台县	Qitai County			17399
吉木萨尔县	Jimsar County	0.10	120.00	2238
木垒哈萨克自治县	Mori Kazak Autonomous County			3310
伊犁哈萨克自治州	**Ili Kazak Autonomous Prefecture**	**0.86**	**2754.86**	**41847**
伊犁州直属县(市)	**Counties (Cities) Direct Under Ili Prefecture**	**0.55**	**2159.30**	**10561**
伊宁市	Yining [Gulja]City			908
奎屯市	Kuytun City			126
伊宁县	Yining [Gulja]County	0.06	72.00	2404
察布查尔锡伯自治县	Qapqal Xibe Autonomous County			695
霍城县	Huocheng [korgas]County	0.10	205.00	758
巩留县	Gongliu [Tokkuzlara]County	0.09	350.00	845
新源县	Xinyuan [kunes]County	0.20	1363.00	3262
昭苏县	Zhaosu [mongolkure]County	0.10	6.30	639
特克斯县	Tekes County		163.00	726
尼勒克县	Nilka County			198
塔城地区	**Tacheng [Tarbagatai] Administrative Offices**			**23993**
塔城市	Tacheng [Qoqek] City			4592
乌苏市	Usu City			2376
额敏县	Emin [Dorbiljin] County			1938
沙湾县	Shawan County			9207
托里县	Toli County			1521
裕民县	Yumin [Qagantokay] County			3135
和布克赛尔蒙古自治县	Hoboksar Mongol Autonomous County			1225
阿勒泰地区	**Altay Administrative Offices**	**0.31**	**595.56**	**7293**
阿勒泰市	Altay City	0.10	184.00	761
布尔津县	Burqin County	0.10	155.00	602
富蕴县	Fuyun [Koktokay] County	0.04	150.00	2521
福海县	Fuhai [Burultokay] County			540
哈巴河县	Habahe [Kaba] County			514
青河县	Qinghe [Qinggil] County	0.07	106.56	1957
吉木乃县	Jeminay County			399

10-9 续表 3 Continued

地　区	Region	乡村及村以下办水电站 HydroPower Station inVillage or Below		农村用电量 (万千瓦小时)
		装机容量(万千瓦) Installed Capacity (10 000 kw)	发电量(万千瓦) Generating Capacity (10 000 kw)	Electricity Consumed in Rural Areas (10 000 kwh)
博尔塔拉蒙古自治州	**Bortala Mongol Autonomous Prefecture**	**0.49**	**1863.00**	**6811**
博乐市	Bole [Bortala] City	0.12	734.00	3495
精河县	Jinghe [Jing] County	0.37	1129.00	2606
温泉县	Wenquan [Araxang] County			710
巴音郭楞蒙古自治州	**Bayangol Mongol Autonomous Prefecture**	**0.11**	**38.00**	**28742**
库尔勒市	Korla City			8831
轮台县	Luntai [Bugur] County			3492
尉犁县	Yuli [Lopnur] County			3271
若羌县	Ruoqiang [Qarkilik] County	0.11	38.00	276
且末县	Qiemo [Qarqan] County			307
焉耆回族自治县	Yanqi Hui Autonomous County			1965
和静县	Hejing County			956
和硕县	Hoxud County			7292
博湖县	Bohu [Bagrax] County			2352
阿克苏地区	**Aksu Administrative Offices**	**0.06**	**96.00**	**27748**
阿克苏市	Aksu City			2734
温宿县	Wensu [Onsu] County	0.06	96.00	3184
库车县	Kuqa County			6064
沙雅县	Xayar County			6185
新和县	Xinhe [Toksu] County			2448
拜城县	Baicheng [Bay] County			1571
乌什县	Wushi [Uxturpan] County			1113
阿瓦提县	Awat County			3592
柯坪县	Kalpin County			857
克孜勒苏柯尔克孜自治州	**Kizilsu Kirgiz Autonomous Prefecture**	**0.12**	**254.35**	**1512**
阿图什市	Artux City	0.11	253.00	1072
阿克陶县	Akto County	0.01	1.35	322
阿合奇县	Akqi County			20
乌恰县	Wuqia [Ulugqat] County			98
喀什地区	**Kashgar [Kaxgar] Administrative Offices**	**0.49**	**73.00**	**16800**
喀什市	Kashgar [Kaxgar] City			765
疏附县	Shufu County	0.30	15.00	1200
疏勒县	Shule County			800
英吉沙县	Yengisar County	0.02	36.00	400
泽普县	Zepu [Poskam] County			795
莎车县	Shache [Yarkant] County			2213
叶城县	Yecheng [Kagilik] County			801
麦盖提县	Makit County			3660
岳普湖县	Yopurga County			726
伽师县	Jiashi [Payzawat] County			3492
巴楚县	Bachu [Maralbexi] County			1926
塔什库尔干塔吉克自治县	Taxkorgan Tajik Autonomous County	0.17	22.00	22
和田地区	**Hotan Administrative Offices**	**1.04**	**967.17**	**17784**
和田市	Hotan City	0.80		3576
和田县	Hotan County	0.03		3185
墨玉县	Moyu [Karakax] County	0.03	42.00	3703
皮山县	Pishan [Guma] County			865
洛浦县	Lop County	0.15	917.00	2862
策勒县	Qira County	0.02	0.07	889
于田县	Yutian [Keriya] County			1965
民丰县	Minfeng [Niya] County	0.01	8.10	739
二、生产建设兵团	**Xinjiang Production and Construction Group**	**5.33**	**17645.00**	**200469**

10-10 灌溉、水库和除涝、治水情况

Irrigation, Reservoirs, Flood Prevention, Water and Soil Conservation

项　　目	Item	2005	2006
灌溉面积(千公顷)	Irrigated Areas (1000 hectares)	3532	3575
有效灌溉面积	Effective Irrigated Areas	2334	2381
林地灌溉面积	Irrigated Wooded-land Areas	556	428
果园灌溉面积	Irrigated Orchard Areas	187	320
牧草灌溉面积	Irrigated Pasture-land Areas	409	383
其他灌溉面积	Other Irrigated Areas	46	63
水库(座)	Number of Reservoirs (unit)	387	365
大型水库	Large-scale Reservoir	9	9
中型水库	Medium-scale Reservoir	90	89
小型水库	Small-scale Reservoir	288	267
水库库容量（亿立方米)	Capacity of Reservoirs (100 million cu.m)	53.08	52.76
大型水库	Large-scale Reservoir	20.51	21.31
中型水库	Medium-scale Reservoir	26.67	25.85
小型水库	Small-scale Reservoir	5.90	5.60
节水灌溉面积（千公顷)	Water-saving Irrigated Areas (1000 hectares)	1460.93	1536.19
除涝面积　(千公顷)	Flooded or Waterlogged Areas (1000 hectares)	36.42	64.82
水土流失治理面积(千公顷)	Area of Soil Erosion under Control (1000 hectares)	211.28	279.14
堤防长度（公里)	Total Length of Dikes (km)	6423.42	6456.47
堤防保护耕地面积（千公顷)	Area of Land Protected by Dikes (1000 hectares)	1409.06	1430.51

注: 1.大型水库库容: 1 亿立方米以上; 中型水库库容: 1 千万至 1 亿立方米;小型水库库容: 10 万至 1 千万立方米。2.本表和 10-11，10-12 表资料由水利厅提供。

Note: a) The capacity of the large reservoirs is over 100 million cubic meters, while that of the medium ones is from 10 million to 100 million cubic meters, and that of the small ones is from 100 000 to 10 million cubic meters. b) The data in the table is offered by the Bureau of Water Conservancy, together with table 10-11,10-12.

10-11 各地、州、市水利设施和除涝面积

Water Conservancy Facilities and Area with Flood Prevention Measures by Prefecture, Autonomous Prefecture and City

(2006 年)

地区	Region	水库数 (座) Number of Reservoirs (unit)	水库总库容量 (万立方米) Capacity of Reservoirs (10 000 cu.m)	除涝面积 (千公顷) Area with Flood Prevention Measures (1000 hectares)	水土流失治理面积 (千公顷) Area of Soil Erosion under Control (1000 hectares)
总计	**Total**	**365**	**527590**	**64.82**	**279.14**
乌鲁木齐市	Urumqi City	17	15491	3.13	18.18
克拉玛依市	Karamay City	7	28440		7.48
吐鲁番地区	Turpan Administrative Offices	17	10317		2.52
哈密地区	Hami [Kumul]Administrative Offices	39	10041		17.26
昌吉回族自治州	Changji HuiAutonomous Prefecture	71	34337		22.81
伊犁州直属县(市)	Counties (Cities) Direct Under Ili Prefecture	11	1560	22.65	52.04
塔城地区	Tacheng [Tarbagatai] Administrative Offices	26	19873	1.50	4.88
阿勒泰地区	Altay Administrative Offices	50	99523	3.33	15.79
博尔塔拉蒙古自治州	Bortala Mongol Autonomous Prefecture	3	5400		10.29
巴音郭楞蒙古自治州	Bayangol Mongol Autonomous Prefecture	4	8220		51.70
阿克苏地区	Aksu Administrative Offices	10	31529	33.61	31.87
克孜勒苏柯尔克孜自治州	Kizilsu Kirgiz Autonomous Prefecture	12	9572		1.40
喀什地区	Kashgar [Kaxgar] Administrative Offices	43	87036		10.88
和田地区	Hotan Administrative Offices	47	28611		21.21
其他	Other	8	137640	0.60	10.83

10-12 各地、州、市农村饮水安全情况

Basic Statistics on Security of Drinking Water in Rural Area by Prefecture, Autonomous Prefecture and City

单位:万人　　(2006 年)　　(10 000 persons)

地区	Region	农村饮水安全达标人口 Reach the Standards in Security of drinking water of Rural population	饮水基本安全人口 Security of drinking water of Rural Population	农村安全饮水不达标人口 Not Reach the Standards in Security of drinking water of Rural Populaition
总计	**Total**	**565.01**	**215.49**	**550.71**
乌鲁木齐市	Urumqi City	5.55	1.15	9.43
克拉玛依市	Karamay City	0.96	0.05	2.57
吐鲁番地区	Turpan Administrative Offices	18.19	6.59	22.93
哈密地区	Hami [Kumul]Administrative Offices	11.07	3.59	8.67
昌吉回族自治州	Changji HuiAutonomous Prefecture	29.44	10.94	55.19
伊犁州直属县(市)	Counties (Cities) Direct Under Ili Prefecture	77.98	30.36	76.27
塔城地区	Tacheng [Tarbagatai] Administrative Offices	26.89	9.92	31.25
阿勒泰地区	Altay Administrative Offices	10.35	3.66	26.18
博尔塔拉蒙古自治州	Bortala Mongol Autonomous Prefecture	15.64	6.24	10.61
巴音郭楞蒙古自治州	Bayangol Mongol Autonomous Prefecture	23.60	8.60	30.24
阿克苏地区	Aksu Administrative Offices	76.30	29.20	76.82
克孜勒苏柯尔克孜自治州	Kizilsu Kirgiz Autonomous Prefecture	21.59	8.65	19.50
喀什地区	Kashgar [Kaxgar] Administrative Offices	156.94	61.45	108.20
和田地区	Hotan Administrative Offices	82.19	32.88	61.69
其他	Other	8.32	2.21	11.16

10-13 主要年份农作物播种面积

Total Sown Areas of Farm Crops in Main Years

单位：千公顷 (1 000 hectares)

年份 Year	农作物播种面积 Total Sown Area	粮食作物播种面积 Sown Area of Grain Crops	谷物 Cereal	#水稻 Rice	#小麦 Wheat	#玉米 Corn	#大麦 Barley	豆类 Soybeans	薯类 Tubers	棉花 Cotton
1978	3021.67	2310.71	2297.44	105.59	1348.82	621.39	50.01	13.27	23.09	150.42
1980	2993.71	2162.37	2147.60	98.39	1354.83	555.79	23.24	14.77	17.55	181.22
1985	2846.63	1853.04	1844.47	74.50	1278.43	418.43	13.63	8.57	10.56	253.52
1990	2979.51	1826.61	1813.16	84.13	1180.11	442.40	42.92	13.45	10.67	435.22
1991	3036.09	1769.99	1741.17	79.93	1149.87	436.56	35.05	28.82	9.52	546.94
1992	3067.85	1730.26	1701.45	76.20	1126.76	429.84	28.12	28.81	12.09	643.30
1993	2995.10	1697.57	1627.10	67.74	1087.14	397.94	36.84	70.47	11.68	606.35
1994	2993.75	1496.04	1396.25	63.25	850.19	387.89	68.69	99.79	10.36	749.82
1995	3051.44	1593.29	1528.62	73.38	952.58	439.16	41.58	64.67	10.34	742.90
1996	3081.15	1648.83	1604.08	75.87	985.39	467.88	54.72	44.75	11.93	799.26
1997	3191.48	1673.73	1618.33	82.06	1017.43	439.83	59.63	55.40	11.58	883.65
1998	3278.55	1573.43	1512.40	69.06	966.80	428.58	31.55	61.03	12.18	999.26
1999	3379.89	1521.65	1453.53	75.56	888.50	432.91	26.02	68.12	17.34	995.93
2000	3388.76	1445.77	1353.99	78.15	838.99	382.45	33.50	91.78	22.59	1012.39
2001	3404.12	1394.96	1281.38	73.28	744.27	410.29	34.11	113.58	20.77	1129.72
2002	3478.37	1493.96	1386.81	74.96	749.74	501.93	36.45	107.15	20.65	943.97
2003	3470.28	1307.02	1202.61	67.16	626.09	454.14	38.25	104.41	23.89	1037.05
2004	3571.89	1378.61	1273.03	66.77	658.08	505.69	24.53	105.58	24.23	1127.55
2005	3728.11	1471.76	1371.89	69.07	761.84	497.64	27.42	99.87	20.51	1157.99
2006	4206.28	1465.82	1369.68	68.00	740.11	496.43	50.96	96.14	22.79	1664.43
2007	4394.25	1379.00	1300.58	70.95	634.02	528.91	55.86	78.42	33.15	1782.60

年份 Year	#长绒棉 Long-Staple Cotton	油料 Oil Bearing Crops	#油菜 Rapeseeds	#胡麻 Flax	#葵花 Helianthus	甜菜 Beetroots	蔬菜 Vegetables	果用瓜 Melon	#甜瓜 Musk-melon	苜蓿 Lucerne
1978	29.05	202.13	90.90	65.49	23.68	17.67	55.12	41.95		174.90
1980	38.50	269.39	107.47	81.85	50.08	24.27	46.99	39.54		191.65
1985	26.28	294.78	89.82	81.12	111.39	15.51	54.91	53.69	27.95	132.07
1990	62.69	269.27	117.35	46.04	96.11	66.87	58.07	28.84	15.09	159.34
1991	55.52	272.22	125.85	38.26	103.57	74.19	55.34	29.29	13.72	142.11
1992	16.96	223.38	102.28	32.67	80.53	84.20	58.40	32.70	14.05	132.83
1993	23.83	232.02	99.16	28.70	84.71	59.86	65.04	32.02	16.47	127.71
1994	9.77	317.32	148.27	30.21	123.43	76.84	63.76	29.03	13.37	127.31
1995	8.35	306.70	130.11	26.75	140.10	71.10	71.54	25.15	9.72	120.25
1996	14.68	194.05	85.24	20.19	82.73	87.41	78.95	23.72	8.19	117.20
1997	39.09	176.01	70.44	17.51	81.88	92.21	75.70	29.70	12.09	113.53
1998	10.74	212.14	84.09	16.48	94.11	110.75	82.62	31.90	14.62	115.27
1999	12.92	327.19	107.65	17.95	161.54	78.54	103.73	52.26	22.21	115.51
2000	49.29	310.07	96.23	24.57	157.05	55.75	127.75	55.99	26.01	120.49
2001	67.69	217.64	72.85	17.10	99.76	85.54	125.96	58.19	26.55	165.06
2002	46.30	215.05	70.00	23.84	96.60	85.32	164.21	82.47	48.47	235.11
2003	70.13	226.38	74.48	22.30	100.07	67.31	163.84	62.45	32.82	294.13
2004	70.63	215.47	67.52	13.74	85.55	59.88	185.60	61.29	36.07	301.10
2005	73.38	185.49	59.92	17.37	84.62	69.90	176.66	70.57	36.02	275.91
2006	106.94	151.73	49.25	14.28	64.29	94.42	186.82	74.02	41.27	242.38
2007	142.53	176.47	59.48	12.32	96.41	94.02	234.88	103.40	62.81	231.36

10-14 各地、州、市、县(市)农作物播种面积

单位：千公顷　　　　　　　　　　　　　　　　　　　　　　　　　　(2007 年)

地　区	Region	农作物播种面积 Total Sown Area	粮食 Grain Crops	谷物 Cereal	#水稻 Rice	#小麦 Wheat	#玉米 Corn	豆类 Soy-beans
总　计	**Total**	**4394.25**	**1379.00**	**1300.58**	**70.95**	**634.02**	**528.91**	**78.42**
一、地 方	**Local Regions**	**2935.70**	**1133.65**	**1063.31**	**42.40**	**545.93**	**429.03**	**70.34**
乌鲁木齐市	**Urumqi City**	**46.86**	**18.23**	**16.98**	**5.93**	**6.19**	**1.33**	**1.25**
#乌鲁木齐县	Urumqi County	20.93	6.30	6.13	0.28	2.47	0.09	0.17
克拉玛依市	**Karamay City**	**10.71**	**0.20**	**0.20**		**0.08**	**0.12**	
吐鲁番地区	**TurpanAdministrative Offices**	**43.52**	**1.75**	**1.73**		**0.61**	**0.24**	**0.02**
吐鲁番市	Turpan City	14.99						
鄯善县	Shanshan [piqan]County	10.39						
托克逊县	Toksun County	18.14	1.75	1.73		0.61	0.24	0.02
哈密地区	**Hami [Kumul]Administrative Offices**	**50.63**	**13.92**	**13.54**		**7.02**	**1.03**	**0.38**
哈密市	Hami [Kumul]City	28.27	3.00	2.95		1.29	0.48	0.05
巴里坤哈萨克自治县	Barkol KazakAutonomous County	17.78	9.27	9.04		5.52	0.01	0.23
伊吾县	Yiwu [Araturuk]County	4.58	1.65	1.55		0.21	0.54	0.10
昌吉回族自治州	**Changji Hui Autonomous Prefecture**	**358.28**	**133.63**	**118.28**	**0.40**	**60.71**	**42.76**	**15.35**
昌吉市	Changji City	64.18	17.07	15.75	0.11	10.45	5.15	1.32
阜康市	Fukang City	24.97	8.96	8.01	0.15	4.44	3.33	0.95
呼图壁县	Hutubi County	46.65	12.12	11.82	0.09	8.32	3.41	0.30
玛纳斯县	Manas County	54.69	10.17	10.08	0.05	2.14	7.75	0.09
奇台县	Qitai County	103.74	52.43	50.73		23.91	14.97	1.70
吉木萨尔县	Jimsar County	30.17	9.14	8.83		5.13	3.24	0.31
木垒哈萨克自治县	Mori Kazak Autonomous County	33.88	23.74	13.06		6.32	4.91	10.68
伊犁哈萨克自治州	**Ili Kazak Autonomous Prefecture**	**815.86**	**341.01**	**293.32**	**9.20**	**146.51**	**119.50**	**47.69**
伊犁州直属县(市)	**Counties (Cities) Direct Under Ili Prefecture**	**330.11**	**192.00**	**160.36**	**8.54**	**75.33**	**69.38**	**31.64**
伊宁市	Yining [Gulja]City	18.61	10.65	10.13		2.61	7.51	0.52
奎屯市	Kuytun City	2.37	0.04	0.04		0.04		
伊宁县	Yining [Gulja]County	69.98	51.56	41.54		10.92	30.40	10.02
察布查尔锡伯自治县	Qapqal Xibe Autonomous County	41.89	22.52	20.72	7.05	8.18	5.49	1.80
霍城县	Huocheng [korgas]County	38.07	18.12	17.09	0.04	7.37	9.64	1.03
巩留县	Gongliu [Tokkuzlara]County	35.95	26.46	16.72	0.85	9.76	6.11	9.74
新源县	Xinyuan [kunes]County	40.40	22.42	14.61	0.57	8.91	4.84	7.81
昭苏县	Zhaosu [mongolkure]County	44.93	21.32	21.32		16.82		
特克斯县	Tekes County	19.10	8.54	8.49		4.26	3.22	0.05
尼勒克县	Nilka County	18.81	10.37	9.70	0.03	6.46	2.17	0.67
塔城地区	**Tacheng [Tarbagatai] Administrative Offices**	**359.79**	**115.50**	**114.81**	**0.66**	**61.64**	**42.55**	**0.69**
塔城市	Tacheng [Qoqek] City	83.38	44.99	44.98		21.76	17.22	0.01
乌苏市	Usu City	65.36	10.53	10.51	0.66	3.73	6.07	0.02
额敏县	Emin [Dorbiljin] County	73.85	25.23	25.19		18.06	4.39	0.04
沙湾县	Shawan County	80.88	15.28	14.83		7.53	6.97	0.45
托里县	Toli County	15.46	8.12	8.00		4.75	2.41	0.12
裕民县	Yumin [Qagantokay] County	30.34	10.89	10.88		5.54	5.34	0.01
和布克赛尔蒙古自治县	Hoboksar Mongol Autonomous County	10.52	0.46	0.42		0.27	0.15	0.04
阿勒泰地区	**Altay Administrative Offices**	**125.96**	**33.51**	**18.15**		**9.54**	**7.57**	**15.36**
阿勒泰市	Altay City	22.64	5.45	2.43		0.51	1.91	3.02
布尔津县	Burqin County	19.91	7.28	1.71		0.38	1.33	5.57
富蕴县	Fuyun [Koktokay] County	19.32	7.24	4.26		1.95	1.78	2.98
福海县	Fuhai [Burultokay] County	20.38	0.84	0.73		0.07	0.66	0.11
哈巴河县	Habahe [Kaba] County	22.53	6.17	2.59		1.47	1.00	3.58
青河县	Qinghe [Qinggil] County	12.60	4.69	4.59		3.80	0.43	0.10
吉木乃县	Jeminay County	8.58	1.84	1.84		1.36	0.46	

Sown Areas of Farm Crops by Prefecture, Autonomous Prefecture, City and County

(1 000 hectares)

薯类 Tubers	棉花 Cotton	#长绒棉 Longstaple Cotton	油料 Oil Bearing Crops	#油菜 Rapeseeds	#胡麻 Flax	#葵花 Helianthus	甜菜 Beetroots	蔬菜 Vegetables	果用瓜 Melon	#甜瓜 Muskmelon	苜蓿 Lucerne
33.15	**1782.60**	**142.53**	**176.47**	**59.48**	**12.32**	**96.41**	**94.02**	**234.88**	**103.40**	**62.81**	**231.36**
26.93	**865.97**	**91.93**	**143.10**	**32.97**	**11.15**	**76.05**	**64.60**	**175.92**	**91.27**	**54.70**	**172.48**
3.70	**2.00**	**0.06**	**3.07**	**0.04**		**2.29**	**0.20**	**11.29**	**0.46**	**0.02**	**4.83**
3.28	0.11		1.06	0.04		1.02	0.05	5.32	0.28		2.78
	9.50	**9.50**						**0.06**	**0.10**	**0.02**	**0.17**
0.01	**18.00**		**0.20**			**0.01**		**4.75**	**7.76**	**5.26**	**1.84**
	4.73							2.64	3.24	1.35	1.25
	5.67							1.06	3.20	2.87	0.14
0.01	7.60		0.20			0.01		1.05	1.32	1.04	0.45
2.22	**13.19**		**1.59**	**1.43**	**0.02**	**0.14**		**1.90**	**4.48**	**4.02**	**5.96**
0.14	13.02		1.41	1.27	0.01	0.13		1.60	2.00	1.54	1.48
2.03	0.12		0.17	0.16		0.01		0.25	0.17	0.17	4.02
0.05	0.05		0.01		0.01			0.05	2.31	2.31	0.46
6.76	**92.98**		**16.59**	**0.25**	**0.23**	**9.40**	**8.71**	**34.22**	**5.70**	**0.82**	**9.61**
0.40	27.22		1.30			0.66	1.70	10.62	2.77	0.20	0.88
0.16	6.93		1.27			1.05	0.06	5.22	0.27	0.05	0.57
0.37	21.83		1.13			0.75	1.46	4.67	1.05	0.17	1.57
0.26	34.69		1.26	0.01		1.25	0.42	3.43	0.36	0.03	1.42
2.43			6.98	0.17	0.03	3.96	4.55	3.98	0.28	0.01	1.89
2.43	2.28		4.01	0.02		1.34	0.31	6.13	0.65	0.07	0.35
0.71	0.03		0.64	0.05	0.20	0.39	0.21	0.17	0.32	0.29	2.93
10.51	**101.60**	**6.53**	**101.59**	**26.78**	**7.63**	**52.14**	**44.66**	**34.95**	**5.13**	**2.40**	**56.59**
7.59	**10.33**		**47.94**	**16.49**	**7.63**	**21.39**	**32.51**	**10.16**	**1.49**	**0.10**	**4.79**
0.23	0.02		1.23	0.32	0.02	0.89	2.16	2.60	0.36		0.36
	2.19		0.10			0.10		0.04			
0.41	0.21		5.19	1.37	0.13	3.34	9.27	1.67	0.56	0.02	0.16
0.05	5.21		2.57		0.57	1.79	2.43	1.10	0.21		0.89
0.25	2.70		4.25		0.08	3.03	9.06	1.80	0.15	0.05	
			2.36	0.25	0.23	1.88	2.33	1.27	0.10	0.02	0.21
2.91			5.03	0.63	0.51	3.32	5.76	0.54	0.10		0.31
1.00			20.46	13.27	4.37	2.82		0.29			
0.12			4.78	0.46	0.34	3.98	0.51	0.52			2.15
2.62			1.97	0.19	1.38	0.24	0.99	0.33	0.01	0.01	0.71
1.16	**91.27**	**6.53**	**32.65**	**10.28**		**9.76**	**10.42**	**23.17**	**0.87**	**0.06**	**25.91**
0.03			4.73	3.58		0.50	1.17	2.62	0.06	0.02	6.93
0.11	41.93		1.80			1.80	0.65	7.07	0.30	0.02	0.97
			10.97	5.61		4.05	6.30	1.31	0.02		8.57
0.69	42.70		2.80			2.58	2.17	11.95	0.49	0.02	1.37
0.13	0.11		2.65	0.84		0.55	0.13	0.07			2.69
0.16			9.49	0.25		0.07		0.01			2.91
0.04	6.53	6.53	0.21			0.21		0.14			2.47
1.76			**21.00**	**0.01**		**20.99**	**1.73**	**1.62**	**2.77**	**2.24**	**25.89**
0.18			5.15			5.15	0.59	0.28	1.91	1.91	3.11
0.07			5.90			5.90		0.17	0.06	0.06	3.08
0.45			4.36	0.01		4.35		0.40	0.36	0.02	3.07
0.03			1.06			1.06	0.81	0.15	0.24	0.19	5.77
0.21			1.33			1.33	0.33	0.47	0.20	0.06	3.47
0.72			0.40			0.40		0.14			5.85
0.10			2.80			2.80		0.01			1.54

10-14 续表

单位：千公顷

地　区	Region	农作物播种面积 Total Sown Area	粮食 Grain Crops	谷物 Cereal	#水稻 Rice	#小麦 Wheat	#玉米 Corn	豆类 Soybeans
博尔塔拉蒙古自治州	**Bortala Mongol Autonomous Prefecture**	**79.19**	**21.65**	**21.09**	**0.16**	**4.70**	**16.23**	**0.56**
博乐市	Bole [Bortala] City	28.91	9.28	8.96	0.16	0.43	8.37	0.32
精河县	Jinghe [Jing] County	25.54	0.40	0.40		0.04	0.36	
温泉县	Wenquan [Araxang] County	24.74	11.97	11.73		4.23	7.50	0.24
巴音郭楞蒙古自治州	**Bayangol Mongol Autonomous Prefecture**	**220.97**	**26.39**	**26.23**	**0.64**	**16.64**	**8.88**	**0.16**
库尔勒市	Korla City	38.56	0.97	0.94		0.64	0.30	0.03
轮台县	Luntai [Bugur] County	30.08	7.50	7.50		4.25	3.25	
尉犁县	Yuli [Lopnur] County	35.72	0.02	0.02			0.02	
若羌县	Ruoqiang [Qarkilik] County	6.46	0.86	0.86		0.48	0.38	
且末县	Qiemo [Qarqan] County	14.33	3.28	3.17		2.09	1.01	0.11
焉耆回族自治县	Yanqi Hui Autonomous County	29.76	6.34	6.33		4.62	1.71	0.01
和静县	Hejing County	20.32	3.16	3.15		2.05	1.10	0.01
和硕县	Hoxud County	26.15	1.35	1.35	0.15	0.75	0.45	
博湖县	Bohu [Bagrax] County	19.59	2.91	2.91	0.49	1.76	0.66	
阿克苏地区	**Aksu Administrative Offices**	**387.17**	**119.55**	**118.67**	**11.02**	**61.14**	**45.06**	**0.88**
阿克苏市	Aksu City	51.28	7.04	7.02	1.92	3.90	1.20	0.02
温宿县	Wensu [Onsu] County	47.15	12.74	12.74	6.88	3.81	1.93	
库车县	Kuqa County	59.97	26.00	26.00		15.60	10.40	
沙雅县	Xayar County	56.24	14.67	14.67		8.00	6.67	
新和县	Xinhe [Toksu] County	37.16	8.85	8.85		4.60	4.25	
拜城县	Baicheng [Bay] County	41.99	24.13	23.84	1.52	10.67	11.39	0.29
乌什县	Wushi [Uxturpan] County	32.97	19.10	18.53	0.70	10.20	6.56	0.57
阿瓦提县	Awat County	52.46	4.62	4.62		2.81	1.81	
柯坪县	Kalpin County	7.95	2.40	2.40		1.55	0.85	
克孜勒苏柯尔克孜自治州	**Kizilsu Kirgiz Autonomous Prefecture**	**41.44**	**29.28**	**29.10**	**0.52**	**15.56**	**12.28**	**0.18**
阿图什市	Artux City	11.88	8.59	8.59	0.07	5.46	2.99	
阿克陶县	Akto County	24.24	18.35	18.35	0.45	9.05	8.64	
阿合奇县	Akqi County	2.73	0.98	0.89		0.24	0.24	0.09
乌恰县	Wuqia [Ulugqat] County	2.59	1.36	1.27		0.81	0.41	0.09
喀什地区	**Kashgar [Kaxgar] Administrative Offices**	**669.73**	**293.62**	**290.11**	**7.02**	**161.71**	**120.51**	**3.51**
喀什市	Kashgar [Kaxgar] City	14.52	7.31	7.31	1.55	3.53	2.23	
疏附县	Shufu County	52.70	32.20	32.20	0.87	18.00	13.33	
疏勒县	Shule County	53.61	26.14	26.14	0.14	16.00	10.00	
英吉沙县	Yengisar County	32.65	18.93	18.93		10.40	8.53	
泽普县	Zepu [Poskam] County	29.13	13.33	11.66	0.53	7.13	4.00	1.67
莎车县	Shache [Yarkant] County	165.84	71.16	70.01	3.33	36.67	30.00	1.15
叶城县	Yecheng [Kagilik] County	75.68	36.79	36.59	0.60	20.00	15.67	0.20
麦盖提县	Makit County	51.56	15.62	15.62		8.36	7.26	
岳普湖县	Yopurga County	35.03	12.66	12.66		7.33	5.33	
伽师县	Jiashi [Payzawat] County	74.25	32.00	32.00		20.00	12.00	
巴楚县	Bachu [Maralbexi] County	80.89	25.33	25.33		13.33	12.00	
塔什库尔干塔吉克自治县	Taxkorgan Tajik Autonomous County	3.87	2.15	1.66		0.96	0.16	0.49
和田地区	**Hotan Administrative Offices**	**211.34**	**134.42**	**134.06**	**7.51**	**65.06**	**61.09**	**0.36**
和田市	Hotan City	13.17	8.82	8.82	0.33	4.82	3.67	
和田县	Hotan County	31.39	22.95	22.92	2.27	11.31	9.17	0.03
墨玉县	Moyu [Karakax] County	51.32	35.44	35.44	2.10	17.53	15.81	
皮山县	Pishan [Guma] County	27.29	15.69	15.53		7.10	8.41	0.16
洛浦县	Lop County	30.10	19.36	19.36	0.01	9.75	9.59	
策勒县	Qira County	20.17	11.30	11.13		5.12	5.81	0.17
于田县	Yutian [Keriya] County	30.54	18.40	18.40	2.80	8.23	7.37	
民丰县	Minfeng [Niya] County	7.36	2.46	2.46		1.20	1.26	
二、生产建设兵团	**Xinjiang Production and Construction Group**	**1010.77**	**195.01**	**186.93**	**28.55**	**80.09**	**63.25**	**8.08**

Continued

(1 000 hectares)

薯类 Tubers	棉花 Cotton	#长绒棉 Longstaple Cotton	油料 Oil Bearing Crops	#油菜 Rapeseeds	#胡麻 Flax	#葵花 Helianthus	甜菜 Beetroots	蔬菜 Vegetables	果用瓜 Melon	#甜瓜 Muskmelon	苜蓿 Lucerne
0.12	**37.16**		**7.81**			**7.81**	**4.09**	**1.18**	**0.48**	**0.02**	**3.07**
	16.11		0.38			0.38	1.39	0.68	0.13	0.01	0.67
	21.05		0.02			0.02	0.20	0.48	0.26	0.01	0.18
0.12			7.41			7.41	2.50	0.02	0.09		2.22
0.29	**139.43**	**16.57**	**2.83**	**0.71**		**2.12**	**4.32**	**22.79**	**4.38**	**3.45**	**4.63**
	36.22							1.02	0.28	0.02	0.06
	17.17							0.64	2.64	2.46	2.13
	35.47							0.09	0.04	0.02	0.10
	4.74							0.02	0.83	0.83	0.01
	9.40	9.40	0.01	0.01				0.23	0.13	0.06	0.95
	2.79		1.35	0.09		1.26	2.16	5.51	0.09	0.03	0.51
0.21	5.14		0.81	0.60		0.21	1.65	7.31	0.13	0.01	0.04
0.08	21.33		0.14	0.01		0.13	0.09	1.83	0.03		0.51
	7.17	7.17	0.52			0.52	0.42	6.14	0.21	0.02	0.32
1.14	**224.02**	**59.27**	**4.08**	**2.83**	**0.94**	**0.30**	**2.62**	**15.14**	**8.38**	**2.24**	**7.70**
0.03	34.07	8.78	0.01					3.83	1.94	0.52	3.82
0.22	30.00		0.65	0.28	0.14	0.23	0.15	1.49	0.79	0.11	0.11
0.18	30.00		0.28	0.28				1.79	1.61	0.66	0.07
0.02	40.00	8.50						0.75	0.65	0.23	0.04
	26.67		0.10	0.10				0.54	0.75	0.30	0.22
0.60	5.33		1.93	1.52	0.34	0.07	2.00	4.35	1.03	0.06	0.34
0.09	9.48		1.11	0.65	0.46		0.47	1.06	0.73	0.09	0.43
	43.33	41.99						0.96	0.84	0.23	2.67
	5.14							0.37	0.04	0.04	
0.05	**6.47**		**0.60**	**0.15**	**0.32**	**0.13**		**0.79**	**0.63**	**0.32**	**3.28**
0.04	1.73		0.09	0.01		0.08		0.29	0.25	0.20	0.62
	4.71		0.05			0.05		0.39	0.38	0.12	0.29
			0.37	0.05	0.32			0.08			1.30
0.01	0.03		0.09	0.09				0.03			1.07
1.47	**196.79**		**3.07**	**0.19**	**1.87**	**0.90**		**36.51**	**50.27**	**34.22**	**46.06**
0.25								6.00	0.36	0.15	0.55
	6.67		0.47	0.19	0.20	0.08		3.61	4.47	0.67	3.15
	11.33							2.07	9.87	8.93	4.20
	6.93		0.07		0.02	0.05		0.76	2.95	2.57	2.03
	10.00							3.00	0.80	0.02	
0.11	46.66		1.73		1.65	0.05		6.06	7.80	4.46	11.66
0.98	9.33		0.60			0.52		5.33	1.32	0.46	8.00
	30.00							0.79	1.98	0.70	2.67
	12.54		0.20			0.20		0.67	4.32	3.66	2.73
	23.33							2.40	11.60	9.93	4.54
	40.00							4.53	4.80	2.67	6.23
0.13								1.29			0.30
0.66	**24.83**		**1.67**	**0.59**	**0.14**	**0.81**		**12.34**	**3.50**	**1.91**	**28.74**
0.03	1.62		0.01		0.01			1.40	0.32	0.09	0.59
0.21	3.27		0.06	0.04	0.02			1.90	0.42	0.20	1.65
0.02	3.96		0.15	0.13	0.02			2.21	0.37	0.12	9.04
0.29	3.75		0.72	0.10		0.62		1.43	0.08	0.03	4.68
	4.63		0.03					1.03	0.37	0.15	4.17
0.03	3.33		0.25	0.01	0.09	0.05		0.61	0.19	0.03	3.17
0.07	3.14		0.37	0.23		0.14		3.46	0.80	0.47	3.01
0.01	1.13		0.08	0.08				0.30	0.95	0.82	2.43
6.22	**514.32**	**50.60**	**38.24**	**12.85**	**1.17**	**20.36**	**29.42**	**58.96**	**12.13**	**8.11**	**58.88**

10-15 主要农作物种植结构
Planting Structure of Major Farm Crops

单位：%　　(%)

项　目	Item	1990	1995	2000	2007
农作物总播种面积	**Total Sown Areas of Farm Crops**	**100**	**100**	**100**	**100**
粮食作物	Grain Crops	61.30	52.21	42.66	31.38
谷 物	Cereal	60.85	50.10	39.95	29.60
稻 谷	Rice	2.82	2.40	2.31	1.61
小 麦	Wheat	39.61	31.22	24.75	14.43
玉 米	Corn	14.85	14.39	11.29	12.04
谷 子	Millet	0.02	0.02	0.04	0.01
高 粱	Jowar	0.72	0.47	0.39	0.13
其它谷物	Other Cereal	2.83	1.59	1.18	1.38
豆 类	Soybeans	0.45	2.12	2.71	1.78
#大 豆	Soja	0.45	0.94	1.85	1.21
杂 豆	Miscellaneous Beans		1.18	0.20	0.29
薯 类	Tubers	0.36	0.34	0.66	0.75
油 料	Oil-bearing Crops	9.04	10.05	9.15	4.02
#花 生	Peanuts	0.01		0.14	0.06
油菜籽	Rapeseeds	3.94	4.26	2.84	1.35
芝 麻	Sesame	0.05		0.02	0.02
胡麻籽	Benne	1.55	0.88	0.72	0.28
向日葵	Helianthus	3.23	4.59	4.63	2.19
棉 花	Cotton	14.61	24.35	29.87	40.57
麻 类	Fiber Crops	0.11	0.14	0.21	0.37
甜 菜	Beetroots	2.24	2.33	1.65	2.14
烟 叶	Tobacco	0.03	0.03	0.08	0.01
药 材	Medicinal Materials	0.04	0.22	0.38	0.41
蔬菜、瓜类	Vegetables and Melon	2.92	3.17	5.42	7.70
#蔬 菜	Vegetables	1.95	2.34	3.77	5.35
其他农作物	Other Farm Crops	9.35	7.16	9.92	12.65
#青饲料	Succulence	0.41	3.94	3.56	7.28

10-16 主要年份农作物产品产量

Output of Major Farm Crops in Main Years

单位：万吨 (10 000 tons)

年份 Year	粮食 Grain Crops	谷物 Cereal	#水稻 Rice	#小麦 Wheat	#玉米 Corn	#大麦 Barley	豆类 Soybeans	薯类 Tubers	棉花 Cotton	#长绒棉 Long-staple Cotton
1978	370.01	367.71	27.39	180.02	134.45	5.01	2.30	22.91	5.50	1.19
1980	386.13	384.16	25.62	213.19	126.43	3.50	1.97	16.03	7.92	1.74
1985	496.65	495.16	30.63	314.52	139.38	1.93	1.49	15.14	18.78	1.40
1990	676.89	673.18	47.27	390.80	209.42	10.51	3.71	22.57	46.88	3.48
1991	672.52	667.82	46.10	382.65	222.25	6.70	4.70	19.81	63.95	3.85
1992	706.27	700.59	43.28	418.62	219.61	7.25	5.68	26.21	66.76	5.65
1993	720.37	703.58	39.12	419.18	219.90	11.44	16.79	23.48	68.00	5.97
1994	666.17	642.89	41.58	337.87	229.49	22.72	23.28	24.95	88.21	1.94
1995	730.16	716.83	48.25	381.21	266.74	12.82	13.33	26.43	93.50	1.13
1996	818.20	808.67	51.49	420.32	312.54	17.39	9.53	32.50	94.04	1.72
1997	825.34	813.07	55.27	437.60	294.31	17.92	12.27	26.73	115.00	3.10
1998	830.00	814.54	49.56	444.00	302.25	11.00	15.46	33.12	140.00	1.39
1999	838.78	821.70	54.14	423.29	323.06	8.00	17.08	46.06	140.75	1.67
2000	808.60	782.93	60.35	405.80	298.22	11.75	25.67	64.01	150.00	6.16
2001	796.00	767.53	56.79	374.14	318.41	11.86	28.47	60.02	157.00	9.71
2002	875.87	849.48	60.62	386.44	379.05	13.78	26.39	62.41	150.00	6.67
2003	801.64	774.62	50.73	335.67	366.25	14.33	27.02	71.80	160.00	10.10
2004	828.53	800.04	51.31	345.94	388.12	8.06	28.49	70.79	175.25	11.22
2005	877.21	852.00	54.18	400.71	380.36	10.23	25.22	65.86	195.70	11.87
2006	895.22	870.21	59.27	400.31	386.80	17.85	25.01	76.50	267.53	18.59
2007	867.04	846.35	62.52	359.22	396.00	24.26	20.69	101.36	290.00	25.02

年份 Year	油料 Oil bearing Crops	#油菜 Rapeseeds	#胡麻 Flax	#葵花 Helianthus	甜菜 Beetroots	蔬菜 Vegetables	果用瓜 Melons	#甜瓜 Muskmelon	苜蓿 Lucerne
1978	10.33	3.30	3.14	2.29	16.37	91.26	44.05		
1980	17.59	5.59	5.17	4.59	38.52	73.44	55.68		
1985	34.25	7.29	8.10	16.90	40.69	111.08	103.18	47.02	49.69
1990	38.96	12.17	6.32	18.17	224.37	187.42	93.38	37.75	89.29
1991	40.49	14.63	5.56	19.16	256.85	172.21	81.68	29.07	76.46
1992	35.62	13.18	5.23	15.93	329.07	193.30	94.17	28.37	75.58
1993	37.02	12.75	4.65	16.65	236.91	191.82	75.49	29.27	73.43
1994	50.76	18.80	4.72	25.05	299.24	210.99	77.12	25.47	77.31
1995	49.41	15.12	3.79	29.06	288.14	269.56	68.75	18.31	82.62
1996	30.95	10.15	3.12	16.91	354.52	301.94	67.16	17.33	75.42
1997	29.95	8.92	2.53	17.69	388.71	295.59	86.78	25.90	70.05
1998	37.52	12.32	2.53	20.82	513.12	321.79	88.32	29.45	67.56
1999	60.46	16.37	2.75	35.69	354.24	406.18	143.49	46.38	69.98
2000	60.14	14.75	3.60	35.47	292.65	527.84	151.03	51.22	76.32
2001	42.64	12.19	2.47	23.31	455.12	486.74	156.87	56.86	103.12
2002	44.37	12.90	3.69	23.26	466.81	674.96	233.40	107.49	149.93
2003	50.13	15.43	3.49	25.80	381.65	761.00	189.32	77.61	249.60
2004	44.54	12.16	2.10	21.90	344.21	919.13	186.06	92.54	273.04
2005	38.94	9.22	2.39	21.69	419.12	862.23	220.65	95.58	295.74
2006	32.82	9.73	2.52	16.17	555.53	958.04	237.28	109.98	240.15
2007	40.30	9.60	1.58	25.39	586.93	1173.99	338.67	192.63	205.47

10-17 各地、州、市、县(市)主要农产品产量

单位：吨 (2007 年)

地区	Region	粮食作物 Grain Crops	谷物 Cereal	#水稻 Rice	#小麦 Wheat	#玉米 Corn	豆类 Soy-beans
总 计	**Total**	**8670400**	**8463525**	**625167**	**3592262**	**3960043**	**206875**
一、地 方	**Local Regions**	**7682100**	**7501376**	**374469**	**3099627**	**3834524**	**180725**
乌鲁木齐市	**Urumqi City**	**117163**	**113018**	**56955**	**31206**	**10309**	**4145**
#乌鲁木齐县	Urumqi County	29754	29192	2776	12405	493	563
克拉玛依市	**Karamay City**	**1145**	**1145**		**335**	**810**	
吐鲁番地区	**TurpanAdministrative Offices**	**8415**	**8389**		**2535**	**1619**	**26**
吐鲁番市	Turpan City						
鄯善县	Shanshan [piqan]County						
托克逊县	Toksun County	8415	8389		2535	1619	26
哈密地区	**Hami [Kumul]Administrative Offices**	**64991**	**64166**		**35912**	**5737**	**825**
哈密市	Hami [Kumul]City	13532	13329		6742	3215	203
巴里坤哈萨克自治县	Barkol KazakAutonomous County	45472	45075		28152	75	397
伊吾县	Yiwu [Araturuk]County	5987	5762		1018	2447	225
昌吉回族自治州	**Changji Hui Autonomous Prefecture**	**819912**	**795209**	**4116**	**329820**	**398984**	**24703**
昌吉市	Changji City	111247	109028	1317	63454	44246	2219
阜康市	Fukang City	57613	55141	1456	26614	26847	2472
呼图壁县	Hutubi County	77562	76331	838	47082	28411	1231
玛纳斯县	Manas County	80463	80125	505	13650	65655	338
奇台县	Qitai County	337330	334336		126118	155599	2994
吉木萨尔县	Jimsar County	64283	63452		29201	32247	831
木垒哈萨克自治县	Mori Kazak Autonomous County	91414	76796		23701	45979	14618
伊犁哈萨克自治州	**Ili Kazak Autonomous Prefecture**	**2356170**	**2218764**	**89290**	**721192**	**1327661**	**137406**
伊犁州直属县(市)	**Counties (Cities) Direct Under Ili Prefecture**	**1351143**	**1259840**	**81790**	**366625**	**781478**	**91303**
伊宁市	Yining [Gulja]City	93754	92392		11588	80782	1362
奎屯市	Kuytun City	102	102		102		
伊宁县	Yining [Gulja]County	436890	409248		51682	356136	27642
察布查尔锡伯自治县	Qapqal Xibe Autonomous County	157278	153629	69404	36090	48135	3649
霍城县	Huocheng [korgas]County	155914	152392	340	40017	111763	3522
巩留县	Gongliu [Tokkuzlara]County	151960	124201	7650	50563	65988	27759
新源县	Xinyuan [kunes]County	140613	115947	4106	51995	58317	24666
昭苏县	Zhaosu [mongolkure]County	96195	96195		77652		
特克斯县	Tekes County	61932	61797		20558	37607	135
尼勒克县	Nilka County	56505	53937	290	26378	22750	2568
塔城地区	**Tacheng [Tarbagatai] Administrative Offices**	**843694**	**841071**	**7500**	**309463**	**476460**	**2623**
塔城市	Tacheng [Qoqek] City	314616	314568		102234	180553	48
乌苏市	Usu City	114387	114000	7500	23035	83316	387
额敏县	Emin [Dorbiljin] County	152852	152722		89516	50666	130
沙湾县	Shawan County	142018	140495		47658	91598	1523
托里县	Toli County	42046	41661		21064	18658	385
裕民县	Yumin [Qagantokay] County	74865	74835		24741	50094	30
和布克赛尔蒙古自治县	Hoboksar Mongol Autonomous County	2910	2790		1215	1575	120
阿勒泰地区	**Altay Administrative Offices**	**161333**	**117853**		**45104**	**69723**	**43480**
阿勒泰市	Altay City	28925	18081		2295	15785	10844
布尔津县	Burqin County	31245	13680		1710	11970	17565
富蕴县	Fuyun [Koktokay] County	30740	27344		6395	19859	3396
福海县	Fuhai [Burultokay] County	7630	7328		313	7015	302
哈巴河县	Habahe [Kaba] County	27900	16790		6820	9750	11110
青河县	Qinghe [Qinggil] County	26029	25766		21066	3019	263
吉木乃县	Jeminay County	8864	8864		6505	2325	

注：各地州市县粮食、棉花产量合计不等于全区总计数(以下同)。

Output of Major Farm Crops by Prefecture, Autonomous Prefecture, City and County

(ton)

薯类 Tubers	棉花 Cotton	#长绒棉 Longstaple Cotton	油料 Oil Bearing Crops	#油菜 Rapeseeds	#胡麻 Flax	#葵花 Helianthus	甜菜 Beetroots	蔬菜 Vegetables	果用瓜 Melon	#甜瓜 Muskmelon	苜蓿 Lucerne
1013598	**2900000**	**250213**	**403000**	**96041**	**15817**	**253872**	**5869300**	**11739880**	**3386652**	**1926261**	**2054692**
819162	**1529809**	**140773**	**316160**	**63340**	**14216**	**194426**	**3902499**	**8088322**	**2941379**	**1686562**	**1645744**
95817	**2523**	**65**	**5904**	**72**	**1**	**5023**	**10440**	**502413**	**12938**	**297**	**38233**
82141	303		1933	66		1866	2645	219331	4424		16801
	15105	**15105**						**2700**	**4050**	**450**	**530**
300	**24789**		**765**			**12**		**186067**	**214223**	**129834**	**31750**
	5562							101410	97530	36618	8171
	7650							52087	81000	66000	9947
300	11577		765			12		32570	35693	27216	13632
61232	**23355**		**2315**	**1928**	**24**	**363**		**76048**	**148138**	**127367**	**50553**
4862	23175		1893	1530	12	351		69610	70020	49249	21357
54810	117		410	398		12		5577	1928	1928	27135
1560	63		12		12			861	76190	76190	2061
243088	**158431**		**34089**	**381**	**219**	**24188**	**481159**	**1916408**	**246468**	**21478**	**100099**
13135	42235		2284			1412	117079	624682	137983	6655	11343
5084	9337		3104			2840	3467	260400	9386	1520	6943
12284	38604		2065			1689	111545	332817	50462	7206	16363
6182	65564		3648	29		3619	34209	222264	23161	1544	20235
85700			14206	257	41	9831	190992	145991	2285	323	14272
93953	2666		7405	37		3656	18527	327134	21353	3292	7633
26750	25		1377	58	178	1141	5340	3120	1838	938	23310
327372	**159743**	**7836**	**228388**	**53735**	**10191**	**133820**	**2690883**	**1840197**	**177038**	**71019**	**439006**
242951	**12240**		**111792**	**35118**	**10191**	**49439**	**1990030**	**454851**	**66271**	**1731**	**46721**
10316	16		2564	642	40	1860	126431	162610	13450		5885
	1610		140			140		3000			
12167	266		13264	2916	215	7562	550418	51157	26831	540	1172
1750	6799		6290		353	2821	151523	28962	9899		7650
8150	3549		11267		331	7270	570436	97600	8710	621	
			7950	431	338	5358	118830	51495	2910	570	9090
110913			15521	1803	944	8248	392662	26655	4331		2981
22965			39547	27676	5849	6022		4461			
4500			11299	1240	459	9600	26355	17675			15158
72190			3950	410	1662	558	53375	11236	140		4785
32716	**147503**	**7836**	**59391**	**18598**		**27195**	**610207**	**1318656**	**25861**	**2262**	**172293**
1012			8401	6109		1508	60619	132603	1483	1062	28886
4361	73173		5610			5610	38992	439775	10864	600	7186
			20997	10528		8984	370441	78932			70333
18992	66362		10552			9037	140155	663003	13514	600	12542
1925	132		4303	1435		1254		1991			19113
5766			8961	526		235		252			17560
660	7836	7836	567			567		2100			16673
51705			**57205**	**19**		**57186**	**90646**	**66690**	**84906**	**67026**	**219992**
5306			16609			16609	34073	15834	50854	50854	27990
3675			15930			15930		10510	2700	2700	19404
13047			10818	19		10799		12859	8715	655	20926
1349			2681			2681	36573	6331	12137	9667	68822
6510			3700			3700	20000	13300	10500	3150	35560
19926			859			859		7550			37681
1892			6608			6608		306			9609

Note: Total yield of grain and cotton by prefecture, city and county is not equal to the total sum of the whole region (the same in the following tables) .

10-17 续表

单位：吨

地　区	Region	粮食作物 Grain Crops	谷物 Cereal	#水稻 Rice	#小麦 Wheat	#玉米 Corn	豆类 Soybeans
博尔塔拉蒙古自治州	**Bortala Mongol Autonomous Prefecture**	**253165**	**251291**	**1703**	**25147**	**224435**	**1874**
博乐市	Bole [Bortala] City	119768	118657	1698	2536	114423	1111
精河县	Jinghe [Jing] County	5295	5295		233	5062	
温泉县	Wenquan [Araxang] County	128102	127339	5	22378	104950	763
巴音郭楞蒙古自治州	**Bayangol Mongol Autonomous Prefecture**	**161001**	**160654**	**3982**	**95582**	**60858**	**347**
库尔勒市	Korla City	4678	4617		3266	1351	61
轮台县	Luntai [Bugur] County	40538	40538		22851	17687	
尉犁县	Yuli [Lopnur] County	135	135		15	120	
若羌县	Ruoqiang [Qarkilik] County	4398	4398		2621	1777	
且末县	Qiemo [Qarqan] County	16684	16444		11732	4480	240
焉耆回族自治县	Yanqi Hui Autonomous County	41102	41086		27258	13828	16
和静县	Hejing County	24233	24203		12889	11314	30
和硕县	Hoxud County	10021	10021	773	4100	5148	
博湖县	Bohu [Bagrax] County	19212	19212	3209	10850	5153	
阿克苏地区	**Aksu Administrative Offices**	**882567**	**879366**	**106629**	**390569**	**378722**	**3201**
阿克苏市	Aksu City	51849	51821	17669	26729	7423	28
温宿县	Wensu [Onsu] County	111231	111231	70795	25918	14272	
库车县	Kuqa County	169413	169413		101813	67570	
沙雅县	Xayar County	101215	101215		53651	47564	
新和县	Xinhe [Toksu] County	61316	61316		29629	31687	
拜城县	Baicheng [Bay] County	210958	210351	12198	64320	133302	607
乌什县	Wushi [Uxturpan] County	131454	128888	5967	60665	59617	2566
阿瓦提县	Awat County	31247	31247		19190	12057	
柯坪县	Kalpin County	13884	13884		8654	5230	
克孜勒苏柯尔克孜自治州	**Kizilsu Kirgiz Autonomous Prefecture**	**160374**	**159800**	**4034**	**77540**	**76530**	**574**
阿图什市	Artux City	49362	49362	407	28585	20180	
阿克陶县	Akto County	102840	102840	3627	44839	53961	
阿合奇县	Akqi County	3211	2856		918	954	355
乌恰县	Wuqia [Ulugqat] County	4961	4742		3198	1435	219
喀什地区	**Kashgar [Kaxgar] Administrative Offices**	**1949466**	**1942893**	**55380**	**996631**	**888965**	**6573**
喀什市	Kashgar [Kaxgar] City	53003	53003	16415	21658	14930	
疏附县	Shufu County	203875	203875	5850	110025	88000	
疏勒县	Shule County	161493	161493	903	102240	58350	
英吉沙县	Yengisar County	126728	126728		67080	59648	
泽普县	Zepu [Poskam] County	90400	87400	3040	51360	33000	3000
莎车县	Shache [Yarkant] County	473068	471068	25500	220550	225000	2000
叶城县	Yecheng [Kagilik] County	277223	276473	3672	125700	146219	750
麦盖提县	Makit County	109109	109109		52919	56190	
岳普湖县	Yopurga County	79000	79000		45640	33360	
伽师县	Jiashi [Payzawat] County	197640	197640		116640	81000	
巴楚县	Bachu [Maralbexi] County	173880	173880		81000	92880	
塔什库尔干塔吉克自治县	Taxkorgan Tajik Autonomous County	4047	3224		1819	388	823
和田地区	**Hotan Administrative Offices**	**907732**	**906681**	**52380**	**393157**	**459895**	**1051**
和田市	Hotan City	68100	68100	2612	30855	34633	
和田县	Hotan County	148068	147981	14817	69605	62981	87
墨玉县	Moyu [Karakax] County	232260	232260	15564	105910	110786	
皮山县	Pishan [Guma] County	112310	111770		40519	71189	540
洛浦县	Lop County	125169	125169	38	59369	65725	
策勒县	Qira County	79051	78627		30670	47385	424
于田县	Yutian [Keriya] County	122927	122927	19349	49522	54056	
民丰县	Minfeng [Niya] County	19847	19847		6707	13140	
二、生产建设兵团	**Xinjiang Production and Construction Group**	**1406511**	**1380361**	**250698**	**492636**	**543729**	**26150**

Continued

(ton)

薯类 Tubers	棉花 Cotton	#长绒棉 Longstaple Cotton	油料 Oil Bearing Crops	#油菜 Rapeseeds	#胡麻 Flax	#葵花 Helianthus	甜菜 Beetroots	蔬菜 Vegetables	果用瓜 Melon	#甜瓜 Muskmelon	苜蓿 Lucerne
3727	**74280**		**21377**			**21377**	**233558**	**41124**	**18970**	**606**	**17792**
	32275		1055			1055	87257	23844	4278	140	4061
	42005		45			45	3000	16035	10539	466	3649
3727			20277			20277	143301	1245	4153		10082
9413	**256729**	**31240**	**4645**	**782**		**3863**	**318964**	**1401874**	**147447**	**104372**	**39232**
	65012							92834	14552	618	595
	32303							22110	87705	83025	8400
	73314							2088	1191	452	1016
	7541							583	16415	16400	147
	18114	18114	21	21				5223	2454	1080	10242
	3720		2564	88		2476	151580	361940	6599	2044	7455
6265	6549		1015	667		348	129471	313347	4790	376	400
3148	37050		69	6		63	5798	124226	1476		5927
	13126	13126	976			976	32115	479523	12265	377	5050
28559	**402558**	**86527**	**8135**	**4788**	**1512**	**661**	**167495**	**537567**	**235782**	**45918**	**118217**
116	66420	13050	34					218310	67217	6655	76757
3317	58019		1024	307	214	503	6770	26530	22882	2970	2063
4275	57960		377	377				42611	26100	11880	1022
515	76836	13126	9	9				9837	15590	5003	840
	51532		102	102				13000	9418	5400	
16961	7419		4339	2633	408	158	129000	177282	34080	1350	6500
3375	12286		2250	1360	890		31725	27507	28335	2700	6035
	63213	60351						16982	31500	9300	25000
	8873							5508	660	660	
1545	**9401**		**723**	**232**	**293**	**198**		**15940**	**11753**	**5255**	**28896**
1365	2897		129	14		115		8318	3666	3050	6541
	6458		83			83		5902	8087	2205	5708
			346	53	293			1140			9120
180	46		165	165				580			7527
35933	**356767**		**5475**	**250**	**1770**	**2174**		**1287911**	**1626114**	**1131280**	**507002**
1700								269111	15218	1720	8300
	10600		875	250	240	385		116600	113550	15150	35720
	21165							83500	269356	251731	63000
	9672		110		30	80		39000	95750	81400	15250
	18000							85500	24000	2600	
94	84700		2600		1500	100		136350	250000	125000	105000
32000	16500		1620			1339		250613	22097	7830	72000
	57150							29631	101677	35383	4000
	19480		270			270		25083	136166	116166	41000
	38500							69000	394300	354300	68100
	81000							165988	204000	140000	93500
2139								17535			1132
12176	**46128**		**4344**	**1172**	**206**	**2747**		**280073**	**98458**	**48687**	**274434**
1196	2688		4		4			65717	9998	2495	11252
7022	6193		101	70	30	1		49736	9786	4237	12791
351	7238		296	253	36			47409	7868	1727	83416
2363	7088		2615	393		2124		15220	11217	720	46734
	8747		41			5		27080	11088	3242	38690
671	6026		491	10	136	267		16496	6400	1206	32975
523	5925		775	425		350		49352	20114	13873	34331
50	2223		21	21				9063	21987	21187	14245
194436	**1194376**	**109440**	**98659**	**32701**	**1601**	**59446**	**2007827**	**3651558**	**445273**	**239699**	**408948**

10-18 各地、州、市、县(市)农作物单位面积产量

Output of Major Farm Products Per Hectare by Prefecture, Autonomous Prefecture, City and County

单位：公斤/公顷　　(2007 年)　　(kg / hectare)

地　区	Region	粮 食 Grain	#谷 物 Cereal	#小 麦 Wheat	#玉 米 Corn	棉 花 Cotton	油 料 Oil-Bearing Crops	甜 菜 Beetroots
总　计	Total	6287	6508	5666	7487	1627	2284	62426
一、地 方	Local Regions	6776	7055	5678	8938	1767	2209	60410
乌鲁木齐市	Urumqi City	6427	6656	5041	7751	1262	1923	52200
#乌鲁木齐县	Urumqi County	4723	4762	5022	5476	2755	1823	52900
克拉玛依市	Karamay City	5725	5725	4188	6750	1590		
吐鲁番地区	TurpanAdministrative Offices	4809	4849	4156	6746	1377	3825	
吐鲁番市	Turpan City					1176		
鄯善县	Shanshan [piqan]County					1349		
托克逊县	Toksun County	4809	4849	4156	6746	1523	3825	
哈密地区	Hami [Kumul]Administrative Offices	4669	4739	5116	5570	1771	1456	
哈密市	Hami [Kumul]City	4511	4518	5226	6698	1780	1343	
巴里坤哈萨克自治县	Barkol KazakAutonomous County	4905	4986	5100	7500	975	2412	
伊吾县	Yiwu [Araturuk]County	3628	3717	4848	4531	1260	1200	
昌吉回族自治州	Changji Hui Autonomous Prefecture	6136	6723	5433	9331	1704	2055	55242
昌吉市	Changji City	6517	6922	6072	8591	1552	1757	68870
阜康市	Fukang City	6430	6884	5994	8062	1347	2444	57783
呼图壁县	Hutubi County	6400	6458	5659	8332	1768	1827	76401
玛纳斯县	Manas County	7912	7949	6379	8472	1890	2895	81450
奇台县	Qitai County	6434	6591	5275	10394		2035	41976
吉木萨尔县	Jimsar County	7033	7186	5692	9953	1169	1847	59765
木垒哈萨克自治县	Mori Kazak Autonomous County	3851	5880	3750	9364	833	2152	25429
伊犁哈萨克自治州	Ili Kazak Autonomous Prefecture	6909	7564	4922	11110	1572	2248	60253
伊犁州直属县(市)	Counties (Cities) Direct Under Ili Prefecture	7037	7856	4867	11264	1185	2332	61213
伊宁市	Yining [Gulja]City	8803	9121	4440	10757	800	2085	58533
奎屯市	Kuytun City	2550	2550	2550		735	1400	
伊宁县	Yining [Gulja]County	8473	9852	4733	11715	1267	2556	59376
察布查尔锡伯自治县	Qapqal Xibe Autonomous County	6984	7415	4412	8768	1305	2447	62355
霍城县	Huocheng [korgas]County	8605	8917	5430	11594	1314	2651	62962
巩留县	Gongliu [Tokkuzlara]County	5743	7428	5181	10800		3369	51000
新源县	Xinyuan [kunes]County	6272	7936	5836	12049		3086	68170
昭苏县	Zhaosu [mongolkure]County	4512	4512	4617			1933	
特克斯县	Tekes County	7252	7279	4826	11679		2364	51676
尼勒克县	Nilka County	5449	5561	4083	10484		2005	53914
塔城地区	Tacheng [Tarbagatai] Administrative Offices	7305	7326	5020	11198	1616	1819	58561
塔城市	Tacheng [Qoqek] City	6993	6994	4698	10485		1776	51811
乌苏市	Usu City	10863	10847	6176	13726	1745	3117	59988
额敏县	Emin [Dorbiljin] County	6058	6063	4957	11541		1914	58800
沙湾县	Shawan County	9294	9474	6329	13142	1554	3769	64588
托里县	Toli County	5178	5208	4435	7742	1200	1624	
裕民县	Yumin [Qagantokay] County	6875	6878	4466	9381		944	
和布克赛尔蒙古自治县	Hoboksar Mongol Autonomous County	6326	6643	4500	10500	1200	2700	
阿勒泰地区	Altay Administrative Offices	4814	6493	4728	9210		2724	52397
阿勒泰市	Altay City	5307	7441	4500	8264		3225	57751
布尔津县	Burqin County	4292	8000	4500	9000		2700	
富蕴县	Fuyun [Koktokay] County	4246	6419	3279	11157		2481	
福海县	Fuhai [Burultokay] County	9083	10038	4471	10629		2529	45152
哈巴河县	Habahe [Kaba] County	4522	6483	4639	9750		2782	60606
青河县	Qinghe [Qinggil] County	5550	5614	5544	7021		2148	
吉木乃县	Jeminay County	4817	4817	4783	5054		2360	

注：个别县(市)油料等作物种植在边角地头，未计面积，故单产偏高。
Note: The oil-bearing crop planted at the edge or margin of fields in small number of counties (cities), whose area is not calculated, thus per-unit output is relatively higher.

10-18 续表 Continued

单位：公斤/公顷 (kg/ hectare)

地　区	Region	粮　食 Grain	#谷　物 Cereal	#小　麦 Wheat	#玉　米 Corn	棉　花 Cotton	油　料 Oil-Bearing Crops	甜　菜 Beet-roots
博尔塔拉蒙古自治州	**Bortala Mongol Autonomous Prefecture**	**11694**	**11915**	**5350**	**13828**	**1999**	**2737**	**57105**
博乐市	Bole [Bortala] City	12906	13243	5898	13671	2003	2776	62775
精河县	Jinghe [Jing] County	13238	13238	5825	14061	1995	2250	15000
温泉县	Wenquan [Araxang] County	10702	10856	5290	13993		2736	57320
巴音郭楞蒙古自治州	**Bayangol Mongol Autonomous Prefecture**	**6101**	**6125**	**5744**	**6853**	**1841**	**1641**	**73834**
库尔勒市	Korla City	4823	4912	5103	4503	1795		
轮台县	Luntai [Bugur] County	5405	5405	5377	5442	1881		
尉犁县	Yuli [Lopnur] County	6750	6750	4883	5985	2067		
若羌县	Ruoqiang [Qarkilik] County	5114	5114	5460	4676	1591		
且末县	Qiemo [Qarqan] County	5087	5187	5613	4436	1927	2100	
焉耆回族自治县	Yanqi Hui Autonomous County	6483	6491	5900	8087	1333	1899	70176
和静县	Hejing County	7669	7683	6287	10285	1274	1253	78467
和硕县	Hoxud County	7423	7423	5467	11440	1737	493	64422
博湖县	Bohu [Bagrax] County	6602	6602	6165	7808	1831	1877	76464
阿克苏地区	**Aksu Administrative Offices**	**7382**	**7410**	**6388**	**8405**	**1797**	**1994**	**63929**
阿克苏市	Aksu City	7365	7382	6854	6186	1950	3400	
温宿县	Wensu [Onsu] County	8731	8731	6803	7395	1934	1575	45133
库车县	Kuqa County	6516	6516	6526	6497	1932	1346	
沙雅县	Xayar County	6899	6899	6706	7131	1921	3166	
新和县	Xinhe [Toksu] County	6928	6928	6441	7456	1932	1020	
拜城县	Baicheng [Bay] County	8743	8823	6028	11703	1392	2248	64500
乌什县	Wushi [Uxturpan] County	6882	6956	5948	9088	1296	2027	67500
阿瓦提县	Awat County	6763	6763	6829	6661	1459		
柯坪县	Kalpin County	5785	5785	5583	6153	1726		
克孜勒苏柯尔克孜自治州	**Kizilsu Kirgiz Autonomous Prefecture**	**5477**	**5491**	**4983**	**6232**	**1453**	**1205**	
阿图什市	Artux City	5746	5746	5235	6749	1675	1433	
阿克陶县	Akto County	5604	5604	4955	6245	1371	1660	
阿合奇县	Akqi County	3277	3209	3825	3975		935	
乌恰县	Wuqia [Ulugqat] County	3648	3734	3948	3500	1533	1833	
喀什地区	**Kashgar [Kaxgar] Administrative Offices**	**6639**	**6697**	**6163**	**7377**	**1813**	**1783**	
喀什市	Kashgar [Kaxgar] City	7251	7251	6135	6695			
疏附县	Shufu County	6332	6332	6113	6602	1589	1862	
疏勒县	Shule County	6178	6178	6390	5835	1868		
英吉沙县	Yengisar County	6695	6695	6450	6993	1396	1571	
泽普县	Zepu [Poskam] County	6782	7496	7203	8250	1800		
莎车县	Shache [Yarkant] County	6648	6729	6014	7500	1815	1503	
叶城县	Yecheng [Kagilik] County	7535	7556	6285	9331	1768	2700	
麦盖提县	Makit County	6985	6985	6330	7740	1905		
岳普湖县	Yopurga County	6240	6240	6226	6259	1553	1350	
伽师县	Jiashi [Payzawat] County	6176	6176	5832	6750	1650		
巴楚县	Bachu [Maralbexi] County	6865	6865	6077	7740	2025		
塔什库尔干塔吉克自治县	Taxkorgan Tajik Autonomous County	1882	1942	1895	2423			
和田地区	**Hotan Administrative Offices**	**6753**	**6763**	**6043**	**7528**	**1858**	**2601**	
和田市	Hotan City	7721	7721	6401	9437	1659	400	
和田县	Hotan County	6452	6456	6154	6868	1894	1683	
墨玉县	Moyu [Karakax] County	6554	6554	6042	7007	1828	1973	
皮山县	Pishan [Guma] County	7158	7197	5707	8465	1890	3632	
洛浦县	Lop County	6465	6465	6089	6853	1889	1367	
策勒县	Qira County	6996	7064	5990	8156	1810	1964	
于田县	Yutian [Keriya] County	6681	6681	6017	7335	1887	2095	
民丰县	Minfeng [Niya] County	8068	8068	5589	10429	1967	263	
二、生产建设兵团	**Xinjiang Production and Construction Group**	**7213**	**7384**	**6151**	**8597**	**2322**	**2580**	**68247**

10-19 各地、州、市林业生产情况

Condition on Forest Products by Prefecture, Autonomous Prefecture, City

单位:公顷　　(2007 年)　　(hectare)

地区	Region	当年造林面积 Planting Area in the Current Year	用材林 Timber Forest	经济林 Economic Forest	防护林 Windbreak	薪炭林 Firewood Forest	特种用途林 Forest for Special Purpose
总计	**Total**	**117299**	**3300**	**51958**	**60704**	**1256**	**81**
一、地方	**Local Regions**	**105027**	**2936**	**50233**	**50601**	**1256**	**1**
乌鲁木齐市	Urumqi City	1283		7	1276		
克拉玛依市	Karamay City	502			502		
吐鲁番地区	Turpan Administrative Offices	8600	1	7103	1496		
哈密地区	Hami [Kumul]Administrative Offices	3500			3500		
昌吉回族自治州	Changji Hui Autonomous Prefecture	15477	292		15185		
伊犁哈萨克自治州	Ili Kazak Administrative Prefecture	21532	2038	2600	16893		1
伊犁州直属县(市)	Counties (Cities) Direct Under Ili Prefecture	8073	2025	2600	3447		1
塔城地区	Tacheng [Tarbagatai] Administrative Offices	6212	13		6199		
阿勒泰地区	Altay Administrative Offices	7247			7247		
博尔塔拉蒙古自治州	Bortala Mongol Autonomous Prefecture	673			673		
巴音郭楞蒙古自治州	Bayangol Mongol Autonomous Prefecture	1936	344		1592		
阿克苏地区	Aksu Administrative Offices	8982		6617	2365		
克孜勒苏柯尔克孜自治州	Kizilsu Kirgiz Autonomous Prefecture	4035	161	304	2903	667	
喀什地区	Kashgar [Kaxgar] Administrative Offices	33248		31647	1458	144	
和田地区	Hotan Administrative Offices	5260	100	1956	2759	445	
二、生产建设兵团	**Xinjiang Production and Construction Group**	**12272**	**364**	**1725**	**10103**		**80**

地区	Region	迹地更新面积 Renewing Area in Slash	当年零星植树(万株) Fragmentary Planting (10 000)	年末实有育苗面积 Actual Sapling Breeding Area	幼林抚育作业面积 Tending Area of Young Growth	成林抚育面积 Tending Area of Full Growth	核桃产量(吨) Walnut Output (ton)	村及村以下木材采伐量(立方米) Timber Felling Output in Village or Below (cu.m)
总计	**Total**	**3422**	**2937.07**	**12448**	**1966277**	**1068030**	**64330**	**518943**
一、地方	**Local Regions**	**2761**	**2177.71**	**10679**	**1717185**	**899471**	**64179**	**476472**
乌鲁木齐市	Urumqi City	8	17.00	573	5632	6444		2125
克拉玛依市	Karamay City		45.00	388	1312	7066		
吐鲁番地区	Turpan Administrative Offices	40		97	11107	11826	144	1794
哈密地区	Hami[Kumul] Administrative Offices	5	4.74	136	84730	16750		1310
昌吉回族自治州	Changji Hui Autonomous Prefecture	364	115.80	1261	278737	134928		30228
伊犁哈萨克自治州	Ili Kazak Administrative Prefecture	755	583.97	982	234766	201286	126	107027
伊犁州直属县(市)	Counties (Cities) Direct Under Ili Prefecture	755	455.50	630	124036	64284	126	69082
塔城地区	Tacheng [Tarbagatai] Administrative Offices		33.00	112	30951	67737		33642
阿勒泰地区	Altay Administrative Offices		95.47	240	79779	69265		4303
博尔塔拉蒙古自治州	Bortala Mongol Autonomous Prefecture	69	31.00	49	15269	32378		15349
巴音郭楞蒙古自治州	Bayangol Mongol Autonomous Prefecture	247	67.39	444	88034	32980		51646
阿克苏地区	Aksu Administrative Offices	406	133.42	1171	352825	205200	10221	65300
克孜勒苏柯尔克孜自治州	Kizilsu Kirgiz Autonomous Prefecture		32.10	93	14589	17247	102	8784
喀什地区	Kashgar [Kaxgar] Administrative Offices	384	632.99	3615	464058	153841	28657	151770
和田地区	Hotan Administrative Offices	482	514.30	1870	166126	79525	24930	41139
二、生产建设兵团	**Xinjiang Production and Construction Group**	**661**	**759.36**	**1769**	**249092**	**168559**	**151**	**42471**

10-20 各地、州、市水果种植面积

Planted Area of Fruits by Prefecture, Autonomous Prefecture, City

单位:公顷 (2007 年) (hectare)

地 区	Region	合 计 Total	苹 果 Apples	梨 Pears	葡 萄 Grapes	#无核葡萄 Seedless Grapes
总 计	**Total**	**610683**	**32482**	**70542**	**109857**	**40891**
一、地 方	**Local Regions**	**516802**	**22758**	**51952**	**82013**	**33456**
乌鲁木齐市	Urumqi City	1218	83	1	940	
克拉玛依市	Karamay City					
吐鲁番地区	TurpanAdministrative Offices	38726	4	69	30144	27830
哈密地区	Hami [Kumul] Administrative Offices	13227	50	102	3731	3290
昌吉回族自治州	Changji Hui Autonomous Prefecture	12152	1214	6	8302	10
伊犁哈萨克自治州	Ili Kazak Autonomous Prefecture	19856	7223	355	2841	
伊犁州直属县(市)	Counties (Cities) Direct Under Ili Prefecture	18546	6787	312	2401	
塔城地区	Tacheng [Tarbagatai] Administrative Offices	1258	426	43	404	
阿勒泰地区	Altay Administrative Offices	52	10		37	
博尔塔拉蒙古自治州	Bortala MongolAutonomous Prefecture	260	67		188	
巴音郭楞蒙古自治州	Bayangol Mongol Autonomous Prefecture	72938	847	32591	7273	455
阿克苏地区	Aksu Administrative Offices	125313	8072	15468	5899	
克孜勒苏柯尔克孜自治州	Kizilsu Kirgiz Autonomous Prefecture	14446	107	48	5819	
喀什地区	Kashgar [Kaxgar] Administrative Offices	170402	3848	2716	6501	150
和田地区	Hotan Administrative Offices	48265	1243	597	10375	1721
二、生产建设兵团	**Xinjiang Production and Construction Group**	**93881**	**9724**	**18590**	**27844**	**7435**

地 区	Region	桃 Peaches	杏 Apricots	红 枣 Jujubes	石 榴 Pomegraniate	其 它 Others
总 计	**Total**	**10626**	**199486**	**137849**	**17749**	**32092**
一、地 方	**Local Regions**	**8057**	**192514**	**111533**	**17350**	**30625**
乌鲁木齐市	Urumqi City	158	12			23
克拉玛依市	Karamay City					
吐鲁番地区	TurpanAdministrative Offices	22	217	7593	664	13
哈密地区	Hami [Kumul] Administrative Offices	8	1538	7739		59
昌吉回族自治州	Changji Hui Autonomous Prefecture	444	1729	37		420
伊犁哈萨克自治州	Ili Kazak Autonomous Prefecture	1034	2745	120	2	5536
伊犁州直属县(市)	Counties (Cities) Direct Under Ili Prefecture	911	2741	120	2	5272
塔城地区	Tacheng [Tarbagatai] Administrative Offices	118	4			263
阿勒泰地区	Altay Administrative Offices	5				1
博尔塔拉蒙古自治州	Bortala Mongol Autonomous Prefecture	5				
巴音郭楞蒙古自治州	Bayangol Mongol Autonomous Prefecture	231	17599	11994	40	2364
阿克苏地区	Aksu Administrative Offices	795	35929	54543	405	4202
克孜勒苏柯尔克孜自治州	Kizilsu Kirgiz Autonomous Prefecture	45	7562	62	193	610
喀什地区	Kashgar [Kaxgar] Administrative Offices	3393	103937	22823	10683	16501
和田地区	Hotan Administrative Offices	1923	21246	6623	5363	897
二、生产建设兵团	**Xinjiang Production and Construction Group**	**2569**	**6972**	**26316**	**399**	**1467**

10-21 各地、州、市水果产量
Output of Fruits by Prefecture, Autonomous Prefecture, City

单位：吨　　(2007 年)　　(ton)

地　区	Region	合 计 Total	苹 果 Apples	梨 Pears	葡 萄 Grapes	#无核葡萄 Seedless Grapes
总　计	**Total**	**4119760**	**388881**	**541451**	**1654581**	**935644**
一、地　方	**Local Regions**	**3456047**	**254165**	**360864**	**1382040**	**821298**
乌鲁木齐市	Urumqi City	16283	817	5	13892	
克拉玛依市	Karamay City					
吐鲁番地区	TurpanAdministrative Offices	780690	25	437	768680	724307
哈密地区	Hami [Kumul] Administrative Offices	72907	35	698	65398	57801
昌吉回族自治州	Changji Hui Autonomous Prefecture	129558	7424	41	115665	108
伊犁哈萨克自治州	Ili Kazak Autonomous Prefecture	124800	64552	2242	35703	
伊犁州直属县(市)	Counties (Cities) Direct Under Ili Prefecture	109704	58194	1466	29657	
塔城地区	Tacheng [Tarbagatai] Administrative Offices	14590	6148	776	5897	
阿勒泰地区	Altay Administrative Offices	506	210		149	
博尔塔拉蒙古自治州	Bortala MongolAutonomous Prefecture	3991	864		3007	
巴音郭楞蒙古自治州	Bayangol Mongol Autonomous Prefecture	284685	11435	177597	28673	3240
阿克苏地区	Aksu Administrative Offices	655715	108100	144457	88796	
克孜勒苏柯尔克孜自治州	Kizilsu Kirgiz Autonomous Prefecture	89226	623	550	60502	
喀什地区	Kashgar [Kaxgar] Administrative Offices	1015393	46367	29918	64416	2475
和田地区	Hotan Administrative Offices	282799	13924	4919	137307	33367
二、生产建设兵团	**Xinjiang Production and Construction Group**	**663713**	**134716**	**180587**	**272541**	**114346**

地　区	Region	桃 Peachs	杏 Apricots	红 枣 Jujubes	石 榴 Pomegranate	其 它 Others
总　计	**Total**	**86137**	**1252036**	**87206**	**48088**	**61379**
一、地　方	**Local Regions**	**48176**	**1240372**	**64339**	**48028**	**58062**
乌鲁木齐市	Urumqi City	1241	222			106
克拉玛依市	Karamay City					
吐鲁番地区	TurpanAdministrative Offices	200	3596	5942	1786	24
哈密地区	Hami [Kumul] Administrative Offices	13	3824	2911		28
昌吉回族自治州	Changji Hui Autonomous Prefecture	2123	3921	18		366
伊犁哈萨克自治州	Ili Kazak Autonomous Prefecture	7522	10880	434		3467
伊犁州直属县(市)	Counties (Cities) Direct Under Ili Prefecture	6406	10788	434		2759
塔城地区	Tacheng [Tarbagatai] Administrative Offices	987	92			690
阿勒泰地区	Altay Administrative Offices	129				18
博尔塔拉蒙古自治州	Bortala MongolAutonomous Prefecture	120				
巴音郭楞蒙古自治州	Bayangol Mongol Autonomous Prefecture	737	48615	14571	230	2827
阿克苏地区	Aksu Administrative Offices	7941	253587	20143	1112	31579
克孜勒苏柯尔克孜自治州	Kizilsu Kirgiz Autonomous Prefecture	156	23585		819	2991
喀什地区	Kashgar [Kaxgar] Administrative Offices	22356	796295	10190	30552	15299
和田地区	Hotan Administrative Offices	5767	95848	10130	13529	1375
二、生产建设兵团	**Xinjiang Production and Construction Group**	**37961**	**11664**	**22867**	**60**	**3317**

10-22 牲畜饲养情况
Number of Livestock

单位：万头(只) (10 000 heads)

年份 Year	大牲畜年底头数 Large Animals (year-end)	牛 Cattle and Buffaloes	马 Horses	驴 Donkeys	骡 Mules	骆驼 Camels	役畜 Draught Animals
1978	446.19	222.39	112.39	96.61	1.61	13.19	148.34
1980	482.55	250.65	106.89	108.88	1.72	14.41	154.86
1985	517.55	293.26	99.54	106.57	2.17	16.05	197.29
1990	575.88	338.22	104.58	112.96	2.69	17.43	209.95
1995	580.04	343.54	100.47	117.04	2.77	16.22	213.61
1996	589.41	349.78	101.16	119.36	2.76	16.34	215.05
1997	600.12	359.81	100.32	120.74	2.87	16.38	207.15
1998	606.79	364.29	100.26	123.45	2.80	15.99	205.31
1999	615.91	370.52	101.47	124.99	2.78	16.15	189.86
2000	632.93	384.98	102.57	125.94	2.74	16.70	173.37
2001	630.67	386.40	99.38	126.06	2.84	15.99	172.08
2002	654.46	414.13	99.71	122.22	2.59	15.81	169.51
2003	694.53	453.06	99.39	124.02	2.48	15.58	163.72
2004	716.56	482.30	95.78	120.82	2.36	15.30	151.49
2005	739.72	504.16	94.19	123.90	2.38	15.09	134.81
2006	736.33	502.86	92.09	124.94	2.14	14.30	145.97
2007	702.03	486.98	86.09	113.92	1.83	13.20	120.79

年份 Year	猪年底头数 Hogs (year-end)	羊年底只数 Sheep and Goats (year-end)	山羊 Goats	绵羊 Sheep	牲畜出栏头数 Slanghtered Fattened Animals withina Year	#猪 Pork Pig	#牛 Beef Cattle	#羊 Mutton Sheep
1978	103.25	1927.34	349.63	1577.91	460.41	50.75	18.75	382.76
1980	84.62	2105.43	388.89	1716.54	584.09	67.32	24.22	477.81
1985	66.58	2431.91	394.79	2037.12	836.39	49.07	42.33	723.51
1990	89.71	2830.81	449.43	2381.38	1242.89	78.93	70.10	1070.43
1995	135.26	3009.02	471.38	2537.64	1709.93	122.32	101.20	1448.72
1996	138.18	3136.21	498.10	2638.11	1859.28	153.75	116.25	1550.65
1997	145.73	3261.81	514.60	2747.21	2096.67	173.06	125.72	1753.88
1998	169.82	3447.38	528.05	2919.33	2222.27	197.39	140.82	1837.57
1999	188.34	3592.29	555.21	3037.08	2223.89	203.87	145.95	1820.71
2000	201.53	3690.21	586.70	3103.51	2455.99	224.46	154.53	2017.36
2001	208.23	3764.88	601.14	3163.74	2633.83	246.00	179.32	2147.31
2002	219.08	3908.23	626.42	3281.81	2878.39	259.05	188.65	2363.02
2003	227.71	4104.30	657.15	3447.15	3201.99	307.74	202.23	2626.94
2004	223.08	4266.73	669.47	3597.26	3437.59	352.83	220.80	2790.53
2005	238.38	4355.50	659.75	3695.75	3756.92	358.71	249.41	3081.88
2006	243.88	4359.50	654.26	3705.20	4063.52	390.82	278.69	3317.99
2007	237.90	4083.44	608.10	3475.34	4108.28	393.70	271.76	3361.99

注：牲畜出栏数 1999 年以后计算口径与 1998 年以前不同。
Note: The calculating norm of cattles out of stock after 1999 was different from that prior to that in 1998.

10-23 各地、州、市、县(市)牲畜年底头数

Number of Livestock at the Year-end by Prefecture, Autonomous Prefecture, City and County

单位：万头(只) (2007 年) (10 000 heads)

地区	Region	合计 Total	#牛 Cattle and Buffaloes	#马 Horses	#驴 Donkeys	#猪 Hogs	#山羊 Goats	#绵羊 Sheep
总　计	**Total**	**5023.37**	**486.98**	**86.09**	**113.92**	**237.90**	**608.10**	**3475.34**
一、地　方	**Local Regions**	**4406.95**	**463.28**	**86.60**	**115.14**	**145.44**	**569.18**	**3012.30**
乌鲁木齐市	**Urumqi City**	**69.76**	**7.54**	**1.68**	**0.30**	**5.07**	**19.14**	**35.81**
#乌鲁木齐县	Urumqi County	27.49	2.67	1.09	0.12	1.46	4.11	18.01
克拉玛依市	**Karamay City**	**12.90**	**0.73**	**0.07**	**0.01**	**6.92**	**1.65**	**3.49**
吐鲁番地区	**TurpanAdministrative Offices**	**114.54**	**5.47**	**0.32**	**4.26**	**0.79**	**14.57**	**88.64**
吐鲁番市	Turpan City	37.98	1.64	0.03	1.21	0.05	8.36	26.66
鄯善县	Shanshan [piqan]County	37.70	0.64	0.11	1.79	0.53	2.29	32.10
托克逊县	Toksun County	38.86	3.19	0.18	1.26	0.21	3.92	29.88
哈密地区	**Hami [Kumul]Administrative Offices**	**115.07**	**6.64**	**1.40**	**1.19**	**5.31**	**21.69**	**77.73**
哈密市	Hami [Kumul]City	40.79	1.97	0.38	0.47	2.26	5.68	29.67
巴里坤哈萨克自治县	Barkol KazakAutonomous County	55.20	3.52	0.60	0.56	2.10	9.79	38.13
伊吾县	Yiwu [Araturuk]County	19.08	1.15	0.42	0.16	0.95	6.22	9.93
昌吉回族自治州	**Changji Hui Autonomous Prefecture**	**363.03**	**30.50**	**4.40**	**1.66**	**32.72**	**44.36**	**247.72**
昌吉市	Changji City	57.02	5.62	0.82	0.24	9.56	9.13	31.48
阜康市	Fukang City	28.77	3.19	0.49	0.06	1.80	6.07	17.01
呼图壁县	Hutubi County	50.34	5.64	0.68	0.04	3.50	2.85	37.50
玛纳斯县	Manas County	47.53	3.45	0.45	0.06	4.71	3.34	35.35
奇台县	Qitai County	77.50	6.86	0.58	0.53	8.22	6.91	54.09
吉木萨尔县	Jimsar County	49.99	3.55	0.52	0.30	3.83	5.64	36.06
木垒哈萨克自治县	Mori Kazak Autonomous County	51.88	2.19	0.86	0.43	1.10	10.42	36.23
伊犁哈萨克自治州	**Ili Kazak Autonomous Prefecture**	**1411.70**	**200.96**	**58.59**	**4.23**	**43.72**	**141.46**	**955.90**
伊犁州直属县(市)	**Counties (Cities) Direct Under Ili Prefecture**	**646.16**	**105.95**	**37.07**	**3.73**	**22.23**	**27.03**	**449.47**
伊宁市	Yining [Gulja]City	26.10	7.10	0.58	0.61	1.50	1.00	15.28
奎屯市	Kuytun City	2.36	0.02			2.00	0.03	0.31
伊宁县	Yining [Gulja]County	76.45	12.55	2.34	0.81	4.59	6.36	49.65
察布查尔锡伯自治县	Qapqal Xibe Autonomous County	42.73	5.18	1.27	1.10	1.85	3.30	30.03
霍城县	Huocheng [korgas]County	71.73	9.34	2.04	0.57	5.33	2.07	52.31
巩留县	Gongliu [Tokkuzlara]County	58.73	10.93	3.50	0.35	2.38	2.30	39.23
新源县	Xinyuan [kunes]County	108.42	20.44	8.63	0.05	1.98	2.58	74.71
昭苏县	Zhaosu [mongolkure]County	94.35	13.33	7.41	0.15	0.58	1.93	70.87
特克斯县	Tekes County	71.31	12.31	3.84	0.03	1.10	3.35	50.66
尼勒克县	Nilka County	93.98	14.75	7.46	0.06	0.92	4.11	66.42
塔城地区	**Tacheng [Tarbagatai] Administrative Offices**	**454.55**	**46.34**	**9.89**	**0.42**	**19.91**	**66.47**	**309.59**
塔城市	Tacheng [Qoqek] City	70.64	6.58	1.21	0.11	2.16	5.73	54.64
乌苏市	Usu City	65.34	4.43	1.38	0.21	4.27	9.69	45.16
额敏县	Emin [Dorbiljin] County	75.68	7.50	1.44		1.06	11.63	53.81
沙湾县	Shawan County	64.59	7.75	0.66	0.04	11.62	6.06	38.38
托里县	Toli County	65.09	8.52	2.01	0.04	0.13	12.32	41.54
裕民县	Yumin [Qagantokay] County	56.19	6.10	1.53		0.55	7.33	40.30
和布克赛尔蒙古自治县	Hoboksar Mongol Autonomous County	57.02	5.46	1.66	0.02	0.12	13.71	35.76
阿勒泰地区	**Altay Administrative Offices**	**310.99**	**48.67**	**11.63**	**0.08**	**1.58**	**47.96**	**196.84**
阿勒泰市	Altay City	56.52	10.98	1.93	0.03	0.20	3.35	39.39
布尔津县	Burqin County	38.00	8.64	1.61		0.20	3.31	23.94
富蕴县	Fuyun [Koktokay] County	74.82	7.11	2.54	0.04	0.31	12.31	51.22
福海县	Fuhai [Burultokay] County	42.35	6.28	0.96		0.45	5.01	28.99
哈巴河县	Habahe [Kaba] County	37.80	9.16	2.02		0.11	6.35	19.75
青河县	Qinghe [Qinggil] County	38.00	3.90	1.72		0.27	14.50	17.03
吉木乃县	Jeminay County	23.50	2.60	0.85	0.01	0.04	3.13	16.52

注：全区总计不等于各地、州汇总数。
Note: Total Livestock of autonomous region is not equal to the sum of Livestock of every prefecture.

10-23 续表 Continued

单位：万头(只) (10 000 heads)

地　区	Region	合 计 Total	#牛 Cattle and Buffaloes	#马 Horses	#驴 Donkeys	#猪 Hogs	#山羊 Goats	#绵羊 Sheep
博尔塔拉蒙古自治州	**Bortala Mongol Autonomous Prefecture**	**118.73**	**7.79**	**2.02**	**0.36**	**2.19**	**12.28**	**93.76**
博乐市	Bole [Bortala] City	42.97	3.50	0.52	0.23	1.39	3.32	33.85
精河县	Jinghe [Jing] County	38.75	1.84	0.64	0.05	0.42	4.93	30.78
温泉县	Wenquan [Araxang] County	37.01	2.45	0.86	0.08	0.38	4.03	29.13
巴音郭楞蒙古自治州	**Bayangol Mongol Autonomous Prefecture**	**309.03**	**21.15**	**4.30**	**5.83**	**17.71**	**66.19**	**193.15**
库尔勒市	Korla City	22.09	1.71	0.06	0.20	4.19	3.66	12.27
轮台县	Luntai [Bugur] County	37.59	1.87	0.03	1.79	0.93	16.00	16.95
尉犁县	Yuli [Lopnur] County	35.88	1.41	0.17	1.13	0.37	19.07	13.71
若羌县	Ruoqiang [Qarkilik] County	12.41	0.70	0.17	0.81	0.67	2.42	7.53
且末县	Qiemo [Qarqan] County	34.95	1.59	0.14	1.22	0.82	8.84	22.12
焉耆回族自治县	Yanqi Hui Autonomous County	19.00	2.02	0.06	0.12	1.18	0.95	14.67
和静县	Hejing County	106.23	9.09	3.37	0.40	3.43	9.74	80.05
和硕县	Hoxud County	23.43	1.34	0.18	0.04	1.67	4.50	15.53
博湖县	Bohu [Bagrax] County	17.45	1.42	0.12	0.12	4.45	1.01	10.32
阿克苏地区	**Aksu Administrative Offices**	**514.58**	**53.77**	**7.50**	**13.24**	**17.75**	**142.55**	**278.03**
阿克苏市	Aksu City	47.42	6.69	0.62	0.81	12.25	6.21	20.83
温宿县	Wensu [Onsu] County	66.36	6.69	1.68	0.82	0.82	15.80	40.47
库车县	Kuqa County	83.39	11.84	1.19	3.47	0.81	21.22	44.55
沙雅县	Xayar County	69.30	4.39	0.89	1.88	1.21	30.81	29.81
新和县	Xinhe [Toksu] County	34.48	4.23	0.71	1.72	0.21	5.77	21.68
拜城县	Baicheng [Bay] County	87.01	7.48	1.02	2.68	1.82	21.95	51.92
乌什县	Wushi [Uxturpan] County	55.29	6.30	1.12	1.06	0.16	20.60	25.75
阿瓦提县	Awat County	53.23	5.90	0.22	0.32	0.47	10.79	35.52
柯坪县	Kalpin County	18.10	0.25	0.05	0.48		9.40	7.50
克孜勒苏柯尔克孜自治州	**Kizilsu Kirgiz Autonomous Prefecture**	**163.83**	**18.24**	**2.70**	**3.93**	**0.05**	**38.17**	**99.88**
阿图什市	Artux City	47.00	4.91	0.37	1.06	0.02	11.01	29.50
阿克陶县	Akto County	49.88	8.41	0.24	2.08	0.03	8.42	30.55
阿合奇县	Akqi County	36.03	3.59	1.65	0.40		10.95	19.21
乌恰县	Wuqia [Ulugqat] County	30.92	1.33	0.44	0.39		7.79	20.62
喀什地区	**Kashgar [Kaxgar] Administrative Offices**	**766.25**	**83.74**	**2.18**	**44.46**	**11.57**	**40.18**	**583.72**
喀什市	Kashgar [Kaxgar] City	25.59	1.40	0.01	1.20	1.50	0.17	21.30
疏附县	Shufu County	98.00	9.75	0.12	3.82	1.05	3.11	80.10
疏勒县	Shule County	73.00	9.75	0.03	4.49	5.35	0.61	52.74
英吉沙县	Yengisar County	37.70	5.60	0.03	2.90	0.18		28.97
泽普县	Zepu [Poskam] County	37.80	5.38	0.18	2.20	1.16	1.36	27.50
莎车县	Shache [Yarkant] County	112.10	12.10	0.58	6.30	0.30	3.04	89.74
叶城县	Yecheng [Kagilik] County	117.00	14.50	0.30	6.88	0.72	6.45	88.03
麦盖提县	Makit County	54.52	6.84	0.24	2.38	0.48	5.88	38.69
岳普湖县	Yopurga County	33.30	4.50	0.08	6.00	0.09	2.70	19.92
伽师县	Jiashi [Payzawat] County	94.70	5.64	0.25	6.50	0.09	5.85	76.36
巴楚县	Bachu [Maralbexi] County	64.13	5.36	0.29	1.30	0.65	5.28	51.25
塔什库尔干塔吉克自治县	Taxkorgan Tajik Autonomous County	18.41	2.92	0.07	0.49		5.73	9.12
和田地区	**Hotan Administrative Offices**	**447.53**	**26.75**	**1.44**	**35.67**	**1.64**	**26.94**	**354.47**
和田市	Hotan City	29.07	2.35	0.07	1.55	0.75	0.56	23.77
和田县	Hotan County	68.92	5.38	0.18	6.41	0.07	2.39	54.43
墨玉县	Moyu [Karakax] County	105.20	7.54	0.26	9.06	0.33	1.62	86.37
皮山县	Pishan [Guma] County	44.42	1.44	0.14	3.47	0.06	2.48	36.74
洛浦县	Lop County	46.75	4.09	0.07	4.13	0.14	1.08	37.21
策勒县	Qira County	47.37	1.22	0.22	3.13	0.08	2.65	39.97
于田县	Yutian [Keriya] County	80.63	4.26	0.42	6.86	0.16	8.05	60.68
民丰县	Minfeng [Niya] County	25.17	0.47	0.08	1.06	0.05	8.11	15.30
二、生产建设兵团	**Xinjiang Production and Construction Group**	**878.04**	**45.86**	**3.33**	**3.60**	**121.93**	**68.68**	**633.95**

10-24 主要年份畜产品产量

Output of Livestock Products in Main Years

年份 Year	肉类产量(万吨) Output of meat (10 000 tons)	#牛 Beef	#马 Horse Meat	#骆驼 Camels	#猪 Pork	#羊 Mutton	#禽兔肉 Poultry and Rabbit Meat
1978	9.65	1.85			2.48	5.32	
1980	12.70	2.20	0.60	0.05	3.29	6.48	
1985	18.37	4.23	0.86	0.15	3.09	9.97	
1990	30.46	7.08	1.18	0.18	4.93	15.75	1.22
1995	52.38	13.14	2.05	0.40	8.37	24.48	3.61
1996	60.31	15.18	2.24	0.38	10.43	26.93	4.82
1997	64.40	16.40	2.55	0.38	11.52	27.72	5.38
1998	75.19	19.19	2.82	0.47	13.60	32.49	6.16
1999	81.36	20.61	2.93	0.62	16.02	33.57	6.94
2000	90.00	22.24	3.57	0.63	17.18	37.50	7.76
2001	97.00	23.99	3.55	0.72	18.36	40.48	8.66
2002	105.44	25.90	3.65	0.68	19.70	43.06	10.38
2003	115.00	28.77	3.88	0.69	22.41	45.54	11.46
2004	128.13	30.42	4.34	0.70	24.58	52.65	13.27
2005	141.46	34.22	4.67	0.77	26.18	59.89	13.46
2006	158.21	39.25	4.80	0.90	28.78	66.99	14.92
2007	160.58	42.25	5.09	0.94	31.73	65.02	13.74

年份 Year	羊毛(万吨) Wool (10 000 tons)	#绵羊毛 Sheep Wool	山羊绒(吨) Cashmere (ton)	驼毛(吨) Camel Hair (ton)	牛奶(万吨) Cow Milk (10 000 tons)	羊奶(万吨) Sheep Milk (10 000 tons)	牛皮(万张) Oxhide (10 000 sheets)	羊皮(万张) Sheep Skin (10 000 sheets)	禽蛋(万吨) Poultry Eggs (10 000 tons)
1978	3.08	3.00	324	371	4.50	0.75	17.36	300.05	
1980	3.31	3.21	263	353	5.84	1.44	18.22	338.32	
1985	7.07	3.91	325	530	16.43	3.27	35.72	587.69	4.29
1990	5.09	4.93	607	656	30.81	4.83	56.76	839.69	6.30
1995	5.66	5.45	716	716	45.21	4.60	91.54	1125.72	9.51
1996	5.99	5.77	780	787	48.76	5.46	92.31	1178.39	10.33
1997	6.25	6.01	813	742	54.18	4.60	96.88	1326.69	12.16
1998	6.48	6.22	811	768	59.96	5.06	110.12	1391.77	13.34
1999	6.76	6.50	849	727	64.81	5.62	118.35	1569.50	16.68
2000	6.98	6.67	893	757	72.54	5.69	125.62	1686.03	18.53
2001	7.30	6.99	973	736	81.09	6.76	143.13	1689.24	20.37
2002	7.78	7.44	1034	824	94.87	5.84	139.87	1801.67	22.64
2003	8.21	7.84	1143	793	113.00	6.21	141.57	1692.35	23.62
2004	8.91	8.49	1228	770	133.32	6.41	150.15	1981.82	24.99
2005	9.38	8.98	1258	730	152.22	5.62	169.53	2022.61	24.99
2006	9.62	8.96	1263	746	179.81	5.60	196.97	2300.73	25.80
2007	9.34	8.92	1265	946	196.23	5.54	191.90	2409.84	28.37

10-25 各地、州、市、县(市)总产肉量

Total Output of Meat by Prefecture, Autonomous Prefecture, City and County

单位：吨 (2007 年) (ton)

地区	Region	合计 Total	#牛 Beef	#马 Horse	#骆驼 Camels	#猪 Pork	#山羊 Goats	#绵羊 Sheep	#禽肉 Poultry Meat	#兔肉 Rabbit Meat
总 计	**Total**	**1605800**	**422539**	**50882**	**9408**	**317278**	**78024**	**572176**	**133479**	**40**
一、地 方	**Local Regions**	**1408987**	**382565**	**49426**	**9193**	**202825**	**72698**	**528619**	**145507**	**1621**
乌鲁木齐市	**Urumqi City**	**47008**	**12611**	**1149**	**132**	**12233**	**2784**	**12116**	**5756**	**28**
#乌鲁木齐县	Urumqi County	11843	2741	595	57	2065	562	4148	1623	2
克拉玛依市	**Karamay City**	**6817**	**465**			**4480**	**288**	**584**	**1000**	**…**
吐鲁番地区	**TurpanAdministrative Offices**	**46636**	**13367**	**143**	**153**	**800**	**4651**	**26443**	**1059**	**20**
吐鲁番市	Turpan City	25159	5590	5		50	3181	16213	119	1
鄯善县	Shanshan [piqan]County	12169	2760	84	75	630	750	7270	600	
托克逊县	Toksun County	9308	5017	54	78	120	720	2960	340	19
哈密地区	**Hami [Kumul]Administrative Offices**	**30591**	**5398**	**588**	**616**	**7420**	**2527**	**12292**	**1157**	**4**
哈密市	Hami [Kumul]City	15195	3458	168	120	2544	1244	6471	891	3
巴里坤哈萨克自治县	Barkol KazakAutonomous County	12265	1550	300	396	3980	876	4648	251	1
伊吾县	Yiwu [Araturuk]County	3131	390	120	100	896	407	1173	15	
昌吉回族自治州	**Changji Hui Autonomous Prefecture**	**247822**	**45820**	**3704**	**2113**	**65366**	**10197**	**68282**	**51303**	**350**
昌吉市	Changji City	44484	10217	914	261	11885	2176	13168	5556	242
阜康市	Fukang City	31671	3867	346	66	3551	1718	8620	13481	11
呼图壁县	Hutubi County	35173	7741	325	176	6681	776	10019	9415	24
玛纳斯县	Manas County	33419	3570	403	100	10581	1049	8644	9032	24
奇台县	Qitai County	59010	8054	262	127	26190	1047	13943	9217	6
吉木萨尔县	Jimsar County	21550	5606	440	43	4923	965	5558	3830	42
木垒哈萨克自治县	Mori Kazak Autonomous County	22515	6765	1014	1340	1555	2466	8330	772	1
伊犁哈萨克自治州	**Ili Kazak Autonomous Prefecture**	**414012**	**134095**	**34035**	**3885**	**54250**	**21152**	**140816**	**22792**	**923**
伊犁州直属县(市)	**Counties (Cities) Direct Under Ili Prefecture**	**193840**	**72661**	**21997**	**306**	**20980**	**3009**	**62059**	**11032**	**123**
伊宁市	Yining [Gulja]City	12932	6964	870	15	1405	149	2453	714	2
奎屯市	Kuytun City	184				77	5	78	24	
伊宁县	Yining [Gulja]County	33656	17168	2415	32	1534	696	8465	2490	
察布查尔锡伯自治县	Qapqal Xibe Autonomous County	12389	4350	810		1428	434	4136	1018	25
霍城县	Huocheng [korgas]County	23015	8251	1035		5220	218	6478	1640	54
巩留县	Gongliu [Tokkuzlara]County	21050	8787	2595	15	3308	299	5260	714	
新源县	Xinyuan [kunes]County	29726	8366	3603	17	4204	322	12066	1125	16
昭苏县	Zhaosu [mongolkure]County	18249	6075	3570	32	323	140	7917	145	2
特克斯县	Tekes County	18397	5518	2824		2505	274	6201	1062	1
尼勒克县	Nilka County	24242	7182	4275	195	976	472	9005	2100	23

注:全区总产肉量不等于各地州市汇总数。
Note: The total output of meat in the whole region does not equal to the total number gathered by different administrative offices, autonomous prefectures and cities.

10-25 续表 1 Continued

单位：吨 (ton)

地区	Region	合计 Total	#牛 Beef	#马 Horse	#骆驼 Camels	#猪 Pork	#山羊 Goats	#绵羊 Sheep	#禽肉 Poultry Meat	#兔肉 Rabbit Meat
塔城地区	**Tacheng [Tarbagatai] Administrative Officess**	**147437**	**37409**	**8683**	**1769**	**28553**	**11338**	**48699**	**10570**	**42**
塔城市	Tacheng [Qoqek] City	19484	7696	1026	120	1584	716	7336	945	1
乌苏市	Usu City	25369	4304	1184	684	9225	2748	5619	1299	17
额敏县	Emin [Dorbiljin] County	28311	6300	2288	126	5899	1723	10835	1140	
沙湾县	Shawan County	38887	8384	1478	163	10564	2245	9193	6811	24
托里县	Toli County	15226	4050	1337	342	520	1995	6954	28	
裕民县	Yumin [Qagantokay] County	9789	3135	845	100	465	550	4374	320	
和布克赛尔蒙古自治县	Hoboksar Mongol Autonomous County	10371	3540	525	234	296	1361	4388	27	
阿勒泰地区	**Altay Administrative Offices**	**72735**	**24025**	**3355**	**1810**	**4717**	**6805**	**30058**	**1190**	**758**
阿勒泰市	Altay City	14352	5441	910	532	608	709	6022	118	4
布尔津县	Burqin County	9255	2349	145	16	1005	616	4720	372	31
富蕴县	Fuyun [Koktokay] County	18431	5565	858	520	1140	1746	7718	174	700
福海县	Fuhai [Burultokay] County	9850	2250	286	354	1535	912	4230	271	12
哈巴河县	Habahe [Kaba] County	9450	4789	378	80	104	725	3184	190	
青河县	Qinghe [Qinggil] County	6833	1965	442	200	285	1851	2029	51	10
吉木乃县	Jeminay County	4564	1666	336	108	40	246	2155	13	
博尔塔拉蒙古自治州	**Bortala Mongol Autonomous Prefecture**	**23977**	**4711**	**896**	**134**	**6074**	**862**	**9889**	**1312**	**8**
博乐市	Bole [Bortala] City	11336	1905	205	29	4527	170	3829	664	
精河县	Jinghe [Jing] County	5948	1397	226	25	408	355	3039	487	8
温泉县	Wenquan [Araxang] County	6693	1409	465	80	1139	337	3021	161	
巴音郭楞蒙古自治州	**Bayangol Mongol Autonomous Prefecture**	**97053**	**27224**	**1567**	**133**	**22395**	**7233**	**29003**	**7913**	**127**
库尔勒市	Korla City	33764	10221	8		8713	990	7539	5877	38
轮台县	Luntai [Bugur] County	8022	1128	2		1057	2014	3407	404	3
尉犁县	Yuli [Lopnur] County	7362	2702	59		630	1575	1789	342	15
若羌县	Ruoqiang [Qarkilik] County	2140	421	43	14	410	182	667	142	9
且末县	Qiemo [Qarqan] County	7403	2227	116	15	525	1048	3088	50	15
焉耆回族自治县	Yanqi Hui Autonomous County	11840	3610	80		3730	325	3570	340	35
和静县	Hejing County	17417	4823	1182	12	3885	667	6473	306	4
和硕县	Hoxud County	4485	984	44	87	1445	291	1352	277	
博湖县	Bohu [Bagrax] County	4620	1108	33	5	2000	141	1118	175	8
阿克苏地区	**Aksu Administrative Offices**	**140027**	**46937**	**3663**	**1097**	**14423**	**11574**	**47796**	**10832**	**26**
阿克苏市	Aksu City	29612	7098	30		7929	1305	7080	5804	
温宿县	Wensu [Onsu] County	13021	4112	387	202	1122	1702	4975	313	2
库车县	Kuqa County	36917	14116	1170		1556	1825	15647	2603	

10-25 续表 2 Continued

单位：吨 (ton)

地区	Region	合计 Total	#牛 Beef	#马 Horse	#骆驼 Camels	#猪 Pork	#山羊 Goats	#绵羊 Sheep	#禽肉 Poultry Meat	#兔肉 Rabbit Meat
沙雅县	Xayar County	12007	3872			1102	2025	3979	370	19
新和县	Xinhe [Toksu] County	7201	3241	288		91	332	2530	720	
拜城县	Baicheng [Bay] County	15100	5212	350	45	1480	1448	5174	115	
乌什县	Wushi [Uxturpan] County	12100	5596	1368	450	198	1160	2579	749	
阿瓦提县	Awat County	11013	3321	50		945	825	4574	102	5
柯坪县	Kalpin County	3055	370	20	400		952	1258	55	
克孜勒苏柯尔克孜自治州	**Kizilsu Kirgiz Autonomous Prefecture**	**29863**	**11870**	**1767**	**576**	**44**	**3322**	**11983**	**301**	
阿图什市	Artux City	10682	4380	295	91	17	1214	4590	95	
阿克陶县	Akto County	10235	5313	260	42	27	692	3762	139	
阿合奇县	Akqi County	4184	1056	732	117		766	1468	45	
乌恰县	Wuqia [Ulugqat] County	4762	1121	480	326		650	2163	22	
喀什地区	**Kashgar [Kaxgar] Administrative Offices**	**265006**	**66907**	**1600**	**145**	**14944**	**6093**	**127391**	**40062**	**102**
喀什市	Kashgar [Kaxgar] City	20260	3575			2448	1066	11814	1066	
疏附县	Shufu County	28500	10000	10	63	256	444	15402	1980	
疏勒县	Shule County	24996	5420			3570	30	12171	2881	
英吉沙县	Yengisar County	13408	6555			128		5652	588	
泽普县	Zepu [Poskam] County	15989	3256	24		3920	79	6261	2252	
莎车县	Shache [Yarkant] County	38917	7400	1085	2	1275	460	22000	6395	50
叶城县	Yecheng [Kagilik] County	38471	8880	120	48	1148	837	17428	8337	38
麦盖提县	Makit County	14675	4503	45		500	403	8315	650	
岳普湖县	Yopurga County	9320	2680	5		102	246	5020	789	8
伽师县	Jiashi [Payzawat] County	29910	5700	194		128	902	13701	6725	
巴楚县	Bachu [Maralbexi] County	26138	6420	90		1470	908	8600	8400	
塔什库尔干塔吉克自治县	Taxkorgan Tajik Autonomous County	4422	2518	27	32		718	1027		
和田地区	**Hotan Administrative Offices**	**60175**	**13160**	**315**	**210**	**395**	**2016**	**42026**	**2021**	**33**
和田市	Hotan City	7809	2810	9		220	62	4304	405	
和田县	Hotan County	7351	1750	27			84	5243	245	3
墨玉县	Moyu [Karakax] County	14099	3050	36		50	135	10205	617	6
皮山县	Pishan [Guma] County	5144	640	27	42	10	202	4095	123	5
洛浦县	Lop County	6996	2140	9		10	73	4541	222	2
策勒县	Qira County	6533	980	81	56	10	274	4988	142	3
于田县	Yutian [Keriya] County	9654	1560	90	56	50	647	7037	200	14
民丰县	Minfeng [Niya] County	2589	230	36	56	45	540	1616	66	
二、生产建设兵团	**Xinjiang Production and Construction Group**	**294575**	**39974**	**1456**	**215**	**114453**	**10799**	**97944**	**25874**	**2297**

10-26 水产品产量和养殖面积
Output of Aquatic Products and Cultured Area

年份 Year	地区 Region	水产品产量(吨) Aquatic Products (ton)	#养殖产量 Cultured Output	养殖面积(公顷) Culture Area (hectare)
1985		8958	3403	32775
1990		23217	15401	68838
1991		25200	17700	57117
1992		26593	19733	60389
1993		28831	22216	68519
1994		35297	27766	68314
1995		44432	35341	72538
1996		47890	38876	79006
1997		52366	42656	75895
1998		53391	44557	67473
1999		55840	48068	70524
2000		60065	50974	69806
2001		60876	50902	63340
2002		63906	55159	62629
2003		67278	57244	67374
2004		73296	60405	74996
2005		79320	65571	76037
2006		84539	71440	76606
2007		88879	78639	77590
一、地　方	**Local Regions**	**66436**	**57977**	**44352**
乌鲁木齐市	Urumqi City	5709	5604	3838
克拉玛依市	Karamay City	632	217	44
吐鲁番地区	Turpan Administrative Offices	359	359	143
哈密地区	Hami [Kumul] Administrative Offices	1156	996	701
昌吉回族自治州	Changji Hui Autonomous Prefecture	12776	12776	2627
伊犁哈萨克自治州	Ili Kazak Autonomous Prefecture	19153	17233	14757
伊犁州直属县(市)	Counties (Cities) Direct Under Ili Prefecture	11887	11833	970
塔城地区	Tacheng [Tarbagatai] Administrative Offices	2416	2368	1299
阿勒泰地区	Altay Administrative Offices	4850	3032	12488
博尔塔拉蒙古自治州	Bortala Mongol Autonomous Prefecture	981	981	293
巴音郭楞蒙古自治州	Bayangol Mongol Autonomous Prefecture	9490	4565	4987
阿克苏地区	Aksu Administrative Offices	7189	6659	1580
克孜勒苏柯尔克孜自治州	Kizilsu Kirgiz Autonomous Prefecture	179	179	310
喀什地区	Kashgar [Kaxgar] Administrative Offices	7207	7207	10757
和田地区	Hotan Administrative Offices	1605	1201	4314
二、生产建设兵团	**Xinjiang Production and Construction Group**	**22443**	**20662**	**33238**

10-27 受灾面积情况

Areas Covered by Natural Disaster

单位：公顷 (hectares)

年 份 Year	地 区 Region	受灾面积 Areas Covered	#水 灾 Flood	#旱 灾 Drought
1990		282787	16900	87040
1991		530933	30733	256000
1992		511067	35333	72067
1993		378833	63538	55778
1994		568782	54413	139366
1995		665580	49812	210422
1996		558297	114905	83547
1997		372060	20200	165400
1998		535900	74990	22340
1999		1290799	145633	36696
2000		932545	49219	461136
2001		740888	82242	151703
2002		493400	128345	16634
2003		440982	80231	21291
2004		524402	35562	368935
2005		482066	93102	210796
2006		515289	35562	359823
2007		557411	68910	273312
乌鲁木齐市	Urumqi City			
克拉玛依市	Karamay City			
石河子市	Shihezi City			
吐鲁番地区	Turpan Administrative Offices	23142		16666
哈密地区	Hami [Kumul] Administrative Offices	8166	6060	2106
昌吉回族自治州	Changji Hui Autonomous Prefecture	29791	17719	2000
伊犁州直属县(市)	Counties (Cities) Direct Under Ili Prefecture	39839	7852	
塔城地区	Tacheng [Tarbagatai] Administrative Offices	58265	21752	8444
阿勒泰地区	Altay Administrative Offices	41783	3229	25988
博尔塔拉蒙古自治州	Bortala Mongol Autonomous Prefecture	12288	1130	7583
巴音郭楞蒙古自治州	Bayangol Mongol Autonomous Prefecture	55286	1646	14148
阿克苏地区	Aksu Administrative Offices	24249	7733	2064
克孜勒苏柯尔克孜自治州	Kizilsu Kirgiz Autonomous Prefecture	20438	1	16154
喀什地区	Kashgar [Kaxgar] Administrative Offices	226285	1788	163452
和田地区	Hotan Administrative Offices	17879	…	14707

10-28 乡镇企业主要指标
Main Indicators of Township Enterprises

单位：万元 (10 000 yuan)

年份 Year	地区 Region	企业个数（个） Number of Enterprises (unit)	企业人数（人） Employees of Enterprises (person)	总产值 Total Output Value	#工业产值 Industrial Output Value
1985		98826	367753	75179	31389
1990		144281	464027	222218	73125
1991		145762	472332	314765	178113
1992		155711	498132	402139	214462
1993		202274	600687	553616	285276
1994		250037	686425	924082	465446
1995		281130	745291	1319217	639617
1996		282733	781784	1622442	796908
1997		43548	355585	1219032	793959
1998		269048	712490	2457410	1112091
1999		297147	749205	2736766	1239596
2000		316524	806368	3022076	1352454
2001		334694	824499	3316049	1479954
2002		307963	866661	3629499	1591886
2003		354640	880874	4119555	1883101
2004		368553	933473	4562898	2211905
2005		366883	954411	4994156	2542138
2006		368724	990365	5574730	3016402
2007		377385	1037023	4265895	3306532
乌鲁木齐市	Urumqi City	25247	64875	748357	599159
克拉玛依市	Karamay City	127	1393	9485	5707
石河子市	Shihezi City	2897	10154	42820	38194
吐鲁番地区	Turpan Administrative Offices	20819	41416	86899	78145
哈密地区	Hami [Kumul] Administrative Offices	15282	32549	113245	73626
昌吉回族自治州	Changji Hui Autonomous Prefecture	36106	109865	908074	804610
伊犁州直属县(市)	Counties (Cities) Direct Under Ili Prefecture	52383	141377	441405	380120
塔城地区	Tacheng [Tarbagatai] Administrative Offices	26408	88504	627882	575532
阿勒泰地区	Altay Administrative Offices	23003	49817	78804	49894
博尔塔拉蒙古自治州	Bortala Mongol Autonomous Prefecture	7643	27211	111956	101002
巴音郭楞蒙古自治州	Bayangol Mongol Autonomous Prefecture	21461	61312	630841	306134
阿克苏地区	Aksu Administrative Offices	36091	102279	208295	154099
克孜勒苏柯尔克孜自治州	Kizilsu Kirgiz Autonomous Prefecture	10507	28592	13189	8797
喀什地区	Kashgar [Kaxgar] Administrative Offices	54627	150910	162244	94229
和田地区	Hotan Administrative Offices	44784	126769	82399	37284

注：总产值、工业产值及增加值全区合计不等于各地、州、市汇总数。

Note: The sum of total output value, gross industrial output value and value-added in the whole region do not equal to collected data by prefecture, autonomous prefecture, country and cities.

10-28 续表 Continued

单位：万元 (10 000 yuan)

年份 Year	地区 Region	营业收入 Business Income	利润总额 Total Profits	国家税金 National Tax	增加值 Added Value
	1985	105072	9357	3136	
	1990	249906	8614	5206	
	1991	299890	25974	13747	
	1992	374810	34644	16976	
	1993	584089	51880	27354	
	1994	957701	75439	69494	
	1995	1493924	110656	76479	
	1996	1927425	136410	76479	
	1997	1128271	43337	48945	
	1998	2455629	156578	82365	
	1999	2742029	164949	93490	
	2000	3071497	191764	100444	745728
	2001	3377589	211439	108864	807174
	2002	3739524	225723	126732	904892
	2003	4276322	264661	137880	1024772
	2004	4757808	304998	152243	1153561
	2005	5164593	294021	164604	1318134
	2006	5806803	332070	190833	1508846
	2007	6776709	318943	228386	1767506
乌鲁木齐市	Urumqi City	852678	37096	23422	208163
克拉玛依市	Karamay City	10016	1047	332	1853
石河子市	Shihezi City	43900	2490	1624	8106
吐鲁番地区	Turpan Administrative Offices	188964	12252	8314	24758
哈密地区	Hami [Kumul] Administrative Offices	115775	7647	5576	28221
昌吉回族自治州	Changji Hui Autonomous Prefecture	1271989	80108	53681	268662
伊犁州直属县(市)	Counties (Cities) Direct Under Ili Prefecture	1264314	33636	24955	107961
塔城地区	Tacheng [Tarbagatai] Administrative Offices	906631	55449	28717	181593
阿勒泰地区	Altay Administrative Offices	315604	7412	8960	24475
博尔塔拉蒙古自治州	Bortala Mongol Autonomous Prefecture	194838	2222	6046.4	19945
巴音郭楞蒙古自治州	Bayangol Mongol Autonomous Prefecture	705915	37913	31385	153341
阿克苏地区	Aksu Administrative Offices	333088	15786	12655	48460
克孜勒苏柯尔克孜自治州	Kizilsu Kirgiz Autonomous Prefecture	29933	1295	1018	3943
喀什地区	Kashgar [Kaxgar] Administrative Offices	351994	17376	12180	45677
和田地区	Hotan Administrative Offices	191070	7214	9520	23721

主要统计指标解释

农林牧渔业总产值 指以货币形式表现的农、林、牧、渔业全部产品的总量，它反映一定时期内农业生产总规模和总成果。农林牧渔业总产值的计算方法通常是按农、林、牧、渔业产品及其副产品的产量分别乘以各自单位产品价格求得;少数生产周期较长，当年没有产品或产品产量不易统计的，则采用间接方法匡算其产值；然后将四业产品产值相加即为农林牧渔业总产值。1957年以前的农林牧渔业总产值中包括了厩肥和农民自给性手工业(如农民自制衣服、鞋、袜，自己从事粮食初步加工等)。1958年及以后，林业中增加了村及村以下竹木采伐产值；牧业中取消了厩肥产值；副业中取消了农民自给性手工业产值，增加了村及村以下办的工业产值;渔业中增加了海洋捕捞水产品产值。1980 年及以后，在副业中增加了农民家庭兼营工业商品部分的产值。从1984年起村及村以下工业产值划归工业。从1993年起取消副业，将野生动物的捕猎划入牧业、野生植物采集和农民家庭兼营商品性工业划归农业。1996 年第一次农业普查以后，由于畜牧业产品年报数据与普查数据之间存在一定的差距，国家统计局对畜牧业年报数据与普查数据进行衔接，相应的畜牧业产值进行调整。

粮食产量 指稻谷、小麦、玉米、高粱等谷物及薯类和豆类的全社会产量。包括国有经济经营的、集体统一经营的和农民家庭经营的粮食产量，还包括工矿企业办的农场和其他生产单位的产量。其产量计算方法，豆类按去豆荚后的干豆计算；薯类(包括甘薯和马铃薯，不包括芋头和木薯)1963年以前按每4 公斤鲜薯折1 公斤粮食计算，从1964年开始改为按5 公斤鲜薯折1 公斤粮食计算。城市郊区作为蔬菜的薯类(如马铃薯等)按鲜品计算，并且不作粮食统计。其他粮食一律按脱粒后的原粮计算。1989年以前全国粮食产量数据的取得主要是靠全面报表取得，1989年以后开始使用抽样调查数据。

棉花产量 指春播棉和夏播棉的全社会产量。产量按皮棉计算。3 公斤籽棉折1 公斤皮棉，不包括木棉。

油料产量 指全部油料作物的生产量。包括花生、油菜籽、芝麻、向日葵籽、胡麻籽(亚麻籽)和其他油料。不包括大豆、木本油料和野生油料。花生以带壳干花生计算。

水产品产量 指人工养殖的水产品和天然生长的水产品的捕捞量。包括海水的鱼类、虾蟹类、贝类和藻类以及内陆水域的鱼类、虾蟹类和贝类，不包括淡水生植物。水产品产量是通过各级水产和统计部门逐级上报取得数据。1995年及以前，贝类中牡蛎按鲜肉计算；蚶、蛤、蛙按 5 斤鲜品折 1 斤计算。1996 年以后则统一按鲜品计算。

猪、牛、羊肉产量 指当年出栏并已屠宰、除去头蹄下水后带骨肉(即胴体重) 的重量。其统计范围为全社会。1996年前为各级逐级上报数据。1996 年第一次农业普查以后，由于畜牧业产品年报数据与普查数据之间存在一定的差距，国家统计局对畜牧业年报数据与普查数据进行了衔接。1999 年以后，国家统计局开展了猪、牛、羊、禽等主要畜禽品种的抽样调查，并用抽样数据作为国家定案数据使用。未开展抽样调查的品种，仍使用各级统计部门逐级上报数据。

期初(末)畜禽存栏头(只)数 指报告期初(末)农村各种合作经济组织和国营农场、农民个人、机关、团体、学校、工矿企业、部队等单位以及城镇居民饲养的大牲畜、猪、羊、家禽等畜禽的存栏数。数据上报方式及数据调整情况同猪、牛、羊肉产量。

常用耕地 指耕地总资源中专门种植农作物并经常进行耕种、能够正常收获的土地。包括当年实际耕种的熟地;弃耕、休闲不满三年，随时可以复耕的地；开荒利用三年以上的土地。在统计口径上包括南方小于1 米、北方小于2 米宽的沟、渠、路和田埂。不包括临时种植农作物的坡度在25度以上的陡坡地；在河套、湖畔、库区临时开发的成片或零星土地；也不包括已列为国家和省(区、市)退耕计划但临时耕种的土地。常用耕地是国家需要重点保护的耕地，可以反映我国农业的综合生产能力。

农作物播种面积 指实际播种或移植有农作物的面积。凡是实际种植农作物的面积，不论种植在耕地上还是种植在非耕地上，均包括在农作物播种面积中。在播种季节基本结束后，因遭灾而重新改种和补种的农作物面积，也包括在内。该指标可以反映我国耕地面积的利用情况。目前，农作物播种面积主要包括粮食、棉花、油料、糖料、麻类、烟叶、蔬菜和瓜类、药材和其它农作物九大类。

有效灌溉面积 指具有一定的水源，地块比较平整，灌溉工程或设备已经配套，在一般年景下当年能够进行正常灌溉的耕地面积。在一般情况下，有效灌溉面积应等于灌溉工程或设备已经配备，能够进行正常灌溉的水田和水浇地面积之和。该指标可以反映我国耕地的抗旱能力。

农用化肥施用量 指本年内实际用于农业生产的化肥数量，包括氮肥、磷肥、钾肥和复合肥。化肥施用量要求按折纯量计算数量。折纯量是指把氮肥、磷肥、钾肥分别按含氮、含五氧化二磷、含氧化钾的百分之百成份进行折算后的数量。复合肥按其所含主要成分折算。公式:
折纯量= 实物量 × 某种化肥有效成份含量的百分比

农业机械总动力 指主要用于农、林、牧、渔业的各种动力机械的动力总和。包括耕作机械、排灌机械、收获机械、农用运输机械、植物保护机械、牧业机械、林业机械、渔业机械和其他农业机械〔内燃机按引擎马力折成瓦(特)计算、电动机按功率折成瓦(特)计算〕。不包括专门用于乡、镇、村、组办工业、基本建设、非农业运输、科学试验和教学等非农业生产方面用的动力机械与作业机械。这个指标的统计数据主要来源于农机部门。

乡村从业人员 指乡村人口中劳动年龄在16 周岁以上实际参加生产经营活动并取得实物或货币收入的人员，包括劳动年龄内经常参加劳动的人员，也包括超过劳动年龄但经常参加劳动的人员，但不包括户口在家的在外学生、现役军人和丧失劳动能力的人，也不包括待业人员和家务劳动者。从业人员按从事主业时间最长(时间相同按收入)分为农业从业人员、工业从业人员、建筑业从业人员、交运仓储及邮电业从业人员、批零贸易及餐饮业从业人员、其它从业人员。

乡镇企业 指农村集体经济组织或者农民投资为主， 在乡镇(包括所辖村)举办的承担支援农业义务的各类企业。投资为主是指农村集体经济组织或农民投资超过百分之五十，或者虽不足百分之五十，但能起到控股或者实际支配作用。其范围包括乡(镇)办企业、村办企业、联户办企业、户(私营、个体)办企业，以及这些企业之间或者这些企业与国有企业、城镇集体企业、私营企业以及外资(包括我国港澳台地区)等多种经济成分联合投资建立的企业。

Explanatory Notes on Main Statistical Indicators

Gross Output Value of Farming, Forestry, Animal Husbandry and Fishery refers to the total value of products of farming, forestry, animal husbandry and fishery, which reflects the total scale and result of agricultural production during a given period. Gross output value of agriculture is obtained by first multiplying the output of each product or by product by its price, resulting in t he output value of each s ingle item. For a small number of products, annual output of which is not available or difficult to get due to the long production growing process involved, t he output value is estimated through an indirect approach. The sum of out put value of all products of farming, forestry, animal husbandry, and fishery is then equal to the gross output value of agriculture. Prior to 1957, Chinas gross agricultural output value included barnyard manure and handicraft products for self-consumption (clothes, shoes, stockings, and initial grain processing undertaken by peasants). Since 1958, cutting and felling of bamboo and trees by villages and other cooperative organizations under villages have been included in forestry; value of barnyard manure has been excluded from animal husbandry; self consumed handicraft s has been excluded from sideline occupations, while the output value of industries run by villages and cooperative organizations under village had been included inside line occupations and the out put value of fish catches by motor fishing boats has been added to fishery. Since 1980, the value of handicraft products made for sale by individuals in households had been added to sideline occupations. Since 1984, industries run by villages and under villages have been included in the sector of industry. Since 1993, the subdivision of sideline occupations has been canceled, and the hunting of wild animals has been classified into animal husbandry, and the gathering of wild plants and commodity industry run by rural household have been included in farming. The firs t agriculture census of China in 1996 revealed some discrepancy between the production of animal products from the annual reports and that from the census. Efforts were made by NBS to adjust the output value of animal husbandry to make the figures from the annual reports consistent with the census data.

Grain Output refers to the total output of rice, wheat, corn, sorghum, millet and other miscellaneous grains as well as tubers and bean in the whole region including grains produced by state farms, collective units, industrial enterprises and mines. Output of beans refers to dry beans without pods. The output of tubers (sweet potatoes and potatoes, not including taros and cassava) was converted into that of grain at the ratio 4:1, i.e. 4 kilograms of fresh tubers was equivalent to 1 kilogram of grain up to 1963. Since 1964 the ratio for conversion has been 5:1.Tubers supplied as vegetables (such as potatoes) in cities and suburbs are calculated as fresh vegetables and their output is not included in the output of grain. Output of all other grains refers to husked grain. Data on grain production before 1989 were obtained through Comprehensive Statistical Reporting System, since then, sample survey data are used.

Cotton Output refers to the cotton production in the whole Region including cotton sown in spring and in autumn. Output is measured as the weight of ginned cotton. Three kilograms of seed-cotton are equivalent to 1 kilogram of ginned cotton, excluding ceiba.

Output of Oil-bearing Crops refers to the total production of oil-bearing crops of various kinds, including peanuts, (dry, in shell) rapeseeds, sesame, sunflower seeds, flax seeds, and other oil-bearing crops. Soybeans, oil-bearing woody plants, and wild oil-bearing crops are not included.

Output of Aquatic Products refers to catches of both artificially cultured and naturally grown aquatic products, including fish, shrimps, crabs and shellfish in sea and inland water as well as seaweed. Freshwater plants are not included. Data on output of aquatic products are reported by aquatic product and statistical agencies level by level. Before 1995, among the shellfish, the oyster was counted as fresh meat; 5 kilograms of ark shell, clams and frogs are equivalent to 1 kilogram of fresh aquatic products; they are all counted as fresh aquatic products since1996.

Output of Pork, Beef, and Mutton refers to the meat of slaughtered hogs, cattle, sheep and goats wit h head, feet, and offal taken away. The statistical scope is of the whole society. The first agriculture census of China in 1996 revealed some discrepancy between the production of animal products from the annual reports and that from the census. Efforts were made by NBS to adjust the output value of animal husbandry to make the figures from the annual rep orts consistent with the census data. Since 1999, NBS conducted sample survey for t he major animal husbandry products, such as hogs, cattle, sheep and goats and fowls, and the data from sample surveys are used as national finalized data. Those products, which are not covered by the sample survey, are still reported by statistical agencies level by level.

Number of Livestock or Poultry in Stock at Beginning (or End) refers to the total number of large animals, pigs, sheep, fowls, etc. raised by rural cooperative organizations, state farms, rural individuals, government agencies, schools, industrial and mining enterprises, army, and urban residents at the beginning (or end) of the reference period. Data reporting system and data adjustment are the same as that in the output of pork, beef and mutton.

Regularly Cultivated Land refers to farmland among the total land resources, which is exclusively used for farming and is under regular cultivation with harvest in normal years. Include dare currently cultivated land, land that has been abandoned or put in idle for less than 3 years and could be re-used for cultivation at any time, and new-claimed land that has been put into cultivation for more than 3 years. According to statistical coverage, it includes the gouges, dykes, roads and ridges of field with 1 meter wide in Southern areas and 2 meters wide in Northern areas. Excluded under this category are steep slope land over 25 degrees under temporary cultivation, land (large or small plots) that is claimed along river bends, lake sides or banks of reservoirs, as well as land that has been designated under the "Green for Grain" programs of the state and provincial governments but is still temporarily under cultivation. The regularly cultivated land is the key protection land of the nation, which reflects the comprehensive productivity of agriculture of China.

Sown Area of Crops refers to area of land sown or transplanted with crops regardless of being in cultivated area or no cultivated area. Area of land re-sown due to natural disasters is also included. The indicator can reflect the utilization condition of the cultivated land in China. At p resent, t he sown area of crops mainly include the following 9 categories of crops: grain, cotton, oil-bearing crops, sugar crops, fiber crops, Tobacco, Vegetables and melons, medicinal materials and other farm crops.

Irrigated Area refers to areas that are effectively irrigated, i.e. level land, which has water source and complete sets of irrigation facilities to lift and move adequate water for irrigation purpose under normal conditions. Under normal conditions, irrigated area is the sum of watered fields and irrigated fields where irrigation systems or equipment have been installed for regular irrigation purpose. This indicator can reflect drought resistance capacity of the cultivated land in China.

Consumption of Chemical Fertilizers in Agriculture refers to the quantity of chemical fertilizers applied in agriculture in the year, including nitrogenous fertilizer, phosphate fertilizer, potash fertilizer, and compound fertilizer. The consumption of chemical fertilizers is required in calculation to convert the gross weight into weight containing 100% effective component (e.g. 100% nitrogen content in nitrogenous fertilizer, 100%phosphorous pent oxide contents in phosphate fertilizer, 100%potassium oxide contents in potash fertilizer). Compound fertilizer is converted with its major component. The formula is:

Volume of effective component = physical quantity X effective component of certain chemical fertilizer (%)

Total Power of Farm Machinery refers to total mechanical power of machinery used in farming, forestry, animal husbandry, and fishery, including ploughing, irrigation and drainage, harvesting, transport, plant protection, stock breeding, forestry and fishery. The power of internal combust ion engines is required to convert horsepower into watts and the power of electric motors is required to be converted into watts. Machinery employed for non-agricultural purposes, such as the machines used in township run and village-run industry, construction, nonagricultural transport, scientific experiments and teaching, is excluded. Data are mainly from agricultural machinery agencies.

Rural Employed Persons refer to rural labor forces aged over 16 years old who are engaged in real production and management activities and receive payment in kind or wages, including those covered within the age frame and regularly participating in production activities, and those who are out of the range of age frame and also participating in production activities regularly. Excluding students studying in other places with their permanent residence registered in local areas, servicemen and persons incapable of working; also excluding those who are waiting for jobs and those engaged in household work. Persons employed are classified as rural employed persons; industrial employed persons; construction industry employed persons; transport, storage and telecommunications industries employed persons; whole sales and retail sales Trades and catering industry employed persons and others according to the longest period of persons engaged in major activities (or using income indicator when periods are the same).

Township Enterprises refer to collective economic organization in rural areas or various enterprises bearing the responsibilities of supporting the agricultural sector in town (including related village), which mainly invested by farmers. The share of rural economic organizations or farmers should account for over50%, if it were below 50%,it should play the leading role or hold the share. Those enterprises include: township enterprises, village enterprises, joint-household enterprises, household (private, individual) enterprises; and also the joint venture enterprises with various ownerships among above-mentioned enterprises, or with state-owned enterprises, urban collective enterprises, private enterprises and foreign funded (including Hong Kong, Macao and Taiwan) enterprises.

第十一篇
工　业

CHAPTER 11
Industry

简要说明
Brief Introduction

本篇资料的主要内容及来源

本篇资料反映新疆维吾尔自治区工业经济方面的基本情况，主要内容包括：全部工业总产值及指数；规模以上工业企业按登记注册类型、轻重工业、企业规模、工业行业大类等分组的主要经济指标和经济效益指标。指标包括：单位数、工业总产值、工业增加值、资产总计、负债合计、产品销售收入、产品销售成本、产品销售税金及附加、利润总额、本年应交增值税、总资产贡献率、资产负债率、成本费用利润率等；主要工业产品产量；规模以上工业主要产品生产能力；国有及国有控股企业主要指标占全部规模以上工业比重；重点行业主要指标占全部规模以上工业比重。

本篇还对国有及国有控股工业企业、股份制工业企业、港澳台及外商投资工业企业、大中型工业企业的主要经济指标和经济效益指标，按工业行业大类、轻重工业、企业规模等主要分组进行了登载。

此外，本篇中主要工业产品产量统计口径为全部工业企业。

本篇资料由新疆维吾尔自治区统计局工交处根据工业统计年度报表中有关资料整理。

Main Content and Source of Data

Data in this chapter reflect the basic condition of industrial sector including the gross industrial output and indices of industrial enterprises; Main indicator on economic and economic benefit of industrial enterprises above designated size by status of registration, light & heavy industries, size of enterprises, industrial sector. Main indicators including number of enterprises, gross industrial output value, value added of industry, total assets, total liabilities, revenue from principal business, cost of principle business, taxes and other charges on principal business, total profits, value added tax payable, ratio of total assets to industrial output value, assets liability ration, ratio of profits to cost, output of major industrial products, production capacity of major products of industrial enterprises above designated size main economic indicator of state-owned and non-state-owned industrial enterprises.

This chapter covers main indicators on economic and economic benefit of all state-owned and non-state-owned industrial enterprises, cooperative enterprises, industrial enterprises with funds from Hong Kong, Macao and Taiwan, foreign funded industrial enterprises, and large & medium-sized enterprises.

Statistical scope of data on output of major industrial products is all industrial enterprises.

Data in this chapter are collected and compiled by the Department of Industry and transport, XBS in accordance with the annual report of industrial statistics.

11-1 工业总产值
Gross Industrial Output Value

单位:亿元 (100 million yuan)

年 份 Year	工业总产值 Gross Industrial Output Value	国有工业 State-owned Enterprises	集体工业 Collective-owned Enterprises	其它经济类型工业 Enterprises of Other Types of Ownership
1978	33.91	30.22	3.69	
1980	40.71	36.20	4.50	0.01
1985	86.78	73.18	11.93	1.67
1990	219.92	176.52	36.72	6.68
1995	593.43	461.31	89.24	42.88
1996	682.24	519.37	94.71	68.16
1997	771.17	580.48	99.49	91.20
1998	758.01	501.08	85.49	171.44
1999	802.09	506.84	74.01	221.24
2000	1061.29	258.93	72.78	729.58
2001	1084.22	155.26	53.31	875.65
2002	1133.38	159.73	46.39	927.26
2003	1330.15	161.94	35.69	1132.52
2004	1756.18	224.63	19.14	1512.41
2005	2358.83	236.18	17.29	2105.36
2006	2894.88	272.06	16.14	2606.68
2007	3471.51	358.28	17.29	3095.94

11-2 工业总产值指数
Indices of Gross Industrial Output Value

(1978 年=100)

年 份 Year	工业总产值 Gross Industrial Output Value	国有工业 State-owned Enterprises	集体工业 Collective-owned Enterprises	其它经济类型工业 Enterprises of Other Types of Ownership
1978	100.0	100.0	100.0	
1980	117.7	118.0	113.2	(1981 年=100)
1985	220.6	199.5	428.2	851.7
1990	380.3	326.0	915.9	2096.1
1995	670.8	506.1	2104.5	7441.5
1996	754.0	551.4	2209.3	13503.8
1997	837.7	597.7	2306.5	18232.1
1998	863.1	530.9	2032.0	31893.5
1999	921.0	538.9	1839.0	36858.5
2000	1000.4	227.3	1763.6	66265.2
2001	1077.8	151.0	1311.5	87376.0
2002	1180.9	149.3	1123.1	99435.1
2003	1306.7	152.9	837.3	113823.3
2004	1567.8	210.4	442.4	135173.5
2005	1821.8	218.2	388.9	160072.4
2006	2057.1	246.3	344.8	180922.4
2007	2322.8	319.9	339.3	201240.8

11-3 规模以上工业企业主要经济指标

单位：万元　　(2007 年)

项　目	Item	企业单位数(个) Number of Enterprises (unit)	#亏损企业 Loss- Suffering Enterprises	工业总产值(当年价格) Gross Industrial Output Value (At Current Prices)
总　　计	**Total**	**1575**	**416**	**32966068.9**
按登记注册类型分	**By Status of Registration**			
内资企业	Domestic Funded Enterprises	1507	397	32347740.3
国有企业	State-owned Enterprises	147	47	3503608.5
#中央企业	Central Enterprises	57	17	2972157.8
地方企业	Local Enterprises	90	30	531450.7
#自治区属企业	Autonomous	33	9	335306.6
地区(州、市)属企业	Prefecture or City	19	9	62192.1
县(市)属企业	County or City	32	11	93029.6
集体企业	Collective-owned Enterprises	30	8	101414.0
#自治区属企业	Autonomous	7		45202.2
地区(州、市)属企业	Prefecture or City	5	2	14519.9
县(市)属企业	County or City	10	5	21652.3
镇属企业	Town	1		710.6
乡属企业	Township	3	1	2971.6
股份合作企业	Cooperative Enterprises	8		10862.8
联营企业	Joint Ownership Enterprises	6	1	32440.3
#国有联营企业	State Joint Ownership Enterprises	1		6981.4
集体联营企业	Collective Joint Ownership Enterprises	3	1	10215.1
国有与集体联营企业	Joint State-collective Enterprises	1		13397.0
其他联营企业	Other Joint Ownership Enterprises	1		1846.8
有限责任公司	Limited Liability Corporations	701	175	7225743.2
#国有独资公司	State Sole funded Corporations	53	15	1670056.3
其他有限责任公司	Other Limited Liability Corporations	648	160	5555686.9
股份有限公司	Share-holding Corporations Ltd.	54	10	18865412.4
私营企业	Private Enterprises	560	156	2607649.1
#私营独资企业	Private-funded Enterprises	39	14	73684.8
私营合伙企业	Private Partnership Enterprises	14	3	34000.6
私营有限责任公司	Private Limited Liability Corporations	489	134	1981002.3
私营股份有限公司	Private Share-holding Corporations Ltd.	18	5	518961.4
港、澳、台商投资企业	Enterprises with Funds from Hong Kong, Macao and Taiwan	23	8	163538.4
外商投资企业	Foreign Funded Enterprises	45	11	454790.2
在总计中：国有控股企业	Of the Total : State-owned and State-holding Enterprises	451	116	26377945.0
在总计中：农村工业	Of the Total : Rural Industry	16	2	47733.7
按轻、重工业分	**Grouped by Light & Heavy Industry**			
轻工业	Light Industry	595	163	4467022.2
以农产品为原料	Using Farm Produces as Raw Materials	530	144	4258930.8
以非农产品为原料	Using Non-Farm Produces as Raw Materials	65	19	208091.4
重工业	Heavy Industry	980	253	28499046.7
采掘工业	Mining and Quarrying	215	36	12638175.8
原料工业	Raw Material Industry	417	133	13465330.3
加工工业	Manufacturing Industry	348	84	2395540.6
按企业规模分	**Grouped by Size of Enterprises**			
大型企业	Large	27	7	20119137.6
中型企业	Medium	230	49	7475708.9
小型企业	Small	1318	360	5371222.4

Main Economic Indicators of Industrial Enterprises above Designated Size

(10 000 yuan)

工业增加值 Added Value of Industry	工业销售产值(当年价) Sales Value of Industry Products (At Current Prices)	出口交货值 Delivery Value of Industry Export	实收资本 Total Capital Hold	资产合计 Total Assets	流动资产合计 Total Working Capitals	#产成品 Finished Product	流动资产年平均余额 Annual Average Balance of Working Capitals	固定资产原价 Original Value of Fixed Assets
13966779.4	**32779858.8**	**615858.6**	**16957893.1**	**43363237.4**	**14507047.5**	**1383752.3**	**12510396.7**	**35929133.1**
13759415.1	32152422.3	550537.6	16663002.5	42430030.6	14046417.8	1308313.1	12127533.9	35375090.9
1158040.2	3487252.1	46939.3	2824202.5	6957611.0	2880715.4	172806.4	2607743.6	4795406.9
951481.2	2952931.2	24108.3	2319097.0	5275686.1	2406820.9	142453.5	2209170.1	3556205.2
206559.0	534320.9	22831.0	505105.5	1681924.9	473894.5	30352.9	398573.5	1239201.7
134631.5	336522.1	3398.5	366001.0	1101331.4	287400.4	8519.0	252536.9	794338.5
20492.6	62823.1		48703.8	221985.4	72689.2	10724.2	65215.4	206678.5
42010.5	90873.3		68698.7	243227.2	71851.9	9744.7	51008.9	201954.0
27606.0	98164.5		13144.1	108294.5	65967.7	6932.6	62965.7	48861.4
8393.7	46598.3		3989.7	27009.0	20140.4	3347.6	21108.1	10031.0
6365.2	13261.7		1352.8	13819.5	10455.9	1605.9	9652.9	8167.2
5868.6	18059.1		3773.5	22194.6	13266.8	1626.1	12926.0	15240.8
388.6	760.0		43.0	3005.5	1845.4		1318.4	1457.5
1836.7	2971.6		603.0	2216.1	619.6	0.7	438.9	2245.4
4367.7	9606.3		9540.3	16590.3	5793.6	912.5	5410.8	16824.1
11243.3	32475.4		9087.6	29187.0	19593.1	536.4	16671.2	11007.7
1797.4	6981.4		1720.0	3704.2	3055.4	0.6	2807.9	1095.5
3562.1	10215.1		6411.4	14412.6	7398.8	316.7	6071.3	7261.0
5254.3	13397.0		810.4	10068.8	8311.1		7145.6	2347.1
629.5	1881.9		145.8	1001.4	827.8	219.1	646.4	304.1
2149523.5	7012324.2	148467.4	3079635.0	10352842.4	4044380.8	498460.3	3668526.8	7329564.2
493947.9	1630143.2	833.6	815307.4	2609643.3	769398.1	52625.6	750818.2	2274780.0
1655575.6	5382181.0	147633.8	2264327.6	7743199.1	3274982.7	445834.7	2917708.6	5054784.2
9703688.7	19057596.3	241819.3	9984302.0	21638056.9	5241252.3	410728.9	4451659.7	22069088.4
704752.6	2454401.4	113311.6	742891.0	3326851.0	1788266.6	217932.6	1314311.3	1104244.0
20923.2	69998.8		21320.5	77037.5	39607.2	7151.5	32777.7	35459.5
11741.5	29213.1		4878.5	20436.3	13287.6	4283.8	12229.1	8412.6
545603.4	1858145.1	77124.3	517392.3	2060736.3	1058158.7	170849.0	930986.9	910014.5
126484.5	497044.4	36187.3	199299.7	1168640.9	677213.1	35648.3	338317.6	150357.4
45659.3	165266.0	6908.5	96005.0	215313.4	114283.9	23113.8	104942.4	174246.8
161705.0	462170.5	58412.5	208885.6	717893.4	346345.8	52325.4	277920.4	379795.4
12024331.8	26454423.5	369483.8	14826419.5	34883239.0	10043920.9	804248.3	8934379.8	32342450.9
15345.2	45966.4		12868.0	47565.0	27537.6	2536.3	24262.1	18299.5
1253759.1	4326117.7	321248.2	1681680.7	6328631.1	3271609.4	665706.1	2848211.5	3523270.1
1183865.3	4120317.7	314190.1	1398228.7	5745205.2	3089256.4	648709.0	2687489.2	3094431.8
69893.8	205800.0	7058.1	283452.0	583425.9	182353.0	16997.1	160722.3	428838.3
12713020.3	28453741.1	294610.4	15286212.4	37034606.3	11235438.1	718046.2	9662185.2	32405863.0
9803653.0	12764616.1	6703.8	8597707.8	17510622.0	4185446.9	115235.8	3860425.2	19465849.3
2299505.5	13390774.9	175523.5	5521639.4	15354483.5	4959778.7	377593.5	4161551.1	11425283.3
609861.8	2298350.1	112383.1	1166865.2	4169500.8	2090212.5	225216.9	1640208.9	1514730.4
9953394.1	20315186.8	95098.0	11787255.4	23978904.8	6334123.8	331800.3	5556469.5	24560019.3
2414359.3	7309020.6	353587.3	2722644.0	11494714.1	4773680.6	549672.4	4051721.5	6867268.4
1599026.0	5155651.4	167173.3	2457993.7	7889618.5	3399243.1	502279.6	2902205.7	4501845.4

11-3 续表

单位：万元

项　目	Item	固定资产净值年平均余额 Annual Average Balance of Net Value of Fixed Assets	流动负债合计 Total Working Liabilities	长期负债合计 Long-term Liabilities	所有者权益合计 Owners' Equities
总　计	**Total**	**20108340.7**	**13724617.8**	**7507726.4**	**21414685.5**
按登记注册类型分	**By Status of Registration**				
内资企业	Domestic Funded Enterprises	19749220.4	13218953.2	7474948.3	21020220.6
国有企业	State-owned Enterprises	2844812.0	2586539.9	1066338.1	3247308.7
#中央企业	Central Enterprises	2063669.6	2140908.1	448301.3	2647408.9
地方企业	Local Enterprises	781142.4	445631.8	618036.8	599899.8
#自治区属企业	Autonomous	512324.1	238133.6	456993.3	406093.5
地区(州、市)属企业	Prefecture or City	132947.9	90589.8	73647.8	48941.8
县(市)属企业	County or City	115736.5	84063.1	52470.3	97254.3
集体企业	Collective-owned Enterprises	23930.8	59327.0	11001.0	37966.2
#自治区属企业	Autonomous	4626.0	13713.0	252.4	13043.6
地区(州、市)属企业	Prefecture or City	3266.1	7005.0	7927.3	-1113.0
县(市)属企业	County or City	7389.0	11721.1	2519.3	7954.1
镇属企业	Town	1343.9	2538.9		466.6
乡属企业	Township	1320.5	1402.9	302.0	511.2
股份合作企业	Cooperative Enterprises	8435.6	6210.7	568.6	9810.9
联营企业	Joint Ownership Enterprises	7653.5	14777.1	33.6	14376.3
#国有联营企业	State Joint Ownership Enterprises	345.9	1645.8		2058.4
集体联营企业	Collective Joint Ownership Enterprises	5625.1	5747.2	30.6	8634.8
国有与集体联营企业	Joint State-collective Enterprises	1485.7	6771.1		3297.7
其他联营企业	Other Joint Ownership Enterprises	196.8	613.0	3.0	385.4
有限责任公司	Limited Liability Corporations	4696995.0	4825549.4	1345342.3	4034370.1
#国有独资公司	State Sole funded Corporations	1383948.0	1202623.7	422344.6	980212.5
其他有限责任公司	Other Limited Liability Corporations	3313047.0	3622925.7	922997.7	3054157.6
股份有限公司	Share-holding Corporations Ltd.	11401384.4	4232210.7	4869060.9	12048971.6
私营企业	Private Enterprises	765936.4	1493890.1	182603.8	1627267.6
#私营独资企业	Private-funded Enterprises	29499.9	43969.9	3977.2	29090.4
私营合伙企业	Private Partnership Enterprises	6248.4	9528.6	1625.6	8987.3
私营有限责任公司	Private Limited Liability Corporations	647682.8	1005866.0	152445.2	885941.3
私营股份有限公司	Private Share-holding Corporations Ltd.	82505.3	434525.6	24555.8	703248.6
港、澳、台商投资企业	Enterprises with Funds from Hong Kong, Macao and Taiwan	81334.2	104354.2	11713.7	99185.0
外商投资企业	Foreign Funded Enterprises	277786.1	401310.4	21064.4	295279.9
在总计中：国有控股企业	Of the Total : State-owned and State-holding Enterprises	17731564.4	9659464.2	6913187.6	17663420.1
在总计中：农村工业	Of the Total : Rural Industry	15915.4	14757.2	2470.9	27554.4
按轻、重工业分	**Grouped by Light & Heavy Industry**				
轻工业	Light Industry	2281518.0	3276540.0	553571.4	2467750.8
以农产品为原料	Using Farm Produces as Raw Materials	1954999.2	3118045.8	476149.8	2125490.2
以非农产品为原料	Using Non-Farm Produces as Raw Materials	326518.8	158494.2	77421.6	342260.6
重工业	Heavy Industry	17826822.7	10448077.8	6954155.0	18946934.7
采掘工业	Mining and Quarrying	10149846.5	3676201.1	3184025.0	10157581.3
原料工业	Raw Material Industry	6754133.8	4927482.3	3347342.1	6929127.2
加工工业	Manufacturing Industry	922842.4	1844394.4	422787.9	1860226.2
按企业规模分	**Grouped by Size of Enterprises**				
大型企业	Large	12689036.5	5358530.8	4643164.6	13485256.4
中型企业	Medium	4207867.7	4856092.1	1643737.2	4865786.0
小型企业	Small	3211436.5	3509994.9	1220824.6	3063643.1

Continued

(10 000 yuan)

主营业务收入 Revenue from Principal Business	#主营业务成本 Cost of Principal Business	主营业务税金及附加 Taes and Other Charges on Principal Business	营业利润 Business Profit	利润总额 Total Profit	亏损企业亏损总额 Losses Value of Loss-Suffering Enterprises	利税总额 Total Profits and Taxes	本年应交增值税 Value-added Taxes Payable	全部从业人员年平均人数(人) Annual Average Employed Persons (person)
34756937.7	**24283121.6**	**667482.3**	**6775696.5**	**6915727.0**	**595186.3**	**9613765.4**	**2030556.1**	**537937**
34096158.9	23780911.0	662345.3	6700500.3	6821639.6	587806.8	9487618.5	2003633.6	526326
4251733.8	3877538.0	81983.8	19261.4	74402.0	68127.5	373921.2	217535.4	152065
3686628.3	3415667.6	78464.2	3291.1	56277.6	45226.0	314745.7	180003.9	130332
565105.5	461870.4	3519.6	15970.3	18124.4	22901.5	59175.5	37531.5	21733
365061.1	307923.7	2398.8	7392.8	8528.4	15746.2	36193.2	25266.0	12325
61003.1	56182.9	332.7	-4049.3	-2714.9	4530.4	847.5	3229.7	3204
95688.5	63919.9	620.5	9599.8	11543.4	2624.7	19349.9	7186.0	5086
112120.3	96123.7	1454.2	5032.5	6751.5	974.9	13215.9	5010.2	4049
49588.0	44186.9	248.6	2032.7	2568.5		5112.5	2295.4	1476
13115.2	10649.1	40.0	908.7	863.2	97.7	1542.8	639.6	558
17377.3	14491.8	98.7	407.0	1029.1	738.1	2062.9	935.1	1256
1367.2	973.4	9.2	233.6	282.2		358.2	66.8	122
2547.7	2060.4	70.8	-80.8	-38.3	139.1	306.3	273.8	265
13341.0	11372.5	156.6	676.8	931.7		1315.3	227.0	400
36066.2	24835.7	700.3	4101.1	4504.7	373.5	7772.3	2567.3	1256
7981.7	3360.3	456.3	869.0	869.0		2150.5	825.2	95
12295.9	8973.1	107.7	1666.2	2068.8	373.5	2516.5	340.0	740
13915.6	11201.1	124.5	1499.3	1500.5		2870.5	1245.5	280
1873.0	1301.2	11.8	66.6	66.4		234.8	156.6	141
7190204.4	5827014.8	63978.7	521994.8	593690.2	106405.7	1014453.0	356784.1	188687
1661299.8	1357117.2	27555.0	94816.5	108341.3	33963.7	223235.7	87339.4	43111
5528904.6	4469897.6	36423.7	427178.3	485348.9	72442.0	791217.3	269444.7	145576
20015811.6	11850408.6	502862.0	5978077.0	5952500.8	388066.5	7802602.0	1347239.2	118185
2476271.6	2093036.1	11209.7	171351.1	188855.7	23858.7	274332.7	74267.3	61654
62721.7	53824.6	295.3	1995.5	1684.2	2386.6	5115.1	3135.6	4810
25125.3	21191.8	118.2	1826.8	1794.4	645.6	3174.7	1262.1	817
1890109.2	1644760.8	9138.5	86409.1	101153.3	19928.1	168602.9	58311.1	49470
498315.4	373258.9	1657.7	81119.7	84223.8	898.4	97440.0	11558.5	6557
170576.0	141910.2	201.7	8863.5	9461.1	1275.5	17561.5	7898.7	5370
490202.8	360300.4	4935.3	66332.7	84626.3	6104.0	108585.4	19023.8	6241
28236850.8	19016030.7	627637.2	6236763.8	6301862.1	533047.2	8718502.7	1789003.4	376062
42554.8	32574.6	184.5	3590.0	3733.1	722.3	5727.4	1809.8	2602
4654199.7	3795480.6	90566.7	277775.1	284559.8	66576.4	539691.8	164565.3	152238
4445900.4	3630508.4	89351.6	277693.6	278029.9	58982.4	523303.7	155922.2	144042
208299.3	164972.2	1215.1	81.5	6529.9	7594.0	16388.1	8643.1	8196
30102738.0	20487641.0	576915.6	6497921.4	6631167.2	528609.9	9074073.6	1865990.8	385699
13540304.6	5638029.3	318512.5	6243241.3	6278555.7	12665.0	7889535.3	1292467.1	173567
14101124.4	12857954.3	246524.0	71912.2	138182.6	492697.6	892170.1	507463.5	156543
2461309.0	1991657.4	11879.1	182767.9	214428.9	23247.3	292368.2	66060.2	55589
21457980.8	13738169.3	514050.2	5652379.3	5679740.7	426422.6	7589302.4	1395511.5	227227
8086058.2	6248747.2	122047.5	827162.7	859180.0	87309.2	1415257.0	434029.5	178135
5212898.7	4296205.1	31384.6	296154.5	376806.3	81454.5	609206.0	201015.1	132575

11-4 按行业分规模以上工业企业主要经济指标

单位: 万元 (2007 年)

行业	Sector	企业单位数(个) Number of Enterprises (unit)	#亏损企业 Loss- Suffering Enterprises	工业总产值(当年价格) Gross Industrial Output Value (At Current Prices)
煤炭开采和洗选业	Mining and Washing of Coal	102	25	542505.5
石油和天然气开采业	Extraction of Petroleum and Natural Gas	20		11228896.1
#天然原油和天然气开采	Extraction of Ores Crude Oil and Natural Gas Extraction	6		9697040.6
黑色金属矿采选业	Processing of Ferrous Metals Ores	41	7	366534.8
有色金属矿采选业	Processing of Nonferrous Metals Ores	38	3	441281.2
非金属矿采选业	Processing of Nonmetal Ores	14	1	58958.2
#采 盐	Extraction of Salt	4		21538.2
农副食品加工业	Processing of Food from Agricultural Products	203	42	1254868.2
#谷物磨制	Grain Grinding	40	5	187009.7
饲料加工	Fodder Processing	27	5	200122.4
制 糖	Sugar Making	14		236332.2
食品制造业	Manufacture of Food	90	21	544893.3
#罐头制造	Manufacture of can	26	6	247826.9
饮料制造业	Manufacture of Beverage	49	21	298038.3
#酒的制造	Manufacture of Wine	35	14	230523.5
烟草制品业	Manufacture of Tobacco	1		140912.3
纺织业	Manufacture of Textile	93	41	1343950.6
#棉、化纤纺织及印染精加工	Cotton, Chemical Fiber, Dyeing, Printing and Processing	71	35	1213650.9
毛纺织和染整精加工	Wool Textile, Dyeing and Printing	4	2	18695.4
纺织服装、鞋、帽制造业	Manufacture of Textile Wearing Apparel, Footware and Caps	5	1	11127.3
皮革、毛皮、羽毛(绒)及其制品业	Leather, Fur, Feather and Related Products Manufacturing	7	1	41325.7
#皮革鞣制加工	Leather Tanning and Processing	6	1	40400.0
皮革制品制造	Manufacture of Leather Products	1		925.7
木材加工及木、竹、藤、棕、草制品业	Processing of Timber, Wood, Bamboo, Cane, Grass Products	19	5	90354.4
家具制造业	Manufacture of Furniture	8	2	88522.5
造纸及纸制品业	Manufacture of Paper and Paper Products	34	13	154057.4
印刷业和记录媒介的复制	Printing and Copying of Medium for Record	26	2	48432.7
石油加工、炼焦及核燃料加工业	Oil Processing, Coking and Nuclear Fuel Processing	55	16	7245490.6
#炼 焦	Coking	23	9	168785.9
化学原料及化学制品制造业	Raw Chemical Material and Chemical Products	112	27	1358330.0
#基础化学原料制造	Basic Chemical Material	33	14	621510.2
肥料制造	Fertilizer Making	13	3	194321.6
医药制造业	Manufacture of Medicine	21	4	69442.4
化学纤维制造业	Manufacture of Chemical Fiber	4		285494.4
橡胶制品业	Manufacture of Rubber Products	4	1	57497.6
塑料制品业	Manufacture of Plastic Products	102	27	382457.3
非金属矿物制品业	Manufacture of Nonmetal Mineral Products	135	29	850989.5
#水泥制造	Manufacture of Cement	55	13	428575.6
黑色金属冶炼及压延加工业	Smelting and Pressing of Ferrous Metals	39	10	2354188.7
有色金属冶炼及压延加工业	Smelting and Pressing of Nonferrous Metals	24	5	430252.6
金属制品业	Manufacture of Metal Products	48	11	225912.0
通用设备制造业	Manufacture of General Purpose Machinery	37	8	90594.9
专用设备制造业	Manufacture of Special Purpose Machinery	24	5	74641.7
交通运输设备制造业	Manufacture of Transport Equipment	10	5	95683.3
电气机械及器材制造业	Manufacture of Electric Equipment and Machinery	28	3	726755.7
通信设备、计算机及其他电子设备制造业	Telecom Equipment, Computer and Other Electronic Equipment	5	1	122997.6
仪器仪表及文化、办公用机械制造业	Measuring Instruments and Machinery for Cultural Activify and Office Work	4		10991.9
工艺品及其他制造业	Art work and Other Manufacturing Sector	2		7514.5
电力、热力的生产和供应业	Electricity and Thermal Production and Supply	138	65	1808364.5
#电力生产和电力供应	Electricity Production and Supply	77	33	1669750.6
燃气生产和供应业	Gas Production and Supply	14	4	78784.2
水的生产和供应业	Water Production and Supply	19	10	35027.0

Main Economic Indicators of Industrial Enterprises above Designated Size by Sectors

(10 000 yuan)

工业增加值 Added Value of Industry	工业销售产值(当年价) Sales Value of Industry Products (At Current Prices)	出口交货值 Delivery Value of Industry Export	实收资本 Total Capital Hold	资产合计 Total Assets	流动资产合计 Total Working Capitals	#产成品 Finished Product	流动资产年平均余额 Annual Average Balance of Circulating Funds	固定资产原价 Original Value of Fixed Assets
323220.2	650519.3		498224.6	1282692.7	474129.1	17774.0	409363.8	701029.9
8976286.6	11251502.3	448.0	7806369.7	15122588.8	3160747.9	38828.5	2981794.2	18341173.8
8486630.5	9727416.8		6303818.0	12139960.3	1460767.8	34310.1	1463137.5	16679870.6
133025.5	353592.2		125934.9	506718.5	260110.4	40548.4	206789.1	210765.7
347177.7	451023.3		144678.2	521102.7	249207.5	10964.5	223113.2	175176.6
23943.0	57979.0	6255.8	22500.4	77519.3	41252.0	7120.4	39364.9	37703.3
7367.0	22048.0	427.6	2376.0	17207.1	8950.8	2430.8	6030.6	9210.7
257782.4	1202245.6	9093.3	251168.8	1311066.9	884082.9	209092.6	680327.6	500738.1
25199.5	182281.7		34948.7	146357.6	82322.5	8284.8	72971.0	59665.1
32482.3	197803.9		33343.4	150585.9	86405.7	8749.3	79108.9	74563.0
66335.5	220502.9		51893.4	269794.8	164466.9	77032.5	129269.2	164431.9
146981.1	546037.9	174017.4	203445.3	871539.6	437919.9	91078.8	401174.6	494199.6
73079.9	254281.4	154165.6	91848.6	489520.0	282751.4	65365.3	268411.3	279726.9
136118.7	282382.4	2775.5	183337.6	587414.2	298290.8	30605.8	278901.7	311900.4
114995.7	215221.4		148608.1	508862.8	270563.1	24639.3	252695.4	251351.1
99927.7	143756.5		18741.7	141073.0	65135.6		68318.8	83494.0
338525.8	1277593.5	56045.2	522701.9	1916279.2	984643.9	233323.4	898858.7	1225451.9
300411.6	1147663.5	23493.4	428580.2	1712524.4	870855.4	206721.9	782273.3	1094979.9
5282.2	21768.0	4982.0	21000.8	42090.8	20169.3	6979.9	20173.6	29116.4
3058.8	10834.2	152.8	3171.5	10155.0	7461.1	365.7	5860.5	4793.8
10351.6	28918.3		12573.8	44516.3	28699.7	6800.4	27825.0	19452.2
9976.2	27976.5		12270.0	43212.7	27804.3	6638.2	26949.5	19130.2
375.4	941.8		303.8	1303.6	895.4	162.2	875.5	322.0
22578.8	86942.5	10910.6	16858.7	71064.3	38267.5	10895.4	35886.3	32372.4
16262.4	89075.3	67787.2	62674.5	225685.9	58299.3	14474.9	57210.4	63448.6
42810.6	148938.8	11.0	61452.5	245368.8	101289.8	21057.6	95660.3	180187.2
17260.3	48097.1		25006.3	74581.2	30031.1	1801.0	26539.6	66663.2
497018.2	7201900.1		2925124.0	4880020.9	1716317.2	145540.2	1361997.9	3186939.7
60827.4	154337.6		47684.0	219473.4	99282.6	11710.2	83662.8	95285.9
410731.6	1326577.3	87809.5	560371.6	2706846.2	976074.3	93293.4	790774.5	1219481.4
176611.7	611482.4	83801.8	180455.0	1288180.4	592434.2	43208.7	446689.1	544825.3
76626.0	191307.3	404.5	130739.3	546120.2	141233.3	6093.6	111931.2	241894.3
26991.3	64226.2	2485.9	39451.1	117807.9	56458.7	11031.2	52498.2	53362.8
96151.4	297424.8	1953.2	40766.9	272163.0	159786.7	32170.8	117364.8	134919.4
11506.2	57270.5	1974.0	14714.2	49021.0	26279.8	9060.7	22235.1	37936.1
95562.3	349468.2	13361.7	372765.8	656339.3	354084.5	66554.9	323051.7	367103.1
269413.6	833322.2	53539.3	623386.0	1754004.4	652922.7	42593.0	642309.5	928522.6
157079.2	422680.2	1248.0	413627.0	960301.4	361581.9	14879.3	345797.7	665894.1
469196.9	2367396.1	79563.1	462437.4	1948498.8	910441.3	112523.7	731952.4	1318576.1
106252.5	429959.8		62434.7	268400.6	123019.5	12010.8	102221.0	173013.0
39639.8	222306.8	2929.4	87406.4	216383.6	111691.6	18511.3	105555.4	67296.2
26299.5	97562.8	2211.0	35153.2	121181.9	85416.2	13162.2	67985.5	39672.9
20461.3	74529.6	1271.0	11913.8	125019.4	85195.2	14982.7	80907.3	47176.5
8629.2	97974.1	571.9	36388.5	88813.1	51385.1	9405.3	46108.0	33163.8
176218.3	695993.0	8284.4	138485.9	1226404.3	869646.5	58050.8	472988.0	135172.8
37124.6	114327.9	32407.4	51554.6	159441.3	60588.7	8926.3	54956.9	128655.3
2653.1	12348.5		3600.0	18776.3	14047.7	466.5	12800.6	3023.0
2705.9	7590.0		1776.0	5656.0	2850.8	327.7	2373.4	3407.5
729896.1	1801060.4		1244840.4	5135979.5	1002633.1	39.1	928562.0	5092974.7
688980.2	1663793.2		1068867.7	4554664.2	840581.1	8.1	779519.7	4535682.5
23319.5	64561.6		74864.7	291190.5	90165.7	370.3	119295.2	187289.2
21696.9	34620.7		221617.5	311923.0	38473.7		37470.6	322896.3

11-4 续表

单位：万元

行业	Sector	固定资产净值年平均余额 Annual Average Balanceof Net Value of Fixed Assets	流动负债合计 Total Working Liabilities	长期负债合计 Long-term Liabilities	所有者权益合计 Creditors' Equities
煤炭开采和洗选业	Mining and Washing of Coal	418623.9	469390.4	165102.6	644071.7
石油和天然气开采业	Extraction of Petroleum and Natural Gas	9463656.7	2811063.9	2950222.6	8882804.5
#天然原油和天然气开采	Extraction of Ores Crude Oil and Natural Gas Extraction	8623911.4	1576889.2	2945288.0	7139292.3
黑色金属矿采选业	Processing of Ferrous Metals Ores	127101.1	195609.1	49579.1	260144.6
有色金属矿采选业	Processing of Nonferrous Metals Ores	116112.9	163806.9	18339.9	330153.2
非金属矿采选业	Processing of Nonmetal Ores	24351.9	36330.8	780.8	40407.3
#采盐	Extraction of Salt	5687.8	7902.9	265.8	9038.2
农副食品加工业	Processing of Food from Agricultural Products	325808.7	820708.9	55154.2	425681.8
#谷物磨制	Grain Grinding	43170.0	76561.6	5817.0	63843.9
饲料加工	Fodder Processing	48769.1	52315.0	19698.1	78513.8
制糖	Sugar Making	83935.0	165072.4	2176.4	101644.0
食品制造业	Manufacture of Food	345026.0	491027.2	56597.2	320824.3
#罐头制造	Manufacture of can	185974.6	321060.2	35726.4	132562.3
饮料制造业	Manufacture of Beverage	198425.9	270408.4	162546.7	152652.2
#酒的制造	Manufacture of Wine	155282.7	239193.6	161174.4	106687.9
烟草制品业	Manufacture of Tobacco	51317.1	63049.5		78023.5
纺织业	Manufacture of Textile	729193.6	1084365.4	139106.1	682112.8
#棉、化纤纺织及印染精加工	Cotton, Chemical Fiber, Dyeing, Printing and Processing	655753.4	1000503.9	123460.0	578140.0
毛纺织和染整精加工	Wool Textile, Dyeing and Printing	17869.4	20877.0	1437.3	19776.4
纺织服装、鞋、帽制造业	Manufacture of Textile Wearing Apparel,Footware and Caps	2640.8	6967.0	213.5	2974.5
皮革、毛皮、羽毛(绒)及其制品业	Leather, Fur, Feather and Related Products Manufacturing	12936.7	16079.9	5007.0	23429.4
#皮革鞣制加工	Leather Tanning and Processing	12810.7	15077.4	5007.0	23128.3
皮革制品制造	Manufacture of Leather Products	126.0	1002.5		301.1
木材加工及木、竹、藤、棕、草制品业	Processing of Timber, Wood, Bamboo, Cane, Grass Products	22267.4	30174.0	8705.8	32181.5
家具制造业	Manufacture of Furniture	47348.0	40186.1	14540.0	170959.8
造纸及纸制品业	Manufacture of Paper and Paper Products	115658.8	124313.6	29496.7	91153.9
印刷业和记录媒介的复制	Printing and Copying of Medium for Record	36440.3	26206.8	8950.6	39423.7
石油加工、炼焦及核燃料加工业	Oil Processing, Coking and Nuclear Fuel Processing	1486166.5	810513.7	922119.7	3091425.8
#炼焦	Coking	87886.3	69934.9	4962.6	88614.3
化学原料及化学制品制造业	Raw Chemical Material and Chemical Products	900781.7	1057487.7	398374.9	1236687.0
#基础化学原料制造	Basic Chemical Material	439072.2	509928.2	167794.4	609143.1
肥料制造	Fertilizer Making	179449.9	210964.3	112306.8	217614.1
医药制造业	Manufacture of Medicine	38973.4	49080.4	11078.5	57649.0
化学纤维制造业	Manufacture of Chemical Fiber	85319.7	142627.6	12720.0	116815.4
橡胶制品业	Manufacture of Rubber Products	17541.8	72455.8	8798.6	-32233.4
塑料制品业	Manufacture of Plastic Products	234311.3	279898.9	14117.4	350790.5
非金属矿物制品业	Manufacture of Nonmetal Mineral Products	532082.5	665996.8	220290.2	841939.7
#水泥制造	Manufacture of Cement	375329.6	371907.2	161313.4	406267.2
黑色金属冶炼及压延加工业	Smelting and Pressing of Ferrous Metals	869761.6	919874.5	278028.6	750525.2
有色金属冶炼及压延加工业	Smelting and Pressing of Nonferrous Metals	57006.5	120786.5	27718.4	119395.4
金属制品业	Manufacture of Metal Products	42116.2	98934.5	3955.4	111275.9
通用设备制造业	Manufacture of General Purpose Machinery	25345.8	63501.1	6227.1	44793.4
专用设备制造业	Manufacture of Special Purpose Machinery	24337.4	100171.1	5296.7	18307.0
交通运输设备制造业	Manufacture of Transport Equipment	13932.8	62608.4	2046.4	24158.3
电气机械及器材制造业	Manufacture of Electric Equipment and Machinery	79708.0	543072.6	125551.1	552251.4
通信设备、计算机及其他电子设备制造业	Telecom Equipment, Computer and Other Electronic Equipment	77949.7	39158.9	49285.0	70279.4
仪器仪表及文化、办公用机械制造业	Measuring Instruments and Machinery for Cultural Activify and Office Work	1813.6	5728.9	1400.0	11647.4
工艺品及其他制造业	Art work and Other Manufacturing Sector	3007.0	1400.6		4255.4
电力、热力的生产和供应业	Electricity and Thermal Production and Supply	3235620.6	1853879.2	1665635.7	1552338.4
#电力生产和电力供应	Electricity Production and Supply	2859640.8	1637176.4	1519729.2	1346863.2
燃气生产和供应业	Gas Production and Supply	97674.9	137836.3	68173.9	80684.9
水的生产和供应业	Water Production and Supply	247979.9	49916.4	22566.0	234700.7

Continued

(10 000 yuan)

主营业务收入 Revenue from Principal Business	#主营业务成本 Cost of Principal Business	主营业务税金及附加 Taes and Other Charges on Principal Business	营业利润 Business Profit	利润总额 Total Profit	亏损企业亏损总额 Losses Value of Loss-Suffering Enterprises	利税总额 Total Profits and Taxes	本年应交增值税 Value-added Taxes Payable	全部从业人员年平均人数(人) Annual Average Employed Persons (person)
520783.6	363301.6	6809.9	51873.2	50269.5	8251.9	112676.5	55597.1	47140
12141578.7	4877026.8	299972.2	5834465.0	5881920.4		7336777.9	1154885.3	108350
10036650.3	2810655.3	283210.1	5890251.3	5868288.3		7197564.1	1046065.7	43246
375044.9	215263.0	6105.3	89915.8	89480.5	803.9	124320.1	28734.3	6469
455698.1	154223.7	4540.5	262734.3	251454.3	2156.2	305154.6	49159.8	7965
47199.3	28214.2	1084.6	4253.0	5431.0	1453.0	10606.2	4090.6	3643
18942.6	11426.0	621.0	1945.4	1889.0		4395.1	1885.1	1529
1284776.6	1106958.5	2674.4	48608.0	65734.4	5638.9	94447.3	26038.5	21040
187603.4	173683.3	176.2	2888.3	4562.6	717.3	5851.9	1113.1	2521
228948.5	199653.0	122.9	5585.3	7311.7	512.4	9184.5	1749.9	2507
242918.1	168856.7	1779.3	29829.4	29069.4		48933.1	18084.4	7466
552658.5	427424.6	2170.3	36762.6	39669.4	3508.6	59206.6	17366.9	11427
258505.7	188651.8	881.6	14596.4	15285.0	1252.7	23252.2	7085.6	3772
272245.0	171548.7	20748.6	14805.9	17803.3	19028.3	60737.6	22185.7	9223
206256.6	122488.5	20582.9	9701.9	11860.3	17829.9	51236.7	18793.5	7959
143756.5	52350.9	54740.1	16366.4	15497.9		86004.2	15766.2	531
1538682.6	1364302.4	6562.3	85653.0	60991.3	23076.3	110261.1	42707.5	81451
1412723.5	1257491.1	6287.5	83275.3	61674.2	11600.3	106257.6	38295.9	70936
24324.5	21677.5	92.5	-307.8	69.4	199.7	967.8	805.9	2079
12045.5	10271.5	22.4	397.0	423.1	13.0	671.6	226.1	886
27286.6	24574.6	63.9	545.2	822.5	519.1	2147.4	1261.0	813
26411.1	23843.3	60.0	550.9	821.4	519.1	2092.9	1211.5	707
875.5	731.3	3.9	-5.7	1.1		54.5	49.5	106
76922.3	71376.3	282.6	409.8	2045.2	722.5	4802.8	2475.0	2506
97795.8	82102.8	30.0	2954.7	4350.7	93.8	4948.9	568.2	2183
141677.8	117366.0	837.8	4854.1	2305.6	7133.4	11308.4	8165.0	7150
48788.7	38311.3	262.8	2977.7	3409.7	61.2	5906.9	2234.4	2988
7418953.9	7152673.0	213934.6	-214891.7	-215752.9	378589.8	147260.4	149078.7	32060
139154.0	104970.1	718.6	24126.9	23632.0	1078.5	34594.7	10244.1	3393
1717169.8	1373991.1	9272.7	143049.7	156504.2	8709.5	233996.6	68219.7	29568
963351.0	787834.7	4278.9	72452.6	74975.7	6970.0	113656.0	34401.4	15031
195431.1	140156.5	832.1	27159.6	35379.0	581.4	42224.0	6012.9	4478
60599.0	37967.4	419.5	7897.9	8617.6	483.3	13292.3	4255.2	2462
283567.2	207556.8	1399.1	53916.3	56784.4		74693.3	16509.8	5191
63800.6	55622.0	1861.9	-1460.4	-1480.7	1586.1	2241.5	1860.3	1621
384213.4	336519.4	2197.9	16689.7	20464.7	6387.4	35517.6	12855.0	14100
822862.0	655729.7	4692.9	38244.9	61110.5	17696.0	113976.8	48173.4	30844
415367.7	318412.3	3095.3	7689.3	26433.0	14399.8	64404.6	34876.3	20072
2402540.9	2102832.8	6414.4	141338.8	144273.1	3948.8	249400.7	98713.2	23634
427392.8	360932.4	1226.4	37990.1	43436.8	1637.2	60273.7	15610.5	5902
231421.3	209455.9	749.9	4840.6	5187.8	1654.9	11147.8	5210.1	6052
91023.6	75600.7	577.2	3412.0	3865.7	840.5	8561.3	4118.4	3628
86813.4	68347.4	212.2	6666.0	7330.0	2066.0	10822.7	3280.5	3774
102705.5	94442.7	126.3	-415.1	-40.4	1809.4	1330.3	1244.4	2756
778789.0	610154.6	2151.7	77749.0	89368.0	1651.8	101378.9	9859.2	4828
115606.2	80685.7	736.8	12603.5	11539.4	2356.0	19213.3	6937.1	2292
12526.5	8092.1	80.2	2237.2	2584.1		3301.3	637.0	324
6386.6	5011.9	0.5	1106.4	1177.7		1418.7	240.5	146
1892054.1	1660547.6	13427.8	-12466.5	20740.8	85665.4	181645.4	147476.8	49905
1745726.0	1525974.2	12875.6	-774.5	20283.2	79320.3	174498.5	141339.7	43450
81919.3	51679.9	851.1	7370.7	13029.3	1020.6	16630.1	2749.7	1828
39652.1	30661.6	241.5	-7758.3	-4621.9	6623.5	-2315.4	2065.0	3257

11-5 各地、州、市、县(市)规模以上工业企业主要经济指标

单位：万元 (2007 年)

地 区	Region	企业单位数(个) Number of Enterprises (unit)	#亏损企业 Loss- Suffering Enterprises	工业总产值(当年价格) Gross Industrial Output Value (At Current Prices)
总 计	**Total**	**1575**	**416**	**32966068.9**
乌鲁木齐市	**Urumqi City**	**362**	**89**	**9701456.6**
#乌鲁木齐县	Urumqi County	5		13297.3
克拉玛依市	**Karamay City**	**77**	**8**	**9429769.4**
石河子市	**Shihezi City**	**58**	**21**	**895405.2**
阿拉尔市	**Aral City**	**10**	**2**	**82018.4**
图木舒克市	**Tumxuk City**	**8**	**1**	**30214.0**
五家渠市	**Wujiaqu City**	**20**	**3**	**85238.9**
吐鲁番地区	**Turpan Administrative Offices**	**59**	**19**	**2010705.0**
吐鲁番市	Turpan City	18	10	244958.2
鄯善县	Shanshan [Piqan] County	31	5	1655609.1
托克逊县	Toksun County	10	4	110137.7
哈密地区	**Hami [Kumul] Administrative Offices**	**74**	**12**	**585580.7**
哈密市	Hami [Kumul] City	57	9	537175.9
巴里坤哈萨克自治县	Barkol Kazak Autonomous County	15	3	33193.5
伊吾县	Yiwu [Araturuk] County	2		15211.3
昌吉回族自治州	**Changji Hui Autonomous Prefecture**	**251**	**84**	**1815318.4**
昌吉市	Changji City	96	32	874845.6
阜康市	Fukang City	28	7	321619.9
呼图壁县	Hutubi County	56	20	203496.5
玛纳斯县	Manas County	36	18	302719.1
奇台县	Qitai County	15	4	63830.7
吉木萨尔县	Jimsar County	14	3	41881.2
木垒哈萨克自治县	Mori Kazak Autonomous County	6		6925.4
伊犁哈萨克自治州	**Ili Kazak Autonomous Prefecture**	**291**	**72**	**2218302.8**
伊犁州直属县(市)	**Counties (Cities) Direct Under Ili Prefecture**	**154**	**32**	**1097526.0**
伊宁市	Yining [Gulja] City	32	4	191146.0
奎屯市	Kuytun City	31	5	300681.9
伊宁县	Yining [Gulja] County	24	3	138867.4
察布查尔锡伯自治县	Qapqal Xibe Autonomous County	13	7	26399.7
霍城县	Huocheng [Korgas] County	21	9	119924.5
巩留县	Gongliu [Tokkuztara] County	7	1	31308.9
新源县	Xinyuan [Kunes] County	8	1	190030.9
昭苏县	Zhaosu [Mongolkure] County	7	1	39313.9
特克斯县	Tekes County	3		10089.7
尼勒克县	Nilka County	8	1	49763.1

Main Economic Indicators of Industrial Enterprises above Designated Size by Prefecture, Autonomous Prefecture, City and County

(10 000 yuan)

工业增加值 Added Value of Industry	工业销售产值(当年价) Sales Value of Industry Products (At Current Prices)	出口交货值 Delivery Value of Industry Export	实收资本 Total Capital Hold	资产合计 Total Assets	流动资产合计 Total Working Capitals	#产成品 Finished Product	流动资产年平均余额 Annual Average Balance of Circulating Funds	固定资产原价 Original Value of Fixed Assets
13966779.4	**32779858.8**	**615858.6**	**16967893.1**	**43363237.4**	**14507047.5**	**1383752.3**	**12510396.7**	**35929133.1**
2657512.0	**9785915.6**	**400537.7**	**4317472.1**	**11769448.7**	**4302934.1**	**466378.0**	**3580002.4**	**8913327.4**
8553.0	12514.2		31620.8	130303.1	23802.0	478.3	20084.9	87058.0
4670872.8	**9425411.8**	**19880.5**	**6095701.9**	**10967378.9**	**3075582.2**	**103141.3**	**2718727.7**	**10692178.6**
250112.5	**864719.6**	**66450.0**	**432154.5**	**2245414.9**	**965531.1**	**108962.5**	**818340.4**	**1242852.5**
23911.7	**70480.3**		**34044.1**	**131063.8**	**72575.1**	**8733.8**	**61803.9**	**63204.1**
5873.3	**23968.2**		**17984.4**	**64523.2**	**30201.0**	**9362.5**	**25705.8**	**29395.6**
18913.1	**79183.0**	**2115.8**	**34021.7**	**161381.0**	**78146.7**	**17412.4**	**59117.6**	**60190.0**
1095314.2	**2002134.2**	**2049.9**	**1234136.6**	**2524056.7**	**743512.3**	**55710.1**	**687103.3**	**2898514.9**
67671.5	244119.4	2049.9	274034.6	287802.1	124929.3	12016.9	102736.5	208326.6
977892.3	1650875.2		926254.3	2063384.9	579179.9	36359.6	544171.4	2553600.8
49750.4	107139.6		33847.7	172869.7	39403.1	7333.6	40195.4	136587.5
239695.7	**571818.7**	**110.7**	**292112.0**	**1018726.5**	**499507.1**	**50584.1**	**414459.1**	**606624.9**
217271.5	524729.2	66.2	281607.3	961778.0	461625.7	46328.1	380229.3	589919.9
12982.7	31589.3	44.5	10375.8	39005.1	21093.6	2259.9	19371.4	14854.2
9441.5	15500.2		128.9	17943.4	16787.8	1996.1	14858.4	1850.8
531478.2	**1784082.9**	**37343.3**	**504060.7**	**2478142.7**	**1118833.5**	**178335.4**	**936934.0**	**1414983.8**
227332.1	872921.6	24297.7	272553.9	1425317.3	673469.2	102064.9	557982.3	660047.0
107030.0	320185.9	1072.5	63662.7	340014.1	129093.5	12350.4	114583.2	213652.3
52579.8	172540.3	1022.2	55987.4	241189.9	106402.8	19085.5	99109.2	142353.3
115203.2	311813.5	10950.9	78943.1	332554.2	139982.2	26659.6	110517.5	323578.3
14085.4	63255.7		15313.4	58726.9	42168.2	8041.3	27819.9	22759.4
13462.3	36679.3		13938.5	69251.7	22939.8	9062.0	22392.8	47297.0
1785.4	6686.6		3661.7	11088.6	4777.8	1071.7	4529.1	5296.5
1020948.2	**2152409.5**	**37857.8**	**954015.9**	**3693114.3**	**1402823.5**	**190382.0**	**1233777.9**	**2300945.2**
470712.3	**1066415.4**	**29945.1**	**567418.0**	**2310285.2**	**849105.7**	**98760.2**	**720144.7**	**1418809.9**
69064.4	185260.1	858.6	65239.8	299114.1	106076.9	7249.4	104613.0	280156.6
148671.2	304991.9	1937.4	89756.9	495720.4	230609.0	17899.5	216824.9	292037.1
52801.5	131258.8	1248.0	71167.3	218823.3	74664.3	10361.4	64612.1	171751.3
7162.8	22644.4		8517.4	39922.7	18252.4	6818.0	14624.7	20261.9
34189.2	119723.2	18608.2	39889.2	155865.8	79947.8	28816.6	59572.4	104226.5
14086.6	30247.7		167249.0	504358.6	118523.5	1817.9	81210.1	187775.1
100470.0	175459.6	7292.9	68310.2	297886.2	158481.9	18487.3	130549.5	111903.3
10063.2	37542.1		8362.4	39066.8	31111.0	5259.5	19422.7	9491.9
4717.0	8813.4		975.0	6876.4	4495.9	1404.5	3274.9	2188.0
29486.4	50474.2		47950.8	252650.9	26943.0	646.1	25440.4	239018.2

11-5 续表 1

单位: 万元

地　　区	Region	企业单位数 (个) Number of Enterprises (unit)	#亏损企业 Loss- Suffering Enterprises	工业总产值 (当年价格) Gross Industrial Output Value (At Current Prices)
塔城地区	**Tacheng [Tarbagatai] Administrative Offices**	**85**	**24**	**622505.5**
塔城市	Tacheng [Qoqek] City	5	3	34274.2
乌苏市	Usu City	21	6	143538.6
额敏县	Emin [Dorbiljin] County	12	3	84981.4
沙湾县	Shawan County	29	8	232919.0
托里县	Toli County	8	2	72431.9
裕民县	Yumin [Qagantokay] County	1		4560.8
和布克赛尔蒙古自治县	Hoboksar Mongol Autonomous County	9	2	49799.6
阿勒泰地区	**Altay Administrative Offices**	**52**	**16**	**498271.3**
阿勒泰市	Altay City	16	7	70785.6
布尔津县	Burqin County	5	1	12553.0
富蕴县	Fuyun [Koktokay] County	14	3	216889.4
福海县	Fuhai [Burultokay] County	7	2	16586.0
哈巴河县	Habahe [Kaba] County	6	2	173355.5
青河县	Qinghe [Qinggil] County	1		5207.4
吉木乃县	Jeminay County	3	1	2894.4
博尔塔拉蒙古自治州	**Bortala Mongol Autonomous Prefecture**	**40**	**16**	**157439.9**
博乐市	Bole [Bortala] City	32	14	140459.0
精河县	Jinghe [Jing] County	6	1	14068.6
温泉县	Wenquan [Araxang] County	2	1	2912.3
巴音郭楞蒙古自治州	**Bayangol Mongol Autonomous Prefecture**	**119**	**32**	**4111121.2**
库尔勒市	Korla City	58	17	3537260.0
轮台县	Luntai [Bugur] County	9	1	220241.4
尉犁县	Yuli [Lopnur] County	9		93668.2
若羌县	Ruoqiang [Qarkilik] County	4		34436.2
且末县	Qiemo [Qarqan] County	2	2	2578.7
焉耆回族自治县	Yanqi Hui Autonomous County	10	2	40859.6
和静县	Hejing County	13	4	135865.4
和硕县	Hoxud County	9	2	23065.9
博湖县	Bohu [Bagrax] County	5	4	23145.8
阿克苏地区	**Aksu Administrative Offices**	**106**	**16**	**1301066.1**
阿克苏市	Aksu City	38	5	324302.1
温宿县	Wensu [Onsu] County	15	2	28356.6
库车县	Kuqa County	22	1	778386.9

Continued

(10 000 yuan)

工业增加值 Added Value of Industry	工业销售产值(当年价) Sales Value of Industry Products (At Current Prices)	出口交货值 Delivery Value of Industry Export	实收资本 Total Capital Hold	资产合计 Total Assets	流动资产合计 Total Working Capitals	#产成品 Finished Product	流动资产年平均余额 Annual Average Balance of Circulating Funds	固定资产原价 Original Value of Fixed Assets
219991.0	**575292.0**	**7912.7**	**161862.2**	**713107.6**	**295574.7**	**71730.1**	**275289.1**	**492370.9**
12527.7	35080.3		9364.0	64283.9	17606.2	751.4	16422.6	73647.5
53117.0	144569.3	7912.7	23095.7	156502.4	74050.7	7361.7	73183.0	92369.8
21908.6	79020.6		32814.1	117670.0	65081.5	24373.5	57857.8	72404.3
74180.7	209128.4		40846.8	191685.5	91978.3	31879.8	78562.4	132353.0
34514.4	57234.8		26495.0	87239.4	25059.9	5113.6	25721.5	46026.9
1993.7	3179.6		300.0	1373.8	1073.2	10.2	1073.2	300.6
21748.9	47079.0		28946.6	94352.6	20724.9	2239.9	22468.6	75268.8
330244.9	**510702.1**		**224735.7**	**669721.5**	**258143.1**	**19891.7**	**238344.1**	**389764.4**
25029.1	71468.4		31078.8	126603.3	32186.2	2168.2	28313.5	124538.4
4622.1	12530.5		14038.7	25906.3	5286.0	156.3	5872.6	24307.9
131544.1	216564.5		106258.3	301794.0	129192.7	11987.9	116929.8	117774.7
6726.3	17777.7		35020.7	45576.4	16018.6	2151.9	14484.7	40600.5
159594.7	183768.4		37053.5	163965.3	72108.2	3311.1	69683.8	77690.3
1628.5	5897.4		180.0	2628.0	716.2	92.2	1014.3	2249.7
1100.1	2695.2		1105.7	3248.2	2635.2	24.1	2045.4	2602.9
40073.2	**143889.1**		**60897.4**	**250031.4**	**112401.6**	**26215.4**	**94382.0**	**156609.3**
35423.3	127122.6		57971.7	229065.4	97396.1	20460.9	82286.1	150323.1
4113.0	14470.3		1914.9	17094.4	12384.2	4269.4	10491.4	5200.3
536.9	2296.2		1010.8	3871.6	2621.3	1485.1	1604.5	1085.9
2876863.5	**4102532.6**	**40577.3**	**2369321.0**	**5606474.0**	**1275956.5**	**80277.8**	**1155466.6**	**5638433.2**
2672271.0	3584199.6	1974.0	2154891.9	4666183.2	886098.2	26467.5	828845.8	5248389.7
88774.8	166272.5		30607.1	152537.0	80477.3	5614.6	67784.1	67087.0
27164.5	96593.7	7500.1	18646.9	114800.0	67257.5	6470.4	60528.1	67268.4
16467.5	34718.4		58640.1	299543.3	59582.2	2837.3	48508.7	43208.0
1179.6	2578.7		1271.7	9938.0	1311.5		1493.5	12058.6
11322.2	37768.5	11367.9	26224.8	74158.5	28488.9	9342.8	25253.1	53862.8
45226.0	130617.6		68872.6	230500.7	120205.5	16905.3	92763.0	102980.8
8827.9	26756.2	4655.4	5756.1	29273.8	18738.8	6994.8	17445.9	14297.1
5630.0	23027.4	15079.9	4409.8	29539.5	13796.6	5645.1	12844.4	29280.8
344053.5	**1265722.9**	**2194.5**	**395495.9**	**1510163.6**	**532358.8**	**60149.7**	**444821.1**	**1080652.9**
107231.2	312569.2		106682.2	652959.7	263361.0	27353.7	223933.7	413259.9
14868.5	28004.3		7310.3	35400.2	14272.2	3166.1	13565.4	18148.4
150898.8	774008.5	2194.5	223760.4	587101.7	137591.0	17545.9	116925.6	500257.1

11-5 续表 2

单位: 万元

地 区	Region	企业单位数（个） Number of Enterprises (unit)	#亏损企业 Loss- Suffering Enterprises	工业总产值（当年价格） Gross Industrial Output Value (At Current Prices)
沙雅县	Xayar County	9	1	52770.5
新和县	Xinhe [Toksu] County	4	1	14874.6
拜城县	Baicheng [Bay] County	13	4	88203.4
乌什县	Wushi [Uxturpan] County	2		3659.9
阿瓦提县	Awat County	3	2	10512.1
柯坪县	Kalpin County			
克孜勒苏柯尔克孜自治州	**Kizilsu Kirgiz Autonomous Prefecture**	**19**	**6**	**52055.2**
阿图什市	Artux City	8	1	27777.4
阿克陶县	Akto County	6	3	16137.7
阿合奇县	Akqi County			
乌恰县	Wuqia [Ulugqat] County	5	2	8140.1
喀什地区	**Kashgar [Kaxgar] Administrative Offices**	**63**	**26**	**414575.6**
喀什市	Kashgar [Kaxgar] City	20	9	253657.2
疏附县	Shufu County	2	2	1522.2
疏勒县	Shule County	10	5	24030.1
英吉沙县	Yengisar County	4	2	8490.0
泽普县	Zepu [Poskam] County	5	1	9468.6
莎车县	Shache [Yarkant] County	6	2	27682.9
叶城县	Yecheng [Kagilik] County	2		17918.0
麦盖提县	Makit County	3		23084.1
岳普湖县	Yopurga County	5	2	14505.0
伽师县	Jiashi [Payzawat] County	2	1	13758.0
巴楚县	Bachu [Maralbexi] County	4	2	20459.5
塔什库尔干塔吉克自治县	Taxkorgan Tajik Autonomous County			
和田地区	**Hotan Administrative Offices**	**18**	**9**	**75801.5**
和田市	Hotan City	9	5	42783.3
和田县	Hotan County	6	2	13717.2
墨玉县	Moyu [Karakax] County	1	1	1200.0
皮山县	Pishan [Guma] County	1	1	5056.5
洛浦县	Lop County	1		13044.5
策勒县	Qira County			
于田县	Yutian [Keriya] County			
民丰县	Minfeng [Niya] County			

Continued

(10 000 yuan)

工业增加值 Added Value of Industry	工业销售产值(当年价) Sales Value of Industry Products (At Current Prices)	出口交货值 Delivery Value of Industry Export	实收资本 Total Capital Hold	资产合计 Total Assets	流动资产合计 Total Working Capitals	#产成品 Finished Product	流动资产年平均余额 Annual Average Balance of Circulating Funds	固定资产原价 Original Value of Fixed Assets
14478.0	47599.6		17041.0	60104.8	37293.2	2389.6	23755.9	26014.3
4262.7	15018.9		5489.7	21247.9	16178.3	2951.0	15486.4	3981.0
47339.2	76459.6		30800.3	133107.7	52595.5	2970.5	41533.8	108092.1
2497.5	3248.1		2300.0	4807.7	2854.1	163.3	2887.4	1686.4
2477.6	8814.7		2112.0	15433.9	8213.5	3609.6	6732.9	9213.7
17497.9	**45779.3**		**17489.1**	**65019.2**	**34438.8**	**3805.2**	**26279.7**	**33978.1**
7593.5	21808.7		10690.2	27847.0	15740.6	2193.0	15487.3	15330.6
6427.7	15764.9		4883.0	28401.9	11971.7	1161.7	5812.0	16684.1
3476.7	8205.7		1915.9	8770.3	6726.5	450.5	4980.4	1963.4
141638.6	**386437.8**	**6741.1**	**73117.1**	**577519.9**	**190545.9**	**13425.5**	**176440.5**	**523076.3**
89343.5	247493.9	6741.1	44041.7	432006.1	108202.4	4164.8	105754.3	452245.1
629.9	1406.2		1976.0	5829.4	1899.6		2245.7	6280.9
8714.7	15948.6		9033.8	23292.8	12113.0	1718.3	9661.5	15495.8
3880.7	6460.9		1619.9	10085.6	3537.1	51.6	3137.9	8071.5
2672.9	11341.7		1177.0	8794.9	5335.7	406.6	4007.5	2592.0
8688.5	28131.0		4921.9	22197.8	8148.9	1120.9	6623.7	14833.2
7508.4	17846.4		2694.2	10794.2	3090.4	89.0	3452.7	6969.6
4945.2	14364.1		4175.7	32192.0	24185.8	2950.5	21523.7	7525.0
3755.0	13369.0		670.0	7434.2	5055.2	94.4	4474.2	1618.4
4236.0	13239.7		445.9	2543.7	1730.1	1282.2	1729.9	1771.5
7263.8	16836.3		2361.0	22349.2	17247.7	1547.2	13829.4	5673.3
32021.0	**75373.3**		**135868.7**	**300778.6**	**71699.3**	**10876.6**	**77034.7**	**274166.3**
15966.8	43392.7		29123.8	160458.5	48304.9	9536.6	45923.6	142214.0
9283.6	13442.6		105056.0	121284.7	11028.1	12.8	19257.8	120482.3
244.3	1300.0		1000.0	1924.1	1241.3		897.0	890.7
2053.7	5283.9		334.9	4765.6	3008.5	364.1	3138.8	3960.0
4472.6	11954.1		354.0	12345.7	8116.5	963.1	7817.5	6619.3

11-5 续表 3

单位: 万元

地区	Region	固定资产净值年平均余额 Annual Average Balance of Net Value of Fixed Assets	流动负债合计 Total Working Liabilities	长期负债合计 Long-term Liabilities	所有者权益合计 Creditors' Equities
总计	**Total**	**20108340.7**	**13724617.8**	**7507726.4**	**21414685.5**
乌鲁木齐市	**Urumqi City**	**5193722.7**	**3770973.1**	**1330638.8**	**6553227.3**
#乌鲁木齐县	Urumqi County	51971.2	87877.6	1535.2	40890.3
克拉玛依市	**Karamay City**	**5123552.3**	**2182492.4**	**2354855.9**	**6418486.4**
石河子市	**Shihezi City**	**953615.8**	**962849.6**	**385008.9**	**890635.1**
阿拉尔市	**Aral City**	**50300.6**	**62794.6**	**14109.7**	**43446.0**
图木舒克市	**Tumxuk City**	**23105.9**	**31987.4**	**14214.5**	**18321.3**
五家渠市	**Wujiaqu City**	**50227.3**	**60365.6**	**472.8**	**47492.2**
吐鲁番地区	**Turpan Administrative Offices**	**1465079.0**	**758554.7**	**88485.4**	**1261165.2**
吐鲁番市	Turpan City	110255.3	118534.0	43306.4	112205.5
鄯善县	Shanshan [Piqan] County	1230448.3	560385.2	6063.8	1097366.1
托克逊县	Toksun County	124375.4	79635.5	39115.2	51593.6
哈密地区	**Hami [Kumul] Administrative Offices**	**354085.0**	**376786.3**	**182797.0**	**451562.1**
哈密市	Hami [Kumul] City	341517.1	349354.1	181429.2	423413.6
巴里坤哈萨克自治县	Barkol Kazak Autonomous County	11638.7	24892.5	1278.9	12833.7
伊吾县	Yiwu [Araturuk] County	929.2	2539.7	88.9	15314.8
昌吉回族自治州	**Changji Hui Autonomous Prefecture**	**829318.3**	**1198851.6**	**467102.9**	**806585.7**
昌吉市	Changji City	427304.3	631462.3	369576.4	420471.2
阜康市	Fukang City	89383.9	181489.5	22918.7	135594.2
呼图壁县	Hutubi County	90450.2	128055.5	17725.8	94261.2
玛纳斯县	Manas County	173852.4	166718.4	55783.3	109455.3
奇台县	Qitai County	13037.0	33750.6	207.7	24729.8
吉木萨尔县	Jimsar County	30522.3	51067.2	579.6	17604.9
木垒哈萨克自治县	Mori Kazak Autonomous County	4768.2	6308.1	311.4	4469.1
伊犁哈萨克自治州	**Ili Kazak Autonomous Prefecture**	**1583084.2**	**1612233.1**	**675919.9**	**1386433.6**
伊犁州直属县(市)	**Counties (Cities) Direct Under Ili Prefecture**	**1006333.0**	**892646.7**	**559315.3**	**856162.9**
伊宁市	Yining [Gulja] City	162546.7	189849.8	26294.1	82731.5
奎屯市	Kuytun City	189068.9	185514.8	117798.1	191556.2
伊宁县	Yining [Gulja] County	100604.4	90313.6	24754.4	102735.2
察布查尔锡伯自治县	Qapqal Xibe Autonomous County	18170.9	18812.7	1428.1	19681.9
霍城县	Huocheng [Korgas] County	63904.9	78718.7	8849.2	68297.8
巩留县	Gongliu [Tokkuztara] County	170656.6	112063.9	222676.5	169618.2
新源县	Xinyuan [Kunes] County	83699.2	145285.9	1767.8	150782.5
昭苏县	Zhaosu [Mongolkure] County	7231.7	28828.6		10238.1
特克斯县	Tekes County	1955.1	4730.9		2145.5
尼勒克县	Nilka County	208494.6	38527.8	155747.1	58376.0

Continued

(10 000 yuan)

主营业务收入 Revenue from Principal Business	#主营业务成本 Cost of Principal Business	主营业务税金及附加 Taes and Other Charges on Principal Business	营业利润 Business Profit	利润总额 Total Profit	亏损企业亏损总额 Losses Value of Loss-Suffering Enterprises	利税总额 Total Profits and Taxes	本年应交增值税 Value-added Taxes Payable	全部从业人员年平均人数(人) Annual Average Employed Persons (person)
34756937.7	**24283121.6**	**667482.3**	**6775696.5**	**6915727.0**	**595186.3**	**9613765.4**	**2030556.1**	**537937**
10088012.3	**8121976.2**	**218025.4**	**861470.1**	**899992.0**	**368880.3**	**1518007.4**	**399990.0**	**144735**
11014.0	5844.4	12.9	1532.9	2259.4		3537.9	1265.6	202
10290668.0	**6940969.7**	**220985.9**	**2516058.1**	**2548498.3**	**72927.7**	**3483388.0**	**713903.8**	**103884**
1205112.9	**986695.3**	**5721.0**	**90755.6**	**96442.1**	**12028.8**	**143019.4**	**40856.3**	**25832**
66220.9	**57896.9**	**120.4**	**3277.3**	**2617.0**	**647.7**	**5964.4**	**3227.0**	**1900**
24309.4	**21539.2**	**17.3**	**972.3**	**949.5**	**212.0**	**1325.9**	**359.1**	**865**
79202.4	**69063.6**	**128.2**	**4281.1**	**5121.9**	**257.4**	**7483.1**	**2233.0**	**2670**
2098427.3	**1307568.6**	**24419.8**	**590002.5**	**602337.5**	**9261.1**	**778726.4**	**151969.1**	**30083**
248812.2	215380.9	1433.4	17848.2	18326.8	7785.1	34177.8	14417.6	7184
1778861.5	1043352.0	22063.5	564983.2	576738.4	500.6	730863.3	132061.4	20348
70753.6	48835.7	922.9	7171.1	7272.3	975.4	13685.3	5490.1	2551
574953.7	**415659.6**	**5004.3**	**83287.1**	**87066.5**	**2964.8**	**134803.0**	**42732.2**	**23961**
527809.1	388758.7	4468.6	75160.5	79408.5	2804.9	122753.2	38876.1	21767
31644.4	22202.4	208.1	1255.3	1198.6	159.9	3884.5	2477.8	2101
15500.2	4698.5	327.6	6871.3	6459.4		8165.3	1378.3	93
1859502.7	**1576213.3**	**7888.9**	**83889.8**	**107599.4**	**43951.0**	**184272.4**	**68784.1**	**40063**
974493.8	864354.3	3436.6	-5972.3	16634.9	35067.6	47146.0	27074.5	16711
309400.2	248072.8	1070.2	40912.4	42425.2	1275.4	58419.6	14924.2	7764
164969.0	145668.6	821.5	2123.1	2617.3	2920.1	7880.8	4442.0	5642
311904.5	237903.6	1672.4	42647.7	41483.7	3601.6	62250.6	19094.5	6635
60313.6	49528.7	406.8	2935.8	3076.3	729.2	5136.7	1653.6	1466
31637.1	25419.5	300.9	852.8	980.1	357.1	2613.7	1332.7	1642
6784.5	5265.8	180.5	390.3	381.9		825.0	262.6	203
2243975.2	**1486202.4**	**79558.4**	**363333.6**	**362039.8**	**37032.9**	**598186.9**	**156588.7**	**70579**
1178808.4	**839551.8**	**68732.5**	**99021.3**	**109334.8**	**23450.3**	**256776.3**	**78709.0**	**37771**
184916.4	151005.5	1644.2	7265.0	4786.6	13755.3	17167.1	10736.3	9383
375505.1	259174.3	55611.8	17099.6	20083.4	3282.2	100621.7	24926.5	7100
139884.7	100532.0	359.8	15515.3	19036.0	1697.9	26886.3	7490.5	6245
23832.2	22024.4	89.8	-868.4	-536.3	1753.8	273.4	719.9	1079
118794.3	92610.5	446.5	10202.1	10532.7	1472.9	17752.1	6772.9	4055
30712.4	23402.6	118.1	1359.9	1755.8	1269.7	4500.8	2626.9	1282
208382.9	123662.6	9917.9	38015.6	40326.3	25.0	67986.8	17742.6	6349
36892.7	33755.8	18.0	1152.7	1562.2	4.1	1908.7	328.5	722
8768.0	6844.0	3.3	888.6	927.4		1381.1	450.4	363
51119.7	26540.1	523.1	8390.9	10860.7	189.4	18298.3	6914.5	1193

11-5 续表 4

单位: 万元

地　　区	Region	固定资产净值年平均余额 Annual Average Balance of Net Value of Fixed Assets	流动负债合计 Total Working Liabilities	长期负债合计 Long-term Liabilities	所有者权益合计 Creditors' Equities
塔城地区	**Tacheng [Tarbagatai] Administrative Offices**	**327754.0**	**465422.8**	**52712.1**	**183930.9**
塔城市	Tacheng [Qoqek] City	45751.7	78386.7	8564.2	-22667.0
乌苏市	Usu City	61051.2	105466.1	10777.4	40170.7
额敏县	Emin [Dorbiljin] County	43843.9	75025.7	4059.9	35506.9
沙湾县	Shawan County	92224.2	133598.5	3767.5	54319.5
托里县	Toli County	36314.1	41739.3	7398.5	38031.7
裕民县	Yumin [Qagantokay] County	300.6	308.7		1065.1
和布克赛尔蒙古自治县	Hoboksar Mongol Autonomous County	48268.3	30897.8	18144.6	37504.0
阿勒泰地区	**Altay Administrative Offices**	**248997.2**	**254163.6**	**63892.5**	**346339.8**
阿勒泰市	Altay City	79972.3	80205.4	18460.5	25038.1
布尔津县	Burqin County	18102.6	7553.7	3857.8	14436.5
富蕴县	Fuyun [Koktokay] County	63804.3	76490.6	24998.0	198239.8
福海县	Fuhai [Burultokay] County	23886.6	11208.3	1991.0	32377.1
哈巴河县	Habahe [Kaba] County	61234.6	76250.7	12417.7	74996.8
青河县	Qinghe [Qinggil] County	1371.1	569.7	1804.0	253.9
吉木乃县	Jeminay County	625.7	1885.2	363.5	997.6
博尔塔拉蒙古自治州	**Bortala Mongol Autonomous Prefecture**	**102669.2**	**105968.4**	**42458.2**	**74511.1**
博乐市	Bole [Bortala] City	98000.2	92925.1	40821.1	68225.7
精河县	Jinghe [Jing] County	3706.3	10514.0	1558.0	5022.3
温泉县	Wenquan [Araxang] County	962.7	2529.3	79.1	1263.1
巴音郭楞蒙古自治州	**Bayangol Mongol Autonomous Prefecture**	**3093227.6**	**1458869.1**	**1588753.4**	**2544329.7**
库尔勒市	Korla City	2858643.5	969031.2	1468179.3	2228039.3
轮台县	Luntai [Bugur] County	51981.6	62391.8	7600.7	76216.1
尉犁县	Yuli [Lopnur] County	27513.5	77606.7	7078.3	30115.0
若羌县	Ruoqiang [Qarkilik] County	27579.2	148117.1	77975.2	72834.1
且末县	Qiemo [Qarqan] County	7633.3	3959.4	243.2	-187.9
焉耆回族自治县	Yanqi Hui Autonomous County	36893.0	43560.4	6044.8	24553.3
和静县	Hejing County	59242.3	114078.0	15397.3	100305.6
和硕县	Hoxud County	8537.5	14246.8	2391.8	12635.2
博湖县	Bohu [Bagrax] County	15203.7	25877.7	3842.8	-181.0
阿克苏地区	**Aksu Administrative Offices**	**754623.7**	**608180.8**	**200402.6**	**694889.6**
阿克苏市	Aksu City	244850.8	307492.6	63776.2	279702.9
温宿县	Wensu [Onsu] County	11500.2	15793.0	3082.4	14579.5
库车县	Kuqa County	407797.4	152256.3	123604.4	311149.2

Continued

(10 000 yuan)

主营业务收入 Revenue from Principal Business	#主营业务成本 Cost of Principal Business	主营业务税金及附加 Taes and Other Charges on Principal Business	营业利润 Business Profit	利润总额 Total Profit	亏损企业亏损总额 Losses Value of Loss-Suffering Enterprises	利税总额 Total Profits and Taxes	本年应交增值税 Value-added Taxes Payable	全部从业人员年平均人数(人) Annual Average Employed Persons (Person)
538784.4	**426114.7**	**4647.1**	**35556.3**	**41640.2**	**8625.0**	**71304.9**	**25017.6**	**22531**
27425.5	26880.6	139.3	-2215.3	-2050.3	2059.1	375.7	2286.7	1581
119401.7	90623.8	1897.2	10629.6	10811.7	2346.5	17924.3	5215.4	3942
88494.6	68639.8	456.1	6285.0	6773.9	933.2	11328.4	4098.4	2313
212215.5	176207.0	1206.1	13499.8	18551.3	1339.4	27620.7	7863.3	5647
51943.7	37147.3	201.7	6008.6	5806.9	56.1	8086.5	2077.9	3952
2632.9	2569.0		13.7	13.7		14.1	0.4	45
36670.5	24047.2	746.7	1334.9	1733.0	1890.7	5955.2	3475.5	5051
526382.4	**220535.9**	**6178.8**	**228756.0**	**211064.8**	**4957.6**	**270105.7**	**52862.1**	**10277**
72483.9	56271.9	450.8	4068.5	3798.1	1237.2	8710.0	4461.1	3045
12578.6	7918.4	89.7	1276.5	1308.9	89.7	2458.6	1060.0	455
233285.0	102348.0	3395.7	86649.1	87399.2	1218.6	116021.3	25226.4	4459
18087.7	15792.5	134.7	570.8	307.6	1128.2	2029.9	1587.6	687
183793.1	33024.4	2086.6	136267.8	118188.1	1243.1	140346.8	20072.1	1222
3564.9	3188.9	9.9	-53.1	75.9		333.7	247.9	134
2589.2	1991.8	11.4	-23.6	-13.0	40.8	205.4	207.0	275
154684.0	**138657.4**	**950.3**	**188.1**	**2665.9**	**5367.6**	**11224.5**	**7608.3**	**7578**
140375.9	126892.8	848.7	-736.5	1861.3	5021.0	9785.8	7075.8	6761
12591.0	10220.7	101.6	914.2	793.1	337.9	1427.2	532.5	768
1717.1	1543.9		10.4	11.5	8.7	11.5		49
4294192.8	**1653052.2**	**79476.9**	**2075653.3**	**2087491.3**	**7287.5**	**2524390.3**	**357422.1**	**40050**
3774421.4	1230528.4	75049.9	2041433.5	2046841.2	3672.2	2460724.4	338833.3	25812
173256.6	153384.1	1973.4	6403.1	6694.5	577.9	12297.1	3629.2	1406
94197.6	77346.7	409.5	5949.4	7742.9		11268.9	3116.5	3066
29878.0	16717.2	815.9	6114.6	7427.7		10176.5	1932.9	2196
1911.8	1882.3	13.7	-260.6	-204.4	204.4	-87.1	103.6	188
39238.4	27320.0	413.1	2214.0	2947.9	1655.5	5245.1	1884.1	1255
130928.2	103228.9	610.3	13028.0	14126.8	441.8	21458.9	6721.8	4719
27323.6	24850.1	86.2	154.8	1055.2	159.8	1990.7	849.3	973
23037.2	17794.5	104.9	616.5	859.5	575.9	1315.8	351.4	435
1278700.8	**1070297.3**	**21702.3**	**95719.2**	**104329.4**	**4600.5**	**179761.1**	**53729.4**	**24090**
322419.2	278506.5	1591.6	8006.8	16760.9	935.4	35673.7	17321.2	12094
26970.3	17265.4	885.5	5139.0	5196.0	176.1	8577.7	2496.2	1777
779311.5	657352.0	18476.1	67361.3	67518.0	173.6	111765.0	25770.9	4156

11-5 续表 5

单位: 万元

地　　区	Region	固定资产净值年平均余额 Annual Average Balance Of Net Value of Fixed Assets	流动负债合　计 Total Working Liabilities	长期负债合　计 Long-term Liabilities	所有者权益合计 Creditors' Equities
沙雅县	Xayar County	11290.3	37463.0	1530.0	21111.8
新和县	Xinhe [Toksu] County	3156.4	14252.8		6995.1
拜城县	Baicheng [Bay] County	68339.7	70940.7	4034.5	55467.0
乌什县	Wushi [Uxturpan] County	1710.4	664.8	1682.4	2460.5
阿瓦提县	Awat County	5978.5	9317.6	2692.7	3423.6
柯坪县	Kalpin County				
克孜勒苏柯尔克孜自治州	**Kizilsu Kirgiz Autonomous Prefecture**	**18413.9**	**25707.2**	**4585.5**	**34203.5**
阿图什市	Artux City	11129.0	6839.8	3787.4	17219.8
阿克陶县	Akto County	6166.7	17356.9	680.3	10364.7
阿合奇县	Akqi County				
乌恰县	Wuqia [Ulugqat] County	1118.2	1510.5	117.8	6619.0
喀什地区	**Kashgar [Kaxgar] Administrative Offices**	**339277.6**	**340672.0**	**141041.1**	**73304.8**
喀什市	Kashgar [Kaxgar] City	286773.8	242817.1	137095.8	35281.8
疏附县	Shufu County	3436.3	3227.2		155.7
疏勒县	Shule County	10738.4	13858.8	345.7	9088.3
英吉沙县	Yengisar County	6777.6	7442.1	320.5	2280.8
泽普县	Zepu [Poskam] County	2335.8	3008.7	118.1	3474.5
莎车县	Shache [Yarkant] County	11670.0	15158.7	620.0	6419.1
叶城县	Yecheng [Kagilik] County	4029.4	7032.2	161.8	2591.9
麦盖提县	Makit County	6852.7	23569.4	150.0	8472.6
岳普湖县	Yopurga County	1189.6	4960.4		2473.8
伽师县	Jiashi [Payzawat] County	813.6	1456.9	45.1	1041.7
巴楚县	Bachu [Maralbexi] County	4660.4	18140.5	2184.1	2024.6
塔什库尔干塔吉克自治县	Taxkorgan Tajik Autonomous County				
和田地区	**Hotan Administrative Offices**	**174037.6**	**167331.9**	**16879.8**	**116091.9**
和田市	Hotan City	98601.8	150187.3	8100.9	2170.3
和田县	Hotan County	69623.0	10486.7	3507.4	107290.6
墨玉县	Moyu [Karakax] County	629.8	1042.2		881.9
皮山县	Pishan [Guma] County	1415.2	3237.2	1209.8	-156.4
洛浦县	Lop County	3767.8	2378.5	4061.7	5905.5
策勒县	Qira County				
于田县	Yutian [Keriya] County				
民丰县	Minfeng [Niya] County				

Continued

(10 000 yuan)

主营业务收入 Revenue from Principal Business	#主营业务成本 Cost of Principal Business	主营业务税金及附加 Taes and Other Charges on Principal Business	营业利润 Business Profit	利润总额 Total Profit	亏损企业亏损总额 Losses Value of Loss-Suffering Enterprises	利税总额 Total Profits and Taxes	本年应交增值税 Value-added Taxes Payable	全部从业人员年平均人数(人) Annual Average Employed Persons (person)
46176.0	43221.7	25.5	709.3	1454.1	81.7	2271.4	791.8	1166
14282.4	11421.6	13.0	167.5	525.9	154.1	809.6	270.7	261
77492.0	51821.3	685.7	14639.3	12925.4	2480.8	20422.8	6811.7	4157
3248.1	1885.3	15.1	551.4	545.6		752.8	192.1	185
8801.3	8823.5	9.8	-855.4	-596.5	598.8	-511.9	74.8	294
52903.2	**33575.8**	**547.7**	**14071.1**	**13667.2**	**1581.4**	**18623.6**	**4408.7**	**2130**
19584.8	14263.9	103.6	3511.5	3569.4	101.8	4988.6	1315.6	618
18319.6	10183.0	153.4	5436.5	4972.4	1440.1	6840.3	1714.5	1065
14998.8	9128.9	290.7	5123.1	5125.4	39.5	6794.7	1378.6	447
371932.2	**341002.6**	**2397.2**	**-7775.6**	**-3610.9**	**17428.5**	**18845.0**	**20058.7**	**13516**
230455.2	213355.6	1967.8	-8079.4	-5341.6	13440.3	12273.8	15647.6	7835
1821.6	1396.6	55.9	-100.4	-106.0	106.0	73.1	123.2	531
15544.0	13058.1	70.8	533.8	991.1	1055.3	1663.4	601.5	1404
6403.1	5575.1	30.1	-335.1	103.2	307.4	638.5	505.2	429
13344.7	8323.0	48.9	583.0	632.7	114.6	1175.7	494.1	210
27977.4	26684.7	100.2	-898.9	-731.6	1214.7	414.5	1045.9	930
7697.5	6124.5	54.2	245.4	289.8		750.0	406.0	683
27473.5	26071.9	0.8	995.4	1077.9		1079.0	0.3	615
8348.3	7312.8	13.9	595.3	277.4	67.3	403.5	112.2	205
11168.9	11524.7	48.2	-1003.9	-1051.4	1059.8	44.7	1047.9	355
21698.0	21575.6	6.4	-310.8	247.6	63.1	328.8	74.8	319
74139.9	**62751.5**	**538.3**	**512.9**	**-1479.9**	**10757.1**	**5744.0**	**6685.6**	**6001**
43156.7	39579.5	337.4	-2662.9	-3098.1	9918.4	762.2	3522.9	3404
13388.1	8763.0	93.6	1982.9	896.8	759.7	2361.1	1370.7	918
1393.9	1234.5	1.6	-42.4	-42.5	42.5	196.0	236.9	100
5266.0	4420.5	57.1	113.8	-36.5	36.5	561.8	541.2	882
10935.2	8754.0	48.6	1121.5	800.4		1862.9	1013.9	697

11-6 规模以上工业企业主要经济效益指标

单位: % (2007 年)

项 目	Item	工业增加值率 Ratio of Value-Added to Gross Industrial Output Value	资金利税率 Ratio of Profits and Taxes to Capital	产值利税率 Ratio of Profits and Taxes to Industrial Output Value
总 计	**Total**	**37.0**	**29.5**	**29.2**
按登记注册类型分	**Grouped by Registry Type**			
内资企业	Domestic Funded Enterprises	37.2	29.8	29.3
国有企业	State-owned Enterprises	29.2	6.9	10.7
#中央企业	Central Enterprises	28.2	7.4	10.6
地方企业	Local Enterprises	35.0	5.0	11.1
#自治区属企业	Autonomous	36.5	4.7	10.8
地区(州、市)属企业	Prefecture or City	29.5	0.4	1.4
县(市)属企业	County or City	40.5	11.6	20.8
集体企业	Collective-owned Enterprises	23.7	15.2	13.0
#自治区属企业	Autonomous	15.7	19.9	11.3
地区(州、市)属企业	Prefecture or City	37.4	11.9	10.6
县(市)属企业	County or City	24.6	10.2	9.5
镇属企业	Town	44.9	13.5	50.4
乡属企业	Township	55.8	17.4	10.3
股份合作企业	Share-holding Cooperative Enterprises	37.3	9.5	12.1
联营企业	Joint Ownership Enterprises	29.5	32.0	24.0
#国有联营企业	State Joint Ownership Enterprises	22.4	68.2	30.8
集体联营企业	Collective Joint Ownership Enterprises	29.2	21.5	24.6
国有与集体联营企业	Joint State-collective Enterprises	33.4	33.3	21.4
其他联营企业	Other Joint Ownership Enterprises	29.1	27.9	12.7
有限责任公司	Limited Liability Corporations	25.9	12.1	14.0
#国有独资公司	State Sole funded Corporations	25.4	10.5	13.4
其他有限责任公司	Other Limited Liability Corporations	26.1	12.7	14.2
股份有限公司	Share-holding Corporations Ltd.	44.9	49.2	41.4
私营企业	Private Enterprises	23.9	13.2	10.5
#私营独资企业	Private-funded Enterprises	25.6	8.2	6.9
私营合伙企业	Private Partnership Enterprises	31.1	17.2	9.3
私营有限责任公司	Private Limited Liability Corporations	24.4	10.7	8.5
私营股份有限公司	Private Share-holding Corporations Ltd.	21.1	23.2	18.8
港、澳、台商投资企业	Enterprises with Funds from Hong Kong, Macao and Taiwan	24.0	9.4	10.7
外商投资企业	Foreign Funded Enterprises	30.4	19.5	23.9
在总计中: 国有控股企业	Of the Total: State-owned and State-holding Enterprises	39.8	32.7	33.1
在总计中: 农村工业	Of the Total: Rural Industry	29.2	14.3	12.0
按轻、重工业分	**Grouped by Light & Heavy Industry**			
轻工业	Light Industry	25.0	10.5	12.1
以农产品为原料	Using Farm Produces as Raw Materials	24.7	11.3	12.3
以非农产品为原料	Using Non-Farm Produces as Raw Materials	29.8	3.4	7.9
重工业	Heavy Industry	38.9	33.0	31.8
采掘工业	Mining and Quarrying	68.5	56.3	62.4
原料工业	Raw Materials Industry	14.7	8.2	6.6
加工工业	Manufacturing Industry	22.3	11.4	12.2
按企业规模分	**Grouped by Size of Enterprises**			
大型企业	Large	43.1	41.6	37.7
中型企业	Medium	28.1	17.1	18.9
小型企业	Small	26.5	10.0	11.3

注：本年度全员劳动生产率是用现价工业增加值计算(以下同)。

Main Indicators on Economic Efficiency of Industrial Enterprises above Designated Size

(%)

总资产贡献率 Ratio of Total Assets to Industrial Output Value	资本保值增值率 Ratio of Capital-hold and Rise	资产负债率 Assets Liability Ratio	流动资产周转次数(次/年) Number of Times of Annual TurnoverWorking Capitals (times/year)	成本费用利润率 Ratio of Profits to Industrial Cost	全员劳动生产率(元/人·年) Overall Labor Productivity (yuan/person-year)	工业经济效益综合指数 Comprehensive Index of Industry Economic Results
25.9	**131.2**	**50.6**	**2.8**	**25.6**	**259636.0**	**372.8**
26.1	131.0	50.5	2.8	25.8	261423.8	375.3
7.0	134.0	53.3	1.6	1.8	76154.3	125.3
7.7	139.0	49.8	1.7	1.5	73004.4	125.0
4.9	115.9	64.3	1.4	3.3	95043.9	133.0
4.9	153.4	63.1	1.5	2.4	109234.5	143.7
2.0	43.9	78.0	0.9	-4.2	63959.4	62.2
7.7	94.3	60.0	1.9	13.5	82600.3	171.8
14.2	151.3	64.9	1.8	6.3	68179.8	153.1
19.2	127.2	51.7	2.4	5.4	56867.9	156.9
11.3		108.1	1.4	6.9	114071.7	142.1
10.6	103.8	64.2	1.3	6.1	46724.5	120.2
8.0	218.1	84.5	1.0	25.1	31852.5	187.5
18.4	212.6	76.9	5.8	-1.5	69309.4	176.9
8.7	86.0	40.9	2.5	7.5	109192.5	170.5
24.9	76.9	50.7	2.2	14.4	89516.7	212.2
22.3	20.5	44.4	2.8	13.1	189200.0	262.0
20.3	145.8	40.1	2.0	19.6	48136.5	206.0
34.8	129.7	67.3	2.0	12.2	187653.6	284.6
25.5	193.9	61.5	2.9	3.7	44645.4	168.4
12.9	134.3	61.0	2.0	9.0	113920.1	189.2
11.1	137.7	62.4	2.2	7.0	114575.8	181.3
13.5	133.3	60.6	1.9	9.6	113725.9	191.9
40.5	126.0	44.3	4.5	45.2	821059.3	830.7
11.4	163.0	51.1	1.9	8.2	114307.7	186.7
8.9	152.4	62.2	1.9	2.8	43499.4	117.0
14.8	86.4	56.0	2.1	7.8	143714.8	199.6
10.7	135.9	57.0	2.0	5.7	110289.8	171.0
13.1	221.8	39.8	1.5	19.8	192900.0	285.2
8.8	106.7	53.9	1.6	5.8	85026.6	145.9
20.3	153.0	58.9	1.8	20.2	259101.1	334.7
28.8	129.1	49.4	3.2	29.9	319743.3	434.4
16.3	220.9	42.1	1.8	9.6	58974.6	174.3
11.3	131.7	61.0	1.6	6.6	82355.2	154.5
12.2	134.8	63.0	1.7	6.8	82188.9	156.6
3.8	115.4	41.3	1.3	3.2	85277.9	124.3
28.4	131.1	48.8	3.1	29.2	329609.9	436.8
49.8	129.3	42.0	3.5	95.1	564833.9	871.6
8.5	139.1	54.9	3.4	1.0	146892.9	186.0
8.7	115.2	55.4	1.5	9.5	109709.1	173.6
35.7	127.8	43.8	3.9	37.9	438037.5	555.9
16.4	150.0	57.7	2.0	12.0	135535.4	223.1
9.8	121.0	61.2	1.8	7.8	120612.9	179.2

Note: Overall labor Productivity is computed on current industrial added value(the same as below).

11-7 分行业规模以上工业企业主要经济效益指标

单位: %　　　　(2007 年)

行业	Sector	工业增加值率 Ratio of Value-Added to Gross Industrial Output Value	资金利税率 Ratio of Profits and Taxes to Capital	产值利税率 Ratio of Profits and Taxes to Industrial Output Value
煤炭开采和洗选业	Mining and Washing of Coal	52.4	13.6	20.8
石油和天然气开采业	Extraction of Petroleum and Natural Gas	70.6	59.0	65.3
#天然原油和天然气开采	Extraction of Ores Crude Oil and Natural Gas Extraction	78.0	71.4	74.2
黑色金属矿采选业	Processing of Ferrous Metals Ores	31.9	37.2	33.9
有色金属矿采选业	Processing of Nonferrous Metals Ores	69.4	90.0	69.2
非金属矿采选业	Processing of Nonmetal Ores	36.3	16.7	18.0
#采　盐	Extraction of Salt	29.9	37.5	20.4
农副食品加工业	Processing of Food from Agricultural Products	18.4	9.4	7.5
#谷物磨制	Grain Grinding	12.0	5.0	3.1
饲料加工	Fodder Processing	16.0	7.2	4.6
制　糖	Sugar Making	24.0	23.0	20.7
食品制造业	Manufacture of Food	24.1	7.9	10.9
#罐头制造	Manufacture of can	27.3	5.1	9.4
饮料制造业	Manufacture of Beverage	39.5	12.7	20.4
#酒的制造	Manufacture of Wine	43.0	12.6	22.2
烟草制品业	Manufacture of Tobacco	60.4	71.9	61.0
纺织业	Manufacture of Textile	22.7	6.8	8.2
#棉、化纤纺织及印染精加工	Cotton, Chemical Fiber, Dyeing, Printing and Processing	22.3	7.4	8.8
毛纺织和染整精加工	Wool Textile, Dyeing and Printing	23.6	2.5	5.2
纺织服装、鞋、帽制造业	Manufacture of Textile Wearing Apparel,Footware and Caps	25.2	7.9	6.0
皮革、毛皮、羽毛(绒)及其制品业	Leather, Fur, Feather and Related Products Manufacturing	22.7	5.3	5.2
#皮革鞣制加工	Leather Tanning and Processing	22.4	5.3	5.2
皮革制品制造	Manufacture of Leather Products	34.9	5.4	5.9
木材加工及木、竹、藤、棕、草制品业	Processing of Timber, Wood, Bamboo, Cane, Grass Products	21.5	8.3	5.3
家具制造业	Manufacture of Furniture	17.2	4.7	5.6
造纸及纸制品业	Manufacture of Paper and Paper Products	24.0	5.4	7.3
印刷业和记录媒介的复制	Printing and Copying of Medium for Record	30.9	9.4	12.2
石油加工、炼焦及核燃料加工业	Oil Processing, Coking and Nuclear Fuel Processing	5.8	5.2	2.0
#炼　焦	Coking	31.6	20.2	20.5
化学原料及化学制品制造业	Raw Chemical Material and Chemical Products	26.5	13.8	17.2
#基础化学原料制造	Basic Chemical Material	24.8	12.8	18.3
肥料制造	Fertilizer Making	35.9	14.5	21.7
医药制造业	Manufacture of Medicine	33.5	14.5	19.1
化学纤维制造业	Manufacture of Chemical Fiber	28.7	36.9	26.2
橡胶制品业	Manufacture of Rubber Products	16.8	5.6	3.9
塑料制品业	Manufacture of Plastic Products	22.0	6.4	9.3
非金属矿物制品业	Manufacture of Nonmetal Mineral Products	27.9	9.7	13.4
#水泥制造	Manufacture of Cement	31.6	8.9	15.0
黑色金属冶炼及压延加工业	Smelting and Pressing of Ferrous Metals	16.9	15.6	10.6
有色金属冶炼及压延加工业	Smelting and Pressing of Nonferrous Metals	21.5	37.9	14.0
金属制品业	Manufacture of Metal Products	15.0	7.6	4.9
通用设备制造业	Manufacture of General Purpose Machinery	25.6	9.2	9.5
专用设备制造业	Manufacture of Special Purpose Machinery	23.4	10.3	14.5
交通运输设备制造业	Manufacture of Transport Equipment	7.6	2.2	1.4
电气机械及器材制造业	Manufacture of Electric Equipment and Machinery	20.9	18.3	14.0
通信设备、计算机及其他电子设备制造业	Telecom Equipment, Computer and Other Electronic Equipment	27.9	14.5	15.6
仪器仪表及文化、办公用机械制造业	Measuring Instruments and Machinery for Cultural Activify and Office Work	20.8	22.6	30.0
工艺品及其他制造业	Art work and Other Manufacturing Sector	32.3	26.4	18.9
电力、热力的生产和供应业	Electricity and Thermal Production and Supply	36.4	4.4	10.0
#电力生产和电力供应	Electricity Production and Supply	37.2	4.8	10.5
燃气生产和供应业	Gas Production and Supply	26.9	7.7	21.1
水的生产和供应业	Water Production and Supply	58.3	-0.8	-6.6

Main Indicators on Economic Efficiency of Industrial Enterprises above Designated Size by Sectors

(%)

总资产贡献率 Ratio of Total Assets to Industrial Output Value	资本保值增值率 Ratio of Capital Hold and Rise	资产负债率 Assets Liability Ratio	流动资产周转次数(次/年) Number of Times of Annual Turnover Working Capitals (times/year)	成本费用利润率 Ratio of Profits to Industrial Cost	全员劳动生产率(元/人·年) Overall Labor Productivity (yuan/person-year)	工业经济效益综合指数 Comprehensive Index of Industry Economic Results
10.5	143.5	49.8	1.3	10.8	68566.0	161.9
53.2	126.0	41.3	4.1	104.5	828452.9	1078.6
64.4	122.9	41.2	6.9	169.7	1962408.2	2059.8
28.4	186.1	48.7	1.8	32.1	205635.3	366.7
70.2	183.2	36.6	2.0	131.6	435879.1	962.2
13.6	99.2	47.9	1.2	12.6	65723.3	163.1
23.7	136.8	47.5	3.1	11.5	48181.8	192.1
10.0	123.7	67.5	1.9	5.4	122520.2	171.0
5.6	110.3	56.4	2.6	2.5	99958.4	145.7
8.3	109.7	47.9	2.9	3.3	129566.4	175.2
20.3	150.8	62.3	1.9	14.0	88850.1	207.0
10.2	136.9	63.2	1.4	7.7	128626.2	182.5
8.6	125.0	72.9	1.0	6.3	193743.1	205.5
12.4	73.9	74.0	1.0	7.6	147586.1	181.3
12.2	65.3	79.0	0.8	6.8	144485.1	171.6
64.8	113.4	44.7	2.1	21.3	1881877.6	1403.8
8.5	185.0	64.4	1.7	4.1	41561.9	121.7
9.4	210.1	66.2	1.8	4.5	42349.7	129.2
2.2	101.3	53.0	1.2	0.3	25407.4	73.8
7.6	113.2	70.7	2.1	3.6	34523.7	106.2
6.3	95.3	47.4	1.0	3.1	127326.0	144.3
6.3	95.4	46.5	1.0	3.2	141106.1	153.1
4.2	87.3	76.9	1.0	0.1	35415.1	72.0
9.0	114.3	54.7	2.1	2.7	90099.0	142.9
3.6	138.4	24.3	1.7	4.6	74495.7	130.0
6.0	81.1	62.9	1.5	1.7	59875.0	103.5
9.1	112.2	47.1	1.8	7.3	57765.4	138.0
3.7	121.5	36.7	5.5	-2.9	155027.5	185.4
19.3	110.8	59.6	1.7	20.6	179273.2	278.1
13.2	177.7	54.3	2.2	10.0	138910.9	217.0
16.5	290.2	52.7	2.2	8.4	117498.3	219.1
9.4	77.9	60.2	1.8	21.1	171116.6	253.7
13.7	123.9	51.1	1.2	16.4	109631.6	206.4
41.2	250.5	57.1	2.4	24.4	185227.1	364.8
4.9		165.8	2.9	-2.4	70982.1	85.0
4.7	76.2	46.6	1.2	5.6	67774.7	117.2
8.4	117.8	52.0	1.3	7.8	87347.2	151.9
8.8	124.2	57.7	1.2	6.7	78257.9	142.7
16.8	142.7	61.5	3.3	6.4	198526.2	252.4
26.8	136.6	55.5	4.2	11.3	180028.0	286.8
6.6	174.2	48.6	2.2	2.3	65498.7	130.9
7.6	73.5	63.0	1.3	4.4	72490.4	123.5
9.3	133.6	85.4	1.1	9.1	54216.5	130.9
1.7	116.6	72.8	2.2		31310.6	81.5
12.1	188.0	55.0	1.7	12.9	364992.3	358.8
15.0	115.4	55.9	2.1	12.1	161974.7	232.7
20.8	139.9	38.0	1.0	25.3	81885.8	239.5
22.6	126.4	24.8	2.7	22.3	185335.6	307.8
6.9	144.2	69.8	2.0	1.1	146257.1	167.5
7.4	155.5	70.4	2.2	1.2	158568.5	179.5
10.5	247.1	72.3	0.7	17.9	127568.4	223.5
-0.3	119.7	24.8	1.1	-9.7	66616.2	55.0

11-8 各地、州、市、县(市)规模以上工业企业主要经济效益指标

单位: %

(2007 年)

地 区	Region	工业增加值率 Ratio of Value Added to Gross Industrial Output Value	资金利税率 Ratio of Profits and Taxes to Capital	产值利税率 Ratio of Profits And Taxes to Industrial Output Value
总 计	**Total**	**37.0**	**29.5**	**29.2**
乌鲁木齐市	**Urumqi City**	**23.8**	**17.3**	**15.7**
#乌鲁木齐县	Urumqi County	56.9	4.9	26.6
克拉玛依市	**Karamay City**	**43.9**	**44.4**	**36.9**
石河子市	**Shihezi City**	**24.5**	**8.1**	**16.0**
阿拉尔市	**Aral City**	**27.0**	**5.3**	**7.3**
图木舒克市	**Tumxuk City**	**17.6**	**2.7**	**4.4**
五家渠市	**Wujiaqu City**	**19.2**	**6.8**	**8.8**
吐鲁番地区	**Turpan Administrative Offices**	**46.8**	**36.2**	**38.7**
吐鲁番市	Turpan City	24.3	16.1	14.0
鄯善县	Shanshan [Piqan] County	50.4	41.2	44.1
托克逊县	Toksun County	41.3	8.3	12.4
哈密地区	**Hami [Kumul] Administrative Offices**	**35.8**	**17.5**	**23.0**
哈密市	Hami [Kumul] City	35.3	17.0	22.9
巴里坤哈萨克自治县	Barkol Kazak Autonomous County	34.7	12.5	11.7
伊吾县	Yiwu [Araturuk] County	56.1	51.7	53.7
昌吉回族自治州	**Changji Hui Autonomous Prefecture**	**26.0**	**10.4**	**10.2**
昌吉市	Changji City	23.1	4.8	5.4
阜康市	Fukang City	29.0	28.6	18.2
呼图壁县	Hutubi County	23.4	4.2	3.9
玛纳斯县	Manas County	33.7	21.9	20.6
奇台县	Qitai County	19.3	12.6	8.1
吉木萨尔县	Jimsar County	29.5	4.9	6.2
木垒哈萨克自治县	Mori Kazak Autonomous County	22.6	8.9	11.9
伊犁哈萨克自治州	**Ili Kazak Autonomous Prefecture**	**40.2**	**21.2**	**27.0**
伊犁州直属县(市)	**Counties (Cities) Direct Under Ili Prefecture**	**36.7**	**14.9**	**23.4**
伊宁市	Yining [Gulja] City	30.4	6.4	9.0
奎屯市	Kuytun City	41.5	24.8	33.5
伊宁县	Yining [Gulja] County	33.9	16.3	19.4
察布查尔锡伯自治县	Qapqal Xibe Autonomous County	24.2	0.8	1.0
霍城县	Huocheng [Korgas] County	25.3	14.4	14.8
巩留县	Gongliu [Tokkuztara] County	39.0	1.8	14.4
新源县	Xinyuan [Kunes] County	44.6	31.7	35.8
昭苏县	Zhaosu [Mongolkure] County	22.4	7.2	4.9
特克斯县	Tekes County	43.9	26.4	13.7
尼勒克县	Nilka County	50.6	7.8	36.8

Main Indicators on Economic Benefit of Industrial Enterprises above Designated Size By Prefecture, Autonomous Prefecture, City and County

(%)

总资产贡献率 Ratio of Total Assets to Industrial Output Value	资本保值增值率 Ratio of Capital Hold And Rise	资产负债率 Assets Liability Ratio	流动资产周转次数(次/年) Number of Times of Annual Turnover Working Capitals (times/year)	成本费用利润率 Ratio of Profits to Industrial Cost	全员劳动生产率(元/人·年) Overall Labor Productivity (yuan/person-year)	工业经济效益综合指数 Comprehensive Index of Industry and Economic Results
25.9	**131.2**	**50.6**	**2.8**	**25.6**	**259636.0**	**372.8**
16.4	**135.5**	**44.3**	**2.8**	**10.0**	**183612.3**	**251.1**
6.1	600.6	68.6	0.6	24.2	423415.8	466.9
34.6	**118.2**	**41.5**	**3.8**	**34.3**	**449623.9**	**545.4**
10.3	**200.5**	**60.3**	**1.5**	**8.7**	**96822.7**	**177.0**
7.5	**202.8**	**66.9**	**1.1**	**4.2**	**125851.1**	**165.2**
4.5	**94.5**	**71.6**	**1.0**	**3.9**	**67899.4**	**105.4**
6.2	**133.2**	**70.6**	**1.3**	**6.8**	**70835.6**	**132.7**
38.6	**202.6**	**50.0**	**3.1**	**42.3**	**364097.4**	**535.2**
15.2	118.9	61.0	2.4	8.0	94197.5	180.5
45.0	219.5	46.8	3.3	51.0	480584.0	654.9
11.6	183.9	70.2	1.8	11.6	195023.1	247.8
15.5	**139.9**	**55.7**	**1.4**	**17.8**	**100035.8**	**214.4**
15.0	140.4	56.0	1.4	17.6	99816.9	212.5
12.4	162.7	67.1	1.6	4.1	61793.0	136.8
48.6	113.6	14.7	1.0	77.8	1015215.1	1051.1
9.3	**94.6**	**67.5**	**2.0**	**6.1**	**132660.6**	**176.0**
5.9	102.6	70.5	1.8	1.7	136037.4	153.1
19.8	109.0	60.1	2.7	15.8	137854.2	246.7
5.7	192.4	60.9	1.7	1.6	93193.6	138.5
21.9	168.4	67.1	2.8	15.4	173629.5	278.4
10.0	167.1	57.9	2.2	5.4	96080.5	166.4
5.4	219.4	74.6	1.4	3.3	81987.2	134.7
8.9	247.8	59.7	1.5	6.2	87950.7	166.0
19.7	**139.7**	**62.5**	**1.8**	**20.2**	**144653.3**	**261.7**
14.1	**127.3**	**62.9**	**1.6**	**10.9**	**124622.7**	**200.3**
8.1	101.5	72.3	1.8	2.8	73605.9	122.4
23.5	115.4	61.4	1.7	6.6	209396.1	253.6
15.8	145.1	53.1	2.2	15.4	84550.0	204.6
2.8	217.3	50.7	1.6	-2.2	66383.7	105.9
13.8	132.2	56.2	2.0	9.8	84313.7	176.7
2.0	143.7	66.4	0.4	5.9	109879.9	138.7
28.4	121.9	49.4	1.6	25.2	158245.4	300.6
8.4	156.1	73.8	1.9	4.4	139379.5	177.0
27.5	191.3	68.8	2.7	13.0	129944.9	252.3
11.9	133.1	76.9	2.0	25.7	247161.8	327.0

11-8 续表 1

单位: %

地　　区	Region	工业增加值率 Ratio of Value Added to Gross Industrial Output Value	资金利税率 Ratio of Profits and Taxes to Capital	产值利税率 Ratio of Profits and Taxes to Industrial Output Value
塔城地区	**Tacheng [Tarbagatai] Administrative Offices**	**32.1**	**11.8**	**11.5**
塔城市	Tacheng [Qoqek] City	32.0	0.6	1.1
乌苏市	Usu City	34.0	13.4	12.5
额敏县	Emin [Dorbiljin] County	22.6	11.1	13.3
沙湾县	Shawan County	28.8	16.2	11.9
托里县	Toli County	45.2	13.0	11.2
裕民县	Yumin [Qagantokay] County	40.7	1.0	0.3
和布克赛尔蒙古自治县	Hoboksar Mongol Autonomous County	40.0	8.4	12.0
阿勒泰地区	**Altay Administrative Offices**	**57.5**	**55.4**	**54.2**
阿勒泰市	Altay City	29.6	8.0	12.3
布尔津县	Burqin County	32.6	10.3	19.6
富蕴县	Fuyun [Koktokay] County	52.3	64.2	53.5
福海县	Fuhai [Burultokay] County	34.9	5.3	12.2
哈巴河县	Habahe [Kaba] County	81.5	107.2	81.0
青河县	Qinghe [Qinggil] County	29.4	14.0	6.4
吉木乃县	Jeminay County	33.3	7.7	7.1
博尔塔拉蒙古自治州	**Bortala Mongol Autonomous Prefecture**	**22.7**	**5.7**	**7.1**
博乐市	Bole [Bortala] City	22.5	5.4	7.0
精河县	Jinghe [Jing] County	26.2	10.1	10.1
温泉县	Wenquan [Araxang] County	17.9	0.5	0.4
巴音郭楞蒙古自治州	**Bayangol Mongol Autonomous Prefecture**	**60.2**	**59.4**	**61.4**
库尔勒市	Korla City	64.6	66.7	69.6
轮台县	Luntai [Bugur] County	36.8	10.3	5.6
尉犁县	Yuli [Lopnur] County	25.2	12.8	12.0
若羌县	Ruoqiang [Qarkilik] County	43.1	13.4	29.6
且末县	Qiemo [Qarqan] County	45.1	-1.0	-3.4
焉耆回族自治县	Yanqi Hui Autonomous County	25.1	8.4	12.8
和静县	Hejing County	28.9	14.1	15.8
和硕县	Hoxud County	32.6	7.7	8.6
博湖县	Bohu [Bagrax] County	23.1	4.7	5.7
阿克苏地区	**Aksu Administrative Offices**	**23.0**	**15.0**	**13.8**
阿克苏市	Aksu City	29.0	7.6	11.0
温宿县	Wensu [Onsu] County	46.4	34.2	30.3
库车县	Kuqa County	16.7	21.3	14.4

Continued

(%)

总资产贡献率 Ratio of Total Assets to Industrial Output Value	资本保值增值率 Ratio of Capital Hold and Rise	资产负债率 Assets Liability Ratio	流动资产周转次数（次/年） Number of Times of Annual Turnover of Circulating Funds (times/year)	成本费用利润率 Ratio of Profits to Industrial Cost	全员劳动生产率（元/人·年） Overall Labor Productivity (yuan/person-year)	工业经济效益综合指数 Comprehensive Index of Industry Economic Results
13.0	**140.3**	**74.2**	**2.0**	**8.5**	**97639.3**	**173.8**
4.4		135.3	1.7	-6.9	79239.1	60.5
14.9	125.4	74.3	1.6	10.4	134746.3	203.0
12.0	113.0	69.8	1.5	8.6	94719.4	164.1
17.7	146.4	71.7	2.7	9.5	131363.0	215.4
12.7	194.4	56.4	2.0	12.7	87334.0	193.2
1.1	134.2	22.5	2.5	0.5	443044.4	336.1
8.6	120.4	60.3	1.6	5.0	43058.6	117.9
46.6	**183.4**	**48.3**	**2.2**	**71.8**	**321343.7**	**624.8**
9.2	160.3	80.2	2.6	5.6	82197.4	154.3
11.7	103.5	44.3	2.1	11.5	101584.6	187.2
48.0	298.5	34.3	2.0	61.0	295008.1	583.7
5.4	154.8	29.0	1.3	1.8	97908.3	135.6
91.2	105.7	54.3	2.6	247.6	1306012.3	1963.0
14.2	121.3	90.3	3.5	2.1	121529.9	177.2
7.7	127.0	69.3	1.3	-0.5	40003.6	88.0
6.2	**165.5**	**70.2**	**1.6**	**1.7**	**52881.0**	**109.8**
6.0	175.1	70.2	1.7	1.3	52393.6	109.2
10.6	82.9	70.6	1.2	6.8	53554.7	123.6
1.8	100.0	67.4	1.1	0.7	109571.4	116.6
50.6	**123.5**	**54.6**	**3.7**	**103.4**	**718318.0**	**998.5**
57.9	121.9	52.3	4.6	132.8	1035282.4	1323.8
10.2	120.8	50.0	2.6	4.2	631399.7	481.0
13.2	115.9	73.8	1.6	8.8	88599.2	164.3
4.8	103.4	75.7	0.6	30.3	74988.6	209.5
-0.4		101.9	1.3	-9.8	62744.7	26.7
9.8	120.3	66.9	1.6	8.1	90216.7	157.3
13.3	239.3	56.5	1.4	12.0	95838.1	198.9
7.7	120.2	56.8	1.6	3.9	90728.7	143.2
8.6		100.6	1.8	3.9	129425.3	140.2
14.6	**135.0**	**54.0**	**2.9**	**9.0**	**142820.1**	**219.3**
7.2	115.8	57.2	1.4	5.4	88664.8	142.2
28.2	155.4	58.8	2.0	24.5	83671.9	261.6
22.7	168.9	47.0	6.7	9.7	363086.6	412.9

11-8 续表 2

单位: %

地　　区	Region	工业增加值率 Ratio of Value Added to Gross Industrial Output Value	资金利税率 Ratio of Profits and Taxes to Capital	产值利税率 Ratio of Profits and Taxes to Industrial Output Value
沙雅县	Xayar County	24.5	6.5	4.3
新和县	Xinhe [Toksu] County	23.2	4.3	5.4
拜城县	Baicheng [Bay] County	47.2	18.6	23.2
乌什县	Wushi [Uxturpan] County	63.5	16.4	20.6
阿瓦提县	Awat County	21.5	-4.0	-4.9
柯坪县	Kalpin County			
克孜勒苏柯尔克孜自治州	**Kizilsu Kirgiz Autonomous Prefecture**	**29.6**	**41.7**	**35.8**
阿图什市	Artux City	24.7	18.7	18.0
阿克陶县	Akto County	35.2	57.1	42.4
阿合奇县	Akqi County			
乌恰县	Wuqia [Ulugqat] County	34.6	111.4	83.5
喀什地区	**Kashgar [Kaxgar] Administrative Offices**	**31.0**	**3.7**	**4.6**
喀什市	Kashgar [Kaxgar] City	31.8	3.1	4.8
疏附县	Shufu County	38.1	1.3	4.8
疏勒县	Shule County	34.4	8.2	6.9
英吉沙县	Yengisar County	40.6	6.4	7.5
泽普县	Zepu [Poskam] County	26.7	18.5	12.4
莎车县	Shache [Yarkant] County	28.3	2.3	1.5
叶城县	Yecheng [Kagilik] County	39.5	10.0	4.2
麦盖提县	Makit County	18.6	3.8	4.7
岳普湖县	Yopurga County	24.2	7.1	2.8
伽师县	Jiashi [Payzawat] County	27.9	1.8	0.3
巴楚县	Bachu [Maralbexi] County	32.6	1.8	1.6
塔什库尔干塔吉克自治县	Taxkorgan Tajik Autonomous County			
和田地区	**Hotan Administrative Offices**	**36.8**	**2.3**	**7.6**
和田市	Hotan City	32.3	0.5	1.8
和田县	Hotan County	60.3	2.7	17.2
墨玉县	Moyu [Karakax] County	17.0	12.8	16.3
皮山县	Pishan [Guma] County	35.5	12.3	11.1
洛浦县	Lop County	30.0	16.1	14.3
策勒县	Qira County			
于田县	Yutian [Keriya] County			
民丰县	Minfeng [Niya] County			

Continued

(%)

总资产贡献率 Ratio of Total Assets to Industrial Output Value	资本保值增值率 Ratio of Capital Hold and Rise	资产负债率 Assets Liability Ratio	流动资产周转次数（次/年） Number of Times of Annual Turnover Working Capitals (times/year)	成本费用利润率 Ratio of Profits to Industrial Cost	全员劳动生产率（元/人·年） Overall Labor Productivity (yuan/person-year)	工业经济效益综合指数 Comprehensive Index of Industry Economic Results
5.4	153.2	64.9	1.9	3.2	124168.1	159.8
8.4	98.0	67.1	0.9	4.1	163321.8	175.8
17.9	104.7	58.3	1.9	20.9	113878.3	237.5
17.5	124.0	48.8	1.1	20.7	135000.0	244.4
-0.6	89.6	77.8	1.3	-6.2	84272.1	69.4
33.1	**207.1**	**47.4**	**2.0**	**35.8**	**82149.8**	**318.0**
17.4	137.2	38.2	1.3	22.0	122872.2	243.3
34.7	299.5	63.5	3.2	40.1	60354.0	347.8
94.6	120.0	24.5	3.0	53.6	77778.5	497.5
6.6	**130.0**	**87.3**	**2.1**	**-1.0**	**104793.3**	**126.8**
6.9	154.1	91.8	2.2	-2.3	114031.3	131.1
4.4	7.2	97.3	0.8	-5.6	11862.5	16.4
7.1	87.6	61.0	1.6	6.6	62070.5	124.2
8.0	567.7	77.4	2.0	1.5	90459.2	188.5
10.7	63.1	60.5	3.3	7.1	127281.0	193.5
3.0	98.2	71.1	4.2	-2.6	93424.7	129.6
9.9	113.3	76.0	2.2	4.0	109932.7	158.2
6.5	742.9	73.7	1.3	4.1	80409.8	204.2
7.2	127.5	66.7	1.9	3.7	183170.7	196.1
1.0	49.8	59.1	6.5	-8.7	119323.9	136.8
2.0	195.8	90.9	1.6	1.1	227705.3	201.2
3.7	**202.2**	**61.4**	**1.0**	**-2.0**	**53359.4**	**93.0**
2.8	36.3	98.7	0.9	-6.9	46906.0	35.9
2.7	246.8	11.5	0.7	7.7	101128.5	160.6
10.6	63.8	54.2	1.6	-3.0	24430.0	74.0
10.6		103.3	1.7	-0.7	23284.6	62.0
16.3	97.3	52.2	1.4	8.2	64169.3	151.4

11-9 国有及国有控股工业企业主要经济指标

单位: 万元 (2007 年)

项目	Item	企业单位数(个) Number of Enterprises (unit)	#亏损企业 Loss- Suffering Enterprises	工业总产值(当年价格) Gross Industrial Output Value (At Current Prices)
总计	**Total**	**451**	**116**	**26377945.0**
按登记注册类型分	**Grouped by Registry Type**			
内资企业	DomesticFunded Enterprises	447	113	26363358.0
国有企业	State-owned Enterprises	147	47	3503608.5
#中央企业	Central Enterprises	57	17	2972157.8
地方企业	Local Enterprises	90	30	531450.7
#自治区属企业	Autonomous	33	9	335306.6
地区(州、市)属企业	Prefecture or City	19	9	62192.1
县(市)属企业	County or City	32	11	93029.6
联营企业	Joint Ownership Enterprises	1		6981.4
#国有联营企业	State Joint Enterprises Ownership	1		6981.4
国有与集体联营企业	Joint State-collective OwnershipEnterprises			
有限责任公司	Limited Liability Corporations	254	57	4431767.1
#国有独资公司	Sole State-funded Corporations	53	15	1670056.3
其他有限责任公司	Other Limited Liability Corporations	201	42	2761710.8
股份有限公司	Share-holding Corporations Ltd.	45	9	18421001.0
港、澳、台商投资企业	Enterprises with Funds from Hong Kong, Macao and Taiwan	2	1	5806.4
外商投资企业	Foreign Funded Enterprises	2	2	8780.6
在总计中: 国有控股企业	Of the Total : State-owned and State-holding Enterprises	451	116	26377945.0
按轻、重工业分	**Grouped by Light & Heavy Industry**			
轻工业	Light Industry	145	38	1952162.4
以农产品为原料	Using Farm Produces as Raw Materials	123	30	1899858.5
以非农产品为原料	Using Non-Farm Produces as Raw Materials	22	8	52303.9
重工业	Heavy Industry	306	78	24425782.6
采掘工业	Mining and Quarrying	66	3	12050965.8
原料工业	Raw Material Industry	165	61	11542096.9
加工工业	Manufacturing Industry	75	14	832719.9
按企业规模分	**Grouped by Size of Enterprises**			
大型企业	Large	25	7	19976716.8
中型企业	Medium	136	34	5005438.0
小型企业	Small	290	75	1395790.2

Main Economic Indicators Efficiency of State-owned and State-holding Industrial Enterprises

(10 000 yuan)

工业增加值 Added Value of Industry	工业销售产值(当年价) Sales Value of Industry Products (At Current Prices)	出口交货值 Delivery Value of Industry Export	实收资本 Total Capital Hold	资产合计 Total Assets	流动资产合计 Total Working Capitals	#产成品 Finished Product	流动资产年平均余额 Annual Average Balance of Circulating Funds	固定资产原价 Original Value of Fixed Assets
12024331.8	**26454423.5**	**369483.8**	**14826419.5**	**34883239.0**	**10043920.9**	**804248.3**	**8934379.8**	**32342450.9**
12021787.6	26440770.6	367851.5	14780238.4	34750864.1	10010758.1	800503.5	8901853.4	32257354.1
1158040.2	3487252.1	46939.3	2824202.5	6957611.0	2880715.4	172806.4	2607743.6	4795406.9
951481.2	2952931.2	24108.3	2319097.0	5275686.1	2406820.9	142453.5	2209170.1	3556205.2
206559.0	534320.9	22831.0	505105.5	1681924.9	473894.5	30352.9	398573.5	1239201.7
134631.5	336522.1	3398.5	366001.0	1101331.4	287400.4	8519.0	252536.9	794338.5
20492.6	62823.1		48703.8	221985.4	72689.2	10724.2	65215.4	206678.5
42010.5	90873.3		68698.7	243227.2	71851.9	9744.7	51008.9	201954.0
1797.4	6981.4		1720.0	3704.2	3055.4	0.6	2807.9	1095.5
1797.4	6981.4		1720.0	3704.2	3055.4	0.6	2807.9	1095.5
1309961.8	4317531.2	125232.7	2139614.9	6989494.7	2273328.6	254132.1	2160731.9	5691709.5
493947.9	1630143.2	833.6	815307.4	2609643.3	769398.1	52625.6	750818.2	2274780.0
816013.9	2687388.0	124399.1	1324307.5	4379851.4	1503930.5	201506.5	1409913.7	3416929.5
9551988.2	18629005.9	195679.5	9814701.0	20800054.2	4853658.7	373564.4	4130570.0	21769142.2
774.1	5098.6		4400.0	9135.3	4714.3	2176.6	4339.6	6949.6
1770.1	8554.3	1632.3	41781.1	123239.6	28448.5	1568.2	28186.8	78147.2
12024331.8	26454423.5	369483.8	14826419.5	34883239.0	10043920.9	804248.3	8934379.8	32342450.9
623464.3	1899818.2	184508.3	963600.0	3239865.6	1589056.1	343781.1	1433677.4	2125881.9
596447.4	1848295.0	184376.9	743811.5	2921703.6	1539448.7	341901.6	1385028.8	1809761.2
27016.9	51523.2	131.4	219788.5	318162.0	49607.4	1879.5	48648.6	316120.7
11400867.5	24554605.3	184975.5	13862819.5	31643373.4	8454864.8	460467.2	7500702.4	30216569.0
9512932.3	12173821.4	875.6	8331138.3	16566568.6	3745108.9	92197.2	3499175.6	19022072.1
1663234.6	11586601.5	160992.4	4849959.2	13369795.7	4016281.0	271998.4	3342930.4	10342128.9
224700.6	794182.4	23107.5	681722.0	1707009.1	693474.9	96271.6	658596.4	852368.0
9906674.1	20171562.4	93426.1	11714788.5	23768849.0	6227683.9	325148.3	5476810.6	24452127.8
1679440.8	4912525.8	210912.0	2051048.8	7657349.5	2802654.3	339775.1	2579822.3	5453292.4
438216.9	1370335.3	65145.7	1060582.2	3457040.5	1013582.7	139324.9	877746.9	2437030.7

11-9 续表

单位: 万元

项　　目	Item	固定资产净值年平均余额 Annual Average Balance of Net Value of Fixed Assets	流动负债合计 Total Working Liabilities	长期负债合计 Long-term Liabilities	所有者权益合计 Creditors' Equities
总　　计	**Total**	**17731564.4**	**9659464.2**	**6913187.6**	**17663420.1**
按登记注册类型分	**By Status of Registration**				
内资企业	Domestic Funded Enterprises	17655549.4	9570861.1	6913187.6	17619648.3
国有企业	State-owned Enterprises	2844812.0	2586539.9	1066338.1	3247308.7
#中央企业	Central Enterprises	2063669.6	2140908.1	448301.3	2647408.9
地方企业	Local Enterprises	781142.4	445631.8	618036.8	599899.8
#自治区属企业	Autonomous	512324.1	238133.6	456993.3	406093.5
地区(州、市)属企业	Prefecture or City	132947.9	90589.8	73647.8	48941.8
县(市)属企业	County or City	115736.5	84063.1	52470.3	97254.3
联营企业	Joint Ownership Enterprises	345.9	1645.8		2058.4
#国有联营企业	State Joint Ownership Enterprises	345.9	1645.8		2058.4
国有与集体联营企业	Joint Statecollective Enterprises				
有限责任公司	Limited Liability Corporations	3559480.8	3096111.6	1111419.5	2680033.8
#国有独资公司	State Sole funded Corporations	1383948.0	1202623.7	422344.6	980212.5
其他有限责任公司	Other Limited Liability Corporations	2175532.8	1893487.9	689074.9	1699821.3
股份有限公司	Share-holding Corporations Ltd.	11250910.7	3886563.8	4735430.0	11690247.4
港、澳、台商投资企业	Enterprises with Funds from Hong Kong, Macao and Taiwan	1871.0	5122.0		4013.3
外商投资企业	Foreign Funded Enterprises	74144.0	83481.1		39758.5
在总计中: 国有控股企业	Of the Total : State-owned and State-holding Enterprises	17731564.4	9659464.2	6913187.6	17663420.1
按轻、重工业分	**Grouped by Light & Heavy Industry**				
轻工业	Light Industry	1342001.9	1646336.7	333022.1	1237808.2
以农产品为原料	Using Farm Produces as Raw Materials	1099131.3	1591189.9	311741.1	1000086.6
以非农产品为原料	Using Non-Farm Produces as Raw Materials	242870.6	55146.8	21281.0	237721.6
重工业	Heavy Industry	16389562.5	8013127.5	6580165.5	16425611.9
采掘工业	Mining and Quarrying	9834789.3	3270759.6	3138285.4	9670229.4
原料工业	Raw Material Industry	6045321.6	3944470.1	3237863.2	6066388.1
加工工业	Manufacturing Industry	509451.6	797897.8	204016.9	688994.4
按企业规模分	**Grouped by Size of Enterprises**				
大型企业	Large	12642839.1	5239025.7	4636086.3	13401784.0
中型企业	Medium	3375681.8	3159960.6	1351266.8	3029038.6
小型企业	Small	1713043.5	1260477.9	925834.5	1232597.5

Continued

(10 000 yuan)

主营业务收入 Revenue from Principal Business	#主营业务成本 Cost of Principal Business	主营业务税金及附加 Taes and Other Charges on Principal Business	营业利润 Business Profit	利润总额 Total Profit	亏损企业亏损总额 Losses Value of Loss-Suffering Enterprises	利税总额 Total Profits and Taxes	本年应交增值税 Value-added Taxes Payable	全部从业人员年平均人数(人) Annual Average Employed Persons (person)
28236850.8	**19016030.7**	**627637.2**	**6236763.8**	**6301862.1**	**533047.2**	**8718502.7**	**1789003.4**	**376062**
28224755.4	19004487.2	627637.2	6239469.3	6304482.1	530364.8	8720557.1	1788437.8	375485
4251733.8	3877538.0	81983.8	19261.4	74402.0	68127.5	373921.2	217535.4	152065
3686628.3	3415667.6	78464.2	3291.1	56277.6	45226.0	314745.7	180003.9	130332
565105.5	461870.4	3519.6	15970.3	18124.4	22901.5	59175.5	37531.5	21733
365061.1	307923.7	2398.8	7392.8	8528.4	15746.2	36193.2	25266.0	12325
61003.1	56182.9	332.7	-4049.3	-2714.9	4530.4	847.5	3229.7	3204
95688.5	63919.9	620.5	9599.8	11543.4	2624.7	19349.9	7186.0	5086
7981.7	3360.3	456.3	869.0	869.0		2150.5	825.2	95
7981.7	3360.3	456.3	869.0	869.0		2150.5	825.2	95
4453184.8	3655113.9	44403.9	287337.1	332399.2	74551.7	618050.9	241247.8	113319
1661299.8	1357117.2	27555.0	94816.5	108341.3	33963.7	223235.7	87339.4	43111
2791885.0	2297996.7	16848.9	192520.6	224057.9	40588.0	394815.2	153908.4	70208
19511855.1	11468475.0	500793.2	5932001.8	5896811.9	387685.6	7726434.5	1328829.4	110006
5255.3	4909.3		-302.3	-198.6	261.0	51.4	250.0	168
6840.1	6634.2		-2403.2	-2421.4	2421.4	-2105.8	315.6	409
28236850.8	19016030.7	627637.2	6236763.8	6301862.1	533047.2	8718502.7	1789003.4	376062
2139226.5	1665481.9	76639.5	146190.1	120425.4	36273.2	289425.0	92360.1	87015
2082854.4	1624072.7	76036.9	153297.6	124554.4	29641.1	289425.3	88834.0	82804
56372.1	41409.2	602.6	-7107.5	-4129.0	6632.1	-0.3	3526.1	4211
26097624.3	17350548.8	550997.7	6090573.7	6181436.7	496774.0	8429077.7	1696643.3	289047
12948054.3	5289047.9	308967.4	6103326.5	6131540.6	3430.9	7686781.3	1246273.3	149594
12308392.9	11377985.7	235959.1	-64845.9	-18645.1	480044.9	642943.3	425629.3	112502
841177.1	683515.2	6071.2	52093.1	68541.2	13298.2	99353.1	24740.7	26951
21318954.8	13621451.1	513654.1	5640635.6	5667863.5	426422.6	7569644.0	1388126.4	222084
5496391.5	4271854.4	104544.8	522794.5	529147.7	72100.9	963098.7	329406.2	114350
1421504.5	1122725.2	9438.3	73333.7	104850.9	34523.7	185760.0	71470.8	39628

11-10 分行业国有及国有控股工业企业主要经济指标

单位: 万元 (2007 年)

行业	Sector	企业单位数(个) Number of Enterprises (unit)	#亏损企业 Loss- Suffering Enterprises	工业总产值(当年价格) Gross Industrial Output Value (At Current Prices)
煤炭开采和洗选业	Mining and Washing of Coal	27	3	349413.5
石油和天然气开采业	Extraction of Petroleum and Natural Gas	8		11113064.2
#天然原油和天然气开采	Extraction of Ores Crude Oil and Natural Gas Extraction	5		9655956.2
黑色金属矿采选业	Processing of Ferrous Metals Ores	9		226695.0
有色金属矿采选业	Processing of Nonferrous Metals Ores	14		318653.7
非金属矿采选业	Processing of Nonmetal Ores	8		43139.4
#采　盐	Extraction of Salt	4		21538.2
农副食品加工业	Processing of Food from Agricultural Products	41	8	396831.7
#谷物磨制	Grain Grinding	10	2	46998.7
饲料加工	Fodder Processing	6	2	55820.0
制　糖	Sugar Making	11		204321.5
食品制造业	Manufacture of Food	23	3	274233.8
#罐头制造	Manufacture of can	11	1	185128.1
饮料制造业	Manufacture of Beverage	10	7	110922.1
#酒的制造	Manufacture of Wine	8	6	105134.7
烟草制品业	Manufacture of Tobacco	1		140912.3
纺织业	Manufacture of Textile	25	9	829457.6
#棉、化纤纺织及印染精加工	Cotton, Chemical Fiber, Dyeing, Printing and Processing	18	7	768678.9
毛纺织和染整精加工	Wool Textile, Dyeing and Printing	3	1	14148.3
纺织服装、鞋、帽制造业	Manufacture of Textile Wearing Apparel,Footware and Caps	3		9066.3
木材加工及木、竹、藤、棕、草制品业	Processing of Timber, Wood, Bamboo, Cane, Grass Products	1	1	2768.3
造纸及纸制品业	Manufacture of Paper and Paper Products	7	3	76722.2
印刷业和记录媒介的复制	Printing and Copying of Medium for Record	10		25885.0
石油加工、炼焦及核燃料加工业	Oil Processing, Coking and Nuclear Fuel Processing	10	2	6604262.8
#炼 焦	Coking	2		38780.2
化学原料及化学制品制造业	Raw Chemical Material and Chemical Products	29	7	1014043.8
#基础化学原料制造	Basic Chemical Material	13	6	523968.9
肥料制造	Fertilizer Making	6		170763.5
医药制造业	Manufacture of Medicine	6	2	37850.5
化学纤维制造业	Manufacture of Chemical Fiber	1		11897.9
橡胶制品业	Manufacture of Rubber Products	2	1	55308.6
塑料制品业	Manufacture of Plastic Products	18	5	157346.6
非金属矿物制品业	Manufacture of Nonmetal Mineral Products	45	7	434687.8
#水泥制造	Manufacture of Cement	28	6	273959.8
黑色金属冶炼及压延加工业	Smelting and Pressing of Ferrous Metals	8	1	1891852.7
有色金属冶炼及压延加工业	Smelting and Pressing of Nonferrous Metals	6	2	223451.8
金属制品业	Manufacture of Metal Products	4	2	57575.7
通用设备制造业	Manufacture of General Purpose Machinery	3		3815.5
专用设备制造业	Manufacture of Special Purpose Machinery	8	1	38536.2
交通运输设备制造业	Manufacture of Transport Equipment	7	2	85513.3
电气机械及器材制造业	Manufacture of Electric Equipment and Machinery	4	1	23205.2
仪器仪表及文化、办公用机械制造业	Measuring Instruments and Machinery for Cultural Activify and Office Work	2		5998.6
电力、热力的生产和供应业	Electric Power and Thermal Production and Supply	92	42	1724922.3
#电力生产和电力供应	Electric Power Production and Supply	65	30	1644525.4
燃气生产和供应业	Gas Production and Supply	3		57938.2
水的生产和供应业	Water Production and Supply	16	7	31972.4

Main Economic Indicators of State-owned and State-holding Industrial Enterprises by Sectors

(10 000 yuan)

工业增加值 Added Value of Industry	工业销售产值(当年价) Sales Value of Industry Products (At Current Prices)	出口交货值 Delivery Value of Industry Export	实收资本 Total Capital Hold	资产合计 Total Assets	流动资产合计 Circulating Funds	#产成品 Finished Product	流动资产年平均余额 Annual Average Balance of Circulating Funds	固定资产原价 Original Value of Fixed Assets
214195.3	459162.1		414887.8	959127.0	355085.3	12388.4	312730.6	540453.0
8936947.3	11135542.8	448.0	7775946.0	14961333.3	3094578.6	38598.9	2924898.8	18227079.9
8467757.5	9686204.8		6288818.0	12079336.7	1454800.1	34190.1	1457055.1	16613556.2
75614.5	207943.5		77644.3	300278.5	155726.8	30817.8	128539.4	116369.8
269476.1	329044.3		51014.4	299060.1	113986.3	6393.9	111315.8	114026.8
16699.1	42128.7	427.6	11645.8	46769.7	25731.9	3998.2	21691.0	24142.6
7367.0	22048.0	427.6	2376.0	17207.1	8950.8	2430.8	6030.6	9210.7
89262.3	373137.7		100046.9	469952.8	285646.4	88510.4	227729.3	244330.5
5698.9	46091.4		13642.8	47047.5	27744.1	3637.6	21752.2	18429.3
10571.9	57438.2		13311.9	72651.7	37459.8	3043.7	37032.2	39579.1
56897.2	191867.3		45633.4	229065.5	140405.0	68890.2	107016.1	139245.2
82968.4	273386.2	142225.6	101415.4	543170.9	294749.2	59471.7	272132.7	317863.3
58745.1	186499.3	132908.8	66908.2	429853.2	251682.5	52627.6	237859.7	241232.7
55416.2	109537.8		109002.3	349279.4	190737.4	9557.7	175142.7	184741.6
53941.1	102488.0		103982.2	338512.5	185230.4	8109.2	172176.8	178156.5
99927.7	143756.5		18741.7	141073.0	65135.6		68318.8	83494.0
215025.4	809144.4	40366.2	340327.3	1137119.2	576455.8	167956.7	523980.7	776539.1
194305.9	748315.5	16081.2	284248.7	1033742.4	517225.1	151929.1	465856.1	707512.4
3877.5	17543.7	4982.0	14302.3	32372.3	15136.1	6320.7	15207.4	19443.3
2515.3	8853.2	152.8	2413.2	8347.5	6099.8	161.8	4606.2	4248.5
498.3	2820.6		27.1	4563.9	1724.3	537.6	1798.8	5288.6
23316.3	77154.9		47912.5	166418.6	61687.2	8036.0	58956.5	136632.9
10640.1	25858.1		14437.8	41747.9	13985.9	1069.4	13185.3	45882.3
285059.1	6625647.1		2834888.8	4501951.3	1513015.3	121362.6	1168098.2	3012218.8
5591.0	37844.8		18000.0	93730.7	31725.0	5106.1	26771.5	34985.9
290247.0	994471.5	84063.4	454029.9	2285074.5	725538.2	70145.7	570521.2	1065597.1
133080.8	516055.9	83757.3	136755.9	1139741.0	504000.7	37161.1	373600.8	501667.9
72720.8	167048.6		120384.7	514642.3	119310.1	1922.4	89773.1	230195.4
17722.4	33688.0	1763.7	20310.1	63377.9	32791.6	8695.3	29678.5	29115.5
5544.4	7857.3		800.0	32336.9	23680.0		23680.0	8618.0
10783.9	55192.4	1974.0	14264.2	47201.5	25124.6	8771.2	21085.8	36987.7
43311.3	136006.6		319794.5	436110.2	213074.6	46555.9	195845.9	286104.6
146140.7	433552.3	19432.5	221691.4	967217.5	419212.3	20641.7	402064.1	552198.5
99561.5	274214.2		162114.9	703220.9	282345.9	8307.2	268309.3	441730.1
317334.2	1937480.9	77235.1	359103.2	1479889.0	645925.0	68860.4	531519.2	1165426.2
55246.1	223635.1		35318.5	128883.6	57711.3	5138.4	43943.6	80150.7
5130.3	53131.6	823.0	47346.9	52260.5	12098.5	4928.1	10923.9	10446.1
971.6	3468.1		1187.9	8112.9	7200.3	3523.5	6865.8	3099.6
10758.1	37474.1		6292.7	72843.6	49314.6	6207.5	46636.8	32732.4
7641.4	89601.5	571.9	28458.5	75843.0	45596.6	9393.3	40279.2	31377.7
3406.3	24776.1		8861.4	16865.7	12165.2	2116.5	11678.0	8703.6
875.0	7355.2		1600.0	7162.4	5992.1	82.3	5564.4	1196.8
696653.1	1718038.7		1151498.8	4823265.3	920761.8	8.1	857699.7	4813473.5
671153.4	1638738.3		1047489.9	4484317.5	823843.2	8.1	766762.9	4482228.8
15196.7	43900.9		44334.2	168340.2	61939.2	319.3	93271.6	82946.9
19807.9	31675.3		211176.0	288261.2	31449.2		29997.3	300964.3

11-10 续表

单位: 万元

行 业	Sector	固定资产净值年平均余额 Annual Average Balance of Net Value of Fixed Assets	流动负债合计 Total Working Liabilities	长期负债合计 Long-term Liabilities	所有者权益合计 Creditors' Equities
煤炭开采和洗选业	Mining and Washing of Coal	308417.7	323773.3	139818.9	495534.5
石油和天然气开采业	Extraction of Petroleum and Natural Gas	9380281.7	2693502.1	2950142.9	8839197.5
#天然原油和天然气开采	Extraction of Ores Crude Oil and Natural Gas Extraction	8569340.8	1522476.4	2945288.0	7133081.5
黑色金属矿采选业	Processing of Ferrous Metals Ores	53317.4	118471.8	34332.7	147473.9
有色金属矿采选业	Processing of Nonferrous Metals Ores	78252.8	110731.3	13488.8	166037.4
非金属矿采选业	Processing of Nonmetal Ores	14519.7	24281.1	502.1	21986.1
#采 盐	Extraction of Salt	5687.8	7902.9	265.8	9038.2
农副食品加工业	Processing of Food from Agricultural Products	140147.3	268220.7	20085.6	175631.7
#谷物磨制	Grain Grinding	12555.9	25127.9	4474.4	17310.2
饲料加工	Fodder Processing	26633.0	17476.9	11621.9	43552.9
制 糖	Sugar Making	69712.1	137688.2	1826.4	88648.9
食品制造业	Manufacture of Food	219421.7	341680.5	40451.5	158011.8
#罐头制造	Manufacture of can	164582.3	287701.4	34474.5	107566.8
饮料制造业	Manufacture of Beverage	111793.5	140170.2	155840.3	51740.7
#酒的制造	Manufacture of Wine	106771.5	139023.1	155840.3	42120.9
烟草制品业	Manufacture of Tobacco	51317.1	63049.5		78023.5
纺织业	Manufacture of Textile	456162.6	650358.4	69851.1	408793.8
#棉、化纤纺织及印染精加工	Cotton, Chemical Fiber, Dyeing, Printing and Processing	421915.4	622222.5	56600.6	347041.5
毛纺织和染整精加工	Wool Textile, Dyeing and Printing	13501.6	11353.2	1327.5	19691.6
纺织服装、鞋、帽制造业	Manufacture of Textile Wearing Apparel,Footware and Caps	2283.8	5888.4	213.5	2245.6
木材加工及木、竹、藤、棕、草制品业	Processing of Timber, Wood, Bamboo, Cane, Grass Products	2938.6	3227.7	3742.8	-2406.6
造纸及纸制品业	Manufacture of Paper and Paper Products	82063.0	77591.4	15728.8	73098.4
印刷业和记录媒介的复制	Printing and Copying of Medium for Record	23843.2	12746.9	4900.3	24100.7
石油加工、炼焦及核燃料加工业	Oil Processing, Coking and Nuclear Fuel Processing	1348480.9	643315.8	914292.1	2891299.4
#炼 焦	Coking	34682.1	20220.0		20466.7
化学原料及化学制品制造业	Raw Chemical Material and Chemical Products	811021.9	862231.2	387855.4	1020805.2
#基础化学原料制造	Basic Chemical Material	410866.1	451302.5	161664.6	525459.5
肥料制造	Fertilizer Making	174744.8	190991.6	110845.8	207569.9
医药制造业	Manufacture of Medicine	20453.4	25699.3	2060.4	35618.2
化学纤维制造业	Manufacture of Chemical Fiber	8500.0	17580.4	4615.0	10141.5
橡胶制品业	Manufacture of Rubber Products	16994.6	71225.0	8798.6	-32822.1
塑料制品业	Manufacture of Plastic Products	174538.8	165008.2	7191.6	253196.9
非金属矿物制品业	Manufacture of Nonmetal Mineral Products	303521.7	363275.4	184600.5	413443.3
#水泥制造	Manufacture of Cement	239944.3	246664.2	147493.0	303316.7
黑色金属冶炼及压延加工业	Smelting and Pressing of Ferrous Metals	746904.7	626471.8	270930.7	582485.9
有色金属冶炼及压延加工业	Smelting and Pressing of Nonferrous Metals	37069.7	52421.9	14848.6	61498.4
金属制品业	Manufacture of Metal Products	7138.1	6677.0		45583.5
通用设备制造业	Manufacture of General Purpose Machinery	862.6	4830.0	400.0	2882.9
专用设备制造业	Manufacture of Special Purpose Machinery	13632.3	76835.1	3889.3	-7881.0
交通运输设备制造业	Manufacture of Transport Equipment	12470.4	56637.3	2046.4	17159.3
电气机械及器材制造业	Manufacture of Electric Equipment and Machinery	3930.1	8622.0	26.9	8216.8
仪器仪表及文化、办公用机械制造业	Measuring Instruments and Machinery for Cultural Activify and Office Work	475.7	3372.9		3789.5
电力、热力的生产和供应业	Electric Power and Thermal Production and Supply	3042603.0	1710574.4	1610686.4	1448784.2
#电力生产和电力供应	Electric Power Production and Supply	2826128.4	1610946.1	1505357.8	1317593.5
燃气生产和供应业	Gas Production and Supply	24179.6	91798.8	32178.2	44363.2
水的生产和供应业	Water Production and Supply	234026.8	39194.4	19668.2	225386.0

Continued

(10 000 yuan)

主营业务收入 Revenue from Principal Business	#主营业务成本 Cost of Principal Business	主营业务税金及附加 Taes and Other Charges on Principal Business	营业利润 Business Profit	利润总额 Total Profit	亏损企业亏损总额 Losses Value of Loss-Suffering Enterprises	利税总额 Total Profits and Taxes	本年应交增值税 Value-added Taxes Payable	全部从业人员年平均人数(人) Ann Employed Persons (person)
358469.4	260412.9	4362.2	25369.9	26095.6	3430.9	71555.1	41097.3	32740
12003225.7	4781142.0	296805.9	5811629.1	5859009.0		7305267.9	1149453.0	106045
9991974.7	2783385.0	282968.3	5874592.5	5852629.5		7178991.5	1043393.7	43116
223065.5	137495.1	3470.5	49261.6	48474.4		67767.7	15822.8	3083
332105.6	89801.8	3494.8	214183.4	195103.3		235589.5	36991.4	4896
31188.1	20196.1	834.0	2882.5	2858.3		6601.1	2908.8	2830
18942.6	11426.0	621.0	1945.4	1889.0		4395.1	1885.1	1529
438648.3	344857.8	1993.2	31861.9	32056.1	2265.9	52406.6	18357.3	10388
47301.1	43614.0	109.0	-300.8	508.7	631.2	1104.1	486.4	912
89910.2	73627.8	122.3	4571.3	4781.3	172.0	6089.3	1185.7	1012
213324.8	147776.5	1540.5	26575.5	25856.2		43230.5	15833.8	6270
272004.7	201026.9	1407.9	22839.3	23603.8	941.3	33736.7	8725.0	4727
187926.5	136355.2	801.4	11077.7	11429.4	805.9	17725.1	5494.3	2659
107634.2	66421.1	12050.0	-3463.7	-2901.9	15948.7	20289.4	11141.3	4397
100953.9	61891.1	12010.3	-4414.3	-3883.0	15936.4	19007.9	10880.6	4189
143756.5	52350.9	54740.1	16366.4	15497.9		86004.2	15766.2	531
982214.8	857520.4	5224.0	72042.2	46379.9	4741.2	76029.9	24426.0	54781
922242.6	804888.2	5127.0	72284.6	45500.1	3686.6	73127.1	22500.0	49973
20092.4	17822.7	92.5	-173.3	153.1	116.0	947.3	701.7	1860
9687.3	7967.9	12.4	382.5	419.3		563.3	131.6	710
2820.6	2842.1	16.2	-586.4	-292.5	292.5	-73.7	202.6	155
74401.8	57322.6	579.8	1959.2	-1879.4	5805.7	4314.5	5614.1	4430
26639.8	19998.7	119.7	1803.1	1854.8		3095.8	1121.3	2034
6891718.4	6691677.4	210862.9	-247981.5	-248969.1	376467.0	94551.8	132658.0	26122
39551.7	36220.9	37.5	1207.3	1880.6		3556.2	1638.1	765
1358708.1	1097148.7	6271.4	110126.0	120398.6	5885.0	178554.7	51884.7	19340
878371.3	727557.5	3756.3	61201.4	62420.1	5713.6	95301.0	29124.6	10501
169271.7	117657.3	790.5	27862.6	35096.8		41514.1	5626.8	3593
31021.1	17412.7	239.5	7219.0	7385.2	321.4	10240.6	2615.9	1279
9954.7	6806.9	46.1	2141.5	2141.5		4342.7	2155.1	416
61769.2	53762.9	1855.9	-1496.9	-1584.1	1586.1	2045.8	1774.0	1465
159282.5	143005.4	1502.6	3529.1	5077.9	5204.7	12060.3	5479.8	8837
421584.2	322793.7	2861.8	12836.4	29550.4	12608.7	59153.9	26741.7	16281
269951.2	206265.7	2175.5	677.5	14323.1	11470.3	38109.0	21610.4	11847
1950592.3	1743020.5	4345.4	88945.5	89198.5	2250.9	170800.5	77256.6	11839
218651.2	182751.3	247.6	25344.6	28400.0	907.9	34394.2	5746.6	2678
52676.8	50876.2	29.4	-599.3	-881.6	895.3	-531.3	320.9	920
3879.3	3264.1	25.3	124.7	152.6		239.7	61.8	359
46528.9	38249.1	157.8	1771.6	1976.3	1614.4	3511.2	1377.1	2368
91974.5	84004.0	110.2	419.5	518.8	1250.2	1615.1	986.1	2531
22857.5	19716.7	79.9	182.3	-1131.1	1468.8	-364.4	686.8	410
7437.4	5585.7	33.7	836.4	850.9		1209.8	325.2	94
1807961.3	1588812.1	13017.2	-11535.8	15220.4	82771.3	172003.0	143765.4	45429
1720318.3	1510322.6	12692.6	-6904.0	13406.3	79099.9	165143.1	139044.2	41946
57893.4	39527.7	612.6	5896.5	11666.0		13771.2	1492.6	1070
36497.7	28259.3	227.2	-7526.8	-4387.7	6389.3	-2244.1	1916.4	2877

11-11 各地、州、市、县(市)国有及国有控股工业企业主要经济指标

单位: 万元 (2007 年)

地　区	Region	企业单位数(个) Number of Enterprises (unit)	#亏损企业 Loss- Suffering Enterprises	工业总产值(当年价格) Gross Industrial Output Value (At Current Prices)
总　计	**Total**	**451**	**116**	**26377945.0**
乌鲁木齐市	**Urumqi City**	**124**	**33**	**8003856.8**
#乌鲁木齐县	Urumqi County	3		11518.1
克拉玛依市	**Karamay City**	**15**	**2**	**9019684.6**
石河子市	**Shihezi City**	**33**	**11**	**683578.6**
阿拉尔市	**Aral City**	**5**	**2**	**51368.5**
图木舒克市	**Tumxuk City**	**5**	**1**	**22843.2**
五家渠市	**Wujiaqu City**	**8**	**1**	**56508.5**
吐鲁番地区	**Turpan Administrative Offices**	**14**	**7**	**1617530.4**
吐鲁番市	Turpan City	6	5	68256.1
鄯善县	Shanshan [Piqan] County	6	1	1522010.6
托克逊县	Toksun County	2	1	27263.7
哈密地区	**Hami [Kumul] Administrative Offices**	**24**	**3**	**427293.8**
哈密市	Hami [Kumul] City	21	3	409596.5
巴里坤哈萨克自治县	Barkol Kazak Autonomous County	1		2486.0
伊吾县	Yiwu [Araturuk] County	2		15211.3
昌吉回族自治州	**Changji Hui Autonomous Prefecture**	**36**	**8**	**563454.7**
昌吉市	Changji City	16	3	233827.3
阜康市	Fukang City	6	1	190670.9
呼图壁县	Hutubi County	6	1	22232.6
玛纳斯县	Manas County	5	2	100488.7
奇台县	Qitai County	1		8325.3
吉木萨尔县	Jimsar County	2	1	7909.9
木垒哈萨克自治县	Mori Kazak Autonomous County			
伊犁哈萨克自治州	**Ili Kazak Autonomous Prefecture**	**86**	**22**	**1188159.3**
伊犁州直属县(市)	**Counties (Cities) Direct Under Ili Prefecture**	**38**	**8**	**574923.5**
伊宁市	Yining [Gulja] City	7	1	95368.7
奎屯市	Kuytun City	10	3	221924.6
伊宁县	Yining [Gulja] County	6	1	61367.5
察布查尔锡伯自治县	Qapqal Xibe Autonomous County	1	1	1617.5
霍城县	Huocheng [Korgas] County	5	1	64559.8
巩留县	Gongliu [Tokkuztara] County	2	1	13086.9
新源县	Xinyuan [Kunes] County	3		87394.3
昭苏县	Zhaosu [Mongolkure] County			
特克斯县	Tekes County	1		1843.6
尼勒克县	Nilka County	3		27760.6

Main Economic Indicators of State-owned and State-holding Industrial Enterprises by Prefecture, Autonomous Prefecture, City and County

(10 000 yuan)

工业增加值 Added Value of Industry	工业销售产值(当年价) Sales Value of Industry Products (At Current Prices)	出口交货值 Delivery Value of Industry Export	实收资本 Total Capital Hold	资产合计 Total Assets	流动资产合计 Total Working Capitals	#产成品 Finished Product	流动资产年平均余额 Annual Average Balance of Circulating Funds	固定资产原价 Original Value of Fixed Assets
12024331.8	**26454423.5**	**369483.8**	**14826419.5**	**34883239.0**	**10043920.9**	**804248.3**	**8934379.8**	**32342450.9**
2286284.2	**8117053.8**	**234678.2**	**3780720.4**	**9437608.7**	**3066270.9**	**331683.8**	**2693750.2**	**8112521.2**
7827.1	10768.1		31272.0	127974.2	22104.8		18289.6	86372.5
4553497.1	**9017169.5**	**19880.5**	**6019968.1**	**10568961.9**	**2827111.3**	**83613.0**	**2491006.4**	**10535412.0**
200147.7	**663141.2**	**62119.0**	**374568.1**	**1955811.7**	**843370.3**	**87213.9**	**708356.9**	**1058824.4**
15998.3	**40972.4**		**18866.3**	**86680.8**	**49500.3**	**6773.8**	**42906.3**	**41908.9**
3236.6	**17905.4**		**15618.7**	**56962.3**	**25130.8**	**7479.9**	**21218.7**	**26854.9**
10268.7	**49665.2**		**28014.9**	**129493.6**	**57953.3**	**14778.6**	**42650.3**	**46901.8**
950925.8	**1618333.8**		**930888.5**	**2101335.5**	**540726.2**	**31172.4**	**518872.0**	**2649994.2**
11703.3	68297.0		19702.4	80126.3	12898.7	217.9	13640.2	99288.5
925687.3	1522978.3		898953.5	1920271.7	519655.5	29428.6	497326.9	2449585.6
13535.2	27058.5		12232.6	100937.5	8172.0	1525.9	7904.9	101120.1
154846.1	**412124.8**		**220957.0**	**707744.4**	**321898.9**	**36324.0**	**289892.0**	**501637.7**
144061.0	394412.3		219989.4	681636.2	300211.0	34320.9	271626.1	497193.8
1343.6	2212.3		838.7	8164.8	4900.1	7.0	3407.5	2593.1
9441.5	15500.2		128.9	17943.4	16787.8	1996.1	14858.4	1850.8
189470.0	**561897.2**	**24833.0**	**163697.1**	**783459.2**	**247026.9**	**42382.8**	**238262.9**	**734556.7**
67245.8	233819.1	14163.4	88178.1	439677.9	152836.9	20147.4	143419.7	372138.3
59060.3	191379.8		20286.6	140881.2	46177.6	4113.1	39898.8	75671.2
6357.9	21133.0		11876.8	29775.7	6814.4	1026.4	6461.7	13564.9
52011.8	100241.7	10669.6	36735.6	129748.3	27141.0	11529.6	35197.8	239039.6
2363.4	8203.7		1000.0	8468.0	4853.6	2421.7	3498.3	7239.5
2430.8	7119.9		5620.0	34908.1	9203.4	3144.6	9786.6	26903.2
656933.0	**1176131.1**	**7912.7**	**623815.0**	**2450790.8**	**754345.3**	**82977.3**	**664811.1**	**1693375.7**
290609.5	**571290.1**		**411448.2**	**1611340.9**	**497320.2**	**45972.2**	**425601.2**	**1057956.1**
45648.6	94289.6		34136.0	192293.7	48371.8	865.2	43682.9	214762.1
130301.7	224690.8		65283.4	389388.4	170216.4	7844.1	162583.1	242590.8
19353.2	54885.1		39085.5	86269.8	30077.4	5526.5	24700.4	69060.1
-145.9	1556.8		302.0	4033.2	2907.0	2313.5	2907.0	708.0
16940.1	69121.0		18447.2	88370.2	48256.0	19861.9	33318.4	63877.3
8424.0	13086.9		161030.0	486663.3	107314.9	172.4	70302.2	178438.7
52845.3	83472.3		48479.9	139330.6	71369.7	8693.9	71407.9	67001.1
880.0	1715.9		299.0	2663.7	2382.7	448.8	1286.0	317.2
16362.5	28471.7		44385.2	222328.0	16424.3	245.9	15413.3	221200.8

11-11 续表 1

单位：万元

地　区	Region	企业单位数（个） Number of Enterprises (unit)	#亏损企业 Loss- Suffering Enterprises	工业总产值（当年价格） Gross Industrial Output Value (At Current Prices)
塔城地区	**Tacheng [Tarbagatai] Administrative Offices**	**25**	**6**	**241875.9**
塔城市	Tacheng [Qoqek] City	1	1	31453.0
乌苏市	Usu City	2	1	20307.8
额敏县	Emin [Dorbiljin] County	4	1	41699.3
沙湾县	Shawan County	7	2	76214.6
托里县	Toli County	4		29553.4
裕民县	Yumin [Qagantokay] County			
和布克赛尔蒙古自治县	Hoboksar Mongol Autonomous County	7	1	42647.8
阿勒泰地区	**Altay Administrative Offices**	**23**	**8**	**371359.9**
阿勒泰市	Altay City	9	5	45533.5
布尔津县	Burqin County	4		11337.0
富蕴县	Fuyun [Koktokay] County	5	1	140477.9
福海县	Fuhai [Burultokay] County	1	1	2231.8
哈巴河县	Habahe [Kaba] County	4	1	171779.7
青河县	Qinghe [Qinggil] County			
吉木乃县	Jeminay County			
博尔塔拉蒙古自治州	**Bortala Mongol Autonomous Prefecture**	**14**	**5**	**93230.0**
博乐市	Bole [Bortala] City	10	3	80828.0
精河县	Jinghe [Jing] County	3	1	10409.0
温泉县	Wenquan [Araxang] County	1	1	1993.0
巴音郭楞蒙古自治州	**Bayangol Mongol Autonomous Prefecture**	**36**	**7**	**3562174.7**
库尔勒市	Korla City	22	5	3448372.3
轮台县	Luntai [Bugur] County			
尉犁县	Yuli [Lopnur] County	1		2256.0
若羌县	Ruoqiang [Qarkilik] County	4		34436.2
且末县	Qiemo [Qarqan] County	1	1	2042.2
焉耆回族自治县	Yanqi Hui Autonomous County	1		11937.0
和静县	Hejing County	2		38434.8
和硕县	Hoxud County	3		6078.1
博湖县	Bohu [Bagrax] County	2	1	18618.1
阿克苏地区	**Aksu Administrative Offices**	**25**	**1**	**904884.4**
阿克苏市	Aksu City	11	1	177100.7
温宿县	Wensu [Onsu] County	5		9783.9
库车县	Kuqa County	7		703000.4

Continued

(10 000 yuan)

工业增加值 Added Value of Industry	工业销售产值(当年价) Sales Value of Industry Products (At Current Prices)	出口交货值 Delivery Value of Industry Export	实收资本 Total Capital Hold	资产合计 Total Assets	流动资产合计 Total Working Capitals	#产成品 Finished Product	流动资产年平均余额 Annual Average Balance of Circulating Funds	固定资产原价 Original Value of Fixed Assets
87114.5	**225143.3**	**7912.7**	**76552.8**	**360075.3**	**113812.7**	**22334.3**	**110882.4**	**316580.3**
11665.4	31453.0		7431.0	53956.9	9612.8		9384.1	71480.0
6253.7	20349.8	7912.7	30.0	30154.4	5657.9	4102.8	6679.2	42961.6
9504.8	39321.0		18300.3	55374.0	31238.4	10157.7	28897.5	27272.1
24121.0	68295.0		13556.7	94685.6	38117.7	4879.7	34819.2	88427.4
18477.4	25797.3		11000.0	47514.5	11473.2	1184.5	12309.8	28624.6
17092.2	39927.2		26234.8	78389.9	17712.7	2009.6	18792.6	57814.6
279209.0	**379697.7**		**135814.0**	**479374.6**	**143212.4**	**14670.8**	**128327.5**	**318839.3**
15175.4	45825.1		24503.8	103261.2	14968.7	988.7	18772.9	117329.5
4566.1	11123.6		13058.7	24384.7	4267.6	156.3	4834.9	23812.7
98153.6	138043.7		33988.7	163140.7	45821.9	10364.7	29512.8	71848.5
2062.0	2231.8		29282.8	28647.0	7043.3		6268.9	30835.4
159251.9	182473.5		34980.0	159941.0	71110.9	3161.1	68938.0	75013.2
24551.7	**93615.5**		**35055.9**	**161767.2**	**60283.4**	**15120.8**	**53675.0**	**128137.1**
20847.5	81051.4		33121.9	149005.6	51413.6	11477.4	46403.9	123727.7
3341.6	11082.5		934.0	9677.2	6813.3	2291.8	6043.2	3502.7
362.6	1481.6		1000.0	3084.4	2056.5	1351.6	1227.9	906.7
2693057.3	**3606326.1**	**20060.4**	**2192013.2**	**4902065.8**	**916448.3**	**39462.5**	**861953.5**	**5338968.8**
2651837.1	3500467.9	1974.0	2118214.1	4490662.2	808969.3	13925.9	768551.7	5193747.7
797.8	1518.6		921.2	2756.5	1071.6	9.0	1383.8	2061.3
16467.5	34718.4		58640.1	299543.3	59582.2	2837.3	48508.7	43208.0
1208.2	2042.2		1183.7	7463.4	363.2		545.2	10080.8
3331.1	9660.9		6754.4	16181.6	7181.6	5186.7	3454.5	16761.4
12432.1	33723.4		3418.0	55758.3	23558.9	9519.7	23723.9	42314.6
2536.7	5177.8	3006.5	2254.6	7946.4	5381.2	2451.6	5343.8	5623.4
4446.8	19016.9	15079.9	627.1	21754.1	10340.3	5532.3	10441.9	25171.6
210537.5	**899787.2**		**273532.7**	**955791.0**	**223517.3**	**14287.8**	**192239.7**	**824884.2**
76218.3	172432.6		74188.8	427000.8	131679.9	4805.4	110659.9	319334.8
6559.7	9207.1		2810.0	16282.9	4758.6	613.9	4610.2	7909.5
120047.4	703178.9		194281.2	491239.7	82815.6	8868.5	73454.7	456809.1

11-11 续表 2

单位：万元

地　　区	Region	企业单位数（个）Number of Enterprises (unit)	#亏损企业 Loss- Suffering Enterprises	工业总产值（当年价格）Gross Industrial Output Value (At Current Prices)
沙雅县	Xayar County			
新和县	Xinhe [Toksu] County			
拜城县	Baicheng [Bay] County	1		13846.0
乌什县	Wushi [Uxturpan] County	1		1153.4
阿瓦提县	Awat County			
柯坪县	Kalpin County			
克孜勒苏柯尔克孜自治州	**Kizilsu Kirgiz Autonomous Prefecture**	**4**	**2**	**7063.1**
阿图什市	Artux City	2	1	1534.1
阿克陶县	Akto County	2	1	5529.0
阿合奇县	Akqi County			
乌恰县	Wuqia [Ulugqat] County			
喀什地区	**Kashgar [Kaxgar] Administrative Offices**	**11**	**6**	**121925.6**
喀什市	Kashgar [Kaxgar] City	5	3	112949.0
疏附县	Shufu County	2	2	1522.2
疏勒县	Shule County	1		3852.8
英吉沙县	Yengisar County	2	1	2980.0
泽普县	Zepu [Poskam] County			
莎车县	Shache [Yarkant] County	1		621.6
叶城县	Yecheng [Kagilik] County			
麦盖提县	Makit County			
岳普湖县	Yopurga County			
伽师县	Jiashi [Payzawat] County			
巴楚县	Bachu [Maralbexi] County			
塔什库尔干塔吉克自治县	Taxkorgan Tajik Autonomous County			
和田地区	**Hotan Administrative Offices**	**11**	**5**	**54388.8**
和田市	Hotan City	7	3	37835.7
和田县	Hotan County	3	1	11496.6
墨玉县	Moyu [Karakax] County			
皮山县	Pishan [Guma] County	1	1	5056.5
洛浦县	Lop County			
策勒县	Qira County			
于田县	Yutian [Keriya] County			
民丰县	Minfeng [Niya] County			

Continued

(10 000 yuan)

工业增加值 Added Value of Industry	工业销售产值(当年价) Sales Value of Industry Products (At Current Prices)	出口交货值 Delivery Value of Industry Export	实收资本 Total Capital Hold	资产合计 Total Assets	流动资产合计 Total Working Capitals	#产成品 Finished Product	流动资产年平均余额 Annual Average Balance of Circulating Funds	固定资产原价 Original Value of Fixed Assets
7118.7	13846.0		1252.7	19574.1	3287.4		2544.2	40380.3
593.4	1122.6		1000.0	1693.5	975.8		970.7	450.5
2647.7	**6919.4**		**1507.0**	**11901.6**	**3131.5**	**197.4**	**2404.6**	**14151.0**
514.4	1657.3		632.0	4031.6	1078.5	106.4	1047.3	4917.7
2133.3	5262.1		875.0	7870.0	2053.0	91.0	1357.3	9233.3
45869.6	**118429.9**		**22966.3**	**305125.6**	**48799.2**	**1057.7**	**47989.8**	**387014.9**
42230.7	108109.0		14721.4	278942.3	41427.7		42641.5	363967.8
629.9	1406.2		1976.0	5829.4	1899.6		2245.7	6280.9
1434.7	5313.1		5000.0	9284.6	4535.8	1053.7	2345.0	5747.2
1249.1	2980.0		1069.9	6645.1	665.5	4.0	469.4	7504.7
325.2	621.6		199.0	4424.2	270.6		288.2	3514.3
26060.5	**54951.0**		**124230.3**	**267738.9**	**58407.0**	**9722.6**	**64390.4**	**247307.4**
15286.3	38445.1		19543.8	143003.1	44856.7	9358.5	42587.1	123579.2
8720.5	11222.0		104351.6	119970.2	10541.8		18664.5	119768.2
2053.7	5283.9		334.9	4765.6	3008.5	364.1	3138.8	3960.0

11-11 续表 3

单位: 万元

地　区	Region	固定资产净值年平均余额 Annual Average Balance of Net Value of Fixed Assets	流动负债合计 Total Working Liabilities	长期负债合计 Long-term Liabilities	所有者权益合计 Creditors' Equities
总　计	**Total**	**17731564.4**	**9659464.2**	**6913187.6**	**17663420.1**
乌鲁木齐市	**Urumqi City**	**4695030.1**	**2852607.8**	**1158295.9**	**5322178.5**
#乌鲁木齐县	Urumqi County	51465.2	87253.0	301.0	40420.2
克拉玛依市	**Karamay City**	**5031763.5**	**1980683.9**	**2350565.7**	**6229009.2**
石河子市	**Shihezi City**	**820793.7**	**803594.3**	**357752.8**	**792516.8**
阿拉尔市	**Aral City**	**32221.9**	**40119.0**	**7051.0**	**28797.4**
图木舒克市	**Tumxuk City**	**20747.4**	**28227.9**	**14214.5**	**14519.9**
五家渠市	**Wujiaqu City**	**40740.8**	**41106.6**	**408.0**	**34939.0**
吐鲁番地区	**Turpan Administrative Offices**	**1303713.6**	**528447.7**	**76435.4**	**1097103.5**
吐鲁番市	Turpan City	55924.7	12248.2	40447.4	27430.7
鄯善县	Shanshan [Piqan] County	1152265.2	461116.5	2230.3	1057377.8
托克逊县	Toksun County	95523.7	55083.0	33757.7	12295.0
哈密地区	**Hami [Kumul] Administrative Offices**	**273712.6**	**252929.3**	**161374.0**	**286699.6**
哈密市	Hami [Kumul] City	270753.4	244068.5	161222.9	269603.3
巴里坤哈萨克自治县	Barkol Kazak Autonomous County	2030.0	6321.1	62.2	1781.5
伊吾县	Yiwu [Araturuk] County	929.2	2539.7	88.9	15314.8
昌吉回族自治州	**Changji Hui Autonomous Prefecture**	**390206.4**	**332043.8**	**307363.2**	**140502.2**
昌吉市	Changji City	223094.1	123188.1	242882.8	70061.0
阜康市	Fukang City	33081.6	76252.6	13557.7	51066.9
呼图壁县	Hutubi County	7827.0	21004.9	3102.9	5667.9
玛纳斯县	Manas County	106433.8	69395.3	47819.8	12533.2
奇台县	Qitai County	2950.8	7711.3		756.7
吉木萨尔县	Jimsar County	16819.1	34491.6		416.5
木垒哈萨克自治县	Mori Kazak Autonomous County				
伊犁哈萨克自治州	**Ili Kazak Autonomous Prefecture**	**1154682.7**	**957797.1**	**616104.8**	**859729.1**
伊犁州直属县(市)	**Counties (Cities) Direct Under Ili Prefecture**	**748302.2**	**516252.9**	**518463.8**	**575311.7**
伊宁市	Yining [Gulja] City	124485.3	127921.6	16763.7	47608.3
奎屯市	Kuytun City	153946.4	130021.3	113264.9	145800.9
伊宁县	Yining [Gulja] County	36647.9	33474.0	6163.8	45670.9
察布查尔锡伯自治县	Qapqal Xibe Autonomous County	1054.3	4155.9		-122.7
霍城县	Huocheng [Korgas] County	34900.8	46792.6	8199.7	33377.9
巩留县	Gongliu [Tokkuztara] County	164667.6	109622.9	219866.9	157173.5
新源县	Xinyuan [Kunes] County	36140.8	38335.5	54.8	100890.3
昭苏县	Zhaosu [Mongolkure] County				
特克斯县	Tekes County	259.0	2356.0		307.7
尼勒克县	Nilka County	196200.1	23573.1	154150.0	44604.9

Continued

(10 000 yuan)

主营业务收入 Revenue from Principal Business	#主营业务成本 Cost of Principal Business	主营业务税金及附加 Taes and Other Charges on Principal Business	营业利润 Business Profit	利润总额 Total Profit	亏损企业亏损总额 Losses Value of Loss-Suffering Enterprises	利税总额 Total Profits and Taxes	本年应交增值税 Value-added Taxes Payable	全部从业人员年平均人数(人) Annual Average Employed Persons (person)
28236850.8	**19016030.7**	**627637.2**	**6236763.8**	**6301862.1**	**533047.2**	**8718502.7**	**1789003.4**	**376062**
8413532.0	**6745364.3**	**210909.9**	**742703.1**	**768120.5**	**359497.9**	**1337480.0**	**358449.6**	**115396**
9236.5	4170.9	6.6	1547.0	2245.9		3438.0	1185.5	104
9810908.7	**6545236.5**	**214976.9**	**2479664.4**	**2508015.5**	**72130.5**	**3418856.8**	**695864.4**	**94549**
990110.9	**806793.8**	**5275.3**	**75324.2**	**76645.9**	**10986.1**	**113144.5**	**31223.3**	**20056**
41469.1	**34732.1**	**108.7**	**2533.0**	**1777.9**	**647.7**	**4640.7**	**2754.1**	**1550**
18511.3	**16997.0**	**4.0**	**52.4**	**29.6**	**212.0**	**238.6**	**205.0**	**633**
49236.6	**42979.0**	**76.0**	**2624.8**	**3716.0**	**196.6**	**5504.7**	**1712.7**	**1970**
1743485.9	**1040683.3**	**22409.9**	**530660.5**	**542182.1**	**7110.4**	**697372.2**	**132780.2**	**19126**
71849.1	73879.5	574.2	-6302.2	-6520.5	7014.5	-1965.5	3980.8	1792
1645189.0	947094.5	21359.9	536025.2	547629.8	78.2	694256.1	125266.4	16936
26447.8	19709.3	475.8	937.5	1072.8	17.7	5081.6	3533.0	398
413394.4	**319592.9**	**3577.4**	**38205.3**	**34197.3**	**1707.1**	**67837.2**	**30062.5**	**18805**
395473.3	313404.2	3190.5	31150.7	27566.3	1707.1	59019.3	28262.5	18566
2420.9	1490.2	59.3	183.3	171.6		652.6	421.7	146
15500.2	4698.5	327.6	6871.3	6459.4		8165.3	1378.3	93
555089.9	**491347.9**	**3079.9**	**7886.5**	**10094.6**	**32612.8**	**46037.7**	**32863.2**	**15184**
229695.8	230439.8	1912.4	-28851.5	-25489.9	31144.5	-8504.4	15073.1	7607
188957.2	151863.0	281.2	30007.5	30589.6	81.7	37436.6	6565.8	3191
21104.6	18310.4	24.2	-19.9	183.8	0.2	996.1	788.1	1074
100580.9	79718.7	795.0	6673.1	4907.2	1102.0	15628.3	9926.1	2526
8149.3	5770.9	35.3	97.6	54.3		530.3	440.7	403
6602.1	5245.1	31.8	-20.3	-150.4	284.4	-49.2	69.4	383
1227238.8	**717357.2**	**70240.6**	**257842.4**	**247839.7**	**18381.2**	**424625.2**	**106544.9**	**36686**
614838.9	**392299.0**	**64572.7**	**53332.5**	**60071.8**	**9143.3**	**178484.6**	**53840.1**	**17164**
91969.2	72385.0	669.8	6327.2	7440.2	3226.8	15718.6	7608.6	4624
256956.6	152576.0	55268.2	14418.4	15188.0	2934.8	91773.2	21317.0	4087
61181.5	39407.4	237.4	7378.2	10010.5	991.0	13223.4	2975.5	2282
1556.8	1528.2		-418.4	-424.7	424.7	-424.7		21
70754.2	50428.2	375.2	8948.5	8586.6	296.3	13945.1	4983.3	2378
13697.2	9366.4	79.6	-1117.4	-560.6	1269.7	1717.1	2198.1	289
88439.3	52287.8	7771.4	16401.4	15855.0		33622.0	9995.6	3108
1751.9	936.1			14.9		359.9	345.0	53
28532.2	13383.9	171.1	1394.6	3961.9		8550.0	4417.0	322

11-11 续表 4

单位: 万元

地区	Region	固定资产净值年平均余额 Annual Average Balance of Net Value of Fixed Assets	流动负债合计 Total Working Liabilities	长期负债合计 Long-term Liabilities	所有者权益合计 Creditors ' Equities
塔城地区	**Tacheng [Tarbagatai] Administrative Offices**	**202051.2**	**247029.1**	**38769.3**	**63393.3**
塔城市	Tacheng [Qoqek] City	43326.7	69113.9	8564.2	-23721.2
乌苏市	Usu City	24703.3	30458.3		-303.9
额敏县	Emin [Dorbiljin] County	18460.9	27272.2	3950.1	21074.3
沙湾县	Shawan County	58546.6	80345.4	3633.0	10707.2
托里县	Toli County	19312.2	19457.9	7398.5	20658.1
裕民县	Yumin [Qagantokay] County				
和布克赛尔蒙古自治县	Hoboksar Mongol Autonomous County	37701.5	20381.4	15223.5	34978.8
阿勒泰地区	**Altay Administrative Offices**	**204329.3**	**194515.1**	**58871.7**	**221024.1**
阿勒泰市	Altay City	76402.1	71010.8	18259.5	11094.6
布尔津县	Burqin County	17627.0	6878.8	3857.8	13646.2
富蕴县	Fuyun [Koktokay] County	34957.4	39469.9	24452.4	97152.9
福海县	Fuhai [Burultokay] County	16301.4	2624.0		26023.0
哈巴河县	Habahe [Kaba] County	59041.4	74531.6	12302.0	73107.4
青河县	Qinghe [Qinggil] County				
吉木乃县	Jeminay County				
博尔塔拉蒙古自治州	**Bortala Mongol Autonomous Prefecture**	**80617.9**	**62334.1**	**31363.1**	**42502.7**
博乐市	Bole [Bortala] City	77210.7	54488.7	29920.7	39029.1
精河县	Jinghe [Jing] County	2649.8	5878.5	1363.3	2435.3
温泉县	Wenquan [Araxang] County	757.4	1966.9	79.1	1038.3
巴音郭楞蒙古自治州	**Bayangol Mongol Autonomous Prefecture**	**2902480.2**	**1112748.5**	**1547670.6**	**2234977.5**
库尔勒市	Korla City	2819147.5	899465.5	1452544.3	2138523.4
轮台县	Luntai [Bugur] County				
尉犁县	Yuli [Lopnur] County	1717.2	1781.3		975.2
若羌县	Ruoqiang [Qarkilik] County	27579.2	148117.1	77975.2	72834.1
且末县	Qiemo [Qarqan] County	6370.1	1737.2		-197.1
焉耆回族自治县	Yanqi Hui Autonomous County	6959.8	14831.6		1350.0
和静县	Hejing County	26118.8	20401.1	13408.3	21948.9
和硕县	Hoxud County	2649.0	5075.6		2870.8
博湖县	Bohu [Bagrax] County	11938.6	21339.1	3742.8	-3327.8
阿克苏地区	**Aksu Administrative Offices**	**594888.4**	**288460.8**	**181904.8**	**484537.8**
阿克苏市	Aksu City	186888.2	157728.0	59000.0	209425.4
温宿县	Wensu [Onsu] County	4079.4	7379.9	2972.9	5930.0
库车县	Kuqa County	386642.4	112078.7	119931.9	259189.0

Continued

(10 000 yuan)

主营业务收入 Revenue from Principal Business	#主营业务成本 Cost of Principal Business	主营业务税金及附加 Taes and Other Charges on Principal Business	营业利润 Business Profit	利润总额 Total Profit	亏损企业亏损总额 Losses Value of Loss-Suffering Enterprises	利税总额 Total Profits and Taxes	本年应交增值税 Value-added Taxes Payable	全部从业人员年平均人数(人) Annual Average Employed Persons (person)
223490.6	**177658.7**	**1778.3**	**8323.8**	**10757.0**	**4961.8**	**24088.1**	**11552.8**	**12587**
23794.3	23326.9	88.2	-1744.3	-1756.3	1756.3	561.4	2229.5	1364
21254.7	20410.2	110.8	-1652.4	-1663.2	1924.2	-630.9	921.5	598
47708.4	41603.0	280.2	3258.5	3432.2	427.3	6203.8	2491.4	914
70791.3	58261.2	428.2	-116.1	1920.5	819.3	3943.3	1594.6	1987
27947.8	14523.4	166.9	5703.1	5518.8		7017.4	1331.7	3369
31994.1	19534.0	704.0	2875.0	3305.0	34.7	6993.1	2984.1	4355
388909.3	**147399.5**	**3889.6**	**196186.1**	**177010.9**	**4276.1**	**222052.5**	**41152.0**	**6935**
45420.3	38903.7	201.4	-806.0	-1047.7	1176.3	1556.6	2402.9	2283
11386.1	6817.8	89.7	1366.2	1398.6		2548.3	1060.0	395
147215.6	66849.3	1518.0	60054.7	59556.5	904.1	78670.0	17595.5	3112
2419.2	2909.0	1.4	-697.4	-1064.7	1064.7	-971.3	92.0	44
182468.1	31919.7	2079.1	136268.6	118168.2	1131.0	140248.9	20001.6	1101
104711.5	**93798.9**	**541.8**	**-46.8**	**2148.0**	**4107.9**	**8191.1**	**5501.3**	**4744**
94597.1	85186.5	460.8	-348.3	1966.3	3761.3	7497.6	5070.5	4078
9119.2	7694.2	81.0	311.3	190.4	337.9	702.2	430.8	645
995.2	918.2		-9.8	-8.7	8.7	-8.7		21
3793771.8	**1229525.9**	**75831.7**	**2047784.7**	**2053854.2**	**2532.7**	**2470005.3**	**340319.4**	**26739**
3688798.9	1157674.7	74602.5	2036974.2	2040700.8	2100.3	2450829.5	335526.2	22008
4321.4	4138.2	0.4	-175.9	10.0		50.2	39.8	175
29878.0	16717.2	815.9	6114.6	7427.7		10176.5	1932.9	2196
1133.3	1093.2	5.6	-139.9	-139.9	139.9	-65.3	69.0	151
10621.0	7330.3	81.5	752.0	721.4		1800.5	997.6	511
34975.0	24807.3	203.2	3242.5	3804.7		5391.8	1383.9	984
5027.3	3848.9	22.3	96.6	186.6		283.8	74.9	376
19016.9	13916.1	100.3	920.6	1142.9	292.5	1538.3	295.1	338
898405.6	**767831.1**	**19202.7**	**60854.5**	**64404.2**	**584.1**	**119310.5**	**35703.6**	**10473**
167337.2	142065.5	968.6	3842.5	8019.7	584.1	21419.4	12431.1	6683
8924.1	3625.4	88.8	3476.6	3270.2		4465.8	1106.8	963
707175.4	609113.6	18027.1	52453.5	52314.1		91065.1	20723.9	2382

11-11 续表 5

单位：万元

地区	Region	固定资产净值年平均余额 Annual Average Balance of Net Value of Fixed Assets	流动负债合计 Total Working Liabilities	长期负债合计 Long-term Liabilities	所有者权益合计 Creditors' Equities
沙雅县	Xayar County				
新和县	Xinhe [Toksu] County				
拜城县	Baicheng [Bay] County	16764.9	10609.4		8964.7
乌什县	Wushi [Uxturpan] County	513.5	664.8		1028.7
阿瓦提县	Awat County				
柯坪县	Kalpin County				
克孜勒苏柯尔克孜自治州	**Kizilsu Kirgiz Autonomous Prefecture**	**4873.4**	**7817.7**	**2695.3**	**1388.6**
阿图什市	Artux City	3026.6	1101.0	2015.0	915.6
阿克陶县	Akto County	1846.8	6716.7	680.3	473.0
阿合奇县	Akqi County				
乌恰县	Wuqia [Ulugqat] County				
喀什地区	**Kashgar [Kaxgar] Administrative Offices**	**230947.6**	**218728.3**	**87170.4**	**-8610.1**
喀什市	Kashgar [Kaxgar] City	214624.7	209194.1	86771.7	-22371.8
疏附县	Shufu County	3436.3	3227.2		155.7
疏勒县	Shule County	4507.6	151.4		9133.2
英吉沙县	Yengisar County	5790.2	5111.5		1491.4
泽普县	Zepu [Poskam] County				
莎车县	Shache [Yarkant] County	2588.8	1044.1	398.7	2981.4
叶城县	Yecheng [Kagilik] County				
麦盖提县	Makit County				
岳普湖县	Yopurga County				
伽师县	Jiashi [Payzawat] County				
巴楚县	Bachu [Maralbexi] County				
塔什库尔干塔吉克自治县	Taxkorgan Tajik Autonomous County				
和田地区	**Hotan Administrative Offices**	**154144.2**	**151817.4**	**12818.1**	**102628.4**
和田市	Hotan City	83595.2	139235.5	8100.9	-4333.3
和田县	Hotan County	69133.8	9344.7	3507.4	107118.1
墨玉县	Moyu [Karakax] County				
皮山县	Pishan [Guma] County	1415.2	3237.2	1209.8	-156.4
洛浦县	Lop County				
策勒县	Qira County				
于田县	Yutian [Keriya] County				
民丰县	Minfeng [Niya] County				

Continued

(10 000 yuan)

主营业务收入 Revenue from Principal Business	#主营业务成本 Cost of Principal Business	主营业务税金及附加 Taes and Other Charges on Principal Business	营业利润 Business Profit	利润总额 Total Profit	亏损企业亏损总额 Losses Value of Loss-Suffering Enterprises	利税总额 Total Profits and Taxes	本年应交增值税 Value-added Taxes Payable	全部从业人员年平均人数(人) Ann Employed Persons (person)
13846.3	12468.4	115.3	868.8	592.9		2150.0	1441.8	410
1122.6	558.2	2.9	213.1	207.3		210.2		35
6792.6	**4267.8**	**74.3**	**1476.7**	**1047.8**	**580.7**	**1744.4**	**622.3**	**379**
1530.5	1149.6	32.0	-20.4	-94.4	101.8	89.4	151.8	183
5262.1	3118.2	42.3	1497.1	1142.2	478.9	1655.0	470.5	196
114867.5	**113391.0**	**872.9**	**-12011.1**	**-11729.9**	**12860.3**	**-1602.7**	**9254.3**	**5187**
105321.2	106275.7	773.5	-12659.0	-12350.7	12461.5	-2686.3	8890.9	4350
1821.6	1396.6	55.9	-100.4	-106.0	106.0	73.1	123.2	531
4940.8	3353.5	30.5	967.3	993.4		1193.0	169.1	63
2242.6	2110.7	10.3	-230.7	-271.0	292.8	-225.5	35.2	161
541.3	254.5	2.7	11.7	4.4		43.0	35.9	82
55324.2	**46132.0**	**455.2**	**1209.2**	**-481.3**	**8899.2**	**5116.5**	**5142.6**	**4585**
38914.1	34771.3	318.2	-905.7	-1355.6	8175.9	2286.8	3324.2	3070
11144.1	6940.2	79.9	2001.1	910.8	686.8	2267.9	1277.2	633
5266.0	4420.5	57.1	113.8	-36.5	36.5	561.8	541.2	882

11-12 国有及国有控股工业企业主要经济效益指标

单位: % (2007 年)

项目	Item	工业增加值率 Ratio of Value-added to Gross Industrial Output Value	资金利税率 Ratio of Profits and Taxes to Capital	产值利税率 Ratio of Profits and Taxes to Industrial Output Value
总计	**Total**	**39.8**	**32.7**	**33.1**
按登记注册类型分	**By Status of Registration**			
内资企业	Domestic Funded Enterprises	39.8	32.8	33.1
国有企业	State-owned Enterprises	29.2	6.9	10.7
#中央企业	Central Enterprises	28.2	7.4	10.6
地方企业	Local Enterprises	35.0	5.0	11.1
#自治区属企业	Autonomous	36.5	4.7	10.8
地区(州、市)属企业	Prefecture or City	29.5	0.4	1.4
县(市)属企业	County or City	40.5	11.6	20.8
联营企业	Joint Ownership Enterprises	22.4	68.2	30.8
#国有联营企业	State Joint Ownership Enterprises	22.4	68.2	30.8
有限责任公司	Limited Liability Corporations	25.6	10.8	14.0
#国有独资公司	State Sole funded Corporations	25.4	10.5	13.4
其他有限责任公司	Other Limited Liability Corporations	25.8	11.0	14.3
股份有限公司	Share-holding Corporations Ltd.	45.2	50.2	41.9
港、澳、台商投资企业	Enterprises with Funds from Hong Kong, Macao and Taiwan	11.5	0.8	0.9
外商投资企业	Foreign Funded Enterprises	18.1	-2.1	-24.0
在总计中: 国有控股企业	Of the Total : State-owned and State-holding Enterprises	39.8	32.7	33.1
按轻、重工业分	**Grouped by Light & Heavy Industry**			
轻工业	Light Industry	28.9	10.4	14.8
以农产品为原料	Using Farm Produces as Raw Materials	28.4	11.7	15.2
以非农产品为原料	Using Non-Farm Produces as Raw Materials	47.0		
重工业	Heavy Industry	40.6	35.3	34.5
采掘工业	Mining and Quarrying	69.6	57.7	63.8
原料工业	Raw Materials Industry	12.4	6.9	5.6
加工工业	Manufacturing Industry	23.8	8.5	11.9
按企业规模分	**Grouped by Size of Enterprises**			
大型企业	Large	43.2	41.8	37.9
中型企业	Medium	29.3	16.2	19.2
小型企业	Small	27.9	7.2	13.3

Main Indicators on Economic Efficiency of State-owened and State-holding Industrial Enterprises

(%)

总资产贡献率 Ratio of Total Assets to Industrial Output Value	资本保值增值率 Ratio of Capital Hold and Rise	资产负债率 Assets Liability Ratio	流动资产周转次数(次/年) Number of Times of Annual Turnover of Circulating Funds (times/year)	成本费用利润率 Ratio of Profits To Industrial Cost	全员劳动生产率(元/人·年) Overall Labor Productivity (yuan/person-year)	工业经济效益综合指数 Comprehensive Index of Industry Economic Results
28.8	**129.1**	**49.4**	**3.2**	**29.9**	**319743.3**	**434.4**
28.9	129.0	49.3	3.2	29.9	320166.9	435.0
7.0	134.0	53.3	1.6	1.8	76154.3	125.3
7.7	139.0	49.8	1.7	1.5	73004.4	125.0
4.9	115.9	64.3	1.4	3.3	95043.9	133.0
4.9	153.4	63.1	1.5	2.4	109234.5	143.7
2.0	43.9	78.0	0.9	-4.2	63959.4	62.2
7.7	94.3	60.0	1.9	13.5	82600.3	171.8
22.3	20.5	44.4	2.8	13.1	189200.0	262.0
22.3	20.5	44.4	2.8	13.1	189200.0	262.0
12.2	140.6	61.7	2.1	8.1	115599.5	187.2
11.1	137.7	62.4	2.2	7.0	114575.8	181.3
13.0	142.3	61.2	2.0	8.7	116228.1	190.9
41.6	125.4	43.8	4.7	46.3	868315.2	867.7
0.2	27.9	56.1	1.2	-3.5	46077.4	54.6
-0.4	714.3	67.7	0.2	-26.2	43278.7	47.2
28.8	129.1	49.4	3.2	29.9	319743.3	434.4
12.2	139.0	61.8	1.5	6.2	71650.2	147.5
13.7	141.9	65.8	1.5	6.6	72031.2	151.4
0.5	128.1	25.3	1.2	-6.5	64157.9	69.1
30.4	128.4	48.1	3.5	32.3	394429.5	494.8
50.9	126.9	41.6	3.7	99.5	635916.7	935.2
7.4	138.9	54.6	3.7	-0.2	147840.5	183.2
6.3	85.7	59.6	1.3	8.7	83373.8	144.1
35.9	127.2	43.6	3.9	38.1	446077.8	562.1
16.5	144.9	60.4	2.1	10.9	146868.5	226.4
7.7	116.9	64.4	1.6	7.8	110582.6	166.5

11-13 分行业国有及国有控股工业企业主要经济效益指标

单位: % (2007 年)

行业	Sector	工业增加值率 Ratio of Value-added to Gross Industrial Output Value	资金利税率 Ratio of Profits and Taxes to Capital	产值利税率 Ratio of Profits and Taxes to Industrial Output Value
煤炭开采和洗选业	Mining and Washing of Coal	52.8	11.5	20.5
石油和天然气开采业	Extraction of Petroleum and Natural Gas	71.0	59.4	65.7
#天然原油和天然气开采	Extraction of Ores Crude Oil and Natural Gas Extraction	78.2	71.6	74.4
黑色金属矿采选业	Processing of Ferrous Metals Ores	29.3	37.3	29.9
有色金属矿采选业	Processing of Nonferrous Metals Ores	74.6	124.3	73.9
非金属矿采选业	Processing of Nonmetal Ores	34.8	18.2	15.3
#采　盐	Extraction of Salt	29.9	37.5	20.4
农副食品加工业	Processing of Food from Agricultural Products	20.0	14.3	13.2
#谷物磨制	Grain Grinding	10.8	3.2	2.4
饲料加工	Fodder Processing	18.9	9.6	10.9
制　糖	Sugar Making	23.8	24.5	21.2
食品制造业	Manufacture of Food	27.7	6.9	12.3
#罐头制造	Manufacture of can	29.6	4.4	9.6
饮料制造业	Manufacture of Beverage	42.5	7.1	18.3
#酒的制造	Manufacture of Wine	43.5	6.8	18.1
烟草制品业	Manufacture of Tobacco	60.4	71.9	61.0
纺织业	Manufacture of Textile	24.3	7.8	9.2
#棉、化纤纺织及印染精加工	Cotton, Chemical Fiber, Dyeing, Printing and Processing	23.8	8.2	9.5
毛纺织和染整精加工	Wool Textile, Dyeing and Printing	22.6	3.3	6.7
纺织服装、鞋、帽制造业	Manufacture of Textile Wearing Apparel, Footware and Caps	25.6	8.2	6.2
木材加工及木、竹、藤、棕、草制品业	Processing of Timber, Wood, Bamboo, Cane, Grass Products	15.3	-1.6	-2.7
造纸及纸制品业	Manufacture of Paper and Paper Products	25.5	3.1	5.6
印刷业和记录媒介的复制	Printing and Copying of Medium for Record	35.9	8.4	12.0
石油加工、炼焦及核燃料加工业	Oil Processing, Coking and Nuclear Fuel Processing	3.7	3.8	1.4
#炼　焦	Coking	11.9	5.8	9.2
化学原料及化学制品制造业	Raw Chemical Material and Chemical Products	25.0	12.9	17.6
#基础化学原料制造	Basic Chemical Material	22.1	12.2	18.2
肥料制造	Fertilizer Making	38.5	15.7	24.3
医药制造业	Manufacture of Medicine	41.3	20.4	27.1
化学纤维制造业	Manufacture of Chemical Fiber	40.8	13.5	36.5
橡胶制品业	Manufacture of Rubber Products	16.3	5.4	3.7
塑料制品业	Manufacture of Plastic Products	23.8	3.3	7.7
非金属矿物制品业	Manufacture of Nonmetal Mineral Products	29.7	8.4	13.6
#水泥制造	Manufacture of Cement	31.3	7.5	13.9
黑色金属冶炼及压延加工业	Smelting and Pressing of Ferrous Metals	14.2	13.4	9.0
有色金属冶炼及压延加工业	Smelting and Pressing of Nonferrous Metals	21.5	42.5	15.4
金属制品业	Manufacture of Metal Products	7.7	-2.9	-0.9
通用设备制造业	Manufacture of General Purpose Machinery	22.3	3.1	6.3
专用设备制造业	Manufacture of Special Purpose Machinery	23.5	5.8	9.1
交通运输设备制造业	Manufacture of Transport Equipment	7.5	3.1	1.9
电气机械及器材制造业	Manufacture of Electric Equipment and Machinery	12.6	-2.3	-1.6
仪器仪表及文化、办公用机械制造业	Measuring Instruments and Machinery for Cultural Activify and Office Work	12.3	20.0	20.2
电力、热力的生产和供应业	Electricity and Thermal Production and Supply	36.4	4.4	10.0
#电力生产和电力供应	Electricity Production and Supply	36.8	4.6	10.0
燃气生产和供应业	Gas Production and Supply	24.1	11.7	23.8
水的生产和供应业	Water Production and Supply	58.3	-0.9	-7.0

Main Indicators on Economic Efficiency of State-owened and State-holding Industrial Enterprises by Sectors

(%)

总资产贡献率 Ratio of Total Assets to Industrial Output Value	资本保值增值率 Ratio of Capital Hold and Rise	资产负债率 Assets Liability Ratio	流动资产周转次数（次/年） Number of Times of Annual Turnover Working Capitals (times/year)	成本费用利润率 Ratio of Profits to Industrial Cost	全员劳动生产率（元/人·年） Overall Labor Productivity (yuan/person-year)	工业经济效益综合指数 Comprehensive Index of Industry Economic Results
8.6	132.6	48.3	1.2	7.9	65423.1	144.2
53.5	126.0	40.9	4.1	106.3	842750.5	1094.7
64.6	122.9	41.0	6.9	170.7	1963947.8	2064.7
25.7	173.9	50.9	1.7	28.5	245262.7	369.0
82.9	126.7	44.5	3.0	166.6	550400.5	1189.6
14.7	119.6	53.0	1.4	9.9	59007.4	155.9
26.1	185.9	47.5	3.1	11.5	48181.8	203.2
14.5	143.7	62.6	1.9	8.0	85928.3	171.4
5.8	217.7	63.2	2.2	1.1	62487.9	127.5
10.4	112.7	40.1	2.4	5.6	104465.4	169.0
21.9	156.4	61.3	2.0	14.2	90745.1	214.5
10.6	127.3	70.9	1.0	9.5	175520.2	211.1
8.5	114.9	75.0	0.8	6.5	220929.3	218.6
8.2	52.0	85.2	0.6	-3.0	126031.8	111.3
7.9	42.9	87.6	0.6	-4.2	128768.4	105.4
64.8	113.4	44.7	2.1	21.3	1881877.6	1403.8
10.5	259.5	64.1	1.9	5.0	39251.8	139.3
11.8	330.1	66.4	2.0	5.2	38882.2	152.0
2.5	102.5	39.2	1.3	0.8	20846.8	75.7
8.1	118.9	73.1	2.1	4.5	35426.8	111.5
4.5		152.7	1.6	-8.6	32148.4	24.6
4.0	77.5	56.1	1.3	-2.6	52632.7	78.0
8.0	101.6	42.3	2.0	7.2	52311.2	132.7
2.6	121.4	35.8	5.9	-3.6	109126.1	157.6
5.1	125.7	78.2	1.5	4.9	73085.0	123.5
12.8	192.3	55.3	2.4	9.7	150076.0	225.7
16.4	318.5	53.9	2.4	7.6	126731.6	227.3
9.7	77.8	59.7	1.9	24.9	202395.8	289.0
21.4	144.0	43.8	1.1	31.3	138564.5	295.6
14.1	100.0	68.6	0.4	27.9	133278.9	248.2
4.7		169.5	2.9	-2.6	73610.2	85.8
2.4	69.5	41.9	0.8	3.2	49011.3	87.2
8.0	118.7	57.3	1.1	7.5	89761.5	149.2
7.4	128.6	56.9	1.0	5.5	84039.4	138.1
14.9	126.9	60.6	3.7	4.8	268041.4	287.2
34.2	166.7	52.3	5.0	14.7	206296.1	341.2
-1.4	518.6	12.8	4.8	-1.7	55764.1	166.1
2.3	31.7	64.5	0.6	4.1	27064.1	68.9
4.9		110.8	1.0	4.4	45431.2	76.3
2.3	108.7	77.4	2.3	0.6	30191.2	82.7
-1.3	863.8	51.3	2.0	-5.0	83080.5	190.1
21.1	157.5	47.1	1.3	13.0	93085.1	207.6
7.0	145.0	70.0	2.1	0.8	153349.9	171.8
7.2	154.4	70.6	2.2	0.8	160004.2	178.5
18.6	50875.2	73.7	0.6	22.2	142025.2	7012.2
-0.4	129.9	21.8	1.2	-9.9	68849.2	58.4

11-14 各地、州、市、县(市)国有及国有控股工业企业主要经济效益指标

单位: %　　　　　　　　　　　　　　　　　　　　　　　　　　　　(2007 年)

地　区	Region	工业增加值率 Ratio of Value Added to Gross Industrial Output Value	资金利税率 Ratio of Profits and Taxes to Capital	产值利税率 Ratio of Profits And Taxes to Industrial Output Value
总　计	**Total**	**39.8**	**32.7**	**33.1**
乌鲁木齐市	**Urumqi City**	**24.7**	**18.1**	**16.7**
#乌鲁木齐县	Urumqi County	60.5	4.9	29.9
克拉玛依市	**Karamay City**	**44.8**	**45.5**	**37.9**
石河子市	**Shihezi City**	**26.2**	**7.4**	**16.6**
阿拉尔市	**Aral City**	**29.4**	**6.2**	**9.0**
图木舒克市	**Tumxuk City**	**12.9**	**0.6**	**1.0**
五家渠市	**Wujiaqu City**	**15.4**	**6.6**	**9.7**
吐鲁番地区	**Turpan Administrative Offices**	**50.2**	**38.3**	**43.1**
吐鲁番市	Turpan City	16.0	-2.8	-2.9
鄯善县	Shanshan [Piqan] County	51.7	42.1	45.6
托克逊县	Toksun County	41.1	4.9	18.6
哈密地区	**Hami [Kumul] Administrative Offices**	**31.7**	**12.0**	**15.9**
哈密市	Hami [Kumul] City	30.7	10.9	14.4
巴里坤哈萨克自治县	Barkol Kazak Autonomous County	45.3	12.0	26.3
伊吾县	Yiwu [Araturuk] County	56.1	51.7	53.7
昌吉回族自治州	**Changji Hui Autonomous Prefecture**	**30.7**	**7.3**	**8.2**
昌吉市	Changji City	26.9	-2.3	-3.6
阜康市	Fukang City	26.9	51.3	19.6
呼图壁县	Hutubi County	25.3	7.0	4.5
玛纳斯县	Manas County	50.2	11.0	15.6
奇台县	Qitai County	24.6	8.2	6.4
吉木萨尔县	Jimsar County	29.0	-0.2	-0.6
木垒哈萨克自治县	Mori Kazak Autonomous County			
伊犁哈萨克自治州	**Ili Kazak Autonomous Prefecture**	**47.9**	**23.3**	**35.7**
伊犁州直属县(市)	**Counties (Cities) Direct Under Ili Prefecture**	**42.9**	**15.2**	**31.0**
伊宁市	Yining [Gulja] City	38.8	9.4	16.5
奎屯市	Kuytun City	49.8	29.0	41.4
伊宁县	Yining [Gulja] County	28.6	21.6	21.6
察布查尔锡伯自治县	Qapqal Xibe Autonomous County	-8.0	-10.7	-26.3
霍城县	Huocheng [Korgas] County	22.6	20.4	21.6
巩留县	Gongliu [Tokkuztara] County	54.7	0.7	13.1
新源县	Xinyuan [Kunes] County	51.4	31.3	38.5
昭苏县	Zhaosu [Mongolkure] County			
特克斯县	Tekes County	44.8	23.3	19.5
尼勒克县	Nilka County	50.2	4.0	30.8

Main Indicators on Economic Efficiency of State-owened and State-holding Industrial Enterprises by Prefecture, Autonomous Prefecture, City and County

(%)

总资产贡献率 Ratio of Total Assets to Industrial Output Value	资本保值增值率 Ratio of Capital Hold And Rise	资产负债率 Assets Liability Ratio	流动资产周转次数（次/年） Number of Times of Annual Turnover of Circulating Funds (times/year)	成本费用利润率 Ratio of Profits to Industrial Cost	全员劳动生产率（元/人·年） Overall Labor Productivity (yuan/person-year)	工业经济效益综合指数 Comprehensive Index of Industry and Economic Results
28.8	**129.1**	**49.4**	**3.2**	**29.9**	**319743.3**	**434.4**
17.5	**128.7**	**43.6**	**3.1**	**10.3**	**198125.1**	**265.2**
6.2	636.8	68.4	0.5	29.7	752605.8	691.7
35.2	**118.1**	**41.1**	**3.9**	**35.9**	**481601.8**	**573.4**
9.9	**219.4**	**59.5**	**1.4**	**8.4**	**99794.4**	**178.9**
9.1	**230.3**	**66.8**	**1.0**	**4.6**	**103214.8**	**158.1**
2.7	**85.6**	**74.5**	**0.9**	**0.2**	**51131.1**	**74.9**
5.5	**128.4**	**73.0**	**1.2**	**7.9**	**52125.4**	**120.3**
41.9	**209.2**	**47.8**	**3.4**	**48.0**	**497190.1**	**647.5**
-0.4	75.0	65.8	5.3	-8.4	65308.6	92.9
46.6	221.5	44.9	3.3	53.4	546579.7	707.5
9.6	117.4	87.8	3.4	4.3	340080.4	306.0
11.5	**130.2**	**59.5**	**1.4**	**9.2**	**82343.1**	**162.5**
10.6	132.4	60.5	1.5	7.6	77594.0	152.4
8.2	57.4	78.2	0.7	8.0	92027.4	134.5
48.6	113.6	14.7	1.0	77.8	1015215.1	1051.1
8.3	**74.8**	**82.1**	**2.3**	**1.8**	**124782.7**	**149.9**
1.1	102.1	84.1	1.6	-9.8	88399.9	66.6
29.6	102.7	63.8	4.7	19.2	185084.0	324.7
5.2	74.5	81.0	3.3	0.9	59198.3	109.6
12.9	85.1	90.3	2.9	5.3	205905.8	224.7
5.7	120.0	91.1	2.3	0.7	58645.2	103.9
0.7	37.2	98.8	0.7	-2.3	63467.4	55.3
20.2	**130.9**	**64.9**	**1.9**	**27.6**	**179069.1**	**310.2**
13.8	**129.6**	**64.3**	**1.4**	**12.1**	**169313.4**	**229.9**
11.0	123.9	75.2	2.1	8.7	98721.0	171.2
27.3	117.3	62.6	1.6	8.1	318819.9	331.0
17.9	166.8	47.1	2.5	19.0	84808.1	227.3
-4.9		103.0	0.5	-21.5	-69476.2	-114.1
17.8	153.5	62.2	2.1	14.2	71236.8	197.3
1.4	148.8	67.7	0.2	-3.8	291487.9	210.2
24.9	106.8	27.6	1.2	24.9	170029.9	294.8
17.0	167.1	88.5	1.4	1.5	166037.7	189.6
8.6	148.0	79.9	1.9	14.7	508152.2	437.4

11-14 续表 1

单位: %

地　　区	Region	工业增加值率 Ratio of Value Added to Gross Industrial Output Value	资金利税率 Ratio of Profits and Taxes to Capital	产值利税率 Ratio of Profits and Taxes to Industrial Output Value
塔城地区	**Tacheng [Tarbagatai] Administrative Offices**	**32.3**	**7.7**	**10.0**
塔城市	Tacheng [Qoqek] City	32.4	1.1	1.8
乌苏市	Usu City	28.2	-2.0	-3.1
额敏县	Emin [Dorbiljin] County	19.8	13.1	14.9
沙湾县	Shawan County	28.3	4.2	5.2
托里县	Toli County	59.1	22.2	23.7
裕民县	Yumin [Qagantokay] County			
和布克赛尔蒙古自治县	Hoboksar Mongol Autonomous County	36.7	12.4	16.4
阿勒泰地区	**Altay Administrative Offices**	**65.9**	**66.8**	**59.8**
阿勒泰市	Altay City	29.7	1.6	3.4
布尔津县	Burqin County	35.7	11.3	22.5
富蕴县	Fuyun [Koktokay] County	60.1	122.0	56.0
福海县	Fuhai [Burultokay] County	86.8	-4.3	-43.5
哈巴河县	Habahe [Kaba] County	82.0	109.6	81.6
青河县	Qinghe [Qinggil] County			
吉木乃县	Jeminay County			
博尔塔拉蒙古自治州	**Bortala Mongol Autonomous Prefecture**	**23.2**	**6.1**	**8.8**
博乐市	Bole [Bortala] City	22.6	6.1	9.3
精河县	Jinghe [Jing] County	28.8	8.1	6.8
温泉县	Wenquan [Araxang] County	18.2	-0.4	-0.4
巴音郭楞蒙古自治州	**Bayangol Mongol Autonomous Prefecture**	**64.7**	**65.6**	**69.3**
库尔勒市	Korla City	65.7	68.3	71.1
轮台县	Luntai [Bugur] County			
尉犁县	Yuli [Lopnur] County	35.4	1.6	2.2
若羌县	Ruoqiang [Qarkilik] County	43.1	13.4	29.6
且末县	Qiemo [Qarqan] County	59.2	-0.9	-3.2
焉耆回族自治县	Yanqi Hui Autonomous County	24.3	17.3	15.1
和静县	Hejing County	27.9	10.8	14.0
和硕县	Hoxud County	40.4	3.6	4.7
博湖县	Bohu [Bagrax] County	23.0	6.9	8.3
阿克苏地区	**Aksu Administrative Offices**	**20.1**	**15.2**	**13.2**
阿克苏市	Aksu City	37.7	7.2	12.1
温宿县	Wensu [Onsu] County	59.7	51.4	45.6
库车县	Kuqa County	14.7	19.8	13.0

Continued

(%)

总资产贡献率 Ratio of Total Assets to Industrial Output Value	资本保值增值率 Ratio of Capital Hold and Rise	资产负债率 Assets Liability Ratio	流动资产周转次数(次/年) Number of Times of Annual Turnover Working Capitals (times/year)	成本费用利润率 Ratio of Profits to Industrial Cost	全员劳动生产率(元/人·年) Overall Labor Productivity (yuan/person-year)	工业经济效益综合指数 Comprehensive Index of Industry Economic Results
9.5	**118.7**	**82.4**	**2.0**	**5.1**	**69209.9**	**132.6**
5.0		144.0	2.5	-6.9	85523.5	73.8
1.6		101.0	3.2	-7.3	104576.9	83.9
11.5	93.2	61.9	1.7	7.7	103991.3	166.6
9.1	104.5	88.7	2.0	2.9	121394.1	151.0
17.0	141.3	56.5	2.3	25.2	54845.4	225.0
10.9	135.8	55.4	1.7	11.6	39247.3	147.6
49.5	**138.5**	**53.9**	**3.0**	**92.5**	**402608.5**	**759.6**
3.8	115.3	89.3	2.4	-2.3	66471.3	95.0
12.7	104.8	44.0	2.4	13.8	115597.5	208.5
51.4	193.8	40.5	5.0	69.6	315403.6	650.4
-4.4	164.2	9.2	0.4	-34.2	468636.4	198.1
92.3	103.1	54.3	2.7	254.6	1446429.6	2076.2
6.5	**111.2**	**73.7**	**2.0**	**2.1**	**51753.2**	**106.9**
6.5	121.4	73.8	2.0	2.1	51121.9	108.8
7.1	40.2	74.8	1.5	2.2	51807.8	95.1
0.7	100.0	66.3	0.8	-0.9	172666.7	144.2
56.0	**120.6**	**54.4**	**4.4**	**132.1**	**1007164.6**	**1298.8**
59.8	121.3	52.4	4.8	139.8	1204942.3	1458.6
1.5	54.5	64.6	3.1	0.2	45588.6	89.1
4.8	103.4	75.7	0.6	30.3	74988.6	209.5
-0.8		102.6	2.1	-11.0	80013.3	39.3
26.3	269.1	91.7	3.1	7.5	65187.9	196.7
10.4	146.4	60.6	1.5	12.0	126342.5	198.9
6.0	154.8	63.9	0.9	3.8	67465.4	118.9
20.4		115.3	1.8	6.4	131562.1	173.7
15.2	**142.9**	**49.3**	**4.7**	**7.9**	**201028.8**	**270.5**
6.7	118.5	51.0	1.5	5.0	114048.0	156.5
30.0	185.3	63.6	1.9	60.7	68117.3	393.8
22.3	181.0	47.2	9.6	8.2	503977.3	522.7

11-14 续表 2

单位: %

地　区	Region	工业增加值率 Ratio of Value Added to Gross Industrial Output Value	资金利税率 Ratio of Profits and Taxes to Capital	产值利税率 Ratio of Profits and Taxes to Industrial Output Value
沙雅县	Xayar County			
新和县	Xinhe [Toksu] County			
拜城县	Baicheng [Bay] County	43.9	11.1	15.5
乌什县	Wushi [Uxturpan] County	51.5	14.2	18.2
阿瓦提县	Awat County			
柯坪县	Kalpin County			
克孜勒苏柯尔克孜自治州	**Kizilsu Kirgiz Autonomous Prefecture**	**34.3**	**24.0**	**24.7**
阿图什市	Artux City	29.7	2.2	5.8
阿克陶县	Akto County	35.6	51.7	29.9
阿合奇县	Akqi County			
乌恰县	Wuqia [Ulugqat] County			
喀什地区	**Kashgar [Kaxgar] Administrative Offices**	**34.1**	**-0.6**	**-1.3**
喀什市	Kashgar [Kaxgar] City	33.8	-1.0	-2.4
疏附县	Shufu County	38.1	1.3	4.8
疏勒县	Shule County	35.9	17.4	31.0
英吉沙县	Yengisar County	37.4	-3.6	-7.6
泽普县	Zepu [Poskam] County			
莎车县	Shache [Yarkant] County	49.5	1.5	6.9
叶城县	Yecheng [Kagilik] County			
麦盖提县	Makit County			
岳普湖县	Yopurga County			
伽师县	Jiashi [Payzawat] County			
巴楚县	Bachu [Maralbexi] County			
塔什库尔干塔吉克自治县	Taxkorgan Tajik Autonomous County			
和田地区	**Hotan Administrative Offices**	**41.6**	**2.3**	**9.4**
和田市	Hotan City	34.9	1.8	6.0
和田县	Hotan County	67.0	2.6	19.7
墨玉县	Moyu [Karakax] County			
皮山县	Pishan [Guma] County	35.5	12.3	11.1
洛浦县	Lop County			
策勒县	Qira County			
于田县	Yutian [Keriya] County			
民丰县	Minfeng [Niya] County			

Continued

(%)

总资产贡献率 Ratio of Total Assets to Industrial Output Value	资本保值增值率 Ratio of Capital Hold and Rise	资产负债率 Assets Liability Ratio	流动资产周转次数(次/年) Number of Times of Annual Turnover of Circulating Funds (times/year)	成本费用利润率 Ratio of Profits to Industrial Cost	全员劳动生产率(元/人·年) Overall Labor Productivity (yuan/person-year)	工业经济效益综合指数 Comprehensive Index of Industry Economic Results
12.7	97.6	54.2	5.4	4.6	173626.8	238.7
11.3	114.9	39.3	1.2	22.7	169542.9	261.6
13.2	**64.7**	**88.3**	**2.8**	**19.6**	**69860.2**	**194.2**
2.4	100.6	77.3	1.5	-5.8	28109.3	48.9
21.8	27.8	94.0	3.9	30.7	108841.8	279.2
3.4		**102.8**	**2.4**	**-9.3**	**88431.9**	**61.7**
3.2		108.0	2.5	-10.5	97082.1	62.5
4.4	7.2	97.3	0.8	-5.6	11862.5	16.4
12.8	100.0	1.6	2.1	24.4	227730.2	336.1
-4.6	120.0	77.6	4.8	-11.0	77583.9	80.3
1.0	54.3	32.6	1.9	0.9	39658.5	80.7
3.8	**236.0**	**61.7**	**0.9**	**-0.9**	**56838.6**	**103.4**
4.4		103.0	0.9	-3.4	49792.5	48.2
2.6	248.0	10.7	0.6	9.8	137764.6	189.3
20.2		103.3	1.7	-0.7	23284.6	80.0

11-15 分行业大中型工业企业主要经济指标

单位: 万元 (2007 年)

行业	Sector	企业单位数(个) Number of Enterp-rises (unit)	#亏损企业 Loss- Suffering Enterprises	工业总产值(当年价格) Gross Industrial Output Value (At Current Prices)
煤炭开采和洗选业	Mining and Washing of Coal	17	2	359922.7
石油和天然气开采业	Extraction of Petroleum and Natural Gas	8		11146330.1
#天然原油和天然气开采	Extraction of Ores Crude Oil and Natural Gas Extraction	4		9655956.2
黑色金属矿采选业	Processing of Ferrous Metals Ores	3		192771.4
有色金属矿采选业	Processing of Nonferrous Metals Ores	6		286190.4
非金属矿采选业	Processing of Nonmetal Ores	2		20246.5
#采 盐	Extraction of Salt	1		9974.5
农副食品加工业	Processing of Food from Agricultural Products	16	1	308117.1
#谷物磨制	Grain Grinding	1		30973.4
饲料加工	Fodder Processing	1		37329.8
制 糖	Sugar Making	12		222872.1
食品制造业	Manufacture of Food	10	2	206790.4
#罐头制造	Manufacture of can	3	1	132653.5
饮料制造业	Manufacture of Beverage	7	2	146003.1
#酒的制造	Manufacture of Wine	7	2	146003.1
烟草制品业	Manufacture of Tobacco	1		140912.3
纺织业	Manufacture of Textile	39	11	1141282.6
#棉、化纤纺织及印染精加工	Cotton, Chemical Fiber, Dyeing, Printing and Processing	32	10	1061665.1
毛纺织和染整精加工	Wool Textile, Dyeing and Printing	2		11993.9
纺织服装、鞋、帽制造业	Manufacture of Textile Wearing Apparel,Footware and Caps	1		7425.9
木材加工及木、竹、藤、棕、草制品业	Processing of Timber, Wood, Bamboo, Cane, Grass Products	1		10752.3
家具制造业	Manufacture of Furniture	3		78871.0
造纸及纸制品业	Manufacture of Paper and Paper Products	3	2	69701.1
印刷业和记录媒介的复制	Printing and Copying of Medium for Record	1		6582.7
石油加工、炼焦及核燃料加工业	Oil Processing, Coking and Nuclear Fuel Processing	11	3	6652856.1
#炼 焦	Coking	4		97998.6
化学原料及化学制品制造业	Raw Chemical Material and Chemical Products	21	5	1030432.9
#基础化学原料制造	Basic Chemical Material	12	5	553855.4
肥料制造	Fertilizer Making	3		140520.4
医药制造业	Manufacture of Medicine	1		8616.7
化学纤维制造业	Manufacture of Chemical Fiber	4		285494.4
橡胶制品业	Manufacture of Rubber Products	1	1	52277.0
塑料制品业	Manufacture of Plastic Products	4	1	118536.7
非金属矿物制品业	Manufacture of Nonmetal Mineral Products	26	4	495444.8
#水泥制造	Manufacture of Cement	19	3	316454.2
黑色金属冶炼及压延加工业	Smelting and Pressing of Ferrous Metals	15	2	2186492.8
有色金属冶炼及压延加工业	Smelting and Pressing of Nonferrous Metals	4		255779.4
金属制品业	Manufacture of Metal Products	6	1	104228.6
通用设备制造业	Manufacture of General Purpose Machinery	1	1	6737.0
专用设备制造业	Manufacture of Special Purpose Machinery	4	1	33559.8
交通运输设备制造业	Manufacture of Transport Equipment	2		62381.7
电气机械及器材制造业	Manufacture of Electric Equipment and Machinery	4		595784.2
通信设备、计算机及其他电子设备制造业	Telecom Equipment, Computer and Other Electronic Equipment	1		107971.6
电力、热力的生产和供应业	Electricity and Thermal Production and Supply	32	16	1407935.5
#电力生产和电力供应	Electricity Production and Supply	30	15	1390534.7
燃气生产和供应业	Gas Production and Supply	1		56363.2
水的生产和供应业	Water Production and Supply	1	1	12054.5

Main Indicators of Large-scale and Medium-scale Industrial Enterprises by Sectors

(10 000 yuan)

工业增加值 Added Value of Industry	工业销售产值(当年价) Sales Value of Industry Products (At Current Prices)	出口交货值 Delivery Value of Industry Export	实收资本 Total Capital Hold	资产合计 Total Assets	流动资产合计 Total Working Capitals	#产成品 Finished Product	流动资产年平均余额 Annual Average Balance of Circulating Funds	固定资产原价 Original Value of Fixed Assets
214218.1	470994.9		410727.0	956347.2	364094.2	12365.6	314730.3	539135.3
8946862.3	11168808.7	448.0	7783491.7	15003243.5	3116824.4	38598.9	2945972.9	18254224.6
8467757.5	9686204.8		6288818.0	12079336.7	1454800.1	34190.1	1457055.1	16613556.2
60776.8	175798.0		72116.3	234553.2	120629.6	26326.2	96444.8	106263.8
247767.3	296618.1		34993.4	245734.3	92045.8	4999.1	89799.7	96243.6
7906.6	20358.1	427.6	3899.9	19888.5	11721.6	2109.0	9200.9	12193.4
3840.2	10193.1	427.6	900.0	9177.3	5407.3	1011.5	2503.0	3828.6
73158.2	289094.6		75456.4	386029.7	230348.0	78109.6	196184.8	206863.9
3382.4	30192.5		7800.0	39098.0	21048.6	2178.2	22280.9	13131.5
8707.2	37994.5		9600.0	61340.4	31946.2	2029.9	32423.2	29649.9
61854.7	205144.1		47243.4	253164.4	154242.4	71482.6	123229.1	152647.9
61469.7	212371.8	81849.4	71628.3	434197.1	244287.6	29907.6	231292.3	199331.5
43625.0	133835.7	74755.1	54746.8	316221.3	202397.7	23023.2	191163.3	137198.1
83088.6	140157.5		100240.5	362259.8	197831.0	5853.5	187177.9	186267.2
83088.6	140157.5		100240.5	362259.8	197831.0	5853.5	187177.9	186267.2
99927.7	143756.5		18741.7	141073.0	65135.6		68318.8	83494.0
293218.1	1085174.7	45842.7	447559.4	1639160.5	839186.9	203276.2	773932.9	1066643.8
270231.0	1007213.6	23493.4	384843.2	1510032.5	762467.0	186700.1	691087.8	983618.3
3277.6	13470.1	3421.0	8283.8	16084.3	10574.1	5842.7	10706.4	6963.3
2015.5	7229.8	152.8	2025.3	5438.6	3655.9	148.8	2227.4	3645.2
1835.1	10777.2		266.5	4134.5	2446.9	846.6	2456.2	3700.8
14611.3	79138.7	63456.2	43047.5	199411.0	52079.0	11610.2	50621.3	58719.4
22082.6	70160.7		43589.0	144788.3	50828.6	5839.7	48672.2	121400.8
3142.3	6484.8		5727.4	17760.5	3589.7	433.0	3842.7	21435.0
326545.2	6675385.5		2862175.4	4601710.9	1555221.7	119173.8	1208285.5	3073567.9
41274.6	86843.3		32039.7	165387.3	67688.5	5290.1	55413.1	72291.9
314300.6	1012651.8	84063.4	471318.9	2360313.6	771454.2	70714.8	609195.8	1092131.0
156355.9	546599.4	83757.3	166985.9	1227229.5	556032.9	37456.1	413981.4	525845.2
65105.0	141500.9		118649.7	493411.9	100215.3	1879.4	76863.4	227487.4
3644.8	8579.9	131.4	4093.4	19776.2	6746.4	1027.3	7805.4	15087.8
96151.4	297424.8	1953.2	40766.9	272163.0	159786.7	32170.8	117364.8	134919.4
10410.0	52369.0	1974.0	14130.0	45170.8	23701.4	8565.0	20131.8	35766.0
36006.0	102790.0		297961.2	353649.1	157984.0	31887.4	151570.4	256450.0
160333.0	491451.6	53479.7	292078.7	1362709.5	484642.1	24383.7	479203.9	648615.1
116487.9	314640.6	1248.0	152562.5	790831.4	303236.1	9417.3	286058.1	509509.1
436192.0	2212496.3	79563.1	426726.4	1809421.7	818640.8	87203.6	654526.1	1273356.5
70755.9	256006.2		37628.6	181246.0	75017.2	7969.8	60158.7	135815.7
20706.0	102566.8		56661.3	110988.2	45931.6	8821.8	43164.2	31740.7
1130.7	15080.8		1994.5	6105.5	3570.7	89.9	3416.5	3412.7
9152.1	32082.4		2250.9	67795.0	45023.5	8335.6	43999.7	32637.3
4550.8	64667.5	571.9	10015.8	48096.7	29519.6	6107.5	24752.6	19215.1
146813.1	566901.6	8169.7	106403.8	1121726.5	797514.8	48197.5	408463.2	109680.5
33867.6	100319.4	26602.2	29805.9	146972.3	53413.2	6072.8	47800.0	122998.6
542977.7	1402115.4		558133.2	2835356.7	611299.9	8.1	601945.4	3220546.6
537812.4	1384714.6		533427.2	2760036.2	577116.3	8.1	562477.9	3144753.2
14953.2	42339.8		44244.2	167734.7	61545.3	319.3	92891.7	82698.8
7183.1	12054.5		140000.0	168662.8	12086.5		12640.2	179085.7

11-15 续表

单位: 万元

行　业	Sector	固定资产净值年平均余额 Annual Average Balance of Net Value of Fixed Assets	流动负债合计 Total Working Liabilities	长期负债合计 Long-term Liabilities	所有者权益合计 Creditors' Equities
煤炭开采和洗选业	Mining and Washing of Coal	307505.9	307180.8	141835.8	504606.5
石油和天然气开采业	Extraction of Petroleum and Natural Gas	9395847.5	2717006.1	2950142.9	8857596.7
#天然原油和天然气开采	Extraction of Ores Crude Oil and Natural Gas Extraction	8569340.8	1522476.4	2945288.0	7133081.5
黑色金属矿采选业	Processing of Ferrous Metals Ores	46470.9	82982.6	28103.1	123467.4
有色金属矿采选业	Processing of Nonferrous Metals Ores	63431.8	98616.2	8803.1	136249.5
非金属矿采选业	Processing of Nonmetal Ores	5766.8	11118.8		8769.7
#采　盐	Extraction of Salt	2011.0	5005.1		4172.2
农副食品加工业	Processing of Food from Agricultural Products	112367.2	211012.6	14005.9	160105.2
#谷物磨制	Grain Grinding	9495.2	21613.8		17484.2
饲料加工	Fodder Processing	21723.2	10724.4	11533.0	39083.0
制　糖	Sugar Making	75918.0	152925.2	1826.4	97510.8
食品制造业	Manufacture of Food	140266.5	236191.2	40444.7	157301.7
#罐头制造	Manufacture of can	100554.1	184138.6	31870.0	100041.8
饮料制造业	Manufacture of Beverage	112340.8	132878.1	153568.7	74086.6
#酒的制造	Manufacture of Wine	112340.8	132878.1	153568.7	74086.6
烟草制品业	Manufacture of Tobacco	51317.1	63049.5		78023.5
纺织业	Manufacture of Textile	618719.0	914648.8	101887.7	614029.9
#棉、化纤纺织及印染精加工	Cotton, Chemical Fiber, Dyeing, Printing and Processing	577592.6	863997.9	100692.8	536985.8
毛纺织和染整精加工	Wool Textile, Dyeing and Printing	5039.3	7801.8	206.9	8075.6
纺织服装、鞋、帽制造业	Manufacture of Textile Wearing Apparel,Footware and Caps	1872.3	4477.1	157.2	804.3
木材加工及木、竹、藤、棕、草制品业	Processing of Timber, Wood, Bamboo, Cane, Grass Products	1446.5	3129.5	385.8	619.2
家具制造业	Manufacture of Furniture	43784.0	35273.3	12900.0	151237.7
造纸及纸制品业	Manufacture of Paper and Paper Products	73674.7	65420.2	15316.8	64051.3
印刷业和记录媒介的复制	Printing and Copying of Medium for Record	12434.6	4677.2	2759.0	10324.3
石油加工、炼焦及核燃料加工业	Oil Processing, Coking and Nuclear Fuel Processing	1393897.9	667833.3	917469.0	2960703.3
#炼　焦	Coking	66845.7	45038.0	3308.3	61335.7
化学原料及化学制品制造业	Raw Chemical Material and Chemical Products	819990.3	895844.4	388290.4	1067231.1
#基础化学原料制造	Basic Chemical Material	425526.7	479803.9	162614.6	583496.6
肥料制造	Fertilizer Making	172979.5	185406.0	110845.8	197160.1
医药制造业	Manufacture of Medicine	12542.5	6886.8	776.5	12112.9
化学纤维制造业	Manufacture of Chemical Fiber	85319.7	142627.6	12720.0	116815.4
橡胶制品业	Manufacture of Rubber Products	16316.7	68818.0	8798.6	-32445.8
塑料制品业	Manufacture of Plastic Products	155311.1	113045.9	5000.0	224889.8
非金属矿物制品业	Manufacture of Nonmetal Mineral Products	345715.2	489711.7	208111.6	659149.1
#水泥制造	Manufacture of Cement	275687.6	300659.1	154499.2	329936.0
黑色金属冶炼及压延加工业	Smelting and Pressing of Ferrous Metals	834288.9	829678.5	271797.1	707876.2
有色金属冶炼及压延加工业	Smelting and Pressing of Nonferrous Metals	35131.8	81198.9	8266.8	91668.6
金属制品业	Manufacture of Metal Products	17893.7	43793.7	1508.6	65205.3
通用设备制造业	Manufacture of General Purpose Machinery	2497.8	5574.7		530.8
专用设备制造业	Manufacture of Special Purpose Machinery	13237.6	74164.9	3180.9	-9550.9
交通运输设备制造业	Manufacture of Transport Equipment	7375.6	41356.1	302.0	6438.6
电气机械及器材制造业	Manufacture of Electric Equipment and Machinery	64511.9	484192.1	123855.0	508150.3
通信设备、计算机及其他电子设备制造业	Telecom Equipment, Computer and Other Electronic Equipment	73201.0	36498.2	48705.0	61769.1
电力、热力的生产和供应业	Electricity and Thermal Production and Supply	1859854.9	1232828.2	778548.4	788596.7
#电力生产和电力供应	Electricity Production and Supply	1820457.5	1198654.2	775357.0	752441.7
燃气生产和供应业	Gas Production and Supply	23992.3	91312.3	32178.2	44244.2
水的生产和供应业	Water Production and Supply	148579.7	21595.6	7083.0	136384.2

Continued

(10 000 yuan)

主营业务收入 Revenue from Principal Business	#主营业务成本 Cost of Principal Business	主营业务税金及附加 Taes and Other Charges on Principal Business	营业利润 Business Profit	利润总额 Total Profit	亏损企业亏损总额 Losses Value of Loss-Suffering Enterprises	利税总额 Total Profits and Taxes	本年应交增值税 Value-added Taxes Payable	全部从业人员年平均人数(人) Ann Employed Persons (person)
363184.5	262545.4	4834.0	24970.4	25125.4	4561.0	71673.0	41713.6	33366
12036874.9	4801028.6	297624.9	5814240.1	5861558.3		7309728.3	1150545.1	106475
9991974.7	2783385.0	282968.3	5874592.5	5852629.5		7178991.5	1043393.7	42928
187576.4	121146.9	2572.1	40214.5	39934.0		55206.3	12700.2	2693
299193.9	77105.5	3392.5	196338.4	177691.3		215416.5	34332.7	4681
15866.1	12219.6	184.7	585.6	679.4		1944.9	1080.8	1539
10602.4	7396.7	101.8	510.5	634.8		1610.7	874.1	739
352148.1	261086.4	1765.0	35053.7	34686.5	652.5	55070.1	18618.6	8746
30913.5	28398.9	15.2	793.4	1038.4		1192.9	139.3	349
69938.2	54832.2	104.5	4744.7	4872.0		5982.9	1006.4	650
229428.9	157528.7	1624.1	29536.9	28818.1		47700.0	17257.8	6918
212187.1	158656.6	660.0	12338.9	12691.5	904.8	21574.4	8222.9	4428
135837.1	95657.9	399.8	9156.7	9307.3	805.9	15402.0	5694.9	1932
136319.0	75640.7	15527.1	10281.6	11486.5	10502.4	42038.2	15024.6	4851
136319.0	75640.7	15527.1	10281.6	11486.5	10502.4	42038.2	15024.6	4851
143756.5	52350.9	54740.1	16366.4	15497.9		86004.2	15766.2	531
1354256.9	1189631.1	6247.9	89655.0	63351.9	15623.8	107585.8	37986.0	70346
1277105.6	1124782.6	6030.7	89170.9	66422.4	5367.0	107211.0	34757.9	62795
15578.4	13659.7	80.5	228.7	269.1		882.3	532.7	1650
8060.4	6755.8	1.7	242.3	309.1		339.9	29.1	642
6491.1	6117.2	29.3	18.5	6.2		342.1	306.6	314
87701.2	72785.0	7.8	2958.7	4360.3		4482.4	114.3	1832
67373.8	51160.3	561.6	2378.3	-1692.7	5569.4	4278.2	5409.3	3390
6467.6	4542.3	40.3	85.8	517.9		961.3	403.1	764
6921557.4	6702987.3	211189.8	-227311.9	-227984.1	376567.8	120170.2	136964.5	28832
72904.6	46103.8	421.1	20385.3	19840.1		26884.2	6623.0	1864
1373228.5	1097216.2	7438.8	119361.9	129462.9	5541.4	189963.6	53061.9	21928
900191.3	736906.1	3921.8	68099.4	69645.1	5541.4	104141.6	30574.7	12862
144567.3	95444.3	790.4	26847.2	33208.5		39625.7	5626.8	3361
8444.2	5437.3	76.9	523.0	378.5		1224.9	769.5	534
283567.2	207556.8	1399.1	53916.3	56784.4		74693.3	16509.8	5191
60804.2	53046.6	1855.6	-1501.9	-1586.1	1586.1	2040.5	1771.0	1405
120393.7	108077.0	1473.1	4072.8	5468.1	4360.6	11068.6	4127.4	7410
485214.7	372618.0	3051.5	25623.5	42444.8	12298.2	76588.6	31092.3	18690
310239.1	233846.0	2288.4	4373.6	19345.2	11159.8	47540.6	25907.0	14354
2237656.2	1947953.3	5968.8	139189.4	141625.8	67.5	242821.1	95226.5	20765
256429.1	205213.8	851.8	36390.8	39901.6		51977.9	11224.5	3832
108590.1	99533.1	346.0	1522.8	1611.4	631.1	4123.6	2166.2	3196
5706.1	5117.3	47.5	-292.1	-511.8	511.8	-344.2	120.1	330
42435.4	35424.4	120.2	1185.4	1232.5	1614.4	2834.1	1481.4	2327
66365.0	62266.4	25.5	863.0	797.5		1156.3	333.3	1296
657073.5	500613.8	1842.5	75143.2	87484.3		96788.7	7461.9	2894
105773.4	71532.5	730.9	14824.0	13658.9		21232.3	6842.5	1930
1458602.6	1305416.6	10795.5	-7587.4	-4447.4	67501.6	122166.2	115818.1	38238
1438595.2	1288186.4	10722.6	-6282.0	-5247.3	67427.6	120468.7	114993.4	37498
56363.2	38164.6	610.6	5863.8	11633.3		13713.1	1469.2	1004
18377.0	15969.2	84.6	-7972.8	-5237.4	5237.4	-4305.0	847.8	962

11-16 分行业大中型工业企业主要经济效益指标

单位: %　　(2007 年)

行　业	Sector	工业增加值率 Ratio of Value-added to Gross Industrial Output Value	资金利税率 Ratio of Profits and Taxes to Capital	产值利税率 Ratio of Profits and Taxes to Industrial Output Value
煤炭开采和洗选业	Mining and Washing of Coal	51.4	11.5	19.9
石油和天然气开采业	Extraction of Petroleum and Natural Gas	70.9	59.2	65.6
#天然原油和天然气开采	Extraction of Ores Crude Oil and Natural Gas Extraction	78.2	71.6	74.4
黑色金属矿采选业	Processing of Ferrous Metals Ores	27.7	38.6	28.6
有色金属矿采选业	Processing of Nonferrous Metals Ores	75.9	140.6	75.3
非金属矿采选业	Processing of Nonmetal Ores	34.9	13.0	9.6
#采　盐	Extraction of Salt	32.7	35.7	16.2
农副食品加工业	Processing of Food from Agricultural Products	20.8	17.9	17.9
#谷物磨制	Grain Grinding	9.7	3.8	3.9
饲料加工	Fodder Processing	23.3	11.1	16.0
制　糖	Sugar Making	23.7	24.0	21.4
食品制造业	Manufacture of Food	26.2	5.8	10.4
#罐头制造	Manufacture of can	29.4	5.3	11.6
饮料制造业	Manufacture of Beverage	48.7	14.0	28.8
#酒的制造	Manufacture of Wine	48.7	14.0	28.8
烟草制品业	Manufacture of Tobacco	60.4	71.9	61.0
纺织业	Manufacture of Textile	23.2	7.7	9.4
#棉、化纤纺织及印染精加工	Cotton, Chemical Fiber, Dyeing, Printing and Processing	23.0	8.5	10.1
毛纺织和染整精加工	Wool Textile, Dyeing and Printing	22.7	5.6	7.4
纺织服装、鞋、帽制造业	Manufacture of Textile Wearing Apparel,Footware and Caps	25.4	8.3	4.6
木材加工及木、竹、藤、棕、草制品业	Processing of Timber, Wood, Bamboo, Cane, Grass Products	15.5	8.8	3.2
家具制造业	Manufacture of Furniture	17.6	4.8	5.7
造纸及纸制品业	Manufacture of Paper and Paper Products	26.6	3.5	6.1
印刷业和记录媒介的复制	Printing and Copying of Medium for Record	41.3	5.9	14.6
石油加工、炼焦及核燃料加工业	Oil Processing, Coking and Nuclear Fuel Processing	4.2	4.6	1.8
#炼　焦	Coking	36.3	22.0	27.4
化学原料及化学制品制造业	Raw Chemical Material and Chemical Products	26.7	13.3	18.4
#基础化学原料制造	Basic Chemical Material	24.7	12.4	18.8
肥料制造	Fertilizer Making	41.0	15.9	28.2
医药制造业	Manufacture of Medicine	36.2	6.0	14.2
化学纤维制造业	Manufacture of Chemical Fiber	28.7	36.9	26.2
橡胶制品业	Manufacture of Rubber Products	16.6	5.6	3.9
塑料制品业	Manufacture of Plastic Products	25.8	3.6	9.3
非金属矿物制品业	Manufacture of Nonmetal Mineral Products	28.2	9.3	15.5
#水泥制造	Manufacture of Cement	31.6	8.5	15.0
黑色金属冶炼及压延加工业	Smelting and Pressing of Ferrous Metals	16.9	16.3	11.1
有色金属冶炼及压延加工业	Smelting and Pressing of Nonferrous Metals	23.9	54.6	20.3
金属制品业	Manufacture of Metal Products	16.7	6.8	4.0
通用设备制造业	Manufacture of General Purpose Machinery	16.8	-5.8	-5.1
专用设备制造业	Manufacture of Special Purpose Machinery	22.7	5.0	8.4
交通运输设备制造业	Manufacture of Transport Equipment	6.1	3.6	1.9
电气机械及器材制造业	Manufacture of Electric Equipment and Machinery	21.2	20.5	16.3
通信设备、计算机及其他电子设备制造业	Telecom Equipment, Computer and Other Electronic Equipment	29.0	17.6	19.7
电力、热力的生产和供应业	Electricity and Thermal Production and Supply	34.9	5.0	8.7
#电力生产和电力供应	Electricity Production and Supply	35.0	5.1	8.7
燃气生产和供应业	Gas Production and Supply	24.4	11.7	24.3
水的生产和供应业	Water Production and Supply	54.6	-2.7	-35.7

Main Indicators on Economic Efficiency of Large-scale and Medium-scale Industrial Enterprises by Sectors

(%)

总资产贡献率 Ratio of Total Assets to Industrial Output Value	资本保值增值率 Ratio of Capital Held and Rise	资产负债率 Assets Liability Ratio	流动资产周转次数(次/年) Number of Times of Annual Turnover Working Capitals (times/year)	成本费用利润率 Ratio of Profits to Industrial Cost	全员劳动生产率(元/人·年) Overall Labor Productivity (yuan/person-year)	工业经济效益综合指数 Comprehensive Index of Industry Economic Results
8.8	146.1	47.2	1.2	7.5	64202.5	144.1
53.5	126.4	41.0	4.1	105.7	840278.2	1091.0
64.6	122.9	41.0	6.9	170.7	1972548.8	2069.9
26.0	195.6	47.4	1.9	27.7	225684.4	359.4
90.3	116.1	44.6	3.3	174.5	529304.2	1222.3
10.7	99.0	55.9	1.7	4.1	51374.9	122.4
22.1	121.2	54.5	4.2	6.3	51964.8	180.5
17.7	162.3	58.5	1.8	11.1	83647.6	189.7
4.1	100.0	55.3	1.4	3.5	96916.9	133.0
11.9	113.4	36.3	2.2	7.5	133956.9	194.0
22.0	172.8	61.5	1.9	14.8	89411.3	216.4
8.9	124.9	63.8	0.9	6.4	138820.5	175.2
8.9	111.9	68.4	0.7	7.4	225802.3	226.4
13.7	56.0	79.6	0.7	10.6	171281.4	203.3
13.7	56.0	79.6	0.7	10.6	171281.4	203.3
64.8	113.4	44.7	2.1	21.3	1881877.6	1403.8
10.0	209.6	62.5	1.8	4.9	41682.3	131.8
11.1	242.0	64.4	1.9	5.5	43033.8	141.4
5.5	115.0	49.8	1.5	1.8	19864.2	85.8
7.0	100.0	85.2	3.6	4.0	31394.1	113.7
9.0	23.1	85.0	2.6	0.1	58442.7	99.9
3.7	128.0	24.2	1.7	5.1	79756.0	134.3
4.8	90.2	55.8	1.4	-2.6	65140.4	89.9
6.5	111.1	41.9	1.7	7.3	41129.6	121.6
3.2	122.4	35.7	5.7	-3.3	113257.9	160.8
23.8	222.8	62.9	1.3	38.0	221430.3	388.0
13.1	192.2	54.8	2.3	10.3	143333.0	223.6
16.4	303.7	52.5	2.2	8.4	121564.2	223.1
9.6	75.7	60.0	1.9	28.4	193707.2	296.5
7.1	99.6	38.8	1.1	4.8	68254.7	122.2
41.7	259.9	57.1	2.4	24.4	185227.1	366.9
4.9		171.8	3.0	-2.7	74092.5	87.3
2.3	65.8	36.4	0.8	4.6	48591.1	91.3
7.8	122.1	51.6	1.0	9.3	85785.5	153.2
8.5	140.1	58.3	1.1	6.5	81153.6	144.6
17.8	144.1	60.9	3.4	6.8	210061.2	264.5
33.1	136.4	49.4	4.3	18.1	184644.8	328.0
4.9	232.1	41.3	2.5	1.5	64787.2	135.3
-3.0	7.8	91.3	1.7	-8.6	34263.6	33.2
4.3		114.1	1.0	3.0	39330.0	65.5
2.6	190.3	86.6	2.7	1.2	35114.2	100.6
14.4	286.2	54.7	1.6	15.2	507301.7	470.8
17.7	122.8	58.0	2.2	16.4	175479.8	264.1
8.0	146.6	72.2	2.4	-0.3	141999.5	165.2
8.1	140.3	72.7	2.6	-0.4	143424.3	166.2
9.3	100.0	73.6	0.6	22.8	148936.3	231.0
-2.5	176.6	19.1	1.5	-19.7	74668.4	29.8

11-17 主要工业产品产量
Output of Major Industrial Products

产品名称	Item	2006	2007
原煤(吨)	Raw Coal (ton)	45185177	50186413
天然原油(吨)	Crude Oil (ton)	24747427	26043117
天然气(万立方米)	Natural Gas (10 000 cu.m)	1642099	2103348
铁矿石原矿量(吨)	Crudeiron Ore (ton)	10950834	12863205
铜选矿含铜量(吨)	Cuproaurite (ton)	64240	61269
硫铁矿(折含 S 35%)(吨)	Pyritel with Content of (S35%)(ton)	345936	243610
原盐(吨)	Salt (ton)	1532068	855424
发电量(万千瓦小时)	Electricity (10 000 kwh)	3571480	4168662
#火 电	Thermalpower	2990073	3521407
水 电	Hydropower	534265	587756
供热量(万百万千焦)	Heat Supply (10 000 million kj)	14015	19271
大米(吨)	Rice (ton)	154841	173330
小麦粉(万吨)	Wheate Flour (10 000 ton)	337	381
精制食用植物油(吨)	Refined Edible Oil (ton)	832663	941247
成品糖(吨)	Sugar (ton)	537880	649409
配混合饲料(吨)	Forage (ton)	1280123	1428511
糖果(吨)	Candy (ton)	3463	4059
乳制品(吨)	Dairy Products (ton)	32752	54389
罐头(吨)	Canned Food (ton)	543484	637403
味精(吨)	Mono Sodium Glutamate (ton)	8825	6243
酱油(吨)	Soy (ton)	23134	28994
方便面(吨)	Instant Noodles(ton)	25182	26432
发酵酒精(千升)	Zymolytic Alcohol (kilo-liter)	30368	28786
饮料酒(千升)	Alcohol Beverage(kilo-liter)	401771	438502
#白 酒	Liquor	64608	66439
啤 酒	Beer	313300	349177
葡萄酒	Grape Wine	22859	21665
软饮料(吨)	Soft Drink (ton)	523763	670141
#碳酸饮料	Carbonic Drink	18592	22567
果汁及果汁饮料	Fruit Juice and Fruit Drink	148360	160398
瓶(罐)装饮用水	Bottled Water	289397	399287
冷冻饮品(吨)	Ice Beverage (ton)	21823	30807
卷烟(万支)	Cigarettes (10 000 pieces)	850000	1000000
纱(吨)	Yarn (ton)	357324	408870
布(万米)	Cloth (10 000 m)	15415	16000
#棉 布	Pure Cotton Cloth	15415	15989
印染布(万米)	Printing and dyeing Cloth (10 000 m)		396
绒线(毛线)(吨)	Knitting Wool (ton)	799	637

注：1.钢材里包括钢材生产中消耗的外购国内钢。2.乳制品里不包括液体乳。
Note: a) Rolled steel contain that manufacture of steel consumed outsourcing of internal steel.. b) Dairy products do not include Total Working milk.

11-17 续表 1 Continued

产品名称	Item	2006	2007
呢绒(万米)	Woolen Cloth Goods (10 000 m)	327	368
丝(吨)	Silk (ton)	35	15
丝织品(万米)	Silk Produces (10 000 m)	134	107
服装(万件)	Garments (10 000 units)	1977	1119
轻革(平方米)	Light Leather (sq.m)	5155977	4496761
皮鞋(万双)	Leather Shoes (10 000 pairs)	35	47
皮革服装(件)	Leather Garments (unit)	28315	26496
人造板(立方米)	Artificial Board (cu.m)	648582	923915
#胶合板	Plywood	117006	174204
纤维板	Fiberboard	442869	580903
刨花板	Chip Board	64055	120584
家具(件)	Furniture (unit)	2905943	3318577
#木制家具	WoodenFurniture	2496357	2912749
金属家具	Steal Furniture	214903	284897
纸浆(吨)	Paper Pulp (ton)	289923	289074
纸制品(吨)	Paper produces (ton)	178574	216135
#瓦楞纸箱(纸箱)	Corrugaled Case	160389	185024
机制纸及纸板(吨)	Machine-made Paper and Paperboard (ton)	295338	252329
本册(万本)	Copy (10 000 copies)	5398	3658
原油加工量(吨)	Processed Crude Oil (ton)	16160756	17054488
汽油(吨)	Gasoline (ton)	2520277	2773428
溶剂油(吨)	Megilp (ton)		131913
煤油(吨)	Kerosene (ton)	347884	306019
柴油(吨)	Diesel Oil (ton)	7594617	8199646
润滑油(吨)	Lubricating Oil (ton)	540138	674193
燃料油(吨)	Fuel Oil (ton)	500780	666735
石油沥青(吨)	Petroleum Bitumen (ton)	1099015	1123734
液化石油气(吨)	Liquefied Petroleum Gas (ton)	795704	905342
焦炭(吨)	Coke (ton)	3105488	4056796
#机械化焦炉生产的焦炭	Coke Turned out by Mechanized Coke Oven	2168601	2775909
煤气(万立方米)	Coal Gas (10 000 cu.m)	790460	594389
硫酸(折 100%)(吨)	Sulfuric Acid (ton)	160073	183484
盐酸(含量 31%以上)(吨)	Hydrochloric Acid (With Content of 31%) (ton)	156678	177496
氢氧化钠(烧碱)(折 100%)(吨)	Caustic Soda (ton)	423901	485880
碳酸钠(纯碱)(吨)	Soda Ash (ton)	127022	127161
碳化钙(电石)(折 300 升/千克)(吨)	Calcium Carbide (ton)	501283	711277
合成氨(吨)	Synthetic Ammonia (ton)	1303586	1325017
农用氮、磷、钾化学肥料(折纯)(吨)	Chemical Fertilizers (ton)	1290802	1385279
#氮肥(折含 N 100%)	Nitrogen Fertilizers	1209392	1319128
#尿 素	Carbamide	1181978	1297888
磷肥(折合 P_2O_5 100%)	Phosphate Fertilizers	18841	7886

11-17 续表 2 Continued

产品名称	Item	2006	2007
乙烯(吨)	Ethylene(ton)	247221	239229
油漆(吨)	Oil Paint (ton)	26431	24464
塑料树脂及共聚物(吨)	Plastics (ton)	976338	1069082
肥皂(吨)	Soap (ton)	4091	4205
合成洗涤剂(吨)	Synthetic Detergents (ton)	45719	61510
火柴(件)	Match (unit)	241516	293485
化学原料药(吨)	Chemical Medicine (ton)	28	51
中成药(吨)	Traditional Chinese Medicine (ton)	11560	3534
轮胎外胎(条)	Outer Tyres (unit)	1071413	1024361
塑料制品(吨)	Plastic Produces (ton)	412032	517069
#塑料薄膜	Plastic Film	114736	145874
#农用薄膜	Farm Plastic Sheet	104679	133262
塑料型材(含板片材)	Plastic Moulding Material	48995	58875
塑料制管子及其附件(吨)	Plastic Pipe and Accessory (ton)	147216	185545
塑料编织袋(吨)	Woven Plastic Bag (ton)	54309	74002
泡沫塑料(吨)	Foamed Plastics (ton)	7645	8408
塑料包装箱及容器(吨)	Plastic Packing Case and Container (ton)	16344	22916
日用塑料制品(吨)	Household Plastic Products (ton)	22416	22665
水泥熟料(万吨)	Cement Chamotte (10 000 ton)	1007	1165
窑外分解窑熟料(预分解窑熟料)(吨)	Clinker Cement (ton)	2281240	5007962
水泥(万吨)	Cement (10 000 tons)	1335	1537
水泥排水管(千米)	Cement Sewage Duct (1000 m)	2007	1721
水泥压力管(千米)	Cement Pressure Duct (1000 m)	1398	547
水泥电杆(吨)	Cement Electric Pole Piece (ton)	107725	195221
建筑涂料(吨)	Architectural Coating (ton)	16040	14005
商品混凝土(立方米)	Commercial Concrete (cb.m)	3855138	5562966
水泥混凝土桩(水泥预制管桩)(吨)	Pile of Cement Concrete (ton)	421865	287373
砖(折标准砖)(万块)	Brick (Standard Brick) (10 000 pieces)	1028604	1334042
瓦(万片)	Tile (10 000 pieces)	955	1351
大理石板材(平方米)	Marble Slab (sq.m)	176025	119926
花岗石板材(平方米)	Granite Sheet (sq.m)	4534542	5184821
石膏板(平方米)	Plasterboard (sq.m)	6864136	8961365
平板玻璃(重量箱)	Plate Glass (weight case)	1315908	1136643
沥青和改性沥青防水卷材(平方米)	Bitumen and Rolled Waterproof Material (sq.m)	1834338	1941897
中空玻璃(平方米)	Insulating Glass (sq.m)	49755	72826
钢化玻璃(平方米)	Toughened Glass (sq.m)	177463	357109
夹层玻璃(平方米)	Laminated Glass (sq.m)	28731	31008
日用玻璃制品(吨)	Household Glass Products (ton)	59826	77773
玻璃保温容器(万个)	Glass Attemperator (10 000 unit)	1464	1096

11-17 续表 3 Continued

产品名称	Item	2006	2007
细炻砖(平方米)	Silica Brick (sq.m)	7740	1700
炻质砖(平方米)	Glaced Brick (sq.m)	1043500	719435
陶质砖(平方米)	Carbonic Bricks (sq.m)	28076633	33060310
卫生陶瓷（件）	Toilet Wares (unit)	124023	130957
日用陶瓷(万件)	Household Ceramics (10 000 pieces)	15	25
耐火材料制品(吨)	Fire Proof Material (ton)	37926	58460
石墨及碳素制品(吨)	Graphite and Carbon Products (ton)	147083	148544
玻璃纤维增强塑料制品(吨)	Glass Fibre Reinforced Plastices Products (ton)	51360	53411
生铁(吨)	Pig Iron (ton)	3240763	3949685
粗钢(吨)	Crude Steel (ton)	3941938	4472394
钢材(吨)	Rolled Steel (ton)	4114505	4709392
中小型型钢	Medium and Small Fasioned Steel	77794	97601
钢　筋	Concrete Iron	1606808	1484675
盘　条(线材)	Wire Rod	1336594	1423672
铁合金(吨)	Ferroalloy (ton)	34562	57897
铜(吨)	Copper (ton)	4690	4400
镍(吨)	Nickel (ton)	3625	4873
铝(吨)	Aluminium (ton)	48341	54089
铝材(吨)	Aluminium Material (ton)	16252	31946
日用不锈钢制品(吨)	Household Steinless Steel Products (ton)	140	93
工业锅炉(蒸发量吨)	Industrial Boiler (Evaporating Quantity ton)	618	576
输送机械(米)	Conveying Machinery (m)	23191	14003
泵(台)	Pump (unit)	5417	5855
风机(台)	Fan (unit)	4194	4627
弹簧(吨)	Springs (ton)	77	128
轴承(万套)	Bearing (10 000 sets)	126	40
铸钢件(吨)	Steel Casting (ton)	5293	10548
铸铁件(吨)	Iron Casting (ton)	14817	19418
金属锻件(吨)	Iron Casting (ton)	630	759
小型拖拉机(台)	Small-Size Tractor (unit)		5408
收获机械(台)	Harvesting Machinery (unit)	3078	4418
汽车(辆)	Motor Vehicles(unit)	981	2309
载货汽车(辆)	Trucks (unit)	981	2309
改装汽车(辆)	Modified Truck (unit)	1494	2128
发电设备(千瓦)	Power Generating Equipment (kw)	387450	818446
变压器(千伏安)	Transformer (kva)	13276083	17812838
电力电缆(公里)	Electric Cable (km)	101300	33170
钢芯铝绞线(吨)	Aluminium Strand Wire with Steel Core (ton)	16777	24701

11-18 各地、州、市主要工业产品产量

年 份 Year	地 区 Region	纱(吨) Yarn (ton)	布(万米) Cloth (10 000 m)	绒线(吨) Knitting Wool (ton)	呢绒(万米) Woolen Piece Goods (10 000 m)	丝(吨) Silk (ton)
	1978	28008	15616	1239	189.37	144
	1980	31272	16931	1614	240.08	86
	1985	39130	21150	2396	680.00	96
	1990	101941	30017	2179	1230.00	190
	1995	244689	30460	2286	1262.00	421
	1996	208526	27186	2202	1361.00	283
	1997	247143	29862	2393	1227.00	352
	1998	220332	26719	1361	979.00	304
	1999	294378	27450	1349	798.00	267
	2000	334307	28060	1184	754.00	149
	2001	302654	25380	843	399.00	214
	2002	316095	20679	811	264.58	201
	2003	292713	15239	744	205.58	110
	2004	291386	13989	980	205.92	39
	2005	340864	14047	1118	283.68	37
	2006	357324	15415	799	326.67	35
	2007	408870	16000	637	367.51	15
乌鲁木齐市	Urumqi City	69000	4690	375	0.38	
克拉玛依市	Karamay City					
石河子市	Shihezi City	82385	3341		183.90	
阿拉尔市	Aral City	10849				
图木舒克市	Tumxuk City					
五家渠市	Wujiaqu City	4649				
吐鲁番地区	Turpan Administrative Offices	9314				
哈密地区	Hami [Kumul] Administrative Offices	19101				
昌吉回族自治州	Changji Hui Autonomous Prefecture	47383	264		183.23	
伊犁哈萨克自治州	Ili Kazak Autonomous Prefecture	45374	2000	262		
伊犁州直属县(市)	Counties (Cities) Direct Under Ili Prefecture	27434	1090			
塔城地区	Tacheng [Tarbagatai] Administrative Offices	17940	910	262		
阿勒泰地区	Altay Administrative Offices					
博尔塔拉蒙古自治州	Bortala Mongol Autonomous Prefecture	16065	287			
巴音郭楞蒙古自治州	Bayangol Mongol Autonomous Prefecture	30136	1128			
阿克苏地区	Aksu Administrative Offices	29497	366			
克孜勒苏柯尔克孜自治州	Kizilsu Kirgiz Autonomous Prefecture					
喀什地区	Kashgar [Kaxgar] Administrative Offices	37552	3522			
和田地区	Hotan Administrative Offices	7565	402			15

注：卷烟计量单位从 2003 年开始改为亿支。

Output of Major Industrial Products by Prefecture, Autonomous Prefecture and City

机制纸及纸板(吨) Machine-made Paper and Paperboard (ton)	原盐(万吨) Salt (10 000 tons)	成品糖(万吨) Sugar (10 000 tons)	饮料酒(千升) Alcohol Beverage (kilo-liter)	卷烟(万箱) Cigarettes (10 000 cases)	原煤(万吨) Coal (10 000 tons)	原油(万吨) Crude Oil (10 000 tons)	天然气(万立方米) Natural gas (10 000 cu.m)	发电量(亿千瓦时) Electricity (100 million kwh)	#水电 Hydropower
19851	51.71	2.08	9336	3.01	1079.01	353.05	25100	21.17	4.64
23838	38.18	4.43	17082	3.11	1136.84	390.58	35298	23.58	5.25
41521	35.09	7.18	74809	8.04	1600.22	499.00	54556	38.11	8.64
90857	159.00	16.84	118585	12.34	2100.00	695.00	50161	69.79	14.25
180440	25.98	30.18	249481	13.61	2720.74	1267.83	114821	120.43	22.82
169789	36.54	36.34	219961	13.56	2986.00	1457.10	140609	136.03	24.49
161659	39.85	42.28	259015	13.21	3021.37	1629.25	213006	150.58	26.97
168799	27.53	47.59	271056	12.04	2926.91	1628.38	237826	157.76	28.23
180138	36.14	46.36	269453	11.00	2778.16	1739.65	310600	169.30	30.06
176477	31.78	30.76	269761	10.50	2798.90	1848.43	353930	182.98	30.53
193389	46.02	41.98	296187	11.04	2819.61	1946.95	417429	197.62	34.10
226950	50.75	51.84	307167	12.00	3098.67	2036.19	485237	212.24	34.67
233365	52.71	45.43	317260	62.50	3482.86	2141.39	502942	234.62	36.20
263066	87.32	37.26	345770	70.00	3749.40	2253.02	574805	266.30	37.08
289318	85.35	42.92	355275	70.00	3898.81	2408.32	1066437	306.92	43.27
295338	153.21	53.79	401771	85.00	4518.52	2474.74	1642099	357.15	53.43
252329	85.54	64.94	438502	100.00	5018.64	2604.31	2103348	416.87	58.78
122514	12.29		171386		1706.68	536.25	95250	121.19	1.68
			18			1217.06	290477	27.34	
21712			35869				1862.8	36.15	2.90
			85						
			15						
	26.49		4127		517.82	207.99	173008	14.73	0.06
130	3.63		13034		526.01			22.55	0.04
17368	0.21	4.30	16552		742.52			65.20	2.64
2491	31.57	42.34	134546	100.00	838.10			52.85	29.48
175		29.15	63856	100.00	399.82			36.59	21.88
719	31.50	11.44	70313		432.60			9.88	2.30
1597	0.07	1.75	377		5.68			6.38	5.30
	4.20	5.40	1421					2.01	1.03
87067	3.18	9.90	10657		66.15	643.01	1541361	23.52	4.05
	2.42	3.00	25754		497.09			28.25	4.81
	1.50				43.04		524	0.08	0.05
1047			24893		13.81		865	17.30	7.30
	0.05		144		67.42			5.70	4.74

Note: The metering unit of tobacco has been changed into 100, 000, 000 from the year 2003.

11-18 续表

年 份 Year	地 区 Region	生 铁 (万吨) Pig Iron (10 000 tons)	粗钢 (万吨) Crude Steel (10 000 tons)	大理石板材 (平方米) Marble Plate (sq.m.)	钢 材 (万吨) Steel Rolled (10 000 tons)
	1978	17.52	8.46		6.83
	1980	15.81	10.74		8.59
	1985	22.87	19.79		16.73
	1990	40.57	36.49	9589	28.48
	1995	69.53	70.59	34169	66.55
	1996	85.64	87.47	6420	86.70
	1997	93.82	97.21	53588	99.89
	1998	100.40	107.67	9197	116.19
	1999	101.30	105.60	7807	117.30
	2000	106.42	109.70	6294	131.26
	2001	111.73	131.83	22786	134.42
	2002	122.78	175.45	34185	173.07
	2003	144.86	204.12	117306	203.10
	2004	193.89	249.13	109663	238.52
	2005	258.66	306.54	78577	326.96
	2006	324.08	394.19	176025	411.45
	2007	394.97	447.24	119926	470.94
乌鲁木齐市	Urumqi City	279.02	415.49	5200	440.98
克拉玛依市	Karamay City				
石河子市	Shihezi City				
阿拉尔市	Aral City				
图木舒克市	Tumxuk City				
五家渠市	Wujiaqu City				
吐鲁番地区	Turpan Administrative Offices	54.28	0.88	17080	
哈密地区	Hami [Kumul] Administrative Offices	5.60			
昌吉回族自治州	Changji Hui Autonomous Prefecture	1.01			0.23
伊犁哈萨克自治州	Ili Kazak Autonomous Prefecture	43.25	2.97	71116	6.27
伊犁州直属县(市)	Counties (Cities) Direct Under Ili Prefecture	36.78		1200	1.01
塔城地区	Tacheng [Tarbagatai] Administrative Offices		2.97		5.26
阿勒泰地区	Altay Administrative Offices	6.47		69916	
博尔塔拉蒙古自治州	Bortala Mongol Autonomous Prefecture	3.15			
巴音郭楞蒙古自治州	Bayangol Mongol Autonomous Prefecture	3.55	27.90	6530	23.46
阿克苏地区	Aksu Administrative Offices			20000	
克孜勒苏柯尔克孜自治州	Kizilsu Kirgiz Autonomous Prefecture				
喀什地区	Kashgar [Kaxgar] Administrative Offices	5.11			
和田地区	Hotan Administrative Offices				

Continued

水 泥 (万吨) Cement (10 000 tons)	硫 酸 (吨) Sulfuric Acid (ton)	烧 碱 (吨) Caustic Soda (ton)	合成氨 (吨)(折纯) Synthetic Ammonia (ton)	农用氮、磷、钾化肥(吨) Farm Nitrogen Phophate and Potassium (ton)	碳化钙 (电石)(吨) Calcium Crbide (ton)	塑料制品 (吨) Plastic Products (ton)	小型拖拉机 (台) Small Tractor (unit)
78.15	20262	4164	33155	20276	4895	3194	843
90.89	19153	3542	13762	9207	4486	2051	137
201.05	23921	5045	85728	58080	5989	17974	11117
285.00	47732	15063	397062	287640	15976	40958	17081
489.88	88491	24732	492754	383279	12344	100739	30352
562.87	76413	28008	488337	372056	15901	129059	26671
628.00	77187	35544	581449	428711	28350	143916	14780
728.94	64836	39614	688069	520681	28999	168372	19017
805.83	68169	42161	896632	685587	40216	139497	17048
895.67	71458	51831	947511	754668	51749	197756	13472
981.29	72511	68589	884340	729034	65763	262873	12672
1029.71	70407	93362	956732	766291	73680	230729	4019
1128.98	85322	114110	1082601	854530	82057	314891	
1212.99	114046	174445	1015630	869795	115991	388270	1407
1241.74	126901	295917	1192001	1285346	290591	349151	5171
1334.50	160073	423901	1303586	1290802	501283	412032	
1536.77	183484	485880	1325017	1385279	711277	517069	5408
372.31	468	255223	740337	587941	120783	188484	5310
						19585	
29.43	28192	226427			303072	75077	
						26057	
2.28						10716	
						24700	
42.97	81268			377	32899	636	
41.33						7976	
146.25	35623			3161	106245	48621	
359.90	15056			200	148278	53101	
139.98	15056				97924	35099	
178.85				200	50354	16810	
41.08						1192	
30.95						5309	
107.12		4230	282695	282427		13338	98
237.79	22778		301985	511173		8175	
0.84						138	
115.16	99					34582	
50.43						573	

11-19 国有及国有控股企业主要指标占全区规模以上工业比重

Percentage of Main Indicators in State-owned and State-holding Enterprises to Enterprises above Designated Size

单位：万元　　(2007 年)　　(10 000yuan)

指　标	Item	全区规模以上工业企业 Enterprises Above Designated Size	国有及国有控股企业 State-Owned and State-Holding Enterprises	比 重 (%) Percentage (%)
从业人员(人)	Employed Person (person)	537937	376062	69.9
工业总产值	Gross Industrial Output Value	32966068.9	26377945.0	80.0
工业增加值	Added Industrial Value	13966779.4	12024331.8	86.1
资产总计	Total Assets	43363237.4	34883239.0	80.4
流动资产年平均余额	Annual Average Balance of Circulating Assets	12510396.7	8934379.8	71.4
固定资产净值年平均余额	Annual Average Balance of Net Fixed Assets	20108340.7	17731564.4	88.2
负债合计	Total Liabilities	21948132.9	17219818.9	78.5
所有者权益	Owner's Right and Interest	21414685.5	17663420.1	82.5
实收资本	Substantial Capital	16967893.1	14826419.5	87.4
主营业务收入	Revenue from Principal Business	34756937.7	28236850.8	81.2
主营业务税金及附加	Taes and Other Charges on Principal Business	667482.3	627637.2	94.0
利润总额	Total Profits	6915727.0	6301862.1	91.1
利税总额	Total Profits and Tax	9613765.4	8718502.7	90.7
全员劳动生产率(元/人)	Productivity of Labor for the Staff (yuan/person)	259636.0	319743.3	123.2
亏损单位数(个)	Number of Loss-suffering Enterprises (unit)	416	116	27.9
亏损企业亏损额	Losses Value of Loss-suffering	595186.3	533047.2	89.6

11-20 重点行业主要指标占全区规模以上工业比重
Percentage of Main Indicators in Key Industrial Sectors to Xinjiang's Industry above Designated Size

(2007 年)

指　标	Item	合　计 Total	占全区比重 (%) Percentage (%)
从业人员(人)	**Employed Person (person)**	**346008**	**64.3**
石油和天然气开采业	Extraction of Petroleum and Natural Gas	108350	20.1
石油加工、炼焦及核燃料加工业	Petroleum Processing,Coking and Nuclear Fuel Processing	32060	6.0
黑色金属冶炼及压延加工业	Smelting and Pressing of Ferrous Metal	23634	4.4
电力、热力的生产和供应业	Electric Power, Thermal Power Production and Supply	49905	9.3
化学原料及化学制品制造业	Raw Chemical Material and Chemical Products	29568	5.5
纺织业	Textile Industry	81451	15.1
农副食品加工业	Processing of Food from Agricultural Products	21040	3.9
工业总产值(万元)	**Gross Industrial Output Value (10 000 yuan)**	**26594088.7**	**80.7**
石油和天然气开采业	Extraction of Petroleum and Natural Gas	11228896.1	34.1
石油加工、炼焦及核燃料加工业	Petroleum Processing,Coking and Nuclear Fuel Processing	7245490.6	22.0
黑色金属冶炼及压延加工业	Smelting and Pressing of Ferrous Metal	2354188.7	7.1
电力、热力的生产和供应业	Electric Power, Thermal Power Production and Supply	1808364.5	5.5
化学原料及化学制品制造业	Raw Chemical Material and Chemical Products	1358330.0	4.1
纺织业	Textile Industry	1343950.6	4.1
农副食品加工业	Processing of Food from Agricultural Products	1254868.2	3.8
工业增加值(万元)	**Added Industrial Output Value (10 000 yuan)**	**11679437.6**	**83.6**
石油和天然气开采业	Extraction of Petroleum and Natural Gas	8976286.6	64.3
石油加工、炼焦及核燃料加工业	Petroleum Processing,Coking and Nuclear Fuel Processing	497018.2	3.6
黑色金属冶炼及压延加工业	Smelting and Pressing of Ferrous Metal	469196.9	3.4
电力、热力的生产和供应业	Electric Power, Thermal Power Production and Supply	729896.1	5.2
化学原料及化学制品制造业	Raw Chemical Material and Chemical Products	410731.6	2.9
纺织业	Textile Industry	338525.8	2.4
农副食品加工业	Processing of Food from Agricultural Products	257782.4	1.8

注：所列行业为工业总产值百亿元以上行业。
Note: Listed sector of gross industrial output value were above ten billion sector.

11-20 续表 Continued

指　标	Item	合　计 Total	占全区比重(%) Percentage(%)
资产总计(万元)	**Total of Assets (10 000 yuan)**	**33021280.3**	**76.2**
石油和天然气开采业	Extraction of Petroleum and Natural Gas	15122588.8	34.9
石油加工、炼焦及核燃料加工业	Petroleum Processing,Coking and Nuclear Fuel Processing	4880020.9	11.3
黑色金属冶炼及压延加工业	Smelting and Pressing of Ferrous Metal	1948498.8	4.5
电力、热力的生产和供应业	Electric Power, Thermal Power Production and Supply	5135979.5	11.8
化学原料及化学制品制造业	Raw Chemical Material and Chemical Products	2706846.2	6.2
纺织业	Textile Industry	1916279.2	4.4
农副食品加工业	Processing of Food from Agricultural Products	1311066.9	3.0
利润总额(万元)	**Total Profits (10 000 yuan)**	**6114411.3**	**88.4**
石油和天然气开采业	Extraction of Petroleum and Natural Gas	5881920.4	85.1
石油加工、炼焦及核燃料加工业	Petroleum Processing,Coking and Nuclear Fuel Processing	-215752.9	-3.1
黑色金属冶炼及压延加工业	Smelting and Pressing of Ferrous Metal	144273.1	2.1
电力、热力的生产和供应业	Electric Power, Thermal Power Production and Supply	20740.8	0.3
化学原料及化学制品制造业	Raw Chemical Material and Chemical Products	156504.2	2.3
纺织业	Textile Industry	60991.3	0.9
农副食品加工业	Processing of Food from Agricultural Products	65734.4	1.0
利税总额(万元)	**Total Profitsand Tax (10 000 yuan)**	**8353789.4**	**86.9**
石油和天然气开采业	Extraction of Petroleum and Natural Gas	7336777.9	76.3
石油加工、炼焦及核燃料加工业	Petroleum Processing,Coking and Nuclear Fuel Processing	147260.4	1.5
黑色金属冶炼及压延加工业	Smelting and Pressing of Ferrous Metal	249400.7	2.6
电力、热力的生产和供应业	Electric Power, Thermal Power Production and Supply	181645.4	1.9
化学原料及化学制品制造业	Raw Chemical Material and Chemical Products	233996.6	2.4
纺织业	Textile Industry	110261.1	1.1
农副食品加工业	Processing of Food from Agricultural Products	94447.3	1.0
主营业务收入(万元)	**Revenue from Principal Business (10 000 Yuan)**	**28395756.6**	**81.7**
石油和天然气开采业	Extraction of Petroleum and Natural Gas	12141578.7	34.9
石油加工、炼焦及核燃料加工业	Petroleum Processing,Coking and Nuclear Fuel Processing	7418953.9	21.3
黑色金属冶炼及压延加工业	Smelting and Pressing of Ferrous Metal	2402540.9	6.9
化学原料及化学制品制造业	Raw Chemical Material and Chemical Products	1717169.8	4.9
电力、热力的生产和供应业	Electric Power, Thermal Power Production and Supply	1892054.1	5.4
纺织业	Textile Industry	1538682.6	4.4
农副食品加工业	Processing of Food from Agricultural Products	1284776.6	3.7

11-21 规模以上工业主要产品生产能力

Production Capacity of Major Industrial Products above Designated Size

(2007 年)

产品名称	Item	2006	2007
原煤(吨)	Raw Coal (ton)	30840328	42851440
天然原油(吨)	Crude Oil (ton)	25281400	26734100
发电设备容量(万千瓦)	Generating Capacity (10000 kw)	714.85	800.47
卷烟(万支)	Cigarettes (10 000 pieces)	850000	1500000
化学纤维(吨)	Chemical Fiber (ton)	99500	90500
棉纺锭(环锭纺)(锭)	Cotton Hasp (unit)	2552783	2880368
气流纺锭(转杯纺)(头)	Airflow Hasp (unit)	65326	70056
棉布织机(台)	Calico Spinning Machine (set)	5209	6633
焦炭(吨)	Coke (ton)	4541000	5496000
炭化钙(电石)(折 300 升/千克)(吨)	Calcium Carbide (ton)	430000	869511
农用氮、磷、钾化学肥料(折纯)(吨)	Chemical Fertilizers (ton)	1592411	1588411
水泥熟料(吨)	Cement Chamotte (ton)		15102380
预分解窑熟料	Decompose Cellar Chamotte		5867500
立窑熟料	Cellar Chamotte		4445923
预热器窑熟料	Preheater Cellar Chamotte		1250000
湿法窑熟料	Wet cellar Chamotte		201000
中空窑熟料	Dished Cellar Chamotte		295000
水泥(吨)	Cement (ton)	18392100	20171665
平板玻璃(重量箱)	Plate Glass (weight case)	1100000	1100000
平拉玻璃(重量箱)	Plate Drawing Glass (weight case)		1100000
生铁(吨)	Pig Iron (ton)	3351000	4338000
粗钢(吨)	Crude Steel (ton)	5350000	5390000
钢材(吨)	Rolled Steel (ton)	5767000	6107879
铁合金(吨)	Ferroalloy (ton)	60500	81000
原铝(电解铝)(吨)	Aluminium (ton)	54100	54200
汽车(辆)	Motor Vehicles(unit)	4500	5000
移动通信手持机(手机)(台)	Mobile Telephones (unit)	250000	250000
彩色电视机(台)	Color TV Set (set)	300000	300000

注：表中水泥熟料及其中品种和平拉玻璃 2006 年没有统计。
Note: Output of products of cement chamotter and it's breed, plate drawing glass in this table did not collected statistics in 2006.

主要统计指标解释

工业　指从事自然资源的开采，对采掘品和农产品进行加工和再加工的物质生产部门。具体包括：(1)对自然资源的开采，如采矿、晒盐等(但不包括禽兽捕猎和水产捕捞)；(2)对农副产品的加工、再加工，如粮油加工、食品加工、缫丝、纺织、制革等；(3)对采掘品的加工、再加工，如炼铁、炼钢、化工生产、石油加工、机器制造、木材加工等，以及电力、自来水、煤气的生产和供应等；(4)对工业品的修理、翻新，如机器设备的修理、交通运输工具(包括小卧车)的修理等。

1984年以前农村的村及村以下办工业归属农业，1984年以后划归工业。

工业统计调查单位为独立核算法人工业企业。

独立核算法人工业企业指从事工业生产经营活动的单位。独立核算法人工业企业应同时具备以下条件：①依法成立，有自己的名称、组织机构和场所，能够承担民事责任；②独立拥有和使用资产，承担负债，有权与其他单位签订合同；③独立核算盈亏，并能够编制资产负债表。

本年鉴中涉及的企业登记注册类型：

国有及国有控股企业　指国有企业加上国有控股企业。国有企业(即原全民所有制工业或国营工业)指企业全部资产归国家所有，并按《中华人民共和国企业法人登记管理条例》规定登记注册的非公司制的经济组织。包括国有企业、国有独资公司和国有联营企业。1957年以前的公私合营和私营工业，后均改造为国营工业，1992年改为国有工业，这部分工业的资料不单独分列时，均包括在国有企业内。国有控股企业是对混合所有制经济的企业进行的"国有控股"分类。它是指这些企业的全部资产中国有资产(股份)相对其他所有者中的任何一个所有者占资(股)最多的企业。该分组反映了国有经济控股情况。

集体企业　指企业资产归集体所有，并按《中华人民共和国企业法人登记管理条例》规定登记注册的经济组织。是社会主义公有制经济的组成部分。包括城乡所有使用集体投资举办的企业，以及部分个人通过集资自愿放弃所有权并依法经工商行政管理机关认定为集体所有制的企业。

股份合作企业　指以合作制为基础，由企业职工共同出资入股，吸收一定比例的社会资产投资组建，实行自主经营，自负盈亏，共同劳动，民主管理，按劳分配与按股分红相结合的一种集体经济组织。

联营企业　指两个及两个以上相同或不同所有制性质的企业法人或事业单位法人，按自愿、平等、互利的原则，共同投资组成的经济组织。联营企业包括：

国有联营企业指国有企业与国有企业间的联营；

集体联营企业指集体企业与集体企业间的联营；

国有与集体联营企业指国有企业与集体企业间的联营。

有限责任公司　指根据《中华人民共和国公司登记管理条例》规定登记注册，由两个以上，五十个以下的股东共同出资，每个股东以其所认缴的出资额对公司承担有限责任，公司以其全部资产对其债务承担责任的经济组织。

有限责任公司包括国有独资公司以及其他有限责任公司。

股份有限公司　指根据《中华人民共和国企业法人登记管理条例》规定登记注册，其全部注册资本由等额股份构成并通过发行股票筹集资本，股东以其认购的股份对公司承担有限责任，公司以其全部资产对其债务承担责任的经济组织。

私营企业　指由自然人投资设立或由自然人控股，以雇佣劳动为基础的营利性经济组织。包括按照《公司法》、《合伙企业法》、《私营企业暂行条例》规定登记注册的私营有限责任公司、私营股份有限公司、私营合伙企业和私营独资企业。

港、澳、台商投资企业　指企业注册登记类型中的港、澳、台资合资、合作、独资经营企业和股份有限公司之和。

外商投资企业　指企业注册登记类型中的中外合资、合作经营企业、外资企业和外商投资股份有限公司之和。

"三资"企业系指港、澳、台商投资企业和外资企业的简称。

轻工业　指主要提供生活消费品和制作手工工具的工业。按其所使用的原料不同，可分为两大类：(1)以农产品为原料的轻工业，是指直接或间接以农产品为基本原料的轻工业。主要包括食品制造、饮料制造、烟草加工、纺织、缝纫、皮革和毛皮制作、造纸以及印刷等工业；(2)以非农产品为原料的轻工业，是指以工业品为原料的轻工业。主要包括文教体育用品、化学药品制造、合成纤维制造、日用化学制品、日用玻璃制品、日用金属制品、手工工具制造、医疗器械制造、文化和办公用机械制造等工业。

重工业　指为国民经济各部门提供物质技术基础的主要生产资料的工业。按其生产性质和产品用途，可以分为下列三类：(1)采掘(伐)工业，是指对自然资源的开采，包括石油开采、煤炭开采、金属矿开采、非金属矿开采等工业；(2)原材料工业，指向国民经济各部门提供基本材料、动力和燃料的工业。包括金属冶炼及加工、炼焦及焦炭、化学、化工原料、水泥、人造板以及电力、石油和煤炭加工等工业；(3)加工工业，是指对工业原材料进行再加工制造的工业。包括装备国民经济各部门的机械设备制造工业、金属结构、水泥制品等工业，以及为农业提供的生产资料如化肥、农药等工业。

根据上述划分原则，修理业中以重工业产品为修理作业对象的划为重工业，反之划为轻工业。

工业总产值

(1)定义：工业总产值是以货币形式表现的，工业企业在一定时期内生产的工业最终产品或提供工业性劳务活动的总价值量。它反映一定时间内工业生产的总规模和总水平。

(2)计算原则：

工业生产的原则，即凡是企业在报告期生产的经检验合格的产品，不管是否在报告期销售，均包括在内。

最终产品的原则，即凡是计入工业总产值的产品，必须是本企业生产的经检验合格的，不需要再进行任何加工的最终产品。如果企业有中间产品(半成品)对外销售，则对外销售的中间产品应视为企业的最终产品。

工厂法原则，即工业总产值是以工业企业作为基本计算(核算)单位，即按企业的最终产品计算工业总产值。按这种方法计算的工业总产值，不允许同一产品价值在企业内部重复计算，不能把企业内部各个车间(分厂)生产的成果相加，但允许企业间的重复计算。

(3)内容及计算方法：1995年全国工业普查对工业总产值(原规定)的内容及计算原则和方法做了某些修订，修订后的工业总产值(新规定)包括三项内容：即本期生产成品价值、对外加工费收入、在制品半成品期末期初差额价值三部分。

本期生产成品价值：指企业本期生产，并在报告期内不再进行加工，经检验、包装入库的全部工业成品(半产品)价值合计，包括企业生产的自制设备及提供给本企业在建工程、其他非工业部门和福利部门等单位使用的成品价值。本期生产成品价值为按自备原材料生产的产品的数量乘以本期不含增值税(销项税额)的产品实际销售平均单价计算；会计核算中按成本价格转帐的自制设备和自产自用的成品，按成本价格计算生产成品价值。生产成品价值中不包括用定货者来料加工的成品(半产品)价值。

对外加工费收入：指企业在报告期内完成的对外承接的工业品加工(包括用定货者来料加工产品)的加工费收入和对外工业修理作业所取得的加工费收入。对外加工费收入按不含增值税(销项税额)的价格计算，可根据会计"产品销售收入"科目的有关资料取得。

对于本企业对内非工业部门提供的加工修理、设备安装的劳务收入，如果企业会计核算基础较好，能取得这部分资料，而且这部分价值所占比重较大，应包括在对外加工费收入中。

自制半成品在制品期末期初差额价值：指企业报告期在制品期末减期初的差额价值，本指标一般可以从会计核算资料中取得。如果会计产品成本核算中不计算半成品、在制品的成本，则总产值中也不包括这部分价值，反之则包括。

(4)工业总产值统计范围变化和计算方法修订情况：

1984年以前工业总产值不包括村办工业，村办工业总产值划归农业。1984年以后工业总产值包括村办工业。

1995年工业普查对工业总产值计算方法做了修订，即从1995年始按新修订(新规定)方法计算工业总产值。新规定与原规定的区别如下：

全价与加工费的计算原则不同：新规定为凡自备原材料，不论其生产繁简程度如何，一律按全价计算工业总产值；凡来料加工，允许按加工费计算工业总产值。原规定则视生产加工的繁简程度不同，规定哪些行业按全价，哪些行业按加工费计算工业总产值。

自制半成品、在产品期末期初差额价值的计算原则不同：新规定要求，凡会计产品成本核算时计算了成本的差额价值，总产值中就应包括，否则可不包括；原规定则按生产周期六个月的界限区分，凡生产周期六个月以上的企业，总产值计算中应包括这部分差额价值，否则可不包括。

计算价格不同：新规定按不含增值税(销项税额)的价格计算；原规定则按含增值税(销项税额)的价格计算。

工业增加值　指工业企业在报告期内以货币表现的工业生产活动的最终成果。

工业增加值有两种计算方法：一是生产法，即工业总产出减去工业中间投入加上应交增值税；二是收入法，即从收入的角度出发，根据生产要素在生产过程中应得到的收入份额计算，具体构成项目有固定资产折旧、劳动者报酬、生产税净额、营业盈余，这种方法也称要素分配法。本年鉴中的工业增加值是以生产法计算的。

生产法工业增加值的计算方法为：

工业增加值=工业总产出-工业中间投入+应交增值税

(1)工业总产出：指工业企业在一定时期内工业生产活动的总成果。工业总产出包括：成品生产价值，对外加工费收入，自制半成品、在产品期末期初差额价值。1995年后用新规定计算的工业总产值代替。

(2)工业中间投入：指工业企业在工业生产活动中消耗的外购物质产品和对外支付的服务费用。服务费用包括支付给物质生产部门(工业、农业、批发零售贸易业、建筑业、运输邮电业)的服务费用和支付给非物质生产部门(如保险、金融、文化教育、科学研究、医疗卫生、行政管理等)的服务费用。工业中间投入的确定须遵循以下原则：必须从外部购入的，并已计入工业总产出的产品和服务价值；必须是本期投入生产，并一次性消耗掉(包括本期摊销的低值易耗品等)的产品和服务价值。

工业中间投入包括直接材料费用、制造费用中的工业中间投入、管理费用中的工业中间投入、销售费用中的工业中间投入和利息支出五部分。

资产总计　指企业拥有或控制的能以货币计量的经济资源，包括各种财产、债权和其他权利。资产按流动性分为流动资产、长期投资、固定资产、无形资产、递延资产和其他资产。该指标根据企业会计"资产负债表"中"资产总计"项目的期末数增列。

流动资产平均余额　指企业在报告期内全部流动资产的平均余额。

固定资产净值年平均余额　指固定资产净值在报告期内余额的平均数。计算公式为：

固定资产净值年平均余额=1至12月各月月初、月末固定资产净值之和/24

该指标根据"资产负债表"中"固定资产原价"、"累计折旧"指标的期初、期末数计算填列。

固定资产净值指固定资产原价减去历年已提折旧额后的净额。计算公式为：

固定资产净值=固定资产原价-累计折旧

负债合计　指企业所承担的能以货币计量，将以资产或劳务偿付的债务，偿还形式包括货币、资产或提供劳务。负债一般按偿还期长短分为流动负债和长期负债。根据会计"资产负债表"中"负债合计"的年末数填列。

所有者权益　指企业投资人对企业净资产的所有权。企业净资产等于企业全部资产减去全部负债后的余额，包括企业投资人对企业的最初投入的实际到位的资产及资本公积金、盈余公积金和未分配利润。所有者权益合计数小于零，表示企业资不抵债。

主营业务收入　指企业销售产品和提供劳务等主要经营业务取得的业务总额。

主营业务成本　指企业销售产品和提供劳务等主要经营业务的实际成本。

主营业务税金及附加　指企业销售产品和提供工业性劳务等主要经营业务应负担的城市维护建设税、消费税、资源税和教育费附加。

利润总额　指企业生产经营活动的最终成果，是企业在一定时期内实现的盈亏相抵后的利润总额(亏损以"-"号表示)，它等于营业利润加上补贴收入加上投资收益加上营业外净收入再加上以前年度损益调整。

本年应交增值税　指企业在报告期内应交纳的增值税额。它等于本年销项税额加上出口退税加上进项税额转出数减去本年进项税额。小规模纳税企业直接按全年计税销售额乘以征收率计算取得。

从业人员平均人数　是指报告期内每天拥有的从业人员人数。其计算公式为：

月平均人数=报告月内每天实有人数之和/报告月日历日数

季平均人数=季内各月平均人数之和/3

年平均人数=年内各月平均人数之和/12

工业经济效益综合指数　是指现行综合评价工业经济效益总体水平及工业经济运行质量的指数。它是以若干项代表性经济效益指标，分别除以各项指标的标准值，再乘以各自的权数，加总后除以总权数求得。其计算公式为：

工业经济效益综合指数=(某项经济效益指标报告期数值/该项指标标准值×权数)÷总权数

上式总权数为100。

总资产贡献率　反映企业全部资产的获利能力，是企业经营业绩和管理水平的集中体现，是评价和考核企业盈利能力的核心指标。计算公式为：

总资产贡献率（%）=利润总额+税金总额+利息支出/平均资金总额×100%

公式中：税金总额为产品销售税金及附加与应交增值税之和；平均资产总额为期初期末资产之和的算术平均值。

资产负债率　该指标既反映企业经营风险的大小，也反映企业利用债权人提供的资金从事经营活动的能力。计算公式为：

资产负债率（%）=负债总额/资产总额×100%

资产与负债均为报告期期末数。

流动资产周转次数　指一定时期内流动资产完成的周转次数，反映投入工业企业流动资金的周转速度。计算公式为：

流动资产周转次数=产品销售收入/全部流动资产平均余额

公式中：全部流动资产平均余额为期初和期末的流动资产之和的算术平均值。

成本费用利润率　反映企业投入的生产成本及费用的经济效益，同时也反映企业降低成本所取得的经济效益。计算公式为：

成本费用利润率（%）=利润总额/成本费用总额×100%

公式中：成本费用总额为产品销售成本、销售费用、管理费用、财务费用之和。

Explanatory Notes on Main Statistical Indicators

Industry refers to the material production sector which is engaged in extraction of natural resources and processing and reprocessing of minerals and agricultural products, including (1) extraction of natural resources, such as mining, salt production (but not including hunting and fishing); (2) processing and reprocessing of farm and sideline produces, such as rice husking, flour milling, wine making, oil pressing, silk reeling, spinning and weaving, and leather making; (3) manufacture of industrial products, such as steel making, iron smelting, chemicals manufacturing, petroleum processing, machine building, timber processing; water and gas production and electricity generation and supply; (4)repairing of industrial products such as the repairing of machinery and means of transport (including cars).

Prior to 1984, the rural industry run by villages and cooperative organizations under village was classified into agriculture. Since 1984, it has been grouped into industry.

Units of industrial statistics survey corporate industrial enterprises with independent accounting system.

Corporate industrial enterprises with independent accounting system refer to enterprises engaging in industrial production activities, which meet the following requirements: ①They are established legally, having their own names, organizations, location, able to take civil liability; ②They possess and use their assets independently, assume liabilities, and are entitled to sign contracts with other units; ③They are financially independent and compile their own balance sheets.

Enterprises covered in the industrial statistics in the Yearbook include following categories by their registration:

State-owned and State-Controlled Enterprises refer to state-owned enterprises plus state-holding enterprises. State-owned enterprises (originally known as state-run enterprises with ownership by the whole society) are non-corporate economic entities registered in accordance with the Regulation of the People's Republic of China on the Management of Registration of Legal Enterprises, where all assets are owned by the state. Included in this category are state-owned enterprises, state-funded corporations and state-owned joint-operation enterprises. Joint state-private industries and private industries, which existed before 1957, were transformed into state-run industries since 1957, and into state-owned industries after 1992. Statistics on those enterprises are included in the state-owned industries instead of grouping them separately. State-controlled enterprises is a sub-classification of enterprises with mixed ownership, referring to enterprises where the percentage of state assets (or shares by the state) is larger than any other single share holder of the same enterprise. This sub-classification illustrates the control of the state over a particular industry.

Collective-owned Enterprises refer to economic entities registered in accordance with the Regulation of the People's Republic of China on the Management of Registration of Legal Enterprises, where assets are owned by collectively. Collective enterprises constitute an integral part of the socialist economy with public ownership. They include urban and rural enterprises invested by collectives, and some enterprises registered in industrial and commercial administration agency as collective units where funds are pulled together by individuals who voluntarily give up their right of ownership.

Share-holding Cooperative Enterprises refer to economic units set up on cooperative basis, with funding partly from members of the enterprise and partly from outside investment, where the operation and management is decided by the members who also participate in the production, and the distribution of income is based both on work (labour input) and on shares (capital input).

Joint-operation enterprises refer to economic units that are established by joint investment by two or more corporate enterprises or institutions of the same or different types of ownership on voluntary, equal and mutual-beneficial basis. They include:

a) state-owned joint-operation enterprises (joint operation between state-owned enterprises);

b) collective joint-operation enterprises (joint operation between collective enterprises; and

c) state-collective joint-operation enterprises (joint operation between state and collective enterprises).

Limited Liability Corporations refer to economic units registered in accordance with the Regulation of the People's Republic of China on the Management of Registration of Corporations, with capitals from 2 to 49 investors, each investor bears limited liability to the corporation depending on his/her holding of shares, and the corporation bears liability to its debt to the maximum of its total assets.

Share-holding Corporations Ltd. refer to economic units registered in accordance with the Regulation of the People's Republic of China on the Management of Registration of Corporate Enterprises, with total registered capitals divided into equal shares and raised through issuing stocks. Each investor bears limited liability to the corporation depending on the holding of shares, and the corporation bears liability to its debt to the maximum of its total assets.

Private Enterprises refer to economic units invested or controlled (by holding the majority of the shares) by natural persons who hire labours for profit-making activities. Included in this category are private limited liability corporations, private share-holding corporations Ltd., private partnership enterprises and private sole investment enterprises registered in accordance with the Corporation Law, Partnership Enterprise Law and Tentative Regulation on Private Enterprises.

Enterprises with Funds form Hong Kong, Macao and Taiwan refers to all industrial enterprises registered as the joint-venture, cooperative, sole (exclusive) investment industrial enterprises and limited liability corporations with funds from Hong Kong, Macao and Taiwan.

Foreign Funded Enterprises refers to all industrial enterprises registered as the joint-venture, cooperative, sole (exclusive) investment industrial enterprises and limited liability corporations with foreign funds.

Light Industry refers to the industry that produces consumer goods and hand tools. It consists of two categories, depending on the materials used:

(1) Industries using farm products as raw materials. These are branches of light industry which directly or indirectly use farm products as basic raw materials, including the manufacture of food and beverages, tobacco processing, textile, clothing, fur and leather manufacturing, paper making, printing, etc.

(2) Industries using non farm products as raw materials. These are branches of light industry which use manufactured goods as raw materials, including the manufacture of cultural, educational articles and sports goods, chemicals, synthetic fiber, chemical products for daily use, glass products for daily use, metal products for daily use, hand tools, medical apparatus and instruments, and the manufacture of cultural and clerical machinery.

Heavy Industry refers to the industry which produces capital goods, and provides various sectors of the national economy with necessary material and technical basis. It consists of the following three branches according to the purpose of production or the use of products:

(1) Mining, quarrying and logging industry refers to the industry that extracts natural resources, including extraction of petroleum, coal, metal and non-metal ores.

(2) Raw materials industry refers to the industry that provides various sectors of the national economy with raw materials, fuels and power. It includes smelting and processing of metals, coking and coke chemistry, chemical materials and building materials such as cement, plywood, and power, petroleum refining and coal dressing.

(3) Manufacturing industry refers to the industry that processes raw materials. It includes machine-building industry which equips sectors of the national economy, industries of metal structure and cement products, industries producing means of agricultural production, such as chemical fertilizers and pesticides.

According to the above principle of classification, the repairing Tradesss, which are engaged primarily in repairing products of heavy industry are classified into heavy industry while these engaged in repairing products of light industry are classified into light industry.

Gross Industrial Output Value

(1) Definition: Gross industrial output value is the total volume of final industrial products produced and industrial services provided during a given period. It reflects the total achievements and overall scale of industrial production during a given period.

(2) Principles for calculation:

Statistics on industrial production follow the principle that all products produced by the enterprises and accepted during the reference period are to be included no matter whether they are sold or not during the reference period.

Determination of final products follow the principle that all products that are included in the calculation of grow industrial output value are the final products of the enterprise which have been accepted through quality check and require no further processing. If an enterprise has intermediate (semi-finished) products to sell, these intermediate products are considered as the final products of the enterprise.

Gross industrial output value is calculated following the principle of factory approach, i.e. industrial enterprise is used as the basic accounting unit in calculating the gross industrial output value. By this approach, value of the same product is not to be double counted, and the output value of different workshops (branch factories) should not be added. However, this approach does not exclude the possibility of double counting between enterprises.

(3) Content and calculation method: The old definition of gross industrial output value was modified during the national industrial census in 1995. The revised (new) definition of gross industrial output value consists of 3 components: value of the finished products during the reference period, income from external processing, and value of change in semi-finished products at the end and at the beginning of the reference period.

Value of the finished products during the reference period: refers to the value of all finished (semi-finished) industrial products that are produced during the reference period without the need for further processing, checked for acceptance, packed and put into the warehouse of the enterprise, including the value of own-produced equipment and the value of products provided to the projects under construction of the enterprise, and to other non-industrial or welfare units. Value of finished products during the reference period is calculated by the quantity of products produced using own materials multiplied by the average unit prices at which products are sold (excluding value-added tax). Own-produced equipment and products produced for own use are value at cost prices as in the case of enterprise accounting. Value of finished products does not include the value of finished products (semi-finished products) that are produced using the materials from the clients who make the orders.

Income from external processing: refers to income from contracted external processing of industrial products (including processing of industrial products using materials from the clients), and the income from industrial repairing work provided to other units. Income from external processing is calculated using information from the item “products sales income” in the enterprise accounting at the prices excluding value-added tax.

For income from services such as processing, repairing and installation of equipment provided to non-industrial units within the enterprise, if the accounting work of the enterprise is good enough to separate it from other records, and the share of such services is significant, it should also be included in the income from external processing.

Value of change in semi-finished products at the end and at the beginning of the reference period: refers to the value of change in semi-finished products at the end and at the beginning of the reference period, which generally can be obtained from accounting records of enterprises. If the enterprise accounting excludes the cost of semi-finished products, then it should not be included in the gross industrial output value, and vice versa.

(4) Changes in the coverage and method of calculation of gross industrial output value

Prior to 1984, the value of rural industry run by villages was classified into agriculture instead of industry. Since 1984, it has been included in the gross industrial output value. Method of calculation for the gross industrial output value was modified in the industrial census in 1995. The difference in the new method as compared with the old one is outlined below:

Principle in using full value vs. processing fee: The new method stipulates that all products produced using own materials are to be calculated with full value in reporting the gross industrial output value irrespective of sophistication of production, and for external processing, it allows calculation using processing fee. In the old method, however, the use of full value or processing fee was determined by the degree of sophistication of production in different branches of industries.

Principle in determining the value of change in semi-finished products: The new method requires that value of the change in semi-finished products should be included in the gross industrial output value if it is included in the accounting record of the enterprise, otherwise it should not be included. By the old method, it is determined by the type of enterprises in terms of production cycle. If the production cycle is over 6 months, the value of change in semi-finished products is included in the gross industrial output value, otherwise it is excluded.

Difference in prices: The new method uses prices excluding value-added tax in the calculation of gross industrial output value, while the old method used prices including value-added tax.

Value-added of Industry refers to the final results of industrial production of industrial enterprises in money terms during the reference period.

Industrial value-added can be calculated by two approaches: the production approach, i.e. gross industrial output value minus intermediate input plus value-added tax, and the income approach, i.e. income for various factors used in the course of production, including depreciation of fixed assets, remuneration of labourers, net of production tax, and operating surplus. Value-added of industry in the Yearbook is calculated by production approach as following:

Value-added of industry = gross industrial output industrial intermediate input + value-added tax

(1) Gross industrial output: refers to the total achievements of industrial production during a given period. Gross industrial output includes value of finished products, income from external processing, and value of change in semi-finished products at the end and at the beginning of the reference period. Since 1995, it was substituted by the gross industrial output value by new method.

(2) Industrial intermediate input: refers to purchased goods and paid services consumed during the industrial production of enterprises. Fees paid for services include fees paid for the services provided by material production sectors (industry, agriculture, wholesale and retail Tradess, construction, transport, post and telecommunications) and by non-material production sectors (insurance, banking, culture, education, scientific research, health and medical care, public administration, etc.). The determination of industrial intermediate input follows the principle that the goods and services must be purchased from outside and included in the gross industrial output, and that the goods and services are inputted into production and consumed (include low-value consumables) during the reference period.

Industrial intermediate input includes 5 components, namely direct consumption of materials, industrial intermediate input in manufacturing cost, industrial intermediate input in management cost, industrial intermediate input in marketing cost and expenditure on interest.

Total Assets refer to all economic resources, in monetary terms, that is owned or controlled by enterprises, including properties, creditors Equities and other economic rights of all forms. Classified by the degree of equitability, total assets include circulating assets, long-term investment, fixed assets, intangible assets and deferred assets, and other assets. Data on this indicator can be obtained by the year-end figures of total assets in the Assets and Liability Table of accounting records of enterprises.

Annual Average Value of Working Capitals refers to the average value of all working capitals of the enterprise during the reference period.

Annual Average of Net Value of Fixed Assets refer to average of the net value of fixed assets during the reference period, calculated with the following formula:

Annual Average of Net Value of Fixed Assets = sum of net value of fixed assets at the beginning and at the end of each month from January to December / 24.

Information on this indicator can be obtained from the beginning and ending figures of the original value of fixed assets and cumulative depreciation from the Assets and Liability Table of enterprises.

Net value of fixed assets refers to the original value of fixed assets minus depreciation over the years, i.e.:

Net value of fixed assets = original value of fixed assets cumulative depreciation

Total Liabilities refer to payable liabilities of enterprises that have to repay in terms of money, assets or labour services. In terms of payment, it can be divided into Total Working liabilities and long-term liabilities. Data on this item is obtained from the ending figures on total liabilities from the Assets and Liability Table from the enterprises.

Owner's Equities refers to the wonershiip of net assets of enterprises by its investors.The net assets equal the total assets minus total liabilities of the enterprise,including the actual assets invested into the enterprise by investors,accumulation of capitals and operating surplus and non-distributed profits.The enterprise's assets is less than its liabilities if the sum of owner's Equities is smaller than zero.

Revenue from Principal Business refers to the annual accumulation of corresponding item in the "profit table"of the accountant. For enterprises that do not follow the 2001 Enterprises Accounting Standards,the year-end accumulation of revenue from the sales of products is used as a substitute.

Cost of Principal Business refers to the annual accumulation of corresponding item in the "profit table" of the accountantForenterprises that do not follow the 2001 Enterprise Accounting Standards,the year-end accumulation of cost for the sales of products is used as a substitute.

Tax and Extra Charges from Principal Business refers to the annual accumulation of correspongding item in the "profit table"of the accountant.For enterprises that do not follow the 2001 Enerprise Accounting Standards,the year-end accumulation of tax and extra charges from the sales of products is used as a substitute.

Total Profits refer to the final achievements of production and operation of the enterprises, represented by the total profits after deducting losses (loss is expressed by the negative figure). It is the sum of profits from operation, income from subsidies, investment earnings, net income from activities other than operation, and adjustment of profits and losses of previous years.

Value-added Tax Payable refers to the amount of the value-added tax which should be paid by the enterprises during the reference period. It is the sum of tax on sales, export rebate, and transferred tax on purchases of the current year, minus the tax on purchases of the current year. Value-added tax payable of small-size enterprises is determined by the taxable sales of the year multiplied by the tax rate.

Aggregative Index on Economic Results of Industry refers to the current comprehensive index to evaluate the general level of economic results of industry and the performance quality of industrial economy. It is calculated as follows:

Aggregative Index on Economic Results of Industry=(Value of an Indicator on Economic Results in Reference Period/Standard Value of the Indicator×Weight) ÷Total Weight

Total Weight=100

Average Annual Number of Employed Persons Employed persons refer to all those who are employed in enterprises and receive remunerations there from, including currently working employees, retirees who are re-employed, teachers of local-run schools, as well as foreigners, staff from Hong Kong, Macao and Taiwan, part-time employees and persons with second job who are employed by the enterprise, and employees of other units temporarily working in the enterprises, but excluding former employees who left the enterprise with their employment records still kept by the enterprises.

Average number of employed persons refers to the number of employees everyday during the reference period, calculated with the following formula:

Monthly average number = sum of actual employees everyday in reference month/number of calendar dates in reference month

Quarterly average number = sum of monthly average number in reference quarter/3

Annual average number = sum of monthly average number in reference year/12

Ratio of Profits, Taxes and Interests to Average Assets reflects the profit-making capability of all assets of the enterprise and is a key indicator manifesting the performance and management and evaluating the profit-making potential of the enterprise. It is calculated as follows:

Ratio of Profits, Taxes and Interests to Average Assets (%) = [(total profits + total taxes + interest payment) / average assets]×100%

In the above formula, total taxes is the sum of tax and extra charges on the sales of products and value-added tax payable; and average assets is the arithmetic mean of the sum of beginning assets and ending assets.

Ratio of Debts to Assets reflect both the operation risk and the capability of the enterprise in making use of the capital from the creditors. It is calculated as follows:

Ratio of Debts to Assets (%) = (total debts / total assets)×100%

Both assets and debts are figures at the end of the reference period.

Turnover of Working Capita refers to the number of times of turnover of working capital in a given period of time, which reflects the speed of the turnover of working capital of industrial enterprises, and is calculated as follows:

Turnover of Working Capital=(sales revenue of products) / (average balance of total working capital)

In the above formula, average balance of total working capital refers to the arithmetic mean of the sum of working capital at the beginning and at the end of the reference period.

Ratio of Profits to Total Industrial Costs refers to the ratio of profits realized in a given period to the total costs in the same period, which reflects the economic efficiency of input cost and is calculated as follows:

Ratio of Profits to Total Industrial Cost (%)=(total profits/ total costs)×100%

Total Costs in the above formula is the sum of cost of products sold, marketing cost, management cost and financial cost.

第十二篇
建筑业

CHAPTER 12
Construction

简要说明
Brief Introduction

本篇资料的主要内容及来源

本篇资料反映在新疆维吾尔自治区注册的建筑法人企业概况及发展情况，包括建筑业企业基本情况和生产经营情况。主要指标有企业个数、从业人员和建筑业总产值、增加值、房屋建筑面积、利润、税金、劳动生产率等。

根据建筑业发展的实际情况，建筑业统计范围从 2002 年起，由原具有建筑业资质等级四级及四级以上的独立核算的建筑业企业调整为具有施工总承包、专业承包和劳务分包的法人建筑业企业。

本篇建筑业企业统计数据是根据国家统计局制定的《建筑业统计报表制度》整理汇总的。建筑业统计数据采取全面调查的方法。资料由新疆维吾尔自治区统计局投资处提供。

Main Content and Source of Data

Data in this chapter show the general situation and the development of the construction in Xinjiang Uygur Autonomous Region. They cover the situation of production and management of the enterprises on construction, including the number of enterprises, number of employed persons, gross output value of construction industry, value added floor space of the buildings, profits and taxes of enterprises and labor productivity, etc.

According to the development of construction industry, starting from 2002,the coverage of construction statistics has been adjusted to include all the construction enterprises of various types of ownership with qualification certificates and with independent accounting system ,instead of the original criteria that required construction enterprises of various types of ownership to have qualification certificates at or above Class 4 with independent accounting system.

Data on construction enterprises are collected in accordance with the Reporting System of Construction Statistics stipulated by the National Bureau of Statistics. Data on the construction industry are collected through comprehensive reporting system and provided by the Department of Investment in Fixed Assets Statistics, Xinjiang Bureau of Statistics.

12-1 建筑企业概况
Main Indicators on Construction Enterprises

年份 Year	地区 Region	企业个数(个) Number of Enterprises (unit)				从业人员(万人) Number of Employed Persons (10 000 persons)			
		合计 Total	国有 State-owned	集体 Collec-Tive-owned	其他 Others	合计 Total	国有 State-owned	集体 Collec-Tive-owned	其他 Others
1985		275	117	158		25.85	19.21	6.64	
1986		326	125	201		22.37	17.42	4.95	
1987		371	135	236		23.97	17.82	6.15	
1988		416	171	245		26.08	20.19	5.89	
1989		348	199	149		21.87	17.67	4.20	
1990		353	183	170		22.86	18.36	4.50	
1991		496	328	168		26.39	21.58	4.81	
1992		526	328	198		28.76	22.77	5.99	
1993		817	441	356	20	34.55	25.75	8.53	0.27
1994		920	496	401	23	31.25	23.29	7.71	0.25
1995		928	481	432	15	35.33	26.33	8.72	0.28
1996		886	478	386	22	24.97	18.53	6.09	0.35
1997		650	313	312	25	30.75	20.39	8.56	1.80
1998		682	269	348	65	22.14	14.83	6.42	0.89
1999		711	272	344	95	19.35	13.00	4.94	1.41
2000		690	226	293	171	26.16	17.69	4.25	4.22
2001		594	175	152	267	25.27	14.77	2.68	7.82
2002		730	146	109	475	23.57	8.64	1.89	13.04
2003		776	112	77	587	20.81	6.16	1.12	13.53
2004		932	105	51	776	33.22	7.21	0.84	25.17
2005		881	107	43	731	34.37	8.70	0.90	24.77
2006		914	102	39	773	33.84	8.81	0.84	24.19
2007		967	103	35	829	37.02	9.63	0.92	26.47
乌鲁木齐市	Urumqi City	481	52	15	414	15.30	5.30	0.44	9.56
克拉玛依市	Karamay City	43	2	5	36	2.56	0.47	0.14	1.95
石河子市	Shihezi City	62	6		56	4.38	1.37		3.01
吐鲁番地区	Turpan Administrative Offices	11	1		10	0.34	0.01		0.33
哈密地区	Hami [Kumul] Administrative Offices	31	3	1	27	0.56	0.13		0.43
昌吉回族自治州	Changji Hui Autonomous Prefecture	65	3	3	59	2.14	0.11	0.17	1.86
伊犁哈萨克自治州	Ili Kazak Autonomous Prefecture	96	15	7	74	3.60	1.65	0.09	1.86
伊犁州直属县(市)	Counties (Cities) Direct Under Ili Prefecture	55	9	4	42	1.93	1.02	0.06	0.85
塔城地区	Tacheng [Tarbagatai] Administrative Offices	22	5	3	14	0.98	0.47	0.03	0.48
阿勒泰地区	Altay Administrative Offices	19	1		18	0.69	0.16		0.53
博尔塔拉蒙古自治州	Bortala Mongol Autonomous Prefecture	20	4	1	15	0.38	0.07	0.06	0.25
巴音郭楞蒙古自治州	Bayangol Mongol Autonomous Prefecture	46	7	1	38	3.20	0.32		2.88
阿克苏地区	Aksu Administrative Offices	49	6		43	1.69	0.16		1.53
克孜勒苏柯尔克孜自治州	Kizilsu Kirgiz Autonomous Prefecture	8		1	7	0.28			0.28
喀什地区	Kashgar [Kaxgar] Administrative Offices	34	2	1	31	1.81	0.02	0.02	1.77
和田地区	Hotan Administrative Offices	21	2		19	0.78	0.02		0.76

注：1.2000 年至 2002 年建筑业所有指标数据均包括克拉玛依石油管理局工业部分，2003 年起将此部分扣除(以下同)。
2.2004 年建筑业所有数据为经济普查数，企业个数及其他指标包括没有工作量或者停业企业，往年未包括(以下同)。

Note: a) All the quota indices in building sector from 2000 to 2002 include the industrial part of Karamay Oil Administration. From the year 2003, this part was omitted. (the same as in the following) . b) All the data in architectural sector are the statistics of economic census, enterprise numbers and other quota exclude work volume or closed enterprises except for previous years. (the same as in the following) .

12-2 按登记注册类型分建筑企业总产值

Total Output Value of Construction Enterprises by Registration Status

单位：万元 (10 000 yuan)

年份 Year	地区 Region	合计 Total	国有经济 State-owned Units	集体经济 Collective -owned Units	其他经济 Others Units
1985		175165	138138	37027	
1986		178237	143634	34594	
1987		197551	155332	42219	
1988		234702	186308	48394	
1989		240076	198912	41164	
1990		273893	220574	53319	
1991		362544	291965	70579	
1992		494945	389230	105715	
1993		811163	618836	180727	11600
1994		910718	694786	202908	13024
1995		1070085	816396	238387	15302
1996		1284669	977358	283776	23535
1997		1141318	828482	288081	24755
1998		1434787	1002235	378956	53596
1999		1569486	1085080	365588	118818
2000		2349506	1436653	362649	550204
2001		2742800	1394099	252076	1096625
2002		3136257	1270601	170319	1695337
2003		3221502	739953	147256	2334293
2004		3439968	910264	89189	2440515
2005		3615674	1138005	102580	2375089
2006		3856223	1269722	88474	2498027
2007		4541026	1548285	97418	2895323
乌鲁木齐市	Urumqi City	1868194	959372	30500	878322
克拉玛依市	Karamay City	453493	112773	23403	317317
石河子市	Shi Hezi City	377796	135867		241929
吐鲁番地区	Turpan Administrative Offices	79238	5768		73470
哈密地区	Hami [Kumul] Administrative Offices	79157	21174	342	57641
昌吉回族自治州	Changji Hui Autonomous Prefecture	228319	13435	20240	194644
伊犁哈萨克自治州	Ili Kazak Autonomous Prefecture	432908	184071	15351	233486
伊犁州直属县(市)	Counties (Cities) Direct Under Ili Prefecture	257120	138045	12084	106991
塔城地区	Tacheng [Tarbagatai] Administrative Offices	98934	35065	3267	60602
阿勒泰地区	Altay Administrative Offices	76854	10961		65893
博尔塔拉蒙古自治州	Bortala Mongol Autonomous Prefecture	49691	15669	2400	31622
巴音郭楞蒙古自治州	Bayangol Mongol Autonomous Prefecture	477790	66035	172	411583
阿克苏地区	Aksu Administrative Offices	229706	29399		200307
克孜勒苏柯尔克孜自治州	Kizilsu Kirgiz Autonomous Prefecture	30961		586	30375
喀什地区	Kashgar [Kaxgar] Administrative Offices	148346	1033	4424	142889
和田地区	Hotan Administrative Offices	85427	3689		81738

12-3 按构成分建筑企业总产值

Total Output Value of Construction Enterprises by Composition

单位：万元 (10 000 yuan)

年份 Year	地区 Region	总产值 Total Output Value	建筑工程 Output Value of Construction Projects	安装工程 Output Value of Installation Projects	其他 Others
	1985	175165	154496	18042	2627
	1986	178237	157204	18359	2674
	1987	197551	174245	20343	2963
	1988	234072	206508	24060	3504
	1989	240076	211747	24728	3601
	1990	273893	241574	28211	4108
	1991	362544	319764	37343	5437
	1992	494945	436542	50979	7424
	1993	811163	715473	83531	12159
	1994	910718	824232	74119	12367
	1995	1070085	942158	106744	21183
	1996	1284669	1124271	132079	28319
	1997	1141318	1009082	105891	26345
	1998	1434787	1270483	139104	25200
	1999	1569486	1398179	146154	25153
	2000	2349506	2073166	214425	61915
	2001	2742800	2403688	279909	59203
	2002	3136257	2637362	405115	93780
	2003	3221502	2708269	336535	176698
	2004	3439968	2836668	396509	206791
	2005	3615674	2981373	487239	147062
	2006	3856223	3209192	510770	136261
	2007	4541026	3822922	564228	153876
乌鲁木齐市	Urumqi City	1868194	1581804	237065	49325
克拉玛依市	Karamay City	453493	241720	180851	30922
石河子市	Shihezi City	377796	352494	23656	1646
吐鲁番地区	Turpan Administrative Offices	79238	18043	39810	21385
哈密地区	Hami [Kumul] Administrative Offices	79157	64694	4773	9690
昌吉回族自治州	Changji Hui Autonomous Prefecture	228319	202432	20882	5005
伊犁哈萨克自治州	Ili Kazak Autonomous Prefecture	432908	408217	15788	8903
伊犁州直属县(市)	Counties (Cities) Direct Under Ili Prefecture	257120	238136	11796	7188
塔城地区	Tacheng [Tarbagatai] Administrative Offices	98934	94148	3071	1715
阿勒泰地区	Altay Administrative Offices	76854	75933	921	
博尔塔拉蒙古自治州	Bortala Mongol Autonomous Prefecture	49691	48077	830	784
巴音郭楞蒙古自治州	Bayangol Mongol Autonomous Prefecture	477790	448598	17522	11670
阿克苏地区	Aksu Administrative Offices	229706	208782	10738	10186
克孜勒苏柯尔克孜自治州	Kizilsu Kirgiz Autonomous Prefecture	30961	27601	1496	1864
喀什地区	Kashgar [Kaxgar] Administrative Offices	148346	136659	9281	2406
和田地区	Hotan Administrative Offices	85427	83801	1536	90

12-4 按行业和登记注册类型分建筑企业总产值

Total Output Value of Construction Enterprises by Registration Status and Sectors

单位：万元 (10 000 yuan)

项　目	Item	2006	2007
总　计	**Total**	**3856223**	**4541026**
#一、二级企业	First, Second Enterprises	2779005	3179365
国有及国有控股	State-owned and State-holding	2421064	2695252
按登记注册类型分组	**Grouped by Registration Status**		
内资企业	Domestic Funede	3855997	4538170
国有企业	State-owned Enterprises	997367	1282349
集体企业	Collective-owned Enterprises	88473	97418
股份合作企业	Share-holding Cooperative	811	6500
有限责任公司	Limited Liability Corporations	2025930	2321366
国有独资公司	Sole State -funded Company	272356	265936
其他有限责任公司	Other Limited Liability Companies	1753574	2055430
股份有限公司	Share-holding Corporations Ltd	162546	92466
私营企业	Private Enterprises	580870	737282
#私营有限责任公司	Private Limited Liability Companies	566460	719351
私营股份有限公司	Private Stock Limited Companies	6970	9119
其他企业	Others		789
港、澳、台及外商企业	Enterprises With Funds from Hong Kong, Macao , Taiwan and Foreign	226	2856
#合资经营企业(港或澳、台资)	Joint-Venture	226	2856
按国民经济行业分组	**Grouped by National Economic Sectors**		
房屋和土木工程建筑业	Buildings and Givil Engineering Construction	3431600	3994824
房屋工程建筑	Building Construction	2256161	2646352
土木工程建筑	Civil Engineering Construction	1175439	1348472
铁路、道路、隧道和桥梁	Railways, Roads, Tunnels and Bridges	677995	802589
水利和港口建筑	Water Conservancy and Seaport Construction	202742	234452
工矿工程建筑	Mine Project	208656	222256
架线和管道工程建筑	Cabling and Piping Project	62099	68512
其他土木工程建筑	Other Civil Engineering	23947	20663
建筑安装业	Construction and Installation	355747	452405
建筑装饰业	Building Decoration	34030	37944
其他建筑业	Others	34846	55853
按隶属关系分组	**Grouped by Subordination**		
中 央	Central Government	1075527	1326141
地 方	Local	2780696	3214885
按企业资质等级分组	**Grouped by Enterprise's Qualification**		
#施工总承包	Undertaking Porjects	3481885	4088152
特　级	Special	89381	96031
一　级	First Class	1578776	1808678
二　级	Second Class	992241	1117018
三级及以下	Third Class	821487	1066425
专业承包	Specialized Undertaking	349235	420162
一　级	First Class	72310	90483
二　级	Second Class	117908	139216
三级及以下	Third Class	159017	190463
劳务分包	Work Subcontractors	25103	32712
一　级	First Class	2557	2343
二　级	Second Class	15213	21627
三级及以下	Third Class	7333	8742

12-5 建筑企业增加值
Value-added of Construction Enterprises

单位：万元 (10 000 yuan)

年份 Year	地区 Region	按注册类型分 Grouped by Ownership 合计 Total	国有企业 State-owned Enterprise	集体企业 Collective-owned Enterprises	其他企业 Others	按隶属关系分 By Administrative Relationship 中央企业 Central Enterprises	地方企业 Local Enterprises
	1985	60152	52022	8130			
	1990	109923	91983	17940			
	1991	142690	121173	21517			
	1992	179949	148759	31190			
	1993	206686	164305	42381			
	1994	239598	178031	58775	2792	75305	164293
	1995	283882	207212	72598	4072	92259	191623
	1996	303370	218532	78973	5865	96996	206374
	1997	380806	284938	87437	8431	133287	247519
	1998	296444	182903	89375	24166	84239	212205
	1999	323714	198463	87477	37774	92459	213255
	2000	587341	386475	84268	116598	274836	312505
	2001	637472	340470	49298	247704	260784	376688
	2002	621430	223509	37383	360538	211988	409442
	2003	672531	143473	29333	499725	161523	511008
	2004	693070	158801	18938	515331	157382	535688
	2005	716063	199645	18265	498153	176697	539366
	2006	790466	230867	20948	538651	215766	574700
	2007	947319	304278	19234	623807	278640	668679
乌鲁木齐市	Urumqi City	391831	177554	6648	207629	134523	257308
克拉玛依市	Karamay City	93941	27222	3484	63235		93941
石河子市	Shi Hezi City	92830	32615		60215	79070	13760
吐鲁番地区	Turpan Administrative Offices	14187	917		13270	9884	4303
哈密地区	Hami [Kumul] Administrative Offices	14234	4699	246	9289	4756	9478
昌吉回族自治州	Changji Hui Autonomous Prefecture	51233	2599	5001	43633	693	50540
伊犁哈萨克自治州	Ili Kazak Autonomous Prefecture	83631	41495	3021	39115	30148	53483
伊犁州直属县(市)	Counties (Cities) Direct Under Ili Prefecture	46411	28681	1824	15906	19338	27073
塔城地区	Tacheng [Tarbagatai] Administrative Offices	21083	9986	1197	9900	7982	13101
阿勒泰地区	Altay Administrative Offices	16137	2828		13309	2828	13309
博尔塔拉蒙古自治州	Bortala Mongol Autonomous Prefecture	8827	1782	651	6394	1571	7256
巴音郭楞蒙古自治州	Bayangol Mongol Autonomous Prefecture	91352	10022	54	81276	15085	76267
阿克苏地区	Aksu Administrative Offices	50521	4244		46277		50521
克孜勒苏柯尔克孜自治州	Kizilsu Kirgiz Autonomous Prefecture	7786		67	7719		7786
喀什地区	Kashgar [Kaxgar] Administrative Offices	36008	730	62	35216	1806	34202
和田地区	Hotan Administrative Offices	10938	399		10539	1104	9834

12-6 建筑企业利税总额
Total Pre-tax Profits of Construction Enterprises

单位：万元 (10 000 yuan)

年 份 Year	地 区 Region	利税总额合 计 Total Pre-tax Profits	利润总额 Total Profits	工程结算税金及附加 Taxes and Extra Charges on Project Settlement Accounts	管理费用中的税金 Taxes in Management Expenses	产 值利税率 (%) Ratio of Pre-tax Profits to Output Value (%)	资 金利税率 (%) Ratio of Pre-tax Profits to Assets (%)
	1994	28199	5535	20195	2469	3.81	4.11
	1995	30156	2974	24916	2266	3.44	3.46
	1996	20752	-8625	26816	2561	1.97	-0.93
	1997	31970	-4347	33360	2957	2.80	2.51
	1998	37596	-5875	41162	2309	2.62	2.41
	1999	64777	13359	48995	2423	4.13	3.72
	2000	19274	-48005	64614	2665	0.82	0.63
	2001	28688	-47485	74206	1967	1.05	0.84
	2002	84833	-11089	92484	3438	2.70	2.18
	2003	169594	67146	96888	5560	5.26	5.51
	2004	174255	65037	102990	6228	5.07	5.65
	2005	165236	46909	112565	5762	4.57	4.91
	2006	177102	54570	116426	6106	4.59	4.83
	2007	221117	67796	145119	8202	4.87	5.40
乌鲁木齐市	Urumqi City	80911	19661	58953	2297	4.33	4.05
克拉玛依市	Karamay City	22137	3459	15116	3562	4.88	3.71
石河子市	Shihezi City	19898	8098	11726	74	5.27	8.40
吐鲁番地区	Turpan Administrative Offices	3608	326	3223	59	4.55	5.17
哈密地区	Hami [Kumul] Administrative Offices	2371	54	2256	61	3.00	3.26
昌吉回族自治州	Changji Hui Autonomous Prefecture	11292	3512	7354	426	4.95	6.01
伊犁哈萨克自治州	Ili Kazak Autonomous Prefecture	19419	5823	13393	203	4.49	6.97
伊犁州直属县(市)	Counties (Cities) Direct Under Ili Prefecture	9741	2600	7042	99	3.79	6.88
塔城地区	Tacheng [Tarbagatai] Administrative Offices	5728	2113	3538	77	5.79	6.83
阿勒泰地区	Altay Administrative Offices	3950	1110	2813	27	5.14	7.43
博尔塔拉蒙古自治州	Bortala Mongol Autonomous Prefecture	1501	-229	1570	160	3.02	4.23
巴音郭楞蒙古自治州	Bayangol Mongol Autonomous Prefecture	31201	16436	14316	449	6.53	12.79
阿克苏地区	Aksu Administrative Offices	16863	8680	7824	359	7.34	9.21
克孜勒苏柯尔克孜自治州	Kizilsu Kirgiz Autonomous Prefecture	1397	-30	1268	159	4.51	4.45
喀什地区	Kashgar [Kaxgar] Administrative Offices	6447	828	5324	295	4.35	5.12
和田地区	Hotan Administrative Offices	4072	1178	2796	98	4.77	12.67

12-7 建筑企业劳动生产率
Labor Productivity of Construction Enterprises

单位：元/人 (yuan/person)

年份 Year	地区 Region	按总产值计算的劳动生产率 Overall Labor Productivity in Terms of Total Output Value	#国有经济 State-owned Enterprises	#集体经济 Collective-owned Enterprises	按增加值计算的劳动生产率 Overall Labor Productivity in Terms of Added-Value	#国有经济 State-owned Enterprises	#集体经济 Collective-owned Enterprises
	1993	25871	27064	23484	6607	7499	4724
	1994	29871	32616	23023	9499	10546	7186
	1995	34668	38483	26617	11238	12505	8673
	1996	32606	36557	25291	10648	12286	7719
	1997	38808	40629	33658	12948	13973	10215
	1998	47698	51465	40819	9855	10044	9627
	1999	55593	61196	44235	11466	11766	10584
	2000	74994	87999	48767	25208	32781	14138
	2001	84666	94344	62458	19678	23041	12215
	2002	86302	108857	66231	17100	19149	14537
	2003	94165	98095	86190	19659	19020	17169
	2004	107150	112145	107185	21588	22365	22759
	2005	112214	137966	127587	22223	23971	22718
	2006	121506	149550	118932	24907	27794	28159
	2007	126303	134275	139988	26349	26389	27640
乌鲁木齐市	Urumqi City	126483	131747	145727	26528	24383	31761
克拉玛依市	Karamay City	193784	239736	171582	40142	57871	25543
石河子市	Shihezi City	87562	99217		21515	23817	
吐鲁番地区	Turpan Administrative Offices	229944	418043		41169	66445	
哈密地区	Hami [Kumul] Administrative Offices	141074	168986	106875	25369	37503	76994
昌吉回族自治州	Changji Hui Autonomous Prefecture	108532	127104	119622	24354	24589	29560
伊犁哈萨克自治州	Ili Kazak Autonomous Prefecture	122964	114872	152286	23755	25896	29969
伊犁州直属县(市)	Counties (Cities) Direct Under Ili Prefecture	135333	139977	171641	24428	29082	25910
塔城地区	Tacheng [Tarbagatai] Administrative Offices	104350	74685	107464	22237	21269	39368
阿勒泰地区	Altay Administrative Offices	114264	74720		23992	19280	
博尔塔拉蒙古自治州	Bortala Mongol Autonomous Prefecture	140610	239232	43636	24978	27213	11831
巴音郭楞蒙古自治州	Bayangol Mongol Autonomous Prefecture	150036	210234	114400	28686	31906	36235
阿克苏地区	Aksu Administrative Offices	139132	204874		30600	29577	
克孜勒苏柯尔克孜自治州	Kizilsu Kirgiz Autonomous Prefecture	111974		234400	28158		26843
喀什地区	Kashgar [Kaxgar] Administrative Offices	84097	49971	245750	20413	35271	3432
和田地区	Hotan Administrative Offices	111117	204911		14227	22167	

12-8 建筑企业技术装备情况

Number and Power of Machinery and Equipment Owned by Construction Enterprises

年 份 Year	地 区 Region	自有机械设备总台数(台) Total number of Self-owned Machinery and Equipment (set)	自有机械设备总功率(万千瓦) Total Power of Self-owned and Equipment Machinery (10 000 kw)	自有机械设备净值(万元) Net Value of Self-owned Machinery and Equipment (10 000 yuan)	技术装备率(元/人) Value of Machines Per Laborer (yuan/ person)	动力装备率(千瓦/人) Power of Machines Per Laborer (kw/person)
	1985	30307	105	29308	1332	6
	1986	25843	67	31983	1535	4
	1987	29369	69	32528	1710	4
	1988	27520	98	35433	1832	4
	1989	32180	97	42183	2387	4
	1990	34806	91	46098	2511	5
	1991	39425	100	52417	2429	5
	1992	38478	116	63719	2798	5
	1993	28800	102	42001	2403	6
	1994	46805	121	93371	3721	5
	1995	55455	138	106383	4211	5
	1996	60567	129	127572	4478	5
	1997	64252	149	139617	4747	5
	1998	72606	148	164157	7415	7
	1999	73735	155	184559	9543	8
	2000	77975	182	224485	8582	7
	2001	85981	177	238142	9425	7
	2002	96116	207	442787	18996	9
	2003	100913	207	395865	11866	6
	2004	98541	239	358397	11389	8
	2005	99324	190	326360	10372	6
	2006	96674	197	348344	11187	6
	2007	103431	203	374396	10650	6
乌鲁木齐市	Urumqi City	29095	71	165140	11753	5
克拉玛依市	Karamay City	7422	28	37540	16041	12
石河子市	Shi Hezi City	5767	12	21560	5019	3
吐鲁番地区	Turpan Administrative Offices	2237	5	7999	23526	16
哈密地区	Hami [Kumul] Administrative Offices	2499	6	9841	18309	11
昌吉回族自治州	Changji Hui Autonomous Prefecture	9636	9	19337	9223	4
伊犁哈萨克自治州	Ili Kazak Autonomous Prefecture	14204	20	27822	7954	6
伊犁州直属县(市)	Counties (Cities) Direct Under Ili Prefecture	6638	9	12886	6835	5
塔城地区	Tacheng [Tarbagatai] Administrative Offices	4073	6	6227	6624	6
阿勒泰地区	Altay Administrative Offices	3493	5	8709	12948	7
博尔塔拉蒙古自治州	Bortala Mongol Autonomous Prefecture	2070	3	7997	22628	8
巴音郭楞蒙古自治州	Bayangol Mongol Autonomous Prefecture	9823	24	36082	11333	8
阿克苏地区	Aksu Administrative Offices	6493	11	22911	13893	7
克孜勒苏柯尔克孜自治州	Kizilsu Kirgiz Autonomous Prefecture	538	1	1726	6243	3
喀什地区	Kashgar [Kaxgar] Administrative Offices	6475	10	10506	5956	5
和田地区	Hotan Administrative Offices	7172	3	5935	7719	4

12-9 按登记注册类型分建筑企业技术装备情况
Number and Power of Machinery and Equipment Owned by Registration Status

(2007 年)

项目	Item	自有机械设备年末总台数(台) Year-end Total of Self-owned Machinery and Equipment (set)	自有机械设备年末总功率(千瓦) Year-end Total Power of Self-Owned Machinery and Equipment (kw)	自有机械设备年末净值(万元) Year-end Net Value of Self-owned Machinery and Equipment (10 000 yuan)
总计	**Total**	103431	2028738	374396
#一、二级企业	First, Second Enterprises	59000	1398471	270809
国有及国有控股	State-owned and State-holding	43933	1191292	230774
按登记注册类型分组	**Grouped by Registration Status**			
内资企业	Domestic Funede	103423	2028408	374386
国有企业	State-owned Enterprises	18971	580711	124870
集体企业	Collective-owned Enterprises	2730	40516	8785
股份合作企业	Share-holding Cooperative	126	3110	2616
有限责任公司	Limited Liability Corporations	51296	1048593	166051
国有独资公司	Sole State -funded Company	4259	150021	18459
其他有限责任公司	Other Limited Liability Companies	47037	898572	147592
股份有限公司	Share-holding Corporations Ltd	1864	21112	3342
私营企业	Private Enterprises	28417	334350	68560
#私营有限责任公司	Private Limited Liability Companies	27546	329902	67098
私营股份有限公司	Private Stock Limited Companies	215	865	827
其他企业	Others	19	16	162
港、澳、台及外商企业	Enterprises With Funds from Hong Kong, Macao, Taiwan and Foreign	8	330	10
#港、澳、台合资经营企业	Joint-Venture	8	330	10
按国民经济行业分组	**Grouped by National Economic Sectors**			
房屋和土木工程建筑业	Buildings and Givil Engineering Construction	89663	1796243	328276
房屋工程建筑	Building Construction	69410	1005567	153078
土木工程建筑	Civil Engineering Construction	20253	790676	175198
铁路、道路、隧道和桥梁	Railways, Roads, Tunnels and Bridges	8089	413588	118314
水利和港口建筑	Water Conservancy and Seaport Construction	7149	170127	26519
工矿工程建筑	Mine Project	3276	160061	22263
架线和管道工程建筑	Cabling and Piping Project	1516	40146	7131
其他土木工程建筑	Other Civil Engineering	223	6754	972
建筑安装业	Construction and Installation	11266	190279	37089
建筑装饰业	Building Decoration	1261	13850	2957
其他建筑业	Others	1241	28366	6074
按隶属关系分组	**Grouped by Subordination**			
中央	Central Government	20533	587190	126265
地方	Local	82898	1441548	248131
按企业资质等级分组	**Grouped by Enterprise's Qualification**			
#施工总承包	Undertaking Porjects	93821	1856029	340983
特级	Special	1361	51926	1314
一级	First Class	27017	749460	155260
二级	Second Class	27100	560330	99780
三级	Third Class	38343	494313	84629
专业承包	Specialized Undertaking	9610	172709	33413
一级	First Class	1909	40446	7011
二级	Second Class	2974	48235	8759
三级	Third Class	4727	84028	17643

12-10 建筑企业签订合同情况
Contracts Signed by Construction Enterprises

单位：万元 (10 000 yuan)

年份 Year	地区 Region	合同总额 Total Value Of Contracts	上年结转合同 Value from Contracts Signed In 2006	本年新签合同 Value from New Contracts Signed In 2007
	2002	3962086	988485	2973601
	2003	4312515	1236887	3075628
	2004	4725501	1351086	3374415
	2005	4857604	1557300	3300304
	2006	5692120	1483664	4208455
	2007	7220300	1986086	5234214
乌鲁木齐市	Urumqi City	3459598	1173704	2285894
克拉玛依市	Karamay City	799542	141511	658031
石河子市	Shihezi City	569541	119230	450311
吐鲁番地区	Turpan Administrative Offices	82988	12720	70268
哈密地区	Hami [Kumul] Administrative Offices	95273	8794	86479
昌吉回族自治州	Changji Hui Autonomous Prefecture	325114	65323	259791
伊犁哈萨克自治州	Ili Kazak Autonomous Prefecture	527659	104925	422734
伊犁州直属县(市)	Counties (Cities) Direct Under Ili Prefecture	312856	63512	249344
塔城地区	Tacheng [Tarbagatai] Administrative Offices	132418	31439	100979
阿勒泰地区	Altay Administrative Offices	82385	9974	72411
博尔塔拉蒙古自治州	Bortala Mongol Autonomous Prefecture	57730	14496	43234
巴音郭楞蒙古自治州	Bayangol Mongol Autonomous Prefecture	656967	212962	444005
阿克苏地区	Aksu Administrative Offices	300472	51170	249302
克孜勒苏柯尔克孜自治州	Kizilsu Kirgiz Autonomous Prefecture	36061	8162	27899
喀什地区	Kashgar [Kaxgar] Administrative Offices	214986	50831	164155
和田地区	Hotan Administrative Offices	94369	22258	72111

注：12-10、12-11、12-16 表口径为总承包和专业承包企业。
Note:The data of the table 12-10、12-11、12-16 refer to all general construction contractors and professional contractors.

12-11 建筑企业承包工程完成情况

Completion of Contracted Projects by Construction Enterprises

单位：万元 (10 000 yuan)

年份 Year	地区 Region	直接从建设单位承揽工程完成产值 Completed Output Value of Projects Contracted Directly from Investors	自行完成施工产值 Own-Completed Output Value	分包出去工程产值 Output Value Of Out-Sourced Projects	从建设单位以外承揽工程产值 Completed Output Value of Projects Contracted From Non-investors
	2002	3141928	3048086	93842	88171
	2003	3238170	3135725	102445	85777
	2004	3443802	3377532	66270	62436
	2005	3634746	3563947	70799	51727
	2006	3856300	3775975	80325	80248
	2007	4534324	4420958	113366	120068
乌鲁木齐市	Urumqi City	1831413	1775803	55610	92391
克拉玛依市	Karamay City	492856	437159	55697	16334
石河子市	Shihezi City	368642	367646	996	10150
吐鲁番地区	Turpan Administrative Offices	79238	79238		
哈密地区	Hami [Kumul] Administrative Offices	79157	79157		
昌吉回族自治州	Changji Hui Autonomous Prefecture	228319	228319		
伊犁哈萨克自治州	Ili Kazak Autonomous Prefecture	432908	432908		
伊犁州直属县(市)	Counties (Cities) Direct Under Ili Prefecture	257120	257120		
塔城地区	Tacheng [Tarbagatai] Administrative Offices	98934	98934		
阿勒泰地区	Altay Administrative Offices	76854	76854		
博尔塔拉蒙古自治州	Bortala Mongol Autonomous Prefecture	49691	49691		
巴音郭楞蒙古自治州	Bayangol Mongol Autonomous Prefecture	477790	477790		
阿克苏地区	Aksu Administrative Offices	229706	228698	1008	1008
克孜勒苏柯尔克孜自治州	Kizilsu Kirgiz Autonomous Prefecture	30961	30961		
喀什地区	Kashgar [Kaxgar] Administrative Offices	148216	148161	55	185
和田地区	Hotan Administrative Offices	85427	85427		

12-12 建筑企业资产及资本金

Assets and Capital Principal of Construction Enterprises

单位：万元 (10 000 yuan)

年份 Year	地区 Region	资产合计 Total of Assets	流动资产合计 Circulating Funds	固定资产合计 Total of Fixed Assets	固定资产净值 Net Value of Fixed Assets	本年折旧 Depreciation in the Year	无形及递延资产 Intangible Assets and deferred Assets	资本金合计 Total of Principal Value	#国家资本金 National Principal
1995		939205	647608	240076	225084	18463	3132	221212	110987
1996		1139380	727336	340195	325229	27386	3837	264390	125332
1997		1368666	896643	396804	377251	27367	5154	309044	219732
1998		1561752	1067004	431263	402995	30168	9103	315532	214300
1999		1740851	1186433	471759	443518	32416	10762	346605	212237
2000		3256421	1855185	1215525	1106384	65383	35063	892851	208214
2001		3740312	2187385	1243161	1048023	82884	138976	1055531	227457
2002		4244587	2527414	1364782	1179599	95565	184827	1327186	227601
2003		3375330	2292828	787690	675947	61335	165349	835618	219826
2004		3810825	2632242	825567	722019	62725	163384	929293	225884
2005		3818087	2665404	826376	700835	72103	150802	936389	184447
2006		4115800	2952267	796558	712740	69191	149062	985436	202670
2007		4611598	3387459	804007	706591	76979	157776	1095997	222967
	乌鲁木齐市 Urumqi City	2212551	1710659	329874	289441	33476	80974	480778	115341
	克拉玛依市 Karamay City	673453	522995	80182	72880	11941	9895	92551	2011
	石河子市 Shihezi City	255636	193903	46647	42856	3241	1937	52919	27779
	吐鲁番地区 Turpan Administrative Offices	81229	53483	20673	16248	1790	3805	19934	2050
	哈密地区 Hami [Kumul] Administrative Offices	88522	54658	18278	18133	2243	1412	26019	4713
	昌吉回族自治州 Changji Hui Autonomous Prefecture	226439	147517	41845	40430	2889	18515	63386	4944
	伊犁哈萨克自治州 Ili Kazak Autonomous Prefecture	313578	212982	77340	65753	6276	6872	97897	28449
	伊犁州直属县(市) Counties (Cities) Direct Under Ili Prefecture	165099	112559	35251	29063	1985	6138	43125	11700
	塔城地区 Tacheng [Tarbagatai] Administrative Offices	88807	70254	15362	13662	2597	20	24530	9149
	阿勒泰地区 Altay Administrative Offices	59672	30170	26728	23028	1694	715	30241	7600
	博尔塔拉蒙古自治州 Bortala Mongol Autonomous Prefecture	37672	24146	12631	11368	728	695	18037	997
	巴音郭楞蒙古自治州 Bayangol Mongol Autonomous Prefecture	274272	175325	79458	68630	7432	6386	90249	16198
	阿克苏地区 Aksu Administrative Offices	209832	145155	48972	37930	3836	5098	76186	9117
	克孜勒苏柯尔克孜自治州 Kizilsu Kirgiz Autonomous Prefecture	35806	22378	9962	9002	584	2522	12879	
	喀什地区 Kashgar [Kaxgar] Administrative Offices	164061	101629	27081	24403	1508	16379	47924	9739
	和田地区 Hotan Administrative Offices	38547	22628	11063	9517	1035	3285	17239	1629

12-13 建筑企业负债及所有者权益

Liability and Owner's Equity of Construction Enterprises

单位：万元 (10 000 yuan)

年 份 Year	地 区 Region	负债合计 Total Liabilities	流动负债 Liquid Liabilities	长期负债 Long-term Liabilities	所有者权益 Owners' Equity
	1994	540403	467895	72508	192618
	1995	699997	614110	84378	239208
	1996	815330	714429	98342	324051
	1997	1018007	901138	115032	350659
	1998	1175839	1044115	131724	385913
	1999	1325825	1205880	119945	415026
	2000	2068439	1941268	127171	1187982
	2001	2300621	2168441	132180	1439690
	2002	2717728	2585374	132354	1526859
	2003	2327382	2206412	120970	1047948
	2004	2631252	2517755	105621	1174864
	2005	2651255	2555028	96227	1159206
	2006	2886203	2797525	88678	1220298
	2007	3240248	3139697	100551	1359137
乌鲁木齐市	Urumqi City	1631929	1587925	44004	570577
克拉玛依市	Karamay City	547064	538298	8766	126389
石河子市	Shihezi City	189780	180945	8835	64765
吐鲁番地区	Turpan Administrative Offices	61080	60859	221	20099
哈密地区	Hami [Kumul] Administrative Offices	53683	51603	2080	34576
昌吉回族自治州	Changji Hui Autonomous Prefecture	141531	136022	5509	84572
伊犁哈萨克自治州	Ili Kazak Autonomous Prefecture	191354	185911	5443	122019
伊犁州直属县(市)	Counties (Cities) Direct Under Ili Prefecture	103709	102216	1493	61281
塔城地区	Tacheng [Tarbagatai] Administrative Offices	59210	57218	1992	29501
阿勒泰地区	Altay Administrative Offices	28435	26477	1958	31237
博尔塔拉蒙古自治州	Bortala Mongol Autonomous Prefecture	17602	15214	2388	20070
巴音郭楞蒙古自治州	Bayangol Mongol Autonomous Prefecture	147687	139554	8133	126432
阿克苏地区	Aksu Administrative Offices	113576	106948	6628	96186
克孜勒苏柯尔克孜自治州	Kizilsu Kirgiz Autonomous Prefecture	21980	21865	115	13826
喀什地区	Kashgar [Kaxgar] Administrative Offices	101917	95370	6547	62144
和田地区	Hotan Administrative Offices	21065	19183	1882	17482

12-14 建筑企业总收入

Total Income of Construction Enterprises

单位：万元 (10 000 yuan)

年份 Year	地区 Region	企业总收入 Total Income of Enterprises	工程结算收入 Revenue of Project Settlement Accounts	#工程结算成本 Costs of Project Settlement Accounts	#工程结算利润 Profits of Project Settle Accounts	其他业务收入 Other Revenue from Business	#其他业务利润 Other Profits from Business
	1994	813369	714469	627830	66444	98900	9332
	1995	898810	821713	713940	82858	77097	9445
	1996	983170	904800	799183	78801	78370	8765
	1997	1210813	1081666	950091	98216	129147	17368
	1998	1454758	1346748	1193276	112310	108010	19146
	1999	1595986	1500818	1320898	130925	95167	14882
	2000	2659696	2514011	2252154	197243	145686	30012
	2001	2961754	2807549	2521902	211441	154205	34532
	2002	3360613	3199880	2854350	254428	160733	30853
	2003	3221521	3090768	2716009	254015	130753	21692
	2004	3395793	3276421	2900842	253783	119372	21601
	2005	3685197	3566042	3202712	238351	119155	23629
	2006	3766819	3643783	3255171	252876	123036	20730
	2007	4584374	4431221	3983622	285041	153154	22186
乌鲁木齐市	Urumqi City	1931532	1851719	1650369	135716	79813	10099
克拉玛依市	Karamay City	591523	562186	510818	32411	29337	2158
石河子市	Shihezi City	360539	345600	314793	18328	14939	1362
吐鲁番地区	Turpan Administrative Offices	64977	64862	60275	1363	115	63
哈密地区	Hami [Kumul] Administrative Offices	72104	71902	63995	4708	202	111
昌吉回族自治州	Changji Hui Autonomous Prefecture	232686	231321	209005	13826	1365	870
伊犁哈萨克自治州	Ili Kazak Autonomous Prefecture	409877	400554	363981	21432	9322	2098
伊犁州直属县(市)	Counties (Cities) Direct Under Ili Prefecture	236303	231223	211302	11552	5079	1913
塔城地区	Tacheng [Tarbagatai] Administrative Offices	96073	95711	85827	5937	362	216
阿勒泰地区	Altay Administrative Offices	77501	73620	66852	3943	3881	-31
博尔塔拉蒙古自治州	Bortala Mongol Autonomous Prefecture	49700	47692	43623	2410	2008	130
巴音郭楞蒙古自治州	Bayangol Mongol Autonomous Prefecture	406964	400283	356540	28857	6682	1347
阿克苏地区	Aksu Administrative Offices	224328	218501	192184	17130	5827	1692
克孜勒苏柯尔克孜自治州	Kizilsu Kirgiz Autonomous Prefecture	30225	29852	27318	1246	373	35
喀什地区	Kashgar [Kaxgar] Administrative Offices	138882	136291	124902	5831	2592	1718
和田地区	Hotan Administrative Offices	71037	70458	65819	1783	579	503

12-15 建筑企业亏损额及从业人数

Losses and Employed Persons of Construction Enterprises

(2007 年)

项　　目	Item	企业数(个) Number of Enterprises (unit)	#亏损企业个数 Number of loss-Suffering Enterprises	亏损额(万元) Amount of Total loss (10 000 yuan)	计算劳动生产率的平均人数(人) Average Number of Staff for Calculation of Labour Productivity (person)	期末从业人数(人) Employees at year-end (person)	#工程技术人员 Engineers and Technicians
总　　计	**Total**	**967**	**346**	**42324**	**359533**	**192249**	**42921**
#一、二级企业	First, Second Enterprises	349	110	29551	246918	135438	28361
#国有及国有控股	State-owned and State-holding	262	86	28259	212182	121420	23693
按登记注册类型分组	**Grouped by Registration Status**						
内资企业	Domestic Funede	962	345	42324	359318	192053	42806
国有企业	State-owned Enterprises	83	27	10019	98608	61602	10448
集体企业	Collective-owned Enterprises	35	14	1207	6959	2807	939
股份合作企业	Share-holding Cooperative	1			438	576	168
有限责任公司	Limited Liability Corporations	343	104	21420	182783	90624	21359
国有独资公司	Sole State -funded Company	20	9	9617	16699	11686	2290
其他有限责任公司	Other Limited Liability Companies	323	95	11803	166084	78938	19069
股份有限公司	Share-holding Corporations Ltd	7	1	119	9948	4969	883
私营企业	Private Enterprises	492	198	9437	60516	31409	8971
#私营有限责任公司	Private Limited Liability Companies	482	195	9376	58743	30910	8776
私营股份有限公司	Private Stock Limited Companies	4	1	4	539	122	77
其他企业	Others	1	1	122	66	66	38
港、澳、台及外商企业	Enterprises With Funds from Hong Kong, Macao , Taiwan and Foreign	5	1		215	196	115
#港、澳、台合资经营企业	Joint-Venture	5	1		215	196	115
按国民经济行业分组	**Grouped by National Economic Sectors**						
房屋和土木工程建筑业	Buildings and Givil Engineering Construction	554	179	32925	319904	165339	36255
房屋工程建筑	Building Construction	345	102	10992	232037	111569	24902
土木工程建筑	Civil Engineering Construction	209	77	21933	87867	53770	11353
铁路、道路、隧道和桥梁	Railways, Roads, Tunnels and Bridges	78	24	6776	53602	27803	6504
水利和港口建筑	Water Conservancy and Seaport Construction	40	12	1129	16736	9978	2191
工矿工程建筑	Mine Project	12	5	10116	11171	11281	1252
架线和管道工程建筑	Cabling and Piping Project	34	13	2752	4348	3428	1081
其他土木工程建筑	Other Civil Engineering	45	23	1160	2010	1280	325
建筑安装业	Construction and Installation	174	64	7264	29091	19278	5039
建筑装饰业	Building Decoration	149	68	1562	4444	3024	766
其他建筑业	Others	90	35	573	6094	4608	861
按隶属关系分组	**Grouped by Subordination**						
中 央	Central Government	68	12	5367	109283	60136	9724
地 方	Local	899	334	36957	250250	132113	33197
按企业资质等级分组	**Grouped by Enterprise's Qualification**						
#施工总承包	Undertaking Porjects	453	121	32556	324040	167029	36835
特　级	Special	1			5200	2994	700
一　级	First Class	44	11	13453	137306	74439	13253
二　级	Second Class	118	24	13802	89377	47090	12127
三　级	Third Class	290	86	5301	92157	42506	10755
专业承包	Specialized Undertaking	373	161	8934	27506	18632	5563
一　级	First Class	14	5	149	4271	2787	898
二　级	Second Class	70	23	1709	8799	5121	1707
三　级	Third Class	289	133	7076	14436	10724	2958

12-16 建筑企业工程施工情况

Condition of Building Works by Construction Enterprise

单位：万平方米 (10 000 sq.m)

年份 Year	地区 Region	房屋建筑施工面积 Floor Space of Buildings Constructing	#本年新开工面积 New-opened Works for This Year	施工面积中实行投标承包面积 Space of Bidding and Contracting	#本年新开工面积 New-opened Works for This Year	房屋建筑竣工面积 Floor Space of Buildings Completed
	1995	1212.45	657.34	214.65	148.22	609.84
	1996	1207.45	673.17	397.83	272.22	645.89
	1997	1400.28	778.14	653.90	400.75	747.24
	1998	1662.36	1032.15	1023.88	678.42	879.67
	1999	1943.05	1068.05	1210.90	807.87	1042.51
	2000	2241.48	1448.34	1666.87	1110.04	1261.42
	2001	2659.69	1679.41	2056.30	1380.07	1467.54
	2002	2572.62	1489.38	2133.56	1274.07	1469.59
	2003	2719.22	1735.19	2411.27	1527.79	1450.80
	2004	2812.30	1791.50	2426.79	1613.19	1483.35
	2005	2767.64	1639.80	2512.79	1517.41	1429.36
	2006	2889.64	1854.91	2687.63	1751.99	1645.02
	2007	3552.36	2421.17	3299.73	2277.87	1849.64
乌鲁木齐市	Urumqi City	1168.91	647.89	1081.77	594.81	500.03
克拉玛依市	Karamay City	100.73	73.08	91.35	69.38	56.70
石河子市	Shihezi City	297.08	206.02	279.94	201.63	164.30
吐鲁番地区	Turpan Administrative Offices	21.33	16.57	17.31	15.92	9.98
哈密地区	Hami [Kumul] Administrative Offices	64.85	49.57	52.45	45.42	44.83
昌吉回族自治州	Changji Hui Autonomous Prefecture	266.88	194.56	247.08	175.96	180.82
伊犁哈萨克自治州	Ili Kazak Autonomous Prefecture	432.01	349.97	401.22	322.52	252.37
伊犁州直属县(市)	Counties (Cities) Direct Under Ili Prefecture	226.26	171.45	218.15	167.75	131.29
塔城地区	Tacheng [Tarbagatai] Administrative Offices	126.93	108.59	104.26	84.84	74.69
阿勒泰地区	Altay Administrative Offices	78.82	69.93	78.82	69.93	46.39
博尔塔拉蒙古自治州	Bortala Mongol Autonomous Prefecture	46.96	36.24	46.96	36.24	35.42
巴音郭楞蒙古自治州	Bayangol Mongol Autonomous Prefecture	541.13	421.02	510.72	418.37	239.02
阿克苏地区	Aksu Administrative Offices	203.16	155.26	195.19	151.39	133.10
克孜勒苏柯尔克孜自治州	Kizilsu Kirgiz Autonomous Prefecture	32.65	28.99	24.33	24.13	24.55
喀什地区	Kashgar [Kaxgar] Administrative Offices	269.30	165.76	250.65	152.84	137.94
和田地区	Hotan Administrative Offices	107.37	76.24	100.75	69.26	70.58

12-17 按登记注册类型分建筑企业工程施工情况
Condition of Building Works by Construction Enterprise by Registration Status

单位：万平方米　　(2007 年)　　(10 000 sq.m)

项目	Item	房屋建筑施工面积 Floor Space of Buildings Constructing	#本年新开工面积 New-opened Works for This Year	施工面积中实行投标承包面积 Space of Buildings and Contracting	#本年新开工面积 New-opened Works for This Year	房屋建筑竣工面积 Floor Space of Buildings Completed
总　计	**Total**	**3552.36**	**2421.17**	**3299.73**	**2277.87**	**1849.64**
#一、二级企业	First, Second Enterprises	2169.61	1363.46	2049.88	1321.05	997.55
#国有及国有控股	State-owned and State-holding	1589.57	948.42	1510.93	895.25	736.80
按登记注册类型分组	**Grouped by Registration Status**					
内资企业	Domestic Funede	3552.36	2421.17	3299.73	2277.87	1849.64
国有企业	State-owned Enterprises	464.86	291.22	444.76	276.68	228.43
集体企业	Collective-owned Enterprises	45.44	40.10	45.22	40.11	28.63
有限责任公司	Limited Liability Corporations	2293.29	1496.00	2135.25	1432.40	1153.10
国有独资公司	Sole State -funded Company	196.69	106.91	192.84	101.86	57.97
其他有限责任公司	Other Limited Liability Companies	2096.60	1389.09	1942.40	1330.54	1095.12
股份有限公司	Share-holding Corporations Ltd	100.17	69.06	97.13	69.06	56.62
私营企业	Private Enterprises	648.60	524.79	577.37	459.62	382.86
#私营有限责任公司	Private Limited Liability Companies	628.36	505.58	557.13	440.42	373.06
私营股份有限公司	Private Stock Limited Companies	9.21	8.73	9.21	8.73	4.83
按国民经济行业分组	**Grouped by National Economic Sectors**					
房屋和土木工程建筑业	Buildings and Givil Engineering Construction	3411.15	2328.50	3174.88	2196.81	1767.23
房屋工程建筑	Building Construction	3254.67	2219.07	3030.52	2092.89	1671.03
土木工程建筑	Civil Engineering Construction	156.48	109.43	144.36	103.92	96.20
铁路、道路、隧道和桥梁	Railways, Roads, Tunnels and Bridges	72.71	53.45	70.91	49.00	41.27
水利和港口建筑	Water Conservancy and Seaport Construction	62.59	45.61	54.14	45.58	39.85
工矿工程建筑	Mine Project	21.13	10.32	19.26	9.29	15.03
架线和管道工程建筑	Cabling and Piping Project	0.05	0.05	0.05	0.05	0.05
建筑安装业	Construction and Installation	130.31	84.62	113.95	74.81	75.47
建筑装饰业	Building Decoration	1.79	1.80	1.80		
其他建筑业	Others	9.10	6.25	9.10	6.25	6.94
按隶属关系分组	**Grouped by Subordination**					
中 央	Central Government	605.20	388.87	574.22	369.66	289.58
地 方	Local	2947.16	2032.30	2725.51	1908.21	1560.06
按企业资质等级分组	**Grouped by Enterprise's Qualification**					
#施工总承包	Undertaking Porjects	3444.37	2350.23	3211.64	2222.74	1790.47
特　级	Special	153.21	75.86	153.21	75.86	40.85
一　级	First Class	1120.32	576.62	1073.51	570.17	469.09
二　级	Second Class	998.36	753.85	925.93	720.19	492.85
三级及以下	Third Class	1172.48	943.90	1058.99	856.52	787.68
专业承包	Specialized Undertaking	107.99	70.94	88.09	55.13	59.17
一　级	First Class	9.07	2.88	8.57	2.38	6.08
二　级	Second Class	41.87	30.10	41.87	28.31	29.52
三级及以下	Third Class	57.05	37.96	37.65	24.44	23.57

12-18 建筑企业竣工房屋建筑面积
Floor Space of Completed Building of Construction Enterprises

单位：万平方米 (10 000 sq.m)

时期(年份)	Period (Year)	合计 Total	厂房 Workshop	住宅 Flat	办公用房 House for Office
"五五"时期	**Fifth Five-Year Plan Period**	**527.31**	**58.53**	**274.62**	**39.81**
"六五"时期	**Sixth Five-Year Plan Period**	**1297.63**	**271.01**	**127.61**	**184.40**
"七五"时期	**Seventh Five-Year Plan Period**	**2120.30**	**324.20**	**925.20**	**193.90**
"八五"时期	**Eighth Five-Year Plan Period**	**2914.41**	**321.35**	**1448.92**	**285.54**
"九五"时期	**Ninth Five-Year Plan Period**	**4576.72**	**262.63**	**2891.37**	**405.71**
	2000	1261.42	55.62	851.49	109.59
"十五"时期	**Tenth Five-Year Plan Period**	**7300.66**	**376.84**	**4380.93**	**637.48**
	2001	1467.54	60.86	1012.33	110.98
	2002	1469.60	60.98	945.33	103.85
	2003	1450.81	70.48	740.17	159.71
	2004	1483.35	97.37	833.23	136.68
	2005	1429.36	87.15	849.87	126.26
"十一五"时期	**Five-Year Plan Period**				
	2006	1645.02	93.82	879.52	181.69
	2007	1849.64	145.11	1096.02	216.88

时期(年份)	Period (Year)	商业、居民服务业用房 House for Commerce and Residents' Services	文化教育业用房 House for Culture and Education	医疗用房 House for Medical Care	科研用房 House for Scientific Research	其他 Others
"五五"时期	**Fifth Five-Year Plan Period**	**22.94**	**56.85**	**11.07**	**4.80**	**58.69**
"六五"时期	**Sixth Five-Year Plan Period**	**106.09**	**263.23**	**51.22**	**22.14**	**271.93**
"七五"时期	**Seventh Five-Year Plan Period**	**140.40**	**258.10**	**51.20**	**24.80**	**202.50**
"八五"时期	**Eighth Five-Year Plan Period**	**261.87**	**246.55**	**60.55**	**12.28**	**277.35**
"九五"时期	**Ninth Five-Year Plan Period**	**351.83**	**287.12**	**63.43**	**13.31**	**301.32**
	2000	86.81	79.86	16.61	3.03	58.42
"十五"时期	**Tenth Five-Year Plan Period**	**832.97**	**565.63**	**122.23**	**12.83**	**371.75**
	2001	121.21	76.50	13.29	1.63	70.74
	2002	160.63	98.16	21.29	2.73	76.63
	2003	217.96	132.84	31.22	3.10	95.33
	2004	192.48	113.95	31.11	3.39	75.14
	2005	140.69	144.18	25.32	1.98	53.91
"十一五"时期	**Five-Year Plan Period**					
	2006	149.41	207.08	44.60	0.97	87.93
	2007	113.16	157.21	44.85	0.92	75.49

主要统计指标解释

建筑业统计单位 指从事房屋、构筑物建造和设备安装活动的法人企业。建筑业法人企业应同时具备的条件是：①依法成立，有自己的名称、组织机构和场所，能够承担民事责任；②独立拥有和使用资产，承担负债，有权与其他单位签订合同；③独立核算盈亏，能够编制资产负债表。

建筑业总产值(即自行完成施工产值) 是以货币表现的建筑安装企业在一定时期内生产的建筑业产品和提供的服务的总和。建筑业总产值包括：

(1)建筑工程产值：指列入建筑工程预算内的各种工程价值。

(2)设备安装工程产值：指设备安装工程价值，不包括被安装设备本身价值。

(3)房屋、构筑物修理产值：指房屋、构筑物修理所完成的价值，但不包括被修理房屋、构筑物本身的价值和生产设备的修理价值。

(4)非标准设备制造产值：指加工制造没有定型的、非标准的生产设备的加工费和原材料价值，以及附属加工厂为本企业承建工程制作的非标准设备的价值。

建筑业增加值 指建筑业企业在报告期内以货币表现的建筑业生产经营活动的最终成果。目前建筑业增加值采用分配法(收入法)计算，即从收入的角度出发，根据生产要素在生产过程中应得的收入份额计算。具体计算公式为：

建筑业增加值＝本年提取的固定资产折旧+主营业务应付工资+主营业务应付福利费+管理费用中的劳动待业保险费、税金+工程结算税金及附加+营业利润

房屋建筑施工面积 指在报告期内施工的全部房屋建筑面积，包括本期新开工的房屋面积、上期施工跨入本期继续施工的房屋面积、上期停缓建在本期恢复施工的房屋面积、本期竣工的房屋面积及本期施工后又停缓建的房屋面积。

房屋建筑竣工面积 指在报告期内房屋建筑按照设计要求全部完工，达到了住人和使用条件，经验收鉴定合格，正式移交使用单位的房屋建筑面积。

自有机械设备年末总台数 指归本企业所有，属于本企业固定资产的生产性机械设备年末总台数。包括施工机械、生产设备、运输设备以及其他设备。

自有机械设备年末总功率 指本企业自有施工机械、生产设备、运输设备以及其他设备等列为在册固定资产的生产性机械设备年末总功率，按设定能力或查定能力计算。包括机械本身的动力和为该机械服务的单独动力设备，如电动机等。计算单位用千瓦，动力换算可按1马力＝0.735千瓦折合成千瓦数。电焊机、变压器、锅炉不计算动力。

工程结算收入 指企业承包工程实现的工程价款结算收入，以及向发包单位收取的除工程价款以外的按规定列作营业收入的各种款项，如临时设施费、劳动保险费、施工机械调迁费等以及向发包单位收取的各种索赔款。

工程结算利润 指已结算工程实现的利润，如亏损以“－”号表示。计算公式为：

工程结算利润＝工程结算收入－工程结算成本－工程结算税金及附加

企业总收入 指与企业生产经营直接有关的各项收入，包括工程结算收入和其他业务收入。计算公式为：

企业总收入＝工程结算收入＋其他业务收入

Explanatory Notes on Main Statistical Indicators

Statistical Unit in Construction refers to corporate enterprise engaged in the construction of buildings and structures and in the installation of equipment.A corporate construction enterprise should have qualification certifieates with independent accounting system,and should meet the following 3 requirements:①being set up in line with relevant legal basis,having its full name,organization and location,and capable of taking civil liabilities;② independently possessing and using its assets and assuming its liabilities,and entitled to sign contracts with other institutions;and ③ making independent accounts of its profits and losses,and capable of compiling its own balance sheet.

Gross Output Value of Construction (Output Value of Projects Under Construction) refers to total of construction products and services, expressed in money terms, completed by construction and installation enterprises during a given period of time. It includes:

(1) Output value of construction projects, that is the value of projects covered by the project budgets;

(2) Output value of installation projects, that is the value of the installation of equipment, (excluding the value of the equipment to be installed);

(3) Output value of repair of buildings and structures, that is the value created through the repairs of buildings or structures,but does not include the value of buildings or structures being repaired and the value of the repair of production equipment;

(4) Output value of manufactured non-standard equipment, that is the value of non-standard production equipment (including raw materials and manufacturing cost) made for the construction project, and the equipment manufactured by subsidiary workshops.

Value-added of Construction refers to the final result of the activities of production and management of construction in monetary terms in the reference period. At present, the value-added of construction is calculated with the income approach. In other words, it is the sum of income of various production factors in the production process. The formula is as follows:

Value-added of construction=depreciation of fixed assets in the year+wages payable+welfare expenses payable+insurance premium and tax for waiting for employment in the administrative expenses +taxes and surcharges on project settlement+profit gained from project settlement.

Floor Space of Buildings Under Construction refers to floor space of buildings under construction during the reference period, including newly started buildings,buildings started earlier and Continued during the reference period,and buildings suspended earlier but restarted during the reference period, buildings completed during the reference period, and buildings under construction and then suspended during the reference period.

Floor Space of Buildings Completed refers to the floor space of buildings that are completed in the reference period in accordance with the requirements of the design, up to the standard for putting them into use, and have been checked and accepted by concerned departments as qualified ones.

Total Number of Machinery and Equipment Owned by the End of Year refers to the number of machines and equipment owned by the enterprises, and listed as the fixed assets of the enterprises by the end of the year, including machinery and equipment for construction, production and transportation.

Total Power of Machinery and Equipment Owned by the End of Year refers to the total power of machinery and equipment owned by the enterprises,and listed as the fixed assets of the enterprises by the end of the year, including machinery and equipment for construction,production and transportation.The power of the machinery is calculated on basis of the designed or verified capacity,covering the power of the machinery/equipment and the separate power equipment serving the machinery/equipment (such as electric motors), but excluding welders, transformers and boilers.The unit used for the calculation of power is kilowatt, with horsepower converted to kilowatt by 1 horsepower=0.735 kilowatt.

Income from Settlement of Projects refers to the income received by the construction enterprise from the contracted project through settlement procedures, and other charges to the contractoree as operational costs in addition to the value of the project, such as temporary facility fee,labour insurance premium,moving cost of construction equipment,as well as various types of claims to the contractee.

Profit from Settlement of Projects refers to profit realized through settled projects. It is calculated with the following formula:

Profit from Settlement of Projects=Income from Settlement of Projects−Settled Cost−Settled Taxes and Other Cost

Total Revenue of Enterprises refers to the sum of income from production and operation of enterprises, including income from settlement of projects and other operational income, namely:

Total Revenue of Enterprises=Income from Settlement of Projects+Other Operational Income

第十三篇
运输和邮电

CHAPTER 13
Transport, Postal and Telecommunication Services

简要说明
Brief Introduction

本篇资料的主要内容及来源

本篇资料反映新疆维吾尔自治区交通运输业和邮政、电信业发展的基本状况。

运输业资料主要包括：铁路、公路、民航、管道四种运输方式的线路条数、里程、总运量及周转量、货物运输平均运距、铁路运输主要技术经济指标；民用机动车辆情况。

邮政、电信业资料主要包括：邮电业务完成情况，邮电业务发展水平等资料。

铁路资料来自乌鲁木齐铁路局；公路资料来自新疆维吾尔自治区交通厅；民航运输数据资料来自中国南方航空股份有限公司新疆分公司；电信资料来自新疆维吾尔自治区通信管理局；邮政数据来自新疆维吾尔自治区邮政公司。

本篇资料由新疆维吾尔自治区统计局工交处收集整理。

Main Content and Source of Data

Data in this chapter cover mainly the basic condition of the development of transportation, post and telecommunications in Xinjiang Uygur Autonomous Region.

Data on transport cover mainly the length of the routes of four means of railway, highways, civil aviation and pipeline. total fright traffic, total freight ton-kilometers, average transport distance of fright, principal economic and technical indicators of railway transport, possession of civil vehicles.

Data on post and telecommunication cover mainly the complete business volume of post and telecommunication services, and the development of the post and telecommunication service, ect.

Data on railways transportation come from the Urumqi Bureau of the Railway. Data on the highways come from the Bureau of Transportation. Data on the civil aviation transport come from the China Southwest Airlines, Xinjiang Branch. Data on telecommunication services come from telecommunication Bureau. Data on post are provided by the Post Bureau.

Data in this chapter are collected and compiled by the Division of Industry and Transport Statistics, Xinjiang Bureau of Statistics.

13-1 运输业基本情况
Basic Conditions of Transport

指　　标	Item	1995	2000	2007
运输线路长度(公里)	**Length of Transport Routes (km)**	**101665**	**236360**	**308498**
国家铁路营业里程	Railways in Operation	1578	3010	2925
公　路	Highways	30298	80875	145219
民用航空	Total Civil Aviation Routes	69789	152941	160354
客运量(万人)	**Total Passenger Traffic (10 000 persons)**	**17533**	**23191**	**38434**
铁　路	Railways	672	1147	1873
公　路	Highways	16739	21877	36159
民用航空	Civil Aviation	122	167	402
旅客周转量(亿人公里)	**Total Passenger-Kilometers (100 million passenger-km)**	**204.89**	**292.80**	**548.10**
铁　路	Railways	58.04	97.40	144.46
公　路	Highways	117.17	158.20	326.70
民用航空	Civil Aviation	29.68	37.20	76.94
货运量(万吨)	**Total Freight Traffic (10 000 tons)**	**25406.0**	**33090.5**	**49009.6**
铁　路	Railways	2733	4199	7430
公　路	Highways	21754	27048	38427
民用航空	Civil Aviation	2.0	3.5	3.6
输油(气)管道	Petroleum and Gas Pipelines	917	1840	3149
货物周转量(亿吨公里)	**Total Freight Ton-kilometers (100 million ton-km)**	**474.39**	**660.88**	**1264.31**
铁　路	Railways	240.88	355.00	678.53
公　路	Highways	219.72	272.90	468.80
民用航空	Civil Aviation	0.57	0.98	0.91
输油(气)管道	Petroleum and Gas Pipelines	13.22	32.00	116.07
民用汽车拥有量(万辆)	**Possession of Civil Motor Vehicles (10 000 units)**	**24.7**	**37.0**	**81.8**
#载客汽车辆数	Buses and Cars	9.4	18.0	45.6
载货汽车辆数	Trucks	14.3	17.5	23.2
#私人汽车拥有量	Privat Vehicles	5.6	13.9	43.7

注：1.2000 年以后公路里程包括兵团数据。2.2006 年起新疆公路通车里程包含村道里程(以下同)。
Note: a) Since 2000 the highway mileage cover the data of XJPCC. b) Length of highways include lenth of backroad since 2006.(the same as in the following table)

13-2 运输线路长度
Length of Transport Routes

单位:公里 (km)

年 份 Year	铁路营业里程 Length of Railways in Operation	#新疆境内 Inside Xinjiang	公 路 Length of Highways	#高级次高级公路 High Grade & Seond High Grade Highways	民用航空 Length of the Civil Aviation	#新疆境内 Inside Xinjiang	管道输油(气)里程 Petrolurn and Gas Pipelines
1978	1031	796	23818	5810	4783	4783	443
1980	1103	868	21148	6390	4412	4412	443
1985	1579	1344	22232	8369	4527	4527	473
1990	1578	1343	25425	12566	36465	5159	740
1991	1578	1343	25697	13270	40538	5159	849
1992	1578	1343	26024	13793	45212	5159	876
1993	2038	1803	27961	15798	48880	5159	876
1994	2038	1803	28611	16888	53715	6693	875
1995	2038	1803	30298	19013	69789	6693	875
1996	2038	1803	31609	20461	122089	9183	928
1997	2038	1803	32053	21495	123664	9717	1373
1998	2038	1803	32762	22485	150473	9717	1955
1999	3008	2780	33484	23214	141872	9719	2496
2000	3010	2775	80875	31059	152941	9719	2696
2001	3010	2774	80947	31635	161814	9719	2965
2002	3010	2775	82929	32541	132483	9898	3153
2003	3009	2775	83633	33891	141456	9898	3008
2004	2999	2763	86824	40679	111768	8664	3003
2005	2925	2761	89531	43803	119481	8664	3003
2006	2925	2761	143736	50119	138564	9064	4631
2007	2925	2761	145219	55080	160354	11363	6793

13-3 运输线路质量
Quality of Transport Routes

单位：公里 (km)

指 标	Item	1995	2000	2006	2007
铁路营业里程	Length of Railways in Operation	2038	3010	2925	2925
#复线里程	Double-Tracking Length		986	906	907
#自动闭塞里程	Automatic Blocking Length	273	685	934	934
公路线路里程	Length of Highways	30298	80875	143736	145219
#水泥沥青路面	Lenth of bituminous Pavement	27982	33035	50119	55080

13-4 客运量及周转量

Passenger Traffic and Passenger kilometers

年 份 Year	客运量(万人) Passenger Traffic (10 000 persons)				旅客周转量(亿人公里) Passenger-Kilometers (100 million passenger-km)			
	总 计 Total	铁 路 Railways	公 路 Highways	民用航空 Civil Aviation	总 计 Total	铁 路 Railways	公 路 Highways	民用航空 Civil Aviation
1978	941	148	786	7	25.23	13.72	10.96	0.55
1980	1356	193	1152	10	30.49	18.83	10.83	0.83
1985	3728	320	3399	9	63.16	33.16	29.13	0.87
1986	4058	362	3674	22	73.87	36.40	34.00	3.74
1987	4439	377	4327	34	83.67	37.14	39.44	7.09
1988	5205	459	4698	48	99.17	42.86	46.35	9.96
1989	8740	453	8240	47	120.69	44.52	66.37	9.80
1990	9602	388	9161	53	103.80	37.96	55.11	10.73
1991	14582	383	14142	56	122.08	41.94	68.05	12.09
1992	14997	425	14490	82	138.24	44.48	75.38	18.38
1993	16352	513	15749	90	174.23	50.04	103.51	20.73
1994	17181	670	16405	106	195.58	58.08	112.50	25.00
1995	17533	672	16739	122	204.89	58.00	117.17	29.68
1996	18858	610	18110	138	218.79	57.80	128.58	32.20
1997	20237	748	19360	129	233.39	64.70	139.00	29.69
1998	21747	878	20735	134	256.90	76.90	149.60	30.40
1999	22763	1000	21618	145	270.74	81.90	157.05	31.79
2000	23191	1147	21877	167	292.80	97.40	158.20	37.20
2001	24344	932	23255	157	309.70	104.10	170.30	35.30
2002	26016	950	24883	183	330.80	106.00	185.60	39.20
2003	26972	879	25878	215	342.00	106.10	195.00	40.90
2004	29782	1023	28473	286	423.80	121.90	249.00	52.90
2005	33220	1134	31747	339	457.42	125.20	271.20	61.02
2006	34471	1272	32835	364	498.30	138.90	292.10	67.30
2007	38434	1873	36159	402	548.10	144.46	326.70	76.94

注：2007 年民航旅客吞吐量为 770.7 万人。
Note: Air passenger handling capacity is 7.707 million persons in 2007.

13-5 货运量及货物周转量
Freight Traffic and Ton-kilometers

年 份 Year	货运量(万吨) Freight Traffic (10 000 tons)				
	总 计 Total	铁 路 Railways	公 路 Highways	民用航空 Civil Aviation	输油(气)管道 Petroleum and Gas Pipelines
1978	6064.12	923	4843	0.12	298
1980	8422.16	884	7209	0.16	329
1985	10681.11	1278	8847	0.11	556
1990	13919.87	1691	11551	0.87	677
1995	25406.00	2733	21754	2.00	917
1996	26676.00	2951	22505	2.00	1218
1997	28790.00	3190	24125	3.00	1472
1998	30484.00	3324	25573	3.00	1584
1999	32076.17	3777	26596	3.17	1700
2000	33090.50	4199	27048	3.50	1840
2001	33589.00	3904	27751	2.00	1932
2002	34966.70	4121	28861	2.70	1982
2003	37485.20	4602	30881	2.20	2000
2004	38885.50	5083	31700	2.50	2100
2005	40600.20	5397	33000	3.20	2200
2006	43096.40	6001	34835	3.40	2256
2007	49009.62	7430	38427	3.62	3149

年 份 Year	货物周转量(亿吨公里) Freight Ton-kilometers (100 million ton-km)				
	总 计 Total	铁 路 Railways	公 路 Highways	民用航空(万吨公里) Civil Aviation (10 000 ton-km)	输油(气)管道 Petroleum and Gas Pipelines
1978	106.96	67.76	32.06	98.10	7.13
1980	121.14	67.27	45.89	137.80	7.97
1985	174.75	102.03	61.26	104.00	11.45
1990	262.29	141.16	108.09	2048.00	12.84
1995	474.39	240.88	219.72	5744.00	13.22
1996	507.15	260.96	229.55	6475.00	16.00
1997	541.40	269.70	247.00	7000.00	24.00
1998	553.60	264.20	262.80	7000.00	25.90
1999	602.94	303.60	270.46	8800.00	28.00
2000	660.88	355.00	272.90	9776.00	32.00
2001	714.43	403.90	275.90	6300.00	34.00
2002	759.62	425.30	298.00	8238.00	35.50
2003	837.04	475.00	325.00	6400.00	36.40
2004	947.24	548.50	361.00	7400.00	37.00
2005	1032.75	586.90	405.00	8500.00	40.00
2006	1143.31	647.10	425.68	8921.00	69.64
2007	1264.31	678.53	468.80	9085.78	116.07

13-6 货物运输平均运距
Average Transport Distance of Freight

单位：公里 (km)

年 份 Year	合 计 Total	铁 路 Railways	公 路 Highways	民用航空 Civil Aviation	输油(气)管道 Petroleum and Gas Pipelines
1978	168	565	66	818	239
1980	139	566	64	861	242
1985	158	624	69	945	206
1990	188	835	94	2354	190
1995	187	881	101	2872	144
1996	190	884	102	3238	131
1997	188	845	102	2333	163
1998	182	795	102	2332	164
1999	188	804	102	2776	165
2000	200	845	101	2857	174
2001	211	1023	99	3150	176
2002	217	1032	103	3051	179
2003	224	865	105	2909	182
2004	244	904	114	2960	176
2005	254	901	122	2656	182
2006	265	894	122	2598	308
2007	257	913	122	2528	368

13-7 铁路运输主要财务指标
Main Financial Indicators of Railway Transport

单位：万元 (10 000 yuan)

指 标	Item	1990	1995	2000	2006	2007
运输总收入	**Total Transport Revenue**	**86686**	**192555**	**509480**	**1136550**	**1052355**
客运收入	Revenue from Passenger Traffic	18763	33560	82121	194913	272729
货运收入	Revenue from Freight Traffic	62516	142168	318485	932146	450969
运输清算收入	**Transportation Claring Revenue**	**59765**		**467142**	**890613**	**998677**
运输总支出	**Toatl Transport Expenditure**	**51875**	**193693**	**418497**	**1036927**	**1165553**
工 资	Wages and Salaries	11163	38429	98293	174111	187327
材 料	Materials	6702	23183	36210	55213	70009
燃 料	Fuel	9308	32996	74487	210657	232222
电 力	Electricity	666	2433	4701	3441	4385
折 旧	Depreciation	17174	13137	60859	94057	100603
营业外收支净额	**Non-operating Net Revenue or Expenditure**	**6886**	**14503**	**23236**	**46547**	**-28218**
实现利润	**Profits**	**6291**	**-12591**	**34130**	**-158948**	**-188563**
运输利润	Transport Profits	5501	-11649	33195	-175170	-189298

13-8 铁路运输技术经济主要指标
Main Technical and Economic Indicators of Railway Transport

指标	Item	2006	2007
货运机车日产量(万吨公里)	Average Daily Ton-kilometers of Freight Locomotives (10 000 ton-km)	111.9	114.0
#内燃机车	Diesel Locomotives	111.9	114.0
货运列车平均总重(吨)	Average Totál Tonnage of Freight Locomotives (ton)	2444	2566
#内燃机车	Diesel Locomotives	2444	2566
货运机车日车公里(公里)	Daily Distance per Freight Locomotive (km)	638	667
客运机车日车公里(公里)	Daily Distance per Passenger Locomotive (km)	638	914
内燃机车每万吨公里耗油(公斤)	Oil Consumption of Diesel Locomotives (kg/10 000 ton-km)	28.2	29.0
货物列车出发正点率(%)	Punctuality Rate of Freight Trains at Departure (%)	99.9	99.1
货物列车运行正点率(%)	Punctuality Rate of Freight Trains in Running (%)	99.7	98.4
旅客列车出发正点率(%)	Punctuality Rate of Passenger Trains at Departure (%)	96.8	99.3
旅客列车运行正点率(%)	Punctuality Rate of Passenger Trains in Running (%)	95.7	98.8
旅客列车技术速度(公里/小时)	Technical Speed of Passenger Trains (km/hr)	61.9	71.6
旅客列车旅行速度(公里/小时)	Travelling Speed of Passenger Trains (km/hr)	54.9	62.4
客运密度(万人公里/公里)	Density of Passenger Transport (10 000 passenger-km/km)	481.5	511.9
货物列车技术速度(公里/小时)	Technical Speed of Freight Trains (km/hr)	46.6	48.9
货物列车旅行速度(公里/小时)	Running Speed of Freight Trains (km/hr)	35.8	38.0
货运密度(万吨公里/公里)	Density of Freight Transport (10 000 ton-km/km)	2207.8	2367.7
货车周转时间(天)	Turning Around Time of Freight Cars (day)	4.72	4.38
一次货物作业时间(小时)	Handling Time of Freight (hour)	20.1	21.5
货车中转停留时间(小时)	Transfer Waiting Time per Car (hour)	4.4	5.0
货车静载重(准轨) (吨)	Static Load of Freight Cars (Standard Gauge) (ton)	55.7	54.8

13-9 民用车辆拥有量
Number of Civil Vehicles Owned

单位：辆 (unit)

指标	Item	2006		2007	
		总计 Total	#私人 Private	总计 Total	#私人 Private
民用汽车	**Civil Vehicles**	**717370**	**365413**	**817722**	**436762**
载客汽车	Passenger Vehicles	383680	222218	456285	280215
#大型	Large	21457	926	23574	1005
中型	Medium	20815	6354	22659	6732
小型	Small	316687	198315	384626	254737
微型	Mini	24721	16623	25426	17741
载货汽车	Trucks	214450	67006	231743	75461
#重型	Large	56178	9431	59439	9354
中型	Medium	42754	9238	43473	9810
轻型	Light	105514	43062	119042	50762
微型	Mini	10004	5275	9789	5535
其它汽车	Others	119240	76189	129694	81086

13-10 邮电事业情况

Basic Conditions of Postal and Telecommunication Services

指　　标	Item	2000	2006	2007
邮政局营业网点(处)	**Number of Post Offices (unit)**		**1444**	**1418**
邮路长度(单程)(公里)	**Length of Postal Routes (km)**	**134109**	**140896**	**113622**
#农 村	Rural	55852	14562	15663
邮电业务总量(万元)	**Business Volume of Post and Telecommunication Services (10 000 yuan)**	**473000**	**2289188**	**3036498**
函件(万件)	Number of Letters (10 000 pcs)	7148	4130	3177
包件(万件)	Number of Parcels (10 000 pcs)	163	179	187
特快专递(万件)	Pieces of Express Mail Services (10 000 pcs)	124	291	323
报刊期发数(万份)	Number of Newspapers and Magazines Circulation (10 000 copies)	535	342	305
长途电话(万次)	Number of Long-distance Calls (10 000 times)	34712	46478	67660
本地电话年末用户(万户)	Local Telephone Subscribers at Year-end (10 000 subscribers)	191.0	706.9	678.1
#城市电话年末数	Urban Telephone Subscribers at Year-end	136.3	533.6	520.6
乡村电话年末数	Number of Rural Telephones Subscribers at Year-end	54.7	154.5	157.5
#住宅电话年末数	Residential Telephone Subscribers	149.3	501.6	495.7
年末移动电话用户(万户)	Number of Mobile Telephones Subscribers at Year-end (10 000 subscribers)	78.0	671.1	808.3
邮电通信电路及长途电信线路	**Telecommunication Lines**			
光缆线路长度(公里)	Length of Long Distance Optical Cable Lines (km)	10828	96796	111000
数字微波线路长度(公里)	Length of Long Distance Microwave Lines (km)	4889	2956	2900
邮电通信设备	**Telecommunication Facilities**			
固定长途交换机容量(路端)	Capacity of long-distance Telephone Excharges (circuit)	102540	219609	286000
本地电话局用交换机容量(万门)	Capacity of Local Office Telephone Exchange (10 000 line)	241.7	912.0	940.6
全区邮电通信水平	**Level of Postal and Telecommunication Services**			
平均每百人每年发函件数(件)	Annual Arerage Number of Letters Mailed Per 100 persons (piece)	387.0	496.0	159.0
平均每百人每年订报刊数(份)	Annual Arerage Number of Newspaper Subscribed Per 100 Persons (piece)	28.9	26.1	15.1
平均每百人拥有电话机数(固定)(部)	Number of Telephone Sets Owned per 100 Persons(stable) (set)	15.0	34.5	33.4
平均每百人拥有电话机数(移动)(部)	Number of Telephone Sets Owned per 100 Persons (mobile) (set)		32.7	38.6
农村邮电通信水平	**Rural Level**			
通电话的乡(镇)比重(%)	Percentage of Townships with Telephone Communication (%)	100	100	100
进入长话自动网的乡(镇)比重(%)	Percentage of Townships with Access to Auto-exchange Net of Long Distance Call (%)	100	100	100

注：1.2000 年后，电信部门取消电话机部数统计；2.2000 年后，电信部门取消长途电话电路中光缆及数字电路统计；3.2004 年后营业网点数及每一局所平均服务人口数均为邮政数。

Note: a) After 2000, the telecommunication authority has cancelled the statistics for telephone subscribers. b) After 2000, the telecommunication authority has cancelled the statistics for optical cable and digital circuit for long-distance telephones. c) Number of business outlets for the year 2004 and average population served by each bureau is postal statistics.

13-11 主要年份邮电业务情况

Conditions of Postal and Telecommunication Services in Main Years

年份 Year	邮电业务总量(万元) Business Volume of Postal and Telecommunication Services (10 000 yuan)	邮政业务总量 Business Volume of Postal Services	电信业务总量 Business Volume of Telecommunication Services	函件(万件) Number of Letters (10 000 pcs)
1978	2122			4842.7
1980	2332			5890.8
1985	4709			7032.6
1990	17372	8203	8312	7380.5
1995	90226	17322	71220	9041.8
1996	132129	20546	111583	8373.0
1997	171552	42144	129408	6985.0
1998	250595	49296	201299	6582.1
1999	347000	56717	290283	6524.0
2000	473000	59370	413630	7148.0
2001	634338	62265	572073	5601.0
2002	947000	68032	878968	6814.0
2003	1144838	72007	1072831	5987.0
2004	1531835	74835	1457000	4756.7
2005	1723759	80500	1643259	4450.0
2006	2289188	94188	2195000	4129.8
2007	3036498	100498	2936000	3177.0

年份 Year	特快专递(万件) Pieces of Express Mail Services (10 000 pcs)	报刊期发数(万份) Issue of Newspapers and Magazines (10 000 copies)	集邮业务(万枚) Stamps for Collection (10 000 pieces)	长途电话(万次) Number of Long Distance Telephone Calls (10 000 times)
1978		223.8		258.8
1980		329.6		276.5
1985		578.9		425.1
1990	…	805.7	1034.5	762.5
1995	93.6	478.1	3086.6	11705.9
1996	102.2	422.3	3634.2	19465.0
1997	96.0	376.0	4497.0	24078.0
1998	96.0	370.6	6412.0	29857.8
1999	103.0	595.6	7537.0	35739.4
2000	124.0	534.5	5766.0	34712.0
2001	147.0	358.0	5491.0	89844.0
2002	163.0	399.0	4620.0	45769.0
2003	199.0	587.3	3112.8	35554.2
2004	238.1	283.0	3141.3	62526.0
2005	266.0	293.0	2072.0	52482.0
2006	291.0	341.7	2205.1	46478.0
2007	324.0	305.0	2134.0	67660.0

注：从 1997 年起，市内电话户数统计口径有了较大调整，故农村电话户数增幅较大。

Note: From 1997, greater readjustment has been made on the Statistic Method about the number of telephone Subscribers and the number of rural Subscribers has gone up by a bigger margin.

13-11 续表 Continued

年 份 Year	移动电话用户(万户) Number of Mobile Telephone Subscribers (10 000 subscribers)	国际互联网络用户(万户) Number of Subscribers of Internet Services (10 000 subscribers)	固定电话年末用户(万户) Number of Subscribers of Local Telephone at Year-end (10 000 subscribers)	#城市电话用户(万户) Number of Urban Telephone Subscribers (10 000 subscribers)
1978			2.9	1.9
1980			3.2	2.1
1985			4.7	3.7
1990			8.9	7.9
1995	2.7		44.6	42.0
1996	4.2		70.5	69.8
1997	7.5		95.0	72.7
1998	15.7		119.4	88.1
1999	32.6		147.5	106.7
2000	78.0		191.0	136.3
2001	180.9	12.8	262.6	196.1
2002	297.0	17.3	337.5	238.3
2003	421.2	60.8	431.0	293.9
2004	489.7	78.0	516.7	387.0
2005	531.3	105.8	612.2	457.5
2006	671.1	123.7	706.9	533.6
2007	808.3	157.8	678.1	520.6

年 份 Year	#住宅电话 Household Fixed Telephone Subscribers	#乡村电话用户(万户) Rural Fixed Telephone Subscribers (10 000 subscribes)	#住宅电话 Household Fixed Telephone Subscribers	公用电话(户) Public Telephone (subscriber)
1978		1.1		
1980		1.0		
1985		1.0		
1990	1.2	1.1		257
1995	26.0	2.6	1.2	5612
1996	49.5	0.7	0.3	11819
1997	54.0	22.4	18.6	22808
1998	65.3	31.3	26.6	38795
1999	79.5	40.8	35.5	46856
2000	101.1	54.7	48.2	70753
2001	124.3	66.5	57.8	84309
2002	179.9	79.5	73.4	166000
2003	180.0	93.5	88.6	281632
2004	194.0	108.2	103.4	432000
2005	318.9	135.2	115.4	570047
2006	369.9	154.5	131.7	668335
2007	359.6	157.5	136.1	675309

主要统计指标解释

铁路营业里程 又称营业长度(包括正式营业和临时营业里程)，指办理客货运输业务的铁路正线总长度。凡是全线或部分建成双线及以上的线路，以第一线的实际长度计算复线、站线、段管线、岔线和特殊用途线以及不计算运费的联络线都不计算营业里程。该指标可以反映铁路运输业基础设施的发展水平，也是计算客货周转量、运输密度和机车车辆运用效率等指标的基础资料。

铁路电气化里程 指在全部铁路营业里程中已安装了供电线路及设备，可以供电力机车牵引列车运行的区段的总里程。

铁路自动、半自动闭塞里程 指装有列车自动或人工完成闭塞状态的铁路设备里程。为保证列车安全运行，在一个区间、同一时间内，一般只允许一列列车运行，这种保证列车在这个区间安全间隔运行的技术方法称为“闭塞”。自动或半自动闭塞里程占铁路营业里程的比重是反映铁路现代化的重要标志之一。

公路里程 指在一定时期内实际达到《公路工程 [WTBZ] 技术标准JTJ01-88》规定的等级公路，并经公路主管部门正式验收交付使用的公路里程数。包括大中城市的郊区公路以及通过小城镇街道部分的公路里程和桥梁、渡口的长度，不包括大中城市的街道、厂矿、林区生产用道和农业生产用道的里程。两条或多条公路共同经由同一路段，只计算一次，不得重复计算里程长度。该指标可以反映公路建设的发展规模，也是计算运输网密度等指标的基础资料。

民用航空航线里程 指民航运输定期班机飞行的航线长度的总和。航线长度按机场之间的距离计算，通常有两种计算方法：一是将每条航线长度相加称为重复计算航线里程;一是将两线或两条以上航线经过同一区段里程，只计算一次航线长度称为不重复计算航线里程。一般常用的是后者，该指标可以确切反映民航运输网的规模，是表明民航事业为国民经济服务和方便人民生活程度的主要指标。

输油(气)管道长度 也称输油(气)里程，指油品(或天然气)的实际输送距离，一般按输油(气)管道的单线长度计算。若包括复线和备用线长度则称为输油(气)管道延展长度，是指管道铺设的实际长度。我们通常使用的是不包括复线的“输油(气)管道里程”，该指标可以反映管道运输的发展规模和水平。

货(客)运量 指在一定时期内，各种运输工具实际运送的货物(旅客)数量。该指标是反映运输业为国民经济和人民生活服务的数量指标，也是制定和检查运输生产计划、研究运输发展规模和速度的重要指标。货运按吨计算，客运按人计算。货物不论运输距离长短、货物类别，均按实际重量统计。旅客不论行程远近或票价多少，均按一人一次客运量统计；半价票、小孩票也按一人统计。

货(客)运密度 指在一定时期内某种运输方式在营运线路的某一区段平均每公里线路通过的货物(旅客)运输周转量。计算公式为：

货(客)运密度=Σ 货物(旅客)周转量/营业线路长度

该指标可以反映交通运输线路上的货物(旅客)运输量运输繁忙程度，是平衡运输线路运输能力和通过能力，规划线路建设及改造、配备技术设备，研究运输网布局的重要依据。

货物(旅客)周转量 指在一定时期内，由各种运输工具运送的货物(旅客)数量与其相应运输距离的乘积之总和。该指标可以反映运输业生产的总成果，也是编制和检查运输生产计划，计算运输效率、劳动生产率以及核算运输单位成本的主要基础资料。计算货物周转量通常按发出站与到达站之间的最短距离，也就是计费距离计算。计算公式为：

货物(旅客)周转量= 货物(旅客)运输量 × 运输距离

铁路货车平均静载重 指铁路货车在始发站静止状态下平均每车装载的货物重量，用以分析货车完成装车时车辆载重力的利用情况。计算公式为：

货车平均静载重=货物发送吨数/装车数

静载重的多少取决于运送货物的性质、种类、车辆的类型和装载技术的高低。根据货车的平均标记载重与静载重进行对比，可以反映货车载重能力的利用程度。计算公式为：

货车载重力利用率(%)=货车平均静载重/货车平均标记载重 × 100%

铁路货运机车日产量 指在一定时期内，平均每台货运机车在一昼夜内所完成的总重吨公里数，包括载运货物的重量和车辆本身的自重。该指标从时间和牵引能力两方面反映了机车运用效率。计算公式为：

货运机车平均日产量=货运总重吨公里数/货运机车台日数

民用汽车拥有量 指报告期末，在公安交通管理部门按照《机动车注册登记工作规范》，已注册登记领有民用车辆牌照的全部汽车数量。汽车拥有量统计的主要分类：根据汽车结构分为载客汽车、载货汽车及其他汽车；根据汽车所有者不同分为个人(私人)汽车、单位汽车；根据汽车的使用性质分为营运汽车、非营运汽车和特种汽车；根据汽车大小规格不同载客汽车分为大型、中型、小型和微型，载货汽车分为重型、中型、轻型和微型。

邮电业务总量 指以价值量形式表现的邮电通信企业为社会提供各类邮电通信服务的总数量。邮电业务量按专业分类包括函件、包件、汇票、报刊发行、邮政快件、特快专递、邮政储蓄、集邮、公众电报、用户电报、传真、长途电话、出租电路、无线寻呼、移动电话、分组交换数据通信、出租代维等。计算方法为各类产品乘以相应的平均单价(不变价)之和，再加上出租电路和设备、代用户维护电话交换机和线路等的服务收入。该指标综合反映了一定时期邮电业务发展的总成果，是研究邮电业务量构成和发展趋势的重要指标。计算公式为：

邮电业务总量= Σ(各类邮电业务量 × 不变单价)+ 出租代维及其他业务收入= 邮电业务总量+ 电信业务总量

移动电话用户 指通过移动电话交换机进入移动电话网、占用移动电话号码的各类电话用户。包括签约用户和智能网预付费用户。一个移动电话号码统计为一户。

本地电话用户 指接入本地电信运营商固定电话网上的电话用户。包括：住宅用户、单位用户、公用电话用户等。按电话用户位置又分为市内电话用户和农村电话用户。1997年以前，“市内电话用户”是指接入县城及县以上城市的电话网上的电话用户；“农村电话用户”是指接入县邮电局农话台及县以下农村电话交换点，以县城为中心(除市话用户外)联通县、乡(镇)、行政村、村民小组的用户。从1997年起，电话用户数分组调整为以用户所在区域划分为“城市电话用户”和“乡村电话用户”，与过去的按市内电话和农村电话划分方法不同。而电话用户总数、电话机总部数统计范围不变。

城市电话用户 指直辖市、省辖市、地级市、县级市的市区、市郊区及县城(包括县人民政府所在地的县城关区或行政建制相当于县人民政府所在地的镇)范围内接入局用交换机的电话用户数，包括分布在农村地区的独立工矿区、林区、驻军等电话用户数。

乡村电话用户 指按行政区划属于城市范围以外的乡(镇)、村的电话用户数。

住宅电话用户 指安装在居民住宅或农民家里并按照住宅电话用户登记注册和收费的电话用户。包括私人付费、单位付费和按规定免费安装的住宅电话用户。

长途电话交换机容量 指用于接入长途电话网的电话交换机设备的额定容量，包括国际电话交换机容量。局用交换机容量指安装在电信运营企业内用于接续本地固定电话的电话交换机容量，包括现用和备用的人工或自动交换机的全部容量。不包括用户交换机容量。

移动电话交换机容量 指移动电话交换机根据一定话务模型和交换机处理能力计算出来的最大同时服务用户的数量。

Explanatory Notes on Main Statistical Indicators

Length of Railways in Operation refers to the total length of the trunk line under passenger and freight transportation (including both full operation and temporary operation). The calculation is based on the actual length of the first line even if this line has a full or partial double track or more tracks, excluding double tracks, station sidings, tracks under the charge of stations, branch lines, special-purpose lines and the non-payable connecting lines. The length of railways in operation is an important indicator to show the development of the infrastructure for the railway transport, and also the essential data to calculate volume of passenger freight transport, traffic density and utilization efficiency of the locomotives and carriages.

Length of Electrified Railways refers to the length of the section of railways in operation in which the power supply lines and other equipment are installed for the running of electrified locomotives. The proportion of the length of electrified railways to the total length of railways in operation is an important indicator to show the modernization of railways.

Automatic-blocking and Semi-automatic-blocking Length of Railways refer to length of railways installed with equipment to perform automatic or manual blocking of trains. Blocking is a spacing technique by which a section of the railway only allows one train to pass at a time in the aim of ensuring the traffic safety. the proportion of automatic/semi-automatic blocking length to the total length of railways in operation is an important indicator to show the modernization of railways.

Length of Highways refers to the length of highways which are built in conformity with the grades specified by the highway engineering standard formulated by the Ministry of Communications, and have been formally checked and accepted by the departments of highways and put into use. The length of highways includes that of the suburb highways at large and medium sized cities, highways passing through streets at small cities and towns, and also the length of bridges and ferries. It does not include the length of streets in big and medium-sized cities and highways built for the production purpose at factories, mines, forest areas and agricultural areas. If two or more highways go the same section of the way, the length of the section is only calculated for once and no duplication is allowed. The length of highways is an important indicator to show the development of the highway construction and to provide essential information to calculate the transport network density.

Length of Civil Aviation Routes refers to the length of all routes for regular civil aviation flights. There are usually two ways to calculate the distance between airports connected by the route length: One is to put the length of all air routes together, called duplicated calculation of the length of the routes; the other is not to allow the duplication in calculation when two or more routes passing the same section of aviation routes. The latter is usually used, as it can precisely show the size of the civil aviation network and indicate the extent of civil aviation serving the national economy and the people.

Length of Oil (Gas) Pipelines used as an indicator to show the development, scale and level of the pipeline transportation, it refers to the actual transport distance of oil (or gas) products, and is in general calculated in the length of single pipeline. If the length of the double pipelines and alternate pipeline are included, it is called the extension length of the oil (gas) pipelines, which indicates the actual length of the pipelines built, excluding double pipelines.

Freight (Passenger) Traffic refers to the volume of freight (passenger) transported with various means. Freight transport is calculated in tons and passenger traffic is calculated in the number of persons. Despite the type of freight and traveling distance, the freight transport is calculated in t he actual weight of the goods: and despite the traveling distance and ticket price, the passenger traffic is calculated by the principle that one person can be counted only once in one travel. The passengers who travel with a half price ticket or a child ticket is also calculate das one person. The freight (passenger) traffic provides a quantitative measure to show how the transport industry serves the national economy and people, and is also an important indicator for planning the transport industry and for studying the development scale and speed of the transport industry.

Freight (Passenger) Traffic Density refers to the freight (passenger) traffic volume carried by a particular means of transportation during a given period through one kilometer of a specific section of transportation route. The formula is as follows:

Freight (Passenger) Traffic Density =[Freight Ton-kilometers (Passenger-kilometers)] / (Length of Rout e in Operation)

Measuring unit: ton-kilometer / kilometer (or person-kilometer/ kilometer)

Freight (passenger) traffic density reflects the degree of business of freight (passenger) traffic on transportation routes, and therefore provides important information for balancing transport cap ability, planning const ruction and up grading of transport routes and studying t he distribution of transport network.

Freight Ton-kilometers (Passenger-kilometers) refer to the sum of the products of the volume of transported cargo (passengers) multiplying by the transport distance. It is an important indicator to reflect the achievement of transportation industry. Normally, the shortest distance between the departure station and the destination station (i.e., the payable distance) is the basis to calculate the freight ton-kilometers. This is an import ant indicator to show the total results of the transport industry, to prepare and examine the transport plan and to measure the efficiency, the lab our productivity and t he unit cost of transport.

The formula is as follows:

Freight Ton-kilometers (Passenger-kilometers) =Σ{Freight(Passenger) Traffic×Distance of Transportation}

Measuring unit: ton-kilometer (person-kilometer)

Static Load of Freight Cars refers to the average cargo weight as loaded by each freight car under the static condition at the departure station. It is used to show the utilization extent of the loading capacity of the freight cars. The formula is:

Static Load (ton) of Freight Car= (Tonnage of Goods Dispatched)/ (Number of Freight Cars Loaded)

The static load of freight cars is determined by the nature and type of goods loaded, the type of vehicles, and the technique of loading. The difference between the average marked load and the static load of freight cars reflects the utilization of loading capacity of freight cars. For its calculation the following formula is app lied:

Utilization Rate of Capacity of Freight Cars(%)=[(Average Static Load)× 100%] / (Average Marked Load)

Average Daily Haul of Freight Locomotives refers to the average total ton-kilometers accomplished by each freight transport locomotive over day and night during a given period of time. It includes both the weight of the goods carried and the deadweight of the train itself. It is a comprehensive indicator reflecting the locomotive efficiency in terms of both time and the pulling force.

Average Daily Haul of Freight Transport Locomotive (ton kilometer)=[(Total Ton/(Kilometers of Freight)) / (Daily Number of Freight Transport Locomotive)

Possession of Civil Motor Vehicles refer to the total numbers of vehicles that are registered and received vehicles' license tags according to the Work Standard for Motor Vehicles Registration formulated by transport management office under department of public security at the end of reference period. They are divided into following categories according to the structure of motor vehicles: passenger vehicles, trucks and others; and private vehicles and vehicles for units use according to ownerships; working vehicles, non-working vehicles and special motor vehicles according to kind of usage; large passenger vehicles, medium passenger vehicles and small passenger vehicles, heavy trucks, light-heavy trucks and light trucks according to sizes of vehicles.

Business Volume of Post and Telecommunications refers to the total amount of post and telecommunication services, expressed in value terms, provided by the post and telecommunications departments for the society. Post and telecommunication services can be classified as letters, parcels, remittance, issue of newspapers and magazines, fast mail service, express mail service, savings deposits, stamps for collection, public and individual telegraph service, facsimiles, long-distance telephone service, leasing of telephone lines, urban paging service, mobile telephone service, data transfer and transmission, etc. The accounting approach is to multiply the service products of all types with their average unit price (constant price) to get sum of business value, plus income from other services such as leasing of telephone lines and equipment, maintenance of telephone switchboards and lines on behalf of customers . This indicator reflects the overall results of post and telecommunications service during a given period, and is important to study the composition of business service and the development of post and telecommunications service.

The formula is as follows:

Business Volume of Post and Telecommunications= Σ(Transaction of Post and Telecommunication Service $\times$ Constant Price) + Income from Leasing, Maintenance and other Services

Mobil e Telephone Subscribers refer to the persons who own mobile telephone numbers and are connected with the mobile telephone communication network through the mobile telephones witch boards, including contracted subscribers and prepaid subscribers for intelligent network. One mobile telephone is taken as a subscriber.

Local Telephone Subscribers refer to subscribers that are connected to the local telecommunication service provider through fix line network, including household subscribers, institutional subscribers and public telephones. They are also classified as city subscribers and rural subscribers according to locations. Before 1997, city subscribers referred to those connected to city telephone networks in county towns and cities, while village subscribers referred to those connected to village telephone stations at and below counties. Since 1997, the classification of telephone subscribers was modified on the basis of physical location of the subscribers as urban telephone subscribers and rural telephone subscribers , which is different from the previous classification of categorizing local telephones and rural telephones , while the definition of total subscribers and total number of telephones remain unchanged.

Urban Telephone Subscribers refer to number of telephone subscribers, located at municipalities, cities under the jurisdiction of province, cities at prefecture level, downtown and suburb of city at county level town and county towns (including country towns where county government located, and towns of count y level according to the administrative organizational system),that are connected to the public line telephone network, including rural mineral area, forest area, military area.

Rural Telephone Subscribers refer to telephone subscribers, located at counties (towns) and villages out side the range of cities according to administrative jurisdiction.

Household Telephone Subscribers refer to telephone sets in stalled in the dwelling units of urban or rural residents, and registered as residence subscribers for payment, including 3 types of payment for the service: private payment, public payment and free service. Capacity of Long Distance Telephone Exchanges: refers to the rated cap a city of telephone exchanges to connect long distance telephone network, including capacity of international telephone exchanges.

Capacity of Office Telephone Exchanges refers to the capacity (measured in gate) of telephone exchanges installed in the offices of telecommunication service providers for communication between fixed telephones. It includes the capacity of both manual and automatic exchanges in use and for stand-by purpose, excluding the capacity of subscribers' exchanges.

Capacity of Mobile Telephone Exchanges refers to the capacity of the maximum services provided to subscribers at onetime basing on a certain model and transacting capacity of the mobile telephone exchanges.

第十四篇
批发和零售业、住宿和餐饮业

CHAPTER 14
Wholesale & Retail Trades, Hotels and Catering Services

简要说明
Brief Introduction

本篇资料的主要内容及来源

本篇资料反映新疆维吾尔自治区商品流通市场发展及批发和零售业、住宿和餐饮业经营情况。主要内容有社会消费品零售额;限额以上批发和零售业、住宿和餐饮业情况;限额以上批发和零售业商品销售及商品分类销售情况;限额以上批发和零售贸易企业及住宿和餐饮企业主要财务情况等。

社会消费品零售额指标的统计范围在 1993 年、1997 年和 2003 年做了较大调整。1993 年及以后不包括农业生产资料;1997 年及以后不包括居民购买住房;2003 年及以后不包括由各种经济类型的制造业法人企业、产业活动单位,直接售给城乡居民(包括本企业职工)和社会集团的商品以及农民在田间地头出售的农产品。

限额以上批发和零售业、住宿和餐饮业统计限额标准：批发业年销售额 2000 万元及以上;零售业年销售额 500 万元及以上;餐饮业年营业额 200 万元及以上,星级住宿业指旅游局认定的星级宾馆。

本篇资料由新疆维吾尔自治区统计局贸易外经处提供。

Main Content and Source of Data

Data in this chapter reflect the development of Xinjiang′s circulation of domestic market and the management situation of wholesale and retail & hotels and catering services, etc.

Adjustments were made for total retail of consumer goods in 1993,1997 and 2003.Total retail sales of consumer goods exclude means of agriculture production since 1993; exclude means of purchase of housing by residents from 1997 ,Total retail sales of consumer goods exclude direct sales of commodities by manufacturing corporations, establishments or self-employed industries to households (including to their employees) or institutions, or sales of farm products by farmers in or beside the fields since 2003(including 2003).

Criteria for wholesale and retail sale trades, hotels and catering services above designated size is defined as follows: wholesale trade has annual sales over 20 million yuan; retail sale trade have annual sale over 5 million yuan; catering services have annual income over 2 million yuan. Enterprise above designated size in accommodation refers to star-rated unit.

Data in this chapter are provided by the Division of Trade Statistics, the Xinjiang Bureau of Statistics.

14-1 限额以上批发和零售业、住宿和餐饮业基本情况

Basic Conditions of Enterprises above Designated Size of Wholesale and Retail Trades, Hotels and Catering Services

指 标	Item	2000	2005	2006	2007
法人机构(个)	**Number of Corporation Unit (unit)**	**394**	**1097**	**1135**	**1198**
批发零售业	Wholesale and Retail Trades	370	800	823	838
住宿餐饮业	Hotels and Catering Servicess	24	297	312	360
#餐饮业	Catering Services	24	65	70	66
产业活动单位(个)	**Number of Establishments (unit)**	**431**	**2396**	**2719**	**3113**
批发零售业	Wholesale and Retail Trades	382	1998	2289	2619
住宿餐饮业	Hotels and Catering Servicess	49	398	430	494
#餐饮业	Catering Services	49	96	112	110
批发零售业	**Wholesale and Retail Trades**				
商品销售总额（亿元)	Total sales (100 million yuan)	478.3	1182.0	1324.1	2228.6
社会消费品零售总额(亿元)	**Total Retail Sales of Consumer Goods (100 million yuan)**	**374.5**	**637.8**	**727.6**	**847.7**
按销售单位所在地分	**By Location of Establishments**				
市	City	233.7	442.3	509.2	599.8
县	County	65.2	95.2	106.9	122.2
县以下	Under County Level	75.6	100.3	111.5	125.7
按行业分	**By Sector**				
批发零售业	Wholesale and Retail Trades	242.3	507.3	577.8	678.1
住宿餐饮业	Hotels and Catering Servicess	38.2	92.5	110.7	129.0
其他行业	Others	94.0	38.0	39.1	40.6

注：2000 年法人机构、产业活动单位、餐饮业零售额不包括住宿业。
Note: The corporation agency, industrial units and retail sales of catering services did not include accommodation in 2000.

14-2 社会消费品零售总额
Total Retail Sales of Consumer Goods

单位：亿元 (100 million yuan)

年 份 Year	社会消费品零售总额 Total Retail Sales of Consumer Goods	按销售单位所在地分 by Location 市 City	县 County	县以下 Under County Level
1978	21.89	7.44	4.80	9.65
1980	29.36	11.06	6.05	12.25
1985	57.38	24.55	10.70	22.13
1990	104.30	57.17	24.27	22.86
1995	253.65	145.74	50.03	57.88
1996	295.36	171.51	55.38	68.47
1997	310.42	186.37	57.54	66.51
1998	327.52	197.89	59.89	69.74
1999	347.40	213.96	61.51	71.93
2000	374.50	233.66	65.15	75.69
2001	406.35	256.58	69.73	80.04
2002	442.88	284.74	74.32	83.82
2003	421.16	311.33	49.20	60.63
2004	563.41	385.81	85.79	91.81
2005	637.78	442.27	95.24	100.27
2006	727.59	509.19	106.86	111.54
2007	847.70	599.80	122.23	125.67

年 份 Year	按行业分 by Sector 批发零售业 Wholesale and Retail Trades	住宿餐饮业 Hotels and Catering Services	其他行业 Others
1978	17.34	0.57	3.98
1980	22.95	0.94	5.47
1985	40.83	2.51	14.04
1990	72.68	6.06	25.56
1995	169.16	17.27	67.22
1996	191.14	19.44	84.78
1997	198.73	22.22	89.47
1998	206.92	27.84	92.76
1999	222.57	32.76	92.07
2000	242.29	38.21	94.00
2001	266.38	44.57	95.40
2002	296.13	53.04	93.71
2003	341.90	60.64	18.62
2004	450.65	76.22	36.54
2005	507.32	92.47	37.99
2006	577.82	110.70	39.07
2007	678.10	129.02	40.58

14-3 分类型、分地区限额以上批发和零售业、住宿和餐饮业基本情况

Basic Conditions of Enterprises above Designated Size in Wholesale and Retail Trades, Hotels and Catering Services by Category and Region

(2007 年)

指标	Item	法人企业数(个) Number of Corporate Enterprises (unit)	产业活动单位数(个) Number of Establishments (unit)	从业人员数(人) Engaged Persons (person)
总计	**Total**	**1198**	**3113**	**125091**
批发业	**Wholesale Trades**	**517**	**1798**	**47959**
内资企业	Domesticfunded Enterprises	511	1788	47178
国有企业	State-owned Enterprises	97	435	15031
集体企业	Collective-owned Enterprises	34	69	4794
股份合作企业	Share-holding Cooperative Enterprises	1	2	34
有限责任公司	Limited Liability Corporations	163	567	15080
股份有限公司	Share-holding Corporations Ltd.	26	445	6733
私营企业	Private Enterprises	189	268	5464
其他企业	Others	1	2	42
港、澳、台投资企业	Enterprises With Funds from Hong Kong, Macao and Taiwan	3	4	280
外商投资企业	Foreign funded Enterprises	3	6	501
零售业	**Retail Trades**	**321**	**821**	**31066**
内资企业	Domesticfunded Enterprises	318	814	29739
国有企业	State-owned Enterprises	43	313	7729
集体企业	Collective-owned Enterprises	2	4	132
股份合作企业	Share-holding Cooperative Enterprises	2	2	248
有限责任公司	Limited Liability Corporations	71	113	5879
股份有限公司	Share-holding Corporations Ltd.	3	7	1775
私营企业	Private Enterprises	196	374	13922
其他企业	Others	1	1	54
港、澳、台商投资企业	Enterprises With Funds from Hong Kong, Macao and Taiwan	1	1	212
外商投资企业	Foreign Funded Enterprises	2	6	1115
住宿业	**Hotels**	**294**	**384**	**34674**
内资企业	Domestic-funded Enterprises	287	376	32048
国有企业	State-owned Enterprises	97	133	12114
集体企业	Collective-owned Enterprises	12	15	1385
股份合作企业	Share-holding Cooperative Enterprises	2	2	166
联营企业	Joint Ownership Enterprises	1	1	100
有限责任公司	Limited Liability Corporations	64	88	9171

14-3 续表 Continued

指　标	Item	法人企业数(个) Number of Corporate Enterprises (unit)	产业活动单位数(个) Number of Economic Active Unit (unit)	从业人员数(人) Engaged Persons (person)
股份有限公司	Share-holding Corporations Ltd.	6	9	691
私营企业	Private Enterprises	98	116	8084
其他企业	Others	7	12	337
港、澳、台商投资企业	Enterprises With Funds from Hong Kong, Macao and Taiwan	6	7	2017
外商投资企业	Foreign Funded Enterprises	1	1	609
餐饮业	**Catering Services**	**66**	**110**	**11392**
内资企业	Domestic-funded Enterprises	64	96	10484
国有企业	State-owned Enterprises	4	4	623
有限责任公司	Limited Liability Corporations	6	9	992
私营企业	Private Enterprises	54	83	8869
外商投资企业	Foreign Funded Enterprises	2	14	908
按地区分	**By Region**			
乌鲁木齐市	Urumqi City	469	803	55576
克拉玛依市	Karamay City	36	105	5490
吐鲁番地区	Turpan Administrative Offices	28	70	2223
哈密地区	Hami [Kumul] Administrative Offices	39	91	2316
昌吉回族自治州	Changji Hui Autonomous Prefecture	40	93	6723
伊犁哈萨克自治州	Ili Kazak Autonomous Prefecture	155	403	12437
伊犁州直属县(市)	Counties (Cities) Direct Under Ili Prefecture	90	152	7780
塔城地区	Tacheng [Tarbagatai] Administrative Offices	34	134	2692
阿勒泰地区	Altay Administrative Offices	31	117	1965
博尔塔拉蒙古自治州	Bortala Mongol Autonomous Prefecture	24	70	1540
巴音郭楞蒙古自治州	Bayangol Mongol Autonomous Prefecture	99	260	8643
阿克苏地区	Aksu Administrative Offices	107	646	8015
克孜勒苏柯尔克孜自治州	Kizilsu Kirgiz Autonomous Prefecture	8	18	569
喀什地区	Kashgar [Kaxgar] Administrative Offices	46	94	7675
和田地区	Hotan Administrative Offices	22	157	1759
生产建设兵团	Xinjiang Production and Construction Corps	125	303	12125

14-4 分行业、分地区限额以上批发零售业商品销售额

Total Sales Values of Enterprises above Designated Size of Wholesale and Retail Trades by Sector and Region

单位：万元 (2007 年) (10 000 yuan)

指　标	Item	销售总额 Total Sales Value	批 发 Wholesale Value	零 售 Retail Value
总　计	**Total**	**22285551**	**19308803**	**2976748**
批发业	**Wholesale Trades**	**19848664**	**19091247**	**757417**
农畜产品批发业	Wholesale of Farm Produce and Livestock Products	3433953	3431061	2892
食品、饮料及烟草制品批发业	Wholesale of Food,Beverages and Tobaccos	1328314	1321209	7105
#米、面制品及食用油批发业	Wholesale of Rice, Flour and Edible Oil	81551	80131	1420
烟草制品批发业	Wholesale of tobaccos	1124133	1119405	4728
纺织、服装及日用品批发业	Wholesale of Textitle, Garments and Daily Consumer Articles	276943	276943	
#服装批发业	Wholesale of Garment	12418	12418	
文化、体育用品及器材批发业	Wholesale of Culture, Sports Goods and Apparatus	156041	141150	14891
医药及医疗器械批发业	Wholesale of Medicines and Medical Appliances	249786	248968	818
矿产品、建材及化工产品批发业	Wholesale of Mineral Products, Building Material and Chemical Products	13054639	12403470	651169
#煤炭及制品批发业	Wholesale of Coal and Related Products	78369	78369	
石油及制品批发业	Wholesale of Petroleum and Related Products	10022667	9375976	646691
金属及金属矿批发业	Wholesale of Metal and Metal Materials	1453111	1452768	343
建材批发业	Wholesale of Building Materials	136797	136797	
化肥批发业	Wholesale of Fertilizer	1012327	1008192	4135
机械设备、五金交电及电子产品批发业	Wholesale of Machinery, Hardware and Electronic Equipments	1022492	942470	80022
#汽车、摩托车及零配件批发业	Wholesale of Motor Vehicles, Motorcycles and Parts	383765	314970	68795
家用电器批发业	Wholesale of Household Electrical Appliances	73703	73703	
计算机、软件及辅助设备批发业	Wholesale of Computer, Software and Accessory Equipment	56424	52694	3730
贸易经纪与代理	Trades Broker and Agent	31081	31081	
其他批发业	Wholesales of Others	295415	294895	520
零售业	**Retail Trades**	**2436887**	**217556**	**2219331**
综合零售业	Integrated Retail	514034	4582	509452
#百货零售业	Retail of Merchandile	296019	1450	294569
超级市场零售业	Retail of Supermarket	211385	2684	208701
食品、饮料及烟草制品专门零售业	Monopoly Retail of Foods, Beverages and Tobacco	17629	2998	14631
纺织、服装及日用品专门零售业	Monopoly Retail of Textile, Garments and Daily Consumer Articles	165431	11931	153500
#服装零售业	Garment Retail	143440	11931	131509

14-4 续表 Continued

单位：万元 (10 000 yuan)

指　　标	Item	销售总额 Total Sales Value	批 发 Wholesale Value	零 售 Retail Value
文化、体育用品及器材专门零售业	Monopoly Retail of Cultural, Sports Goods And Apparatus	89300	928	88372
#体育用品零售业	Retail of Sports Goods	2540		2540
图书零售业	Retail of Books	76846	928	75918
医药及医疗器材专门零售业	Monopoly Retail of Medicine and Medical-care Apparatus	213173	27152	186021
#药品零售业	Retail of Medcine	213173	27152	186021
汽车、摩托车、燃料及零配件专门零售业	Monopoly Retail of Car, Motor, Fuel and Parts as Well as Components	1061841	124793	937048
#汽车零售业	Retail of Car	716305	22400	693905
机动车燃料零售业	Retail of Auto Fuel	335911	102222	233689
家用电器及电子产品专门零售业	Monopoly Retail of House hold Electric Appliancesound Electronic Products	307600	11600	296000
#家用电器零售业	Retail of Electric Appliances	194768	2746	192022
计算机、软件及辅助设备零售业	Retail of Cumputers,Software and Office Appliances	49215	3898	45317
通讯设备零售业	Retail of Telecommunication Equipments	59408	4957	54451
五金、家俱及室内装修材料专门零售业	Monopoly Retail of Hardware, Furniture and Indoor Decorating Material	43220	32084	11136
无店铺及其他零售业	Retail of Storeless and others	24659	1488	23171
按地区分	**By Region**			
乌鲁木齐市	Urumqi City	14059537	12222540	1836997
克拉玛依市	Karamay City	318058	197147	120911
吐鲁番地区	Turpan Administrative Offices	155662	125951	29711
哈密地区	Hami [Kumul] Administrative Offices	233880	146197	87683
昌吉回族自治州	Changji Hui Autonomous Prefecture	385312	314610	70702
伊犁哈萨克自治州	Ili Kazak Autonomous Prefecture	1147563	1040737	106826
伊犁州直属县(市)	Counties (Cities) Direct Under Ili Prefecture	464046	406586	57460
塔城地区	Tacheng [Tarbagatai] Administrative Offices	575191	543983	31208
阿勒泰地区	Altay Administrative Offices	108326	90168	18158
博尔塔拉蒙古自治州	Bortala Mongol Autonomous Prefecture	438480	426059	12421
巴音郭楞蒙古自治州	Bayangol Mongol Autonomous Prefecture	628096	488688	139408
阿克苏地区	Aksu Administrative Offices	768573	614582	153991
克孜勒苏柯尔克孜自治州	Kizilsu Kirgiz Autonomous Prefecture	40962	28039	12923
喀什地区	Kashgar [Kaxgar] Administrative Offices	577530	482311	95219
和田地区	Hotan Administrative Offices	120549	88690	31859
生产建设兵团	Xinjiang Production and Construction Group	3411349	3133252	278097

14-5 限额以上餐饮企业销售情况
Sales Value of Enterprises Above Designated Size of Catering Services

单位：万元 (2007 年) (10 000 yuan)

项 目	Item	法 人 企业数 (个) Number of Corporate Enterprise (unit)	产业活动 单 位 数 (个) Number of Establishments (unit)	营业额 Business Revenue	#商品零售额 Retail Sales of Commodities
总 计	**Total**	**66**	**110**	**83493**	**78729**
正 餐	Dinner	63	83	66015	61251
快 餐	Snack	3	27	17478	17478
按地区分	**By Region**				
乌鲁木齐市	Urumqi City	47	76	67263	62838
克拉玛依市	Karamay City	2	13	3717	3643
哈密地区	Hami [Kumul] Administrative Offices	1	1	345	345
昌吉回族自治州	Changji Hui Autonomous Prefecture	3	4	2149	2057
巴音郭楞蒙古自治州	Bayangol Mongol Autonomous Prefecture	10	13	7645	7588
喀什地区	Kashgar [Kaxgar] Administrative Offices	1	1	310	194
生产建设兵团	Xinjiang Production and Construction Corps	2	2	2064	2064

14-6 限额以上住宿企业经营情况
Operation of Enterprises Above Designated Size in Hotels Services

单位：万元 (2007 年) (10 000 yuan)

项目	Item	营业额 Business Revenue	客房收入 From Hotel Rooms	餐费收入 From Meals
总计	**Total**	**287043**	**138559**	**111954**
按星级分	**By Stars**			
一星	One-Star	8602	4405	3478
二星	Two-Star	32277	18978	10917
三星	Three-Star	116968	63798	43430
四星	Four-Star	69854	33690	28475
五星	Five-Star	59342	17688	25654
按地区分	**By Region**			
乌鲁木齐市	Urumqi City	159193	69182	63108
克拉玛依市	Karamay City	13888	5624	7227
吐鲁番地区	Turpan Administrative Offices	4867	2894	1700
哈密地区	Hami [Kumul] Administrative Offices	7965	3715	3760
昌吉回族自治州	Changji Hui Autonomous Prefecture	5027	2455	2228
伊犁哈萨克自治州	Ili Kazak Autonomous Prefecture	34070	18294	12667
伊犁州直属县(市)	Counties (Cities) Direct Under Ili Prefecture	20670	10478	7759
塔城地区	Tacheng [Tarbagatai] Administrative Offices	3527	1695	1543
阿勒泰地区	Altay Administrative Offices	9873	6121	3365
博尔塔拉蒙古自治州	Bortala Mongol Autonomous Prefecture	2413	1149	979
巴音郭楞蒙古自治州	Bayangol Mongol Autonomous Prefecture	14289	7886	4988
阿克苏地区	Aksu Administrative Offices	7942	5467	2223
克孜勒苏柯尔克孜自治州	Kizilsu Kirgiz Autonomous Prefecture	756	327	418
喀什地区	Kashgar [Kaxgar] Administrative Offices	6593	4189	1924
和田地区	Hotan Administrative Offices	3622	2251	1289
生产建设兵团	Xinjiang Production and Construction Group	26418	15126	9443

注：限额以上住宿企业指星级以上宾馆。
Note: The enterprises above designated size in accommodation services refer to started hotels.

14-6 续表 Continued

单位：万元 (10 000 yuan)

项　目	Item	商品销售收入 From Commodities	其他收入 Others	床位数（张） Number of beds
总　计	**Total**	**12778**	**23752**	**78615**
按星级分	**Classified by Star**			
一 星	One-Star	214	505	3739
二 星	Two-Star	797	1585	16437
三 星	Three-Star	2796	6944	42235
四 星	Four-Star	1625	6064	12941
五 星	Five-Star	7345	8655	3263
按地区分	**By Region**			
乌鲁木齐市	Urumqi City	9430	17473	29560
克拉玛依市	Karamay City	281	756	2591
吐鲁番地区	Turpan Administrative Offices	59	214	2697
哈密地区	Hami [Kumul] Administrative Offices	238	252	2399
昌吉回族自治州	Changji Hui Autonomous Prefecture	35	309	2451
伊犁哈萨克自治州	Ili Kazak Autonomous Prefecture	1783	1326	13609
伊犁州直属县(市)	Counties (Cities) Direct Under Ili Prefecture	1313	1120	7034
塔城地区	Tacheng [Tarbagatai] Administrative Offices	205	84	1036
阿勒泰地区	Altay Administrative Offices	265	122	5539
博尔塔拉蒙古自治州	Bortala Mongol Autonomous Prefecture	164	121	1181
巴音郭楞蒙古自治州	Bayangol Mongol Autonomous Prefecture	579	836	4973
阿克苏地区	Aksu Administrative Offices	74	178	4201
克孜勒苏柯尔克孜自治州	Kizilsu Kirgiz Autonomous Prefecture		11	283
喀什地区	Kashgar [Kaxgar] Administrative Offices	62	418	3244
和田地区	Hotan Administrative Offices		82	1575
生产建设兵团	Xinjiang Production and Construction Group	73	1776	9851

14-7 各地、州、市、县(市)社会消费品零售总额

Total Retail Sales of Consumer Goods by Prefecture, Autonomous Prefecture, City and County

单位：万元　　(2007 年)　　(10 000 yuan)

地区	Region	社会消费品零售总额 Total Retail Sales of Consumer Goods	市 City	县 County	县以下 Under County Level
总　计	**Total**	**8477044**	**5998014**	**1222287**	**1256743**
乌鲁木齐市	**Urumqi City**	**3217648**	**3192178**		**25470**
#乌鲁木齐县	Urumqi County	44603	19133		25470
克拉玛依市	**Karamay City**	**230656**	**184617**	**44181**	**1858**
吐鲁番地区	**TurpanAdministrative Offices**	**178119**	**72372**	**56188**	**49559**
吐鲁番市	Turpan City	89229	72372		16857
鄯善县	Shanshan [piqan]County	66454		40445	26009
托克逊县	Toksun County	22436		15743	6693
哈密地区	**Hami [kumul]Administrative Offices**	**250075**	**222839**	**13722**	**13514**
哈密市	Hami [kumul]City	228240	222839		5401
巴里坤哈萨克自治县	Barkol KazakAutonomous County	15823		9355	6468
伊吾县	Yiwu [Araturuk]County	6012		4367	1645
昌吉回族自治州	**Changji Hui Autonomous Prefecture**	**666480**	**258056**	**213565**	**194859**
昌吉市	Changji City	286323	196448		89875
阜康市	Fukang City	86581	61608		24973
呼图壁县	Hutubi County	78538		55465	23073
玛纳斯县	Manas County	81920		61648	20272
奇台县	Qitai County	73168		52087	21081
吉木萨尔县	Jimsar County	35300		27150	8150
木垒哈萨克自治县	Mori Kazak Autonomous County	24650		17215	7435
伊犁哈萨克自治州	**Ili Kazak Autonomous Prefecture**	**1097915**	**420224**	**415122**	**262569**
伊犁州直属县(市)	**Counties (Cities) Direct Under Ili Prefecture**	**606218**	**279967**	**189130**	**137121**
伊宁市	Yining [Gulja]City	202407	195970		6437
奎屯市	Kuytun City	83997	83997		
伊宁县	Yining [Gulja]County	52224		29739	22485
察布查尔锡伯自治县	Qapqal Xibe Autonomous County	9150		4537	4613
霍城县	Huocheng [korgas]County	72772		48255	24517
巩留县	Gongliu [Tokkuzlara]County	23905		16410	7495
新源县	Xinyuan [kunes]County	79746		35168	44578
昭苏县	Zhaosu [mongolkure]County	21611		13206	8405
特克斯县	Tekes County	32747		22784	9963
尼勒克县	Nilka County	27659		19031	8628
塔城地区	**Tacheng [Tarbagatai] Administrative Offices**	**268729**	**81949**	**100192**	**86588**
塔城市	Tacheng [Qoqek] City	59497	41934		17563
乌苏市	Usu City	58355	40015		18340
额敏县	Emin [Dorbiljin] County	52005		29432	22573
沙湾县	Shawan County	62874		46138	16736
托里县	Toli County	9334		6164	3170
裕民县	Yumin [Qagantokay] County	11059		7270	3789
和布克赛尔蒙古自治县	Hoboksar Mongol Autonomous County	15605		11188	4417
阿勒泰地区	**Altay Administrative Offices**	**222968**	**55208**	**128900**	**38860**
阿勒泰市	Altay City	73418	55208		18210
布尔津县	Burqin County	57855		50856	6999
富蕴县	Fuyun [Koktokay] County	29531		25126	4405
福海县	Fuhai [Burultokay] County	23899		20637	3262
哈巴河县	Habahe [Kaba] County	20218		17568	2650
青河县	Qinghe [Qinggil] County	12731		10708	2023
吉木乃县	Jeminay County	5316		4005	1311

14-7 续表 Continued

单位：万元 (10 000 yuan)

地区	Region	社会消费品零售总额 Total Retail Sales of Consumer Goods	市 City	县 County	县以下 Under County Level
博尔塔拉蒙古自治州	**Bortala Mongol Autonomous Prefecture**	**126292**	**73978**	**19182**	**33132**
博乐市	Bole [Bortala] City	87169	73978		13191
精河县	Jinghe [Jing] County	25607		14708	10899
温泉县	Wenquan [Araxang] County	13516		4474	9042
巴音郭楞蒙古自治州	**Bayangol Mongol Autonomous Prefecture**	**350930**	**244042**	**68769**	**38119**
库尔勒市	Korla City	256402	244042		12360
轮台县	Luntai [Bugur] County	17815		10459	7356
尉犁县	Yuli [Lopnur] County	8690		6142	2548
若羌县	Ruoqiang [Qarkilik] County	3744		2733	1011
且末县	Qiemo [Qarqan] County	4888		3310	1578
焉耆回族自治县	Yanqi Hui Autonomous County	24651		20325	4326
和静县	Hejing County	13542		10756	2786
和硕县	Hoxud County	8064		4873	3191
博湖县	Bohu [Bagrax] County	13134		10171	2963
阿克苏地区	**Aksu Administrative Offices**	**428691**	**174317**	**170590**	**83784**
阿克苏市	Aksu City	180461	174317		6144
温宿县	Wensu [Onsu] County	25300		18615	6685
库车县	Kuqa County	79861		58491	21370
沙雅县	Xayar County	41329		27828	13501
新和县	Xinhe [Toksu] County	21510		13042	8468
拜城县	Baicheng [Bay] County	41947		27190	14757
乌什县	Wushi [Uxturpan] County	8800		5799	3001
阿瓦提县	Awat County	25783		17418	8365
柯坪县	Kalpin County	3700		2207	1493
克孜勒苏柯尔克孜自治州	**Kizilsu Kirgiz Autonomous Prefecture**	**50760**	**31004**	**15308**	**4448**
阿图什市	Artux City	32602	31004		1598
阿克陶县	Akto County	9108		7636	1472
阿合奇县	Akqi County	4231		3989	242
乌恰县	Wuqia [Ulugqat] County	4819		3683	1136
喀什地区	**Kashgar [Kaxgar] Administrative Offices**	**465040**	**211600**	**158844**	**94596**
喀什市	Kashgar [Kaxgar] City	211600	211600		
疏附县	Shufu County	6434		3123	3311
疏勒县	Shule County	26258		10514	15744
英吉沙县	Yengisar County	14816		8882	5934
泽普县	Zepu [Poskam] County	18440		13114	5326
莎车县	Shache [Yarkant] County	48763		28776	19987
叶城县	Yecheng [Kagilik] County	40143		30129	10014
麦盖提县	Makit County	23860		17046	6814
岳普湖县	Yopurga County	12456		8621	3835
伽师县	Jiashi [Payzawat] County	15600		8763	6837
巴楚县	Bachu [Maralbexi] County	41000		24367	16633
塔什库尔干塔吉克自治县	Taxkorgan Tajik Autonomous County	5670		5509	161
和田地区	**Hotan Administrative Offices**	**142199**	**69100**	**29963**	**43136**
和田市	Hotan City	87766	69100		18666
和田县	Hotan County	7711		135	7576
墨玉县	Moyu [Karakax] County	12087		7476	4611
皮山县	Pishan [Guma] County	6318		4316	2002
洛浦县	Lop County	8413		6007	2406
策勒县	Qira County	8550		4455	4095
于田县	Yutian [Keriya] County	9196		6086	3110
民丰县	Minfeng [Niya] County	2158		1488	670
生产建设兵团	**Xinjiang Production andConstruction Group**	**1301564**	**779761**	**32557**	**489246**

14-8 各地、州、市、县(市)社会消费品零售总额(按行业分)

Total Retail Sales of Consumer Goods by Sector and Prefecture, Autonomous Prefecture, City and County

单位：万元 (2007 年) (10 000 yuan)

地区	Region	社会消费品零售总额 Total Retail Sales of Consumer Goods	批发零售业 Wholesale And Retail Sale Trades	住宿餐饮业 Hotels and Catering Services	其他行业 Others
总计	**Total**	**8477044**	**6781033**	**1290258**	**405753**
乌鲁木齐市	**Urumqi City**	**3217648**	**2609708**	**546092**	**61848**
#乌鲁木齐县	Urumqi County	44603	10622	33883	98
克拉玛依市	**Karamay City**	**230656**	**186429**	**42413**	**1814**
吐鲁番地区	**TurpanAdministrative Offices**	**178119**	**142360**	**35280**	**479**
吐鲁番市	Turpan City	89229	69308	19584	337
鄯善县	Shanshan [piqan]County	66454	55470	10842	142
托克逊县	Toksun County	22436	17582	4854	
哈密地区	**Hami [kumul]Administrative Offices**	**250075**	**189158**	**40694**	**20223**
哈密市	Hami [kumul]City	228240	170750	37946	19544
巴里坤哈萨克自治县	Barkol KazakAutonomous County	15823	13645	1716	462
伊吾县	Yiwu [Araturuk]County	6012	4763	1032	217
昌吉回族自治州	**Changji Hui Autonomous Prefecture**	**666480**	**522766**	**109520**	**34194**
昌吉市	Changji City	286323	217946	49690	18687
阜康市	Fukang City	86581	65858	17620	3103
呼图壁县	Hutubi County	78538	61839	13521	3178
玛纳斯县	Manas County	81920	67747	10022	4151
奇台县	Qitai County	73168	60783	10111	2274
吉木萨尔县	Jimsar County	35300	29240	5500	560
木垒哈萨克自治县	Mori Kazak Autonomous County	24650	19353	3056	2241
伊犁哈萨克自治州	**Ili Kazak Autonomous Prefecture**	**1097915**	**862330**	**194264**	**41321**
伊犁州直属县(市)	**Counties (Cities) Direct Under Ili Prefecture**	**606218**	**480722**	**99840**	**25656**
伊宁市	Yining [Gulja]City	202407	160955	32782	8670
奎屯市	Kuytun City	83997	71755	9376	2866
伊宁县	Yining [Gulja]County	52224	43310	4446	4468
察布查尔锡伯自治县	Qapqal Xibe Autonomous County	9150	6885	2088	177
霍城县	Huocheng [korgas]County	72772	57811	13653	1308
巩留县	Gongliu [Tokkuzlara]County	23905	16924	3735	3246
新源县	Xinyuan [kunes]County	79746	65182	13851	713
昭苏县	Zhaosu [mongolkure]County	21611	16967	1493	3151
特克斯县	Tekes County	32747	28084	3834	829
尼勒克县	Nilka County	27659	12849	14582	228
塔城地区	**Tacheng [Tarbagatai] Administrative Offices**	**268729**	**206107**	**50461**	**12161**
塔城市	Tacheng [Qoqek] City	59497	43206	11905	4386
乌苏市	Usu City	58355	40355	14993	3007
额敏县	Emin [Dorbiljin] County	52005	47183	3416	1406
沙湾县	Shawan County	62874	47609	13730	1535
托里县	Toli County	9334	7689	1498	147
裕民县	Yumin [Qagantokay] County	11059	7260	3124	675
和布克赛尔蒙古自治县	Hoboksar Mongol Autonomous County	15605	12805	1795	1005
阿勒泰地区	**Altay Administrative Offices**	**222968**	**175501**	**43963**	**3504**
阿勒泰市	Altay City	73418	59028	13315	1075
布尔津县	Burqin County	57855	38544	18366	945
富蕴县	Fuyun [Koktokay] County	29531	24448	4161	922
福海县	Fuhai [Burultokay] County	23899	20719	2976	204
哈巴河县	Habahe [Kaba] County	20218	16914	3126	178
青河县	Qinghe [Qinggil] County	12731	11397	1265	69
吉木乃县	Jeminay County	5316	4451	754	111

14-8 续表 Continued

单位：万元 (10 000 yuan)

地　区	Region	社会消费品零售总额 Total Retail Sales of Consumer Goods	批发零售业 Wholesale And Retail Sale Trades	住宿餐饮业 Hotels and Catering Services	其他行业 Others
博尔塔拉蒙古自治州	**Bortala Mongol Autonomous Prefecture**	**126292**	**99379**	**17626**	**9287**
博乐市	Bole [Bortala] City	87169	73336	9766	4067
精河县	Jinghe [Jing] County	25607	15178	6135	4294
温泉县	Wenquan [Araxang] County	13516	10865	1725	926
巴音郭楞蒙古自治州	**Bayangol Mongol Autonomous Prefecture**	**350930**	**274736**	**46621**	**29573**
库尔勒市	Korla City	256402	211946	27329	17127
轮台县	Luntai [Bugur] County	17815	13081	4245	489
尉犁县	Yuli [Lopnur] County	8690	5791	1982	917
若羌县	Ruoqiang [Qarkilik] County	3744	2719	948	77
且末县	Qiemo [Qarqan] County	4888	2787	1215	886
焉耆回族自治县	Yanqi Hui Autonomous County	24651	17218	2856	4577
和静县	Hejing County	13542	9009	2822	1711
和硕县	Hoxud County	8064	4515	3534	15
博湖县	Bohu [Bagrax] County	13134	7670	1690	3774
阿克苏地区	**Aksu Administrative Offices**	**428691**	**285583**	**60613**	**82495**
阿克苏市	Aksu City	180461	152867	13848	13746
温宿县	Wensu [Onsu] County	25300	15355	3853	6092
库车县	Kuqa County	79861	40360	20773	18728
沙雅县	Xayar County	41329	21059	11673	8597
新和县	Xinhe [Toksu] County	21510	11357	1603	8550
拜城县	Baicheng [Bay] County	41947	24844	2922	14181
乌什县	Wushi [Uxturpan] County	8800	5910	1151	1739
阿瓦提县	Awat County	25783	12543	4516	8724
柯坪县	Kalpin County	3700	1288	274	2138
克孜勒苏柯尔克孜自治州	**Kizilsu Kirgiz Autonomous Prefecture**	**50760**	**44584**	**5303**	**873**
阿图什市	Artux City	32602	30154	2113	335
阿克陶县	Akto County	9108	7013	1781	314
阿合奇县	Akqi County	4231	3670	514	47
乌恰县	Wuqia [Ulugqat] County	4819	3747	895	177
喀什地区	**Kashgar [Kaxgar] Administrative Offices**	**465040**	**344034**	**58177**	**62829**
喀什市	Kashgar [Kaxgar] City	211600	172732	8376	30492
疏附县	Shufu County	6434	4404	826	1204
疏勒县	Shule County	26258	13500	7438	5320
英吉沙县	Yengisar County	14816	10304	2966	1546
泽普县	Zepu [Poskam] County	18440	11023	2305	5112
莎车县	Shache [Yarkant] County	48763	36761	7846	4156
叶城县	Yecheng [Kagilik] County	40143	28075	10190	1878
麦盖提县	Makit County	23860	17072	3705	3083
岳普湖县	Yopurga County	12456	7841	4533	82
伽师县	Jiashi [Payzawat] County	15600	8133	2849	4618
巴楚县	Bachu [Maralbexi] County	41000	28704	7090	5206
塔什库尔干塔吉克自治县	Taxkorgan Tajik Autonomous County	5670	5485	53	132
和田地区	**Hotan Administrative Offices**	**142199**	**113803**	**25459**	**2937**
和田市	Hotan City	87766	71563	13912	2291
和田县	Hotan County	7711	5543	2168	
墨玉县	Moyu [Karakax] County	12087	10254	1833	
皮山县	Pishan [Guma] County	6318	5662	656	
洛浦县	Lop County	8413	6835	1578	
策勒县	Qira County	8550	5542	2362	646
于田县	Yutian [Keriya] County	9196	6747	2449	
民丰县	Minfeng [Niya] County	2158	1657	501	
生产建设兵团	**Xinjiang Production and Construction Group**	**1301564**	**1039298**	**170338**	**91928**

14-9 限额以上批发企业资产及负债情况

Assets and Liabilities of Enterprises above Designated Size of Wholesale Trades

单位：万元 (2007 年) (10 000 yuan)

指标	Item	资产合计 Total Assets	#流动资产 Working Capitals	#固定资产 Fixed Assets	负债合计 Total Liabilities
总　计	**Total**	**6848148**	**5306304**	**1222197**	**5654073**
按登记注册类型分	**By Type of Registration**				
内资企业	Domestic-funded Enterprises	6730427	5240562	1195920	5589443
国有企业	State-owned Enterprises	2291848	1867535	404462	2000105
集体企业	Collective-owned Enterprises	500185	386301	108608	425351
股份合作企业	Cooperative Enterprises	1461	743	483	705
有限责任公司	Limited Liability Corporations	2574316	2120824	361232	1988518
股份有限公司	Share-holding Corporations Ltd	617262	301211	179058	656061
私营企业	Private Enterprises	744574	563212	142029	518107
其他企业	Others	781	736	48	596
港、澳、台投资企业	Enterprises With Funds from Hong Kong, Macao and Taiwan	7981	6164	2720	7173
外商投资企业	Foreign funded Enterprises	109740	59578	23557	57457
按国民经济行业分	**By Sector**				
农畜产品批发业	Wholesale of Farm Produce and Livestock Products	3112504	2605684	522243	2610214
食品、饮料及烟草制品批发业	Wholesale of Food, Beverages and Tobaccos	408200	289080	129526	236751
#米、面制品及食用油批发业	Wholesale of Rice, Flour and Edible Oil	151181	123020	35716	116837
烟草制品批发业	Wholesale of tobaccos	109222	67872	51898	24022
纺织、服装及日用品批发业	Wholesale of Textitle, Garments and Daily Consumer Articles	124093	34741	11163	110223
#服装批发业	Wholesale of Garment	5669	5336	177	5538
文化、体育用品及器材批发业	Wholesale of Culture, Sports Goods and Apparatus	80813	50359	34688	51789
医药及医疗器械批发业	Wholesale of Medicines and Medical Appliances	103939	88025	12644	75791
矿产品、建材及化工产品批发业	Wholesale of Mineral Products, BuildingMaterial and Chemical Products	2305806	1696366	432844	2087946
#煤炭及制品批发业	Wholesale of Coal and Related Products	107022	54143	7752	41221
石油及制品批发业	Wholesale of Petroleum and Related Products	797826	454170	304857	970819
金属及金属矿批发业	Wholesale of Metal and Metal Materials	461340	397930	25593	295842
建材批发业	Wholesale of Building Materials	31525	30180	1070	24454
化肥批发业	Wholesale of Fertilizer	813686	680490	82798	692046
机械设备、五金交电及电子产品批发业	Wholesale of Machinery, Hardware and Electronic Equipments	499563	349216	67371	353812
#汽车、摩托车及零配件批发业	Wholesale of Motor Vehicles, Motorcycles and Parts	209021	134478	37851	130602
家用电器批发业	Wholesale of Household Electrical Appliances	8364	7583	731	9064
计算机、软件及辅助设备批发业	Wholesale of Computer, Software and Accessory Equipment	10220	10049	280	9149
贸易经纪与代理	Trades Broker and Agent	12296	6445	3204	7080
其他批发业	Wholesales of Others	200934	186388	8514	120467
按地区分	**By Region**				
乌鲁木齐市	Urumqi City	2244656	1778399	268988	1648164
克拉玛依市	Karamay City	40822	18365	35220	85375
吐鲁番地区	Turpan Administrative Offices	74261	58270	18388	78101
哈密地区	Hami [Kumul] Administrative Offices	61322	46085	18120	86798
昌吉回族自治州	Changji Hui Autonomous Prefecture	287052	207684	65390	272341
伊犁哈萨克自治州	Ili Kazak Autonomous Prefecture	546639	403995	110667	539539
伊犁州直属县(市)	Counties (Cities) Direct Under Ili Prefecture	221695	140757	71912	237302
塔城地区	Tacheng [Tarbagatai] Administrative Offices	303661	250953	25989	260713
阿勒泰地区	Altay Administrative Offices	21283	12285	12766	41524
博尔塔拉蒙古自治州	Bortala Mongol Autonomous Prefecture	197710	171048	19301	142834
巴音郭楞蒙古自治州	Bayangol Mongol Autonomous Prefecture	324547	213508	124585	236463
阿克苏地区	Aksu Administrative Offices	451903	319334	126520	395161
克孜勒苏柯尔克孜自治州	Kizilsu Kirgiz Autonomous Prefecture	19171	17642	2538	18769
喀什地区	Kashgar [Kaxgar] Administrative Offices	327618	229758	98857	308906
和田地区	Hotan Administrative Offices	71664	30086	24908	59985
生产建设兵团	Xinjiang Production and Construction Group	2200783	1812130	308715	1781637

14-10 限额以上零售企业资产及负债情况

Assets and Liabilities of Enterprises above Designated Size of Retail Trades

单位：万元　　(2007 年)　　(10 000 yuan)

指　　标	Item	资产合计 Total Asset	#流动资产 Working Capitals	#固定资产 Fixed Asset	负债合计 Total Liabilities
总　计	**Total**	**1153225**	**720832**	**362279**	**822245**
按登记注册类型分	**By Type of Registration**				
内资企业	Domestic-funded Enterprises	1116110	705673	338670	797913
国有企业	State-owned Enterprises	185933	86145	114898	157468
集体企业	Collective-owned Enterprises	1213	1110	292	982
股份合作企业	Cooperative Enterprises	3626	2426	2014	2325
有限责任公司	Limited Liability Corporations	219242	153779	58565	149190
股份有限公司	Share-holding Corporations Ltd	162786	39763	59780	82580
私营企业	Private Enterprises	514588	397947	99283	399123
其他企业	Others	28722	24503	3838	6245
港、澳、台投资企业	Enterprises With Funds from Hong Kong, Macao and Taiwan	12164	6506	5023	7685
外商投资企业	Foreign Funded Enterprises	24951	8653	18586	16647
按国民经济行业分	**By Sector**				
综合零售业	Integrated Retail	367546	155723	154996	279539
百货商店	Retail of Merchandile	278800	95949	124527	208459
超级市场	Retail of Supermarket	85940	57520	29740	69388
食品、饮料及烟草制品专门零售业	Monopoly Retail of Foods, Beverages and Tobacco	14434	10688	4756	20573
纺织、服装及日用品专门零售业	Monopoly Retail of Textile, Garments and Daily Consumer Articles	111735	72384	31949	98797
#服装零售业	Garment Retail	110536	71210	31927	97583
文化、体育用品及器材专门零售业	Monopoly Retail of Cultural, Sports Goods And Apparatus	91271	44457	59335	50415
#体育用品零售业	Retail of Sports Goods	1071	888	242	886
图书零售业	Retail of Books	78350	37707	49593	41056
医药及医疗器材专门零售业	Monopoly Retail of Medicine and Medical-care Apparatus	109693	89076	21182	79529
#药品零售业	Retail of Medcine	109693	89076	21182	79529
汽车、摩托车、燃料及零配件专门零售业	Monopoly Retail of Car, Motor, Fuel and Parts as Well as Components	298009	224838	58102	203302
#汽车零售业	Retail of Car	280447	214345	49940	193354
机动车燃料零售业	Retail of Auto Fuel	13513	8043	6885	7324
家用电器及电子产品专门零售业	Monopoly Retail of Household Electric Appliancesound Electronic Products	120401	93061	25301	73653
#家用电器零售业	Retail of Electric Appliances	64957	59921	2402	48557
计算机、软件及辅助设备零售业	Retail of Cumputers,Software and Office Appliances	17510	15621	2742	11948
通讯设备零售业	Retail of Telecommunication Equipments	36854	17246	19982	12876
五金、家俱及室内装修材料专门零售业	Monopoly Retail of Hardware, Furniture and Indoor Decorating Material	35937	28155	4817	13768
无店铺及其他零售业	Retail of Storeless and others	4199	2450	1841	2669
按地区分	**By Region**				
乌鲁木齐市	Urumqi City	863833	537684	245327	615956
克拉玛依市	Karamay City	24093	15670	9363	19306
吐鲁番地区	Turpan Administrative Offices	6473	4277	2385	4288
哈密地区	Hami [Kumul] Administrative Offices	22566	17163	5844	17770
昌吉回族自治州	Changji Hui Autonomous Prefecture	34641	15465	24747	24880
伊犁哈萨克自治州	Ili Kazak Autonomous Prefecture	30868	20614	13498	19249
伊犁州直属县(市)	Counties (Cities) Direct Under Ili Prefecture	21428	14487	8873	13570
塔城地区	Tacheng [Tarbagatai] Administrative Offices	6701	4476	3033	4419
阿勒泰地区	Altay Administrative Offices	2739	1651	1592	1260
博尔塔拉蒙古自治州	Bortala Mongol Autonomous Prefecture	3312	1896	1629	1983
巴音郭楞蒙古自治州	Bayangol Mongol Autonomous Prefecture	48194	33093	16130	37665
阿克苏地区	Aksu Administrative Offices	47158	27246	17707	28501
克孜勒苏柯尔克孜自治州	Kizilsu Kirgiz Autonomous Prefecture	1565	821	535	835
喀什地区	Kashgar [Kaxgar] Administrative Offices	27003	17172	10830	20702
和田地区	Hotan Administrative Offices	5298	3400	1746	2891
生产建设兵团	Xinjiang Production and Construction Group	38221	26331	12538	28219

14-11 限额以上餐饮企业资产及负债情况

Assets and Liabilities of Enterprises above Designated Size of Catering Services

单位：万元 (2007 年) (10 000 yuan)

指 标	Item	资产合计 Total Asset	#流动资产 Working Capitals	#固定资产 Fixed Asset	负债合计 Total Liabilities
总 计	**Total**	**71860**	**21993**	**48200**	**35437**
按登记注册类型分	**By Status of registration**				
内资企业	Domestic-funded Enterprises	66938	21208	41891	32382
国有企业	State – owned Enterprises	29050	3164	26864	3229
有限责任公司	Limited Liability Corporations	6621	3616	2394	3784
私营企业	Private Enterprises	31267	14428	12633	25369
外商投资企业	Foreign Funded Enterprises	4922	785	6309	3055
按国民经济行业分	**By sector**				
正 餐	Dinner	66630	20914	41883	32241
快 餐	Snack	5230	1079	6317	3196
按地区分	**By Region**				
乌鲁木齐市	Urumqi City	64049	19614	42404	29560
克拉玛依市	Karamay City	195	108	103	58
哈密地区	Hami [Kumul] Administrative Offices	1400	262	1118	1664
昌吉回族自治州	Changji Hui Autonomous Prefecture	2178	348	1557	1048
巴音郭楞蒙古自治州	Bayangol Mongol Autonomous Prefecture	3693	1365	2920	2785
喀什地区	Kashgar [Kaxgar] Administrative Offices	7	7	5	24
生产建设兵团	Xinjiang Production and Construction Group	338	289	93	298

14-12 限额以上住宿企业资产及负债情况

Assets and Liabilities of Enterprises above Designated Size of Accommodation Services

单位：万元 (2007 年) (10 000 yuan)

指标	Item	资产合计 Total Assets	#流动资产 Working Capitals	#固定资产 Fixed Assets	负债合计 Total Liabilities
总计	**Total**	**698898**	**140027**	**688519**	**414378**
按登记注册类型分	**By Status of registration**				
内资企业	Domestic-funded Enterprises	625113	122536	602574	345083
国有企业	State-owned Enterprises	257580	45438	247974	134408
集体企业	Collective-owned Enterprises	23780	3614	31353	30474
股份合作企业	Cooperative Enterprises	3471	265	1719	3071
联营企业	Joint Ownership Enterprises	2826	1394	2786	946
有限责任公司	Limited Liability Corporations	188829	36204	196770	70913
股份有限公司	Share-holding Corporations Ltd	8477	1192	9067	5289
私营企业	Private Enterprises	137881	34398	110560	99895
其他企业	Others	2269	31	2345	87
港、澳、台投资企业	Enterprises With Funds from Hong Kong, Macao and Taiwan	72258	15964	85945	67754
外商投资企业	Foreign funded Enterprises	1527	1527		1541
按国民经济行业分组	**By Sector**				
旅游饭店	Tourist Hotel	659453	134285	653101	393491
一般旅馆	Ordinary Hotel	26184	3566	23834	9095
其他住宿服务	Other	13261	2176	11585	11792
按星级等级分	**Classified by Stars**				
一 星	One-Star	5167	1039	5573	3939
二 星	Two-Star	79319	17014	75000	54528
三 星	Three-Star	288183	64776	265010	164752
四 星	Four-Star	156269	34228	157956	94886
五 星	Five-Star	169960	22970	184980	96273
按地区分	**By Region**				
乌鲁木齐市	Urumqi City	346731	73877	354796	216038
克拉玛依市	Karamay City	6893	776	7286	3827
吐鲁番地区	Turpan Administrative Offices	13231	3493	14666	8282
哈密地区	Hami [Kumul] Administrative Offices	17497	2564	18915	8792
昌吉回族自治州	Changji Hui Autonomous Prefecture	10545	2036	12058	8929
伊犁哈萨克自治州	Ili Kazak Autonomous Prefecture	96013	15784	90559	48303
伊犁州直属县(市)	Counties (Cities) Direct Under Ili Prefecture	67316	9941	64744	32487
塔城地区	Tacheng [Tarbagatai] Administrative Offices	8760	1539	7709	5365
阿勒泰地区	Altay Administrative Offices	19937	4304	18106	10451
博尔塔拉蒙古自治州	Bortala Mongol Autonomous Prefecture	6266	1217	6913	2370
巴音郭楞蒙古自治州	Bayangol Mongol Autonomous Prefecture	48055	7265	41480	32535
阿克苏地区	Aksu Administrative Offices	32005	4787	30827	19619
克孜勒苏柯尔克孜自治州	Kizilsu Kirgiz Autonomous Prefecture	2271	337	2034	502
喀什地区	Kashgar [Kaxgar] Administrative Offices	25242	10680	14856	21157
和田地区	Hotan Administrative Offices	11389	2027	9450	3737
生产建设兵团	Xinjiang Production and Construction Group	82760	15184	84679	40287

14-13 限额以上批发企业主要财务指标
Main Financial Indicators of Wholesale Enterprises above Designated Size

单位：万元 (2007 年) (10 000 yuan)

指 标	Item	商品销售收入 Revenue of Product Sales	商品销售成本 Cost of Product Sales	商品销售税金及附加 Sales Tax and Extra Changes	商品销售利润 Profits of Product Sales
总 计	**Total**	**16221044**	**15244918**	**14758**	**774666**
按登记注册类型分	**By status of registration**				
内资企业	Domestic-funded Enterprises	16050542	15087097	14650	763858
国有企业	State-owned Enterprises	8939323	8456751	5148	344296
集体企业	Collective-owned Enterprises	386459	356713	65	17128
股份合作企业	Cooperative Enterprises	9673	9269	4	401
有限责任公司	Limited Liability Corporations	3785631	3535376	3089	226813
股份有限公司	Share-holding Corporations Ltd	1280881	1175366	4416	95679
私营企业	Private Enterprises	1637620	1542950	1924	79262
其他企业	Others	10955	10672	4	279
港、澳、台投资企业	Enterprises With Funds from Hong Kong, Macao and Taiwan	24207	21184	10	1468
外商投资企业	Foreign funded Enterprises	146295	136637	98	9340
按国民经济行业分	**By Sector**				
农畜产品批发业	Wholesale of Farm Produce and Livestock Products	3200643	2905885	1039	191112
食品、饮料及烟草制品批发业	Wholesale of Food, Beverages and Tobaccos	734719	645520	1409	73995
#米、面制品及食用油批发业	Wholesale of Rice, Flour and Edible Oil	81819	74769	21	6312
烟草制品批发业	Wholesale of tobaccos	531004	466831	682	53520
纺织、服装及日用品批发业	Wholesale of Textitle, Garments and Daily Consumer Articles	237565	219303	91	17042
#服装批发业	Wholesale of Garment	11273	10648	9	616
文化、体育用品及器材批发业	Wholesale of Culture, Sports Goods and Apparatus	139365	107068	145	9455
医药及医疗器械批发业	Wholesale of Medicines and Medical Appliances	215519	201315	202	13581
矿产品、建材及化工产品批发业	Wholesale of Mineral Products, BuildingMaterial and Chemical Products	10487245	10036047	10080	405436
#煤炭及制品批发业	Wholesale of Coal and Related Products	64330	52300	3055	8722
石油及制品批发业	Wholesale of Petroleum and Related Products	7778545	7491074	5307	258461
金属及金属矿批发业	Wholesale of Metal and Metal Materials	1332847	1267011	1077	63696
建材批发业	Wholesale of Building Materials	108458	104969	41	3339
化肥批发业	Wholesale of Fertilizer	899787	834148	100	56734
机械设备、五金交电及电子产品批发业	Wholesale of Machinery, Hardware and Electronic Equipments	895705	838213	1664	46151
#汽车、摩托车及零配件批发业	Wholesale of Motor Vehicles, Motorcycles and Parts	353945	328033	478	20002
家用电器批发业	Wholesale of Household Electrical Appliances	35018	33057	94	1867
计算机、软件及辅助设备批发业	Wholesale of Computer, Software and Accessory Equipment	48308	47045	20	1025
贸易经纪与代理	Trades Broker and Agent	29457	27969	6	1452
其他批发业	Wholesales of Others	280826	263598	122	16442
按地区分	**By Region**				
乌鲁木齐市	Urumqi City	9233535	8874790	10032	309412
克拉玛依市	Karamay City	202251	188139	558	13553
吐鲁番地区	Turpan Administrative Offices	131044	120497	126	9682
哈密地区	Hami [Kumul] Administrative Offices	156544	146368	185	9991
昌吉回族自治州	Changji Hui Autonomous Prefecture	342985	306680	206	23335
伊犁哈萨克自治州	Ili Kazak Autonomous Prefecture	1034331	968077	491	57511
伊犁州直属县(市)	Counties (Cities) Direct Under Ili Prefecture	394915	370395	260	23864
塔城地区	Tacheng [Tarbagatai] Administrative Offices	546556	512260	123	26608
阿勒泰地区	Altay Administrative Offices	92860	85422	108	7039
博尔塔拉蒙古自治州	Bortala Mongol Autonomous Prefecture	429309	379242	650	46870
巴音郭楞蒙古自治州	Bayangol Mongol Autonomous Prefecture	446592	410587	440	32653
阿克苏地区	Aksu Administrative Offices	604241	552640	460	37786
克孜勒苏柯尔克孜自治州	Kizilsu Kirgiz Autonomous Prefecture	22651	21302	286	904
喀什地区	Kashgar [Kaxgar] Administrative Offices	582196	454248	219	28458
和田地区	Hotan Administrative Offices	99474	90627	117	8508
生产建设兵团	Xinjiang Production and Construction Group	2935891	2731721	988	196003

14-14 限额以上零售企业主要财务指标

Main Financial Indicators of Retail Enterprises above Designated Size

单位：万元　　(2007 年)　　(10 000 yuan)

指　标	Item	商品销售收入 Revenue of Product Sales	商品销售成本 Cost of Product Sales	商品销售税金及附加 Sales Tax and Extra Changes	商品销售利润 Product Sales Profits
总　计	**Total**	**1820870**	**1616339**	**5340**	**176196**
按登记注册类型分	**By status of registration**				
内资企业	Domestic-funded Enterprises	1758379	1567182	5132	165668
国有企业	State-owned Enterprises	165340	130231	1079	27956
集体企业	Collective-owned Enterprises	3418	3011	7	361
股份合作企业	Cooperative Enterprises	8025	6895	12	1118
有限责任公司	Limited Liability Corporations	387719	349699	718	34260
股份有限公司	Share-holding Corporations Ltd	121057	94959	1131	23000
私营企业	Private Enterprises	1043179	955062	2109	76733
其他企业	Others	29641	27325	76	2240
港、澳、台投资企业	Enterprises With Funds from Hong Kong, Macao and Taiwan	21242	17475	128	3611
外商投资企业	Foreign Funded Enterprises	41249	31682	80	6917
按国民经济行业分	**By Sector**				
综合零售业	Integrated Retail	439283	369634	2141	60702
#百货商店	Retail of Merchandile	243379	199339	1871	39231
超级市场	Retail of Supermarket	189272	164600	263	20543
食品、饮料及烟草制品专门零售业	Monopoly Retail of Foods, Beverages and Tobacco	13725	10689	7	1408
纺织、服装及日用品专门零售业	Monopoly Retail of Textile, Garments and Daily Consumer Articles	101404	82734	631	16457
#服装零售业	Garment Retail	100262	81714	631	16333
文化、体育用品及器材专门零售业	Monopoly Retail of Cultural, Sports Goods And Apparatus	93859	70323	356	19798
#体育用品零售业	Retail of Sports Goods	2171	1838	17	316
图书零售业	Retail of Books	77521	58717	67	17116
医药及医疗器材专门零售业	Monopoly Retail of Medicine and Medical-care Apparatus	182943	164073	262	15999
#药品零售业	Retail of Medcine	182943	164073	262	15999
汽车、摩托车、燃料及零配件专门零售业	Monopoly Retail of Car, Motor, Fuel and Parts as Well as Components	676010	632752	810	38070
#汽车零售业	Retail of Car	624127	585797	750	33274
机动车燃料零售业	Retail of Auto Fuel	42961	38610	53	4241
家用电器及电子产品专门零售业	Monopoly Retail of Household Electric Appliances and Electronic Products	261588	238974	780	20359
#家用电器零售业	Retail of Electric Appliances	162878	149039	282	12940
计算机、软件及辅助设备零售业	Retail of Cumputers,Software and Office Appliances	44034	40296	94	2983
通讯设备零售业	Retail of Telecommunication Equipments	51078	46285	400	4197
五金、家俱及室内装修材料专门零售业	Monopoly Retail of Hardware, Furniture andIndoor Decorating Material	47230	43265	320	2791
无店铺及其他零售业	Retail of Storeless and others	4828	3895	33	612
按地区分	**By Region**				
乌鲁木齐市	Urumqi City	1347101	1198108	4112	136128
克拉玛依市	Karamay City	58876	54196	121	4558
吐鲁番地区	Turpan Administrative Offices	8746	7630	13	1039
哈密地区	Hami [Kumul] Administrative Offices	47172	43989	150	3030
昌吉回族自治州	Changji Hui Autonomous Prefecture	35573	29455	284	1648
伊犁哈萨克自治州	Ili Kazak Autonomous Prefecture	49345	41632	56	6895
伊犁州直属县(市)	Counties (Cities) Direct Under Ili Prefecture	36455	31469	48	4939
塔城地区	Tacheng [Tarbagatai] Administrative Offices	8884	6784	6	1331
阿勒泰地区	Altay Administrative Offices	4006	3379	2	625
博尔塔拉蒙古自治州	Bortala Mongol Autonomous Prefecture	3566	2792	3	702
巴音郭楞蒙古自治州	Bayangol Mongol Autonomous Prefecture	89385	82785	147	4609
阿克苏地区	Aksu Administrative Offices	72995	63047	334	6525
克孜勒苏柯尔克孜自治州	Kizilsu Kirgiz Autonomous Prefecture	1456	1276		141
喀什地区	Kashgar [Kaxgar] Administrative Offices	43869	34768	32	5135
和田地区	Hotan Administrative Offices	10355	9134	15	962
生产建设兵团	Xinjiang Production and Construction Group	52431	47527	73	4824

14-15 限额以上餐饮企业主要财务指标
Main Financial Indicators of Catering Enterprises above Designated Size

单位：万元 (2007 年) (10 000 yuan)

指　　标	Item	主营业务收入 Revenue from Principal Business	主营业务成本 Cost of Principal Business	主营业务税金及附加 Tax and Addition of Major Business	主营业务利润 Profit From Principal Business
总　　计	**Total**	**72973**	**37088**	**4264**	**29112**
按登记注册类型分	**By Status of registration**				
内资企业	Domestic-funded Enterprises	59534	32181	3592	21253
国有企业	State – owned Enterprises	3121	1162	125	1833
有限责任公司	Limited Liability Corporations	9057	4365	579	4112
私营企业	Private Enterprises	47356	26654	2888	15308
外商投资企业	Foreign Funded Enterprises	13439	4907	672	7859
按国民经济行业分	**By sector**				
正　餐	Dinner	58121	31350	3500	20763
快　餐	Snack	14852	5738	764	8349
按地区分	**By Region**				
乌鲁木齐市	Urumqi City	60382	29886	3324	25336
克拉玛依市	Karamay City	1600	1081	105	414
哈密地区	Hami [Kumul] Administrative Offices	351	259	16	76
昌吉回族自治州	Changji Hui Autonomous Prefecture	1631	890	84	656
巴音郭楞蒙古自治州	Bayangol Mongol Autonomous Prefecture	6635	3528	606	1900
喀什地区	Kashgar [Kaxgar] Administrative Offices	310	192	12	36
生产建设兵团	Xinjiang Production and Construction Group	2064	1252	117	694

14-16 限额以上住宿企业主要财务指标
Main Financial Indicators of Hotels Enterprises above Designated

单位：万元 (2007 年) (10 000 yuan)

指 标	Item	主营业务收入 Revenue from Principal Business	主营业务成本 Cost of Principal Business	主营业务税金及附加 Tax and Addition of Major Business	主营业务利润 Profit From Principal Business
总 计	**Total**	**228553**	**87529**	**13106**	**108639**
按登记注册类型分	**By Status of registration**				
内资企业	Domestic-funded Enterprises	208109	83359	12102	93400
国有企业	State – owned Enterprises	79545	31105	4249	32594
集体企业	Collective-owned Enterprises	9218	1974	500	6102
股份合作企业	Cooperative Enterprises	1249	409	69	771
联营企业	Joint Ownership Enterprises	637	119	35	483
有限责任公司	Limited Liability Corporations	66838	32092	4133	25404
股份有限公司	Share Holding Limited Corporations Ltd.	3010	878	163	1964
私营企业	Private Enterprises	47305	16506	2935	26068
其他企业	Others	307	276	18	14
港、澳、台投资企业	Enterprises With Funds from Hong Kong, Macao and Taiwan	15741	3118	773	11819
外商投资企业	Foreign Funded Enterprises	4703	1052	231	3420
按国民经济行业分组					
旅游饭店	Tourist Hotel	218857	83604	12584	104602
一般旅馆	Ordinary Hotel	7503	3247	418	2850
其他住宿服务	Other	2193	678	103	1188
按星级等级分	**Classified by Stars**				
一 星	One-Star	1758	650	103	984
二 星	Two-Star	22128	9261	1207	10074
三 星	Three-Star	88525	31551	4812	44356
四 星	Four-Star	57020	18940	3373	32237
五 星	Five-Star	59122	27127	3611	20988
按地区分	**By Region**				
乌鲁木齐市	Urumqi City	130253	49675	7758	59382
克拉玛依市	Karamay City	4216	1778	200	2238
吐鲁番地区	Turpan Administrative Offices	4244	1218	272	2707
哈密地区	Hami [Kumul] Administrative Offices	5751	2844	280	2508
昌吉回族自治州	Changji Hui Autonomous Prefecture	3078	1349	160	1569
伊犁哈萨克自治州	Ili Kazak Autonomous Prefecture	29378	10667	1646	15620
伊犁州直属县(市)	Counties (Cities) Direct Under Ili Prefecture	19563	6338	1124	12101
塔城地区	Tacheng [Tarbagatai] Administrative Offices	3374	1981	203	768
阿勒泰地区	Altay Administrative Offices	6441	2348	319	2751
博尔塔拉蒙古自治州	Bortala Mongol Autonomous Prefecture	2407	1666	115	559
巴音郭楞蒙古自治州	Bayangol Mongol Autonomous Prefecture	11406	4214	641	4942
阿克苏地区	Aksu Administrative Offices	6613	2193	358	3299
克孜勒苏柯尔克孜自治州	Kizilsu Kirgiz Autonomous Prefecture	746	620	56	16
喀什地区	Kashgar [Kaxgar] Administrative Offices	5843	2469	369	2371
和田地区	Hotan Administrative Offices	3622	1395	121	1428
生产建设兵团	Xinjiang Production and Construction Group	20996	7441	1130	12000

14-17 限额以上批发零售业商品销售类值

Total Sales of Enterprises above Designated Size in Wholesale and Retail Trades by Category of Commodities

单位：万元 (10 000 yuan)

项 目	Item	销售合计 Total Sales		批 发 Wholesale Trades		零 售 Retail Trades	
		2006	2007	2006	2007	2006	2007
总 计	**Total**	**11801236**	**20425838**	**9516296**	**17669665**	**2284940**	**2756177**
食品、饮料、烟酒类	Foods, Beverages, Tobacco and Liquor	1448315	1734647	1277880	1520608	170435	214039
服装、鞋帽类、针、纺织品类	Garments, Shoes and Hats, Knitted Goods and Textiles	268073	299697	80046	29055	188027	270642
化妆品类	Cosmetics	49005	63571	14314	18649	34691	44922
金银珠宝类	Gold, Silver and Jewelry	20786	36472			20786	36472
日用品类	Articles for Daily Use	52303	68737	7495	8354	44808	60383
五金、电料类	Hardwares, Electrc Appliances	30439	25563	26633	20583	3806	4980
体育、娱乐用品类	Sports and Recreational Articles	4079	5477		4	4079	5474
书报杂志类	Books and Newspapers	141522	164841	86400	89114	55122	75727
电子出版物及音像制品类	E-journal and Video Products	923	1196		76	923	1120
家用电器及音像器材类	Household Appliances and Video Equipments	203977	211434	65224	44169	138753	167265
中西药品类	Chinese Traditional medicine and Western Medicines	309687	447356	155850	270163	153837	177193
文化办公用品类	Office Articles	95881	166149	51992	105036	43889	61113
家俱类	Furnitures	29918	35355	2567	13585	27351	21771
通讯器材类	Telecommunication Apparatus	119575	120683	44939	39439	74636	81244
煤炭及制品类	Coal and Related Products	33686	60126	28696	54168	4990	5957
木材及制品类	Wood and Wooden Products	2529	1534	2529	1525		9
石油及制品类	Petroleum and Petroleum Products	2248261	9450756	1400126	8662480	848135	788276
化工材料及制品类	Raw Chemical Materials and Products	1473093	1281325	1470883	1280776	2210	549
金属材料类	Metal Materials	1100996	1212941	1100623	1212522	373	419
建筑装潢材料类	Building and Decorative Materials	50353	89397	47311	86302	3042	3096
机电产品及设备类	Mechanical and Electrical Products and Accessories	162257	250994	156479	242871	5778	8124
汽车类	Automobile	692862	1020914	258022	315384	434840	705530
种子饲料类	Seeds and Forage	48349	59445	48349	59445		
棉麻类	Cotton and Flax	2637602	3065618	2637602	3065618		
其他类	Others	576765	551610	552336	529739	24429	21872

主要统计指标解释

社会消费品零售总额 指批发和零售业、餐饮业、新闻出版业、邮政业和其他服务业等，售予城乡居民用于生活消费的商品和社会集团用于公共消费的商品之总量。社会消费品零售总额包括：

1、批发和零售业企业（单位）：

(1)售予城乡居民的各种生活消费品；(2)售予入境旅游的外国人、华侨、港澳台同胞的各类商品；(3)售予行政事业单位、社会团体、军队和武警等机构的商品，以及以零售方式售予各类企业的商品。具体包括：用于非生产和社会交往的办公用品，如通讯设备、计算器具和设备、电讯网络设备、文印设备、音像视听器材和设备、纸张、本册、文具及装订文印材料、家具、日用电器、针纺织品、清洁卫生用品、文体用品、奖品、纪念品、礼品等；供内部人员乘坐的交通工具和燃料；用于办公设施修缮的各类配件、材料、工具等；用于取暖和防暑降温的设备、燃料、材料及食品等；专用于教学的用品和设备；非营利医疗机构的中、西药品、中药材和医疗设备器材；非专用的劳动保护用品；不对外营业的内部食堂用的餐具、炊具、设备、清洁卫生工具和食品、燃料等；军队、武警用于其人员生活的衣着品和个人用品；其他各类非生产性设备和用品。

2、餐饮业出售的主食、菜肴、烟酒饮料和其他商品。

3、新闻出版业、邮政业售予城乡居民、企事业单位、军队和武警等机构的书报杂志、音像制品、邮品等。

4、其他服务业出售的食品、烟酒饮料、服装鞋帽、日常生活用品、医药保健用品、艺术品、工艺美术品、玩具、殡葬用品以及其他消费品。

批发零售贸易业商品购、销、存总额 指各种登记注册类型的批发、零售业企业(单位)以本企业(单位)为总体的，从国内、国外市场购进的商品总量，销售和出口的商品总量、库存商品总量等情况。该指标可以反映商品流转过程中商品的购进、销售、库存之间的比例关系和存在的问题。

批发零售贸易业商品购、销、存总额 指各种登记注册类型的批发、零售贸易业企业(单位)以本企业(单位)为总体的，从国内、国外市场购进的商品总量、销售和出口的商品总量、库存商品总量等情况。该指标对促进工农业生产发展、活跃市场、平抑物价、保障供给、满足需求具有举足轻重的作用。该指标可以反映商品流转过程中商品的购进、销售、库存之间的比例关系和存在的问题。

商品购进总额 指从本企业(单位)以外的单位和个人购进(包括从境外直接进口)作为转卖或加工后转卖的商品总额。它反映批发零售贸易业从国内、国外市场上购进商品的总量。商品购进总额包括：(1)从工农业生产者购进的商品；(2)从出版社、报社的出版发行部门购进的图书、杂志和报纸；(3)从各种登记注册类型的批发零售贸易企业(单位)购进的商品；(4)从其他单位购进的商品，如从机关、团体、企业等单位购进的剩余物资，从餐饮业、服务业购进的商品，从海关、市场管理部门购进的缉私和没收的商品，从居民手中收购的废旧商品等；(5)从国(境)外直接进口的商品。不包括企业(单位)为自身经营用和未通过买卖行为而收入的商品以及销售退回、商品升溢等。

商品销售总额 指对本企业(单位)以外的单位和个人出售(包括对境外直接出口)的商品总额。它反映批发零售贸易业在国内市场上销售商品以及出口商品的总量。商品销售总额包括：(1)售给城乡居民和社会集团消费用的商品；(2)售给工业、农业、建筑业、运输邮电业、批发零售贸易业、餐饮业、服务业等作为生产、经营使用的商品；(3)售给批发零售贸易业作为转卖或加工后转卖的商品；(4)对国(境)外直接出口的商品。不包括出售本企业(单位)自用的废旧包装用品；未通过买卖行为付出的商品；经本单位介绍，由买卖双方直接结算，本单位只收取手续费的业务；购货退出的商品以及商品损耗和损失等。

批发零售贸易业库存 指报告期末各种登记注册类型的批发零售贸易企业(单位)已取得所有权的商品。它反映批发零售贸易企业(单位)的商品库存情况和对市场商品供应的保证程度。期末库存包括：(1)存放在批发零售贸易业经营单位(如门市部、批发站、经营处)仓库、货场、货柜和货架中的商品；(2)挑选、整理、包装中的商品；(3)已记入购进而尚未运到本单位的商品，即发货单或银行承兑凭证已到而货未到的部分；(4)寄放他处的商品，如因购货方拒绝承付而暂时存放在购货方的商品和已办完加工成品收回手续而未提回的商品；(5)委托其他单位代销(未作销售或调出)尚未售出的商品；(6)代其他单位购进尚未交付的商品。不包括所有权不属于本单位的商品、拨付除批发零售贸易业以外的其他行业所属独立核算加工厂等加工生产尚未收回成品的商品、代国家物资储备部门保管的商品等。

库存总额采用的计算价格是：农副产品采购单位按购进价计算；批发单位按进货价计算；零售单位按核算价格计算，即按什么价格核算就按什么价格计算。

餐饮业商品零售额 指餐饮企业、活动单位或个体户直接对居民和社会集团零售的各种商品。包括：(1)经烹饪、调制加工后出售的各种食品，如主食、炒菜、凉拌菜等；(2)不经加工直接转卖的各种外购商品，如卷烟、酒、饮料、熟食、水果等；(3)附设非独立核算的专门销售商品的小卖部出售的各种食品及其他商品。

连锁企业（或称连锁店、连锁公司） 指在核心企业或总店的领导下，由分散的、经营同类商品或服务的企业或活动单位，采取共同方针，实行集中采购和分散销售的有机结合，通过规范化经营，实现规模效益的经济联合组织形式。一般连锁店应由若干个分店组成。其经营特征：(1)经营同类商品；(2)使用统一商号；(3)统一采购配送，采购与销售相分离（部分商品可根据物流合理和保质保鲜原则，由供应商直接送货到门店，其余均由总部统一配送）。

连锁门店包括下列两种形式：

直营连锁：指正规连锁。连锁门店均由总部独资或控股开设，在总部的直接领导下统一经营。

加盟连锁：指特许连锁。各连锁门店（被特许人）通过合同形式，取得使用总部（特许人）商标、商号、经营技术和销售总部开发的商品的特许权，各加盟连锁门店为独立法人，在总部指导下统一经营。

Explanatory Notes on Main Statistical Indicators

Total Retail Sales of Consumer Goods refer to the sum of retail sales of commodities sold by wholesale, retail, catering, publishing, post and telecommunications and other service industries to urban and rural households for private consumption and to social institutions for public consumption. Retail sales of consumer goods include:

1) Sales by wholesale and retail units: a) of consumer goods sold to urban and rural households ; b) of commodities sold to foreigners, overseas Chinese and Chinese compatriots from Hong Kong, Macao and Taiwan visiting in China ; c) of commodities sold to government agencies, institutions, social organizations, military and armed police units, and commodities sold to enterprises in the form of retail sales. More specifically, they include: office facilities and articles for non-production purposes such as communications equipment, computing equipment and instruments, TV and network equipment, printing and copying equipment, audio-visual equipment and instruments, paper, notebooks, stationeries, furniture, electric appliances, knitwear, sanitation and cleaning articles, cultural and sport articles, articles for prizes, souvenirs, etc.; transport vehicles and fuels for employees; materials, spare parts and tools for the maintenance of office facilities; equipment, fuels, materials and food for winter heating or summer cooling purposes; articles and equipment for teaching purpose; Chinese and western medicines and medical equipment and facilities purchased by non profit-making medical institutes; non-specialized work safety articles; cooking utensils, tableware, equipment, cleaning articles, food and fuels purchased by internal cafeterias; clothes and personal articles purchased by military or armed police units for their officials and soldiers; and other equipment and articles for non-production purposes.

2) Sales of stable food, cooked dishes, beverages, tobaccos and other articles by catering units.

3) Sales of books, newspapers, magazines, audio-visual products and post products by publishing, post and telecommunications departments to urban and rural households and to enterprises, institutions, military and armed police units.

4) Sales of food, beverages, tobaccos, clothing, hats, footwear, articles for daily use, medicines, medical and health articles, work of art, handicrafts, toys, funeral articles and other articles by other service industries.

Purchase, Sales and Stock of Commodities by Wholesale and Retail Trades refer to the total volume of commodities purchased, total volume of sales and exports, and the stock of commodities by wholesale and retail enterprises (establishments) of different status of registration from domestic and overseas markets. This indictor plays an important role in promoting industrial and agricultural production, thriving market, stabilizing prices, ensuring market supply and meeting the needs of consumers. It also reflects the relationship among purchase, sales and stock of commodities in the circulation of goods and reveals the existing problems.

Total Purchases of Commodities refer to the total value of purchases of commodities by the enterprises (establishments) from other establishments or individuals (including direct import from abroad) for the purpose of re-selling, either with or without further processing of the commodities purchased. This indicator is us ed to show the total value of purchases of commodities by wholes ale and retail establishments from domes tic and overseas markets. The total purchases include: (1) agricultural and industrial products purchased from producers; (2) books, magazines and news papers purchased from distribution departments of the publishers; (3) commodities purchased from wholesale and retail establishments of different status of registration; (4) commodities purchased from other units, such as surplus materials purchased from government agencies, enterprises or institutions, commodities purchased from catering and service establishments, confiscated goods purchased from customs authorities or market management agencies, second-hand goods and wastes purchased from resident s; and (5) commodities directly imp ort ed from abroad. Excluded are commodities purchased by enterprises (establishments) for use in their own business operation, commodities obtained without buying or selling procedures, rejected commodities, etc.

Total Sales of Commodities refer to value of commodities old by the establishments to other establishments and individuals (including direct export). This indicator is used to show the total value of sales of commodities at domestic market sand export. The total sales include: (1) commodities sold to urban and rural residents and social groups for their consumption; (2) commodities sold to establishments in industry, agriculture, construction, transportation, post and telecommunications, wholesale and retail Trades, Catering Services and public utility for their production and operation; (3) commodities sold to wholesale and retail establishments for re selling, with or without further processing; and (4) commodities for direct export to other countries. Excluded are selling of waste packaging materials used by the establishments (units) themselves, commodities transferred without buying or selling procedures, commission income from brokerage in trans actions whose settlement is directly handled by buyers and sellers, rejected commodities in the purchase, loss in commodities, etc.

Commodity Stock of Wholesale and Retail Enterprises refers to total commodities possessed by wholesale and retail enterprises (units) of various types of registration status at the end of the reference period, which reflects the commodity stock level of various wholesale and ret ail enterprises and the potential for market supply. It includes: (1) commodities located in storage, garages, counters, and shelves of operating units (such as sale stores, wholesale centers, and operating offices) of wholesale and ret ail enterprises; (2) commodities in the process of selecting, sorting, and packing; (3) commodities not arrived but recorded as purchase in t he account, i.e. commodities not arrived but payment receipts for the commodities from the sellers or the banks arrived; (4) commodities deposited in other p laces rather than places mentioned above, for instance: commodities in the hold of purchasers temporarily due t o the refusal of payment and commodities not taken back after going through the formalities;(5) commodities entrusted to other units to sell but not sold yet; (6) commodities purchased for other units but not delivered yet. Commodities not included as stock are those not owned by the enterprises (unit s), those allocated to financially in dependent factories rather than wholesale and retail enterprises for processing but not taken back yet, and finally those put in stock by wholesale and retail enterprises on behalf of t he state material reserves units.

For the calculation of the value of commodities stock, the value is calculated at purchasing prices in agricultural goods purchasing units and wholesale units, and at the accounting prices in retail units.

Retail Sales of Commodities in Catering Industry refer to retail sales to residents and social groups by catering enterprises, establishments and individual, including: (1) various food sold after cooking and processing, such as: staple food, cooked dishes, cold and dressed dishes and so on. (2) re-selling commodities without further processing, such as: cigarettes, liquor, beverage, cooked food, fruit s and son on. (3) various food and other commodities sold in and ascent buffets with dependant accounting system.

Chain Enterprises (also called chain stores or chain corporations) refer to a form of joint economic entities under which scattered enterprises or establishments engaged in providing homogeneous commodities or services, with the central leadership of core enterprise or headquarters and guided by common policies, conduct centralized purchase and distributed selling of commodities, in order to gain better efficiency through standardized operation. Consisting of a number of branch stores, the chain stores have in general following features: 1) homogeneous commodities, 2) unique name of stores, 3) centralized purchase and delivery which is separated from distributed selling operation (most commodities are delivered from the headquarters except some items which, from logistics, quality or freshness considerations, might be delivered by the suppliers directly).

Chain stores have two categories:

a) Chain stores under direct management: These are formal chain stores invested or controlled by the headquarters. They operate under the direct and unified management from the headquarters.

b) Chain stores through license arrangement: Through contracts, chain stores (their owners) obtain licenses from the headquarters to use designated Trades marks, names, operation know-how, and to sell the commodity developed by the headquarters. Under this arrangement, each store in the chain is an independent legal entity and operates under the guidance from the headquarters.

第十五篇
能源生产和消费

CHAPTER 15
Production and Consumption of Energy

简要说明
Brief Introduction

本篇资料的主要内容及来源

本篇包括的主要内容有能源生产、消费总量及品种构成，综合能源平衡表和主要能源品种单项平衡表，分行业、分主要能源品种的消费量，能源生产和消费弹性系数，能源加工转换效率及生活用能源消费量等。

从 2006 年度开始，能源生产、消费等指标需经国家审定后方可公布，因国家审定、公布各省的这部分指标数据为每年的八月份，时间在年鉴出版时间之后，为此，这部分数据采取错年上，即 2007 年上 2006 年数据。

本篇资料由新疆维吾尔自治区统计局能源处依据能源年报整理提供。

Main Content and Source of Data

Data in this chapter cover mainly the energy production and consumption and their composition, the overall balance of energy and the balance by different types of energy, the consumption of energy by sector and by types of energy the elasticity ratio of energy production and consumption, efficiency of energy conversion and the consumption of energy for non-production uses.

Since 2006, data on production and consumption of energy are announced after NBS authorized. Time of publication is August every year. So the data on energy in 2007 Statistical Yearbook is data in 2006.

Data in this chapter are provided and processed in accordance with the statistical reporting scheme on energy by the Department of Energy of the Xinjiang Bureau of Statistics.

15-1 能源生产总量及构成

Total Production of Energy and Its Composition

年份 Year	能源生产总量(万吨标准煤) Total Energy Production (10 000 tons of SCE)	占能源生产总量的比重(%) Percentage of Total Energy Production (%)			
		原煤 Coal	原油 Crude Oil	天然气 Natural Gas	水风电 Hydro- Power and Wind Power
1978	1410.75	60.0	35.8	2.4	1.8
1980	1527.72	58.4	36.5	3.1	2.0
1985	2092.47	60.0	34.1	3.5	2.4
1990	2801.57	58.8	35.8	2.4	3.0
1995	4266.06	50.1	43.5	3.6	2.8
1996	4755.50	49.3	44.1	3.9	2.7
1997	5130.60	46.2	45.4	5.5	2.9
1998	5095.18	45.1	45.7	6.2	3.0
1999	5246.28	41.8	47.4	7.9	2.9
2000	5419.77	40.6	48.7	7.9	2.8
2001	5720.04	38.7	48.6	9.7	3.0
2002	6156.05	39.5	47.3	10.5	2.7
2003	6657.43	41.1	46.0	10.2	2.7
2004	7112.95	41.4	45.3	10.7	2.6
2005	8175.74	37.9	42.1	17.3	2.7
2006	9528.72	37.3	37.1	22.9	2.7

注：电力折算标准煤的系数根据当年平均发电煤耗计算，并将历史资料做了调整，下表同。
Note: The coefficient for conversion of electric power into SCE (standard coal equivalent) is calculated on the basic of the data on the average coal consumption in generating electric power in the same year. The same is as in the following tables.

15-2 能源消费总量及构成

Total Consumption of Energy and Its Composition

年份 Year	能源消费总量(万吨标准煤) Total Energy Consumption (10 000 tons of SCE)	占能源消费总量的比重(%) As percentage of Total Energy Consumption (%)			
		煤炭 Coal	石油 Crude Oil	天然气 Natural Gas	水风电 Hydro- Power and Wind Power
1978	979.27	72.5	21.5	3.4	2.6
1980	1026.45	71.3	21.1	4.6	3.0
1985	1410.84	72.0	19.3	5.1	3.6
1990	1924.38	69.6	22.5	3.5	4.4
1995	2733.04	66.2	23.8	5.6	4.4
1996	3045.16	65.1	24.8	6.0	4.1
1997	3208.24	63.3	24.3	7.8	4.6
1998	3279.75	62.2	24.9	8.2	4.7
1999	3215.02	62.9	23.1	9.2	4.8
2000	3316.03	63.6	23.3	8.6	4.5
2001	3496.44	60.4	21.6	13.2	4.8
2002	3622.40	62.2	20.5	12.7	4.6
2003	4064.43	60.3	21.7	13.1	4.9
2004	4784.83	61.0	20.1	15.0	3.9
2005	5506.49	56.1	26.2	13.7	4.0
2006	6047.27	56.7	24.7	14.3	4.3

15-3 综合能源平衡表
Overall Energy Balance Sheet

单位:万吨标准煤 (10 000 tons of SCE)

项　　目	Item	1990	1995	2000	2005	2006
可供消费的能源总量	**Total Energy Available for Consumption**	**2045.32**	**2883.61**	**3430.05**	**5349.17**	**5956.66**
一次能源生产量	Primary Energy Output	2801.57	4266.06	5419.77	8175.74	9528.72
进口量	Imports			107.39	130.80	339.75
外省调入量	Inflow from other Provinces (Autonomons Regions and Municipalities)	2.26	8.29	25.59	58.17	58.86
出口量(-)	Exports (-)	4.84	1.04	31.90	60.80	45.74
本区调出量(-)	Outflow (-)	694.89	1414.05	2144.79	3172.41	3977.93
年初年末库存差额	Stock Changes in the Year	-58.78	24.35	53.99	95.71	-12.42
能源消费总量	**Total Energy Consumption**	**1924.45**	**2733.01**	**3316.03**	**5506.49**	**6047.27**
在总量中:	Consumption by Sector					
农、林、牧、渔、水利业	Agriculture, Forestry, Animal Husbandry, Fishery and Water Conservancy	134.91	189.13	274.97	314.25	337.18
工　业	Industry	1095.22	1571.88	1860.26	3440.83	4199.53
建筑业	Construction	41.16	63.01	81.73	43.22	53.30
交通运输和邮电通讯业	Transportation, Post and Telecommunications Services	99.72	152.77	189.76	413.77	487.87
商业、饮食、物资供销和仓储业	Commerce, Catering Services, Materials Supply, Marketing and Storage	26.28	51.37	93.83	138.39	167.66
其　他	Others	99.12	205.04	164.57	177.51	189.08
生活消费	Household Consumption	428.04	499.84	650.91	978.54	612.66
在总量中:	Consumption by Sector					
终端消费	End-use Consumption	1825.44	2587.35	3148.77	5086.96	5661.80
#工　业	Industry	996.27	1426.22	1692.96	3021.27	3814.06
加工转换损失量	Losses in Processing and Transformation	27.90	62.06	91.25	228.26	123.62
#炼　焦	Coking	13.00	27.56	72.05	77.60	61.02
炼　油	Petroleum Refining	13.16	33.49	75.99	62.18	55.54
损失量	Energy Losses	71.05	83.60	76.05	191.27	261.85
平衡差额	**Balance**	**120.87**	**150.60**	**114.02**	**-157.32**	**-90.61**

注：1.村办工业包括在工业中(下同)。
2.电力、热力按等价热值折算，因此加工转换损失量中不包括发电、供热损失量。
3.进口量包括新疆飞机在国外加油量，出口量包括外国飞机在新疆的加油量。

Note: a) Energy consumption of industry include that of village in dustry. (The same is as in the following tables).
b) Electric power and heat are converted on the basic of equal caloric value. Therefore, losses in processing and transformation exclude losses in power generation and heating.
c) The refueling by Xinjang airplanes abroad is include in imports.The refueling by foreign airplanes in Xinjiang is include in Exports.

15-4 石油平衡表
Petroleum Balance Sheet

单位:万吨 (10 000 tons)

项目	Item	1990	1995	2000	2005	2006
可供量	**Total Energy Available for Consumption**	**333.19**	**496.35**	**616.14**	**1021.31**	**1042.95**
生产量	Output	701.26	1299.83	1848.43	2408.32	2474.74
进口量	Imports			75.16	91.54	237.61
外省调入量	Inflow from other Provinces (Autonomons Regions and Municipalities)	1.44	3.31	10.85	14.85	14.35
出口量(-)	Exports (-)	3.29	0.63	11.17	5.18	2.26
本区调出量(-)	Outflow (-)	353.59	849.63	1285.38	1525.72	1677.86
年初年末库存差额	Stock Changes in the Year	-12.63	43.47	-21.75	37.50	-3.63
消费量	**Total Energy Consumption**	**300.16**	**451.26**	**527.71**	**1014.84**	**1038.63**
在消费量中：	Consumption by Sector					
农、林、牧、渔、水利业	Agriculture, Forestry, Animal Husbandry, Fishery And Water Conservancy	42.46	44.56	63.65	70.68	79.18
工业	Industry	171.96	269.79	273.95	611.18	572.87
建筑业	Construction	16.87	16.67	32.10	15.36	21.50
交通运输和邮电通讯业	Transportation, Post and Telecommunications Services	48.30	76.55	86.89	210.00	251.03
商业、饮食、物资供销和仓储业	Commerce, Catering Services, Materials Supply, Marketing and Storage	3.66	8.80	18.78	31.91	36.33
其他	Others	8.48	20.25	32.70	46.20	47.66
生活消费	Household Consumption	8.43	14.64	19.64	29.51	30.06
在消费量中：	Consumption by Usage					
终端消费	End-use Consumption	257.06	411.94	457.99	936.88	907.87
#工业	Industry	128.86	230.47	204.23	533.22	442.11
中间消费(用于加工转换)	Intermediate Consumption	15.69	10.01	17.34	47.37	35.06
#发电	Power Generation	15.69	10.01	2.10	8.65	1.38
供热	Heating			1.24	1.04	0.85
此外：当年炼油投入量	Petroleum Refining Input	464.29	692.40	1001.32	1531.68	1610.35
平衡差额	**Balance**	**33.03**	**45.09**	**88.43**	**6.47**	**4.32**

注：1.生产量为原油产量。
2.进口量包括新疆飞机在国外加油量，出口量包括外国飞机在新疆的加油量。

Note: a) Data on output refer to the output of crude oil.
b) The refueling by Xinjiang airplanes abroad is included in imports. The refueling by foreign airplane in Xinjiang is included in export.

15-5 煤炭平衡表
Coal Balance Sheet

单位:万吨 (10 000 tons)

项 目	Item	1990	1995	2000	2005	2006
可供量	**Total Energy Available for Consumption**	**1816.32**	**2444.21**	**2702.81**	**3702.32**	**4314.06**
生产量	Output	2100.20	2720.74	2798.90	3942.29	4518.52
外省调入量	Inflow from other Provinces (Autonomons Regions and Municipalities)		1.40	10.70	30.40	41.44
出口量(-)	Exports (-)	0.01	0.14	0.22	0.01	0.01
本区调出量(-)	Outflow (-)	232.76	221.00	203.12	323.47	245.63
年初年末库存差额	Stock Changes in the Year	-51.11	-56.79	96.55	53.08	-0.39
消费量	**Total Energy Consumption**	**1716.11**	**2327.52**	**2702.40**	**3859.91**	**4436.21**
在消费量中:	Consumption by Sector					
农、林、牧、渔、水利业	Farming, Forestry, Animal Husbandry, Fishery and Water Conservancy	23.96	80.44	100.00	103.30	99.24
工 业	Industry	1080.07	1452.19	1801.40	3110.44	3974.07
建筑业	Construction	11.67	26.02	26.00	17.00	17.30
交通运输和邮电通讯业	Transportation, Post and Telecommunications Services	25.42	32.56	55.00	56.60	57.57
商业、饮食、物资供销和仓储业	Commerce, Catering Services, Materials Supply, Marketing and Storage	20.50	33.00	40.00	31.78	36.23
其 他	Others	79.48	176.31	90.00	40.00	40.80
生活消费	Residential Consumption	479.37	527.00	590.00	500.79	211.00
在消费量中:	Consumption by Usage					
终端消费	End-use Consumption	1163.46	1427.87	1502.63	1503.83	1730.12
#工 业	Industry	523.06	552.54	601.63	754.36	1267.98
中间消费(用于加工转换)	Intermediate Consumption	525.51	842.96	1199.77	2356.08	2705.79
#发 电	Power Generation	372.01	575.88	849.20	1363.96	1556.14
供 热	Heating	32.32	102.93	204.46	585.51	640.08
炼 焦	Coking	111.39	158.93	137.77	380.90	482.90
平衡差额	**Balance**	**100.21**	**116.69**	**0.41**	**-157.59**	**-122.15**

注：生产量为原煤产量。
Note: Data on output refer to the output of raw coal.

15-6 电力平衡表
Electricity Balance Sheet

单位:亿千瓦小时 (100 million kwh)

项目	Item	1990	1995	2000	2005	2006
可供量	**Total Energy Available for Consumption**	**69.79**	**120.43**	**182.98**	**310.14**	**357.15**
生产量	Output	69.79	120.43	182.98	310.14	357.15
水电	Hydropower	14.25	22.82	30.54	46.49	53.43
风电	Wind Power	0.08	0.34	1.73	2.32	4.71
火电	Thermal Power	55.46	97.27	150.71	261.33	299.01
消费量	**Total Energy Consumption**	**69.79**	**120.37**	**182.98**	**310.14**	**356.15**
在消费量中:	Consumption by Sector					
农、林、牧、渔、水利业	Agriculture, Forestry, Animal Husbandry, Fishery and Water Conservancy	9.16	11.50	22.30	28.72	32.62
工业	Industry	48.86	83.53	118.85	221.67	248.47
建筑业	Construction	1.18	3.20	3.50	1.44	1.91
交通运输和邮电通讯业	Transportation, Post and Telecommunications Services	1.48	2.73	4.00	4.74	8.09
商业、饮食、物资供销和仓储业	Commerce, Catering Services, Materials Supply, Marketing and Storage	0.81	2.30	6.90	11.09	15.37
其他	Others	4.08	7.00	9.83	15.38	17.79
生活消费	Household Consumption	4.22	10.11	17.60	27.10	31.90
在消费量中:	Consumption by Usage					
终端消费	End-use Consumption	65.74	112.87	170.86	282.42	327.93
#工业	Industry	44.81	76.03	106.73	193.95	220.25
输配电损失量	Losses in Transmission	4.05	7.50	12.12	27.72	28.22

15-7 分行业能源消费总量和主要能源消费量

(2006 年)

行　　业	Sector	能源消费总量(万吨标准煤) Total Energy Consumption (10 000 tons of SCE)	煤炭消费量(万吨) Coal Consumption (10 000 tons)	焦炭消费量(万吨) Coke Consumption (10 000 tons)
消费总量	**Total Consumption**	**6047.27**	**4436.21**	**230.60**
农、林、牧、渔业	**Farming, Forestry, Animal Husbandry, and Fishery**	**337.18**	**99.24**	
工　业	**Industry**	**4199.53**	**3974.07**	**230.60**
采 矿 业	**Mining and Quarrying**	**1171.67**	**182.12**	**3.25**
煤炭开采和洗选业	Mining and Washing of Coal	92.07	130.99	
石油和天然气开采业	Extraction of Petroleum and Natural Gas	1019.45	23.71	
黑色金属矿采选业	Processing of Ferrous Metals Ores	24.64	11.36	1.19
有色金属矿采选业	Processing of Nonferrous Metals Ores	22.36	5.35	2.06
非金属矿采选业	Processing of Nonmetal Ores	13.14	10.71	
制 造 业	**Manufacturing**	**2669.65**	**1969.49**	**227.35**
农副食品加工业	Processing of Food from Agricultural Products	106.46	105.61	3.12
食品制造业	Food Manufacturing	61.32	53.17	
饮料制造业	Beverage Manufacturing	22.94	23.27	
烟草制品业	Tobacco Manufacturing	1.31	0.97	
纺织业	Textile Industry	105.64	53.42	
纺织服装、鞋、帽制造业	Textile Wearing Apparel,Footware and Caps Manufacturing	0.31	0.09	
皮革、毛皮、羽绒及其制品业	Leather, Fur, Feather and Related Products Manufacturing	0.78	0.65	
木材加工及木、竹、藤、棕、草制品业	Timber Production, Wood, Bamboo, Cane and Grass	13.70	10.19	
家具制造业	Furniture Manufacturing	1.61	0.81	
造纸及纸制品业	Paper and Paper Products Manufacturing	58.26	53.18	
印刷业和记录媒介的复制	Printing and Copying of Medium for Record	1.68	0.55	
文教、体育用品制造业		0.23	0.05	
石油加工、炼焦及核燃料加工业	Oil Processing, Coking and Nuclear Fuel Processing	802.31	632.79	

Consumption of Total Energy and Its Main Varieties by Sector

原油消费量(万吨) Crude Oil Consumption (10 000 tons)	汽油消费量(万吨) Gasoline Consumption (10 000 tons)	煤油消费量(万吨) Kerosene Consumption (10 000 tons)	柴油消费量(万吨) Diesel Oil Consumption (10 000 tons)	燃料油消费量(万吨) Fuel Oil Consumption (10 000 tons)	天然气消费量(亿立方米) Natural Gas Consumption (100 million cu.m)	电力消费量(亿千瓦小时) Electricity Consumption (100 million kwh)
1813.64	**117.82**	**30.88**	**341.01**	**19.31**	**65.04**	**356.15**
	11.32	**0.53**	**63.51**			**32.62**
1813.64	**7.80**	**0.10**	**56.11**	**19.31**	**57.84**	**248.47**
250.44	**3.46**		**35.65**	**0.02**	**40.93**	**39.08**
	0.46		3.53			4.96
250.44	2.36		28.25	0.02	40.93	27.78
	0.32		1.56			2.68
	0.27		0.95			3.24
	0.05		1.36			0.42
1563.18	**3.29**	**0.09**	**17.61**	**19.29**	**14.20**	**149.75**
	0.26		0.70		0.01	4.13
	0.19		0.47		0.01	2.11
	0.08		0.05			0.89
	0.01					0.10
	0.15	0.02	0.12			13.08
	0.01					0.02
	0.01		0.02			0.05
	0.02		0.06			1.26
	0.05		0.06			0.22
0.05	0.05	0.01	0.06		0.02	2.71
	0.06	0.01	0.01			0.14
			0.01			0.04
1563.13	0.40	0.01	2.15	19.15	6.81	20.54

15-7 续表

行业	Sector	能源消费总量（万吨标准煤） Total Energy Consumption (10 000 tons of SCE)	煤炭消费量（万吨） Coal Consumption (10 000 tons)	焦炭消费量（万吨） Coke Consumption (10 000 tons)
化学原料及化学制品制造业	Raw Chemical Material and Chemical Products	331.67	144.80	14.29
医药制造业	Medicine Manufacturing	5.17	5.27	
化学纤维制造业	Chemical Fiber Manufacturing	17.83	7.50	
橡胶制品业	Rubber Products Manufacturing	8.67	9.35	
塑料制品业	Plastic Products Manufacturing	136.30	23.15	15.42
非金属矿物制品业	Nonmetal Mineral Products Manufacturing	393.44	378.61	1.74
黑色金属冶炼及压延加工业	Smelting and Pressing of Ferrous Metals	489.49	369.07	187.89
有色金属冶炼及压延加工业	Smelting and Pressing of Nonferrous Metals	46.53	38.90	0.89
金属制品业	Metal Products Manufacturing	14.99	2.95	3.53
通用设备制造业	General Purpose Machinery Manufacturing	3.26	1.25	0.31
专用设备制造业	Special Purpose Machinery Manufacturing	2.01	5.06	0.12
交通运输设备制造业	Transport Equipment Manufacturing	2.67	1.52	0.04
电气机械及器材制造业	Electric Equipment and Machinery Manufacturing	4.58	0.53	
通信设备、计算机及其他电子设备制造业	Communication Equipment, Computer and Other Electronic Equipment	35.63	46.78	
仪器仪表及文化办公用机械制造业	Equipment, Meter, Culture and Office Machinery	0.13		
工艺品及其他制造业	Arts and Handicraft, Other Manufacturing Sector	0.66		
废弃资源和废旧材料回收加工业	Recycling and Processing of Deserted Resources and Waste Material	0.09		
电力、燃气及水的生产和供应业	**Electric Power, Gas and Water Production and Supply**	**358.20**	**1822.46**	
电力、热力的生产和供应业	Production and Distribution of Power, Steam and Hot Water	351.59	1821.78	
燃气生产和供应业	Gas Production and Distribution	0.69		
水的生产和供应业	Water Production and Distribution	5.92	0.68	
建筑业	**Construction**	**53.30**	**17.30**	
交通运输、仓储及邮电通信业	**Transportation, Storage, Post & Telecommunications Services**	**487.87**	**57.57**	
批发和零售贸易业、餐饮业	**Wholesale, Retail Trades and Catering Services**	**167.66**	**36.23**	
其他行业	**Others**	**189.08**	**40.80**	
生活消费	**Residential Consumption**	**612.66**	**211.00**	

Continued

原油消费量 (万吨) Crude Oil Consumption (10 000 tons)	汽油消费量 (万吨) Gasoline Consumption (10 000 tons)	煤油消费量 (万吨) Kerosene Consumption (10 000 tons)	柴油消费量 (万吨) Diesel Oil Consumption (10 000 tons)	燃料油消费量 (万吨) Fuel Oil Consumption (10 000 tons)	天然气消费量 (亿立方米) Natural Gas Consumption (100 millioncu.m)	电力消费量 (亿千瓦小时) Electricity Consumption (100 millionkwh)
	0.61	0.01	4.13		6.97	21.75
	0.02		0.04			0.13
	0.02		0.02			1.35
	0.01		0.02			0.29
	0.18		0.37	0.14	0.22	21.00
	0.30		4.24		0.04	18.10
	0.39	0.02	3.23			25.56
	0.05		1.13		0.03	6.99
	0.09		0.24		0.08	1.67
	0.10	0.01	0.17			0.25
	0.06		0.05		0.01	0.17
	0.03		0.06			0.13
	0.12		0.09			0.41
	0.02		0.11			6.60
						0.02
						0.02
						0.02
0.02	**1.05**	**0.01**	**2.85**		**2.71**	**59.64**
0.02	0.95	0.01	2.78		2.70	58.40
	0.01		0.01		0.01	0.10
	0.09		0.06			1.14
	3.40		**12.60**			**1.91**
	58.00	**28.30**	**153.73**		**3.00**	**8.09**
	9.60	**0.50**	**22.80**		**1.10**	**15.37**
	18.50	**0.90**	**26.20**		**0.50**	**17.79**
	9.20	**0.55**	**6.06**		**2.60**	**31.90**

15-8 能源生产弹性系数

Elasticity Ration of Energy Production

年 份 Year	能源生产比上年增长(%) Growth Rate of Energy Production Over Preceding Year(%)	电力生产比上年增长(%) Growth Rate of Electricity Production over Preceding Year(%)	新疆生产总值比上年增长(%) Growth Rate of Gross Domestic Product (GDP) over Preceding Year(%)	能源生产弹性系数 Elasticity Cofficient of Energy Production	电力生产弹性系数 Elasticity Ratio of Electricity Production
1980	7.8	3.6	7.2	1.08	0.50
1985	11.6	11.5	16.9	0.69	0.68
1990	5.8	10.8	11.7	0.50	0.92
1995	7.8	13.4	9.0	0.87	1.49
1996	11.5	12.9	6.4	1.80	2.02
1997	7.9	10.7	11.0	0.72	0.97
1998	-0.7	4.8	7.3		0.66
1999	3.0	7.3	7.1	0.42	1.03
2000	3.3	8.1	8.2	0.40	0.99
2001	5.5	8.0	8.1	0.68	0.99
2002	7.6	7.4	8.1	0.94	0.91
2003	8.1	10.5	10.8	0.75	0.97
2004	6.8	13.3	11.1	0.61	1.20
2005	14.9	16.6	10.9	1.37	1.52
2006	16.6	15.2	11.0	1.51	1.38

注：新疆生产总值按可比价格计算，下表同。

Note: The Gross Production Value is calculated at comparable prices and the same as in the following tables.

15-9 能源消费弹性系数

Elasticity Ration of Energy Consumption

年 份 Year	能源消费比上年增长(%) Growth Rate of Energy Consumption Over Preceding Year(%)	电力消费比上年增长(%) Growth Rate of Electricity Consumption over Preceding Year(%)	新疆生产总值比上年增长(%) Growth Rate of Gross Domestic Product (GDP) over Preceding Year(%)	能源消费弹性系数 Elasticity Ration of Energy Consumption	电力消费弹性系数 Elasticity Ration of Electricity Consumption
1980	4.5	3.6	7.2	0.63	0.50
1985	13.6	11.5	16.9	0.80	0.68
1990	9.3	10.8	11.7	0.79	0.92
1995	4.9	13.4	9.0	0.54	1.49
1996	11.4	12.9	6.4	1.78	2.02
1997	5.4	10.7	11.0	0.49	0.97
1998	2.2	4.8	7.3	0.30	0.66
1999	-2.0	7.3	7.1		1.03
2000	3.1	8.1	8.2	0.38	0.99
2001	5.4	8.0	8.1	0.67	0.99
2002	3.6	7.4	8.1	0.44	0.91
2003	12.2	10.5	10.8	1.13	0.97
2004	17.7	13.3	11.1	1.59	1.20
2005	15.1	16.6	10.9	1.39	1.52
2006	9.8	14.8	11.0	0.89	1.35

15-10 能源加工转换效率
Efficiency of Energy Conversion

单位：% (%)

年 份 Year	总效率 Total Efficiency	发 电 Electricity Generation	供 热 Heating	炼 焦 Coking	炼 油 Petroleum Refining
1980	73.9	21.2		72.0	96.9
1985	74.9	21.1		75.5	98.1
1990	73.9	20.9	69.4	85.5	98.0
1995	72.7	23.6	71.2	78.6	96.6
1996	71.0	24.3	57.0	79.5	94.5
1997	70.6	22.9	54.7	90.0	95.5
1998	71.9	23.6	58.8	94.8	95.9
1999	72.3	25.4	69.8	92.2	94.0
2000	73.6	26.6	75.0	89.4	94.7
2001	73.7	26.1	74.6	78.2	97.4
2002	73.6	26.8	73.5	83.4	96.8
2003	73.8	26.0	78.0	92.0	97.9
2004	70.2	25.9	70.3	78.8	96.2
2005	72.3	27.0	77.7	75.7	97.1
2006	74.8	27.8	76.7	85.0	97.6

15-11 平均每天各种能源消费量
Average Daily Energy Consumption by Type of Energy

能源品种	Variey of Energy	1990	1995	2000	2005	2006
总计(万吨标准煤)	**Total (10 000 tons of SCE)**	**5.41**	**7.60**	**9.09**	**15.09**	**16.57**
煤炭(万吨)	Coal (10 000 tons)	5.04	6.67	7.48	10.58	12.15
焦炭(万吨)	Coke (10 000 tons)	0.16	0.20	0.20	0.50	0.63
原油(万吨)	Crude Oil (10 000 tons)	1.33	1.99	2.94	4.46	4.97
燃料油(万吨)	Fuel Oil (10 000 tons)	0.25	0.32	0.16	0.50	0.05
汽油(万吨)	Gasoline (10 000 tons)	0.20	0.28	0.28	0.29	0.32
煤油(万吨)	Kerosene (10 000 tons)	0.01	0.04	0.06	0.07	0.08
柴油(万吨)	Diesel Oil (10 000 tons)	0.24	0.33	0.43	0.83	0.93
天然气(万立方米)	Natural Gas (10 000 cu.m)	137.53	314.52	642.19	1546.85	1781.92
电力(亿千瓦时)	Electricity (100 million kwh)	0.19	0.33	0.50	0.85	0.98

15-12 分品种生活能源年消费总量

Average Annual Energy Consumption for Households by Variety

年 份 Year	合 计（万吨标准煤） Total (10 000 tons of SCE)	煤 炭（万吨） Coal (10 000 tons)	煤 油（万吨） Kerosene (10 000 tons)	液化石油气（万吨） Liquefied Petroleum Gas (10 000 tons)	天然气（亿立方米） Natural Gas (100 million cu.m)	热 力（万百万千焦） Heat (10 billion kilo-joule)	电 力（亿千瓦小时） Electricity (100 million kwh)
1980	330.44	404.10					1.70
1985	355.65	421.72	0.71	3.00			2.38
1990	428.04	479.37	0.58	5.35		160.02	4.22
1995	499.84	527.00	0.50	8.94		177.29	10.11
1996	522.59	537.33	0.56	9.59		180.55	12.35
1997	594.82	549.00	0.50	8.66		1000.00	14.06
1998	617.55	570.00	0.65	9.82	0.05	1000.00	15.98
1999	609.22	580.00	0.75	10.10	0.11	864.00	16.83
2000	650.91	590.00	0.75	10.89	0.13	1611.81	17.60
2001	703.97	600.00	0.67	12.31	0.46	2209.66	19.50
2002	752.10	610.00	0.10	14.22	0.32	3112.58	19.20
2003	782.21	625.04		16.62	0.60	3191.14	20.37
2004	901.88	605.00		17.00	1.00	3363.45	24.26
2005	978.54	500.79	0.55	12.96	1.92	6219.00	27.10
2006	612.66	211.00	0.55	14.10	2.60	5008.00	31.90

注：表 15-12 和 15-13 中，除 2006 年，其余年份数据未按新口径进行调整。
Note: Figures in table15-12and 5-13 did not made adjustment at new coverage, except for figures in 2006.

15-13 每人年平均生活用能源

Annual Average Per Capital Energy Consumption of Households

年 份 Year	平均每人生活消费能源（公斤标准煤/人） Annual Per Capita Consumption for Household (kg of SCE/person)	煤 炭（公斤） Coal (kg)	电 力（千瓦小时） Electricity (kwh)	煤 油（公斤） Kerosene (kg)	液化石油气（公斤） Liquefied Petroleum Gas (kg)	天然气（立方米） Natural Gas (cu.m)
1980	258	315	13.25			
1985	261	310	17.49	0.52	2.20	
1990	268	313	27.60	0.38	3.50	
1995	301	317	65.60	0.30	5.33	
1996	299	318	73.10	0.33	5.67	
1997	330	331	81.80	0.29	5.04	
1998	353	326	91.45	0.37	5.61	0.03
1999	343	327	94.82	0.42	5.69	0.62
2000	353	320	95.33	0.41	5.90	0.70
2001	375	320	103.93	0.36	6.56	2.45
2002	395	320	100.78	0.05	7.46	1.68
2003	404	323	105.33		8.59	3.10
2004	459	308	123.58		8.66	5.09
2005	487	249	134.80	0.27	6.45	9.55
2006	302	104	157.13	0.27	6.95	12.81

15-14 各地、州、市规模以上工业能源消费量

Energy Consumption of Industry above Designated Size by Prefecture, Autonomous Prefecture and City

(2006 年)

能源品种	Item	合 计 Total	乌鲁木齐市 Urumqi City	克拉玛依市 Karamay City	吐鲁番地区 Turpan Administrative Offices
原煤(吨)	Coal (ton)	33677192	11981568	1922962	658521
洗精煤(吨)	Washed Coal(ton)	2456136	1826839		
其他洗煤(吨)	Other Washed Coal (ton)	95876	95876		
焦炭(吨)	Coke (ton)	2251815	1392033		171801
焦炉煤气(万立方米)	Coke Oven Gas (10 000 cu.m)	29440	22645		
高炉煤气(万立方米)	High Oven Gas (10 000 cu.m)	42409	42409		
天然气(万立方米)	Natural Gas (10 000 cu.m)	514502	81720	231480	52295
原油(吨)	Coal (ton)	17101174	5105416	8947793	156814
汽油(吨)	Gasoline (ton)	41708	10556	10595	681
煤油(吨)	Kerosene (ton)	80	36		
柴油(吨)	Diesel Oil (ton)	248752	39715	109755	12260
燃料油(吨)	Fuel Oil (ton)	375243	366746	5846	20
液化石油气(吨)	Liquefied Petroleum Gas (ton)	160071	65520	9039	19147
炼厂干气(吨)	Refinary Dry Gas (ton)	479765	178877	204160	
其他石油制品(吨)	Other Oil Product (ton)	137072	64424		44507
热力(百万千焦)	Heat (million KJ)	47440765	10577371	12050236	
电力(万千瓦时)	Electricity (10 000 kwh)	2067838	710845	252367	65039
其他燃料(吨标准煤)	Other (tons of SCE)	48217	17858		3915
能源合计(吨标准煤)	Energy Total (tons of SCE)	66361788	22420825	18540429	1755033

能源品种	Item	哈密地区 Hami [kumul] Administrative Offices	昌吉回族自治州 Changji Hui Autonomous Prefecture	博尔塔拉蒙古自治州 Bortala Mongol Autonomous Prefecture	伊犁州直属县(市) Counties (Cities) Direct Under Ili Prefecture
原煤(吨)	Coal (ton)	1901468	4955540	272671	2587097
洗精煤(吨)	Washed Coal (ton)				304075
其他洗煤(吨)	Other Washed Coal (ton)				
焦炭(吨)	Coke (ton)	64191	13676	1733	276968
焦炉煤气(万立方米)	Coke Oven Gas (10 000 cu.m)				6795
高炉煤气(万立方米)	High Oven Gas (10 000 cu.m)				
天然气(万立方米)	Natural Gas (10 000 cu.m)		1055		36
原油(吨)	Coal (ton)		25764		
汽油(吨)	Gasoline (ton)	1655	5547	275	1755
煤油(吨)	Kerosene (ton)		20		13
柴油(吨)	Diesel Oil (ton)	12927	13880	591	5510
燃料油(吨)	Fuel Oil (ton)		38		
液化石油气(吨)	Liquefied Petroleum Gas (ton)		65309		
炼厂干气(吨)	Refinary Dry Gas (ton)				
其他石油制品(吨)	Other Oil Product (ton)		901		16461
热力(百万千焦)	Heat (million KJ)		4103778	159751	207449
电力(万千瓦时)	Electricity (10 000 kwh)	75678	196575	10597	101614
其他燃料(吨标准煤)	Other (tons of SCE)		16541		
能源合计(吨标准煤)	Energy Total (tons of SCE)	1555778	4182448	226588	2545938

注：1.本表为全部国有及年产品销售收入 500 万元以上的非国有工业企业；2.各地区数含兵团工业在内。

Note: a) This table is for all the state-owned and non-state owned enterprises with sales revenue of over 5 million yuan;
b) Figures in different prefectures include XPCG enterprises.

15-14 续表 Continued

名　称	Variey of Energy	塔城地区 Tacheng [Tarbagatai] Administrative Office	阿勒泰地区 Altay Administrative Offices	巴音郭楞蒙古自治州 Bayangol Mongol Autonomous Prefecture	阿克苏地区 Aksu Administrative Offices
原煤(吨)	Coal (ton)	1258852	314837	1468654	2359540
洗精煤(吨)	Washed Coal (ton)			69140	256082
其他洗煤(吨)	Other Washed Coal (ton)				
焦炭(吨)	Coke (ton)	13506	24348	113311	7483
焦炉煤气(万立方米)	Coke Oven Gas (10 000 cu.m)				
高炉煤气(万立方米)	High Oven Gas (10 000 cu.m)				
天然气(万立方米)	Natural Gas (10 000 cu.m)			95715	49848
原油(吨)	Coal (ton)			1033507	1831880
汽油(吨)	Gasoline (ton)	1518	1553	3841	1440
煤油(吨)	Kerosene (ton)			11	
柴油(吨)	Diesel Oil (ton)	3234	3819	30435	7912
燃料油(吨)	Fuel Oil (ton)			11	1598
液化石油气(吨)	Liquefied Petroleum Gas (ton)	6		4	1046
炼厂干气(吨)	Refinary Dry Gas (ton)			29559	67169
其他石油制品(吨)	Other Oil Product (ton)		41	9413	1325
热力(百万千焦)	Heat (million KJ)	1083707		12909453	1821768
电力(万千瓦时)	Electricity (10 000 kwh)	66675	43080	166294	87784
其他燃料(吨标准煤)	Other (tons of SCE)				
能源合计(吨标准煤)	Energy Total (tons of SCE)	1038171	309386	4738515	5524179

名　称	Variey of Energy	克孜勒苏柯尔克孜自治州 Kizilsu Kirgiz Autonomous Prefecture	喀什地区 Kashgar [kaxgar] Administrative Offices	和田地区 Hotan Administrative Offices	石河子市 Shihezi City
原煤(吨)	Coal (ton)	9033	759737	169395	2726173
洗精煤(吨)	Washed Coal (ton)				
其他洗煤(吨)	Other Washed Coal (ton)				
焦炭(吨)	Coke (ton)		2657		170108
焦炉煤气(万立方米)	Coke Oven Gas (10 000 cu.m)				
高炉煤气(万立方米)	High Oven Gas (10 000 cu.m)				
天然气(万立方米)	Natural Gas (10 000 cu.m)		934	31	1388
原油(吨)	Coal (ton)				
汽油(吨)	Gasoline (ton)	188	303	471	1039
煤油(吨)	Kerosene (ton)				
柴油(吨)	Diesel Oil (ton)	870	971	2378	2947
燃料油(吨)	Fuel Oil (ton)				984
液化石油气(吨)	Liquefied Petroleum Gas (ton)				
炼厂干气(吨)	Refinary Dry Gas (ton)				
其他石油制品(吨)	Other Oil Product (ton)				
热力(百万千焦)	Heat (million KJ)				4475564
电力(万千瓦时)	Electricity (10 000 kwh)	1324	34153	9032	236612
其他燃料(吨标准煤)	Other (tons of SCE)		2845	7058	
能源合计(吨标准煤)	Energy Total (tons of SCE)	9624	604826	140470	2510521

主要统计指标解释

能源生产总量 指一定时期内一次能源生产量的总和，是观察能源生产水平、规模、构成和发展速度的总量指标。一次能源生产量包括原煤、原油、天然气、水电、核能及其他动力能(如风能、地热能等)发电量，不包括低热值燃料生产量、生物质能、太阳能等的利用和由一次能源加工转换而成的二次能源产量。

能源消费总量 指一定时期内物质生产部门、非物质生产部门和生活消费的各种能源的总和，是观察能源消费水平、构成和增长速度的总量指标。能源消费总量包括原煤和原油及其制品、天然气、电力，不包括低热值燃料、生物质能和太阳能等的利用。能源消费总量分为终端能源消费量、能源加工转换损失量和损失量三部分。

(1)终端能源消费量：指一定时期内生产和生活消费的各种能源在扣除了用于加工转换二次能源消费量和损失量以后的数量。

(2)能源加工转换损失量：指一定时期内投入加工转换的各种能源数量之和与产出各种能源产品之和的差额，是观察能源在加工转换过程中损失量变化的指标。

(3)能源损失量：指一定时期内能源在输送、分配、储存过程中发生的损失和由客观原因造成的各种损失量，不包括各种气体能源放空、放散量。

能源生产弹性系数 是研究能源生产增长速度与国民经济增长速度之间关系的指标。计算公式为：

能源生产弹性系数＝能源生产总量年平均增长速度／国民经济年平均增长速度

国民经济年平均增长速度，可根据不同的目的或需要，用国民生产总值、国内生产总值等指标来计算，本年鉴是采用国内生产总值指标计算的。

电力生产弹性系数 是研究电力生产增长速度与国民经济增长速度之间关系的指标。一般来说，电力的发展应当快于国民经济的发展，也就是说电力应超前发展。计算公式为：

电力生产弹性系数＝电力生产量年平均增长速度／国民经济年平均增长速度

能源消费弹性系数 是反映能源消费增长速度与国民经济增长速度之间比例关系的指标。计算公式为：

能源消费弹性系数＝能源消费量年平均增长速度／国民经济年平均增长速度

电力消费弹性系数 反映电力消费增长速度与国民经济增长速度之间比例关系的指标。计算公式为：

电力消费弹性系数＝电力消费量年平均增长速度／国民经济年平均增长速度

能源加工转换效率 指一定时期内能源经过加工、转换后，产出的各种能源产品的数量与同期内投入加工转换的各种能源数量的比率。它是观察能源加工转换装置和生产工艺先进与落后、管理水平高低等的重要指标。计算公式为：

能源加工转换效率＝能源加工、转换产出量／能源加工、转换投入量×100%

单位国内生产总值能耗 指一定时期内，一个国家或地区每生产一个单位的国内生产总值所消耗的能源。计算公式为：

单位国内生产总值能耗=能源消费总量/国内生产总值

单位国内生产总值电耗 指一定时期内，一个国家或地区每生产一个单位的国内生产总值所消耗的电力。计算公式为：

单位国内生产总值电耗=全社会用电量/国内生产总值

单位工业增加值能耗 指一定时期内，一个国家或地区每生产一个单位的工业增加值所消耗的能源。计算公式为：

单位工业增加值能耗=工业能源消费量/工业增加值

单位地区生产总值能耗 指一定时期内，一个国家或地区每生产一个单位的地区生产总值所消耗的能源。计算公式为：

单位地区生产总值能耗=能源消费总量/地区生产总值

单位地区生产总值电耗 指一定时期内，一个国家或地区每生产一个单位的地区生产总值所消耗的电力。计算公式为：

单位地区生产总值能耗=全社会用电量/地区生产总值

单位工业增加值能耗 指一定时期内，一个国家或地区每生产一个单位的工业增加值所消耗的能源。计算公式为：

单位工业增加值能耗=工业能源消费量/工业增加值

Explanatory Notes on Main Statistical Indicators

Total Energy Production refers to the total production of primary energy by all energy producing enterprises in the region in a given period of time. It is a comprehensive indicator to show the capacity, scale, composition and development of energy production of the region. The production of primary energy includes that of coal, crude oil, natural gas, hydropower and electricity generated by nuclear energy and other means such as wind power and geothermal power. However, it excludes the production of fuels of low calorific value, bio-energy, solar energy and the secondary energy converted from the primary energy.

Total Domestic Energy Consumption refers to the total consumption of energy of various kinds by material production sectors, non material production sectors and households in the region in a given period of time. It is a comprehensive indicator to show the scale, composition and development of energy consumption. The total energy consumption includes that of coal, crude oil and their products, natural gas and electricity. However it excludes the consumption of fuel of low calorific value, bio-energy and solar energy. Total domestic energy consumption can be divided into three parts:

(1) Final Energy Consumption: It refers to the total energy consumption by material production sectors, non material production sectors and households in the region (region) in a given period of time, but excludes the consumption in conversion of the primary energy into the secondary energy and the loss in the process of energy conversion.

(2) Loss During the Process of Energy Conversion: It refers to the total input of various kinds of energy for conversion, minus the total output of various kinds of energy in the region in a given period of time. It is an indicator to show the loss that occurs during the process of energy conversion.

(3) Energy Loss: It refers to the total of the loss of energy during the course of energy transport, distribution and storage and the loss caused by any objective reason in a given period of time. The loss of various kinds of gas due to gas discharges and stocktaking is excluded.

Elasticity Ratio of Energy Production is an indicator to show the relationship between the growth rate of energy production and the growth rate of the national economy. The formula is:

Elasticity Ratio of Energy Production=Average Annual Growth Rate of Energy Production/Average Annual Growth Rate of National Economy

The average annual growthrate of the national economy can be shown by the gross national product, gross domestic product and other indicators, depending upon the purposes or needs. The gross domestic product is used in calculation of the ratio in this chapter.

Elasticity Ratio of Electricity Production is an indicator to show the relationship between the growth rate of electricity production and the growth rate of the national economy. Generally speaking, the growth rate of electricity production should be higher than that of the national economy.

Its formula is:

Elasticity Ratio of Electricity Production=Average Annual Growth Rate of Electricity Production/Average Annual Growth Rate of National Economy

Elasticity Ratio of Energy Consumption is an indicator to show the relationship between the growth rate of energy consumption and the growth rate of the national economy. The formula is:

Elasticity Ratio of Energy Consumption=Average Annual Growth Rate of Energy Consumption/Average Annual Growth Rate of National Economy

Elasticity Ratio of Electricity Consumption is an indicator to show the relationship between the growth rate of electricity consumption and the growth rate of the national economy. The formula is:

Elasticity Ratio of Electricity Consumption=Average Annual Growth Rate of Electricity/Average Annual Growth Rate of National Economy

Efficiency of Energy Processing and Conversion refers to the ratio of the total output of energy products of various kinds after processing and conversion and the total input of energy of various kinds for processing and conversion in the same reference period. It is an important indicator to show the current conditions of energy processing and conversion equipment, production technique and management. The formula is:

Efficiency of Energy Processing & Conversion=Output of Energy After Processing & Conversion/Input of Energy for Processing & Conversion×100%

Energy Consumption per Unit of GDP refers to the energy consumption per unit of gross domestic production in a country or the gross region production in a region in the same reference period. The formula is:

Energy Consumption per Unit of GDP=Total Energy Consumption/Gross Domestic Production

Electricity Consumption per Unit of GDP refers to the electricity consumption per unit of gross domestic production in a country or the gross region production in a region in the same reference period. The formula is:

Electricity Consumption per Unit of GDP=Total Electricity Consumption/Gross Domestic Production

Electricity Consumption per Unit of Industrial Value-added refers to the energy consumption per unit of industrial value-added in a country or region in the same reference period. The formula is:

Energy Consumption per Unit of Industrial Value-added=Total Energy Consumption/Industrial Value-added

Energy Consumption per Unit of GDP refers to the energy consumption per unit of gross domestic production in a country or the gross region production in the same reference period. The formula is:

Energy Consumption per Unit of GDP=Total Energy Consumption/Gross Domestic Production

Electricity Consumption per Unit of GDP refers to the electricity consumption per unit of gross domestic production in a country or the gross region production in the same reference period. The formula is:

Electricity Consumption per Unit of GDP=Total Electricity Consumption/Gross Domestic Production

Energy Consumption per Unit of Industrial Value-added refers to the energy consumption per unit of industrial value-added in a country or region in the same reference period. The formula is:

Electricity Consumption per Unit of Industrial Value-added=Total Energy Consumption/Industrial Value-added

第十六篇
对外经济贸易和旅游

CHAPTER 16
Foreign Trade & Economic Cooperation and Tourism

简要说明
Brief Introduction

本篇资料的主要内容及来源

本篇内容包括海关进出口额、主要进出口商品数量及金额、对外承包工程和劳务合作、利用外资、外国和港澳台地区在新疆直接投资情况、新疆在国外和港澳台地区直接投资、经济技术开发(合作)主要情况、旅游情况等。

海关进出口额、利用外资、旅游资料由新疆维吾尔自治区统计局贸易外经处分别根据乌鲁木齐海关、新疆维吾尔自治区对外经济贸易厅、新疆维吾尔自治区工商管理局和新疆维吾尔自治区旅游局的有关资料加工整理。

Main Content and Source of Data

Data in this chapter cover mainly total imports and exports at customs, main imports and exports in volume and value, contracted projects and labor services cooperation, utilization of foreign capital, basic condition of direct investment in Xinjiang by foreign countries and compatriots from Hong Kong, Macao and Taiwan, main condition of economic and technological development and cooperation zones, condition of tourism.

Data on imports and exports, utilization of foreign capitals, tourism are collected and processed by the Department of Trade Statistics, the Xinjiang Bureau of Statistics in accordance with the data from custom of Urumqi, Foreign Economic and Trade Commission of Xinjiang,Xinjiang Administration for Industry and Commerce, Tourist Bureau of Xingjiang.

16-1 进出口贸易总额

Total Value of Imports and Exports

单位：万美元 (USD 10 000)

年份 Year	地区 Region	进出口总额 Total Imports and Exports	出口额 Exports	#一般贸易 Ordinary Trades	#边境贸易 Border Trades	进口额 Imports	#一般贸易 Ordinary Trades	#边境贸易 Border Trades
	1978	2346	937			1409		
	1985	29197	18020			11177		
	1990	41025	33530		3506	7495		3416
	1991	45933	36317		5025	9616		4931
	1992	75039	45386		16474	29653		15555
	1993	92210	49509		28906	42701		28806
	1994	104053	57612	29106	23932	46441	16036	27335
	1995	142798	76880	44550	27562	65918	17640	41888
	1996	140367	54975	30281	18647	85392	25982	54484
	1997	144667	66547	36061	22962	78120	24061	52031
	1998	153214	80789	32268	37599	72425	20972	49354
	1999	176534	102743	37120	57329	73791	25723	44976
	2000	226399	120408	55060	58020	105991	28020	73950
	2001	177148	66849	29523	18418	110299	24895	79661
	2002	269186	130849	54404	47218	138337	26028	107152
	2003	477198	254221	71115	160411	222977	72510	143504
	2004	563563	304658	50194	223782	258905	101540	147058
	2005	794189	504024	88036	386237	290165	108894	167648
	2006	910327	713923	158842	522038	196404	61915	126429
	2007	1371623	1150311	294000	806885	221312	75418	134778
乌鲁木齐市	Urumqi City	377467	345127			32340		
克拉玛依市	Karamay City	11664	5544			6120		
石河子市	Shihezi City	28083	22642			5441		
吐鲁番地区	Turpan Administrative Offices	554	386			168		
哈密地区	Hami [Kumul] Administrative Offices	5993	4083			1910		
昌吉回族自治州	Changji Hui Autonomous Prefecture	240269	229998			10271		
伊犁哈萨克自治州	Ili Kazak Autonomous Prefecture	345634	312275			33359		
伊犁州直属县(市)	Counties (Cities) Direct Under Ili Prefecture	259253	233427			25826		
塔城地区	Tacheng [Tarbagatai] Administrative Offices	81019	74927			6092		
阿勒泰地区	Altay Administrative Offices	5362	3921			1441		
博尔塔拉蒙古自治州	Bortala Mongol Autonomous Prefecture	171173	50290			120883		
巴音郭楞蒙古自治州	Bayangol Mongol Autonomous Prefecture	24446	23766			680		
阿克苏地区	Aksu Administrative Offices	2651	2041			610		
克孜勒苏柯尔克孜自治州	Kizilsu Kirgiz Autonomous Prefecture	31560	23705			7855		
喀什地区	Kashgar [Kaxgar] Administrative Offices	131564	129932			1632		
和田地区	Hotan Administrative Offices	565	522			43		

注：1.1998 年以前的资料由外经贸厅提供，1998 年以后资料由乌鲁木齐海关提供(16-2、16-3、16-4 表相同)。
2.补充了 1990—1993 年的边境贸易进口、出口数。由于 1990—1993 年新疆进出口只按大贸和边贸分类，故没有一般贸易数。

Note: a) The data prior to 1998 is offered by the Bureau of Foreign Economic and Trades , data after 1998 is offered by Urumqi Customs House (The same in the 16-2, 16-3, 16-4 tables). b) The figures of frontier-Trades import and export from 1990 to 1993 have been supplanted. As Xinjiang import and export Trades were classified by international Trades and frontier Trades during that period, no general Trades figures are available.

16-2 主要进出口商品数量和金额
Main Imports and Exports in Volume and Value

项　　目	Item	2007		2007年比2006年增减% Increase Rate in 2007 Over 2006 Decrease(%)	
		数　量 Volume	金　额 (万美元) Value (USD 10 000)	数　量 Volume	金　额 Value
主要出口商品	**Main Export Commodities**				
棉花(原棉)(吨)	Cotton，Raw Cotton (ton)	2390	519	1.0 倍	92.3
棉纱(吨)	Cotton Yarn (ton)	3285	1495	-10.0	-2.1
棉坯布(千米)	Cotton Clothing (thousand m)	176	31	-61.7	-39.4
肠衣(吨)	Casings (ton)	381	966	-11.0	-5.2
番茄酱(万吨)	Tomato jam (10 000 tons)	53	31372	39.1	57.7
电视机(万台)	TV sets (10 000 sets)	13	1557	-69.0	-32.6
地毯(百平方米)	Carpets (100 sp.m)	29742	889	-12.7	32.1
药材(吨)	Medical Materials (ton)	761	156	-57.3	-42.0
鞋　类	Shoes		124457		30.2
主要进口商品	**Main Import Commodities**				
羊毛及条(吨)	Wool and Wool Tops (ton)	6895	995	70.3	64.6
钢材(万吨)	Rolled Steel (10 000 tons)	14	8083	-26.3	1.6
纸及纸板(未切成型的)(吨)	Paper and Paperboard in Rolls (ton)	458	143	1.4 倍	2.5 倍
原木(万立方米)	Logs (10 000 cu.m)	10	1075	25.0	41.5
医疗仪器及器械	Medical Equipment and Apparatus		1869		-8.5
肥料(万吨)	Fertilizers (10 000 tons)	27	6440	-6.9	11.3
原油(万吨)	Crude Oil (10 000 tons)	173	87156	64.8	79.2
成品油(万吨)	Oil Product (10 000 tons)	11	3787	-15.4	-27.5
牛皮革及马皮革(吨)	Cattle and Horse Leather (ton)	17960	2690	-25.3	-25.5

16-3 新疆同各国(地区)海关进出口总额

Value of Xinjiang's Imports and Exports with Related Countries and Territories (Customs Statistics)

单位：万美元 (USD 10 000)

国别（地区）	Country (Territory)	2006			2007		
		进出口总额 Total Value Imports and Exports	出口额 Exports	进口额 Imports	进出口总额 Total Value Imports and Exports	出口额 Exports	进口额 Imports
总 计	**Total**	**910327**	**713923**	**196404**	**1371623**	**1150311**	**221312**
亚 洲	**Asia**	**814356**	**647040**	**167316**	**1192887**	**1022404**	**170483**
阿富汗	Afghanistan	1075	1075		2216	2216	
巴 林	Bahrain	107	107		74	74	
孟加拉国	Bangladesh	23	23		47	47	
缅 甸	Myanmar	10	10		143	143	
柬埔寨	Cambodia	157	37	120	37	2	35
塞浦路斯	Cyprus				1	1	
中国香港	Hong Kong, China	4684	4583	101	3949	3855	94
印 度	India	2257	1928	329	2599	1539	1060
印度尼西亚	Indonesia	3384	3275	109	4618	4028	590
伊 朗	Iran	305	276	29	3388	664	2724
伊拉克	Iraq	27	27		6	6	
以色列	Israel	642	121	521	677	210	467
日 本	Japan	8843	4332	4511	11119	6903	4216
约 旦	Jordan	80	80		87	86	1
科威特	Kuwait	77	77		73	73	
黎巴嫩	Lebanon	61	61		176	176	
马来西亚	Malaysia	2448	2259	189	2654	2449	205
蒙 古	Mongolia	1338	1090	248	1890	1708	182
尼泊尔	Nepal	19	19		73	73	
阿 曼	Aman	397	397		384	384	
巴基斯坦	Pakistan	34330	34185	145	41409	41056	353
巴勒斯坦	Palestine	14	14		3	3	
菲律宾	The Philippines	650	534	116	1359	1114	245
卡塔尔	Qatar	71	71		38	38	
沙特阿拉伯	Saudi Arbia	1198	1166	32	2403	2388	15
新加坡	Singapore	1506	239	1267	1877	1436	441
韩 国	Republic of Korea	4780	1511	3269	5002	2077	2925
斯里兰卡	Sri Lanka	76	64	12	141	136	5
叙利亚	Syria	117	117		151	151	
泰 国	Thailand	885	759	126	1296	1093	203
土耳其	Turkey	518	183	335	1154	712	442
阿拉伯联合酋长国	Unitd Arab Emirates	2168	2130	38	2857	2853	4
也门共和国	Arab Republic of Yemen	539	539		696	696	
越 南	Viet Nam	102	78	24	522	480	42
中华人民共和国	China	364		364	434		434
中国台湾	Taiwan, China	1134	767	367	1709	1400	309
哈萨克斯坦	Kazakhstan	501472	370757	130715	697377	562463	134914
吉尔吉斯斯坦	Kirghizia	185729	174737	10992	325021	314099	10922
塔吉克斯坦	Tadzhikistan	21810	21217	593	37717	37479	238
土库曼斯坦	Turkmenistan	4328	4193	135	3956	3734	222
乌兹别克斯坦	Uzbekistan	26631	14002	12629	33554	24359	9195
非 洲	**Africa**	**6375**	**6336**	**39**	**10601**	**9700**	**901**
阿尔及利亚	Algeria	813	813		1018	1018	
安哥拉	Angola	9	8	1	7	7	
贝 宁	Benin	12	12		49	49	
喀麦隆	Cameroon	2	2		58	58	
刚 果	Congo	27	27		34	34	
吉布提	Djibouti	40	40		31	31	
埃 及	Egypt	488	486	2	1734	1732	2
埃塞俄比亚	Ethiopia	511	511		21	21	

16-3 续表 1 Continued

单位：万美元 (USD 10 000)

国 别 (地 区)	Country (Territory)	2006			2007		
		进出口总额 Total Value Imports and Exports	出口额 Exports	进口额 Imports	进出口总额 Total Value Imports and Exports	出口额 Exports	进口额 Imports
加 纳	Gambia	86	86		388	388	
冈比亚	Gambia	61	61		90	90	
加 蓬	Gabon	12	12		18	18	
几内亚	Guinea	3	3		2	2	
可特迪瓦共和国	Cote d'ivoir	19	19		2	2	
肯尼亚	Kenya	23	23		71	71	
利比里亚	Liberia				14	14	
利比亚	Libya	8	8		52	52	
马达加斯加	Madagascar				40	40	
毛里塔尼亚	Mauritania	1	1		9	9	
毛里求斯	Mauritius	412	412		259	259	
摩洛哥	Morocco	76	76		39	39	
莫桑比克	Mozambique	15	15		53	53	
纳米比亚	Mozanmbique	72	72		143	143	
尼日利亚	Nigeria	292	292		890	889	1
留尼汪	Reunion				1	1	
塞内加尔	Senegal	50	50		298	298	
塞拉利昂	SierraLeone				8	8	
南 非	South Africa	969	960	9	2323	2322	1
苏 丹	Sudan	2061	2061		1435	1435	
坦桑尼亚	Tanzania	97	97		130	130	
多 哥	Togo	83	83		380	380	
突尼斯	Tunisia				79	79	
乌干达	Uganda	1	1		5	5	
赞比亚	Zambia				897		897
津巴布韦	Zimbabwe	2	2		23	23	
欧 洲	**Europe**	**64681**	**46834**	**17847**	**137020**	**100596**	**36424**
比利时	Belgium	425	333	92	885	626	259
丹 麦	Denmark	118	20	98	741	46	695
英 国	United Kingdom	1987	1151	836	2915	1673	1242
德 国	Federal Republic of Germany	4908	2016	2892	10470	3034	7436
法 国	France	1720	131	1589	2246	616	1630
爱尔兰	Ireland	106	58	48	178	107	71
意大利	Italy	5248	2559	2689	12395	5345	7050
荷 兰	Netherlands	1160	819	341	2827	2220	607
希 腊	Greece	31	31		107	107	
葡萄牙	Portugal	13	7	6	122	89	33
西班牙	Spain	1233	1145	88	1796	1696	100
奥地利	Austria	136	68	68	69	26	43
保加利亚	Bulgaria	15	15		122	122	
芬 兰	Finland	662	372	290	1375	291	1084
匈牙利	Hungary	61	44	17	6	6	
冰 岛	Iceland				1	1	
马尔他	Malta	54	54		90	90	
挪 威	Norway	256	216	40	385	307	78
波 兰	Poland	490	490		921	916	5
罗马尼亚	Romania	512	512		877	877	
瑞 典	Sweden	850	189	661	478	55	423
瑞 士	Switzerland	878	463	415	2956	423	2533
爱沙尼亚	Estonia	63	63		7	7	
拉脱维亚	Latvia	50	50		73	70	3
立陶宛	Lithuania	78	78		240	240	

16-3 续表 2 Continued

单位：万美元 (USD 10 000)

国别(地区)	Country (Territory)	2006 进出口总额 Total Value Imports and Exports	2006 出口额 Exports	2006 进口额 Imports	2007 进出口总额 Total Value Imports and Exports	2007 出口额 Exports	2007 进口额 Imports
格鲁吉亚	Georgia	163	159	4	98	76	22
亚美尼亚	Argentina	3	3		1	1	
阿塞拜疆	Azerbajan	24899	24870	29	32129	32077	52
白俄罗斯	Belorussia	93	15	78	190	33	157
俄罗斯	Russia	16926	9387	7539	60160	47308	12852
乌克兰	Ukraine	1105	1086	19	1629	1600	29
南斯拉夫联盟	Yugoslavia	223	223		13	13	
斯洛文尼亚	Slovenia	55	55		39	39	
克罗地亚	Croatia	13	13		72	72	
捷　克	Czecho	145	137	8	293	273	20
马其顿	Macedonia				10	10	
塞尔维亚	Serbia				97	97	
黑山	Montenegro				7	7	
拉丁美洲	**Latin America**	**2577**	**2320**	**257**	**3452**	**3280**	**172**
阿根廷	Argentina	242	119	123	649	548	101
巴哈马	Bahamas	8	8		7	7	
巴巴多斯	Barbados	1	1		1	1	
巴　西	Brazil	133	133		650	620	30
智　利	Chile	88	88		211	211	
哥伦比亚	Colombia	5	5		135	135	
多米尼克	Dominica				3	3	
哥斯达黎加	Costarica	138	138		253	253	
古　巴	Cuba	38	38		13	13	
多米尼加共和国	Dominica Rep.	306	306		10	10	
厄瓜多尔	Ecuador	34	34		70	70	
格林纳达	Granada	3	3		1	1	
洪都拉斯	Honduras	32	32		13	13	
危地马拉	Guatemala	13	13		89	89	
海　地	Hayti	35	35		158	158	
牙买加	Jamaica	27	27		76	76	
墨西哥	Mexico	268	256	12	234	194	40
尼加拉瓜	Nicaragua	3	3		3	3	
巴拿马	Panama	131	131		334	334	
巴拉圭	Paraguay	42	42		84	84	
秘　鲁	Peru	159	159		163	162	
波多黎各	Puerto Rico	233	233		167	167	
圣卢西亚	Saint Lucia				1	1	
萨尔瓦多	El. Salvador	31	31		4	4	
苏里南	Surinam				3	3	
特立尼达和多巴哥	Trinidada and Tobago	9	9		28	28	
乌拉圭	Uruguay	104	104		26	26	
委内瑞拉	Venezuela	41	17	24	65	65	
拉美其他国家(地区)	Other countries(regions) in Latin America				1	1	
北美洲	**North America**	**20154**	**10673**	**9481**	**24928**	**13221**	**11707**
加拿大	Canada	1017	613	404	1330	813	517
美　国	United States	19137	10060	9077	23598	12408	11190
大洋洲	**Oceania**	**2184**	**720**	**1464**	**2735**	**1110**	**1625**
澳大利亚	Australia	1544	497	1047	2035	877	1158
斐　济	Fiji	16	16		11	11	
新喀里多尼亚	New Caledonia	7	7		17	17	
新西兰	New Zealand	612	195	417	628	195	433
巴布亚新几内亚	Papua New Guinea	5	5		44	10	34

16-4 按贸易方式和登记注册类型分的海关进出口额

Total Imports and Exports by Trades Mode and Registration (Customs Statiatics)

单位：万美元 (USD10 000)

项 目	Item	2006			2007		
		进出口总额 Total Imports and Exports	出口额 Exports	进口额 Imports	进出口总额 Total Imports and Exports	出口额 Exports	进口额 Imports
总 计	**Total**	**910327**	**713923**	**196404**	**1371623**	**1150311**	**221312**
按贸易方式分	**By Trades Mode**						
一般贸易	Ordinary Trades	220757	158842	61915	369418	294000	75418
加工贸易	Processing Trades	31773	27044	4729	39565	36670	2895
边境小额贸易	Petty-volume Border Trades	648467	522038	126429	941663	806885	134778
其它贸易	Other Trades	9330	5999	3331	20977	12756	8221
按登记注册类型分	**By Registration Status**						
国有经济	State-owned Units	337642	209667	127975	426485	261412	165073
集体经济	Collective-owned Units	76359	58485	17874	37389	33786	3603
私营经济	Private-owned Units	477959	431508	46451	879596	833495	46101
三资企业	Enterprises with Hong kong,Macao, Taiwan and Foreign Funds	18242	14260	3982	28119	21600	6519
其它经济	Other Types of Ownership	125	3	122	34	18	16

16-5 人民币对主要外币年平均汇价(中间价)

Average Exchange Rate of RMB Yuan Against Main Convertible Currences (Medium Rate)

单位：人民币元 (RMB yuan)

年 份 Year	100 美元 100 US Dollars	100 日元 100 JapaneseYen	100 港元 100 Hong Kong Dollars	100 欧元 100 Euros
1985	293.66	1.25	37.57	
1990	478.32	3.32	61.39	
1995	835.10	8.92	107.96	
1996	831.42	7.64	107.51	
1997	828.98	6.86	107.09	
1998	827.91	6.35	106.88	
1999	827.83	7.29	106.66	
2000	827.84	7.69	106.18	
2001	827.70	6.81	106.08	
2002	827.70	6.62	106.07	800.58
2003	827.70	7.15	106.24	936.13
2004	827.68	7.66	106.23	1029.00
2005	819.17	7.45	105.30	1019.53
2006	797.18	6.86	102.62	1001.90
2007	760.40	6.46	97.46	1041.75

16-6 对外承包工程和劳务合作

Contracted Projects in Foreign Countries or Territories

项　　目	Item	2006	2007
承包工程	**Contracted Projects**		
新签合同数(个)	Number of Newly Signed Contracts (unit)		113
新签合同金额(万美元)	Newly Signed Contracted Value (USD 10 000)	42233	52830
实际营业额(万美元)	Actual Business Volume (USD 10 000)	10840	36639

16-7 外商直接投资

Foreign Direct Investments

单位：个、万美元　　(unit, USD 10 000)

指　　标	Item	2006			2007		
		项　目 Number of Projects	合同金额 Contract Value	实际使用金额 Investment Actually Utilized	项　目 Number of Projects	合同金额 Contract Value	实际使用金额 Investment Actually Utilized
总　　计	**Total**	**99**	**36439**	**10366**	**91**	**45679**	**12484**
独资经营企业	Foreign Investment Enterprises	51	9924	2340	53	24617	8497
合资经营企业	Joint Ventures Enterprises	33	12334	6907	30	19826	3000
合作经营企业	Cooperative Operation Enterprises	13	12812	1034	7	1121	987
股份制企业	Share-holding Corporations Ltd.	2	1369	85	1	115	

16-8 外国和港澳台地区在华直接投资情况

Basic Conditions of Direct Investment in China by Foreign Countries and Compatriots From Hongkong，Macao and Taiwan

单位：个、万美元　　(2007 年)　　(unit, USD 10 000)

项　目	Item	签订协议情况 Signed Agreements		客商实际投资额	年末实有企业个数
		合同数 Number of Contracts	客商投资额 Actually Used Amount of Region Investment	Used Amount of Foreign Investment	Year-end Number of Enterprises
总　计	**Total**	**91**	**45679**	**12484**	**341**
按投资方式分	**Grouped by Investment Mode**				
独资经营企业	Foreign Investment Enterprises	53	24617	8497	131
合资经营企业	Joint Ventures Enterprises	30	19826	3000	174
合作经营企业	Cooperative Operation Enterprises	7	1121	987	29
外商投资股份制企业	Foreign Investment Share Enterprises	1	115		7
按国民经济行业分	**Grouped by Economic Sector**				
农、林、牧、渔业	Farming, Forestry, Animal Husbandry and Fishery	3	1024	3222	32
采掘业	Mining and Quarrying	14	18977	1222	14
制造业	Manufacturing	24	15935	2302	163
电力、煤气及水的生产和供应业	Production and Distribution of ElectiCity, Gas and Water			1114	9
建筑业	Construction				6
交通运输、仓储及邮电通讯业	Transport, Storage, Post and Telecommunications	2	-1529	1016	6
信息传输、计算机服务和软件业	Information Transmission, Computer Service and Software	1	6	25	1
批发和零售业	Wholesale and Retail Trades	38	7809	2534	38
住宿和餐饮业	Accommodation and Catering Service	4	1267	33	21
金融业	Finance				1
房地产业	Real Estate	2	2620	869	12
租赁和商务服务业	Social Services		6	60	6
科学研究、技术服务和地质勘察业	Scientific Research, Technical Service and Geological Survey	2	-471	71	13
水利、环境和公共设施管理业	Water Conservancy, Environment and Public Facility Management				2
居民服务和其他服务业	Community Service and Other Services	1	35	9	8
卫生、社会保障和社会福利业	Health Care, Sports and Social Welfare				
文化、体育和娱乐业	Education, Culture and Arts			7	5
其他行业	Others Sectors				4
按国别、地区分	**By Country or Territory**				
中国香港	Hong Kong，China	23	26115	4246	117
中国澳门	Macao，China		160		2
中国台湾	Taiwan，China	2	377	178	18
日　本	Japan	1	432	269	8
美　国	United States	3	3715	31	24
加拿大	Canada	1	-644	200	5
丹　麦	Denmark	1	353	53	1
意大利	Italy		-160	6	2
德　国	Federal Republic of Germany	1	3		4
土耳其	Turkey	2	11	65	5
英　国	United Kingdom	1	29	13	9
泰　国	Thailand				3
新加坡	Singapore	2	3497	150	12
澳大利亚	Australia	4	643	312	13
独联体	Commonwealth of Independent States	30	5848	2540	48
马来西亚	Malaysia			4	3
韩　国	Republic of Korea	2	173	26	8

16-9 各地、州、市利用外商直接投资情况

Conditons of Conditions of Foreign Direct Investment Used by Prefecture, Autonomous Prefecture and City

单位：个、万美元 (unit, USD 10 000)

地区	Region	2006			2007		
		签订合同数 Number of Contracts	合同金额 Contract Value	实际利用投资 Amount of Foreingn Capital Actually Used	签订合同数 Number of Contracts	合同金额 Contract Value	实际利用投资 Amount of Foreingn Capital Actually Used
总计	**Total**	**99**	**36439**	**10366**	**91**	**45679**	**12484**
乌鲁木齐市	Urumqi City	64	23698	7866	52	16707	10942
克拉玛依市	Karamay City				1	3	3
石河子市	Shihezi City	5	260	655	8	3897	232
吐鲁番地区	Turpan Administrative Offices	4	1812		1	150	38
哈密地区	Hami [Kumul] Administrative Offices	4	2005	364	2	7851	67
昌吉回族自治州	Changji Hui Autonomous Prefecture	7	2155	445	7	3979	638
伊犁哈萨克自治州	Ili Kazak Autonomous Prefecture	5	569	294	11	5412	189
伊犁州直属县(市)	Counties (Cities) Direct Under Ili Prefecture	1	-27	209	5	2244	174
塔城地区	Tacheng [Tarbagatai] Administrative Offices	4	596	85	2	386	15
阿勒泰地区	Altay Administrative Offices				4	2782	
博尔塔拉蒙古自治州	Bortala Mongol Autonomous Prefecture		-119		2	1508	
巴音郭楞蒙古自治州	BayangolMongol Autonomous Prefecture		9	616	4	-519	13
阿克苏地区	Aksu Administrative Offices	4	2198	70		3479	
克孜勒苏柯尔克孜自治州	Kizilsu Kirgiz Autonomous Prefecture	2	300		3	3661	73
喀什地区	Kashgar [Kaxgar] Administrative Offices	2	411	56		-425	289
和田地区	Hotan Administrative Offices	1	621			-24	

16-10 新疆在外国和港澳台地区直接投资

Direct Investment in Foreign Countries and Hong Kong，Macao and Talwan Made by Xinjiang Partner

单位：个、万美元 (unit, USD 10 000)

项目	Item	2006		2007	
		合同数 Number of Contracts	我方投资额 National Investment	合同数 Number of Contracts	我方投资额 National Investment
总计	**Total**	**17**	**1690**	**24**	**25267**
独资经营企业	Foreign Investment Enterprises	8	1254	12	25059
合资经营企业	Joint Ventures Enterprises	9	436	12	208

16-11 经济技术开发(合作)区主要情况

Main Conditions of Economic and Technological Development and Cooperation Zones

项　目	Item	2007
工业总产值(现价)(万元)	**Gross Industrial Output Value (10 000 yuan)**	**4572317**
#外商投资企业	Foreign Funded Enterprises	593571
工业企业销售收入(万元)	**Sales Revenue of Industral Enterprises (10 000 yuan)**	**4438979**
#外商投资企业	Foreign Funded Enterprises	609616
税收总额 (万元)	**Total Tax Rerenue (10 000 yuan)**	**424144**
#外商投资企业	Foreign Funded Enterprises	21870
工业企业	Industrial Enteprises	188486
财政收入(万元)	**Government Revenue (10 000 yuan)**	**292164**
出口总额(万美元)	**Total Exports (USD 10 000)**	**230625**
#外商投资企业	Foreign Funded Enterprises	23568
进口总额(万美元)	**Total Imports (USD 10 000)**	**32543**
#外商投资企业	Foreign Funded Enterprises	4703
外商投资企业利润总额(万元)	**Total Profit of Foreign Investment Enterprises (10 000 yuan)**	**46464**
#盈利额	Profit Volume	54016
外引内联	**Introduce i nvestment from abroad and establish lateral Cooperation**	
#外商投资企业	Foreign Funded Enterprises	
新签合同数(个)	New Signed Number of Countracts (unit)	19
新签投资总额(万美元)	New Signed Contracted Value (USD 10 000)	20826
#外资金额(万美元)	Foreign Capital (USD 10 000)	12824
实际利用外资(万美元)	Amount of Foreign Capital Actually Utilized (USD 10 000)	8741
#内联企业	Internal United Enterprise	
新签合同数(个)	Number of New signed Contracts (unit)	310
注册资本(万元)	Registered Capital (10 000 yuan)	469287
吸引外省资金(万元)	Absorb Fund from Other Provinces (10 000 yuan)	1030700
年末全部投产企业数(个)	**Total Number of Operated Enterprises Year-end (unit)**	**4759**
#外商投资企业	Foreign Funded Enterprises	106
内联企业	Internal United Enterprise	2297
从业人员平均人数(人)	**Average Numbers of Employees (person)**	**176675**
#外商投资企业	Foreign Funded Enterprises	11924
基本建设完成投资额(万元)	**Investment in Capital Construction Completed (10 000 yuan)**	**1203269**
#基础设施	Infrastructure	140682
#水	Watar	28286
电	Electricity	6828
路	Road	49351
通 信	Correspondence	1214
其 他	Other	15533
在固定资产投资完成额中	**The completetd sum of investment in Fixed Assets**	
房屋建设投资额 (万元)	Investment in Building Construction (10 000 yuan)	398490
房屋竣工面积(万平方米)	Space of Buildings Completed （10 000 sq.m）	136.70
出让土地面积(万平方米)	**Sold Land Areas (10 000 sq.m)**	**899.30**
吸取土地出让金(万元)	**Absorbing Money For Land Sold (10 000 yuan)**	**95250**

16-12 旅游事业发展情况
Development of Tourism

项目	Item	1995	2000	2007
旅行社总数（个）	**Total Number of Travel Agencies (unit)**	**79**	**130**	**426**
国际旅行社	International Travel Agencies	27	38	51
国内旅行社	Domestic Travel Agencies	52	92	375
入境旅游人数（人）	**Number of Overseas Visitor Arrivals (person)**	**203579**	**256082**	**438436**
外国人	Foreigners	185514	208374	402673
#日　本	Japan	43983	51974	25449
新加坡	Singapore	2048	5137	3753
美　国	United States	5595	10231	9907
英　国	United Kingdom	2422	3702	3129
法　国	France	3062	5218	7819
德　国	Federal Republic of Germany	4892	6310	6083
独联体	Commonwealth of Independent States	93578	76966	217149
香港同胞	Compatriots from Hong Kong		12710	11680
澳门同胞	Compatriots from Macao		1387	638
台湾同胞	Compatriots from Taiwan	8816	33611	23445
按地区分	**By Regions**			
乌鲁木齐市	Urumqi City	63275	144830	232250
克拉玛依市	Karamay City		505	1152
石河子市	Shihezi City		532	2142
吐鲁番地区	Turpan Administrative Offices	27230	43641	50741
哈密地区	Hami [Kumul] Administrative Offices	1220	624	12866
昌吉回族自治州	Changji Hui Autonomous Prefecture	224	213	56
伊犁哈萨克自治州	Ili Kazak Autonomous Prefecture	68948	18204	85961
伊犁州直属县(市)	Counties (Cities) Direct Under Ili Prefecture	67651	15356	49024
塔城地区	Tacheng [Tarbagatai] Administrative Offices	1297	298	1735
阿勒泰地区	Altay Administrative Offices		2550	35202
博尔塔拉蒙古自治州	Bortala Mongol Autonomous Prefecture	354	672	686
巴音郭楞蒙古自治州	BayangolMongol Autonomous Prefecture	1738	7313	4939
阿克苏地区	Aksu Administrative Offices	5737	6028	1372
克孜勒苏柯尔克孜自治州	Kizilsu Kirgiz Autonomous Prefecture	2485	2100	8399
喀什地区	Kashgar [Kaxgar] Administrative Offices	31102	27510	30435
和田地区	Hotan Administrative Offices	1266	3910	7437
国内旅游人数（万人）	**Number of Domestic Visitors (10 000 persons)**	**514**	**758**	**2126**
疆内居民出境游（人）	**Total Number of Domestic Resident Outbound (person)**	**591**	**4535**	**20544**
旅游收入	**Tourism Earnings**			
国际旅游收入(万美元)	Earnings from International Tourism (USD 10 000)	5268	9494	16190
国内旅游收入(亿元)	Earnings from Domestic Tourism (100 million yuan)	7.10	62.67	192.92

注：1998 年以后的旅游外汇收入根据抽样调查取得。
Note: The Foreign Exchange Earnings from Tourism after 1998 are obtained from Sampled Survey.

16-13 各地、州、市国际旅行社及旅游宾馆(酒店)基本情况
Accommodation of International Travel Agencies and Tourist Hotels by Prefecture, Autonomous Prefecture and City

(2007 年)

地 区	Region	国际旅行社 (个) Number of International Travel Agencies (unit)	星级宾馆 (个) Number of Tourist Hotels (unit)	客房 (间) Number of Rooms (unit)	床位 (张) Number of Beds (unit)
总 计	**Total**	**51**	**432**	**41974**	**82236**
乌鲁木齐市	Urumqi City	32	119	16438	31117
克拉玛依市	Karamay City	3	19	1436	2712
石河子市	Shihezi City		4	605	1178
吐鲁番地区	Turpan Administrative Offices	1	21	1443	3105
哈密地区	Hami [Kumul] Administrative Offices	1	16	1461	2856
昌吉回族自治州	Changji Hui Autonomous Prefecture	1	31	2393	5200
伊犁哈萨克自治州	Ili Kazak Autonomous Prefecture	4	108	8748	17195
伊犁州直属县(市)	Counties (Cities) Direct Under Ili Prefecture	2	53	4659	8998
塔城地区	Tacheng [Tarbagatai] Administrative Offices	1	13	906	1778
阿勒泰地区	Altay Administrative Offices	1	42	3183	6419
博尔塔拉蒙古自治州	Bortala Mongol Autonomous Prefecture		12	917	2036
巴音郭楞蒙古自治州	Bayangol Mongol Autonomous Prefecture		31	2891	5778
阿克苏地区	Aksu Administrative Offices	1	24	2083	4248
克孜勒苏柯尔克孜自治州	Kizilsu Kirgiz Autonomous Prefecture		2	96	201
喀什地区	Kashgar [Kaxgar] Administrative Offices	6	27	2406	4531
和田地区	Hotan Administrative Offices	2	18	1057	2079

16-14 各地、州、市旅游收入情况

Income of Tourism by Prefecture, Autonomous Prefecture and City

(2007 年)

地 区	Region	入境旅游收入 (万美元) Earnings International Tourism (USD 10 000)	国内旅游收入 (万元) Domestic Tourism (10 000 yuan)
总 计	**Total**	**16190**	**1929175**
乌鲁木齐市	Urumqi City	10587	819097
克拉玛依市	Karamay City	19	49830
石河子市	Shihezi City	57	68050
吐鲁番地区	Turpan Administrative Offices	2479	113085
哈密地区	Hami [Kumul] Administrative Offices	366	63320
昌吉回族自治州	Changji Hui Autonomous Prefecture	2	64515
伊犁哈萨克自治州	Ili Kazak Autonomous Prefecture	606	390099
伊犁州直属县(市)	Counties (Cities) Direct Under Ili Prefecture	382	144117
塔城地区	Tacheng [Tarbagatai] Administrative Offices	40	42800
阿勒泰地区	Altay Administrative Offices	184	203182
博尔塔拉蒙古自治州	Bortala Mongol Autonomous Prefecture	16	26850
巴音郭楞蒙古自治州	BayangolMongol Autonomous Prefecture	190	74133
阿克苏地区	Aksu Administrative Offices	25	74315
克孜勒苏柯尔克孜自治州	Kizilsu Kirgiz Autonomous Prefecture	134	13531
喀什地区	Kashgar [Kaxgar] Administrative Offices	1482	129309
和田地区	Hotan Administrative Offices	227	43041

16-15 国际旅游外汇收入及构成
Foreign Exchange Earnings and Its Composition

单位：万美元、% (USD 10 000,%)

指 标	Item	2006 金 额 Value	2006 比 重 Percentage	2007 金 额 Value	2007 比 重 Percentage
总 计	**Total**	**12800**	**100**	**16190**	**100**
长途交通费	Long Distance Transportation	3114	24.3	2511	15.5
民 航	Air	2537	19.8	2053	12.7
铁 路	Railway	477	3.7	253	1.5
汽 车	Highway	100	0.8	205	1.3
游 览	Visiting	465	3.6	332	2.0
住 宿	Accommodation	1168	9.1	1106	6.8
餐 饮	Food and Beverage	640	5.0	884	5.5
商品销售	Commodity Sales	5124	40.0	8498	52.5
娱 乐	Entertainment	854	6.7	253	1.6
邮电通信	Postal and Communication Services	100	0.8	426	2.6
市内交通	Local Transportation	239	1.9	253	1.6
其他服务	Other Services	854	6.7	1532	9.5
一日游	One-day Tourism	242	1.9	395	2.4

16-16 接待外国旅游人数(按国别分)
Number of Foreign Tourists Received by Country

单位：人 (person)

国 别	Country	2006	2007
总 计	**Total**	**313101**	**402673**
亚 洲	**Asia**	**105228**	**132600**
印 度	India	329	211
印度尼西亚	Indonesia	726	806
日 本	Japan	33775	25449
马来西亚	Malaysia	3384	3428
蒙 古	Mongolia	218	223
菲律宾	The Philppines	303	298
新加坡	Singapore	4211	3753
韩 国	Republic of Korea	11072	11340
泰 国	Thailand	969	1384
巴基斯坦	Pakistan	20755	9190
其 他	Other	29486	76518
非 洲	**Africa**	**240**	**362**
欧 洲	**Europe**	**183204**	**247272**
英 国	United Kingdom	3679	3129
德 国	Federal Republic of Germany	4657	6083
法 国	France	6476	7819
意大利	Italy	2065	1879
西班牙	Spain	618	806
瑞 典	Sweden	316	541
瑞 士	Switzerland	1042	1286
独联体	Commonwealth of Independent States	154182	217149
其 他	Other	10169	8580
北美洲	**North America**	**15044**	**13900**
加拿大	Canada	3097	2508
美 国	United States	10564	9907
其 他	Other	1383	1485
大洋洲	**Oceania**	**4304**	**4768**
澳大利亚	Australia	3539	3822
新西兰	New Zealand	357	392
其 他	Other	408	554
其他小计	**Other sub-total**	**5081**	**3771**

主要统计指标解释

进出口总额 指实际进出我国国境的货物总金额。包括对外贸易实际进出口货物，来料加工装配进出口货物，国家间、联合国及国际组织无偿援助物资和赠送品，华侨、港澳台同胞和外籍华人捐赠品，租赁期满归承租人所有的租赁货物，进料加工进出口货物，边境地方贸易及边境地区小额贸易进出口货物(边民互市贸易除外)，中外合资企业、中外合作经营企业、外商独资经营企业进出口货物和公用物品，到、离岸价格在规定限额以上的进出口货样和广告品(无商业价值、无使用价值和免费提供出口的除外)，从保税仓库提取在中国境内销售的进口货物，以及其他进出口货物。进出口总额用以观察一个国家在对外贸易方面的总规模。我国规定出口货物按离岸价格统计，进口货物按到岸价格统计。

商品经营单位所在地进、出口额 指所在地海关注册登记的有进出口经营权的企业实际进、出口额。

商品目的地进口额和商品货源地出口额、目的地进口额 指进口货物的消费、使用或最终抵运地的实际进口额，货源地出口额是指出口货物的产地或原始发货地的实际出口额。

利用外资 指我国各级政府、部门、企业和其他经济组织通过对外借款、吸收外商直接投资以及用其他方式筹措的境外现汇、设备、技术等。

对外借款 是我国利用外资的重要部分。指通过对外正式签订借款协议，从境外筹措的资金，包括外国政府贷款、国际金融组织贷款、外国银行商业贷款、出口信贷以及对外发行债券等。1996年及以前还包括对外发行股票。

外商直接投资 指外国企业和经济组织或个人(包括华侨、港澳台胞以及我国在境外注册的企业)按我国有关政策、法规，用现汇、实物、技术等在我国境内开办外商独资企业、与我国境内的企业或经济组织共同举办中外合资经营企业、合作经营企业或合作开发资源的投资(包括外商投资收益的再投资)，以及经政府有关部门批准的项目投资总额内企业从境外借入的资金。

外商其他投资 指除对外借款和外商直接投资以外的各种利用外资的形式。包括企业在境内外股票市场公开发行的以外币计价的股票(目前主要是在香港证券市场发行的H股和在境内证券市场发行的B股)发行价总额，国际租赁进口设备的应付款，补偿贸易中外商提供的进口设备、技术、物料的价款，加工装配贸易中外商提供的进口设备、物料的价款。

对外承包工程 指各对外承包公司以招标议标承包方式承揽的下列业务：(1)承包国外工程建设项目，(2)承包我国对外经援项目，(3)承包我国驻外机构的工程建设项目，(4)承包我国境内利用外资进行建设的工程项目，(5)与外国承包公司合营或联合承包工程项目时我国公司分包部分，(6)对外承包兼营的房屋开发业务。对外承包工程的营业额是以货币表现的本期内完成的对外承包工程的工作量，包括以前年度签订的合同和本年度新签订的合同在报告期内完成的工作量。

对外劳务合作 指以收取工资的形式向业主或承包商提供技术和劳动服务的活动。我国对外承包公司在境外开办的合营企业，中国公司同时又提供劳务的，其劳务部分也纳入劳务合作统计。劳务合作营业额按报告期内向雇主提交的结算数(包括工资、加班费和奖金等)统计。

对外设计咨询 指以服务成果向业主收费的技术服务项目。包括承担地形地貌测绘，地质资源勘探与普查，建设区域规划，提供设计文件、图纸、生产工艺技术资料和工程技术经济咨询，工程项目的可行性考察、研究和评估，进行技术指导和培训人员等；也包括承担国(境)内利用外资进行建设的工程项目的上述规定的设计咨询项目的收取外币部分。

旅游者人数 包括入境国际旅游者人数、出境居民人数和国内旅游者人数。

(1)入境国际旅游者人数：指来中国参观、访问、旅行、探亲、访友、休养、考察、参加会议和从事经济、科技、文化、教育、宗教等活动的外国人、华侨、港澳同胞和台湾同胞的人数。不包括外国在我国的常驻机构，如使领馆、通讯社、企业办事处的工作人员；来我国常住的外国专家、留学生以及在岸逗留不过夜人员。

(2)出境居民人数：指大陆居民因公务活动或私人事务短期出境的人数。公务活动出境居民人数包括在国际交通工具上的中国服务员工，因私出境居民人数不包括在国际交通工具上的中国服务员工。

(3)国内旅游者人数：指我国大陆居民和在我国常住1年以上的外国人、华侨、港澳台同胞离开常住地在境内其他地方的旅游设施内至少停留一夜，最长不超过6个月的人数。

国际旅游(外汇)收入 指入境旅游的外国人、华侨、港澳同胞和台湾同胞在中国大陆旅游过程中发生的一切旅游支出，对于国家来说就是国际旅游(外汇)收入。

国际旅行社 指经营对外招徕并接待外国人、华侨、港澳同胞和台湾同胞来中国、归国或回内地旅游业务的旅行社。

国内旅行社 指负责经营招徕、组团、接待国内旅客的旅游业务，以及不对外招徕，负责经营接待国际旅行社或其它涉外部门组织的外国人、华侨、港澳同胞和台湾同胞来中国、归国或回内地的旅游业务的旅行社。

涉外饭店 指经有关部门批准，允许接待外国人、华侨、港澳同胞和台湾同胞的饭店。

Explanatory Notes on Main Statistical Indicators

Total Imports and Exports at Customs refer to the value of commodities imported into and exported from the boundary of China. They include the actual imports and exports through foreign Trades, imported and exported goods under the processing and assembling Trades and materials, supplies and gifts as aid given gratis between governments and by the United Nations and other international organizations, and contributions donated by overseas Chinese, compatriots in Hong Kong and Macao and Chinese with foreign citizenship, leasing commodities owned by tenant at the expiration of leasing period, the imported and exported commodities processed with imported materials, commodities trading in border areas(excluding mutual exchange goods), the imported and exported commodities and articles for public use of the Sino-foreign joint ventures, cooperative enterprises and ventures exclusively with foreign own investment .Also included are import or export of samples and advertising goods for whose CIF or FOB value are beyond the permitted ceiling (excluding goods of no trading or use value and free commodities for export),imported goods sold in China from bonded warehouses and other imported or exported goods.The indicator of the total imports and exports at customs can be used to observe the total size of external Trades in a country.In accordance with the stipulation of the Chinese government,imports are calculated at CIF, while exports are calculated at FOB

Import Export Value by Location of China Foreign Trades Managing Units refers to actual value of imports and exports carried out by corporations which have been registered by the local customhouse and are vested with right to run import export business.

Import Value of Commodities by the Places of their Destination and Export Value of Commodities by the Places of their Origin in China: The former indicator refers to the value of import commodities of the places of their consumption, utilization or the places of their final destination. The latter indicator refers to the value of export commodities of the places of their origin or the places of the commodities dispatched.

Utilization of Foreign Capital refers to remittance, equipment and technology financed from abroad, by loans, foreign direct investment and other forms undertaken by the Chinese governments at all levels, by various departments, enterprises and other economic units.

Foreign Borrowings an important part of China扭 utilization of foreign capital,it refer to funds borrowed from abroad through formal signing of borrowing agreements with foreign institutions, including loans of foreign governments, loans of international financial institutions,commercial loans of foreign banks, export credit, and funds raised by Chinese bonds (and shares before 1996) issued abroad.

Foreign Direct Investment refers to the investments inside China by foreign enterprises and economic organizations or individuals(including overseas Chinese,compatriots from Hong Kong and Macao,and Chinese enterprises registered abroad), following the relevant policies and laws of China, for the establishment of ventures exclusively with foreign own investment, Sino-foreign joint ventures and cooperative enterprises or for co-operative exploration of resources with enterprises or economic organizations in China. It includes the re investment of the foreign entrepreneurs with the profits gained from the investment and the funds that enterprises borrow from abroad in the total investment of projects which are approved by the relevant department of the government.

Other Investment by Foreign Entrepreneurs refers to all forms of utilization of foreign capitals other than foreign borrowings and foreign direct investment. It includes the total value of stock shares in foreign currencies issued by enterprises at domestic or foreign stock exchanges (now mainly consisting of H shares issued at Hong Kong Security Market and B shares issued at domestic security markets), rent payable for the imported equipment through international leasing arrangement, cost of imported equipment, technology and materials provided by foreign counterparts in compensation Trades and processing and assembly Trades.

Contracted Projects with Foreign Countries refer to projects undertaken by Chinese contractors (project contracting companies)through bidding process.They include: (1)overseas civil engineering construction projects financed by foreign investors; (2)overseas projects financed by the Chinese government through its foreign aid programs; (3)construction projects of Chinese diplomatic missions,Trades offices and other institutions stationed abroad; (4)construction projects in China financed by foreign investment; (5)sub-contracted projects to be taken by Chinese contractors through a joint umbrella project with foreign contractor(s); (6)housing development projects.The business income from international contracted projects is the work volume of contracted projects completed during the reference period, expressed in monetary terms, including completed work on projects signed in previous years.

Service Cooperation with Foreign Countries refers to the activities of providing technology and labour services to employers or contractors in the forms of receiving salaries and wages. Labour services providing by contractual joint ventures of Chihe statistics of service co operation with foreign countries.The business income of labour service co operation is the income in the form of wages and salaries, overtime pay, bonuses and other remuneration received from the employers during the reference period.

Overseas Design and Consultation Service refers to projects with charges for technical services from overseas operators. It includes geographic and topographic mapping, geological resource prospecting and survey, planning of construction areas, provision of design documents, blueprints, materials on production process and techniques, as well as engineering, technical and economic consultation, and feasibility study, research and evaluation of projects. Also included under this category are the above-mentioned services of foreign-financed projects in China that are paid in foreign currencies.

Number of Tourists include international tourists entering into China, Chinese residents going abroad and domestic tourists.

(1) International tourists refer to foreigners, overseas Chinese, Chinese compatriots from Hong Kong, Macao and Taiwan coming to China for sightseeing, visits, tours, family reunions, vacations, study tours, conferences and other activities of a business, scientific and technological, cultural, educational and religious nature. It does not include representatives and employees of resident institutions of foreign countries in China such as embassies, consulates, news agencies and offices of foreign companies and organizations, nor does it include long-term foreign experts or students residing in China, or persons in transition without spending a night in China.

(2) Chinese residents going abroad refer to Chinese residents going abroad for short terms for either public business or private purposes. Chinese employees working on international transport carriers are included in those going abroad for public business purpose, not in those for private purpose.

(3) Domestic tourists refer to residents of the mainland of China who stay for one night at least but no more than 6 months at tourist facilities in other places than their permanent residence within the territory of the mainland China, including foreigners, overseas Chinese and Chinese compatriots from Hong Kong, Macao and Taiwan who have resided in China for over one year.

Foreign Exchange Earnings from International Tourism refer to the total expenditures of foreigners, overseas Chinese, Chinese compatriots from Hong Kong, Macao and Taiwan during their stay in the mainland of China, which are earnings of foreign exchange from international tourism from the point of view from China.

International Travel Agencies refer to travel agencies engaged in the promotion, solicitation, organization and reception of tours to the mainland of China by foreigners, overseas Chinese, Chinese compatriots from Hong Kong, Macao and Taiwan.

Domestic Travel Agencies refer to travel agencies engaged in the promotion, solicitation, organization and reception of domestic tourists, and in the reception of foreigners, overseas Chinese, Chinese compatriots from Hong Kong, Macao and Taiwan organized by international travel agencies or other departments concerned, without their own promotion and solicitation programmes.

Tourist Hotels refer to hotels that are able, with the approval of departments concerned, to accommodate foreigners, overseas Chinese, Chinese compatriots from Hong Kong, Macao and Taiwan Province.

第十七篇
教育、科技和文化

CHAPTER 17
Education,Science & Technology and Culture

简要说明
Brief Introduction

本篇资料的主要内容及来源

教育统计资料包括研究生教育(高等学校研究生教育、科研机构研究生教育);普通高等学校本专科教育;普通中等教育(中等专业教育、技工学校、普通中学、职业高中、工读学校);初等教育(小学)、学前教育、特殊教育(盲聋哑和弱智儿童学校等)以及教育经费等资料。

教育部分资料由新疆维吾尔自治区统计局人口与社会科技处根据科技专业年报以及新疆维吾尔自治区教育厅所提供资料整理。

科技统计资料包括科技活动基本情况、县级以上政府部门属研究与开发机构及科技信息与文献机构人员数、重大科学技术研究成果及奖励、专利申请和批准情况、高等学校科技活动情况、企事业单位专业技术人员情况、大中型工业企业科技活动情况、各类技术合同鉴定及执行情况、技术经济合同成交情况、技术流向地域情况等。

科技统计范围包括新疆地区有科技活动的企事业单位,具体涵盖规模以上工业企业(标准见工业篇)、各级各部门所属国有独立核算的科学研究与技术开发机构及科技情报与文献机构、普通高等学校等。

科技部分资料由新疆维吾尔自治区统计局人口与社会科技处根据新疆维吾尔自治区科技厅提供资料整理。

文化部分主要包括艺术表演团体、艺术表演场所、公共图书馆、博物馆、文化馆、档案馆、文化站、广播、电影、电视以及文物等文化单位的机构、人员、经费和业务活动情况。

文化部分资料是由新疆维吾尔自治区统计局人口与社会科技处根据部门统计报表制度加工整理而成。艺术事业、图书馆事业、群众文化事业的资料主要来自新疆维吾尔自治区文化厅;档案馆资料来新疆维吾尔自治区档案局;文物资料来自新疆维吾尔自治区文物局;广播、电影、电视资料来自新疆维吾尔自治区广播电视局。

Main Content and Source of Data

The data on education cover the situation on postgraduate, normal higher education, popular secondary education, elementary education (primary schools), preschool education, special education(schools for the blind, deaf-mutes and the retarded) and expenditure on education. The main indicators cover the number of schools, the number of students enrolled, the number of new students enrolled, the number of graduates, the number of staff and workers, the number of full-time teachers, sources and outlay of education fund, education expenditure from the state budget.

Statistical data on education compiled by the Statistics Bureau of Xinjiang in accordance with the data from the Bureau of Education.

Data on technology mainly include: condition of scientific and technological activities, state-owned research and development institutions and information and literature institutions at and above county level and persons engaged; the situation of science and technological achievements & prizes and patent applications, basic statistics on scientific and technological activities of high education, condition of professional scientific and technological personnel of enterprises and institutions, statistics on signing and implementing technical contracts, statistics on transaction in technical and economic contract, statistics on location of technical contract.

Statistical scope on technology include scientific and technical activities in enterprises and institution, they are mainly: industrial enterprises above designated size, state-owned research and development institutions and information and literature institutions at and above county level and persons engaged, regular institutions of high

Data on technology compiled by the Statistics Bureau of Xinjiang in accordance with the data from the Bureau of Science &Technology.

Data on culture cover mainly the situations on institutions, personal and business activities of arts (performing groups and venues), libraries, museums, cultural centers, archives, cultural stations, broadcasting, films, televisions, news and publication.

Data on culture are collected and tabulated in accordance with the statistical reporting schemes stipulated by the Statistical Bureau of Xinjiang. Data on the causes of arts, libraries, mass culture are provided by the Xinjiang Bureau of Culture; Data on archives are from Xinjiang Bureau of Archives; Data on broadcasting, film and television are mainly from Xinjiang Bureau of Broadcasting.

17-1 各级各类学校数

Number of Schools by Level and Type

单位：所 (unit)

年 份 Year	普通高等学校 Regular Institutions of Higher Education	中等学校 Secondary Schools	普通中等职业学校 Specialized Secondary Schools	普通中学 Regular Secondary Schools	#高 中 Senior Secondary Schools	职业中学 Vocational Secondary Schools	技工学校 Technical Schools	小 学 Primary Schools	盲聋哑学校 Special Schools
1978	10	2078	78	1997	673		10	9891	1
1980	12	2197	96	2032	720	21	48	9006	2
1985	14	2360	97	2147	794	65	51	8104	3
1990	21	2274	112	1958	766	134	70	7247	6
1995	21	2121	115	1792	554	145	69	7086	6
2000	20	2000	112	1711	484	112	65	6718	7
2001	21	2179	99	1929	472	89	62	6221	7
2002	24	2173	87	1945	507	83	58	6043	7
2003	26	2154	78	1932	500	86	58	5832	8
2004	28	2186	78	1965	498	84	59	5451	8
2005	31	2185	79	1961	503	87	58	5209	10
2006	31	2101	67	1891	486	84	59	4815	9
2007	32	2040	74	1830	454	75	61	4589	9

注：从 2006 年起，职业初中并入普通中学统计。(以下同)
Note: Number of regular secondary schools include the number of junion vocational secondary schools from 2006.(The same applies to the tables follows)

17-2 各级各类学校教师数

Number of Teachers by Level and Type of School

单位：人 (person)

年 份 Year	普通高等学校 Regular Institutions of Higher Education	中等学校 Secondary Schools	普通中等职业学校 Specialized Secondary Schools	普通中学 Regular Secondary Schools	#高 中 Senior Secondary Schools	职业中学 Vocational Secondary Schools	技工学校 Technical Schools	小 学 Primary Schools	盲聋哑学校 Special Schools
1978	2458	44417	2543	41661	8064		213	82616	28
1980	3149	50056	3459	45232	9292	77	1288	98027	54
1985	5473	69185	4554	60942	15059	1567	2122	98294	67
1990	7002	78596	6158	65814	19318	3117	3507	95060	139
1995	7687	76584	6540	62934	14434	3494	3616	106001	162
2000	7924	89211	6786	75895	16069	3104	3426	131259	183
2001	9123	93126	6842	79419	17025	2546	4319	132137	187
2002	10369	96469	6031	84714	19031	2399	3325	132435	200
2003	11237	124132	5157	89332	20976	2440	6227	132284	237
2004	12239	106839	5494	94381	22809	3079	3885	134915	257
2005	12733	112941	4993	102168	25153	2163	4084	134768	262
2006	13783	120777	4339	106975	26815	2832	6631	134718	286
2007	15096	123246	5553	108232	27970	2295	7166	133626	298

17-3 各级各类学校在校学生数

Number of Students Enrollment by Level and Type of School

单位：人 (person)

年 份 Year	普通高等学校 Regular Institutions of Higher Education	中等学校 Secondary Schools	普通中等职业学校 Specialized Secondary Schools	普通中学 Regular Secondary Schools	#高 中 Senior Secondary Schools	职业中学 Vocational Secondary Schools	技工学校 Technical Schools	小 学 Primary Schools	盲聋哑学校 Special Schools
1978	10229	838560	23696	806386	128376		8478	2028771	270
1980	14308	886740	42362	823161	147446	1416	19801	2055513	371
1985	26500	1054293	33251	955356	223405	41825	23861	1966306	706
1990	31271	1015214	45985	863118	251067	65862	40249	1857246	610
1995	44918	912597	68586	749788	141330	54122	40101	2301274	643
2000	74063	1311845	105255	1132912	198639	51270	22408	2477413	674
2001	109815	1390360	97321	1228566	225411	47673	16800	2435667	922
2002	134831	1493580	83902	1338836	272381	50787	20055	2359788	3876
2003	151256	1584700	71499	1448531	315178	45330	19340	2289066	1863
2004	168247	1676971	71324	1517948	359147	61502	26197	2218109	2549
2005	188752	1717403	86744	1587850	387763	63158	26219	2143833	4961
2006	207672	1739422	108131	1572502	402321	23488	35301	2097975	4843
2007	226012	1742947	141162	1529092	413452	31741	40952	2058884	6396

注：1.17-3、17-4、17-5 表中高等学校含研究生数。2.盲聋哑学校 2002 年新增随班就读。(以下同)

Note: a) Institntions of higher education include the number of postgraduates with table 17-3,17-4,17-5.

b) In Special Schools for the blind,deaf, mute, new comers may follow the classes accordingly from the year 2002 (The same as follows).

17-4 各级各类学校招生数

Number of New Students Enrollment by Level and Type of School

单位：人 (person)

年 份 Year	普通高等学校 Regular Institutions of Higher Education	中等学校 Secondary Schools	普通中等职业学校 Specialized Secondary Schools	普通中学 Regular Secondary Schools	#高 中 Senior Secondary Schools	职业中学 Vocational Secondary Schools	技工学校 Technical Schools	小 学 Primary Schools	盲聋哑学校 Special Schools
1980	3767	336402	14688	310931	73959	792	10531	433089	90
1985	9298	386074	13919	341123	93692	20429	10603	374643	91
1990	8034	356615	15586	297641	84567	27968	15420	335552	103
1995	12307	356814	25260	286318	58203	25643	19593	419717	165
2000	30689	486763	38866	418790	76744	20027	9080	364193	175
2001	42253	510469	26763	459878	93519	16621	7207	352975	135
2002	42808	551353	22241	501824	113366	16746	10442	346386	874
2003	44733	583033	24016	532987	126163	15378	10652	347619	369
2004	53204	606666	27990	536405	138315	27585	14686	347364	390
2005	58653	602335	34882	539922	145044	12416	15115	338539	847
2006	62395	599748	45536	522425	142853	13017	18770	337994	780
2007	68999	619218	65290	510080	146449	19201	24647	340108	1158

17-5 各级各类学校毕业生数

Number of Graduates by Level and Type of School

单位：人 (person)

年 份 Year	普通高等学校 Regular Institutions of Higher Education	中等学校 Secondary Schools	中等专业学校 Specialized Secondary Schools	普通中学 Regular Secondary Schools	#高中 Senior Secondary Schools	职业中学 Vocational Secondary Schools	技工学校 Technical Schools	小学 Primary Schools	盲聋哑学校 Special Schools
1978	1509	205862	8801	195542	53970		1519	388359	195
1980	814	264626	11946	246382	60370	341	5957	292515	37
1981	779	280171	17039	257478	67114	367	5287	397524	37
1982	4108	269927	17201	244853	69504	385	7488	310025	32
1983	4823	283120	11584	260906	77546	1144	9486	317227	27
1984	3426	275788	8130	257833	72191	2764	7061	295993	48
1985	3511	290077	8097	267302	68096	7424	7254	289045	73
1986	4797	296360	11551	268402	58585	8543	7864	307047	52
1987	8001	321981	10623	289556	73947	12280	9522	317820	101
1988	7792	346072	12026	311224	85718	12758	10064	288594	68
1989	6900	347719	12441	308467	86489	14650	12161	249888	57
1990	8603	343313	14260	297235	81062	17938	13880	259301	98
1991	7919	324031	15571	274913	79664	17505	16042	183350	159
1992	8402	310076	14950	260953	84518	18999	15174	268074	157
1993	7741	312284	16760	261502	78675	18558	15464	259468	104
1994	7734	250909	16206	198839	57090	18100	17764	262215	55
1995	10505	271992	18981	215756	44589	16490	20765	271227	57
1996	12272	271267	21701	215295	43478	15424	18847	279866	39
1997	10908	284580	21936	228287	37966	17181	17176	294420	71
1998	11401	313807	23090	259910	49702	18038	12769	321044	100
1999	11886	341434	25118	282486	52403	18826	15004	357801	84
2000	11220	363503	25879	308225	54985	17341	12058	371758	70
2001	16121	380946	26403	329801	59251	13881	10861	395010	104
2002	16380	410299	31598	356203	61932	15087	7411	411626	848
2003	25785	434523	31304	379269	70824	15685	8265	421443	264
2004	31013	468849	24758	420583	84418	15475	8033	417588	382
2005	37920	520798	19559	474621	103928	19492	7126	397592	714
2006	45810	541729	22515	501697	115422	5510	12007	373862	684
2007	48372	557512	25735	515494	127129	5943	10340	361921	716

17-6 研究生数

Number of Postgraduates

单位：人 (person)

年份 Year	招生数 New Enrollment	在校学生数 Total Enrollment	攻读博士学位 Working for Doctor's Degree	攻读硕士学位 Working for Master's Degree	毕业生数 Graduates	攻读博士学位 Working for Doctor's Degree	攻读硕士学位 Working for Master's Degree
1978	16	16		16			
1980	15	66		66			
1985	120	179		174	21		21
1990	73	256	3	253	112		112
1995	180	509	14	295	91		91
1996	217	535	16	519	142	3	139
1997	234	647	18	629	158	3	155
1998	276	747	19	728	173	7	166
1999	386	901	29	872	229	5	224
2000	544	1196	48	1148	235	5	230
2001	827	1749	80	1669	277	8	269
2002	1104	2495	112	2383	355	11	344
2003	1664	3629	186	3443	521	18	503
2004	2336	5120	283	4837	832	30	802
2005	2902	6938	415	6523	1066	35	1031
2006	3147	8421	489	7932	1628	90	1538
2007	3491	9623	549	9074	2244	110	2134

17-7 高等学校基本情况

Basic Statistics on Institutions of Higher Education

单位：人 (2007 年) (person)

项目	Item	学校数(所) Schools (unit)	毕业生数 Graduates	招生数 New Enrollment	在校学生数 Total Enrollment	教职工数 Staff and Teachers	#专任教师 Full-time Teachers
总计	**Total**		**46128**	**65508**	**216389**	**31544**	**17982**
普通高等学校	Regular Institutions of Higher Education	32	44167	64437	211498	26490	15096
综合大学	Multiversity	6	12011	17494	61631	8414	4506
理工院校	Science Engineering	11	9980	16205	41850	4809	3110
农业院校	Agriculture	4	6926	9618	34988	3813	2305
医药院校	Medicine	3	1953	4755	14733	2293	1276
师范院校	Teacher Training	4	9093	10515	38297	4150	2528
财经学院	Economics and Finance	1	2649	3585	12661	1598	863
政法院校	Politics & Law	2	1214	1457	4159	715	275
艺术院校	Art	1	341	808	3179	443	233
总计中：高职学院	In total: Vocational Training	16	11405	21055	54292	7081	4575
成人高等学校	Ordinary Class for Adult Higher Education	3	1961	1071	4891	5054	2886

17-8 中等专业学校基本情况
Basic Statistics on Specialized Secondary Schools

单位: 人 (2007 年) (person)

项 目	Item	毕业生数 Graduates	招 生 数 New Student Enrollment	在校学生数 Student Enrollment	专业课教师 Teachers of Various Subjects
总 计	**Total**	**25735**	**65290**	**141162**	**5553**
农业类	Agriculture	1501	8633	11036	284
资源与环境类	Resource and Environment		225	658	64
能源类	Energy	1095	1813	4820	82
土木水利工程类	Civil and Hydraulic Engineering	2013	3222	6378	174
加工制造类	Processing and Manufacturing	4959	15123	30743	194
交通运输类	Transportation and Communication	1462	2345	5687	138
信息技术类	Information Technologies	2008	4896	8593	166
医药卫生类	Medcine and Health	5197	10991	34451	437
商贸与旅游类	Trades and Tourism	1855	3014	7018	99
财经类	Economics and Finance	504	1778	3152	307
文化艺术与体育类	Culture Arts and Physical Education	2373	3716	9815	442
社会公共事业类	Scoial and Public Affairs	809	1308	3094	255
师范类	Teacher Training	1146	2503	5774	528
其 他	Others	813	5723	9943	2383

17-9 普通中学和其他学校基本情况
Basic Statistics on Regular Secondary Schools and Other Schools

单位: 人 (2007 年) (person)

项 目	Item	学校数(所) Schools (unit)	毕业生数 Graduates	招 生 数 New Enrollment	在校学生数 Total Enrollment	教职工数 Staff and Teachers	#专任教师 Full-time Teachers
普通中学	Regular Secondary Schools	1830	515494	510080	1529092	126880	108232
高 中	Senior Secondary Schools	454	127129	146449	413452		27970
初 中	Junior Secondary Schools	1376	388365	363631	1115640		80262
职业中学	Vocational Secondary Schools	75	5943	19201	31741	3391	2295
技工学校	Technical Shools	61	10340	24647	40952	8057	3547
小 学	Primary Schools	4589	361921	340108	2058884	149286	133626
盲聋哑学校	Special Schools	9	716	1158	6396	385	298

17-10 各类成人教育情况
Basic Statistics on Adult Education by Type

单位：人 (2007 年) (person)

项 目	Item	学校数(所) Schools (unit)	毕业生数 Graduates	在校学生数 Total Enrollment	教职工数 Staff and Teachers	#专任教师 Full-time Teachers
成人高等教育	Adult Education Schools	8	32127	63816	5054	2886
广播电视大学	Radio and TV Universities	2	420	1013	3260	1781
职工大学	Schools of Higher Education for Staff Workers	1	90	206	102	73
教育学院	Pedagogical Colleges	5	4225	5115	1692	1032
普通高校办的成人班	Adult Classes run by Ordinary Colleges and Universities		27392	57482		
成人中等教育	Secondary Schools for Adults	22	5445	20181	2258	1910
成人中学	Secondary Schools for Adults	16	3672	4294	120	23
成人技术培训学校	Technical adult college	1521	1543911	1774999	2853	895
成人初等学校	Primary Schools for Adults	454	43374	64230	2308	402
#扫盲班	Literacy Courses		15735	34861	1176	275

17-11 教育发展水平
Development Level of Education

年份 Year	各类学校在校生占全区人口比重(%) Students as Percentage of Total Population (%)	平均每万人口中(人) Number of Students per 10 000 Population (person)			大中小学生各占学生总数的比重(%) Students of Different Level as Percentage of Total Students(%)		
		大学生 University and College Students	中学生 Secondary School students	小学生 Primary School Students	大学生 University and College Students	中学生 Secondary School Students	小学生 Primary School Students
1978	23.34	8.30	654.00	1645.38		28.02	70.50
1980	23.04	11.15	641.47	1601.82		27.80	69.52
1985	22.39	19.47	701.88	1444.60		31.35	64.52
1990	18.99	20.45	564.44	1208.01	1.08	29.72	63.94
1995	19.61	26.84	453.23	1330.61	1.38	23.00	70.60
1996	19.62	26.60	475.85	1362.56	1.36	24.26	69.46
1997	20.44	26.97	510.29	1408.37	1.32	24.96	68.89
1998	21.02	27.16	548.49	1432.28	1.29	26.10	68.15
1999	21.39	30.96	598.52	1412.62	1.45	27.98	66.05
2000	22.84	41.05	638.26	1395.72	1.82	27.93	61.09
2001	20.98	58.53	654.84	1298.22	2.79	31.21	61.87
2002	23.14	70.04	702.72	1238.61	3.21	31.87	56.18
2003	22.53	76.33	749.00	1183.62	3.39	33.25	52.54
2004	21.91	83.09	773.23	1129.89	4.18	38.92	56.90
2005	21.96	90.44	766.67	1066.40	4.70	39.86	55.44
2006	21.78	97.20	767.07	1023.40	5.10	40.64	54.26
2007	21.21	103.28	729.81	982.67	5.69	40.19	54.12

17-12 各级学校教师负担学生数
Student-Teacher Ratio by Level of School

单位：人 (person)

年份 Year	高等学校 University and College		普通中学 Secondary Schools		小学 Primary Schools	
	教师数 Number of Teachers	平均每个教师负担学生数 Student-Teacher Ratio	教师数 Number of Teachers	平均每个教师负担学生数 Student-Teacher Ratio	教师数 Number of Teachers	平均每个教师负担学生数 Student-Teacher Ratio
1978	2458	4.16	41661	19.36	82616	24.56
1980	3149	4.54	45232	18.20	89027	23.09
1985	5473	4.84	60942	15.68	98294	20.00
1990	7002	4.47	65814	13.12	95060	19.54
1995	7687	5.78	62934	11.91	106001	20.77
2000	7924	9.34	75895	14.92	131259	18.87
2001	9123	12.04	79419	15.47	132137	18.43
2002	10369	13.00	84714	15.80	132435	17.82
2003	11237	13.46	89332	16.22	132284	17.30
2004	12239	13.74	94381	16.08	134915	16.44
2005	12733	14.82	101701	15.16	134768	15.91
2006	13783	15.07	106975	14.70	134718	15.57
2007	15096	14.33	108232	14.13	133626	15.41

17-13 各级学校女学生和女教师数
Number of Female Students and Teachers by Level of School

单位：人 (person)

项目	Item	1995	2000	2007
女学生	**Number of Female Students**	**1553655**	**1889552**	**1985993**
高等学校	Institutions of Higher Education	21268	38419	113793
中等专业学校	Specialized Secondary Schools	35927	49892	78770
普通中学	Regular Secondary Schools	379171	568060	769873
职业中学	Vocational Secondary Schools	28495	23670	16943
技工学校	Technical Shools	12191	8740	12028
小学	Primary Schools	1076333	1200513	992061
盲聋哑学校	Special Schools for the Blind, Mute and Deaf	270	258	2525
女学生占学生总数的比重(%)	**Percentage of Female Students to Total Students (%)**	**49.2**	**48.9**	**49.2**
女教师	**Number of Female Teachers**	**106877**	**134563**	**165238**
高等学校	Institutions of Higher Education	2857	3192	9044
中等专业学校	Specialized Secondary Schools	3079	3408	2966
普通中学	Regular Secondary Schools	30508	40030	61666
职业中学	Vocational Secondary Schools	1613	1601	1213
技工学校	Technical Schools	1085	1264	3378
小学	Primary Schools	67617	84944	90118
盲聋哑学校	Special Schools for the Blind, Mute and Deaf	118	124	231
女教师占教师总数的比重(%)	**Percentage of Female Teachers to Total Teachers (%)**	**56.5**	**58.9**	**60.7**

17-14 初中毕业生和小学生升学率及小学学龄儿童入学率

Percentage of Graduates of Junior Secondary Schools and Primary Schools Entering Higher Level Schools, Enrollment Rate of School-age Children

单位：人、% (person,%)

年份 Year	初中毕业生升高中情况 Student of Graduates of Junior Secondary Schools Entering Senior Secondary Schools			小学毕业生升学情况 Student of Graduates of Primary Schools Entering Junior Secondary Schools			小学学龄儿童入学情况 Student of School-Age Children Enrolled		
	初中毕业生数 Graduates of Junior Secondary Schools	高中招生数 Students Entering Senior Secondary Schools	升学率 Percentage of Graduates of Primary Schools Entering Junior Secondary Schools	小学毕业生数 Graduates of Primary Schools	初中招生数 Students Entering Junior Secondary Schools	升学率 Percentage of Graduates of Primary Schools Entering Junior Secondary Schools	学龄儿童数 School-Age Children	已入学学龄儿童数 School-Age Children Enrolled in Schools	入学率 Enrollment Rate
1978	141572	68261	48.22	788359	255687	88.67	1541148	1480400	96.00
1980	186012	73989	39.76	292515	236432	80.83	1637610	1548653	94.57
1985	199206	93692	47.03	289045	247431	85.60	1645055	1569328	95.40
1990	216173	84567	39.12	259301	213074	82.17	1502163	1465325	97.50
1995	171167	58203	34.00	271227	228115	84.10	2036541	1976120	97.03
2000	253240	76744	30.30	371758	342046	92.01	2313890	2245190	97.03
2001	270550	93519	34.56	395010	366359	92.75	2257795	2212477	97.41
2002	294271	113366	38.52	411626	388558	94.39	2184260	2136643	97.82
2003	308445	126163	40.90	421443	406824	96.53	2122900	2087775	98.34
2004	336165	138315	41.14	417588	398090	95.33	2063210	2038258	97.79
2005	370693	145044	39.13	397592	394878	99.33	2007742	1981569	98.70
2006	386275	142853	36.98	373862	379572	101.53	1957604	1941068	99.15
2007	388365	146449	37.71	361921	363631	100.47	1930074	1916265	99.28

17-15 各级各类学校少数民族在校学生数

Number of Students Enrollment of Minority Nationalities by Level and Type of School

单位：人 (person)

年份 Year	高等学校 Institutions of Higher Education	中等学校 Secondary Schools	中等专业学校 Specialized Secondary Schools	职业中学 Vocational Secondary Schools	技工学校 Technical Schools	普通中学 Regular Secondary Schools	#高中 Senior Secondary Schools	#初中 Junior Secondary Schools	小学(万人) Primary Schools (10 000 persons)
1978	7890	310987	10807			300180	38837	261343	106.58
1980	6455	311213	22263	592	4514	283844	50340	233504	101.73
1985	13996	346833	17888	4915	7649	316381	71199	245182	116.43
1990	17542	439140	23897	13577	13685	387981	94579	293402	126.78
1995	24125	477379	33264	20013	16040	408012	52570	355492	157.84
2000	31989	834390	62572	34992	12260	724566	91843	632723	171.44
2001	47689	867582	58971	37013	9191	762407	103658	658749	165.83
2002	61610	913720	51204	40938	10971	810607	121523	689084	158.25
2003	65394	950853	38025	34863	9898	868067	137714	730353	151.52
2004	70340	985148	31566	49693	13407	890482	148398	742084	143.62
2005	75744	993338	32698	54773	13371	892501	152244	740257	136.94
2006	77627	975346	36393	13216	18002	907735	149963	757772	132.94
2007	81978	958643	55224	19181	20476	863762	156478	707284	131.32

17-16 各地、州、市各级各类学校数

Number of Schools by Level, Type and by Prefecture, Autonomous Prefecture and City

单位：所 (2007 年) (unit)

地区	Region	普通高等学校 Regular Institutions of Higher Education	中等专业学校 Specialized Secondary Schools	#中等师范学校 Teacher Training Secondary Schools
总计	**Total**	**32**	**74**	**13**
乌鲁木齐市	Urumqi City	17	20	1
克拉玛依市	Karamay City	1	1	1
石河子市	Shihezi City	1	5	1
吐鲁番地区	Turpan Administrative Offices		1	
哈密地区	Hami [Kumul] Administrative Offices		2	1
昌吉回族自治州	Changji Hui Autonomous Prefecture	3	1	
伊犁哈萨克自治州	Ili Kazak Autonomous Prefecture	2	10	3
伊犁州直属县(市)	Counties (Cities) Direct Under Ili Prefecture	2	6	1
塔城地区	Tacheng [Tarbagatai] Administrative Offices		1	1
阿勒泰地区	Altay Administrative Offices		3	1
博尔塔拉蒙古自治州	Bortala Mongol Autonomous Prefecture		3	1
巴音郭楞蒙古自治州	Bayangol Mongol Autonomous Prefecture	1	2	1
阿克苏地区	Aksu Administrative Offices	1	1	1
克孜勒苏柯尔克孜自治州	Kizilsu Kirgiz Autonomous Prefecture		2	1
喀什地区	Kashgar [Kaxgar] Administrative Offices	1	6	
和田地区	Hotan Administrative Offices	2	3	1
生产建设兵团	Production and Construction Group	3	17	1

地区	Region	普通中学 Regular Secondary Schools	#高中 Senior Secondary Schools	小学 Primary Schools	盲聋哑学校 Special Schools
总计	**Total**	**1830**	**454**	**4589**	**9**
乌鲁木齐市	Urumqi City	137	58	159	2
克拉玛依市	Karamay City	21	16	32	1
石河子市	Shihezi City	11	4	14	
吐鲁番地区	Turpan Administrative Offices	89	19	116	
哈密地区	Hami [Kumul] Administrative Offices	72	17	50	1
昌吉回族自治州	Changji Hui Autonomous Prefecture	92	24	130	1
伊犁哈萨克自治州	Ili Kazak Autonomous Prefecture	415	99	718	1
伊犁州直属县(市)	Counties (Cities) Direct Under Ili Prefecture	225	58	437	
塔城地区	Tacheng [Tarbagatai] Administrative Offices	99	24	188	1
阿勒泰地区	Altay Administrative Offices	91	17	93	
博尔塔拉蒙古自治州	Bortala Mongol Autonomous Prefecture	37	10	79	
巴音郭楞蒙古自治州	Bayangol Mongol Autonomous Prefecture	115	22	246	1
阿克苏地区	Aksu Administrative Offices	157	44	710	1
克孜勒苏柯尔克孜自治州	Kizilsu Kirgiz Autonomous Prefecture	37	10	173	
喀什地区	Kashgar [Kaxgar] Administrative Offices	232	43	1157	1
和田地区	Hotan Administrative Offices	152	16	740	
生产建设兵团	Production and Construction Group	263	72	265	

17-17 各地、州、市各级各类学校教职工数

Number of Teachers and Staff by Level and Type of School and by Prefecture, Autonomous Prefecture and City

单位：人 (2007 年) (person)

地区	Region	普通高等学校 Regular Institutions of Higher Education	中等专业学校 Specialized Secondary Schools	#中等师范学校 Teacher Training Secondary Schools
总计	**Total**	**26490**	**8971**	**1738**
乌鲁木齐市	Urumqi City	16040	2535	135
克拉玛依市	Karamay City	509	259	177
石河子市	Shihezi City	251	618	53
吐鲁番地区	Turpan Administrative Offices		279	
哈密地区	Hami [Kumul] Administrative Offices		543	148
昌吉回族自治州	Changji Hui Autonomous Prefecture	1664	153	
伊犁哈萨克自治州	Ili Kazak Autonomous Prefecture	1749	1265	373
伊犁州直属县(市)	Counties (Cities) Direct Under Ili Prefecture	1749	635	233
塔城地区	Tacheng [Tarbagatai] Administrative Offices		383	95
阿勒泰地区	Altay Administrative Offices		247	45
博尔塔拉蒙古自治州	Bortala Mongol Autonomous Prefecture		72	32
巴音郭楞蒙古自治州	Bayangol Mongol Autonomous Prefecture	431	349	204
阿克苏地区	Aksu Administrative Offices	501	131	61
克孜勒苏柯尔克孜自治州	Kizilsu Kirgiz Autonomous Prefecture		322	185
喀什地区	Kashgar [Kaxgar] Administrative Offices	951	599	
和田地区	Hotan Administrative Offices	526	340	259
生产建设兵团	Production and Construction Group	3868	1506	111

地区	Region	普通中学 Regular Secondary Schools	小学 Primary Schools	盲聋哑学校 Special Schools
总计	**Total**	**126880**	**149286**	**385**
乌鲁木齐市	Urumqi City	12016	10367	175
克拉玛依市	Karamay City	2461	2104	17
石河子市	Shihezi City	1187	692	
吐鲁番地区	Turpan Administrative Offices	4583	4990	
哈密地区	Hami [Kumul] Administrative Offices	3423	3778	18
昌吉回族自治州	Changji Hui Autonomous Prefecture	8152	7700	38
伊犁哈萨克自治州	Ili Kazak Autonomous Prefecture	23715	31773	9
伊犁州直属县(市)	Counties (Cities) Direct Under Ili Prefecture	13509	17941	
塔城地区	Tacheng [Tarbagatai] Administrative Offices	5986	7784	9
阿勒泰地区	Altay Administrative Offices	4220	6048	
博尔塔拉蒙古自治州	Bortala Mongol Autonomous Prefecture	2753	3270	
巴音郭楞蒙古自治州	Bayangol Mongol Autonomous Prefecture	7396	9664	47
阿克苏地区	Aksu Administrative Offices	10666	15221	25
克孜勒苏柯尔克孜自治州	Kizilsu Kirgiz Autonomous Prefecture	3238	5041	
喀什地区	Kashgar [Kaxgar] Administrative Offices	20228	25855	56
和田地区	Hotan Administrative Offices	9152	11732	
生产建设兵团	Production and Construction Group	17910	17099	

注：2005 年起石河子大学、塔里木农大数据列入生产建设兵团。(以下同)
Note: Since 2005 data of Production and construction group include data of Shihezi University and Tarim University.

17-18 各地、州、市各级各类学校教师数

Number of Teachers by Level and Type of School and by Prefecture, Autonomous Prefecture and City

单位：人 (2007 年) (person)

地区	Region	普通高等学校 Regular Institutions of Higher Education	中等专业学校 Specialized Secondary Schools	#中等师范学校 Teacher Training Secondary Schools
总计	**Total**	**15096**	**5553**	**1186**
乌鲁木齐市	Urumqi City	8813	1459	93
克拉玛依市	Karamay City	271	94	64
石河子市	Shihezi City	140	325	22
吐鲁番地区	Turpan Administrative Offices		197	
哈密地区	Hami [Kumul] Administrative Offices		318	90
昌吉回族自治州	Changji Hui Autonomous Prefecture	1108	101	
伊犁哈萨克自治州	Ili Kazak Autonomous Prefecture	939	781	265
伊犁州直属县(市)	Counties (Cities) Direct Under Ili Prefecture	939	417	177
塔城地区	Tacheng [Tarbagatai] Administrative Offices		216	65
阿勒泰地区	Altay Administrative Offices		148	23
博尔塔拉蒙古自治州	Bortala Mongol Autonomous Prefecture		35	17
巴音郭楞蒙古自治州	Bayangol Mongol Autonomous Prefecture	329	262	164
阿克苏地区	Aksu Administrative Offices	284	119	61
克孜勒苏柯尔克孜自治州	Kizilsu Kirgiz Autonomous Prefecture		251	148
喀什地区	Kashgar [Kaxgar] Administrative Offices	645	421	
和田地区	Hotan Administrative Offices	301	253	189
生产建设兵团	Production and Construction Group	2266	937	73

地区	Region	普通中学 Regular Secondary Schools	#高中 Senior Secondary Schools	小学 Primary Schools	盲聋哑学校 Special Schools
总计	**Total**	**108232**	**27970**	**133626**	**298**
乌鲁木齐市	Urumqi City	9440	3583	9569	140
克拉玛依市	Karamay City	1982	766	1839	13
石河子市	Shihezi City	944	477	602	
吐鲁番地区	Turpan Administrative Offices	4062	1047	4670	
哈密地区	Hami [Kumul] Administrative Offices	2963	1104	3407	9
昌吉回族自治州	Changji Hui Autonomous Prefecture	6924	2395	7369	32
伊犁哈萨克自治州	Ili Kazak Autonomous Prefecture	20307	5764	27892	8
伊犁州直属县(市)	Counties (Cities) Direct Under Ili Prefecture	11566	3167	15816	
塔城地区	Tacheng [Tarbagatai] Administrative Offices	5256	1566	6910	8
阿勒泰地区	Altay Administrative Offices	3485	1031	5166	
博尔塔拉蒙古自治州	Bortala Mongol Autonomous Prefecture	2291	678	2890	
巴音郭楞蒙古自治州	Bayangol Mongol Autonomous Prefecture	6414	1922	8874	36
阿克苏地区	Aksu Administrative Offices	9276	1783	13944	18
克孜勒苏柯尔克孜自治州	Kizilsu Kirgiz Autonomous Prefecture	2820	723	4224	
喀什地区	Kashgar [Kaxgar] Administrative Offices	18369	2628	23278	42
和田地区	Hotan Administrative Offices	8211	847	10342	
生产建设兵团	Production and Construction Group	14229	4253	14726	

17-19 各地、州、市各级各类学校在校学生数

Number of Students Enrollment by Level and Type of School and by Prefecture, Autonomous Prefecture and City

单位：人 (2007 年) (person)

地区	Region	高等学校 Regular Institutions of Higher Education	普通中等职业学校 Specialized Secondary Schools	#中等师范学校 Teacher Training Secondary Schools
总计	**Total**	**216389**	**141162**	**3877**
乌鲁木齐市	Urumqi City	126923	68750	730
克拉玛依市	Karamay City	5075	1350	
石河子市	Shihezi City	1864	16358	455
吐鲁番地区	Turpan Administrative Offices		1903	
哈密地区	Hami [Kumul] Administrative Offices		1046	73
昌吉回族自治州	Changji Hui Autonomous Prefecture	16621	7625	
伊犁哈萨克自治州	Ili Kazak Autonomous Prefecture	12082	10532	1159
伊犁州直属县(市)	Counties (Cities) Direct Under Ili Prefecture	12082	8069	1059
塔城地区	Tacheng [Tarbagatai] Administrative Offices		640	
阿勒泰地区	Altay Administrative Offices		1823	100
博尔塔拉蒙古自治州	Bortala Mongol Autonomous Prefecture		866	
巴音郭楞蒙古自治州	Bayangol Mongol Autonomous Prefecture	1563	7824	716
阿克苏地区	Aksu Administrative Offices	2142	3489	
克孜勒苏柯尔克孜自治州	Kizilsu Kirgiz Autonomous Prefecture		780	110
喀什地区	Kashgar [Kaxgar] Administrative Offices	11225	5692	
和田地区	Hotan Administrative Offices	3986	3677	402
生产建设兵团	Production and Construction Group	34908	11270	232

地区	Region	普通中学 Regular Secondary Schools	#高中 Senior Secondary Schools	小学 Primary Schools	盲聋哑学校 Special Schools
总计	**Total**	**1529092**	**413452**	**2058884**	**6396**
乌鲁木齐市	Urumqi City	141627	57096	180967	798
克拉玛依市	Karamay City	23932	8693	26451	59
石河子市	Shihezi City	17347	8407	13246	10
吐鲁番地区	Turpan Administrative Offices	36164	10903	52281	26
哈密地区	Hami [Kumul] Administrative Offices	32133	13151	35120	157
昌吉回族自治州	Changji Hui Autonomous Prefecture	81071	33134	90307	208
伊犁哈萨克自治州	Ili Kazak Autonomous Prefecture	257928	85115	351946	630
伊犁州直属县(市)	Counties (Cities) Direct Under Ili Prefecture	154607	47157	226935	389
塔城地区	Tacheng [Tarbagatai] Administrative Offices	66169	24404	80178	186
阿勒泰地区	Altay Administrative Offices	37152	13554	44833	55
博尔塔拉蒙古自治州	Bortala Mongol Autonomous Prefecture	25889	10072	30797	78
巴音郭楞蒙古自治州	Bayangol Mongol Autonomous Prefecture	76569	27991	94939	280
阿克苏地区	Aksu Administrative Offices	159140	32989	224903	511
克孜勒苏柯尔克孜自治州	Kizilsu Kirgiz Autonomous Prefecture	38237	10152	50457	51
喀什地区	Kashgar [Kaxgar] Administrative Offices	300352	42753	438175	1668
和田地区	Hotan Administrative Offices	131935	9289	216482	1239
生产建设兵团	Production and Construction Group	206768	63707	252813	681

17-20 各地、州、市各级各类学校招生数

Number of New Students Enrollment by Level and Type of School and by Prefecture, Autonomous Prefecture and City

单位：人 (2007 年) (person)

地 区	Region	高等学校 Regular Institutions of Higher Education	中等专业学校 Specialized Secondary Schools	#中等师范学校 Teacher Training Secondary Schools
总 计	**Total**	**65508**	**65290**	**1984**
乌鲁木齐市	Urumqi City	37813	35681	303
克拉玛依市	Karamay City	1774	312	
石河子市	Shihezi City	1042	7112	194
吐鲁番地区	Turpan Administrative Offices		941	
哈密地区	Hami [Kumul] Administrative Offices		343	
昌吉回族自治州	Changji Hui Autonomous Prefecture	5470	2689	
伊犁哈萨克自治州	Ili Kazak Autonomous Prefecture	3879	5111	707
伊犁州直属县(市)	Counties (Cities) Direct Under Ili Prefecture	3879	3974	607
塔城地区	Tacheng [Tarbagatai] Administrative Offices		210	
阿勒泰地区	Altay Administrative Offices		927	100
博尔塔拉蒙古自治州	Bortala Mongol Autonomous Prefecture		475	
巴音郭楞蒙古自治州	Bayangol Mongol Autonomous Prefecture	714	2707	265
阿克苏地区	Aksu Administrative Offices	823	1008	
克孜勒苏柯尔克孜自治州	Kizilsu Kirgiz Autonomous Prefecture	2930	204	
喀什地区	Kashgar [Kaxgar] Administrative Offices	1314	1917	
和田地区	Hotan Administrative Offices	9749	1055	368
生产建设兵团	Production and Construction Group		5735	147

地 区	Region	普通中学 Regular Secondary Schools	#高中 Senior Secondary Schools	小学 Primary Schools	盲聋哑学校 Special Schools
总 计	**Total**	**510080**	**146449**	**340108**	**1158**
乌鲁木齐市	Urumqi City	48516	18838	30977	135
克拉玛依市	Karamay City	8450	2908	4387	6
石河子市	Shihezi City	6212	3031	2091	1
吐鲁番地区	Turpan Administrative Offices	11979	3752	9172	2
哈密地区	Hami [Kumul] Administrative Offices	10619	4261	5585	8
昌吉回族自治州	Changji Hui Autonomous Prefecture	25906	10309	14037	25
伊犁哈萨克自治州	IliKazak Autonomous Prefecture	88064	29834	59940	64
伊犁州直属县(市)	Counties (Cities) Direct Under Ili Prefecture	54007	16842	38528	40
塔城地区	Tacheng [Tarbagatai] Administrative Offices	22244	8407	13162	12
阿勒泰地区	Altay Administrative Offices	11813	4585	8250	12
博尔塔拉蒙古自治州	Bortala Mongol Autonomous Prefecture	8364	3459	5040	8
巴音郭楞蒙古自治州	Bayangol Mongol Autonomous Prefecture	26569	9739	16573	39
阿克苏地区	Aksu Administrative Offices	50528	13208	37941	110
克孜勒苏柯尔克孜自治州	Kizilsu Kirgiz Autonomous Prefecture	12853	4254	8857	11
喀什地区	Kashgar [Kaxgar] Administrative Offices	100155	18064	72105	277
和田地区	Hotan Administrative Offices	41047	3401	35071	173
生产建设兵团	Production and Construction Group	70818	21391	38332	298

17-21 各地、州、市各级各类学校毕业生数

Number of Graduates by Level and Type of School and by Prefecture, Autonomous Prefecture and City

单位：人 (2007 年) (person)

地区	Region	高等学校 Regular Institutions of Higher Education	中等专业学校 Specialized Secondary Schools	#中等师范学校 Teacher Training Secondary Schools
总计	**Total**	**46128**	**25735**	**670**
乌鲁木齐市	Urumqi City	26955	12286	139
克拉玛依市	Karamay City	1482	774	
石河子市	Shihezi City	137	2212	75
吐鲁番地区	Turpan Administrative Offices		234	
哈密地区	Hami [Kumul] Administrative Offices		254	59
昌吉回族自治州	Changji Hui Autonomous Prefecture	4107	2389	
伊犁哈萨克自治州	Ili Kazak Autonomous Prefecture	2379	1326	27
伊犁州直属县(市)	Counties (Cities) Direct Under Ili Prefecture	2379	942	
塔城地区	Tacheng [Tarbagatai] Administrative Offices		80	
阿勒泰地区	Altay Administrative Offices		304	27
博尔塔拉蒙古自治州	Bortala Mongol Autonomous Prefecture		224	105
巴音郭楞蒙古自治州	Bayangol Mongol Autonomous Prefecture	216	1076	72
阿克苏地区	Aksu Administrative Offices	169	433	
克孜勒苏柯尔克孜自治州	Kizilsu Kirgiz Autonomous Prefecture		249	98
喀什地区	Kashgar [Kaxgar] Administrative Offices	2826	1327	
和田地区	Hotan Administrative Offices	1173	314	42
生产建设兵团	Production and Construction Group	6684	2637	53

地区	Region	普通中学 Regular Secondary Schools	#高中 Senior Secondary Schools	小学 Primary Schools	盲聋哑学校 Special Schools
总计	**Total**	**515494**	**127129**	**361921**	**716**
乌鲁木齐市	Urumqi City	44128	18744	28627	102
克拉玛依市	Karamay City	7038	2933	4164	13
石河子市	Shihezi City	4289	2095	2262	
吐鲁番地区	Turpan Administrative Offices	13455	3821	8630	3
哈密地区	Hami [Kumul] Administrative Offices	10927	4366	6108	5
昌吉回族自治州	Changji Hui Autonomous Prefecture	26246	9745	14976	20
伊犁哈萨克自治州	Ili Kazak Autonomous Prefecture	86570	27164	59855	69
伊犁州直属县(市)	Counties (Cities) Direct Under Ili Prefecture	50028	15012	37995	46
塔城地区	Tacheng [Tarbagatai] Administrative Offices	22553	8269	13705	14
阿勒泰地区	Altay Administrative Offices	13989	3883	8155	9
博尔塔拉蒙古自治州	Bortala Mongol Autonomous Prefecture	8649	3464	5223	12
巴音郭楞蒙古自治州	Bayangol Mongol Autonomous Prefecture	25122	8917	15469	15
阿克苏地区	Aksu Administrative Offices	58380	8314	37867	61
克孜勒苏柯尔克孜自治州	Kizilsu Kirgiz Autonomous Prefecture	15994	3037	8866	11
喀什地区	Kashgar [Kaxgar] Administrative Offices	109822	11067	83254	186
和田地区	Hotan Administrative Offices	40033	3149	38894	183
生产建设兵团	Production and Construction Group	64841	20313	47726	36

17-22 各类学校教育经费情况
Educational Funds in Various Schools

单位：万元　　(2007 年)　　(10 000 yuan)

指　标	Item	合 计 Total	国家财政性教育经费 Government Appropriation for Education	#预算内教育经费 Budgetary Education Expense	民办学校中举办者投入 Investor Donation	社会捐资 Donations	事业收入 Income from Under-takings	其 他 Others
总　计	**Total**	**1929180**	**1554296**	**1453498**	**1345**	**7085**	**296052**	**70403**
高等学校	**Institutions of Higher Education**	**307546**	**147038**	**139256**		**24**	**125087**	**35397**
普通高等学校	Regular Institutions of Higher Education	276412	132549	124782		21	111844	31999
成人高等学校	Institutions of Higher Education for Adults	31134	14489	14474		3	13243	3398
中等职业学校	**Technical Schools**	**110056**	**70007**	**64889**	**56**	**1713**	**35194**	**3087**
中等专业学校	Specialized Secondary Schools	66429	39875	36324		1610	23469	1476
职业高中	Professional Senior High School	16067	13124	11699	56	13	2701	174
技工学校	Technical Schools	19729	11893	11764		58	6752	1026
成人中专学校	Specialized Secondary Schools for Adults	7831	5116	5102		33	2272	411
中　学	**Secondary Schools**	**673200**	**566332**	**533840**	**717**	**3123**	**89358**	**13671**
普通中学	Regular Secondary Schools	672969	566130	533637	717	3123	89329	13671
普通高中	Senior high school	228912	161530	149138	163	2248	59272	5700
#农 村	Rural Areas	4781	4225	4042		101	199	256
普通初中	Junior high school	444057	404600	384499	554	875	30057	7971
#农 村	Rural Areas	230609	223408	217652	1	258	4160	2782
小　学	**Primary Schools**	**647030**	**618721**	**594547**	**572**	**1070**	**20158**	**6510**
普通小学	Regular Primary Schools	647030	618721	594547	572	1070	20158	6510
#农 村	Rural Areas	410067	403127	395384	38	729	3231	2944
特殊教育	**Special Education Schools**	**2150**	**1816**	**1767**		**17**	**271**	**46**
幼儿园	**Kindergartens**	**45093**	**37353**	**36846**		**492**	**6772**	**475**
教育行政单位	**Education administrative unit**	**46333**	**36278**	**35509**		**327**	**4197**	**5531**
教育事业单位	**Education institution**	**71592**	**54926**	**25260**		**118**	**11868**	**4679**
其　他	**Others**	**26181**	**21826**	**21586**		**200**	**3148**	**1007**

17-23 科技活动基本情况
Basic Statistics on Scientific and Technological Activities

指　　标	Item	2006	2007
科技活动人员(人)	**Personal Engaged in Scientific and Technological Activities (person)**	**28398**	**30239**
#科学家与工程师	Scientists and Engineers	18924	20976
研究与试验发展全时人员(人年)	**Full-time Equivalent of Rearch and Development Personnel (person year)**	**7377**	**8832**
#科学家与工程师	Scientists and Engineers	6457	7888
科技经费筹集额(万元)	**Funding for Scientific and Technological Activities (10 000 yuan)**	**338666**	**362948**
#政府资金	Government Appropriation Funds	60492	87478
企业资金	Enterprises'Own Funds	231003	229661
银行贷款	Bank Loans	13826	15939
科技经费内部支出(万元)	**Internal Expenditures on Scientific and Technological Activities (10 000 yuan)**	**280141**	**328246**
#劳务费	Service Fees	71714	86838
固定资产购建费	Purchases or Construction of Fixed Assets	92973	112461
#研究与试验发展经费支出	Expenditure on Research and Development	84764	100174
基础研究	Basic Research	5664	9009
应用研究	Applied Research	17194	27980
试验发展	Experimental Development	61906	59953
研究与试验发展经费支出占新疆生产总值比重(%)	**Proportion of Expenditure on Research and Development to GDP of Xinjiang (%)**	**0.28**	**0.28**

17-24 县级以上政府部门属研究与开发机构及科技信息与文献机构数、人员数
State-Owned Research and Development Institutions and Information and Literature Institutions at and Above County Level and Persons Engaged

(2007 年)

指　　标	Item	合　计 Total	自然科学技术领域 Field of Natural Sciences and Technology	社会、人文科学技术领域 Field of Social Sciences and Humanities	科技信息和文献机构 Scientific-technical Information and Document Institutions
机构数(个)	**Institutions (unit)**	**106**	**91**	**7**	**8**
科技活动人员(人)	**Personal Engaged in Scientific and Technological Activities (person)**	**5685**	**5076**	**368**	**241**
#科学家与工程师	Scientists and Engineers	4784	4300	296	188
研究与试验发展全时人员(人·年)	**Full-time Equivalent of Rearch and Development Personnel (person.year)**	**2280**	**2056**	**206**	**18**
#科学家与工程师	Scientists and Engineers	1890	1700	172	18
科技经费筹集额(万元)	**Sources of Funds for S&T(10 000 yuan)**	**72396**	**64924**	**4064**	**3407**
#政府拨款	Government Funds	57204	50509	3761	2934
科技经费内部支出额(万元)	**Internal Expenditures on Scientific and Technological Activities (10 000 yuan)**	**56536**	**50592**	**3600**	**2344**
#劳务费	Service Fees	18788	16758	1213	817
固定资产购建费	Purchases or Construction of Fixed Assets	6632	6113	188	331
#研究与发展经费支出	Expenditure on Research and Development	20890	18232	2527	132
基础研究	Basic Research	4400	2036	2364	
应用研究	Applied Research	8525	8473	34	18
试验发展	Experimental Development	7965	7723	129	113

17-25 重大科学技术研究成果及奖励数

Number of Major Achievements in Scientific and Technological Research and Awarded Prizes

单位：项 (item)

年 份 Year	自治区级重大科技成果 Number of Major Achievements in Science and Technology of Autonomous Region	奖励情况 Awarded Prizes					
		国家级 National	自治区级 Autonomous Regional	一等奖 Frist Class Awards	二等奖 Second Class Awards	三等奖 Third Class Awards	四等奖 Fourth Class Awards
1978 年以前	1551	88	610				
1980-1985	1173	16	356	5	31	102	218
1990	444	3	129		18	56	55
1995	218	3	137	4	26	53	54
1996	276	15	135	2	27	46	60
1997	230	9	131	5	25	47	54
1998	219	4	105	2	27	38	38
1999	215	5	108	9	32	49	18
2000	250	2	90	5	18	67	
2001	285	6	92	4	23	65	
2002	207	5	99	5	30	64	
2003	232	3	111	8	34	69	
2004	218	4	108	4	33	71	
2005	225	3	101	6	27	68	
2006	110	3	107	8	37	62	

17-26 专利申请和批准数

Number of Patent Applications Accepted and Approved

单位：件 (case)

年 份 Year	申请数 Number of Patent Applications Accepted				批准数 Number of Patent Applications Granted				代理机构（个） Agency (unit)
	合计 Total	发明 Inventions	实用新型 Utility Models	外观设计 Designs	合计 Total	发明 Inventions	实用新型 Utility Models	外观设计 Designs	
1985	36								
1990	250	38	203	9	139	3	135	1	5
1995	609	92	467	50	312	11	285	16	6
1996	713	113	531	69	362	9	316	37	7
1997	799	139	544	116	328	12	246	70	7
1998	978	166	600	212	462	14	337	111	7
1999	881	139	552	190	859	32	630	197	7
2000	1088	179	699	210	717	66	475	176	7
2001	1088	189	683	216	755	90	522	143	5
2002	1239	216	779	244	627	61	407	159	4
2003	1472	253	940	279	751	75	520	156	5
2004	1492	272	870	350	792	75	530	187	5
2005	1851	320	1117	414	921	88	537	296	5
2006	2256	381	1166	709	1187	107	805	275	5
2007	2270	476	1255	539	1534	90	1035	409	5

17-27 高等学校科技活动情况

Basic Statistics on Scientific and Technological Activities of Higher Education School

指　　标	Item	2006	2007
科技活动人员(人)	**Personnel Engaged in Scientific and Technological Activities (person)**	**3203**	**4430**
#科学家与工程师	Scientists and Engineers	2774	3913
研究与发展机构(个)	**Agencies of Research and Development (unit)**	**25**	**47**
研究与发展人员全时当量(人·年)	**Full-time Equivalent of R&D Personnel (person.year)**	**1446**	**1998**
#科学家与工程师	Scientists and Engineers	1418	1962
#基础研究	Basic Research	613	764
应用研究	Applied Research	640	816
试验发展	Experimental Development	194	418
科技经费筹集额(万元)	**Funding for Scientific and Development Activities(10 000 yuan)**	**12737**	**13241**
#政府拨款	Government Funds	7143	11464
科技经费内部支出额(万元)	**Internal Expenditure on Scientific and Technological Activities (10 000 yuan)**	**10872**	**10087**
#劳务费	Service Fees	1964	3044
固定资产购建费	Purchases or Construction of Fixed Assets	5569	2341
#研究与发展经费支出	Expenditure on Research and Development	5964	7629
基础研究	Basic Research	2436	2902
应用研究	Applied Research	2450	3009
试验发展	Experimental Development	1078	1714

17-28 企事业单位主要专业技术人员数

Number of Main Scientific and Technical Personnel in Enterprises and Institutions

单位：人 (person)

年 份 Year	合 计 Total	工程技术人员 Engineering	农业技术人员 Agriculture	卫生技术人员 Health Care	科学研究人员 Scientific Researcn	教学人员 Teaching
1978.6 月末	85063	22198	13141	31741	3042	14941
1985	158709	51636	20730	57559	3416	25368
1990	241524	92383	25089	71906	4326	47820
1995	437209	109463	28096	79014	4825	215811
1996	325286	58108	22306	55332	2691	186849
1997	345273	60324	24434	58787	2933	198795
1998	355878	59009	27727	6008	2701	206433
1999	367125	75276	25856	57054	2515	206424
2000	368262	58576	27764	62338	2409	217175
2001	385129	59913	30043	65585	2492	227096
2002	387726	58011	31867	65364	2337	230147
2003	385705	57506	30808	65622	2236	229533
2004	398318	55421	32831	68604	2928	238534
2005	402404	51915	32744	67945	2451	247349
2006	412977	52702	34131	68231	2460	255453
2007	411590	50680	33859	69101	2453	255497

注: 1.1991 年起专业技术人员包括企事业单位(不含行政机关)人员数,教学人员包括社会和自然科技领域及小学教师人数。

2.1996 年后数据不包括中央单位的专业技术人员数，故人员减少较多。

Note: a) The Specialezed and technical personnel include those who work in enterprises and institutions (excluding administrative organs), teaching Staff, those work in social and nature scientific fields as well as elementary school teachers from 1991 on.

b) After 1996, the data exclude the figure of professionals with national establishments stationed to Xinjiang and thus the number of staff is reduced a lot.

17-29 企事业单位主要专业技术人员比重

Proportion of Scientific and Technical Personnel in Enterprises and Institutions

单位：% (%)

年 份 Year	合 计 Total	工程技术 Engineering	农业技术 Agriculture	卫生技术 Health Care	科学研究 Scientific Research	教 学 Teaching
1978.6 月末	100	26.10	15.45	37.31	3.58	17.56
1985	100	32.54	13.06	36.27	2.15	15.98
1990	100	38.25	10.39	29.77	1.79	19.80
1995	100	25.04	6.43	18.07	1.10	49.36
1996	100	17.86	6.86	17.01	0.83	57.44
1997	100	17.47	7.08	17.03	0.85	57.57
1998	100	16.58	7.79	16.86	0.76	58.00
1999	100	20.50	7.04	15.54	0.69	56.23
2000	100	15.91	7.54	16.93	0.65	58.97
2001	100	15.55	7.80	17.03	0.65	58.97
2002	100	14.96	8.22	16.86	0.60	59.36
2003	100	14.91	7.99	17.01	0.58	59.51
2004	100	13.91	8.24	17.22	0.74	59.89
2005	100	12.90	8.14	16.89	0.61	61.46
2006	100	12.76	8.26	16.52	0.60	61.86
2007	100	12.31	8.22	16.79	0.60	62.08

17-30 大中型工业企业科技活动情况

(2007 年)

项　目	Item	企业数(个) Nnmber of Industrial Enterprises (unit)	科技机构(个) Number of Scientific Technological Agencies (unit)	从事科技活动人员数(人) Number of Persons Engaged in Scientific and Technological Activities (person)
总　计	**Total**	**255**	**71**	**11546**
按登记注册类型分	**Grouped by Ownership**			
内资企业	Domestic-funded Enterprises	245	71	11470
国有企业	State-owned	43	19	2550
集体企业	Collective-owned Enterprises	2		
联营企业	Joint Ownership Enterprises	1		
集体联营企业	Collective Joint-Ownership Enterprises	1		
有限责任公司	Limited Liability Corporations	135	31	2627
国有独资公司	Sole State-funded Corporations	25	3	79
其他有限责任公司	Limited Liability Corporations	110	28	2548
股份有限责任公司	Share-holding Corporations Ltd	39	20	6239
私营企业	Private Enterprises	25	1	54
私营独资企业	Private-funded Enterprises	1		
私营有限责任公司	Private Limited Liability Corporations	21	1	54
私营股份有限公司	Private Stock Ltd. Co.	3		
港澳台商投资企业	Enterprises With Funds from Hong Kong, Macao and Taiwan	6		
合资经营企业(港或澳、台资)	Joint-ventures Enterprises	2		
港、澳、台商独资经营企业	Enterprises with Funds from Hong Kong, Macao and Taiwan	4		
外商投资企业	Foreign Funded Enterprises	4		76
中外合资经营企业	Joint-venture Enterprises	4		76
按工业行业大类分	**Grouped by Sector**			
采矿业	Mining and Quarrying	35	18	6225
煤炭开采和洗选业	Coal Extracting and Dressing	17	3	199
石油和天然气开采业	Petroleum and Natural Gas Extraction	7	14	5939
黑色金属矿采选业	Processing of Ferrous Metals Ores	3		
有色金属矿采选业	Processing of Nonferrous Metals Ores	6	1	87
非金属矿采选业	Processing of Nonmetal Ores	2		
制造业	Manufacturing	186	50	4891
农副食品加工业	Processing of Food from Agricultural Products	16	2	100
食品制造业	Food Manufacturing	10	4	188
饮料制造业	Beverage Manufacturing	7	1	348
烟草制品业	Tobacco Manufacturing	1		
纺织业	Textile Industry	38	7	636
纺织服装、鞋、帽制造业	Leather, Fur, Feather and Related Products Manufacturing	1	1	33
木材加工及木、竹、藤、棕、草制品业	Processing of Timber, Wood, Bamboo, Cane, Grass Products	1		
家具制造业	Furniture Manufacturing	3		26
造纸及纸制品业	Paper and Paper Products Manufacturing	3	1	93

Statistics on Science and Technical Activities of Large and Medium-Sized Industrial Enterprises

科学家工程师 Scientists and Engineers	研究与试验发展人员 Number of Persons in Research and Experiment	机构中从事科技活动人员 Number of Persons Engaged in Scientific and Technological Activities	经费筹集额(万元) Funding for Scientific and Technological Activities (10 000 yuan)	#企业资金 Self-raised Funds by Enterprise	支出总额(万元) Funding for Scientific and Technological Expenses (10 000 yuan)	#研究与试验发展经费 Expenditure on Research and Development	科技项目数(项) Number of Science and Technology (item)	#新产品项目数 Number of Research and Development
8121	**4802**	**5984**	**231561**	**201915**	**219096**	**70055**	**1256**	**206**
8070	4802	5984	226734	199112	215944	70055	1251	201
2082	1236	1209	22473	16844	32711	6727	235	27
1566	742	908	35424	28448	43370	12105	200	101
52	22	27	415	390	678	27	22	13
1514	720	881	35009	28058	42692	12078	178	88
4380	2824	3854	158137	153321	127495	51224	814	72
42		13	10700	500	12367		2	1
42		13	10700	500	12367		2	1
51			4826	2804	3152		5	5
51			4826	2804	3152		5	5
4740	3312	3467	123094	117648	90221	35823	623	8
97	14	79	1581	1576	1388	23	13	2
4578	3298	3371	120935	115494	88249	35800	597	2
65		17	578	578	584		13	4
2983	1490	2304	102372	79231	121887	34232	616	182
60	20	76	1968	1768	1389	546	7	5
126	58	67	3405	2715	4496	1168	27	23
83	80	17	6352	4328	4678	1526	9	9
321	84	329	7417	4175	11213	2728	32	18
24	8	4	220	195	560	4	20	11
14					21			
42	19	45	2222	1857	8761	1576	8	4

17-30 续表

项　目	Item	企业数(个) Nnmber of Industrial Enterprises (unit)	科技机构数(个) Number of Scientific Technological Agencies (unit)	从事科技活动人员数(人) Number of Persons Engaged in Scientific and Technological Activities (person)
印刷业和记录媒介的复制	Printing and Copying of Medium for Record	1		
石油加工、炼焦及核燃料加工业	Oil Processing, Coking and Nuclear Fuel Processing	11	4	751
化学原料及化学制品制造业	Raw Chemical Material and Chemical Products	21	5	681
医药制造业	Medicine Manufacturing	1		
化学纤维制造业	Chemical Fiber Manufacturing	4	1	84
橡胶制品业	Rubber Products Manufacturing	1	1	35
塑料制品业	Plastic Products Manufacturing	4	4	198
非金属矿物制品业	Nonmetal Mineral Products Manufacturing	26	10	550
黑色金属冶炼及压延加工业	Smelting and Pressing of Ferrous Metals	15	1	209
有色金属冶炼及压延加工业	Smelting and Pressing of Nonferrous Metals	4		11
金属制品业	Metal Products Manufacturing	5	2	118
通用设备制造业	General Purpose Machinery Manufacturing	2	1	31
专用设备制造业	Special Purpose Machinery Manufacturing	4	1	66
交通运输设备制造业	Transport Equipment Manufacturing	2	1	258
电气机械及器材制造业	Electric Equipment and Machinery Manufacturing	4	2	350
通信设备、计算机及其他电子设备制造业	Telecom Equipment, Computer and Other Electronic Equipment	1	1	125
电力、燃气及水的生产和供应业	Production and Suppoly of Electric Power,Gas and Water	34	3	430
电力、热力的生产和供应业	Electric Power and Thermal Production and Supply	32	3	430
燃气生产和供应业	Gas Production and Supply	1		
水的生产和供应业	Water Production and Supply	1		
按企业所在地区划分	**Grouped by Region**			
乌鲁木齐市	Urumqi City	66	14	1849
克拉玛依市	Karamay City	16	19	4966
吐鲁番地区	Turpan Administrative Offices	13	1	893
哈密地区	Hami [Kumul] Administrative Offices	7	5	100
昌吉回族自治州	Changji Hui Autonomous Prefecture	24	8	704
伊犁州直属县(市)	Counties (Cities) Direct Under Ili Prefecture	23	4	413
塔城地区	Tacheng [Tarbagatai] Administrative Offices	17		
阿勒泰地区	Altay Administrative Offices	8	1	87
博尔塔拉蒙古自治州	Bortala Mongol Autonomous Prefecture	9	1	82
巴音郭楞蒙古自治州	Bayangol Mongol Autonomous Prefecture	16	3	925
阿克苏地区	Aksu Administrative Offices	18	4	445
克孜勒苏柯尔克孜自治州	Kizilsu Kirgiz Autonomous Prefecture	1		
喀什地区	Kashgar [Kaxgar] Administrative Offices	6		155
和田地区	Hotan Administrative Offices	5		3
自治区直辖行政单位	Administrative unite of municipality directly under the central government	26	11	924

Continued

科学家工程师 Scientists and Engineers	研究与试验发展人员 Number of Persons in Research and Experiment	机构中从事科技活动人员 Number of Persons Engaged in Scientific and Technological Activities	经费筹集额(万元) Funding for Scientific and Technological Activities (10 000 yuan)	#企业资金 Self-raised Funds by Enterprise	支出总额(万元) Funding for Scientific and Technological Expenses (10 000 yuan)	#研究与试验发展经费 Expenditure on Research and Development	科技项目数(项) Number of Science and Technology (item)	#新产品项目数 Number of Research and Development
535	415	521	18137	18137	16799	10289	153	7
390	323	185	8909	7156	13433	7239	30	10
30		11	1230	1200	1160		2	2
6		35	1265	1265	1268		25	16
181	77	147	1593	1591	4440	2161	33	8
464	214	178	13745	3965	15844	1514	46	25
119	44	44	756	303	756	104	15	5
2			2968	1500	4396		1	
64	26	26	785	685	845	135	2	
22	5	4	180	105	120	33	6	
25		66	455	245	457		4	4
69		246	1752	1752	1752		12	12
321	117	216	23915	21390	24448	5211	170	18
85		87	5100	4900	5050		14	5
398		213	6095	5037	6989		17	16
398		213	6095	5037	6989		17	16
1251	199	1046	42763	36527	39932	2798	189	66
3958	3248	2567	78477	74417	85189	43849	561	2
593	407	605	4001	4001	1842	1842	60	
71	41	50	505	455	648	187	10	10
526	294	363	13481	11254	13655	6758	234	52
88	114	116	6621	4624	9401	1586	15	12
65		17	578	578	584		13	4
39		13	7793	90	9439		5	
514	138	494	55997	54381	20210	643	79	16
346	30	125	6555	3880	6789	39	17	12
149	23		500	462	2728	2028	7	6
3	3		10	10	10	10	1	
518	305	588	14280	11236	28669	10315	65	26

17-31 各类技术合同签定及执行情况

Statistics on Signing and Implementing Technical Contracts by Type

单位：项、万元 (item,10 000yuan)

项　目	Item	合同数 Number of Contracts		合同金额 Revenue from Fulfilment of Contracts		#技术交易额 Transaction Value in Technical Market	
		2006	2007	2006	2007	2006	2007
总　计	**Total**	**1764**	**3049**	**76084.17**	**71724.42**	**53300.79**	**65983.90**
技术开发合同	Technology Development	166	319	5118.21	16373.85	4455.43	15821.05
技术转让合同	Technology Transfer	191	175	2187.87	2645.47	2091.21	2557.88
技术咨询合同	Technology Consultation	797	1046	17301.11	11836.92	10316.23	11747.65
技术服务合同	Technology Service	610	1509	51476.98	40868.19	36437.92	35857.33

17-32 各级技术计划项目进入技术市场情况

Statistics on Projects for Technical Plan Entering Technical Market by Level

单位：项、万元 (2007 年) (item,10 000 yuan)

项　目	Item	合　计 Total		国家计划 National Plans		部门计划 Department Plans	
		项　数 Number of Items	金　额 Values	项　数 Number of Items	金　额 Values	项　数 Number of Items	金　额 Values
总　计	**Total**	**3049**	**71724.42**	**17**	**1430.95**	**152**	**6333.37**
机关法人	Government Agency Legal Person	1	7.00				
事业法人	Institntion Legal Person	1773	14354.62	12	336.92	36	613.95
社团法人	Corporation Aggregate	24	256.00				
企业法人	Business Entity	1250	57103.20	5	1094.03	116	5719.41
自 然 人	Person	1	3.60				

项　目	Item	省、自治区计划 单列市计划 Provinces, Municipality Plans		地、市、县计划 Area City and County Plans		计划外 Out of Plan	
		项　数 Number of Items	金　额 Values	项　数 Number of Items	金　额 Values	项　数 Number of Items	金　额 Values
总　计	**Total**	**128**	**2295.37**	**281**	**2839.69**	**2471**	**58825.04**
机关法人	Government Agency Legal Person					1	7.00
事业法人	Institntion Legal Person	89	913.03	217	2321.25	1419	10169.46
社团法人	Corporation Aggregate	8	38.00	11	59.00	5	159.00
企业法人	Business Entity	31	1344.34	53	459.44	1045	48485.98
自 然 人	Person					1	3.60

17-33 技术流向地域情况

Statistics on Location of Technical Contract

单位：项、万元 (2007 年) (item, 10 000 yuan)

地 区 Region	合同类别合计 Contracts of Classification Total		技术开发 Technology Development		技术转让 Technology Transfer		技术咨询 Technology Consultation		技术服务 Technology Service	
	项 数 Number of Items	金 额 Values	项 数 Number of Items	金 额 Values	项 数 Number of Items	金 额 Values	项 数 Number of Items	金 额 Values	项 数 Number of Items	金 额 Values
总 计 Total	**3049**	**71724.42**	**319**	**16373.85**	**175**	**2645.47**	**1046**	**11836.92**	**1509**	**40868.19**
北京市 Beijing	31	2941.85	8	338.40	2	192.20	7	298.00	14	2113.25
天津市 Tianjing	2	57.10			1	43.50			1	13.60
河北省 Hebei	15	198.43			1	65.00	1	10.00	13	123.43
内蒙古 Neimengu	3	49.00	1	2.00			2	47.00		
辽宁省 Liaoning	9	1320.51	3	180.00			1	150.00	5	990.51
黑龙江省 Heilongjiang	2	240.00					2	240.00		
上海市 Shanghai	4	36.20	2	10.00	1	1.20	1	25.00		
江苏省 Jiangsu	7	498.10	1	4.69			2	126.00	4	367.40
浙江省 Zhejiang	5	101.00					2	15.00	3	86.00
安徽省 Anhui	1	12.00							1	12.00
福建省 Fujian	6	83.76			1	1.20			5	82.56
江西省 Jiangxi	3	3.00			3	3.00				
山东省 Shandong	1	1.20			1	1.20				
河南省 Henan	6	143.45			1	1.20	2	49.00	3	93.25
湖北省 Hubei	2	1.70			2	1.70				
湖南省 Hunan	2	4.20			1	1.20			1	3.00
广东省 Guangdong	8	67.50	2	62.00	6	5.50				
重庆市 Chongqing	2	28.00							2	28.00
四川省 Sichuan	4	21.78			2	2.40			2	19.38
云南省 Yunnan	2	1.70			2	1.70				
陕西省 Shaanxi	2	11.00					1	6.00	1	5.00
甘肃省 Gansu	10	1240.00	1	60.00			5	280.00	4	900.00
青海省 Qinghai	2	28.52					1	5.00	1	23.52
宁夏回族自治区 Ningxia	1	20.00					1	20.00		
新疆维吾尔自治区 Xinjiang	2910	62213.95	300	15635.35	151	2324.47	1017	10550.62	1442	33703.51
其 他 Others	9	2400.48	1	81.40			1	15.30	7	2303.78

17-34 技术经济合同成交情况
Statistics on Transaction in Technical and Economic Contract

单位：项、万元 (2007 年) (item, 10 000 yuan)

买方类别 Classification of Buyers \ 卖方类别 Classification of Sellers		合 计 Total		#机关法人 Government Agency Legal Person		#事业法人 Institntion Legal Person		#社团法人 Corporation Aggregate		#企业法人 Business Entity	
		项 数 Number of Items	金 额 Values	项 数 Number of Items	金 额 Values	项 数 Number of Items	金 额 Values	项 数 Number of Items	金 额 Values	项 数 Number of Items	金 额 Values
总 计	**Total**	**3049**	**71724**	**1**	**7**	**1773**	**14355**	**24**	**256**	**1250**	**57103**
机关法人	Government Agency Legal Person	385	6627			279	3293	18	91	88	3243
事业法人	Institntion Legal Person	361	3770			247	1857			114	1913
社团法人	Corporation Aggregate	4	19			3	19			1	…
企业法人	Business Entity	2159	60653	1	7	1138	8551	6	165	1013	51926
自然人	Person	110	30			86	29			24	…
其他组织	Others	30	627			20	606			10	21

17-35 文化产业基本情况
Basic Statistics on Culture

项 目	Item	1995	2000	2007
文化产业机构数(个)	**Number of Culture Institutions (unit)**	**1174**	**7848**	**12052**
文化部门	Culture Departments	366	1055	1623
其他部门	Other Departments	808	6793	10429
文化产业人员数(人)	**Number of Person in Culture (person)**	**8348**	**26621**	**38203**
文化部门	Culture Departments	7372	9801	12526
其他部门	Other Departments	976	16820	25677
各类文化艺术事业单位数(个)	**Number of Institutions on Various Culture and Art (unit)**			
文化馆、艺术馆	Cultural Centers, Art Centers	107	108	109
公共图书馆	Public Libraries	66	80	94
博物馆	Museums	12	23	32
艺术表演场所	Art Performance Places	26	23	30
艺术表演团体	Art Performance Troupes	87	88	120
戏剧、电影观众(万人次)	**Spectators of Theater and Movie (10 000 person-times)**			
戏 剧	Theater	20	14	51
电 影	Movie	319	35	136
按总人口平均每人观看(次)	**Average Per-Capital Watch by Total Population (times)**			
戏 剧	Theater	0.01	0.01	0.02
电 影	Movie	0.20	0.02	0.06

17-36 文化艺术、文物事业机构和人员情况
Number of Institutions and Personnel in Culture, Art and Cultural Relics

(2007 年)

项　目	Item	机构数（个） Number of Institutions (unit)	从业人员数（人） Number of Persons Engaged (person)
艺术事业	**Art Institutions**	**150**	**4624**
艺术表演团体	Art Performance Troupes	120	4174
话剧、儿童剧、滑稽剧团	Drama, Children Plays and Comedy Troupes	2	122
歌剧、舞剧、歌舞剧团	Opera, Ballet and Dance Troupes	6	463
歌舞团、轻音乐团	Song and Dance Troupe, Light Music Troupe	63	2183
文工团、文宣队、乌兰牧骑	Cultural and Performance Troupes and Ulanmuchi (equestrain art troupes)	35	850
戏曲剧团	Local Opera Troupes	12	432
#京 剧	Local Beijing Opera Troupes	2	88
曲艺、杂技、木偶、皮影团	Recitation and Ballad Troupes, Acrobatics and Circus Troupes, Puppet Show Troupes and Shadow Play Troupes	2	124
艺术表演场所	Art Centers	30	450
剧场、影剧院	Theaters and Music Halls	29	442
图书馆事业	**Libraries**	**94**	**971**
群众文化事业	**Mass Culture**	**1160**	**3409**
群众艺术馆	Mass Art Centers	15	321
文化馆	Cultural Centers	94	1043
文化站	Cultural Stations	1051	2045
#乡镇文化站	Township Cultural Stations	941	1859
艺术教育事业	**Culture and Education**	**3**	**215**
艺术科研机构	**Art Research Institutions**	**1**	**27**
文化市场经营单位	**Entertainment Operators**	**10385**	**25058**
文化娱乐业	Entertainment Operators	4176	12757
文化市场其他经营单位	Cultural Market Operators	6209	12301
其他文化事业	**Other Cultural Units**	**17**	**166**
艺术创作机构	Art Creation Institutions	2	34
艺术展览机构	Art Exhibition Institutions	1	5
其　他	Others	14	127
文物事业	**Cultural Relics**	**121**	**1131**
文物机构	Historical Relics Agency	88	761
文物保护管理机构	Agency of Historical Relics Preservation	85	623
文物科研机构	Scientific and Research Historical Relics Agency	2	122
其他文物机构	Other Historical Relics Agency	1	16
博物馆	Museums	32	335
#历史类	History Museum	20	161
文物商店	Cultural Relics Store	1	35

17-37 电影、电视、广播事业基本情况

Basic Statistics on Feature Film, Television and Broadcasting

项　目	Item	2007
电影制片厂(个)	**Number of Film Studios (unit)**	**1**
广播电台(座)	**Number of Broadcasting Stations (unit)**	**6**
中短波发射台及转播台(座)	Transmission and Relaying Stations of MW&SW (unit)	47
中短波广播发射功率(千瓦)	Power of MW & SW Transmitters (kw.)	2711
调频发射台及转播台(座)	FM Transmission and Relaying Stations (unit)	1006
调频发射功率(千瓦)	Power of FM Transmitters (kw.)	261.243
节目(套)	Program (set)	115
制作广播节目(小时)	Production of Broadcasting (hour)	214615
#新闻资讯类节目	News Programs	33011
专题服务类节目	Feature Programs	67239
综艺类节目	Variety Show	65322
广播剧类节目	Radio Play	5403
广告类节目	Advertisement Programs	21344
其他类节目	Other Programs	22296
广播人口覆盖率((%)	Listener Rate (%)	93.53
电视台(座)	**Number of Television Stations (unit)**	**9**
广播电视台(座)	**Radio and TV Stations (unit)**	**31**
#县级广播电视台(座)	Radio and TV Station at County-Level (unit)	23
电视发射台及转播台(座)	TV Transmission Stations and Relaying Stations (unit)	934
电视发射机功率(千瓦)	Power of TV Transmitters (kw.)	372.796
节目(套)	Program (set)	139
制作电视节目(小时)	Production of TV Programs (hour)	53984
#新闻资讯类节目	News Programs	15150
专题服务类节目	Feature Programs	9643
综艺类节目	Variety Show	6171
影视剧类节目	Film and TV Play Programs	932
广告类节目	Advertisement Programs	15904
其他类节目	Other Programs	6184
电视人口覆盖率(%)	Viewer Rate (%)	93.48
有线电视用户(万户)	Numbe of Users of CATV (10 000 households)	1620424
#数字电视用户	Number of users Digital TV	176744
卫星地球站(座)	Eearth Satellite Station (unit)	1
卫星收转站(座)	Satellite Receiving Stations (unit)	17355

注：影视剧类节目不包括译制节目。
Note:Number of film and television programs did not include number of film dubbing program .

主要统计指标解释

普通高等学校 指按照国家规定的设置标准和审批程序批准举办的，通过全国普通高等学校统一招生考试，招收高中毕业生为主要培养对象，实施高等教育的全日制大学、独立设置的学院和高等专科学校、高等职业学校和其他机构。

大学、独立设置的学院主要实施本科层次以上教育，高等专科学校、高等职业学校实施专科层次教育，其他机构是承担国家普通招生计划任务不计校数的机构。包括普通高等学校分校和批准筹建的普通高等学校等。

成人高等学校 指按照国家规定的设置标准和审批程序批准举办的，通过全国成人高等学校统一招生考试，招收具有高中毕业或同等学历的在职从业人员为主要培养对象，利用函授、业余、脱产等多种形式对其实施高等学历教育的学校。包括职工高等学校、农民高等学校、管理干部学院、教育学院、独立函授学院、广播电视大学、其他机构等。其他机构是承担国家成人招生计划任务不计校数的机构。

小学学龄儿童入学率 指调查范围内已入小学学习的学龄儿童占校内外学龄儿童总数(包括弱智儿童，不包括盲聋哑儿童)的比重。计算公式为:

小学学龄儿童入学率=已入小学学习的学龄儿童数/按内外学龄儿童总数 × 100%

科技活动 指在自然科学、农业科学、医药科学、工程与技术科学、人文与社会科学领域(简称科学技术领域)中，与科技知识的产生、发展、传播和应用密切相关的有组织的活动。可分为研究与试验发展(R&D)、研究与试验发展成果应用及相关的科技服务三类活动。该定义是联合国教科文组织考虑成员国特别是发展中国家开展科技统计工作的需要，而对科技活动所作的统计界定。

科技活动人员 指直接从事科技活动、以及专门从事科技活动管理和为科技活动提供直接服务，累计的实际工作时间占全年制度工作时间10%及以上的人员。(1)直接从事科技活动的人员包括：在独立核算的科学研究与技术开发机构、高等学校、各类企业及其他事业单位内设的研究室、实验室、技术开发中心及中试车间(基地)等机构中从事科技活动的研究人员、工程技术人员、技术工人及其它人员；虽不在上述机构工作，但编入科技活动项目(课题)组的人员；科技信息与文献机构中的专业技术人员；从事论文设计的研究生等。(2)专门从事科技活动管理和为科技活动提供直接服务的人员，包括：独立核算的科学研究与技术开发机构、科技信息与文

献机构、高等学校、各类企业及其他事业单位主管科技工作的负责人，专门从事科技活动的计划、行政、人事、财务、物资供应、设备维护、图书资料管理等工作的各类人员，但不包括保卫、医疗保健人员、司机、食堂人员、茶炉工、水暖工、清洁工等为科技活动提供间接服务的人员。该指标用来反映投入科技活动人力的规模。

科学家与工程师 指科技活动人员中具有高、中级技术职称(职务)的人员和不具有高、中级技术职称(职务)的大学本科及以上学历人员。该指标用来反映投入科技活动人力的素质。

研究与试验发展(R&D) 指在科学技术领域，为增加知识总量、以及运用这些知识去创造新的应用进行的系统的创造性的活动，包括基础研究、应用研究、试验发展三类活动。国际上通常采用R&D 活动的规模和强度指标反映一国的科技实力和核心竞争力。

基础研究 指为了获得关于现象和可观察事实的基本原理的新知识(揭示客观事物的本质、运动规律，获得新发现、新学说)而进行的实验性或理论性研究，它不以任何专门或特定的应用或使用为目的。其成果以科学论文和科学著作为主要形式。用来反映知识的原始创新能力。

应用研究 指为获得新知识而进行的创造性研究，主要针对某一特定的目的或目标。应用研究是为了确定基础研究成果可能的用途，或是为达到预定的目标探索应采取的新方法(原理性)或新途径。其成果形式以科学论文、专著、原理性模型或发明专利为主。用来反映对基础研究成果应用途径的探索。

试验发展 指利用从基础研究、应用研究和实际经验所获得的现有知识，为产生新的产品、材料和装置，建立新的工艺、系统和服务，以及对已产生和建立的上述各项作实质性的改进而进行的系统性工作。其成果形式主要是专利、专有技术、具有新产品基本特征的产品原型或具有新装置基本特征的原始样机等。在社会科学领域，试验发展是指把通过基础研究、应用研究获得的知识转变成可以实施的计划(包括为进行检验和评估实施示范项目)的过程。人文科学领域没有对应的试验发展活动。主要反映将科研成果转化为技术和产品的能力，是科技推动经济社会发展的物化成果。

研究与试验发展人员 指参与研究与试验发展项目研究、管理和辅助工作的人员， 包括项目(课题)组人员， 企业科技行政管理人员和直接为项目(课题)活动提供服务的辅助人员。反映投入从事拥有自主知识产权的研究开发活动的人力规模。

研究与试验发展人员全时当量 指全时人员数加非全时人员按工作量折算为全时人员数的总和。例如：有两个全时人员和三个非全时人员(工作时间分别为20%、30% 和70%)，则全时当量为2+0.2+0.3+0.7=3.2 人年。为国际上比较科技人力投入而制定的可比指标。

专业技术人员 指从事专业技术工作和专业技术管理工作的人员，即企事业单位中已经聘任专业技术职务从事专业技术工作和专业技术管理工作的人员，以及未聘任专业技术职务，现在专业技术岗位上工作的人员。包括工程技术人员，农业技术人员，科学研究人员，卫生技术人员，教学人× 100%员，经济人员，会计人员，统计人员，翻译人员，图书资料、档案、文博人员，新闻出版人员，律师、公证人员，广播电视播音人员，工艺美术人员，体育人员，艺术人员及企业政治思想工作人员，共十七个专业技术职务类别。用来反映科技人力资源情况。

科技活动经费筹集 指从各种渠道筹集到的计划用于科技活动的经费，包括政府资金、企业资金、事业单位资金、金融机构贷款、国外资金和其他资金等。反映各社会经济主体对促进科技进步所做的努力。

政府资金 指从各级政府部门获得的计划用于科技活动的经费，包括科学事业费、科技三项费、科研基建费、科学基金、教育等部门事

业费中计划用于科技活动的经费以及政府部门预算外资金中计划用于科技活动的经费等。

企业资金 指从自有资金中提取或接受其他企业委托的、科研院所和高校等事业单位接受企业委托获得的，计划用于科研和技术开发的经费。不包括来自政府、金融机构及国外的计划用于科技活动的资金。

金融机构贷款 指从各类金融机构获得的用于科技活动的贷款。

科技活动经费内部支出 指报告年内用于科技活动的实际支出，包括劳务费、科研业务费、科研管理费，非基建投资购建的固定资产、科研基建支出以及其他用于科技活动的支出。不包括生产性活动支出、归还贷款支出及转拨外单位支出。反映科技投入实际完成情况。

劳务费 指以货币或实物形式直接或间接支付给从事科技活动人员的劳动报酬及各种费用。包括各种形式的工资、津贴、奖金、福利、离退休人员费用、人民助学金等。反映改善科技人员待遇情况。

固定资产购建费 指报告年内使用非基建投资购建的固定资产和用于科研基建投资的实际支出额，即固定资产实际支出和科研基建投资实际完成额之和。固定资产是指长期使用而不改变原有实物形态的主要物资设备、图书资料、实验材料和标本以及其他设备和家具、房屋、建筑物。反映用于改善科研条件和科研手段方面的投入情况。

新产品 指采用新技术原理、新设计构思研制、生产的全新产品，或在结构、材质、工艺等某一方面比原有产品有明显改进，从而显著提高了产品性能或扩大了使用功能的产品。既包括政府有关部门认定并在有效期内的新产品，也包括企业自行研制开发，未经政府有关部门认定，从投产之日起一年之内的新产品。用来反映科技产出及对经济增长的直接贡献。

专利 是专利权的简称，是对发明人的发明创造经审查合格后，由专利局依据专利法授予发明人和设计人对该项发明创造享有的专有权。包括发明、实用新型和外观设计。反映拥有自主知识产权的科技和设计成果情况。

发明 指对产品、方法或者其改进所提出的新的技术方案。是国际通行的反映拥有自主知识产权技术的核心指标。

实用新型 指对产品的形状、构造或者其结合所提出的适于实用的新的技术方案。反映具有一定技术含量的技术成果情况。

外观设计 指对产品的形状、图案、色彩或者其结合所作出的富有美感并适于工业上应用的新设计。反映拥有自主知识产权的外观设计成果情况。

文化事业机构 指从事专业文化工作和为专业文化工作服务的独立建制的单位。不包括这些单位另外举办独立核算的其他机构和各部门的业余文化组织。该指标主要反映文化事业机构发展规模水平。

艺术表演团体 指从事戏曲、音乐、舞蹈、杂技等专业艺术表演，有独立帐户的单位，不包括半工半艺、半农半艺和民间职业剧团。该指标主要反映全国专业艺术表演团体发展规模水平。

艺术表演观众人数(人次) 指售票、包场演出或民族地区免费演出的艺术表演观众人次数，不包括彩排审查和内部观摩演出的观看人次数。该指标主要反映全国观看专业艺术表演团体演出的效益规模。

Explanatory Notes on Main Statistical Indicators

Regular Institutions of Higher Learning refer to educational establishments set up according to the government evaluation and approval procedures, enrolling graduates from senior secondary schools and providing higher education courses and training for senior professionals. They include full-time universities, colleges, high professional schools, high professional vocational schools and others.

Universities and colleges are mainly providing undergraduate courses; those high professional schools and high professional vocational schools are mainly providing professional trainings; and others refer to educational establishments, which hare responsible for enrolling students but not covered in the total number of schools, including: branch schools of universities and colleges, and universities and colleges that have been proved and prepared to construct.

Institutions of Higher Learning for Adults refer to educational establishments, set up in line with relevant rules approved by the government, enrolling staff and workers wit h senior secondary school or equivalent education, and providing higher education courses in many forms of correspondence, spare time, or full time for adults. Professionals thus trained receive a qualification equivalent to graduates studying regular courses at regular universities, colleges and professional colleges. Institutions of higher learning for adults include schools of high education for staff and workers, schools of high education for peasants, colleges for management cadres, pedagogical colleges, independent correspondence colleges, Radio and TV universities and other educational establishments. Other educational establishments are responsible for enrolling adult students but not covered in the number of schools.

Enrollment Rate of Primary School Age Children refers to the proportion of school age children enrolled at schools to the total number of school age children both in and outside schools (including retarded children, but excluding blind, deaf and mute children). The formula is:

Enrollment Rate of Primary School-age Children = (Total Primary School-age Children at Schools)/(Total Primary School-age Children Both at and Outside Schools) × 100%

Scientific and Technological Activities (S&T Activities) refer to organized activities which are closely related with the creation, development, dissemination and application of the scientific and technical knowledge in the fields of natural sciences, agricultural science, medical science, engineering and technological science, humanities and social sciences (referred to as scientific and technological fields). S&T activities can be classified into 3 categories: research and development (R&D) activities, application of R&D results, and related S&T services. This statistical definition is made by UNICHIEF for scientific and technological activities to meet the need of carrying out statistical work in this field for its member countries in particular those developing countries.

Personnel Engaged in S&T Activities refer to personnel directly engaged in S&T activities, in the management of S&T activities, and in providing direct service to S&T activities, who sp end over 10% of the total working hours in a year in S&T activities. (1) Personnel directly engaged in S&T activities include researchers, engineers, technicians and other related personnel engaged in S&T activities in independent-accounting R&D institutions, institutions of higher learning, and in research institutes, laboratories, technology development centers and central experiment workshops under enterprises and institutions. Also included are people working in S&T research project teams, professional and technical personnel working in S&T information archiving institutes, and graduate students working on the design of their thesis. (2) Personnel engaged in the management of S&T activities and in providing direct service to S&T activities include senior management people responsible for S&T activities in independent -accounting R&D institutions, S&T information archiving institutes, institutions of higher learning, and in enterprises and institutions where S&T activities are undertaken. Also included are people responsible for the planning, administration, personnel management, financial management, logistics supply, equipment maintenance, information and library management that are related with S&T activities. People providing indirect services are excluded, such as security, medical service, drivers, plumbers, cleaners and those providing catering and related service. This indicator reflects the size of personnel engaged in S&T activities.

Scientists and Engineers refer to persons engaged in S&T activities who have obtained titles of senior and middle level professional positions, and those without such position but have completed university or higher education. This indicator reflects the quality of personnel engaged in S&T activities.

Research and Development (R&D) refers to systematic and creative activities in the field of science and technology aiming at increasing the knowledge and using the knowledge for new application. R&D includes 3 categories of activities: basic research, applied research and experiments and development. The scale and intensity of R&D are widely used internationally to reflect the strength of S&T and the core competitiveness of a country in the world.

Basic Research refers to empirical or theoretical research aiming at obtaining new knowledge on the fundament al principles of phenomena of observable facts to reveal the nature and law of movement of objects and to acquire new discoveries or new theories. Basic research takes no specific or designated application as the aim of the research. Results of basic research are mainly released or disseminated in the form of scientific papers or monographs. This indicator reflects the original innovation capacity of knowledge.

Applied research refers to creative research aiming at obtaining new knowledge on a specific objective or target. Purpose of the applied research is to identify the possible use of results from basic research, or to explore new (fundamental) methods or new approaches. Results of applied research are expressed in the form of scientific papers , monographs, fundamental models or invention patents. This indicator reflects the exploration of ways to apply the results of basic research.

Experiments and Development refer to systematic activities aiming at using the knowledge from basic and applied researches or from practical experience to develop new products, materials and equipment, to establish new production process, systems and services, or to make substantial improvement on the existing products, process or services. Results of experiment and development activities are embodied in patents, exclusive technology, and monotype of new products or equipment. In social sciences, experiment and development activities refer to the process of converting the knowledge from basic or applied researches in to feasible programs (including conduct of demonstration projects for assessment and evaluation). There are no experiment and development activities in the science of humanities. This indicator reflects the capability of transferring the results of S&T into technique and products, which is the materialized measurement of S&T pushing forward the economic and social development.

R&D Personnel refer to persons engaged in research, management and supporting activities of R&D, including persons in the project teams, persons engaged in the management of S&T activities of enterprises and sup porting staff providing direct service to the research projects. This indicator reflects the size of personnel engaged in R&D activities with independent intellectual property.

Full-time Equivalent of R&D Personnel refers to the sum of the full-time persons and the full-time equivalent of part time persons converted by workload. For instance, if there are 2full-time persons and 3 part time workers (20%, 30% and 70%of working hours respectively on R&D activities), the full-time equivalent is 2+0.2+0.3+0.7=3.2 person-years. This is an internationally comp arable indicator of input of personnel in S&T activities.

Professional and Technical Personnel refer to persons engaged in professional and technical work or in the management of professional and technical activities, i.e., people with professional or technical posit ions who are engaged in professional and technical work or in the management of professional and technical activities, and people without professional or technical positions but are working on professional or technical posts. They include professionals and technicians working in 17 categories of technical occupations including engineering, agriculture, scientific researches, medical service, teaching, economic research and application, accounting, statistics, translation, libraries, archives, cultural and museum service, journalism and publication, lawyers, notarization service, radio and television broadcasting, handicraft and fine arts, sports, performing art, and political workers in enterprises. This indicator reflects the condition of human resources in S&T.

Funding for S&T Activities refers to funds obtained from various sources for S&T activities, including government funds, self-raised funds by enterprises, self-raised funds by institutions, loans from financial institutions, foreign funds and other funds . This indicator reflects the efforts made by various social economic entities in promoting the development of S&T.

Government Funds refer to funds obtained from government agencies at all levels to be used for S&T activities, including fund for scientific undertakings, 3 kinds of fund for S&T activities, fund for capital const ruction for scientific researches, science fund, funds from education expenditures by education departments for S&T activities, and extra-budget fund from government agencies for S&T activities.

Self-raised Funds by Enterprises refers to self-raised funds by enterprises from their own expenditure or from other enterprises and funds received by universities or research institutions from enterprises for scientific research or technical development projects. Excluded in this category are funds from government agencies, financial institutions or from foreign institutions.

Loans from Financial Institutions refer to loans from various financial institutions for S&T activities.

Internal Expenditures on S&T activities refer to the actual expenditures on S&T activities during the reference year, including service fees, expenditure on research activities, expenditure on research management, purchase or const ruction of fixed assets not included in the investment for capital const ruction, expenditure on capital construction for scientific researches, and other expenditures on S&T activities. Not included are expenditure on production activities, repayment of loans and transfer expenditure. This indicator reflects the real accomplishment of input in S&T.

Service Fees refer to direct or indirect payment, in cash or in kind, made to personnel engaged in S&T activities as remuneration and other fees. They include, in various forms, salaries, subsidies, bonus, benefits, retirement pension, stipend, etc. This indicator reflects the improvement of treatment toward S&T personnel.

Purchase or Construction of Fixed Assets refers to the fixed assets purchased or constructed using funds other than the investment in capital construction, and the actual expenditure on capital construction for scientific researches. In other words, it is the sum of the actual expenditure on fixed as sets and the accomplished investment in capital construction for scientific researches. Fixed as sets refer to main materials and equipment, literatures and documents in libraries, materials for experiments, specimen, instruments, furniture, buildings and constructions that can be used for a long time without changing t he form and shape of those articles or constructions. This indictor reflects the input in improving t he condition of S&T and the means of scientific research.

New Products refer to new products produced with new technology and new design, or products that represent noticeable improvement in terms of structure, material, or production process so as to imp rove significantly the character or function of the older versions. They include new products certified by relevant government agencies within the period of certification, as well as new products designed and produced by enterprises within a year without certification by government agencies. This indictor reflects the direct contribution of S&T output to economic growth.

Patent is an abbreviation for the patent right and refers to the exclusive right of ownership by the inventors or designers for the creation or inventions, given from the patent offices after due process of assessment and approval in accordance wit h the Patent Law. Patents are grant ed for inventions, utility model sand designs. This indicator reflects the achievements of S&T and design with in dependent intellectual property.

Inventions refer to the new technical proposals to the products or methods or their modifications. This is universal core Indicator reflecting the technologies with independent intellectual property.

Utility Models refer to t he practical and new technical proposals on the shape and structure of the product or the combination of both. This indicator reflects the condition of technological results with certain technical content.

Designs refer to the aesthetics and industrially applicable new designs for the shape, pattern and color of the product, or their combinations. This indicator reflects the appearance design achievements with independent intellectual property.

Cultural Institutions refer to units, which have their own organizational system and independent accounting system and specialize in or serve cultural development. They exclude other establishments run by these cultural institutions and amateur cultural groups established by various departments. This indicator reflects the development of cultural units.

Art Troupe refers to t he troupe which is engaged in drama, opera, music, dance, acrobatics or other art performance, opens independent accounts with banks and has self-supporting accounting system; excluding the troupes which are engaged partly in industrial or agricultural activities, partly in art performance and the professional troupes organized by the people. This indicator reflects the development of national professional art troupes.

Number of Spectators at Art Performance refers to the number of attendants at commercial shows, completely booked shows or free shows given in minority national areas, and does not include the number of spectators at rehearsals for examination and internal shows for study. This indicator reflects beneficial results of.

第十八篇
体育、卫生及其他

CHAPTER 18
Sports, Public Health and Others

简要说明
Brief Introduction

本篇资料的主要内容及来源

本篇资料主要包括卫生事业、体育事业、民政事业、公安机关案件受理处治情况、安全生产情况、道路交通事故和火灾事故等内容，由新疆维吾尔自治区统计局人口与社会科技处与综合处根据有关部门资料整理提供。

卫生资料来自新疆维吾尔自治区卫生厅，体育资料来自新疆维吾尔自治区体育局，民政部分资料由新疆维吾尔自治区民政厅提供，治安、刑事案件资料由新疆维吾尔自治区公安厅提供，安全生产情况来自新疆维吾尔自治区安全生产监督管理局，道路交通事故和火灾事故分别由新疆维吾尔自治区公安交通管理局和新疆维吾尔自治区消防总队提供。

Main Content and Source of Data

Data in this chapter mainly include the development of public health, sports, civil affairs, offense cases against public order handled by public Security organs, traffic accidents and fires. These statistics are provided by Department of Population and Social Science &Technology in Statistics Bureau of Xinjiang according to the data from the related Department of Statistics Bureau.

Data on public health are from the Bureau of Public Health; Data on sports are from the Bureau of Sports; Data on public security, statistics on procuratorial, legal and judicial affairs are provided by the Bureau of Public Security. Data on production safety are come from Xinjiang Administration of Work Safety. Data on traffic accident and fire are respectively provided by the Xinjiang Traffic Management Bureau and the Xinjiang Fire Department.

18-1 体育局系统从业人员数
Number of Staff and Workers in Sports Bureau

单位：人 (2007 年) (person)

项 目	Item	合 计 Total	公 务 员 Government Officials	教 练 员 Coaches	运 动 员 Athletes	科研人员 Scientific Research Personnel
总 计	**Total**	**2629**	**521**	**657**	**379**	**21**
体育行政机关	Sports Administration	653	521			
优秀运动队	Excellent Sports Teams	630		65	371	1
体育运动学校	Physical Education and Sports Schools	484		156		3
业余体校	Spare-time Sports Schools	596		425	6	
体育场馆	Gymnasium	109		10	1	
训练基地	Training Bases	6		1		
其他事业单位	Other Institutions	151			1	17

项 目	Item	医务人员 Medical Personnel	文化教师 Culture Teachers	管理人员 Administrative Personnel	其他人员 Others
总 计	**Total**	**30**	**156**	**451**	**414**
体育行政机关	Sports Administration			64	68
优秀运动队	Excellent Sports Teams	19		116	58
体育运动学校	Physical Education and Sports Schools	8	153	93	71
业余体校	Spare-time Sports Schools	1	3	65	96
体育场馆	Gymnasium	2		39	57
训练基地	Training Bases			3	2
其他事业单位	Other Institutions			71	62

18-2 按项目分等级裁判员发展人数

Number of Referees in Levels by Type of Sports

单位：人　　　　(2007 年)　　　　(person)

项 目	Item	合 计 Total	国家级裁判员 National Level Referee 小 计 Sub-total	男 Male	女 Female	一级裁判员 First Level Referee 小 计 Sub-total	男 Male	女 Female	二级裁判员 Second Level Referee 小 计 Sub-total	男 Male	女 Female
总 计	**Total**	**702**	**4**	**3**	**1**	**156**	**124**	**32**	**542**	**334**	**208**
田 径	Track and Field	138				51	30	21	87	54	33
拳 击	Boxing	21				20	19	1	1	1	
国际式摔跤	InternationalWrestling	34				29	23	6	5	5	
信 鸽	Horning Pigeon	30							30	26	4
足 球	Football	20				15	15		5	5	
篮 球	Basketball	164				32	28	4	132	89	43
排 球	Volleyball	5							5	5	
乒乓球	Table Tennis	19							19	16	3
门 球	Croquet	89							89	34	55
武 术	Martial Art	47							47	27	20
跆拳道	Taikuangdao	56	1	1					55	33	22
射 箭	Archery	2	2	1	1						
无线电测向	Radio direction	1	1	1							
围 棋	L-go	5				5	5				
桥 牌	Bridge	4				4	4				
轮 滑	Skidding of wheel	52							52	26	26
钓 鱼	Fishing	15							15	13	2

18-3 按项目分等级运动员发展人数

Number of Athletes at Levels by Type of Sports

单位：人　　　　(2007 年)　　　　(person)

项 目	Item	合 计 Total	国际级运动健将 InternationalLevel 小 计 Sub-total	#男 Male	国家级运动健将 National Level 小 计 Sub-total	#男 Male	一级运动员 First Grade 小 计 Sub-total	#男 Male	二级运动员 Second Grade 小 计 Sub-total	#男 Male
总 计	**Total**	**285**	**3**	**2**	**9**	**6**	**62**	**40**	**211**	**132**
田 径	Track and Field	91			2	1	10	8	79	44
拳 击	Boxing	11	2	2					9	9
国际式摔跤	InternationalWrestling	14			2	2	7	6	5	4
柔 道	Judo	10							10	7
射 击	Shooting	15					7	6	8	5
射 箭	Archery	11					3	3	8	4
篮 球	Basketball	26			3	3			23	18
乒乓球	Table Tennis	30							30	19
手 球	Handball	6					6			
速度滑冰	Speed Skating	1							1	1
航空模型	Model Airplane	2					2	2		
武 术	Martial Art	12			1		2		9	6
沙滩排球	Sand wolleyball	1	1							
游 泳	Swimming	2							2	2
马 术	Horsemanship	1					1			
足 球	Football	16					15	7	1	1
排 球	Volleyball	6							6	3
登 山	mountaineering	6					6	6		
跆拳道	Taikuangdao	24			1		3	2	20	9

18-4 各地、州、市体育局系统机构数
Number of Institutions in Sports Committees by Region

单位：个 (2007 年) (unit)

地区	Region	合计 Total	行政机关 Administration	优秀运动队 Excellent Sports Teams	体育运动学校 Physical Education and Sports Schools
总计	**Total**	**219**	**106**	**7**	**6**
自治区直属	Under Autonomous Region	16	1	5	1
乌鲁木齐市	Urumqi City	18	9		1
克拉玛依市	Karamay City	3	1		
吐鲁番地区	Turpan Administrative Offices	8	4		
哈密地区	Hami [Kumul] Administrative Offices	10	4		
昌吉回族自治州	Changji Hui Autonomous Prefecture	11	8		1
伊犁哈萨克自治州	Ili Kazak Autonomous Prefecture	50	27	2	1
伊犁州直属县(市)	Counties (Cities) Direct Under Ili Prefecture	20	11	1	1
塔城地区	Tacheng [Tarbagatai] Administrative Offices	13	8		
阿勒泰地区	Altay Administrative Offices	17	8	1	
博尔塔拉蒙古自治州	Bortala Mongol Autonomous Prefecture	8	4		
巴音郭楞蒙古自治州	Bayangol Mongol Autonomous Prefecture	16	10		
阿克苏地区	Aksu Administrative Offices	20	10		1
克孜勒苏柯尔克孜自治州	Kizilsu Kirgiz Autonomous Prefecture	12	5		
喀什地区	Kashgar [Kaxgar] Administrative Offices	27	13		1
和田地区	Hotan Administrative Offices	18	9		
自治区直辖行政单位	Administrative Units under Autonomous Region	2	1		

地区	Region	业余体校 Spare-time Sports Schools	体育场馆 Gymnasium	训练基地 Training Bases	其他事业单位 Other Institutions
总计	**Total**	**77**	**9**	**1**	**13**
自治区直属	Under Autonomous Region		1		8
乌鲁木齐市	Urumqi City	5	2		1
克拉玛依市	Karamay City	1			1
吐鲁番地区	Turpan Administrative Offices	4			
哈密地区	Hami [Kumul] Administrative Offices	3	1		2
昌吉回族自治州	Changji Hui Autonomous Prefecture	1	1		
伊犁哈萨克自治州	Ili Kazak Autonomous Prefecture	19	1		
伊犁州直属县(市)	Counties (Cities) Direct Under Ili Prefecture	7			
塔城地区	Tacheng [Tarbagatai] Administrative Offices	5			
阿勒泰地区	Altay Administrative Offices	7	1		
博尔塔拉蒙古自治州	Bortala Mongol Autonomous Prefecture	4			
巴音郭楞蒙古自治州	Bayangol Mongol Autonomous Prefecture	5	1		
阿克苏地区	Aksu Administrative Offices	8	1		
克孜勒苏柯尔克孜自治州	Kizilsu Kirgiz Autonomous Prefecture	5		1	1
喀什地区	Kashgar [Kaxgar] Administrative Offices	12	1		
和田地区	Hotan Administrative Offices	9			
自治区直辖行政单位	Administrative Units under Autonomous Region	1			

18-5 各地、州、市体育局系统机构从业人员数

Number of Staff & Workers in Sports Bureau by Region

单位：人 (2007 年) (person)

地 区	Region	合 计 Total	行政机关 Administration	#公务员 Government Officials	优秀运动队 Excellent Sports Teams
总 计	**Total**	**2629**	**653**	**521**	**630**
自治区直属	Under Autonomous Region	914	56	47	597
乌鲁木齐市	Urumqi City	279	46	40	
克拉玛依市	Karamay City	26	11	11	
吐鲁番地区	Turpan Administrative Offices	95	56	51	
哈密地区	Hami [Kumul] Administrative Offices	103	42	37	
昌吉回族自治州	Changji Hui Autonomous Prefecture	65	41	38	
伊犁哈萨克自治州	Ili Kazak Autonomous Prefecture	433	145	100	33
伊犁州直属县(市)	Counties (Cities) Direct Under Ili Prefecture	214	56	29	12
塔城地区	Tacheng [Tarbagatai] Administrative Offices	71	29	19	
阿勒泰地区	Altay Administrative Offices	148	60	52	21
博尔塔拉蒙古自治州	Bortala Mongol Autonomous Prefecture	63	32	28	
巴音郭楞蒙古自治州	Bayangol Mongol Autonomous Prefecture	104	43	42	
阿克苏地区	Aksu Administrative Offices	145	36	23	
克孜勒苏柯尔克孜自治州	Kizilsu Kirgiz Autonomous Prefecture	106	48	29	
喀什地区	Kashgar [Kaxgar] Administrative Offices	219	63	49	
和田地区	Hotan Administrative Offices	48	31	23	
自治区直辖行政单位	Administrative Units under Autonomous Region	29	3	3	

地 区	Region	体育运动学校 Physical Education and Sports Schools	业余体校 Spare-time Sports Schools	体育场馆 Gymnasium	训练基地 Training Bases	其他事业单位 Other Institutions
总 计	**Total**	**484**	**596**	**109**	**6**	**151**
自治区直属	Under Autonomous Region	132		17		112
乌鲁木齐市	Urumqi City	123	81	24		5
克拉玛依市	Karamay City		7			8
吐鲁番地区	Turpan Administrative Offices		39			
哈密地区	Hami [Kumul] Administrative Offices		33	13		15
昌吉回族自治州	Changji Hui Autonomous Prefecture	12	6	6		
伊犁哈萨克自治州	Ili Kazak Autonomous Prefecture	71	160	24		
伊犁州直属县(市)	Counties (Cities) Direct Under Ili Prefecture	71	75			
塔城地区	Tacheng [Tarbagatai] Administrative Offices		42			
阿勒泰地区	Altay Administrative Offices		43	24		
博尔塔拉蒙古自治州	Bortala Mongol Autonomous Prefecture		31			
巴音郭楞蒙古自治州	Bayangol Mongol Autonomous Prefecture		50	11		
阿克苏地区	Aksu Administrative Offices	68	38	3		
克孜勒苏柯尔克孜自治州	Kizilsu Kirgiz Autonomous Prefecture		41		6	11
喀什地区	Kashgar [Kaxgar] Administrative Offices	78	67	11		
和田地区	Hotan Administrative Offices		17			
自治区直辖行政单位	Administrative Units under Autonomous Region		26			

18-6 主要年份卫生机构数
Number of Health Institutions in Main Years

单位：个 (unit)

年 份 Year	合 计 Total	医院、卫生院 Hospitals And Township Hospitals	#县及县以上医院 At and Above County Level	疗养院 Sanatoriums	门诊部 Clinics	专科防治所、站 Specialized Prevention & Treatment Centers or Stations	疾病防控中心 Sanitation and Antiepidemic Agencies	妇幼保健所、站 Maternity and Child Care Centers	社区卫生服务中心 Community Sanitation Service Center	医学科学研究机构 Research Institutes of Medical Science	其他卫生机构 Other Institutions	诊所、医务保健室、医务室 Clinics Health Care Room Infirmary	#私营、个体机构 Institutions of Privately Owned & Individual
1978	2581	806		2	1609	1	104	12		1	46		
1980	2818	884		4	1756	4	102	12		1	55		
1985	3320	947		5	2125	2	139	27		2	73		
1990	3945	1049		6	2536	13	191	59		3	88		
1995	3932	1292		8	2247	16	216	69		6	78		
2000	7314	1352	522	8	154	16	210	74		7	89	5404	3653
2005	8087	1516	685	6	224	8	197	88	46	3	140	5859	4183
2006	8175	1560	699	6	220	7	211	92	62	3	129	5885	4227
2007	7465	1629	756	7	240	7	214	87	250	3	139	4889	4093

注：1. 从 1996 年起含私营、个体机构。2.2002 年起卫生部新制度规定持有"医疗执业许可证"所有卫生机构算为一个机构,兵团连队卫生室统计到卫生所中,所以卫生机构总数增加。3. 2007 年报卫生部门实行网络直报，数据与往年出入较大。

Note: 1.Since 1996 Institutions of privately owned and individuals has been contained.
2.From 2002, in line with new regulations of ministry of public health,all the health institutions that have medical service permit shall be counted as one and health care rooms shall be counted in health clinics,therefore the total number of health institutions increased.
3.So the statistics are not fully comparable with historical statistics.

18-7 主要年份卫生人员数
Number of Persons Engaged in Health Institutions in Main Years

单位：人 (person)

年 份 Year	合 计 Total	#卫生技术人员 Medical Technical Personnel	#医 生 Doctors	执业医师 Doctors with License	执业助理医师 Assistant Doctors with License	#注册护士 Registered Nurses	平均每万人医生数 Number of Doctors per 10 000 Population	在合计中私人个体开业人员 Persons of Privately Owned & Individual
1978	66252	51050	16898	7368	9530	10765	14	
1980	74627	57949	20614	10092	10522	12077	16	
1985	88460	68961	25721	13330	12391	17136	19	188
1990	102053	79853	33683	24967	8716	23386	22	2034
1995	116856	92028	39636	30038	9598	26350	24	4252
2000	122064	98093	45402	34892	10510	30850	25	5835
2005	117165	96266	41426	32563	8863	30657	21	13562
2006	121400	99839	42775	33988	8787	32119	21	13256
2007	127621	104671	43551	34838	8713	34662	21	14689

注：2002 年以前执业医师为中医师、西医师、中西医结合医师，执业助理医师为中医士、西医士、中西医结合医士，注册护士为护师、护士。(以下同)

Note: Prior to 2002,doctors with license were doctors trained in Western medicine,assistant doctors are practioners with Secondary Western medical education,and registered nurses are master nurses and nurses (The following is the same as below) .

18-8 卫生机构、床位、人员数

(2007 年)

项　目	Item	机构数（个） Number of Institutions (unit)	床位数（张） Beds (unit)	卫生人员合计（人） Total Number of Medical Personnel (person)	卫生技术人员 Medical Technical Personnel
总　计	**Total**	**7465**	**90329**	**127621**	**104671**
按市县分	**By City and County**				
市	City	4304	56407	83667	68546
县	County	3161	33922	43954	36125
按经济类型分	**By Economic Sectors**				
国　有	State-owned	2890	77848	104853	84960
集　体	Couective-owned	355	2298	4159	3507
联　营	Joint Operation	36	1351	1133	902
私　营	Private-owned	4093	6476	14689	13117
其　他	Others	91	2356	2787	2185
按设置主办单位分	**By sponsors**				
政府办	Government sponsored	2509	74944	100264	81328
社会办	Society sponsored	989	8312	12256	9970
个人办	Individual sponsored	3967	7073	15101	13373
按机构分	**By Organizations**				
医院合计	Total Number of Hospitals	756	71496	84203	67726
市	City	469	51763	62005	49821
县	County	287	19733	22198	17905
综合医院	Comprehensive Hospitals	602	57146	70613	57366
中医医院	Hospitals of Traditional Chinese Medicine	39	4210	4628	3594
中西医综合医院	TCM and Western Medicine Hospital	3	615	489	371
民族医院	Hospitals for Nationalities	44	3047	2997	2295
专科医院	Specialist Hospitals	68	6478	5476	4100
口腔医院	Nonnasality Hospitals	2	42	195	165
眼科医院	Ophthalmology Hospitals	4	90	101	68
耳鼻喉科医院	Otolaryngology Hospitals	2	65	161	115
肿瘤医院	Tumour Hospital	2	1379	1222	989
心血管病医院	Cardiovascular Hospitals	1	310	516	363
胸科医院	Chest Hospital	1	245	336	253
妇产(科)医院	Hospitals for Gynaecology and Obsterics	11	319	361	290
儿童医院	Hospital for Children	1	30	29	21
精神病医院	Mental Hospitals	12	2530	1182	793
传染病医院	Infectous Diseases Hospitals	4	322	256	184
结核病医院	Tubercuiosis Hospitals	1	160	142	122
骨科医院	Hospital of Orthopedics	5	220	252	195
康复医院	Recovery Hospitals	3	210	123	81
整形外科医院	Plastic surgical holpital	2	30	47	30
其他专科医院	Other Specialist Hospitals	17	526	553	431
疗养院	Sanatoriums	7	793	390	192
社区卫生服务中心	Community Sanitation Service Center	250	343	1597	1419
卫生院合计	Total Number of Public Health Center	873	15635	17484	14540
街道卫生院	Public Health Center in Neighbourhood	5	77	134	125
乡、镇卫生院	Public Health Center in Township and Towns	868	15558	17350	14415
中心卫生院	Public Health Center in Rural Area	122	3220	3141	2653
乡卫生院	Public Health Center in Township	746	12338	14209	11762
门诊部	Out-patients Department	240	523	1875	1559
诊所、卫生所、医务室	Clinics and Health Centers	4889	7	10372	10202
急救中心(站)	First-Aid-Stations(Center)	3		71	48
采供血机构	Blood Collection & Supply Organs	21		468	110
妇幼保健院(所、站)	Hospitals for Maternity and Child Care	87	1525	3007	2431
专科疾病防治院(所、站)	Specialized Stations	7	7	148	77
疾病预防控制中心(防疫站)	Diseases Preventing & Controlling Center (Epidemic Prevention Station)	214		6441	4971
卫生监督所	Sanitation Superintendence Office	112		1540	1178
卫生监督检验(监测、检测)所(站)	Sanitation Superintendence & Examining(monitoring,testing)office(station)	1		10	10
医学科学研究机构	Research Institutes of Medical Sciences	3			
其它卫生事业机构	Other Health Institutions	3		25	18

Number of Health Institutions, Beds and Persons Engaged by Type of Institutons

执业医师 Doctors with License	执业助理医师 Assistant Doctors with License	注册护士 Registered Nurses	药剂人员 Druggist of Medicine	技师(士) Technician (artificer)	检验人员 Laboratory Technicians	其他 Others	其他技术人员 Other Technicians	管理人员 Managerial Personnel	工勤人员 Logistics Workers
34838	**8713**	**34662**	**5647**	**6701**	**4746**	**14110**	**5276**	**7143**	**10531**
25041	3855	24174	3813	4477	3230	7186	3351	4712	7058
9797	4858	10488	1834	2224	1516	6924	1925	2431	3473
26767	7181	28612	4577	5741	4098	12082	4509	6096	9288
1231	350	1210	228	169	121	319	118	250	284
438	17	286	92	47	32	22	85	40	106
5694	1038	3775	632	592	399	1386	387	536	649
708	127	779	118	152	96	301	177	221	204
25354	7042	27255	4374	5462	3895	11841	4332	5773	8831
3701	625	3559	629	603	425	853	513	781	992
5783	1046	3848	644	636	426	1416	431	589	708
22310	3693	25709	4482	4513	2886	7019	3619	5154	7704
17201	2147	19403	3249	3199	2108	4622	2632	3828	5724
5109	1546	6306	1233	1314	778	2397	987	1326	1980
18760	3188	22324	3551	3828	2447	5715	2602	4415	6230
1416	121	1155	372	264	169	266	365	268	401
107	41	140	16	17	11	50	41	33	44
791	207	540	344	153	95	260	244	117	341
1236	136	1550	199	251	164	728	367	321	688
89	7	47	4	3	2	15	3	14	13
21	4	21	6	3	3	13	10	12	11
47	5	43	8	5	3	7	5	4	37
274	2	353	18	29	17	313	61	21	151
95	2	127	8	9	8	122	70	55	28
70	8	115	12	27	13	21	26	7	50
79	30	103	19	30	20	29	9	31	31
5	1	3	3	2	1	7	4	3	1
203	26	423	41	42	28	58	101	54	234
65	7	45	8	20	9	39	3	30	39
46	9	47	6	12	7	2	5	5	10
45	10	74	18	13	9	35	13	26	18
38	4	18	7	5	3	9	18	11	13
14	1	11	1	3	3		5	10	2
145	20	120	40	48	38	58	34	38	50
63	11	65	13	18	11	22	9	57	132
551	97	511	90	62	44	108	64	61	53
2910	2870	3839	569	611	475	3741	864	854	1226
31	13	31	11	6	5	33	5	2	2
2879	2857	3808	558	605	470	3708	859	852	1224
552	491	760	134	140	104	576	147	147	194
2327	2366	3048	424	465	366	3132	712	705	1030
637	134	307	121	246	98	114	89	144	83
5137	908	3075	207	88	88	787			170
21		18	1	1		7	5	3	15
50	10	80	8	76	123	38	43	35	80
904	299	625	93	210	149	300	148	181	247
19	19	4	1	1		33	9	51	11
2227	668	326	62	926	872	762	365	399	706
						1178	56	203	103
5	3	2							
13	9	4				1	5	1	1

18-9 卫生机构床位数
Number of Beds in Health Institutions

单位：张 (unit)

年 份 Year	合 计 Total	医 院 卫生院 Hospitals and Health Centers	#县及县以上医院 At and above County Level	疗 养 院 Sanatoriums	其他卫生机构 Other Health Institutions	每万人医院、卫生院床位数 Number of Hospital Beds per 10 000 Population
1978	57647	39179		108	18360	31.8
1980	61075	47236		682	13157	36.8
1985	60930	55298		870	4762	40.6
1990	67414	60707	47924	1010	5697	40.5
1995	72955	66696	53336	1233	5026	40.1
2000	70542	65916	52438	1301	3325	35.7
2005	79753	76002	63013	830	2921	37.8
2006	83722	80090	65589	860	2772	39.1
2007	90329	87131	71496	793	2405	41.6

18-10 医疗机构病床使用情况
Utilization of Beds in Medical Institutions

(2007 年)

项 目	Item	实际开放总床日数(日) Beds Open to Patients (day)	平均开放病 床(张) Average Beds Open to Patients (unit)	病床周转次 数(次) Turnover of Beds (times)	病床工作日(日) Number of Days per Bed in Use in a Year (day)	病 床使用率(%) Utilization Rate of Beds (%)	出院者平均住 院 日(日) Average Stay Days in Hospital (day)
总 计	**Total**	**30644644**	**83958**	**27.40**	**276.60**	**75.77**	**9.30**
医 院	Total Number of Hospitals	24778006	67885	25.80	291.20	79.79	10.60
疗养院	Sanatoriums	182199	499	37.20	116.80	31.99	3.00
社区卫生服务中心	Community Sanitation Service Center	100079	274	9.50	225.60	61.80	13.80
卫生院	Total Number of Public Health Center	4996431	13689	35.50	219.80	60.22	5.10
门诊部	Out-patients Department	118893	326	8.60	127.90	35.05	9.60
妇幼保健院(所、站)	Hospitals for Maternity and Child Care	469036	1285	35.00	218.30	59.81	5.50

18-11 医疗机构、诊疗人次及入院出院人数

Number of Visits Inpatients and Patients Discharged in Medical Institutions

(2007 年)

项 目	Item	机构数(个) Number of Institutions (unit)	诊疗人次(万人次) Total Number of Patients Treated (10 000 patient-times)	#门、急诊人次 Out-patients and Emergency Patients	#急诊人次 Emergency Patients
总 计	**Total**	**2220**	**5434.40**	**4382.93**	**175.80**
医 院	Total Number of Hospitals	756	3854.33	2900.87	161.96
疗养院	Sanatoriums	7	3.18	2.40	…
社区卫生服务中心	Community Sanitation Service Center	250	214.95	205.09	1.12
卫生院	Total Number of Public Health Center	873	1068.74	997.72	10.97
门诊部	Out-patients Department	240	136.95	126.86	1.08
妇幼保健院(所、站)	Hospitals for Maternity and Child Care	87	154.11	148.15	0.67
专科疾病防治院(所、站)	Specialized Stations	7	2.14	1.84	…

项 目	Item	门、急诊诊次占总诊次的比重(%) Percentage of Clinic Case and Emergence Case Among the Total Cases (%)	入院人数(万人) Hospital Admissions (10 000 patients)	出院人数(万人) Patients Discharged (10 000 patients)	治愈率(%) Cure rate (%)
总 计	**Total**	**80.65**	**232.37**	**230.37**	**59.36**
医 院	Total Number of Hospitals	75.26	176.00	174.82	56.48
疗养院	Sanatoriums	75.49	1.86	1.86	33.78
社区卫生服务中心	Community Sanitation Service Center	95.41	0.26	0.26	74.86
卫生院	Total Number of Public Health Center	93.35	49.52	48.65	67.76
门诊部	Out-patients Department	92.63	0.28	0.28	75.75
妇幼保健院(所、站)	Hospitals for Maternity and Child Care	96.13	4.45	4.50	88.89
专科疾病防治院(所、站)	Specialized Stations	86.15			

18-12 各地、州、市卫生机构、床位和人员数

Number of Health Institutions, Beds and Personnel by Prefecture, Autonomous Prefecture and City

(2007 年)

地区	Region	机构数(个) Number of Institutions (unit)	床位数(张) Beds (unit)	卫生人员合计(人) Total Number of Medical Personnel (person)	卫生技术人员 Medical Technical Personnel
总计	**Total**	**7465**	**90329**	**127621**	**104671**
乌鲁木齐市	Urumqi City	1606	20204	30068	24410
克拉玛依市	Karamay City	91	1582	3336	2739
石河子市	Shihezi City	505	4161	6071	4937
吐鲁番地区	Turpan Administrative Offices	201	1970	3545	2947
哈密地区	Hami [Kumul] Administrative Offices	223	2687	4587	3876
昌吉回族自治州	Changji Hui Autonomous Prefecture	777	7603	10837	8979
伊犁哈萨克自治州	Ili Kazak Autonomous Prefecture	1685	16188	25881	21435
伊犁州直属县(市)	Counties (Cities) Direct Under Ili Prefecture	1004	10193	15277	12482
塔城地区	Tacheng [Tarbagatai] Administrative Offices	438	3676	5798	4882
阿勒泰地区	Altay Administrative Offices	243	2319	4806	4071
博尔塔拉蒙古自治州	Bortala Mongol Autonomous Prefecture	278	2031	3699	3038
巴音郭楞蒙古自治州	Bayangol Mongol Autonomous Prefecture	395	6513	8799	7346
阿克苏地区	Aksu Administrative Offices	443	8714	9610	7620
克孜勒苏柯尔克孜自治州	Kizilsu Kirgiz Autonomous Prefecture	96	2061	2691	2247
喀什地区	Kashgar [Kaxgar] Administrative Offices	891	11293	12980	10727
和田地区	Hotan Administrative Offices	274	5322	5517	4370

地区	Region	其他技术人员 Other Technicians	管理人员 Managerial Personnel	工勤人员 Logistics Workers	平均每万人床位数(张) Number of Beds per 10000 Population (unit)
总计	**Total**	**5276**	**7143**	**10531**	**43.11**
乌鲁木齐市	Urumqi City	1166	1956	2536	95.47
克拉玛依市	Karamay City	98	123	376	59.21
石河子市	Shihezi City	297	346	491	40.67
吐鲁番地区	Turpan Administrative Offices	170	132	296	32.80
哈密地区	Hami [Kumul] Administrative Offices	147	215	349	49.20
昌吉回族自治州	Changji Hui Autonomous Prefecture	368	765	725	49.03
伊犁哈萨克自治州	Ili Kazak Autonomous Prefecture	1095	1361	1990	37.28
伊犁州直属县(市)	Counties (Cities) Direct Under Ili Prefecture	657	866	1272	37.72
塔城地区	Tacheng [Tarbagatai] Administrative Offices	198	274	444	36.95
阿勒泰地区	Altay Administrative Offices	240	221	274	35.95
博尔塔拉蒙古自治州	Bortala Mongol Autonomous Prefecture	73	294	294	42.95
巴音郭楞蒙古自治州	Bayangol Mongol Autonomous Prefecture	414	404	635	53.21
阿克苏地区	Aksu Administrative Offices	528	514	948	39.55
克孜勒苏柯尔克孜自治州	Kizilsu Kirgiz Autonomous Prefecture	122	108	214	41.22
喀什地区	Kashgar [Kaxgar] Administrative Offices	577	663	1013	30.57
和田地区	Hotan Administrative Offices	221	262	664	28.25

18-13 各地、州、市卫生技术人员数

Number of Medical Technical Personnel by Prefecture, Autonomous Prefecture and City

单位:人 (2007 年) (person)

地 区	Region	卫生技术人员合计 Medical Technical Personnel	执业医师 Certified Doctors	执业助理医师 Assistant Doctors with Licence	注册护士 Registered Nurses
总 计	**Total**	**104671**	**34838**	**8713**	**34662**
乌鲁木齐市	Urumqi City	24410	9470	868	9015
克拉玛依市	Karamay City	2739	1007	57	1082
石河子市	Shihezi City	4937	1853	401	1726
吐鲁番地区	Turpan Administrative Offices	2947	906	310	1023
哈密地区	Hami [Kumul] Administrative Offices	3876	1328	343	1377
昌吉回族自治州	Changji Hui Autonomous Prefecture	8979	2994	770	2953
伊犁哈萨克自治州	Ili Kazak Autonomous Prefecture	21435	7074	2184	6701
伊犁州直属县(市)	Counties (Cities) Direct Under Ili Prefecture	12482	4128	1104	3977
塔城地区	Tacheng [Tarbagatai] Administrative Offices	4882	1491	612	1505
阿勒泰地区	Altay Administrative Offices	4071	1455	468	1219
博尔塔拉蒙古自治州	Bortala Mongol Autonomous Prefecture	3038	1009	326	946
巴音郭楞蒙古自治州	Bayangol Mongol Autonomous Prefecture	7346	2278	593	2282
阿克苏地区	Aksu Administrative Offices	7620	2169	727	2579
克孜勒苏柯尔克孜自治州	Kizilsu Kirgiz Autonomous Prefecture	2247	548	272	646
喀什地区	Kashgar [Kaxgar] Administrative Offices	10727	2980	1353	3255
和田地区	Hotan Administrative Offices	4370	1222	509	1077

地 区	Region	药剂人员 Druggist of Medicine	技师(士) Technician (artificer)	检验人员 Laboratory Technicians	其 他 Others	平均每万人医生数 Number of Doctors per 10 000 Population
总 计	**Total**	**5647**	**6701**	**4746**	**14110**	**20.79**
乌鲁木齐市	Urumqi City	1247	1426	1035	2384	48.85
克拉玛依市	Karamay City	162	143	98	288	39.82
石河子市	Shihezi City	294	324	229	339	22.03
吐鲁番地区	Turpan Administrative Offices	171	233	148	304	20.25
哈密地区	Hami [Kumul] Administrative Offices	216	246	192	366	30.59
昌吉回族自治州	Changji Hui Autonomous Prefecture	644	629	420	989	24.28
伊犁哈萨克自治州	Ili Kazak Autonomous Prefecture	1039	1434	1079	3003	21.32
伊犁州直属县(市)	Counties (Cities) Direct Under Ili Prefecture	654	870	677	1749	19.36
塔城地区	Tacheng [Tarbagatai] Administrative Offices	212	301	225	761	21.14
阿勒泰地区	Altay Administrative Offices	173	263	177	493	29.81
博尔塔拉蒙古自治州	Bortala Mongol Autonomous Prefecture	188	208	155	361	28.23
巴音郭楞蒙古自治州	Bayangol Mongol Autonomous Prefecture	364	499	306	1330	23.45
阿克苏地区	Aksu Administrative Offices	394	532	351	1219	13.15
克孜勒苏柯尔克孜自治州	Kizilsu Kirgiz Autonomous Prefecture	99	113	84	569	16.40
喀什地区	Kashgar [Kaxgar] Administrative Offices	551	684	488	1904	11.73
和田地区	Hotan Administrative Offices	278	230	161	1054	9.19

18-14 分市县医院床位和专业卫生技术人员数
Hospital Beds and Medical Technical Personnel by City and County Areas

年 份 Year	医院、卫生院床位(张) Number of Hospital Beds (unit)		专业卫生技术人员(人) Number of Medical Technical Personnel (person)		#执业医师、执业助理医师 Cevtified Doctors & Assistant Doctors with Licence		#注册护士 Registered Nurses	
	市 City	县 County	市 City	县 County	市 City	县 County	市 City	县 County
2000	38398	27518	44115	31138	18408	13225	16805	9918
2001	38323	27685	44113	31055	18811	13271	16714	10105
2002	38700	26178	41850	27932	16689	10578	15965	8840
2003	42880	26915	44678	28228	17883	10916	17015	9087
2004	46300	27722	46956	28552	19207	10583	17185	9054
2005	50238	29515	54188	31132	23191	12323	18240	9289
2006	52275	31125	56701	32178	24033	13049	19365	9538
2007	54595	32536	68546	36125	28896	14655	24174	10488

18-15 全区法定报告传染病发病及死亡情况
Confirmed Incidence and Death from Infectious Diseases in Xinjiang

(2007 年)

项 目	Item	发病率(1/10 万) Incidence Disease Rate (1/100 000)	死亡率(1/10 万) Death Rate (1/100 000)	病死率(%) Mortality Rate (%)
总 计	**Total**	**860.90**	**1.68**	**0.20**
肝 炎	Viral Hepatitis	310.62	0.10	0.03
痢 疾	Dysentery	71.94	0.01	0.02
伤 寒	Typhoid	3.93		
艾滋病	AIDS	1.23	0.19	15.42
淋 病	Gonorrhea	16.50		
梅 毒	Syphilis	28.32		0.02
麻 疹	Measles	12.91	0.02	0.19
百日咳	Pertussis	3.35		
流 脑	Epidemic Encephalitis	1.15	0.09	8.09
猩红热	Scarlet Fever	5.49		
布氏杆菌病（简称布病）	Brucellosis	1.46		
炭 疽	Anthrax	0.25		
黑热病	Kala-Azar	0.57	0.01	1.71
新生儿破伤风	Newborn Baby Tetanus	0.22	0.02	8.96
肺结核	Pulmonary Tuberculosis	199.99	1.20	0.60

18-16 城市前十位疾病死亡原因及构成

Death Causes and Percentage of Top 10 Diseases in Urban Areas

(2007 年)

疾病死亡原因	Cause of Death	占死亡总人数的比重 (%) Percentage to Total Deaths (%)
十种死因合计	**Total**	**95.64**
循环系统	Circulatory system	31.56
肿瘤	Malignant Tumour	25.48
呼吸系统	Diseases of the Respiratory System	14.05
诊断不明	Diagnosis in nubibus	6.20
损伤和中毒	Trauma and Toxicosis	4.93
内分泌	Internal secretion	3.49
消化系统	Disease of the Digestive System	3.35
传染病	Infections Disease	3.21
泌尿生殖系统	Disease of the Genifourinary system	1.86
起源于围生期的某些情况	Diseases of the Nervous system	1.51

注：统计范围包括乌鲁木齐市及辖区资料。
Note: Statistics in Data Covers Urumqi and its Districts.

18-17 安全生产情况

Basic Statistics on Work Safety

项　　目	Item	2006	2007
亿元新疆生产总值生产安全事故死亡率	Mortality Rate of Work Safety Accident Average 100 Billion Yuan GDP	1.01	0.77
工矿商贸企业就业人员生产安全事故十万人死亡率	Mortality Rate of Work Safety Accident of Employment in Industrial & Mining and Commercial & Tradal Enterprises Average 100 000 Persons	9.68	8.64
煤矿百万吨死亡率	Mortality Rate of Coal Procution Average 1 Million Tons	3.15	2.71
道路交通万车死亡率	Mortality Rate of Highway Traffic Accident Average 10 000 Vehicles	14.20	11.00

18-18 社会福利事业单位基本情况
Basic Statistics on Social Welfare Institutions

(2007 年)

指　标	Item	院　数(个) Number of Homes (unit)	工作人员数(人) Number of Persons Engaged (person)	床位数(张) Number of Beds (unit)	年末收养人数(人) Number of Persons Housed (person)	#女性 Female
总　计	**Total**	**498**	**2943**	**25106**	**22280**	**4973**
社会福利院	Social Welfare Homes	33	505	3044	2577	529
儿童福利院	Children Welfare Homes	38	525	3192	3180	1352
光荣院	Homes for Disabled Veterans	7	39	274	204	87
社会福利医院	Psychopathy Welfare Homes	8	515	1380	1467	408
城镇老年性福利机构	Urban Elderly Welfare Units	31	331	2469	1188	521
农村老年性福利机构	Rural Elderly Welfare Units	380	991	14647	13654	2076
荣誉军人康复医院	Recuperative Hospital for Soldiers with Honour	1	37	100	10	

18-19 社会福利事业、企业单位数和工作人员数
Number of Social Welfare Institutions and Enterprises and Persons Engaged

(2007 年)

项　目	Item	机构数(个) Number of Institutions or Enterprises (unit)	工作人员数(人) Number of Persons Engaged (person)
收养性福利事业单位	Adopting Social Welfare Institutions	498	2943
编制部门	Organization Department	383	2531
民政部门	Civil Administration Department	115	412
社会福利企业	Social Welfare Enterprises	109	6169
优抚安置事业单位	Administration Agencies for Martyrs	39	398
救助类单位情况	Condition on Salvaged Deparement	28	250
殡葬服务事业单位	Funeral and Interment Institutions	118	635
福利彩票发行单位	Welfare Lottery-Ticked Issuance Unit	24	167
社区服务中心	Community Service Institutions	50	609

18-20 社会救济情况
Basic Statistics on Social Relief Funds

指　标	Item	2007
城镇居民最低生活保障人数(人)	**Number of Persons Receiving Lowest Cost-of-living in Urban Area (person)**	**615464**
老年人	Old Folks	121201
成年人	Adult	291922
在职人员	Full Employed Staff and Workers	13717
灵活就业人员	Flexible Employed Persons	77766
登记就业人员	Registered Employed Persons	88218
未登记就业人员	Unregistered Employed Persons	112221
未成年人	Minors	202341
在校生	Enrollment	132830
其 他	Others	69511
城镇居民最低生活保障家庭数(户)	**Number of Family Receiving Lowest Cost-of-living in Urban Area (household)**	**250131**
农村最低生活保障人数(人)	**Number of Persons Receiving Lowest Cost-of-living in Rural Area (person)**	**1298787**
农村最低生活保障家庭数(户)	**Number of Family Receiving Lowest Cost-of-living in Rural Area (household)**	**428414**

18-21 工会组织情况
Basic Statistics on Trades Unions

年　份 Year	工会基层组织个数(个) Number of Grassroots Unions (unit)	全区已建工会组织的基本单位职工与会员人数(万人) Membership and Number of Staff and Workers in Grassroots Unions (10 000persons)				专职工会干　部(万人) Number of Full-time Personnel of Unions (10 000 persons)
		职工人数 Number of Staff and Workers	#女 Female	会员人数 Number of Membership	#女 Female	
1980	3255	84.20	30.25	67.13	20.42	0.48
1985	6165	189.48	73.84	151.93	59.03	0.50
1990	10685	231.48	90.64	196.58	76.97	0.79
1995	14457	271.43	114.13	254.49	104.97	1.19
2000	13016	211.73	90.80	200.80	84.93	0.59
2001	18219	234.84	100.71	215.31	91.07	0.73
2002	20806	236.58	99.65	220.85	93.11	0.49
2003	11263	230.24	93.43	220.55	87.05	0.45
2004	11979	224.52	94.49	219.35	90.62	0.48
2005	11721	232.78	97.50	232.03	97.20	0.41
2006	13163	302.05	130.12	263.80	115.64	0.69
2007	15040	323.37	139.45	289.65	124.23	0.60

18-22 残疾人事业基本情况
Basic Information of Person with Disabilities

项　　目	Item	2006	2007
康 复	**Rehabilitation**		
白内障复明	Sight-restoring of Cataract Surgery		
白内障复明手术(万例)	Sight-restoring of Cataract Surgeries (10 000 cases)	1.10	1.30
低视力配用助视器(人)	Vision-aids Provided for Individuds with Low-vision (person)	260	322
聋儿康复	Rehabilitation of Children With Hearing Disability		
年收训聋儿(人)	Hearing and Speech Training (person)	98	149
聋儿入普幼普小率(%)	Enrollment Rate to General Infant School or Elementary School (%)	31	25
培训家长(人)	Parents Trained (person)	130	210
精神病防治康复	Prevention and Treatment of Psychiatric Diseases		
开展精神病防治康复工作市县数(个)	Number of Counties Carried on the Works (unit)	5	15
综合防治康复精神病人数(万人)	Number of Psychosis Sicks Synthetically Prevented, Cured and Rehabilitated (10 000 persons)	1.12	1.07
监护率(%)	Guardianship Rate (%)	88.89	62.33
显好率(%)	Rate of Getting Better (%)	60.48	75.86
社会参与率(%)	Social Participation Rate (%)	48.27	55.82
肇事率(%)	Violent Everds Rate (%)	0.17	0.06
救济贫困患者数(人)	Number of Poor Sufferer Relieved (person)	2665	3855
用品用具供应件数(万件)	Number of Appliances Supplied (10 000 units)	1.09	1.10
康复训练与服务(人)	Rehabilitation Training and Service (person)		
肢体残疾康复训练数	Rehabilitation Training of Body Disabilities	1731	1647
智力残疾儿童康复训练数	Rehabilitation Training of Mental Disabilities Children	223	265
教 育	**Education**		
未入学适龄残疾儿童(万人)	School-age Disabled Children without Schooling (10 000 persons)	0.78	0.68
职业教育与培训机构数(个)	Vocational Education and Training Facilities (unit)		
独立建制	Self Help	49	24
依托社会	Supported by Society	96	71
教育与培训人数(万人)	Number of Educated and Trained (10 000 persons)	1.35	1.34

18-22 续表 Continued

项　目	Item	2006	2007
就 业	**Employment**		
城镇残疾人就业状况(万人)	Employment of Urban Handicappeds (10 000 persons)		
当年安排就业	Persons Employed in the Year	0.29	0.44
按比例就业	Employment by Quota Scheme	0.13	0.17
集中就业	Employment at Welfare Enterprises	0.05	0.10
个体就业	Self-employed	0.11	0.17
未安排就业	Unemployment	2.33	1.89
农村残疾人就业状况(万人)	Employment of Rural Handicapped (10 000 persons)		
就　业	Employed	16.91	17.40
未就业	Unemployed	4.81	5.32
残疾人就业服务机构(个)	Employment Service Institutions for Handicapped (unit)		
省	Provinces	1	1
地	Prefectures	12	12
市(含县级市)	Cities (Cities at County Level)	19	18
县	County	69	68
市辖区	Districts under the Jurisdiction of Cities	11	11
实施分散按比例就业的地区数(个)	Number of Regions Implemented the Policy of the Disperse Employment by Proportion (unit)		
省	Provinces	1	1
地	Prefectures	12	12
市(含县级市)	Cities (Cities at County Level)	19	18
县	County	69	69
市辖区	Districts under the Jurisdiction of Cities	11	11
扶 贫	**Poverty Alleviation**		
扶贫开发解决温饱(万人)	Disabled Persons Overcoming Poverty through Government's Poverty Reduction Program (10 000 persons)	1.33	1.79
尚未解决温饱贫困残疾人(万人)	Number of Handicappeds Remained in Poverty(10 000 persons)	8.45	
可扶持贫困残疾人(万人)	Number of Handicappeds Can Be Supported (10 000 persons)	1.66	1.99
残联组织建设	**Organization of the Disabled Persons's Federation**		
残疾人工作者(万人)	Workers Working for the Disabled (10 000 persons)	0.19	0.13

18-23 历届全区人民代表大会代表人数

Number of Deputies to all the Previous People's Congresses of Xinjiang

项　目 Item	第一届 (1954) First Congress	第二届 (1959) Second Congress	第三届 (1964) Third Congress	第四届 (1975) Fourth Congress	第五届 (1978) Fifth Congress	第六届 (1983) Sixth Congress	第七届 (1988) Seventh Congress	第八届 (1993) Eighth Congress	第九届 (1998) Ninth Congress	第十届 (2003) Tenth Congress	第十一届 (2008) Eleventh Congress
代表总数(人) Total Number of All Deputies (person)	**376**	**386**	**453**	**809**	**672**	**550**	**550**	**542**	**550**	**550**	**550**
#中国共产党党员 Deputies from the Communist Party of China	178		240			374	357	381	396	396	352
占总数比重(%) As Percentage to Total Deputies (%)	47.3		53.0			68.0	64.9	70.3	72.0	72.0	64.0
#少数民族 Deputies from National Minorities	331		383	510	430	357	363	355	363	363	363
占总数比重(%) As Percentage to Total Deputies (%)	88.0		84.5	63.8	64.0	64.9	66.0	65.5	66.0	66.0	66.0
#妇　女 Female Deputies	52	61	89	200	146	17	126	123	135	135	143
占总数比重(%) As Percentage to Total Deputies (%)	13.8	15.8	19.6	24.7	21.7	21.3	22.9	22.7	24.5	24.5	26.0

18-24 历届全区政治协商会议委员人数

Number of Deputies to all the Previous People's Political Consultative Conferences of Xinjiang

项　目 Item	第一届 (1954) First Congress	第二届 (1959) Second Congress	第三届 (1964) Third Congress	第四届 (1978) Fourth Congress	第五届 (1983) Fifth Congress	第六届 (1988) Sixth Congress	第七届 (1993) Seventh Congress	第八届 (1998) Eighth Congress	第九届 (2003) Ninth Congress	第十届 (2008) Tenth Congress
委员总数(人) Total Number of All Deputies (person)	**141**	**275**	**303**	**407**	**441**	**429**	**416**	**444**	**470**	**515**
#中国共产党党员 Deputies from the Communist Party of China	28	57	65	149	158	157	161	183	196	225
占总数比重(%) As Percentage to Total Deputies (%)	19.9	20.7	21.5	36.6	35.8	36.6	38.7	41.2	41.7	43.7
#少数民族 Deputies from National Minorities (%)	121	196	205	221	253	245	204	246	246	263
占总数比重(%) As Percentage to Total Deputies (%)	85.8	71.3	67.7	54.3	57.4	57.0	49.0	55.4	52.3	51.1
#妇　女 Female Deputies	10	28	28	40	49	63	66	82	95	125
占总数比重(%) As Percentage to Total Deputies (%)	7.1	10.2	9.2	9.8	11.1	14.7	15.9	18.5	20.2	24.3

18-25 律师、公证、调解工作基本情况
Basic Statistics on Lawyers, Notarization and Mediation

项目	Item	1985	1990	1995	2000	2007
律师工作	**Lawyers**					
律师事务所(个)	Number of Law Offices (unit)	113	130	169	227	264
律师(人)	Number of Lawyers (person)	694	780	1705	2414	2228
专职律师(人)	Full-time Lawyers (person)	280	435	1209	1508	2075
兼职和特邀律师(人)	Part-time Lawyers (person)	414	345	336	418	94
聘请担任常年法律顾问的单位(处)	Number of Units with Permanent Legal Advisors (unit)	1263	1748	2560	2613	3076
民事诉讼代理(件)	Agent of Civil Cases (case)	1937	6306	6380	16165	28295
刑事辩护及代理(件)	Defender and Agent of Criminal Cases (case)	2310	6237	5850	5826	6682
非诉讼法律事务(件)	Agent of Non-Litigious Legal Affairs (case)	979	614	5357	4810	2992
解答法律咨询(万件)	Agent of Legal Advisory Services (10 000 cases)	1.83	4.62	4.21	7.45	8.06
代写法律事务文书(万件)	Agent of Legal Documents Written on Behalf of Clients (10 000 cases)	0.43	0.69	1.06	1.94	2.64
公证工作	**Notarization**					
公证处(个)	Number of Notary Offices (unit)	90	113	126	131	124
公证员(人)	Notaries (person)	101	173	266	332	402
公证员助理(人)	Assistant Notaries (person)	22	76	49	43	95
办理公证文书(万件)	Number of Notarized Document (10 000 cases)	5.18	6.79	10.11	18.85	24.61
人民调解工作	**Number of People's Mediation**					
专职司法助理员(人)	Number of Full-time Judicial Assistants (person)	1061	939	1515	1750	1808
人民调解委员会(个)	Number of People's Mediation Committees (unit)	16070	17422	19045	22294	14988
调解人员(万人)	Number of Mediators (10 000 persons)	7.88	7.11	12.04	10.04	7.85
调解民间纠纷(万件)	Number of Civil Disputes Mediated (10 000 cases)	8.43	11.86	9.18	8.09	12.98

18-26 调解民间纠纷分类
Number of Civil Disputes Mediated by Type

(2007 年)

项　目	Item	调解纠纷(件) Civil Disputes (case)	各类纠纷所占比重(%) Percentage (%)
总　计	**Total**	**129799**	**100.00**
婚姻家庭	Disputes and Family	31891	24.57
合　同	Contract	8926	6.88
劳　动	Labor	7091	5.46
村务管理	Village-affair Management	2061	1.59
土　地	Land	14251	10.98
征地拆迁	Requisitioned Land Demolition	2071	1.60
房屋宅基地	Housing and Housing Sites	4884	3.76
计划生育	Family Planning	901	0.69
邻　里	Neighbour	25138	19.37
损害赔偿	Compensation for Damages	9790	7.54
施工扰民	Construction Noise	1439	1.11
其　他	Others	21356	16.45

18-27 火灾事故发生情况
Basic Statistics on Fire Accidents

(2007 年)

指　标	Item	合　计 Total	按事故发生程度分 By Serious Dgree of Fires		
			特　大 Extraordinarily Serious	重　大 Serious	一　般 Ordinary
发生起数(起)	Fires (case)	6215	2	7	6206
死亡(人)	Death (person)	37		4	33
受伤(人)	Injuries (person)	66			66
损失折款(万元)	Losses Converted into Cash (10 000 yuan)	2385	217	340	1828
平均每起事故损失(元)	Average Loss per Fire (yuan)	3837	1083500	485680	2945

18-28 交通事故发生情况
Basic Statistics on Traffic Accidents

指　标	Item	2005	2006	2007
发生起数(起)	Traffic Accidents (case)	9527	7427	6487
死亡(人)	Death (person)	3111	2588	2152
受伤(人)	Injuries (person)	10436	8843	7499
损失折款(万元)	Losses Converted into Cash (10 000 yuan)	2845	1663	1261
平均每起事故损失(元)	Average Loss per Fire (yuan)	2986	2239	1943

18-29 公安机关受理查处治安案件情况
Cases of Offense Against Public Order Handled by Public Security Organs

单位：起 (2007 年) (case)

案件类别	Category of Cases	受理 Number of Cases Accepted to be Treated	查处 Number of Cases Investigated and Treated
总 计	**Total**	**133420**	**114510**
扰乱工作、公共秩序	Disturbing Work or Public Order	3708	3377
扰乱单位秩序	Disturbing Business Orders	629	612
扰乱公共场所秩序	Disturbing the Orders in Public Places	679	669
寻衅滋事	Causing Quarrels and Making Troubles	1500	1246
其 他	Others	900	850
妨害公共安全	Disorderly Cordnct	1328	1205
非法携带枪支、弹药、管制刀具	Violation of Firearms Control Regulations	295	287
盗窃、损毁公共设施	Stealing and Damaging Public Facilities	749	649
其 他	Others	284	269
侵犯他人人身权利、财产权利	Offences Against, Citizens'Personal and Property Rights	109399	91150
侮辱、诽谤、诬告陷害	Insult, Slander and Circumvention	1145	1011
殴打他人	Beating Other Body	65861	58865
故意伤害	Wilfully Injuring Others	2640	2210
盗 窃	Stealing Property	28830	19764
诈 骗	Swindling, Seizing and Extorting Property	1564	1140
抢 夺	Robbery and Snatch	791	516
敲诈勒索	Extertion and Blackmail	713	595
其 他	Others	7855	7049
妨害社会管理	Disorderly Social Management	18985	18778
阻碍执行职务	Obstructing Government Workers in Performing Their Duties	1128	1106
违反旅馆业管理	Violating the Hotel Management Regulations	1265	1253
违反房屋出租管理	Violating the Rent Control Regulations	3662	3657
卖淫、嫖娼	Prostitution or Going Whoring	1365	1350
赌博或为赌博提供条件	Gambling	1407	1341
毒品违法活动	Illegal Drug Related Action	7431	7429
其 他	Others	2727	2642

18-30 刑事案件中青少年犯罪情况
Juvenile Delinquency Among Criminal Cases

单位：人 (person)

年份 Year	刑事罪犯总数 Offenders	#青少年罪犯 Young Offenders	#不满 18 岁 Less than 18	#18 岁至 25 岁 Between 18 to 25	青少年罪犯占刑事罪犯 (%) Percentage to Total (%)
2005	40856	21750	7966	13784	53.24
2006	40492	20259	7583	12676	50.00
2007	38878	19838	7142	12696	51.03

主要统计指标解释

等级运动员人数　指经考核正式批准授予等级运动员称号的人数。运动员等级分为国际级运动健将、运动健将、一级运动员、二级运动员、三级运动员、少年级运动员。该指标主要反映运动员队伍的技术质量水平。

等级裁判员人数　指经考核正式批准授予等级裁判员称号的人数。裁判员等级分为国际裁判、国家级裁判、一级裁判、二级裁判、三级裁判。该指标主要反映裁判员队伍的技术质量水平。

体育场　指有400米跑道(中心含足球场)，有固定道牙，跑道6条以上，并有固定看台的室外田径场地。体育场按看台容纳观众人数分为：甲级25000人以上，乙级15000-25000人，丙级5000-15000人，丁级5000人以下。该指标主要反映大中型体育场数量水平。

体育馆　指有固定看台，可供篮球、排球、羽毛球、乒乓球、体操等项目训练比赛活动用的室内运动场地。体育馆按看台容纳观众人数分为：甲级6000人以上，乙级4000-6000人，丙级2000-4000人，丁级2000人以下。该指标主要反映大中型体育馆数量水平。

卫生机构　包括医疗机构、疾病预防控制中心(防疫站)、采供血机构、卫生监督及监测(检验)机构、医学科研和在职培训机构、健康教育所等。医疗机构包括医院、社区卫生服务中心(站)、疗养院、卫生院、门诊部、诊所(卫生所、医务室)、妇幼保健院(所、站)、专科疾病防治院(所、站)、急救中心(站)和临床检验中心。医疗机构分为非赢利性医疗机构和赢利性医疗机构。

医院　包括综合医院、中医医院、中西医结合医院、民族医院、各类专科医院和护理院。

卫生技术人员　指卫生机构中医生、护理人员、药剂人员、检验人员等卫生技术人员。

医生　指在医疗、预防保健机构工作且取得《执业医师证书》的执业医师和执业助理医师。

卫生服务总费用　反映全国当年用于医疗卫生保健服务所消耗的资金总额，用筹资来源法测算。政府预算卫生支出指各级政府用于卫生事业的财政预算拨款。社会卫生支出指政府预算外的卫生资金投入，主要表现为社会医疗保险。其中包括如企事业单位和乡村集体经济单位举办医疗卫生机构设施建设费，企业职工医疗卫生费，行政事业单位负担的职工公费医疗超支部分等。居民个人卫生支出指城乡居民用自己可支配的经济收入支付的各项医疗卫生费用和医疗保险费用。

社会福利事业单位　指集中收养社会孤老、残、幼的机构，包括由民政部门管理的社会福利院、儿童福利院、精神病人福利院和城镇集体举办的福利院及农村集体举办的敬老院以及优抚医院和具有收养能力的社区服务中心等。该指标主要反映我国在社会福利性单位投入的水平。

社会福利事业单位收养人数　包括民政部门管理和城镇、农村集体举办的社会福利事业单位中收养的老人、少年儿童、缺乏生活自理能力的残疾人员和精神病人。该指标主要反映收养性社会福利单位的收养能力。

社会福利企业单位　指以安置城镇有一定劳动能力的盲、聋、哑和肢体残疾人员就业为目的，享受国家减免税待遇的国有或集体企业。包括福利工厂、福利商业和服务业、假肢厂和安置农场等单位。该指标主要反映我国对残疾人照顾的特殊政策。

农村五保户　指农村中既无劳动能力，又无经济来源的老、弱、孤、残的农民，其生活由集体供养，实行保吃、保穿、保住、保医、保葬(孤儿保教)，简称"五保"，享受五保待遇的家庭叫五保户。该指标主要反映农村弱势群体的人员数量。

聋儿入普幼普小率　指本年度内进入普通幼儿园、普通小学的聋儿数与在训聋儿数(不含当年新收训聋儿数)之比。该指标主要反映经过康复训练的聋儿进入普通幼儿园和普通小学的情况。

综合防治康复精神病人数　指在开展精神病防治康复工作地区，采取不同形式，接受综合性防治康复措施、开放式管理的精神病人数。该指标主要反映精神病患者接受治疗康复情况。

监护率　指通过监护小组、家庭病床、工疗站、社会就业以及精神卫生机构，接受社会化、综合性、开放式治疗与康复的精神病人占经调查摸底、登记在册的精神病人数的百分比。该指标主要反映对精神病患者落实治疗康复措施的情况。

精神病人社会参与率　指生活能自理，并参加生产劳动和社会生活的精神病人数占监护精神病人数的百分比。该指标主要反映精神病人康复状况和参与社会的情况。

未入学适龄残疾儿童少年　指根据义务教育法规定应接受义务教育，但因各种原因未能入学的适龄视力残疾、听力与言语残疾、智力残疾、肢体残疾、精神残疾、多重残疾儿童少年。适龄残疾儿童少年的年龄段参照各省级人民政府依照义务教育法规定的入学年龄。该指标主要反映因各种原因未能入学的适龄残疾儿童的年度变化，为制定残疾儿童义务教育发展规划及其应采取的方针、政策和措施提供依据，同时为各地开展资助残疾儿童就学工作提供依据。

律师　指依法取得律师执业证书，担任法律顾问，民事(刑事、行政)案件代理人、刑事案件辩护人、办理非诉讼业务，解答法律询问，代写法律事务文书等，为社会提供法律服务的人员。

公证人员　指在公证处工作的人员总称，包括公证处主任、副主任、公证员、公证员助理(助理公证员)和其他从事辅助性工作的人员。

公证文书　指公证处根据当事人申请，依照事实和法律，按照法定程序制作的，具有法律效力的司法证明文书。根据公证书用途和使用地，公证书分为国内公证书、国内经济公证书、涉外民事公证书、涉外经济公证书四类。

调解员　指在人民调解委员会担负调解民间纠纷工作的人员，包括调解委员会的委员和调解小组的调解员。该指标主要反映从事人民调解工作的人员数量。

调解民间纠纷　指调解委员会按照法律规定，根据自愿原则，用说服教育的方法调解民间发生的有关民事权利和义务争执的件数，包括调解成功数和调解未成功数。该指标主要反映人民调解委员会的工作量。

立案　指人民检察院对受理的报案、控告、举报或自首及自行发现的犯罪线索、犯罪嫌疑人进行初步调查后，认为存在职务犯罪事实和应追究刑事责任，并决定作为刑事案件进行侦查的诉讼活动，是追究犯罪的开始。该指标主要反映人民检察院依法将职务犯罪线索作为刑事案件进行侦查的诉讼活动。

大案　指贪污、贿赂案数额在5万元以上，挪用公款案数额在10万元以上，集体私分、巨额财产来源不明、隐瞒境外存款案数额在50万元以上以及按照《人民检察院直接受理的渎职、侵权重、特大案件标准(试行)》认定的案件。该指标主要反映人民检察院立案查办的职务犯罪案件中经济损失大、社会危害严重的案件。

要案　指县、处级以上干部的犯罪案件。该指标主要反映国家工作人员中县、处级以上干部因职务犯罪被人民检察院依法立案侦查的情况。

决定逮捕　指人民检察院对直接受理、自行侦查的案件，认为需要逮捕犯罪嫌疑人时，依据法律做出的逮捕决定。该指标主要反映人民检察院对直接受理的案件行使决定逮捕权的情况。

批准逮捕　指人民检察院对公安机关、国家安全机关、监狱管理机关提出逮捕的犯罪嫌疑人进行审查，根据事实，依法做出逮捕决定。该指标主要反映人民检察院对提请逮捕机关提请逮捕犯罪嫌疑人进行审查后依法做出批准逮捕决定的情况。

决定起诉　指人民检察院对公安机关、国家安全机关、监狱管理机关和检察机关内设机构反贪污贿赂部门等移送起诉的案件进行审查，根据事实，做出提起公诉的案件。该指标主要反映人民检察院对各种刑事案件向人民法院提起公诉的情况。

受理劳动争议案件数　指劳动争议仲裁委员会根据国家有关规定，对劳动争议当事人的申请予以审查，符合受理条件而正式立案、准备处理的劳动争议案件数。

Explanatory Notes on Main Statistical Indicators

Number of Athletes in Grades refers to the number of athletes who have been given titles through examination. The titles of athletes include international masters of sports, masters of sports, first-grade, second- grade and third-grade sportsmen and young athletes. This indicator reflects skill of the athletes.

Number of Referees in Grades refers to the number of referees who have been given titles after examination. They are classified as international referees, national referees and referees of the first, second and third grades. This indicator reflects the skill of referees.

Stadiums refer to stadiums for track and field events with six lane 400-meter tracks around soccer fields, permanent track marks and permanent bleachers. Stadiums are classified according to seating capacity. They include: Class A stadiums have the capaCity of seating 25000 people each. Class B stadiums have the capaCity of seating 15000 to 25000 people each. Class C stadiums have the capaCity of s eating 5000 to 15000 people each, and Class D stadiums have the capaCity of seating fewer than 5000 people. This indicator reflects numbers of large and medium-sized stadiums.

Gymnasiums refer to indoor sports grounds with permanent seats in which basketball, volleyball. Badminton, table tennis and gymnastics competitions can be held. Gymnasiums are classified according to seating capaCity. They include: Class Agymnasiums with seating over 6000 people. Class B gymnasiums with seating 4000 to 6000 people. Class Cgymnasiums with seating 2000 to 4000 people, and Class D gymnasiums with eating fewer than 2000 people. This indicator reflects the total number of large and medium-sized gymnasiums Health Care Institutions include: medical institutions, disease prevent ion and control centers (epidemic prevention stations), blood gathering and supplying institutions, health supervision and inspection (checkup) institutions, medicinal scientific research and on-job training institutions, health education and son on.

Health Care Institutions include: medical institutions,disease prevention and control centers(epidemic prevention stations),blood gathering and supplying Institutions,health supervision and inspection(check up)institutions,medical scientific research and on-job training institutions,health education and so on.

Hospitals include: polyclinics, traditional Chinese medical hospitals, hospitals integrated with traditional Chinese therapeutics and western therapeutics, ethical hospitals, various specialties hospitals and nursing hospitals.

Medical Technical Personnel refers to doctors, assistant nurses, pharmacists, and laboratory technicians working in medical institutions.

Doctors refer to certified physicians and certified assistant physicians with certifications working in medical and health care and prevention agencies.

Total Cost of Health Services reflects the total expenditures on medical and health care services for the whole country, calculated on basis of sources of funding. Health expenditure from government budget refers to budgetary allocation for health undertakings by governments at all levels. Social health expenditure refers to non-government budgetary cap ital input, mainly the health insurance. It includes expenditure on health institutions run by enterprises and rural collective entities, expenditure on medical and health care of employees of enterprises, and excessive health expenditure of government employees that could be covered by the government health care system. Health expenditure on individuals refers to expenditure on health service and health insurance paid by residents from their disposable income.

Social Welfare Institutions refer to institutions taking care of old pople without children, handicapped people and orphans. They include social welfare institutions run by civil affairs departments, children welfare institutions, social welfare institutions for mental patients, collective-owned old peoples homes in rural areas, convalescent homes and community service centers with the capaCity of receiving those people. This indicator reflects the input in social welfare institutions.

Number of People Taken in by Social Welfare Institutions refers to the number of old people, children, totally dependent handicapped people and mental patients taken in by social welfare institutions run by civil affairs departments and those run by collective units in urban and rural areas. This indicator reflects the cap a City of social welfare institutions.

Social Welfare Enterprises are collective owned enterprises which employ the blind, deaf-mute, and other handicapped people who are able to work in cities and towns and enjoy exemption from state taxes, including welfare plants, welfare commercial services, artificial limb plants and farms, etc. This indicator reflects the preferential policies toward disabled persons.

Rural Households with Livelihood Guaranteed in Five Aspects refer to the households in which there are old people without child, orphans and handicapped people who are unable to work and without financial resources in rural areas. They are taken care of by the collective units and their food, clothing, housing, medical care, funeral expenses (or schooling for orphans) are guaranteed to be provided for. This indicator reflects the total number of disadvantageous groups of rural population.

Proportion of Deaf Children Enrolled in Ordinary Preschool and Primary Education refers to the proportion of deaf children who are enrolled in ordinary kindergartens or primary schools during the year in the total number of deaf children under rehabilitation programs (not including new comers into the rehabilitation programs during the year). This indicator mainly reflects number of rehabilitated deaf children entering ordinary kindergartens or primary schools.

Number of Mental Patients under Integrated Prevention and Rehabilitation Program refers to mental disease patients receiving integrated prevention and rehabilitation treatment of various forms under open environment in areas with mental disease rehabilitation programs. This indicator reflects the condition of metal patients receiving rehabilitation treatment.

Supervision Rate refers to the percentage of patients among the total number of registered mental disease patients, who participate in social integrated and open treatment and rehabilitation programs through various forms such as supervision groups, family treatment, employment or guidance from psychiatric institutions. This indicator reflects the implementation of various measures aimed at rehabilitating those metal patients.

Social Participation Rate of Mental Patients refers to proportion of mental disease patients who are able to manage their daily life and participate in economic activities to the total number of mental disease patients under supervision. This indicator reflects the condition of recovery of those metal patient sand their participation in social activities.

School-age Disabled Children not in Schools refer to children with disability in sight, listening, speaking, mentality, limbs or multi-disability who are obliged to compulsory education by law but have not been enrolled in schools due to various reasons. The definition of school age for disabled children is decided by the definition of school age as specified by provincial governments in line wit h the local laws on compulsory education. This indicator reflects the annual change of school-age disable children not entering schools by various reasons. It will provide foundation for the formulation of development plans of compulsory education for those disable children, and for related principles, policies and measures as well. It is also t he base for the job of funding t hose disabled children back to schools across the countries.

Lawyers are certified legal workers according to law, and who are employed by legal counseling firms to act as legal advisers, agents in criminal or civil lawsuits, or defenders in criminal lawsuits, or to handle non-litigious legal affairs, to advise on matters of law or t o write legal papers for others, and provide service to the public.

Notary Personnel refers to people working for notary offices including: directors, deputy direct or, notaries, assistant notaries, and other people providing assistance.

Notary Documents refer to the judicatory notary documents drawn up by the request of the party and are in accordance with facts and laws and following certain legal proceedings. According to usage and locality, the notary documents are divided into following 4 types: domestic notary documents, domestic economic notary documents, foreign-related civil notary documents and foreign-related economic notary documents.

Mediators refer to workers on peoples mediation committees responsible for mediating in civil disputes and cases of slight infraction of the law. They include members of the mediation committees and mediators of mediation groups. This indicator reflects the number of people engaged in meditation.

Mediation of Civil Disputes refers to number of cases made by mediation committees in mediating in civil disputes concerning civil rights and duties through persuasion and education in accordance wit h t he provisions of law on a voluntary basis, so as t o solve disputes by helping the parties involved come to an agreement and understanding, including those unsuccessful ones. This indicator reflects the workload of the mediation committees.

Acceptance of Case refers t o t he decision made by the people's procurator ate office on reported cases, prosecution, impeachment, surrender, self-found criminal clues or suspects after initial investigation to confirm t he act of crime and to start legal proceedings of the case as criminal case.

Large Case refers to the case involves a corruption or bribery of over 50,000 yuan, or a misappropriation of over 100,000 yuan. Cases of collectively illegal possess ion of public funds, unstated sources of large properties, or disguised overseas savings deposits involving 500,000 yuan, or a case that has been defined by the "Standard on Serious and Large Cases of Misconduct and Tortious that Directly Accepted by People's Procurators Office (try out)". This indicator mainly reflects number of accepted cases of job-related criminals that caused serious economic losses or extremely harmful to the society.

Key Case refers to a case committed by government officials with a ranking of division director or county administrator. This indicator mainly reflects the recorded and spied on cases by the people's procurators offices toward government official with a ranking of division director or county administrator.

Decision on Arrest refers to decision made by people's procurators office, in accordance with laws, to arrest the suspect (s) in the cases that are accepted and to be investigated by procurators office. This indicator mainly reflects the implementation of the decision on arrest by people's procurators office.

Approval for Arrest refers to the decision made by people's procurators office, in accordance with laws and relevant facts, to approve t he arrest of the suspect(s) that is propos ed by the public security departments, state security departments or authority of prisons. This indicator reflects approved arrests made by people's procurators office that are proposed by related departments.

Decision on Prosecution refers to the decision made by people's procurators office, in accordance with laws and relevant facts, to institute proceedings to the people's court against the suspect (s) of criminal cases handed over by the public security departments, state security departments or authority of prisons, or by t he anti-corruption department s within the procurators office. This indicator reflects t he condition of the prosecutions made by people's procurators office toward the people's court.

Number of Labor Dispute Cases Accepted refers to the number of cases of labor dispute submitted that, after being reviewed by the labor dispute arbitration committees in line with the relevant stat e regulations, are accepted and registered or treatment.

第十九篇
企业集团及企业景气指数

CHAPTER 19
Enterprises Group and Prosperity Index on Enterprises

简要说明
Brief Introduction

本篇资料的主要内容及来源

本篇资料主要包括企业集团主要经济指标、企业集团主要财务情况、企业家信心指数、企业景气指数。

企业集团及企业景气指数资料由国家统计局新疆调查总队统计监测处提供。

Main Content and Source of Data

The data in this chapter mainly include main indicator of enterprises group, main indicators in finance of enterprises group, entrepreneur confidence index and enterprises business climate index. Data on the business group and enterprises business climate index are provided by the Department of Monitoring Statistics , NBS Survey Office in Xinjiang.

19-1 企业集团基本情况
Basic Condition of Enterprise Group

指　　标	Item	2006	2007
企业集团单位数(个)	**Number of Enterprises(unit)**	**67**	**85**
按集团审批部门分	**Grouped by Examining and Approving Department**		
自治区人民政府	Government of Autonomous Region	10	9
自治区政府主管部门	Responsible Government Department of Autonomous Region	22	23
其　他	Others	35	53
按集团主营行业分	**Grouped by Sector of Major Business**		
农、林、牧、渔业	Farming, Forestry, Animal Husbandry and Fishery	2	6
采掘业	Mining and Quarrying	3	3
制造业	Manufacturing	19	23
电力、燃气及水的生产和供应业	Production and Distribution of Electricity,Gas and Water	1	2
建筑业	Construction	8	10
交通运输、仓储和邮政业	Transport, Storage and post	6	7
批发和零售业	Wholesale and Retail Trades	16	16
住宿和餐饮业	Hotels and Catering Services		
房地产业	Real Estate	11	17
其　他	Others	1	1
按母公司控股情况分	**Grouped by Share- holding Situation Parent Company**		
国有控股	State-holding Enterprises	20	19
集体控股	Collective- holding Enterprises	14	10
私人控股	Private- holding Enterprises	33	56
按母公司登记注册类型分	**Grouped by Registration Status of Parent Company**		
国有企业	State-owned	2	2
国有独资公司	State-owned Exclusive Investment Company	11	10
其他有限责任公司	Other Limited Liability Corporations	48	67
股份有限公司	Share-holding Corporation Ltd.	5	4
其　他	Others	1	2
从业人员（人）	**Employment (person)**	**178387**	**182785**
在岗职工	Fully-employed Staff and Workers	169513	174736
其他从业人员	Other Employed Persons	8874	8049
从业人员劳动报酬(万元)	**Remuneration Payment of Employment (10 000 yuan)**	**320078**	**386801**
在岗职工	Fully-Employed Staff and Workers	311105	377524
其他从业人员	Other Employed Persons	8973	9277

19-2 企业集团主要财务指标
Main Indicators in Finance of Enterprises Group

单位：万元 (2007 年) (10 000yuan)

指 标	Item	年末资产总计 Total Assets	固定资产 Value of Fixed Assets	累计折旧 Accumu-Lative Depre-ciation	累计对外投资 Accumulative External Investment
总 计	**Total**	**13933216**	**4116715**	**1696814**	**269021**
按集团审批部门分	**Grouped by Examining and Approving Department**				
自治区人民政府	Government of Autonomous Region	3878622	1300906	624057	84094
自治区政府主管部门	Responsible Government Department of Autonomous Region	6544778	1884801	693925	82001
其 他	Others	3509816	931008	378832	102926
按集团主营行业分	**Grouped by Sector of Major Business**				
农、林、牧、渔业	Farming, Forestry, Animal Husbandry and Fishery	93375	37317	9016	488
采掘业	Mining and Quarrying	763424	271865	136537	19563
制造业	Manufacturing	6297411	2163321	965427	124373
电力、燃气及水的生产和供应业	Production and Distribution of Electricity,Gas and Water	147053	89282	33895	27205
建筑业	Construction	1004510	164230	94542	15287
交通运输、仓储和邮政业	Transport, Storage and Post	276366	93619	42966	4574
批发和零售业	Wholesale and Retail Trades	3979742	941278	330845	50031
房地产业	Real Estate	824879	184779	46856	23205
其 他	Others	546456	171024	36730	4295
按母公司控股情况分	**Grouped by Share- holding Situation Parent Company**				
国有控股	State-holding Enterprises	6469108	2119453	1069769	114952
集体控股	Collective- holding Enterprises	2588966	600528	213454	14101
私人控股	Private- holding Enterprises	4875142	1396734	413591	139968
按母公司登记注册类型分	**Grouped by Registration Status of Parent Company**				
国有企业	State-owned	78448	28204	12763	1550
国有独资公司	State-owned Exclusive Investment Company	2698209	683829	330054	8403
其他有限责任公司	Other Limited Liability Corporations	9165711	2796830	1081717	232102
股份有限公司	Share-holding Corporation Ltd.	1776098	534409	250559	17034
其 他	Others	214750	73443	21721	9932

注：企业集团的财务指标来源于企业集团母公司按财政部门制定的“企业集团合并会计报表”的有关数据，合并会计报表中没有的指标按母公司与各子公司相加汇总的数据。

Note：The data sources of enterprises group financial indicators are obtained by parent company in accordance with Merge Financial Report Forms compiled by the Ministry of Finace, with the indicators excluded from Merge Financial Report Forms according to data collected from parent company and all subsidiary company.

19-2 续表 1 Continued

单位：万元 (10 000yuan)

指 标	Item	流动资产年平均余额 Average Balance of Circulating Funds	年末负债合计 Total Liabilites at Year-end	年末少数股东权益 Minority Share-holder's Equity at Year-end	年末股东(所有者)权益 Share-holder's (or Owner's) Equity at Year-end
总 计	**Total**	**6674963**	**8264773**	**1328639**	**5668443**
按集团审批部门分	**Grouped by Examining and Approving Department**				
自治区人民政府	Government of Autonomous Region	1748003	2626426	225668	1252196
自治区政府主管部门	Responsible Government Department of Autonomous Region	3084630	3449304	911147	3095474
其 他	Others	1842330	2189043	191824	1320773
按集团主营行业分	**Grouped by Sector of Major Business**				
农、林、牧、渔业	Farming, Forestry, Animal Husbandry and Fishery	23245	41615	2871	51760
采掘业	Mining and Quarrying	309716	334968	45758	428456
制造业	Manufacturing	2668081	3506376	691521	2,791035
电力、燃气及水的生产和供应业	Production and Distribution of Electricity,Gasand Water	29701	76589	11784	70464
建筑业	Construction	668042	713942	53172	290568
交通运输、仓储和邮政业	Transport, Storage and post	197603	213294	4005	63072
批发和零售业	Wholesale and Retail Trades	2363568	2598453	483264	1381289
房地产业	Real Estate	403686	524687	11562	300192
其 他	Others	11321	254849	24702	291607
按母公司控股情况分	**Grouped by Share- holding Situation Parent Company**				
国有控股	State-holding Enterprises	2904386	3662482	615029	2806626
集体控股	Collective- holding Enterprises	1738229	1913880	102949	675086
私人控股	Private- holding Enterprises	2032348	2688411	610661	2186731
按母公司登记注册类型分	**Grouped by Registration Status of Parent Company**				
国有企业	State-owned	49061	65037	1669	13411
国有独资公司	State-owned Exclusive Investment Company	1385832	1179957	388626	1518252
其他有限责任公司	Other Limited Liability Corporations	4189639	5718,830	824922	3446881
股份有限公司	Share-holding Corporation Ltd.	936571	1165497	113422	610601
其 他	Others	113860	135452		79298

19-2 续表 2 Continued

单位：万元 (10 000yuan)

指标	Item	营业收入 Business Income	营业成本 Cost of Business	#营业税金及附加 Tax and Addition for Business	新产品销售收入 Sales Income of New Products	出口销售总额 Total Exports
总计	**Total**	**8928328**	**7261088**	**110105**	**462527**	**366625**
按集团审批部门分	**Grouped by Examining and Approving Department**					
自治区人民政府	Government of Autonomous Region	2308133	1848964	27732	138786	35809
自治区政府主管部门	Responsible Government Department of Autonomous Region	4139317	3365354	42152	75322	199480
其他	Others	2480878	2046770	40221	248419	131336
按集团主营行业分	**Grouped by Sector of Major Business**					
农、林、牧、渔业	Farming, Forestry, Animal Husbandry and Fishery	40837	34113	253		
采掘业	Mining and Quarrying	359730	280741	8208		34376
制造业	Manufacturing	3774360	2888470	30328	387096	328208
电力、燃气及水的生产和供应业	Production and Distribution of Electricity, Gas and Water	27843	19169	146		
建筑业	Construction	730413	638710	22241	109	
交通运输、仓储和邮政业	Transport, Storage and post	160102	138286	2142		
批发和零售业	Wholesale and Retail Trades	3435520	2981831	28275	75322	4041
房地产业	Real Estate	317130	249220	15795		
其他	Others	82393	30548	2717		
按母公司控股情况分	**Grouped by Share- holding Situation Parent Company**					
国有控股	State-holding Enterprises	3575206	2791746	45226	138786	179270
集体控股	Collective- holding Enterprises	2095680	1800462	6836	240431	129614
私人控股	Private- holding Enterprises	3257442	2668880	58043	83310	57741
按母公司登记注册类型分	**Grouped by Registration Status of Parent Company**					
国有企业	State-owned	38650	31630	791		155
国有独资公司	State-owned Exclusive Investment Company	1431192	1149368	19423		12310
其他有限责任公司	Other Limited Liability Corporations	5906362	4863433	81671	222096	93242
股份有限公司	Share-holding Corporation Ltd.	1368417	1068150	6974	240431	260918
其他	Others	183707	148507	1246		

19-2 续表 3 Continued

单位：万元 (10 000yuan)

指 标	Item	投资收益 Investment Income	利润总额 Total Profits	应交所得税 Due Income Tax	应交增值税 Due Value-adding Tax	固定资产投资完成额 Sum of Completed Investment in Fixed Asset
总 计	**Total**	**73731**	**514217**	**75133**	**203097**	**800272**
按集团审批部门分	**Grouped by Examining and Approving Department**					
自治区人民政府	Government of Autonomous Region	9792	62976	10047	105591	331416
自治区政府主管部门	Responsible Government Department of Autonomous Region	51287	304271	42508	72566	291074
其 他	Others	12652	146970	22578	24940	177782
按集团主营行业分	**Grouped by Sector of Major Business**					
农、林、牧、渔业	Farming, Forestry, Animal Husbandry and Fishery	3	2246	211	117	2044
采掘业	Mining and Quarrying	3711	14604	4291	27966	48243
制造业	Manufacturing	68247	276970	22242	140313	479336
电力、燃气及水的生产和供应业	Production and Distribution of Electricity,Gas and Water	2623	3448	247	921	5965
建筑业	Construction	2648	21999	8790	1269	31217
交通运输、仓储和邮政业	Transport, Storage and Post	78	2521	251	529	7127
批发和零售业	Wholesale and Retail Trades	206	159657	33858	30965	115946
房地产业	Real Estate	-3128	14326	3717	1017	92736
其 他	Others	-657	18446	1526		17658
按母公司控股情况分	**Grouped by Share- holding Situation Parent Company**					
国有控股	State-holding Enterprises	51801	204295	17249	168434	475308
集体控股	Collective- holding Enterprises	10123	92729	11061	9055	47032
私人控股	Private- holding Enterprises	11807	217193	46823	25608	277932
按母公司登记注册类型分	**Grouped by Registration Status of Parent Company**					
国有企业	State-owned	89	69	20	43	2760
国有独资公司	State-owned Exclusive Investment Company	41202	117568	11447	59341	104536
其他有限责任公司	Other Limited Liability Corporations	14826	275094	51370	132443	579081
股份有限公司	Share-holding Corporation Ltd.	17614	102277	12194	5377	97728
其 他	Others		19209	102	5893	16167

19-3 企业家信心指数
Entrepreneur Confidence Index

(2007 年)

经济类型及行业	Ownership and Sector	一季度 First Quarter		二季度 Second Quarter	
		本期实际 Index	比上年同期增减 as±of Last Same Period Index	本期实际 Index	比上年同期增减 as±of Last Same Period Index
企业家信心指数	**Entrepreneur Confidence Index**	**136.5**	**4.5**	**136.6**	**3.5**
按企业登记注册类型分	**Grouped by Status of Registration**				
国有企业	State-owned Enterprises	136.1	5.3	133.8	5.5
集体企业	Collective-owned Enterprises	127.6	2.3	123.7	-13.5
股份合作企业	Cooperative Enterprises	128.6	-8.9	171.4	21.4
有限责任公司	Limited-Liability Corporations	126.2	0.2	130.1	5.0
股份有限公司	Share Holding Corporations Ltd.	164.4	7.8	163.6	1.9
私营企业	Private Enterprises	143.0	16.7	128.2	1.2
外商及港澳台投资企业	Enterprises with Funds from Hogkong, Macao and Taiwan	132.3	20.7	129.0	-1.7
按行业分	**Grouped by Sector**				
工　业	Industry	137.1	2.8	142.6	2.3
建筑业	Construction	133.0	9.4	127.1	8.7
交通运输、仓储和邮政业	Transportation, Storage,Post and Telecommunications	124.8	0.2	113.1	5.4
批发和零售业	Wholesale and Retail Trades	138.5	4.9	131.0	5.3
房地产业	Real Estate	146.5	30.2	147.0	16.2
社会服务业	Social Services	129.3	-5.2	117.9	-25.5
信息传输、计算机服务和软件业	Information Transmission, Computer Servcie and Software Industries	166.0	2.0	155.6	-9.4
住宿和餐饮业	Accommodation and Catering Services	119.2	-1.9	115.4	-13.5
按企业规模分	**Grouped by Size of Enterprises**				
大　型	Large	160.7	1.9	164.5	10.9
中　型	Medium	138.9	7.8	137.1	3.8
小　型	Small	122.3	0.6	122.6	-0.2
按特殊群体分	**Grouped by Special Group**				
乡镇企业	Town and Township Enterprises	132.4	-6.0	140.7	4.6
上市公司	Listed Companies	180.1	19.2	183.6	14.5
国有控股企业	State-owned and State-holding Enterprises	139.7	3.9	141.5	6.8

19-3 续表 Continued

经济类型及行业	Ownership and Sector	三季度 Third Quarter		四季度 Fourth Quarter	
		本期实际 Index	比上年同期增减 as±of Last Same Period Index	本期实际 Index	比上年同期增减 as±of Last Same Period Index
企业家信心指数	**Entrepreneur Confidence Index**	**140.2**	**6.3**	**140.8**	**7.0**
按企业登记注册类型分	**Grouped by Status of Registration**				
国有企业	State-owned Enterprises	136.1	2.3	135.8	2.6
集体企业	Collective-owned Enterprises	135.3	7.3	116.7	-12.6
股份合作企业	Cooperative Enterprises	157.1	32.1	157.1	32.1
有限责任公司	Limited-Liability Corporations	134.0	7.3	133.1	7.8
股份有限公司	Share Holding Corporations Ltd.	164.6	10.6	171.4	10.0
私营企业	Private Enterprises	134.1	-8.2	129.6	4.2
外商及港澳台投资企业	Enterprises with Funds from Hogkong, Macao and Taiwan	138.7	0.3	122.6	3.4
按行业分	**Grouped by Sector**				
工　业	Industry	145.6	6.3	148.2	8.9
建筑业	Construction	131.9	11.8	127.8	11.7
交通运输、仓储和邮政业	Transportation, Storage,Post and Telecommunications	118.3	-1.8	122.6	-6.8
批发和零售业	Wholesale and Retail Trades	133.4	9.5	132.2	2.8
房地产业	Real Estate	148.9	14.9	139.6	7.3
社会服务业	Social Services	144.1	3.1	129.9	18.9
信息传输、计算机服务和软件业	Information Transmission, Computer Servcie and Software Industries	144.9	-13.4	155.4	-3.5
住宿和餐饮业	Accommodation and Catering Services	136.5	-1.9	115.4	-5.8
按企业规模分	**Grouped by Size of Enterprises**				
大　型	Large	167.6	9.4	171.1	11.9
中　型	Medium	137.5	3.7	135.9	3.9
小　型	Small	131.4	7.0	128.9	5.3
按特殊群体分	**Grouped by Special Group**				
乡镇企业	Town and Township Enterprises	136.5	7.2	136.5	5.5
上市公司	Listed Companies	186.9	27.0	187.6	21.0
国有控股企业	State-owned and State-holding Enterprises	145.4	8.5	146.8	9.3

19-4 企业景气指数
Prosperity Index on Enterprises

(2007 年)

经济类型及行业	Ownership and Sector	一季度 First Quarter		二季度 Second Quarter	
		本期实际 Index	比上年同期增减 as±of Last Same Period Index	本期实际 Index	比上年同期增减 as±of Last Same Period Index
企业景气指数	**Enterprises Business Climate Index**	**123.9**	**6.1**	**135.0**	**6.7**
按企业登记注册类型分	**Grouped by Status of Registration**				
国有企业	State-owned Enterprises	119.6	3.0	126.2	-4.2
集体企业	Collective-owned Enterprises	107.7	18.4	108.4	-0.9
股份合作企业	Cooperative Enterprises	114.3	-23.2	128.6	-21.4
有限责任公司	Limited-Liability Corporations	122.5	8.1	128.1	8.6
股份有限公司	Share Holding Corporations Ltd.	149.4	12.5	165.7	22.7
私营企业	Private Enterprises	123.7	16.3	127.2	7.1
外商及港澳台投资企业	Enterprises with Funds from Hogkong, Macao and Taiwan	116.1	8.4	129.0	-9.4
按行业分	**Grouped by Sector**				
工　业	Industry	123.7	4.4	141.2	5.5
建筑业	Construction	109.0	6.3	127.2	9.8
交通运输、仓储和邮政业	Transportation, Storage, Posts and Telecommunications	124.1	5.4	116.9	17.8
批发和零售业	Wholesale and Retail Trades	132.9	12.0	125.0	5.0
房地产业	Real Estate	133.6	26.3	135.2	12.3
社会服务业	Social Services	121.3	1.6	118.4	-15.6
信息传输、计算机服务和软件业	Information Transmission, Computer Servcie and Software Industries	165.7	5.8	159.8	-0.6
住宿和餐饮业	Accommodation and Catering Services	94.2	-3.9	101.9	-25.0
按企业规模分	**Grouped by Size of Enterprises**				
大　型	Large	143.4	14.2	162.5	34.1
中　型	Medium	124.5	7.5	130.7	-6.1
小　型	Small	114.3	4.3	122.6	6.4
按特殊群体分	**Grouped by Special Group**				
乡镇企业	Town and Township Enterprises	116.8	-13.9	144.9	17.8
上市公司	Listed Companies	159.1	21.0	182.3	30.6
国有控股企业	State-owned and State-holding Enterprises	125.2	9.5	138.6	10.4
按观察指标分	**Grouped by Indicator Observed**				
生　产	Production (Operation)	95.9	-2.3	133.4	-1.8
盈利(亏损)变化	Changes of Profit(Loss)	102.0	6.6	115.7	-7.5
流动资金	Funds	82.3	9.4	87.2	9.2
货款拖欠	Paymeny for Goods in Arrears	112.9	0.4	110.0	5.0
劳动力需求	Demond on Labors	96.8		115.8	-1.8
固定资产投资	Investment	96.3	-2.9	129.9	5.0
企业融资	Financing of Enterprises	75.8	7.7	77.7	11.8

19-4 续表 Continued

经济类型及行业	Ownership and Sector	三季度 Third Quarter		四季度 Fourth Quarter	
		本期实际 Index	比上年同期增减 as±of Last Same Period Index	本期实际 Index	比上年同期增减 as±of Last Same Period Index
企业景气指数	**Enterprises Business Climate Index**	**135.8**	**2.1**	**133.8**	**6.3**
按企业登记注册类型分	**Grouped by Status of Registration**				
国有企业	State-owned Enterprises	131.6	-3.5	133.9	4.2
集体企业	Collective-owned Enterprises	108.4	-12.9	116.0	10.7
股份合作企业	Cooperative Enterprises	185.7	35.7	171.4	-16.1
有限责任公司	Limited-Liability Corporations	130.7	3.3	128.5	7.0
股份有限公司	Share Holding Corporations Ltd.	156.4	3.8	146.6	2.9
私营企业	Private Enterprises	131.4	6.2	126.0	22.9
外商及港澳台投资企业	Enterprises with Funds from Hogkong, Macao and Taiwan	135.5	-3.0	122.6	-0.5
按行业分	**Grouped by Sector**				
工　业	Industry	137.9	3.4	137.9	8.8
建筑业	Construction	136.8	6.0	128.9	10.3
交通运输、仓储和邮政业	Transportation, Storage, Posts and Telecommunications	125.4	3.6	115.4	-8.6
批发和零售业	Wholesale and Retail Trades	125.0	-2.1	133.1	5.2
房地产业	Real Estate	133.6	7.0	133.6	13.2
社会服务业	Social Services	137.7	3.7	127.0	7.7
信息传输、计算机服务和软件业	Information Transmission, Computer Servcie and Software Industries	150.9	-18.6	156.0	-15.5
住宿和餐饮业	Accommodation and Catering Services	134.6	-17.3	101.9	3.8
按企业规模分	**Grouped by Size of Enterprises**				
大　型	Large	150.9	2.3	151.1	18.0
中　型	Medium	134.1	-0.5	130.9	5.4
小　型	Small	126.5	-0.5	122.2	1.8
按特殊群体分	**Grouped by Special Group**				
乡镇企业	Town and Township Enterprises	136.5	1.5	140.7	19.6
上市公司	Listed Companies	167.8	13.6	156.1	19.8
国有控股企业	State-owned and State-holding Enterprises	137.9	-0.8	135.4	8.6
按观察指标分	**Grouped by Indicator Observed**				
生　产	Production (Operation)	134.6	-3.2	112.7	0.1
盈利(亏损)变化	Changes of Profit(Loss)	122.2	0.2	118.1	0.3
流动资金	Funds	86.2	5.8	87.1	7.8
货款拖欠	Paymeny for Goods in Arrears	108.1	4.6	112.8	6.2
劳动力需求	Demond on Labors	118.6	0.1	98.0	3.9
固定资产投资	Investment	126.5	3.7	113.5	1.3
企业融资	Financing of Enterprises	80.3	13.2	82.8	13.7

主要统计指标解释

企业集团：是以母子公司为主体，通过投资及生产经营协作等多种方式，与众多的企事业单位共同组成的经济联合体。

母 公 司：是企业集团中起主导作用的核心企业，通过投资和生产经营协作等多种联结纽带，决定和影响着集团内其他成员企业，是居于控制地位的控股公司。

所属成员企业(单位)：指企业集团所属的成员企事业单位，包括企业集团的母公司、全资子公司(单位)、绝对控股子公司(单位)、相对控股子公司(单位),不包括参股企业、协作企业(单位)。但如果企业集团的子公司(单位)是一个纯粹管理型的公司,那么该子公司的二级控股子公司(单位)可作为企业集团所属成员单位进行统计。上述企业集团的各类子公司(单位)中应包括在中国境内和境外的子公司(单位)。

登记注册类型：是指在工商行政管理机关登记注册的具有法人资格的各类企业。包括国有企业、国有独资公司、其他有限责任公司、股份有限公司、中外合资企业、港澳台合资企业、其它。

国有企业：是指企业全部资产归国家所有,并按《中华人民共和国企业法人登记管理条例》规定登记注册的非公司制的经济组织。不包括有限责任公司中的国有独资公司。

国有独资公司：是指国家授权的投资机构或者国家授权的部门单独投资设立的有限责任公司。

其他有限责任公司：是指根据《中华人民共和国公司登记管理条例》规定登记注册,由两个以上,五十个以下的股东共同出资,每个股东以其所认缴的出资额对公司承担有限责任,公司以其全部资产对其债务承担责任的经济组织。其他有限责任公司不包括国有独资公司。

股份有限公司：是指根据《中华人民共和国公司登记管理条例》规定登记注册,其全部注册资本由等额股份构成并通过发行股票筹集资本,股东以其认购的股份对公司承担有限责任,公司以其全部资产对其债务承担责任的经济组织。

中外合资企业：是指外国企业或外国人与中国内地企业依照《中华人民共和国中外合资经营企业法》及有关法律的规定，按合同规定的比例投资设立，分享利润和分担风险的企业。

港澳台合资企业：是指港澳台地区投资者与内地企业依照《中华人民共和国中外合资经营企业法》及有关法律的规定，按规定的比例投资设立，分享利润和分担风险的企业。

少数股东权益：指子公司所有者权益中由母公司以外的其他投资者拥有的份额,在合并资产负债表中应单独列示。

股东(所有者)权益合计：指企业集团投资人对企业净资产的所有权,企业集团净资产等于企业集团全部资产减去负债合计和少数股东权益后的余额,其中包括企业投资人对企业的最初投入以及资本公积金、盈余公积金和未分配利润。

股本(实收资本)：指股份制企业集团以发行股票的方式筹集的资本。非股份制企业集团指实际收到的投资人投入的资本。

主营业务收入：指企业集团从事某种主要生产、经营活动所取得的营业收入。本项指标在各行业会计制度中的名称叫法不同,但一律按各行业会计制度或报表定义的口径进行填报。农业企业是指“主营业务收入”；工业企业是指“产品销售收入”；交通运输企业指“主营业务收入”；建筑企业指“工程结算收入”；批发零售贸易企业指“商品销售收入”；房地产企业指“房地产经营收入”；其他企业指“经营(营业)收入”。

从业人员：指在企业集团(包括母公司和子公司)工作并领取工资或其他形式的劳动报酬的全部人员数,包括在岗职工、再就业的离退休人员以及在企业集团中工作的外方人员和港澳台方人员、兼职人员、借用的外单位人员和第二职业者。不包括离开本企业集团仍保留劳动关系的职工。

企业景气调查：是通过对部分企业家定期进行问卷调查，并根据企业家对企业经营状况及宏观经济形势的判断和预期来编制景气指数，从而对现实经济运行状况及其发展趋势进行分析和预测的一种统计调查方法。

景气指数：又称为景气度，它是对企业景气调查中的定性指标通过定量方法加工汇总，综合反映某一特定调查群体或某一社会经济现象所处的状态或发展趋势的一种指标。通过其上升和下降的动态变化，反映经济发展状态及其变化过程。景气指数取值于 0--200 之间，100 为景气指数的临界值；当景气指数大于 100 时，表明经济状况趋于上升或改善，处于景气状态；当景气指数小于 100 时，表明经济状况趋于下降或恶化，处于不景气状态。

企业家信心指数：也称宏观经济景气指数，是根据企业家对企业外部市场经济环境与宏观政策的认识、看法、判断与预期而编制的指数，用以综合反映企业家对宏观经济环境的感受与信心。

企业景气指数：也称企业综合生产经营景气指数，是根据企业家对本企业综合生产经营情况的判断与预期而编制的指数，用以反映企业的综合生产经营状况。

Explanatory Notes on Main Statistical Indicators

Enterprises Group an economic association consists of numerous enterprises and institution, with parent company and subsidiary company as its main body, they join together by means of various methods, investment and business cooperation, etc.

Parent Company the nuclear enterprise, which plays a leading role in enterprises group. It occupies the holding company position, determines and affects other members of group by various ties of join, investment and business cooperation, etc.

Subordinate Enterprises (Units) refer to enterprises and institutions under enterprises group, include parent company of enterprises group, subsidiary companies(units) with exclusive investment, absolutely holding shares companies(units), relatively holding shares companies(units), exclude own shares enterprises, cooperate enterprises(units), If the subsidiary company(unit) is a pure management company, the companies(units) under the subsidiary company can be statistics as subordinate enterprises(units). The above-mention subsidiary company (units) include all companies those within and out of the boundaries of China.

Registration Status of Enterprises refer to different enterprises, which have registered in industrial and commercial administration agencies. Include state-owned enterprises, Sole State-Funded enterprises, other limited liability corporation, share-holding corporation Ltd. Joint-venture enterprises with foreign investment, Joint-venture enterprises with funds from Hong Kong, Macao and Taiwan, and Others.

State-owned Enterprises refer to non-corporation economic units where the entire assets are owned by the state and which have registered in accordance with the Regulation of the People's Republic of China on the Management of Registration of Corporation Enterprises. Excluded from this category are sole state-funded corporation in the limited liability corporations.

Exclusive State-Funded Company refer to limited liability corporations established with exclusive investment from investment institutions or departments authorized by the state.

Other Limited Liability Corporations refer to economic units established with investment from 2-50 investors and registered in accordance with the Regulation of the People's Republic of China on the Management of Registration of Corporations, each investor bearing limited liability to the corporation depending on its share of investment, and the corporation bearing liability to its debt to the maximum of its total assets. Excluded from this category are exclusive state-funded corporations.

Share-holding Corporations Ltd. Refer to economic units registered in accordance with the Regulation of the People's Republic of China on the Management of Registration of Corporations, with total registered capitals divided into equal shares and raised through issuing stocks. Each investor bears limited liability to the corporation depending on the holding shares, and the corporation bears liability to its debt to the maximum of its total assets.

Joint-venture Enterprises with Foreign Investment refer to enterprises jointly established by foreign enterprises or foreigners with enterprises in the mainland of China in accordance with the Low of the People's Republic of China on Sino-foreign Joint Venture Enterprises and other relevant lows, where the share of investment, profits and risks is stipulated in the contract.

Joint-venture Enterprises with Funds from Hong Kong, Macao and Taiwan refer to enterprises jointly established by investor from Hong Kong, Macao and Taiwan with enterprises in the mainland of China in accordance with the Low of the People's Republic of China on Sino-foreign Joint Venture Enterprises and other relevant lows, where the share of investment, profits and risks is stipulated in the contract.

Minority Share-holder's Equity refer to the owner shares of subsidiary company which not owned to parent company but to other investors, it must be arranged independently on merge balance sheet.

Total of Share-holder's (or Owner's) Equity refer to enterprises group investor's title to net funds, the balance of total liabilities and minority share-holding equity from entire funds is net funds, it includes initial investment, accumulation fund, surplus of accumulation and undistributed profits.

Capital Stock (Capital Obtained) refer to capital raised through issuing stocks by the joint-stock enterprises group. It refers to capital actually received from investors in non-joint-stock enterprises group.

Major Business Revenue refer to the revenue earned from certain major action of production and management by enterprises group. This indicator has different account name in various sectors, but it must be filled and submitted in accordance with account system of various sector, or the concepts, definitions and coverage of report schedule. It refers to major business revenue in agriculture enterprises; It refers to production sales revenue in industry enterprises; It refers to major business revenue in transport enterprises; It refers to revenue of project settle accounts in construction; It refers to commodity sales revenue in wholesale and retail Trades enterprises; It refers to real estate operation revenue in real estate Trades enterprises; In other enterprises it refers to business revenue.

Employed Persons refer to all persons who work in ,and receive wages or other remuneration payment from enterprises group(include parent company and subsidiary company), they include fully employed staff and workers, re-employed retirees, foreigners and Chinese compatriots from Hong Kong, Macao and Taiwan part-time employees, employees of other units working temporarily at current posts, and employees holding the second job, but exclude staff and workers who have left their work units while keeping their labour contract (employment relation) unchanged.

Enterprises Climate Survey It is a statistics survey, which compile the climate index by regular paper survey to a section of entrepreneurs, based on entrepreneur's judgement and forecast to the production situation of their own enterprises and the macro-economy situation, and thus we can analyse and predict the current situation and future trend of the economic performance.

Business climate index It is the quantitative disposition and compilation of the qualitative economic indicators of the business climate survey, which can improve a comprehensive description of the real situation or the future trend of a special survey group or a social and economic phenomenon. The business climate index is ranging from 0 to 200. 100 is the critical value, when the climate index is larger than 100, it shows that the economic performance is picking up or improving. When it is lower than 100, it shows that the economic performance is declining or worsening.

Entrepreneur confidence index also called as the macro-economy climate index. It is a index based on entrepreneur's recognition, opinion, judgement and forecast to the market circumstances and macro-policies, It is a comprehensive description of the entrepreneur's impression and confidents of the macro-economy circumstances .

Business climate index also called as the comprehensive production and management climate index of enterprises. It is compiled basing on entrepreneur's judgement on production situation of their own expectation for the future performance. It is the description of the comprehensive production and management situation of the enterprises.

第二十篇
各地州市主要经济指标排序

CHAPTER 20
Ranking of Main Economic Indicators By Region of Xinjiang

简要说明
Brief Introduction

本篇资料的主要内容及来源

本篇反映2007年新疆各地州(市)主要经济指标排序情况。

本篇资料由新疆维吾尔自治区统计局综合处根据新疆维吾尔自治区统计局各相关专业处提供资料整理。

Main Content and Source of Data

Data in this chapter mainly include main social economic statistics by prefecture, autonomous prefecture, city and county in 2007.

Data on this chapter are compiled by the Department of Comprehensive Statistic, XBS according to the data provided by the related department of Statistics Bureau of Xinjiang Uygur Autonomous Region.

20-1 各地、州、市生产总值

Gross Domestic Product by Prefecture, Autonomous Prefecture and City

单位：万元 (2007 年) (10 000 yuan)

地区	Region	地区生产总值 Gross Domestic Product	位次 Rank	第一产业增加值 Primary Industry	位次 Rank
乌鲁木齐市	Urumqi city	8202800	1	162659	10
克拉玛依市	Karamay city	5151297	2	25445	14
石河子市	Shihezi city	732468	12	50878	13
吐鲁番地区	Turpan Administrative Offices	1720268	8	164631	9
哈密地区	Hami [Kumul] Administrative Offices	919912	10	142197	11
昌吉回族自治州	Changji Hui Autonomous Prefecture	3131995	4	973960	1
伊犁哈萨克自治州	Ili Kazak Autonomous Prefecture	5396630		1559727	
伊犁州直属县(市)	Counties (Cities) Direct Under Ili Prefecture	2364705	5	592900	5
塔城地区	Tacheng [Tarbagatai] Administrative Offices	2039121	7	748599	3
阿勒泰地区	Altay Administrative Offices	992804	9	218228	8
博尔塔拉蒙古自治州	Bortala Mongol Autonomous Prefecture	770414	11	246439	7
巴音郭楞蒙古自治州	Bayangol Mongol Autonomous Prefecture	4690028	3	688644	4
阿克苏地区	Aksu Administrative Offices	2315179	6	850624	2
克孜勒苏柯尔克孜自治州	Kizilsu Kirgiz Autonomous Prefecture	237132	14	59928	12
和田地区	Hotan Administrative Offices	636962	13	255785	6

地区	Region	第二产业增加值 Secondary Industry	位次 Rank	第三产业增加值 Tertiary Industry	位次 Rank	人均地区生产总值（元/人） Per-capital GDP (yuan/person)	位次 Rank
乌鲁木齐市	Urumqi city	3165857	3	4874284	1	31140	3
克拉玛依市	Karamay city	4615056	1	510796	7	98398	1
石河子市	Shihezi city	349172	10	332418	11	23797	5
吐鲁番地区	Turpan Administrative Offices	1174061	5	381576	10	28907	4
哈密地区	Hami [Kumul] Administrative Offices	318520	11	459195	8	16910	8
昌吉回族自治州	Changji Hui Autonomous Prefecture	1196734	4	961301	3	20893	6
伊犁哈萨克自治州	Ili Kazak Autonomous Prefecture	1896660		1940243		12349	
伊犁州直属县(市)	Counties (Cities) Direct Under Ili Prefecture	806274	6	965531	2	9534	12
塔城地区	Tacheng [Tarbagatai] Administrative Offices	635049	7	655473	6	15451	10
阿勒泰地区	Altay Administrative Offices	455337	9	319239	12	17412	7
博尔塔拉蒙古自治州	Bortala Mongol Autonomous Prefecture	104095	13	419880	9	16437	9
巴音郭楞蒙古自治州	Bayangol Mongol Autonomous Prefecture	3184905	2	816479	5	37466	2
阿克苏地区	Aksu Administrative Offices	618047	8	846508	4	9898	11
克孜勒苏柯尔克孜自治州	Kizilsu Kirgiz Autonomous Prefecture	43512	14	133692	14	4712	13
和田地区	Hotan Administrative Offices	111942	12	269235	13	3405	14

20-2 各地、州、市人口状况

Population Status by Prefecture, Autonomous Prefecture and City

(2007 年)

地 区	Region	总人口（万人） Total Population (10 000 person)	位 次 Rank	城镇人口（万人） Urban Population (10 000 person)	位 次 Rank
乌鲁木齐市	Urumqi City	231.30	3	224.41	1
克拉玛依市	Karamay City	26.72	15	26.72	15
石河子市	Shihezi City	63.61	10	63.61	8
吐鲁番地区	Turpan Administrative Offices	60.06	11	43.27	11
哈密地区	Hami [Kumul] Administrative Offices	54.62	12	48.02	10
昌吉回族自治州	Changji Hui Autonomous Prefecture	135.37	6	112.37	5
伊犁哈萨克自治州	Ili Kazak Autonomous Prefecture	434.22		246.91	
伊犁州直属县(市)	Counties (Cities) Direct Under Ili Prefecture	270.23	2	137.94	3
塔城地区	Tacheng [Tarbagatai] Administrative Offices	99.48	8	73.56	7
阿勒泰地区	Altay Administrative Offices	64.51	9	35.41	13
博尔塔拉蒙古自治州	Bortala Mongol Autonomous Prefecture	47.29	14	37.95	12
巴音郭楞蒙古自治州	Bayangol Mongol Autonomous Prefecture	122.41	7	94.80	6
阿克苏地区	Aksu Administrative Offices	220.31	4	138.55	2
克孜勒苏柯尔克孜自治州	Kizilsu Kirgiz Autonomous Prefecture	50.00	13	28.86	14
喀什地区	Kashgar [Kaxgar] Administrative Offices	369.43	1	134.03	4
和田地区	Hotan Administrative Offices	188.39	5	60.16	9

地 区	Region	乡村人口（万人） Rural Population (10 000 person)	位 次 Rank	人口自然增长率(‰) Natural Growth Rate (‰)	位 次 Rank
乌鲁木齐市	Urumqi City	6.88	12	5.42	13
克拉玛依市	Karamay City			5.21	14
石河子市	Shihezi City			0.51	15
吐鲁番地区	Turpan Administrative Offices	16.80	10	16.06	4
哈密地区	Hami [Kumul] Administrative Offices	6.60	13	7.87	11
昌吉回族自治州	Changji Hui Autonomous Prefecture	23.00	8	6.75	12
伊犁哈萨克自治州	Ili Kazak Autonomous Prefecture	187.30		15.10	
伊犁州直属县(市)	Counties (Cities) Direct Under Ili Prefecture	132.29	2	17.74	2
塔城地区	Tacheng [Tarbagatai] Administrative Offices	25.91	7	9.68	9
阿勒泰地区	Altay Administrative Offices	29.10	5	12.49	6
博尔塔拉蒙古自治州	Bortala Mongol Autonomous Prefecture	9.35	11	9.49	10
巴音郭楞蒙古自治州	Bayangol Mongol Autonomous Prefecture	27.61	6	10.48	8
阿克苏地区	Aksu Administrative Offices	81.76	4	17.19	3
克孜勒苏柯尔克孜自治州	Kizilsu Kirgiz Autonomous Prefecture	21.14	9	19.22	1
喀什地区	Kashgar [Kaxgar] Administrative Offices	235.42	1	16.05	5
和田地区	Hotan Administrative Offices	128.23	3	10.76	7

注：城镇、乡村人口按公安年报口径计算。
Note: The urban and rural population in Prefecture, Autonomous Prefecture and City are calculated on the annals of public security.

20-3 各地、州、市城镇固定资产投资
Investmment in Fixed Assets by Prefecture, Autonomous Prefecture City and Town

单位：万元 (2007 年) (10 000 yuan)

地 区	Region	合计 Total	位次 Rank	国有经济 State-owned Economy	位次 Rank	集体经济 Collective-owned Economy	位次 Rank
乌鲁木齐市	Urumqi City	3150310	1	1312521	3	20531	1
克拉玛依市	Karamay City	2861913	2	1586081	1	829	14
石河子市	Shihezi City	549008	10	438597	7		
吐鲁番地区	Turpan Administrative Offices	613575	9	176668	13	3730	8
哈密地区	Hami [Kumul] Administrative Offices	397082	12	185550	12	1099	12
昌吉回族自治州	Changji Hui Autonomous Prefecture	1125342	6	383360	8	14085	2
伊犁哈萨克自治州	Ili Kazak Autonomous Prefecture	1940315		1027660		11745	
伊犁州直属县(市)	Counties (Cities) Direct Under Ili Prefecture	881789	7	483133	6	4100	7
塔城地区	Tacheng [Tarbagatai] Administrative Offices	676355	8	308034	9	6655	5
阿勒泰地区	Altay Administrative Offices	382171	13	236493	11	990	13
博尔塔拉蒙古自治州	Bortala Mongol Autonomous Prefecture	264830	14	173397	14	1202	11
巴音郭楞蒙古自治州	Bayangol Mongol Autonomous Prefecture	2100681	3	1413978	2	1680	9
阿克苏地区	Aksu Administrative Offices	1133263	5	580675	5	4952	6
克孜勒苏柯尔克孜自治州	Kizilsu Kirgiz Autonomous Prefecture	121096	15	55221	15	9205	4
喀什地区	Kashgar [Kaxgar] Administrative Offices	1158147	4	689185	4	10374	3
和田地区	Hotan Administrative Offices	434951	11	300721	10	1286	10

地 区	Region	股份制经济 Share-Holding Economy	位次 Rank	私营个体经济 Private and Individuals Economy	位次 Rank	其他经济 Other Economy	位次 Rank
乌鲁木齐市	Urumqi City	823801	2	742795	1	250662	1
克拉玛依市	Karamay City	1260595	1	14110	15	298	13
石河子市	Shi Hezi City	65631	12	34764	12	10016	9
吐鲁番地区	Turpan Administrative Offices	402132	5	27045	13	4000	12
哈密地区	Hami [Kumul] Administrative Offices	132207	10	55999	8	22227	5
昌吉回族自治州	Changji Hui Autonomous Prefecture	528693	3	191711	3	7493	10
伊犁哈萨克自治州	Ili Kazak Autonomous Prefecture	579232		288091		33587	
伊犁州直属县(市)	Counties (Cities) Direct Under Ili Prefecture	217606	9	162876	5	14074	8
塔城地区	Tacheng [Tarbagatai] Administrative Offices	260294	8	81859	7	19513	6
阿勒泰地区	Altay Administrative Offices	101332	11	43356	9		
博尔塔拉蒙古自治州	Bortala Mongol Autonomous Prefecture	48340	14	36935	11	4956	11
巴音郭楞蒙古自治州	Bayangol Mongol Autonomous Prefecture	428009	4	239720	2	17294	7
阿克苏地区	Aksu Administrative Offices	353741	6	163472	4	30423	4
克孜勒苏柯尔克孜自治州	Kizilsu Kirgiz Autonomous Prefecture	42005	15	14415	14	250	14
喀什地区	Kashgar [Kaxgar] Administrative Offices	275218	7	135396	6	47974	2
和田地区	Hotan Administrative Offices	52674	13	37880	10	42390	3

20-4 各地、州、市农林牧渔业总产值

Gross Output Value of Agriculture, Forestry, Animal Husbandry and Fishery by Prefecture, Autonomous Prefecture and City

单位：万元 (2007 年) (10 000 yuan)

地 区	Region	农林牧渔业总产值 Total	位次 Rank	农业 Agriculture	位次 Rank	林业 Forestry	位次 Rank
乌鲁木齐市	Urumqi City	189911	11	86706	12	1570	14
克拉玛依市	Karamay City	59070	14	23015	14	5133	9
吐鲁番地区	Turpan Administrative Offices	267171	9	207266	8	2652	12
哈密地区	Hami [Kumul] Administrative Offices	159272	12	97442	11	4354	10
昌吉回族自治州	Changji Hui Autonomous Prefecture	1192472	2	600042	4	21362	4
伊犁哈萨克自治州	Ili Kazak Autonomous Prefecture	1936796		1087816		30542	
伊犁州直属县(市)	Counties (Cities) Direct Under Ili Prefecture	819352	5	415061	6	14236	5
塔城地区	Tacheng [Tarbagatai] Administrative Offices	805674	6	531388	5	8919	7
阿勒泰地区	Altay Administrative Offices	311770	8	141367	10	7387	8
博尔塔拉蒙古自治州	Bortala Mongol Autonomous Prefecture	267120	10	192689	9	2832	11
巴音郭楞蒙古自治州	Bayangol Mongol Autonomous Prefecture	912405	4	656675	3	11050	6
阿克苏地区	Aksu Administrative Offices	1055781	3	787950	2	41328	3
克孜勒苏柯尔克孜自治州	Kizilsu Kirgiz Autonomous Prefecture	115514	13	62858	13	2034	13
喀什地区	Kashgar [Kaxgar] Administrative Offices	1723347	1	1096608	1	110079	1
和田地区	Hotan Administrative Offices	517983	7	346427	7	51680	2

地 区	Region	牧业 Animal Husbandry	位次 Rank	渔业 Fishery	位次 Rank	农林牧渔服务业 Agriculture, Forestry, Animal Husbandary and Fishery	位次 Rank
乌鲁木齐市	Urumqi City	88672	9	3962	7	9001	9
克拉玛依市	Karamay City	14677	14	466	12	15779	6
吐鲁番地区	Turpan Administrative Offices	52359	12	307	13	4587	13
哈密地区	Hami [Kumul] Administrative Offices	53416	11	1258	11	2803	14
昌吉回族自治州	Changji Hui Autonomous Prefecture	542356	1	9755	1	18957	5
伊犁哈萨克自治州	Ili Kazak Autonomous Prefecture	760814		16051		41573	
伊犁州直属县(市)	Counties (Cities) Direct Under Ili Prefecture	362840	3	7968	3	19247	4
塔城地区	Tacheng [Tarbagatai] Administrative Offices	247537	4	3446	8	14384	7
阿勒泰地区	Altay Administrative Offices	150437	7	4637	6	7942	11
博尔塔拉蒙古自治州	Bortala Mongol Autonomous Prefecture	63316	10	1662	9	6621	12
巴音郭楞蒙古自治州	Bayangol Mongol Autonomous Prefecture	204652	5	6802	4	33226	3
阿克苏地区	Aksu Administrative Offices	163410	6	5884	5	57209	1
克孜勒苏柯尔克孜自治州	Kizilsu Kirgiz Autonomous Prefecture	41523	13	168	14	8931	10
喀什地区	Kashgar [Kaxgar] Administrative Offices	453068	2	8758	2	54834	2
和田地区	Hotan Administrative Offices	109116	8	1605	10	9155	8

注：本表按当年价格计算。

Notes：The data in this table is caculated at current price.

20-5 各地、州、市主要农产品产量

Output of Major Farm Crops by Prefecture, Autonomous Prefecture and City

单位：吨 (2007 年) (ton)

地　区	Region	粮食 Grain	位次 Rank	棉花 Cotton	位次 Rank	油料 Oil Bearing Crops	位次 Rank	甜菜 Beetroots	位次 Rank
乌鲁木齐市	Urumqi City	117163	11	2523	13	5904	7	10440	8
克拉玛依市	Karamay City	1145	14	15105	10				
吐鲁番地区	Turpan Administrative Offices	8415	13	24789	8	765	12		
哈密地区	Hami [Kumul] Administrative Offices	64991	12	23355	9	2315	11		
昌吉回族自治州	Changji Hui Autonomous Prefecture	819912	6	158431	4	34089	4	481159	3
伊犁哈萨克自治州	Ili Kazak Autonomous Prefecture	2356170		159743		228388		2690883	
伊犁州直属县(市)	Counties (Cities) Direct Under Ili Prefecture	1351143	2	12240	11	111792	1	1990030	1
塔城地区	Tacheng [Tarbagatai] Administrative Offices	843694	5	147503	5	59391	2	610207	2
阿勒泰地区	Altay Administrative Offices	161333	8		14	57205	3	90646	7
博尔塔拉蒙古自治州	Bortala Mongol Autonomous Prefecture	253165	7	74280	6	21377	5	233558	5
巴音郭楞蒙古自治州	Bayangol Mongol Autonomous Prefecture	161001	9	256729	3	4645	9	318964	4
阿克苏地区	Aksu Administrative Offices	882567	4	402558	1	8135	6	167495	6
克孜勒苏柯尔克孜自治州	Kizilsu Kirgiz Autonomous Prefecture	160374	10	9401	12	723	13		
喀什地区	Kashgar [Kaxgar] Administrative Offices	1949466	1	356767	2	5475	8		
和田地区	Hotan Administrative Offices	907732	3	46128	7	4344	10		

20-6 各地、州、市规模以上工业总产值和工业增加值

Gross Industrial Ouput Value and Added-Value of Industrial Enterprises above Designated Size By Prefecture, Autonomous Prefecture and City

单位：万元 (2007 年) (10 000 yuan)

地　区	Region	工业总产值(当年价格) Gross Industrial Output Value (At Current Prices)	位次 Rank	工业增加值 Added-value of Industry	位次 Rank
乌鲁木齐市	Urumqi City	9701457	1	2657512	3
克拉玛依市	Karamay City	9429769	2	4670873	1
石河子市	Shihezi City	895405	8	250113	9
吐鲁番地区	Turpan Administrative Offices	2010705	4	1095314	4
哈密地区	Hami [Kumul] Administrative Offices	585581	10	239696	10
昌吉回族自治州	Changji Hui Autonomous Prefecture	1815318	5	531478	5
伊犁哈萨克自治州	Ili Kazak Autonomous Prefecture	2218303		1020948	
伊犁州直属县(市)	Counties (Cities) Direct Under Ili Prefecture	1097526	7	470712	6
塔城地区	Tacheng [Tarbagatai] Administrative Offices	622506	9	219991	11
阿勒泰地区	Altay Administrative Offices	498271	11	330245	8
博尔塔拉蒙古自治州	Bortala Mongol Autonomous Prefecture	157440	13	40073	13
巴音郭楞蒙古自治州	Bayangol Mongol Autonomous Prefecture	4111121	3	2876864	2
阿克苏地区	Aksu Administrative Offices	1301066	6	344054	7
克孜勒苏柯尔克孜自治州	Kizilsu Kirgiz Autonomous Prefecture	52055	15	17498	15
喀什地区	Kashgar [Kaxgar] Administrative Offices	414576	12	141639	12
和田地区	Hotan Administrative Offices	75802	14	32021	14

20-7 各地、州、市规模以上工业企业主要经济效益指标

Main Indicators on Economic Benefit of Industrial Enterprises above Designated Size By Prefecture, Autonomous Prefecture and City

单位：% (2007 年) (%)

地　区	Region	工　业 增加值率 Ratio of Value Added to Gross Industrial Output Value	位 次 Rank	资　金 利税率 Ratio of Profits And Taxes to Capital	位 次 Rank
乌鲁木齐市	Urumqi City	23.8	13	17.3	7
克拉玛依市	Karamay City	43.9	4	44.4	3
石河子市	Shihezi City	24.5	12	8.1	12
吐鲁番地区	Turpan Administrative Offices	46.8	3	36.2	5
哈密地区	Hami [Kumul] Administrative Offices	35.8	7	17.5	6
昌吉回族自治州	Changji Hui Autonomous Prefecture	26.0	11	10.4	11
伊犁哈萨克自治州	Ili Kazak Autonomous Prefecture	40.2		21.2	
伊犁州直属县(市)	Counties (Cities) Direct Under Ili Prefecture	36.7	6	14.9	9
塔城地区	Tacheng [Tarbagatai] Administrative Offices	32.1	8	11.8	10
阿勒泰地区	Altay Administrative Offices	57.5	2	55.4	2
博尔塔拉蒙古自治州	Bortala Mongol Autonomous Prefecture	22.7	15	5.7	13
巴音郭楞蒙古自治州	Bayangol Mongol Autonomous Prefecture	60.2	1	59.4	1
阿克苏地区	Aksu Administrative Offices	23.0	14	15.0	8
克孜勒苏柯尔克孜自治州	Kizilsu Kirgiz Autonomous Prefecture	29.6	10	41.7	4
喀什地区	Kashgar [Kaxgar] Administrative Offices	31.0	9	3.7	14
和田地区	Hotan Administrative Offices	36.8	5	2.3	15

地　区	Region	总资产 贡献率 Ratio of Total Assets To Industrial OutputValue	位 次 Rank	资本保值 增 值 率 Ratio of Capital Holding And Rise	位 次 Rank
乌鲁木齐市	Urumqi City	16.4	6	135.5	9
克拉玛依市	Karamay City	34.6	4	118.2	14
石河子市	Shihezi City	10.3	11	200.5	4
吐鲁番地区	Turpan Administrative Offices	38.6	3	202.6	2
哈密地区	Hami [Kumul] Administrative Offices	15.5	7	139.9	8
昌吉回族自治州	Changji Hui Autonomous Prefecture	9.3	12	94.6	15
伊犁哈萨克自治州	Ili Kazak Autonomous Prefecture	19.7		139.7	
伊犁州直属县(市)	Counties (Cities) Direct Under Ili Prefecture	14.1	9	127.3	12
塔城地区	Tacheng [Tarbagatai] Administrative Offices	13.0	10	140.3	7
阿勒泰地区	Altay Administrative Offices	46.6	2	183.4	5
博尔塔拉蒙古自治州	Bortala Mongol Autonomous Prefecture	6.2	14	165.5	6
巴音郭楞蒙古自治州	Bayangol Mongol Autonomous Prefecture	50.6	1	123.5	13
阿克苏地区	Aksu Administrative Offices	14.6	8	135.0	10
克孜勒苏柯尔克孜自治州	Kizilsu Kirgiz Autonomous Prefecture	33.1	5	207.1	1
喀什地区	Kashgar [Kaxgar] Administrative Offices	6.6	13	130.0	11
和田地区	Hotan Administrative Offices	3.7	15	202.2	3

20-7 续表 Continued

单位：% (%)

地　区	Region	资产负债率 Assets Liability Ratio	位次 Rank	成本费用利润率 Ratio of Profits to Industrial Cost	位次 Rank
乌鲁木齐市	Urumqi City	44.3	14	10.0	8
克拉玛依市	Karamay City	41.5	15	34.3	5
石河子市	Shihezi City	60.3	7	8.7	10
吐鲁番地区	Turpan Administrative Offices	50.0	11	42.3	3
哈密地区	Hami [Kumul] Administrative Offices	55.7	8	17.8	6
昌吉回族自治州	Changji Hui Autonomous Prefecture	67.5	4	6.1	12
伊犁哈萨克自治州	Ili Kazak Autonomous Prefecture	62.5		20.2	
伊犁州直属县(市)	Counties (Cities) Direct Under Ili Prefecture	62.9	5	10.9	7
塔城地区	Tacheng [Tarbagatai] Administrative Offices	74.2	2	8.5	11
阿勒泰地区	Altay Administrative Offices	48.3	12	71.8	2
博尔塔拉蒙古自治州	Bortala Mongol Autonomous Prefecture	70.2	3	1.7	13
巴音郭楞蒙古自治州	Bayangol Mongol Autonomous Prefecture	54.6	9	103.4	1
阿克苏地区	Aksu Administrative Offices	54.0	10	9.0	9
克孜勒苏柯尔克孜自治州	Kizilsu Kirgiz Autonomous Prefecture	47.4	13	35.8	4
喀什地区	Kashgar [Kaxgar] Administrative Offices	87.3	1	-1.0	14
和田地区	Hotan Administrative Offices	61.4	6	-2.0	15

地　区	Region	全员劳动生产率(元/人年) Overall Labor Productivity (yuan/person-year)	位次 Rank	工业经济效益综合指数 Comprehensive Index of Industry Economic Results	位次 Rank
乌鲁木齐市	Urumqi City	183612	5	251.1	6
克拉玛依市	Karamay City	449624	2	545.4	3
石河子市	Shihezi City	96823	12	177.0	10
吐鲁番地区	Turpan Administrative Offices	364097	3	535.2	4
哈密地区	Hami [Kumul] Administrative Offices	100036	10	214.4	8
昌吉回族自治州	Changji Hui Autonomous Prefecture	132661	7	176.0	11
伊犁哈萨克自治州	Ili Kazak Autonomous Prefecture	144653		261.7	
伊犁州直属县(市)	Counties (Cities) Direct Under Ili Prefecture	124623	8	200.3	9
塔城地区	Tacheng [Tarbagatai] Administrative Offices	97639	11	173.8	12
阿勒泰地区	Altay Administrative Offices	321344	4	624.8	2
博尔塔拉蒙古自治州	Bortala Mongol Autonomous Prefecture	52881	15	109.8	14
巴音郭楞蒙古自治州	Bayangol Mongol Autonomous Prefecture	718318	1	998.5	1
阿克苏地区	Aksu Administrative Offices	142820	6	219.3	7
克孜勒苏柯尔克孜自治州	Kizilsu Kirgiz Autonomous Prefecture	82150	13	318.0	5
喀什地区	Kashgar [Kaxgar] Administrative Offices	104793	9	126.8	13
和田地区	Hotan Administrative Offices	53359	14	93.0	15

20-8 各地、州、市主要工业产品产量

Output of Major Industrial Products by Prefecture, Autonomous Prefecture and City

(2007 年)

地　区	Region	纱(吨) Yarn (ton)	位次 Rank	布(万米) Cloth (10 000 m)	位次 Rank	呢绒(万米) Woolen Piece Goods (10 000 m)	位次 Rank
乌鲁木齐市	Urumqi City	69000	2	4690	1	0.38	3
克拉玛依市	Karamay City						
石河子市	Shihezi City	82385	1	3341	3	183.90	1
吐鲁番地区	Turpan Administrative Offices	9314	11				
哈密地区	Hami [Kumul] Administrative Offices	19101	8				
昌吉回族自治州	Changji Hui Autonomous Prefecture	47383	3	264	10	183.23	2
伊犁哈萨克自治州	Ili Kazak Autonomous Prefecture	45374		2000			
伊犁州直属县(市)	Counties (Cities) Direct Under Ili Prefecture	27434	7	1090	5		
塔城地区	Tacheng [Tarbagatai] Administrative Offices	17940	9	910	6		
阿勒泰地区	Altay Administrative Offices						
博尔塔拉蒙古自治州	Bortala Mongol Autonomous Prefecture	16065	10	287	9		
巴音郭楞蒙古自治州	Bayangol Mongol Autonomous Prefecture	30136	5	1128	4		
阿克苏地区	Aksu Administrative Offices	29497	6	366	8		
克孜勒苏柯尔克孜自治州	Kizilsu Kirgiz Autonomous Prefecture						
喀什地区	Kashgar [Kaxgar] Administrative Offices	37552	4	3522	2		
和田地区	Hotan Administrative Offices	7565	12	402	7		

地　区	Region	成品糖(万吨) Sugar (10 000 ton)	位次 Rank	饮料酒(千升) Alcohol Beverage (kilo-liter)	位次 Rank	塑料制品(吨) Plastic Products (ton)	位次 Rank
乌鲁木齐市	Urumqi City			171386	1	188484	1
克拉玛依市	Karamay City			18	14	19585	6
石河子市	Shihezi City			35869	4	75077	2
吐鲁番地区	Turpan Administrative Offices			4127	10	636	13
哈密地区	Hami [Kumul] Administrative Offices			13034	8	7976	10
昌吉回族自治州	Changji Hui Autonomous Prefecture	4.30	5	16552	7	48621	3
伊犁哈萨克自治州	Ili Kazak Autonomous Prefecture	42.34		134546		53101	
伊犁州直属县(市)	Counties (Cities) Direct Under Ili Prefecture	29.15	1	63856	3	35099	4
塔城地区	Tacheng [Tarbagatai] Administrative Offices	11.44	2	70313	2	16810	7
阿勒泰地区	Altay Administrative Offices	1.75	7	377	12	1192	12
博尔塔拉蒙古自治州	Bortala Mongol Autonomous Prefecture	5.40	4	1421	11	5309	11
巴音郭楞蒙古自治州	Bayangol Mongol Autonomous Prefecture	9.90	3	10657	9	13338	8
阿克苏地区	Aksu Administrative Offices	3.00	6	25754	5	8175	9
克孜勒苏柯尔克孜自治州	Kizilsu Kirgiz Autonomous Prefecture					138	15
喀什地区	Kashgar [Kaxgar] Administrative Offices			24893	6	34582	5
和田地区	Hotan Administrative Offices			144	13	573	14

20-8 续表 Continued

地区	Region	机制纸及纸板(吨) Machine-made Paper and Paper board (ton)	位次 Rank	原煤(万吨) Coal (10 000 tons)	位次 Rank	原油(万吨) Crude Oil (10 000 tons)	位次 Rank
乌鲁木齐市	Urumqi City	122514	1	1706.68	1	536.25	3
克拉玛依市	Karamay City					1217.06	1
石河子市	Shihezi City	21712	3				
吐鲁番地区	Turpan Administrative Offices			517.82	4	207.99	4
哈密地区	Hami [Kumul] Administrative Offices	130	9	526.01	3		
昌吉回族自治州	Changji Hui Autonomous Prefecture	17368	4	742.52	2		
伊犁哈萨克自治州	Ili Kazak Autonomous Prefecture	2491		838.10			
伊犁州直属县(市)	Counties (Cities) Direct Under Ili Prefecture	175	8	399.82	7		
塔城地区	Tacheng [Tarbagatai] Administrative Offices	719	7	432.60	6		
阿勒泰地区	Altay Administrative Offices	1597	5	5.68	12		
博尔塔拉蒙古自治州	Bortala Mongol Autonomous Prefecture						
巴音郭楞蒙古自治州	Bayangol Mongol Autonomous Prefecture	87067	2	66.15	9	643.01	2
阿克苏地区	Aksu Administrative Offices			497.09	5		
克孜勒苏柯尔克孜自治州	Kizilsu Kirgiz Autonomous Prefecture			43.04	10		
喀什地区	Kashgar [Kaxgar] Administrative Offices	1047	6	13.81	11		
和田地区	Hotan Administrative Offices			67.42	8		

地区	Region	水泥(万吨) Cement (10 000 tons)	位次 Rank	发电量(亿千瓦小时) Electricity (100 million kwh)	位次 Rank	农用化肥(吨) Chemical Fertilizers (ton)	位次 Rank
乌鲁木齐市	Urumqi City	372.31	1	121.19	1	587941	1
克拉玛依市	Karamay City			27.34	6		
石河子市	Shihezi City	29.43	13	36.15	4		
吐鲁番地区	Turpan Administrative Offices	42.97	9	14.73	10	377	5
哈密地区	Hami [Kumul] Administrative Offices	41.33	10	22.55	8		
昌吉回族自治州	Changji Hui Autonomous Prefecture	146.25	4	65.20	2	3161	4
伊犁哈萨克自治州	Ili Kazak Autonomous Prefecture	359.9		52.85		200	
伊犁州直属县(市)	Counties (Cities) Direct Under Ili Prefecture	139.98	5	36.59	3		
塔城地区	Tacheng [Tarbagatai] Administrative Offices	178.85	3	9.88	11	200	6
阿勒泰地区	Altay Administrative Offices	41.08	11	6.38	12		
博尔塔拉蒙古自治州	Bortala Mongol Autonomous Prefecture	30.95	12	2.01	14		
巴音郭楞蒙古自治州	Bayangol Mongol Autonomous Prefecture	107.12	7	23.52	7	282427	3
阿克苏地区	Aksu Administrative Offices	237.79	2	28.25	5	511173	2
克孜勒苏柯尔克孜自治州	Kizilsu Kirgiz Autonomous Prefecture	0.84	14	0.08	15		
喀什地区	Kashgar [Kaxgar] Administrative Offices	115.16	6	17.30	9		
和田地区	Hotan Administrative Offices	50.43	8	5.70	13		

20-9 各地、州、市社会消费品零售总额
Total Retail Sales of Consumer Goods by Prefecture, Autonomous Prefecture and City

单位：万元 (2007 年) (10 000 yuan)

地区	Region	社会消费品零售总额 Total Retail Sales of Consumer Goods	位次 Rank	市 City	位次 Rank
乌鲁木齐市	Urumqi City	3217648	1	3192178	1
克拉玛依市	Karamay City	230656	9	184617	7
吐鲁番地区	Turpan Administrative Offices	178119	11	72372	11
哈密地区	Hami [Kumul] Administrative Offices	250075	8	222839	5
昌吉回族自治州	Changji Hui Autonomous Prefecture	666480	2	258056	3
伊犁哈萨克自治州	Ili Kazak Autonomous Prefecture	1097915		420224	
伊犁州直属县(市)	Counties (Cities) Direct Under Ili Prefecture	606218	3	279967	2
塔城地区	Tacheng [Tarbagatai] Administrative Offices	268729	7	81949	9
阿勒泰地区	Altay Administrative Offices	222968	10	55208	13
博尔塔拉蒙古自治州	Bortala Mongol Autonomous Prefecture	126292	13	73978	10
巴音郭楞蒙古自治州	Bayangol Mongol Autonomous Prefecture	350930	6	244042	4
阿克苏地区	Aksu Administrative Offices	428691	5	174317	8
克孜勒苏柯尔克孜自治州	Kizilsu Kirgiz Autonomous Prefecture	50760	14	31004	14
喀什地区	Kashgar [Kaxgar] Administrative Offices	465040	4	211600	6
和田地区	Hotan Administrative Offices	142199	12	69100	12

地区	Region	县 County	位次 Rank	县以下 Under County Level	位次 Rank
乌鲁木齐市	Urumqi City			25470	11
克拉玛依市	Karamay City	44181	9	1858	14
吐鲁番地区	Turpan Administrative Offices	56188	8	49559	6
哈密地区	Hami [Kumul] Administrative Offices	13722	13	13514	12
昌吉回族自治州	Changji Hui Autonomous Prefecture	213565	1	194859	1
伊犁哈萨克自治州	Ili Kazak Autonomous Prefecture	415122		262569	
伊犁州直属县(市)	Counties (Cities) Direct Under Ili Prefecture	189130	2	137121	2
塔城地区	Tacheng [Tarbagatai] Administrative Offices	100192	6	86588	4
阿勒泰地区	Altay Administrative Offices	128900	5	38860	8
博尔塔拉蒙古自治州	Bortala Mongol Autonomous Prefecture	19182	11	33132	10
巴音郭楞蒙古自治州	Bayangol Mongol Autonomous Prefecture	68769	7	38119	9
阿克苏地区	Aksu Administrative Offices	170590	3	83784	5
克孜勒苏柯尔克孜自治州	Kizilsu Kirgiz Autonomous Prefecture	15308	12	4448	13
喀什地区	Kashgar [Kaxgar] Administrative Offices	158844	4	94596	3
和田地区	Hotan Administrative Offices	29963	10	43136	7

20-10 各地、州、市海关进出口总额
Total Value of Imports and Exports by Prefecture, Autonomous Prefecture and City

单位：万美元 (2007 年) (USD 10 000)

地 区	Region	进出口总额 Total value of Imports and Exports	位 次 Rank	出口额 Exports	位 次 Rank	进口额 Lmports	位 次 Rank
乌鲁木齐市	Urumqi City	377467	1	345127	1	32340	2
克拉玛依市	Karamay City	11664	10	5544	10	6120	6
石河子市	Shihezi City	28083	8	22642	9	5441	8
吐鲁番地区	Turpan Administrative Offices	554	15	386	15	168	14
哈密地区	Hami [Kumul] Administrative Offices	5993	11	4083	11	1910	9
昌吉回族自治洲	Changji Hui Autonomous Prefecture	240269	3	229998	3	10271	4
伊犁哈萨克自治州	Ili Administrative Offices	345634		312275		33359	
伊犁州直属县(市)	Counties (Cities) Direct Under Ili Prefecture	259253	2	233427	2	25826	3
塔城地区	Tacheng [Tarbagatai] Administrative Offices	81019	6	74927	5	6092	7
阿勒泰地区	Altay Administrative Offices	5362	12	3921	12	1441	11
博尔塔拉蒙古自治州	Bortala Mongol Autonomous Prefecture	171173	4	50290	6	120883	1
巴音郭楞蒙古自治州	Bayangol Mongol Autonomous Prefecture	24446	9	23766	7	680	12
阿克苏地区	Aksu Administrative Offices	2651	13	2041	13	610	13
克孜勒苏柯尔克孜自治州	Kizilsu Kirgiz Autonomous Prefecture	31560	7	23705	8	7855	5
喀什地区	Kashgar [Kaxgar] Administrative Offices	131564	5	129932	4	1632	10
和田地区	Hotan Administrative Offices	565	14	522	14	43	15

20-11 各地、州、市在岗职工工资总额和平均工资
Total Wages of Employed Staff and Workers and Average Wage by Prefecture, Autonomous Prefecture and City

(2007 年)

地 区	Region	在岗职工工资总额(万元) Total Wages of Staff and Workers (10 000 yuan)	位 次 Rank	在岗职工平均货币工资(元) Average On-the-Job Wage (yuan)	位 次 Rank
乌鲁木齐市	Urumqi City	1463601	1	29483	2
克拉玛依市	Karamay City	424259	3	29706	1
石河子市	Shihezi City	185790	10	19215	9
吐鲁番地区	Turpan Administrative Offices	231334	9	29415	3
哈密地区	Hami [Kumul] Administrative Offices	165900	13	22422	5
昌吉回族自治州	Changji Hui Autonomous Prefecture	390283	5	19085	10
伊犁哈萨克自治州	Ili Kazak Autonomous Prefecture	944421		15888	
伊犁州直属县(市)	Counties (Cities) Direct Under Ili Prefecture	430600	2	16590	13
塔城地区	Tacheng [Tarbagatai] Administrative Offices	330023	8	14534	15
阿勒泰地区	Altay Administrative Offices	183798	11	17049	12
博尔塔拉蒙古自治州	Bortala Mongol Autonomous Prefecture	131984	14	15456	14
巴音郭楞蒙古自治州	Bayangol Mongol Autonomous Prefecture	360358	7	19345	8
阿克苏地区	Aksu Administrative Offices	397962	4	18207	11
克孜勒苏柯尔克孜自治州	Kizilsu Kirgiz Autonomous Prefecture	78788	15	22990	4
喀什地区	Kashgar [Kaxgar] Administrative Offices	377626	6	19897	7
和田地区	Hotan Administrative Offices	180089	12	20936	6

20-12 各地、州、市地方财政一般预算收支

The General Budgetary Revenue and Expenditures of Local Finance by Prefecture, Autonomous Prefecture and City

单位：万元 (2007 年) (10 000 yuan)

地　区	Region	地方财政一般预算收入 Local Financial Revenue	位次 Rank	地方财政一般预算支出 Local Financial Expenditure	位次 Rank
乌鲁木齐市	Urumqi City	734279	1	683153	1
克拉玛依市	Karamay City	364826	2	428248	5
石河子市	Shihezi City	66656	10	84440	15
吐鲁番地区	Turpan Administrative Offices	93214	8	165740	12
哈密地区	Hami [Kumul] Administrative Offices	60955	12	163823	13
昌吉回族自治州	Changji Hui Autonomous Prefecture	138018	6	344146	8
伊犁哈萨克自治州	Ili Kazak Autonomous Prefecture	335217		1134352	
伊犁州直属县(市)	Counties (Cities) Direct Under Ili Prefecture	146961	5	555788	3
塔城地区	Tacheng [Tarbagatai] Administrative Offices	125913	7	323630	9
阿勒泰地区	Altay Administrative Offices	62343	11	254934	10
博尔塔拉蒙古自治州	Bortala Mongol Autonomous Prefecture	48082	13	153008	14
巴音郭楞蒙古自治州	Bayangol Mongol Autonomous Prefecture	196444	4	396809	6
阿克苏地区	Aksu Administrative Offices	255818	3	538450	4
克孜勒苏柯尔克孜自治州	Kizilsu Kirgiz Autonomous Prefecture	12294	15	178392	11
喀什地区	Kashgar [Kaxgar] Administrative Offices	81220	9	607616	2
和田地区	Hotan Administrative Offices	31843	14	351057	7

注:各地、州、市合计不等于总计。
Note: The total amount of different administrative office, autonomous prefectures and cities is not equal to the total.

20-13 分城镇居民消费价格指数和商品零售价格指数

General Retail Price and Consumer Price Index by City/County

(上年=100) (2007 年)(抽样调查) (Sampled Survey) (preceding year=100)

地　区	Region	商品零售价格指数 General Retail Price Index	位次 Rank	居民消费价格指数 General Consumer Price Index	位次 Rank
乌鲁木齐市	Urumqi City	104.6	11	104.6	12
喀什市	Kashgar [Kaxgar] City	104.4	13	104.3	16
伊宁市	Yining [Gulja] City	104.6	11	104.5	13
和田市	Hotan City	104.8	10	104.5	13
克拉玛依市	Karamay City	105.5	6	106.1	6
哈密市	Hami [Kumul] City	103.7	19	103.8	17
昌吉市	Changji City	104.1	17	103.7	19
库尔勒市	Korla City	104.2	15	105.2	9
阿克苏市	Aksu City	106.4	2	106.5	3
焉耆回族自治县	Yanqi Hui Autonomous County	105.5	6	106.3	5
塔城市	Tacheng [Qoqek] City	103.9	18	103.8	17
阿勒泰市	Altay City	104.4	13	104.8	10
乌苏市	Usu City	105.0	9	104.4	15
博乐市	Bole [Bortala] City	104.2	15	105.6	8
吐鲁番市	Turpan City	106.4	2	106.4	4
库车县	Kuqa County	105.6	5	108.4	2
阿图什市	Artux City	105.9	4	106.1	6
莎车县	Shache [Yarkant] County	107.4	1	108.5	1
奎屯市	Kuytun City	103.5	20	103.6	20
石河子市	Shihezi City	105.1	8	104.8	10

20-14 各地、州、市各类学校在校学生数

Number of Students Enrollment by Type of School and by Prefecture, Autonomous Prefecture and City

单位：人 (2007 年) (person)

地区	Region	普通高等学校 Regular Institutions of Higher Education	位次 Rank	中等专业学校 Specialized Secondary Schools	位次 Rank
乌鲁木齐市	Urumqi City	126923	1	68750	1
克拉玛依市	Karamay City	5075	5	1350	11
石河子市	Shihezi City	1864	8	16358	2
吐鲁番地区	Turpan Administrative Offices			1903	9
哈密地区	Hami [Kumul] Administrative Offices			1046	12
昌吉回族自治州	Changji Hui Autonomous Prefecture	16621	2	7625	5
伊犁哈萨克自治州	Ili Kazak Autonomous Prefecture	12082		10532	
伊犁州直属县(市)	Counties (Cities) Direct Under Ili Prefecture	12082	3	8069	3
塔城地区	Tacheng [Tarbagatai] Administrative Offices			640	15
阿勒泰地区	Altay Administrative Offices			1823	10
博尔塔拉蒙古自治州	Bortala Mongol Autonomous Prefecture			866	13
巴音郭楞蒙古自治州	Bayangol Mongol Autonomous Prefecture	1563	9	7824	4
阿克苏地区	Aksu Administrative Offices	2142	7	3489	8
克孜勒苏柯尔克孜自治州	Kizilsu Kirgiz Autonomous Prefecture			780	14
喀什地区	Kashgar [Kaxgar] Administrative Offices	11225	4	5692	6
和田地区	Hotan Administrative Offices	3986	6	3677	7

地区	Region	普通中学 Regular Secondary Schools	位次 Rank	小学 Primary Schools	位次 Rank
乌鲁木齐市	Urumqi City	141627	4	180967	5
克拉玛依市	Karamay City	23932	14	26451	14
石河子市	Shihezi City	17347	15	13246	15
吐鲁番地区	Turpan Administrative Offices	36164	11	52281	9
哈密地区	Hami [Kumul] Administrative Offices	32133	12	35120	12
昌吉回族自治州	Changji Hui Autonomous Prefecture	81071	6	90307	7
伊犁哈萨克自治州	Ili Kazak Autonomous Prefecture	257928		351946	
伊犁州直属县(市)	Counties (Cities) Direct Under Ili Prefecture	154607	3	226935	2
塔城地区	Tacheng [Tarbagatai] Administrative Offices	66169	8	80178	8
阿勒泰地区	Altay Administrative Offices	37152	10	44833	11
博尔塔拉蒙古自治州	Bortala Mongol Autonomous Prefecture	25889	13	30797	13
巴音郭楞蒙古自治州	Bayangol Mongol Autonomous Prefecture	76569	7	94939	6
阿克苏地区	Aksu Administrative Offices	159140	2	224903	3
克孜勒苏柯尔克孜自治州	Kizilsu Kirgiz Autonomous Prefecture	38237	9	50457	10
喀什地区	Kashgar [Kaxgar] Administrative Offices	300352	1	438175	1
和田地区	Hotan Administrative Offices	131935	5	216482	4

20-15 各地、州、市每万人口医院床位数和医生数
Number of Doctors and Hospital Beds Per 10 000 Population by Prefecture, Autonomous Prefecture and City

(2007 年)

地 区	Region	每万人医院、卫生院床位数(张) Number of Hospital Beds per 10 000 Population (unit)	位 次 Rank	平均每万人医生数(人) Number of Doctors Per 10 000 Population (person)	位 次 Rank
乌鲁木齐市	Urumqi City	95.47	1	48.85	1
克拉玛依市	Karamay City	59.21	2	39.82	2
石河子市	Shihezi City	40.67	8	22.03	8
吐鲁番地区	Turpan Administrative Offices	32.80	13	20.25	10
哈密地区	Hami [Kumul] Administrative Offices	49.20	4	30.59	3
昌吉回族自治州	Changji Hui Autonomous Prefecture	49.03	5	24.28	6
伊犁哈萨克自治州	Ili Kazak Autonomous Prefecture	37.28		21.32	
伊犁州直属县(市)	Counties (Cities) Direct Under Ili Prefecture	37.72	10	19.36	11
塔城地区	Tacheng [Tarbagatai] Administrative Offices	36.95	11	21.14	9
阿勒泰地区	Altay Administrative Offices	35.95	12	29.81	4
博尔塔拉蒙古自治州	Bortala Mongol Autonomous Prefecture	42.95	6	28.23	5
巴音郭楞蒙古自治州	Bayangol Mongol Autonomous Prefecture	53.21	3	23.45	7
阿克苏地区	Aksu Administrative Offices	39.55	9	13.15	13
克孜勒苏柯尔克孜自治州	Kizilsu Kirgiz Autonomous Prefecture	41.22	7	16.40	12
喀什地区	Kashgar [Kaxgar] Administrative Offices	30.57	14	11.73	14
和田地区	Hotan Administrative Offices	28.25	15	9.19	15

20-16 各地、州、市卫生技术人员和医生数
Medical Technical Personnel and Doctors by Prefecture, Autonomous Prefecture and City

单位：人 (2007 年) (person)

地 区	Region	卫生技术人员 Medical Technical Personnel	位 次 Rank	#医 生 Doctors	位 次 Rank
乌鲁木齐市	Urumqi City	24410	1	10338	1
克拉玛依市	Karamay City	2739	14	1064	14
石河子市	Shihezi City	4937	7	2254	7
吐鲁番地区	Turpan Administrative Offices	2947	13	1216	13
哈密地区	Hami [Kumul] Administrative Offices	3876	11	1671	11
昌吉回族自治州	Changji Hui Autonomous Prefecture	8979	4	3764	4
伊犁哈萨克自治州	Ili Kazak Autonomous Prefecture	21435		9258	
伊犁州直属县(市)	Counties (Cities) Direct Under Ili Prefecture	12482	2	5232	2
塔城地区	Tacheng [Tarbagatai] Administrative Offices	4882	8	2103	8
阿勒泰地区	Altay Administrative Offices	4071	10	1923	9
博尔塔拉蒙古自治州	Bortala Mongol Autonomous Prefecture	3038	12	1335	12
巴音郭楞蒙古自治州	Bayangol Mongol Autonomous Prefecture	7346	6	2871	6
阿克苏地区	Aksu Administrative Offices	7620	5	2896	5
克孜勒苏柯尔克孜自治州	Kizilsu Kirgiz Autonomous Prefecture	2247	15	820	15
喀什地区	Kashgar [Kaxgar] Administrative Offices	10727	3	4333	3
和田地区	Hotan Administrative Offices	4370	9	1731	10

附　录
各省、市、区主要经济指标排序

APPENDIX
Ranking of Main Economic Indicators By Region

XINJIANG STATISTICAL YEARBOOK 2008

新疆统计年鉴

XINJIANG STATISTICAL YEARBOOK 2008

各省市区主要经济指标排序
Ranking of Main Economic Indicators by Region

(2007 年)

省市区	Region	地区生产总值(亿元) Gross Regional Product (100 million yuan)	位次 Rank	地区生产总值比上年增长(%) Increase Rate of Gross Regional Product over the previous year(%)	位次 Rank
全　国	**China**	**249529.9**		**11.9**	
北　京	Beijing	9006.2	13	12.3	27
天　津	Tianjin	5018.3	22	15.1	4
河　北	Hebei	13863.5	6	12.9	24
山　西	Shanxi	5696.2	18	14.2	17
内蒙古	Inner Mongolia	6018.8	16	19.0	1
辽　宁	Liaoning	11021.7	8	14.5	8
吉　林	Jilin	5226.1	21	16.1	2
黑龙江	Heilongjiang	7077.2	15	12.1	30
上　海	Shanghai	12001.2	7	13.3	22
江　苏	Jiangsu	25560.1	3	14.8	7
浙　江	Zhejiang	18638.4	4	14.5	8
安　徽	Anhui	7345.7	14	13.9	20
福　建	Fujian	9160.1	10	15.1	4
江　西	Jiangxi	5469.3	19	13.0	23
山　东	Shandong	25887.7	2	14.3	16
河　南	Henan	15058.1	5	14.4	13
湖　北	Hubei	9150.0	11	14.5	8
湖　南	Hunan	9145.0	12	14.4	13
广　东	Guangdong	30673.7	1	14.5	8
广　西	Guangxi	5885.9	17	14.9	6
海　南	Hainan	1229.6	28	14.5	8
重　庆	Chongqing	4111.8	24	15.6	3
四　川	Sichuan	10505.3	9	14.2	17
贵　州	Guizhou	2710.3	26	13.7	21
云　南	Yunnan	4721.8	23	12.3	27
西　藏	Tibet	342.2	31	14.0	19
陕　西	Shaanxi	5369.9	20	14.4	13
甘　肃	Gansu	2699.2	27	12.1	30
青　海	Qinghai	761.0	30	12.5	25
宁　夏	Ningxia	834.2	29	12.4	26
新　疆	Xinjiang	3523.2	25	12.2	29

续表 1

省市区	Region	第一产业增加值(亿元) Value-added of the Primary Industry (100 million yuan)	位次 Rank	第二产业增加值(亿元) Value-added of the Secondary Industry (100 million yuan)	位次 Rank	第三产业增加值(亿元) Value-added of the Tertiary Industry (100 million yuan)	位次 Rank
全　国	**China**	**28095.0**		**121381.3**		**100053.6**	
北　京	Beijing	101.3	28	2479.3	20	6425.6	5
天　津	Tianjin	102.9	26	2891.3	18	2024.1	18
河　北	Hebei	1971.2	4	7252.5	6	4639.8	7
山　西	Shanxi	313.0	25	3394.7	14	1988.5	20
内蒙古	Inner Mongolia	784.1	18	3079.8	16	2154.9	17
辽　宁	Liaoning	1178.4	11	5829.5	7	4013.8	9
吉　林	Jilin	813.5	17	2389.9	21	2022.7	19
黑龙江	Heilongjiang	892.5	15	3779.5	13	2405.2	15
上　海	Shanghai	101.8	27	5675.5	8	6223.9	6
江　苏	Jiangsu	1726.1	6	14285.8	3	9548.2	2
浙　江	Zhejiang	1025.3	13	10092.0	4	7521.1	4
安　徽	Anhui	1214.7	10	3282.6	15	2848.4	14
福　建	Fujian	1038.4	12	4508.0	10	3613.7	13
江　西	Jiangxi	910.0	14	2827.3	19	1732.0	24
山　东	Shandong	2509.1	1	14773.4	2	8605.2	3
河　南	Henan	2365.9	2	8280.3	5	4411.9	8
湖　北	Hubei	1422.8	8	4094.2	11	3633.0	11
湖　南	Hunan	1611.5	7	3901.2	12	3632.3	12
广　东	Guangdong	1746.2	5	15938.2	1	12989.3	1
广　西	Guangxi	1264.6	9	2335.4	22	2285.9	16
海　南	Hainan	382.8	24	363.8	30	483.0	28
重　庆	Chongqing	531.7	21	1832.1	24	1748.0	23
四　川	Sichuan	2092.1	3	4595.5	9	3817.7	10
贵　州	Guizhou	455.7	22	1145.6	27	1109.0	26
云　南	Yunnan	868.1	16	2040.4	23	1813.3	22
西　藏	Tibet	55.3	31	96.6	31	190.3	31
陕　西	Shaanxi	594.7	20	2917.0	17	1858.3	21
甘　肃	Gansu	386.4	23	1282.2	26	1030.6	27
青　海	Qinghai	85.9	30	396.6	29	278.5	30
宁　夏	Ningxia	97.9	29	420.3	28	316.0	29
新　疆	Xinjiang	628.7	19	1647.6	25	1246.9	25

Continued

第一产业占 GDP 比重 (%) Composition of Primary Industry Product to GDP(%)	位 次 Rank	第二产业占 GDP 比重 (%) Composition of Secondary Industry Product to GDP(%)	位 次 Rank	第三产业占 GDP 比重 (%) Composition of Tertiary Industrial Product to GDP(%)	位 次 Rank
11.3		**48.6**		**40.1**	
1.1	30	27.5	31	71.4	1
2.0	29	57.7	2	40.3	8
14.2	15	52.3	10	33.5	28
5.5	27	59.6	1	34.9	25
13.0	16	51.2	14	35.8	23
10.7	23	52.9	9	36.4	21
15.6	12	45.7	20	38.7	15
12.6	18	53.4	8	34.0	27
0.8	31	47.3	18	51.9	3
6.8	25	55.9	4	37.3	19
5.5	27	54.1	7	40.4	7
16.5	9	44.8	20	38.8	13
11.3	20	49.2	16	39.5	11
16.6	8	51.7	13	31.7	30
9.7	24	57.1	3	33.2	29
15.7	11	55.0	5	29.3	31
15.5	13	44.8	20	39.7	9
17.6	6	42.7	26	39.7	9
5.7	26	52.0	12	42.3	5
21.5	2	39.7	28	38.8	13
31.1	1	29.6	29	39.3	12
12.9	17	44.6	23	42.5	4
19.9	3	43.8	24	36.3	22
16.8	7	42.3	27	40.9	6
18.4	4	43.2	25	38.4	16
16.2	10	28.2	30	55.6	2
11.1	22	54.3	6	34.6	26
14.3	14	47.5	17	38.2	17
11.3	20	52.1	11	36.6	20
11.7	19	50.4	15	37.9	18
17.8	5	46.8	19	35.4	24

续表 2

省市区	Region	总人口（万人） Total Population (10 000 persons)	位次 Rank	地方财政收入（亿元） Local Government Revenue (100 million yuan)	位次 Rank	地方财政支出（亿元） Local Government Expenditures (100 million yuan)	位次 Rank
全国	**China**	**132129**		**23565.04**		**38120.36**	
北京	Beijing	1633	26	1492.6	6	1646.9	9
天津	Tianjin	1115	27	540.1	16	674.3	27
河北	Hebei	6943	6	788.9	10	1478.5	10
山西	Shanxi	3393	19	597.6	13	1042.6	18
内蒙古	Inner Mongolia	2405	23	492.3	17	1083.6	16
辽宁	Liaoning	4298	14	1082.0	8	1763.0	7
吉林	Jilin	2730	21	320.5	24	883.8	22
黑龙江	Heilongjiang	3824	15	440.2	21	1187.3	14
上海	Shanghai	1858	25	2102.6	3	2201.9	4
江苏	Jiangsu	7625	5	2237.7	2	2506.4	2
浙江	Zhejiang	5060	10	1649.5	5	1806.9	6
安徽	Anhui	6118	8	543.5	15	1219.4	13
福建	Fujian	3581	18	700.3	11	901.2	21
江西	Jiangxi	4368	13	389.6	23	902.6	20
山东	Shandong	9367	2	1674.5	4	2262.5	3
河南	Henan	9360	3	861.5	9	1868.4	5
湖北	Hubei	5699	9	590.4	14	1256.4	12
湖南	Hunan	6355	7	606.6	12	1341.6	11
广东	Guangdong	9449	1	2785.4	1	3147.3	1
广西	Guangxi	4768	11	418.8	22	977.3	19
海南	Hainan	845	28	108.3	28	245.4	30
重庆	Chongqing	2816	20	442.7	20	769.7	25
四川	Sichuan	8127	4	1395.7	7	1760.9	8
贵州	Guizhou	3762	16	284.9	26	787.6	24
云南	Yunnan	4514	12	486.7	18	1134.7	15
西藏	Tibet	284	31	20.1	31	275.4	29
陕西	Shaanxi	3748	17	475.2	19	1054.0	17
甘肃	Gansu	2617	22	190.6	27	675.1	26
青海	Qinghai	552	30	56.7	30	282.3	28
宁夏	Ningxia	610	29	80.0	29	241.5	31
新疆	Xinjiang	2095	24	285.9	25	795.2	23

Continued

居民消费价格指数 Consumer Price Index	位次 Rank	在岗职工平均货币工资(元) Average moneyWage of Staff and workers (yuan)	位次 Rank	#国有单位在岗职工平均货币工资(元) Average Wage of Staff in State-owned Units (yuan)	位次 Rank	城镇居民年人均可支配收入(元) Per Capita Annual Disposable Income of Urban households (yuan)	位次 Rank	城镇居民年人均消费性支出(元) Per Capita Annual living Expenditures for Consumption (yuan)	位次 Rank
104.8		**24932**		**26620**		**13786**		**9997**	
102.4	31	46507	2	50524	2	21989	2	15330	2
104.2	26	34938	4	37654	5	16357	6	12029	5
104.7	20	19911	27	20900	28	11690	14	8235	19
104.6	22	21525	18	22309	22	11565	15	8102	21
104.6	22	21884	16	22822	18	12378	10	9281	11
105.1	14	23202	10	24748	13	12300	11	9430	10
104.8	17	20513	25	21688	25	11286	21	8560	15
105.4	9	19386	29	19635	29	10245	30	7519	30
103.2	30	49310	1	55547	1	23623	1	17255	1
104.3	25	27374	7	33411	7	16378	5	10715	7
104.2	26	31086	5	48857	3	20574	3	14091	4
105.3	12	22180	14	22428	19	11474	19	8532	16
105.2	13	22283	13	28011	9	15505	7	11055	6
104.8	17	18400	31	19624	30	11452	20	7811	27
104.4	24	22844	12	27290	10	14265	8	9667	9
105.4	9	20935	23	22345	20	11477	18	7827	25
104.8	17	19818	28	21971	24	11486	17	8701	13
105.6	6	21534	17	23336	16	12294	12	8991	12
103.7	28	29443	6	36396	6	17699	4	14337	3
106.1	3	21898	15	23369	15	12200	13	8151	20
105.0	16	19357	30	18937	31	10997	24	8293	18
104.7	20	23098	11	25365	12	12591	9	9890	8
105.9	4	21312	20	24365	14	11098	23	8692	14
106.4	2	20668	24	22106	23	10678	27	7759	28
105.9	4	20481	26	22884	17	11496	16	7922	22
103.4	29	46098	3	47757	4	11131	22	7532	29
105.1	14	21296	21	21653	26	10763	26	8427	17
105.5	7	20987	22	22314	21	10012	31	7876	23
106.6	1	26166	9	29683	8	10276	29	7512	31
105.4	9	26210	8	26687	11	10859	25	7817	26
105.5	7	21434	19	21369	27	10313	28	7874	24

续表 3

省市区	Region	农民人均纯收入(元) Annual Per Capita Disposable Income of Rural Households (yuan)	位次 Rank	农民人均现金收入(元) Annual Per Capita Cash Income of Rural Households (yuan)	位次 Rank	农民人均生活消费支出(元) Annual Per Capita Living Expenditure of Rural Households (yuan)	位次 Rank
全　国	**China**	**4140**		**4958**		**3224**	
北　京	Beijing	9440	2	10859	1	6399	3
天　津	Tianjin	7010	4	8961	4	3538	8
河　北	Hebei	4293	10	5371	13	2787	16
山　西	Shanxi	3666	19	4040	22	2683	20
内蒙古	Inner Mongolia	3953	15	5483	12	3256	11
辽　宁	Liaoning	4773	9	6854	6	3368	10
吉　林	Jilin	4191	11	5530	11	3065	14
黑龙江	Heilongjiang	4132	12	6675	7	3117	12
上　海	Shanghai	10145	1	10772	2	8845	1
江　苏	Jiangsu	6561	5	7392	5	4786	4
浙　江	Zhejiang	8265	3	10497	3	6802	2
安　徽	Anhui	3556	20	4092	21	2754	17
福　建	Fujian	5467	7	6136	10	4053	6
江　西	Jiangxi	4045	13	4452	17	2994	15
山　东	Shandong	4985	8	6434	8	3622	7
河　南	Henan	3852	17	4109	20	2676	21
湖　北	Hubei	3997	14	4499	15	3090	13
湖　南	Hunan	3904	16	4455	16	3377	9
广　东	Guangdong	5624	6	6256	9	4202	5
广　西	Guangxi	3224	23	3770	24	2747	18
海　南	Hainan	3791	18	4452	18	2557	24
重　庆	Chongqing	3509	22	3406	25	2527	26
四　川	Sichuan	3547	21	3940	23	2747	19
贵　州	Guizhou	2374	30	2347	31	1914	31
云　南	Yunnan	2634	29	3191	27	2637	22
西　藏	Tibet	2788	26	2576	29	2218	29
陕　西	Shaanxi	2645	28	3300	26	2560	23
甘　肃	Gansu	2329	31	2567	30	2017	30
青　海	Qinghai	2684	27	2905	28	2447	27
宁　夏	Ningxia	3181	25	4317	19	2529	25
新　疆	Xinjiang	3183	24	5249	14	2351	28

注：现金收支为不含储蓄借贷后的现金收支。
Note: The cash income and expenditure refer to the one abscent of deposit loan.

Continued

农林牧渔业总产值(亿元) Gross Output Value of Agriculture, Forestry, Animal Husbandry and Fishery (100 million yuan)	位 次 Rank	农林牧渔业总产值比上年增长(%) Output Value Increase Rate in 2007 over 2006 of Agriculture,Forestry, Animal Husbandry and Fishery(%)	位 次 Rank	粮食产量(万吨) Grain (10 000 ton)	位 次 Rank	棉花产量(万吨) Cotton (10 000 ton)	位 次 Rank	油料产量(万吨) Oilbearing Crops (10 000 ton)	位 次 Rank
48893.0		**3.9**		**50148.3**		**762.4**		**2548.9**	
272.3	26	0.8	30	102.1	30	0.2	18	2.2	30
240.7	28	1.5	27	147.2	27	9.3	12	0.5	31
3075.8	4	3.9	16	2841.6	7	72.5	4	138.1	7
498.4	25	0.1	31	1007.1	20	11.5	11	13.5	25
1276.4	18	4.0	15	1810.7	13	0.4	16	79.4	10
2128.0	9	4.1	14	1835.0	12	0.2	18	26.4	21
1359.8	16	1.2	29	2453.8	9	0.1	21	28.7	19
1700.6	12	1.9	26	3462.9	3			21.3	24
256.0	27	1.5	27	109.2	28	0.3	17	3.6	29
3064.7	5	3.1	24	3132.2	4	34.8	7	145.1	6
1597.2	14	2.3	25	728.6	23	2.6	14	33.0	17
2070.1	10	3.8	19	2901.4	6	37.4	6	179.4	5
1692.2	13	4.2	12	635.1	24	0.1	21	23.3	22
1426.9	15	4.2	12	1904.0	11	12.8	10	82.7	9
4766.2	1	3.3	22	4148.8	2	100.1	2	328.6	2
3879.9	2	3.9	16	5245.2	1	75.0	3	484.0	1
2296.8	8	3.9	16	2185.4	10	55.7	5	254.8	3
2632.2	7	4.9	9	2692.2	8	24.4	8	110.1	8
2821.2	6	3.3	22	1284.7	16			77.7	11
2026.2	11	5.8	7	1396.6	15	0.2	18	33.8	16
548.3	24	8.3	2	177.5	26			6.8	27
720.7	21	9.5	1	1088.0	18			30.7	18
3377.0	3	3.5	20	3027.0	5	1.7	15	204.3	4
697.0	22	3.4	21	1100.9	17	0.1	21	69.7	12
1331.7	17	5.6	8	1448.7	14			22.1	23
79.8	31	4.8	10	93.9	31			5.2	28
1002.9	20	6.3	6	1067.9	19	9.0	13	39.1	15
686.1	23	4.3	11	824.0	22	12.9	9	42.4	13
121.3	30	8.2	3	106.2	29			28.0	20
182.9	29	7.0	5	323.5	25			7.7	26
1063.5	19	8.2	3	867.0	21	290.0	1	40.3	14

续表 4

省市区	Region	工业增加值(亿元) Value-added of Industry (100 million yuan)	位 次 Rank	原 煤(万吨) Raw Coal (10 000 tons)	位 次 Rank	原 油(万吨) Crude Oil (10 000 tons)	位 次 Rank
全 国	**China**	**107367.2**		**253600.0**		**18665.7**	
北 京	Beijing	2053.4	21	633.3	23		
天 津	Tianjin	2669.0	16			1924.3	5
河 北	Hebei	6566.8	6	8389.9	8	660.0	8
山 西	Shanxi	3098.2	14	57056.9	1		
内蒙古	Inner Mongolia	2668.6	17	34885.9	2		
辽 宁	Liaoning	5179.4	8	6320.0	11	1237.8	7
吉 林	Jilin	2085.8	20	3157.8	17	623.9	9
黑龙江	Heilongjiang	3412.0	12	7997.1	9	4169.8	1
上 海	Shanghai	5295.9	7			20.7	15
江 苏	Jiangsu	13000.1	3	2480.2	19	198.9	12
浙 江	Zhejiang	9040.0	4	12.3	26		
安 徽	Anhui	2752.1	15	9112.4	7		
福 建	Fujian	3980.7	9	1991.7	21		
江 西	Jiangxi	2264.1	19	2379.8	20		
山 东	Shandong	13411.2	2	14518.3	5	2793.1	2
河 南	Henan	7508.3	5	18917.2	3	485.1	10
湖 北	Hubei	3588.9	11	610.0	24	85.5	13
湖 南	Hunan	3360.6	13	4852.4	13		
广 东	Guangdong	14910.0	1			1261.1	6
广 西	Guangxi	2001.2	22	597.9	25	2.9	18
海 南	Hainan	278.4	30			10.7	17
重 庆	Chongqing	1514.7	24	2711.7	18		
四 川	Sichuan	3868.6	10	7758.8	10	18.1	16
贵 州	Guizhou	1006.0	27	10864.2	6		
云 南	Yunnan	1701.8	23	3738.9	14		
西 藏	Tibet	25.7	31				
陕 西	Shaanxi	2498.2	18	18313.3	4	2265.9	4
甘 肃	Gansu	1066.7	26	3555.1	16	82.9	14
青 海	Qinghai	324.1	29	896.1	22	220.7	11
宁 夏	Ningxia	348.7	28	3729.9	15		
新 疆	Xinjiang	1405.1	25	5018.6	12	2604.3	3

Continued

社会消费品零售总额(亿元) Total Retail Sales of Consumer Goods (100 million yuan)	位 次 Rank	社会消费品零售总额比上年增长(%) Increase Rate in 2007 over 2006of Total Retail Sales of Consumer Goods(%)	位 次 Rank	进出口总额(亿美元) Total Value of Imports and Exports (USD 100 million)	位 次 Rank	#出口总额(亿美元) Total Exports (USD 100 million)	位 次 Rank
89210.0		**16.8**		**21738.3**		**12180.1**	
3800.2	11	16.0	29	1929.5	4	489.2	7
1603.7	23	18.2	14	715.2	8	381.5	8
3986.2	9	17.3	20	255.3	10	170.1	10
1914.1	17	18.6	5	115.7	17	65.3	17
1904.1	18	19.4	2	77.4	23	29.5	25
4030.1	6	17.3	20	594.7	9	353.3	9
1999.2	16	19.3	3	103.0	18	38.6	24
2331.1	15	16.7	24	173.1	11	122.7	11
3847.8	10	14.5	31	2829.1	3	1438.9	3
7838.1	3	18.3	12	3495.6	2	2037.0	2
6214.0	4	16.7	24	1768.3	5	1282.9	4
2403.7	14	18.4	9	159.3	12	88.2	13
3187.9	13	17.9	16	744.6	7	499.4	6
1683.1	21	17.9	16	94.8	20	54.6	19
8438.8	2	18.5	7	1225.0	6	751.3	5
4597.5	5	18.5	7	128.0	16	83.9	15
4028.5	7	18.1	15	148.6	13	81.7	16
3356.5	12	18.4	9	96.9	19	65.2	18
10598.1	1	16.2	27	6340.7	1	3692.6	1
1897.9	19	18.6	5	92.7	21	51.1	20
362.0	28	17.4	18	35.1	27	13.6	28
1661.2	22	18.4	9	74.4	24	45.1	23
4015.6	8	17.4	18	143.8	14	86.1	14
821.8	27	19.1	4	22.7	28	14.7	27
1394.5	24	17.3	20	87.8	22	47.4	21
112.0	31	24.9	1	3.9	31	3.3	31
1800.9	20	18.3	12	68.9	25	46.7	22
833.3	26	16.1	28	55.0	26	16.6	26
208.3	30	15.7	30	6.1	30	3.9	30
233.3	29	17.3	20	15.8	29	10.9	29
847.7	25	16.5	26	137.2	15	115.0	12

续表 5 Continued

省市区	Region	国际旅游人数（万人）Total Number of Oversea Visitor Arrivals (10 000 persons)	位次 Rank	#外国人 Foreigners	位次 Rank	旅游外汇收入（亿美元）Earnings from International Tourism (USD 100 million)	位次 Rank
全国	**China**	**13187.3**		**2611.0**		**419.2**	
北京	Beijing	435.5	5	382.6	3	45.80	3
天津	Tianjin	103.2	18	95.2	16	7.79	10
河北	Hebei	81.8	20	73.8	19	3.09	21
山西	Shanxi	73.8	23	44.8	23	2.22	23
内蒙古	Inner Mongolia	149.5	12	147.4	8	5.45	15
辽宁	Liaoning	200.1	10	170.7	7	12.28	8
吉林	Jilin	54.4	25	44.2	24	1.79	25
黑龙江	Heilongjiang	141.4	13	134.4	10	6.43	11
上海	Shanghai	520.1	2	442.6	2	46.73	2
江苏	Jiangsu	512.5	3	369.2	4	34.69	4
浙江	Zhejiang	511.2	4	343.6	5	27.08	5
安徽	Anhui	106.4	17	74.3	18	3.44	19
福建	Fujian	268.7	6	100.8	14	21.69	6
江西	Jiangxi	66.5	24	23.9	27	1.96	24
山东	Shandong	249.6	7	202.0	6	13.52	7
河南	Henan	88.1	19	55.6	22	3.18	20
湖北	Hubei	131.8	14	107.7	12	4.13	17
湖南	Hunan	120.6	16	87.5	17	6.42	12
广东	Guangdong	2460.9	1	628.5	1	87.06	1
广西	Guangxi	205.5	9	124.5	11	5.77	14
海南	Hainan	75.3	22	59.3	21	3.02	22
重庆	Chongqing	76.2	21	62.2	20	3.82	18
四川	Sichuan	170.9	11	107.4	13	5.12	16
贵州	Guizhou	43.0	27	15.5	29	1.29	28
云南	Yunnan	221.9	8	144.7	9	8.60	9
西藏	Tibet	36.5	28	33.9	26	1.35	27
陕西	Shaanxi	123.1	15	98.2	15	6.12	13
甘肃	Gansu	33.1	29	23.4	28	0.70	29
青海	Qinghai	5.0	30	3.6	30	0.16	30
宁夏	Ningxia	0.9	31	0.8	31	0.03	31
新疆	Xinjiang	43.8	26	40.3	25	1.62	26

New Published Statistical Yearbook by China Statistics Press

以新型工业化建设为主线　全力开创我区经贸工作新局面

新疆维吾尔自治区经济贸易委员会

（新疆维吾尔自治区国防科技工业办公室）

2007 年，在自治区党委、人民政府的正确领导下，全区经贸系统紧紧围绕年初确定的目标任务，坚持实施优势资源转换战略，加快推进新型工业化进程，工交商贸经济继续保持了稳步发展的良好态势。

全年完成工业增加值 1378 亿元，增长 15%，其中地方工业增长 25%以上；

规模以上工业企业实现利润 681 亿元，增长 17.7%，其中除石油外其它工业实现利润增幅 70%以上；

工业领域投资完成 942 亿元，增长 38.1%；

社会消费品零售总额 848 亿元，增长 16.5%；

全年铁路和石油管输运量完成 7000 万吨以上。

2008 年，全区经贸系统将坚持以邓小平理论和“三个代表”重要思想为指导，深入贯彻落实科学发展观，全面贯彻落实党的十七大、国务院 32 号文件精神，紧紧抓住和用好重要战略机遇期，充分发挥比较优势，坚定不移地实施以市场为导向的优势资源转换战略，加快推进新型工业化进程。

主要预期目标：

工业增加值增长 17%，工业占生产总值的比重提高 1 个百分点；

工业领域投资增长 25%；

工业企业效益平稳增长；

工业产品销售率 97%以上；

社会消费品零售总额增长 14%以上；

单位生产总值能耗降低 4%左右；

铁路货物发送量及出疆石油管线运量力争达到 8000 万吨。

1

2

3

4

1.自治区政协副主席、经贸委主任王永明

2.深入企业调研

3.丰富多彩的职工活动

4.表彰年度先进集体

积极开展审计监督 为自治区经济发展保驾护航

朱登云厅长代表政府向自治区人大作审计工作报告

原自治区常务副主席陈雷到审计厅调研

召开自治区审计工作会议

2007年，在自治区党委、人民政府的正确领导下，全区各级审计机关以邓小平理论和“三个代表”重要思想为指导，认真贯彻党的十六届五中、六中全会和自治区第七次党代会精神，全面落实科学发展观，切实履行审计监督职责，积极开展效益审计，审计质量和工作水平进一步提高，为促进各级政府依法行政，确保自治区经济又好又快发展，建设社会主义新农村，维护和谐社会发挥了重要作用。

一年来，全区各级审计机关共审计单位2538个，专项审计调查单位532个，查出各类违规违纪问题资金44.5亿元，损失浪费3.11亿元，侵害人民群众利益问题资金1646万元，增加财政收入5.52亿元，已追还被侵占的资金1.05亿元；移送司法纪检监察机关53人，涉案金额5.34亿元。提出的审计建议被采纳2973条，被审计单位制定整改措施236项，建立健全规章制度105个(份)；提交的审计专题报告、综合性报告和信息简报被党政领导和有关部门批示、采用1242篇次。

召开自治区审计项目告知会

举办自治区地厅级领导干部财务与审计研讨班

农业开发项目审计现场

创新监管机制　提高执法效能

2007年自治区工商行政管理局工作剪影

近年来，自治区工商行政管理系统认真贯彻党的路线、方针、政策，按照全面落实科学发展观和构建和谐社会的要求，在自治区党委、政府和国家工商总局的正确领导下，坚持“一手抓执法，一手抓服务”的工作思路，积极推进“五型”工商（学习型、和谐型、服务型、数字型、创新型）建设，切实履行法定职能，努力做到“四个统一”（监管与发展、监管与服务、监管与维权、监管与执法的统一），开拓创新，务实奋进，各项工作取得了新的显著成绩，为自治区经济社会又好又快发展作出了积极贡献。

2007年，自治区工商局在系统全体干部的共同努力下，工作有了新成绩、新亮点，与历年相比业绩更加突出。国家工商总局周伯华局长来疆视察工作，对该局的工作给予了非常高的评价。周伯华局长称赞自治区工商局在队伍建设、服务经济发展等方面走在了全国前列。

2007年，全区工商系统各项工作取得了显著的成绩。在2008年2月20日召开的全国工商行政管理工作会议上，自治区工商局局长吐尔逊·阿布都热衣木（左前一）受到时任国务院副总理吴仪（右前一）的亲切接见。

国家工商总局周伯华局长（左前二）在自治区副主席胡伟（右二）、自治区工商局党组书记王新怀（右一）、局长吐尔逊·阿不都热衣木（左后二）陪同下参观自治区工商局12315指挥中心。

2007年，自治区工商局被自治区区直机关工委授予“党建工作先进单位”荣誉称号。图为自治区工商局党组书记王新怀（右前一）在颁奖大会上接受颁奖。

在自治区工商行政管理工作会议上，荣获系统“双先”荣誉称号的代表受到自治区政协主席艾斯海提·克里木拜（右前二）、自治区副主席胡伟（右前一）等自治区领导的亲切接见。

新疆交通加快科学发展步伐

自治区交通厅是自治区人民政府主管全区公路、水路交通的职能部门。主要负责和指导全区交通基础设施建设、公路管理与养护、道路与水路运输、交通规费征收、海事安全监管等方面的行业管理工作。交通厅下设交通建设局、公路管理局、道路运输管理局、征稽局、海事局、路政局等6个具有行政管理职能的事业局，以及公路设计院、交通科研院、交通职业技术学院等3个事业单位。对自治区各地、州、市和县(市)103个交通局进行行业指导和管理。

长期以来，落后的交通运输一直是制约新疆经济和社会发展的主要因素之一。解放初期，新疆仅有3361公里简易公路，汽车不足100辆。改革开放以来，在党中央、国务院的亲切关怀和自治区党委、政府的正确领导下，在国家交通部和有关部委的大力支持下，交通系统各级党组织和广大交通干部职工，以邓小平理论和“三个代表”重要思想为指导，艰苦奋斗，团结奉献，拼搏进取，经过数十年艰苦不懈的努力，新疆交通事业发生了天翻地覆的变化。全疆15个地、州、市首府城市通达二级以上公路，89个县市通达三级以上油路。形成了以乌鲁木齐市为中心，以国道干线为主骨架，环绕两大盆地，辐射地、州、市、县、乡和农牧团场，东联甘肃、青海，南接西藏，西出中亚、西亚各国，北达蒙古国的干支线公路交通网。

2008年自治区交通工作会议

2007 年 10 月 30 日，新藏公路举行通车 50 年庆典

2007 年 11 月 1 日阿拉尔 – 和田沙漠公路正式通车

2008 年 3 月 27 日，中哈举行签字仪式同意开通 7 条直达国际道路客货运输新线路

2007 年 8 月 21 日至 22 日，联合国亚太经社委员会八成员国磋商亚欧区域便利化运输

特别是党的十六大以来，交通干部职工牢固树立和落实科学发展观，进一步加快新疆交通建设和发展步伐，交通基础设施建设投资达到 480 亿元，带动社会投入累计达 1000 亿元以上。截止 2007 年底，全区公路总里程达到 14.5 万公里，高速公路突破 1000 公里，国省干线公路好路率达到 85.5%；全区农村公路里程达到 12 万公里，乡镇通公路率达 98.6%，建制村通公路率 73.5%；全区国际客货运输线路 101 条，具全国各省区市之首，2008 年将再开通 9 条；全区客运班线 2935 条，乡镇客运班车通达率 99.9%，行政村客运班车通达率 70%。2007 年全区民用机动车保有量达到 244 万辆，完成营业性道路运输客运量 2.63 亿人次、旅客周转量 242 亿人公里；货运量 2.68 亿吨、货物周转量 366.2 亿吨公里。前 3 项指标在自治区综合运输体系中居首位，交通基础和主导地位进一步增强。为自治区实施优势资源转换战略，加快新型工业化进程，推进社会主义新农村建设，扩大全方位对内对外开放，加强石油、天然气、煤炭、有色矿产资源等的开发利用，扩大交通投资，引导交通消费，推动自治区经济社会又好又快发展，全面建设小康社会，提供了有效的交通服务和保障。同时，交通系统党的建设、交通科技教育、交通职工队伍建设、交通文明行业建设、交通文化建设都取得了可喜的成绩。

新疆交通系统举办大型文艺演唱会

交通系统大众运动会

自治区农村公路建设质量年活动启动

特大件炼油设备行驶在新疆境内的高速公路上

天山公路深处，养路段职工为即将通车紧张地清理冰雪

公交车直通农民家门口

2007 年 1 月 7 日司法厅召开全区司法行政工作会议，安排部署 2007 年司法行政工作

司法厅党委书记杜建锡调研基层司法行政工作

自治区司法行政工作

2007 年，新疆各级司法行政机关坚持以邓小平理论、“三个代表”重要思想为指导，全面贯彻落实科学发展观，紧紧围绕国家和自治区关于全面建设小康社会、构建和谐社会的重大工作部署和要求，坚持改革创新，锐意进取，真抓实干，各项工作都有了进一步发展。

坚持“稳定压倒一切”的方针，监狱、劳教工作持续发展。罪犯脱逃率、非正常死亡率和狱(所)内发案率均较上年有所下降；罪犯、劳教人员教育改造转化质量明显提高。2007 年，监狱系统总体安全稳定，劳教系统连续第六年保持“四无”。人民调解工作进一步加强，调解力度进一步加大。全年，各类人民调解组织共调解矛盾纠纷 129799 件，调解纠纷数比上年上升 78%，调解成功率达到 94.5%，有力地维护了基层社会的稳定。以“法治六进”为抓手，普法依法治理工作进一步加强。“法治六进”活动在全疆广泛开展，形式不断创新，效果明显增强。法律服务工作不断发展。全区已有律师事务所 264 个，执业律师 2169 名；公证处 124 个，执业公证员 403 名；司法鉴定机构 47 家，专职注册司法鉴定人员 628 人；基层法律服务所 816 个，执业法律服务工作者 2417 名；法律援助机构 111 个，法律援助工作人员 286 人。司法行政基层基础工作特别是司法所建设进一步加强，全区各乡镇(街道)已建立司法所 1030 个，有司法助理员 2148 人。积极开展了司法所规范化建设达标活动，有 164 个司法所被评为自治区级规范化司法所。队伍建设不断加强，党风廉政建设和反腐败斗争进一步深化。

司法厅召开“法治六进”活动新闻发布会

司法厅办公室副主任肉孜·尼牙孜当选 2006 年度新疆十大法治人物

新疆维吾尔自治区环保局

2007 年，自治区环保工作围绕贯彻落实党的十七大、国务院 32 号文件和自治区党委七届五次全委（扩大）会议精神，按照全国环保厅局长会议确定的工作重点，结合新疆实际，采取有力措施，加大污染防治力度，一些关系民生的突出环境问题得到解决，部分主要污染物排放量增速明显减缓，环境质量基本保持稳定，各项环保工作取得积极进展。

污染防治工作。2007 年，全区环境污染治理投资 41.16 亿元，占当年生产总值的 1.18%。其中，老工业污染源治理投资 6.01 亿元，“三同时”项目环保投资 8.75 亿元，两项合计占当年生产总值的 0.42%；城市环境基础设施建设投资 26.40 亿元，占当年生产总值的 0.76%。

环境监督管理。完成了 22 个工业园区、口岸等规划环境影响评价。各级环保部门办理项目审批手续 3072 个，审批的大中型建设项目环境影响报告书比上年增加 29.09%。拟实施项目环保投资 44.10 亿元，占申报项目总投资的 6.03%。

环境执法。自治区人大开展了“加快村镇规划，促进新农村建设”天山环保世纪行执法检查活动，自治区人民政府组织了“整治违法排污企业保障群众健康环保专项行动”，检查企业 7184 家、重点建设项目 191 个，查处违法企业 216 家，确定挂牌督办企业 140 家。全区共受理信访投诉案件 2875 件，办结 2820 件，办结率 98%。全区受理环境行政处罚案件共计 2655 起，做出行政处罚决定的 2233 起；受理复议案件 8 起，做出行政复议决定的 8 起；无行政诉讼案件发生。

排污费征收。2007 年，全区征收排污费 24786.68 万元（不含兵团），其中自治区本级直接征收 8263.35 万元，各地、州、市征收 16523.33 万元。

环境污染事故。2007 年，全区未发生较大环境污染事故。

自然保护区管理。全区共建立各级、各类自然保护区 34 个，其中国家级 9 个，自治区级 19 个，兵团 1 个，地、县级 5 个。总面积 22.58 万平方公里，占新疆国土总面积的 13.6%。

自治区党委副书记、自治区主席努尔·白克力讲话

自治区环保局局长牛晓萍到东山区考察生态建设情况

自治区环保局党组书记艾努瓦尔讲话

2005年12月14日上午，中共中央政治局委员、自治区党委书记王乐泉向困难群众捐款。

自治区民政工作成就辉煌

近年来，新疆维吾尔自治区各级民政部门，深入贯彻“以民为本、为民解困”的民政工作宗旨，在改革中探索，在创新中发展，各项工作实现整体推进取得了辉煌成就。

救灾救助工作切实有效。全区建立了救灾工作分级负责、救灾经费分级负担和专户管理体制，提高了救灾工作的时效性。规范了救灾工作程序，拓宽了救灾资金来源渠道，开展了经常性的社会捐助活动，推动了救灾工作的社会化进程。加强救灾物资储备设施建设，提高了灾害紧急救助能力。

社会救助工作全面推进。规范城市低保工作程序，建立健全低保机构。目前全区61万低保对象享受最低生活保障，基本实现了应保尽保；加大在农村医疗救助工作力度；稳妥推进城市医疗救助试点工作；积极抓好农村低保试点工作。

基层政权和城市社区建设工作初见成效。深入开展了村务公开和民主管理示范活动，在全区成功地进行了村民委员会换届选举，全区有1个县(市)被民政部命名为“全国村务公开示范市”，有2个城

港商向新疆灾区捐献御寒物品

社区各族群众踊跃捐款捐物

自治区党委常委肖开提·依明视察新疆福利彩票发行中心机房

自治区副主席贾帕尔·阿比布拉前往困难家庭了解情况

区被命名为“全国社区建设示范城区”，有7个县被命名为“全国村民自治示范县”；有8个县被命名为“自治区村民自治示范县”，有9个市（区）被命名为“自治区社区建设示范城区”。

双拥优抚安置工作向纵深发展。全区有12个县市先后18次被命名为全国双拥模范城(县)，有28个县市被命名为自治区双拥模范城(县)；在全区开展了“爱心献功臣行动”，为在乡老复员军人新建改建维修住房5万余间；落实优抚安置政策和军休人员安置政策。

民间组织管理工作得到加强。对社会团体进行了总量控制和结构调整，优先培育和发展为经济建设服务的行业性协会和社会中介组织，目前全区有各类社团约3200个，民办非企业单位达到1601家，已登记农民用水户协会559个。

社会福利和社会事务工作扎实推进。目前，全区有敬老院423所、社会福利院25所、精神病福利院7所、儿童福利院36所、SOS儿童村1所。组织实施了“星光计划”、“微笑列车”和“明天计划”。深化殡葬改革，做好救助管理工作和福利彩票发行工作。

区划地名工作稳步发展。完成了省区、地州、县(市)区、乡镇四级行政区域界线的勘界工作。完成了全疆城市地名设标工作。开展了公共地名服务工程工作。

自治区民政厅党组书记莫涓到南疆调研社会福利工作

自治区民政厅厅长吾买尔江·米孜艾合买提
在和田地区敬老院看望老人们

自治区人口和计划生育工作取得新进展

2007年，在自治区党委、政府的正确领导和大力支持下，我区人口和计划生育工作坚持推进综合改革，重点强化和完善利益导向机制，基层基础工作得到全面加强，全区人口出生率低于国家规定的控制指标。

新疆人口问题得到中央和自治区领导高度重视。温家宝总理在新疆视察时特别强调，要加大计划生育家庭奖励扶助力度，提高奖励扶助标准。王乐泉书记亲自带队专程赴北京与国家人口计生委商谈新疆人口计生工作。自治区召开高规格的人口和计划生育工作会议，国家人口计生委主任张维庆专程来疆参加会议并作关于落实中央《决定》的专题辅导。2007年至今年初，国家人口计生委5位领导先后来疆调研指导工作。自治区党委、政府先后5次听取人口计生工作汇报，研究解决人口计生工作的重大问题。

以财政资金为主渠道的人口计生事业经费投入大幅增长。国家发改委确定"十一五"期间对我区投入国债资金1.3

2008年1月7日，国家人口计生委在我区举行"三下乡"活动，自治区党委常委、自治区副主席努尔兰·阿不都满金与国家人口计生委主任李斌共同为"新家庭文化屋"揭牌

2008 年 2 月 27 日，自治区召开人口和计划生育工作会议，安排部署人口计生工作

亿元集中解决基层计划生育服务机构基础设施建设，现已投入资金 2985 万元。2007 年全区财政投入计划生育工作的经费达到 82690 余万元，比上年增长 59.2%。其中国家和自治区投入达 3.8 亿元，用于基层工作和落实惠民政策的资金达 94%以上。全区兑现农牧民奖励的资金总额达 2.69 亿元，农牧民领取计划生育光荣证家庭 2000 元兑现率达到 90%，提高 31.6 个百分点。

利益导向机制建设取得突破。初步形成以国家、自治区计划生育奖励政策为主体，各地计划生育奖励优惠优先政策为补充的计划生育利益导向政策体系。国家西部地区“少生快富”工程实施后，我区已有 9 万余户农村计划生育家庭得到一次性 3000 元奖励；南疆三地州实施农村计划生育家庭特殊奖励政策当年符合奖励条件的近 3 万户；全区享受国家农村部分计划生育家庭奖励扶助制度的人数达 46399 人；享受自治区农村独生子女死亡伤残救助政策有 2602 人；符合农村领证家庭子女升学加分政策的有 4672 人。2007 年全区领取《独生子女光荣证》和《计划生育光荣证》的家庭达 10.53 万户。

基层基础工作进一步巩固和加强。2007 年利用国债项目总投资 3195 万元，对 28 个县（市）计划生育服务站进行了改扩建；安排 780 万元经费专项补助地县计划生育服务站改扩建，对 56 个乡级服务站进行了改造。加强人口信息网络建设，全区有 10 个县（市）开展了数字化服务站试点，完成计算机“综合统计应用系统”，实现人口计生报表、流动人口计生报表网络直报。加强计生服务队伍建设，2007 年全区新增加技术服务人员 355 人，安排专业技术人员参加各类培训进修达 1895 人次。

2008 年 2 月 26 日，自治区人民政府副主席艾尔肯·吐尼亚孜到自治区人口计生委调研工作

2008 年 1 月 8 日，国家人口计生委在喀什启动《南疆三地州农村计划生育特殊奖励仪式》，使计划生育家庭得到更多实惠

新疆对外贸易实现跨越式发展

党的十六大以来，自治区外经贸厅坚持以邓小平理论和“三个代表”重要思想为指导，坚持用科学发展观统揽外经贸发展全局，以实施自治区党委提出的建设西部国际商贸中心战略为主线，充分发挥向西开放的区位优势，坚持“东联西出、西来东去”的方针，努力拓展中亚、西亚、俄罗斯、东欧等市场，着力推动外向型经济发展，促进外经贸实现持续、快速增长。

对外贸易持续快速增长。“十五”期间，全区进出口贸易额年均递增 28.5%，出口年均递增 33.2%。2005 年，全区实现进出口额 79.4 亿美元，比上年增长 40.9%；2006 年，全区进出口总额 91 亿美元，增长 14.6%，居全国第 16 位，比 2000 年上升了 6 位，居西部十二省区第二位。2007 年，全区完成进出口额 137.16 亿美元，增长 50.7%，高于全国平均增幅 27.2 个百分点。其中出口 115.03 亿美元，增长 61.1%；进口 22.13 亿美元，增长 12.7%。

（一）外经贸对全区经济社会发展的贡献和促进作用明显

自治区经济对外贸的依存度提高。自治区 GDP 对外贸依存度达 24.2%，其中出口达 19%。出口扩大增加了税收收入。据初步测算，2006 年自治区对外贸易实现税收 65 亿元人民币，其中：上交中央财政的税收为 54.3 亿元；上缴地方财政的税收为 10.7 亿元（其中 22.1 亿美元地产品出口实现的地方税收为 7.1 亿元），平均出口 1 美元实现地方财政收入 0.15 元。外向型企业的蓬勃兴起，促进了经济结构调整和产业技术升级，有力地支持了优势资源转换和新型工业化发展，对全区增加就业、繁荣市场、拉动内需和发展第三产业都发挥了重要作用。据统计，2006 年全区直接为进出口服务的人员达 28 万多人。

（二）进出口商品结构进一步优化，贸易质量和效益不断提高。

2006 年工业制成品出口比重达 93.3%。机电产品及高新技术产品出口 12.2 亿美元，同比增长 56.2%，占出口总额的17.1%。新疆当地生产的商品，如：石油石化产品、番茄制品、钢材、特种变压器、电线电缆、甲乙酮、太阳能发电设备、电子铝箔、玻璃钢管材、焦炭、建材等成为出口新的增长点。2006年地产品出口占出口总额的35%。

（三）不断扩大与周边国家经贸合作，促进了国家向西开放战略的实施

我区外经贸企业抓住近年来周边国家经济全面复苏，特别是哈萨克斯坦、俄罗斯等经济快速发展的机遇，通过多种方式拓展外经贸业务，实现了对周边国家贸易在高基数上的大幅增长。

2006年中国与中亚、俄罗斯等周边十国贸易额772亿美元，占当年中国进出口额的4.4%。2006年新疆与周边十国进出口额达79.6亿美元，占当年新疆进出口总额的87.5%。其中，对哈萨克斯坦进出口50.1亿美元，占全区贸易额的55%，占我国对哈贸易额的60%。

新疆从周边各国吸引外资发展势头看好，对外经济技术合作领域扩大。截止2006年，周边国家在新疆投资41项目，合同外资2860万美元，实际投资1032万美元。其中哈萨克斯坦在我区共投资31家企业，合同外资总额2747万美元，实际投资1030万美元。

新疆的对外经济技术合作和对外投资主要集中在哈萨克斯坦，合作领域扩大，石油、机电等行业成为对外工程承包的主力军。2006年，新疆与哈萨克斯坦的工程承包完成营业额8084万美元，占全区承包工程营业额的62%。新疆在哈萨克斯坦有30家境外投资企业，中方协议投资实现了结构调整的目标，由以往的贸易型公司到参与中亚地区的资源开发和利用国内成熟技术在中亚地区开展加工业，有力地促进经贸合作的深化和拓展。

就对哈贸易而言，新疆对哈贸易实现税收37.6亿元，其中：上交中央财政的税收为32亿元，上交地方财政的税收为5.6亿元，对哈贸易可提供14.8万个就业岗位。

新疆对外贸易为全国经济发展做出了贡献。我区出口商品中，地产品占35%，65%为外购产品。进口商品的80%多的消费市场在内地。我们依托国内大市场，大力拓展中亚等周边国家市场，出口拉动了内地沿海地区经济增长，进口满足了国内对能源原材料的旺盛需求，每年40多亿元的关税收入为国家税收增长做了努力。目前哈萨克斯坦各类基础建设已进入高潮，而我国的大型机械设备在技术和质量上已接近国际先进水平，但价格却远低于欧美、日韩等国家。我区一些外贸企业凭借多年与哈国开展贸易的经验，积极参与哈萨克斯坦基础设施建设招投标，从而带动工程设备等机电产品出口。引导企业努力扩大进口，促进了原油、废钢、各类矿砂、化肥、锌锭、铜、成品油、氧化铝、棉花、皮革等资源性产品进口的增长。2006年以资源性产品为主的初级产品进口占进口总额的40%。虽然新疆进出口额仅占全国进出口总额的0.56%，但新疆资源性产品进口在全国的重要性已日益显现出来，如新疆原油进口已居国内陆路口岸第二（第一为满洲里口岸）。

外经贸厅举办全疆外贸领导干部“人才强商”培训班

厅党组书记张野代表党组慰问贫困牧民

新疆维吾尔自治区旅游局

2007 年是我区旅游业实现“十一五”战略发展目标，加快旅游业发展极为重要的一年，在自治区党委、政府的正确领导和国家旅游局的有力指导下，全区旅游业认真落实科学发展观，紧密围绕胡锦涛总书记关于“把新疆建设成为中国西部旅游胜地”的重要指示精神和自治区党委、政府确立的“把旅游业培育成为自治区重要的支柱产业”的奋斗目标，把旅游工作与全面建设小康社会、构建和谐新疆紧密结合起来，主动服从和服务于自治区经济社会发展大局，自觉融入自治区经济社会发展全局，坚持科学发展，坚持改革开放，坚持统筹协调，坚持重点推进，使全区旅游业继续保持了旺盛的发展势头。入境旅游增幅明显，国内旅游发展强劲，出境旅游健康有序，假日旅游经济效益和社会效益显著增长，旅游环境和服务质量都有明显提高。圆满并超额完成了全年的工作任务。

2007 年，全区接待海外旅游者 43.84 万人次，创汇 1.62 亿美元，分别同比增长 20.96%和 26.48%。接待国内旅游者 2126 万人次，旅游收入 192.92 亿元人民币，同比分别增长 27.99%和 29.35%。全年累计接待游客总数达 2170 万人次，旅游总收入 205.27 亿元人民币。

截止 2007 年底，全区已有旅行社 426 家(自治区 314 家，兵团 12 家)，其中国际旅行社 51 家，国内旅行社 375 家，旅游星级饭店 403 家，其中五星级 8 家，在全国省会城市中名列前位，客房 3.7 万余间，床位数 6.8 万余张；旅游景区(点)468 个，国家 A 级景区 152 家；持证导游员 9425 人，(其中兵团 1668 人)，汉族导游员 7917 人，少数民族导游员 1508 人；全国工农业旅游示范点 34 家(工业旅游示范点 13 爱，农业旅游示范点 21 家)；旅游

中共中央政治局委员、自治区党委书记王乐泉会见我区首批获得国家 5A 级景区代表

原自治区党委副书记、自治区主席司马义·铁力瓦尔地考察新疆国际大巴扎

自治区党委副书记、自治区主席努尔·白克力等领导同志参加2008年自治区旅游工作会议并会见先进个人代表

国家旅游局邵琪伟局长在自治区副主席胡伟陪同下参观天池景区

自治区党委副书记、自治区政协主席艾斯海提·克里木拜出席自治区旅游局成立三十周年座谈会并与先进代表合影留念

自治区副主席胡伟在自治区旅游局和吐鲁番地区领导陪同下调研吐鲁番旅游业发展情况

股份公司7家，优秀旅游城市13座，旅游汽车5800多辆；设有旅游专业的高等院校17家，旅游学院3家，中等专科学校20家，旅游规划设计资质单位19家；旅游直接从业人员16万人，间接从业人员65万人。

2008年要以邓小平理论和“三个代表”重要思想为强大思想动力，以科学发展观统领旅游发展全局，深入贯彻党的“十七大”精神和国发32号文件精神，按照把新疆建设成为“中国西部旅游胜地”和把新疆旅游业建设成为自治区重要支柱产业的奋斗目标，强化精神建设，狠抓品牌促销，深化行业改革，加强工作指导，着力提升旅游经济运行质量，促进旅游市场繁荣发展，全面增强产业素质、努力推动全区旅游业又好又快发展。

自治区党委副书记、自治区主席努尔·白克力等领导同志参加2008年自治区旅游工作会议

时任自治区党委副书记，自治区主席司马义·铁力瓦尔地接见民族团结进步模范个人和集体代表

2007 年 10 月 13 日，自治区副主席库热西·买合苏提，自治区民委(宗教局)党组书记刘振强等共同点点燃第八届全国民运会新疆传递火炬

开展民族团结教育活动 推进民族团结进步事业

民族团结是新疆各族人民的生命线，是做好一切工作的根本前提和保证。自 1983 年以来，自治区连续二十五年开展“民族团结教育月”活动，并做到有计划、有动员、有检查、有总结，年年有新内容，年年有新发展。在民族团结教育月中，利用各种形式，向各族干部群众大力宣传加强民族团结、反对民族分裂的重要意义，宣传党的民族政策和国家法律法规，努力把民族团结教育纳入全民道德教育和社会主义精神文明建设全过程，与为群众办好事、办实事结合起来，使“三个离不开”的思想深入人心，增强了各族干部群众珍惜和维护民族团结的坚定性和自觉性，进一步增强了军政、军民、民族团结。为促进民族团结教育具体化、经常化、制度化和规范化，广泛开展了创建民族团结模范单位、民族团结大院、民族团结家庭和军民共建、警民共建、工农共建、地方与兵团共建等多种形式的民族团结创建活动，大力表彰宣传涌现出来的先进典型。1982 年以来，自治区先后 4 次、各地各单位也多次召开了民族团结进步表彰大会。目前，全区受到国务院、国家民委、自治区三级表彰的民族团结进步模范单位 821 个(次)，模范个人 1368 人(次)。自 1998 年起，在国家民委的支持下，自治区先后组织 9 批民族团结进步模范代表赴发达地区考察学习，取得了很好的效果。通过大量工作，维护了民族和睦、宗教和顺、社会和谐，为各民族共同团结奋斗，共同繁荣发展，创设了良好的社会环境。

2007 年 1 月 29 日，在中国少数民族和民族地区综合扶贫示范项目新疆项目区第一期培训班上，自治区民委(宗教局)党组书记刘振强等陪同国家民委项目办主任铁木尔参观手工艺品展

2007 年 5 月，自治区民族团结模范参观团在内地参观考察

黄文玉局长带队（左二）到北疆塔城、博乐等地调研

加帕尔副局长（左六）带队到吐库二线铁路施工现场勘察，为自治区铁路建设提供通信保障

围绕一个“中心”，突出两个“重点”，落实三个“坚持”

为实现全区电信行业又好又快发展保驾护航

2007年是实施电信业“十一五”规划的重要一年。新疆维吾尔自治区通信管理局以邓小平理论和“三个代表”重要思想为指导，认真贯彻自治区和原信息产业部各项工作部署，落实科学发展观和构建社会主义和谐社会的目标要求，围绕“深入贯彻十六届六中全会精神，团结和带领全行业为构建和谐新疆做出积极贡献”这个中心，突出抓好“通信服务质量”、“网络与信息安全”两个重点，坚持科学管理，加强队伍和作风建设，提高整体素质，适应形势发展和任务要求；坚持以人为本、监管为民，营造公平有序的市场竞争环境，着力解决人民群众关注的热点问题；坚持依法行政，推进电信业战略转型，保障我区电信行业实现又好又快发展。

2007年，全区电信业务总量完成293.6亿元，同比增长33.7%，电信业务收入完成103.2亿元，增长13.1%。固定资产投资完成41.1亿元。电信综合资费水平较上年下降15.5%，五年下降60.9%。非话业务收入比例达到30.6%。全区固定电话用户达到696.2万户，移动电话用户达到808.3万户，互联网用户达到157.8万户。固定电话普及率达到33.7部/百人，移动电话普及率达到39.4部/百人。全年实现新增通电话的自然村289个，兵团连队、牧业点、边防点等845个；新增45个乡镇、426个行政村开通了宽带互联网。

新疆电信行业“诚信服务放心消费”活动拉开序幕

与自治区外宣办、教育厅联合举办“让信息通信技术惠及下一代”活动

新疆维吾尔自治区招商发展局

2007年3月19日，自治区党委副书记、自治区政协主席艾斯海提·克里木拜点击开通新疆招商网

2007年3月19日，自治区人大常委会主任艾力更·依明巴海为自治区区外投资企业服务中心成立揭牌

奠基

新疆维吾尔自治区招商发展局（新疆维吾尔自治区人民政府经济技术协作办公室）主要负责我区招商引资等相关政策法规及实施办法的研究、起草、修订、解释、督查和协调落实；负责全区招商引资、经济技术协作运行情况的监测、调研、考核评价和综合分析；协调和服务全区招商引资和经济技术协作工作；负责外省（区、市）政府和大型企业驻疆办事机构管理工作；研究提出招商引资重点产业和重点项目；组织或参与重大招商引资项目论证工作等。

2006年自治区招商发展局在自治区党委和政府的正确领导下，积极开展区域合作与招商引资工作，取得丰硕成果。全区共引进区外企业投资项目到位资金510.38亿元，比上年增长23.16%，占全社会固定资产投资的31.99%；实际利用外资3.01亿美元，增长29.6%。

新疆与内地党政高层互访频繁，有力推动了区域经济合作与发展。自治区党政主要领导先后率团到北京、上海、江苏、广东等省市考察和招商，促成和签订了一批合作项目。韩国SK、美国迪尔、中粮集团等19家世界500强企业落户新疆；仅招商系统就引进苏宁电器、大连实德、浙江华孚等国内知名企业21家。

通过举办乌洽会、旅交会、华凌国际建材博览会、喀交会等区内会展活动，吸引内地省市及企业参与新疆开发。2006年乌洽会，上海、天津、山东、河南、山西等30个省区组团参加，签订内联合作项目和内贸合同790.21亿元，较上届增长32.39%。

上海、天津、山东等10个省市政府在新疆设立了办事处，各地企业先后在新疆建立了浙江、福建、广东等10家企业联合会（商会），成为推进区域合作的重要组织形式。

自治区招商局书记姚建新在第十一届中国东西部合作投资贸易洽谈会签字仪式上致开幕词

部分知名企业家汇聚新疆座谈会

认真贯彻落实党的十七大精神　努力提升食品药品监管工作水平

自治区食品药品监督管理局

自治区食药监局党组书记于胜德同志在策勒县人民政府领导陪同下考察零售药店。

2007年4月，新疆维吾尔自治区食品药品监管局党组书记于胜德在和静县利华食品厂调研。

自治区食品药品监督管理局，是自治区人民政府的直属机构，肩负着全区药品、医疗器械、药包材的研究、生产、流通、使用全过程的监管和食品、保健品、化妆品安全管理的综合监督、组织协调及依法组织对重大安全事故查处的职责。2007年，在自治区党委、政府领导下，区局党组团结带领全系统广大干部职工认真贯彻党的十七大精神，落实科学发展观，实践科学监管理念，深入开展食品药品专项整治行动，为保障公众饮食用药安全、构建和谐新疆做出了积极贡献。

一年来，集中力量对药品医疗器械研制、生产、流通、使用环节和广告开展全方位整治，共查获假药173个品种、计9147瓶（盒），查处案件3992起，罚没款1238.8万元，移送司法机关9起13人，整治规模、力度和成效是前所未有的。通过整治，全面完成了780个药品批准文号清理工作，“一药多名”问题得到有效治理；严厉打击查处从非法渠道购进药品等严重违反GMP、GSP违法违规行为，依法收回GMP证书2个、GSP证书73家，取缔无证挂靠经营92家，责令限期改正2164家，药品生产经营秩序明显好转；向工商部门移送违法广告998件，对18种虚假广告药品采取暂停销售和下架处理的行政强制措施，违法药品广告与整治初期相比下降了80%，主流媒体播发公众人物代言药品广告基本消除；全年药品监督抽验的不合格率达27.9%，同比提高了12.5个百分点，药品抽验针对性、靶向性和技术性显著提高；农村药品药品供应网和监督网覆盖率分别达到92.86%和98.93%，农牧区药品质量状况明显改善，药价平均降幅10%～20%，最高达30%，以现代物流业为主渠道的农村药品供应网正在形成。

我们积极履行食品安全“三项职能”，加强食品安全综合监管，高位推进食品安全责任制的落实，以“食品放心工程”为重点，开展综合评价、食品安全信用体系建设试点和食品安全示范县创建工作，全年各级监管部门查处各类食品违法案件5002起、货值1.1亿元，取缔无照经营1万余家，捣毁制假售假窝点97个，食品安全形势明显好于往年，消费者满意度达到合格等级。

我们积极推进依法行政，制定《行政执法评议考核标准》等10余项制度，47项行政审批事项全部实现了受理、认证、审批三分离，形成了执法有依据、行为有规范、权力有制约、过程有监控、违法有追究的行政执法责任体系。区局被评为自治区依法行政先进单位；我们以推进“作风建设年”为契入点，加强干部队伍思想政治建设，着力解决“为谁监管、怎样监管”的问题，提升了监管效能和质量。加大干部交流和培训力度，为监管事业发展注入了新的活力。坚持标本兼治，强化监督，党风廉政建设进一步加强，15个单位被评为自治区“行风建设示范窗口”单位；围绕创建自治区“文明行业”，加强精神文明建设，全系统各级文明单位创建率达100%，地区级文明行业3个，自治区级文明单位45个。

在新的一年中，我们将迎来改革开放30周年和举世瞩目的北京奥运会，大事多，喜事多，食品药品监管的任务十分繁重和艰巨。面对新形势新任务，我们将深入贯彻落实党的十七大精神，全面落实科学发展观，大力实践科学监管理念，求真务实，创新监管思路和方法，巩固提高专项整治成果，着力解决监管中的难点问题，建立完善食品药品安全长效机制，推进“十一五”规划的实施，以勤政建设为重点，抓好各级班子、队伍的作风建设，扎实推进精神文明建设，加大反腐倡廉力度，努力把食品药品监管工作提高到新的水平，为北京奥运会的成功举办、促进自治区经济社会又好又快发展创造良好的食品药品安全环境。

新疆维吾尔自治区道路运输管理局

自治区道路运输管理局党组书记任存新（左三）到基层调研。

道路运输是国民经济的基础产业，由于我区独特的地理环境，决定了道路运输在我区综合运输体系中的主导地位。截止2007年底，全区机动车保有量195万辆，其中民用汽车保有辆82万辆。经营性客货运输车辆25.03万辆，比上年增长13.88%，其中经营性客车4.42万辆、经营性货车20.61万辆，分别比上年增长9.15%、14.94%；全区共有道路运输经营业户78265户，比上年增长15.83%，其中拥有客运经营业户6664户、货运经营业户65880户、客运站573个、货运站（场）506个，国际道路运输经营企业66家、机动车维修业户7601户、机动车驾驶员培训学校265所、其他经营业户511户。从事营业性道路运输及相关人数已达45万人。随着我区经济的蓬勃发展，道路运输在自治区经济建设中显示出越来越重要的作用。

新疆维吾尔自治区道路运输管理局是新疆道路运输行业的管理部门，负责全区道路旅客运输、货物运输、道路运输相关业务、国际道路运输管理等工作。其主要职责是执行国家和自治区有关道路运输行业的方针、政策、法规和规章，制定相应的规定和办法，负责行业的调查研究、分析预测、信息交流、拟定道路运输市场发展规划，搞好宏观调控，对道路运输市场进行监督检查。近几年，道路运输管理局在自治区交通厅的领导下，以道路运输发展为第一要务，以实现全区道路运输业的全面、协调、可持续发展为目标，开拓创新，求真务实，全面落实道路运输科学发展观，着力提高道路运输服务保障能力、依法行政和市场监管能力、运输安全监督管理和运输应急处置能力，使道路运输各项工作取得了显著的成绩。道路运输生产大幅上升，道路运输有效供给能力明显提升；道路运输市场基础设施得以改善，各种运输方式迅速发展，道路运输公共服务能力明显提高；对外交流取得显著成效，国际道路运输生产持续大幅增长；依法行政和市场监管能力明显提高，为民服务意识明显增强；道路运输应急处置体系初步建立，应对突发性事件能力得以提升；道路运输文明行业创建工作取得丰硕成果。

整齐待发的长途客车

新疆维吾尔自治区妇女联合会

自治区妇联党组书记王建玲（右一）在哈密调研基层组织建设情况

在自治区党委、政府的正确领导下，自治区妇联紧紧围绕全区的工作大局，坚持统筹协调促进发展，完善机制强化维权，倾情服务关爱儿童，借力运作扩大宣传，关注民生热心公益，夯实基础增强能力，扎实工作，开拓进取，积极为全面建设小康社会、构建社会主义和谐新疆贡献力量。

2007年，自治区妇联以促进农村妇女增收致富和城镇妇女就业创业为重点，围绕“三农”问题，不断拓展农民增收致富途径，积极争取政策、协调资源、搭建平台、提供服务，为妇女增收致富搭建平台。创新发展“三学三比”竞赛活动，推动妇女小额信贷促增收、农牧区妇女劳动力转移就业、城镇妇女创业就业等工作，推动形成了城乡互动、统筹发展、共同进步的妇女工作发展格局，营造城乡妇女发展的良好环境。同时，自治区妇联把维护好、实现好、发展好妇女群众的利益作为参与构建和谐新疆的切入点，发挥职能，在加大源头参与、畅通妇女儿童诉求表达渠道、有效调处妇女儿童权益问题、推动“两纲”实施等方面取得了新突破。把建设社会主义核心价值体系的要求贯穿于妇女和家庭群众性精神文明创建活动之中，加强未成年人思想道德建设，推动家庭教育工作取得新进步，积极开展公益活动，服务于各族妇女群众，在引导各族妇女群众在倡导和谐精神、弘扬文明风尚和维护民族团结、社会稳定中发挥了积极作用。

自治区妇联妇联副主席郑平（左三）在和田调研家庭暴力情况

自治区妇联副主席库来惜·阿不都拉（左三）在伊犁调研妇女参与新农村建设情况

自治区残联在自治区党委,人民政府的正确领导和中国残联的有力指导下,认真贯彻党的十七大精神,及全国第二十次残疾人工作会议和自治区党代会精神,各项工作开局良好。圆满完成了年初制定的工作任务。

牢固树立和落实为本,全面、协调、可持续的科学发展观,以构建社会主义和谐新疆,全面推进我区残疾人事业又好又快地发展为目标,团结奋进,研拓进取,经全区残疾系统广大干部职工和广大残疾人的共同努力,我区残疾事业长远发展的重点工作相继启动实施或顺利完成。

继续实施了为期三年的“视觉第一中国行动”项目,免费为一万名贫困白内障患者实施复明手术的“彭年光明行动”项目,2006 年,完成白内障复明手术 11000 例,其中免费为贫困白内障患者实施 3217 例,分别完成国家下达任务的 107.8%和 200%。为 250 名低视力者佩带了助听器并进行视力功能训练,完成任务的 147%。培训低视力儿童家长 85 名,完成任务的 167%,新建低视力康复部 2

自治区残疾人联合会

中共中央政治局委员、自治区党委书记王乐泉亲切接见参加全国特奥会的运动员,教练员。

自治区人民政府副主席,自治区人民政府残疾人工作委员会主任贾帕尔·阿比布拉亲临赛场看望特奥运动会,教练员。

我区残疾人运动员在各届运动会上取得了丰硕的成果,在第九届“远南”残疾人运动会中,我区 5 名运动员共夺得 10 金 1 银 1 铜,刷新了我区运动员在国际大赛中取得金牌总数的纪录;在荷兰世界残疾人体育运动会上取得 1 金 3 银;组团参加了在哈尔滨举办的第四届全国特奥运动会,获 7 金,11 银,12 铜的好成绩。

自治区第四届残疾人运动会暨首届特奥会在首府乌鲁木齐隆重开幕

个。

在市辖区新建康复站 4 个，县（市）康复站 12 个，全年各级残联完成肢体残疾人康复训练 201 名，培训智力残疾儿童家长 168 名。

深入残疾人就业服务，全区共安排城镇残疾人就业 1863 人，残疾人职业技能培训工作取得了可喜的成绩，培训各类残疾人 13508 人，将义务教育阶段的残疾学生全部纳入了自治区“两免一补”政策范围，近万名残疾学生和残疾人家庭子女得到资助。

自治区残联在新的一年里继续发扬团结协作，奋发进取的精神，把我区的残疾人工作不断向前推进，为构建和谐新疆做出更大的贡献。

自治区人大常委会主任艾力更·依明巴海在刘林亭理事长的陪同下慰问新市区贫困残疾人家庭

自治区残联党组书记、理事长刘林亭在托克逊县慰问贫困残疾人生活情况

自治区残疾人体育训练基地在奎屯体育中心挂牌成立

开展第七次全国爱耳日活动

“彭年光明行动”启动仪式在首府乌鲁木齐市举行

原中共中央政治局
常委宋平在题词

新疆地矿局第一地质大队

新疆地矿局第一地质大队于1964年在四川建队，转战湘、川、滇，1976年响应地质部号召奉调进疆，1982年划归新疆地矿局，专业从事地质勘查和工程勘查，先后发现并评价各类大、中、小型矿产地166处，是一支特别能吃苦、特别能战斗、特别能出成果的功勋地质队。所荣获的地矿部和国家有关部委颁发的地质找矿和科技成果奖30余次，荣获了“全国地质勘察功勋单位”称号，2005年光荣的跨入了首批“全国文明单位”行列，2006年获得了“全国五一劳动”奖状。

进疆以来，大队扎跟火焰山脚底，历经三十余年的洗礼，在荒无人烟的戈壁建起了一个集勘查开发、生产科研于一体的现代地质苑。上个世纪80年代至90年代初期，由第一地质大队完成的吐哈聚煤田盆地和准噶尔南部煤田西段的煤田远景调查，取得了丰硕的地质成果，其中吐哈煤田位列世界十大煤田之中，准噶尔煤田成为自治区煤电煤化工产业的主要能源基地。进入地质工作体制改革以来，第一地质大队主动转变思路，谋求发展，在固体矿产资源勘查迈出了成功的步伐，取得了一批如伊宁市阿希特大型金矿、哈密市土屋特大型铜矿、鄯善县维权大型银铜矿、哈密市裤子山大型钾盐矿、昌吉市萨日达拉大型金矿、鄯善县彩霞山大型铅锌矿的重大找矿成果，2005年又在鄯善县境内发现世界级钠硝石矿产地。

第一地质大队坚持实施“人才强队、科技兴企”战略，走出了一条“勘查开发一体化，探采工贸一条龙”的经营之路。经济壮大的同时积极融入地域经济发展，先后投资市政基础设施、社会主义新农村、交通电力、中小学校舍等工程建设，取得了良好的社会效益。

近年来，大队继续解放思想，与时俱进，先后与神华集团、国投公司、中国万向集团、新华联公司、中亚华金公司、山东鲁能集团、宝钢集团新疆八一钢铁公司等疆内外“大企业、大集团”合作开发矿产资源，为自治区实施优势资源转换战略，促进新疆经济“大开发、大发展”，走新型工业化道路作出重要贡献。

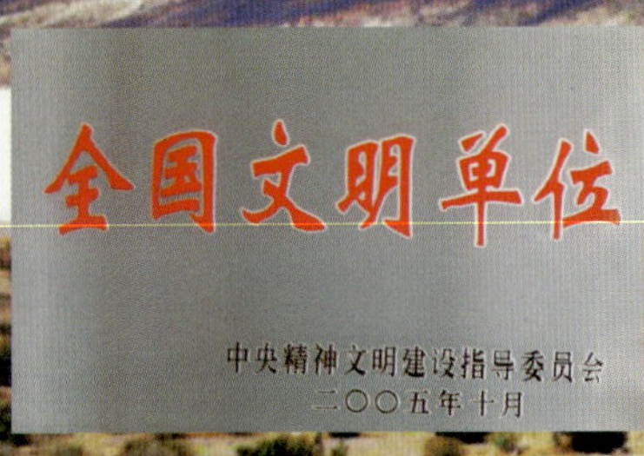

进疆以来评价的特大型阿希金矿勘探全景

中共中央政治局委员、自治区党委书记王乐泉来队检查工作

自治区党委常委、自治区副主席努尔兰·阿不都满金来队检查工作

落实十七大精神到基层

团结奋进的领导班子

坚持科学发展观　发展公益性文化事业

新疆维吾尔自治区图书馆始建于 1930 年 8 月，原名新疆省立图书馆。1949 年新中国成立，改名为新疆省人民图书馆。1955 年新疆维吾尔自治区成立，正式定名为新疆维吾尔自治区图书馆。在自治区党委和政府的关怀下，自治区图书馆事业得到了不断的发展和壮大。1999 年 10 月 23 日，图书馆新馆大楼竣工开始。

新馆坐落于乌鲁木齐环境幽雅的北京路上，总建筑面积 24700 平方米，可容纳藏书 300 万册，阅览席位 2500 个。经过长期建设与积累，新疆维吾尔自治区图书馆已形成了以少数民族文献及新疆地方文献为特色藏书体系。目前，共有纸质文献 110 余万册，其中汉文普通图书 60 万册，少数民族文献 12 万册、外文图书 21 万册、古籍图书 8 万册、少儿图书 10 万册，报纸期刊近 3000 种。电子图书 20 万册。

2007 年是该馆各项工作，特别是业务建设得到深入拓展的重要时期。该馆以深化改革为动力，以不断提高创新能力为保障，以全面构建和谐社会为目标，坚持科学发展观，坚持“求真务实”的馆训、“读者之上，服务第一”的宗旨和“建章立制抓管理，提高素质抓服务；开门办馆抓规模，开发资源抓效益；求真务实讲奉献，拓展思路求发展”的办馆方针，使图书馆事业得到了新发展。在全年工作中提出了“坚持一条主线、一个标准、达到两个提高、完成六项任务”的工作思路：即以争创文明单位为主线；以“全国省级公共图书馆评估达标工作”为标准；提高基础业务水平、提高员工整体素质；重点完成评估达标准备工作、资源加工任务、古籍保护普查工作、读书进社区工程、发展读者工作、理论科研工作。经过不懈的努力，2007 年度该馆圆满完成了各项工作任务，荣获了文化厅系统先进基层党组织、文化厅系统先进集体、综合治理先进单位、全民读书月活动先进单位等光荣称号，汉文流通部和少数民族文献部荣获自治区“五一文明岗”。

宽敞明亮的图书馆大厅

新疆维吾尔自治区有色地质勘查局

召开地质立项会

新疆维吾尔自治区有色地质勘查局是集地质调查、矿产勘查、地理物理勘查、地球化学勘查、测量、科研、综合测试、矿业开发为一体的综合地质勘查队伍。全局拥有固体矿产勘查甲级资质四个，物化探甲级资质一个，国家级化验室一个。全局现有 9 个基层单位，分别为 701 队、703 队、704 队、705 队、706 队、物探队、地研所、测试中心、地勘院，分布在乌鲁木齐市、昌吉市、哈密市、阿勒泰市、伊犁、库车等地。

局长杨有明（右二）在南疆大青山考察

2007 年是我局各项工作取得显著成绩的一年。全局各族干部职工紧密围绕有色集团公司资源控制战略，开拓进取，努力工作，全年完成国家投资地质项目 19 项，总费用 3678.69 万元，承揽商业地质项目 70 项，合同金额达 10709 万元，并取得了一批重要的地质成果。产业经济不断发展，经济效益明显提高，全年实现利润 1546.42 万元。精神文明建设稳步推进，创建“文明单位“活动再结硕果，全面实现了局 2007 年工作会议确定的各项工作目标。这些成果的取得，既是各级党政领导高度的责任心和使命感的体现，更是广大干部职工辛勤工作的结果。

党委书记徐华工（左三）在琼吉项目组考察

我局自成立以来共找到有色、黑色、稀有、贵金属等矿床 120 处，其中举世闻名的可可托海三号脉稀有金属矿，为我国稀有金属的生产和国防事业的发展作出了重大贡献。近年来我局先后勘探发现了阿勒泰地区可可塔勒铅锌矿、蒙库铁矿、博乐地区喇嘛苏铜矿、喀什地区的契列克其铁矿，特别是近年来又在哈密图拉尔根地区发现并探明一处较大型铜镍矿，在托里县包谷图地区发现了斑岩型铜矿，在布尔津县发现了铜锌矿。五十年来，我局探明的矿产储量黑色金属 3.7 亿吨，有色金属 300 余万吨，稀有金属 30 多万吨，非金属 3 亿多吨。为新疆的地质找矿事业和实施资源转换战略及经济发展作出了重要贡献。

近几年，我局积极拓展视野，加强对外技术合作和项目合作，分别与加拿大、澳大利亚、吉尔吉斯等国的矿业公司建立了合作关系。2005 年在吉尔吉斯组建了铁岭矿业公司，这是我区跨出国门找矿的第一支队伍，得到了自治区和国家有关部门的高度重视。

邮传万里 信达天下

腾飞奋起的乌鲁木齐邮区中心局

乌鲁木齐邮区中心局是中国邮政集团公司确定的新疆境内的二级中心局，1999 年 5 月成立以来，一直致力于建设适应区域经济发展和市场竞争需要的紧密衔接的快速邮运网，为全疆各族人民提供优质快捷的通信服务。

自治区党委常委、纪委书记符强等一行在 3.8 前夕看望慰问日夜奋战在邮运生产一线的劳模

在新疆邮政公司的关心指导下，9 年多来乌鲁木齐邮区中心局外树形象，提升企业竞争力；内强素质，激发职工创新力，将“持续优化”原则凝聚在企业管理的各个方面，大力推行生产管理扁平化、作业流程标准化、生产操作规范化的“三化”改革，全面推行生产现场“8S”管理，促进了生产力的发展。截止目前，汽车邮路已达 20 条幅射全疆；火车邮路 9 条，通达全国 34 个直辖市、省会、自治区首府；航空干线邮路 37 条，通航全国 28 个大中城市，已基本形成了火车、汽车、航空运输功能齐全，分拣封发快速高效，与全国邮政网紧密衔接通达全国 34 个大中城市的集散立体运输网。

乘着邮政体制改革的春风，踏着经济蓬勃发展的前进步伐，历经市场激烈竞争的风雨洗礼，乌鲁木齐邮区中心局散发出前所未有的青春活力和蓬勃生机。在全国“安康杯”竞赛中乌鲁木齐邮区中心局连续 5 年夺冠；连续 8 年保持自治区级文明单位，2006－2007 年连续两年获得全国通信行业质量管理活动推进优秀企业，T69/70 次邮车连续 8 年荣获全国文明邮车称号。

邮传万里，信达天下，一肩承担国家赋予的圣神光荣使命，乌鲁木齐邮区中心局英姿勃发，昂首阔步，风劲扬帆正当时！

持续挖潜、持续改造、不断创新的交叉带磁悬浮自动包裹分拣机

散发出蓬勃生机青春活力的邮政员工风采

折射人文关爱的乌鲁木齐邮区中心局员工茶吧开业

繁忙的阿拉山口口岸

州党委书记、人大常委会主任史少林（左三）、州党委副书记、州长奥曲尔（右二）调研温泉县冷水鱼加工产业

博尔塔拉蒙古自治州

中国优秀旅游城市——博乐市

博州位于新疆西北部，与哈萨克斯坦共和国接壤，总面积2.7万平方公里，辖博乐市、精河县、温泉县、阿拉山口口岸行政管理区、赛里木湖风景名胜区管理区，境内驻有新疆生产建设兵团农五师及其所属11个团场。全州有蒙古、汉、维吾尔、哈萨克、回等35个民族，总人口47.29万人，少数民族占33%。“博尔塔拉”系蒙古语，意为“青色的草原”，其悠久的历史可上溯到春秋战国时期。全州水土光热资源丰富，宜农、宜牧、宜林、宜渔，是全国枸杞生产基地、全国冷水鱼育种生产基地和全疆重要的优质棉出口基地。全州已探明矿种39种，其中石灰岩、石英岩、湖盐、芒硝、花岗岩、铜、钨、钼、地热等矿产资源尤为丰富。旅游资源种类齐全，风光秀丽。著名的自然风景有：国家重点风景名胜区、国家湿地公园赛里木湖，中国西部最后一片净土夏尔西里自然保护区，亚洲规模最大的怪石群、国家AAAA级景区哈布图哈怪石峪等。新疆三大旅游节之一——博尔塔拉“那达慕”草原节在传承蒙古族传统文化的同时，不断融入汉、维吾尔、哈萨克等民族文化，精彩纷呈，每年吸引着数万游客。

多年来，在党的民族区域自治政策的光辉照耀下，博州始终保持着政治稳定、经济发展、民族团结、边防巩固、社会不断进步的良好局面。随着国家一类口岸——阿拉山口口岸铁路、公路、管道运输能力的不断提升和基础设施功能的不断完善，博州由封闭的西部边陲，一跃成为向西开放连接中亚和欧洲的最前沿，成为国家资源能源陆路安全大通道和重要的交通枢纽。

海内存知己，天涯若比邻。一个物华天宝、人杰地灵的博州，热忱欢迎五湖四海的宾客前来观光旅游、投资创业，我们会以更加宽松的环境、更加优惠的政策、更加高效的服务，与您精诚合作，共谋发展。

迷人的赛里木湖

龟兹故地、西域精萃

柔美的龟兹乐舞

水韵之城、人居最佳的阿克苏市一角

库车县石化工业园区夜景

蓬勃发展的棉纺织业

阿克苏地委书记朱昌杰(右一)、阿克苏地区行政公署专员吉尔拉·伊萨姆丁(左一)陪同自治区党委常委朱海仑视察社会稳定工作

阿克苏地区位于新疆天山南麓、塔里木盆地北缘,东经 78° 03′ 至 84° 07′,北纬 39° 30′ 至 42° 41′ 间,总面积 13.25 万平方公里。全地区辖库车、沙雅、新和、拜城、温宿、阿瓦提、乌什、柯坪 8 个县和阿克苏市。新疆生产建设兵团农一师及所属阿拉尔市和 16 个团场分布在地区境内。总人口 231.02 万人,由 36 个民族组成,是一个以维吾尔族为主体的多民族聚居地区。

阿克苏地区气候宜人,水草丰茂,农牧业发达,是我国重要长绒棉和优质商品棉生产基地,是全疆最大的绒山羊基地和品质最好的细毛羊基地,也是“中国白杏之乡”、“中国红富士之乡”和新疆薄皮核桃、红枣及香梨等优质特色果品的主产区。阿克苏地区石油天然气资源十分丰富,目前在地区境内已探明的油气资源占环塔里木盆地油气总量的 88.58%和 93%以上。煤炭储量 109.6 亿吨,占南疆已探明储量的 90%以上;水能资源理论蕴藏量为 379.28 万千瓦,可开发水能资源为 220.307 万千瓦。矿产资源丰富,探明储量的矿产 46 种,矿产资源潜在价值达 1.75 万亿元。阿克苏地区区位优势明显。随着阿

——阿克苏

豪迈的多浪文化

拉尔市至和田第二条沙漠公路的全线通车，乌什口岸开放顺利推进，阿克苏、库车机场改扩建完成，阿克苏地区在南疆交通枢纽中的关键地位将进一步突出。

近年来，地区提出了以经济建设为中心，大力实施以市场为导向的优势资源转换战略，深入推进“6122”工程建设，即：“六大基地、一个旅游目的地、两座龙头城市和两大文化品牌”。具体说就是：努力把阿克苏建成新疆的重要石油化工基地、煤电基地、煤焦化基地、棉产业基地、以红枣、核桃为主的优质果品基地和优质商品粮基地，提升地区产业化、工业化水平；在整合旅游资源基础上，改善旅游设施，加大旅游宣传，努力打造阿克苏“龟兹故地、西域精萃”的整体形象，使地区成为新疆乃至我国西部知名度较高的重要旅游目的地；重点抓好阿克苏市和库车两座“龙头城市”建设，使之成为地区东西两大区域经济辐射中心，提升地区城市化水平；重点挖掘、整理、研究、宣传、打造“龟兹文化”、“多浪文化”两大地方特色文化品牌，提升地区文化品位。

地区各族人民在地委、行署的正确领导下，以邓小平理论和“三个代表”重要思想为指导，全面落实科学发展观，继续大力推进“6122”工程建设，地区国民经济保持了持续、健康、快速、协调发展，实现了“十一五”的良好开局。预计地区生产总值386.5亿元（含一师和石油开采作业区），同比增长18.1%。地方生产总值174.4亿元，同比增长13.9%，其中第一产业完成增加值54.8亿元，增长8%，第二产业完成增加值48.9亿元，增长20.5%，第三产业完成增加值70.7亿元，增长14.7%，三次产业结构比为31.41:28.02:40.57。万元生产总值能耗降低4.7%，二氧化硫和化学需氧量排放完成年度减排目标。地方财政收入29.23亿元，同比增长41.07%，其中一般预算收入25.58亿元，同比增长37.83%；地方财政支出57.06亿元，同比增长33.04%。完成固定资产投资89.90亿元，同比增长19.2%。农牧民人均纯收入3868元、增加483元，城镇居民人均可支配收入10036元。这些成就表明，地区在全面建设小康社会的征途上又迈出了坚实的一步。

阿克苏地区优质红枣基地

阿克苏地区优质红富士苹果基地

军垦新城

阿拉尔市市委书记、人大主任刘向松（右二）与阿拉尔市委副书记、市长王平海（右一）规划阿拉尔市政建设

阿拉尔市位于塔里木河上游南北两岸，维吾尔语意为“绿色的岛屿”。2002 年 9 月，经国务院批复设立为自治区县级直辖市，2004 年 1 月 19 日正式挂牌。行政区划面积 4196 平方公里，城市中心区规划面积 21 平方公里，辖 10 个团、2 个处、1 个乡等 120 余家单位，总人口 20 余万人。S207 省道阿（克苏）塔（里木）公路与 314 国道和南疆铁路相接，阿和（田）、阿图（木舒克）、阿沙（雅）、玉（尔滚）阿公路汇集于此，使阿拉尔市成为南疆地区重要的交通枢纽。

屯垦 50 年来，阿拉尔已成为棉、粮、果、畜、水产品综合产区，尤以盛产优质棉著称。“塔里木河”牌棉种荣获“中国名牌”，“新农”牌棉花先后评为“中国棉花市场公认十佳畅销品牌”和“新疆著名商标”，年产皮棉 20 万吨左右，生产的长绒棉占国家出口总量的一半以上。“天山雪”米荣获“中国最具市场竞争力品牌”称号；香梨、灰枣等优质果品，曾荣获全国农业博览会金奖；“天山雪”蟹获国家绿色有机食品认证。“新农开发”、“塔河种业”等农业产业化龙头企业全面带动了现代农业发展。

阿拉尔市文化公园

建设中的阿拉尔市富苑商住小区

通车后的自治区第二条沙漠公路：阿拉尔至和田沙漠公路

——阿拉尔市

鸟瞰阿拉尔市

阿拉尔市是兵团新建3座城市之一。城市建设充分体现“大绿地、大水面、大空间”的现代城建时尚，城市总体规划获自治区一等奖。围绕“西部棉业纺织城、南疆农副产品加工集散城、生态旅游城、屯垦文化城和兵团南疆石化工业城”的五大城市定位，阿拉尔市立足农业产业化建市、发展工业化强市、兴办服务业富市，以科学发展观经营、发展城市，城市基础设施建设不断完善；按照创建“最低收费、最优服务、最高效率”的“三个最”要求，投资环境不断优化，项目和招商引资累计40余亿元，30多家企业在工业园区落户，初步形成棉纺、电力、农用化工和农副产品加工等产业体系。

阿拉尔市是新疆三座拥有综合性大学的城市之一。塔里木大学是全国著名的国家部属高等院校，为加快阿拉尔市的全面发展，注入了厚实的文化底蕴。城市旅游资源十分丰富，依托库容总量近5亿立方米三座大型平原水库的8000余公顷水域，已开发建成国家3A级旅游风景区祥龙湖风景区和多浪湖“银沙湾”度假村；拥有保护良好的2万余公顷胡杨林。

2007年，阿拉尔市完成生产总值30.71亿元，职均收入1.98万元。军垦新城阿拉尔，将成为新疆乃至中国西部最具特色、最具活力、最为美丽的城市。

棉纺生产线

中国棉花市场公认十佳畅销品牌“新农”牌棉花生产基地

阿拉尔市辖区多浪、上游、胜利三座平原水库，水域面积8000余公顷

国家农业产业化龙头企业、上市公司“新农开发”大厦

彭家瑞在塔城市调研

地区代表团到哈国签订农产品购销协议

大棚芹菜

新疆塔城

塔城地区位于新疆西北部，辖五县二市，辖区总面积10.45万平方公里，地方总人口90.2万人，有哈萨克、汉、维吾尔、蒙古、柯尔克孜、达斡尔、锡伯、俄罗斯等29个民族。总播面积500多万亩。地区所在地塔城市是国家沿边进一步对外开放城市，巴克图口岸是国家一类陆路口岸，已有200多年通商历史。塔城地区大农业资源丰富，绿色农产品、畜产品品质优良，被农业部确定为"国家级绿色农业示范区"；矿产资源种类繁多，已发现50多个矿种，目前已开采的有：煤、金、铬、石油、天然气、池盐、石灰石、花岗岩、膨润土等，探明储量的有36种，有着广阔的发展前景。

近年来，塔城地委、行署牢固树立和全面落实科学发展观，坚持"三大经济板块"分类指导，围绕"三大核心目标"，大力实施优势资源转换战略，坚定不移地走特色经济发展之路，地区经济发展速度加快，运行质量和效益大幅度提高。2007年，完成地区生产总值164.6亿元，增长18.5%。一、二、三产业比重为26:37:37。地方财政一般预算收入12.59亿元，增长24%。工业经济增势强劲，完成增加值43.7亿元，增长52.5%，工业经济已成为支撑地区经济的主导力量。第三产业蓬勃发展，实现社会消费品零售总额26.9亿元，增长15.1%。基础设施建设力度加大，完成地方固定资产投资60.17亿元，增长30.4%。对内对外开放深入推进，进出口贸易总额6亿美元（不含转口贸易），增长29.9%，实现顺差4.4亿美元。人民生活质量和水平进一步提高，城镇居民人均可支配收入9353元，增长12.4%，农牧民人均纯收入5571元，增加529元。地区经济社会发展呈现出速度加快、质量提高、和谐健康、团结稳定的良好态势。

双塔组合

国家级伊宁边境经济合作区

GUOJIAJI YINING BIANJING JINGJI HEZUOQU

伊宁边境经济合作区作为中国最西部的国家级合作区，紧紧依托邻近的霍尔果斯、都拉塔、木扎尔特三个对外开放的一类口岸和合作区内的伊宁二类口岸的地缘优势及伊犁独特的资源优势，近年来通过"环境立区、工业强区、商贸兴区"三大发展战略，围绕"工业、商贸流通业、房地产业"三大产业板块，全力发展绿色食品、生物制药、新型纺织、新型建材四大产业，建成了一批以绿色食品加工、乳制品、生物制药、新型建材、房地产开发、商贸物流为主的企业群体。

截至2007年末，建成区面积达6平方公里，项目入区承载辐射面达9.6平方公里，道路建设40公里，地面建筑面积110多万平方米，入区企业已达近300余家；全区实现生产总值5.13亿元，同比增长30.3%；完成工业总产值9.65亿元，增长31.9%；工业增加值3.49亿元，增长36.7%；财政一般预算收入突破亿元大关，完成1.09亿元，招商引资到位资金7.01亿元，增长31.3%。

为深入贯彻落实党的十七大、国务院32号文件精神，抢抓新的发展机遇，积极对接和储备了62个重点跟踪项目，确定了今后三年合作区实现GDP和招商引资翻两番的发展目标。根据自治州产业发展格局和伊宁市自身的优势，努力构建四大基地（伊犁河谷大项目大企业聚集发展基地、特色农产品加工产业聚集发展基地、出口加工产业聚集发展基地、科技型就业型产业聚集发展基地），做大做强四大支柱产业（绿色食品、生物制药、新型建材、纺织），积极培育两大新兴产业（汽车制造、精细化工）的工业发展格局。

合作区现代工业

现代化流水线

宽敞明亮的生产车间

正在崛起的首府中心商贸区
——沙依巴克区

沙依巴克区是乌鲁木齐市的中心城区之一，总面积为 427 平方公里，西傍雅玛里克山，东隔河滩公路与天山区为邻，南起乌拉泊与乌鲁木齐县相接，北到新医路与新市区相连。全区总人口 52.8 万人，居住着汉、维吾尔、回、哈萨克、满、蒙古、锡伯、俄罗斯等 38 个民族，是一个团结和睦的民族大家庭。沙依巴克区维吾尔语意为“戈壁滩上的花园”，是乌鲁木齐市唯一用维吾尔语命名的城区。

沙依巴克区办公地点位于乌鲁木齐市扬子江路 101 号，区属党政机关 36 个部门，下属 10 个街道办事处、1 个村、114 个社区居委会；驻区单位达 5000 余家。

改革开放以来，沙依巴克区各族人民，在区委、政府的领导下，团结一心，开拓进取，社会经济不断发展，各项事业欣欣向荣，成为乌鲁木齐市的对外窗口区、商贸繁荣区、科技发达区、治安模范区和生态示范区。

沙依巴克区交通便利，通讯发达，得天独厚的地缘、地理环境使沙区具备了优越的经济发展条件，欧亚大陆桥的兰新铁路与南北疆铁路横贯城区，321 国道、216 国道、吐乌大高速、乌奎高速与通往南北疆各地的公路及市区道路纵横交错，形成了铁路线、国道线、公路线四通八达的交通网络。南北交通枢纽火车站、长途汽车客运站、民航售票处和全疆大部分地州政府驻乌办事处聚集区内，特别是近几年商贸城国际二类口岸、国际客运二类口岸、邮电国际二类口岸发展的日益成熟，使沙依巴克区成为国内外人们观察审视乌鲁木齐建设与发展的重要窗口。

几年来，全区围绕“把沙区建设成为现代国际商贸城中心商贸区”和“全疆最大制造业基地中心服务区”的奋斗目标和“科教兴区”、“商贸富区”、“依法治区”、

“环境优区”的强区战略，突出发展第三产业，大力发展区域融合经济和非公有制经济，使全区经济取得长足进步，成为乌市商贸繁荣活跃的城区。区内现已形成了分别以火车南站、红山、友好为核心的三大商业旺圈，以新疆商贸城、德汇置业、火车头、北园春市场等为重点大型专业化市场，共同构建了全区有一定规模和档次的市场网格。目前，全区拥有各类市场85处，其中销售收入超亿元的10余个，是全疆亿元市场的三分之一，占据了乌鲁木市亿元市场的半边天，成为区域经济发展的重要支撑。2007年全区实现生产总值147亿元，实现财政收入5.42亿元。

经过这些年的发展，全区已形成以商贸为基础，科技为先导，区域经济、融合经济、非公有制经济大发展的格局，经济实力显著增强，实现了精神文明建设、物质文明建设和政治文明建设的全面协调发展。

新疆广播电视大学

新疆电大系统代表大会现场

新疆广播电视大学（以下简称“新疆电大”）1978 年 10 月经新疆维吾尔自治区革命委员会批准筹建，1979 年 1 月正式成立，新疆电大是一所从事现代远程教育的新型高等学校。建校 28 年来，新疆电大在中央电大的指导下，在自治区党委、人民政府的领导下，在自治区教育厅的支持下，在全疆电大系统教职工的共同努力下，始终坚持“面向地方、面向基层、面向农村、面向边远少数民族地区”的办学方向，主动适应新疆经济建设和社会发展对各民族人才培养的需求，综合运用基于计算机网络、卫星电视网络、文字教材、音像教材、多媒体课件及网络课件等多种媒体和教学手段组织教学，充分发挥现代远程教育的优势，迄今为止已建立了覆盖全疆 15 个地州市、52 个县市的“天地网结合、三级平台互动”的传输系统，初步构建了立体式网络化的教学、教学管理和支持服务系统，基本具备了数字化、多媒体、交互式双向反馈的现代远程教育教学环境，形成了具有边疆少数民族地区特色的、符合实际的教学和教学管理模式，以多层次、多规格、多形式的人才培养方式，培养了大批满足新疆经济社会发展的各民族人才，特别是少数民族应用型人才，已经成为新疆发展现代远程教育的骨干力量。建校 29 年来，累计培养大中专毕业生 104053 人（其中少数民族毕业生 15845 人），非学历教育近 40 万人次。现有在校生 42143 人（其中少数民族学生 6788 人）。全疆电大系统现共有教职工 2620 名，其中专职教师 1423 名。

29 年来，新疆电大对远程教育进行了不断探索和实践，先后开展了“自学视听生”、“大学基础教育”、“注册视听生”、“专升本”、“开放教育”等试点，共开设开放教育本科经济学、法学、教育学、文学、理学、工学、管理学 7 个学科 10 门类 20 专业（少数民族语言专业 3 个），开放教育专科 9 科 19 类 35 个专业（少数民族语言专业 3 个），成人 8 类 13 个专业（民、汉），重点建设少数民族学科和专业课程。承担全国试点高校网络教育 8 门公共基础课的统一考试考务工作。

1999 年 6 月，新疆电大被批准成为全国首批开展“中央广播电视大学人才培养模式改革和开放教育试点”项目（以下简称“试点项目”）的省级电大之一。

2000 年秋季，经中央电大批准，新疆电大开始了少数民族专科小学教育专业的开放教育试点工作，之后又开展了部分本科试点，从而揭开了新疆少数民族现代远程开放教育发展史上的新篇章。2002 年我校顺利通过了教育部“试点项目”中期评估。

少数民族双语本专科开放教育试点是新疆电大依托系统优势，满足地方少数民族人才培养需求的统筹规划、分级办学、分级管理、分级服务、协调运作”运行机制为保证重大举措。特别是新疆电大投入大量人力、物力和财力开发出了“双语远程教学平台”并及时使用，不仅为少数民族学生提供了基于网络条件下的教学环境，使他们能够用本民族语言通过网络来进行个别化的自主学习，更重要的是加速了少数民族教师对现代教育技术的掌握，提高了现代远程教学能力，对开展少数民族现代远程开放教育，确保教学质量起到了十分重要的作用。这为新疆电大系统利用现代远程教育网络，参与自治区的中小学少数民族教师双语培训奠定了基础。

少数民族教师培训班

丰富多彩的多媒体教室

积极承担社会责任
助力和谐新疆建设

新疆移动成立9年来，在自治区党委政府的正确领导下，紧紧依靠社会各界和广大客户的大力支持，成长为自治区通信业界的骨干企业。在快速发展的进程中，新疆移动注重企业与社会的和谐发展，企业与客户的共同成长，把服从于新疆稳定、发展的大局，服务于客户的需求，始终作为企业发展的宗旨，尽最大努力，积极承担社会责任，主动为新疆经济社会发展做贡献。

2008年5月18日，白志刚总经理代表新疆移动向残奥会新疆健儿捐款30万元

一、实现跨越发展，积极承担社会责任

截至2007年底，公司累计投入120亿元，围绕自治区发展布局，建成了技术先进、保障有力、可持续改进的通信网络，实现对全疆91%人口的网络覆盖。为党政部门、公安、教育、医疗、石化、电力、金融、矿业等单位和行业提供了多种信息化解决方案；经过总部连续3年"村通工程"政策支持，我们共解决480个行政村、770个等同于行政村、135个自然村的通信覆盖，"农信通"业务得到了广大农民朋友的欢迎，农业信息化实现规模发展。

新疆移动全体员工为汶川地震灾区捐款

在九年跨越发展的进程中，新疆移动为自治区重大政治、经济、社会活动和抗击各类自然灾害等突发事件提供了通信保障；累计上缴税金14亿多元；直接提供8千余个就业岗位，间接为产业链相关企业提供5万多个就业岗位；在助学、环保、助残、脱贫、救灾等各个领域，结合新疆实际开展公益活动。实施以回收废旧手机和电池为主要内容的"绿箱子环保计划"、以节能减排为主旨的"绿色行动计划"。

二、关注弱势群体，让信息通信技术普惠残疾人

新疆移动尤其关注弱势群体，关注残疾人事业。2003年5月17日，新疆移动与自治区残联签署了"新疆移动盲童基金"捐赠协议书，向聋哑孩子捐赠100张关闭语音业务的爱心卡，为盲童基金预支人民币1万元，并在之后的一年里，从每位彩信用户发送一条彩信的费用中抽出0.2元钱注入盲童基金账户。

2004年5月16日，新疆移动举行了"放飞希望——畅想新生活"大型风筝义卖活动，通过义卖和企业、员工捐赠的方式共募得公益金10余万元。

2008年5月，新疆移动又推出了大型、系列化的帮助残疾人事业活动。

新疆移动开展助残活动

新疆移动将吉祥号码拍卖的全部款项捐赠慈善事业

一是推出特殊业务。在国家政策允许的范围内，针对残疾人降低资费，分别推出爱心语音卡、爱心短信卡和爱心卡。

二是提供爱心服务。对全区自办营业厅外部台阶进行统一改造，建立无障碍交通通道；在自办营业厅设立无障碍业务办理通道，残疾人无须等待可直接办理业务，并对行动不便的残障客户提供代办服务；请专业教师对自办营业厅员工进行手语基本沟通培训，使营业员通过手语沟通向聋哑人提供各项服务。

三是扩展“金牌服务，满意100”内涵，开展与残疾人客户的交流互动活动。

四是参加“牵手残疾人，走进残奥会”活动。新疆移动将为北京残奥会新疆体育健儿捐款30万元，用于资助新疆残奥代表团运动队、二线运动员及演员的训练，为备战2008残奥会的残疾人运动员改善训练、生活条件以及解决他们家庭子女上学等问题。

五是号召、组织公司干部员工个人开展“奉献爱心”捐助活动，充实公司“爱心基金”，向当地残疾人捐款，以改善他们的生活状况。同时，为汶川地震灾区捐款，帮助灾区同胞度过难关，重建家园。

三、深化企业责任，助力和谐新疆建设

2007年1月9日，中国移动创建了企业社会责任管理体系，提出了以“以天下之至诚而尽己之性、尽人之性、尽物之性”为核心的企业社会责任观，把履行企业社会责任贯穿于企业经营和管理的各个环节，推动企业社会责任管理的科学化、规范化。

新疆移动慰问为社会作出贡献的盲人王旗生

按照中国移动的总体部署，结合自治区实际，新疆移动确定了近期着力推进企业社会责任“五大工程”。

一是深化实施“农村工程”。继续提高行政村、自然村覆盖率，完成“村村通电话”工程任务，推进农村信息网全国联网工作，提升农村信息网服务和支撑能力。持续推进“边防110”工程，为边境地区的安全稳定构筑一道重要的高科技防线。

二是全面推进“绿色工程”。以节能、减排、降耗为核心，紧密结合新疆实际，因地制宜，将谐波治理、专用机房空调乙二醇改造、SIM卡回收、智能抄表、电子渠道自助终端、绿箱子环保、照明改造等作为“绿色行动计划”年度重点项目，将“绿色行动计划”转化为员工的行为规范。通过构建全员、全过程“绿色行动计划”，努力成为全社会节能减排的倡导者和推动者。

三是继续强化“生命工程”。不断完善应急通信保障体系建设，提高对突发事件的应急通信反应速度和保障能力；关爱生命健康、关注弱势群体，积极开展公益慈善活动，组织、配合中国移动组织的各项重大公益慈善活动，落实“中国温暖12.1爱心基金—中国移动关爱行动”计划。

新疆移动克拉玛依分公司开展党员奉献日活动

四是大力实施“文化工程”。继续开展爱心图书馆、农村教师培训、贫困学生资助等文化公益活动。

五是积极推动“志愿工程”。建立员工公益志愿活动的保障和激励机制，培育员工责任意识，营造热心公益、关注社会的良好氛围。

新疆移动将在实施“五大工程”的整体框架下，号召广大员工积极关注残疾人事业，把扶弱助残活动深入持久的开展下去，为自治区加快发展残疾人事业添砖加瓦，为构建和谐新疆作出更大的贡献。

福利彩票送温暖、献爱心慰问活动仪式

新疆维吾尔自治区福利彩票发行中心

新疆维吾尔自治区福利彩票发行中心成立于 1991 年 2 月(时称新疆维吾尔自治区募委办),隶属于自治区民政厅,同时,受中国福利彩票发行管理中心的业务领导,是全疆福利彩票销售业务的主办机构。工作职责是:在全疆发行和销售福利彩票,为国家筹集公益资金,促进社会福利事业发展。

在各级党委、政府的大力支持下,十七年来,新疆维吾尔自治区福利彩票发行中心协同各地(州、市)福利彩票发行机构解放思想,以创新为先导,与时俱进,全疆福利彩票发行工作得到了稳步发展。2000 年至 2006 年,全疆福利彩票年销售额持续保持六年稳步增长,2005 年至 2007 年,全疆累计销售福利彩票 40.46 亿元,累计给国家筹集公益金 14.16 亿元,代扣代缴中奖者个人所得税 7900 余万元。目前,市场定型的常规电脑型彩票玩法有:35 选 7、25 选 7、18 选 7、趣味偶数 10 选 7、“时时彩”以及全国性玩法——“七乐彩”、双色球和 3D。

根据福利彩票“扶老、助残、救孤、济困”的发行宗旨,在自治区党委、自治区人民政府和民政厅党组的大力支持下,2005 年至 2007 年底,新疆福利彩票发行中心共计使用福利彩票公益金“爱心关注”资金 1253 万余元,对 80 个“爱心关注”项目、19485 人次进行了资助,受到了社会各界的普遍好评。

自治区党委常委肖开提·依明在和田师专参加“福利彩票送温暖、献爱心,三年资助和田师专贫困生活动”座谈会暨“和田师专慈善爱心超市”揭牌仪式

新疆维吾尔自治区人民政府副主席贾帕尔·阿比布拉一行在新疆福利彩票发行中心机房视察工作

新疆福利彩票 25 选 7 玩法开奖现场

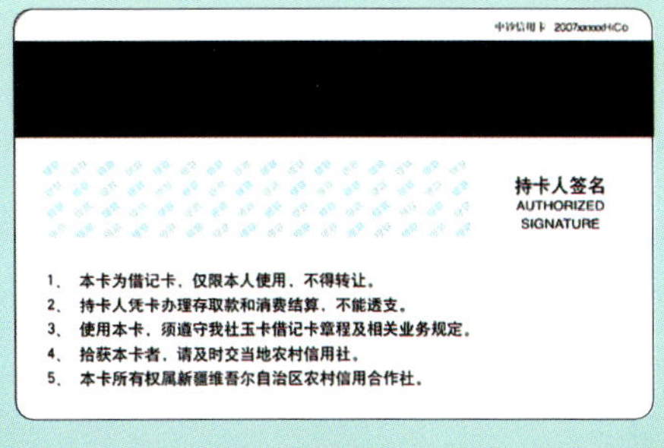

卡片正面主图采用世界独有的新疆和田羊脂玉，雕做成“如意”与“新疆”相连相拥的图景造型，寓意新疆维吾尔自治区这块沃土永远与美玉、如意紧密相连，新疆维吾尔自治区农村信用社将像和田美玉一样，用它温润、细腻、纯洁、忠诚、高贵的凝脂，默默滋润和回报孕育、滋养它的这块美丽沃土，并通过它遍布新疆大地各个角落的农信网脉，秉承“立足三农、服务三农”的经营宗旨，以其如玉般高品质、高品位的金融服务，伴随新疆各族人民生活的更加富足、滋润、如意和幸福，共同奔向光辉灿烂的明天。

卡片背景运用浑厚、高贵的灰黑色衬托，使得卡片更加庄重、高贵、优雅和静逸。

2007 年新疆农村信用社各项业务经营成果显著

2007 年，在自治区党委、自治区人民政府的正确领导下，新疆农村信用社以科学发展观为统领，实施“规模、质量、结构、效益可持续发展”战略，经过全社干部员工的共同努力，各项业务经营指标均创历史新高。

截至 2007 年 12 月 31 日，新疆农村信用社各项存款达 403 亿元，比年初增加 51 亿元；各项贷款 220 亿元，比年初增加 64 亿元，增长 41%，农户贷款覆盖率达 94%，比年初增加 26 个百分点。据中国银监会统计显示，2007 年新疆农村信用社农户小额贷款覆盖率、贷款净投放在全国农村信用社系统分别名列第一位与第二位，全疆农牧民贷款难问题得到进一步缓解；实现经营利润 7.5 亿元，比上年增加 3.4 亿元；税后利润 1.7 亿元，比上年增加 1.4 亿元，增长 415%；增提风险拨备 5.5 亿元，较上年增加 1.7 亿元，增幅 47%；中间业务收入 3 876 万元，增长 223%。与此同时，管理基础进一步夯实，全年实现安全运营，无重特大案件事故发生，全疆信合人精心打造的信用卡产品——玉卡正式面世。各项工作呈现又好又快发展态势，社会影响力和综合竞争力明显提升，实现了自身效益和社会效益的“双赢”。

在新的一年里，新疆农村信用社将认真贯彻党的十七大精神、中央经济工作、农村工作会议以及自治区党委七届五次全委（扩大）会议精神，坚持为“三农”服务、为中小企业服务、为县域经济服务的经营宗旨，落实好科学的金融发展观，在 2007 年工作的基础上再上新台阶，为自治区经济社会发展做出新的、更大的贡献。

自治区副主席胡伟在玉卡发行仪式上致贺辞

在中国县域经济最具影响力银行颁奖典礼上

新疆社情民意调查中心

随着社会经济的发展，尤其是十六届四中全会以来，政府职能发生了巨大的转变。执政为民，立党为公的理念不断深入，舆情信息成为党委政府重大决策的重要参考依据。党政机关不断通过多种渠道广泛听取群众意见，听民声，查民情，解民忧，问政于民。如何运用科学手段全面深入地了解民情民意，及时反映百姓对当前社会热点、焦点问题的看法和建议。在落实科学发展观，构建和谐社会大背景下，建立一个系统性强，题材多样，覆盖面广，反应迅速的社情民意调查系统势在必行，把政府需要，百姓心声和社会需求有机结合起来，在百姓和政府之间架起一座沟通的桥梁，使民调中心成为"深入了解民情，充分反映民意，广泛集中民智，切实珍惜民力"的一条重要渠道。

新疆社情民意调查中心首条计算机辅助电话访问系统已正式建立。该系统拥有 30 条电话专线和 30 个工作机位，使用国内最先进的专用技术软件，配备了几十名经过严格专业训练的访问员和督导员。它是将传统的调查技术与现代计算机和通讯技术相结合的一种全新的调查作业系统。通过电话访问系统、访谈、入户等调查手段，广泛地对外承接各类业务、政务等调查活动。

社情民意调查中心的宗旨是：为政府及部门、企事业单位、社会组织在社情民意调查及统计调查业务等方面提供相关服务。业务范围是：负责对政府及部门、企事业单位、社会组织委托的各类社情民意调查及相关统计调查业务提供服务，开展舆情调查分析，提供或上报相关统计调查结果。

地址：乌鲁木齐市解放北路 339 号
（酒花大厦 21 楼）
电话：0991-8878697　8877490
8873003　2844866
传真：0991-8878697
邮编：830002
邮箱：zyx_xj@stats.gov.cn

新疆统计书店

2007年2月9日,新疆统计书店隆重开业,在开业庆典仪式上,中国统计出版社刘科总编辑发表了热情洋溢地致辞,对新疆统计书店的开业表示热烈地祝贺,同时,对新疆统计局在统计信息咨询服务、统计信息对外提供方面的大胆尝试,给予了充分地肯定。自治区统计局党组成员、副局长王忠山希望统计书店今后在自身不懈努力,开拓创新的同时,能够继续得到社会各界更加一如既往的支持和关心,努力使统计书店的事业蒸蒸日上,欣欣向荣,力求取得社会效益和经济效益双丰收,并能够充分利用统计书店这个平台,这个良好地环境,不断提高统计工作的社会影响,扩大统计工作社会服务领域,拓展统计咨询服务发展空间,使其切实履行好统计的信息、咨询和监督职能,努力使统计信息更好地服务于各级党政,服务于社会,服务于经济建设。

新疆统计书店面积60余平方米,藏书丰富,主要包括统计教材、统计工具书、统计年鉴、统计研究分析成果类书籍等,并在书店内设置了统计信息查询室,为社会各界提供全疆乃至全国各行各业统计信息的查询服务。

地址:乌鲁木齐和平北路80号(自治区统计局办公大楼旁)
电话:0991-8877855

牧在天山　　　　黄永中 摄影